Principles of
Comparative Politics
Third Edition

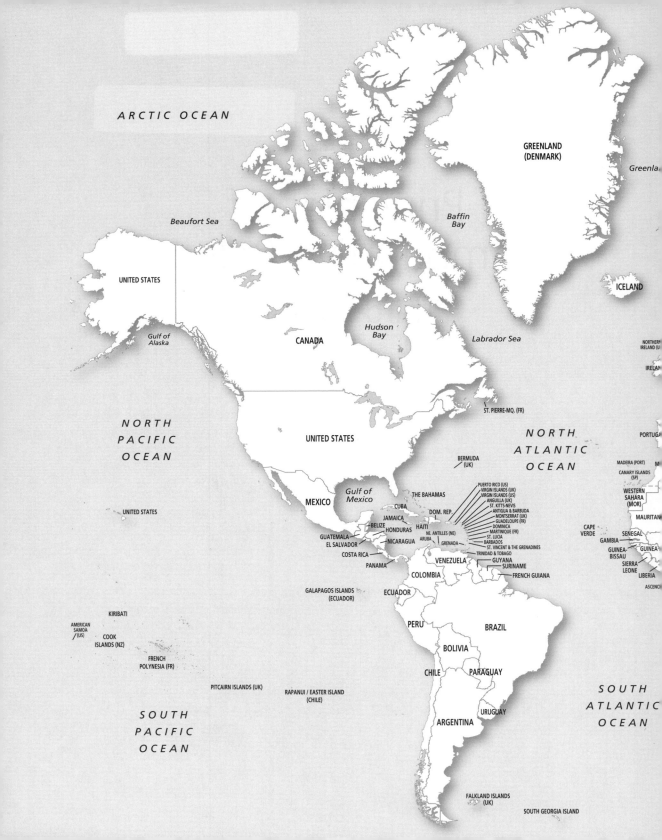

ARCTIC OCEAN

SVALBARD
(NORWAY)

gian

Baltic Sea
Gulf of Bothnia

SEN
FINLAND

ESTONIA
LATVIA
LITHUANIA
RUS.

BELARUS

POLAND

SLOVAKIA
HUNGARY
ROMANIA
SERBIA
ALBANIA
GREECE

MOLDOVA
UKRAINE

Black Sea

GEORGIA
ARMENIA
AZERBAIJAN

TURKEY

Terranean

CYPRUS
LEBANON
ISRAEL
SYRIA
IRAQ
JORDAN

KUWAIT

RUSSIA

KAZAKHSTAN

Aral Sea

UZBEKISTAN

Caspian Sea

TURKMENISTAN

KYRGYZSTAN

TAJIKISTAN

MONGOLIA

Sea of Okhotsk

Bering Sea

NORTH
KOREA
SOUTH
KOREA

Sea of Japan

JAPAN

NORTH
PACIFIC
OCEAN

LIBYA

EGYPT

SAUDI
ARABIA

BAHRAIN
QATAR
U.A.E.

Persian Gulf

Gulf of Oman

OMAN

IRAN

AFGHANISTAN

PAKISTAN

CHINA

NEPAL

BHUTAN

East China Sea

TAIWAN

Red Sea

CHAD

SUDAN

ERITREA
YEMEN

DJIBOUTI

ETHIOPIA

Gulf of Aden

Arabian Sea

INDIA

BANGLADESH
MYANMAR
LAOS
THAILAND
CAMBODIA
VIETNAM

South China Sea

Philippine Sea

NORTHERN MARIANAS
(US)

CENTRAL AFRICAN
REPUBLIC

SOUTH
SUDAN

UGANDA

SOMALIA

KENYA

Bay of Bengal

MALDIVES

SRI LANKA

BRUNEI

PHILIPPINES

GUAM
(US)

PALAU

MICRONESIA

MARSHALL
ISLANDS

DEMOCRATIC
REPUBLIC
OF THE CONGO

RWANDA
BURUNDI
TANZANIA

SEYCHELLES

MALAYSIA

SINGAPORE

NGOLA

ZAMBIA
MALAWI

COMOROS

MAYOTTE
(FR)

INDIAN OCEAN

INDONESIA

PAPUA
NEW GUINEA

NAURU

SOLOMON
ISLANDS

TUVALU

KIRIBATI

TOKELAU (NZ)

MOZAMBIQUE

MIBIA

ZIMBABWE

MADAGASCAR

MAURITIUS

RÉUNION (FR)

COCOS
(KEELING ISLANDS)
(AUSTRALIA)

CHRISTMAS ISLAND
(AUSTRALIA)

Timor Sea

EAST
TIMOR

Coral Sea

VANUATU

WALLIS & FUTUNA
ISLANDS (FR)

NEW CALEDONIA (FR)

FIJI

SAMOA

TONGA

BOTSWANA

SWAZILAND

SOUTH
AFRICA

LESOTHO

AUSTRALIA

NORFOLK ISLAND
(AUSTRALIA)

Tasman Sea

NEW ZEALAND

CHATHAM ISLANDS
(N.Z.)

Sara Miller McCune founded SAGE Publishing in 1965 to support the dissemination of usable knowledge and educate a global community. SAGE publishes more than 1000 journals and over 800 new books each year, spanning a wide range of subject areas. Our growing selection of library products includes archives, data, case studies and video. SAGE remains majority owned by our founder and after her lifetime will become owned by a charitable trust that secures the company's continued independence.

Los Angeles | London | New Delhi | Singapore | Washington DC | Melbourne

Principles of Comparative Politics

Third Edition

WILLIAM ROBERTS CLARK

Texas A&M University

MATT GOLDER

Pennsylvania State University

SONA NADENICHEK GOLDER

Pennsylvania State University

FOR INFORMATION:

CQ Press
An Imprint of SAGE Publications, Inc.
2455 Teller Road
Thousand Oaks, California 91320
E-mail: order@sagepub.com

SAGE Publications Ltd.
1 Oliver's Yard
55 City Road
London EC1Y 1SP
United Kingdom

SAGE Publications India Pvt. Ltd.
B 1/I 1 Mohan Cooperative Industrial Area
Mathura Road, New Delhi 110 044
India

SAGE Publications Asia-Pacific Pte. Ltd.
3 Church Street
#10-04 Samsung Hub
Singapore 049483

Acquisitions Editor: Carrie Brandon
Development Editor: Elise Frasier
eLearning Editor: John Scappini
Production Editor: Jane Haenel
Editorial Assistant: Duncan Marchbank
Copy Editor: Patrice Sutton
Typesetter: C&M Digitals (P) Ltd.
Proofreader: Scott Oney
Indexer: Nancy Fulton
Cover Designer: Candice Harman
Marketing Manager: Amy Whitaker

Printed in Great Britain by Ashford Colour Press Ltd.

Library of Congress Cataloging-in-Publication Data

Names: Clark, William Roberts, 1962– author. | Golder, Matt, author. | Golder, Sona Nadenichek, author.

Title: Principles of comparative politics / William Roberts Clark, Texas A&M University, Matt Golder Pennsylvania State University, Sona Nadenichek Golder, Pennsylvania State University.

Description: Third edition. | Washington DC : SAGE/CQ Press, [2017] | Includes index.

Identifiers: LCCN 2016052425 | ISBN 9781506389790 (pbk. : alk. paper)

Subjects: LCSH: Comparative government. | Democracy. | Political science—Research—Methodology.

Classification: LCC JF51 .C53 2017 | DDC 320.3—dc23
LC record available at https://lccn.loc.gov/2016052425

This book is printed on acid-free paper.

18 19 20 21 10 9 8 7

To our most important students: Meaghan, Brian, Liam, Cameron, and Sean.

About the Authors

William Roberts Clark is the Charles Puryear Professor of Liberal Arts in the department of political science at Texas A&M University. He is the author of *Capitalism, Not Globalism,* and his articles have appeared in the *American Political Science Review,* the *British Journal of Political Science, Comparative Political Studies, Political Analysis, International Organization,* and *European Union Politics,* among other journals. He has taught at a wide variety of public and private schools, including William Paterson College, Rutgers University, Georgia Tech, Princeton, New York University, the University of Essex, the University of Michigan, and Texas A&M University.

Matt Golder is associate professor of political science at Pennsylvania State University. His articles have appeared in the *American Journal of Political Science,* the *Journal of Politics,* the *British Journal of Political Science, Political Analysis, Comparative Political Studies,* and *Electoral Studies,* among other journals. He has taught classes on comparative politics, quantitative methods, game theory, and European politics at the University of Iowa, Florida State University, the University of Essex, and Pennsylvania State University.

Sona Nadenichek Golder is associate professor of political science at Pennsylvania State University. She is the author of *The Logic of Pre-electoral Coalition Formation* and articles published in journals such as the *American Journal of Political Science,* the *Journal of Politics, Comparative Political Studies, Political Analysis, Politics & Gender,* and the *British Journal of Political Science.* She has taught courses on game theory, political institutions, comparative politics, and quantitative analysis at Florida State University, the University of Essex, and Pennsylvania State University.

Brief
Contents

Contents

Preface

This book began as a syllabus for an introductory comparative politics class taught by a newly minted PhD—one of the book's authors, Bill Clark—at Georgia Tech in the early 1990s. The class had three goals: (1) to introduce students to the major questions in comparative politics, (2) to acquaint them with the field's best answers to those questions, and (3) to give them the tools to think critically about the answers. The decision to write this textbook was born out of the frustration caused by our inability, ten years later, to find a single text that accomplished these goals. The intervening period, however, allowed us to conduct what turned out to be a useful experiment, because along the way, our frustration led us to gradually develop an ambitious syllabus from research monographs and refereed journal articles. The benefit of this approach has been our ability to respond flexibly to the changes in the discipline of political science and the field of comparative politics that have, for the most part, not made their way into textbooks. As a result, we have had the satisfaction of introducing many students to exciting work being done at the cutting edge of this field. And we learned that students were by and large up to the task. Nonetheless, we have also recognized the frustration of students confronting material that was not written with them in mind. The goal of this text is to try to maximize these upside benefits while minimizing the downside risks of our previous approach. We want students to be challenged to confront work being done at the cutting edge of the field, and we believe we have packaged this work in a way that is comprehensible to ambitious undergraduates with no prior training in political science.

THE APPROACH OF THIS BOOK

With these goals in mind, we have organized the book around a set of questions that comparative scholars have asked repeatedly over the past several decades:

- What is the state, and where did it come from?
- What is democracy?
- Why are some countries democracies whereas others are dictatorships?

- How might we explain transitions to democracy?
- Does the kind of regime a country has affect the material well-being of its citizens?
- Why are ethnic groups politicized in some countries but not in others?
- Why do some countries have many parties whereas some have only a few?
- How do governments form, and what determines the type of governments that take office?
- What are the material and normative implications associated with these different types of government?
- How does the type of democracy in a country affect the survival of that regime?

Using the latest research in the field of comparative politics, we examine competing answers to substantively important questions such as these and evaluate the proposed arguments for their logical consistency and empirical accuracy. At times our approach requires us to present substantial amounts of original research, although we believe that this research is closely tied to existing studies in the field.

The book itself is designed and organized to build upon the questions asked above, starting with a section that defines comparative politics. In Part I, after an overview of the book and its goals in Chapter 1, we define the parameters of our inquiry in Chapters 2 and 3 in a discussion of the fundamental questions of "What Is Science?" and "What Is Politics?" In Chapters 4 through 9 in Part II, "The Modern State: Democracy or Dictatorship?," we look at the origins of the modern state, measurements of democracy and dictatorship, the economic and cultural determinants of democracy and dictatorship, the issue of democratic transitions, and whether regime type makes a material difference in people's lives. We explore the varieties of democracy and dictatorship in Part III, beginning with a chapter exploring the varieties of dictatorship that we observe around the world. In Chapter 11 we present the problems of democratic group decision making and the implications of Arrow's Theorem. In Chapter 12 we look at the major types of democracies and the forms of government that they have, in Chapter 13 at elections and electoral systems, in Chapter 14 at social cleavages and party systems, and in Chapter 15 at institutional veto players. In Part IV, Chapter 16, we investigate the relationships between types of democracy and economic and political outcomes.

As we explain in greater length in the first chapter, we adopt a strategic approach to politics. We believe that the behavior of rulers and the ruled is most easily understood as the interaction between individuals seeking goals in an environment in which goal attainment is complicated by the choices of other actors. Game theory is a useful tool for understanding such interactions, and it will be used wherever we think it illuminating. We also believe that explanations should be confronted with as much potentially falsifying evidence as possible. Consequently, we make every effort to present students with information about rigorous empirical tests of the theoretical arguments we offer and try to give them tools to begin to critically engage with such evidence themselves. We view comparative politics as a subfield of political science, which, like all of science, is about comparison. And the only bad comparison is one that shelters a hypothesis from disconfirming evidence. As the cover illustration suggests, one can compare apples and oranges. Indeed, the claim that "you cannot compare apples and oranges" seems contradictory. How would you support this claim without conducting such a comparison—an act that would contradict the very claim being asserted.

Of course, the usefulness of such a comparison depends on the question one is asking. In this book we make many comparisons across disparate contexts and attempt to use such comparisons to test claims made about the political world. In doing so, we highlight the similarities and differences among countries. We also aim to show the conditions under which some claims about the political world apply or do not apply. Policymakers and writers of constitutions are forced to make comparisons when forming expectations about the consequences of the choices they make. For scholars, exactly what should or should not be compared is a question of research design, not a matter of religion. In sum, there are no invalid comparisons, only invalid inferences.

METHODOLOGY

In addressing the substantive questions that form the backbone of this textbook, we introduce students to a variety of methods that have become central to the study of comparative politics. For example, students will be exposed to tools such as decision theory, social choice theory, game theory, experiments, and statistical analysis, although we have written this book under the assumption that students have no prior knowledge of any of these. Basic high school algebra is the only mathematical prerequisite. We show students how to calculate expected utilities, how to solve complete information games in strategic and extensive form, how to solve repeated games, how to analyze simple games with incomplete information, how to evaluate one-dimensional and two-dimensional spatial models, and how to interpret simple statistical results. Although the tools that we employ may appear sophisticated, we believe (and our experience teaching this material tells us) that students beginning their college careers have the necessary skills to learn them and apply them to new questions of more direct interest to themselves personally. Given the relative youth of the scientific approach to politics, we believe that students can successfully contribute to the accumulation of knowledge in comparative politics if they are given some basic tools. In fact, on more than one occasion we have made contributions to the literature through collaborations with our own comparative politics undergraduate students (Brambor, Clark, and Golder 2006, 2007; Clark and Reichert 1998; Golder and Lloyd 2014; Golder and Thomas 2014; Uzonyi, Souva, and Golder 2012).

PEDAGOGY

Although this book differs in content and approach from other comparative politics text-books, we do appreciate the usefulness of textbook features that genuinely assist the reader in digesting and applying the ideas presented. To that end, we have created chapter-opener overviews that help orient the reader toward each chapter's main goals. To establish a common understanding of the most important concepts we discuss, we've defined each new key term in a box near its first mention. Lists of those same terms appear at the end of each chapter along with page references to aid in review and study. We have schematized a great deal of our data and information in tables, charts, and maps, thereby allowing students to better visualize the issues and arguments at hand.

Two important features are unique to this book and in keeping with our focus on methods and current research. The first is extensive class-tested problem sets at the end of each chapter. Our emphasis on problem sets comes from the belief that there is a lot of art in science and one learns an art by doing, not by simply watching others do. Developing a command over analytical materials and building a capacity to engage in analysis require practice and repetition, and the problem sets are meant to provide such opportunities for students. We, together and separately, have been assigning these problem sets and others like them in large introductory classes for several years now and find they work particularly well in classes with discussion sections. We have consistently found that students who seriously engage with the problem sets perform better on tests and appear grateful for the opportunity to apply what they have learned. We suspect they also perform better in upper-division classes and graduate school as well, although we admit that we have only anecdotes to support this claim. Graduate students who lead discussion sections in such classes seem to welcome the direction provided by the problem sets while also being inspired to contribute to the ever-expanding bank of questions. We believe that the best way to learn is to teach, and we have the distinct impression that this approach to undergraduate education has contributed directly to the training of graduate students. (A solutions manual for the problems is available via download at **https://edge.sagepub.com/principlescp3e**.)

The second important feature of the book is the set of online resources for students and instructors. New to this edition is a series of online tutorials that walk students through how to use many of the methods they come across in the book. If students want to get a better understanding of how to solve extensive or strategic form games, for example, or if they want to review spatial models or how to distinguish between valid and invalid arguments, they can watch one or more short videos on each of these topics. In addition to these new online tutorials, the free student companion website at **https://edge.sagepub.com/principlescp3e** also features quiz questions, flashcards, brief chapter summaries for each chapter, and links to important data for further research. Finally, to help instructors "tool up," we offer a set of downloadable resources, materials we've developed for our own classes over the years. These include test bank questions, PowerPoint lecture slides, downloadable graphics from the book, a glossary of key terms that can be used as handouts or for quizzing, and more at **https://edge.sagepub.com/principlescp3e**.

NEW FOR THE THIRD EDITION

We have made a number of changes in the third edition of the book. For example, the "Varieties of Dictatorship" chapter has been reorganized to focus on the two problems of authoritarian rule: (a) the problem of authoritarian power-sharing, and (b) the problem of authoritarian control. The "Cultural Determinants of Democracy and Dictatorship" chapter now includes a more extensive overview of cultural modernization theory and a discussion of new survey techniques that scholars are using to examine attitudes toward sensitive topics. We have added a detailed discussion of electoral integrity to the chapter on elections and electoral systems. We have also tried to incorporate a discussion of gender-related issues into various chapters and their Problems sections. For example, the "What Is Science" chapter includes a discussion of why diversity is important to science, and the "Consequences of Democratic Institutions" chapter examines how institutions, such as electoral rules, affect the descriptive and substantive representation of women. We have also added a new intuitive take on understanding statistical analyses and a clearer description of how to interpret regression results in Chapter 6. In addition to updating our empirical examples and our maps showing the geographic distribution of different institutions, we have also streamlined most chapters to highlight key explanations and offer a more coherent overview of the literature. The problem sets at the end of each chapter have been significantly expanded to allow students more opportunity to work through the theoretical, conceptual, and methodological material covered in the book.

ACKNOWLEDGMENTS

Given the long gestation of this text, we have accumulated many, many debts and would like to acknowledge just a few of them. Dong-Hun Kim, Korea University; Amy Linch, Pennsylvania State University; Will Moore, Arizona State University; Laura Potter, University of Michigan; Joel Simmons, Stonybrook University; Jeff Staton, Emory University; and various graduate students at the University of Michigan and Florida State University were kind enough to assign trial versions of chapters in their classes and offer us feedback and constructive criticism. In addition, André Blais, Sabri Ciftci, Courtenay Conrad, Charles Crabtree, Kostanca Dhima, Rob Franzese, Steffen Ganghof, Brad Gomez, Mark Hallerberg, Indriði Indriðason, Marek Kaminski, Kiril Kalinin, Özge Kemahlioglu, Masayuki Kudamatsu, Jerry Loewenberg, Monika Nalepa, Chris Reenock, Tyson Roberts, David Siegel, Mark Souva, Mike Thies, Josh Tucker, Tom Walker, Carol Weissert, and Joe Wright read portions of the manuscript and offered helpful comments. In addition to helping to produce the online tutorials that accompany this book, Charles Crabtree also created many of the maps showing the global distribution of different institutions and political outcomes. Cristina Crivelli provided additional questions for the problem sets at the end of the chapters.

We would also like to thank the reviewers CQ Press commissioned to vet the book at the proposal, manuscript, and post-adoption stages and who have helped shape this project over the past several years: Kathleen Bawn, University of California, Los Angeles; Charles Blake,

James Madison University; Douglas Blair, Rutgers University; Pamela Camerra-Rowe, Kenyon College; Clifford Carrubba, Emory University; Karen Ferree, University of California, San Diego; Tracy Harbin, St. John Fisher College; William Heller, SUNY Binghamton; Erik Herron, University of Kansas; Indriði Indriðason, University of California, Riverside; Monika Nalepa, University of Chicago; Irfan Nooruddin, Georgetown University; Tim Rich, Indiana University; Andrew Roberts, Northwestern University; Sarah Sokhey, University of Colorado, Boulder; Boyka Stefanova, University of Texas, San Antonio; Joshua Tucker, New York University; and Christopher Way, Cornell University. Finally, we should thank the thousands of undergraduate students at the Georgia Institute of Technology, the University of Iowa, New York University, the University of Michigan, Florida State University, Pennsylvania State University, and Texas A&M University who forced us to find better ways of explaining the material in this book by asking questions and challenging our presentation of this material.

We are hugely indebted to the entire team at CQ Press. Nancy Matuszak, Carrie Brandon, Elise Frasier, and John Scappini were all one could hope for in editors: insightful, patient, critical, encouraging, and honest coaches. We appreciate their efforts to keep the revisions process moving forward while allowing us to take the time to get it right, and Duncan Marchbank for his editorial assistance. Patrice Sutton did a wonderful job of copyediting the manuscript. Jane Haenel served as production editor and did a terrific job helping us find photographs and maps.

On a more personal note, we are grateful to the comparative politics scholars who inspired us and trained us at both the undergraduate and graduate levels (Neal Beck, André Blais, Maya Chadda, Mike Gilligan, Robert Kaufman, Anand Menon, Jonathan Nagler, Bing Powell, Adam Przeworski, Michael Shafer, Stephen Rosskam Shalom, Daniel Verdier, Richard W. Wilson, and Vincent Wright [and a couple of us would include Bill Clark in this list]). By declaring the truth clearly, while encouraging heresy, they have given us direction at the same time as giving us the freedom to grow. We are also grateful to New York University's Department of Politics, where much of this book was formed in us, and our current departments at Pennsylvania State University and Texas A&M University. They say that iron sharpens iron, and although we've been rubbed in uncomfortable ways at times, we are grateful for being shaped by such competent hands. Our thanks go out to our colleagues, teachers, and mentors of various stripes for their criticism, encouragement, inspiration, and companionship over the years, including André Blais, Robert Bates, Jenna Bednar, Fred Boehmke, Ted Brader, Lawrence Broz, Bruce Bueno de Mesquita, George Downs, Rob Franzese, Jeff Frieden, Mary Gallagher, Jen Gandhi, Mike Gilligan, Brad Gomez, Anna Gryzmala-Busse, Anna Harvey, Allen Hicken, Ron Inglehart, Stathis Kalyvas, Orit Kedar, Ken Kollman, Jack Levy, Michael Lewis-Beck, Jerry Loewenberg, Skip Lupia, Fiona McGillivray, Rob Mickey, Sara McLaughlin Mitchell, Burt Monroe, Will Moore, Jim Morrow, Rebecca Morton, Scott Page, Chris Reenock, Sebastian Saiegh, Rob Salmond, Shanker Satyanath, Chuck Shipan, Dave Siegel, Alastair Smith, Jeff Staton, George Tsebelis, Ashu Varshney, John Vasquez, Leonard Wantchekon, Libby Wood, Joe Wright, and Bill Zimmerman.

Introduction

My purpose is to consider if, in political society, there can be any legitimate and sure principle of government, taking men as they are, and laws as they might be. I shall try always to bring together what right permits with what interest prescribes so that justice and utility are in no way divided.

Jean-Jacques Rousseau, *The Social Contract*

OVERVIEW

- Political science is the study of politics in a scientific manner. Whereas international politics is the study of politics predominantly between countries, comparative politics is the study of politics predominantly within countries.

- In this chapter, we outline the central questions in comparative politics that we address in the remainder of this book. These questions are all related to the causes and consequences of democracy and dictatorship, as well as to the tremendous variety of democratic and dictatorial institutions seen in the world.

- We argue that attempts to engineer democracy, should they occur, should rest on foundations provided by the study of comparative politics.

- We also discuss why we adopt an explicitly cross-national approach to introduce students to the study of comparative politics.

On December 17, 2010, twenty-six-year-old Mohamed Bouazizi set fire to himself to protest his treatment by local officials who had confiscated the produce he had gone into debt to sell on the streets of Sidi Bouzid, Tunisia. While permits are not needed to sell produce on the streets of Sidi Bouzid, police and local officials had been harassing Mr. Bouazizi—apparently in attempts to extract bribes—ever since he left high school as a teenager to help feed his extended family. On this day, the police also confiscated the electronic scales that Mr. Bouazizi used to weigh the fruit he sold and, by some accounts, beat him and made slurs against his deceased father. Mr. Bouazizi appealed to the local governor's office and, when ignored, stood in traffic outside the governor's office, doused himself with gasoline, and lit himself on fire. He died—having survived eighteen days in a coma—on January 5, 2011. In the weeks that followed Mr. Bouazizi's self-immolation, mass protests, in which scores of demonstrators were killed, spread from his hometown to the capital city, Tunis. On January 15, after controlling the country for almost a quarter of a century, President Zine al-Abidine Ben Ali was forced to flee to Saudi Arabia, making him the first Arab leader in generations to leave office in response to public protests.

Over the next few months, expressions of discontent spread across the Middle East and North Africa (MENA) region. The first signs of contagion came in mid-January in the form of self-immolations in Egypt and Algeria, but in the following weeks mass protests would be held in more than a dozen countries across the region. For example, on January 23, protests spread to Yemen where thousands took to the streets in support of Tawakul Karman, an activist who was jailed after she called for an end to President Ali Abdullah's thirty-two-year control of the country. Organized protests, coordinated through social networking sites such as Facebook and Twitter, occurred across Egypt on January 25. In the weeks that followed, the Egyptian military showed a marked reluctance to open fire on protesters. Despite this, many protesters were injured or killed, frequently in clashes with bands of pro-regime thugs. Protesters were not placated when President Hosni Mubarak, who had ruled Egypt longer than any modern Egyptian leader, first fired his cabinet and then promised to step down before elections in the fall. Mubarak eventually resigned on February 11 and was tried and found guilty of corruption. On February 16, protests erupted in Libya—a month after Libyan leader Muammar al-Qaddafi had gone on television to bemoan the ouster of Tunisian president Zine al-Abidine Ben Ali. Within a few weeks, mass protests had turned into a full-scale insurrection that was aided by North Atlantic Treaty Organization (NATO) air strikes. On February 25, protests referred to as a "day of rage" occurred throughout the MENA region. These protests were followed in March by government crackdowns on protesters in both Saudi Arabia and Syria. By the end of March 2011, significant protests, frequently accompanied by violent government crackdowns, had occurred in seventeen countries throughout the Middle East and North Africa.

The fact that at least some of these popular movements led to the removal of long-standing dictators raised the prospect that we might be observing the beginning of a wave of liberalization, perhaps even a new wave of democratization, in a region that has long been dominated by resilient authoritarian regimes. A brief look at history, though, suggests that such optimism may have been unwarranted.

Beginning with a revolt in Palermo, Sicily, in January 1848, a wave of nearly fifty revolts spread across Europe, challenging dynasties that had ruled for decades in France, Austria, Prussia, and almost all of the lesser known states in Germany and Italy. This revolutionary period is known as the Spring of Nations. As with the 2011 Arab Spring, some of Europe's leaders were forcibly removed from power, some went into exile when their armies refused to fire on protesting citizens, and some used the coercive power of the state to put down rebellions. In many ways, the rebellions of 1848 shared a common set of causes with the revolts of 2011. For example, rapid changes in social structure brought about by the Industrial Revolution gave middle-class groups new power, often in coalition with working-class groups who were newly mobilized by economic crises. In many countries, rulers attempted to placate the masses by firing unpopular ministers, promising constitutional reforms, and adopting universal male suffrage. Although the rebellions often had local antecedents, they tended to share the goal of wresting power from the nobility and vesting authority in constitutional republics dedicated to the protection of individual liberties. In Frankfurt, for instance, a parliament known as the Frankfurt National Assembly wrote a constitution for what it declared to be the German Empire—a constitutional monarchy founded on eloquently expressed nineteenth-century liberal ideals including democracy and national unity.

Such changes brought about a wave of euphoria that expressed the hope that government was finally going to be put under the control of the people. Tyrants were to be sent packing, and rational self-rule was to replace tradition and prejudice. National self-determination movements would produce self-rule for oppressed groups long under the thumb of monarchies such as the Habsburg Empire. In nearly all instances, though, the hope produced by the 1848 Spring of Nations had turned to disappointment and recrimination by the autumn. A chilling example can be found in Austria, where the emperor's military forces, which had been cooperating with the "constituent assembly" formed in Vienna, put down the "October Rising" (the third wave of radical insurrection that year) by bombarding and then occupying the city. The constituent assembly was exiled, and many radical leaders were executed on the spot. Although Emperor Ferdinand I was convinced to step down, ceding his throne to his nephew Francis Joseph I, little else had changed. In the words of the historian Charles Breunig (1971, 1012), "to all intents and purposes the revolution in Vienna had been defeated by October, 1848."

The reversal suffered by reformers in Vienna was not unusual. By April 1849, the answer to the question that Tsar Nicholas I had posed to Queen Victoria—"What remains standing in Europe?"—was not, as he had suggested a year earlier, "Great Britain and Russia" but, instead, "almost everything." Revolution had swiftly been followed by reaction. Political reforms that seemed promising turned out, in practice, to change little (at least in the short term). Power remained vested in largely the same hands as before the revolutions of the previous spring.

In the previous 2012 edition of this book, we emphasized that the optimism expressed by some observers of the Arab Spring should be tempered by an understanding that "democratic" revolutions, like those in the 1848 Spring of Nations, are often followed by reaction and repression. We argued that regime change and political reform are difficult to predict, but that an understanding of such political change can be enhanced by the knowledge of the economic and cultural determinants of democracy, the strategic interaction between autocratic rulers and reform-minded opposition groups, the institutional determinants of policy outcomes in autocracies and democracies, and the effect of constitutional design on democratic consolidation, party competition, fiscal policy, and ethnic conflict.

Since 2012, comparative politics scholars have attempted to explain why the Arab Spring has not blossomed into a new wave of democracy. Of the fourteen countries that experienced widespread uprisings in 2011, only three—Egypt, Tunisia, and Yemen—have seen an incumbent autocrat removed as a result of domestic political pressure.[1] And of the three countries that saw an incumbent autocrat removed, only Tunisia has made progress toward becoming a democracy. Brownlee, Masoud, and Reynolds (2015) argue that the authoritarian regimes in the MENA region were, for the most part, able to withstand widespread uprisings because so many of them had significant oil wealth and systems of hereditary rule. They claim that oil wealth and hereditary rule "were each individually sufficient for authoritarian continuity—unless external powers intervened on behalf of the opposition" (p. 61). Importantly, the reasons why oil wealth and hereditary rule might help dictatorial leaders fend off challenges from below have been well understood by comparative politics scholars for some time, as evidenced by the discussion of the "resource curse" in Chapter 6 and the consequences of monarchy in Chapter 10 of this book.

Every generation seems to have its own motivation for studying comparative politics. The unfortunate truth is that each generation seems beset by a problem that is both devastatingly complex and extraordinarily urgent. For example, the Great Depression and the rise of fascism in Europe compelled comparative politics scholars in the middle of the last century to address two important topics. The

Photo by Christopher Furlong/Getty Images

Tunisian protesters demand the removal from office of government ministers associated with the ousted president in front of the ruling party's headquarters in Tunis on January 20, 2011.

---

1. The removal of Muammar al-Qaddafi from his position as leader of Libya in 2011 was heavily reliant on foreign intervention. It was only thanks to the sustained aerial bombing campaign conducted by NATO forces as part of Operation Unified Protector that Libyan rebels were able to topple Gaddafi.

Box 1.1   WHAT IS COMPARATIVE POLITICS?

Traditionally, the field of comparative politics has been characterized by many related, but distinct, endeavors. An influential comparative politics textbook by Joseph LaPalombara (1974) is titled *Politics Within Nations*. LaPalombara's title distinguishes **comparative politics** from **international politics**, which Hans Morgenthau (1948) famously calls *Politics Among Nations*. This definition of comparative politics, with its complementary definition of international politics, has one of the desirable features of all good scientific typologies in that it is logically exhaustive. By defining comparative and international politics in this way, these scholars have exhausted the logical possibilities involved in the study of politics—political phenomena occur either within countries or between countries.

> **Comparative politics** is the study of political phenomena that occur predominantly within countries. **International politics** is the study of political phenomena that occur predominantly between countries.

Still, all good scientific typologies should also be mutually exclusive. Whereas logical exhaustion implies that we have a place to categorize every entity that is observed, mutual exclusivity requires that it not be possible to assign any single observation to more than one category. Unfortunately, the typology just presented does not satisfy mutual exclusivity. A quick glance at today's newspapers clearly reveals that many contemporary political issues contain healthy doses of both "within country" and "between country" factors. As a consequence, the line between comparative and international politics is often blurred. This is particularly the case when it comes to studying how politics and economics interact. For example, ask yourself whether it is possible to fully understand American trade policy, say, toward China, without taking account of US domestic politics or to fully understand the ongoing crisis in the Euro zone without taking into account the domestic political situation in Greece. Similarly, many environmental issues involve factors both within and across a country's borders. In addition, because many violent antistate movements receive support from abroad, it is hard to categorize the study of revolutions, terrorism, and civil war as being solely in the domain of either comparative or international politics. Indeed, many insurgency movements have a separatist component that raises the very question of where the boundary between the "domestic" and "international" should lie.

Nonetheless, it is possible to retain the basic insights of LaPalombara and Morgenthau by simply saying that comparative politics is the study of political phenomena that are predominantly within country relationships and that international politics is the study of political phenomena that are predominantly between country relationships. This view of comparative politics, and political science more generally, is illustrated in Figure 1.1. As you can see, international politics addresses things like conflict, foreign policy, and international organizations that shape the relationships between countries. In contrast, comparative politics focuses on issues such as party systems, elections, identity politics, and interest group relations within countries like Brazil, China, France, and Nigeria. Scholars interested in political economy issues, such as migration, trade, central bank independence, and exchange rate policy, cross the divide between international and comparative politics.

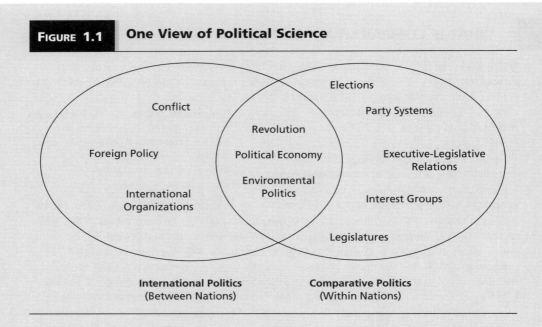

FIGURE 1.1   One View of Political Science

International Politics
(Between Nations)

Comparative Politics
(Within Nations)

Students in the United States may wonder where American politics fits into this description. In most political science departments in the United States, American politics is considered a separate subfield. Does the fact that American politics focuses predominantly on politics within the United States mean that it should be considered part of comparative politics? This is a question that, for some reason, generates quite heated debate among political scientists. Historically, a second traditional definition of comparative politics has been that it is the study of politics in every country except the one in which the student resides. Thus, according to this definition, comparative politics is the study of what economists often like to call "the rest of the world." This definition, however, seems rather silly to us because it means that the study

first was what governments can and should do to encourage stable economic growth. In other words, what, if anything, can governments do to protect their citizens from the devastating consequences of market instability? The second was how to design electoral institutions in such a way as to reduce the likelihood that political extremists who oppose democracy, like the Nazi Party in Germany's Weimar Republic, might be elected. Both of these topics remain central to the field of comparative politics today.

In the aftermath of World War II, decolonization and the onset of the Cold War combined to drive many comparative politics scholars to focus on the question of "political development." What, if anything, could be done to reduce political and economic instability of Nigerian politics is part of comparative politics unless one happens to be studying it in Nigeria, in which case it is simply "Nigerian politics." We leave it up to you to decide whether you think American politics should be considered part of comparative politics or not.

In addition to the two definitions just outlined, comparative politics has sometimes been defined as the study of politics using the method of comparison. In fact, as seen in Box 2.2, "The Comparative Method: An Overview and Critique" in Chapter 2, scholars of comparative politics who seek to define their subject in this way typically have a particular type of comparative method in mind. This tradition, which dates back at least as far as Aristotle's attempt to classify constitutional forms, seeks to answer questions about politics by comparing and contrasting attributes of different polities (predominantly city-states in Aristotle's day but nation-states today). Although this third definition is, to some extent, descriptively accurate, it is not particularly useful. As we show in Chapter 2, comparison is central to any and all scientific endeavors. As a result, defining comparative politics in terms of a "comparative" method would make it synonymous with political science itself. If this is the case, it makes one wonder why there are two phrases—*comparative politics* and *political science*—to describe the same thing.

We believe that comparative politics is best understood as the study of politics occurring predominantly within countries. As such, it is a rather vast field of research. For reasons that we explain later in this chapter, we choose not to focus on the politics of a single nation or a particular collection of nations in this book. Instead, we try to understand political behavior through the explicit comparison of important national-level attributes. In other words, we compare domestic political behavior from a cross-national perspective. As an example of our approach, we prefer to ask why some countries have two parties (like the United States) but others have many (like the Netherlands) rather than examine the party systems in the United States and the Netherlands separately. By taking this approach, we do not mean to suggest that the study of politics within individual countries should be excluded from the field of comparative politics. Nor do we mean to imply that cross-national comparison is a more worthy endeavor than studying a single country. Having said that, we believe that a comparison of national-level attributes is a reasonable introduction to comparative politics and one that will set a broad framework for the closer study of politics within individual polities at an advanced level.

in poor and underdeveloped countries? Research conducted at that time frequently focused on the proper relationship between the government and the market, with the central concerns of the day perhaps being best summarized in the title of Joseph Schumpeter's 1942 classic *Capitalism, Socialism, and Democracy*. The Cold War between the United States and the Soviet Union only heightened the urgency with which scholars struggled to understand the causes and consequences of communist revolutions in China and Cuba, as well as the political turmoil in places like Vietnam and Chile.

By the 1970s, economic instability, brought on by the Middle East oil crisis, returned to wealthy industrial countries. As a result, many comparative politics scholars revisited questions raised during the interwar years on their home turf of Western Europe. By now, however, the discussion had been narrowed somewhat because many scholars had come to accept the "postwar settlement" or "class compromise" that had essentially seen workers accept a capitalist economy and free trade in return for the expansion of the welfare state and other benefits. With the widespread acceptance of capitalist economies across Western Europe, researchers now turned their attention to how the specific variety of capitalism that existed in a particular country might influence that country's capacity to weather economic storms created elsewhere.

In the waning days of the twentieth century, attention turned to the fallout created by the end of the Cold War. Suddenly, dozens of countries in Eastern and Central Europe were negotiating the twin transitions from centrally planned economies to market-based ones and from one-party dictatorships to democracy. Now, in the twenty-first century, attention appears to be turning to the question of state authority. The Islamic State in Iraq and the Levant (ISIL), alternatively known as the Islamic State in Iraq and Syria (ISIS), proclaimed a worldwide caliphate in June 2014. In effect, ISIL now claims religious, political, and military authority over Muslims wherever they live in the world. Such a claim is a direct challenge to the primary organizing principle of the international system—sovereign states—that has been operative since the Peace of Westphalia in 1648. ISIL currently controls portions of Iraq and Syria, and has imposed Sharia law on the millions of people who live in these regions. The ensuing persecution, chaos, and violence, in combination with the fallout from the Syrian Civil War, have led many to flee the region, causing an immigration crisis in Europe.

As we discuss in Chapter 4, the "modern state" is understood as an organization that uses coercion and the threat of force to control the inhabitants in a given territory. ISIL's declaration of a worldwide caliphate, and, indeed, the behavior of violent insurgency groups around the world, constitutes a direct challenge to this conception of the modern state. It remains to be seen whether such developments constitute a lasting threat to the idea that a state is an entity that can successfully control the inhabitants in a well-defined territory. Recent developments suggest, though, that we should not take political order for granted. Research by anthropologists and archaeologists reminds us that the vast majority of our experience as a species has occurred within relatively small groups of hunter-gatherers and that violence within and between these groups was commonplace (Gat 2006). Societal order in large groups is something that needs to be explained, rather than assumed.

OVERVIEW OF THE BOOK

Political science is the study of politics in a scientific manner. It is easy to see that, as it stands, this definition of political science is not particularly informative. For example, what is politics? What is science? We explicitly address these questions in Chapters 2 and 3 of Part I. With these preliminaries out of the way, we begin to examine the substantive questions relating to the causes and consequences of democracy and dictatorship that are the book's central focus. In Part II we contrast democracies and dictatorships. Specifically, we explore the origins of the modern state and ask two questions that have been central to the study of comparative politics. First, why are some countries democracies and others dictatorships? And second, does it matter? In Part III we turn our attention to the different types of democracies and dictatorships that exist around the world. In particular, we examine the sometimes dizzying array of institutional forms that countries can adopt. Finally, in Part IV, we investigate how different types of democracy affect government performance and the survival of democracy itself.

Our goal in writing this book is to provide answers that are relevant to the problems motivating the study of comparative politics today and that are reliable—that is, built on the best practices of contemporary political scientists. In what follows, we highlight some of the questions and issues that we address in the upcoming chapters. These issues have been of long-standing interest to comparative political scientists and remain vitally important for understanding the contemporary world.

State Failure

Although state failure has long been recognized as one of the key sources of political and economic instability around the globe, the horrific events of September 11, 2001, have lent a new urgency to the need to understand the conditions under which states fail and the conditions under which such power vacuums might foster international terrorism. The reason for this is that the September 11 terrorist attacks were planned from Afghanistan—a failed state in which the Taliban provided sanctuary for al-Qaida to train terrorists and plan attacks against various targets around the world. In Chapter 4 we define what political scientists mean when they speak of the "state" and describe what life is like in two failed states, Somalia and Syria. To understand how one might fill the power vacuum that exists in failed states, it is necessary to understand the historical development of the modern state. What distinguishes the modern state from other forms of political organization? What led to its development? The rest of Chapter 4 focuses on addressing these types of questions.

Economic Determinants of Democracy

In October 2001 the United States responded to the September 11 terrorist attacks by invading Afghanistan to overthrow the Taliban. In addition to trying to capture Osama bin Laden and destroy al-Qaida's terrorist infrastructure, one of the stated goals of this attack was to replace the Taliban with a more democratic form of government. In order to establish democracy intentionally and successfully in countries like Afghanistan and Iraq, however, it is important that we first understand the factors that encourage or discourage the emergence and survival of democracy. Similarly, to comprehend the prospects for democracy in the MENA region, we must take account of both the specific political background of the countries in this part of the world and the considerable body of theoretical and empirical evidence that comparative political scientists have compiled on the determinants of democracy.

In Chapter 6 we examine how economic development and the structure of the economy influence the likelihood that a country will become and remain democratic. Some scholars have argued that countries are more likely to democratize as their economies become more modern—that is, less reliant on natural resource exports, more productive, more industrial, more highly educated, and so on. Other scholars have argued that such modernization may affect the survival of democracy but does not influence the emergence of democracy. In other words, they argue that modernization helps democracies stay democratic but does not help dictatorships become democratic. Although debate continues over the precise relationship between economic modernization and democracy, the fact that most of the countries affected by the Arab Spring do not fulfill many of the basic requirements of "modernization" means that comparative politics scholars on both sides of the debate would reach essentially the same conclusion regarding the prospects for democracy in the MENA region—they are poor. On a related note, many political scientists have argued that democracy is unlikely to arise in countries whose economies are dependent on natural resource extraction. If you find such arguments persuasive after reading Chapter 6, then the vast reservoirs of oil found in countries like Iraq and Libya should be viewed as a cause for concern, rather than hope, in regard to attempts to build democracy in these countries.

Cultural Determinants of Democracy

Over the years, many scholars have argued that democracy is incompatible with particular cultures. Exactly which cultures are thought to be bad for democracy tend to change from one time period to the next, depending on which countries in the world are democratic at a particular point in time. For example, Catholicism was seen as a hindrance to democracy during the 1950s and 1960s when few Catholic countries in the world were democratic. As Catholic countries in southern Europe and Latin America became democratic in the 1970s and 1980s, the earlier view began to wane. Today, of course, the culture that is deemed most antithetical to democracy is Islam. Again, the basic reason why people commonly view Islam as bad for democracy tends to be that they do not see many contemporary Islamic democracies. In fact, this is one of the reasons why the rapid rise in mass movements in many Muslim majority countries during the Arab Spring caught many observers by surprise. In Chapter 7 we examine the theoretical and empirical evidence behind arguments that some cultures are more suited for dictatorship than democracy. In doing so, we suggest that the type of after-the-fact (post hoc) theorizing that leads people to conclude, for example, that there must be something about Islam that discourages democracy because there aren't many predominantly Muslim democracies in the contemporary world should be treated with considerable skepticism.

If, after reading Chapters 6 and 7, you believe that the economic and cultural factors in countries like Iraq and Libya make democratization feasible, you might begin to wonder whether military force is the best way to bring it about. We do not examine the attempts of foreign countries to impose democracy by force in any great detail, but we do examine the process by which countries transition from dictatorship to democracy in Chapter 8. In particular, we look at bottom-up transitions to democracy, in which the people rise up as part of a popular revolution to overthrow the dictator, and top-down transitions, in which authoritarian elites introduce liberalization policies that ultimately lead to democracy. Our discussion in this chapter offers an explanation for why dictatorships frequently appear so stable, why popular revolutions are so rare, and why revolutions, when they do occur, nearly always come as a surprise even though they often appear so inevitable in hindsight. By focusing on the strategic interaction of elites and masses involved in top-down transitions, we also emphasize the important role that information, beliefs, and uncertainty can play in these types of democratic transitions.

What's So Good about Democracy Anyway?

Our time has been referred to as the "age of democracy." Even dictatorships spend a fair amount of time and energy paying lip service to the wonders of democracy. The benefits of democracy that many people speak of may be real, but political scientists like to reach conclusions on the basis of logic and evidence rather than conventional wisdom and ideology. As a result, we devote considerable effort in Chapters 9 through 11 to examining whether or not there is a sound basis for pursuing democracy in the first place.

In Chapter 9 we examine whether democracy makes a material difference in people's lives. Is economic growth higher in democracies than dictatorships? Do people live longer, healthier, and more educated lives in democracies than dictatorships? As we demonstrate, the picture that emerges from this literature is significantly more nuanced than the rhetoric that politicians around the world typically employ. Although democracies seldom perform poorly in regard to the level of material well-being that they provide their citizens, they frequently fail to outperform a substantial number of dictatorships.

One of the reasons why it is difficult to compare democracies and dictatorships and come up with clear-cut answers as to which perform better has to do with the fact that dictatorships come in many different forms. For example, personalist dictatorships, such as the one in North Korea under Kim Jong-un, function quite differently from, say, the hereditary monarchies of the Gulf states or the military juntas found in countries like Thailand. Accordingly, we devote Chapter 10 to examining how the institutional variation among dictatorships influences things like economic performance, regime stability, and the likelihood of democratic transitions.

In Chapter 11, we take a slightly different tack and examine whether the actual *process* of democracy has some inherently attractive properties that would make it morally or normatively appealing over and above any material benefits it might produce. The picture that emerges from the comparative politics literature on this matter may surprise you. The bottom line is that there is no support for the idea that there is an ideal form of political organization—and this includes democracy.

Institutional Design

If one were convinced that democracy was the best alternative for a country like Iraq, Egypt, or Libya, then the next logical question is how one should design such a democracy. Designing a democracy presumes that we know both how various democratic institutions work and what their consequences will be. In the remainder of this book, we examine what the comparative politics literature has to say in these regards.

In Chapter 12 we explore the significant differences that exist between parliamentary, presidential, and semi-presidential types of democracy. We pay particular attention to how governments form and survive in parliamentary and presidential democracies. In Chapter 13 we look at the dizzying variety of electoral systems that have been employed around the world and attempt to understand each of their strengths and weaknesses with respect to things like proportionality, ethnic accommodation, accountability, and minority representation. In Chapter 14 we examine party systems. In particular, we focus on how the choice of electoral system in a country combines with attributes of that country's social structure to determine both the number and types of parties that are likely to exist. In Chapter 15 we briefly examine other institutional ways in which democracies vary. Democracies can be federal or unitary, bicameral or unicameral, and they can differ in the extent to which they exhibit judicial independence. Federalism, bicameralism, and judicial independence can all be thought of as forms of checks and balances that create institutional veto players in a political system. As such, their causes and consequences are closely related, and it is for this reason that we consider them in the same chapter.

As Chapters 12 through 15 indicate, democracies around the world exhibit many different institutional forms. But do these different institutional forms produce different outcomes? This is what we examine in Chapter 16 in Part IV of the book. We begin by looking at the normative and material consequences associated with different types of democracies. Are the governments in some types of democracy more accountable, representative, and responsive than the governments in other types of democracy? What are the expected economic consequences associated with different types of democracy? We then review what the comparative politics literature has to say about how the institutions adopted by a country affect the survival of democracy. Many scholars have argued that the kind of ethnic and religious diversity observed in countries like Iraq is a destabilizing force in democracies. But do these types of divisions make democratic stability impossible, or are there institutional mechanisms that can be put in place that might mitigate the effects of ethnic and religious differences? In addition to examining how institutions might mitigate the effects of ethnic and religious diversity, we also look at whether a country's choice of democratic regime—parliamentary or presidential—influences the prospects for democratic survival. There is considerable evidence that parliamentary democracies survive significantly longer than presidential democracies. But if this is true, one might wonder, what explains the persistence of democracy in the United States? Comparative politics scholars have an answer to this question, but to appreciate it, we must be willing to travel through both time and space.

THE APPROACH TAKEN IN THIS BOOK

Many introductory comparative politics texts are organized around a sequence of individual country studies. Typically, one starts with Britain, before moving on to France and Germany. Next it's on to Russia, Japan, India, Brazil, and, nearly always, Nigeria. Occasionally, China and Mexico might make an appearance somewhere along the line. We believe that this approach has some limitations if the goal of an introductory class is to teach something other than descriptive information about a tiny fraction of the world's countries. The eight countries that make up the domain of a typical comparative politics textbook constitute little more than 4 percent of the world's 193 widely recognized independent states. Why should we focus on these countries and not others? The response from the authors of these textbooks might be that these countries are, in some sense, either the most important or the most representative countries in the world. We find the first of these claims—that they are the most important countries—to be displeasing and the second—that they are the most representative countries—to be questionable.

An introductory class in comparative politics has many goals. We believe that it should stimulate students' interest in the particular subject matter and introduce them to the principal concerns and findings of the field. It should also give students an insight into the extent to which there is consensus or ongoing debate concerning those findings. Consequently, we have endeavored to focus our attention on the questions that comparative politics scholars have historically considered vitally important and those on which there is some growing consensus. It is undeniable that the causes and consequences of democracy and dictatorship are a central issue in comparative politics. It is for this reason that they are a central concern of our book. Less obvious perhaps is a growing consensus regarding the causes and consequences of particular sets of autocratic and democratic institutions. We endeavor both to make this emerging consensus clearer and to provide the analytical tools required to critically engage it.

In light of the types of research questions that we want to address here, the traditional series of country studies found in most textbooks would not provide the most useful approach. First, very few countries exhibit sufficient variation across time with their experience of democracy to allow questions about democracy's causes and consequences to be answered by a single country study. Similarly, very few countries experience sufficient variation in their institutions across time to give us much leverage in gaining an understanding of their causes and consequences. For example, countries that adopt presidentialism or a particular set of electoral laws tend to retain these choices for long periods of time. In fact, when forced to choose those institutions again (for example, at the end of an authoritarian interruption), countries frequently make the same choice. It is for these reasons that comparisons across countries are important for understanding the research questions that are at the heart of this book—they provide the much-needed variation not often found in any one country.

Second, we—personally—do not possess the required memory and attentiveness to remember the relevant details of particular countries' institutions and cultures across many weeks, and we, perhaps incorrectly, do not expect our students to either. Overall, we are not hopeful that we, or our students, can be expected in week ten of the semester when studying the intricacies of the Russian Duma to make comparisons with the Japanese Diet or the British House of Commons studied weeks earlier. Even if we could retain the relevant information across the course of a semester, it is not obvious that eight or ten countries would produce a sufficiently large variety of socioeconomic and institutional experiences to allow us to adequately evaluate the hypotheses that are central to the comparative politics subfield and this book. Given that our primary concern in this textbook surrounds institutional, social, economic, and cultural factors that remain fairly constant across time within countries, the most a comparison of a relatively small number of observations could accomplish is to provide a collection of confirming cases. In Chapter 2 we discuss why such a practice is problematic from the standpoint of the scientific method.

We also believe that the traditional approach adopted by most textbooks has the unfortunate consequence of creating a significant disjuncture between what comparative political scientists teach students and what these scholars actually do for a living. Comparative politics scholars do sometimes engage in descriptive exercises such as detailing how laws are made, how institutions function, or who has power in various countries. This is the traditional subject matter of most textbooks. However, it is much more common for comparative scholars to spend their time constructing and testing theories about political phenomena in the world. In reality, they are primarily interested in explaining, rather than describing, why politics is organized along ethnic lines in some countries but class lines in others, or why some countries are democracies but others dictatorships. Some textbook authors seem reluctant to present this sort of material to students because they believe it to be too complicated. However, we strongly believe that comparative political science is not rocket science. The fact that it is only relatively recently that the scientific method has begun to be applied to the study of political phenomena suggests to us that students should be able to engage the political science literature with relative ease. Indeed, we believe that, compared with other disciplines such as physics or mathematics, there is unusual room for students actually to make significant contributions to the accumulation of knowledge in comparative political science. As a result, one of the goals of our book is to introduce you to what comparative political scientists spend most of their time doing and to begin to give you the tools to contribute to the debates in our discipline.[2]

KEY CONCEPTS

comparative politics *5*
international politics *5*

---

2. Brambor, Clark, and Golder (2006, 2007); Clark and Reichert (1998); Uzonyi, Souva, and Golder (2012); Golder and Lloyd (2014); and Golder and Thomas (2014) are examples of original research published in scientific journals in which our own undergraduate students have played significant roles.

2 What Is Science?

The wrong view of science betrays itself in the craving to be right; for it is not his possession of knowledge, of irrefutable truth, that makes the man of science, but his persistent and recklessly critical quest for truth.

Sir Karl Popper, *The Logic of Scientific Discovery*

So I left him, saying to myself, as I went away: Well, although I do not suppose that either of us knows anything really beautiful and good, I am better off than he is—for he knows nothing, and thinks that he knows. I neither know nor think that I know. In this latter particular, then, I seem to have slightly the advantage of him.

Socrates, in Plato's *Apology*

Test everything. Keep what is good.

Saint Paul, *First Letter to the Thessalonians*

OVERVIEW

- Comparative politics is the subfield of political science that focuses primarily on politics within countries. In Chapter 3 we define and examine the nature of politics. In this chapter we define and examine the nature of science.

- Science is a strategy for understanding and explaining the social and natural world that emphasizes the use of statements that can be examined to see whether they are wrong.

- Scientific explanations should explain previously puzzling facts, be logically consistent, and produce (many) potentially falsifiable predictions.

- All scientific explanations are tentative. We accept some explanations as provisionally true when they have withstood vigorous attempts at refutation more successfully than competing explanations.

Consider the following five statements. What do they all have in common?

1. Science is a collection of facts that tell us what we know about the world.
2. A scientific theory is one that has been proven.
3. "The sun revolves around the earth" is not a scientific statement.
4. If my theory is correct, then I should observe that rich countries are more likely to be democracies. I do observe that rich countries are more likely to be democracies. Therefore, my theory is correct.
5. Politics cannot be studied in a scientific manner.

The common element in these statements is that they are all, in some sense, wrong. Science is not a collection of facts that tell us what we know about the world. Scientific theories cannot be proven; thus, a scientific theory is not one that has been proven. The statement that the sun revolves around the earth is a scientific statement (even though it is false). The argument outlined in statement 4 is logically invalid; therefore, I cannot conclude that my theory is correct. And finally, politics can be studied in a scientific manner. We suspect that many of you will have thought that at least some of these statements were correct. To know why all of these statements about science are wrong, you will need to continue reading this chapter.

Science certainly has its detractors, largely because of what was experienced in the twentieth century. Some horrendous things were either done in the name of science or "justified" on scientific grounds or, at a minimum, made possible by science. Although we should never close our eyes to the harm that is sometimes done with science, we believe that it is as much a mistake to blame science for what some scientists have done in its name as it is to blame religion for what some believers have done in its name.

But what is science? First and foremost, science is a method; however, it is also a culture. The epigraphs at the start of this chapter are meant to capture what we might call the "culture" of science. Some of the negative views of science come from what people perceive the culture of science to be—cold, calculating, self-assured, arrogant, and, perhaps, even offensive. We believe, however, that at its best, the culture of science displays the characteristics encouraged by the otherwise very different thinkers who are quoted. The scientific method is, at its very core, a critical method, and those reflective individuals who use it are much more likely to be humbled than emboldened. Sir Karl Popper ([1959] 2003) reminds us that science is not a static set of beliefs to be conserved and that all knowledge is tentative. Socrates reminds us that an acute awareness of our own ignorance is always the first step toward knowledge. Saint Paul offers hope that our willingness to test all of our ideas will leave us something good to hang on to. As we'll demonstrate in this chapter, science isn't about certainty, it isn't merely about the orderly collection of facts, and it isn't about invoking authority to protect our ideas from uncomfortable evidence. Instead, science is about asking tough questions and providing answers that invite criticism. Science is about recognizing the limits of our knowledge without lapsing into irresponsible cynicism. And science is about using the best logic, methods, and evidence available to provide answers today, even though we recognize that they may be overturned tomorrow.

Comparative politics is a subfield of political science. But what exactly is political science? Well, it is the study of politics in a scientific way. How's that for a tautology? It is easy to see that, as it stands, this definition is not particularly informative. For example, what is politics? And what is science? In the next chapter we answer the first of these questions and seek to demarcate politics from other forms of social phenomena. In this chapter, though, we focus on the second question—what is science? Our goal is to provide an answer that resembles the way most practicing scientists would answer this question.

WHAT IS SCIENCE?

Is science simply a body of knowledge or a collection of facts, as many of us learn in high school? While there was a time when many scientists may have defined science in this way, this definition is fundamentally unsatisfactory. If this definition of science were accurate, then many of the claims about how the universe worked, such as those developed through Newtonian physics, would now have to be called unscientific, because they have been replaced by claims based on more recent theories, such as Einstein's theory of relativity. Moreover, if science were simply a collection of statements about how the world works, then we would not be able to appeal to science to justify our knowledge of the world without falling into the following circular reasoning:

> "Science is a collection of statements about how the world works."
> "How do we know if these statements are accurate?"
> "Well, of course they're accurate! They're scientific!"

The body of knowledge that we call "scientific" may well be a product of science, but it is not science itself. Rather, science is a method for provisionally understanding the world. The reason for saying "provisionally" will become clear shortly. Science is one answer to the central question in epistemology (the study of knowledge): "How do we know what we know?" The scientist's answer to that question is, "Because we have subjected our ideas to the scientific method." Science, as Karl Popper indicates in one of the epigraphs at the start of this chapter, is the quest for knowledge. At this point, you might say that there are many ways to seek knowledge. Does this mean that meditation, reading scripture, and gazing at sunsets are all scientific activities? Although we agree that these are all ways of seeking knowledge, none of them is scientific. Science is a particular quest for knowledge. To use Popper's phrase, it is the "recklessly critical" pursuit of knowledge, in which the scientist continually subjects her ideas to the cold light of logic and evidence.

Although science is not the only route to knowledge, it may be unique in its emphasis on self-criticism. Scientists, like other scholars, can derive their propositions from an infinite number of sources. For example, Gregory Derry (1999) tells the story of how August Kekulé made an extremely important scientific breakthrough while hallucinating—half asleep—in front of the fireplace in his laboratory one night. He had spent days struggling to understand the spatial arrangement of atoms in a benzene molecule. In a state of mental and physical exhaustion, his answer appeared to him as he "saw" swirls of atoms joined in a particular formation dancing among the embers of his fireplace. In a flash of inspiration, he saw how the pieces of the puzzle with which he had been struggling fit together. This inspired understanding of the physical properties of organic compounds did not become a part of science that night, though. It did so only after the implications of his vision had withstood the critical and sober onslaught that came with the light of day. Thus, although flashes of insight can come from a variety of sources, science begins only when one asks, "If that is true, what else ought to be true?" And it ends—if ever—when researchers are satisfied that they have taken every reasonable pain to show that the implications of the insight are false and have failed to do so. Even then, however, the best answer is not the final answer—it is just the best "so far."

So, science is the quest for knowledge that relies on criticism. The thing that allows for criticism is the possibility that our claims, theories, hypotheses, ideas, and the like could be wrong. Thus, what distinguishes science from "non-science" is that scientific statements must be **falsifiable**—there must be some imaginable observation or set of observations that could falsify or refute them. This does not mean that a scientific statement will ever be falsified, just that there must be a possibility that it could be falsified if the "right" observation came along. Only if a statement is potentially testable is it scientific. We deliberately say "potentially testable" because a statement does not have to have been tested to be scientific; all that is required is that we can conceive of a way to test it.[1]

> Scientific statements must be **falsifiable**. This means that they are potentially testable—there must be some imaginable observation that could falsify or refute them.

What sorts of statements are not falsifiable? Tautologies are not falsifiable because they are true by definition. For example, the statement "Triangles have three sides" is a **tautology**. It is simply not possible ever to observe a triangle that does not have three sides because *by definition* if an object does not have three sides, it is not a triangle. It is easy to see that this statement is not testable and hence unscientific. Tautologies, though, are not always so easy to spot. Consider the following statement: "Strong states are able to overcome special interests in order to implement policies that are best for the nation." Is this a tautology? This statement may be true, but unless we can think of a way to identify a strong state without referring to its ability to overcome special interests, then it is just a definition

> A **tautology** is a statement that is true by definition.

---

1. Indeed, a statement can be scientific even if we do not currently have the data or the technical equipment to test it. Our upcoming discussion of Einstein's special theory of relativity illustrates this point quite clearly.

and is, therefore, unscientific. In other words, whether this particular statement is scientific depends on how strong states are defined.

Other statements or hypotheses are not falsifiable, not because they are tautological, but because they refer to inherently unobservable phenomena. For example, the claims "God exists" and "God created the world" are not falsifiable because they cannot be tested; as a result, they are unscientific. Note that these claims may well be true, but it is important to recognize that science has nothing to do with the truth or falsity of statements. All that is required for a statement to be scientific is that it be falsifiable. It should be clear from this that we are not claiming that "nonscience" is nonsense or that it lacks meaning—this would clearly be a mistake. Nonfalsifiable statements like "God exists" may very well be true and have important and meaningful consequences—our claim is simply that they do not form a part of science. Having defined science as a critical method for learning about the world, we can now evaluate the basic elements of the scientific method in more detail.

THE SCIENTIFIC METHOD

Although there is no **scientific method** clearly written down that is followed by all scientists, it is possible to characterize the basic features of the scientific method in the following manner.

> The **scientific method** describes the process by which scientists learn about the world.

Step 1: Question

The first step in the scientific process is to observe the world and come up with a question or puzzle. The very need for a theory or explanation begins when we observe something that is so unexpected or surprising that we ask, "Why did that occur?" Note that the surprise that greets such an observation, and that makes the observation a puzzle worth exploring, implies that the observation does not match some prior expectation or theory that we held about how the world works. Thus, we always have a preexisting theory or expectation when we observe the world; if we did not have one, we could never be surprised, and there would be no puzzles.

Step 2: Theory or Model

Once we have observed something puzzling, the next step is to come up with a theory or model to explain it. In what follows, we will talk of theories, models, and explanations interchangeably. Scientists use the word **theory** to describe a set of logically consistent state-

> A **theory** is a set of logically consistent statements that tell us why the things that we observe occur. A theory is sometimes referred to as a model or an explanation.

ments that tell us why the things that we observe occur. It is important that these statements be logically consistent; otherwise we have no way of determining what their empirical predictions will be and, hence, no way to test them. Put differently, theories that are logically inconsistent should not, indeed cannot, be tested, because we have no way of knowing what observations would truly falsify them.

Most philosophers of science assume that all phenomena occur as a result of some recurring process. The principle of the **uniformity of nature** asserts that nature's operating mechanisms are unchanging in the sense that if X causes Y today, then it will also cause Y tomorrow and the next day and so on. If it does not, then we should not consider X a cause. Be careful to note that the principle of uniformity is a statement not that nature is unchanging, only that the laws of nature do not change (although our understanding of those laws will likely change over time). This is an important principle, because if this principle is rejected, we must accept the possibility that things "just happen." That is, we must accept that things happen for no reason. Casual observation of the sometimes maddening world around us suggests that this may, indeed, be true, but it is the job of scientists to attempt to impose order on the apparent chaos around them. In the social world, this process often begins by dividing the behavior we observe into systematic and unsystematic components. The social scientist then focuses her attention on explaining only the systematic components.[2]

> The principle of the **uniformity of nature** asserts that nature's operating mechanisms are unchanging in the sense that if X causes Y today, then it will also cause Y tomorrow and the next day and so on.

So what should theories or models look like? It is useful to think of our starting puzzle or observation as the end result of some previously unknown process (Lave and March 1975). We can then speculate about what (hidden) processes might have produced such a result. In effect, we try to imagine a prior world that, if it had existed, would have produced the otherwise puzzling observation before us. This prior world then becomes our model explaining the observation.

Notice that this process of imagining prior worlds is one place—but surely not the only one—where imagination and creativity enter the scientific process. What scientists do to stimulate this creative process is itself not part of the scientific method. Essentially, anything goes. Nobel Prize–winning physicist Richard Feynman, who himself spent a lot of time hanging out in bars and playing Brazilian hand drums, describes science as "imagination in a straightjacket"—it is imagination constrained by what we already know about the world (Feynman 1967). Consequently, he suggests that there is no point engaging in flights of fancy about things that we know cannot exist (like antigravity machines). Whatever means we use to stimulate speculation about a prior world, if we can show through logical deduction that *if* that prior world existed, it would have produced the puzzling observation we started with, then we have a theory, or model. Note that we have only *a* theory; we do not necessarily have *the* theory. This is why we continually test the implications of our theory.

The model that we end up with will necessarily be a simplified picture of the world. It is impossible to have a descriptively accurate model of the world as an infinite number of

---

2. This suggests that you should be wary of anyone who tells you that you need to know everything before you can know anything.

details would have to be captured in such a model. Pure description is impossible—models are always going to leave many things out. As with all arts, much of the skill of modeling is in deciding what to leave out and what to keep in. A good model contains only what is needed to explain the phenomenon that puzzles us and nothing else. If we made our models too complex, we would have no way of knowing which elements were crucial for explaining the puzzling observation that we started with and which were superfluous. The purpose of a model is not to describe the world but to explain it, so descriptive accuracy is not a core value in model building. Details are important only to the extent that they are crucial to what we are trying to explain. For example, if we are interested in explaining an aircraft's response to turbulence, it is not important whether our model of the aircraft includes LCD screens on the back of the passengers' seats. In fact, such inconsequential details can easily distract our attention from the question at hand. Another benefit of simple models is that they invite falsification because they make it very clear what we should not observe. The more amendments and conditions placed on an explanation, the easier it is for scholars to dismiss apparently contradictory evidence.

It is important to remember that models are always developed with a specific goal in mind. This means that we should evaluate models in terms of how useful they are for achieving that goal. As the late Dutch economist Henri Theil (1971) once said, "models should be used, not believed." To emphasize this point, it can be helpful to think of models as being similar to maps. Like models, maps are simplified pictures of the world designed for a specific purpose. Consider the subway map of any city. The subway map is always a simplification of the city and, indeed, an inaccurate simplification in the sense that it provides inaccurate information about the relative distances between, and geographic positions of, particular locations. Despite this, the map is incredibly useful if one's goal is to move efficiently around the city using the subway system—the purpose for which the map was designed. Of course, this map would be less useful if one's goal was to walk above ground from one location to another. As with a map, one must not judge the value of a model in some abstract sense but in terms of how well it helps us understand some particular aspect of the world and explain it to others.

Step 3: Implications (Hypotheses)

Once we have a model, the third step in the scientific process is to deduce implications from the model other than those that we initially set out to explain. Why do we say "other than those that we initially set out to explain"? Well, presumably the model that we construct will provide a logical explanation for the puzzling observation that we started with; after all, that is what it was designed to do! In other words, there is no way that a model can ever be falsified if only the observations that were employed to develop the model in the first place are used to test it. To actually test the model and allow for the possibility that it will be falsified, we will have to find other implications that can be deduced from it. We must ask ourselves, "If the prior world that we created to explain the phenomena that we originally found puzzling really did exist, what else ought to exist? What else should we be able to observe?"

As before, there is often room for incredible imagination here, because the complete list of logical implications of a model is seldom self-evident.

Good models are those that produce many different implications. This is so because each prediction represents another opportunity for the model to fail and, therefore, makes the model easier to falsify. This is good because if the model fails to be falsified, we gain more confidence in its usefulness. Fertile models—models with many implications—are also desirable because they encourage the synthesis of knowledge by encouraging us to see connections between ostensibly disparate events. Good models also produce surprising implications—they tell us something we would not know in the absence of the model. Models are not particularly useful if they tell us only what we already know. Surprise, however, is best appreciated in small doses. If every implication of a model is surprising, then either everything we thought about the world is wrong, or the model is.

Step 4: Observe the World (Test Hypotheses)

The fourth step is to examine whether the implications of the model are consistent with observation. Remember that the goal is not to dogmatically uphold the implications of our model or defend them in order to prove how right they are. On the contrary, we should try our best to falsify them, because it is only after a theory has withstood these attempts to overthrow it that we can reasonably start to have confidence in it. Although as many of the model's implications as possible should be tested, testing those that are most likely to be falsified is particularly important. Always submit a model to the harshest test that you can devise.

It is standard practice to stop and ask if other models—models that describe altogether different processes—might also explain the phenomena of interest. When this is the case (and it almost always is), it is incumbent upon the scientist to compare the implications of those other models with the implications of her own model. Although it is always the case that competing models have some of the same implications (otherwise they could not explain the same observations to begin with), it is typically the case that they will differ in some of their implications (otherwise they are not different models). The trick for a researcher is to identify these points of conflict between the different models and identify the relevant observations in the real world that would help her decide between them. This is what scientists refer to as a **critical test**. Ultimately, if a critical test is possible, observation will prove decisive in choosing between the models. This is because we know that there is only one world and the creative scientist has managed to get competing theories to say contradictory things about it—only one of the models can be consistent with the real world.

> A **critical test** allows the analyst to use observation to distinguish between two or more competing explanations of the same phenomenon.

Step 5: Evaluation

If we observe the implications deduced from our theory, we say that our theory has been corroborated. Note that we cannot say that our theory has been verified or proven. This

Box 2.1

AN EXAMPLE OF THE SCIENTIFIC PROCESS

The Case of Smart Female Athletes

Because student athletes often miss classes to compete out of state, they frequently submit a letter from the athletic director asking for cooperation from their professors. Over the years, a certain professor has noticed through casual observation that women engaged in athletic competition frequently perform better academically than the average student. It is puzzling why female athletes would perform better in spite of missing classes. Can you think of a model—a process—that might produce such a puzzling observation?

You might start with the following conjecture:

- Female athletes are smart.

This is an explanation, but it is not a particularly good one. For example, it comes very close to simply restating the observation to be explained. One thing that could improve the explanation is to make it more general. This might lead you to a new explanation:

- Athletes are smart.

This model is certainly more general (but not necessarily more correct). Still, there are at least two problems with this model as things stand. First, it has no sense of process; it basically says that athletes share some inherent quality of smartness that leads them to perform better academically. In effect, this only pushes the phenomenon to be explained back one step; that is, we now need to know why athletes are smart. Second, the model comes close to being a tautology. It essentially says that athletes perform better academically because they are defined as being smart. This is problematic, as we saw earlier, because tautologies are not falsifiable—they cannot be tested; hence, they are not part of the scientific endeavor.

This might lead you to look for a new explanation or model that includes some sort of process that makes female athletes appear smart. You might come up with the following model:

- Being a good athlete requires a lot of hard work; performing well academically in college requires a lot of work. Students who develop a strong work ethic in athletics are able to translate this to their studies.

This is a much more satisfying model because it provides a process or mechanism explaining why female athletes might be more academically successful than other students. An appealing feature of the model is that the logic of the argument applies not only to female athletes but to any athlete. Indeed, it applies to any person involved in an activity that rewards hard work. Thus, we might generalize this model by removing the specific reference to athletes:

- **Work Ethic Theory:** Some activities provide a clear, immediate, and tangible reward for hard work—in fact, they may provide an external stimulus to work hard (coaches shouting through bullhorns, manipulating rewards and punishments based on effort, and so on). Individuals who engage in these activities develop a habit of working hard and so will be successful in other areas of life as well.

At this point, you should stop and ask yourself whether there are any alternative explanations for why female athletes are successful. Can you think of any? One alternative explanation is the following:

- **Excellence Theory:** Everyone wants to feel successful, but some people go long periods without success and become discouraged. Those individuals who experience success in one area of their life (perhaps based on talent, rather than hard work) develop a "taste" for it and devise strategies to be successful in other parts of their life. Anyone who achieves success in nonacademic areas, such as athletics, will be more motivated to succeed in class.

Another alternative explanation is the following:

- **Gender Theory:** In many social and academic settings, women are treated differently from men. This differential treatment often leads women to draw inferences that certain activities are "not for them." Because many athletic endeavors are gender specific, they provide an environment for women to develop their potential free from the stultifying effects of gender bias. The resulting sense of efficacy and autonomy encourages success when these women return to gendered environments like the classroom.

We now have three different or competing models, all of which explain the puzzling observation that we started with. But how can one evaluate which model is best? One way is to test some of the implications that can be derived from these theories. In particular, we would like to find some new question(s) to which the three models give different answers. In other words, we would like to conduct a critical test that would allow us to choose among the alternative reasonable models.

We might start by wondering whether being an athlete helps the academic performance of women more than men. Whereas the Work Ethic Theory and the Excellence Theory both predict that being an athlete will help men and women equally, the Gender Theory predicts that female athletes will perform better than nonathletic women but that male athletes will have no advantage over nonathletic men. Thus, collecting information on how well male and female athletes perform in class relative to male and female nonathletes, respectively, would allow us to distinguish between the Gender Theory and the other theories.

But how can we distinguish between the Excellence Theory and the Work Ethic Theory? One difficulty frequently encountered when trying to devise critical tests is that alternative theories do not always produce clearly differentiated predictions. For example, we just saw that the Excellence Theory and the Work Ethic Theory both predict that athletics will help men and women academically. It turns out that these two theories have other predictions in common as well. The Excellence Theory clearly suggests that success in any nonacademic area of life is likely to encourage academic success. In other words, the Excellence Theory predicts that academic success will be associated with success in other areas of life. The problem is that success in many of these nonacademic areas may require hard work. As a result, if we observe, for instance, accomplished musicians performing well in our political science classes, it will be difficult to discern whether this is because they learned the value of hard work in music and transferred it to political science (Work Ethic Theory) or because they developed a "taste" for success as musicians that then inspired success in political science (Excellence Theory). In effect, the Excellence Theory and the Work Ethic Theory both predict that academic success will be associated with success in other areas of life.

If we want to distinguish between the Work Ethic Theory and the Excellence Theory, we need to imagine observations in which they produce different expectations. Sometimes, this requires further development of a theory. For example, we might expand the Excellence Theory to say that those people who develop a taste for excellence also develop a more competitive spirit. If this is true, then the Excellence Theory would predict that student athletes are likely to be more competitive and will perform better than other students even when playing relatively frivolous board games. Since even the most driven athletes are not likely to devote time to training for board games, the Work Ethic Theory predicts that athletes will perform the same as nonathletes in such trivial pursuits. Thus, we could look at the performance of athletes and nonathletes at board games to distinguish between the Excellence Theory and the Work Ethic Theory.

The three critical tests that we have come up with and their predictions are listed in Table 2.1. All that is now required is to collect the appropriate data and decide which model, if any, is best.

It is worth noting that there is considerable overlap between the predictions of our three theories. This is often the case in political science settings as well. The crucial point is not that each theory should yield a complete set of unique predictions, but that our theories should have sufficiently many distinct predictions that we can use observation to help us make decisions about which theories to embrace, however tentatively. Table 2.1 lists just some of the predictions that might help us to distinguish between the three theories outlined above. Can you think of any more?

Table 2.1   Three Critical Tests

Question	Theory		
	Gender	Excellence	Work ethic
Will athletics help women more than men?	Yes	No	No
Is academic success associated with success in other areas of life?	No	Yes	Yes
Are female athletes more successful at board games than women who are not athletes?	Yes	Yes	No

important point is one that we will return to in more detail in the next section of this chapter.[3] The fact that we can never prove a scientific explanation is why we earlier called science a method for "provisionally" understanding the world. Our theory may or may not be true. All we can conclude, if observations are consistent with our theoretical implications, is that our theory has not yet been falsified; we cannot rule out that it will not be falsified the next time it is tested. As you can see, the scientific method is an inherently critical method when it is "successful" (when a theory's predictions seem to be borne out), because it is precisely under these circumstances that it is most cautious in the claims that it makes.

Although we cannot ever prove our theories, we can claim that some theories are better corroborated than others. As a result, we can have more confidence in their conclusions. One might think that a theory that has been subjected to multiple tests is better corroborated than one that has not been subjected to many tests at all. However, this is not always the case. If we keep testing the same implication over and over again, it is not clear how much an additional test actually adds to the degree to which the theory is corroborated. What really matters is not so much how many times a theory has been corroborated, but the severity and variety of the tests to which it has been subjected. This, in turn, will depend on the degree to which the theory is falsifiable. Again, this is why we like our models to be simple and have multiple implications. In general, we will have more confidence in a theory that has survived a few harsh tests than a theory that has survived many easy ones. This is why scientists often talk about the world as if it were black-and-white rather than gray. Bold statements should be interpreted not as scientific hubris but rather as attempts to invite criticism—they are easier to falsify.

What happens if we do not observe the implications deduced from our theory? Can we conclude that our theory is incorrect based on one observation? The answer is "probably not." It is entirely possible that we have not observed and measured the world without error. Moreover, if we believe that human behavior is inherently probabilistic, then we might not want to reject theories on the basis of a single observation. In a world in which our tests are potentially fallible, we should not relegate a theory to the dustbin of intellectual history the minute one of its implications is shown to be false. Instead, we must weigh the number, severity, and quality of the tests that the theory's implications are subjected to and make a judgment. And most important, this judgment should be made with an eye toward what would replace the theory should we decide to discard it. This is why some scientists say that it takes a theory to kill a theory. Further, if we do embrace a new theory and disregard an alternative, it should be because the new theory is more consistent with all of the implications of both theories. Developing a new theory that explains the facts that the old theory found

---

3. Many scientists, however, slip into the language of verification when reporting their results. Instead of simply saying that their test has failed to falsify their hypotheses or is consistent with their theory, they will claim that the test has shown that their theory is correct. For example, they might claim that their test shows that wealth causes democracies to live longer when, in fact, all they can conclude is that they were unable to falsify the claim that wealth causes democracies to live longer.

inconvenient without also explaining the many facts that the old theory accurately predicted is called *ad hoc* explanation. Because this practice does not expose the new theory to falsification as strenuously as it does the old theory, it is not consistent with sound scientific practice.

AN INTRODUCTION TO LOGIC

In the previous section, we talked in a rather casual way about constructing and testing scientific explanations. In order to better appreciate the important connection between theory construction and theory testing, it is useful to devote some time to the study of logic. The study of logic is, first and foremost, about learning to be careful about how we construct and evaluate arguments.

Throughout our lives, we are confronted by people trying to convince us of certain things through arguments. Politicians make arguments as to why we should vote for their party rather than the party of their opponents. National leaders provide arguments for why certain policies should be implemented or abandoned. Lawyers make arguments as to why certain individuals should be found guilty or innocent. Professors make arguments as to why students should spend more time in the library and in class rather than at parties. It is important for you to know when these arguments are logically valid and when they are not. If you cannot distinguish between a valid and an invalid argument, other people will be able to manipulate and exploit you. You will be one of life's suckers. In this section, we give you some tools to determine whether an argument is valid or not.

Valid and Invalid Arguments

What is an argument? An **argument** is a set of logically connected statements, typically in the form of a set of **premises** and a **conclusion**. An argument is **valid** when accepting its premises compels us to accept its conclusions. An argument is **invalid** if, when we accept the premises of an argument, we are free to accept or reject its conclusions. One way to represent an argument is in the form of a **categorical syllogism** that consists of a major premise, a minor premise, and a conclusion. The major premise is typically presented as a conditional statement, such as "If *P*, then *Q*." The "if" part of the conditional statement (in this case "If *P*") is called the *antecedent*, whereas the "then" part of it (in this case "then *Q*") is called the *consequent*. An example of a conditional statement is "If a country is wealthy [antecedent], then it will be a democracy [consequent]." The minor premise consists of a claim about either the antecedent or the consequent in the conditional statement (major premise). The conclusion is a claim that is thought to be supported by the premises.

> An **argument** is a set of logically connected statements, typically in the form of a set of premises and a conclusion. A **premise** is a statement that is presumed to be true within the context of an argument leading to a conclusion. A **conclusion** in an argument is a claim that is thought to be supported by the premises. A **valid argument** is one in which, if you accept the premises, you are compelled to accept the conclusion. An **invalid argument** is one in which, if you accept the premises, you are free to accept or reject the conclusion. A **categorical syllogism** is a specific type of argument that consists of a major premise, a minor premise, and a conclusion.

TABLE 2.2	Affirming the Antecedent: A Valid Argument	
	General form	**Specific example**
Major premise	If *P*, then *Q*	If a country is wealthy, then it will be a democracy.
Minor premise	*P*	The country is wealthy.
Conclusion	Therefore, *Q*.	Therefore, the country will be a democracy.

Four types of conditional argument can be represented with a syllogism—arguments that affirm or deny the antecedent and those that affirm or deny the consequent. Which of these four types of argument are valid, and which are invalid? Recall that a valid argument is one such that if you accept that the premises are true, then you are compelled to accept the conclusion as true. Let's start by considering what happens when we affirm the antecedent. An example is shown in Table 2.2.

The major premise states, "If *P* is true, then *Q* must be true." The minor premise says that "*P* is true." Together, these premises compel us to accept that the conclusion is true. As a result, the argument is valid. In other words, the major premise states, "If a country is wealthy [antecedent], then it will be a democracy [consequent]." The minor premise says, "The observed country is wealthy." It logically follows from this that the observed country must be a democracy. To see why this type of argument is valid, consider the general form of this argument in set-theoretic form. This is shown in Figure 2.1. The major premise indicates that the set of cases where *P* occurs is a subset of the cases where *Q* occurs. The minor premise maintains that *P* does occur. Figure 2.1 clearly shows that if the case in question is in *P*, as the minor premise affirms, then the case must also be in *Q*. Thus, the argument is valid—we are compelled to conclude *Q*.

FIGURE 2.1	Major Premise: If *P*, Then *Q*

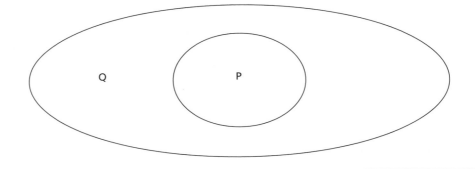

TABLE 2.3	Denying the Antecedent: An Invalid Argument	
	General form	**Specific example**
Major premise	If *P*, then *Q*	If a country is wealthy, then it will be a democracy.
Minor premise	Not *P*	The country is not wealthy.
Conclusion	Therefore, not *Q*.	Therefore, the country will not be a democracy.

Now let's consider what happens when we deny the antecedent. An example is shown in Table 2.3. Once again, the major premise can be represented in set-theoretic terms by Figure 2.1. The difference from the previous example is that the minor premise now asserts that *P* is not the case; that is, it denies the antecedent. If we accept this, does it necessarily follow that *Q* is not the case, as the conclusion maintains? Figure 2.1 clearly illustrates that even if our case is not in *P*, it could still be in *Q*. As a result, it does not logically follow from observing "not *P*" that *Q* is not the case. Therefore, this is an invalid argument. This is because we can contradict the conclusion (not *Q*) without running into a contradiction with either the major premise or the minor premise. Since a valid argument compels us to accept its conclusion given that its premises are true, this is sufficient to demonstrate that arguments that deny the antecedent are invalid.

In the context of our running example, does it follow from the fact that the observed country is not wealthy that it will not be a democracy? Intuitively, we can imagine that there may be other reasons why a country is a democracy even though it is not wealthy. Indeed, one example of a nonwealthy democracy is India. An important point here, though, is that the argument is invalid, not because we can come up with an example of a real democracy that is not wealthy (India), but rather because we are not compelled to accept the conclusion based on the truthfulness of the major and minor premises. It may be confusing for readers that there is no direct connection between the factual accuracy of an argument's conclusion and the validity of the argument itself—a valid argument can have a conclusion that is factually false, and an invalid argument can have a conclusion that is factually true. If we restrict our attention only to whether the argument is valid as it applies to our democracy example, we must ask, "Does the major premise claim that wealth is the only reason why a country will be a democracy?" The answer is clearly no. The major premise states only what will happen if a country is wealthy. It makes no claim as to what might happen if a country is not wealthy. It is for this reason, and this reason alone, that the argument is invalid.

Now let's consider what happens when we affirm the consequent. An example is shown in Table 2.4. As before, the major premise can be represented in set-theoretic terms by Figure 2.1. The difference this time is that the minor premise now asserts that *Q* is the case; that is, it affirms the consequent. If we accept that the premises are true, are we compelled to accept the conclusion that *P* is the case? Figure 2.1 clearly illustrates that the fact that our

TABLE 2.4	**Affirming the Consequent: An Invalid Argument I**

	General form	Specific example
Major premise	If *P*, then *Q*	If a country is wealthy, then it will be a democracy.
Minor premise	*Q*	The country is a democracy.
Conclusion	Therefore, *P*	Therefore, the country is wealthy.

case is in *Q* does not necessarily mean that it is also in *P*. As a result, the argument is invalid—we are not compelled to accept the conclusion based on the premises.

In the context of our running example, an argument that affirms the consequent confuses necessity and sufficiency. Although the major premise states that wealth is sufficient for democracy—wealthy countries will be democracies—it does not assert that wealth is necessary for democracy. In other words, the major premise does not state that wealth is the only cause of a country's democracy. Consequently, we cannot make a valid inference from the fact that a country is a democracy to the claim that the country must be wealthy—it may be wealthy, or it may not be. Recall that to show that an argument is invalid, it is not necessary to show that its conclusion is false; we have to show only that it doesn't have to be true.

Finally, let's consider what happens when we deny the consequent. An example is shown in Table 2.5. As always, the major premise can be represented in set-theoretic terms by Figure 2.1. The difference this time is that the minor premise now denies that *Q* is the case; that is, it denies the consequent. If we accept that the premises are true, are we compelled to accept the conclusion that "not *P*" is the case? Figure 2.1 clearly shows that the fact that our case is not in *Q* necessarily means that it is not in *P*. As a result, the argument is valid—we are compelled to accept the conclusion based on the premises. In the context of our running example, the major premise indicates that all wealthy countries are democracies and the minor premise states that the country is not a democratic one. If these premises are both true, then it logically follows that our country cannot be wealthy.

Our brief foray into the study of logic indicates that if complex arguments can be broken down into categorical syllogisms, then it is possible to classify all arguments into one of four types according to whether they affirm or deny the consequent or antecedent. Two of these

TABLE 2.5	**Denying the Consequent: A Valid Argument I**

	General form	Specific example
Major premise	If *P*, then *Q*	If a country is wealthy, then it will be a democracy.
Minor premise	Not *Q*	The country is not a democracy.
Conclusion	Therefore, not *P*	Therefore, the country is not wealthy.

TABLE 2.6	**What Types of Conditional Arguments Are Valid?**	
	Antecedent	**Consequent**
Affirm	Valid	Invalid
Deny	Invalid	Valid

arguments are valid, but the other two are invalid. Specifically, affirming the antecedent and denying the consequent are valid arguments—if you accept the major and minor premises, you are compelled to accept the conclusion. In contrast, denying the antecedent and affirming the consequent are invalid arguments—if you accept the major and minor premises, you are not compelled to accept the conclusion. These results are summarized in Table 2.6.

Testing Theories

We obviously think that it is important for you to be able to distinguish between valid and invalid arguments so that you are not manipulated or exploited by others. However, this brief introduction to logic is also important because it tells us something about the way that scientists test their theories and explanations. Suppose we want to explain why rich countries are much more likely to be democracies than poor countries. One possible explanation for why this might be the case is given in the following statements:[4]

1. Living in a dictatorship is risky—if you are one of the dictator's friends, you will do extremely well; but if you are not, you will do extremely poorly.
2. Living in a democracy is less risky—democratic leaders have to spread the goodies (and the pain) around more evenly. This means that you are less likely to do extremely well or extremely poorly in a democracy.
3. Rich people are less likely to take risks than poor people because they have more to lose. This means that countries with lots of rich people are more likely to be democracies than dictatorships.

This short explanation provides reasons why rich countries might be more likely to be democracies than poor countries. How good is this explanation, though? Does this argument have any testable implications? One implication is that rich democracies should live longer than poor democracies. This is because people in rich democracies should be less likely to take the "risk" of becoming a dictatorship; in contrast, people in poor democracies might wonder what they have to lose.

How can we use observations of the real world to evaluate our proposed explanation? It is often the case that the implications of an explanation are more readily observable than the

---

4. This is a simplified version of an argument presented by Przeworski (2001). It will be discussed more fully in Chapter 6.

TABLE 2.7	Affirming the Consequent: An Invalid Argument II	
General form	**Example**	**Specific example**
If P, then Q	If our theory T is correct, then we should observe some implication I.	If our theory is correct, then we should observe that rich democracies live longer than poor democracies.
Q	We observe implication I.	Rich democracies live longer than poor democracies.
Therefore, P	Therefore, our theory T is correct.	Therefore, our theory is correct.

elements of the explanation itself. Consider the example we are using. Although it may be possible to compare the distribution of good and bad outcomes in dictatorships and democracies, the claims that people differ in their propensity to take risks and that this propensity is related to their level of income are difficult to observe. This is because the propensity to take risks is an internal and psychological attribute of individuals. For similar reasons, scholars typically evaluate their explanations by observing the real world to see if the implications of their explanations appear to be true based on the assumption, "If my theory is true, then its implications will be true." If we take this to be our major premise and the truth or falsity of the theory's implications as the minor premise, then we might be able to use observations to draw inferences about our theory or explanation.

Suppose our theory's implications were borne out by our observation that rich democracies live longer than poor democracies. Can we conclude that our theory is true? Note that if we were to do so, we would be engaging in reasoning that affirmed the consequent. This fact is shown more clearly in Table 2.7. As you know by now, affirming the consequent is an invalid form of argument. The major premise says only that if the theory is correct, then the implications should be observed. It never says that the only way for these implications to be produced is if the theory is correct. In other words, processes other than those described in our theory may produce the observation that rich countries live longer than poor countries. Put differently, the mere fact of observing the predicted implication does not allow us to categorically accept or reject our theory.

Suppose now that our observations did not bear out our theory's implications; that is, we did not observe that rich democracies live longer than poor democracies. Can we conclude that our theory is incorrect? Note that if we were to do so, we would be engaging in reasoning that denies the consequent. This fact is shown more clearly in Table 2.8. As you know by now, denying the consequent is a valid form of argument. In other words, by accepting the premises, we are compelled to accept the conclusion that our theory is not correct.

If we compare the two previous examples, we can see an important asymmetry as regards the logical claims that can be made on the basis of "confirming" and "disconfirming" observations. When an implication of our theory is confirmed, the most we can say is that the

TABLE 2.8	Denying the Consequent: A Valid Argument II	
General form	**Example**	**Specific example**
If *P*, then *Q*	If our theory *T* is correct, then we should observe some implication *I*.	If our theory is correct, then we should observe that rich democracies live longer than poor democracies.
Not *Q*	We do not observe implication *I*.	Rich democracies do not live longer than poor democracies.
Therefore, not *P*	Therefore, our theory *T* is incorrect.	Therefore, our theory is incorrect.

theory may be correct. This is because neither of the two possible conclusions—our theory is correct or our theory is not correct—contradicts our major and minor premises. In other words, we cannot say that our theory is correct or verified. In contrast, if we find that an implication of our theory is inconsistent with observation, then we are compelled by logic to accept that the theory is false—this is the only conclusion that is consistent with our observation. Thus, although we can know that a theory must be incorrect in light of a disconfirming case, all that we can say in light of a confirming case is that a theory may be correct (it may also be wrong). What does this mean? It means that we are logically justified in having more confidence when we reject a theory than when we do not. This, in turn, implies that the knowledge encapsulated in theories that have not been rejected remains tentative and can never be proven for sure—scientific theories can never be proven. Even if we are utterly convinced that our major and minor premises are true, all that we can logically conclude from a confirming instance is that the theory has not yet been falsified.

This asymmetry between confirming and disconfirming cases led the philosopher of science Sir Karl Popper ([1959] 2003, 280–81) to conclude:

> The old scientific ideal of *episteme*—of absolutely certain, demonstrable knowledge—has proved to be an idol. The demand for scientific objectivity makes it inevitable that every scientific statement must remain *tentative for ever*. . . . With the idol of certainty . . . there falls one of the defenses of obscurantism which bar the way to scientific advance. For the worship of this idol hampers not only the boldness of our questions, but also the rigor and integrity of our tests. The wrong view of science betrays itself in the craving to be right; for it is not his *possession* of knowledge, of irrefutable truth, that makes the man of science, but his persistent and recklessly critical *quest* for truth.

If confirming observations do not prove that our theory is correct, does this mean that they are of no use whatsoever? The answer is no. Imagine that we start with a set of implications derived from a theory and then observe some facts. In other words, let's start with the theory and then observe the world. If we do this, then it is possible that our observations will contradict our theory. If it turns out that our observations are consistent with our theory, then we can have a greater measure of confidence in our theory because it withstood the very real chance of being falsified. We cannot say that our theory is verified or confirmed, just that we have more confidence in it. If our observations are inconsistent with our theory, then we can draw valid inferences about the truthfulness of our theory—we can conclude that it is wrong. This approach to doing science, which forms the basis of the scientific method described earlier, is called falsificationism. **Falsificationism** is an approach to science in which scientists generate or "deduce" testable hypotheses from theories designed to explain phenomena of interest. It emphasizes that scientific theories are constantly called into question and that their merit lies only in how well they stand up to rigorous testing. Falsificationism forms the basis for the view of science employed in this book.

> **Falsificationism** is an approach to science in which scientists generate testable hypotheses from theories designed to explain phenomena of interest. It emphasizes that scientific theories are constantly called into question and that their merit lies only in how well they stand up to rigorous testing.

The approach to science that we have described here takes a clear stance in the debate between "deductive" and "inductive" approaches to learning. The **deductive approach to learning** formulates an expectation about what we ought to observe in light of a particular theory about the world and then sets out to see if our observations are consistent with that theory. The **inductive approach to learning**, on the other hand, starts with a set of observations and then tries to ascertain a pattern in the observations that can be used to generate an explanation for the observations. Induction is problematic because in order to be successful it must rest at some point on the fallacy of affirming the consequent—the fact that observation precedes theory construction means that the theory is never exposed to potential falsification! Popper ([1959] 2003) suggests that, in fact, the biggest problem with induction is not so much that it is wrong but that it is impossible. Observational facts do not just present themselves to observers—we always decide which facts to pay attention to and which to ignore. As we noted earlier, the hunch that tells us what to observe and what to ignore, that is, what constitutes a puzzle worth explaining, constitutes a theory. In this respect, scholars who claim to be engaged in an inductive inquiry are actually engaged in an implicit deductive endeavor. If it is true that we are "all deductivists" as Popper claims, then the argument for deduction amounts to a claim that it is better to use theory explicitly than to use it implicitly.

> The **deductive approach to learning** involves formulating an expectation about what we ought to observe in light of a particular theory about the world and then sets out to see if observation is consistent with that theory. With deduction, theory precedes observation. The **inductive approach to learning** starts with a set of observations and then tries to ascertain a pattern in the observations that can be used to generate an explanation for the observations. With induction, observation precedes theory.

Having described the scientific method, we would like to briefly dispel certain myths that have developed about science. Some of these myths have been promoted by opponents of the scientific project, but others, unfortunately, have been sustained by scientists themselves.

Box 2.2

THE COMPARATIVE METHOD

An Overview and Critique

An undated portrait of John Stuart Mill.

Hader, Ernst, Artist; Williams, Sophus, photographer. J. Stuart Mill/E. Hader, pinxit; phot. u. verl. v. Sophus Williams, Berlin W. Berlin: Sophus Williams, 1884. Image. Retrieved from the Library of Congress, https://www.loc.gov/item/2004678579/. (Accessed October 26, 2016.)

You will, undoubtedly, encounter excellent work by scholars who claim to be proceeding inductively. The most common method of inductive research in comparative politics is known as the **comparative method**. It is also known as Mill's methods because it is based on a formal set of rules outlined by John Stuart Mill in his 1872 book, *A System of Logic.* Mill actually outlined two different methods. One is called the Method of Agreement, and the other is called the Method of Difference. Political scientists who employ these methods collect observations of the world and then use these observations to develop general laws and theories about why certain political phenomena occur.[5] In employing these methods, the goal is to identify the causes of political events.

The **comparative method**, also known as Mill's methods, involves the systematic search for the necessary and sufficient causes of political phenomena. The comparative method comprises the Method of Agreement and the Method of Difference. The **Method of Agreement** compares cases that "agree" in regard to the phenomenon to be explained.

Mill's **Method of Agreement** compares cases that "agree" in regard to the political phenomenon to be explained. To see how this works, suppose that we want to explain the occurrence of democracy. Common sense might suggest that if we want to know what causes democracy, we should study democracies.[6] We could observe two or more contemporary democracies and take note of their features. For example, we might compare the United Kingdom, Belgium, and the United States, as we do in Table 2.9. All three countries "agree" in regard to the outcome to be explained—they are all democracies.

TABLE 2.9 Mill's Method of Agreement

Country	Democracy	Wealth	Ethnically homogeneous	Parliamentary system
UK	Yes	Yes	Yes	Yes
Belgium	Yes	Yes	No	Yes
US	Yes	Yes	Yes	No

5. For example, Weber ([1930] 1992) employs Mill's methods to explain the rise of capitalism; Moore ([1966] 1999) to determine why some countries are democracies but others are dictatorships; Skocpol (1979) to examine social revolutions; Katznelson (1985) to analyze the variation in the organizational patterns of the working class in the United States and the United Kingdom; and Kalyvas (1996) to explain the rise of Christian democracy in western Europe.

6. As we will see, the kind of sense needed to do good science often turns out to be very "uncommon."

What, if anything, can we infer from such a comparison? Well, we observe that the United Kingdom is a wealthy, relatively homogeneous parliamentary democracy. Belgium is a wealthy, heterogeneous parliamentary democracy.[7] And the United States is a wealthy, relatively homogeneous presidential democracy. Assuming that the classification of our observations is correct, we can conclude that ethnic homogeneity is not a **necessary condition** for democracy. This is because Belgium is a democracy despite being ethnically diverse. We can also conclude that having a parliamentary system is not a necessary condition for democracy. This is because the

A **necessary condition** is a circumstance in whose absence the phenomenon in question cannot occur. A **sufficient condition** is a circumstance in whose presence the phenomenon in question must occur.

United States is a democracy despite having a presidential system. Wealth alone survives as a potential necessary condition for democracy in our three observations—all three democracies are wealthy. Based on the evidence in this simple example, then, a scholar using Mill's Method of Agreement would conclude that democracy is caused by wealth, or economic development.

Note that Mill's Method of Agreement does not allow us to determine whether wealth is a **sufficient condition** for democracy. To determine this, you would need to look for wealthy countries that are not democracies. If you found such a country, you would know that wealth is not sufficient for democracy. Thus, to evaluate whether wealth is sufficient for democracy, we need to examine nondemocracies as well as democracies. This obviously cannot be done with Mill's Method of Agreement because the outcome to be explained would not "agree" for all of the cases. It turns out, though, that we can evaluate claims about sufficient (and necessary) causes using Mill's Method of Difference.

The **Method of Difference** compares cases that "disagree" in regard to the outcome to be explained.

Mill's **Method of Difference** compares cases that "differ" in regard to the outcome to be explained. To evaluate whether wealth is a sufficient condition for democracy, we must go back out into the real world to observe some nondemocracies.[8] Imagine that the first nondemocracy that we observe is Mexico prior to 1990. As Table 2.10 indicates, Mexico was a relatively wealthy, ethnically homogeneous presidential country in this period. The case of Mexico prior to 1990 tells us that wealth is not a sufficient condition for democracy. This is because Mexico is wealthy but not a democracy. Not only does Mill's Method of Difference allow us to determine whether certain features are sufficient to produce democracy but it also allows us to find out if those features are necessary for democracy. In this sense, it is "stronger" than the Method of Agreement.

From the set of four observations in Table 2.10, we can make the following conclusions:

- Wealth is not sufficient for democracy in light of the Mexican case. It may, however, be a necessary condition.

---

7. Belgium's population is fairly evenly split between Dutch-speaking Flemish and French-speaking Walloons. There is also a sizable German-speaking population in the east of the country and a nontrivial number of non-European immigrants.

8. Here's an example of science depending on uncommon sense. Note the somewhat surprising implication that if you want to know what is sufficient to produce democracy, you must study nondemocracies.

| TABLE 2.10 | Mill's Method of Difference | | | |

Country	Democracy	Wealth	Ethnically homogeneous	Parliamentary system
UK	Yes	Yes	Yes	Yes
Belgium	Yes	Yes	No	Yes
US	Yes	Yes	Yes	No
Mexico	No	Yes	Yes	No

- Ethnic homogeneity is neither necessary for democracy in light of the Belgian case nor sufficient for democracy in light of the Mexican case.
- A parliamentary system is not necessary for democracy in light of the United States case. It may, however, be a sufficient condition based on the Belgium and United Kingdom cases.

Mill's methods are widely employed in comparative political science, where they form the basis of the popular "most similar systems" and "most different systems" research designs (Collier 1993; Lijphart 1971, 1975; Przeworski and Teune 1970).[9]

It is easy to see why the comparative method is so appealing—it claims to be able to identify the necessary and sufficient conditions for political phenomena. The problem, as many scholars have noted, though, is that certain fairly restrictive assumptions must be met before analysts can draw valid inferences from Mill's methods (Lieberson 1991, 1994; Sekhon 2004). For example, one must assume that there is only one cause for a political phenomenon like democracy and that this cause is deterministic; that is, it *always* produces the political phenomenon (democracy). One must also assume that all potential causes have been identified and that all causal factors work independently of each other. These assumptions are particularly problematic given that the comparative method does not provide us with any help in determining when they will be met. In our view, at least one of these assumptions is likely to be violated in almost any social scientific application. Mill (1872) himself recognized this and warned scholars against using his methods to explain the political world. As he put it,

> Nothing can be more ludicrous than the sort of parodies on experimental reasoning which one is accustomed to meet with, not in popular discussion only, but in grave treatises, when the affairs of nations are the theme. "How," it is asked, "can an institution be bad, when the country has prospered under it?" "How can such or such causes have contributed to the prosperity of one country, when another has prospered without them?" Whoever

---

9. Somewhat confusingly, the most similar systems design is equivalent to Mill's Method of Difference. It requires that the analyst find cases that are identical to each other except in regard to the outcome to be explained and one key condition. The most different systems design is equivalent to Mill's Method of Agreement. It requires the analyst to choose cases that are as different as possible except in regard to the outcome to be explained and one key condition.

makes use of an argument of this kind, not intending to deceive, should be sent back to learn the elements of some of the more easy physical sciences. (p. 324)

These reservations are sufficiently worrisome on their own that analysts should be reluctant to accept uncritically claims based on the application of Mill's methods. A more fundamental problem is at issue here, however. Even if the analyst could be satisfied that the assumptions underpinning the comparative method were met, she would have established only that certain phenomena occur together; she would not have provided an explanation of the outcome in question. That is, Mill's methods are empirical methods—they tell us what happens, not why the phenomena occur together. Put differently, all they say is that Y happened when X was present; this is roughly equivalent to saying that the sun came up because the rooster crowed. An essential missing ingredient is a sense of process, a story about why Y appears to happen when X happens. The story about the process that produces the outcomes we see is what scientists call a *theory,* and these stories cannot necessarily be reduced to a set of circumstances that covary with the outcome we wish to explain.

Finally, we should note that the asymmetry between confirmation and falsification that we noted previously has important implications for the methods we use to build knowledge. When scholars use the comparative method, they go out into the real world to collect observations and look for patterns in the data. Those factors that cannot be eliminated as potential causes by Mill's methods become our explanation. Each new case that exhibits the same pattern in the data confirms or verifies our conclusion. Note that because the comparative method starts with observations, it relies entirely on the process of affirming the consequent. If we identify causes only after we have observed the data, as the comparative method requires, we have no chance of ever coming across disconfirming observations. This is because our "theory" is essentially just a restatement of the patterns in our observations.[10] This is a real problem, whether the researcher is employing the comparative method on a small number of cases or analyzing large data sets looking for patterns. No matter how many cases these researchers observe that appear to exhibit the predicted pattern, they are never logically justified in claiming that their conclusions have been confirmed or verified.

You might wonder whether there is any way to avoid these problems. The answer is yes. Imagine that we start with a set of implications derived from a theory and then observe some facts. In other words, let's start with the theory and then observe the world rather than the other way around. It is now at least possible for our observations to contradict our theory. If it turns out that our observations are consistent with our theory, then we can have a greater measure of confidence in our theory because it withstood the very real chance of being falsified. If our observations are inconsistent with our theory, then we can draw valid inferences about the truthfulness of our theory—we can conclude that it is wrong. This approach to doing science, as we have seen, is called falsificationism, and it forms the basis for the view of science employed in this book.

---

10. This suggests that the comparative method is, at most, suitable only for developing theories and not for testing them.

MYTHS ABOUT SCIENCE

The first myth is that science proves things and leads to certain and verifiable truth. This is not the best way to think about science. It should be clear by now from our discussion that the best science can hope to offer are tentative statements about what seems reasonable in light of the best available logic and evidence. It may be frustrating for students to realize this, but science can speak with more confidence about what we do not know than what we do know. In this sense, the process of scientific accumulation can be thought of as the evolution of our ignorance. We use the scientific method because it is the best tool available to interrogate our beliefs about the (political) world. If we hold on to any beliefs about the (political) world, it is because, after we have subjected them to the most stringent tests we can come up with, they remain the most plausible explanations for the phenomena that concern us.

The second myth is that science can be done only when experimental manipulation is possible. This is clearly false. For theories to be scientific, they need only be falsifiable. There is no claim that the tests of these theories need to be carried out in an experimental setting. Many of the natural sciences engage in research that is not susceptible to manipulation. For example, all research on extinct animals, such as dinosaurs, must be conducted without the aid of experimental manipulation because the subjects are long dead. In fact, there is also no claim that a theory must be tested before it can be called scientific. Einstein presented a special theory of relativity in 1905 that stated, among other things, that space had to be curved, or warped. It took fourteen years before his theory was tested with the help of a solar eclipse. No scientist would claim that Einstein's theory was unscientific until it was tested. Put simply, scientific theories must be potentially testable, but this does not mean that they stop being scientific if they are yet to be actually tested.

The third myth is that scientists are value neutral. It is necessary here to distinguish between the method of science and the individuals—the scientists—who engage in science. The scientific method itself is value neutral. As we have indicated in this chapter, science is simply a method that involves generating and evaluating logically consistent sets of falsifiable statements about the world. Scientists, though, may not be value neutral (Longino 1987; Haraway 1988). It is important to remember that the pursuit of knowledge about the world is closely entangled with attempts by people to change the world. As a result, the types of research questions that are asked and the interpretation of scientific results are likely to be infused with the specific values and biases held by individual scientists and those who use their research. The lack of diversity in most scientific disciplines, whether in terms of gender, race, income, class, sexuality, religion, ethnicity, and so on, along with the power structure that exists in many societies, means that some research areas are less studied than others and that certain viewpoints are excluded or less privileged than others when it comes to interpreting scientific evidence (Smith 1974; Collins 1986, 1989; Carroll and Zerilli 1993). In effect, the knowledge that is produced by science is socially constructed. This is one of the many reasons for trying to promote the diversity of those involved in the scientific endeavor. The fact that scientists may not be value neutral means that we should be very clear about the limits of our knowledge and not encourage others to act upon knowledge that is not highly corroborated. Moreover, we should try to conduct our studies in such a way that someone who does not share our biases can determine if our arguments and evidence are reasonable.

It has been argued that science is predicated on two rules (Rauch 1993). First, no one gets the final say on any issue—all knowledge claims are, for the reasons outlined in this chapter, open to criticism. Second, no individual has a personal claim of authority about whether scientific statements are true or not. Taken together, these two rules create a social system that makes it possible that even though individual scientists will have biased perspectives, others, who hold different biases, will have incentives to check their work. As a community, scientists with many different biases will use the scientific method to check the claims that are being made in an attempt to reach a consensus that is independent of the biases held by individual scholars. This is yet another reason why having a diverse group of scientists is valuable.

The fourth myth, that politics cannot be studied in a scientific manner, can easily be dispelled by now. Our description of the scientific method clearly shows that this myth is false. The study of politics generates falsifiable hypotheses and hence generates scientific statements. These theories of politics can be tested just like any other scientific theory. We will further demonstrate that politics can be studied in a scientific manner in the remaining chapters of this book. The fact, though, that our subjects can read our work and change their behavior makes our job quite a bit harder than if we were working in one of the natural sciences.

CONCLUSION

In this chapter we have argued that it is useful to think about politics in a scientific manner. We have also tried to offer a clear view of what most practicing scientists have in mind when they use the word *science*. It is a fairly minimalist view. What unites all scientists is the idea that one ought to present one's ideas in a way that invites refutation (Popper 1962). It is incumbent upon the scientist to answer the question "What ought I to observe if what I claim to be true about the world is false?" This view of science recognizes that scientific knowledge is tentative and should be objective. Although it is certainly likely that our prejudices and biases motivate our work and will creep into our conclusions, the goal of science is to present our conclusions in a way that will make it easy for others to determine whether it is reasonable for people who do not share those prejudices and biases to view our conclusions as reasonable.

KEY CONCEPTS

argument *27*
categorical syllogism *27*
comparative method *35*
conclusion (in an argument) *27*
critical test *22*
deductive approach to learning *34*
falsifiable *18*
falsificationism *34*
inductive approach to learning *34*
invalid argument *27*

Method of Agreement *35*
Method of Difference *36*
necessary condition *36*
premise *27*
scientific method *19*
sufficient condition *36*
tautology *18*
theory *19*
uniformity of nature *20*
valid argument *27*

PROBLEMS

This section includes various questions designed to evaluate your comfort with some of the more important concepts, issues, and methods introduced in this chapter.

Logic: Valid and Invalid Arguments

1. Consider the following argument.

Major Premise: If a country has a strong economy, the government will be popular.

Minor Premise: The government is not popular.

Conclusion: Therefore, the country does not have a strong economy.

    a. What form of categorical syllogism is this (affirming the antecedent/consequent or denying the antecedent/consequent)?

    b. Is this a valid or an invalid argument?

2. Consider the following argument.

Major Premise: If the president commits a criminal act, then he can be impeached.

Minor Premise: The president does not commit a criminal act.

Conclusion: Therefore, the president cannot be impeached.

    a. What form of categorical syllogism is this?

    b. Is this a valid or an invalid argument?

3. Consider the following argument.

Major Premise: If a country employs proportional representation electoral rules, it will have many parties.

Minor Premise: The country does employ proportional representation electoral rules.

Conclusion: Therefore, the country will have many parties.

    a. What form of categorical syllogism is this?

    b. Is this a valid or an invalid argument?

4. Consider the following argument.

Major Premise: If a county has a participant culture, then democracy in that country will be stable.

Minor Premise: Democracy in country X is unstable.

Conclusion: Therefore, country X does not have a participant culture.

    a. What form of categorical syllogism is this?

    b. Is this a valid or an invalid argument?

5. Consider the following argument.

Major Premise: If Islam is incompatible with democracy, then Muslim majority countries are more likely to be dictatorships than democracies.

Minor Premise: Muslim majority countries are more likely to be dictatorships than democracies.

Conclusion: Therefore, Islam is incompatible with democracy.

    a. What form of categorical syllogism is this?

    b. Is this a valid or an invalid argument?

6. Consider the following argument.

Major Premise: If I work hard in this class, then I will get a good grade.

Minor Premise: I did not work hard in this class.

Conclusion: Therefore, I will not get a good grade.

    a. What form of categorical syllogism is this?

    b. Is this a valid or an invalid argument?

7. Consider the following argument.

Major Premise: If theory T is correct, all rich countries will be democracies.

Minor Premise: All rich countries are democracies.

Conclusion: Therefore, theory T is correct.

    a. What form of categorical syllogism is this?

    b. Is this a valid or an invalid argument?

    c. If you wanted to demonstrate that theory T is wrong, what would you have to observe?

8. Come up with an example of your own categorical syllogism. Demonstrate why the argument is either valid or invalid.

Scientific Statements

9. A statement is scientific if it is falsifiable. Which of the following statements are scientific and why?

- Smoking increases the probability of getting cancer.
- A square is a two-dimensional figure with four equal straight sides and four right angles.
- The sun revolves around the earth.
- It always rains in England during the winter.
- Education spending increases under left-wing governments.
- Religious faith assures a person a place in the afterlife.
- Democracies are less likely to go to war than dictatorships.

- The unexamined life is not worth living.

- Voter turnout is higher among citizens living in rural areas than for citizens in urban areas.

10. Some statements are nonscientific because they are tautologies and some because they refer to inherently unobservable phenomena. Come up with an example of both types of nonscientific statement.

11. Sometimes it is hard to know whether a statement is scientific or not. Much depends on how we define certain terms. Consider the following statement.

- All good students get high grades.

Whether this statement is falsifiable depends on how we define "good students." On the one hand, if we define good students as those who get high grades, then this statement becomes tautological or true by definition—no observation could falsify it. This is easy to see if we swap in our definition of good students in the statement above. If we did this, we would have "All students with high grades get high grades." It should be obvious that this statement could never be falsified because it is impossible to ever find a student with high grades who does not have high grades! With this particular definition of good students, the statement above is not scientific. On the other hand, if we define good students as those who work hard, then the statement above is scientific. This is easy to see if we swap in our new definition of good students. If we did this, we would have "All students who work hard get good grades." It should be obvious that this statement could be falsified. It would be falsified if we observed a student who worked hard but received a low grade.

Consider the following statement.

- All mainstream US senators agree that the House bill is unacceptable.

    a. Is this statement scientific if "mainstream US senators" are defined as those who find the House bill unacceptable?

    b. Is this statement scientific if "mainstream US senators" are defined as those who share a middle-of-the-road ideology?

Now consider the following statement.

- If the Affordable Care Act (sometimes referred to as "Obamacare") is successfully implemented, then health care outcomes in the United States will improve.

    a. Is this statement scientific if the "successful implementation of the Affordable Care Act" is defined in terms of improved health care outcomes?

    b. Is this statement scientific if the "successful implementation of the Affordable Care Act" is defined in terms of the Affordable Care Act actually being passed in Congress?

Necessary and Sufficient Conditions

12. Consider the following statements. After looking at the structure of each statement, would you say that the conditions shown in boldface type are necessary or sufficient to produce the effects shown?

- If a person contracts measles, then she was **exposed to the measles virus**.
- If a **democracy is rich**, then it will stay a democracy.
- If **a democracy has a participant culture**, then it will stay a democracy.
- A country cannot maintain democracy unless **it has a participant culture**.
- Countries have many parties only when they employ proportional electoral rules.
- Countries always have few parties when they employ majoritarian electoral rules.
- Students will receive a good grade only if they work hard.

Model Building in the Scientific Method

13. It has frequently been observed that students coming into a lecture hall tend to fill up the rear of the hall first (Lave and March 1975; Schelling 1978). Here are two possible explanations, or models, that predict this kind of behavior.

    Minimum Effort Theory: People try to minimize effort; having entered at the rear of the hall, they sit there rather than walk to the front.

    "Coolness" Theory: General student norms say that it is not cool to be deeply involved in schoolwork. Sitting in front would display interest in the class, whereas sitting in the rear displays detachment.

    a. Make up two facts (that is, derive two specific predictions) that, if they were true, would tend to support the Minimum Effort Theory. Do the same thing for the "Coolness" Theory.

    b. Make up a critical fact or experiment (specific prediction) that, if it were true, would tend to support one theory and contradict the other.

    c. Propose a third theory to explain student seating results and explain how you might test it against the other two theories.

14. It has frequently been observed that democracies do not go to war with each other. This has come to be known as the Democratic Peace.

    a. Make up two theories or models that would account for this observation.

    b. Generate a total of three interesting predictions from the two models and identify from which model they were derived.

    c. Find some critical fact/situation/observation/prediction that will distinguish between the two models. Be explicit about how it simultaneously confirms one model and contradicts the other.

15. A casual look around the world reveals that some governments treat their citizens better than other governments do.

    a. Make up two theories or models that would account for this observation.

b. Generate a total of three interesting predictions from the two models and identify from which model they were derived.

c. Find some critical fact/situation/observation/prediction that will distinguish between the two models. Be explicit about how it simultaneously confirms one model and contradicts the other.

Implicit Bias

In the chapter, we pointed out that scientists are not always value neutral. As with any individual, scientists are likely to have biases that influence how they evaluate, interpret, and act in the world around them. If they are aware of their biases, they can take steps, if they so choose, to minimize the impact of their biases. However, a growing body of research indicates that all individuals have biases of which they are unconscious. These "implicit biases" are activated involuntarily and without an individual's conscious control or even awareness. These implicit biases can be positive or negative, they often have to do with things like race, gender, age, and appearance, and they develop over the course of one's lifetime in response to the direct and indirect messages that one receives from different sources. Due to their different cultural backgrounds, individuals from different countries or regions can often have different implicit biases. What the research tells us, though, is that implicit biases are pervasive and that everyone has them. It also indicates that our implicit biases do not always line up with our conscious attitudes and beliefs. Among other things, implicit biases have been shown to affect which groups gain most from medical research (Romm 2014) and who gets hired to do science in the first place (Moss-Racusin et al. 2012). Unlike explicit biases, implicit biases are not accessible through introspection and, as a result, are much harder to overcome.

Scientists at *Project Implicit* have developed an Implicit Association Test to determine the extent to which people have implicit biases. Take one or more of these tests at https://implicit.harvard.edu/implicit/takeatest.html to see how these scientists try to capture people's implicit biases with respect to things like race, age, and gender.

16. Explain the strategy used by the researchers to try to measure implicit bias. That is, how does the test work?

17. Although the researchers in this example are psychologists, not political scientists, they face the same problem that you'll see again and again in later chapters—how can we measure concepts that are hard to observe? Do you find the approach taken by the scientists who designed the Implicit Association Test to be reasonable? Why or why not? If you find this approach to be unsatisfying, can you think of an alternative?

3 | What Is Politics?

OVERVIEW

- Political science is the study of politics in a scientific manner. Politics comprises the subset of human behavior that involves the use of power. Power is involved whenever individuals cannot accomplish their goals without either trying to influence the behavior of others or trying to wrestle free from the influence exerted by others.

- We introduce an Exit, Voice, and Loyalty (EVL) Game that captures key elements of many political situations. We use the game to analyze the balance of power between citizens and governments.

- Among other things, the EVL Game helps us think about when citizens will take direct action against the government, when governments will respond positively to the demands of their citizens, and how citizens can strengthen their position vis-à-vis the government. In other words, it helps us think about the role of power in politics: Who has it? Why do they have it? and How and when is it used?

olitical science is the study of politics in a scientific manner. In the previous chapter we described what we mean by science and examined the various components that constitute the scientific process. In this chapter we define what we mean by politics. What makes one situation political and another not? What is politics? Although many answers have been given to these questions over the years, most share the intuition that **politics** comprises the subset of human behavior that involves the use of power. Broadly speaking, power is involved whenever individuals cannot accomplish their goals without either trying to influence the behavior of others or trying to wrestle free from the influence exerted by others. That all forms of social interaction, whether at home, at work, or at play, typically involve some person or group trying to influence, or avoid the influence of, others illustrates that politics is a key aspect of much of our everyday lives.

> **Politics** comprises the subset of human behavior that involves the use of power or influence.

In this chapter, we introduce a simple model that captures what we think are the key elements of many political situations.[1] Our model represents a reformulation and extension of an argument put forth in a famous book by Albert Hirschman (1970) titled *Exit, Voice, and Loyalty: Responses to Decline in Firms, Organizations, and States*. Whereas Hirschman primarily addresses the relationship between consumers and firms, we focus here on the power relationship between citizens and governments. The model helps us understand when citizens will take direct action against the government, when governments will respond positively to the demands of their citizens, and when governments will ignore their citizens. More generally, the model throws light on who has power, when and why they have it, and how they use it. In other words, it helps us think about what politics is and how politics works.

THE EXIT, VOICE, AND LOYALTY GAME

Throughout our lives we will all experience changes to our environment that we do not like. Below are examples of what some people might consider negative changes to their environment:

- The government increases taxes.
- The state imposes a ban on handguns.
- The Supreme Court rules that prayer in public schools is unconstitutional.
- The national currency drops in value.
- Fuel-efficient cars are imported from a foreign country.
- The quality of peaches at your local fruit stand declines.

---

1. This chapter draws heavily on the ideas presented in Clark, Golder, and Golder (forthcoming).

Note that although some people will not like these changes and will see them as bad, others will see them as improvements. For example, those people who have to pay higher taxes will be unhappy when the government raises the tax rate, but recipients of government benefits might be better off. Although consumers in the domestic market are likely to suffer when the national currency drops in value because imports are now more expensive, exporters are likely to benefit because their goods are now more competitive. The importation of fuel-efficient cars may well have negative consequences for domestic car manufacturers who can no longer compete, but it provides benefits for consumers who are struggling with high gas prices. Similarly, the decision by the Supreme Court that prayer in schools is unconstitutional would obviously upset some people, but it would just as likely make others happy. On the whole, political situations nearly always involve some individuals or groups benefiting at the expense of other individuals and groups. As we'll see, politics is frequently about winners and losers.

Let's say that there has been some change in your environment that you do not like. What can you do about it? Broadly speaking, there are three possible responses that you might have—you can **exit**, use **voice**, or demonstrate **loyalty**. Choosing to exit means that you accept the negative change in your environment and alter your behavior to achieve the best outcome possible given your new environment. For example, if you do not like the fact that your state has introduced a ban on handguns, you could accept the policy change as inevitable and simply move to another state where handguns are allowed. Similarly, if you do not like a decline in the quality of peaches at your local fruit stand, you could accept the decline in peach quality and either go to a different fruit stand to buy your peaches or start buying mangoes instead. Choosing to use voice means complaining, protesting, lobbying, or taking other forms of direct action to try to change the environment back to its original condition. For example, if the government increases your tax rate, you might join an antitax protest to pressure the government to reverse its tax hike. Similarly, if the importation of fuel-efficient cars is having negative effects on your automobile firm, you could consider lobbying the government to place import restrictions or tariffs on these cars. Choosing to demonstrate loyalty means that you accept the negative change in your environment and you make no change to your preexisting behavior. For example, if the Supreme Court rules that prayer in public schools is unconstitutional, you could accept the situation and keep your children in the public school system. In Table 3.1, we illustrate what it means to use exit, voice, or loyalty in response to several potentially negative changes in your environment.

Consider the situation in which the government introduces a policy—say, a tax hike—that negatively affects the environment of one of its citizens. How should the citizen respond? When should the citizen choose to exit, use voice, or remain loyal? The citizen's choice will

> **Exit:** You accept that there has been a negative change in your environment, and you alter your behavior to achieve the best outcome possible given your new environment.
>
> **Voice:** You use your "voice" (complain, protest, lobby, or take direct action) to try to change the environment back to its original condition.
>
> **Loyalty:** You accept the fact that your environment has changed and make no change to your preexisting behavior.

TABLE 3.1	Exit, Voice, and Loyalty		
Stimulus	**Exit**	**Voice**	**Loyalty**
The government increases taxes.	Reallocate portfolio to avoid tax increase	Organize tax revolt	Continue to pay taxes, keep your mouth shut
There is a decline in the quality of peaches at the local fruit stand.	Buy mangoes, or buy peaches somewhere else	Complain to the store owner	Continue to eat peaches, keep your mouth shut
The Supreme Court rules that prayer in public schools is unconstitutional.	Homeschool your children	Lobby the government to change the Constitution	Keep your children in the public school system, keep your mouth shut
Your state outlaws handguns.	Move to a different state	Join the NRA or a militia group to put pressure on the state to allow handguns	Turn in your handguns, keep your mouth shut

depend on what she expects to happen when she chooses one of these options. In order for the citizen to know what to do, she needs to know what the government would do if she used voice. On the one hand, the fact that the citizen complains or protests might cause the government to respond positively to the citizen. This would lead to a tax reduction and the restoration of the citizen's original environment. On the other hand, the government might simply ignore the citizen's use of voice. If the government did ignore her, then the citizen would have to decide what to do next. After all, even though the citizen's use of voice failed, she would still have the choice of exiting or remaining loyal. What should the citizen do? What should the government do?

Game theory is a fundamental tool for analyzing strategic situations.

In a **strategic situation**, the choices of one actor depend on the choices made by other actors.

The problem facing the citizen and government is complicated because the citizen's choice of what to do depends on what she thinks the government will do, and the government's choice of what to do depends on what it thinks the citizen will do. This strategic aspect of social interactions is the essence of politics. **Game theory** is a fundamental tool that political scientists use for analyzing these types of **strategic situations** in which the choices of one actor depend on the choices made by other actors.[2] Throughout

2. In addition to its usage in political science, game theory is also widely applied in biology, economics, anthropology, sociology, social psychology, computer science, philosophy, and many other fields. Those students interested in learning more about game theory might want to begin by consulting Dixit, Skeath, and Reiley (2015), Dutta (1999), or Osborne (2004).

this book, we will use game theory as a conceptual tool to analyze, and better understand, a variety of strategic situations relating to things like the emergence of the state (Chapter 4), how the socioeconomic structure of a country affects the emergence and survival of democracy (Chapter 6), how culture affects bargaining behavior (Chapter 7), transitions to democracy (Chapter 8), and the electoral coordination of political parties (Chapter 14).

We can think of the decisions to be made by the citizen and the government as a **game**. A game is a situation in which an individual's ability to achieve his or her goals depends on the choices made by other identifiable actors. It is important to recognize that there is nothing trivial about political games; as will be seen throughout this book, the way they are "played" may mean the difference between life and death. Games have a set of players, and each player has a set of possible choices to make. There are two players in the story that we are presenting in this chapter—a citizen and the government. The citizen has to choose whether to exit, use voice, or remain loyal. If the citizen uses voice, then the government has to choose whether to respond positively to it or ignore it. And if the government ignores the citizen's voice, then the citizen has to choose whether to exit or remain loyal.

> A **game** is a situation in which an individual's ability to achieve her goals depends on the choices made by other actors.

Games have rules about how decisions are made. The basic rule is that players choose to do what they believe is in their best interest. The interests of the players are reflected in the **payoffs** associated with each possible outcome of the game. Players prefer outcomes with higher payoffs to outcomes with lower payoffs. A game can be represented by a game tree (extensive form games) or by a payoff table (normal, or strategic, form games). **Extensive form games** allow us to examine strategic situations in which players take turns to make decisions, that is, situations in which players make choices sequentially. **Normal, or strategic, form games** allow us to examine strategic situations in which players make their decisions at the same time, that is, situations in which players make choices simultaneously. In this chapter, we are going to use an extensive form game to examine the balance of power between citizens and governments. In the next chapter, we employ a strategic form game to think about the emergence of the state.

> The **payoffs** in a game indicate how the players value each of the possible outcomes.
>
> In an **extensive form game**, players can make their choices sequentially. In a **normal, or strategic, form game**, players make their choices simultaneously.

An extensive form game consists of **choice nodes** linked in a sequence. Choice nodes are points at which a player must choose an action. Each choice node is marked by the name of the player making the choice at that point in the game. The first choice node in a game, the place where the game starts, is called the **initial node**. The choice nodes are linked to other choice nodes or outcomes by branches. The **branches** represent the actions that can be taken at each choice node.

> A **choice node** is a point in an extensive form game at which a player must choose an action. The **initial node** is the place where the game begins. The **branches** represent the actions that can be taken at choice nodes.

A **game tree** is the entire specification of choice nodes, branches, and payoffs that comprise an extensive form game.

A branch that is not followed by another choice node leads to one of the potential outcomes of the game. Each of the potential outcomes of the game is labeled with the payoffs earned by each player in that outcome. The entire specification of choice nodes, branches, and payoffs is called a **game tree** because it resembles a tree.

Figure 3.1 illustrates a game in extensive form between two players—a citizen and the government—going from top to bottom. The choice nodes are identified by the name of the player making a choice at that point of the game. Branches are shown as lines that link choice nodes to other choice nodes or to one of the possible outcomes in the game. The "prehistory," or background, to the game is that the government has caused a negative change in the environment of the citizen that resulted in a transfer of some benefit from the citizen to the government. For example, the government might have introduced a tax hike leading to an increase in revenue for the government and less income for the citizen. It is at this point that the game displayed in Figure 3.1 begins.

The game starts at the topmost choice node, the initial node, with the citizen deciding whether to exit, use voice, or remain loyal. If the citizen decides to exit, then the government gets to keep the benefit that it seized in the game's prehistory, and the citizen opts for some substitute. This is outcome 1 (O1). If the citizen chooses to remain loyal, then the

FIGURE 3.1 | **Exit, Voice, and Loyalty (EVL) Game without Payoffs**

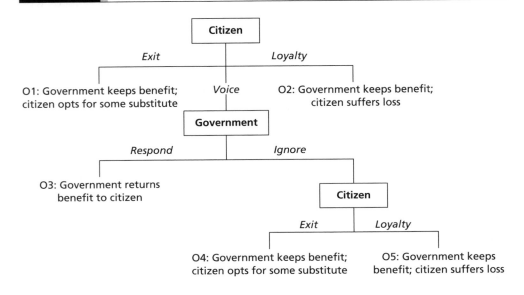

government gets to keep the benefit that it seized, and the citizen just suffers the loss in silence. This is outcome 2 (O2). If the citizen chooses to use voice, then the government must decide whether to respond positively to the citizen or ignore her. If the government responds positively, then the government returns the benefit to the citizen. This is outcome 3 (O3). If the government ignores the citizen's use of voice, then the citizen must decide whether to remain loyal or exit.[3] If the citizen chooses to exit, then the government gets to keep the benefit, but the citizen opts for some substitute. This is outcome 4 (O4). If the citizen remains loyal, the government gets to keep the benefit that it took, and the citizen suffers the loss. This is outcome 5 (O5).

What do you expect the players to do in this game? This is actually an unfair question because you cannot really answer it without knowing how much each of the players values the different possible outcomes. In Table 3.2, we indicate the payoffs for the players that are associated with each of the five possible outcomes. If the citizen chooses to exit at any point in the game, then she gets what we call her "exit payoff." We arbitrarily set the value of the citizen's exit payoff at E. The precise value of E in any specific situation will depend on the attractiveness of the citizen's exit option. Some citizens will have attractive exit options (E will be high), whereas others will not (E will be low). If the citizen chooses to remain loyal at any point in the game, then she accepts the loss of her benefit, and she gets nothing, 0. We assume that the use of voice is costly for the citizen, because protesting, complaining, lobbying, and taking direct action all require effort that could be put to an alternative use. Depending on the country in which she lives, voice might be costly in other respects as well. For example, one's involvement in a protest might be met by imprisonment, loss of employment, or even death. In other words, the degree of government repression will likely affect the citizen's cost of using voice. For these reasons, the citizen must pay a cost, c, where $c > 0$, whenever she chooses to use voice.

If the government gets to keep the benefit that it transferred from the citizen in the prehistory of the game, then the government gets a payoff of 1.[4] We could have chosen any positive number to represent this payoff, but 1 is the easiest for presentational purposes. Whenever the citizen chooses to remain loyal, the government also receives a loyalty payoff, L, where $L > 0$. This additional loyalty payoff captures the notion that governments value having a loyal citizenry and can be thought of in at least a couple of ways. One is that loyal citizens can make life easier for government officials by providing them with support to help them stay in power or by providing them with what could be thought of as "legitimacy." The

---

3. You might be wondering why the citizen cannot choose to use her voice again at this point. Well, obviously, she could. But ask yourself whether the government would behave any differently this time around if nothing else has changed. If the government ignored the citizen's voice before, it will do so again. Thus, allowing the citizen to use her voice at this point in the game does not add anything substantively new. This is why we allow the citizen to choose only between exiting and remaining loyal if the government decides to ignore her use of voice.

4. In effect, the citizen had a payoff of 1 in the prehistory of the game but the government took it from her, leaving her with nothing. This is why the citizen receives a payoff of 0 when she chooses to remain loyal in the game.

TABLE 3.2	Turning Outcomes into Payoffs		
Outcome	Description	Citizen	Government
O1	The government keeps the benefit but loses the support of the citizen. The citizen opts for some substitute.	E	1
O2	The government keeps both the benefit and the support of the citizen. The citizen suffers her loss in silence.	0	$1 + L$
O3	The government returns the benefit to the citizen and keeps her support.	$1 - c$	L
O4	The government keeps the benefit but loses the support of the citizen. Having used her voice, the citizen opts for some substitute.	$E - c$	1
O5	The government keeps both the benefit and the support of the citizen. Having used her voice, the citizen suffers her loss.	$0 - c$	$1 + L$

Note: E = citizen's exit payoff; 1 = value of benefit taken from the citizen by the government; L = government's value from having a loyal citizen who does not exit; c = cost of using voice.

other is that loyal citizens continue to invest in the economy or other activities that provide meaningful resources and support to the government. Whatever the precise source of this additional loyalty payoff, its size will obviously vary across governments and citizens. Some governments desire or require more support from their citizenry than others, and some citizens are more important to government officials than others.

We can now put these payoffs together to see what the citizen and government get in each of the five possible outcomes. These are the payoffs shown in Table 3.2. In outcome 1 (O1), the citizen's payoff is E, because she exits; the government's payoff is 1, because it gets to keep the benefit it took from the citizen. In outcome 2 (O2), the citizen's payoff is 0, because she remains loyal; the government's payoff is $1 + L$, because it gets to keep the benefit it took from the citizen and it retains a loyal citizen. In outcome 3 (O3), the citizen's payoff is $1 - c$, because the government returns the benefit to the citizen, but the citizen had to use her voice to get it; the government's payoff is L, because the government retains a loyal citizen. In outcome 4 (O4), the citizen's payoff is $E - c$, because she exits but only after using her voice; the government's payoff is 1, because it gets to keep the benefit that it took from the citizen. In outcome 5 (O5), the citizen's payoff is $0 - c$, because the citizen chooses to remain loyal but only after using her voice; the government's payoff is $1 + L$, because it gets to keep the benefit it took

FIGURE 3.2 Exit, Voice, and Loyalty (EVL) Game with Payoffs

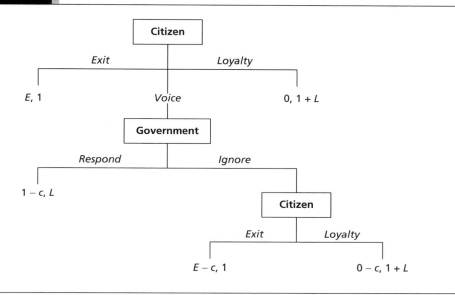

Note: E = citizen's exit payoff; 1 = value of benefit taken from the citizen by the government; *L* = government's value from having a loyal citizen who does not exit; *c* = cost of using voice. It is assumed that *c, L* > 0, and that *E* < 1 − *c*. The citizen's payoffs are shown first because she is the first player to make a choice; the government's payoffs are shown second. A comma separates the payoffs for the players associated with *each* outcome.

from the citizen as well as retain a loyal citizen. We can now add these payoffs to the game tree shown in Figure 3.1. The new game tree with the payoffs is shown in Figure 3.2. The citizen's payoffs are shown first because she is the first player to make a choice; the government's payoffs are shown second. A comma separates the payoffs for the players associated with each outcome.

We are almost ready to determine what the citizen and government will do in this game. Before we do this, however, we make one final assumption. Specifically, we assume that $E < 1 - c$. Think about what this assumption means for a moment. This assumption states that the value the citizen gets from exiting is less than the value that the citizen gets from successfully using her voice and regaining the benefit taken by the government. This assumption simply says that we are considering only the set of social situations in which exit is sufficiently unattractive that the value of the government's responding positively minus the cost of using voice is greater than the value offered by exit. If this assumption were not made, then the citizen would always exit irrespective of how the government would respond to the use of voice. We believe that this assumption makes the situation we are examining between the citizen and the government more interesting from a political point of view because there is now at least the possibility that the citizen might try to exert influence over the government by choosing to use her voice.

SOLVING THE EXIT, VOICE, AND LOYALTY GAME

Now that we know the players, the choices available to them, and how they value each possible outcome, we are ready to "solve" the game. To solve the game we have to identify the choices that a rational decision maker who is trying to do as well as possible would make. By *rational*, all we mean is that the player does what she believes is in her best interest given what she knows at the time of choosing.[5] By solving a game, it becomes possible to say something about what we expect the players to do in the type of strategic situation being examined. Typically, political scientists solve extensive form games like the Exit, Voice, and Loyalty Game shown in Figure 3.2 for something called a **subgame perfect equilibrium** (SPE). We can find subgame perfect equilibria by using a method known as **backward induction**. Although this sounds a little complicated, it really isn't. We will go through it with you step-by-step with our EVL Game. We will also walk you through another example, the Senate Race Game, at the end of the chapter just before the Problems section begins.

A **subgame perfect equilibrium** (SPE) is an important solution concept for extensive form games in which all actors do the best they can at every point where they could possibly make a decision. SPE can be found using a method known as backward induction.

Backward induction is the process of reasoning backward, from the end of a game or situation to the beginning, in order to determine an optimal course of action.

Players in a game care about the consequences of their choices and therefore think ahead. They try to think about and anticipate how the other players will respond to their choices. For example, a player might ask herself how some other player would respond if she chooses action *A* and how that same player would respond if she chooses action *B*. The player then chooses the action, *A* or *B,* that is expected to give her the highest payoff. This process is quite familiar to chess players. Before making a move in a chess game, a player takes into consideration what she thinks the other player will do if she takes each of the possible moves open to her. Based on how she thinks the other player will respond to each of these possible moves, she then chooses the move that she thinks will be the best. The logical extension of this thought process leads players to begin at the end of the game and reason backward. This process is called backward induction and is probably something that most of us do when making decisions in our everyday lives without even thinking about it.

In the context of a game tree, backward induction requires starting at the end of the game tree and working our way back to the beginning of the game tree. By doing this, each player can decide which choices are optimal in regard to obtaining the best possible payoff given how she expects the other player to respond. The players must exhaust the choices first at the final choice

---

5. We provide a more detailed definition of rationality in Chapter 11.

nodes, then at all of the choice nodes that come before these nodes, then at all of the choice nodes that come before these nodes, and so on until they reach the initial choice node. At each choice node, the players will choose the action that provides them with the highest payoff given how they expect the other players to respond farther down the game tree. At the final choice node, the players simply choose the action that provides them with the highest payoff.

So, how does this work in practice? We now solve the EVL Game shown in Figure 3.2 by backward induction. The final choice node of the game has the citizen deciding whether to exit or remain loyal. If the citizen chooses to exit, she will receive a payoff of $E - c$. If the citizen chooses to remain loyal, she will receive a payoff of $0 - c$. It is easy to see that the decision as to whether to exit or remain loyal will depend on whether $0 - c$ is larger or smaller than $E - c$. For now, let us assume that $E > 0$; that is, the citizen's exit payoff is greater than her loyalty payoff. One way to interpret this is to say that the citizen has a credible exit threat, because if the game reaches this final node, she has an incentive to exit. Had the citizen's exit payoff been smaller than her loyalty payoff, $E < 0$, the citizen would never choose to exit as she can always do at least as well by remaining loyal. Once we make the assumption that $E > 0$, it becomes clear that $E - c > 0 - c$. As a result, the citizen will choose to exit rather than remain loyal. We indicate this choice by making the exit branch at this final choice node bold. This is shown in Figure 3.3.

FIGURE 3.3	Solving the Exit, Voice, and Loyalty Game When the Citizen Has a Credible Exit Threat ($E > 0$): Step 1

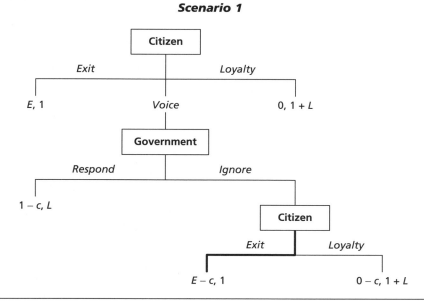

Scenario 1

Note: E = citizen's exit payoff; 1 = value of benefit taken from the citizen by the government; L = government's value from having a loyal citizen who does not exit; c = cost of using voice. It is assumed that c, $L > 0$; $E < 1 - c$; $E > 0$.

Now we move backward to the choice node prior to the final choice node. At this choice node, the government has to decide whether to respond positively to the citizen or ignore her. If the government responds positively, then it receives a payoff of L. If the government ignores the citizen, then it can look down the game tree (follow the bold line) and see that the citizen will choose to exit at the final choice node and that its payoff will be 1. The decision whether to respond positively to the citizen or ignore her will obviously depend on whether L is larger or smaller than 1. For now, let us assume that $L > 1$. One way to interpret this is to say that the government is *dependent* on the citizen—the government values having the loyalty of the citizen more than the benefit that it took from her. Once we make this assumption, it becomes clear that the government will choose to respond positively. We indicate this choice by making the respond branch at this choice node bold. This is shown in Figure 3.4.

FIGURE 3.4   **Solving the Exit, Voice, and Loyalty Game When the Citizen Has a Credible Exit Threat ($E > 0$) and the Government Is Dependent ($L > 1$): Step 2**

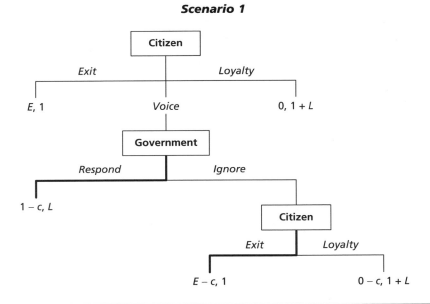

Scenario 1

Note: E = citizen's exit payoff; 1 = value of benefit taken from the citizen by the government; L = government's value from having a loyal citizen who does not exit; c = cost of using voice. It is assumed that c, $L > 0$; $E < 1 - c$; $E > 0$; $L > 1$.

Now we move backward to the choice node prior to this one. In this particular game, this is the initial node. At this node, the citizen has to choose whether to exit, remain loyal, or use her voice. If the citizen chooses to exit, then she receives a payoff of E. If the citizen chooses to remain loyal, then she receives a payoff of 0. And if the citizen chooses to use her voice, then she can look down the game tree (follow the bold lines) and see that the government will respond positively and that her payoff will be 1 − c. As always, the citizen will choose the action that provides her with the highest payoff. Remember that we have assumed in this particular example that the citizen has a credible exit threat (E > 0) and that E < 1 − c. Given these assumptions, it is easy to see that the citizen will choose to use voice to get a payoff of 1 − c instead of E or 0. Again, we indicate this choice by making the voice branch at the initial node bold. This is shown in Figure 3.5.

FIGURE 3.5	Solving the Exit, Voice, and Loyalty Game When the Citizen Has a Credible Exit Threat (E > 0) and the Government Is Dependent (L > 1): Third and Final Step

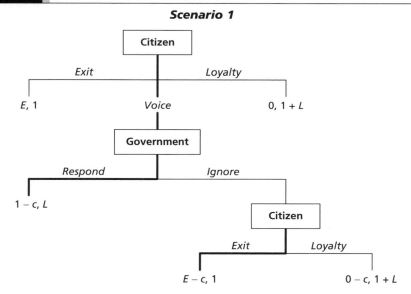

Scenario 1

The subgame perfect equilibrium is (Voice, Exit; Respond)

Note: E = citizen's exit payoff; 1 = value of benefit taken from the citizen by the government; *L* = government's value from having a loyal citizen who does not exit; *c* = cost of using voice. It is assumed that *c, L* > 0; *E* < 1 − *c*; *E* > 0; *L* > 1.

We have now solved the game using backward induction. Once we have solved a game, we are often interested in identifying three things: the expected outcome of the game, the payoffs that each player receives, and, of course, the subgame perfect equilibrium. Let's start by identifying the expected outcome of the game. We do this by starting at the beginning of the game and following the bold lines until we reach one of the possible outcomes of the game. The path that we move along when we do this is what we expect to happen. Thus, the expected outcome of the game in Figure 3.5 is that the citizen uses her voice and the government responds positively (Voice, Respond). The payoffs associated with the expected outcome indicate the payoffs that each player will receive. In this case, the citizen obtains $1 - c$ and the government obtains L, that is, $(1 - c, L)$.

To determine the subgame perfect equilibrium, we must list the choices made by the players at all of the choice nodes in the game. These choices are the ones that we identified during the process of backward induction—the bold branches. Backward induction essentially identifies the best choices available to the players at each of the choice nodes in the game. There are three choice nodes in the EVL Game, so the SPE must list three choices. By convention, the SPE first lists all of the choices that the first player (citizen) makes at each of the choice nodes with which she is associated; then it lists all of the choices that the second player (government) makes at each of the choice nodes with which it is associated. The two sets of choices are separated by a semicolon and placed within parentheses. In our EVL Game, the citizen is associated with two choice nodes, and the government is associated with one choice node. As a result, the SPE first lists the two choices made by the citizen (Voice, Exit); then it lists the one choice made by the government (Respond). The SPE for the EVL Game shown in Figure 3.5 is therefore written as (Voice, Exit; Respond). This equilibrium indicates that the citizen chooses to use voice at her first choice node and would choose exit at her second choice node if the game ever arrived at this choice node; the government chooses to respond positively at its one and only choice node.

You are probably wondering why we bother to list what the citizen does at her second choice node in the SPE given that the citizen never actually gets to make a choice at this node because the government chooses to respond positively earlier in the game. Ask yourself, however, exactly why the game never reaches this node. In other words, why does the government choose to respond positively to the citizen's use of voice rather than ignore it? The answer to this question is that the government chooses to respond positively because it anticipates that the citizen will exit at her second choice node if it chooses to ignore her. In other words, knowledge about what the citizen will choose at her second choice node if this node were to be reached is crucial in determining the outcome of the game. This is one of the reasons why an SPE always includes the choices of each actor at all of the choice nodes even if these choice nodes are never actually reached when the game is played. An important point to take away from this, more generally, is that choices that are not taken are often as important to understanding the outcomes of strategic interactions as choices that we actually observe. As seen later in the chapter, power is often most effective when it is least observable. One of the benefits of game theory is that it forces the analyst to consider the influence of anticipated events. These anticipated events can have a tremendous impact on people's behavior even though they might never actually occur; they never occur precisely because people anticipate them and change their behavior to avoid them.

The SPE of the EVL Game shown in Figure 3.5 indicates that the citizen's use of voice will be successful. However, this particular equilibrium rests on the assumptions that the citizen has a credible exit threat, $E > 0$, and that the government is dependent, $L > 1$. What happens if we change these assumptions? What happens, for example, if we retain the assumption that the government is dependent, $L > 1$, but now assume that the citizen does not have a credible exit threat, $E < 0$? In other words, let's assume that, as unhappy as the citizen may be with the government's behavior in the prehistory of the game, remaining loyal is preferred to exiting. The solution to this game is shown in Figure 3.6.

FIGURE 3.6	Solving the Exit, Voice, and Loyalty Game When the Citizen Does Not Have a Credible Exit Threat ($E < 0$) and the Government Is Dependent ($L > 1$)

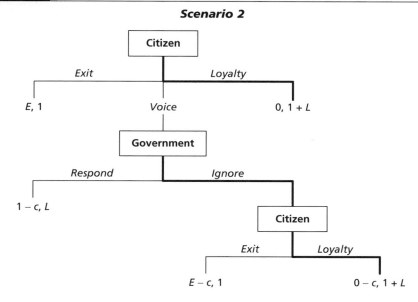

Scenario 2

The subgame perfect equilibrium is (Loyalty, Loyalty; Ignore)

Note: E = citizen's exit payoff; 1 = value of benefit taken from the citizen by the government; *L* = government's value from having a loyal citizen who does not exit; *c* = cost of using voice. It is assumed that *c, L* > 0; *E* < 1 − *c*; *E* < 0; *L* > 1.

At the final choice node, the citizen has to choose whether to remain loyal with a pay-off of $0 - c$ or exit with a payoff of $E - c$. Because $E < 0$ in this second scenario, the citizen will receive a higher payoff if she remains loyal. As a result, the loyalty branch from the final choice node is bold. At the choice node prior to the final one, the government must choose whether to respond positively to the citizen's use of voice or ignore it. If the government responds positively, then it receives a payoff of L. If the government ignores the citizen, then it can look down the game tree (follow the bold line) and see that the citizen will choose to remain loyal at the final choice node and that its payoff will be $1 + L$. No matter what the value of L, the government will always choose to ignore the citizen because $1 + L > L$. As a result, the ignore branch from this choice node is bold. At the initial choice node, the citizen must choose whether to exit, remain loyal, or use voice. If she exits, her payoff will be E. If she remains loyal, her payoff will be 0. And if she uses voice, she can look down the game tree (follow the bold lines) and see that her payoff will be $0 - c$. Because the citizen does not have a credible exit threat, $E < 0$, in this scenario, she will get her highest payoff, 0, by remaining loyal. As a result, the loyalty branch from the initial choice node is bold. We have now solved this new scenario of the EVL game using backward induction. The SPE for the EVL Game shown in Figure 3.6 is (Loyalty, Loyalty; Ignore). This indicates that the citizen will choose to be loyal from the beginning of the game. If the citizen had used her voice, the government would have ignored her, at which point the citizen would have remained loyal. The expected outcome of this game is that the citizen remains loyal and the government gets to keep the benefit it took from her. The payoffs associated with this outcome are 0 for the citizen and $1 + L$ for the government, that is, $(0, 1 + L)$.

What happens if we change the assumptions again? What happens, for example, if we assume that the citizen has a credible exit threat ($E > 0$) but that the government is autonomous and does not depend on the citizen ($L < 1$)? The solution to this game is shown in Figure 3.7. At the final choice node, the citizen has to choose whether to remain loyal with a payoff of $0 - c$ or exit with a payoff of $E - c$. Since the citizen has a credible exit threat once again, $E > 0$, she will receive a higher payoff if she exits because $E - c > 0 - c$. As a result, the exit branch from the final choice node is bold. At the choice node prior to this, the government must choose whether to respond positively to the citizen's use of voice or ignore it. If the government responds positively, its payoff will be L. If the government ignores the citizen, it can look down the game tree (follow the bold line) and see that the citizen will exit and that its payoff will be 1. Because the government is now autonomous, $L < 1$, it will choose to ignore the citizen. As a result, the ignore branch from this choice node is bold. At the initial choice node, the citizen must choose whether to exit, remain loyal, or use voice. If she exits, her payoff will be E. If she remains loyal, her payoff will be 0. And if she uses voice, she can look down the game tree (follow the bold lines) and see that her payoff will be $E - c$. Because the citizen has a credible exit threat, $E > 0$, she will receive her highest payoff by choosing to exit. As a result, the exit branch from the initial

FIGURE 3.7	Solving the Exit, Voice, and Loyalty Game When the Citizen Has a Credible Exit Threat (*E* > 0) and the Government Is Autonomous (*L* < 1)

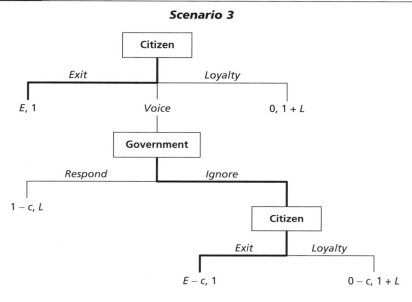

Scenario 3

The subgame perfect equilibrium is (Exit, Exit; Ignore)

Note: E = citizen's exit payoff; 1 = value of benefit taken from the citizen by the government; *L* = government's value from having a loyal citizen who does not exit; *c* = cost of using voice. It is assumed that *c*, *L* > 0; *E* < 1 − *c*; *E* > 0; *L* < 1.

choice node is bold. The SPE is, therefore, (Exit, Exit; Ignore). This indicates that the citizen will choose to exit at the beginning of the game. If the citizen had used her voice, the government would have ignored her, at which point the citizen would have exited. The expected outcome of this third version of the game is that the citizen simply exits and the government gets to keep the benefit. The payoffs associated with this outcome are *E* for the citizen and 1 for the government, that is, (*E*, 1).

What happens if we change the assumptions one last time? For example, what happens if we assume that the citizen does not have a credible exit threat, *E* < 0, and that the government is autonomous, *L* > 1? The solution to this game is shown in Figure 3.8. At the final choice node, the citizen has to choose once again whether to remain loyal with a payoff of 0 − *c* or exit with a payoff of *E* − *c*. Because the citizen does not have a credible exit threat, *E* < 0, she will receive a higher payoff if she remains loyal. As a result, the loyalty branch from the final choice node is bold. At the choice node prior to this, the government must choose whether to respond positively to the citizen's use of voice or ignore it. If the government responds positively, its payoff will be L. If the government ignores the citizen, it can look down the game tree (follow the bold line) and see that its payoff will be $1 + L$. It is easy to see that no matter what the value of L, the government will always choose to ignore the citizen. As a result, the ignore branch from this choice node is bold. At the initial choice node, the citizen must choose whether to exit, remain loyal, or use voice. If the citizen exits, her payoff will be E. If she remains loyal, her payoff will be 0. And if she uses voice, she can look down the game tree (follow the bold lines) and see that her payoff will be $0 - c$. Because the citizen has no credible exit threat, $E < 0$, she will receive her highest payoff if she remains loyal. As a result, the loyalty branch from the initial choice node is bold. Thus, the SPE is (Loyalty, Loyalty; Ignore). This indicates that the citizen will choose to remain loyal at the beginning of the game. If the citizen had used her voice, the government would have ignored

FIGURE 3.8   **Solving the Exit, Voice, and Loyalty Game When the Citizen Does Not Have a Credible Exit Threat ($E < 0$) and the Government Is Autonomous ($L < 1$)**

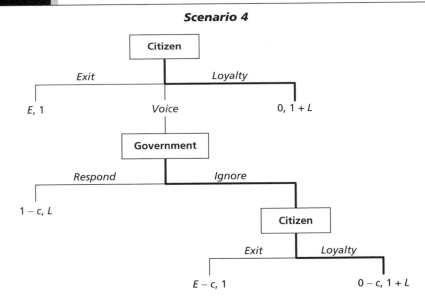

The subgame perfect equilibrium is (Loyalty, Loyalty; Ignore)

Note: E = citizen's exit payoff; 1 = value of benefit taken from the citizen by the government; L = government's value from having a loyal citizen who does not exit; c = cost of using voice. It is assumed that c, $L > 0$; $E < 1 - c$; $E < 0$; $L < 1$.

her, at which point the citizen would have decided to remain loyal. The observed outcome of this game is that the citizen remains loyal from the beginning and the government gets to keep the benefit. The payoffs associated with this outcome are 0 for the citizen and $1 + L$ for the government, that is, $(0, 1 + L)$.

EVALUATING THE EXIT, VOICE, AND LOYALTY GAME

What can we learn from these various scenarios in the EVL Game about the balance of power between citizens and the government? A summary of the subgame perfect equilibria with their expected outcomes is shown in Table 3.3. Several important conclusions about the power relationship between citizens and governments can be learned from this game. The first is that the government will be willing to respond positively to the citizen only when two conditions are met—the citizen must have a credible exit threat, $E > 0$, and the government must be dependent on the citizen, $L > 1$. You might have thought that a citizen would have a significant advantage *over the government* whenever she has a credible exit threat. This is clearly not the case, however. The government must also be dependent for the citizen with a credible exit threat to be able to influence it. A citizen with a credible exit threat does have an advantage in relation to one without such a threat, because the citizen with a credible exit threat has the realistic option of exiting, whereas the other citizen does not. Our point here, though, is that having a credible exit option itself is not sufficient for the citizen to be able to influence the government. Put differently, an autonomous government will never respond positively even if the citizen has a credible exit threat.

Think about what this means for your life more generally. If you want to be able to influence others (say, for example, you want your employer to give you a pay raise), then you should try to make sure that you have a credible exit threat (there are other jobs you could do or other firms that would hire you) and that the person you are interacting with depends on you in some way (perhaps you are the only one who knows how the firm's accounts work).

TABLE 3.3	**Summary of Subgame Perfect Equilibria and Outcomes**	
	The Government	
The citizen	Is Autonomous ($L < 1$)	Is Dependent ($L > 1$)
Has a Credible Exit Threat ($E > 0$)	(Exit, Exit; Ignore) Outcome 1	(Voice, Exit; Respond) Outcome 3
Has no Credible Exit Threat ($E < 0$)	(Loyalty, Loyalty; Ignore) Outcome 2	(Loyalty, Loyalty; Ignore) Outcome 2

If other firms are willing to hire you but your employer does not depend on you, then your employer will feel free to ignore you. Similarly, if your employer depends on you but other firms are not willing to hire you, then your employer will again feel free to ignore you. The only way to have power and be able to influence others is if you have a credible exit threat and the person or group that you want to influence depends on you. Think about how this applies to other relationships in your life. What about the relationship between you and your parents, you and your professors, or you and your friends? Do you have a credible exit threat in these relationships? Does the actor on the other side of these relationships depend on you? Your answers to these questions will indicate whether you have power and influence in these relationships.

The second important conclusion is that, in the absence of a credible exit option, $E < 0$, the citizen is, in some sense, a sitting duck. Under these conditions, the government can take away the citizen's benefits, and there is nothing that the citizen can do about it but accept the new state of affairs. How can we see this conclusion at work in the real world? Well, some have argued that the Democratic Party in the United States has not done enough to take account of the concerns of African American voters. If this is true—and we do not wish to enter that particular debate—then our EVL Game throws some light on why this might be the case. Clearly, Democrats depend on African American voters. Without their vote, Democrats have little chance of winning national office as things stand. But ask yourself whether African American voters have a credible exit option. In other words, is there another party that African Americans could credibly threaten to vote for instead of the Democrats? Some might argue that the fact that African Americans rarely vote for the Republican Party sends a signal to the Democratic Party that African Americans do not have a credible exit threat. Think about it this way. If the Republican Party were a credible option for African Americans, wouldn't more of them vote for it? Observing this signal, the Democratic Party can, to some extent, ignore (and exploit) African Americans even though it depends heavily on this particular constituency for its electoral success. The bottom line is that we should always strive to make sure that we have credible exit options in our life because they are a necessary, though not sufficient, condition to make sure we are not exploited. Going back to our example, this suggests, perhaps somewhat counterintuitively, that African Americans who want the Democratic Party to pay more attention to their concerns and to treat them better should start voting for the Republican Party as a way of signaling that they have a credible exit option. Only then will the Democratic Party feel that it has to take African Americans seriously.

On the other side of the political spectrum, conservative religious voters in the United States are often dissatisfied with the policies supported by the Republican Party. However, they are even less satisfied with the policies promoted by the Democratic Party. What are their options? If we follow the same logic as before, then these conservative religious voters should start voting for the Democratic Party to signal to the Republican Party that they have a credible exit option. In both of these cases, though, you might argue that voting for a different party is not the only available exit option for voters who are unsatisfied with the policies offered by their political party. Eligible voters could simply refuse to vote, or they could temporarily withhold their vote as a signal to their party that its candidates need to take their concerns more seriously. These potential voters need to ask themselves if it would be worth having their less-preferred party be in office for now, if this meant that their preferred party would be more responsive to them later. The answer to that question will obviously depend on how much the voters value present-day policy versus future policy.

We have argued that the government is free to take away the citizen's benefits whenever the citizen does not have a credible exit threat. Note, though, that we can think of the "benefits" that the government takes away in the game's prehistory in many ways. It could be that the government has denied the citizen some of her civil rights or liberties. Alternatively, it could be that the government has taken property away from the citizen through either taxation or appropriation. In our discussion to this point, it has implicitly been assumed that the government has taken something away from the citizen that in some sense rightfully belonged to her. That need not be the case for this model to be useful in understanding the role of power in the relationship between the citizen and the government. For example, it could be the case that the government has taken away the citizen's ability to seize an unfair advantage over other citizens—say, through a licensing agreement that grants the holder of the license a market advantage. Thus, there is nothing inherently good about the government's being responsive to the citizen's use of voice; nor is it necessarily loathsome for the government to turn a deaf ear to citizen demands. In fact, we often refer to the demands that some people make on the government as "special interests," and government officials are as likely to be applauded as lambasted for ignoring them.

A third point made by our model is that it is often difficult to learn very much from observing real-world political situations. Consider the following. It is always possible to infer whether a citizen has a credible exit threat from observing her action. This is because the decision to exit or use voice requires a credible exit threat, whereas the decision to demonstrate loyalty implies the lack of such a threat. It is not so easy to learn whether a government is dependent or autonomous when the citizen has no credible exit threat, however, because both types of government will respond to the use of voice by this type of citizen in exactly the same way—they will simply ignore her. It is precisely because she expects to be ignored in these circumstances that the citizen without a credible exit threat always chooses to remain loyal in the first place. This is an important point. It means that we should not make the mistake of inferring that governments that experience little use of voice or public opposition, such as those in contemporary China, Iran, and North Korea, are autonomous or that they do not rely on the support of their citizenry. These governments may be very dependent yet feel entirely free to ignore their citizens because their citizens lack credible exit threats.

The history of the collapse of the Communist regime in East Germany is consistent with this logic. For example, one can argue that, with the exception of the Berlin Uprising in 1953, the East German population was very loyal prior to 1989 because it lacked a credible exit threat. To many outsiders (and insiders), it appeared that the Communist regime was very stable and relatively autonomous from its citizens (Kuran 1991). The opening of the Hungarian border to Austria and hence the West in May 1989, however, provided East Germans with a credible exit option for the first time since the construction of the Berlin Wall in 1961.[6] The seemingly "loyal" and rather docile East German population was transformed into enthusiastic protesters who used voice in large numbers on the streets of Leipzig and East Berlin (Garton Ash 1999). One can argue that it was precisely because the East German Communist Party did depend on its citizens, despite all evidence to the contrary for almost three decades, that the Communist regime eventually responded by opening the Berlin Wall. This particular historical example should make us wary of inferring that a government is autonomous when its citizens have no credible exit threat—it might be, but it also might not be.

Similarly, our model suggests that it is also inappropriate to use political mobilization (voting, lobbying, campaign contributions, and so on), or the lack thereof, as a straightforward revelation of citizen preferences. Citizens may remain silent on particular issues either because they are satisfied with the status quo or because they do not expect their use of voice to be effective.

The EVL Game raises a fourth important point. If the government is responsive to those citizens on whom it depends for loyalty whenever those citizens possess credible exit threats, why would the government ever take a benefit away from these citizens in the first place? This question cannot be answered with the game as it stands. It is relatively easy, however, to think about how we might answer this question if we were to incorporate the prehistory of the game into the game itself. For example, imagine that we added a move at the beginning of the game in which the government decides whether or not to take the benefit away from the citizen. We can think of this as a decision by the government about whether to exploit the citizen by taking away some of her resources or not. If the government chooses to seize the citizen's resource, then the version of the EVL Game that we have just examined begins. If the government chooses not to exploit the citizen, then the citizen gets to keep her resource, and she remains loyal. You will get the opportunity to investigate this "extended" EVL game in one of the problems at the end of this chapter. What you'll find when you do this is that the government will not choose to exploit the citizen if it depends on her and she has a credible exit threat. This in turn means that the citizen will never have to use her voice. Why? Well, put yourself in the shoes of the dependent government. You can see that if you attempt to exploit a citizen with a credible exit option, the citizen will use her voice, and because you depend on her, you will respond positively to her demands. Because you know that you will eventually have to respond positively, you will choose not to seize the citizen's

---

6. By 1961 the East German government had come to recognize that it relied on its citizens to keep the economy afloat and itself in power. By building the Berlin Wall and removing the one credible exit option available to its citizens, the Communist regime was able to deprive its citizens of any influence that they had over it.

resources in the first place. As a result, the citizen will never have to use her voice (Clark, Golder, and Golder, forthcoming).

An important point to note here is that those citizens who have credible exit options wield considerable power without ever needing to open their mouths (use voice) whenever the government depends on them. Consider the epigraph attributed to the former British prime minister Margaret Thatcher at the beginning of this chapter: "Being powerful is like being a lady. If you have to tell people you are, you aren't." Thatcher's major insight was that sufficiently powerful people never need to use their voice because they are already getting other people to do what they want. This insight corresponds exactly to the results that we have just discussed from the extended version of the EVL model that incorporates the game's prehistory.

There are striking similarities between the argument we have just presented and the so-called structural Marxist view of the state (Althusser 1969; Poulantzas 1975, 1980). According to this view, capitalists exercise tremendous power over the government despite speaking in a soft voice because they possess credible exit threats and the government is dependent on them for the deployment of investment that fosters job creation, economic growth, and tax revenues (Przeworski and Wallerstein 1988). It is precisely because capital is generally more mobile than labor (has more credible exit options) that capitalists typically have significantly more influence over the government than workers. This is the case even if the government depends equally on both labor and capital. We examine the structural Marxist view of the state in more detail in Chapter 9.

This central insight—that powerful people never need to use their voice—poses a particularly troubling problem for political scientists and other scholars who wish to empirically evaluate who has power in a given society. In many cases, the most powerful actors are precisely those citizens who are least likely to take action or use their voice—in other words, the political scientist will never be able to observe them using their power. Our EVL Game suggests that it might be misleading to infer that citizens who do not engage in protests, strikes, lobbying, advertising, and so forth have no significant influence over government policy. To provide a specific example, our game indicates that it would be wrong to infer that presidents lack power because they rarely use their right to veto legislation. The possibility that presidents will veto legislation is enough to ensure that legislatures send presidents only the bills that the president wants. In effect, the president gets what he wants without having to use his veto power (Cameron 2000). The basic point here is that it is difficult to determine who has power and who does not simply by observing the world. This is one reason game theory, which allows us to analyze the way strategic dynamics may encourage nonaction, has become central to the scientific study of politics.

Finally, the EVL Game is as noteworthy for what it does not explain as for what it does. Notice that in the game as it stands, citizens use voice only when they expect it to be effective. This means that the model cannot explain why we sometimes see governments being unresponsive to the demands of their citizens. One reason governments might ignore their

Box 3.1 **A COMPARISON OF BAILOUTS IN THE US FINANCIAL AND AUTO SECTORS**

Many observers were surprised that the US government moved quickly and enthusiastically to bail out "rich" New York banks during the 2008 global financial crisis while moving more slowly and with greater reluctance to come to the aid of troubled car manufacturers. While a full assessment of the prudence of the US policy response to the financial crisis is beyond the scope of our discussion, it should be noted that the EVL model can help to explain why governments might respond differently to the desires of different sectors of the economy.

On Monday, September 15, 2008, Lehman Brothers, the fourth largest bank on Wall Street, declared bankruptcy. On the same day, in a deal engineered by Treasury Secretary Henry Paulson Jr., it was announced that Merrill Lynch, the troubled Wall Street financial giant, would be purchased by the Bank of America. Secretary Paulson's attempt to stem financial contagion and calm financial markets failed. The Dow Jones Industrial Average experienced its biggest decline since the aftermath of 9/11. The very next day Paulson and Chairman of the Federal Reserve Ben Bernanke informed members of Congress that the Federal Reserve intended to bail out the troubled insurance giant American International Group with an $85 billion loan. Lawmakers from both parties expressed support for the rescue plan. By the end of the week, Paulson and Bernanke briefed congressional leaders on a much broader plan to support the financial industry. The Troubled Asset Relief Program, or TARP, which authorized the Treasury to spend up to $700 billion to help financial firms get "toxic assets" off their books, was signed into law by President George W. Bush two weeks later on October 3.

In contrast, on Wednesday, September 17, two months after an ailing economy and a rise in gas prices brought car sales to a ten-year low, the chief executive officers of the "Big Three" auto manufacturers (General Motors, Ford, and Chrysler) met with House Speaker Nancy Pelosi to ask for loan guarantees to help the industry through the deepening economic crisis. They emerged from their talks with the promise that aid would be forthcoming, but with few concrete commitments from the government. By the end of the month, the situation had grown worse for the automakers as the credit crunch made it more difficult for the few consumers interested in buying new cars during a recession to find easy finance. By early October, a week after TARP came into law, Chrysler and GM were exploring a merger, something that many saw as an alternative to bankruptcy. At this point, aid was still "forthcoming."

On Tuesday, November 18, the heads of the Big Three returned to Washington to plead with lawmakers for a $25 billion piece of the $700 billion TARP funds; they received a chilly reception. Treasury Secretary Paulson urged lawmakers to resist the temptation to use any of the TARP funds to bail out the auto industry. Congress, doubtful that the $25 billion would be anything more than a lifeline tossed to a dying industry, gave the auto executives twelve days to develop a convincing plan showing how the money could be used to turn the Big Three firms into viable enterprises.

On December 4, the auto executives returned to Washington with a request for $34 billion in TARP funds and a plan for how the funds would be used to turn the firms around. Once again, they were not treated warmly. The Bush administration eventually announced that $13.4 billion of what little of the TARP funds had not already been promised to financial firms would be made available. Many observers at the time believed that this amount was just enough to delay bankruptcy until Bush left office in January 2009.

Clearly, there are striking differences in the way the US government responded to the 2008 crises in the financial and auto sectors of the economy. Most obvious is the magnitude of the dollar amounts involved. The size of the financial sector bailout dwarfed that of the auto industry bailout, despite the fact that, in the words of GM CEO Rick Wagoner, "The societal costs [of auto industry collapse] would be catastrophic—three million jobs lost within the first year, US personal income reduced by $150 billion and a government tax loss of more than $156 billion over three years" (Vlasic and Herszenshorn 2008, para. 11). Furthermore, the auto industry's call for support came from an industry concentrated in battleground states like Michigan and Ohio just weeks before a presidential election.

Somewhat less obvious, perhaps, was the way in which the leaders of the two sectors were treated by government officials. The heads of the auto industry were publicly chastised for flying in corporate jets to Washington to ask for taxpayer money. They were rebuffed, and when they returned twelve days later to once again supplicate Congress, they first performed an act of contrition by carpooling from Detroit to Washington. In contrast, when it became clear that Lehman Brothers was in trouble, Treasury Secretary Paulson flew in a private jet to New York when summoned by New York's Federal Reserve Bank President Timothy Geithner. A few weeks later, when Paulson decided that the United States should inject capital into the banks, he summoned the heads of the country's biggest banks to Washington the next day; there was no discussion about how they would get there. Once assembled, the bank chiefs were told "you won't leave this room until you agree to take this money." Notice that the auto industry executives went to Washington to ask for money. In contrast, Washington first went to New York to solve the financial sector's problems and then invited the leaders of the financial sector to Washington to accept the funds the government had proactively decided to bestow upon them. The auto industry repeatedly and publicly asked for funds from Congress. Financial industry leaders were summoned to a private meeting where Bush administration officials insisted on loaning them billions of dollars—in much the way a generous dinner host might insist on picking up the tab.

While it is difficult to establish whether the government was equally dependent on the auto and financial sectors of the economy, there is little doubt that a collapse of either sector would have been extremely costly for the incumbent government. The EVL model suggests

Rick Wagoner, chief executive of General Motors (*left*), returns to Washington in an electric car, two weeks after being chastised, along with the heads of Ford and Chrysler, for flying to Washington in corporate jets to ask for access to federal bailout funds.

that the difference in the bargaining relationship between the government and firms in both sectors can be attributed to the credibility of exit threats. The aftermath of the Lehman Brothers bankruptcy demonstrated the speed and magnitude with which liquid asset holders could respond to negative changes in their environment. Millions of stockholders suffered serious losses when the value of the stocks they held declined during the sell-off that occurred after the bankruptcy announcement. No one had to tell the government that it was in their interest to prevent a reoccurrence of this event. In fact, the government had already engaged in dramatic activity to try to prevent the Lehman Brothers bankruptcy in the first place. In contrast, while the Big Three automakers have gradually moved production offshore and can threaten to do so more in the future, the relatively fixed nature of the assets they own makes it hard to do this in a time frame that is relevant to the calculations of survival-maximizing politicians who generally focus on short-term interests such as getting reelected. The comparison illustrates that the government will anticipate the needs of liquid asset holders upon whom it depends, but it will be relatively unresponsive when actors with less credible exit threats are similarly imperiled. This is an issue that we will return to in more detail in Chapter 6.

citizens is that the citizens may not view the use of voice as costly. It is not altogether hard to imagine, at least in university towns, that some citizens might derive intrinsic benefits from the use of voice. For example, some citizens might welcome the opportunity simply to express themselves. Alternatively, they might use protest rallies as an opportunity to network with other like-minded individuals. Or they might feel a certain pride in the fact that they are living up to their civic responsibilities. If citizens do indeed derive such "consumption" benefits from the use of voice, we could capture this in our model by relaxing the assumption that $c > 0$. In effect, we could assume that $c < 0$ and treat these "negative costs" as benefits. If we do this, it is relatively easy to see that the citizen will always get a higher payoff from using voice than from choosing to either exit or remain loyal regardless of what the government does. In other words, the citizen will always use her voice even when she knows that it will not be successful.[7]

Another reason for sometimes seeing a government ignore its citizens has to do with information. The EVL Game that we present in this chapter is currently one of complete information—each player knows everything about the game and about the preferences of all the other players. More advanced game-theoretic models, some of which are presented later in this book (Chapter 8), relax the assumption that the actors know enough about each other's preferences to be able to predict each other's responses perfectly. These more advanced games contain incomplete information. Perhaps the government does not know whether the citizen has a credible exit threat or not. Or perhaps the citizen does not know whether the government is dependent or not. A citizen with a credible exit option might overestimate the value of her loyalty to the government and might find out the hard way that the government is perfectly happy to let her exit. Conversely, a government may believe that a citizen who uses voice is bluffing—that the citizen does not intend to make good on her threat to exit.

CONCLUSION

We spend a fair amount of time in later chapters critically evaluating some of the claims that we have just made. Our goal in this chapter, though, was to demonstrate that the EVL Game can be used to reveal something about what politics is and how politics works. Human interactions are considered political whenever actors cannot accomplish their goals without considering the behavior of other actors. Under such circumstances, the attempt to influence—or to avoid the influence of—others becomes relevant. It is here that power can, and will, be exercised. Attempts to influence, or break free of the influence of, others involve three basic strategies. Political actors can, as in the primordial response of "fight or flight," attempt to change their environment by using voice or change their location by using exit. *Voice* and *exit*

---

7. Of course, this only leaves us with a different puzzle, namely, why citizens sometimes choose not to use voice when the government negatively affects their environment.

are to be understood metaphorically here. A citizen's use of exit in response to a government policy need not involve emigration. Instead, a citizen might change industries, production processes, or political parties. Similarly, a citizen's use of voice might come as one of a host of behaviors, ranging from a ballot to a bullet. Finally, a citizen's best response to government policy might be to "keep on keepin' on." That is, throughout most of human history, the vast majority of humanity has often found itself between a rock and a hard place. Under such circumstances, it is possible that neither voice nor exit is a feasible or palatable option. It should be clear that here, too, the term *loyalty* is being used metaphorically—indeed, euphemistically.

KEY CONCEPTS

backward induction *56*

branches *51*

choice node *51*

exit *49*

extensive form game *51*

game *51*

game theory *50*

game tree *52*

initial node *51*

loyalty *49*

normal, or strategic, form game *51*

payoffs *51*

politics *48*

strategic situation *50*

subgame perfect equilibrium *56*

voice *49*

PREPARATION FOR THE PROBLEMS

As we have noted, game theory is a useful tool for examining strategic situations in which decision makers interact with one another. But how do we use it? We start by identifying a strategic situation of interest. Let's suppose that this strategic situation involves actors making sequential choices as in this chapter. The next step is to write an extensive form game that captures our strategic situation.

1. Writing the game

    a. Identify the players involved in the strategic situation.

    b. Draw the game tree to indicate what choices each player has and the order in which the players make the choices. Label the choice nodes where players must make a choice with the names of the players making them.

    c. Determine the payoffs that the players receive for each of the possible outcomes that could occur in the game.

    d. Write the payoffs for each player in the game tree next to the appropriate potential outcome. By convention, start by writing the payoffs belonging to the player who moves first in the game, then write the payoffs belonging to the player who moves second, then write the payoffs belonging to the player (if there is one) who moves third, and so on. Use a comma to distinguish between the players' payoffs.

Once written, the game must be solved by backward induction.

2. Solving the game by backward induction

    a. Start at the end of the game tree. At each final choice node, determine which of the available actions provides the highest payoff to the player making the choice. Highlight the branch of the game tree associated with this "most preferred" action by making it bold.
    b. Now go to the previous choice node. Again, determine which of the available actions provides the highest payoff to the player now making the choice. Highlight this branch of the game tree by making it bold.
    c. Continue this process of backward induction all the way back to the initial node and the beginning of the game.

After the game has been solved by backward induction, it is often interesting to identify three things: the expected outcome of the game, the payoffs that each player receives, and the subgame perfect equilibrium of the game.

3. Identifying the outcome, payoffs, and subgame perfect equilibrium

    a. Start at the beginning of the game and follow the bold lines until you reach one of the potential outcomes of the game. The path that you have just followed is called the equilibrium path. The potential outcome that you reach, or the path along which you travel, is the expected outcome.
    b. The payoffs associated with the expected outcome indicate the payoffs that each player will receive.
    c. To determine the subgame perfect equilibrium, you must list the choices made by the players at all of the choice nodes in the game. These choices are the ones that you identified during the process of backward induction—the bold branches. There will be as many choices listed in the SPE as there are choice nodes in the game. By convention, the SPE first lists all of the choices that the first player makes at each of the choice nodes with which she is associated, then it lists all of the choices that the second player makes at each of the choice nodes with which she is associated, then it lists all of the choices that the third player (if there is one) makes at each of the choice nodes with which she is associated, and so on. The sets of choices made by each player are separated by a semicolon and placed within parentheses.

Example: Potential Entry in a Senate Race

Suppose the strategic situation that we are interested in is a US Senate race between an incumbent senator called Staton and a potential challenger called Reenock.[8] Imagine that Staton (incumbent) must decide whether to start a preemptive advertising campaign for the Senate seat and that Reenock (potential challenger) must decide whether to enter the race or not. We will assume that Staton chooses whether to launch a preemptive advertising campaign first and that Reenock then decides whether or not to enter the race. Now that we have identified our strategic situation, we can go through the steps outlined earlier.

The game tree for the Senate Race Game going from left to right is shown in Figure 3.9. At the beginning of the game, Staton must decide whether to advertise or not. Whatever Staton decides, Reenock must then choose whether to enter the race or stay out. The choice nodes in the game tree indicate who is making the choice at each point in the game, and the branches coming from each choice node indicate what actions are available to the named player. As you can see, there are four possible outcomes: (a) Staton advertises and Reenock enters (advertise; enter); (b) Staton advertises and Reenock stays out (advertise; stay out); (c) Staton does not advertise and Reenock enters (don't advertise; enter); and (d) Staton does not advertise and Reenock stays out (don't advertise; stay out).

How do we determine the payoffs that the players associate with each outcome? One way to do this is to think about how each of the players would rank the four possible outcomes. Let's start by thinking about how Staton might rank the possible outcomes. If you know anything about US senatorial races, you will know that there is a large incumbency advantage—incumbents typically enjoy a reelection rate of over 90 percent (Jacobson 2001). As a result, Staton can probably expect to be reelected no matter whether he advertises or not. Given that advertising is costly, this means that the best outcome for Staton is for him not to advertise and for Reenock to stay out of the race. The worst outcome for him would probably be to advertise and for Reenock to enter the race anyway. Of the remaining two outcomes, we might think that Staton prefers the situation in which he advertises and Reenock stays out to the situation in which he does not advertise and Reenock enters, because running unopposed (even with the cost of advertising) increases his reputation more than winning a tightly contested race in which he does not advertise. Thus, Staton's preference ordering, or ranking, of the four possible outcomes might be

- (don't advertise; stay out) > (advertise; stay out) > (don't advertise; enter) > (advertise; enter), where ">" means "is strictly preferred to."

How might Reenock rank the four possible outcomes? Reenock knows that he is probably going to lose if he enters. Let's assume, however, that he would like to do as well as possible so as to build name recognition in his party for the future. This suggests that the best outcome for Reenock is for Staton not to advertise and for him to enter. His worst

---

8. The following example is based on a strategic situation described in Dixit and Skeath (1999, 44–47).

outcome would probably be for Staton to advertise and for him to enter, because he is likely to be trounced and see his reputation severely damaged. Of the remaining two outcomes, we might think that Reenock prefers the situation in which Staton advertises and he stays out to the one in which Staton does not advertise and he stays out. Why? Well, Reenock can plausibly tell his party leaders that he did not enter because he had no chance of winning because of Staton's advertising, whereas he comes across as a bit of a wimp if he did not enter and Staton did not advertise. Thus, Reenock's preference ordering, or ranking, of the four possible outcomes might be

- (don't advertise; enter) > (advertise; stay out) > (don't advertise; stay out) > (advertise; enter).

Because there are four possible outcomes, we can assign the value 4 to each player's most preferred outcome, 3 to their second preferred outcome, 2 to their third preferred outcome, and 1 to their least preferred outcome. These are called "ordinal payoffs" because they tell us how the players order the possible outcomes.

Now that we have written the game, we must solve it by backward induction. We start by looking for the final choice nodes. As you can see in Figure 3.9, the Senate Race Game has two final choice nodes. At the top one, Reenock must choose whether to enter or stay out

---

FIGURE 3.9   Senate Race Game

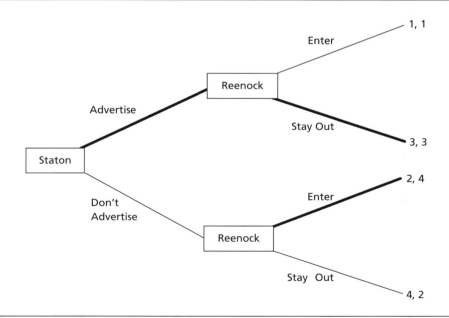

after Staton has decided to advertise. If Reenock enters, his payoff is 1. If Reenock stays out, his payoff is 3. Because 3 is bigger than 1, Reenock will choose to stay out. We indicate this choice by making the "stay out" branch bold. At the bottom final choice node, Reenock must choose whether to enter or stay out after Staton has decided not to advertise. If Reenock enters, his payoff is 4. If Reenock stays out, his payoff is 2. Because 4 is bigger than 2, Reenock will choose to enter. We indicate this choice by making the "enter" branch bold. Now we move backward to the previous choice node, which in this game is the initial choice node. At this choice node, Staton must choose whether to advertise or not. If he advertises, he can see that Reenock will stay out and his payoff will be 3. If he does not advertise, he can see that Reenock will enter and his payoff will be 2. Because 3 is bigger than 2, Staton will choose to advertise. We indicate this choice by making the "advertise" branch bold. We have now solved the Senate Race Game by backward induction.

We now need to identify the expected outcome of the game, the payoffs that each player receives, and the subgame perfect equilibrium of the game. In order to find the expected outcome, we start at the beginning of the game and follow the highlighted branches until we reach one of the possible outcomes. As you can see, the expected outcome of the Senate Race Game is that the incumbent, Staton, advertises and the potential challenger, Reenock, stays out (advertise, stay out). In order to find the payoffs that each player receives in this game, we simply look at the payoffs associated with the expected outcome. In this case, we can see that Staton receives 3 and Reenock receives 3, that is, (3, 3). This indicates that both players obtained their second-best outcome. In order to determine the subgame perfect equilibrium, we must list the choices made by each of the players at all of the choice nodes in the game. There are three choice nodes in the Senate Race Game, so the SPE will list three choices, one for each choice node. Recall that we must first list the choices made by Staton at all of the choice nodes with which he is associated and then list the choices made by Reenock at all of the choice nodes with which he is associated. The process of backward induction indicates that Staton will choose "advertise" at the one choice node where he gets to make a decision and that Reenock will choose "stay out" at his top choice node and "enter" in his bottom choice node. As a result, the subgame perfect equilibrium for this game is (advertise; stay out, enter).

As you will notice, the Senate Race Game offers a potential explanation for why incumbents might choose to run an advertising campaign even when they do not face any challengers. In effect, the incumbent launches a preemptive advertising game in order to deter the entry of a potential challenger. The Senate Race Game is a generic type of Entry Deterrence Game. Epstein and Zemsky (1995) offer a slightly different version of our Senate Race Game to explain entry deterrence in electoral contests. In their model, a potential challenger would like to enter an electoral contest but only if the incumbent is politically weak. If the incumbent is strong, the potential challenger would prefer to stay out. As you can imagine, incumbents may want to signal to potential challengers that they are strong by raising large amounts of campaign money. If this "war chest" convinces the potential challenger that the incumbent is strong, then he is deterred from entering. As you can see, the Epstein and Zemsky game is, in its basic form, very similar to the Senate Race Game examined here.

PROBLEMS

1. Backward Induction: Some Generic Games to Solve

We now present some generic extensive form games. As always, higher-valued payoffs are preferred to lower-valued payoffs. Solve each of the games by backward induction. For each game, write down the expected outcome, the payoffs that each player receives, and the subgame perfect equilibrium.

> a. Generic Game I: Figure 3.10
> b. Generic Game II: Figure 3.11
> c. Generic Game III: Figure 3.12
> d. Generic Game IV: Figure 3.13

FIGURE 3.10   **Generic Game I**

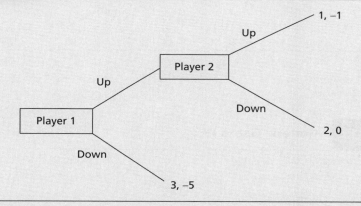

FIGURE 3.11   **Generic Game II**

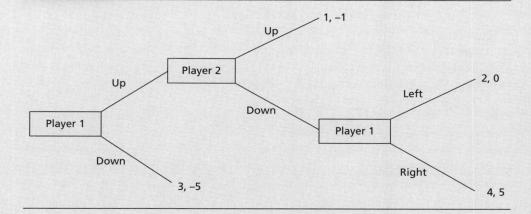

FIGURE 3.12 **Generic Game III**

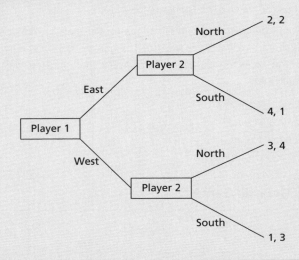

FIGURE 3.13 **Generic Game IV**

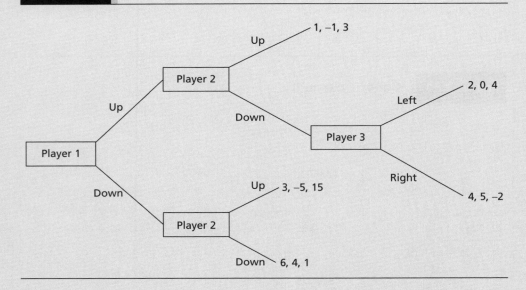

2. Senate Race Game Revisited

Earlier we solved the Senate Race Game assuming that the incumbent, Staton, first decided whether or not to advertise and that the potential challenger, Reenock, then decided whether to enter or stay out. What happens, though, if we reverse the order in which the choices are made? In other words, what happens if Reenock has to decide whether to enter or stay out before Staton decides whether to advertise or not? The game tree for this scenario is shown in Figure 3.14. Assume that the two players have the same preference orderings as before; that is, Reenock's preference ordering is

- (enter; don't advertise) > (stay out; advertise) > (stay out; don't advertise) > (enter; advertise).

Staton's preference ordering is

- (stay out; don't advertise) > (stay out; advertise) > (enter; don't advertise) > (enter; advertise).

    a. Put the payoffs for each player associated with the four possible outcomes into the game tree in Figure 3.14. Use the numbers 4, 3, 2, and 1 to indicate the preference ordering for each player as we did with the original Senate Race Game.

FIGURE 3.14 **New Senate Race Game**

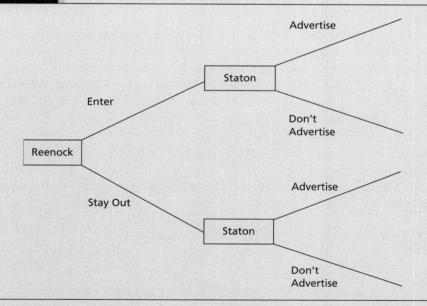

    b. Solve the game by backward induction. Write down the expected outcome of the game, the payoffs that each player receives, and the subgame perfect equilibrium.

    c. Based on what you have found, does it matter which player gets to move first? If it does matter, explain why it matters. If it does not matter, explain why it does not matter.

3. Terrorism Game

Terrorism is a problem that afflicts countries around the world, from Spain to Chechnya to Mali to Pakistan to Iraq. We can use game theory to think about the circumstances in which groups in society might engage in terrorist activities.[9] Imagine that there are two types of groups in society who might become terrorists and who can be distinguished by their preference for negotiations or violence. One type might be called "True Believers." These are fanatics who wish to engage in violent acts even if governments are willing to negotiate with them. We might think of al-Qaida members when we think of this type of social group. The second type might be called "Reluctant Terrorists" or "Freedom Fighters." These are people who would prefer to solve problems through negotiation but who will engage in terrorist acts if they are repressed by the government. One could argue that members of the Palestine Liberation Organization (PLO) or the Irish Republican Army (IRA) fall into this category. Imagine also that there are two types of governments that can be distinguished by their preference for negotiations or repression. One type of government might be called "Repressive Governments" because they wish to repress all social groups that oppose them. The second type of government might be called "Responsive Governments" because they are willing to listen to the demands of opposition groups and enter good faith negotiations with them.

    We can think of a strategic situation in which a group in society must decide whether to request some policy concession from the government that will satisfy them politically or engage in a violent terrorist act. If the social group chooses violence, then the game ends with a terrorist act that leads to no cooperative negotiations and no change in the government position. If the social group requests some policy concession, the government must decide whether to repress the social group now that it has identified itself or enter good faith negotiations with it. As you can see, this Terrorism Game has three possible outcomes: Terrorist act, Repression, or Good faith negotiations. The basic game tree for the Terrorism Game is shown in Figure 3.15.

    Based on the story that we have just told, the preference ordering for the True Believers over the three possible outcomes might be

- Terrorist act > Good faith negotiations > Being repressed.

---

9. The following terrorism game is based on a game found in Bueno de Mesquita (2006, 395–401).

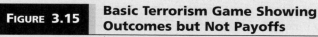

FIGURE 3.15   **Basic Terrorism Game Showing Outcomes but Not Payoffs**

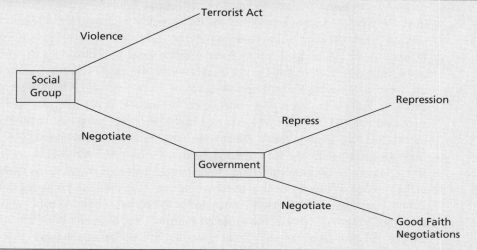

The preference ordering for the Reluctant Terrorists might be

- Good faith negotiations > Terrorist act > Being repressed.

The preference ordering for the Repressive Government might be

- Repression > Good faith negotiations > Terrorist act.

The preference ordering for the Responsive Government might be

- Good faith negotiations > Repression > Terrorist act.

    a. Draw the game tree for the Terrorism Game with the social group True Believers and a Repressive Government. Using the preference orderings shown above, write in the appropriate payoffs for each possible outcome. Use the numbers 3, 2, and 1 to indicate the preference ordering for the players as we did with the Senate Race Game. Solve the game using backward induction. What is the expected outcome of the game? What are the payoffs that each player receives? What is the subgame perfect equilibrium?

    b. Draw the game tree for the Terrorism Game with the social group True Believers and a Responsive Government. Using the preference orderings shown above, write in the appropriate payoffs for each possible outcome. As before, use the numbers 3, 2, and

1 to indicate the preference ordering for the players. Solve the game using backward induction. What is the expected outcome of the game? What are the payoffs that each player receives? What is the subgame perfect equilibrium?

c. Does the type of government matter for the expected outcome of the Terrorism Game if the social group is True Believers?

d. Draw the game tree for the Terrorism Game with the social group Reluctant Terrorists and a Repressive Government. Using the preference orderings shown above, write in the appropriate payoffs for each possible outcome. As before, use the numbers 3, 2, and 1 to indicate the preference ordering for the players. Solve the game using backward induction. What is the expected outcome of the game? What are the payoffs that each player receives? What is the subgame perfect equilibrium?

e. Draw the game tree for the Terrorism Game with the social group Reluctant Terrorists and a Responsive Government. Using the preference orderings shown above, write in the appropriate payoffs for each possible outcome. As before, use the numbers 3, 2, and 1 to indicate the preference ordering for the players. Solve the game using backward induction. What is the expected outcome of the game? What are the payoffs that each player receives? What is the subgame perfect equilibrium?

f. Does the type of government matter for the expected outcome of the Terrorism Game if the social group is Reluctant Terrorists?

g. It is commonly assumed that terrorist acts are always committed by crazy, irrational fanatics. According to the various versions of the Terrorism Game that you have examined, are fanatics the only type of people who conduct terrorist attacks?

h. The common assumption that terrorist acts are committed by crazy, irrational fanatics helps to explain why so many countries such as the United States and the United Kingdom make public declarations that they will never negotiate with terrorists under any circumstances. Given that governments do not want terrorist acts, think about whether making such declarations matters for whether terrorist acts actually occur. What if the social group is made up of True Believers? What if the social group is made up of Reluctant Terrorists? *Hint:* Think about how these declarations influence the perception of the social group about whether the government they are interacting with is responsive or repressive. Does it make sense to make these kinds of statements? If so, why? If not, why not?

4. Legislative Pay Raise Game

Imagine a strategic situation in which three legislators vote sequentially on whether they should receive a pay raise. Let's assume that decisions are made by majority rule. This means that if at least two legislators vote yes, then each legislator will receive a pay raise. Although all the legislators would like to receive a pay raise, they know that they will pay a cost with their constituents if they are seen to vote for the raise. From the perspective of each legislator, four possible outcomes can occur. The most preferred outcome for all three legislators is that they get the pay raise even though they personally vote no. The worst possible outcome is that they do not get the pay raise and they voted yes. Of the remaining two outcomes, let us assume that the legislators prefer the outcome in which they get the pay raise when they voted yes to the outcome in which they do not get the pay raise when they voted no. As a result, the preference ordering for each legislator is

- Get raise, vote no > Get raise, vote yes > No raise, vote no > No raise, vote yes.

    a. Imagine that you are one of the legislators. Would you prefer to vote first, second, or third? Explain your answer.
    b. The game tree for the Legislative Pay Raise Game is shown in Figure 3.16. Using the preference orderings shown above, we have written in appropriate payoffs for some, but not all, of the outcomes. As before, we have used the numbers 4, 3, 2, and 1 to

FIGURE 3.16   Legislative Pay Raise Game

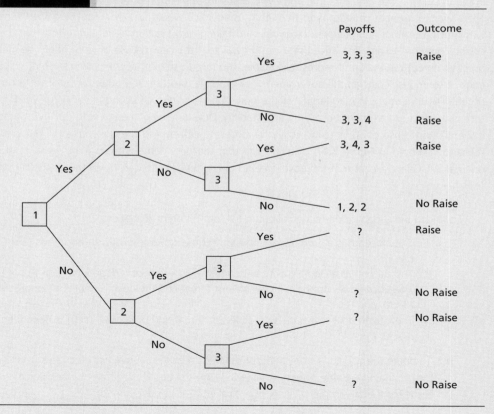

Payoffs	Outcome
3, 3, 3	Raise
3, 3, 4	Raise
3, 4, 3	Raise
1, 2, 2	No Raise
?	Raise
?	No Raise
?	No Raise
?	No Raise

indicate the preference ordering of the players. Legislator 1's payoff is shown first, Legislator 2's payoff is shown second, and Legislator 3's payoff is shown third. Fill in the missing payoffs to complete the game.

c. Solve the game by backward induction. Be careful to make sure that you are comparing the payoffs of the correct legislator. What is the expected outcome of the game? What are the payoffs that each player receives? What is the subgame perfect equilibrium?

d. Imagine that you are one of the legislators again. Now that you have solved the game, would you prefer to vote first, second, or third? Explain your answer. Did your answer change from before?

e. Does the Legislative Pay Raise Game have any implications for whether you would want to be in a position to set the rules or the agenda in business meetings or other official settings? Explain your answer.

5. EVL Game Extension I

In the EVL Game, we assumed that voice was costly for the citizen but not for the government. There were a number of reasons to think that using voice would be costly for the citizen. One was that protesting, complaining, lobbying, and taking direct action all require effort that the citizen could put to an alternative use. Another was that the citizen's use of voice might be met by government repression. It seems reasonable, though, to think that the citizen's use of voice might also impose costs on the government. For example, protests and other forms of voice can potentially undermine the legitimacy of the government or disrupt economic activity, which in turn can affect government popularity and stability. Does anything change with our EVL Game if we allow the use of voice to be costly for both the citizen and the government? This new scenario is shown in Figure 3.17. You'll notice that the new game is exactly the same as our original EVL Game except that the government now suffers a cost, $c_g > 0$, whenever the citizen uses her voice.

a. Find the subgame perfect equilibrium for four different scenarios:

   (i) The citizen has a credible exit threat and the government is autonomous ($E > 0$, $L < 1$)

   (ii) The citizen has a credible exit threat and the government is dependent ($E > 0$, $L > 1$)

   (iii) The citizen does not have a credible exit threat and the government is autonomous ($E < 0$, $L < 1$)

   (iv) The citizen does not have a credible exit threat and the government is dependent ($E < 0$, $L > 1$)

b. Compare the equilibria from the four different scenarios above with the ones from the original EVL Game shown in Table 3.3. Are the equilibria different when voice is costly for the government? If so, how and why? If not, why not?

FIGURE 3.17	EVL Game Extension I: Voice Is Costly for the Citizen and the Government

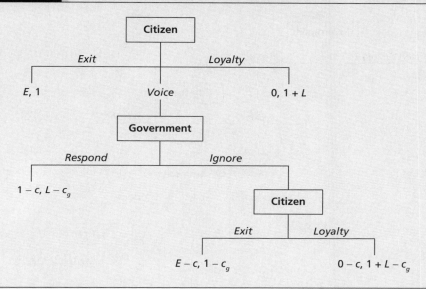

Note: E = citizen's exit payoff; 1 = value of benefit taken from the citizen by the government; L = government's value from having a loyal citizen who does not exit; c = cost of using voice for the citizen; c_g = cost imposed on the government by the citizen's use of voice. It is assumed that c, c_g, $L > 0$ and that $E < 1 - c$.

6. EVL Game Extension II

In the chapter, we discussed what it would look like to incorporate the EVL Game's prehistory into the game itself. In effect, we would have to add a move at the beginning of the game in which the government decides whether or not to take the benefit away from the citizen. We can think of this as a decision by the government about whether to exploit the citizen by taking away some of her resources or not. The game tree for this "extended" version of the EVL Game is shown in Figure 3.18. In addition to adding the prehistory into the game itself, we also assume, as we did in the last problem, that voice is costly for both the citizen and the government. As before, the cost of voice for the citizen is $c > 0$, and the cost imposed on the government by the citizen's use of voice is $c_g > 0$. It is important to note that the government is now the first player to move in the game, and so the government's payoffs are now listed first and the citizen's payoffs are listed second.

a. Find the subgame perfect equilibrium for four different scenarios:

   (i) The citizen has a credible exit threat and the government is autonomous ($E > 0$, $L < 1$)

   (ii) The citizen has a credible exit threat and the government is dependent ($E > 0$, $L > 1$)

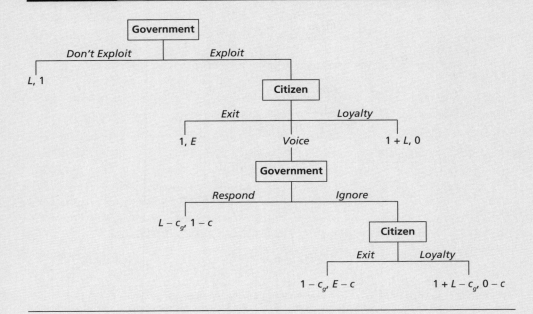

FIGURE 3.18   **EVL Game Extension II: Incorporating the Prehistory**

    (iii) The citizen does not have a credible exit threat and the government is autonomous ($E < 0$, $L < 1$)

    (iv) The citizen does not have a credible exit threat and the government is dependent ($E < 0$, $L > 1$)

  b. Under what conditions will the government seek to exploit the citizen? Under what conditions will the government not seek to exploit the citizen? Does the citizen ever use her voice in equilibrium? If so, when and why? And if not, why not?

7. Writing and Solving Your Own Games

  a. Think of a strategic situation in which two players make choices sequentially. Write down the game tree, establish preferences, and solve by backward induction. What is the expected outcome? What are the payoffs that each player receives? What is the subgame perfect equilibrium?

  b. Think of a strategic situation in which three players make choices sequentially. Write down the game tree, establish preferences, and solve by backward induction. What is the expected outcome? What are the payoffs that each player receives? What is the subgame perfect equilibrium?

4 The Origins of the Modern State

- A state is an entity that relies on coercion and the threat of force to rule in a given territory. A failed state is a state-like entity that cannot coerce and is unable to successfully control the inhabitants of a given territory.

- We present two views of the state: a contractarian view and a predatory view. According to the contractarian view, the creation of the state helps to resolve political disputes that citizens might have with one another. Although the emergence of the state helps to solve these sorts of problems, it creates a potential new problem between the citizens and the state itself: if the state has sufficient power to prevent conflict between its citizens, what is to stop the state from using this power against the citizens?

- The predatory view of the state focuses on the potential conflicts of interest that exist between citizens and the state. According to the predatory view, states emerge as an unintended consequence of the strategies employed by actors like lords and kings to seize and maintain their hold on power. In many respects, a state can be viewed as an "extortion racket" that threatens the well-being of its citizens and then sells them protection from itself.

OVERVIEW

In the previous chapter, we defined the domain of politics as the subset of human behavior that involves the use of power. This includes any situation in which individuals cannot accomplish their goals without either trying to influence the behavior of others or trying to wrestle free from the influence exerted by others. As anyone who has tried to get her room-mate to wash the dishes or her professor to change a grade knows, political behavior is ubiquitous. Politics affects virtually every aspect of our lives, but the study of comparative politics typically focuses on political behavior that occurs at the level of the state. In this chapter, we focus on the state; we explain what it is, where it comes from, and what its function is. To do this, we concentrate on two common views of the state—the contractarian view of the state and the predatory view of the state. According to the contractarian view, the state emerges to help individuals in cases where decentralized cooperation is likely to be difficult. Although those who subscribe to this view see the creation of the state as a solution to conflicts of interest between citizens, it leads to a new problem—a conflict of interest between citizens and the state itself. The predatory view of the state looks squarely at this new conflict of interest. We will use the predatory view of the state as a lens through which to study the historical origins of the state in early modern Europe. We begin, though, by examining standard definitions of the state.

WHAT IS A STATE?

The most famous definition of the **state** comes from the German sociologist Max Weber ([1918] 1958, 78). The state, he said, "is a human community that (successfully) claims the *monopoly of the legitimate use of physical force* within a given territory" (p. 78, italics original). Weber's definition has several different components. One is that a state requires a "given territory." In some sense, this component of Weber's definition distinguishes states from nations. At a basic level, a **nation** is a group of people who share some sort of common identity like a language, a religion, or an ethnicity—there is no obvious requirement that the nation be geographically located in a particular place, as a state must. For example, many Jews believed that they belonged to a nation long before the current state of Israel was established; indeed, many Jews in the interwar period in Europe advocated an extraterritorial view of the Jewish nation (Mendelsohn 1983). Of course, the gradual emergence of the **nation-state** since the eighteenth century has led many to associate nations with states and, hence, with a given territory. It is important to recognize, however, that although the nation-state has become by far the most predominant political entity in the world, there are still "stateless nations," like the Kurds in Iraq, and "diasporic nations" without a clearly identified homeland, such as the Roma. As a result, nations and states remain distinct concepts even if they increasingly seem to occur together. On the whole, all definitions of a state since Weber's have retained his assertion that

> A **state** is an entity that uses coercion and the threat of force to rule in a given territory. A **nation** is a group of people who share some sort of common identity like a language, a religion, an ethnicity, or a shared history. A **nation-state** is a state in which a single nation predominates and the legal, social, demographic, and geographic boundaries of the state are connected in important ways to that nation.

some kind of "given territory" is a required characteristic for a state.

A second component of Weber's definition is that the state must have a "monopoly on the *legitimate* use of physical force." This focus on "legitimacy" has troubled many scholars over the years because it is not always easy to determine what is, and is not, a legitimate use of force. In fact, we can all probably think of situations in which the use of force by the state lacks legitimacy. For example, many of you will think that the violence perpetrated by state officials on the civil rights protesters of the 1960s in the United

AP Photo

Members of the Cambridge Nonviolent Action Committee watched by members of the National Guard at a protest on July 21, 1963, in Cambridge, Maryland.

States was illegitimate. Martin Luther King Jr. clearly considered certain actions by the US state to be illegitimate when he criticized it for being "the greatest purveyor of violence in the world" during an anti-Vietnam War speech in New York City in 1967. These examples suggest that a state's use of force need not always be legitimate, at least in the minds of some of its citizens. It is because of this that subsequent scholars have largely dropped any reference to legitimacy in their definitions of the state.

A third component of Weber's definition is that the state must have a "*monopoly* on the legitimate use of physical force." This focus on "monopoly" has also troubled many scholars. The primary reason for this is that it is relatively easy to think of examples in which nonstate actors have the ability to use physical force and in which this use of force might be considered legitimate. For instance, many people believe that the use of force by groups such as the Irish Republican Army in Northern Ireland, Hamas and Islamic Jihad in the Palestinian territories, or al-Qaida in Iraq and Afghanistan is a legitimate response to foreign occupation and repression. Similarly, many people believe that the violent resistance by the Islamic mujahideen to Soviet control in Afghanistan during the 1980s was legitimate. Of course, one man's freedom fighter is another man's terrorist, and whether you agree that the violent actions of these nonstate groups are legitimate or not will probably depend on which side of the conflict you are on. Thus, it is not obvious that a state always has a "monopoly" on the legitimate use of force. It is for this reason that subsequent scholars have tended to shy away from using the term *monopoly* when defining the state's use of physical force.

Below are two more recent definitions of a state. The first is by a sociologist named Charles Tilly, and the second is by the Nobel-laureate economist Douglass North.

> [States are] relatively centralized, differentiated organizations, the officials of which, more or less, successfully claim control over the chief concentrated means of violence within a population inhabiting a large contiguous territory. (Tilly 1985, 170)

> A state is an organization with a comparative advantage in violence, extending over a geographic area whose boundaries are determined by its power to tax constituents. (North 1981, 21)

Although these definitions differ from that provided by Weber in that they no longer refer to legitimacy or a monopoly over the use of force, they share his belief that all states must have a given territory and that they inherently rely on the threat of force to rule. That states rely on the threat of forceful coercion cannot be overemphasized. The economic historian Frederick Lane (1958) even refers to a state as a violence-producing enterprise. All states use at least the threat of force to organize public life. This is true whether we are referring to the harshest of dictatorships or the most laudable of democracies. The more obvious use of force by dictatorships should not hide the fact that state rule in democracies is also based on the threat of force (and often the use of force). To see this, think about how many of us would actually pay our taxes in full if the threat of imprisonment from the state for tax avoidance was not implicit. Even if the state uses force in the best interests of society and is authorized to use force by its citizens, we should never forget that it still rules by coercion.

That states rule through the use of force does not mean that they are all-powerful. As we noted earlier, states never perfectly monopolize force in any country. This explains why North claims only that states must have a "comparative advantage in violence" and Tilly that they have control "over the chief concentrated means of violence." Nor does the state's ability to use force necessarily mean that it can always enforce its will. All states tolerate some noncompliance. For example, the state does not punish every driver who runs a red light or every underage student who drinks alcohol. At some point, the marginal cost of enforcing laws becomes so great for any state that it prefers to allow some degree of noncompliance rather than spend more resources on improving law enforcement. The bottom line is that although various states justify coercion in different ways (through elections, through birthright, through religion, and so on), although they may use coercion for different purposes (to improve social welfare or to enrich themselves, and so on), and although their use of coercion may have different effects (higher levels of investment and economic growth or increased poverty and conflict, and so on), all states rely on, and use, coercion to rule.

States that cannot coerce and are unable to use force to successfully control the inhabitants of a given territory are often described as **failed states** (King and Zeng 2001; Milliken 2003; Rotberg 2002). For example, contemporary observers frequently refer to countries such as Afghanistan,

A **failed state** is a state-like entity that cannot coerce and is unable to successfully control the inhabitants of a given territory.

the Central African Republic, Iraq, Syria, Somalia, Sudan, and Yemen as failed states. Note that these states are not "failing" because they are unable to meet some policy objective; they are "failing" because they are unable to provide the functions that define them as states—they are unable to coerce or successfully control the inhabitants in their territory. In effect, states in these countries fail to exist.

SOMALIA AND SYRIA: TWO FAILED STATES

But what does a failed state look like exactly? In what follows, we briefly describe the history of two failed states in Somalia and Syria.

Somalia

In a 2006 US congressional hearing, it was pointed out that the African country of Somalia had become synonymous with "chaos" and, for the past fifteen years, had been considered to be a "classic failed state."[1] One scholar of failed states writes the following about his experience in Somalia:

> In 1993 I did emergency relief work in Baidoa, Somalia. This was a time when the Somali state had truly collapsed: there was no army, no state bureaucracy, no police force or courts, and no state to provide electricity, water, road maintenance, schools, or health services. I have a passport full of immigration exit and entry stamps from Wilson Airport in Nairobi [Kenya], the departure point for Baidoa, but there is no evidence that I was ever in Somalia because there was no immigration service to stamp my passport. I would get off the plane, and simply walk through the airport gates and go to town. As journalists often remarked, Somalia during this era had similarities with the *Mad Max/Road Warrior* movies: water wells [were] guarded by armed gangs, diesel fuel was society's most precious commodity, and ubiquitous "technicals"—4WD vehicles with heavy machine guns mounted onto their rear trays—cruised the streets hoping for trouble. (Nest 2002, vi)

Since 1991 there have been at least fifteen attempts to establish a national government in Somalia, but none has been successful (Kasaija 2010). The Somali Federal Government, installed in 2012, is generally recognized by foreign countries and the United Nations as the legitimate government in Somalia. As of February 2016, though, the Somali Federal Government's authority is not universally accepted throughout the country. Even in the regions that it controls, the federal government is heavily reliant on external military intervention from the African Union Mission in Somalia (Mosley 2015).

The collapse of the Somali state can be dated back to January 1991 when several Somali clans coalesced to overthrow the longtime dictator Siad Barre (Kasaija 2010). These clans

---

1. For the full report of the hearing, see US Congress (2006).

soon fell out with each other, though, once their common enemy had been removed. At this point, various militia leaders and "warlords" fought to take control in the post-Siad Barre era. The conflict that ensued resulted "in a protracted bloodbath, killing an estimated 14,000 and wounding three times that number. . . . Ferocious fighting extended outside [the capital] Mogadishu, spreading devastation and starvation through most of southern Somalia" (Lewis 2002, 264).

In March 1992, a United Nations humanitarian mission was organized to help the Somali population. Later that year, a military coalition backed by the United Nations and led by American troops went into Somalia under the code name "Operation Restore Hope" to provide humanitarian support. The international coalition soon met violent resistance from various Somali warlords. In October 1993, eighteen American soldiers were killed when two American helicopters were shot down. This incident became known as the "Battle of Mogadishu." Readers may be familiar with this event from the book *Black Hawk Down* by the war correspondent Mark Bowden. At the time, the media broadcast images of an American soldier being dragged through the streets of Mogadishu. The American public responded by calling for an immediate withdrawal of US forces from Somalia (Anderson 2009).[2] Without US support, the rest of the UN coalition also decided to leave.

Fighting between different Somali militias continued, with new factions continually emerging to claim power. The most important of these new factions was the Islamic Courts Union (ICU). The ICU was a collection of previously autonomous local Islamic courts and associated militias that had formed in the mid-1990s to improve law and order in their respective regions (Barnes and Hassan 2007; Ibrahim 2010).[3] These local courts gradually unified under the umbrella of the Islamic Courts Union.

In the years that followed the withdrawal of the UN mission, a series of unsuccessful peace talks were held (Kasaija 2010). Eventually, in August 2004, a Transitional Federal Government (TFG) was sworn in. The ICU provided the main opposition to the TFG. The US government claimed that the ICU was a serious terrorist threat and actively supported opposition to it (Barnes and Hassan 2007; Ibrahim 2010). Indeed, some in the US government believed that the ICU was sheltering the individuals behind the 1998 bombings of the US embassies in Tanzania and Kenya (International Crisis Group 2006). In 2006, the United States backed several "secular" warlords in Mogadishu who opposed the expansion of ICU rule. These warlords had banded together as a counterterrorism coalition called the Alliance for the Restoration of Peace and Counter-Terrorism (International Crisis Group 2006). Despite US backing, though, the warlords were eventually defeated by the ICU in what became known as the "Second Battle of Mogadishu."

---

2. The Battle of Mogadishu led to a profound change in US foreign policy at the time, with the Clinton administration increasingly reluctant to intervene militarily in developing-country conflicts, such as the genocide of 800,000 Tutsis by Hutu militia groups in Rwanda in 1994 (Gourevitch 1998).

3. For more information on the ICU, see Stanford University's *Mapping Militants Project* (Militant Mapping Organizations 2010–2016) at https://web.stanford.edu/group/mappingmilitants/cgi-bin/.

By June 2006, the ICU controlled much of southern Somalia and had become the first group in sixteen years to control the whole of the capital Mogadishu (Barnes and Hassan 2007). With the removal of the warlords, law and order improved, schools began to open, garbage was collected, and new businesses opened (Anderson 2009).[4] In many ways, the ICU had begun the difficult task of reestablishing a Somali state.

Fearing the rise of an Islamic state led by the ICU on its borders, Ethiopia, with the implicit support of the United States, sent troops into Somalia in December 2006 to support the Transitional Federal Government (Ibrahim 2010). Although the ICU was quickly driven from the capital, Mogadishu, the TFG and its Ethiopian allies were unable to exert much control (Barnes and Hassan 2007). In September 2007, the ICU reconstituted itself as the Alliance for the Re-Liberation of Somalia (ARS). More militant elements, such as al-Shabab ("The Youth"), which had been the hard-line military youth movement within the ICU, remained outside the ARS and began fighting a guerrilla war against the Ethiopian troops.[5] Al-Shabab's radical tactics, which involved suicide terrorism, attracted numerous foreign fighters to their cause, including several people from the United States (Ibrahim 2010). By January 2009, al-Shabab and other militias had forced the Ethiopian troops to withdraw from the country. Only a small African Union peacekeeping force (AMISOM) remained to protect the UN-sponsored Djibouti peace agreement that had been signed in 2008 between the TFG and the more moderate elements within the Alliance for the Re-Liberation of Somalia (Kasaija 2010).[6]

Al-Shabab is committed to global jihadism (Ibrahim 2010) and has been designated a terrorist organization by numerous countries, including Australia, Canada, Norway, Sweden, the United Kingdom, and the United States. In July 2010, al-Shabab committed its first terrorist attacks outside Somalia when it carried out two suicide bombings against

MOHAMED ABDIWAHAB/AFP/Getty Images

A Somali soldier patrols in Afgooye, near Mogadishu, on October 19, 2016. The previous day, an attack by members of the al-Qaida-linked al-Shabab group killed policemen, soldiers, and civilians.

---

4. See also "Ethiopian Troops on Somali Soil." July 20, 2006. BBC News. http://news.bbc.co.uk/2/hi/africa/5198338.stm.

5. For more information on al-Shabab, see Stanford University's *Mapping Militants Project* ("Al Shabab" 2010–2016) at http://web.stanford.edu/group/mappingmilitants/cgi-bin/groups/view/61.

6. For more information, see African Union Mission in Somalia (AMISOM), "Somali Peace Process: The Djibouti Process." (n.d.) http://amisom-au.org/about-somalia/somali-peace-process/.

crowds watching screenings of the 2010 World Cup final in Kampala, Uganda. These attacks were purportedly in retaliation for Ugandan support for the AMISOM peacekeeping force in Somalia. More recently, al-Shabab has also targeted Kenya for its support of the Somali government—it carried out brutal attacks at the Westgate Mall in Nairobi in 2013 and at Garissa University College in 2015 ("Kenya al-Shabab Attack" 2015).

What is the current political situation in Somalia? September 2012 saw the Transitional Federal Government replaced by the Somali Federal Government (SFG). This government was the first in more than two decades not to be qualified by the term "transitional" (Bryden 2013). The formation of this government was viewed optimistically by international leaders. In a 2013 joint statement with the President of Somalia, the EU High Representative for Foreign Affairs and Security Policy even went so far as to say that "Somalia is no longer a failed state" (Mohamud and Ashton 2013). As we have seen, though, al-Shabab, which has officially been associated with al-Qaida since 2012, continues to engage in terrorist activities and remains a significant force. Indeed, as of February 2016, al-Shabab retains control over large portions of southern and central Somalia and has imposed its own harsh form of Sharia law in these regions. According to Human Rights Watch, the actions of both al-Shabab and the Somali Federal Government are contributing to the ongoing humanitarian crisis and severe human rights violations ("World Report 2015, Somalia" 2015). Despite the optimistic claims made by some international leaders, the establishment of a Somali state still remains a long way off.

Syria

The collapse of the Syrian state is much more recent and has its roots in the 2011 Arab Spring. Syria, like the other countries in the Middle East and North Africa region that experienced pro-democracy protests, had long been a dictatorship. The president of Syria Bashar al-Assad came to power in 2000, following the death of his father, Hafez al-Assad, who had previously ruled Syria for thirty years. In March 2011, protests broke out in response to the arrest and torture of some teenagers who, inspired by events taking place in Tunisia and Egypt, had sprayed anti-regime slogans on a wall (Fahim and Saad 2013). The protests were met by gunfire from the regime's security forces and several protesters were killed. This incident led to more demonstrations, which were met by further violence and repression, which in turn prompted larger protests. By July, hundreds of thousands of Syrians were out on the streets protesting. It was not long before some of the protesters began to take up arms.

Violent confrontations between protesters and regime forces soon transformed into an open civil war between rebel groups and the Syrian government. According to a 2012 UN Report, the conflict has a sectarian element, with Syria's minority Allawite community and other Shia groups on the government side fighting against the majority Sunni community on the rebels' side (United Nations High Commissioner for Human Rights 2013). Numerous foreign countries have been drawn into the conflict. The Syrian government has received support from Russia, Iran, Iraq, and the Lebanese group Hezbollah, while the rebels have received support from the United States, Turkey, Saudi Arabia, and a variety of other Arab nations. Some have claimed that the conflict between the Syrian government and the rebels is a proxy war between regional Sunni and Shia powers, especially Saudi Arabia and Iran (Gerges 2013).

The conflict took on a second dimension when the Islamic terrorist group, the Islamic State in Iraq and the Levant (ISIL), sought to expand its influence beyond Iraq into Syria.[7] The United States

People walk over the rubble following an air strike on a rebel-held neighborhood in Aleppo, Syria, on April 28, 2016.

AMER ALHALBI/AFP/Getty Images

is particularly concerned with the rise of ISIL. Indeed, US air strikes in Syria are primarily targeted at ISIL forces rather than forces controlled by the Syrian government. The United States has been joined in its fight against ISIL by Turkey, Australia, France, Canada, the United Kingdom, and a variety of Arab countries that believe that ISIL is a threat to their own security. Kurdish ground forces have been America's main ally in the fight against ISIL. With the help of US air strikes, Kurdish forces have gained control of territory along the Turkish border in the north of Syria. This, though, has created tension between the United States and Turkey, which has been fighting a Kurdish separatist movement for several decades. Although Russia claims to also be concerned about ISIL, its bombing raids have mainly targeted areas held by antigovernment rebels instead of ISIL. Some commentators have claimed that "what started as a popular uprising against the Syrian government . . . has become a proto-world war with nearly a dozen countries embroiled in two overlapping conflicts" (Peçanha, Almukhtar, and Lai 2015).

The collapse of the Syrian state has been devastating for all Syrians. Since the violence began, a quarter of a million Syrians have been killed and almost thirteen million are in need of humanitarian assistance ("Syria: The Story of the Conflict" 2016). Despite claims

---

7. People use many different names to refer to this particular terrorist group. Some, like us, refer to it as the Islamic State in Iraq and the Levant (ISIL). However, others refer to it as the Islamic State in Iraq and al-Sham or the Islamic State in Iraq and Syria (ISIS). After it announced the restoration of a caliphate in the Middle East in June 2014, the group itself started using the name the Islamic State (IS). More recently, a few countries have begun referring to the terrorist group as Daesh, an acronym derived from the group's original Arabic name. Some commentators have noted that the name Daesh sounds like the Arabic word Daes, meaning "one who crushes something underfoot," and Dahes, meaning "one who sows discord."

to the contrary by the Syrian government, international observers believe that the Syrian government has used chemical weapons against its opponents. In addition to the deaths that it has caused, the Syrian civil war has also left about eleven million people displaced. Of the displaced persons, four and a half million have fled Syria. Most are in poorly resourced refugee camps in bordering countries, such as Turkey, Jordan, and Lebanon. Others, maybe 10 percent, have managed to travel to Europe, where their presence has become a major political issue and contributed to the European refugee crisis ("Migrant Crisis" 2016). In 2015, the European Union member states received almost one and a quarter million asylum applications, with the majority of these coming from Syria (48%), Afghanistan (21%), and Iraq (9%). The topic of Syrian refugees has even become a political issue in the United States, despite the fact that relatively few refugees have attempted to go there. As of October 2015, the United States had accepted only 1,500 Syrian refugees since 2011 (Yan 2015). In November 2015, over half of US state governors said that they opposed letting Syrian refugees into their states (Fantz and Brumfield 2015). Of the citizens who remain in Syria, it is estimated that 80 percent live in poverty and 70 percent lack satisfactory drinking water. As is the case with Somalia, the establishment of a functioning Syrian state seems a long way off.

How Unusual Are Somalia and Syria?

We have described the failed states that currently exist in Somalia and Syria in some detail. But how typical is the situation in Somalia and Syria? Although these two countries stand out as particularly disturbing cases of state failure, they are, unfortunately, not unique. According to the 2015 Fragile States Index, calculated by the think tank The Fund for Peace, South Sudan, Somalia, the Central African Republic, Sudan, the Democratic Republic of Congo, Chad, Yemen, Syria, Afghanistan, and Guinea have the ten most fragile states in the world.[8] Each year the Fragile States Index classifies countries into one of four categories— Alert, Warning, Stable, Sustainable—based on the scores they get on twelve social, economic, and political indicators. The scores for each indicator run from 0 to 10, with higher numbers indicating greater state fragility. The social indicators take account of demographic pressures, refugees, group grievances, and human flight. The economic indicators look at economic development and poverty, while the political indicators focus on state legitimacy, public services, human rights, the security apparatus, factionalized elites, and external intervention. In 2015, Somalia had a score of 114 and Syria had a score of 107.9 out of 120 on the Fragile States Index.

In Map 4.1 we provide a graphic look at state fragility around the world and how it has changed over the last decade. The top panel shows the geographic distribution of state fragility in 2015. The darker the shade of gray, the greater the fragility of the state. As you can see, "sustainable" states are quite rare and "stable" states are not much more common. Much of the world, and the vast majority of the world's population, comes under the jurisdiction of a state that has either an "alert" or "warning" designation. The bottom

---

8. For more information on the Fragile States Index, go to the website for the Fund for Peace at http://fsi.fundforpeace.org/.

Map 4.1   State Fragility in 2015

a. State Fragility in 2015

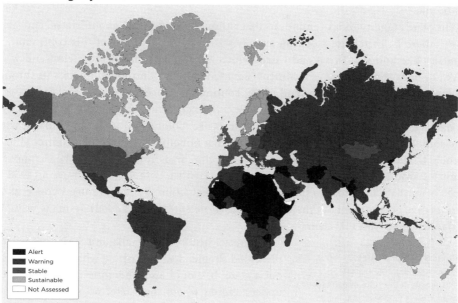

Legend:
- Alert
- Warning
- Stable
- Sustainable
- Not Assessed

b. Change in State Fragility, 2006–2015

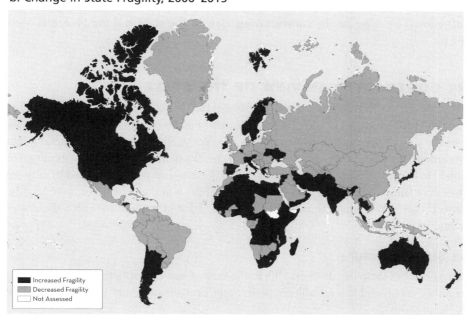

Legend:
- Increased Fragility
- Decreased Fragility
- Not Assessed

Source: Data come from the Fragile States Index 2015, which is provided by the Fund for Peace at http://www.fsi .fundforpeace.org/rankings-2015.

panel shows whether a country's state fragility score has increased or decreased from 2006 to 2015. The countries shown in dark gray have seen their states become more fragile during this period, whereas countries shown in light gray have seen their states become less fragile.

The State Fragility Index reminds us that although we often talk about "states" and "failed states," there is, in reality, a continuum of "stateness." At one end of this continuum are countries like Somalia, Syria, and Chad, which are almost completely stateless and whose weak or nonexistent central governments are ineffective at controlling inhabitants throughout their territory. At the other end of the continuum are countries like Finland, Norway, and Sweden, which have strong and effective central governments that rule in an effectively unchallenged manner. In between are countries like Colombia, Russia, and Turkey, which have somewhat effective central governments that nonetheless fail to fully control all parts of their territory and that frequently leave specific areas ungoverned. When comparing countries around the world, a famous political scientist, Samuel P. Huntington (1968, 1), once wrote that "the most important political distinction among countries concerns not their form of government but their *degree of government*" (italics added). In many ways, it is hard to disagree with this claim.

The **contractarian view of the state** sees the creation of the state as resulting from a social contract between individuals in the state of nature in which the state provides security in exchange for obedience from the citizen.

The brief history of Somalia and Syria that we have presented should clearly illustrate what life is like without a state. It should also underline the importance of understanding where the "state" actually comes from. This is a question that has drawn the attention of political theorists and political scientists for centuries. In what follows, we examine the **contractarian view of the state** and the predatory view of the state.

THE CONTRACTARIAN VIEW OF THE STATE

Early modern political thinkers like Hobbes ([1651] 1994), Locke ([1690] 1980), and Rousseau (1762) engaged in thought experiments in order to help them think more clearly about the role of the state in contemporary life. What, they asked, would social relationships among men (and, we would add, women) be like in a world without states or governments? How would people behave if they did not have to fear being punished by authorities if they stole things or engaged in opportunistic behavior at the expense of their neighbors? In effect, they asked what life would be like in a "state of nature," in which there was no government.

The State of Nature

Thomas Hobbes famously described life in the state of nature as a "war of every man against every man" in which life was "solitary, poor, nasty, brutish, and short" (Hobbes [1651] 1994, chap. 13).[9] He believed that individuals in the **state of nature** faced a dilemma. Given a certain degree of equality between individuals, each citizen recognized

> The **state of nature** is a term used to describe situations in which there is no state.

that he could gain by attacking his neighbor in a moment of vulnerability (say, while his neighbor slept). Each citizen knew, however, that his neighbors were probably thinking exactly the same thing about him. Hobbes believed that even the weakest individual in the state of nature had enough power to overcome the strongest, either by trickery or by joining forces, if he chose (chap. 13). In this type of situation, it is clear that the individuals in the state of nature would all be better off if they abstained from taking advantage of their neighbors than they would be in a "war of all against all." Still, if an act of violence or theft were to take place, it would obviously be far better to be the attacker or thief than the victim. Without a "common power to keep them all in awe," this was the dilemma that faced individuals in the state of nature (chap. 13).

You might think that this discussion is really about barbarous individuals and that it is, therefore, quite remote from the concerns of elevated individuals such as ourselves. It is important to recognize, however, that social contract theorists like Hobbes, Locke, and Rousseau did not claim that life in the state of nature was problematic because of any particular moral failing on the part of the individuals involved. In fact, Jean-Jacques Rousseau worried about "modern" man and had quite romantic notions about the "noble savages" that we might expect to find in the state of nature. Social contract theorists argued that there was something fundamental about the very structure of the situation characterizing the state of nature that made it difficult for citizens to behave themselves.

Game theory can be used to shed light on the structural aspects of the state of nature that might lead to problems. We begin by describing a stylized interaction between two individuals in the state of nature using Hobbes's own language. Imagine that there are two individuals who both desire "the same thing [say, a plot of land], which nevertheless they cannot both enjoy." In the absence of protection from a third-party enforcer, an "invader hath no more to fear than another man's single power" (Hobbes [1651] 1994, chap. 13). Consequently, "if one plants, sows, builds, or possesses a convenient seat, others may probably be expected to come prepared with forces united, to dispossess and deprive him, not only of the fruit of his labour, but also of his life or liberty. And the invader again is in the like danger of another" (chap. 13). Under these conditions, "there is no place for industry" because the industrious have no confidence that they will be able to control the fruit of their labor (chap. 13).

---

9. Hobbes's notion of the "state of nature" is remarkably similar to the notion of "anarchy" used by realist international relations scholars today. Just as Hobbes referred to the condition in which individuals lived in the absence of government as the state of nature, realist international relations scholars refer to the international environment in which individual states live in the absence of a world government as anarchy (Waltz 1979). Like Hobbes, realist international relations scholars believe that anarchy is characterized by a security dilemma in which states are constantly engaged in conflict as they seek to increase their power.

What is Hobbes really saying here? In this stylized interaction, both individuals have essentially two actions that they can take: they can choose to "steal" or they can choose to "refrain" from stealing.[10] If an individual refrains from stealing, then he is essentially choosing to earn a living by doing something productive rather than by stealing. What should the individuals do? The choice facing each individual is complicated because one individual's choice of what to do depends on what he thinks the other individual will do. As we saw in the last chapter, game theory is an extremely useful tool for analyzing these types of strategic situations. We can think of this interaction between two people in the state of nature as a game. In the previous chapter, we used an extensive form game to examine how individuals respond to negative changes in their environment. In this chapter, we are going to use a normal, or strategic, form game to examine how individuals might behave in the state of nature. Recall that an extensive form game employs a game tree that allows us to see what happens when the players take turns to make decisions; that is, there is a specific sequence of play as illustrated by the branches and choice nodes in the game tree. In contrast, a normal, or strategic, form game employs a **payoff table** or **payoff matrix** that allows us to see what happens when the players make decisions at the same time; that is, decisions are made simultaneously in normal form games rather than sequentially.

A **payoff table** or **payoff matrix** represents the strategies and payoffs available to players in strategic, or normal, form games.

Figure 4.1 illustrates the "empty" payoff table of the normal form game that captures our stylized interaction between two individuals, whom we'll call *A* and *B*, in the Hobbesian state

---

FIGURE 4.1   **State of Nature Game without Payoffs**

---

10. To the extent that *steal* presupposes the concept of property, this choice in the state of nature is slightly inaccurate. This is because Hobbes explicitly denies that the concept of property can exist in the state of nature. A more accurate term, then, might be *dispossess*.

of nature. Each player must decide whether to steal or refrain. There are four possible outcomes: both players refrain (top left cell), both players steal (bottom right cell), player *A* steals but player *B* refrains (bottom left cell), and player *A* refrains but player *B* steals (top right cell).

What do you expect the players to do in this game? As before, you cannot really answer this question without knowing how much each of the players values the possible outcomes. In other words, you need to know the payoffs that the players associate with each outcome. Based on what Hobbes says, how do you think that the players might rank each outcome? One interpretation is that each player's best outcome is to steal the other actor's belongings and to keep his own. In other words, a player's best outcome occurs when he steals and the other player refrains. The worst outcome is the exact opposite of this; that is, he refrains and the other player steals his belongings. Between these two fates are the outcomes in which both players refrain and both steal. It seems clear from Hobbes's description of the state of nature that individuals would prefer the former (both refrain) to the latter (both steal). They would prefer this outcome because when both actors choose to "steal" they live in a state of war, which prevents them from engaging in productive activities and makes them reluctant to invest in things that would make their lives better.

Based on Hobbes's view of the state of nature, we can provide a **preference ordering** for each player over the four possible outcomes; that is, we can determine how both players would rank the outcomes. Player *A*'s preference ordering over the four outcomes is

> A **preference ordering** indicates how a player ranks the possible outcomes of a game.

- (Steal; Refrain) > (Refrain; Refrain) > (Steal; Steal) > (Refrain; Steal),

and player *B*'s preference ordering is

- (Refrain; Steal) > (Refrain; Refrain) > (Steal; Steal) > (Steal; Refrain),

where player *A*'s action is given first, player *B*'s action is given second, and ">" means "is strictly preferred to." Given that there are four possible outcomes, we can assign the number 4 to each player's most preferred outcome, 3 to the second preferred outcome, 2 to the third preferred outcome, and 1 to the least preferred outcome. These payoffs are called **ordinal payoffs** because they tell us about the order in which the players rank each of the outcomes. Note that ordinal payoffs can tell us only whether one outcome is preferred by a player to another

> **Ordinal payoffs** allow us to know how a player ranks the possible outcomes; they do not tell us how much more a player prefers one outcome to another.

(the one with the higher number); they cannot tell us how much more the player prefers one outcome to the other.[11] In other words, we can say that an outcome worth 4 is preferred to

---

11. As a result, we could use any sequence of numbers that retains the theorized ranking of the outcomes. For example, we could have chosen the numbers 50, 12, 1, and –10 to indicate how the players rank the four possible outcomes in the game, because these numbers retain the correct preference ordering. Using the numbers 4, 3, 2, and 1 is just simpler.

an outcome worth 1; however, we cannot say that the outcome worth 4 is preferred four times as much as the outcome worth 1.

We can now add these payoffs to the normal form game shown in Figure 4.1. The new game is shown in Figure 4.2. Player A's (the row player's) payoffs are shown first in each cell; player B's (the column player's) payoffs are shown second. A comma separates the payoffs for the players in each cell. Thus, player A receives a payoff of 1 if he refrains and player B steals; player B receives a payoff of 4 in this situation. Player A receives a payoff of 4 if he steals and player B refrains; player B receives a payoff of 1 in this situation. Each player receives a payoff of 3 if they both refrain, and they each receive a payoff of 2 if they both steal.

Solving the State of Nature Game

Now that we know the players, the choices available to them, and how they value each possible outcome, we are ready to solve the State of Nature Game.[12] In the previous chapter, we saw that political scientists solve extensive form games, like the Exit, Voice, and Loyalty Game, for something called a subgame perfect equilibrium (SPE). When it comes to strategic, or normal, form games like the State of Nature Game, though, political scientists solve them for something called a Nash equilibrium (NE). A **Nash equilibrium** is a combination of strategies, one for each player, such that each player in the game would not want to

---

FIGURE 4.2   **State of Nature Game with Payoffs**

		B	
		Refrain	Steal
A	Refrain	3, 3	1, 4
	Steal	4, 1	2, 2

Note: Player A's (the row player's) payoffs are shown first in each cell; player B's (the column player's) payoffs are shown second. A comma separates the payoffs for the players in each cell.

---

12. We refer to this game as a State of Nature Game because of the topic under discussion. As we note later in the chapter (pp. 122–125), however, games with this same payoff structure are more familiarly known as Prisoner's Dilemma games. Prisoner's Dilemma games are used widely in political science to examine a whole host of phenomena, ranging from arms races and democratic transitions to resource exploitation and international cooperation. They are also commonly used in other disciplines such as biology, economics, and sociology.

unilaterally change her strategy given the strategy adopted by the other player. A **strategy** specifies the choices that are made by a player at every point in a game where that player has a choice to make. In the State of Nature Game, each player has only one choice to make, either to refrain or to steal. As a result, each player's equilibrium strategy will have only one choice in it. To form the Nash equilibrium, we simply have to put the two equilibrium strategies together to form a strategy combination. By convention, a NE first lists the equilibrium strategy of the row player, in this case player A, and then the equilibrium strategy of the column player, in this case player B. We separate the players' equilibrium strategies with a semicolon and place them both within parentheses.

> A **Nash equilibrium** is a combination of strategies, one for each player, such that each player in the game does not want to unilaterally change her strategy given the strategy adopted by the other player. The equilibrium strategy for each player is a best reply for that player.
>
> A **strategy** specifies the choices that are made by a player at every point in a game where that player has a choice to make.
>
> A player's **best replies** indicate the choices that are "best" for *each* of the possible choices that the other player might make. "Best" refers to the choice that yields the highest payoff.

The key to solving strategic, or normal, form games is therefore identifying the equilibrium strategies of the players. There are several ways to do this. We are going to focus here on a technique that involves finding each player's "**best replies**." A player's "best replies" indicate the choices that are "best" for *each* of the possible choices that the other player might make. As always, "best" refers to the choice that yields the highest payoff. To identify the best replies for player A, we need to determine which of player A's choices (refrain or steal) is best if player B refrains and which of player A's choices (refrain or steal) is best if player B steals. Similarly, to identify the best replies for player B, we need to determine which of player B's choices (refrain or steal) is best if player A refrains and which of player B's choices (refrain or steal) is best if player A steals. A Nash equilibrium occurs when a strategy combination consists of a strategy (a choice) that is considered a best reply for player A and a strategy (a choice) that is considered a best reply for player B. If both players are doing the best that they can given the strategy adopted by the other player, then neither player wants to unilaterally change her strategy; therefore we have a Nash equilibrium. We're going to walk through this process with the State of Nature Game now, but note that we also walk you through this whole process again for a different normal form game at the end of the chapter just before the Problems section begins.

Let's start by identifying the best replies for player A. What is player A's best reply (refrain or steal) if player B refrains? Note that we're now looking only at the left-hand column of the payoff table where player B refrains. If player A refrains, he will get a payoff of 3, and if he steals, he will get a payoff of 4. Thus, player A's best reply to player B's refraining is for him to steal. We indicate this by placing a line under the 4 in the bottom left cell of the payoff table. This is shown in Figure 4.3. What is player A's best reply if player B steals? We are now just looking at the right-hand column of the payoff table where player B steals. If player A chooses to refrain, he will get a payoff of 1, and if he steals, he will get a payoff of 2. Thus, player A's best reply to player B's stealing is for him to steal as well. We indicate this by placing

FIGURE 4.3   **Solving the State of Nature Game I**

		B	
		Refrain	Steal
A	Refrain	3, 3	1, 4
	Steal	<u>4</u>, 1	2, 2

Note: Player *A*'s (the row player's) payoffs are shown first in each cell; player *B*'s (the column player's) payoffs are shown second. A comma separates the payoffs for the players in each cell. Payoffs associated with the best replies for player *A* are underlined.

a line under the 2 in the bottom right cell of the payoff table. This is shown in Figure 4.4. We have now identified the best replies for player *A* to any choice made by player *B*.

Now let's identify the best replies for player *B*. What is player *B*'s best reply if player *A* refrains? We are now just looking at the top row of the payoff table where player *A* refrains. If player *B* refrains, she will get a payoff of 3, and if she steals, she will get a payoff of 4 (recall that we are now looking at the second number in each cell, because we are trying to identify

FIGURE 4.4   **Solving the State of Nature Game II**

		B	
		Refrain	Steal
A	Refrain	3, 3	1, 4
	Steal	<u>4</u>, 1	<u>2</u>, 2

Note: Player *A*'s (the row player's) payoffs are shown first in each cell; player *B*'s (the column player's) payoffs are shown second. A comma separates the payoffs for the players in each cell. Payoffs associated with the best replies for player *A* are underlined.

FIGURE 4.5 Solving the State of Nature Game III

		B	
		Refrain	Steal
A	Refrain	3, 3	1, ④
	Steal	<u>4</u>, 1	<u>2</u>, 2

Note: Player *A*'s (the row player's) payoffs are shown first in each cell; player *B*'s (the column player's) payoffs are shown second. A comma separates the payoffs for the players in each cell. Payoffs associated with the best replies for player *A* are underlined. Payoffs associated with the best replies for player *B* are circled.

player *B*'s best replies). Thus, player *B*'s best reply to player *A*'s refraining is for her to steal. We indicate this by drawing a circle around the 4 in the top right cell of the payoff table.[13] We show this in Figure 4.5. What is player *B*'s best reply if player *A* steals? We are now just looking at the bottom row in the payoff table where player *A* chooses to steal. If player *B* refrains, she will get a payoff of 1, and if she steals, she will get a payoff of 2. Thus, player *B*'s best reply to player *A*'s stealing is for her to steal as well. We indicate this by drawing a circle around the 2 in the bottom right cell of the payoff table. This is shown in Figure 4.6. We have now identified the best replies for player *B* to any choice made by player *A*

Recall that a Nash equilibrium is a combination of strategies, one for each player, where each player's strategy is a best reply for that player. To locate any Nash equilibria, we therefore need to find cells in the payoff table in Figure 4.6 in which both payoffs are marked as being produced by best replies. As you can see, the one cell in which both numbers are marked as being produced by best replies is the one in which both players choose to steal. Thus, the strategy combination that represents the unique Nash equilibrium in our State of Nature Game is (Steal; Steal).[14] The expected outcome of the game is that both players steal and the payoff to each player is 2.

An interesting feature of this particular game is that both players choose to steal (because they are better off doing so) no matter what the other player chooses. When this occurs, we

---

13. We circle the best replies for player *B* rather than underline them as we did for player *A* for presentational purposes only. By doing this, we are able to easily distinguish the best replies of each player.

14. In this particular game, there is only one Nash equilibrium. Other games with different payoff structures, however, may have no equilibria or multiple equilibria—there is no rule that there will always be a unique equilibrium.

FIGURE 4.6	Solving the State of Nature Game IV

		B	
		Refrain	Steal
A	Refrain	3, 3	1, ④
	Steal	<u>4</u>, 1	<u>2</u>, ②

Note: Player *A*'s (the row player's) payoffs are shown first in each cell; player *B*'s (the column player's) payoffs are shown second. A comma separates the payoffs for the players in each cell. Payoffs associated with the best replies for player *A* are underlined. Payoffs associated with the best replies for Player *B* are circled.

> A player has a **dominant strategy** if that strategy is a best reply to all of the other player's strategies. A **dominant-strategy Nash equilibrium** occurs when both players have a dominant strategy.

say that both players have a **dominant strategy**—in this case their dominant strategy is to steal. The row player in a strategic form game has a dominant strategy whenever his best replies (underlined payoffs) are all in the same row and the column player has a dominant strategy whenever her best replies (circled payoffs) are all in the same column. Because *both* players in the State of Nature Game have dominant strategies, we have what is known as a **dominant-strategy Nash equilibrium**. The bottom line is that the expected outcome from our State of Nature Game is that refraining will be unlikely and that theft will be endemic.[15] This is precisely why Hobbes described life in the state of nature as a "war of every man against every man" in which life was "solitary, poor, nasty, brutish, and short."

Keep in mind that we have simplified the state of nature quite considerably here in order to isolate only the most important aspects of the environment in which player *A* and player *B* find themselves. For example, it is hard to imagine a world in which theft and mutual predation are constantly occurring. In the real world, even the weak are able to fend off attack some of the time. When both actors are equal in strength, attacks will be successful only in moments of temporary vulnerability. Nevertheless, in the absence of someone to keep the actors in a permanent state of "awe," attacks will come when the opportunity arises. As a

---

15. This is the expected outcome when the State of Nature Game is played once. But what do you think happens if player *A* and player *B* get to play the game over and over again? Do you think things change? To find out, you'll have to look at Box 4.1, "Can Cooperation Occur without the State?" at the end of the chapter (pp. 140–144).

result, individuals will live in a persistent state of fear that can be debilitating, even in moments of relative calm.

Although this "abstract" state of nature probably seems remote from many of our own experiences, recall the troubled recent histories of Somalia and Syria. Many commentators have described the environment in Somalia and Syria as a modern-day version of Hobbes's state of nature. Similar descriptions might be given of other situations in which no single actor is able to "awe" everyone in society, such as Iraq during the US occupation, the Darfur region and the "Two Areas" (South Kordofan and Blue Nile) in Sudan today, south central Los Angeles and New York City in the 1980s, New Orleans directly after Hurricane Katrina in 2005, or suburban New Jersey in the world of the Sopranos. In fact, according to the economic historian and Nobel laureate Robert Fogel (2004), the world described by Hobbes as absent of invention, trade, arts, and letters fairly accurately describes most of human history. Similarly, Azar Gat (2006) argues that humans have spent almost their entire evolutionary history in small bands of hunter-gatherers where looting and violent death were about as commonplace as the Hobbesian state of nature would suggest.

When we solved the State of Nature Game for the Nash equilibrium, you may have noticed something that seemed odd. The Nash equilibrium outcome from this game happens to be the second worst outcome for both players. Indeed, both players could be made better off if they chose to refrain—they would both get a payoff of 3 instead of the 2 they get from both stealing in the Nash equilibrium. For this reason, the absence of cooperation represents a dilemma—individual rationality leads actors to an outcome that they both agree is inferior to an alternative outcome. The class of problems in which individual rationality produces outcomes that everyone in society recognizes as inferior has fascinated political thinkers since at least the time of Hobbes. One of the many ways in which it is interesting is that it doesn't seem to be enough for the players to recognize their mutually destructive behavior for cooperation to occur. Ask yourself what would happen if player *A* and player *B* met with each other one sunny afternoon and promised not to steal from each other because this would make them both better off. Do you think that they would feel comforted by such promises as they lay down to sleep that night?

Part of the problem is that each actor may come to feel that he is being taken advantage of. What if you are the only one who is sticking to your promise of good behavior? If your opponent breaks his promise and starts to steal, your best response is to stop refraining and start stealing as well. As the State of Nature Game illustrates, you will increase your payoff from 1 to 2 by doing this. But part of the problem is that you also have an incentive to steal even if you think that your opponent is going to keep his promise. Say you knew for sure that your opponent was going to refrain and that, under these circumstances, you could benefit. What would you do? As the State of Nature Game illustrates, you would choose to break your promise to refrain and start stealing, because this would increase your payoff from 3 to 4. Thus, promising to stop stealing because it is mutually destructive is not sufficient to actually stop the players from stealing. As Garrett Hardin (1968) points out, relying on promises of good behavior or moral suasion may actually have perverse evolutionary consequences in any case. If the world is truly set up as in the State of Nature Game, then individuals who are swayed by entreaties to "behave" and to "do unto others as you would have them do unto you" are not likely to survive long enough to pass such ideas on to their progeny (whether one thinks that the mechanism of transmission is genetics or socialization). In effect, Hardin suggests that to rely on moral suasion is to run the risk that moral people will be eliminated from society.

Civil Society and the Social Contract

Hobbes's solution to the problems that individuals experience in the state of nature was to create someone or something—the "Sovereign"—that had sufficient force that people would stand in awe of it. Like us, Hobbes realized that simply promising not to steal would be insufficient to prevent people from stealing. Instead, he believed that "there must be some coercive power to compel men equally to the performance of their covenants, by the terror of some punishment greater than the benefit they expect by breach of their covenant" (Hobbes [1651] 1994, chap. 15). In other words, Hobbes wanted a sovereign that could "force" people to refrain—for their own good, of course. The sovereign was to be created by an implicit **social contract** between individuals in the state of nature. Individuals would "contract" with each other to give up their **natural rights** (rights given to them by nature) in exchange for **civil rights** (rights given to them by laws) that would be protected by the sovereign. In effect, individuals would give up what they had to the sovereign in return for protection.

> A **social contract** is an implicit agreement among individuals in the state of nature to create and empower the state. In doing so, it outlines the rights and responsibilities of the state and the citizens in regard to each other.
>
> A **natural right** is a universal right that is inherent in the nature of living beings; as such, a natural right can exist even in the state of nature. A **civil right** does not arise naturally but is instead created by the state through laws; as such, a civil right cannot exist in the state of nature.

Hobbes believed that life in the state of nature was sufficiently bad that individuals would, and should, be willing to transfer everything they had to the sovereign in exchange for protection. In many ways, Hobbes's pessimistic view of the state of nature helps to explain why so many Afghans and Somalis were quick to welcome the "law and order" brought by the Taliban and the Islamic Courts Union in their respective countries even though they may have strongly disagreed with the ideologies of these particular movements. Other social contract theorists, like Jean-Jacques Rousseau and John Locke, were more hopeful that individuals in the state of nature could find ways to achieve limited degrees of cooperation. As a result, these latter theorists believed that the extent to which individuals in the state of nature should delegate authority to a "third-party enforcer" such as the sovereign should always be evaluated in light of the particular conditions in which they found themselves. Although there are important differences between them, social contract theorists all view the state as a third-party enforcer who can dole out punishments to individuals who engage in socially destructive behavior that violates the social contract. These punishments were to be structured in such a way that "steal" would no longer be a dominant strategy for individuals in society. How does this happen?

Figure 4.7 illustrates the exact same stylized interaction between two people, A and B, as we saw in the state of nature, except that now there is a "passive player"—the state—lurking in the background who has sufficient physical force to punish those people if they choose to steal rather than refrain. We refer to this as the Civil Society Game because social contract theorists use the term *civil society* to describe the situation in which individuals live with a state. Again, each player must decide whether to steal or refrain. The state will dole out a punishment of value p to anyone who steals. We assume, for simplicity, that the state can see every infraction by the players and always doles out this punishment in response. The four possible outcomes are the same as before: both players refrain, both players steal, player A steals but player B refrains, and player A refrains but player B steals. To keep the discussion that follows as simple as possible, we will now treat the payoffs in the Civil Society Game as though they were **cardinal payoffs**. Unlike ordinal payoffs, cardinal payoffs tell us exactly how much more a player values one

> **Cardinal payoffs** allow us to know how much more the players prefer one outcome to another.

outcome compared with another. In other words, a player values an outcome with a payoff of 4 four times as much as an outcome with a payoff of 1. Now that we have determined the payoff table for the Civil Society Game, we can examine whether the creation of a state that can dole out punishments is sufficient to induce good behavior on the part of the individuals in question. As is often the case in this book, the answer is "it depends."

We can see exactly what it depends on by solving the Civil Society Game for Nash equilibria in the same way that we solved the State of Nature Game earlier. Recall that we start by identifying the best replies for player A. What is player A's best reply if player B refrains? We are now

---

FIGURE 4.7   Civil Society Game

		B	
		Refrain	Steal
A	Refrain	3, 3	1, 4 − p
	Steal	4 − p, 1	2 − p, 2 − p

Note: p = the value of the punishment doled out by the state to anyone who steals.

looking at the left column of the payoff table where player B refrains. If player A refrains, he will get a payoff of 3, and if he steals, he will get a payoff of 4 − p. It is relatively easy to see that he will refrain if 3 > 4 − p. This means that player A can be encouraged to give up his criminal ways if the state sets the punishment for stealing sufficiently high. How high is sufficiently high? A tiny bit of algebra should convince you that as long as the punishment is greater than 1 (that is, bigger than the difference between 4 and 3), then player A will refrain.

Presumably, the state has a relatively easy job in getting player A to refrain if player B is going to refrain. But what if player B steals? We are now looking at the right column of the payoff table where player B steals. If player A refrains, he will get a payoff of 1, and if he steals, he will get a payoff of 2 − p. It is easy to see that he will refrain if 1 > 2 − p. This means that as long as the state chooses a punishment greater than 1 (that is, bigger than the difference between 2 and 1), then player A will "do the right thing" and refrain.

Because player B's payoffs are symmetrical to player A's—they are the same in the equivalent situation—we know that player B will also refrain under the same conditions under which player A refrains, namely, when p > 1. Figure 4.8 indicates the best replies for players A and B when p > 1. As you can see, when the punishment doled out by the state is sufficiently high, p > 1, the unique Nash equilibrium is (Refrain; Refrain). The expected outcome is that both players refrain and the payoff to each player is 3. Note that both players now have a dominant strategy to refrain. In other words, as long as the punishment level imposed by the state is sufficiently high, players will refrain no matter what the other player decides to do.

It seems that by creating a third-party enforcer, the state, that dutifully doles out punishments for bad behavior, we can get individuals to give up the sorts of behavior that made life in the state of nature "solitary, poor, nasty, brutish, and short." Problem solved, right? Well, as you might suspect, the fact that we're still studying politics some three hundred and fifty

---

FIGURE 4.8   Civil Society Game When p > 1

		B	
		Refrain	Steal
A	Refrain	**3**,③	**1**, 4 − p
	Steal	4 − p,①	2 − p, 2 − p

Note: p = the value of the punishment doled out by the state to anyone who steals. Payoffs associated with the best replies of player A are underlined. Payoffs associated with the best replies of player B are circled.

years after Hobbes wrote suggests that there are some problems with his solution. Start by asking yourself why anyone would want to be the sovereign and why she would be willing to do us all a favor by acting as our policeman.

One common answer to this question portrays the members of civil society as being engaged in an exchange relationship with the sovereign. In effect, the sovereign agrees to police us in exchange for taxes that citizens pay.[16] One of the uses of this taxation will be to build up the state's "comparative advantage in violence" (North 1981) and its "control over the chief concentrated means of violence" (Tilly 1985) so that it can keep the citizens in awe and carry out its duties as a state. Given that a sovereign will demand tax revenue to carry out his job, it is not immediately obvious that the citizens will choose to leave the state of nature for civil society; much will depend on the level of taxation imposed by the state. In other words, citizens will not always choose to create a state.

To illustrate this point, compare our State of Nature Game and our Civil Society Game in Figure 4.9. The Civil Society Game now illustrates that the state will impose a tax of size t on the citizens for allowing them to live in civil society. We indicate this by subtracting t from the payoffs of each player in each cell. Note that because the citizen must pay the tax in every cell of the game, the expected outcome of the Civil Society Game does not change—both

| FIGURE 4.9 | **Choosing between the State of Nature and Civil Society** |

Note: p = the value of the punishment doled out by the state to anyone who steals; t = the value of the tax imposed by the state. It is assumed that $p > 1$. Payoffs associated with the best replies of player A are underlined. Payoffs associated with the best replies of player B are circled. The expected outcomes of the two games are shown in the shaded cells.

---

16. Most obviously, we can think of these "taxes" as money that citizens give to the state in return for security. It is possible, however, to conceptualize these taxes more broadly. For example, we might think of required behavioral patterns—such as regularly attending religious institutions or following dress codes, such as wearing a burqa—as a kind of taxation that citizens give in exchange for state-provided security.

players will still choose to refrain (check this for yourself). The expected outcomes of the two games are shown in the shaded cells.

Now ask yourself, "Under what conditions will citizens prefer to leave the state of nature and enter civil society?" The citizen can decide whether to leave the state of nature by comparing the payoffs she expects to receive from playing each game. As you can see, the citizen will get a payoff of 2 if she chooses to remain in the state of nature and a payoff of $3 - t$ if she chooses to live in civil society. It is easy to see that the citizen will prefer to leave the state of nature and live in civil society if $3 - t > 2$. This means that as long as the state does not charge a tax rate larger than 1 (that is, bigger than the difference between 3 and 2), the citizen will prefer to create a state and live in civil society.

Thus, for the state to be a solution to the state of nature as social contract theorists claim, it must be the case that (a) the punishment imposed by the state for stealing is sufficiently large that individuals prefer to refrain rather than steal and (b) the taxation rate charged by the state for acting as the policeman is not so large that individuals prefer the state of nature to civil society. With the particular cardinal payoffs that we have used in our State of Nature Game and Civil Society Game (Figure 4.9), this requires that $p > 1$ and $t < 1$.

This comparison between the responsibilities that the state imposes on its citizens (here thought of in terms of a level of taxation) and the benefits that the citizen can obtain from living in civil society is central to the very nature of politics. Thinkers who see the state of nature as dire are going to expect citizens to accept a draconian set of responsibilities in exchange for the "protection" that the state provides. In contrast, those who see civil society as a mere convenience over a workable, if inefficient, state of nature are going to place much greater restrictions on what the state can ask of its citizens. It is, perhaps, not an accident that Hobbes was writing at the end of a long period of religious war in Europe and civil war in his home country. It was because he had had a firsthand glimpse of what the "war of every man against every man" looked like that he believed that the difference between civil society and the state of nature was effectively infinite. For Hobbes, almost any level of taxation that the state might choose to levy on its citizens in exchange for protection looked like a good deal. You might think that many of the people living in Somalia and Syria right now share a similar view of the world. In contrast, Thomas Jefferson—borrowing from social contract theorists like John Locke—believed, from the relative calm of Monticello, that we had a natural right (that is, the possibility of obtaining in the state of nature) to "life, liberty, and the pursuit of happiness" and that our commitment to the state was so conditional that we should probably engage in revolution, or at least the rewriting of the Constitution, every couple of decades.

The reader is likely to have noticed that contemporary disputes in the United States and elsewhere over whether we should reduce civil liberties by giving more power to the state in an attempt to better protect ourselves against terrorist threats directly echo this historical debate between scholars such as Hobbes and Jefferson. Those politicians who argue that the threat of terrorism warrants a reduction in our civil liberties on the grounds that freedom means little without security are taking a distinctly Hobbesian view of the world.

Whether you ultimately agree more with Hobbes or Jefferson, it seems clear that although the creation of the state may solve the political problem we have with each other, it may also create a potential new problem between us and the state. Put simply, if we surrender control over the means of violence to the state, what is to prevent the state from using this power against us? As some have put it, "Who will guard the guardian?"[17] At the very least, once the state has developed a "comparative advantage" in the use of violence, we would expect a renegotiation of the social contract that, at a minimum, would set the tax rate so high as to leave the citizen indifferent between living in the state of nature and living in civil society. It is the fear that this might occur that drives civil libertarians around the world to challenge ongoing attempts to locate ever-increasing amounts of power in the hands of the state. As you can see, one of the grim, but true, implications of many game-theoretic models is that solutions to political problems frequently lead to changes in behavior that erase the benefits of those solutions. The sovereign: can't live with him, can't live without him.

THE PREDATORY VIEW OF THE STATE

Whereas the contractarian view of the state focuses on the conflicts of interest that exist between individuals, the **predatory view of the state** focuses more on the potential conflicts of interest that exist between individuals and the state. Scholars who employ a predatory view of the state seek to understand the conditions under which the state can be expected to enforce rules

> The **predatory view of the state** holds that states that exercise an effective control over the use of violence are in a position to threaten the security of citizens. This makes it possible for them to exploit the citizens that, according to the contractarian view of the state, they have a duty to protect.

and foster cooperation rather than use its "comparative advantage in violence" to prey upon the citizenry. According to the predatory view of the state, rulers can be viewed as similar to individuals in the state of nature. This is because rulers face their own sort of security dilemma in that they have potential rivals constantly vying to take their place. The concern for security on the part of rulers leads them to use their power to extract resources from others, both because these resources can be used to help ensure their continued existence and because leaving these resources in the hands of rivals is potentially dangerous.

The sociologist Charles Tilly (1985) went as far as to say that states resemble a form of organized crime and should be viewed as extortion rackets. Why? As with the contractarian theory of the state, the predatory approach to the state sees the state as an organization that trades security for revenue. The difference, though, is that the seller of the security in the predatory view of the state happens to represent a key threat to the buyer's continued security. In other words, the state resembles an extortion racket in that it demands tribute (taxes and obedience) from citizens within its jurisdiction in return for protection from, among other things, itself. The British comedy troupe Monty Python's Flying Circus once performed

---

17. The original quotation, "Quis custodiet ipsos custodies?" is from Juvenal, *Satire IV* ("On Women").

a skit in which members of an organized crime group walked into the office of a British army colonel and said, "Nice operation you have here, colonel. It would be a shame if something should happen to it." The implication here was a thinly veiled threat that if the army didn't pay for "protection," then the criminal organization would take actions that would result in damage to the army's resources. According to the predatory view of the state, the role of the crime group in this sketch is precisely the role that the state is thought to play in relation to its own citizens. Proponents of the predatory theory of the state are essentially pointing out that if we don't think that individuals are trustworthy and public-spirited (if they were, there would be no need for a state in the first place), then why would we imagine that representatives of the state, who wield a near monopoly on the use of force, would be? In this regard, those who take a predatory view of the state are arguing that Rousseau's (1762) admonition to "take men as they are and laws as they might be" applies at least as much to rulers as to the ruled.

Tilly (1985) argues that the level of predation inflicted by rulers in early modern Europe on their subjects varied from place to place because rulers faced a complex set of cross-pressures. To some extent, these rulers emerged out of what would look to us like a period of lawlessness during the Middle Ages. After the decline of the Roman Empire, Europe comprised a hodgepodge of local lords who offered protection to peasants in exchange for rents paid either in kind or in service on the lord's land. Like the heads of organized crime syndicates, feudal lords were constantly trying to put rivals down. These rivals included external competitors, such as other lords seeking to expand their territory, as well as internal challengers from within their own ranks. In part because of changes in military technology, lords who could seize control over larger numbers of peasants and more extensive areas of land were able to gain competitive advantages over their rivals. In time, feudal lands were consolidated into larger holdings under the control of feudal kings. For some time, feudal kings coexisted somewhat uneasily with local lords; although the kings controlled some lands themselves, they often relied on local lords to control other territories on their behalf. As time went on, however, the balance of power tended to tilt toward feudal kings, and local lords eventually became their subjects. The lands controlled by these kings gradually began to look like the territories that we would recognize as the political geography of contemporary Europe.

This change in the balance of power between local lords and feudal kings in early modern Europe was aided by a change in the "economies of scale" in the use of violence. A production process is said to exhibit "economies of scale" if unit costs decline as the number of units produced increases. When economies of scale exist, big producers of, say, violence are advantaged over small producers. Holding the amount of agricultural land constant, population growth in the "high middle ages" (from the tenth to the thirteenth century) led to a decline in the marginal productivity of labor. In other words, it was not as profitable as it once was for a lord to simply increase the number of serfs working on his land. At the same time, changes in military technology (armored cavalry, crossbows, better fortification, and siege weapons) raised the fixed costs of providing protection (Bartlett 1993). Together, these factors increased the "economies of scale" of protection and violence. Feudal lords could restore profitability by expanding the amount of land they controlled. In effect, the decreasing marginal productivity of labor caused by population growth could be mitigated if new lands could be cultivated. In addition, investments made in the tools to protect one manor could be profitably redeployed to protect other holdings when they came under attack.

Bargaining between lords and serfs also led to a dynamic that encouraged larger protection organizations. If a serf thought his lord's demands were unreasonable, the only alternative was to flee to a neighboring lord's manor and hope for better treatment. Although lords tried to cooperate in the return of serfs, they were often tempted to keep runaway serfs for use on their own land. This implicit competition for the services of serfs could erode the lord's bargaining power in a way that advantaged serfs. This would be more difficult, however, if a particular lord could centralize coercive authority over a wide range of local manors (North and Thomas 1971). The desire to exploit the "economies of scale in protection" created incentives for entrepreneurial rulers to conquer neighboring rulers, and the availability of underutilized arable land created incentives for them to settle new lands. Because competition was fierce and the fighting was costly, it was also important for rulers to become efficient in the administration of their territories and the extraction of revenues from their subjects. Viewed in this way, the political geography of modern Europe is essentially an unintended consequence of the strategies employed by lords and kings to keep a grasp on power (Tilly 1985). To remain in power, lords and kings engaged in four primary activities:

1. *War making:* Eliminating or neutralizing their own rivals outside the territories in which they had clear and continuous priority as wielders of force.
2. *State making:* Eliminating or neutralizing their rivals inside those territories.
3. *Protection:* Eliminating or neutralizing the enemies of their clients.
4. *Extraction:* Acquiring the means of carrying out the first three activities.

As Tilly (1985, 172) notes,

> Power holders' pursuit of war involved them [the state] willy-nilly in the extraction of resources for war making from the populations over which they had control and in the promotion of capital accumulation by those who could help them borrow and buy. War making, extraction, and capital accumulation interacted to shape European state making. Power holders did not undertake those three momentous tasks with the intention of creating national states—centralized, differentiated, autonomous, extensive political organizations. Nor did they ordinarily foresee that national states would emerge from war making, extraction, and capital accumulation. Instead, the people who controlled European states and states in the making warred in order to check or overcome their competitors and thus to enjoy the advantages of power within a secure or expanding territory. To make more effective war, they attempted to locate more capital. In the

short run, they might acquire that capital by conquest, by selling off their assets, or by coercing or dispossessing accumulators of capital. In the long run, the quest inevitably involved them in establishing regular access to capitalists who could supply and arrange credit and in imposing one form of regular taxation or another on the people and activities within their spheres of control.

In this sense, the modern state arose as a by-product of the attempts of leaders to survive. External geopolitical pressures and changes in military technology meant that lords needed to increase their war-making capacity to protect themselves and their subjects from the attack of external rivals. At the same time, this greater war-making capacity could be turned against their own subjects in order to increase their capacity to extract more resources—which, in turn, were needed to put their rivals down. The act of extraction

> entailed the elimination, neutralization, or cooptation of the great lord's [internal] rivals; thus it led to state making. As a by-product, it created organization in the form of tax-collection agencies, police forces, courts, exchequers, account keepers; thus it again led to state making. To a lesser extent, war making likewise led to state making through the expansion of military organization itself, as a standing army, war industries, supporting bureaucracies, and (rather later) schools grew up within the state apparatus. All of these structures checked potential rivals and opponents. (Tilly 1985, 183)

In effect, "war makes states" (Tilly 1985, 170). The "kill or be killed" dynamic that, to a large extent, underpins the predatory view of the state makes it abundantly clear that those states that exist today do so only because they managed to outcompete their rivals who are now gone.

The need to extract resources from their subjects placed constraints on the predation of some early modern leaders (Levi 1988; North 1981). Rulers could extract the resources they needed to respond to geopolitical pressures in one of two ways. On the one hand, they could simply seize the assets of their subjects outright. We can think of this as the strategy that a predatory state would adopt. On the other hand, rulers could try to extract the resources they needed through what Levi (1988, 52) terms "quasi-voluntary compliance." Quasi-voluntary compliance refers to a situation in which the subject feels that he is getting something—maybe policy concessions or limits on future state behavior—in return for the tax dollars that the state is extracting. We can think of this as the strategy that a limited state would adopt. As you might expect, quasi-voluntary compliance has several positive advantages over outright predation. For example, rulers would need to use fewer resources to coerce their subjects if their subjects voluntarily complied with their demands. Moreover, subjects might feel freer to invest and innovate in ways that expanded the tax base if the state limited its level of predation. In this way, leaders who managed to build quasi-voluntary compliance could succeed in extracting the resources they needed to meet external challenges without "killing the goose that laid the golden egg." By taming their predatory instincts, rulers could opt, in effect, to increase their net extractive capacity by reducing the costs of conducting business and by taking a smaller portion of a larger pie. As it turned out, not all states were successful in limiting their predation in this way, and as a result, the character and consequences of rule exhibited quite a variety across early modern Europe. We return to the question of why some leaders chose to limit their predation more than others in Chapter 6.

Inspired by the work of Tilly, Jeffrey Herbst (2000) argues that the modern state has developed later and less completely in sub-Saharan Africa because the return from agricultural activity was modest, and the rough physical geography of the region makes the administration of large holdings difficult. In effect, the payoff to effective state protection has not always been worth the cost. In addition, the large distances between populated areas and interference from outside actors has limited geopolitical competition between independent units. As a result, there are large portions of sub-Saharan Africa which, although nominally under the control of states that were established at the end of the colonial period, appear "stateless." State failure, in other words, may occur when the nominal size of states exceeds, for historical reasons such as the process of colonization and decolonization, the "economy of scale" of protection otherwise implied by political, economic, and geographic conditions.

CONCLUSION

In this chapter, we have examined different definitions of the state, as well as two conceptions of where the state comes from. The contract theory of the state explains how the state resolves conflict between members of society. Although the literature on the evolution of cooperation points out that a state isn't strictly necessary for resolving conflicts between members of society (see Box 4.1, "Can Cooperation Occur without the State?" at the end of this chapter), it does not conclusively show that decentralized cooperation is sufficient to ensure optimal outcomes. Although the contract theory of the state does identify key functions played by the state, it has little to say about the conflicts of interest that are likely to arise between rulers and the ruled. The predatory theory of the state assumes that such conflicts exist and attempts to explain why states do not always exploit their monopoly on the use of force to run roughshod over the citizens they came into being to protect.

Because the predatory view of the state both recognizes the possibility of exchange between rulers and the ruled *and* explains the nature and character of that exchange relationship, philosophers of science would call it a "progressive problem shift." That is, it seems to explain all of what the contract theory of the state explains while also answering at least some of the questions that the contract theory of the state raises. It should be noted, however, that the predatory theory of the state is almost exclusively "positive" in its orientation—that is, it seeks to explain the way that states and citizens behave without necessarily answering questions about what rulers or their citizens ought to do. In contrast, the contract theory of the state arose largely as a way of exploring the moral responsibilities of citizens to the state.

The predatory approach to the state has several other advantages over the contract theory of the state. First, it views rulers as egoistic, maximizing, rational actors. Consequently, we can imagine integrating explanations of leaders' behavior with other models of human behavior that have a similar view of humans. Political leaders are not qualitatively different from the rest of us—they are concerned about their survival, their livelihood, and so on. Second, it shows how goal-oriented behavior leads to changes in the institutional environment in which political actors operate and, in addition, how changes in the institutional environment alter leader behavior. For example, it can explain why political units grew large over time: so that they might benefit from economies of scale in the production of violence. Finally, it has the potential to explain why some rulers share power or limit their extractive activity whereas others do not. This is an issue that we return to in Chapter 6 when we examine economic explanations for why some states are democracies and others are not. In Chapter 5 we investigate how it is that we know a democracy when we see one—that is, how we conceptualize and measure democracy and dictatorship.

KEY CONCEPTS

best reply *105*
cardinal payoffs *111*
civil right *110*
contractarian view of the state *100*
discount factor *140*
dominant strategy *108*
dominant-strategy Nash equilibrium *108*
failed state *92*
Nash equilibrium *105*
nation *90*
nation-state *90*

natural right *110*
ordinal payoffs *103*
payoff table/payoff matrix *102*
predatory view of the state *115*
preference ordering *103*
present value *141*
social contract *110*
state *90*
state of nature *101*
strategy *105*

PREPARATION FOR THE PROBLEMS

As we have sought to demonstrate throughout this book, game theory is a useful tool for examining strategic situations in which decision makers interact with one another. In the previous chapter, we employed extensive form games to examine strategic situations where actors make sequential choices. In this chapter, we introduced normal form, or strategic form, games to examine strategic situations in which actors make simultaneous choices. We now review how to construct and solve normal form games. The first thing to do is identify a strategic situation of interest. The next step is to draw a payoff table that captures our strategic situation.

1. Drawing the payoff table
   a. Identify the players involved in the strategic situation.
   b. Draw the payoff table to indicate the choices available to each player.

    c. Determine the payoffs that the players receive for each of the possible outcomes that could occur in the game.

    d. Write the payoffs for each player in the appropriate cell of the payoff table. By convention, the payoffs belonging to the row player come first and the payoffs belonging to the column player second. Use a comma to distinguish between the players' payoffs.

Once you have drawn the payoff table, you must solve the game.

2. Solving the game

    a. Identify the "best replies" for the row player. Find the row player's best choice for *each* of the possible choices available to the column player. Indicate these choices by underlining the payoffs that the row player will receive.

    b. Identify the "best replies" for the column player. Find the column player's best choice for *each* of the possible choices available to the row player. Indicate these choices by circling the payoffs that the column player will receive.

Once you have solved the game, you will be able to identify any Nash equilibria that exist.

3. Identifying Nash equilibria

    a. To find any Nash equilibria, identify those cells in the payoff table in which both payoffs are marked as best replies. In parentheses, list the choices made by each player that together lead to those cells. By convention, the choice made by the row player comes first and the choice made by the column player second. Use a semi-colon to distinguish between the players' choices.

    b. Note that there may be multiple Nash equilibria. In other words, there may be more than one cell in which both payoffs are marked as best replies. List each of these equilibria separately in its own set of parentheses.

    c. If there are no cells in the payoff table in which both players' payoffs are marked as best replies, then there are no Nash equilibria.[18]

Sometimes, we are interested in determining whether any of the players in the strategic situation have a dominant strategy.

4. Identifying a player who has a dominant strategy

    a. The row player has a dominant strategy if his best replies are all in the same row, that is, if his best choice is always the same no matter what the column player might do. The column player has a dominant strategy if her best replies are all in the same column, that is, if her best choice is always the same no matter what the row player might do.

    b. If both players have a dominant strategy, then there is a dominant-strategy Nash equilibrium.

---

18. Technically, there are no Nash equilibria if players use pure strategies. If players use something called "mixed strategies," which we do not introduce in this book, we would be able to find a Nash equilibrium.

Example: Prisoner's Dilemma Game

One of the most well-known strategic form games employed by political scientists is called the Prisoner's Dilemma. The name *Prisoner's Dilemma* comes from the fact that it was originally used to describe a strategic interaction between two criminals. Here's the basic story. Two suspects in a major crime are arrested and placed in separate cells. Although there is enough evidence to convict each of them of some minor offense, there is not enough evidence to convict either of them of the major crime unless one of them rats the other one out (Talk). If they both stay quiet (Quiet), each will be convicted of the minor offense. If one and only one of them talks, then the one who talks will be freed and used as a witness against the other, who will be convicted of the major crime. If they both talk, then each will be convicted of the major crime, but some leniency will be shown for their cooperation. The situation that the prisoners find themselves in is clearly strategic because the outcome of any action taken by suspect 1 depends on the choices made by suspect 2 and vice versa. Now that we have identified the strategic situation, we can go through the steps outlined earlier.

The payoff table for the Prisoner's Dilemma Game is shown in Figure 4.10. There are two players, suspect 1 and suspect 2. Both players must decide whether to keep quiet or talk. As you can see, there are four possible outcomes: both suspects keep quiet, both suspects talk, suspect 1 talks but suspect 2 keeps quiet, and suspect 1 keeps quiet but suspect 2 talks. How are the payoffs that the players associate with each outcome determined? One way to do this is to think about how each of the players would rank the four possible outcomes in the game. Based on the strategic situation that the prisoners find themselves in and the story that we have just told, the best outcome for each player would be for him to talk and for his partner to keep quiet, because this means that he would be set free. The worst outcome for each player would be for him to keep quiet and for his partner to rat him out, because he would be convicted of the major crime. Of the remaining two outcomes, both players prefer the outcome in which they both keep quiet and get convicted of the minor crime to the one in which they both talk and get convicted of the major crime with some leniency for talking. Based on this, we can write suspect 1's preference ordering as

- (Talk; Quiet) > (Quiet; Quiet) > (Talk; Talk) > (Quiet; Talk)

and suspect 2's preference ordering as

- (Quiet; Talk) > (Quiet; Quiet) > (Talk; Talk) > (Talk; Quiet),

where suspect 1's action is given first, suspect 2's action is given second, and ">" means "is strictly preferred to." Because there are four possible outcomes, the value 4 can be assigned to each player's most preferred outcome, 3 to his second preferred outcome, 2 to his third preferred outcome, and 1 to his least preferred outcome. These numbers are the ordinal payoffs shown in the payoff table in Figure 4.10.

FIGURE 4.10	**Prisoner's Dilemma Game**

		Suspect 2	
		Quiet	Talk
Suspect 1	Quiet	3, 3	1, ④
	Talk	<u>4</u>, 1	<u>2</u>, ②

Note: Suspect 1's (the row player's) payoffs are shown first in each cell; suspect 2's (the column player's) payoffs are shown second. A comma separates the payoffs for the players in each cell. Payoffs associated with the best replies of suspect 1 are underlined. Payoffs associated with the best replies of suspect 2 are circled.

Now that you have drawn the payoff table, you must solve the game. You start by identifying the best replies for suspect 1. What is suspect 1's best reply (Quiet or Talk) if suspect 2 is quiet? You are now looking at the left-hand column of the payoff table where suspect 2 is quiet. If suspect 1 is quiet, he will get a payoff of 3, and if he talks, he will get a payoff of 4. Thus, suspect 1's best reply to suspect 2 being quiet is to talk. You can indicate this by placing a line under the 4 in the bottom left cell of the payoff table. What is suspect 1's best reply if suspect 2 talks? You are now looking at the right-hand column of the payoff table where suspect 2 talks. If suspect 1 is quiet, he will get a payoff of 1, and if he talks, he will get a payoff of 2. Thus, suspect 1's best reply to suspect 2 talking is to talk. You can indicate this by placing a line under the 2 in the bottom right cell of the payoff table.

You must now identify the best replies for suspect 2. What is suspect 2's best reply (Quiet or Talk) if suspect 1 is quiet? You are now looking at the top row of the payoff table where suspect 1 is quiet. If suspect 1 is quiet, then suspect 2 will get a payoff of 3 if she is quiet and a payoff of 4 if she talks. Thus, suspect 2's best reply to suspect 1 being quiet is to talk. You can indicate this by circling the 4 in the top right cell of the payoff table. What is suspect 2's best reply if suspect 1 talks? You are now looking at the bottom row of the payoff table where suspect 1 is talking. If suspect 1 is talking, then suspect 2 will get a payoff of 1 if she is quiet and a payoff of 2 if she talks. Thus, suspect 2's best reply to suspect 1 talking is to talk. You can indicate this by circling the 2 in the bottom right cell of the payoff table. At this stage, you have found the best replies for both suspect 1 and suspect 2.

To identify any Nash equilibria, you simply look for cells in which both payoffs are marked as best replies. The only cell in which this is the case in the Prisoner's Dilemma

Game is the one in which suspect 1 talks and suspect 2 talks. Thus, the unique Nash equilibrium for the Prisoner's Dilemma Game is (Talk; Talk). The expected outcome is that both players talk. The payoff to both players is 2.

Do either of the players have a dominant strategy? You can see that suspect 1 has a dominant strategy as his best replies are all in the same row. Talk is suspect 1's dominant strategy as talking is his best reply to all of the choices available to suspect 2. You can also see that suspect 2 has a dominant strategy as her best replies are all in the same column. Talk is suspect 2's dominant strategy as talking is her best reply to all of the choices available to suspect 1. The fact that both players have a dominant strategy means that the Nash equilibrium (Talk; Talk) in the Prisoner's Dilemma Game is a dominant-strategy Nash equilibrium.

Interestingly, both players in the Prisoner's Dilemma Game would be better off if they kept quiet (their payoffs would be 3) than if they played their equilibrium strategies (their payoffs would be 2). Given this, you might wonder why it is not an equilibrium for both players to keep quiet. Think about this for a moment. If you were suspect 1 and you knew that suspect 2 was going to keep quiet, would you talk (payoff of 4) or keep quiet (payoff of 3)? You would talk. And if you were suspect 2 and you knew that suspect 1 was going to keep quiet, would you talk (payoff of 4) or keep quiet (payoff of 3)? You would talk as well. In other words, no player will want to keep quiet if he thinks that the other player is going to keep quiet. The criminals probably promised each other prior to committing the crime that if they were both caught, they would keep quiet. The problem is that these promises are not credible. Once they are caught, the criminals have a dominant strategy to talk. It is in their interests to talk if they think their partner will keep quiet, and it is in their interests to talk if their partner talks. The end result is that both criminals talk even though this means that they get a lower payoff than if they both keep quiet. This is one of the central characteristics of the Prisoner's Dilemma Game—the Nash equilibrium is suboptimal from the perspective of the players; both players prefer another outcome.

The importance of the Prisoner's Dilemma Game and the reason why it is so frequently used by political scientists has to do with the huge variety of strategic situations in which people face similar incentives to those faced by the suspects in the crime story we have just described. As we noted earlier, the State of Nature Game has the same basic structure as a Prisoner's Dilemma Game. In addition to helping to explain the origins of the state, the Prisoner's Dilemma Game has also been used to explain a whole host of things, including arms races (Powell 1999). To see how it might throw light on arms races, think about the Cold War strategic situation in which the United States and the Soviet Union had to decide whether to reduce or increase their nuclear arsenals. Arguably, the best outcome for the United States and the Soviet Union was the one in which one country built up its nuclear weapons but the other country did not; this would give the first country a military advantage. The worst outcome for both countries, of course, was one in which one country reduced its weapons, while its opponent built up its arsenal. Of the other two possible outcomes, each country preferred the outcome in which they both reduced their nuclear

FIGURE 4.11   Nuclear Arms Race Game as a Prisoner's Dilemma Game

		Soviet Union	
		Reduce Arms	Continue Buildup
United States	Reduce Arms	3, 3	1, ④
	Continue Buildup	**4**, 1	**2**, ②

Note: The United States' (the row player's) payoffs are shown first in each cell; the Soviet Union's (the column player's) payoffs are shown second. A comma separates the payoffs for the players in each cell. Payoffs associated with the best replies of the United States are underlined. Payoffs associated with the best replies for the Soviet Union are circled.

weapons (lower cost and maintained security) to the one in which they both increased their nuclear weapons (higher cost and no increased security). If you write out the preference orderings for the United States and the Soviet Union in this Nuclear Arms Race Game, you will see that they have the same basic structure as the preference orderings in the Prisoner's Dilemma Game. We illustrate the payoff table for the Nuclear Arms Race Game in Figure 4.11. The Nash equilibrium is (Continue Buildup; Continue Buildup), and the expected outcome is a nuclear arms race.

PROBLEMS

The problems that follow address some of the more important concepts and methods introduced in this chapter.

States and Failed States

1. A state is an entity that uses coercion and the threat of force to rule in a given territory. Choose a country that you know reasonably well. To what extent does a state exist in this country? Is the state able to coerce or successfully control the inhabitants in its territory? Explain your answers.

2. Go to The Fund for Peace website at http://fsi.fundforpeace.org/ and examine the latest Fragile States Index data and map. Choose four countries, one from each of the four

general classifications: alert, warning, stable, and sustainable. Identify the overall state fragility score out of 120 for each of these countries. Now look at the separate scores that these four countries received on the twelve indicators that make up their overall state fragility score. What factors are contributing the most to state fragility in your four countries?

3. The bottom panel of Map 4.1 on page 99 shows whether a country's state fragility score has increased or decreased in the last decade. Choose a country whose fragility has increased in the last decade and one whose fragility has decreased. On the website for The Fund for Peace, click on the page that allows you to conduct an "FSI Country-by-Country Trend Analysis." On this page, you will be able to see exactly how the state fragility score for your two countries has changed over time. Indicate the highest and lowest state fragility scores that your two countries received in the last decade and the years in which those particular scores occurred. Look at how the separate scores that each of your two countries received on the twelve indicators that make up their overall state fragility score have changed over the last decade. Use this information to explain exactly why state fragility has increased over the last decade in one of your countries and decreased in the other.

Strategic Form Games

The Prisoner's Dilemma Game is just one type of strategic form game. Below, we present other strategic form games and ask various questions.

4. The Game of Chicken

Footloose is a 1984 rock musical film about a Chicago teenager called Ren McCormack, played by Kevin Bacon, who moves to a small conservative town in Iowa. Ren's love of dancing and partying to rock music causes friction with the straitlaced townspeople, who have passed a law prohibiting dancing within the town limits. Much of the film centers on the competition between Ren and a local tough guy named Chuck for the affections of the local reverend's daughter, Ariel. At one stage, Chuck challenges Ren to a "tractor face-off." In this face-off, Ren and Chuck have to drive tractors directly at each other as Ariel and others watch. Whoever swerves out of the way first is considered a "chicken."

As you can see, this part of the film captures a strategic situation in which Ren and Chuck both have to decide whether to "swerve" or "drive straight." Political scientists generally call the strategic situation described here the Game of Chicken. The best outcome for both characters is one in which they continue to drive straight but their competitor swerves; their status among their peers rises, and the other character is seen as a wimp. The worst possible outcome is the one in which neither of them swerves, because they will end up dead or badly injured. Of the other two possible outcomes, both Ren and Chuck prefer the outcome in which they both swerve to the one in which one swerves but the other does not. If they both swerve, neither of them gains or loses anything; they may both even gain some credit simply for participating in the face-off in the first place. If one swerves and the other does not, then

FIGURE 4.12   **A Game of Chicken: The Tractor Face-Off**

		Chuck	
		Swerve	Drive Straight
Ren	Swerve	3, 3	2, 4
	Drive Straight	4, 2	1, 1

Note: Ren's (the row player's) payoffs are shown first in each cell; Chuck's (the column player's) payoffs are shown second. A comma separates the payoffs for the players in each cell.

the one who swerved loses face. The payoff table for this Game of Chicken is shown in Figure 4.12.

 a. Use the numbers in each cell of the payoff table in Figure 4.12 to write out the preference ordering for Ren and Chuck over the four possible outcomes.

 b. Solve the Game of Chicken for Nash equilibria. *Hint:* There are actually two possible Nash equilibria.

 c. Does either Ren or Chuck have a dominant strategy? If so, what is it?

 d. What strategic situations in comparative politics might fit the basic structure of the Game of Chicken? In other words, provide a specific example in which actors might have preferences and interactions like those in the Game of Chicken.

5. The Stag Hunt Game

In *Discourse on the Origin and Foundations of Inequality among Men*, the French philosopher Jean-Jacques Rousseau ([1755] 1997, 163) describes a strategic situation in which a group of hunters are trying to catch a stag. To keep things simple, imagine that there are just two hunters. The hunters have two options: They can work together and pursue the stag, or they can hunt independently and catch a hare. If both hunters pursue the stag, they catch it and share it equally. If either of the hunters chooses to go after the hare, they catch one but the stag escapes. Each hunter prefers a share of the stag to a hare. The strategic situation that Rousseau describes has come to be known by political scientists as the Stag Hunt Game. The payoff table for the Stag Hunt Game is shown in Figure 4.13.

FIGURE 4.13   The Stag Hunt Game

		Hunter 2	
		Stag	Hare
Hunter 1	Stag	4, 4	1, 3
	Hare	3, 1	2, 2

Note: Hunter 1's (the row player's) payoffs are shown first in each cell; hunter 2's (the column player's) payoffs are shown second. A comma separates the payoffs for the players in each cell.

a. Use the numbers in each cell of the payoff table in Figure 4.13 to write out the preference ordering for the two hunters over the four possible outcomes.

b. Solve the game in Figure 4.13 for all Nash equilibria.

c. Does either of the hunters have a dominant strategy? If so, what is it?

d. What strategic situations in comparative politics might fit the basic structure of the Stag Hunt Game? In other words, provide a specific example in which actors might have preferences and interactions like those in the Stag Hunt Game.

6. *Pure Coordination Game*

People often find themselves in strategic situations in which they must agree on adopting just one of several potential solutions to their problems. For example, it does not really matter whether cars drive on the left of the road, as they do in the United Kingdom, or on the right of the road, as they do in France. All that really matters is that all the drivers in a given country choose to drive on the same side of the road. Strategic situations like this have come to be known by political scientists as Pure Coordination Games. Figure 4.14 shows an empty payoff table for a situation in which two drivers are deciding to drive on the left or right of the road. Driver 1's preference ordering over the four possible outcomes is

- (Left; Left) = (Right; Right) > (Left; Right) = (Right; Left),

and driver 2's preference ordering over the four possible outcomes is

- (Left; Left) = (Right; Right) > (Left; Right) = (Right; Left).

a. Allocate appropriate payoffs (numbers) to these preference orderings and enter them into the relevant cells of the payoff table in Figure 4.14.

| FIGURE 4.14 | **Pure Coordination Game** |

b. Solve the game in Figure 4.14 for all Nash equilibria.

c. Does either of the drivers have a dominant strategy? If so, what is it?

d. What strategic situations in comparative politics might fit the basic structure of the Pure Coordination Game? In other words, provide a specific example in which actors might have preferences and interactions like those in the Pure Coordination Game.

7. Asymmetric Coordination Game

Consider the following strategic situation. Archie and Edith are two people who would like to go on a date with each other. Archie likes going bowling, and Edith likes going to movies. Unfortunately, Archie and Edith work on different sides of town, and for some reason, they have no way of contacting each other to decide whether the date will be at the bowling alley or the movie theater. The most important thing for both Archie and Edith is that they be together in the evening. In other words, they prefer to go to the same venue, whether it is the bowling alley or the movie theater, rather than miss each other. Of course, if they could guarantee being together, Archie would prefer to be together at the bowling alley, and Edith would prefer to be together at the movies. Similarly, if it was going to be the case that they were not together, then Archie would prefer to be at the bowling alley whereas Edith would prefer to be at the movie theater. Political scientists call strategic situations like this Asymmetric Coordination Games because both actors want to coordinate on some outcome, but their preferences conflict over what that outcome should be. The empty payoff table for the Asymmetric Coordination Game is shown in Figure 4.15.

a. Write down Archie's preference ordering over the four possible outcomes in the game. Now write down Edith's preference ordering over the four possible outcomes in the game. Once you have done this, allocate appropriate payoffs (numbers) to these preference orderings and enter them into the relevant cells of the payoff table in Figure 4.15.

FIGURE 4.15   **Asymmetric Coordination Game**

		Archie	
		Movie	Bowling
Edith	Movie		
	Bowling		

b. Solve the game in Figure 4.15 for all Nash equilibria.

c. Does either Edith or Archie have a dominant strategy? If so, what is it?

d. What strategic situations in comparative politics might fit the basic structure of the Asymmetric Coordination Game? In other words, provide a specific example, in which actors might have preferences and interactions like those in the Asymmetric Coordination Game.

e. If you solved the Pure Coordination Game from the previous question and the Asymmetric Coordination Game from this question correctly, you should have found that each game has two possible Nash equilibria. In the real world, actors must try to "coordinate" on one of these equilibria. Use your intuition to say whether you think actors will generally find it easier to coordinate when they are in a strategic situation characterized by a Pure Coordination Game or one characterized by an Asymmetric Coordination Game. Explain your answer.

8. *Rock, Paper, Scissors Game*

All of the strategic form games that we have looked at so far involve actors deciding between two choices. There is no reason, however, why actors in strategic form games cannot have more than two potential choices. Consider the famous children's game of Rock, Paper, Scissors. In this game, two children simultaneously choose to play "rock," "paper," or "scissors." "Rock" beats "scissors," "paper" beats "rock," and "scissors" beats "paper." If the two children ever choose the same thing, then there is a draw. Let's assume that you get one point for a win, you lose one point for a loss, and you get 0 for a draw. The payoff table for this version of the Rock, Paper, Scissors Game is shown in Figure 4.16.

a. Solve the game in Figure 4.16 by identifying the best replies for Player 1 and Player 2. Unlike in the previous games where you had to identify which of the two actions

FIGURE 4.16	**Rock, Paper, Scissors Game**

		Player 2		
		Scissors	Paper	Rock
	Scissors	0, 0	1, −1	−1, 1
Player 1	Paper	−1, 1	0, 0	1, −1
	Rock	1, −1	−1, 1	0, 0

Note: Player 1's (the row player's) payoffs are shown first in each cell; player 2's (the column player's) payoffs are shown second. A comma separates the payoffs for the players in each cell.

available to each player was best for each possible choice of the other player, you now have to identify which of the three actions available to each player is best for each possible choice of the other player. Are there any Nash equilibria in this game?

b. Imagine that you were going to play this game over and over again. Would you choose to play rock, paper, or scissors, or would you randomize over all three choices? Explain your answer.

9. American Football Game

Another example of a strategic situation in which actors have more than two choices might be called the American Football Game. In an American Football Game, we can think that the offense has four possible strategies to progress down the field: run the ball, make a short throw, make a medium throw, and make a long throw. The defense has three strategies to try to stop this: counter the run, counter the pass, or blitz the quarterback. Let's say that after studying many games, statisticians have come up with the payoff table shown in Figure 4.17, in which the numbers in each cell indicate the expected number of yards either gained by the offense or lost by the defense. As you can see, every yard gained by the offense is a yard lost by the defense. As always, the players prefer higher numbers to lower numbers.

a. Solve the game in Figure 4.17 for all Nash equilibria.

b. Does the offense or defense have a dominant strategy? If so, what is it?

FIGURE 4.17 | **American Football Game**

		Defense		
		Counter Run	Counter Pass	Blitz
Offense	Run	2, –2	5, –5	13, –13
	Short Pass	6, –6	5.6, –5.6	10.5, –10.5
	Medium Pass	6, –6	4.5, –4.5	1, –1
	Long Pass	10, –10	3, –3	–2, 2

Note: The offense's (the row player's) payoffs are shown first in each cell; the defense's (the column player's) payoffs are shown second. A comma separates the payoffs for the players in each cell.

10. *Mafia Game*

Earlier we described the Prisoner's Dilemma Game, in which two prisoners had to choose between ratting out their partner or keeping quiet. The Nash equilibrium in this game involved both prisoners deciding to talk even though they would both have been better off keeping quiet. This scenario will probably be familiar to anyone who watches the TV show *Law and Order*. As many of you are probably aware, however, certain types of criminals in the real world rarely talk or rat out their accomplices. In particular, it is well known that members of the Mafia rarely provide incriminating evidence against their accomplices. Why is this? The answer is that the Mafia organization imposes a cost, c, often physical and deadly, on anyone who talks to the police. This additional cost changes the structure of the strategic situation in which the two prisoners find themselves. Rather than playing the traditional Prisoner's Dilemma Game, we can think that the prisoners are playing a Mafia Game with a payoff table like the one shown in Figure 4.18.

a. Solve the game in Figure 4.18 for any Nash equilibria assuming that $c = 0$. We have looked at a variety of normal form games by this stage. What type of game is this version of the Mafia Game more commonly known as?

FIGURE 4.18	**Mafia Game**

		Mafia Suspect 2	
		Quiet	Talk
Mafia Suspect 1	Quiet	30, 30	10, 40 − c
	Talk	40 − c, 10	20 − c, 20 − c

Note: c = the cost imposed by the Mafia on a suspect who talks. Suspect 1's (the row player's) payoffs are shown first in each cell; suspect 2's (the column player's) payoffs are shown second. A comma separates the payoffs for the players in each cell.

  b. Given the cardinal payoffs shown in the payoff table in the Mafia Game, what is the minimum cost that the Mafia needs to impose on its members who talk in order for the Nash equilibrium to be one in which both suspects keep quiet? Explain your answer.

  c. The role of the Mafia in the Mafia Game can be thought of as that of a third-party enforcer. What do we mean by that? How is this role that the Mafia plays in this game related to the role that the state plays in the Civil Society Game examined earlier?

11. Counterterrorism Games

On September 11, 2001, nineteen terrorists affiliated with al-Qaida hijacked four commercial passenger jets and flew them into two American landmarks (the World Trade Center in New York City and the Pentagon in Washington, DC) in coordinated terrorist attacks. Since 9/11, governments around the world have spent tens of billions of dollars on a variety of counterterrorism policies.

  Counterterrorism policies generally fall into two types: preemption and deterrence. Preemption involves proactive policies such as destroying terrorist training camps, retaliating against state sponsors of terrorism, infiltrating terrorist groups, freezing terrorist assets, and the like. The goal of preemption is to curb future terrorist attacks. One thing to note about preemption policies is that they not only make the country that carries out the preemptive strike safer but they also make all countries that are potential targets safer. Deterrence involves defensive policies, such as placing bomb detectors in airports, fortifying potential targets, and securing borders. The goal is to deter an attack either by making success more difficult or by increasing the likely negative consequences for the terrorists. One thing to note about deterrence policies is that they often end up displacing terrorist attacks away from the country introducing the defensive measures to other countries or regions where targets are now relatively more vulnerable (Enders and Sandler 1993; Sandler and Enders 2004).

In an article titled "Counterterrorism: A Game-Theoretic Analysis," Arce and Sandler (2005) use strategic form games to examine these two types of counterterrorism policies. They argue that governments around the world overinvest in deterrence policies at the expense of preemption policies and that this results in a socially suboptimal outcome from the perspective of world security. The following questions deal with some of the strategic form games examined by Arce and Sandler.

Let's start with preemption policies. Imagine that the United States and the European Union must decide whether to preempt a terrorist attack or do nothing. A terrorist group is a "passive player" in this game and will attack the weaker of the two targets. For illustrative purposes, let's suppose that each preemptive action provides a public benefit worth 4 to the United States and the European Union. Recall that preemptive action increases the safety of all countries. Preemptive action comes at a private cost of 6 to the preemptor, though. Consider an outcome in which only the United States preempts. In this situation, the United States will get –2 (i.e., 4 – 6) and the European Union will get 4. If the United States and the European Union both preempt, they each get a payoff of 2 (i.e., 8 – 6). If both the United States and the European Union do nothing, they each get 0. The payoff table for this Counterterrorism Preemption Game is shown in Figure 4.19.

a. Use the numbers in each cell of the payoff table in Figure 4.19 to write out the preference ordering for the United States and the European Union over the four possible outcomes.

b. Solve the game in Figure 4.19 for all Nash equilibria.

FIGURE 4.19 **Counterterrorism Preemption Game**

		European Union	
		Preempt	Do Nothing
United States	Preempt	2, 2	–2, 4
	Do Nothing	4, –2	0, 0

Note: The United States' (the row player's) payoffs are shown first in each cell; the European Union's (the column player's) payoffs are shown second. A comma separates the payoffs for the players in each cell.

c. Does either the United States or the European Union have a dominant strategy? If so, what is it?

Now let's look at deterrence policies. Imagine that the United States and the European Union must decide whether to deter a terrorist attack or do nothing. Terrorists will attack the weaker of the two targets. For illustrative purposes, let's suppose that deterrence is associated with a cost of 4 for both the deterring country and the other country. The deterrer's costs arise from the actual deterrence action that it takes, whereas the nondeterrer's costs arise from now being the terrorists' target of choice. Each deterrence action provides a private benefit worth 6 (prior to costs being deducted) to the deterring country because it is now safer. Recall that deterrence increases the safety only of the deterring country. Consider an outcome in which only the United States deters. In this situation, the United States will get 2, that is, 6 − 4, and the European Union will get −4. Net benefits are 0 if the United States and the European Union do nothing, whereas each receives a net payoff of −2, that is, 6 − (2 × 4), from mutual deterrence, because costs of 8 are deducted from private gains of 6. The payoff table for this Counterterrorism Deterrence Game is shown in Figure 4.20.

d. Use the numbers in each cell of the payoff table in Figure 4.20 to write out the preference ordering for the United States and the European Union over the four possible outcomes.

e. Solve the game in Figure 4.20 for all Nash equilibria.

f. Does either the United States or the European Union have a dominant strategy? If so, what is it?

FIGURE 4.20   Counterterrorism Deterrence Game

		European Union	
		Do Nothing	Deter
United States	Do Nothing	0, 0	–4, 2
	Deter	2, –4	–2, –2

Note: The United States' (the row player's) payoffs are shown first in each cell; the European Union's (the column player's) payoffs are shown second. A comma separates the payoffs for the players in each cell.

Instead of assuming that governments can implement only preemption or only deterrence policies, let's now look at a situation in which they can implement both types of counterterrorism policy. We can do this by combining the last two games. The only thing we need to do is determine the payoffs that the countries receive when one preempts and the other deters. In this situation, the deterrer gets a payoff of 6, that is, 6 + 4 − 4. In other words, the deterrer gets 6 from the private benefit associated with the deterrence policy, −4 from the cost of the deterrence policy, and 4 from the public benefit associated with the other country's taking a preemptive action. The preemptor receives a payoff of −6, that is, 4 − 6 − 4. In other words, the preemptor gets 4 from the public benefit associated with the provision of preemption, −6 from the cost of the preemption policy, and −4 from the deflected costs associated with becoming the target country. The payoff table for this more general Counterterrorism Preemption and Deterrence Game is shown in Figure 4.21.

g. Solve the game in Figure 4.21 for all Nash equilibria.

h. Does either the United States or the European Union have a dominant strategy? If so, what is it?

i. Is the Nash equilibrium in this game suboptimal? In other words, are there other outcomes that both countries would prefer? If so, what are they?

j. If you have solved these games correctly, you will see that states overinvest in counterterrorism deterrence policies and underinvest in counterterrorism preemption

FIGURE 4.21   Counterterrorism Preemption and Deterrence Game

		European Union		
		Preempt	Do Nothing	Deter
United States	Preempt	2, 2	−2, 4	−6, 6
	Do Nothing	4, −2	0, 0	−4, 2
	Deter	6, −6	2, −4	−2, −2

Note: The United States' (the row player's) payoffs are shown first in each cell; the European Union's (the column player's) payoffs are shown second. A comma separates the payoffs for the players in each cell.

policies. This is not only a theoretical prediction but something that terrorist experts have observed in the real world. Looking at the structure of these three games, can you explain why states do this? *Hint:* The answer to this question has something to do with what political scientists call the "free-rider problem" and is something that we examine in more detail in Chapter 8.

12. *Free Trade Game*

Free trade occurs when goods and services between countries flow unhindered by government-imposed restrictions such as tariffs, quotas, and antidumping laws that are often designed to protect domestic industries. Although it is well known that free trade creates winners and losers, a broad consensus exists among most economists that free trade has a large and unambiguous net gain for society as a whole. For example, Robert Whaples (2006) finds in a survey of economists that "87.5% agree that the US should eliminate remaining tariffs and other barriers to trade" and that "90.1% disagree with the suggestion that the US should restrict employers from outsourcing work to foreign countries." Despite this consensus, it is not at all clear that countries will actually adopt policies promoting free trade.

Consider the following strategic situation in which the United States and the European Union are engaged in trade negotiations. Both countries must decide whether to reduce their tariffs or impose new tariffs. The best outcome for both countries is for one side to impose new tariffs and the other side to reduce tariffs; the first country can export more easily to the other country and obtain increased revenue from the new tariffs. The worst outcome for both countries is for one country to reduce tariffs and the other country to increase tariffs; one country will lose jobs due to reduced exports, and the other country will benefit from the lower tariffs. Of the remaining two outcomes, both countries would prefer the reduction of tariffs to the imposition of new tariffs. If both countries reduce their tariffs, then each country can benefit from increased free trade. If both countries impose new tariffs, a trade war begins in which each country sees a decline in trade and a loss of jobs. Based on this story, the preference ordering for the European Union over the four possible outcomes is

- (Impose; Reduce) > (Reduce; Reduce) > (Impose; Impose) > (Reduce; Impose),

and the preference ordering for the United States is

- (Reduce; Impose) > (Reduce; Reduce) > (Impose; Impose) > (Impose; Reduce),

where the European Union's action is given first, the United States' action is given second, and ">" means "is strictly preferred to." An empty payoff table for this Free Trade Game is shown in Figure 4.22.

   a. Use the preference orderings shown above to fill in the payoff table shown in Figure 4.22 with the payoffs for each player. Use the numbers 4, 3, 2, and 1 to indicate the preference ordering for the players.

   b. Based on the preference orderings in the Free Trade Game, what is this sort of game more generally called?

FIGURE 4.22   **Free Trade Game**

		United States	
		Reduce Tariffs	Impose New Tariffs
European Union	Reduce Tariffs		
	Impose New Tariffs		

c. Solve the game in Figure 4.22 for all Nash equilibria. What is the expected outcome of the game?

d. Does either the European Union or the United States have a dominant strategy? If so, what is it?

So far, you have solved the Free Trade Game assuming that it is played only once. In reality, though, countries often trade with each other many times and engage in multiple rounds of trade negotiations. We now examine the Free Trade Game assuming that it is played over and over again. In order to answer the following questions, you should first read Box 4.1 "Can Cooperation Occur without the State" on pages 140 to 144 at the end of this chapter. The European Union and the United States must now decide how to play the Free Trade Game in each round. Let's assume that both countries play grim trigger strategies. In the present context, recall that a grim trigger strategy means that a country will continue to reduce tariffs as long as the other country reduces its tariffs; but if the other country ever imposes new tariffs, it will impose new tariffs in the next round and in all future rounds.

e. Using the payoffs from the Free Trade Game, what is the present value of reducing tariffs?

f. Using the payoffs from the Free Trade Game, what is the present value of imposing new tariffs?

g. Is there a discount factor, d, at which it is possible to sustain the strategy combination (Reduce Tariffs; Reduce Tariffs) as a Nash equilibrium in this repeated Free Trade Game if the European Union and the United States use grim trigger strategies? What is this discount rate?

h. Interpret the results from the "one-shot" Free Trade Game and the infinitely repeated Free Trade Game. In other words, what do they mean for free trade in substantive terms?

13. *Writing and Solving Your Own Games*

a. Think of a strategic situation in which two players must simultaneously choose between two possible actions. Establish preference orderings over the four possible outcomes and use them to write down a payoff table. Solve the game for any Nash equilibria.

b. Think of a strategic situation in which two players make choices simultaneously. At least one player should have to choose between more than two possible actions. Write down a payoff table for this strategic situation. Solve the game for any Nash equilibria.

Box 4.1   ## CAN COOPERATION OCCUR WITHOUT THE STATE?

According to Hobbes ([1651] 1994), life in the state of nature is "solitary, poor, nasty, brutish, and short." This seemed to be confirmed when we found that both players in our State of Nature Game had a dominant strategy to steal rather than refrain—both players were better off stealing no matter what the other player was doing. Hobbes believed that the only way to get individuals in the state of nature to cooperate and refrain was to create a state with sufficient power to "awe" them. As we saw in our Civil Society Game, the threat of a large enough punishment by the state was sufficient to get the players to refrain. In fact, both players now had a dominant strategy to cooperate and refrain. In effect, this is Hobbes's justification for the existence of the state. Some scholars, however, have challenged this justification by arguing that cooperation can emerge through a decentralized process in the state of nature; you do not always need to create a sovereign or a state (Axelrod 1981, 1984; Taylor 1976). These scholars claim that cooperation can occur without a sovereign as long as the individuals in the state of nature repeatedly interact with each other and care sufficiently about the future benefits of cooperation. Earlier in the chapter, we saw that cooperation or refraining was not possible when the State of Nature Game was played once. But let's now examine what happens if the individuals in the state of nature play the game over and over again.

A **discount factor** tells us the rate at which future benefits are discounted compared with today's benefits; in effect, it tells us how much people value the future.

Before we do this, we need to introduce two new concepts that will come in handy. The first is called the **discount factor**. A discount factor essentially tells us how much people care about the future. Specifically, the discount factor tells us how much future benefits are discounted compared with today's benefits. Low discount factors mean that people do not value the future very much—they value the benefits they receive today much more than the benefits they will get tomorrow. High discount factors mean that people value the future a lot—they value the benefits they will receive tomorrow almost as much as the benefits they receive today. This probably all sounds a little abstract. To make the idea of a discount factor more concrete, consider the following numerical example. Imagine that you had a choice of receiving $1,000 today or $1,000 in a month's time. If it didn't matter to you whether you received the money today or in a month's time, your discount factor, d, would be 1; that is, future payoffs are worth as much to you as today's payoffs. In contrast, if receiving the money in a month's time was worthless to you, perhaps because you will be dead in a month's time, then your discount factor would be 0; that is, future payoffs are worth nothing to you. And if the $1,000 in a month's time was worth something to you, but not as much as getting it today, then your discount factor would be $0 < d < 1$. As you can see, the discount factor is always bounded between 0 and 1; that is, $0 \leq d \leq 1$. A slightly different, but complementary, way to think about a discount factor is that it indicates the probability that you will be around in the next period to enjoy the "future" payoff. The important point to remember is that the higher the discount factor, the more you care about the future; the lower the discount factor, the less you care about the future.

The second concept is called the **present value** of some stream of payoffs. This concept is most easily explained with an example. Imagine that your parents promise to give you $1 every day from now into the future. How much is this promise

> The **present value** of a stream of benefits tells us how much this stream of future benefits is worth to us today.

of a stream of payments into the future worth to you today? In other words, what is the "present value" of this stream of future payments? The $1 you receive today is obviously worth $1 to you today. But what about all the dollars that you expect to receive in the future? How much are they worth to you today? The $1 you expect to receive tomorrow is not going to be worth quite as much to you as if you had received it today—it will be discounted by your discount factor. Thus, the $1 you expect to get tomorrow is worth only 1d$ today. The $1 you expect to receive in two days' time is worth even less to you today because it will be discounted by your discount factor a second time. Thus, the $1 you receive in two days' time is worth only $1d^2$ today. Similarly, the $1 you expect to get in three days' time is worth only $1d^3$ today. Continuing with this logic, it is easy to see that the present value of the stream of payments promised to you by your parents is

$$\text{Present Value (Promise)} = 1 + 1d + 1d^2 + 1d^3 + 1d^4 + 1d^5 + \ldots + 1d^\infty, \qquad (4\text{--}1)$$

or

$$\text{Present Value (Promise)} = 1 + d + d^2 + d^3 + d^4 + d^5 + \ldots + d^\infty. \qquad (4\text{--}2)$$

Although we don't show it here, it turns out that this sum of numbers is equal to $1 / (1 - d)$:

$$\text{Present Value (Promise)} = 1 + d + d^2 + d^3 + d^4 + d^5 + \ldots + d^\infty = 1 / (1 - d). \qquad (4\text{--}3)$$

What if your parents had promised you $5 every day indefinitely into the future instead of $1? In this case, the present value of their promise would be $5 / (1 - d)$. If they had promised you $3, the present value would be $3 / (1 - d)$, and so on.

Now that we know what a discount factor is and how to calculate the present value of a future stream of payments, we can examine what happens when the State of Nature Game is played over and over again. The State of Nature Game is shown in Figure 4.23.

Now that players A and B have to play the State of Nature Game over and over again, they have to decide how to play the game in each round (or period). One strategy that the players might employ is called a grim trigger strategy. A grim trigger strategy says that a player will refrain (cooperate) as long as the other player refrains; but if the other player ever steals instead, the first player will steal from him in the next round and in all future rounds. Imagine that both players decide to use a grim trigger strategy when playing the State of Nature Game. How much will the players get if they both choose to refrain? The present value of refraining is

$$\text{Present Value (Refrain)} = 3 + 3d + 3d^2 + 3d^3 + 3d^4 + 3d^5 + \ldots + d^\infty = 3 / (1 - d). \qquad (4\text{--}4)$$

FIGURE 4.23   **State of Nature Game Revisited**

		B	
		Refrain	Steal
A	Refrain	3, 3	1, 4
	Steal	4, 1	2, 2

Where do these numbers come from? If both players refrain, we can see from the payoff table in Figure 4.23 that they will get a payoff of 3 in every period; this payoff will be discounted by the discount rate, d, every time the game is played. This leads to equation 4–4.

What we want to know is whether it is ever a Nash equilibrium for both players to refrain now that the State of Nature Game is infinitely repeated. Recall that a Nash equilibrium requires that no player wishes to unilaterally change his strategy given the strategy adopted by the other player. Well, we know that the players will get a payoff of $3 / (1 - d)$ if they always refrain. But how much would a player get if he changed his strategy from refrain to steal while the other player continued to refrain? Let's imagine that player A unilaterally changed his strategy and started to steal. As the payoff table in Figure 4.23 illustrates, player A would get 4 in the first period—this is the payoff from stealing while player B refrains. The fact that player B is using a grim trigger strategy, however, means that he will respond to player A's stealing by stealing himself in all the future rounds of the game. Given that player B is always going to steal, the best that player A can do now is to continue stealing. As a result, player A will get a payoff of 4 in the first period but a payoff of only 2 discounted by the discount factor in every period thereafter. Thus, player A's present value of unilaterally changing his strategy from refrain to steal is given by equation 4–5.

$$\text{Present Value (Steal)} = 4 + 2d + 2d^2 + 2d^3 + 2d^4 + 2d^5 + \ldots + 2d^\infty. \tag{4–5}$$

Notice that equation (4–5) can be rewritten as

$$\text{Present Value (Steal)} = 4 + 2d(1 + d + d^2 + d^3 + d^4 + d^5 + \ldots + d^\infty). \tag{4–6}$$

We saw earlier in equation (4–3) that $1 + d + d^2 + d^3 + d^4 + d^5 + \ldots + d^\infty = 1 / (1 - d)$. Thus, we can rewrite and simplify equation (4–6) as

Present Value (Steal) $= 4 + 2d / (1 - d)$. (4–7)

Player A will choose not to unilaterally change his strategy to steal if the present value of refraining is greater than the present value of stealing. This will occur when $3 / (1 - d)$ is greater than $4 + 2d / (1 - d)$. A little algebra (equations 4–8 through 4–13) indicates that player A will prefer to refrain rather than steal when $d > 1/2$. Given that player B has the same payoffs as player A, he will also prefer to refrain rather than steal when $d > 1/2$.

Present Value (Refrain) > Present Value (Steal)

$$\Rightarrow 3 / (1 - d) > 4 + 2d / (1 - d) \qquad (4\text{–}8)$$

$$\Rightarrow 3 / (1 - d) > (4 - 4d + 2d) / (1 - d) \qquad (4\text{–}9)$$

$$\Rightarrow 3 / (1 - d) > (4 - 2d) / (1 - d) \qquad (4\text{–}10)$$

$$\Rightarrow \qquad 3 > 4 - 2d \qquad (4\text{–}11)$$

$$\Rightarrow \qquad 2d > 1 \qquad (4\text{–}12)$$

$$\Rightarrow \qquad d > 1/2 \qquad (4\text{–}13)$$

What we have just shown is that the strategy combination (Refrain; Refrain) can be sustained as a Nash equilibrium in the infinitely repeated State of Nature Game when both players use a grim trigger strategy and the discount factor is greater than a half. The condition that the discount rate must be greater than a half is something specific to the payoffs that we have chosen for our particular State of Nature Game. The result, however, is quite general. Players using a grim trigger strategy in an infinitely repeated State of Nature Game can sustain cooperation as part of a Nash equilibrium as long as the discount factor is sufficiently high.[19] It turns out that other strategies can also sustain cooperation. One of the most famous strategies is called the tit-for-tat strategy, or TFT. According to TFT, players will start by cooperating and will then choose whatever action the other player did in the last period to determine how they will behave in subsequent rounds. Thus, if one player chose to cooperate the last time the game was played, the other player will cooperate in the next round. In contrast, if the first player chose to steal the last time the game was played, the other player will steal in the next round. And so on. If the players care enough about the future (if the discount factor is sufficiently high), then cooperation can be sustained in an infinitely repeated State of Nature Game using TFT. The important point here is that cooperation can occur in the

---

19. That the game is infinitely repeated (or, alternatively, that the players do not know when the game will end) is very important. If the players know that the game will be played for a finite or fixed number of periods, it is no longer possible to sustain cooperation. We do not actually show this, but here is the basic logic. In whatever is the last period, the best reply for both players will be to steal as there is no future period in which the other player can punish them for stealing. Because both players know that they will both steal in the last period, however, the best they can do in the penultimate period is also to steal. Knowing that they will both steal in the penultimate period leads them to steal in the period before that and so on. This logic continues to the point that both players steal from the very first period.

state of nature without needing to create a state. In effect, cooperation can evolve in the state of nature as long as the players are sufficiently concerned about the potential benefits of future cooperation. This conclusion runs directly counter to the claims of social contract theorists like Hobbes and provides support for groups like anarchists who believe that society can survive, and thrive, without a state.

That cooperation can be sustained in equilibrium without a state does not necessarily mean that we should all become anarchists, though. It turns out that cooperation is only one of a whole host of possible equilibria in the infinitely repeated State of Nature Game. For example, it is also a Nash equilibrium for both players to steal. This is relatively easy to see. If your opponent is always going to steal, then you never have an incentive to unilaterally change your strategy—you will always steal as well. Thus, the strategy combination (Steal; Steal) is another Nash equilibrium. Game theory cannot tell us which equilibrium is most likely to occur in these circumstances. As a result, there is no reason to believe that the cooperative outcome will be any more likely to occur than any of the other equilibrium outcomes. That cooperation can be sustained in equilibrium without a state does not guarantee that cooperation will, in fact, occur. Moreover, it actually takes a lot of effort for the players to sustain cooperation in the state of nature because everyone has to monitor everyone else to see who is stealing and who is not. It also requires that the individuals get together to punish those people who have been caught stealing. In sum, although it is possible for cooperation to occur in the state of nature without a state, relying on it to emerge through some decentralized process may not be the best thing to do—the creation of a state may be a more preferable and reliable route to cooperative outcomes.

5 Democracy and Dictatorship

Conceptualization and Measurement

> If you can think about something, you can conceptualize it; if you can conceptualize it, you can operationalize it; and if you can operationalize it, you can measure it.

J. David Singer

> If you can not measure it, you can not improve it.

Lord Kelvin

> Not everything that counts can be counted, and not everything that can be counted counts.

From a sign in Einstein's office at Princeton

- Although a strong consensus exists that democracy is the most desirable form of political regime, this has not always been the case. In fact, historically, democracy was commonly viewed as an obsolete system that was both dangerous and unstable.

- Given the current widespread agreement concerning the importance and desirability of democracy, one might wonder how a country becomes a democracy and about the sorts of things that influence democratic survival. Answering these types of questions presupposes that we can conceptualize and measure democracy and dictatorship.

- In this chapter, we look at the types of issues that arise when social scientists try to conceptualize and measure abstract political phenomena. We do so in the context of democracy and dictatorship. What exactly is it that makes a democracy a democracy? Should we conceptualize and measure democracy in substantive or minimalist terms? Should we

OVERVIEW

conceptualize and measure democracy and dictatorship as two separate categories or two ends of a single democratic-dictatorial continuum?

- We also discuss different criteria—validity, reliability, and replicability—that political scientists employ to evaluate empirical measures of their theoretical concepts. We do so by examining three different measures of democracy and dictatorship commonly employed by comparative scholars.

- Issues having to do with conceptualization and measurement are important, but often underemphasized, elements in the process by which social scientists test their theories.

We live in a world in which there is now strong agreement concerning the importance and desirability of democracy. It is important to recognize, however, that this has historically not always been the case. "For two millennia politicians and philosophers regarded democracy as an inferior form of politics" dominated by mob rule and class warfare (Hanson 1989, 70). As C. B. Macpherson (1966, 1) puts it,

> Democracy used to be a bad word. Everybody who was anybody knew that democracy, in its original sense of rule by the people or government in accordance with the will of the bulk of the people, would be a bad thing—fatal to individual freedom and to all graces of civilized living. That was the position taken by pretty nearly all men of intelligence from the earliest historical times down to about a hundred years ago. Then, within fifty years, democracy became a good thing.

It is only relatively recently, then, that democracy has come to be considered a political system to be championed and exported around the world. It is for this reason that we begin this chapter by briefly examining how the meaning and appeal of democracy has changed over time.

Given the consensus that now exists in favor of democracy, we might ask ourselves what causes democracy to emerge and survive. In the last chapter, we examined contractarian and predatory views of the state. We argued that the predatory view of the state had the potential to explain why some rulers share power or limit their extractive activity whereas others do not. Put differently, the predatory view of the state has the potential to explain why some states adopt democratic regimes but others adopt dictatorial ones. In the next two chapters, we take a closer look at this issue by analyzing economic and cultural explanations for the emergence and survival of democracy. Empirical tests of these arguments, however, presuppose that we know a democracy when we see one. But is it obvious which countries are democracies and which are not? How do we know which ones are democracies? What makes a democracy a democracy and a dictatorship a dictatorship? In the second half of this chapter, we investigate how comparative politics scholars have tried to conceptualize and measure democratic and dictatorial regimes.

Although we deliberately focus on democracy and dictatorship in this chapter, it is important to recognize that all political scientists interested in theory testing must ultimately wrestle with how best to conceptualize and measure whatever abstract political phenomena they are examining. How should scholars conceptualize and measure representation, government performance, material well-being, societal development, culture, identity, accountability, and so on? The conceptualization and measurement issues that we raise here with respect to democracy and dictatorship apply equally well to these other types of political phenomena, many of which will be examined in subsequent chapters. Thinking about the issues that arise when scholars operationalize abstract political concepts is important because good measures are a prerequisite for good theory testing, a key part of the scientific process.

DEMOCRACY AND DICTATORSHIP IN HISTORICAL PERSPECTIVE

Democracy acquired a highly positive connotation during the second half of the twentieth century. Even countries widely considered dictatorships have professed their support for democracy and simply adjusted their definition of democracy so that the word could be applied to their form of regime (see Box 5.1, "States, Regimes, and Governments"). Indeed, many acknowledged dictatorships make reference to "people" or "democracy" in their very name—the Democratic People's Republic of Korea, the Democratic Republic of Congo, and the Lao People's Democratic Republic—as if this would somehow make them democratic. As we will see in later chapters, these countries often go so far as to adopt seemingly democratic institutions, such as elections, legislatures, and political parties. Still, until the middle of the nineteenth century, democracy was commonly viewed as an obsolete and ancient political system that was both dangerous and unstable. Of course, one reason for this view of democracy is that the debate concerning the appropriate form that regimes should take typically occurred among elites rather than the common people.

The earliest debates surrounding the merits of different forms of regime, including democracy, can be dated to around 520 B.C. in Persia (Herodotus [440 BCE] 2005, bk. 3, pp. 80–83).[1] It was perhaps Plato and Aristotle, however, who first began to think systematically about the different forms that regimes could take. In *The Republic,* Plato ([360 BCE] 1991) makes the case that political decision making should be based on expertise and that "ochlocracy," or "mob rule," would result from allowing all people to rule in a democracy (427e–29a). In effect, Plato believed that just as only trained pilots should fly airplanes, only

---

1. The earliest use of the word *demokratia* is in the *Histories* written by Herodotus sometime in the 440s to 420s B.C. (Rhodes 2003, 19). In this work, Herodotus mentions a debate among the Persians as to the relative merits of democracy, oligarchy, and monarchy. Although Athens is often considered the first recorded democracy (sixth century B.C.), some scholars argue that democracy existed in a recognizable form even earlier in the republics of ancient India (Muhlberger and Paine 1993).

Box 5.1   STATES, REGIMES, AND GOVERNMENTS

What is the difference between a state, a regime, and a government? Although it is common to see people use these terms interchangeably, they do in fact refer to distinct things. As we saw in the last chapter, the **state** is an entity that uses coercion and the threat of force to rule in a given territory. One can talk, for example, of the French state, the Iranian state, the Malaysian state, the Indian state, and so on. With the exception of relatively rare cases in which states merge (the formation of the United Arab Emirates in 1971) or break up (East Timor in 2002, South Sudan in 2011), the states that comprise the contemporary world system are generally quite stable.

A **state** is an entity that uses coercion and the threat of force to rule in a given territory. A **government** is the set of people who run the state or have the authority to act on behalf of the state at a particular point in time. A **regime** is the set of rules, norms, or institutions that determine how the government is constituted, how it is organized, and how major decisions are made.

In a very general sense, the **government** is the set of people who run the state or have the authority to act on behalf of the state at a particular point in time. That is, governments are the means through which state power is exercised. As examples, the governments of the United States, Saudi Arabia, and Japan in 2016 were headed by President Barack Obama, King Salman of the Saud family, and Prime Minister Shinzō Abe, respectively. While states are generally stable over time, governments come and go.

A **regime** is the set of rules, norms, or institutions that determine how the government is constituted, how it is organized, and how major decisions are made. Regimes are generally classified as being either democratic or dictatorial, and are the focus of this chapter. As we will see in subsequent chapters, democratic and dictatorial regimes actually come in different types. For example, democracies are often classified in terms of whether they are presidential, parliamentary, or semi-presidential (Chapter 12), and dictatorships are frequently classified in terms of whether they are run by the military, a monarchy, or civilians (Chapter 10).

To put all of these definitions together, consider the following two examples. The Tunisian state came into existence in its current form in 1956 when Tunisia achieved independence from France. Tunisia had a civilian dictatorial regime from 1956 to 1987, and the government was led by President Habib Bourguiba. From 1987 to 2011, Tunisia had a military dictatorial regime, and the government was led by President Zine al-Abidine Ben Ali. Mass demonstrations, which were part of the Arab Spring, forced President Ben Ali to resign and flee to Saudi Arabia in January 2011. A Constituent Assembly was created after the October 2011 election to write a new constitution. The new constitution, which was adopted in January 2014, established Tunisia as a semi-presidential democratic regime. The Tunisian government as of 2016 is led by Prime Minister Habib Essid and the head of state is President Beji Caid Essebsi.

The Australian state emerged in its current form in 1901 when the Commonwealth of Australia was established. Since forming, the Australian state has always had a parliamentary democratic regime. There have been numerous Australian governments over the last century, led by thirty-five different prime ministers. The government as of 2016 is led by Prime Minister Malcolm Turnbull.

trained statesmen should guide the ship of state. The Greek word **demokratia** often gets translated as "rule by the people" with no mention about who these people are. In Plato and Aristotle's time, **demos** referred primarily to the "common people"—those people with little or no economic independence who were politically uneducated (Hanson 1989, 71). Ultimately, Plato thought that

> **Demokratia** is a Greek word meaning "rule by the demos." Although the Greek word **demos** often gets translated as "the people," it refers more specifically to the "common people"—those people with little or no economic independence who are politically uneducated.

democracy would not be rule by the people but instead would be rule by the poor and uneducated against the rich and educated. In addition, he believed that the uneducated mass would be open to demagoguery, leading to short-lived democracies in which the people quickly surrender power to a tyrant (Baradat 2006, 63).

Aristotle ([350 BCE] 1996) disagreed with Plato to the extent that he believed that there were some conditions under which the will of the many could be equal to or wiser than the will of the few (1281b). This is not to say, however, that he thought highly of democracy. In his *Politics,* Aristotle ([350 BCE] 1996) classified regimes in regard to the number of rulers that they had, stating that government "must be in the hands of one, or of a few, or of the many" (1279a.27–28). His classification is shown in Table 5.1. He believed that regimes come in good and bad forms. In good forms of regime the rulers govern for the good of all, whereas in bad forms they govern only for the good of themselves (Aristotle [350 BCE] 1996, 1279a.17–21). The good forms of regime were monarchy, aristocracy, and *politeia;* the bad forms were tyranny, oligarchy, and democracy (Aristotle [350 BCE] 1996, 1279b.4–10).

The concern for Aristotle was that each of the good forms of regime could be corrupted in that the common good could be replaced by the good of the rulers. For example, a corrupted monarchy would become a tyranny, a corrupted aristocracy would become an oligarchy, and a corrupted *politeia* would become a democracy. Aristotle argues that we should choose the type of regime that had the least dangerous corrupt form. For Aristotle, this was aristocracy. Like Plato, Aristotle believed that democracy would be the most dangerous form of regime because it is characterized by class rule, in which poor and uneducated citizens govern for themselves rather than the commonweal. Some of the same fears about democracy—that it would result in class warfare, attempts by the poor to expropriate the rich, and so forth—were just as strong in the eighteenth and nineteenth centuries, when

TABLE 5.1   Aristotle's Classification of Regimes

Number of rulers	Good form "For the Good of All"	Bad form "For the Good of the Rulers"
One	Monarchy	Tyranny
Few	Aristocracy	Oligarchy
Many	Politeia	Democracy

people were debating whether to extend the suffrage (Offe 1983; Roemer 1998). For example, Marx ([1850] 1952, 62) stated that universal suffrage and democracy inevitably "unchain the class struggle." These fears have also motivated efforts to restrict voting by certain categories of individuals during the twentieth century in the United States (Piven and Cloward 1988, 2000).

It should be noted that democracy at the time of Plato and Aristotle looked very different from what we understand democracy to be today. The most obvious difference is that democracy had nothing to do with elections when they wrote. In fact, leaders were chosen by elections in aristocratic regimes, whereas they were decided by lot (that is, by drawing names from a hat) in democracies. As Montesquieu writes in his *Spirit of the Laws* ([1752] 1914, 2:2), "suffrage by lot is natural to democracy; as that by choice is to aristocracy." The notion that democracy was a system in which political offices were determined by lot continued all the way into the eighteenth century, and it is partly for this reason that many political theorists argued for the benefits of monarchy over democracy. Those people who were arguing for representative government in the eighteenth century did not see themselves as proponents of democracy. For them, democracy was associated with direct legislation by the people and, hence, was possible only in the city-states of the ancient world. In effect, democracy was seen as obsolete (Rosanvallon 1995, 141).

Only with the establishment of a major fault line between democracy and aristocracy in the age of revolution—French and American—did representative government and democracy come to be synonymous with each other (Hanson 1989; Rosanvallon 1995). Until this time, moves away from absolutism were motivated by attempts to get rid of unjust rulers rather than a desire to shift power to the people (Rhodes 2003, 28). In fact, lords and other members of the nobility would often side with commoners to get rid of unjust rulers. In this sense, corrupt monarchs, rather than the monarchy per se, were the target of opposition groups. This situation began to change during the French Revolution (1789) as the two opposing forces in the conflict solidified around the distinction between the aristocracy and the people. From this point on in time, the contemporary notion of democracy took on many of the characteristics that are familiar to us today. It was also at this point that Aristotle's three-way distinction of government by one, a few, and many was replaced by a simple dichotomy between democracy (many) and autocracy/dictatorship (one or a few). As with the conception of democracy, that of dictatorship has also evolved a great deal over time (see Box 5.2, "Dictatorships").

CLASSIFYING DEMOCRACIES AND DICTATORSHIPS

As political scientists, we often want to address questions such as why some countries are democracies but others are dictatorships, what factors influence democratic survival, and whether democracies or dictatorships produce better economic performance. To answer these questions, we need to be able to measure democracy and classify countries as either democratic or dictatorial.

Box 5.2

DICTATORSHIPS

It was only after World War I that people began to commonly refer to autocracies as dictatorships. Historically, dictatorships have not always been seen as bad things. Although tyranny, despotism, and autocracy have always had negative connotations, this is not the case with dictatorships. A "dictator" was an extraordinary Roman magistrate nominated under exceptional emergency circumstances from about 500 B.C. to the third century A.D. This magistrate or dictator was nominated only for the duration of the extraordinary task entrusted to him. In his *Discourses*, Machiavelli ([1531] 1998, 34) argued that "dictatorial authority did good, not harm, to the republic of Rome." Likewise, Rousseau, in *The Social Contract,* also suggested that dictators might be required in emergencies. He writes that "if the danger is such that the apparatus of law is itself an obstacle to safety, then a supreme head must be nominated with power to silence all laws and temporarily suspend the sovereign authority" (Rousseau [1762] 1987, bk. 4, chap. 6). Clearly, this positive connotation of a dictatorship has disappeared. Today, dictatorships are seen as largely synonymous with autocracy, tyranny, and despotism.

Theories about the world are based on abstract **concepts**—mental categories that capture the meaning of objects, events, or ideas. Think about what your concept of democracy is. What does democracy mean to you? We imagine that some picture of what democracy "is" or means to you is forming in your mind. This is your concept of democracy. By their very nature, theoretical concepts cannot be observed—they exist in our heads, not in the real world. When we want to test our

> A **concept** is a mental category or construct that captures the meaning of objects, events, or ideas.
>
> A **measure** or **indicator** is a quantification of the concept or thing in which we are interested.
>
> **Operationalization** is the process by which abstract theoretical concepts are translated into concrete and observable measures or indicators.

theoretical claims, we have to translate our concepts into concrete measures or indicators that we can actually observe. A **measure** or **indicator** is a quantification of the thing we are interested in. The process by which we translate a concept into a measure is called **operationalization**—we use a particular measure to operationalize a theoretical concept. It is important to recognize, then, that when we conduct empirical tests of our theories, we get to evaluate only indicators or measures of our concepts, not the concepts themselves. It should quickly become obvious that our empirical tests are good only to the extent that our selected indicators accurately capture the concept that we intend to measure. It is for this reason that measurement is so important to the scientific endeavor. In this section, we examine some of the various ways in which scholars have operationalized the abstract concept of democracy and discuss their strengths and weaknesses. Before you read on, though, you should stop and think about how you would operationalize the concept of democracy. What observable indicators would you use?

Dahl's View of Democracy and Dictatorship

Although our understanding of democracy has changed over time, the central notion underlying our contemporary concept of democracy is that "the people" rather than some subset of the people should rule. Exactly how this abstract concept is translated into a practical set of criteria for classifying political regimes varies enormously in political science (Collier and Levitsky 1997). In a highly influential book, Robert Dahl (1971) cautioned scholars against employing a substantive view of democracy. A **substantive view of democracy** classifies political regimes in regard to the outcomes that they produce and not just the institutions that they have. To a large extent, Aristotle's view of democracy that we described earlier can be seen as substantive, because he distinguishes between good and bad forms of regimes based on the degree to which they serve the public good. Dahl argued that if scholars used normatively derived or substantive definitions of "ideal democracy"—that "true" democracies should rule in certain ways and should produce certain outcomes such as economic justice or government accountability—then they may find it difficult to find real-world examples of such regimes. For example, ask yourself how many regimes in the world actually produce economic justice. Dahl believed that researchers should employ a **minimalist**, or **procedural**, **view of democracy**, which classifies political regimes only in regard to their institutions and procedures.

> A **substantive view of democracy** classifies political regimes in regard to the outcomes that they produce. A **minimalist**, or **procedural**, **view of democracy** classifies political regimes in regard to their institutions and procedures.

Dahl identified two dimensions as being particularly important for classifying political regimes—**contestation** and **inclusion**. Contestation captures the extent to which citizens are free to organize themselves into competing blocs in order to press for the policies and outcomes they desire. Aspects of contestation include the freedom to form political parties, freedom of speech and assembly, and the extent to which leaders are chosen in free and fair elections. Contestation is, therefore, largely concerned with the procedures of democratic competition. Inclusion has to do with who gets to participate in the democratic process. Political regimes in which barriers to the naturalization of immigrants are low and all adult citizens are permitted to vote will rank high in regard to inclusion. In contrast, countries that have property requirements or that deny the effective right to vote based on place of birth, ethnicity, or gender would be considered less inclusive. We illustrate the two dimensions of contestation and inclusion in Figure 5.1.

> Dahl conceptualizes democracy along two dimensions: contestation and inclusion. **Contestation** captures the extent to which citizens are free to organize themselves into competing blocs in order to press for the policies and outcomes they desire. **Inclusion** has to do with who gets to participate in the democratic process.

The former Soviet Union is an example of a country that had high levels of inclusion because everyone was allowed to vote and participate, but it had low levels of contestation because there was only one political party. China has low levels of both inclusion and contestation because there is only one party and there are no elections above the municipal

FIGURE 5.1	**Dahl's Two Dimensions of Democracy: Contestation and Inclusion**

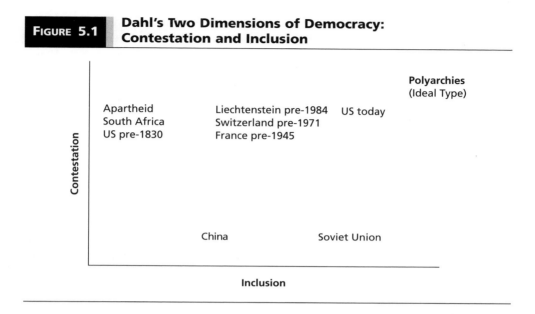

level. Although contestation was high in South Africa under apartheid and in the United States prior to 1830 because there were multiparty elections, inclusion was low because vast segments of the population were not allowed to vote or participate. The expansion of the franchise in the United States during the 1830s represented an increase in inclusion, but substantial barriers to full inclusion remained in place until at least 1964, when the Voting Rights Act gave many African Americans de facto access to the vote for the first time. As countries located in the top left of Figure 5.1 expand the right to vote, they begin to move rightward along the inclusion dimension. For example, Liechtenstein pre-1984, Switzerland pre-1971, and France pre-1945 had high levels of contestation due to multiparty elections, but they had only moderate levels of inclusion because universal suffrage applied only to men. Most of the countries that we immediately recognize as being democracies today would be in the top right-hand corner of Figure 5.1 with high levels of both contestation and inclusion.

Dahl (1971) conceded that contestation and inclusion are only two aspects of what people take into account when they think of the concept of democracy. As a result, he was willing to drop the use of the term *democracy* altogether. Instead, he used the word **polyarchy** to describe a political regime with high levels of both contestation and inclusion. Another reason for preferring the term *polyarchy* was that he did not believe that any large country exhibited, or could exhibit, sufficient levels of contestation or inclusion to rightfully

A **polyarchy** is a political regime with high levels of both contestation and inclusion.

be considered a true democracy—countries could be closer or farther away from the ideal type of democracy, but they could never actually get there. Although the emphasis on contestation and inclusion has stuck and been incorporated into many of the subsequent measures of regime type, the term *polyarchy* has not. Comparative politics scholars continue to talk about democracy even when their operational definitions are no more ambitious (and frequently less ambitious) than Dahl's. We follow the practice of the comparative politics literature in using the word *democracy* even when discussing the procedural, or minimalist, definitions inspired by Dahl.

Three Measures of Democracy and Dictatorship

How have comparative scholars operationalized the concept of democracy? What are the strengths and weaknesses of these operationalizations? Although there are several different measures of democracy and dictatorship (Coppedge et al. 2011; Munck and Verkuilen 2002; Pemstein, Meserve, and Melton 2010), we focus here on three that are commonly used in the comparative politics literature—Democracy-Dictatorship (DD), Polity IV, and Freedom House. All three measures build on Dahl's insights.

The Democracy-Dictatorship (DD) Measure

Cheibub, Gandhi, and Vreeland (2010) provide an annual measure of democracy and dictatorship for 199 countries from January 1, 1946 (or independence) to December 31, 2008. We refer to this as the Democracy-Dictatorship (DD) measure.[2] According to the conceptualization of democracy underlying the DD measure, democracies are "regimes in which governmental offices are filled as a consequence of contested elections" (Cheibub, Gandhi, and Vreeland 2010, 69). This simple conceptualization of democracy has two primary components: (i) governmental offices and (ii) contestation. For a regime to be considered democratic, it must be that both the chief executive office and the legislature are elected. Contestation requires that there exists an opposition that has some chance of winning office as a consequence of elections. Specifically, contestation entails the following three elements: (a) *ex ante* uncertainty: the outcome of the election is unknown before it happens, (b) *ex post* irreversibility: the winner of the election actually takes office, and (c) repeatability: elections that meet the first two criteria must occur at regular and known intervals (Przeworski 1991). *Ex ante* uncertainty rules out those countries, such as Iraq under Saddam Hussein, in which there was absolutely no uncertainty as to which candidate or party was going to win before the voters went to the polls. *Ex post* irreversibility rules out countries like Algeria in 1991, when the army intervened to prevent the Islamic Salvation Front from taking office following its success in the first round of legislative elections. And repeatability rules out countries like Weimar Germany in the 1930s when the Nazi Party came to power through democratic elections but then canceled further electoral contests.

---

2. The DD measure is a revised and updated version of the PACL measure of democracy and dictatorship first developed by Przeworski, Alvarez, Cheibub, and Limongi (1996, 2000).

The authors who constructed the DD measure employ four rules for operationalizing their conceptualization of democracy and dictatorship. A country is classified as a democracy if all of the following conditions apply:

1. The chief executive is elected.
2. The legislature is elected.
3. There is more than one party competing in the elections.
4. An alternation in power under identical electoral rules has taken place.

A country is classified as a dictatorship if any of these four conditions do not hold.

The first two conditions follow in a straightforward way from the authors' conceptualization of democracy—governmental offices must be elected. The third condition is also relatively straightforward—for a contested election to take place, voters must have at least two alternatives to choose from. Elections in which only one party competes or in which voters are confronted with a single party list as in Vietnam are therefore not considered contested. The inclusion of the third (and fourth) rule is a clear recognition of the fact that elections, in and of themselves, are not sufficient to distinguish between democracies and dictatorships. Virtually every country in the world has held legislative or presidential elections at one time or another (Bormann and Golder 2013). In other words, elections cannot fully distinguish between political regimes because almost all countries in the contemporary world would have to be considered democratic by this standard.

The fourth condition is less straightforward: An alternation in power under identical electoral rules must take place before a regime can be considered democratic. An alternation in power means that the individual who is the chief executive is replaced through the electoral process by someone else. Thus, an alternation occurred in Mexico when Enrique Peña Nieto of the Institutional Revolutionary Party (PRI) took over the presidency from Felipe Calderón of the National Action Party (PAN) in 2012. The authors who constructed the DD measure believe that unless the incumbent ruler has demonstrated that he is willing to give up power after losing an election, then we have no way of truly knowing whether the country is a dictatorship or a democracy. For example, it is impossible without an alternation in power to distinguish between regimes in which the incumbents are always in power because they are popular (but would give up power if they lost) and those in which incumbents hold elections only because they know they will not lose—these two scenarios are observationally equivalent; that is, they look the same. Examples of this type of situation have occurred in several countries in which one party has been in power for long periods of time—Botswana, Japan, Malaysia, and Mexico (see Box 5.3, "Alternation in Power").

The DD measure builds on Dahl's insights in two respects. First, it is based on a purely procedural, or minimalist, view of democracy and dictatorship, because the classification rules make no mention of the substantive outcomes produced by different political regimes. Second, it focuses strongly on Dahl's notion of contestation. One obvious difference from Dahl is that the DD measure completely ignores Dahl's dimension of inclusion.

Box 5.3 **ALTERNATION IN POWER**

Multiparty elections have been held in Botswana, Japan, Malaysia, and Mexico. In each of these countries, however, a single party has been in power for long periods of time. Until the incumbents lost in Japan (Liberal Democratic Party [LDP]) and Mexico (PRI) and willingly gave up power, it was unclear whether these countries should be considered democracies or dictatorships.

The difficulty in deciding whether these countries were democracies is illustrated by Malaysia, in which three multiparty elections were held between 1957 and 1969. The incumbent government (Alliance Party coalition) won the first two multiparty elections. When it lost the third election, however, it declared a state of emergency, closed parliament, and rewrote the constitution such that it, and its successor, the National Front coalition, never lost another election (Ahmad 1988). Clearly, the holding of contested multiparty elections did not mean that Malaysia was a democracy. That the incumbent government was unwilling to give up power when it lost the third election suggests that it would have been unwilling to give up power if it had lost either of the two previous ones.

Now consider Botswana. The incumbent government (Botswana Democratic Party) has never lost an election since the country became independent in 1966. Should we consider Botswana to be a democracy? Many scholars do. According to the DD measure, though, Botswana is coded as a dictatorship precisely because it is impossible to know for certain whether the incumbent government would willingly give up power if it lost—we have never seen it lose, so how would we know? In effect, the authors who constructed the DD measure prefer to potentially mistake a democracy for a dictatorship rather than mistake a dictatorship for a democracy. This is a choice that all scholars have to make.

One justification for this is that countries around the world exhibit almost no variation in their level of inclusion for the time frame (1946–2008) considered by the DD measure—by 1946 all but a handful of countries had adopted universal suffrage for their elections. The biggest difference, though, between the DD measure and Dahl's classification scheme is that the DD measure treats regime type as a dichotomy—countries are either a democracy or a dictatorship—whereas Dahl treats regime type as a continuum with strong dictatorships at one end and strong democracies at the other. Although the DD authors accept that some regimes are more democratic than others, they believe that those countries with uncontested political offices, such as China and North Korea, should not be considered even partly democratic. Put differently, the DD authors assume that there is a qualitative difference between democracies and dictatorships and that it does not make sense to think that there is a point at which a regime is equally democratic and dictatorial as implied by **continuous measures** of democracy. The abstract concepts of democracy proposed by

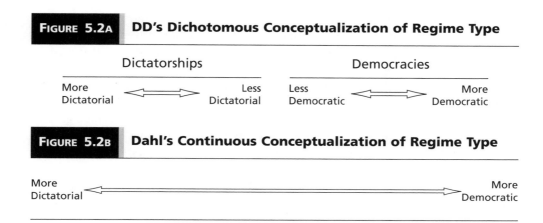

FIGURE 5.2A **DD's Dichotomous Conceptualization of Regime Type**

Dictatorships   Democracies

More   Less   Less   More
Dictatorial   Dictatorial Democratic   Democratic

FIGURE 5.2B **Dahl's Continuous Conceptualization of Regime Type**

More   More
Dictatorial   Democratic

Dahl and the DD authors are compared in Figures 5.2a and 5.2b. It is important to recognize that it is because their conceptual view of regime type is dichotomous that the DD authors choose to employ a **dichotomous measure** to capture it, not because they think it is impossible to determine or measure whether some regimes are more democratic than others as some have implied (Elkins 2000).

> A **continuous measure** can take on any intermediate value within a given range (for example, "height in centimeters").
>
> A **dichotomous measure** has only two discrete categories or values (for example, "tall" or "short").

Polity IV

An alternative measure of democracy comes from Polity IV (Marshall, Gurr, and Jaggers 2016). Polity IV provides an annual measure of democracy and autocracy for 167 countries from 1800 to 2015. The Democracy and Autocracy scores for each country both range from 0 to 10. From these two measures, a Polity Score is constructed for each country. The Polity Score is calculated as the Democracy Score minus the Autocracy Score. As a result, the Polity Score for each country ranges from a minimum of –10 (as autocratic or dictatorial as possible) to a maximum of 10 (as democratic as possible). Polity IV follows Dahl in conceptualizing and measuring democracy along a continuum like the one illustrated in Figure 5.2b. In practice, though, many scholars choose to code countries as democracies if their Polity Score is +6 to +10, dictatorships if their Polity Score is –6 to –10, and as an "anocracy" or "mixed regime" if the Polity Score is between –5 and 5.[3] Polity IV also follows Dahl in providing a largely minimalist, or procedural, measure of democracy.

---

3. Other scholars pick different cut-points for deciding whether a country should be considered a democracy or an autocracy. The decision of where to place the cut-points is rarely, if ever, justified in a theoretical manner. Unfortunately, there is reason to believe that the choice of where to place the cut-points matters in empirical tests (Coppedge 1997; Elkins 2000; Pemstein, Meserve, and Melton 2010).

What are the precise rules that generate the Polity Score? A country's Polity Score is based on five different attributes or dimensions: (a) the competitiveness of executive recruitment, (b) the openness of executive recruitment, (c) the constraints that exist on the executive, (d) the regulation of political participation, and (e) the competitiveness of political participation. Together, these dimensions capture Dahl's notion of both contestation and inclusion. By including "constraints that exist on the executive," Polity IV actually adds an additional dimension to Dahl's concept of democracy—that democratic governments must be limited governments.[4] Each of Polity IV's five attributes contributes a different number of points to a country's Democracy and Autocracy scores. As an illustration, consider the "competitiveness of political participation" dimension (an indicator of the degree of contestation) and the "regulation of political participation" dimension (an indicator of the degree of inclusion) in the political system. The possible scores for these dimensions are shown in Tables 5.2 and 5.3.

If political participation is considered competitive in a country by those scholars coding it, then that country will have 3 added to its Democracy Score and 0 to its Autocracy Score.[5]

TABLE 5.2   Competitiveness of Political Participation

	Contribution to Democracy Score	Contribution to Autocracy Score	Contribution to Polity Score
Competitive	3	0	3
Transitional	2	0	2
Factional	1	0	1
Suppressed	0	1	−1
Repressed	0	2	−2

TABLE 5.3   Regulation of Political Participation

	Contribution to Democracy Score	Contribution to Autocracy Score	Contribution to Polity Score
Sectarian	0	1	−1
Restricted	0	2	−2

---

4. It is interesting to note that most of the variation in Polity Scores across countries actually comes from this additional "constraints on the executive" dimension (Gleditsch and Ward 1997).

5. To know precisely what is meant by *competitive, transitional, factional,* and so on, see the Polity IV Dataset Users' manual at http://www.systemicpeace.org/inscr/p4manualv2015.pdf (Marshall, Gurr, and Jaggers 2016).

In contrast, if political participation is considered suppressed by the coders, then 2 will be added to its autocracy score and 0 to its democracy score. If a country's political participation is considered restricted by the coder, then 2 will be added to that country's Autocracy Score and 0 to its Democracy Score. Note that the numbers or "weights" vary across these two dimensions. The scores from each of these dimensions are added together to come up with a country's overall Democracy, Autocracy, and Polity scores.

Freedom House

Freedom House is an independent, nongovernmental organization that has, among other things, provided an annual measure of "global freedom" for countries around the world since 1972.[6] The 2015 Freedom in the World survey covers 195 countries and fifteen related and disputed territories. Although the measure provided by Freedom House is not technically a measure of democracy, many scholars use it as if it were, presumably under the assumption that democracy and freedom are synonymous. We leave it up to you to decide whether it is reasonable to assume that the more freedom exhibited by a country, the more democratic it is.

A country's Freedom House score is based on two dimensions that capture a country's level of political rights and civil rights. The amount of freedom on the political rights dimension is measured by a series of ten questions, each worth between 0 and 4 points.[7] Zero indicates the lowest level of freedom and 4 indicates the highest level of freedom. The ten questions dealing with political rights cover three primary categories: (i) the electoral process, (ii) political pluralism and participation, and (iii) the functioning of government. The following are examples of the types of questions asked on the political dimension: Is the head of state elected through free and fair elections? Is there pervasive corruption? Is the government open, accountable, and transparent between elections? Do people have the right to organize? Is there a competitive opposition? Do minorities have reasonable autonomy? Whatever score a country gets out of the possible 40 points is then converted to a 7-point scale. Thus, each country ultimately receives a score of 1 to 7 on the political rights dimension. You have to be careful, though, because Freedom House now reverses the scale so that 1 indicates the highest level of freedom and 7 indicates the lowest level of freedom.

The amount of freedom on the civil rights dimension is measured by a series of fifteen questions, each worth between 0 and 4 points, covering four primary categories: (i) freedom of expression and belief, (ii) associational and organizational rights, (iii) rule of law, and (iv) personal autonomy and individual rights. The following are examples of the types of questions asked on the civil rights dimension: Is the media free and independent? Are there

---

6. You can find Freedom House online at http://www.freedomhouse.org.

7. There are two additional "discretionary" questions that can add or subtract up to four points. The maximum score that a country can receive on the political rights dimension, though, is 40.

free religious organizations? Is there an independent judiciary? Is there equal treatment under the law? Are there free trade unions? Is there equality of opportunity? Do citizens have the right to own property? Whatever civil rights score a country gets out of the possible 60 points is also converted to a 7-point scale. Thus, each country ultimately receives a score of 1 to 7 on the civil rights dimension as well. A country's overall Freedom House score is simply the average of its scores on the political rights and civil rights dimensions.

The questions relating to the political rights and civil rights dimensions take into account Dahl's concern with the levels of both contestation and inclusion in a country. Freedom House also follows Dahl in conceptualizing regime type along a continuum like the one illustrated in Figure 5.2b. In practice, though, many scholars choose to code countries as Free (Democratic), Partly Free (Mixed), or Not Free (Dictatorship) based on their Freedom House score. If a country scores 1 to 2.5, it is considered Free; if it scores 3 to 5.5, it is considered Partly Free; and if it scores 5.5 to 7, it is considered Not Free. In stark contrast to the procedural view of democracy adopted by Polity IV, DD, and Dahl, Freedom House employs a substantive view of democracy. Freedom House believes that although particular institutions are necessary for democracy, they are not sufficient. As a result, Freedom House takes into account the substantive outcomes produced by different political regimes, such as whether there is academic freedom, freedom from war, and freedom from socioeconomic inequalities.

Comparing DD, Polity IV, and Freedom House Scores

In Map 5.1, we graphically illustrate how DD (top panel), Polity IV (middle panel), and Freedom House (bottom panel) classify countries around the world as democratic, mixed, or dictatorial in 2015.[8] Several scholars have noted that the three different measures of democracy and dictatorship are highly correlated; that is, there is a large degree of overlap between them. To some extent, this is confirmed by Map 5.1, which illustrates that there is general agreement among all three measures that most countries in North America, Europe, and Australasia are democracies, and that most countries in the Middle East are dictatorships. This high degree of correlation across the three measures is largely driven by uncontroversial cases in which it is clear that a regime is either democratic or dictatorial. For example, it is not surprising that all three measures classify countries like the United States, Australia, and Sweden as democracies and countries like China, Saudi Arabia, and North Korea as dictatorships—these are the easy cases. It turns out, though, that there is considerable disagreement among the measures when it comes to classifying the mixed regimes, that is, the countries that occupy the middle of the distribution of the Polity IV and Freedom House measures (Coppedge et al. 2011, 252). This can be clearly seen again in Map 5.1 by looking at the different ways in which Polity IV and Freedom House classify countries in much of Africa and

---

8. The DD data set runs only from 1946 to 2008. To obtain the 2015 DD scores shown in Map 5.1, we updated the DD data based on the coding rules shown earlier.

MAP 5.1 Comparing Democracy and Dictatorship Scores in 2015

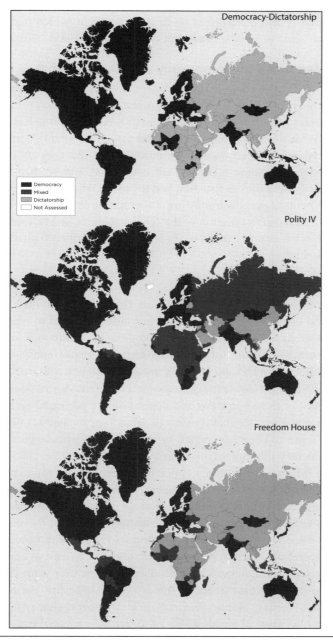

Source: Author created based on data from Cheibub, Gandhi, and Vreeland (2010); Marshall, Gurr, and Jaggers (2016); http://www.freedomhouse.org.

South America. These differences in how countries are classified would not be too problematic if they did not lead to different conclusions when scholars use these measures to test their theories. Unfortunately, there is growing evidence that the results from empirical tests relating to democracy and dictatorship do in fact depend on which particular measure is employed (Casper and Tufts 2003; Cheibub, Gandhi, and Vreeland 2010; Elkins 2000).

Evaluating Measures of Democracy and Dictatorship

In order to test our theories about abstract concepts such as democracy and dictatorship, we need to find measures of those concepts. The process by which scholars operationalize their measures will always involve some simplification or loss of meaning. It is important to recognize, however, that simplification is an essential part of the scientific process, for without it, empirical tests of our theories would be impossible. Still, this does not mean that all measures are created equal. Some measures are better than others. It is incumbent upon researchers to justify both the construction and the use of whatever measure they employ in their research. Whether a particular measure is appropriate or not will depend heavily on the specific objective or research question of the scholar (Collier and Adcock 1999). With this in mind, we also often evaluate measures in terms of their conceptualization, validity, reliability, and replicability.

Conceptualization

Our three measures—DD, Polity IV, and Freedom House—differ in their conceptualization of democracy and dictatorship. In particular, they differ in regard to whether they employ (a) a minimalist or substantive and (b) a dichotomous or continuous view of democracy. Let's begin by considering the distinction between minimalist and substantive views of democracy. Recall that the DD and Polity IV measures adopt a minimalist view of democracy, whereas the Freedom House measure adopts a more substantive view. To some extent, the appropriateness of these two views will depend on the particular research question the scholar asks. For example, a substantive view of democracy runs into considerable problems if the researcher wants to know how regime type influences particular outcomes. Why? Well, if we define democracy substantively in regard to, say, accountability, socioeconomic equality, and freedom from war, as Freedom House does, then using a country's Freedom House score to empirically examine whether democracy affects these very same things involves circular reasoning. Empirical tests will always suggest that a country's level of democracy increases accountability and the like in this situation because of the way the measure of democracy is constructed. As we saw in the previous chapter, you cannot test tautologies. Substantive measures of democracy, however, are arguably at least as appropriate as minimalist measures if the research question addressed by the scholar is unrelated to any of the attributes that go into the construction of the democracy measure. For example, we might legitimately use the Freedom House score to examine whether regime type affects a country's proclivity to join international organizations or to sign international treaties.

Irrespective of the research question, the very fact that minimalist views of democracy are *minimal* means that they have potential advantages when it comes to isolating causal processes. For example, if a study using Freedom House scores finds that democracy increases levels of economic development, how can the scholar determine which of the twenty-five underlying attributes (ten political rights questions and fifteen civil rights questions) is driving this observed relationship? The bottom line is that many substantive measures of democracy conflate institutional and procedural factors with the outcomes they are thought to produce.

Finally, it should be noted that minimalist views of democracy do not place importance on things such as how the judiciary is organized or how the state intervenes in the economy. In effect, minimalist views recognize that democracies can be organized in many different ways. In contrast, Freedom House considers a country more free (democratic) if there is equality of opportunity, an independent judiciary, a right to own property, free trade unions, and so on. These are certainly important factors, but are they a part of what makes something a democracy, or are they characteristics that vary from democracy to democracy that we might want to explain? In many ways, a free and democratic country according to Freedom House looks remarkably similar to an idealized version of the United States. Is this simply an accident or an example of analysts allowing what they view to be normatively appealing characteristics to color an ostensibly objective measure?

Now let's consider the distinction between dichotomous and continuous views of democracy. Recall that DD employs a dichotomous conceptualization of democracy and dictatorship, whereas both Polity IV and Freedom House employ a continuous conceptualization. There has been much debate about the relative merits of these two approaches (Collier and Adcock 1999; Elkins 2000). On the one hand, Bollen and Jackman (1989, 612, 618) argue for a continuous view of democracy, claiming that "democracy is always a matter of degree" and that treating it as dichotomous is a "flawed" practice. On the other hand, other scholars claim that Bollen and Jackman are "confused," because political regimes "cannot be half-democratic: there is a natural zero point" (Alvarez et al. 1996, 21). The debate essentially hinges on whether you think Figure 5.2a or 5.2b is the more appropriate conceptualization of regime type. In our opinion, scholars may reasonably disagree about this.

As with the distinction between minimalist and substantive views of democracy, though, the appropriateness of a dichotomous or continuous conceptualization of democracy will depend to some extent on the researcher's question. On the one hand, the study of democratic transitions would suggest that a dichotomous conceptualization is more appropriate, because a transition seems to imply movement from one distinct regime to another. This is, in fact, why we employ DD's dichotomous measure of democracy when we examine the economic and cultural determinants of democratic transitions in Chapters 6 and 7. Similarly, research that examines whether parliamentary or presidential regimes affect democratic stability also seems to implicitly assume a dichotomy because parliamentary and presidential regimes are typically thought to exist only in democracies. On the other hand, studies that examine, say, the effect of foreign intervention on a country's level of democracy don't seem to necessarily imply a dichotomous concept of democracy in the same way.

Validity

When we conduct empirical tests of our theories, we do not actually evaluate our abstract concepts. Instead, we compare only indicators or measures of those concepts. Consequently, our ability to use observations to understand the world is constrained by our ability to iden-

> **Validity** refers to the extent to which our measures correspond to the concepts that they are intended to reflect.

tify useful indicators or measures. This raises the question of what makes some indicators or measures more desirable than others. One thing that scholars would like their measures to be is valid. **Validity** refers to the extent to which our measures correspond to the concepts that they are intended to reflect (Adcock and Collier 2001). Does our indicator actually measure the thing that it is supposed to measure? Several issues arise when we think about validity. Here, we briefly consider three: attributes, aggregation issues, and measurement level.

One of the initial tasks when constructing a measure is to determine the attributes that make up the abstract concept under consideration. You might ask whether a particular measure includes the "correct" attributes, whether it includes enough attributes to fully capture the concept, or whether it includes too many attributes. Unfortunately, there are no hard-and-fast rules for determining which attributes must be included when measuring a particular concept. Nonetheless, there are certain issues that scholars can take into account when constructing their measures. One issue has to do with having too many attributes. This is a particular concern with substantive measures of democracy, such as the Freedom House measure. For example, Dahl was worried that there would be no actual countries in the world that could be classified as true democracies if too many attributes were included. Even if some countries can be classified as democracies, measures that employ many attributes may be of little analytical use. As we mentioned earlier, the inclusion of attributes such as accountability and socioeconomic equality in Freedom House's measure limits the scope of research questions that the measure can be used to answer. Of course, having too few attributes may also be problematic. Minimalist or procedural measures of democracy, such as those constructed by DD and Polity IV, are open to the criticism that they do not really capture all of what we think of when we think of democracy. For example, some scholars criticize the DD measure for not taking into account Dahl's notion of inclusion.

Even when the researcher has decided upon the attributes that constitute the abstract concept under consideration, she still has to decide on how to aggregate or combine these attributes into a single measure of the concept. The measure of regime type from DD does not require aggregation rules—a country is either a democracy or a dictatorship based on whether it passes a set of necessary and sufficient conditions. In contrast, the measures of democracy and dictatorship from both Freedom House and Polity IV require aggregation rules to combine scores on multiple attributes into a single overall regime score. None of the individual attributes used by Polity IV or Freedom House is explicitly necessary for a country to be considered democratic; instead, a country is classified as democratic whenever it scores a high enough number of points across the range of included dimensions. A consequence of requiring aggregation is that there can be numerous ways of obtaining the same Freedom House or Polity IV score. For example, there are seventeen distinct combinations of the five dimensions underlying the Polity IV regime measure that result in a Polity IV score of 0 (Cheibub, Gandhi, and Vreeland 2010, 93).[9] As a good political scientist, you should ask yourself whether the aggregation rules employed by Freedom House and Polity IV are appropriate and justified.

Consider the aggregation rules used by Freedom House. Is it appropriate for Freedom House to weight each of the attributes (twenty-five questions) that make up a country's level of civil rights and political rights equally? Is academic freedom as important to democracy as an independent judiciary? Is it appropriate for Freedom House to weight the civil rights and political rights dimensions equally when coming up with a country's overall score? Now consider the aggregation rules employed by Polity IV. Is it appropriate for Polity IV to assume that moving from a 1 to a 2 on one of its five attributes will have the same effect on a country's level of democracy as, say, moving from a 3 to a 4? Is Polity IV right to assume that all of its attributes measure democracy equally well? In other words, should Polity IV assume that moving from a 1 to a 2 on one attribute (competitiveness of political participation) will have the same impact on a country's level of democracy as moving from a 1 to a 2 on a different attribute (competitiveness of executive recruitment)? Is it appropriate for both Freedom House and Polity IV to assume that the different attributes of democracy can be aggregated along a single dimension? This last assumption would seem to run counter to Dahl's claim that democracy is inherently multidimensional. Although it is extremely rare to see scholars explicitly address these types of questions, Treier and Jackman (2008) examined aggregation issues as they relate to the Polity IV measure. They conclude that "skepticism as to the precision of the Polity democracy scale is well-founded, and that many researchers have been overly sanguine about the properties of the Polity democracy scale in applied statistical work" (Treier and Jackman 2008, 201).

Once a scholar has determined the best way to aggregate the attributes of a particular concept, she has to decide upon the most appropriate measurement level. There are three different measurement levels: nominal, ordinal, and interval. A **nominal measure** classifies observations into discrete categories that must be mutually exclusive and collectively exhaustive. This means that it must not be possible to assign any single case into more than one category (mutually exclusive) and that the categories must be set up so that all cases can be assigned to some category (collectively exhaustive). Essentially, a nominal measure is just a

---

9. The fact that there are literally hundreds of possible combinations that can lead to Polity IV and Freedom House scores that result in a country being classified as a "mixed regime" has led some scholars to wonder exactly what it is that mixed regimes have in common conceptually.

different way of naming cases. The DD measure of regime type is a nominal measure in that it classifies, or "names," countries as either democracies or dictatorships. This is a valid way to measure regime type given the way the authors of the measure conceptualize democracy and dictatorship as a dichotomy.

An **ordinal measure** allows us to rank-order cases along some dimension. As a result, an ordinal measure allows us to know whether a case has more or less of the thing we are measuring. Thus, an ordinal measure of democracy would allow us to say whether country A was more or less democratic than country B. Note that we cannot say how much more or less democratic a country is using an ordinal measure. In contrast, an **interval measure** can allow us to determine exactly how much more or less a case has of the thing we are measuring. In other words, the distance between values is interpretable with an interval measure. The claim that country A has two more units of democracy than country B is a meaningful statement only if we have an interval measure of democracy. Obviously, an **interval measure** requires that there be a standard unit of measurement. Both Polity IV and Freedom House are widely considered to be interval measures of democracy and dictatorship.[10] This is a valid way of measuring democracy given the way that they conceptualize democracy as a continuum.

> A **nominal measure** classifies observations into discrete categories that must be mutually exclusive and collectively exhaustive. An **ordinal measure** rank-orders observations along some dimension. An **interval measure** places observations on a scale so that we can tell how much more or less of the thing being measured it exhibits.

Reliability

When conducting empirical tests, we not only want our measures to be valid but also reliable. A reliable measure is one that repeatedly and consistently produces the same score for a given case when we apply the same measurement process (Shively 1990, 48). A reliable measure of democracy would be one in which several people, when given the same rules for measuring democracy, all produce the same democracy score for a given country.

> **Reliability** refers to the extent to which the measurement process repeatedly and consistently produces the same score for a given case.

What is the relationship between validity and **reliability**? A reliable measure does not necessarily imply a valid measure. Although a measurement process might produce results that do not change when repeated (reliability), this does not necessarily mean that the measure is an accurate reflection of the concept under consideration (validity). For example, an invalid measure might be reliable because it repeatedly and consistently produces the same "poor" score for a given case (Figure 5.3 left panel). Similarly, a measure may be

---

10. Although Polity IV and Freedom House both employ a continuous conceptualization of democracy, their measures are technically categorical rather than continuous (Cheibub, Gandhi, and Vreeland 2010, 77; Gleditsch and Ward 1997). For example, the Polity IV measure has only 21 possible values, and each of the two civil and political rights dimensions from Freedom House has only 7 possible values. Arguably, the Polity IV and Freedom House measures should be considered (polychotomous) nominal measures rather than interval measures given the aggregation rules that underpin them.

| FIGURE 5.3 | Comparing the Reliability and Validity of Three Measures |

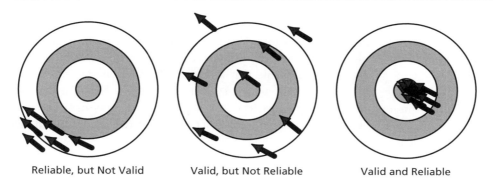

Reliable, but Not Valid   Valid, but Not Reliable   Valid and Reliable

valid in the sense that on "average" it captures the underlying concept, but unreliable in the sense that there might be a big difference in any two attempts to measure the phenomenon (Figure 5.3 center panel). Obviously, we would like our measures to be both valid and reliable (Figure 5.3 right panel).

The reliability of a measure is likely to vary with the extent to which the measure depends on observable facts or subjective judgments. The DD measure of regime type is likely to be highly reliable because it is based entirely on observables. For example, one only has to know whether the chief executive and legislature are elected, whether there is more than one party, and whether there has been an alternation in power under identical electoral rules to be able to code a country as a democracy or a dictatorship. Given the ease with which we can observe elections, political parties, and so on, it is highly unlikely that two individuals would code the same country differently using DD's rules. In contrast, the measures provided by Freedom House and Polity IV are likely to be less reliable because of their reliance on the subjective judgments of the individuals coding each country. For example, Freedom House asks country experts to code countries based on things such as *fair* electoral rules, *equal* campaigning opportunities, *free* and *independent* media, and *reasonable* self-determination. The fact that two individuals could reasonably disagree as to the meanings of the italicized words suggests that they might code the same country differently and, hence, that the resultant measure would be unreliable. A useful way to determine whether a measure suffers from reliability problems is to empirically assess interobserver reliability by examining the degree to which different observers give consistent estimates of the same phenomenon. While Polity IV has conducted some checks for intercoder reliability in recent years, we know of no such checks from Freedom House (Coppedge et al. 2011, 251).

Replicability

Another way to evaluate different measures is in regard to their replicability. **Replicability** refers to the ability of third-party scholars to reproduce the process through which a measure is created. King (1995, 2003) has been one of the strongest proponents of replication. He argues that for "any empirical work enough information should be made available that a third party can comprehend, analyze, replicate, and evaluate the results without further information from the original author" (King 2003, 72). Replicability is important because it allows researchers who were not party to the construction of a particular measure to independently evaluate its reliability and validity.

> **Replicability** refers to the ability of third-party scholars to reproduce the process through which a measure is created.

At a minimum, replicability requires that scholars provide clear coding rules and make their disaggregated data available. The three measures of regime type that we have examined vary in the extent to which they are replicable. For example, DD and Polity IV provide much more detailed and clear coding rules for constructing their measures of regime type than Freedom House does. In fact, Freedom House provides no coding rules for why a country might be given, say, a 3 on one of its twenty-five questions instead of any other score. Disaggregated data refer to the scores given to each observation on the different attributes that are combined to produce a country's overall democracy or dictatorship score. Although Polity IV makes all of the disaggregated data on each of its five attributes available to the public, Freedom House has not historically provided the disaggregated data from its twenty-five questions. In other words, there is no way to know what score a country was given on, say, the questions about academic freedom or personal autonomy. This has led Munck and Verkuilen (2002, 21) to conclude that "the aggregate data offered by Freedom House has to be accepted largely on faith."

In the last few years, a movement has emerged in political science calling for greater "data access and research transparency," or DA-RT.[11] There are three components to DA-RT: (i) data access, (ii) production transparency, and (iii) analytic transparency. The *data access* component calls on scholars who have published research to make their data publicly available so long as doing so does not endanger human subjects, violate ethical norms and confidentiality agreements, or break the law. The *production transparency* component calls on scholars to be transparent about how their data were collected and how their measures were constructed. The *analytic transparency* component calls on scholars to be clear about exactly how their data and analyses support their evidence-based claims and inferences. The hope is that an increased focus on these issues will lead to better research and will maintain, or even increase, the public's confidence in the scientific endeavor.

---

11. For more information about the DA-RT movement, see Lupia and Elman (2014); Büthe and Jacobs (2015); Golder and Golder (2016); and http://www.dartstatement.org/.

CONCLUSION

In this chapter, we have illustrated some of the difficulties that political scientists face when they try to transform abstract concepts such as democracy and dictatorship into measures or indicators that can be used to empirically test theories. Democracy has many meanings in our everyday language, and it is just not possible to capture them all in a single measure; nor would we necessarily want to do this even if we could. Measurement implies simplification, and simplification implies choices and trade-offs on the part of the scholar. Scholars should ask themselves what their research question is before creating or using a particular measure. Some measures will be appropriate for some research projects but not for others. You might think that it is always better to have the most multifaceted measure possible, but this is not always the case. As we have suggested, "minimalist" measures may be able to answer more questions, and more interesting questions at that, even though they do not perhaps capture the full complexity of the abstract concept under consideration. The validity and reliability of our measures will often be constrained by the practicalities of the measurement process. Unlike in most areas of the natural sciences, many of the measures in political science require subjective evaluations. This brings with it the danger of nonvalidity and poor reliability. Without these measures, however, we would be unable to test many of our most interesting and important theoretical claims.

Ultimately, we believe that political scientists should be aware of measurement issues and do the best that they can. This involves being aware of the limitations of their measures and not overstating the generality of theoretical claims made on the basis of these measures. The exact details of the process by which various measures are constructed should be made publicly available so that other scholars can replicate them and better evaluate their validity and reliability. At the same time, it is important for readers like you not to immediately reject measures because they appear to be poor reflections of the concept that they are trying to capture. Instead, ask yourself whether you can come up with a better measure. How can the measure be improved? Does the perceived quality of the measure affect the conclusions reached by the author, and in what way? Just as we do not reject an existing theory until a better one comes along, we should not immediately reject a particular measure until a better measure comes along. We hope that political scientists and students like you will construct better measures. Political scientists often spend their time developing better theories, but it may be better to spend a little more time developing better measures first.

KEY CONCEPTS

concept *151*
contestation *152*
continuous measure *157*
demokratia *149*
demos *149*

dichotomous measure *157*
government *148*
inclusion *152*
interval measure *166*
measure (indicator) *151*

PROBLEMS

The problems that follow address some of the more important concepts and methods introduced in this chapter.

Conceptualizing and Measuring Democracy

1. Name some of the things that you associate with democracies and dictatorships. Would these things form part of a minimalist or a substantive view of regime type? Are these things observable or based on subjective evaluations? Do you think that the things you name enable you to classify countries as democracies or dictatorships in an unambiguous manner?

2. Do you think that a dichotomous or a continuous view of democracy and dictatorship is most appropriate? Does it depend? If so, on what does it depend?

3. Discuss the advantages and disadvantages of the three measures of regime type addressed in this chapter.

4. In ancient Greece, democracy was not associated with elections. Instead, it was associated with selecting leaders by lot. In other words, democracies chose their leaders by drawing names out of a hat. What are the benefits or costs of this method as opposed to selecting our leaders through elections?

5. Say we wanted to test the following hypothesis:

    - Citizens in democracies have more equality of opportunity than citizens in dictatorships.

    If we want our hypothesis to be falsifiable, would it matter whether we used Freedom House or DD to measure regime type? If so, why? If not, why not?

6. Say we wanted to test the following hypothesis:

    - Democracies are more likely to sign international treaties with other democracies than they are with dictatorships.

If we want our hypothesis to be falsifiable, would it matter whether we used Freedom House or DD to measure regime type? If so, why? If not, why not?

7. Go to the Freedom House website (https://freedomhouse.org/) and find the page that provides information on "Freedom in the World." You may have to click on the Reports tab. You should be able to examine specific countries. Find two countries whose Freedom House scores have changed by at least 2 points over the last ten years. Based on the descriptions of the two countries provided by Freedom House, what specific changes in these countries led to the change in their Freedom House scores?

8. On the "Freedom in the World" section of the Freedom House website, consider the regions used by Freedom House (Americas, Europe, North Africa & Middle East, sub-Saharan Africa, Eurasia, and Asia-Pacific). Do any of these regions comprise only countries considered to be "Free"? Is there much variation in the percentage of "Free" countries in each region, or do you think that regional patterns are similar across the globe?

9. A recent international data-gathering effort, the Varieties of Democracy (V-Dem) project, has led to the creation of a new dataset designed to provide researchers with "a new approach to conceptualizing and measuring democracy." The V-Dem data set contains information on about 400 different indicators of democracy for 173 countries from 1900 to the present. More information about the project can be found on the project website, https://v-dem.net/en/. On the project website, you can click on the Analysis tab to see how the different indicators of democracy change over time within specific countries ("V-Dem: Global Standards, Local Knowledge" 2016).

    a. After clicking on the Analysis tab, click on Variable Graph on the left. Use the online analysis tools to graph how one of the available indicators or indices changes over time in four different countries. You may wish to save the graph.

    b. Now create another graph with the same four countries as before but a different indicator variable. What do you observe about the changes over time?

    c. What changes do you observe over time, across indicators, and between countries?

Conceptualization and Measurement

10. As you have seen in this chapter, there are different ways to think about democracy. This is also true of other important concepts in political science. As an example, there are many ways to think about political representation. Some scholars argue that representation is high when political representatives share the same ideological preferences as their constituents. In these cases, we say that the political representatives are "ideologically congruent" with their constituents. Obtain a copy of Matt Golder and Jacek Stramski's 2010 article, "Ideological Congruence and Electoral Institutions," from the *American Journal of Political Science* (54:90–106) using your institution's library resources. Read the article and then answer the following questions.

a. Golder and Stramski graphically present three different ways to conceptualize ideological congruence in their Figure 1. Describe these three different ways of conceptualizing ideological congruence.

b. In their section on measuring congruence, Golder and Stramski operationalize two of the three conceptualizations of ideological congruence. Briefly describe the measures of ideological congruence that they come up with. How well do they capture the two underlying concepts of ideological congruence?

11. In a famous book, *The Concept of Representation*, Hanna Fenichel Pitkin (1967) offers four different ways of conceptualizing political representation: (i) descriptive representation, (ii) substantive representation, (iii) formalistic representation, and (iv) symbolic representation. With *descriptive representation*, we're interested in the extent to which representatives resemble those being represented. Do representatives look like or share certain experiences with the represented? With *substantive representation*, we're interested in whether representatives take actions in the interests of the represented. Do representatives advance the policy preferences that serve the interests of the represented? With *formalistic representation*, we're interested in whether the representatives have been selected or authorized in an appropriate manner and whether they can be held accountable for their actions. How are representatives selected and what sanctioning mechanisms are available to constituents? With *symbolic representation*, we're interested in the symbolic ways that a representative "stands for" the represented. Are the representatives "accepted" by the represented as being "their" representatives? We examine Pitkin's four different concepts of representation in more detail in Chapter 16.

a. How would you operationalize each of these four concepts of representation? In other words, how would you measure descriptive, substantive, formalistic, and symbolic representation?

b. Which form of representation do you think is the most important and why?

c. In Question 10, we indicated that many scholars argue that political representation is high when political representatives share the same ideological preferences as their constituents. Which of Pitkin's four concepts of representation are these scholars focusing on?

12. Can you think of other abstract concepts like democracy and representation that might be of interest to political scientists and difficult to measure? How do you think political scientists measure these concepts in practice?

Measures

13. In this chapter, we introduced different levels of measurement—nominal, ordinal, and interval.

a. The economic growth rate in Bangladesh in 2014 was 6.1 percent. Is this an example of a nominal, an ordinal, or an interval measure of economic growth?

b. If we classified national economies as "open" or "closed," then would we be creating a nominal, an ordinal, or an interval measure?

c. Surveys such as the American National Election Studies frequently ask respondents to say how much they like a particular party or candidate. If the possible responses are "Very much," "Sort of," "Not really," and "Not at all," then is the measure nominal, ordinal, or interval?

d. We often measure an individual's level of education in terms of the number of years that she has spent in school. As a result, is our measure of education nominal, ordinal, or interval?

e. If we were to measure someone's eye color, would we typically use a nominal, an ordinal, or an interval measure? Could we measure eye color at more than one level of measurement? If so, explain how.

f. Say we wanted to measure temperature. What might a nominal measure of temperature be? What might an ordinal measure be? What might an interval measure be?

14. Describe the difference between validity and reliability in your own words.

15. Imagine that the true value of democracy in country X is 5 on a scale of 0 to 10. Say there are four people who code the level of democracy in country X using two different measures of democracy, A and B. Measure A yields values of 4, 3, 6, and 4. Measure B yields values of 6, 6, 7, and 6. Is measure A or measure B a more reliable measure of democracy in country X? Why?

16. Imagine that the true level of human rights violations in country X is 5 on a scale of 0 to 10. Say there are four people who code the level of human rights violations in country X using two different measures, A and B. Measure A yields values of 3, 4, 6, and 7. Measure B yields values of 6, 5, 7, and 6. Is measure A or measure B a more valid measure of human rights violations? Why?

6 The Economic Determinants of Democracy and Dictatorship

> **Democracy endures only if it is self-enforcing. It is not a contract because there are no third parties to enforce it. To survive, democracy must be an equilibrium at least for those political forces which can overthrow it.**
>
> Przeworski (2006, 312)

> **The capacity for strategic calculations by maximizing monarchs results in the owners of *mobile* factors, which the monarch seeks to tax, being . . . given greater voice over the policy choices of governments.**
>
> Bates and Lien (1985, 61)

OVERVIEW

- Classic modernization theory argues that countries are more likely to become democratic and to stay democratic as they develop economically. We present empirical evidence to support these claims. Specifically, we show that democracy is more likely to emerge and survive in high-income countries.

- One criticism of classic modernization theory is that it lacks a strong causal mechanism linking national income with democracy. A more recent variant of modernization theory offers a potential solution to this criticism. The theory posits that changes in the socioeconomic structure of a country that accompany economic development in the modernization process (not high income per se) promote the emergence and survival of democracy.

- This variant of modernization theory explains why democracies are more likely to emerge and survive in high-income countries. It also helps to explain why countries that are dependent on revenue from natural resources, such as oil, diamonds, and minerals, tend to be dictatorships.

- The theory also has important insights for the role that foreign aid, economic inequality, and economic performance play in the democratization process. Specifically, it offers an explanation for why foreign aid is often detrimental to democratization efforts though it can sometimes promote limited democratic reforms, why economic inequality does not necessarily hinder the emergence and survival of democracy, and why economic performance in dictatorships is much more varied than in democracies.

In the previous chapter, we examined the criteria that political scientists use to classify a country as democratic or dictatorial. With this knowledge in hand, we can now address the following two questions: Why do some states become democratic but not others? Why does democracy survive in some states but fail in others? In this chapter, we focus on so-called economic arguments for democracy. In particular, we investigate how economic development and the structure of the economy influence the likelihood that a country will become democratic and remain democratic. In doing so, we illustrate how the predatory view of the state discussed in Chapter 4 can help to explain why some states are democratic and others dictatorial. In the next chapter, we turn to so-called cultural arguments for democracy.

CLASSIC MODERNIZATION THEORY

Most economic explanations for democracy can be linked to a paradigm—a family of explanations—called "modernization theory." Modernization theory argues that all societies pass through the same historical stages of economic development. The claim in the aftermath of post–World War II decolonization was that contemporary underdeveloped countries were merely at an earlier stage in this linear historical process of development than more developed countries. For example, economic historians, such as Rostow (1960) and Gerschenkron (1962), believed that countries in Africa, Asia, and Latin America in the 1950s and 1960s were just "primitive" versions of European nations and that they would eventually "develop" and come to look like Western Europe and the United States.[1] These primitive or immature societies were characterized by large agricultural sectors and small industrial and service sectors. Eventually, these countries would "grow up" and become mature societies characterized by small agricultural sectors, large industrial and service sectors, rising urbanization, higher educational attainment, and increasing societal "complexity."

Although modernization theory was originally developed by economists and economic historians, it was later taken up by political scientists, most famously by Seymour Martin Lipset (1959, 1960). Modernization theorists in political science claim that as a society

---

1. Modernization scholars eventually came to believe that countries could jump stages by copying and learning from countries further ahead of them. This was important because it helped to explain how the Soviet Union could advance so quickly during the middle of the twentieth century.

moves from being immature or "traditional" to being mature or "modern," it needs to change to a more appropriate type of government. Dictatorships might be sustainable in immature societies, but this is no longer the case in mature societies once they develop economically. Przeworski and colleagues (2000, 88) summarize modernization theory in the following way:

> As a country develops, its social structure becomes complex, new groups emerge and organize, labor processes require the active cooperation of employees, and, as a result, the system can no longer be effectively run by command: The society is too complex, technological change endows the direct producers with autonomy and private information, civil society emerges, and dictatorial forms of control lose their effectiveness. Various groups, whether the bourgeoisie, workers, or just the amorphous "civil society," rise against the dictatorial regime, and it falls.

In effect, democracy is "secreted" out of dictatorship by economic development. Although Przeworski and colleagues (2000) highlight modernization theory's claim that countries will become democratic as they develop economically, Lipset (1959, 75) argues that modernization theory also implies that democracy will be more likely to survive in economically developed countries—as he puts it, "the more well-to-do a nation, the greater the chances that it will sustain democracy." In sum, classic modernization theory predicts that economic development will help both (a) the emergence of democracy and (b) the survival of democracy. The basic outline of classic modernization theory is shown in Figure 6.1.

For many people, the terminology used by modernization theory and its implications are unsettling. After all, the theory suggests that all countries, once they mature, will eventually come to look like the United States and Western Europe. In effect, countries just need to grow up—rather like a baby growing up into a responsible adult. Attempts have since been made to change the terminology used to describe these "primitive" countries. These countries used to be called primitive, but scholars started to refer to them as "backward." As this

---

FIGURE 6.1   Classic Modernization Theory

"Traditional" society		"Modern" society
Large agriculture	→	Small agriculture
Small industry	→	Large industry
Small service	→	Large service
Dictatorship	→	Democracy

new terminology took on negative connotations of its own, "backward" countries soon became "third world" countries. With the collapse of the Berlin Wall (see Box 8.3, "A Brief History of East Germany, 1945–1990"), this new term began to seem outmoded because the "second world" countries—the command economies behind the "iron curtain"—were no longer set apart from the rest of the world in the way they once were. In addition, "third world" began to take on negative connotations because the term *third* implied that these countries were somehow behind the "first" and "second" worlds. As a result, scholars started referring to these countries as "underdeveloped." This too has recently changed to "developing" countries. Although scholars have changed the terminology of classic modernization theory and felt disturbed by the implication that all countries will eventually come to look like the United States and Western Europe, we should not let political correctness stop us from asking whether this theory is actually falsified or not in the real world. Just because we do not like some of the implications of our theory is not a good reason to reject it—we have to ask what the empirical evidence says. Is classic modernization theory falsified or not?

One of the central implications of modernization theory is that there should be a strong relationship between how economically developed a country is and whether it is a democracy. But is there a positive relationship between income and democracy? Let's look at some data. Figure 6.2 graphs the proportion of countries that are democratic at different levels of

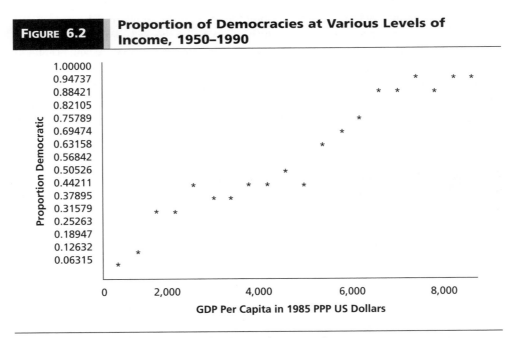

| FIGURE 6.2 | **Proportion of Democracies at Various Levels of Income, 1950–1990** |

Source: Data are from Przeworski and colleagues (2000, 80).

income. In this case, income is measured by **GDP per capita** calculated in 1985 PPP US dollars (see Box 6.1, "Comparing Income Across Countries"). Figure 6.2 clearly indicates that a country is much more likely to be a democracy if its average income is high rather than low. Although virtually all countries with a GDP per capita above $8,000 are democratic (the proportion is close

> **GDP per capita** stands for gross domestic product per capita. Gross domestic product measures the value of all goods and services produced in a country during a specified period, usually one year. GDP per capita is a country's gross domestic product divided by the size of the population. It is a common measure of economic development.

to 1), only 12 percent of the countries with a GDP per capita of less than $1,500 are democracies; that is, 88 percent of these countries are dictatorships.

Clearly, there seems to be a strong positive relationship between income and democracy. But does this necessarily mean that classic modernization theory is correct? Recall that modernization theory predicts that increases in income promote both the emergence and the survival of democracy. The data in Figure 6.2 are certainly consistent with modernization theory, but it turns out that they are also consistent with a slightly different story, which we will call the "survival story." According to the survival story, increasing income promotes the survival of democracy but does not affect whether a country becomes democratic in the first place. But which story is more accurate? Does increased income help only the survival of democracy, or does it also help the emergence of democracy? In recent years, scholars have conducted a great deal of research in an attempt to answer this question (Boix 2011; Boix and Stokes 2003; Epstein et al. 2006; Inglehart and Welzel 2005; Przeworski 2005; Przeworski et al. 1996, 2000; Przeworski and Limongi 1997).

This new round of research began when a well-known comparative political scientist, Adam Przeworski, argued that increased income helps democracies survive but does not help countries become democratic. Why does Przeworski think that income helps democracy to survive? Well, he argues that the decision to choose democracy or dictatorship depends on the types of outcomes that citizens expect democracy or dictatorship to produce for them. Whereas Przeworski describes democracy as a system in which citizens can expect at least a moderate level of consumption, he describes dictatorship as a system in which they might win or lose everything. In democracies, citizens are normally guaranteed at least some minimal standard of living because resources are distributed relatively broadly. In a dictatorship, though, citizens are likely to do extremely well if they are part of the dictator's circle but extremely poorly if they are not. Not only is a dictatorship a world of extremes, but it is also a world in which the probability of being part of the dictator's circle is very small.

Imagine that you are a wealthy person living in a democracy. Consider what life would be like for you in a dictatorship. There is a small probability that you would be in the dictator's circle, and you might become richer. Still, there is a very large possibility that you would not be in the dictator's circle and that you would lose everything and become much, much poorer. Thus, switching to a dictatorship is very much a gamble if you are wealthy. According to Przeworski, this is why most wealthy people prefer to stay in democracies and, hence, why countries where the average person has a high income tend to remain democratic.

Box 6.1   COMPARING INCOME ACROSS COUNTRIES

In order to study economic development, we need to measure it. One commonly used indicator of economic development is the amount of income per person in an economy, or "GDP per capita." GDP stands for gross domestic product and measures the value of all goods and services produced in a country during a specified period, usually one year. GDP per capita is a country's gross domestic product divided by the size of the population. While development is typically thought of as broader than mere income, income is the most commonly used indicator of development because countries tend to become richer as they develop.

In this chapter, we measure income as GDP per capita *calculated in 1985 PPP US dollars.* But what exactly does this mean? GDP per capita is normally measured in each country's own currency. So GDP per capita would be measured in pounds in the United Kingdom, pesos in Mexico, dinars in Iraq, rupees in India, euros in France, and so on. If we want to compare one country's income with that of another, we have to express both countries' GDP per capita in the same currency. One way to do this would be to use one country's actual exchange rate to transform it into the currency of the other country. However, this method is considered problematic by most scholars because a country's exchange rate does not appropriately reflect price differences on goods and services between countries. As a result, the standard method employed by economists and political scientists to transform each country's GDP per capita into the same currency is to use what is known as purchasing power parity (PPP) exchange rates. How does this work?

PPP calculates the price of a particular bundle of goods in each country using each country's local currency. To calculate the exchange rate between two countries, one simply takes the ratio of the two prices. A simple example of a measure of PPP is the Big Mac index popularized by the *Economist* magazine. The Big Mac index looks at the prices of a Big Mac burger in McDonald's restaurants in different countries. If a Big Mac costs US$4 in the United States and GB£3 in Britain, then the PPP exchange rate would be £3 for $4. The *Economist* magazine uses this Big Mac PPP exchange rate to see how much a country's actual exchange rate is under- or overvalued. Obviously, economists and political scientists use a much more representative bundle of goods than just a Big Mac, but the idea is the same.

The most common PPP exchange rate comes from comparing goods in each country with equivalent goods in the United States. As a result, we get what is known as a PPP US dollar exchange rate. These PPP exchange rates are calculated at specific points in time—in our case, 1985. This is important because, over time, inflation can change the value of a currency even within countries. We hope that you are now able to understand what we mean when we say that a country's income is measured as the gross domestic product (GDP) per capita calculated in 1985 purchasing power parity (PPP) US dollars.

Now imagine that you are a poor person living in a democracy. Consider what life would be like for you in a dictatorship. There is a large possibility that you would remain poor. There is, however, a small possibility that you could become very rich if you were in the dictator's group. Given that you are already poor and really have nothing to lose, you might want to take a gamble and switch to a dictatorship. According to Przeworski, this is why poor people may be more willing to take a chance with dictatorship and, hence, why democracy tends to be unstable in poor countries. As you can see, this line of reasoning implies that democracy is more likely to survive in a rich country than in a poor country.

Notice that Przeworski's "survival story" looks at the situation from the standpoint of decision makers who already find themselves in a democracy. He argues that the process by which countries become democratic may be unknowable, but if actors find themselves in a democracy at any given point in time, then the level of income will, for the reasons just indicated, influence whether they stay in a democracy. This has led Przeworski and various coauthors (1996, 1997, 2000, 2005) to argue that the emergence of democracy may be entirely unrelated to the level of income in a country but that we will still observe a long-run positive relationship between increased income and democracy because rich democracies survive longer than poor ones. Why? Well, imagine that a country flips between dictatorship and democracy at random. Sometimes a country will flip to democracy when it has a high income. Even though, from this perspective, increased income did not cause this country to become democratic, it will help it stay democratic. Sometimes a country will flip to democracy when it is poor. Because the country is poor, it will likely collapse back into dictatorship. If this story is correct, then we will end up with a world in which nearly all the rich countries are democratic but in which the poor countries continue to alternate between democratic and dictatorial episodes. Unless countries for some unknown reason flip more frequently to democracy than they flip to dictatorship, democracies will—on average—be richer than dictatorships.

As you can now see, the evidence presented in Figure 6.2 showing a positive relationship between income and democracy is consistent with (a) **modernization theory** and its prediction that high income promotes both the emergence and the survival of democracy and (b) the **survival story**, in which income has no effect on the emergence of democracy but does help democracy to survive once it is established. The reason is that both of these stories predict that democracy is more likely in high-income countries than in poor ones. As a result, we cannot simply look to see if democracy and high levels of income go together as we did in Figure 6.2 to determine whether modernization theory is consistent with the observed world.

> **Modernization theory** predicts that democracy is more likely to emerge and survive as countries develop and become richer. Przeworski's **survival story** predicts that democracy is more likely to survive as countries develop and become richer, but it is not more likely to emerge.

You may remember from our discussion of the scientific method back in Chapter 2 that political scientists often have competing theories to explain the same empirical observation. This is exactly what we have here, because modernization theory and the survival story both explain the observed positive relationship between income and democracy. When political scientists find themselves in this type of situation, they must try to deduce additional hypotheses from their theories in the hope that these additional hypotheses will help them decide which of the competing theories is most consistent with the observed world. As we saw in Chapter 2, competing stories will always share some implications in common (otherwise they would not be explanations for the same phenomena), but they must always differ in others (otherwise they would not be different explanations). It is up to the political scientist to identify these divergent and discriminating implications and come up with a critical test to identify which story is most consistent with the observed world.

Boix and Stokes (2003) graphically show how modernization theory and the survival story expect increased income to affect the probability of transitioning to democracy and the probability of transitioning to dictatorship. We reproduce their basic plot in Figure 6.3. Note that both modernization theory and the survival story predict that the probability of a transition to dictatorship decreases as income increases (the solid lines in both panels slope down). In other words, both stories predict that increased income helps democratic survival. What about the emergence of democracy? Although modernization theory predicts that a transition to democracy increases with income (the dotted line in the left panel slopes up), the survival story predicts that the probability of a transition to democracy is unaffected by increasing income (the dotted line in the right panel is flat).

Note that the probability of any type of transition is simply the sum of the probability of a transition to dictatorship and the probability of a transition to democracy weighted by the

| FIGURE 6.3 | **Expected Probability of Regime Transitions as Income Increases according to Modernization Theory and the Survival Story** |

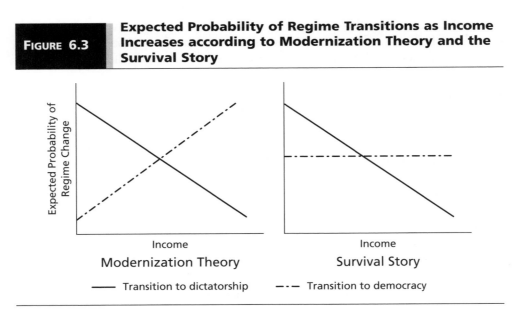

Modernization Theory — Transition to dictatorship — Transition to democracy — Survival Story

Source: Adapted from Boix and Stokes (2003).

frequency of each type of transition. According to the survival story, the probability that a country will experience any kind of regime transition declines with increased income. This is because the survival story predicts that increased income increases democratic stability (fewer transitions to dictatorship) but has no effect on the stability of dictatorships (no effect on transitions to democracy). In contrast, the effect of increased income on the probability of any kind of regime transition is ambiguous in modernization theory. This is because higher average incomes increase the stability of democracies but reduce the stability of dictatorships—modernization theory does not tell us which effect is stronger. In sum, then, modernization theory and the survival story share two implications in common but differ on two as well. All four implications are summarized in Table 6.1.

We now evaluate the implications of both modernization theory and the survival story using data from Przeworski and colleagues (2000). As predicted by both stories, democracies are more common in rich countries than poor countries (Implication 1). We saw this earlier in Figure 6.2, which showed that the proportion of countries that were democratic at different levels of income was larger when income was high than when income was low. This result is further confirmed by Figure 6.4, which plots the number of years that all countries (country years) have lived under democracy or dictatorship at different levels of income between 1950 and 1990. As you can see, when countries are very poor (say, when GDP per capita is below $2,000), almost 9 out of every 10 country years in the data set are lived under dictatorship. When countries are relatively rich, however (say, when GDP per capita is above $8,000), virtually all the country years in the data set are lived under democracy. For a broad swath of countries in between (say, when GDP per capita is between $4,000 and $6,000), there are about as many country years under democracy as there are under dictatorship.

The two critical implications that allow us to distinguish between modernization theory and the survival story concern (a) the frequency of regime transitions in general and (b) the effect of increased income on the probability of democratic transitions in particular. The probability of a regime transition, given a particular level of income, is calculated as follows:

TABLE 6.1	**Implications from Modernization Theory and the Survival Story**

Modernization theory and survival story
1. Democracy is more common in rich countries than poor countries.
2. Transitions to dictatorship become less likely as income increases.

Modernization theory	Survival story
3a. Transitions to democracy become more likely as income increases.	3b. Transitions to democracy are unaffected by increases in income.
4a. Regime transitions may or may not become less likely as countries become richer.	4b. Regime transitions become less likely as countries become richer.

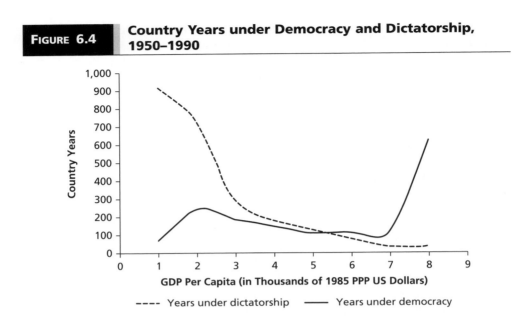

FIGURE 6.4   **Country Years under Democracy and Dictatorship, 1950–1990**

Source: Data are from Przeworski and colleagues (2000).

Note: The figure plots the number of years that all countries (country years) have lived under democracy or dictatorship at different levels of income.

Pr (Regime Transition | Income Level) =

$$\left. \frac{\text{Number of Transitions to Democracy or Dictatorship}}{\text{Number of Country Years}} \right|\text{Income Level}$$

This equation tells us that the probability of a regime transition given a particular level of income is equal to the total number of transitions at that income level divided by the number of cases (or country years) that could have transitioned at that income level.

In Figure 6.5, we plot the *probability* of a regime transition at different levels of income. As you can see, there is no strong relationship between income and the probability of a regime transition. Specifically, it does not appear that the probability of a regime transition decreases linearly with income as the survival story predicts. Thus, the evidence presented in Figure 6.5 would seem to falsify one of the implications of the survival story (Implication 4b, Table 6.1). In contrast, an increase in the probability of a regime transition when levels of income are low, as shown in Figure 6.5, is consistent with modernization theory; a certain amount of resources may be necessary for any change to take place. A decrease in the probability of a regime transition at high levels of income, as shown in Figure 6.5, is also consistent with modernization theory; by this point democracy should have emerged in nearly all countries, and there is no reason according to modernization theory for it not to survive.

| FIGURE 6.5 | **Probability of Regime Transitions as a Function of Income, 1950–1990** |

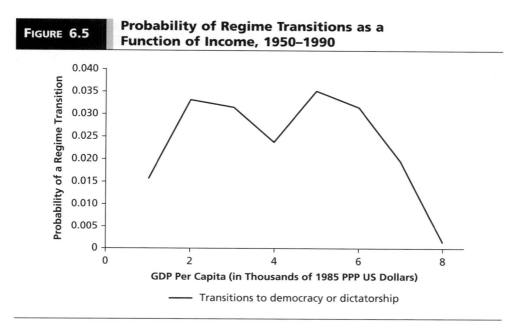

Source: Data are from Przeworski and colleagues (2000).

Although the evidence suggests that the survival story is incorrect when it predicts that the frequency of regime transitions declines linearly with income, the key implication that allows us to discriminate between the survival story and modernization theory has to do with whether increases in income actually make democratic transitions more likely. In Figure 6.5, we looked only at the effect of increases in income on regime transitions in general. We now need to examine the effect of increased income on transitions to democracy and transitions to dictatorship separately. The probability of transitioning to democracy is calculated as

Pr (Transition to Democracy | Income Level) =

$$\frac{\text{Number of Transitions to Democracy}}{\text{Number of Dictatorial Country Years}} \Bigg| \text{Income Level}$$

and the probability of transitioning to dictatorship is calculated as

Pr (Transition to Dictatorship | Income Level) =

$$\frac{\text{Number of Transitions to Dictatorship}}{\text{Number of Democratic Country Years}} \Bigg| \text{Income Level}$$

In Figure 6.6, we plot the probability that a country will transition to democracy and the probability that it will transition to dictatorship at different levels of income. The numbers in the figure indicate how many times more likely it is for a country to transition one way rather than the other. The numbers are gray whenever a country is more likely to transition to dictatorship than democracy and black whenever a country is more likely to transition to democracy than dictatorship. Figure 6.6 clearly shows that the kind of regime transition that countries experience is a function of income. As predicted by both the survival story and modernization theory, the probability of transitioning to dictatorship (the gray dotted line) declines as income increases. In other words, the downward-sloping dotted line indicates that high levels of income encourage democratic survival (Implication 2, Table 6.1).

In direct contradiction to the survival story but entirely consistent with modernization theory, the probability of a democratic transition increases with income (the solid black line slopes upward). In other words, countries are more likely to become democratic as income increases (Implication 3a, Table 6.1). Note that the likelihood that a country transitions to democracy rather than dictatorship clearly increases with income. For example, transitions to dictatorship are eighteen times more likely than transitions to democracy when GDP per capita is less than $2,000. The reverse is true in rich countries, however—transitions to

| FIGURE 6.6 | **Probability of Transitions to Democracy and Dictatorship as a Function of Income, 1950–1990** |

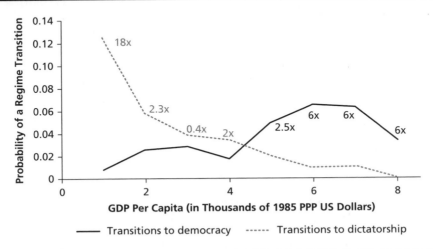

Source: Data are from Przeworski and colleagues (2000).

Note: The numbers in the figure indicate how many times more likely it is for a country to transition one way or another. For example, the gray "2x" indicates that a country is twice as likely to transition to dictatorship as transition to democracy when its GDP per capita is $4,000.

TABLE 6.2	**Modernization Theory and the Survival Story: A Summary of the Evidence**

Modernization theory and survival story

1. Democracy is more common in rich countries than poor countries: YES
2. Transitions to dictatorship become less likely as income increases: YES

Modernization theory	**Survival story**
3a. Transitions to democracy become more likely as income increases: YES	3b. Transitions to democracy are unaffected by increases in income: NO
4a. Regime transitions may or may not become less likely as countries become richer: YES	4b. Regime transitions become less likely as countries become richer: NO

Note: The hypotheses in the shaded cells are supported by the data, whereas those in the nonshaded cells are not.

democracy are much more likely to occur than transitions to dictatorship. For instance, the probability of becoming democratic is six times larger than the probability of becoming dictatorial when GDP per capita is greater than $6,000.

In sum, the evidence we have just presented suggests that the observed world looks more like the one envisioned by modernization theory than the one envisioned by the survival story. The bottom line is that additional income is positively associated with both the emergence and survival of democracy. This is entirely consistent with the predictions of classic modernization theory.[2] Later in the chapter, we show that these results continue to hold even when we take account of other factors that might affect the emergence and survival of democracy. We summarize our findings for now in Table 6.2. Those implications supported by the data are shown in the shaded cells.

A VARIANT OF MODERNIZATION THEORY

In the previous section, we examined the claim made by classic modernization theorists that countries are more likely to become democratic and stay democratic as they become wealthier. One common criticism of classic modernization theory is that it lacks a strong causal mechanism and that it simply relies on an empirical correlation between income and democracy (Acemoglu and Robinson 2006; Rueschemeyer, Stephens, and Stephens 1992). We now examine a variant of classic modernization theory that explicitly provides a causal mechanism linking economic development and democracy.[3]

2. Evidence in support of the theoretical predictions of classic modernization theory has been provided by a whole host of empirical analyses in recent years (Ansell and Samuels 2014; Barro 1999; Boix 2003, 2011; Boix and Stokes 2003; Epstein et al. 2006; Inglehart and Welzel 2005; Londregan and Poole 1996; Ross 2001).

3. The remaining material in this chapter draws on Clark, Golder, and Golder (forthcoming).

This variant of modernization theory says that it is not income per se that encourages democracy but rather changes in the socioeconomic structure of a country that accompany economic development. This variant of modernization theory incorporates a predatory view of the state and helps to show why some rulers share power or limit their extractive activity (democracy) whereas others do not (dictatorship). As such it helps to answer one of the puzzles that we were confronted with at the end of Chapter 4 when we examined the origins of the modern state. Not only does this variant of modernization theory explain why democracies are more likely to emerge and survive in rich countries, but it also helps to explain why countries that are dependent on revenue from natural resources, such as oil, diamonds, and minerals, tend to be dictatorships rather than democracies. The theory also has important insights for the role that foreign aid, economic inequality, and economic performance play in the democratization process. Specifically, it offers an explanation for why foreign aid tends to be detrimental to democratization efforts but can sometimes promote limited democratic reforms, why economic inequality does not necessarily impede the emergence and survival of democracy, and why economic performance in dictatorships is much more heterogeneous than in democracies.

Economic Development and Democracy

As we mentioned earlier, one of the central features of modernization theory is the idea that all societies proceed through a similar series of economic and political stages. As a society proceeds through these stages, it undergoes structural changes. A key structural change has to do with the relative size of the "sectors" in the economy. According to this view, and illustrated in Figure 6.1, all economies can be divided into the same set of sectors—agricultural (the "traditional" sector) and manufacturing and services (the "modern" sector). Just as the relative sizes of a human's body parts change as they mature, so too—according to some modernization theorists—do the relative sizes of a society's economic sectors. Specifically, countries tend to have large agricultural sectors but relatively small manufacturing and service sectors in the early stages of development. As the modernization process brings about efficiencies in the agricultural sector, resources are freed up for use in manufacturing and service sectors. Over time, and as countries continue to develop and mature, the manufacturing and service sectors become larger and larger relative to the agricultural sector. A consequence of these changes is that the economy increasingly comprises actors with mobile assets.

Many scholars have argued that this is precisely what started to happen in early modern Europe. As agriculture became more efficient, fewer peasants were needed to work the land, and traditional feudal bonds that tied peasants to the land were torn asunder. This, eventually, led to a population shift from rural areas to urban ones. This shift occurred at both the top and bottom of the social spectrum. Peasants found themselves dispossessed of lands to which they had had traditional claims, and members of the gentry found themselves drawn into the commercial activities of the towns. A key feature of the commercialization of the agricultural gentry in England at this time was the shift from grain production to the grazing of sheep to feed the growing demand of wool producers (Moore [1966] 1999). As Bates and Lien (1985) have argued, this change in the composition of the British economy played a crucial role in the creation of representative government in England.

By the seventeenth century, the modernization process in England had brought about a shift in economic power from a relatively small number of traditional agricultural elites, who controlled large domains producing easily quantifiable agricultural products, to a rising class of wool producers, merchants, and financial intermediaries, who controlled assets that were much more difficult for the state to count—and, hence, more difficult for the state to tax. In contrast to the traditional agricultural elites, who were unable to hide their fields from the Crown's tax collectors, wool producers and the new commercialized gentry could better hide their sheep (by moving them around) and their business profits. According to Bates and Lien (1985), the ability of the gentry to hide their assets from state predation changed the balance of power between modernizing social groups and the traditional seats of power—specifically, the Crown. Suddenly, the kings and queens of England, who needed money to keep hold of power at home and to wage their wars abroad, found themselves in a position in which predation no longer worked; instead, they had to negotiate with economic elites in order to extract revenues. Because the growth of towns and the rise of the wool trade had also led to an increase in the number of economic decision makers whose actions determined the share of revenues available to the Crown, it was, perhaps, natural for these actors to use their new-found bargaining power to increase the strength of institutions such as the Parliament that helped aggregate their interests. The result was the supremacy of Parliament and the withering away of old avenues of representation, such as the Star Chamber, that had formerly served the traditional elites. Note that the increased mobility of assets—the ability to move and hide sheep or the ability to invest money in the Netherlands rather than in England, for example—can be thought of as equivalent to an increase in the value of the "exit option" possessed by economic elites. We return to this later in the chapter.

North and Weingast (1989) present a similar argument, in which they claim that the development of economic actors who could hide their assets led the Crown to look for ways to credibly commit to honoring its financial obligations to the emerging financial class from whom it wished to borrow money to fund its external wars. One way to do this was by strengthening the power of Parliament in relation to the king. To see how this argument works, imagine a king who has a temporary need to raise resources above and beyond what existing tax revenues can cover. Perhaps the king is conducting an expensive foreign war against a rival power. Although the king might like to simply exploit his citizens and take the money he needs by force as he did in the past, this option is less realistic now that the new gentry can hide their assets. Instead, it is likely that the king must borrow the money he needs from the gentry and promise to pay it back with interest at a later date. The problem is that the king controls the use of violence within his territory. As a result, private capital holders always have to worry that the king will default on his debts after the war is over and that they won't get their money back. In contrast to a student who takes on large amounts of debt while in college, there is no authority over the king who can threaten to forcefully col-

> **Sovereign debt** refers to debt that is accrued by the sovereign, that is, the government.
>
> A **credible commitment problem**, or a time-inconsistency problem, occurs when (a) an actor who makes a promise today may have an incentive to renege on that promise in the future and (b) power is in the hands of the actor who makes the promise and not in the hands of those expected to benefit from the promise.

lect the debt once the smoke has cleared and the battles have been fought. In other words, **sovereign debt**—debt accrued by the sovereign, or Crown—creates what is known as a **credible commitment problem** (see Box 6.2, "Credible Commitment Problems"). Although the king would like to credibly commit, or promise, to pay back the money he borrows from the gentry, he cannot do this because there is nothing that the gentry can do to force the king to pay the debt back once the money has been borrowed. Knowing that they cannot force the king to pay the debt back, the lenders are unwilling to lend the king any money in the first place. As North and Weingast (1989) suggest, one solution to this problem is to make the Crown's potential financial backers more powerful by strengthening the role and importance of the Parliament vis-à-vis the king. If the king reneges on his debts now, he will suffer punishment at the hands of the Parliament. This is precisely the explanation proposed by many scholars to explain the institutional reforms that led to the establishment of modern parliamentary democracy in Britain during the Glorious Revolution of 1688 (Acemoglu and Robinson 2000, 2006; Stasavage 2002).

Bates and Lien (1985) argue that the introduction of this more limited state occurred earlier and more definitively in England than it did in France because of the unique structure of the economy that early modernization had produced in England. To see why this is the case, it is useful to return to the Exit, Voice, and Loyalty Game we first analyzed in Chapter 3. In the prehistory of the game, the Crown, under the exigencies of war, has confiscated or taxed the assets of a segment of the elite represented by Parliament. We shall refer to this segment of the elite as the Parliamentarians. At this point, the Crown is still behaving in its usual predatory fashion as though the economic development sweeping through English society does not concern it directly. However, the Parliamentarians are operating from a newfound position of strength vis-à-vis the Crown. The Parliamentarians have three options. The first option is to take what assets remain and do everything they can to shield them from further confiscation—in part by taking their assets out of production or by consuming them (exit). If the Parliamentarians no longer invest their assets, the economy is likely to stagnate, and there will be less for the Crown to tax or confiscate in the future. The second option is to petition the Crown for protections against future confiscations in exchange for a promise to continue investing their assets in the economy (voice). We will assume that the petition calls for the Crown to accept limits on future predatory behavior, say, by granting Parliament the right to veto all future increases in taxation or by constructing an independent judiciary capable of policing the Crown's behavior. The third option is for the Parliamentarians to continue investing their assets as they did before the confiscation (loyalty).

Box 6.2

CREDIBLE COMMITMENT PROBLEMS

North and Weingast (1989) suggest that kings who wish to borrow money from economic elites may have difficulty credibly committing or promising to repay any loans that they obtain. The basic reason is that although the king may promise today to repay the loans in the future, the king might use his power to renege on his promise when the loans actually come due. Credible commitment problems like the one outlined here have (at least) two basic characteristics. One is that they always involve a temporal dimension: what is in your interest to promise today may not be in your interest to promise in the future. Some people refer to credible commitment problems as "time-inconsistency problems" for this very reason. The second is that they always involve situations in which power is in the hands of those who make the promise and not in the hands of those who expect to benefit from the promise. For instance, it is the king who has the power and not the economic elites in North and Weingast's example.

Credible commitment problems are not confined to politics; in fact, they occur in many areas of our lives. For example, consider an employer who promises to pay a worker at the end of the month for the work that she does. The worker must do her work before she actually gets paid. A commitment problem arises if the employer promises to pay the worker at the end of the month, but when payday comes, it is no longer in the interests of the employer to make the payment. You should immediately be able to see why the employer might have an incentive to not pay the worker once the work is done.

Society has developed at least three ways to deal with credible commitment problems like this: (1) contracts, (2) repeated interactions, and (3) institutions that alter the distribution of power (Acemoglu and Robinson 2006, 134).

1. *Enforceable contracts:* One of the most common ways to deal with a credible commitment problem like the one in our employer–worker example is with an enforceable contract. In effect, the worker and the employer could sign a contract in which the employer promises to pay the worker for her work. If the employer reneges, the worker can file a complaint with an outside agency such as a court of law that can force the employer to pay up. Although contracts can help in the economic sphere, they are not always useful in more political settings. This is primarily because the outside agency that typically enforces the contract in a political setting (the state or the king perhaps) may well be one of the actors involved. For instance, it should be obvious that the economic elites and the king in North and Weingast's example cannot write a contract to solve their credible commitment problem for the simple reason that it would be the king—who has an incentive to renege—who would have to enforce it.

2. *Repeated interactions:* Another solution to potential credible commitment problems occurs when the two sets of actors are involved in repeated interactions. For example, employers may be deterred from reneging on their promise to pay workers at the end of the month if they need those workers (or others) to work the following month. In effect, employers do not want to develop a bad reputation because they need people to be

willing to work for them in the future. Note that this solution to the credible commitment problem assumes that the actors making the promise care enough about the future that they are willing to forgo the benefits that they could get today from reneging on their promise. This assumption helps to explain why the repeated interactions solution to potential credible commitment problems is often not very useful in political settings. For example, the king's promise to repay his loans in the North and Weingast story is not particularly credible even though the king and the economic elites are likely to be involved in repeated interactions. The reason has to do with the fact that the king is often under financial stress, and hence in need of loans, precisely when foreign wars threaten his continued survival. In these circumstances, the king may not be particularly forward looking. In other words, he may come to discount the future so steeply that he is relatively unconcerned with the implications of his behavior on his future reputation. After all, we are only really concerned with our future reputation when we are reasonably confident that we will have a future.

3. *Institutions that alter the distribution of power:* Recall that one of the reasons why certain promises suffer from a credibility problem is that the actor making the promise has power and the beneficiary of the promise does not. It is this asymmetric distribution of power that allows the promiser to renege. Given this, one solution to potential credible commitment problems is to create institutions that transfer power from the actor making the promise to the beneficiary of the promise. In our employer–worker example, one could create a trade union that would give workers the power to punish employers who renege on their promises through things like strikes. It is this ability to punish the employer that (a) encourages the employer to stick to his promise to pay the worker at the end of the month and (b) makes the worker believe that the employer will follow through with his promise and thus provide labor in the first place. This solution to potential credible commitment problems is quite common in political settings and is precisely the solution that the king of England employs in North and Weingast's example to make his promise to repay the loans from the economic elites credible. By transferring power to Parliament, which represents the interests of the economic elites and which could realistically punish the king if he reneges, the king is able to solve his credible commitment problem.

Despite these potential solutions, the difficulty in solving credible commitment problems should not be underestimated in politics. Consider the following examples.

1. *Northern Ireland:* Imagine that you are a member of the Irish Republican Army (IRA) in the early 1990s. At this time, the IRA was involved in violent activities designed to force the British government to give up control of Northern Ireland. Suppose that the British government promises to sit down and negotiate a political settlement as long as you first give up your weapons. The problem is that this promise is not necessarily credible. If you give up your weapons, you are likely to lose any leverage that you would have in the upcoming negotiations. What's to stop the British government from ignoring or

repressing you as soon as you give up your weapons? It is this credible commitment problem that made it so difficult to negotiate an end to the decades-long civil war in Northern Ireland. Attempts to solve the problem involved both sides making small, incremental steps toward peace in an attempt to develop a reputation for following through on their word. For example, the IRA periodically allowed an independent monitoring commission to verify that it had put increasing numbers of its weapons beyond use. At the same time, the British government periodically responded by removing army posts from Northern Ireland or making reforms to the Protestant-dominated Royal Ulster Constabulary (the Northern Irish police force) that had traditionally been closely linked to the British government in the minds of many Catholics. These incremental steps, which were necessary to develop reputations for not reneging on promises, help to explain why moves toward a peaceful resolution of the civil war in Northern Ireland were so slow.

2. *South Africa:* Imagine that you are a member of the white minority that controlled South Africa during the apartheid era. Apartheid was a system of racial segregation that was enforced from 1948 to 1994 to ensure the economic and political dominance of whites over the indigenous African population. Suppose that you have come to believe that apartheid is unsustainable and that you think full democracy should be introduced in South Africa. The problem is that in a democratic South Africa, the indigenous African population would represent a clear majority of the electorate and could pass policies to redistribute income and assets from the rich white minority to the poor black majority. This is likely to make you reluctant to introduce democracy. Imagine that the indigenous Africans, led by the African National Congress (ANC), promise that they will not redistribute too much if you allow democracy. Is this promise credible? Not really. Once democracy is established, what's to stop the ANC from reneging on its promise and using its large majority to redistribute wealth away from the white minority? This credible commitment problem may well help to explain why the apartheid system lasted so long. Note that the inability of the ANC to credibly promise not to redistribute too much may have prolonged the life of the apartheid system even if both the white minority and the black majority preferred to live in a low-redistributive democracy. You may be wondering why the apartheid regime finally came to an end in 1994. One answer is that the credible commitment problem faced by the ANC was solved by structural changes in the South African economy (Wood 2000). These changes included the increased mobility of the economic assets of the white minority that resulted from the globalization of the South African economy during the 1980s and early 1990s. In effect, this change in the mobility of the assets controlled by the white minority altered the power relationship between the white minority and the ANC. Now, if the ANC reneged on any promise not to redistribute too much, members of the white minority had the ability to simply remove their assets from South Africa and take them somewhere else. Because the economic performance of the South African economy depended heavily on these assets, the ANC's promise not to redistribute them became credible. This helps to explain why the transition to democracy in South Africa occurred when it did.

If the Parliamentarians decide to use voice and petition the Crown, the Crown can respond in one of two ways. First, it can accept the new limits on its power to tax (accept). In this case, we assume that the Parliamentarians will happily continue to invest their assets and the economy will grow. Second, it can reject the new limits (reject). If the Crown rejects the limits, then the Parliamentarians must choose whether to continue investing as before (loyalty) or withdraw substantial portions of their assets from the market (exit). Depending on whether the Parliamentarians continue investing their assets, the economy will either stagnate or grow. This strategic interaction between the Parliamentarians and the Crown is shown in Figure 6.7, going from top to bottom.

As you may recall from our analysis of game-theoretic models in Chapters 3 and 4, we cannot say what we expect the actors to do unless we can make statements about how they evaluate the potential outcomes. In what follows, we use the same payoffs as we did when evaluating the EVL Game in Chapter 3.[4]

According to the story we have been telling, the Crown is dependent on the Parliamentarians—the Crown needs their money. In regard to the payoffs in our model, this means that $L > 1$. For now, let us assume that the Parliamentarians have credible exit threats, $E > 0$. In other words, the Parliamentarians have mobile assets and the value they get from

| FIGURE 6.7 | **Exit, Voice, and Loyalty (EVL) Game without Payoffs between the Parliamentarians and the Crown** |

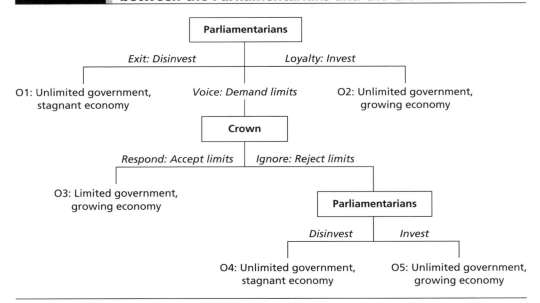

---

4. To see where these payoffs come from, we encourage the reader to refer back to Table 3.2 in Chapter 3.

their assets when they hide them from the Crown is higher than it is when they continue to invest them in a confiscatory environment. In Figure 6.8, we solve the EVL Game for the situation in which the Crown is dependent and the Parliamentarians have a credible exit option. The subgame perfect equilibrium is (Demand limits, Disinvest; Accept limits), and the observed outcome is a limited government with a growing economy. In effect, the Crown decides to accept limits on its predatory behavior because it knows that it is dependent on the Parliamentarians for its money and because it knows that the Parliamentarians will disinvest and exit if it rejects the limits. Knowing that their petition will be effective, the Parliamentarians use voice and demand limits from the Crown. This particular scenario helps to explain why the Crown in England, which was dependent on a social group with a credible exit threat (mobile assets), agreed to accept limits on its power.

Bates and Lien (1985) argue that, in contrast to England, the agricultural sector in France had undergone considerably less modernization and, as a result, the engine of the economy continued to be a traditional oligarchy that derived its wealth from agricultural production

FIGURE 6.8	**Solving the EVL Game When the Parliamentarians Have a Credible Exit Threat, *E* > 0, and the Crown Is Dependent, *L* > 1**

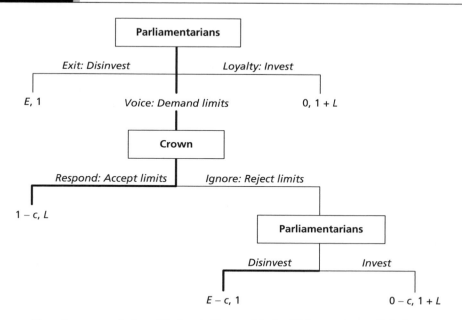

The subgame perfect equilibrium is (Demand limits, Disinvest; Accept limits).

Note: E = Parliamentarians' exit payoff; 1 = value of benefit taken from the Parliamentarians by the Crown; *L* = Crown's value from having loyal Parliamentarians who do not exit; *c* = cost of using voice for the Parliamentarians. It is assumed that $c > 0$; $E < 1 - c$; $E > 0$; and $L > 1$.

based on quasi-feudal processes that were easy to observe and therefore easy to tax. In the terminology of our EVL Game, the relevant elites in France did not possess credible exit threats, $E < 0$. The French Crown, though, was as dependent on its economic elites as the English Crown. In Figure 6.9, we solve the EVL Game for the situation in which the Crown is dependent and the Parliamentarians do not have a credible exit option. The subgame perfect equilibrium is (Invest, Invest; Reject limits), and the observed outcome is an unlimited government with a growing economy. In effect, the Crown will reject any demands to limit its predatory behavior in this situation. This is because it knows that, although it is dependent on the Parliamentarians for money, the Parliamentarians will continue to invest and pay their taxes even in a predatory environment due to the fact that they do not have a credible exit option. Knowing that the Crown will ignore their petitions, the Parliamentarians simply continue to invest and pay their taxes at the beginning of the game. This scenario helps to explain why the French Crown remained absolutist at a time when the English monarchy was accepting limits on its predatory behavior. For example, the Estates General, the chief

FIGURE 6.9 | **Solving the EVL Game When the Parliamentarians Do Not Have a Credible Exit Threat, $E < 0$, and the Crown Is Dependent, $L > 1$**

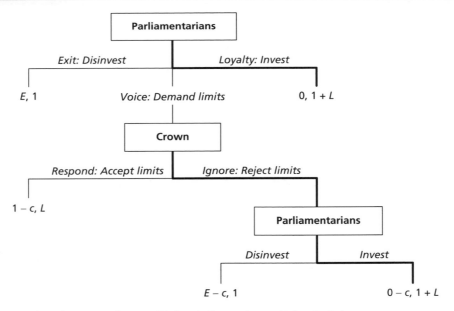

The subgame perfect equilibrium is (Invest, Invest; Reject limits).

Note: E = Parliamentarians' exit payoff; 1 = value of benefit taken from the Parliamentarians by the Crown; L = Crown's value from having loyal Parliamentarians who do not exit; c = cost of using voice for the Parliamentarians. It is assumed that $c > 0$; $E < 1 - c$; $E < 0$; and $L > 1$.

French representative body at the time, did not meet between 1614 and May 1789, by which point financial crises had reached such proportions that the French Revolution may have been unavoidable. For nearly two centuries, then, French elites had little choice but to try to influence the Crown's behavior through the intricacies of court politics rather than through a parliament.

Up to this point, we have assumed that the Crown depends on the Parliamentarians for money and other resources. What happens, though, if the Crown is autonomous—it has other sources of money—and does not depend on the Parliamentarians? There are two scenarios to consider—one in which the Parliamentarians do not have a credible exit option and one in which they do. Instead of explicitly solving the EVL Game for these two scenarios— we leave that for you to do—we simply describe the expected outcomes of the game. If the Parliamentarians do not have a credible exit option (they have immobile assets), then they will respond to state predation by continuing to invest and paying their taxes. They will do this because they know that the Crown does not depend on them in any way and so will ignore any of their petitions. In this scenario, the fact that the Parliamentarians continue to invest their assets means that the economy will grow. If the Parliamentarians do have a credible exit option (they have mobile assets), though, then they will choose to exit and disinvest in the economy—they realize that there is no point in petitioning the Crown to limit its predatory behavior because the Crown does not depend on them. In this scenario, the fact that the Parliamentarians disinvest means that the economy stagnates.

The outcomes of the four different scenarios are shown in Table 6.3. Note that we expect democracy (limited government) to emerge and survive only when the state (Crown) depends on economic elites (Parliamentarians) who have credible exit options (mobile assets). This was the case during the Glorious Revolution in England. The English Crown found itself dependent on a set of societal elites with whom it was forced to bargain. It had to bargain with them because a sufficient number of these elites possessed assets that were mobile and, hence, difficult to tax. It was as a result of this that the Crown ultimately accepted serious limitations on its power, thereby bringing limited and representative government into being in England. This central argument can be stated more broadly: representative government (of which democracy is an example) is more likely to emerge and survive when the rulers of a country depend on a segment of society that comprises a relatively large number of people holding mobile assets.[5] Barrington Moore Jr. ([1966] 1999, 418) essentially stated the same argument quite succinctly in his book about the social origins of democracy and dictatorship—"No bourgeois, no democracy."

---

5. Governments that are dependent on actors with mobile assets will not necessarily be democratic in the sense that they respond to the preferences of the majority. Our argument indicates only that they will be responsive to those citizens with credible exit threats. However, the fact that the number of people with credible exit threats typically increases with development means that dependent governments are likely to become responsive to larger and larger sections of their society over time.

TABLE 6.3	Summary of Outcomes in the Exit, Voice, and Loyalty Game	
	Crown	
Parliamentarians	**Is autonomous** $L < 1$	**Is dependent** $L > 1$
Have a credible exit threat (mobile assets) $E > 0$	Poor dictatorship (unlimited government, stagnant economy)	Rich democracy (limited government, growing economy)
Have no credible exit threat (fixed assets) $E < 0$	Rich dictatorship (unlimited government, growing economy)	Rich dictatorship (unlimited government, growing economy)

The argument we have just made helps alleviate some of the concern that political theorists, such as Locke, had with Hobbes's solution to the state of nature. Recall from our discussion in Chapter 4 that Hobbes saw the creation of a powerful state that would hold its citizens in "awe" as the solution to the "war of all against all" and the "solitary, poor, nasty, brutish, and short" life that characterizes the state of nature. Although theorists such as Locke recognized that the creation of the state might solve the problem that citizens have with each other, they thought that it created a potentially more troubling problem between the citizens and the state. By surrendering control over the means of violence to the state, what was to prevent the state from using its power against its citizens? The argument we have just presented illustrates that there are some conditions under which the state will *voluntarily* agree to accept limits on its predatory behavior: when the state depends on a segment of society with mobile assets. Under these conditions, the citizens need not fear state predation.

Natural Resources and Democracy

In addition to providing a causal mechanism linking the process of modernization to the emergence of representative government, our variant of modernization theory also provides an explanation for something called the **political resource curse** (Barro 1999; Ross 2001, 2012). According to the political resource curse, countries that depend on revenue from **natural resources**, such as oil, diamonds, and minerals, will find it difficult to democratize. You might think that having natural resources would be a blessing as these resources provide access to "free" or "unearned" income that can be used to build democracy and improve the material well-being of citizens. The empirical evidence, though, consistently

According to the **political resource curse**, countries that rely heavily on revenue from natural resources are unlikely to democratize. They are also prone to corruption, poor governance, and civil war.

Natural resources are naturally occurring substances that are usually considered valuable, such as oil, diamonds, and minerals.

shows that leaders in countries with natural resources do not use their "unearned" income in this way. Not only are countries that rely on natural resources more likely to be dictatorships than democracies, but they are also more prone to corruption, poor governance, and civil war (P. Collier and Hoeffler 2002, 2005; Dunning 2005; Fearon 2005; Humphreys 2005; Karl 1997; Ross 1999; Shafer 1994). Far from being a blessing, natural resources appear to be a curse.

But why? Political scientists have proposed what they call demand-side and supply-side explanations for the political resource curse (Uhlfelder 2007). Demand-side explanations emphasize how resource revenues reduce both the citizens' demand for democratic reform and government responsiveness to that demand. Governments with access to natural resources do not need to raise revenue by taxing their citizenry—they can simply dig it out of the ground (Beblawi 1987; Karl 1997; Mahdavy 1970; Ross 2001). As our discussion of the emergence of representative institutions in early modern Europe indicates, there is often a close connection between taxation and representation (Bates and Lien 1985; Levi 1988; North and Weingast 1989). Citizens often demand greater representation and accountability when their leaders want to raise taxes. The fact that governments with access to natural resources have a stream of unearned income means that they can afford to keep taxes low. A consequence of this is that the demand from citizens for greater representation is lower than it otherwise would be.

Governments with access to natural resources are unlikely to respond positively to demands for greater representation even if citizens were to make them. The fact that governments can simply dig revenue out of the ground means that they are *autonomous* from the citizens and do not need to accept institutional limits on their political power in exchange for revenue. Does it matter if the natural resources are "controlled" or "owned" by private actors rather than the state? Not really. Natural resources are your quintessential immobile asset. Oil rigs and diamond mines, for example, are not movable. Governments are free to predate on this sector of the economy safe in the knowledge that private actors do not have a credible exit option and thus cannot exert influence over them. As you can see, the underlying logic of demand-side explanations is evident in our EVL Game. By increasing the autonomy of the government in a context where assets are immobile, resource revenues undermine a government-citizen bargaining dynamic that might otherwise culminate in democratic reforms (Wiens, Poast, and Clark 2014).

Supply-side explanations, in contrast, focus on how resource revenues enable dictators to resist pressure to democratize and help them to consolidate their hold on power. These explanations highlight how resource revenue can be distributed as patronage to preempt or co-opt opposition groups, or used to repress them (Al-Ubaydli 2012; Bueno de Mesquita and Smith 2009; Dunning 2008; Jensen and Wantchekon 2004; Morrison 2007, 2009; Paler 2013; Ross 2004; Smith 2006; Wantchekon 2001). For example, oil-funded leaders like those in the Middle East are able to placate opposition groups "by offering new handouts, lowering taxes, or both—and this usually works" (Ross 2011, 3). In response to the Arab Spring in 2011,

"Algeria announced plans to invest $156 billion in new infrastructure and to cut taxes on sugar; Saudi Arabia directed $130 billion toward increasing wages in the public sector, unemployment benefits, and housing subsidies; Kuwait offered each of its citizens a cash gift of 1,000 dinars (about $3,600) and free food staples for fourteen months" (Ross 2011, 3–4). Revenues from natural resources are particularly helpful for buying the loyalty of the armed forces. For example, "Iranian president Mahmoud Ahmadinejad . . . has given billions of dollars in no-bid contracts to businesses associated with the elite Revolutionary Guards. . . . Some of the world's biggest oil producers, including Oman, Saudi Arabia, and the United Arab Emirates, are also some of the biggest military spenders. When the citizens of Oman and Saudi Arabia took to the streets [in 2011], their armies proved relatively willing and able to suppress the protests" (Ross 2011, 4).

We can see the importance of natural resource revenue for maintaining the loyalty of the military by comparing what happened in Libya and Egypt during the Arab Spring. In Libya, Muammar al-Qaddafi was able to use oil revenue to hire mercenaries from countries like Chad, Niger, Mali, and Sudan to fight rebel groups. It is widely believed that without the intervention of NATO forces in March 2011, these mercenaries, along with the rest of the Libyan military, would have easily defeated the rebels. As we indicate toward the end of this chapter, the per capita revenues generated by oil and gas were considerably lower in Egypt than in Libya. As a result, it was much harder for the longtime dictatorial leader in Egypt, Hosni Mubarak, to keep the support of his military. Mubarak had historically relied on two mechanisms to ensure the loyalty of his military. One mechanism involved transferring vast amounts of aid provided by the United States to the military. Since 1979, the United States had provided Egypt an average of $2 billion a year, much of it in the form of military aid. The other mechanism was to allow the military to take over large parts of the Egyptian economy. The Egyptian military owns companies that sell everything from fire extinguishers and medical equipment to laptops, televisions, bottled water, and olive oil. Exactly how much of the economy is controlled by the military is unclear, with estimates varying from a low of 5 percent to a high of 45 percent (Fadel 2011). With the United States threatening to reconsider its military aid to Egypt and the military viewing the people camped out in Tahrir Square more as "customers" than "protesters," it is perhaps unsurprising that the military was reluctant to fire on the people and began to distance itself from Mubarak. Without the support of the Egyptian military, it was not long before Mubarak was forced to step down.

The existence of dictatorships that are rich due to the presence of natural resource revenue is inconsistent with classic modernization theory's claim that increased income leads to democracy. Although the existence of a few wealthy dictatorships, such as Saudi Arabia or Oman, is anomalous in the context of classic modernization theory, it should be easy to see that it is entirely compatible with the political resource curse and the variant of modernization theory that we have presented.

Two things are worth noting about the political resource curse. First, the political resource curse does not say that having an *abundance* of natural resources is necessarily bad for democratization. Instead, what matters is the extent to which the government depends on natural resources for its revenue. Recall that the relative bargaining power of the actors in our EVL Game is based on whether the government depends on actors with mobile assets. If a sizable proportion of the government's revenue comes from citizens with mobile assets, then the government needs to commit to policies that favor these citizens if it wants to ensure their continued investment. However, if the government's revenue comes from natural resource extraction, then its incentive to make credible commitments to its citizens by establishing representative institutions declines. This implies that it is a country's *dependence* on natural resource revenue that affects its regime type, not simply whether there is an *abundance* of natural resources. In other words, a country with an abundance of natural resources can still have a good chance at democratizing so long as the income that the government earns from this sector of the economy is small relative to what it earns from other sectors of the economy with more mobile assets.

Second, the political resource curse is about the *emergence* of democracy, not the *survival* of democracy. In our EVL game, one of the ways that resource revenue reduces the likelihood of democratization is by making governments autonomous from the demands of their citizens. Although resource revenue hurts the emergence of democracy, it doesn't have to harm democratic stability. There are two reasons for this. One is that the discovery of natural resources in a democracy occurs after the emergence of institutions that are capable of holding the government accountable. The second is that the popular oversight that occurs in democracy will help to prevent governments from spending natural resource revenue on patronage and coercion. This helps to explain why natural resource revenue has not been a "curse" in countries like Canada, Norway, the United Kingdom, or the United States. In these countries, the flow of resource revenue began only after democratic institutions were well established.

Foreign Aid and Democracy

How does **foreign aid** affect democratization? Scholars who examine the effect of foreign aid on the democratization process can be divided into "aid optimists," who think that foreign aid can spur democratization efforts, and "aid pessimists," who think that foreign aid has a negative effect on democratization reforms (Wright and Winters 2010). Our EVL Game highlights one way in which foreign aid hinders democratization. However, it also suggests that there may be conditions under which foreign aid can encourage limited democratic reforms.

> **Foreign aid** is aid—in the form of money, food, technical assistance, military weapons, and the like—that people in one country give to another. This aid can come from national governments, intergovernmental organizations, or private donations.

As the outcomes to our EVL Game in Table 6.3 indicate, democracy is unlikely to emerge when governments are autonomous from their citizens. By freeing governments from the need to raise taxes and providing them with access to "slack resources" that can be strategically used to reward supporters and co-opt opposition groups, foreign aid increases the autonomy of recipient governments from the demands of their citizens (Ahmed 2012; Bueno de Mesquita and Smith 2009; Kono and Montinola 2009; Smith 2008). In addition, the low taxes and increased spending that foreign aid makes possible reduces the citizenry's

On March 27, 2009, US president Barack Obama announces a new strategy of increasing foreign aid to Pakistan in hopes of weakening al-Qaida.

demand for democratic reforms (Remmer 2004; Morrison 2007, 2009). In these ways, foreign aid hinders the emergence of democracy. Although it may be hard to see citizens living in destitution under harsh dictatorial rule, attempting to ease their pain by providing foreign aid to their governments may simply result in their prolonged suffering. The argument here is consistent with many studies showing that foreign aid to dictatorships harms the welfare of the average citizen and helps dictators stay in office through corruption and exploitation rather than through the production of effective public policy (Bräutigam and Knack 2004; Knack 2004; Djankov, Montalvo, and Reynal-Querol 2008; Moyo 2009).

If the argument here reminds you of the reasoning behind the political resource curse, you are not alone. Many scholars claim that income from foreign aid is essentially the same as income from natural resources—both represent forms of unearned income that increase the autonomy of governments relative to their citizens (Bueno de Mesquita and Smith 2009; Morrison 2007, 2009; Smith 2008). Indeed, some people speak of a foreign aid curse, similar to a resource curse (Djankov, Montalvo and Reynal-Querol 2008). This line of reasoning, though, overlooks some significant differences between natural resources and foreign aid (Altincekic and Bearce 2014; Bermeo 2016; Wright and Winters 2010). Importantly, these differences suggest that a foreign aid curse, while likely, is not inevitable.

The key thing to note is that while natural resource revenue makes governments more autonomous in a general sense, this is not the case with foreign aid revenue. While foreign aid makes governments less dependent on their citizens, it makes them more dependent on their foreign aid donors. As we know from our EVL Game, aid donors will be able to exert influence on these dependent recipient countries whenever the donors can credibly threaten to withdraw their aid. But what exactly do donor countries want when they give aid? And when can they credibly threaten to withdraw their aid?

Donor countries often value achieving strategic goals with their foreign aid at least as much as they value obtaining democratic reforms in recipient countries (Bearce and Tirone

2010). For example, donor countries might use foreign aid to encourage recipient countries to attack terrorist groups, such as ISIL and the Taliban, to prop up "friendly" regimes in hostile regions of the world, or to obtain privileged access to economic markets for their domestic companies. If aid is driven by strategic concerns, then we shouldn't expect it to promote democratization (Wright and Winters 2010). However, many donor countries do demand democratic and other political reforms as a condition for continued foreign aid. Empirical evidence, though, suggests that these types of conditions are rarely enforced by the donor country (Svensson 2003).[6] This has led some scholars to claim that foreign aid is effectively "unconditional" in practice (Morrison 2012). If this is true, then there is again no reason to believe that foreign aid would promote democratization.

As our EVL Game highlights, the extent to which aid donors can enforce their conditions for democratic reform depends on whether they have credible exit threats. When the aid donor has a strategic interest in the recipient country, threats to withhold aid are not credible (Bearce and Tirone 2010; Bermeo 2016). It is hard to imagine, for example, that the United States would withdraw significant amounts of aid from countries such as Iraq and Afghanistan if they fail to democratize. This is because the governments in these countries are strategically important to the United States in terms of fighting international terrorism and achieving stability in the Middle East. Recipient countries that are strategically important are often aware of this fact and feel that they can safely ignore any demands for political reform. All of this suggests that foreign aid will be effective at promoting democratic reform only when the donor country has no strategic interests in the "dependent" recipient country. Our argument here is supported by studies showing that foreign aid is more associated with democratic reforms in the post–Cold War period than during the Cold War period when alliance politics was more strategically important (Dunning 2005; Wright 2009).

What we can see, then, is that foreign aid can promote democratization, but only under extremely demanding conditions. Specifically, foreign aid will promote democratization only when (a) the recipient country is dependent on the foreign aid, (b) the aid donor wants to promote democratic reform in the recipient country, and (c) the aid donor can credibly threaten to withdraw aid if its demands for reform are not met. If any of these conditions fail to hold, then we can expect foreign aid to hinder democratization efforts. Moreover, if political reforms do actually occur in the recipient country, they are likely to be limited in scope. Most dictatorial leaders in recipient countries will try to avoid introducing meaningful reforms that put their authority in jeopardy. Instead, they will try to implement superficial reforms that are sufficient to satisfy their foreign aid donors (it seems like they are responding to donor demands) but do not actually threaten their hold on power. Dietrich and Wright (2014) present evidence consistent with this expectation. They find that foreign

---

6. One reason for this is that donor countries, while publicly stating that they desire democratization, often have little actual interest in recipient countries becoming democratic. This is because it is typically cheaper to get a dictatorship rather than a democracy to adopt "friendly" policies.

aid tends to increase de jure political competition in the recipient country but not de facto political competition. In effect, there is more competition on paper but not so much in practice. For example, they find that while foreign aid might encourage the emergence of multiparty politics, the resulting multiparty politics are characterized by weak opposition parties and the incumbent leaders continuing to dominate.

Inequality and Democracy

It is commonly argued that economic inequality undermines democracy (Acemoglu and Robinson 2000, 2001, 2006; Boix 2003; Houle 2009; Huntington 1991; Reenock, Bernard, and Sobek 2007; Rosendorf 2001). The claim that inequality is bad for democracy actually goes back at least as far as Tocqueville ([1835] 1988, 49–55, 128–136), who argued that economic equality was important for the introduction and persistence of democratic institutions. The basic argument is that inequality produces political competition between the rich and the poor. This is because it provides incentives for the poor to redistribute wealth from the rich. The ability of the poor to take wealth away from the rich simply by voting makes democracy appealing to the poor but costly to the rich. As a result, the expectation is that economic elites will step in to block attempts at democratization or to conduct coups to reverse democratization in highly unequal societies.

Although the argument sounds compelling, it lacks strong empirical support. Some studies find a negative relationship between inequality and democracy, but most find no relationship at all (Barro 1997; Bollen and Jackman 1985, 1995; Przeworski et al. 2000). In terms of the causal story itself, there is little evidence that the demand for redistribution increases with inequality or that democracies redistribute more than dictatorships (Przeworski 1985; Roemer 1998; Scheve and Stasavage 2009; Shelton 2007). Moreover, Haggard and Kaufman (2012) find that redistributive conflict between the rich and the poor is evident in only about half of the recent transitions to democracy. The key actor in most democratic transitions is not the poor, but the middle class (bourgeoisie). That is, the key actor is a group whose income is higher than that of the average income earner and who would therefore be a net contributor, not beneficiary, from any tax and redistribution system (Ansell and Samuels 2014).

The logic inherent in our variant of modernization theory provides one explanation for why existing studies fail to find a consistent negative relationship between inequality and democracy. We saw earlier that economic elites who have credible exit options (mobile assets) can force a dependent state to accept limits on its predatory behavior. That these economic elites have credible exit options and can realistically withdraw their much-needed investment in the economy also helps to explain why the poor will not vote to expropriate them. In effect, the poor "depend" on the economic elites for the economy to grow. If this is true, then existing empirical studies examining the link between economic inequality and democracy need to be modified. Economic inequality should be bad for democracy only in countries where the economic elites have immobile assets and therefore lack credible exit threats. In countries where they have mobile assets, the elites should be willing to accept democracy safe in the knowledge that the poor will have incentives to curb their demands for redistribution.

Evidence in support of this line of reasoning comes from Freeman and Quinn (2010), who find that unequal dictatorships that are financially integrated into the global economy are much more likely to experience democratic transitions than unequal dictatorships that are financially closed. Additional sup-

AP Photo/Denis Farrell

People queuing outside the polling station in the black township of Soweto, in the southwest suburbs of Johannesburg, South Africa, on Wednesday, April 27, 1994, during South Africa's first all-race elections.

port comes from Ansell and Samuels (2014), who find that *income* inequality promotes democratization but that *land* inequality hinders it. The reason is that income inequality generally increases along with the creation of a large middle class, whereas land inequality usually goes hand in hand with a large landed aristocracy. A large middle class is a group that tends to have mobile assets, but the landed aristocracy primarily holds immobile assets. Landed elites have more to fear from democratization due to the immobile nature of their assets. As Box 6.2, "Credible Commitment Problems," indicates, Wood's (2000) account of the democratic transition in South Africa in 1994 also fits with our variant of modernization theory. As the South African economy globalized in the 1980s and early 1990s, the economic assets of the white minority became more mobile. She argues that it was the increased mobility of the white South Africans' assets that made them willing to accept a democratic transition despite the high levels of inequality in the country.

Economic Performance

In addition to providing predictions about whether countries are likely to be democratic or dictatorial, our EVL Game also offers predictions about whether they will have growing or stagnant economies. The outcomes of our EVL Game shown in Table 6.3 indicate that the economic performance of democracies will be good, whereas that of dictatorships will be much more varied. Countries in which the government is dependent on citizens with a credible exit threat are likely to be democratic and have a strong and growing economy. The economy grows because the citizens freely invest their assets safe in the knowledge that the government will not predate on them. Countries in which citizens lack credible exit threats are likely to be dictatorial and have a weak but growing economy. The economy grows because citizens have little option but to continue investing, making the best of what they have and hoping that the government does not exploit them too much. Countries in which the government is autonomous and the citizens have a credible exit threat are likely to be dictatorial with a stagnant economy. The economy is stagnant because the citizens will use their assets elsewhere to avoid government predation. The prediction that dictatorships will exhibit more variation in economic performance than democracies is consistent with several theoretical and empirical studies (Alesina and Perotti 1994; Bueno de Mesquita et al. 2003).

That some dictatorships are expected to have growing economies may help to explain why so many economists and political scientists have been unable to find compelling evidence that democracies routinely produce better economic performance than dictatorships (Przeworski and Limongi 1993; Sirowy and Inkeles 1991; Ross 2006; see also Chapter 9 of this book). The variant of modernization theory that we have examined here would suggest that it is inappropriate simply to compare the economic performance of democracies and dictatorships, because economic performance across these regimes should depend on the presence or absence of credible exit options. Specifically, regime type should have little impact on growth when immobile asset holders dominate the economy. We look in more detail at the theoretical reasons as to why some dictatorships have incentives to produce good economic performance but others do not in Chapter 10.

SOME MORE EMPIRICAL EVIDENCE

Before turning to cultural explanations for the emergence and survival of democracy in the next chapter, we first evaluate some of the arguments that have been presented in this chapter, using statistical analyses. We begin by examining how a country's status as an oil producer, its income, and its economic growth affect the probability that it will become a democracy. In what follows, we briefly describe how to interpret key pieces of information typically found in a table of statistical results. We strongly encourage you to read the Appendix, "An Intuitive Take on Statistical Analyses," at the end of this chapter for a more detailed discussion of statistical analyses and significance tests.

A **dependent variable** is an outcome or thing we want to explain. An **independent**, or **explanatory**, **variable** is what we think will explain, or determine the value of, the dependent variable.

The results of our statistical analyses are shown in Table 6.4. The **dependent variable**, which is listed at the top of the table, is the thing we want to explain. It is the effect in a proposed cause-and-effect relationship. In this case, the dependent variable is the probability that a country becomes a democracy given that it was a dictatorship in the previous year. The **independent**, or **explanatory**, **variables,** which are listed in the first column, are the things we hypothesize might affect the emergence of democracy. These are the causes in a proposed cause-and-effect relationship. In this case, our independent variables are income (GDP per capita), economic growth, and oil production.

| TABLE 6.4 | **Economic Determinants of Democratic Emergence** |

Dependent variable: Probability that a country will be a democracy this year if it was a dictatorship last year.

Independent Variables	1946–1990	1946–1990	
GDP per capita	0.00010***	0.00010***	← Coefficient
	(0.00003)	(0.00003)	← Standard error
Growth in GDP per capita		−0.02***	
		(0.01)	
Oil production		−0.48**	
		(0.24)	
Constant	−2.30***	−2.27***	
	(0.09)	(0.09)	
Number of observations	2,407	2,383	
Log-likelihood	−233.01	−227.27	

**p < 0.05; ***p < 0.01

Note: Data are from Przeworski and colleagues (2000) and cover all countries from 1946 to 1990. The results shown in Table 6.4 come from a dynamic probit model. Standard errors are shown in parentheses.

Next to each independent variable (in the other columns) is a coefficient with a corresponding standard error beneath it in parentheses. The sign of the coefficient is important because it tells us the slope of the relationship between the independent variable and the dependent variable. A positive coefficient indicates that an increase in the independent variable is associated with an increase in the probability that a country will become a democracy. A negative coefficient indicates that an increase in the independent variable is associated with a reduction in the probability that a country will become a democracy. If the statistical analysis reveals that there is no relationship between an independent variable and the probability that a country will become a democracy, then the coefficient will be zero. The coefficients basically describe particular patterns (positive, negative, none) in the data between the independent variables and the dependent variable.

Are the patterns described by the coefficients likely to be found outside of this data set? One concern is that the pattern indicated by the coefficients could have arisen because of chance elements in this particular data set, rather than because they capture some relationship in a broader sense. This is where the standard errors come in. The standard errors are measures of uncertainty, and they help us to determine how confident we should be in our results. We tend to be confident that we have found a pattern in the data that is likely to be found more generally when the standard error is small relative to the size of its corresponding coefficient. Typically, as a rule of thumb, we say that we have found a statistically significant relationship whenever the coefficient is bigger than twice the size of the standard error. It is common practice for political scientists to place stars next to the coefficients of variables that are considered statistically significant; more stars signal higher statistical significance. Independent variables that do not have a coefficient with stars—where the size of the coefficient is not sufficiently large relative to the size of its standard error—are considered statistically insignificant. An independent variable is considered statistically insignificant if we don't feel confident ruling out the possibility that the observed pattern (the slope) between this variable and the dependent variable arose by chance. For a more detailed discussion of how we determine whether an observed pattern in the data is "real" or not, see the material on significance tests covered in the Appendix, "An Intuitive Take on Statistical Analyses," at the end of this chapter.

So what do the results in Table 6.4 tell us? First, we can see that the coefficient on GDP per capita is positive and statistically significant. This indicates that the probability that a dictatorship becomes a democracy increases with income as measured by GDP per capita. This result is entirely consistent with classic modernization theory. Second, we can see that the coefficient on growth is negative and statistically significant. This indicates that a dictatorship that produces economic growth is less likely to become a democracy. In other words, dictatorships that do well with the economy are rewarded, as it were, by being allowed to continue to control the economy. This implies that dictatorships have an incentive to produce good economic performance. As we'll see in Chapter 10, some dictatorships have more of an incentive to produce good economic performance than others. Third, we can see that the coefficient on being an oil producer is negative and significant. This indicates that a dictatorship is less likely to become a democracy if it is an oil producer. This result is consistent with the political resource curse and its claim that countries that depend on immobile assets are less likely to become democracies.

At this point you might be wondering exactly how much income, economic growth, and oil production really matter for the emergence of democracy. For example, how much more likely would it be for a dictatorship to transition to democracy if its GDP per capita rose by a certain amount? Take a country in Africa like Burkina Faso. In 1987 Burkina Faso was a dictatorship with a GDP per capita of $500; it was not an oil producer, and it had a negative growth rate of –2.15 percent. The average GDP per capita in the world in 1987 was $4,022. How much more likely would a country like Burkina Faso have been to become a democracy in 1988 if its GDP per capita had been $4,022 instead of $500? Although we do not show exactly how to do this here, it is possible to answer this question using the results in Table 6.4. The answer is that it would have been 3.07 times more likely to become a democracy if its GDP per capita had increased from $500 to $4,022. As this example illustrates, income is quite an important determinant for the emergence of democracy.

Let's continue with the example of Burkina Faso. How much less likely would it be for a country like Burkina Faso in 1987 to have become a democracy in 1988 if its growth rate had been the same as that of the United States (2.55 percent) instead of –2.15 percent? Again using the results in Table 6.4, the answer is 23 percent less likely. In other words, increasing the growth rate of a dictatorial country like Burkina Faso in 1987 from –2.15 percent to 2.55 percent could be expected to reduce the probability of a democratic transition by 23 percent. Finally, how much less likely would it be for a country like Burkina Faso in 1987 to have become a democracy in 1988 if it were an oil producer? The answer is 66 percent less likely. In other words, a dictatorship with a GDP per capita of $500 and a growth rate of −2.15 percent is 66 percent less likely to become a democracy if it is an oil producer than if it is not an oil producer.

Throughout the chapter, we claimed, in line with classic modernization theory, that economic development affects not only the emergence of democracy but also the survival of democracy. In contrast, we argued that the political resource curse applies only to the emergence of democracy and not to the survival of democracy. Using the same data as before, we now examine how a democratic country's status as an oil producer, its income, and its economic growth affect the probability that it will remain a democracy. The results of our new statistical analyses are shown in Table 6.5.

The dependent variable is the probability of democratic survival. As a result, whether a coefficient is positive or negative now tells us whether an increase in our independent variables is associated with an increase or decrease in the probability of democratic survival. So what do the results tell us? First, we can see that the coefficient on GDP per capita is positive and statistically significant. This indicates that increased income, as measured by GDP per capita, increases the probability of democratic survival. This result is consistent with the claim made by classic modernization theory that higher levels of income help democracies survive. Second, the coefficient on growth is positive and significant. This indicates that economic growth helps democracies survive. In other words, good economic performance

| TABLE 6.5 | **Economic Determinants of Democratic Survival** |

Dependent variable: Probability that a country will be a democracy this year if it was a democracy last year.

Independent Variables	1946–1990	1946–1990
GDP per capita	0.00020***	0.00020***
	(0.00004)	(0.00004)
Growth in GDP per capita		0.04***
		(0.01)
Oil production		−0.21
		(0.269)
Constant	1.13***	1.12***
	(0.13)	(0.13)
Number of observations	1,584	1,576
Log-likelihood	−149.71	−144.11

***$p < 0.01$

Note: Data are from Przeworski and colleagues (2000) and cover all countries from 1946 to 1990. The results shown in Table 6.5 come from a dynamic probit model. Standard errors are shown in parentheses.

appears to help both dictatorial and democratic regimes survive. Finally, the coefficient on oil production is negative but statistically insignificant. This indicates that, although being an oil producer helps dictatorships to survive (see the result in Table 6.4), we do not feel confident ruling out the possibility that oil has no effect on the survival of democracies. This is consistent with the claim of the political resource curse that immobile assets impede the emergence of democracy but not necessarily democratic stability.

But how much do income and economic growth really matter for democratic survival? To address this issue, let's return to the example of Burkina Faso. Let's imagine that Burkina Faso was a democracy in 1987. How would making it richer or improving its economic growth affect the chances that a country like this would still be a democracy in 1988? What if we increased GDP per capita from $500 to the world average in 1987 of $4,022? The results in Table 6.5 indicate that an increase like this would increase the probability of democratic survival by 12 percent. What if we increased the economic growth rate from –2.15 percent to that of the United States in 1987 (2.55 percent)? The answer is that the probability of democratic survival would increase by 4 percent.

CONCLUSION

There is considerable evidence to support the claim made by classic modernization theory that countries are more likely to become democratic and remain democratic as their economies become more "modern." Higher levels of income encourage both the emergence and the survival of democracy. Changes in economic structure that accompany changes in income also matter. We have shown that limited government in early modern Europe was more likely to arise in polities in which the Crown was dependent on elites with mobile assets. This argument can be generalized to account for the emergence and survival of democracy in more contemporary periods. States that are more dependent on revenue from immobile assets are less likely to democratize. In support of this claim, we cited considerable evidence that democracy is less likely to arise in countries that are heavily dependent on oil production. In our own statistical analyses, income and economic growth continue to be important contributors to the emergence and survival of democracy even after taking account of oil production. In a more detailed study than the one presented here, Ross (2001) shows that increased income affects democratization by bringing about additional changes such as increased occupational differentiation, improved education, and the growth of the service economy. All of these changes can be thought of as parts of a broader process of modernization. Moreover, all of these changes can be expected to increase the "exit options" available to citizens.

Arguments linking the prospects for democracy to the structure of a nation's economy are not popular with democratic activists. If democracy arose in Great Britain as a result of a gradual change in the British economy that took centuries to unfold, then what hope is there for people living under authoritarian regimes today? We wrote the second edition of this book shortly after the Arab Spring in 2011. At the time, many people were optimistic that a wave of democracy was washing over the Middle East and North Africa. We were less optimistic. Many, though certainly not all, of the regimes in this region of the world were dependent on oil revenue. In an age of Twitter and the Internet, we recognized that protest could spread quickly, but it was not clear to us that the process of democratization could be sped up appreciably. In an opinion piece written at the time, Michael Ross (2011, 5) reminded us that "no country with more oil wealth than Venezuela had in 1958" when it transitioned to democracy "has ever successfully democratized." Our knowledge of the political resource curse led us to claim that there was little hope that many of the regimes that had faced widespread opposition during the Arab Spring would transition into stable democracies.

We finished this chapter in the second edition of our book by showing estimates of per capita oil and gas production in several countries in the Middle East and North Africa (Ross 2012). We reproduce these estimates here in Table 6.6. We noted at the time that if the structure of a nation's economy places constraints on the propensity to democratize, then, all other things being equal, we would expect countries near the top of this list to be much less likely to democratize than countries near the bottom of this list. Removing autocrats from office is a necessary, but not sufficient, condition for democratization. We were not surprised that it was the rulers of Tunisia and Egypt—countries with the lowest levels of per capita oil and gas production in Table 6.6—who were the first leaders to lose their grip on power

TABLE 6.6	**Estimated Value of Oil and Gas Produced Per Capita in 2009 in Current Dollars**
Country	**Oil Income Per Capita (2009 Dollars)**
Qatar	$24,940
Kuwait	$19,500
United Arab Emirates	$14,100
Oman	$7,950
Saudi Arabia	$7,800
Libya	$6,420
Bahrain	$3,720
Algeria	$1,930
Iraq	$1,780
Iran	$1,600
Syria	$450
Yemen	$270
Egypt	$260
Tunisia	$250

Source: Ross (2012).

during the Arab Spring. Unfortunately, the events of the past half decade since the Arab Spring have seen our predictions further borne out. As we mentioned in the previous chapter, only Tunisia out of the countries listed in Table 6.6 can be considered a democracy today.

If changes to the structure of the economy are prerequisites for democratization, change is likely to come slowly—even in today's fast-paced world. In the next chapter, we move away from economic arguments about democracy to consider whether cultural traits influence the emergence and survival of democracy. Unfortunately, for those who would like to speed the pace of democratization, culture too changes slowly.

KEY CONCEPTS

credible commitment problem *190*
dependent variable *206*
foreign aid *201*
GDP per capita *179*
independent (explanatory) variable *206*
modernization theory *181*

natural resources *198*
political resource curse *198*
significance test (in Appendix) *215*
sovereign debt *190*
survival story *181*

APPENDIX: AN INTUITIVE TAKE ON STATISTICAL ANALYSES

As you'll see throughout this book, comparative political scientists use a variety of methods for evaluating their theoretical claims. One of the most common methods that they employ involves using some form of statistical analysis. Earlier in this chapter, we briefly described how to begin interpreting statistical results like those shown in Tables 6.4 and 6.5. Here, we try to provide you with an intuitive and conceptual understanding of statistical analyses.

The starting point for any statistical analysis is a theoretically derived hypothesis. A hypothesis makes some falsifiable claim about the world. For example, a hypothesis might state that an increase in X leads to an increase in Y. In this example, X is the independent variable and Y is the dependent variable. To be more concrete, a "democratization hypothesis" might state that more economic development (independent variable, X) is associated with higher levels of democracy (dependent variable, Y). To evaluate a hypothesis, we must first collect data on X and Y for each of our units of analysis. The units of analysis refer to the entities that we're talking about in our theory—they may be individuals, groups, countries, and so on. In our democratization hypothesis, country-years (i.e., United States 2016, Nigeria 2016, and so on) are the unit of analysis—we want to know whether economic development (X) affects the level of democracy (Y) *in a country-year* (unit of analysis).

Once we have the relevant data, we put them into a spreadsheet so that we can start the statistical analysis. A spreadsheet essentially stores data in a tabular form. If you are familiar with Excel, you will already have a good idea about what a spreadsheet looks like. A spreadsheet contains columns and rows. Each row corresponds to a particular unit of analysis; they are our observations. For example, the rows might correspond to different countries or individuals. Each column refers to some category that contains information about each observation. For example, one column might contain the names of the units of analysis. Other columns might contain the values for the dependent variable or the values for an independent variable. Rows and columns intersect to form cells. Each cell contains a particular piece of information about a particular observation. We typically refer to the information in a spreadsheet as the data set.

Suppose we want to test the hypothesis that an increase in X leads to an increase in Y. And let's suppose that we have collected information about X and Y for 100 observations or units. A snapshot of our data set is shown in Table 6.7. We can see that the value of Y is 0.92 for observation 1 and 2.28 for observation 100. The value of X is 2.37 for observation 3 and 0.13 for observation 98. Had we collected other pieces of information about our units other than just Y and X, we would have put them in separate columns to the right or left of the X column.

Recall that we want to see whether there is a positive relationship between X and Y. Are higher values of X associated with higher values of Y? One place to start is by producing a scatterplot that plots the Y values in our data set against the X values. This is precisely what we do in Figure 6.10. Each of the 100 circles shown in gray represents one of the (X, Y) pairs, say $(X = 0.50, Y = 0.92)$, in our data set. As you can see, higher Y values do tend to be associated with higher X values—the circles slope upward to the right. This is consistent with our hypothesis.

While there appears to be a clear pattern in the scatterplot, we can see that not all observations with a high X value are associated with a high Y value, and not all observations with a low X value are associated with a low Y value. To better summarize the observed relationship between X and Y, we can add a line that "best fits" the cloud of points in the scatterplot.

TABLE 6.7	A Snapshot of a Data Set	
Observation	**Y**	**X**
1	0.92	0.50
2	0.71	0.96
3	3.24	2.37
⋮	⋮	⋮
98	0.44	0.13
99	2.80	1.65
100	2.28	1.63

FIGURE 6.10 **A Scatterplot of Y against X**

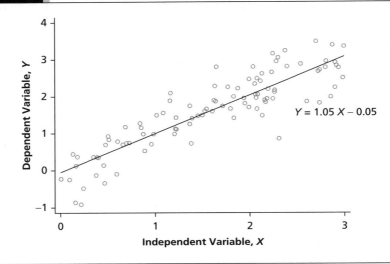

Note: Each of the 100 circles shown in the scatterplot represents one of the (X, Y) pairs in our data set. The solid black line sloping upward is the line that "best fits" the data. The equation for the line is $Y = 1.05 X - 0.05$.

This is the solid black line that slopes upward in Figure 6.10.[7] You'll remember from your middle school or high school classes that the equation for a line is

$$Y = mX + b.$$

The "m" is called the "coefficient" and indicates the slope of the line. A positive coefficient, m > 0, indicates that the line slopes upward to the right, suggesting that there is a positive relationship between X and Y. This is the scenario depicted in Figure 6.10. A negative coefficient, m < 0, indicates that the line slopes downward to the right, suggesting a negative relationship between X and Y. A zero coefficient, m = 0, indicates a horizontal line, suggesting that there is no relationship between X and Y. As you can see, the sign of the coefficient gives us a sense of the relationship that exists between X and Y. The "b" is the "constant" and indicates the value of Y when X is 0; it is sometimes referred to as the intercept as this is the point where the line "intercepts" the vertical Y-axis.

The equation for the line shown in Figure 6.10 is $Y = 1.05 X - 0.05$. If we were to report the pattern shown in Figure 6.10 in a table of statistical results, it would look like that shown

7. If you take a statistics class, you'll learn the mathematics that goes into finding the line that best fits the data in examples like this.

in Table 6.8.[8] The key thing to note here is that the coefficients you see in a table of statistical results essentially describe slope relationships—each coefficient describes the slope of the relationship between some independent variable X and the dependent variable Y. So the next time you see a table of statistical results, look at the sign of the coefficients (positive, negative, or zero) and think slope relationships.

In parentheses beneath the coefficient (and the constant) is something called the standard error. The standard error is essentially a measure of uncertainty. The sloping line in Figure 6.10 is the line that best fits our data, but it's only an estimate of the relationship that exists between X and Y more generally. The standard error gives us a sense of how certain we are that the "best-fit" line we find in our data reflects the more general relationship. The smaller the standard error relative to the size of the coefficient, the less likely it is that a relationship that exists in our data does not exist more generally. We will return to the role of the standard error shortly.

We've clearly identified a pattern in our data. There appears to be a positive relationship between X and Y. But how confident are we that we've identified a real relationship that is not driven by the peculiarities of our data? Our data are "noisy" and perhaps the pattern we have observed has arisen by chance. Perhaps there is no relationship between X and Y outside of our data set. This is where statistical significance tests come in. Whenever we've identified a pattern in our data like the one in Figure 6.10, it is incumbent on us to conduct a **significance test** to see how likely it is that we've identified a real relationship.[9]

> A **significance test** is used to see how likely it is that we've identified a real relationship or pattern in our data.

If you take a statistics class, you'll find out that there are many, many different types of significance tests. However, they all have the same basic structure.[10]

TABLE 6.8	A Table of Statistical Results Capturing the Pattern Shown in Figure 6.10

Independent Variables	Model 1
X	1.05*** ⟵ Coefficient, m
	(0.06)
Constant	−0.05 ⟵ Constant, b
	(0.10)
Number of Observations	100

***$p < 0.01$

---

8. For those who are interested, the statistical results shown in Table 6.8 come from an ordinary least squares regression model where we regress Y on X.

9. The discussion that follows adopts a frequentist understanding of traditional null-hypothesis significance tests.

10. The following discussion draws on a blog post by Stephen Heard (2015), "Why do we make statistics so hard for our students?"

- Step 1: Measure the strength of the pattern in our data.
- Step 2: Ask whether the pattern is strong enough to be believed.

Step 1 requires identifying a "test statistic." We'll call the test statistic T. In our particular example, the test statistic is calculated as the coefficient—the slope—divided by the standard error (i.e., 1.05/0.06 = 17.5).[11] This is where the standard error comes in. The fact that this is how we mathematically calculate the test statistic in our particular example is not important here. What matters is that however the test statistic is calculated, it is a measure of the strength of the pattern in our data. The larger the test statistic, the stronger the pattern in the data. At least three factors influence the strength of the pattern in our data: (i) the raw effect size, (ii) the amount of noise in the data, and (iii) the amount of data in our sample.[12]

To intuitively see how these factors influence the strength of the pattern in our data, consider the various panels in Figure 6.11. There are three columns in Figure 6.11, with each column depicting two patterns in the data. The patterns in the bottom panels are always more convincing—they are stronger—than the corresponding patterns in the top panels.

The first column looks at the importance of *raw effect size*. Raw effect size refers to how much Y changes when we change the value of X. The reason why the pattern in the bottom panel is more convincing than the pattern in the top panel is because the slope of the relationship between X and Y—how much Y changes when X changes—in the bottom panel is twice as large as that in the top panel. If there were no relationship between X and Y outside of our data, it is more likely that we would observe a pattern like that in the top panel (where the slope of the line is closer to zero) than in the bottom.

The second column looks at the importance of noise in the data. Both panels show a "best-fit" line with the same slope (i.e., the same raw effect size). The reason why the pattern in the bottom panel is more convincing than the pattern in the top panel is because there is less noise in the data—the circles (observations) are much closer, on average, to the "best-fit" line in the bottom panel. Thus, knowing something about the value of X for an observation allows us to predict its value for Y with a greater degree of accuracy in the bottom panel than in the top panel.

The third column looks at the importance of sample size, or how many data points we have. Both panels have the same amount of noise in the data and show a "best-fit" line with the same slope. The reason why the pattern in the bottom panel is more convincing than the pattern in the top panel is because our "best-fit" line is based on 100 observations instead of just twenty-five observations. Our inferences about the relationship between X and Y would be much more sensitive to the removal of a few observations in the top panel than in the bottom panel.

---

11. In what follows, we focus on the slope coefficient rather than the constant. However, the same reasoning that we apply to the slope coefficient also applies to the constant.

12. For those of you who have taken a statistics class, you'll immediately see how these three factors feed into the mathematical formulas used to calculate test statistics.

FIGURE 6.11 Intuitive Ideas about the Strength of Patterns in Our Data

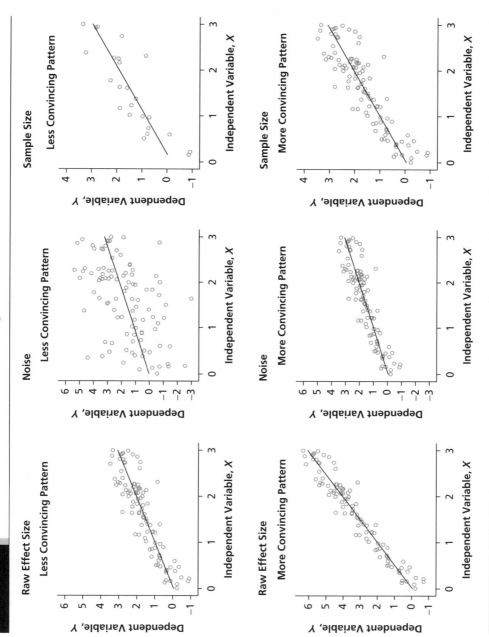

Note: The three columns each depict two slightly different patterns between *X* and *Y*. The pattern in the top panel is always weaker than the corresponding pattern in the bottom panel. The two patterns in each column indicate how raw effect size (left column), the noise in the data (middle column), and sample size (right column) influence the observed strength of the relationship between *X* and *Y*.

If we were to calculate them, the test statistics (T) for the patterns (slope coefficients) shown in the bottom panels of Figure 6.11 would be larger than the test statistics for the patterns shown in the top panels.

Step 2 concerns identifying something called the "p-value." We want to know how likely it is that we would observe a pattern as strong (or stronger) than the one we see in our data if, in fact, there were no pattern in general. This is precisely what the "p-value" tells us. The p-value indicates the probability of observing a test statistic as large (or larger) than T if there were no relationship between X and Y beyond our data set; that is, if the true slope of the relationship between X and Y were 0. If this probability is sufficiently low, then we rule out the possibility that the pattern we observe in our data occurred by chance. In our particular example, we would look up the p-value associated with our test statistic of $T = 17.5$ in something called a t-distribution table. If we did this, we would find that the p-value associated with a test statistic as large or larger than $T = 17.5$ is incredibly small, smaller than 0.0001. Exactly how we calculated this particular p-value is, again, not important here. The point is that all significance tests provide you with a p-value. When the p-value is very small, like it is in our particular example, we rule out the possibility that the pattern we observe in our data occurred by chance.[13]

In practice, political scientists often use cutoffs in the p-value to determine whether they have identified a "statistically significant" relationship. For example, it is common for political scientists to say that they have identified a "statistically significant" relationship if the p-value associated with a test statistic for a particular variable, X, is less than 0.05 (i.e., $p < 0.05$); sometimes, they use a cutoff of $p < 0.01$ or $p < 0.10$ instead.[14] To help readers determine if a particular pattern in the data, such as a slope coefficient, is statistically significant, political scientists will often place stars next to the relevant coefficient in the table of results. Whenever we present tables of statistical results in this book (see, for example, Table 6.4), we have used three stars to indicate $p < 0.01$, two stars to indicate $p < 0.05$, one star to indicate $p < 0.10$, and no stars to indicate that $p \geq 0.10$. If a pattern is not considered statistically significant (no stars), then we are saying that we do not consider the p-value to be sufficiently small for us to rule out the possibility of no relationship between X and Y; that is, we are unwilling to rule out the possibility that the pattern we observe in the data may have arisen by chance.

Statistical analyses provide a very powerful tool for testing our claims about the world. If you are interested in learning more about statistical analyses after reading this, and we hope that you are, we encourage you to sign up for a statistics or quantitative methods class.

_____

13. Hopefully you can see the connection between statistical tests and the approach to science that we outlined in Chapter 2. In effect, statistical tests are designed to see if we can falsify the possibility that the pattern we observe in our data occurred by chance. When the p-value is very small, we deem that this possibility has been falsified.

14. This practice of using cutoffs to determine statistical significance is controversial. This is because these cutoffs are essentially arbitrary. Would we really want to say, for example, that a p-value of 0.049 is evidence of a statistically significant relationship because it falls below the conventional cutoff of $p = 0.05$ but that a p-value of 0.051 is not because it falls just above the cutoff?

You will almost certainly learn about lots of different significance tests in such a class. Remember, though, that all of these significance tests have the same basic structure. First, determine the strength of the pattern in the data; then, determine how likely it is that we would observe a pattern as strong (or stronger) than this if there were, in fact, no pattern in the observations outside of our data set.

PROBLEMS

The problems that follow address some of the more important concepts and methods introduced in this chapter.

Classic Modernization Theory

1. In this chapter we discussed classic modernization theory, which suggests that economic development is positively related to democracy. Answer the following questions.

   a. The basic idea with classic modernization theory is that as countries develop from traditional societies into modern societies, they shift from dictatorial forms of government to democratic ones. What are the general characteristics of "traditional societies" and "modern societies"?

   b. One implication of classic modernization theory is that rich countries tend to be democracies and poor countries tend to be dictatorships. In the chapter, we argue that this association between income and democracy can be explained by both modernization theory and the survival story. Outline how these two stories explain the observed relationship between income and democracy.

   c. Why does Przeworski say that increased income should help democratic survival?

   d. Does the evidence presented in this chapter suggest that increased income makes the emergence of democracy more likely or less likely?

   e. Does the evidence presented in this chapter suggest that increased income makes democratic survival more likely or less likely?

A Variant of Modernization Theory

2. In this chapter we discussed a variant of modernization theory. Answer the following questions.

   a. According to the variant of modernization theory that we examined, why does democracy emerge as economies develop?

   b. In early modern Europe, why did England develop a limited form of government while France developed an absolutist and autocratic form of government?

   c. Country A is characterized by the following features: it is wealthy, it has an abundance of natural resources, and its population is poorly educated. Country B is characterized by the following features: it is wealthy, its economy is dominated by the financial service sector, and its population is well educated. Based on the variant of modernization theory that we examined, which country is most likely to be democratic and why?

d. Why might globalization encourage democratization around the world?

e. Many people have recently argued that countries with high levels of economic inequality are unlikely to become democratic. What is their basic argument? Based on the variant of modernization theory that we examined, do you expect economic inequality to always harm the prospects for democracy? Explain your answer.

Exit, Voice, and Loyalty Game

3. Earlier in the chapter we solved the Exit, Voice, and Loyalty Game for (a) the scenario in which the Crown was dependent and the Parliamentarians had a credible exit threat, and (b) the scenario in which the Crown was dependent and the Parliamentarians had no credible exit threat. We did not explicitly solve the EVL Game for scenarios when the Crown was autonomous. The game tree for the Exit, Voice, and Loyalty Game is shown in Figure 6.12. Answer the following questions.

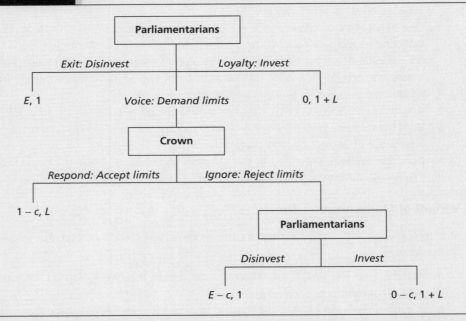

| FIGURE 6.12 | **EVL Game with Payoffs** |

*Note: E = Parliamentarians' exit payoff; 1 = value of benefit taken from the Parliamentarians by the Crown; L = Crown's value from having loyal Parliamentarians who do not exit; c = cost of using voice for the Parliamentarians. It is assumed that $c > 0$ and that $E < 1 - c$.

a. Use backward induction to solve the game for the scenario in which the Crown is autonomous, $L < 1$, and the Parliamentarians have a credible exit threat, $E > 0$. What is the subgame perfect equilibrium? Do we get a democracy or a dictatorship? Do we get good economic performance or bad economic performance?

b. Use backward induction to solve the game for the scenario in which the Crown is autonomous, $L < 1$, and the Parliamentarians do not have a credible exit threat, $E < 0$. What is the subgame perfect equilibrium? Do we get a democracy or a dictatorship? Do we get good economic performance or bad economic performance?

c. In the chapter we claim that foreign aid can hinder democratization. Based on the outcomes from the two scenarios in the EVL Game that you have just examined, explain why we make this claim.

Credible Commitment Problems

4. In the chapter we introduce the concept of credible commitment problems. Answer the following questions about them.

a. What two factors characterize credible commitment problems?

b. Describe a nonpolitical (everyday) situation in which actors face a credible commitment problem? Can you think of a way to solve this problem?

c. Describe a political situation in which actors face a credible commitment problem? Can you think of a way to solve this problem?

Dependent and Independent Variables

5. In this chapter we introduce the concept of dependent and independent variables. Dependent variables are the outcomes or things we want to explain. They are the "effects" in cause-and-effect relationships. Independent variables are the factors we think might explain or determine the value of the dependent variable. They are the "causes" in cause-and-effect relationships. Look at the following statements and identify the independent variable and the dependent variable.

a. Smoking causes cancer.
b. Incumbents lose elections when economic performance is bad.
c. When a country develops economically, it will become a democracy.
d. Obesity is caused by eating too much food.
e. Democracy is stable in rich countries.
f. If citizens have mobile assets, then the government will not exploit them.
g. Crime is caused by poverty.
h. Economic inequality is bad for democracy.
i. Countries with high levels of natural resources are less likely to be democratic.
j. A good grade in class is the result of hard work.
k. Voter turnout is lower when it rains.

l. A change in the partisan control of the government, from a right-wing party to a left-wing party, will lead to higher government spending.

m. Governments with more parties will have higher levels of government spending.

Oil and Democracy: The Political Resource Curse

6. Obtain a copy of Michael L. Ross's 2001 article, "Does Oil Hinder Democracy?" from the journal *World Politics* (53:325–361) using your institution's library resources. Read the article and then answer the following questions.[15]

   a. What is Ross's dependent variable? How is it measured? What is the main independent variable? How is it measured?

   b. What is the main hypothesis of this article? What evidence would falsify this hypothesis?

   c. Why does Ross believe that having oil might be detrimental to the development of democracy? Summarize the argument's three proposed causal mechanisms in a couple of sentences.

   d. Ross tests his theory using statistical analyses. Given his dependent variable, what sign (positive or negative) does Ross predict for the coefficient on his primary explanatory variable? (*Hint:* See your answers to parts a and b.) What sign does he find? Is the coefficient on this variable statistically significant? How do you know? (*Hint:* The answer is in Table 3.3, column 1, page 341.)

   e. Does Ross find that being an oil producer hinders the development of democracy only in the Middle East?

   f. Does Ross find any evidence that nonfuel (not oil or gas) minerals help or hinder the development of democracy?

---

15. The following series of questions is based on several similar questions posed by Powner and Bennett (2005, 118–20).

7 The Cultural Determinants of Democracy and Dictatorship

> **There was a time when many said that the cultures of Japan and Germany were incapable of sustaining democratic values. Well, they were wrong.**
>
> George W. Bush, in a speech to the American Enterprise Institute, Washington Hilton Hotel, February 26, 2003

> **I am a democrat only on principle, not by instinct—nobody is that. Doubtless some people say they are, but this world is grievously given to lying.**
>
> Mark Twain, Notebook, entry for February–March 1898

OVERVIEW

- Does democracy require a "democratic culture"? Are certain cultures incompatible with democracy? Does culture affect the emergence and survival of democracy?

- According to cultural modernization theory, economic development produces certain cultural changes, and it is these cultural changes that lead to democracy. A key cultural change is the emergence of a "civic culture." For many, the existence of a civic culture is seen as a prerequisite for the successful emergence and survival of democracy. As we demonstrate, the empirical evidence in support of cultural modernization theory is somewhat mixed.

- We investigate recent claims that particular religions such as Islam are incompatible with democracy. As we indicate, all religions have some doctrinal elements that can be seen as compatible with democracy and others that can be seen as incompatible; Islam is no exception. Our empirical evidence suggests that there is little reason to believe that majority Muslim countries cannot sustain democracy once we take account of their wealth.

- We examine evidence from a series of experiments conducted around the world that throws light on why culture may be important for the emergence and survival of democracy.

In the previous chapter, we examined the vast literature linking economic factors to the emergence and survival of democracy. The literature addressing the relationship between culture and democracy is equally large and is the subject of this chapter. The notion that cultural differences drive significant elements of political and economic life is commonplace and has a long history. But does democracy really require a "democratic culture"? Are certain cultures incompatible with democracy? How does culture affect the emergence and survival of democracy? The claim that culture plays any role with respect to democracy obviously has important implications for those wishing to spread democracy to regions of the world such as the Middle East, Africa, and Asia.

> **Primordialist arguments** treat culture as something that is objective and inherited—something that has been fixed since "primordial" times.
>
> **Constructivist arguments** treat culture as something that is constructed or invented rather than inherited.

Cultural arguments regarding democracy typically fall into two categories: primordialist and constructivist (Laitin 1983, 1986; Przeworski, Cheibub, and Limongi 1998). **Primordialist arguments** treat culture as something that is objective and inherited—something that has been fixed since "primordial" times. For example, Geertz (1973, 259–260) describes primordial cultural attachments, which for him include things like bloodlines, language, race, religion, and customs, as stemming "from the givens . . . of social existence. . . . For virtually every person, in every society, at almost all times, some attachments seem to flow more from a sense of natural—some would say spiritual—affinity than from social interaction." According to primordialists, culture exists prior to, and remains unchanged by, political interaction. Put differently, it is culture that affects political behavior by providing ideological guidelines for collective action rather than political behavior that shapes culture. As a result, political institutions, such as democracy, may not be compatible with all cultures. In effect, primordialist arguments imply that democracy is not for everyone.

Constructivist arguments treat culture as something that is constructed or invented rather than inherited. Like primordialist arguments, constructivist arguments claim that culture has a causal effect and that a democratic culture is required for democracy to emerge and prosper. Constructivists recognize, however, that cultures are malleable and are not given once and for all—cultures can change in response to social, economic, and political actors. As a result, cultures do not necessarily represent impenetrable barriers to democratization. Although cultures may not act as impenetrable barriers to democratization as they do in primordialist arguments, constructivists recognize that the speed with which cultures can change is likely to vary from culture to culture. In this sense, some cultures will find it easier to adopt democracy than others.

CLASSICAL CULTURAL ARGUMENTS: MILL AND MONTESQUIEU

The notion that political institutions, such as democracy and dictatorship, are more suited to some cultures than others is not new (Przeworski, Cheibub, and Limongi 1998). As long ago as 472 B.C., Aeschylus contrasted the authoritarianism associated with the people of Asia with the democracy found in Athenian Greece in his play *The Persians* (Emmerson 1995, 96). The views of Aeschylus would later be echoed in what would become known as the Asian values debate in the 1990s. Although vague references to the compatibility of certain cultures with democracy have been around for some time, the first person to write in any great detail about the importance of culture to political institutions was Montesquieu in the eighteenth century. He claimed that monarchy was most suited to European states, that despotism was most suited to the Orient, and that democracy was most suited to the ancient world. He believed that the best government for a given country was that which "leads men by follow-ing their propensities and inclinations" (Montesquieu [1721] 1899, Persian Letter 81) and which "best agrees with the humor and disposition of the people in whose favor it is estab-lished" (Montesquieu [1752] 1914, 1:3). What did this entail exactly? He stated that political institutions "should be in relation to the climate of each country, to the quality of its soil, to its situation and extent, to the principal occupation of the natives, whether husbandmen, huntsmen, or shepherds: they should have relation to the degree of liberty which the consti-tution will bear; to the religion of the inhabitants, to their inclinations, riches, numbers, commerce, manners, and customs" (Montesquieu [1752] 1914, 1:3). He goes on to claim that it can be only by chance that the political institutions of one country can successfully be exported to another.

In his discussion "To What Extent Forms of Government Are a Matter of Choice," John Stuart Mill also argued that different cultures were suited to different political institutions. He stated, "No one believes that every people is capable of working every sort of institutions" (Mill [1861] 2001, 7). To illustrate this, he claimed, "Nothing but foreign force would induce a tribe of North American Indians to submit to the restraints of a regular and civilized gov-ernment" (Mill [1861] 2001, 8). Mill believed that even those people who recognized the benefits of a civilized government might still have to live under authoritarianism if they did not have the required characteristics to support a better system of government. These neces-sary characteristics included "moral" or "mental habits," such as the willingness to "co-operate actively with the law and the public authorities in the repression of evil-doers" (Mill [1861] 2001, 9). They also included a certain degree of development characterized, for example, by a press capable of propagating public opinion and a tax system "sufficient for keeping up the force necessary to compel obedience throughout a large territory" (Mill [1861] 2001, 11). Mill ([1861] 2001) was clearly a strong believer that legislators should take account of "pre-existing habits and feelings" when creating political institutions in a country (11).

It is important, however, not to interpret Mill's statements as if they are arguments that certain cultures are incompatible with political institutions, such as democracy. In fact, Mill was highly critical of those who believe that culture prevents political actors from choosing the institutions they desire. Although he thought that "people are more easily induced to do, and do more easily, what they are already used to," he also believed that "people . . . learn to do things new to them. Familiarity is a great help; but much dwelling on an idea will make it familiar, even when strange at first" (Mill [1861] 2001, 11). Ultimately, Mill did not see particular cultural traits as necessary conditions for democracy. This is because he thought that culture is inherently malleable and that, as a result, people could learn to live with democracy. As you can see, Mill asserted a constructivist cultural argument regarding the prospects for democracy.

Cultural modernization theory argues that socioeconomic development does not directly cause democracy; instead, economic development produces certain cultural changes, such as the emergence of a civic culture, and it is these cultural changes that ultimately produce democratic reform.

The cultural arguments put forth by both Montesquieu and Mill were later incorporated into strands of **cultural modernization theory**. As you'll remember from the previous chapter, modernization theory predicts that "immature" societies (those with large agricultural sectors and authoritarian institutions) will eventually become "mature" societies (those with large industrial and service sectors and democratic institutions) as they develop economically. Cultural modernization theory states that socioeconomic development transforms societies with primitive cultures into societies with civilized cultures—only when this happens are societies ready for democracy. In other words, cultural modernization theory argues that socioeconomic development does not directly cause democracy; instead, economic development produces certain cultural changes, and it is these cultural changes that produce democratic reform. As Inglehart and Welzel (2005, 15) put it, "socioeconomic development brings roughly predictable cultural changes . . . [and] these changes make democracy increasingly likely to emerge where it does not yet exist, and to become stronger and more direct where it already exists."

The claims made by Montesquieu and Mill regarding culture and democracy illustrate several potential problems that characterize some cultural arguments to this day (Przeworski, Cheibub, and Limongi 1998). How would you test the claims made by Mill and Montesquieu? What exactly would the hypotheses be? Try to state one of them in a way that can be tested. One obvious problem is that neither scholar specifically states exactly what it is about culture that matters for democracy. Both men provide a whole host of cultural things that might affect the emergence and survival of democracy—religion, customs, morals, manners, marital institutions, and so on. Indeed, most of these things are left quite vague. For example, what particular morals are incompatible with democracy? Which customs are problematic? Moreover, both scholars point to numerous noncultural things that also affect democracy such as the climate of a country, the quality of the soil, and the economy. The key point here is that cultural arguments must specify exactly what it is about culture that matters, otherwise it will never be possible to conclude that culture does not matter. Put simply, one of the problems with cultural arguments such as those made by Montesquieu and Mill is that they are so vague or nonspecific that they become nonfalsifiable (Przeworski, Cheibub, and Limongi 1998). In effect, they become "nonscientific" in the terms we outlined in Chapter 2.

The second problem relates to the purported causal relationship between cultural, economic, and political factors. Does culture cause political institutions, such as democracy, to emerge and survive? Does it also cause economic development? Or do political institutions and economic development cause culture? In other words, which way does the causal arrow go? If culture does cause democracy, is it a necessary or a sufficient condition? If culture is a cause, does it cause the emergence of democracy, or does it affect only the survival of democracy? In Figure 7.1, we illustrate some of the causal arguments that scholars have made concerning the interaction between culture, economic development, and democracy.

| FIGURE 7.1 | **Culture, Economic Development, and Democracy: Some Potential Causal Relationships** |

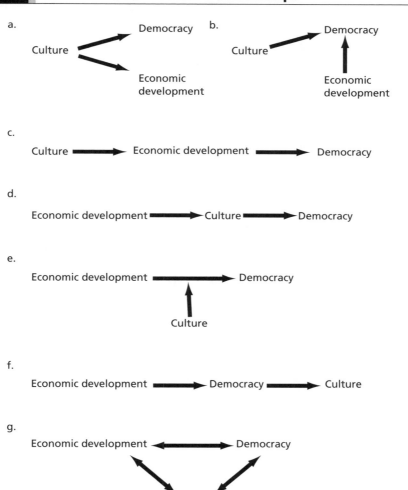

Mill and Montesquieu clearly believed that economic development and culture both matter for democracy. From what they wrote, however, it is hard to discern what they thought the exact causal relationship was between these factors.

DOES DEMOCRACY REQUIRE A CIVIC CULTURE?

Gabriel Almond and Sidney Verba reopened the debate about culture and democracy in the 1960s with their book *The Civic Culture*. Although they recognized the importance of economic development for democracy, they believed that only a "civic culture" could provide the "psychological basis of democratization" and that without this, the prospects for democratic survival were slim (Almond and Verba [1963] 1989, 9). Almond and Verba claimed that there were three basic types of political culture in the world—parochial, subject, and participant/civic. According to them, the civic culture was the only culture compatible with democracy. In contrast, parochial cultures were compatible with the traditional political systems of African tribes, and subject cultures were compatible with centralized authoritarian institutions like those seen in Soviet-dominated Eastern Europe (Almond and Verba [1963] 1989, 20, 33).

A political culture, for Almond and Verba, was something that captured how individuals think and feel about the political system. They believed that it was possible to study culture by conducting surveys and asking individuals about their feelings toward political institutions, actors, and processes. The idea was that the distribution of responses to these survey questions would identify a nation's political culture. In this conceptualization, a political culture simply refers to a relatively coherent cluster of attitudes in society. According to Almond and Verba, a civic culture reflects a particular cluster of attitudes that includes (a) the belief on the part of individuals that they can influence political decisions, (b) positive feelings toward the political system, (c) high levels of interpersonal trust, and (d) preferences for gradual societal change. In contrast, parochial and subject political cultures reflect different clusters of attitudes on these same issues. Applying their methodology to the study of Germany, Italy, Mexico, the United States, and the United Kingdom, Almond and Verba found that the United States and the United Kingdom were not only the most stable democracies in their sample but also the countries that most closely resembled their ideal civic culture. As a result, they concluded that a **civic culture** was necessary for democratic stability (see Box 7.1, "Does Good Democratic Performance Require a Civic Culture?").

> Broadly speaking, a **civic culture** refers to a shared cluster of attitudes that are thought to promote democracy and democratic performance.

Inglehart (1990) reached a similar conclusion after studying survey responses from 25 industrial nations in the 1980s. Like Almond and Verba ([1963] 1989), he believed that "different societies are characterized to very different degrees by a specific syndrome of political cultural attitudes; that these cultural differences are relatively enduring, but not immutable; and that they can have major political consequences, one being that they are closely linked

| ox 7.1 | **DOES GOOD DEMOCRATIC PERFORMANCE REQUIRE A CIVIC CULTURE?** |

In this chapter, we are primarily interested in how political culture affects the emergence and survival of democracy. Several scholars have argued that political culture is also important for the overall *performance* of democracy. In *Making Democracy Work: Civic Traditions in Modern Italy*, Robert Putnam (1993) argues that cultural norms affect the variation in economic and political performance exhibited by regional governments in Italy. In accordance with a long line of scholarship on Italy, Putnam found that regional governments in the north of Italy functioned far more effectively than those in the south. Putnam's research goal was to explain this variation across Italian regional governments and to determine the causes behind variation in governmental performance in democracies more generally.

Putnam argued that institutions couldn't possibly be the explanation for the variation in government performance between the north and south of Italy, as Italian regional governments all shared a similar institutional structure.

Instead, he looked at cultural explanations and focused on the presence or absence of a civic culture. For Putnam, the key to a civic culture was **social capital**. Social capital refers to the collective value of social networks and shared norms that promote reciprocity, trust, and social cooperation. In his work on Italy, Putnam (1993, 167) argued that social capital and, in particular, "norms of reciprocity and networks of civic engagement," were the key to good government performance.

> **Social capital** refers to the collective value of social networks and shared norms that promote reciprocity, trust, and social cooperation.

In line with his expectations, Putnam found that regions with more social capital had better government performance than regions with less social capital. In effect, Putnam showed that the high performing regions in the north of Italy were characterized by a "good" civic culture that encouraged working for the common good and that the low-performing regions in the south were characterized by a "bad" culture of "amoral familism," in which norms of reciprocity and engagement were limited to one's family and in which self-interest was the primary motivating force behind individual actions. According to Putnam, the civic culture in the north could be traced back to the communal relations exhibited by republican towns in this region in Italy's medieval past, whereas the culture of amoral familism in the south could be traced back to this region's monarchic past.

Putnam's work on Italy has energized many in the policymaking community. "From the World Bank to city hall, the creation of social capital [and civic culture] has been embraced as a solution for social problems as diverse as promoting economic development in Africa and stemming urban decay in Los Angeles" (Boix and Posner 1996). Putnam's study of Italy has also been a catalyst for research on political culture in the United States. In *Bowling Alone*, Putnam (2000) argues that the number of people participating in voluntary associations—one place in which social networks can be built—has been falling in the United States and that people have become disconnected from family, friends, and neighbors. Putnam's book created quite a stir, because the decline in social capital that it described was seen to have potentially negative consequences for the state of American democracy.

to the viability of democratic institutions" (Inglehart 1990, 15). According to Inglehart, political culture is determined by, among other things, the levels of overall life satisfaction, the levels of interpersonal trust, and the support for gradual societal change among the individuals of a nation. Clearly, these determinants of political culture are very similar to those proposed by Almond and Verba. In his analysis, Inglehart (1990, 43) found that countries in which levels of life satisfaction, interpersonal trust, and support for gradual societal change were high were more likely to be stable democracies. In other words, he too found that some kind of civic culture is required for stable democracy.

There has never been complete agreement on the precise cluster of attitudes thought to compose a civic culture. In their recent work, Inglehart and Welzel (2005) claim that there are two major dimensions of cross-cultural variation in the world today. The first dimension has to do with whether countries exhibit traditional values or secular-rational values. Traditional values emphasize the importance of religion, traditional family roles, and deference to authority. Individuals who hold traditional values typically exhibit national pride and reject things like divorce, euthanasia, suicide, and abortion. Secular-rational values place less emphasis on religion, traditional family roles, and deference to authority. Individuals who hold these values typically find things like divorce, euthanasia, suicide, and abortion more acceptable. The second dimension has to do with whether countries exhibit survival values or self-expression values. Survival values emphasize the importance of physical and economic security. Individuals who hold survival values typically hold an ethnocentric worldview and exhibit low levels of interpersonal trust and tolerance. Self-expression values emphasize the importance of gender, racial, and sexual equality; environmental protection; tolerance of diversity; civic activism; and life satisfaction. Individuals who hold these values often exhibit high levels of interpersonal trust and demand a greater say in how political and economic decisions are made.

Like Almond and Verba, Inglehart and Welzel (2005) use survey responses to determine the extent to which different societies exhibit traditional versus secular-rational values and the extent to which they exhibit survival versus self-expression values. With these survey responses, it is possible to create a "cultural map" of the world. Figure 7.2 shows a cultural map of the world based on data from the 2010–2014 World Values Survey. Moving upward on this map represents a shift from traditional to secular-rational values, while a move to the right represents a shift from survival to self-expression values. Countries that exhibit high levels of traditional and survival values (bottom left) include Jordan, Yemen, and Morocco. Countries that exhibit high levels of traditional and self-expression values (bottom right) include Mexico, Colombia, and Ecuador. Countries that exhibit high levels of secular-rational and survival values (top left) include Russia, Belarus, and Ukraine. Countries that exhibit high levels of secular-rational and self-expression values (top right) include Sweden, Norway, and Denmark. Figure 7.2 identifies nine subjective "cultural zones." The countries in these cultural zones are thought to share similar cultural values and hence exhibit distinct political cultures.

In line with cultural modernization theory, Inglehart and Welzel (2005) argue that socio-economic development generally produces a change in cultural values that sees countries move from the bottom left quadrant in Figure 7.2 where they are poor and authoritarian to the top right quadrant where they are rich and democratic. According to Inglehart and Welzel (2005), the modernization process is not linear; instead, it occurs in two distinct phases. The first phase—the industrialization phase—sees countries move upward in Figure 7.2 away from traditional values to secular-rational values. In the pre-industrial world, most people earn their living from agriculture and rely on God to provide them with good weather and good health. Social interactions with outsiders are limited, reputation rests on ties of kinship, tradition is valued, and comfort is sought in religion. The shift to an industrial society changes things. Technology gives people more control over their environment

| FIGURE 7.2 | **A Cultural Map of the World** |

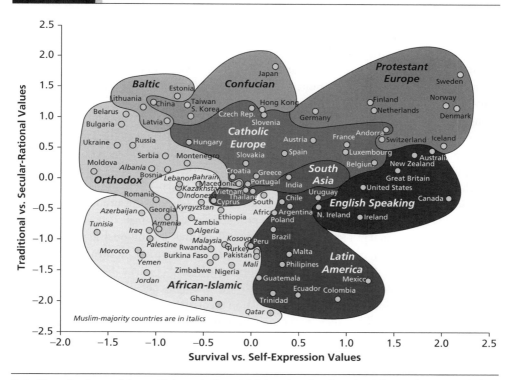

Note: The cultural map of the world shown in Figure 7.2 is based on data from the sixth wave (2010–2014) of the World Values Survey. The different clusters indicate countries that Inglehart and Welzel identify as sharing similar cultural values—they represent distinct political cultures.

Source: http://www.worldvaluessurvey.org/WVSContents.jsp

and science provides a rational explanation for the previously inexplicable. The result is a decline in the importance of religion and the rise of secular authorities. The modernization process is, in this sense, a secularization process (Norris and Inglehart 2004; Gaskins, Golder, and Siegel 2013a, b).

The second phase—the post-industrialization phase—sees countries move rightward in Figure 7.2 away from survival values to self-expression values. While industrialization brings certain changes, people generally remain poor, and they continue to be concerned about their physical and economic security. They worry about putting a roof over their head and food on the table. As socioeconomic development continues and societies become wealthier, though, existential security concerns recede and people can begin to focus on expanding their opportunities for self-expression and personal autonomy. In his earlier work, Inglehart (1977) refers to this change as a "silent revolution" in which materialist worries are replaced by post-materialist concerns. A growing sense of human autonomy leads people to question authority, hierarchies, and dogmatism. As self-expression values spread, so do demands for political liberalization, greater emancipation, and a greater say in how political and economic decisions are made. This puts pressure on authoritarian regimes to democratize and for democratic regimes to act more effectively. As you can see, Inglehart and Welzel (2005) see self-expression and secular-rational values as the core components of a civic culture.

Over the years, there has been considerable debate about the exact causal relationship between culture, economic development, and democracy. On one side of the debate are scholars who argue that economic development produces cultural change and that it is cultural change that produces democracy (Inglehart 1990, 1997; Inglehart and Welzel 2003, 2005). This potential causal relationship, which as we have seen forms the basis for cultural modernization theory, is illustrated in Figure 7.1d. According to this story, cultural values act on, shape, and cause political institutions. We might call this the "values story." On the other side of the debate are scholars who argue that this causal story is backward (Barry 1970; Muller and Seligson 1994; Seligson 2002). These scholars argue that economic development produces democracy and that it is experience with democracy that produces cultural change. This potential causal relationship is illustrated in Figure 7.1f. We might call this the "institutional story." According to the institutional story, cultural values are a *consequence*, not a *cause*, of democracy.

There is, however, no reason to think that both stories can't be true. It seems reasonable to us that societal development might increase the likelihood of democracy through its effects on cultural values as cultural modernization theorists propose—and that it could also increase the likelihood of democracy through other mechanisms such as those examined in Chapter 6. This means that whatever the existing cultural values are in some country, an increasingly modern social structure will increase that country's probability of experiencing democracy. This experience with democracy can, in turn, contribute to cultural change that reinforces democratic practice in the future. Thus, we are not forced to choose between the institutional and values stories. Perhaps these stories work together to create a virtuous cycle tying changes in social structure to increasingly democratic outcomes.

Surveys and Comparative Research

One of the major impacts of Almond and Verba's ([1963] 1989) *Civic Culture* was to encourage the use of surveys to examine the relationship between culture and democracy. The most commonly used survey today is the World Values Survey. This is the survey that provided the data for the cultural map of the world shown in Figure 7.2. Scholars who are particularly interested in the relationship between culture and democracy are frequently drawn to the following question from the World Values Survey:

> Democracy may have problems, but it's better than any other form of government. Could you please tell me if you strongly agree, agree, neither agree nor disagree, disagree, or strongly disagree?

Many people believe that mass support for a particular system of government, and mass confidence in specific institutions, provides political systems with the legitimacy they need to operate effectively (Newton and Norris 2000). In effect, mass support for democracy is seen by some as essential in delegitimizing dictatorial rule and legitimizing democratic rule. Thus, when a low level of public support is reported in questions like this one from the World Values Survey, it is often seen as a harbinger of democratic instability or collapse.

Surveys such as the World Values Survey are increasingly being used to examine many important questions in comparative politics. Researchers who use surveys often confront certain problems, two of which we briefly discuss here. The first problem arises when surveys address sensitive topics. One of the implicit assumptions in survey research is that respondents are answering the survey questions truthfully (Blair 2015). Unfortunately, respondents often have incentives to lie or conceal their true beliefs. For example, a respondent in a dictatorship may not feel comfortable revealing her true preferences when asked about the value of democracy. This is because democracy is a sensitive topic in most authoritarian regimes. We discuss the issue of "preference falsification" in dictatorships in more detail in the next chapter. Similarly, respondents may feel unwilling to express negative attitudes toward particular ethnic, racial, religious, or sexual groups if these attitudes run counter to social norms. **Social desirability bias**, in which individuals tend to overreport "good behavior" and underreport "bad behavior,"

helps to explain why surveys often underestimate the support for extremist anti-immigrant parties in Europe or overestimate the degree of support for minority political candidates in the United States. Social pressure, potential legal sanctions, and fear of retaliation can create incentives for respondents

> **Social desirability bias** refers to the tendency of individuals to overreport "good behavior" and underreport "bad behavior."

to lie on surveys. Indeed, these concerns can even lead to certain types of people not participating in surveys in the first place, with the result that these surveys are no longer "representative." It is easy to see how surveys might produce biased and misleading estimates in these circumstances. For example, if citizens in authoritarian societies underreport their enthusiasm for democracy because they believe they will be punished for expressing their sincere beliefs, cross-national surveys will overstate the positive association between attitudes toward democracy and democratic persistence.

The second problem, which applies in particular to cross-national surveys, such as the World Values Survey, has to do with the fact that respondents don't always comprehend survey questions in the same way. Consider the following example about self-reported health in India and the United States. Sen (2002, 860–861) writes:

> The state of Kerala has the highest rates of literacy . . . and longevity . . . in India. But it also has, by a very wide margin, the highest rate of reported morbidity among all Indian states. . . . At the other extreme, states with low longevity, with woeful medical and educational facilities, such as Bihar, have the lowest rates of reported morbidity in India. Indeed, the lowness of reported morbidity runs almost fully in the opposite direction to life expectancy, in interstate comparisons. . . . In disease by disease comparisons, while Kerala has much higher reported morbidity rates than the rest of India, the United States has even higher rates for the same illnesses. If we insist on relying on self-reported morbidity as the measure, we would have to conclude that the United States is the least healthy in this comparison, followed by Kerala, with ill provided Bihar enjoying the highest level of health. In other words, the most common measure of the health of populations is negatively correlated with actual health.

Differential item functioning (DIF) refers to the fact that different items, such as particular survey questions, may function differently across individuals or groups. DIF exists when individuals or groups understand survey items differently or evaluate survey items using different scales.

Clearly, the respondents in the different regions of India and in the United States either understood the survey questions differently or evaluated their levels of health on very different scales. This problem is commonly referred to as **differential item functioning**. A key point here is that measuring or inferring reality by comparing people's attitudes or perceptions across different regions, countries, or cultures can often be "extremely misleading" (Sen 2002). This particular issue is especially relevant for survey research related to democracy. This is because democracy means different things to different people around the world. For example, democracy may conjure up images of economic and political equality for some, but it may simply mean holding competitive elections for others. These different views of democracy should not come as a surprise, given that we have already seen in Chapter 5 that political scientists disagree about whether to employ a minimalist or substantive view of democracy in their own work. If experts can't agree on what they mean by democracy, why would we expect individuals in different countries to have the same concept in mind when answering survey questions about it?

Political scientists are increasingly aware of these problems with surveys and have begun to develop ingenious methods to get around them. Blair (2015) describes four basic methods for addressing sensitive topics with surveys. The first method focuses on survey administration. The core idea here is to adopt practices that build trust with respondents. Some scholars recommend using interviewers who share similar demographic characteristics, such as age, gender, or ethnicity, with the respondent. Adida and colleagues (2016) find that respondents in Africa give systematically different answers to survey questions if the people who interview them are coethnics as opposed to non-coethnics. Others have highlighted the importance of allowing respondents to report their answers in private rather than aloud to an interviewer (Krysan 1998; Krysan and Couper 2003). In a study of caste-sensitive attitudes in India, Chauchard (2013) provided his respondents with MP3 players so that they could self-report their answers in private.

The second method involves the use of randomized response techniques (Gingerich 2010; Blair, Imai, and Zhou 2015). The core feature of these techniques is the introduction of a randomizing device, such as a coin or a die, into the survey response process to guarantee the confidentiality of individual responses. For example, before answering a sensitive survey question that requires a "yes" or "no" answer, a respondent might be asked to roll a die in private. If the die shows a 1, the respondent is told to report "yes." If the die shows a 6, the respondent is told to report "no." If the die shows a 2, 3, 4, or 5, then the respondent is told to answer the question truthfully, either "yes" or "no." As you can see, the interviewer never knows whether a given individual response is true or not; hence, the confidentiality of the individual response is guaranteed. The key, though, is that the interviewer knows the probability with which truthful answers are given (if the respondents follow the instructions) and can therefore calculate the overall numbers of respondents who said "yes" and "no" to the sensitive question. Randomized response techniques have been used to study a variety of phenomena, such as corruption within bureaucracies (Gingerich 2013), cheating by undergraduates (Fox and Meijer 2008), sexual attitudes (De Jong, Pieters, and Stremersch 2012), and the prevalence of xenophobia and anti-Semitism (Krumpal 2012).

The third method involves the use of list experiments. The core idea in list experiments is to protect the confidentiality of individual responses by mixing sensitive items into lists that include nonsensitive "control" items. In a list experiment, some survey respondents are presented with a list of nonsensitive control items and are then asked to indicate the number with which they agree. Another set of survey respondents are presented with the same list of control items except that a sensitive item is now also included. These respondents are also asked to indicate the number of items with which they agree. By comparing the number of items that respondents agree with across these two randomly selected groups, it is possible to identify the level of support for the sensitive item. As you may have realized, this method does not always guarantee that individual responses are kept confidential. This is because a respondent who answers that she agrees with none or all of the items in the list containing the sensitive item reveals her preferences about the sensitive item. As a result, researchers need to be careful about what items they include in the list of control items. List experiments have been used to study a variety of phenomena such as public support for coalition forces in Afghanistan (Blair, Imai, and Lyall 2014), vote buying in Nicaragua (Gonzalez-Ocantos et al. 2012), and the impact of citizen preferences on policy in China (Meng, Pan, and Yang, forthcoming).

The fourth method involves the use of endorsement experiments. The core idea in endorsement experiments is to protect the confidentiality of individual responses by mixing attitudes toward a sensitive political actor with attitudes toward one or more policies. In an endorsement experiment, some survey respondents are asked to give their attitudes toward a policy that a "sensitive" political actor has endorsed. The responses to this question mix the preferences of the respondents toward the policy and their preferences toward the sensitive actor. Other survey respondents are asked to give their attitudes toward the same policy but without any mention of the endorsement. The responses to this question isolate the preferences of the respondents toward the policy. By comparing the responses across the two groups, it is possible to identify just the preferences toward the sensitive political actor. Endorsement experiments have been used to study a variety of phenomena such as attitudes toward the Taliban in Afghanistan (Lyall, Blair, and Imai 2013) and militants in Pakistan (Blair et al. 2013).

The fact that respondents don't always comprehend survey questions in the same way, perhaps because they come from different cultures, is problematic. This is particularly the case if one wants to compare survey responses to learn about cultural differences. One way in which political scientists attempt to deal with this issue is through the use of anchoring vignettes (King et al. 2004; King and Wand 2007). Anchoring vignettes are useful for survey questions that use an ordinal scale—say, strongly disagree, disagree, neutral, agree, strongly agree—such as the "democracy" question seen earlier from the World Values Survey. Anchoring vignettes use additional survey questions to create "anchors" that allow for a common scale of measurement across respondents. Respondents are asked to provide a self-assessment of a particular issue. They are then asked to provide an assessment of a vignette (short story) that depicts a particular outcome of that issue. For example, respondents might be asked to judge their own political efficacy, that is, their belief that they can get their representatives to address issues important to them. They are then confronted with a vignette that includes information about some other individual's political efficacy. The vignette provides a common reference point, or "anchor," for the respondents and therefore allows the researcher to place the respondents' self-assessments on a common scale. For example, the researcher could code the respondent self-assessments as "less than," "equal to," or "greater than" the efficacy depicted in the vignette (King and Wand 2007). Anchoring vignettes have been used in numerous settings. For example, the World Health Organization has used them to examine various health indicators, the World Bank has used them to investigate economic welfare, and other scholars have used them to look at things like corruption, political efficacy, and women's autonomy.[1]

The development of these new techniques for overcoming the challenges of using survey responses to measure cultural differences is promising. But their application to the study of

---

1. For examples of the types of vignettes used in these studies, see King, "Examples," at http://gking.harvard.edu/vign/eg.

political culture is in its infancy, and only time will tell whether the canonical findings of political culture scholars will stand up to this more careful analysis.

RELIGION AND DEMOCRACY

Recent arguments linking culture and democracy have increasingly focused on religion. Unlike many of their predecessors, these cultural arguments have strongly influenced public discourse and shaped the direction of public policy. For example, Samuel Huntington's (1996) book *The Clash of Civilizations and the Remaking of World Order,* in which he argues that Islamic and Confucian cultures are incompatible with democracy (see Box 7.2, "The Clash of Civilizations"), was reportedly recommended reading for many of the soldiers heading to Iraq during the second Gulf War in 2003. More recently, the issue of Islam and democracy has

---

ox 7.2 | **THE CLASH OF CIVILIZATIONS**

In 1992 Francis Fukuyama famously declared the "end of history." With the end of the Cold War, Fukuyama believed that liberal democracy had finally won the battle with other rival ideologies such as fascism and communism. Liberal democracy was the "end point of mankind's ideological evolution" and hence the "end of history." Although Samuel Huntington (1993, 1996) took issue with the claim that we were witnessing the end of history, he agreed with the claim that conflict in the world would no longer be based on ideological divisions. He wrote,

> It is my hypothesis that the fundamental source of conflict in this new world will not be primarily ideological or primarily economic. The great divisions among humankind and the dominating source of conflict will be cultural. Nation states will remain the most powerful actors in world affairs, but the principal conflicts of global politics will occur between nations and groups of different civilizations. The clash of civilizations will dominate global politics. The fault lines between civilizations will be the battle lines of the future. (Huntington 1993, 22)

For Huntington (1993, 24), a civilization is the "highest cultural grouping of people and the broadest level of cultural identity people have short of that which distinguishes humans from other species." Huntington identifies many different civilizations in the world today—Western Christian, Confucian, Japanese, Islamic, Hindu, Slavic-Orthodox, Latin American, African, and others. The exact number is ambiguous because he refers to different civilizations in different studies. It is not always obvious how Huntington moves from his definition of a civilization to an indicator of them. On the whole, civilizations seem to be coded primarily in regard to religion, although linguistic differences and geographic proximity seem to play a role in some cases.

Continued

Continued

Huntington argues that the widespread Western belief in the universality of the West's values and its insistence on imposing these values through democratization efforts will only antagonize other civilizations and lead to conflict. He believes that these conflicts will be less amenable to diplomacy and peaceful resolution than previous economic and ideological conflicts because cultural differences are less mutable and less easy to compromise. In effect, Huntington argues that certain cultures are incompatible with democracy. In particular, Islamic and Confucianist countries cannot support democracy; even Catholic countries will find it hard to sustain democratic regimes. He also notes that violent conflict will be "particularly prevalent between Muslims and non-Muslims" because Muslims are prone to violence (Huntington 1996, 256–258).

come up in the 2016 US presidential elections, with the Republican Party's candidate, Donald Trump, calling for a ban on Muslims entering the United States as well as a national database and ID cards for Muslims (Matharu 2015; Pilkington 2015). It is worth noting, however, that these contemporary debates concerning the relationship between religion and democracy actually have a long and storied history—a history that should perhaps make us wary of unthinkingly accepting claims that certain religions are incompatible with democracy.

Are Some Religions Incompatible with Democracy?

Historically, scholars have argued that Protestantism encourages democracy but that Catholicism, Orthodox Christianity, Islam, and Confucianism inhibit it (Lipset [1960] 1994, 5). Max Weber ([1930] 1992) is commonly thought to have provided the first argument linking Protestantism with democracy in his book *The Protestant Ethic and the Spirit of Capitalism.* For example, Lipset ([1960] 1994, 57) writes, "It has been suggested, by Weber among others, that a historically unique concatenation of elements produced both democracy and capitalism in this area [northwest Europe, America, and Australasia]. . . . Protestantism's emphasis on individual responsibility furthered the emergence of democratic values in these countries." The causal story connecting Protestantism to democracy is the following: Protestantism encourages economic development, which in turn creates a bourgeoisie, whose existence is a necessary condition for democracy (Moore [1966] 1999). In effect, the causal relationship mirrors the one shown earlier in Figure 7.1c. The notion that Protestantism promotes democracy was later taken up by other scholars such as Inglehart (1990), for whom the percentage of Protestants in a country is one element of his civic culture.

Rodney Stark (2004a, 2004b) has criticized the Weberian emphasis on Protestantism by pointing out that many of the attributes of modern capitalism were present in the Italian city-states before the Protestant Reformation. Stark's controversial study suggests that it is Christianity in general, not Protestantism per se, that encouraged the growth of capitalism and democracy. He argues that because Christianity focuses on orthodoxy (correct belief) rather than orthopraxy (correct practice, which is the focus of Islam and Judaism) and posits a rational and personal God, a brand of science and philosophy arose in predominantly Christian countries that supported the development of democratic self-rule.

Other scholars have suggested that Protestantism really is a key determinant for contemporary levels of democracy, but not for the reasons suggested by Weber. For example, Woodberry (2004, 2012; Woodberry and Shah 2004) has argued that it is the depth and breadth of Protestant missionary activity during colonial periods that helps to explain why certain countries are democracies today and others are not. The reason has to do with the emphasis that Protestants placed on teaching people to read the scripture in their own language. These missionary efforts spearheaded mass education and the introduction of modern printing to colonial regions, which in turn unleashed many modernizing forces that encouraged democracy, such as increased literacy, greater equality, a more independent workforce, and a larger middle class. Whatever the causal process, Protestantism has historically been seen by many as a religion that encourages democracy.

In contrast to Protestantism, Catholicism has traditionally been seen as antithetical to democracy. For example, Lipset ([1960] 1994, 72) has argued that Catholicism's emphasis on there being only one church and one truth is incompatible with democracy's need to accept different and competing ideologies as legitimate. The hierarchy in the Catholic Church and the clear distinction between the clergy and laity are also thought to pose particular problems for the acceptance of more egalitarian institutions, such as democracy. Those who believe that democracy is difficult to establish in Catholic countries often point to the support that the Catholic Church has given to dictatorships around the world in the past. For example, the Catholic Church was an open supporter of fascist Italy under Mussolini and of authoritarian Spain under Franco. The Catholic Church has historically also supported several dictatorships in South America and Asia.

Confucianism and Islam have come to be seen as posing even bigger problems for the successful establishment of democracy than Catholicism. Huntington (1993) is perhaps the most vocal proponent of this belief. He argues that we are currently observing a clash of civilizations and that "Western concepts differ fundamentally from those prevalent in other civilizations. Western ideas of individualism, liberalism, constitutionalism, human rights, equality, liberty, the rule of law, democracy, free markets, the separation of church and state, often have little resonance in Islamic, Confucian, Japanese, Hindu, Buddhist or Orthodox cultures" (40).

He goes so far as to say that Confucian democracy is a contradiction in terms and that "almost no scholarly disagreement exists regarding the proposition that traditional Confucianism was either undemocratic or anti-democratic" (Huntington 1993, 24). Huntington is not alone in claiming that Confucianism is incompatible with democracy. In what became known as the Asian values debate in the 1990s, scholars argued that Confucianism's respect for authority and its emphasis on communalism and consensus rather than individual rights and competition made it incompatible with democracy (Kim 1997; Pye 1985; Scalapino 1989). To a large extent, the catalyst for this debate was the Bangkok Declaration that was signed in April 1993 by the political leaders of China, Indonesia,

Malaysia, and Singapore. This declaration stated that Asian values justify a different way of understanding human rights and democracy. Along these lines, Lee Kuan Yew (1994), Singapore's prime minister from 1959 to 1990, has suggested that Confucianism's respect for authority and its emphasis on the community are antithetical to Western images of liberalism. This line of reasoning was used by various authoritarian leaders in Asia to justify the ongoing existence of their nondemocratic forms of government (Dalton and Ong 2004, 3).

As with Confucianism, numerous reasons have been proposed for why Islam might be incompatible with democracy. One of the earliest arguments dates to Montesquieu, who claimed that Islam had a violent streak that predisposed Muslim societies to authoritarianism. While comparing Christianity and Islam, Montesquieu ([1752] 1914, 24:3–4) writes that "the Christian religion is a stranger to mere despotic power. The mildness so frequently recommended in the Gospel is incompatible with the despotic rage with which a prince punishes his subjects, and exercises himself in cruelty. . . . The Mahometan [Islam] religion, which speaks only by the sword, acts still upon men with that destructive spirit with which it was founded." Huntington (1996, 256–258) is a modern-day proponent of the same idea. He too argues that one of the reasons democracy is so difficult to establish in Islamic countries is that Muslims are prone to political violence. A second proposed reason for the incompatibility of Islam and democracy concerns the purported inability of Islam to disassociate religious and political spheres. The recognition in Islam that God is sovereign and the primary lawgiver has led some to argue that the Islamic state is in principle a theocracy (Lewis 1993) or, as Huntington (1996, 70) puts it, that "in Islam God is Caesar." A third proposed argument for the incompatibility of Islam and democracy concerns Islam's unequal treatment of women (Fish 2002; Norris and Inglehart 2004). Some believe that the repressiveness and dominance of the father in the family and of men in relation to women more generally in Islamic culture replicate themselves in the larger society, thereby creating a culture suitable for authoritarianism. Others claim that the social marginalization of women in the political sphere leaves society susceptible to dictatorship because men hold attitudes that are more conducive to domination.

Although arguments that particular religions are incompatible with democracy have strong supporters around the world (notably among the authoritarian leaders of certain countries), there is good reason to doubt their veracity. Why might these arguments be flawed? Note that many of the arguments presented so far rest on claims that there is something about the doctrine of each religion that makes them particularly compatible or incompatible with democracy. One problem with this is that virtually all religions have some doctrinal elements that can be seen as compatible with democracy and others that are not (Stepan 2000, 44). This is true even of "pro-democratic" Protestantism. For example, Przeworski and colleagues (1998, 132) argue that Protestantism's legitimization of economic inequality and the ethic of individual self-interest associated with it provide "a poor moral basis for living together and resolving conflicts in a peaceful way."

What about Confucianism and Islam? Well, many people argue that these religions have elements that make them compatible with democracy. For example, some claim that

Confucianism's meritocratic system and its emphasis on the importance of education and religious tolerance suggest that it can sustain democracy (Fukuyama 1995a). Indeed, Taiwan's president from 1988 to 2000, Lee Teng-hui, even claims that traditional Confucianism calls for limited government. In addition, the existence of a public sphere in Korea during the Joseon (Chosun or Choson) dynasty from 1392 to 1910 would seem to contradict those who assert that Confucianism cannot sustain democracy because it has no concept of civil society (Im 1997). Thus, despite claims to the contrary by some authoritarian leaders in Asian countries, there seems to be nothing explicit in Confucianism itself that would necessitate an authoritarian government. In fact, many of the elements of Confucianism mentioned above seem quite well suited to a democratic form of government. Indeed, Friedman (2002) even suggests that "Buddhist and Confucian cultures may actually have more democratic elements than Greco-Christian culture."

Many scholars have also taken issue with the claim that Islam is incompatible on doctrinal grounds with democracy (Abootalebi 1999; Esposito and Voll 1996; Filali-Ansary 1999; Hefner 2000; Price 1999; Rahman 1979; Sachedina 2000). For example, several scholars find a basis for democracy in the Koran's emphasis on *shura* (consultation). Shura requires that even the messenger of Allah should consult with his people in earthly matters and that Muslims should consult with each other in their secular affairs. This process of consultation is in many respects similar to the process of consultation that underpins elections and legislatures in democracies. Indeed, many Islamic scholars "have come to the conclusion that general elections and a parliament properly serve that concept of consultation" (Yazdi 1995, 18). Other scholars have interpreted Islamic concepts such as *ijma* (consensus of the community) and *ijtihad* (reinterpretation), as well as legal principles, such as *maslaha* (public welfare), as providing a basis for Islamic forms of parliamentary governance, representative elections, and religious reform (Esposito 2003).

Still others have suggested that those who portray the rule of law in a democratic state ("law of man") as being inherently in conflict with sharia, or Islamic law ("law of God"), are creating a false dichotomy. It is true that the primary lawgiver in Islam is God and that God's agents such as the Islamic state enjoy only marginal autonomy to implement and enforce God's laws. In other words, it is true that sovereignty lies in different places in democracy (with the people) and Islam (with God). Still, the reason this distinction should not be overemphasized is that, in practice, it is the state, and not God, that actually exercises sovereignty in Islam. Worth noting here is that one of the underlying concerns in both Islam and democracy is the need to limit the power of the state and the people who rule. That this is achieved in Islam by arguing that God is the primary lawgiver and that the state should simply implement God's laws, whereas it is achieved in democracy by holding elections and implementing checks and balances, should not be allowed to hide the fact that both Islam and democracy share the same goal of limited government.

We should also point out that there is nothing inherent in democratic theory that requires a democratic state to be secular anyway (Stepan 2000, 40). It may be true that most contemporary democracies tend to separate church and state (although there is considerable variation even in this), but it is important to recognize that this is a choice and not necessarily part and parcel of democratic theory. Indeed, it is illuminating to remember that until the eighteenth century, many leaders of the Christian church vehemently opposed both democracy and secularism, just like many proponents of Islam today. For decades, there was a great struggle between the church and princely rulers on the one hand and between Christians and secularists on the other. It was only during the nineteenth century that democracy and secularism became broadly acceptable within Western Christian society. Even today, some Christians believe that the strict separation of church and state should be relaxed. In sum, Islamic doctrine, like the doctrines of other religions, contains elements that make it compatible with many traditional aspects of democracy.

Some Empirical Evidence

Given that almost all religions seem to contain doctrinal elements that can be seen as detrimental to democracy and others that can be seen as conducive to it, it becomes an empirical question as to whether certain religions pose particular difficulties for the establishment and survival of democracy (Przeworski, Cheibub, and Limongi 1998). So what does the empirical evidence say?

The growing empirical evidence that cultures are invented, constructed, and malleable rather than primordial, inherited, and unchanging suggests that it is inappropriate to view particular religions or civilizations as being permanently incompatible with democracy. For example, Eickelman and Piscatori (1996) point out that Islamic doctrine has historically been interpreted in various ways to justify many different types of government. As to Confucianism, the fact that the comments of Singapore's former prime minister, Lee Kuan Yew, concerning the relationship between Confucianism and democracy run directly counter to the comments of Taiwan's former president, Lee Teng-hui, suggests that Confucianism can be interpreted differently by different people and that it can be adapted to suit different purposes.

Considerable evidence supports the claim that the stance of different religions toward political institutions often depends less on the content of religious doctrine and more on the interests of religious leaders. For example, Kalyvas (1996) shows in his study of the rise of European Christian democracy that the relationship between Catholicism and democracy had less to do with the actual content of Catholic faith and more to do with the strategic considerations of elites in the Catholic Church. Balmer (2006) makes a similar point with respect to Protestants in his account of the rise of the "religious right" in the United States. Elsewhere, Kalyvas (1998, 2000) examines why Catholic fundamentalism proved compatible with the successful establishment of democracy in nineteenth-century Belgium but Islamic fundamentalism did not in Algeria during the 1990s. He argues that the reasons for the different outcomes in the two countries had little to do with actual doctrinal issues and more to do with the different organizational structures of the two religions (see the Religious Party Game in the Problems section at the end of Chapter 8 for more details). Numerous other scholars have similarly highlighted the role played by "cultural entrepreneurs" in producing cultural change, thereby suggesting that conflicts over culture tend to be matters of interest and strategy rather than any primordially given cultural content (Laitin 1983, 1986, 1992; Posner 2004, 2005). In other words, a vast amount of empirical evidence undermines the implication made by scholars such as Huntington that the antidemocratic tendencies of certain religions and civilizations are given once and for all.

The empirical reality is that all religions have historically been compatible with a broad range of political institutions. For example, Fukuyama (1995b,

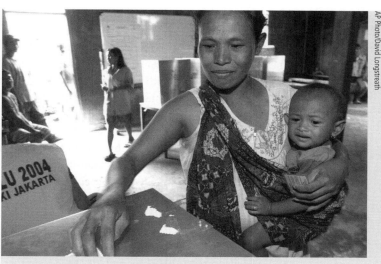

AP Photo/David Longstreath

A Jakarta mother carries her child as she votes Monday, July 5, 2004, in the first direct presidential election in the vast archipelago of Indonesia, the world's most populous Muslim-majority country.

12) claims that many different types of political institutions are compatible with Confucianism. The fact that it is possible to distinguish between "political" and "everyday" Confucianism helps to explain why the imperial system mandated by traditional political Confucianism could be abolished relatively easily in China in 1911 and replaced with a variety of different political institutions without the loss of Chinese society's essential coherence. According to Fukuyama, the important legacy of traditional Confucianism is not its political teaching but rather the personal ethic that regulates attitudes toward family, work, education, and other elements of everyday life. This helps to explain why Confucian society can exist easily in democracies like Japan, South Korea, and Taiwan, in semi-authoritarian regimes like Singapore, or in more authoritarian regimes like China and North Korea.

Islamic countries also have considerable experience with different forms of political systems. Despite the claim that Islam requires an Islamic state, it should be noted that, with the exception of Iran since the 1979 revolution and of Afghanistan during the period of Taliban rule in the 1990s, there have been few historical precedents for mullahs, or religious leaders, controlling political power in Islamic countries. On the whole, secular political elites have controlled political power in Islamic countries for the roughly 1,400 years since the Prophet Muhammad died in 632. Despite claims that Islam is incompatible with democracy, it is important to remember that hundreds of millions of Muslims live today in such democratic countries as Canada, France, Germany, India, the Netherlands, the United Kingdom, and the United States (Stepan 2000, 49). Indeed, several countries with majority Muslim populations are considered democracies—Albania, Indonesia, Mali, Niger, Senegal, and Turkey. Clearly, being Muslim does not preclude someone from living a peaceful and constructive life in a democratic society.

Not only can we find evidence for the compatibility of Islam and democracy by looking at the world today, but we can also find evidence of at least quasi-democratic institutions and practices in Islam's past. Perhaps the most notable example is the Constitution of Medina. In 622 the Prophet Muhammad established the first Islamic state when he migrated from Mecca to Medina. Medina was a highly diverse city—45 percent of the residents were non-Muslim Arabs, 40 percent were Jews, and 15 percent were Muslims. Whereas the Muslim population accepted that Muhammad had the right to rule over them by divine decree, this was not the case for the majority non-Muslim population. Rather than rule by force, Muhammad explicitly sought the consent of the people he would govern by having them agree to and sign a constitution. Interestingly, this means that Jews were constitutional partners in making the first Islamic state (M. Khan 2001). As you can see, the Constitution of Medina represents a social contract between the ruler and his people, one that occurred almost six centuries earlier than the much more famous Magna Carta in England (A. Khan 2006). Social contract theorists, such as Hobbes and Rousseau, have typically portrayed the social contract as a "fictional" document that helps to explain the emergence of the modern state (see Chapter 4). The Constitution of Medina represents one of the few real-world examples of such a document (A. Khan 2006, 2–3).

In addition to highlighting the importance of having the people's consent and cooperation for governance, the Constitution of Medina is also a symbol of pluralism and religious tolerance in Islam (Shah 2012). The constitution created a pluralistic state with a common citizenship that guaranteed identical rights and duties across the various religious and tribal communities in Medina. Among other things, the constitution guaranteed social, legal, and economic equality; cooperation; freedom of conscience; and other human rights. Importantly, Muslims and non-Muslims were free to practice their own religions and were duty bound to come to each other's defense. As A. M. Khan (2010, 6) notes, the Constitution of Medina "was the first document in history to establish religious freedom as a fundamental constitutional right." In effect, the constitution envisioned a religiously pluralistic Islamic state.

Despite the fact that cultures tend to be malleable and that all religions have been compatible with a variety of political institutions throughout history, one might still wonder whether certain religions are *more* or *less* compatible with democracy than others. In this vein, several empirical studies have suggested that Islam is particularly bad for democracy—Islamic countries seem to have lower Freedom House scores than non-Islamic countries. For example, Karatnycky (2002) finds that there was only one Islamic country in 2001 that was coded as Free, whereas there were twenty-eight that were coded as Not Free. In contrast, eighty-five non-Islamic countries were coded as Free and only twenty-one were coded as Not Free. Fish (2002) argues that the reason Islam is so bad for democracy has to do with its treatment of women. Why? First, he finds that Islamic countries tend to be characterized by a wider literacy gap between men and women, fewer women in government, and lower measures of overall gender empowerment. Second, he finds that all of these measures of women's status are associated with lower Freedom House scores. This leads him to infer that it is the poor treatment of women in Islamic countries that leads to their low democracy scores.

Despite the evidence presented in these studies, we should be cautious in concluding that Islam is bad for democracy. One reason for such caution is that several of the studies mentioned above examine the effect of Islam on democracy at a fixed point in time. For example, Karatnycky (2002) examines the effect of Islam on a country's Freedom House score in 2001, while Fish examines the effect of Islam on a country's average Freedom House score in the 1990s. Why might this be problematic? What do you think a researcher would find if she examined the relationship between Catholicism and democracy in 1976? She would find that of the forty-seven countries with a Catholic majority, fourteen were coded as Free and sixteen were coded as Not Free. In contrast, eleven of the sixteen countries with a Protestant majority were coded as Free and only one was coded as Not Free. This would suggest that Catholicism is bad for democracy, at least in comparison with Protestantism. However, if the same researcher examined the relationship between Catholicism and democracy in 2004, her conclusion would be very different. Of the fifty-seven countries with a Catholic majority in 2004, forty were coded as Free and only three were coded as Not Free. As you can see, whereas Catholicism seemed to pose some difficulties for democracy from the perspective of 1976, this was no longer the case from the perspective of 2004. Our point here is that it can be dangerous to draw strong inferences about the incompatibility of a religion with democracy from a single point in time.

Note that it would be equally dangerous to draw inferences about the compatibility of a *civilization* with democracy from a single point in time as well. For example, consider Huntington's assertion that Western civilization is obviously compatible with democracy. Such a claim might seem eminently reasonable from our perspective today. However, it would hardly seem this way to someone living in Europe during the 1930s. As Mazower (2000, 5) notes,

> It is hard to see the inter-war experiment with democracy for the novelty that it was: yet we should certainly not *assume* that democracy is suited to Europe. . . . Triumphant in 1918, it was virtually extinct twenty years on. . . . Europe found other, authoritarian, forms of political order no more foreign to its traditions. (italics in original)

It turns out that most of the arguments claiming that particular religions or civilizations are incompatible with democracy are implicitly based on observations of the world at a particular point in time. For example, arguments linking Protestantism to democracy and Catholicism to authoritarianism tended to be made most frequently when Protestant countries around the world were predominantly democratic and when Catholic countries were largely authoritarian. This observed variation encouraged some scholars to look for reasons why Protestantism might promote democracy and why Catholicism might impede it. In other words, theory construction came after observing the world. Because explanation always begins with a puzzling observation, there is nothing inherently wrong with this. But if the explanation does not suggest testable implications other than those that led to it, we call this an *ex post,* or ad hoc, explanation. Such explanations violate the norms of science because they do not invite falsification.[2] Of course, the argument that Catholic countries are inherently antidemocratic has now lost most of its force because Catholic countries today are predominantly democratic. In fact, one might now even argue that Catholicism helps democratization, given the important role that the Catholic Church played in aiding democratic transitions in countries like Chile, Paraguay, the Philippines, and Poland in the 1980s. Despite this, the exact same type of argument that used to be made about Catholicism is now frequently made about Islam: we observe that there are few democratic Islamic countries at this point in time, and we therefore conclude that there must be something about Islam that is antidemocratic. The history of arguments concerning Catholicism (and Confucianism) should make us wary of accepting this type of reasoning.

What about the evidence that Islam is particularly bad for democracy because of its treatment of women (Fish 2002)? Unfortunately, because of the author's decision to use Freedom House as his measure of democracy, it is hard to know if his evidence is truly compelling. If you remember our discussion in Chapter 5 of the Freedom House measure of democracy, you might recall that it is based on a series of questions regarding the level of political rights and civil liberties in a country. Countries that have more political rights and civil liberties are considered more free and, hence, more democratic. The problem is that some of these questions take into account, at least implicitly, the treatment and status of women. In other words, the overall Freedom House score for each country automatically varies with that country's treatment of women simply because of the way it is constructed. As a result, it is inappropriate to test to see whether the measure of the treatment of women affects a country's Freedom House score—we already know that it will by construction. Thus, the question as to whether Islam is bad for democracy because of its treatment of women remains an open question in our eyes.

Are Some Religions Incompatible with Democracy? A New Test

Given that questions remain about the compatibility of certain religions with democracy, it might be useful to reexamine the issue here. Let's start with what we know. We know that Protestant and Catholic countries tend to be democratic today and that Muslim countries tend to be authoritarian. This has already been demonstrated by some of the studies we just mentioned (Fish 2002; Karatnycky 2002). In and of itself, however, this does not establish a

---

2. Some of you may have noticed that this type of analysis is similar to employing Mill's Method of Difference (See Box 2.2, "The Comparative Method," in Chapter 2). The analyst begins by observing democracies and dictatorships in the world. She then looks for things that only democracies have in common (such as Protestantism) and for things that only dictatorships have in common (Catholicism). From this pattern of observations, the analyst then generates a general theory claiming that Protestantism causes democracy and that Catholicism impedes democracy. The fact that Catholic countries are largely democratic today clearly illustrates the central problem with this mode of scientific analysis; that is, no matter how many times you observe a Catholic dictatorship, it does not logically follow that Catholicism causes dictatorship.

clear link between these religions and the prospects for democracy. We also know that democracy originated in Protestant countries. But our question is not about where democracy originated. What we really want to know is whether democracy can be transplanted to countries dominated by different religions. The evidence to answer this question is not whether more Protestant countries are democratic than Catholic or Muslim countries at some specific moment in time. Instead, what we need to know is whether democracy is more or less likely to emerge and survive in countries that are dominated by Protestants, Muslims, or Catholics. In other words, we need to examine the effect of these religions on democracy *across time*. To do this, we need to know what effect being a Protestant, Catholic, or Muslim country has on (a) the probability of becoming democratic and (b) the probability of staying democratic. In other words, we would like to test the following hypotheses:

> *Catholic hypothesis:* Countries with a majority Catholic population are less likely to become and stay democratic.
>
> *Protestant hypothesis:* Countries with a majority Protestant population are more likely to become and stay democratic.
>
> *Islamic hypothesis:* Countries with a majority Muslim population are less likely to become and stay democratic.

In Table 7.1, we list the countries with majority Catholic, Protestant, and Muslim populations.

Although we have not addressed cultural diversity in this chapter, there is reason to think that high levels of cultural diversity may make countries less compatible with democracy. For example, Weingast (1997) argues that democracy can be sustained only if citizens can coordinate their beliefs about when the government has transgressed and when they should do something about this transgression. In many ways, this coordination of beliefs might be considered a "democratic culture"—something that is necessary for democracy to emerge and survive. It seems reasonable to think that this type of coordination is likely to be more difficult when there are many cultural groups in society. Other scholars have argued that ethnic diversity is particularly bad for democracy because it makes reaching compromises difficult and because it raises the risk of intercommunal violence (Dahl 1971; Horowitz 1993; Lijphart 1977; Rabushka and Shepsle 1972). We might suspect that countries with a large number of religious groups or a large number of cultural groups might also be problematic for democracy on similar grounds. As a result, we also evaluate the following hypotheses in our upcoming empirical analyses:

> *Ethnic group hypothesis:* Countries with a large number of ethnic groups are less likely to become and stay democratic.
>
> *Religious group hypothesis:* Countries with a large number of religious groups are less likely to become and stay democratic.

TABLE 7.1	**Countries with a Majority Muslim, Protestant, or Catholic Population**
Religion of majority	**Countries**
Muslim	Afghanistan, Albania, Algeria, Azerbaijan, Bahrain, Bangladesh, Brunei, Comoros, Djibouti, Egypt, Eritrea, Gambia, Guinea, Indonesia, Iran, Iraq, Jordan, Kuwait, Kyrgyzstan, Lebanon, Libya, Malaysia, Maldive Islands, Mali, Mauritania, Morocco, Niger, Oman, Pakistan, Qatar, Saudi Arabia, Senegal, Somalia, Sudan, Syria, Tajikistan, Tunisia, Turkey, Turkmenistan, United Arab Emirates, Uzbekistan, (Republic of) Yemen
Protestant	Angola, Antigua, Bahamas, Barbados, Denmark, Fiji, Finland, Iceland, Liberia, Marshall Islands, Namibia, Norway, Papua New Guinea, St. Kitts and Nevis, St. Vincent, Solomon Islands, South Africa, Sweden, Tonga, United Kingdom, United States, Vanuatu, Western Samoa
Catholic	Andorra, Argentina, Armenia, Austria, Belgium, Belize, Bolivia, Brazil, Burundi, Cape Verde, Chile, Colombia, Congo, Costa Rica, Croatia, Cyprus, Dominica, Dominican Republic, Ecuador, El Salvador, Equatorial Guinea, France, Gabon, Greece, Grenada, Guatemala, Haiti, Honduras, Hungary, Ireland, Italy, Kiribati, Liechtenstein, Lithuania, Luxembourg, Macedonia, Malta, Mexico, Micronesia, Nicaragua, Panama, Paraguay, Peru, Philippines, Poland, Portugal, Romania, Rwanda, St. Lucia, San Marino, Sao Tomé and Principe, Seychelles, Slovakia, Slovenia, Spain, Uruguay, Venezuela, Yugoslavia

Note: "Catholic" includes both Roman Catholic and Orthodox religions.

Source: Data are from Przeworski and colleagues (2000). Their data are based on *Atlas Narodov Mira* (1964; open library.org/).

Cultural group hypothesis: Countries with a large number of cultural groups are less likely to become and stay democratic.

Let's start by looking at the emergence of democracy. In order to test our hypotheses about the cultural determinants of democracy, we conduct a similar statistical analysis to the one we did in Chapter 6 when we examined the economic determinants of democracy. The results of our statistical analysis are shown in Table 7.2. The dependent variable, which is listed at the top of the table, is the thing we want to explain. In this case, the dependent variable is the probability that a country becomes a democracy given that it was a dictatorship in the previous year. In other words, our dependent variable concerns the *emergence* of democracy. Our independent, or explanatory, variables, which are listed in the first column, are the things we think might affect the emergence of democracy. Next to each independent variable (in the other columns) is a coefficient with a corresponding standard error beneath it in parentheses. Recall that the sign of the coefficient is important because it tells us the

TABLE 7.2 Cultural and Economic Determinants of Democratic Emergence

Dependent variable: Probability that a country will be a democracy this year if it was a dictatorship last year

Independent Variables	Model 1	Model 2	Model 3	Model 4	Model 5
Muslim majority	−0.28**	−0.18	−0.23	−0.25	−0.18 ← Coefficient
	(0.12)	(0.16)	(0.17)	(0.19)	(0.16) ← Standard error
Protestant majority	−0.56	−0.42	−0.40	−0.45	−0.43
	(0.35)	(0.38)	(0.38)	(0.39)	(0.38)
Catholic majority	0.33***	0.31***	0.26**	0.26**	0.31**
	(0.10)	(0.12)	(0.12)	(0.13)	(0.13)
GDP per capita		0.00004*	0.00003*	0.00003*	0.00004*
		(0.00002)	(0.00002)	(0.00002)	(0.00002)
Growth in GDP per capita		−0.02**	−0.02**	−0.02**	−0.02**
		(0.01)	(0.01)	(0.01)	(0.01)
Oil production		−0.15	−0.12	−0.13	−0.15
		(0.18)	(0.19)	(0.19)	(0.18)
Effective number of ethnic groups			−0.02		
			(0.02)		
Effective number of religious groups				−0.06	
				(0.09)	
Effective number of cultural groups					0.02
					(0.08)
Constant	−2.06***	−2.05***	−1.94***	−1.91***	−2.06***
	(0.07)	(0.10)	(0.13)	(0.23)	(0.19)
Number of observations	4,379	2,578	2,563	2,578	2,563
Log-likelihood	−418.75	−318.64	−317.85	−318.46	−318.35

$*p < 0.10; **p < 0.05; ***p < 0.01$

Note: Data on religious groups and whether a country is a democracy are from Przeworski and colleagues (2000), updated through 2000; data on GDP per capita and growth in GDP per capita are from the Penn World Tables 6.1 (2004; datacentre.chass.utoronto.ca/pwt61/); and data on ethnic and cultural groups are from Fearon (2003). The results shown in Table 7.2 come from a dynamic probit model. Standard errors are shown in parentheses.

slope of the relationship between the independent variable and the dependent variable. A positive coefficient indicates that an increase in the independent variable is associated with an increase in the probability that a country will become a democracy. A negative coefficient indicates that an increase in the independent variable is associated with a reduction in the probability that a country will become a democracy. If the statistical analysis reveals that there is no relationship between an independent variable and the probability that a country will become a democracy, then the coefficient will be zero.

Recall also that the standard error beneath the coefficient helps us to determine how confident we should be in our results. We tend to be confident that we have found a pattern in the data that is likely to be found more generally when the standard error is small relative to the size of its corresponding coefficient. Typically, as a rule of thumb, we say that we have found a statistically significant relationship whenever the coefficient is bigger than twice the size of the standard error. It is common practice for political scientists to place stars next to the coefficients of variables that are considered statistically significant; more stars signal higher statistical significance. Independent variables that do not have a coefficient with stars—where the size of the coefficient is not sufficiently large relative to the size of its standard error—are considered statistically insignificant. An independent variable is considered statistically insignificant if we don't feel confident ruling out the possibility that the observed pattern between this variable and the dependent variable arose by chance.[3]

So, what do the results in Table 7.2 tell us? Model 1 in the first column examines how having a Muslim, Catholic, or Protestant majority affects the emergence of democracy without taking anything else into account. As predicted, the coefficient on "Muslim majority" is negative and statistically significant. This means that countries with a Muslim majority are less likely to become democratic. The coefficient on "Protestant majority" is statistically insignificant, meaning that we cannot confidently rule out the possibility that there is no relationship between Protestantism and the emergence of democracy. The coefficient on "Catholic majority" is positive and statistically significant. This coefficient indicates that, contrary to the claims of scholars such as Huntington (1993), Catholicism is positively associated with the emergence of democracy.

If we looked only at the results from Model 1, we would have to conclude that majority Muslim countries are bad for the emergence of democracy. We know, however, that these countries tend to be poorer than most other countries. We also know that poor countries are less likely to become democratic than rich countries (see Chapter 6). Thus, it might be the case that Muslim countries are less likely to become democratic not because they are Muslim but because they are poor. To test this possibility, we include in Model 2 the three economic variables that were used in Chapter 6 to examine the economic determinants of democracy: GDP per capita, economic growth, and oil production. Once we take these economic factors

---

3. For a more detailed discussion of how we determine whether an observed pattern in the data is "real" or not, see the material on significance tests covered in the Appendix at the end of Chapter 6, "An Intuitive Take on Statistical Analyses."

into account, we see that the coefficient on "Muslim majority" is no longer statistically significant. This means that we can no longer be confident in ruling out the possibility that there is no relationship between Islam and the emergence of democracy. The evidence suggests that Muslim countries are less likely to become democratic not because they are Muslim but because they are poor. If these countries can develop economically and become wealthier, then there is no reason to think, based on the evidence presented here, that being majority Muslim will pose a significant barrier to them becoming democratic.

What about our other cultural hypotheses? Does having more ethnic, religious, or cultural groups decrease the likelihood that a country will become democratic? None of the coefficients on our ethnic, religious, and cultural diversity variables are statistically significant. As a result, we cannot confidently rule out the possibility that these forms of diversity are unrelated to the emergence of democracy.

Having examined how various cultural factors affect the emergence of democracy, we now investigate how they influence the survival of democracy. The results of our analysis are shown in Table 7.3. The dependent variable is now the probability of democratic *survival*. As a result, whether a coefficient is positive or negative tells us whether an increase in our independent variables is associated with an increase or decrease in the probability of democratic survival. So what do the results tell us? Model 1 in the first column examines how having a Muslim, Protestant, or Catholic majority affects the probability of democratic survival without taking anything else into account. It turns out that there were no democracies with a Protestant majority that ever collapsed into dictatorship in our sample of countries and time period. As a result, it was not possible to include this variable in the analysis. What this indicates, though, is that having a Protestant majority is strongly associated with democratic survival. What about having a Muslim or Catholic majority? The coefficient on "Muslim majority" is negative and statistically significant. This means that countries with a Muslim majority are less likely to survive as democracies. The coefficient on "Catholic majority" is not statistically significant, meaning that we cannot confidently rule out the possibility that there is no relationship between Catholicism and the survival of democracy.

If we looked only at the results from Model 1, we would have to conclude that having a Muslim majority is bad for the survival of democracy. But again, it is important to remember that majority Muslim countries tend to be poorer than most other countries. We know that poor countries are less likely to survive as democracies than rich countries (see Chapter 6). Thus, it might be the case that Muslim countries are less likely to survive as democracies not because they are Muslim but because they are poor. To test this possibility, we again include in Model 2 the three economic variables that were used in Chapter 6 to examine the economic determinants of democracy. Once we take account of these economic determinants, we see that the coefficient on "Muslim majority" is no longer statistically significant. This means that we can no longer be confident in ruling out the possibility that there is no relationship between Islam and the survival of democracy. The evidence suggests that Muslim countries are less likely to survive as democracies not because they are Muslim but because

TABLE 7.3 Cultural and Economic Determinants of Democratic Survival

Dependent variable: Probability that a country will be a democracy this year if it was a democracy last year

Independent Variables	Model 1	Model 2	Model 3	Model 4	Model 5
Muslim majority	−0.61***	−0.30	−0.46	−0.48	−0.39
	(0.18)	(0.26)	(0.28)	(0.30)	(0.27)
Protestant majority[†]					
Catholic majority	0.02	−0.27*	−0.41**	−0.43*	−0.39**
	(0.13)	(0.16)	(0.20)	(0.22)	(0.18)
GDP per capita		0.0001***	0.0001***	0.0001***	0.0001***
		(0.00003)	(0.00003)	(0.00003)	(0.00003)
Growth in GDP per capita		0.02*	0.02*	0.02*	0.02*
		(0.01)	(0.01)	(0.01)	(0.01)
Oil production		0.29	0.43	0.35	0.40
		(0.31)	(0.31)	(0.29)	(0.31)
Effective number of ethnic groups			−0.09*		
			(0.05)		
Effective number of religious groups				−0.19	
				(0.15)	
Effective number of cultural groups					−0.23***
					(0.12)
Constant	2.06***	1.50***	1.88***	1.92***	1.99***
	(0.10)	(0.16)	(0.28)	(0.37)	(0.30)
Number of observations	2,408	1,784	1,784	1,784	1,784
Log-likelihood	−252.28	−163.19	−161.41	−162.33	−161.74

*p < 0.10; **p < 0.05; ***p < 0.01

† No democracy with a Protestant majority ever failed to survive in this time period. As a result, it is not possible to include this variable.

Note: Data on religious groups and whether a country is a democracy are from Przeworski and colleagues (2000), updated through 2000; data on GDP per capita and growth in GDP per capita are from the Penn World Tables 6.1 (2004; datacentre.chass.utoronto.ca); and data on ethnic and cultural groups are from Fearon (2003). The results shown in Table 7.3 come from a dynamic probit model. Standard errors are shown in parentheses.

they are poor. If these countries can develop economically and become wealthier, then there is no reason to think, based on the evidence presented here, that being majority Muslim will pose a significant barrier to democratic survival.

What about the other hypotheses? Does ethnic, religious, or cultural diversity decrease the likelihood of democratic survival? The results in Models 3 through 5 indicate that countries with a large number of ethnic or cultural groups are less likely to stay democratic. This is because the coefficients on the variables capturing ethnic and cultural diversity are both negative and statistically significant. We cannot confidently rule out that there is no relationship between the number of religious groups in a country and the survival of democracy. This is because the coefficient on the variable capturing religious diversity is not statistically significant.

So what conclusions can we draw from our "cultural" analysis of the emergence and survival of democracy? First, there is no compelling evidence that predominantly Muslim countries are less likely to become democratic or less likely to stay democratic. It is true that Muslim countries typically have authoritarian forms of government at present. However, there is reason to believe that this has more to do with the fact that they tend to be poor than because they are Muslim.

Second, majority Protestant countries do not seem more likely to become democratic than other countries. Still, if a majority Protestant country does become democratic for some reason, then it is likely to stay democratic. This is illustrated by the fact that there are no examples in our data set (1950–2000) of a majority Protestant democracy ever collapsing into dictatorship. It is difficult to determine, though, whether this is the result of religion or wealth, as Protestant democracies tend to be wealthy.

Third, predominantly Catholic countries are significantly more likely to become democratic than other countries. This runs counter to the traditional argument that Catholic countries do not provide fertile terrain for the emergence of democracy. It is unclear why having a Catholic majority might increase the likelihood of transitioning to democracy. Still, even though Catholic countries are more likely to become democratic, they seem to have a hard time staying democratic. The results in Table 7.3 when we take account of economic factors indicate that majority Catholic countries are less likely to remain democratic than other countries. In this book's concluding chapter, we will explore the possibility that particular types of political institutions may make democratic consolidation difficult. These institutions have been linked to democratic instability in Latin American countries, many of which have Catholic majorities. Thus, there are reasons to believe that the negative association between Catholicism and democratic stability that we have observed here is not causal in nature.

Fourth, ethnically, religiously, or culturally diverse countries do not seem less likely to undergo a democratic transition than homogeneous countries. In other words, diversity of these kinds does not seem to destabilize dictatorships. In contrast, ethnic and cultural diversity do seem to destabilize democracies. Democracy is significantly less likely to survive in countries that have many ethnic or cultural groups; the number of religious groups does not seem to matter. One interpretation of these results is that some sort of shared values or beliefs is required for democracy, but not for authoritarianism, to persist (Weingast 1997).

Finally, economic factors continue to have an important impact on democracy even when we take account of various cultural features. As modernization theory would predict, and as we found in Chapter 6, wealthy countries are more likely to become democratic and stay democratic. Economic growth is good for both dictatorships and democracies—economic growth reduces the likelihood of a democratic transition, and it reduces the likelihood of democratic collapse. One result that differs somewhat from those in the previous chapter is that we are no longer confident of ruling out the possibility that there is no relationship between being an oil producer and the emergence of democracy once we take account of various cultural features. This is a result that requires more study.

EXPERIMENTS AND CULTURE

So far we have examined how culture might affect democracy using survey evidence and statistical analyses. We now turn to some experimental results that also suggest that culture might be important for the establishment and survival of democracy. The experiments that we are going to examine involve individuals playing what are known as Ultimatum Games and Dictator Games.

In an Ultimatum Game, individuals (known as subjects or players) are paired together. The first player, often called the "proposer," is provisionally allotted a divisible "pie" (usually money). The proposer then offers a portion of the total pie to the second player, called the "responder." The responder, knowing both the offer and the total amount of the pie, can then either accept or reject the proposer's offer. If the responder accepts, then he receives the amount offered, and the proposer gets the remainder (the pie minus the offer). If the responder rejects the offer, then neither receives any money. In either case, the game ends, and the two subjects receive their winnings and leave. In the experiments, the players are anonymous to each other, and the games use substantial sums of money. An example might help. Imagine that the proposer is given $100 and offers $40 to the responder. If the responder accepts the offer, then the responder keeps the $40, and the proposer keeps the remaining $60. If the responder rejects the offer, then both the responder and the proposer get nothing. The Dictator Game is essentially the same as the Ultimatum Game except that responders are not given an opportunity to reject the offer; they simply get whatever the proposer dictates. You should think about how much of the pie you would offer if you were the proposer. What types of offers would you accept or reject if you were the responder? Would the offer you make depend on whether you were playing the Ultimatum Game or the Dictator Game?

Why might a researcher want to compare the behavior of individuals in the Ultimatum Game with their behavior in a Dictator Game? To answer this question, think about why someone might make a positive offer in the Ultimatum Game. There are two potential reasons. First, the proposer might make a positive offer out of a sense of fairness. In other words, the proposer realizes that he was randomly chosen to receive the pie and thinks it only fair that he should offer some of it to the responder. Second, the proposer might make a positive offer because of fear of rejection. In other words, the proposer makes only a positive offer in order to reduce the risk that he would get nothing if the responder rejects it. In the Dictator Game, there is no fear of rejection, because the responder cannot reject the proposer's offer. As a result, any positive offer in the Dictator Game must be from a sense of fairness. Thus, the Dictator Game allows the experimenter to distinguish between proposers who make positive offers out of a sense of fairness and those who make positive offers out of a fear of rejection.

What would you expect individuals who care only about their own share of the pie to do if they acted as the proposer in an Ultimatum Game? What would they do if they acted as the responder? We sometimes refer to individuals who care only about their own share of the pie as *Homo economicus*. It turns out that we would expect a proposer who cares only about his own share of the pie to offer ε to the responder, where ε is only slightly larger than 0. We would then expect the responder to accept this offer because receiving ε is clearly better than getting nothing, which is what both players get if the responder refuses. Thus, if we continue our example from above and assume that we are in the world of *Homo economicus,* we would expect the proposer to get $100 - \varepsilon$ and the responder to get ε. Things look only slightly different in the Dictator Game. Now we would expect a proposer who cares only about his own share of the pie not to offer anything to the responder and to simply keep all of the $100 for himself. Remember, these are the theoretical predictions if we were in the world of *Homo economicus.* But what do we actually observe when individuals play this game in an experimental setting?

Both the Ultimatum and Dictator Games have been played in numerous experimental settings in virtually all of the industrialized democracies in the world. Typically, the experiment involves a group of students who are paired up anonymously in a computer lab. One student is randomly chosen to be the proposer and the other becomes the responder. The game then begins. What do you think happens in these games? Somewhat remarkably, there is a great deal of similarity in the results produced by these experiments despite the fact that they are conducted in different countries around the world. It turns out that the modal offer—the most common offer—in student populations playing the Ultimatum Game is almost always 50 percent, with the mean, or average, offer varying somewhere between 40 percent and 45 percent. Offers of less than 20 percent of the pie are rejected by responders about half the time. In contrast, the modal offer in student populations playing the Dictator Game is normally 0 percent. The large difference in the modal offers between the two games would suggest that many of the positive offers in the Ultimatum Game come about because of a fear of rejection, rather than a sense of fairness, on the part of the proposer. Although this is certainly true, the mean offer in the Dictator Game is still typically in the 20 percent to 30 percent range. In other words, some individuals still make quite large positive offers even when they know that their offers cannot be rejected. These proposers are clearly acting out of a sense of fairness; they exhibit what some call a prosocial behavior. Overall, the results from these experiments indicate that a substantial portion of the students playing these games do not approximate the theoretical *Homo economicus*.

Several scholars began to wonder whether these deviations from the theoretical predictions for *Homo economicus* were evidence of a universal pattern of human behavior or whether the deviations varied with an individual's economic and cultural setting. Do some cultures exhibit behavior that more closely resembles that of *Homo economicus* than the behavior of other cultures? Of course, these questions cannot be answered with any satisfaction simply by looking at experimental results from student populations around the world. Although there are cultural differences among students in different countries, these differences are quite small compared with the range of cultural environments that exist in the world. As a result, a group composed primarily of anthropologists and economists decided to conduct experiments using Ultimatum and Dictator Games in fifteen small-scale societies in twelve countries on five continents (Gintis 2003; Henrich et al. 2001, 2005). These societies exhibited a wide range of cultural and economic environments: foraging societies, slash-and-burn horticulture groups, nomadic herding groups, and sedentary, small-scale agriculturalist societies. Information on these societies is shown in Table 7.4.

How did the individuals in these societies act in the Ultimatum and Dictator Games? The offers made in the Ultimatum Game are shown in a bubble plot in Figure 7.3. Data from an experiment using students at the University of Pittsburgh are included as a benchmark against which to compare the results from the fifteen small-scale societies. The size of the bubble at each location along each row represents the proportion of the sample that made a particular offer. The right edge of the lightly shaded horizontal gray bar gives the mean offer for that group. For example, if you look at the row associated with the Machiguenga from Peru, you can see that the mode (the most common offer) is 0.15, the secondary mode is 0.25, and the mean is 0.26.

The information in Figure 7.3 illustrates that no society conforms well to the predictions for *Homo economicus*. The second thing to note, though, is that there is much more variation in the offers made in the fifteen small-scale societies than in the student populations of the advanced industrial countries. Remember that the mean offer among students varies from about 40 to 45 percent in Ultimatum Games. In contrast, the range for the mean offers in the fifteen small-scale societies is much larger, varying from 26 percent for the Machiguenga in Peru to 58 percent for the Lamelara in Indonesia. Whereas the modal offer among students is 50 percent, the modal offer among the fifteen small-scale societies ranges from 15 percent to 50 percent.

Although we do not show any evidence here, it turns out that the rejection rates in these fifteen societies also vary quite considerably between the groups. Whereas offers below 20 percent in industrial democracies are rejected with a probability of 0.4 to 0.6, the experimenters found that rejections of very low offers such as this are quite rare in some groups.

TABLE 7.4	**Fifteen Small-Scale Societies**		
Group	**Country**	**Environment**	**Economic base**
Machiguenga	Peru	Tropical forest	Horticulture
Quichua	Ecuador	Tropical forest	Horticulture
Achuar	Ecuador	Tropical forest	Horticulture
Hadza	Tanzania	Savanna-woodlands	Foraging
Aché	Paraguay	Semi-tropical woodlands	Foraging and horticulture
Tsimané	Bolivia	Tropical forest	Horticulture
Au	Papua New Guinea	Mountainous tropical forest	Foraging and horticulture
Gnau	Papua New Guinea	Mountainous tropical forest	Foraging and horticulture
Mapuche	Chile	Temperate plains	Small-scale farming
Torguud	Mongolia	High-altitude desert, seasonally flooded grassland	Pastoralism
Khazax	Mongolia	High-altitude desert, seasonally flooded grassland	Pastoralism
Sangu (farm/herd)	Tanzania	Savanna-woodlands, seasonally flooded grassland	Agro-pastoralists
Orma	Kenya	Savanna-woodlands	Pastoralism
Lamelara	Indonesia	Tropical island coast	Foraging-trade
Shona	Zimbabwe	Savanna-woodlands	Farming

For example, the Machiguenga rejected only one offer even though 75 percent of the offers made were below 30 percent. In some groups, though, the experimenters found that rejection rates were quite high even when offers were over 50 percent of the pie. For example, the Au and the Gnau in Papua New Guinea were equally likely to reject offers that were below or above 50 percent. The results from the Dictator Game also showed considerable variation. Among student populations, the distribution of offers has a mode at zero and a secondary mode at 50 percent. In contrast, the Orma had a mode at 50 percent, and the Hadza had a mode at 10 percent. There were no zero offers among the Tsimané; the mean was 32 percent, and the mode was 25 percent.

What explains this large variation in behavior between the different cultural groups? The researchers found that individual level characteristics such as the proposer's (or responder's)

FIGURE 7.3   **Offers from an Ultimatum Game**

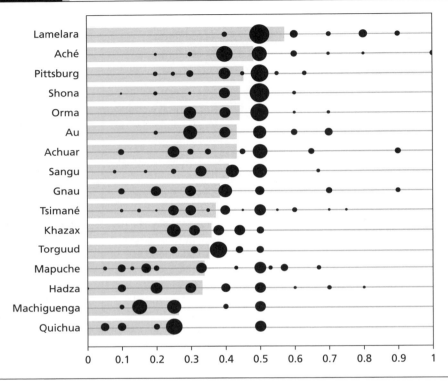

Note: The size of the bubble at each location along each row represents the proportion of the sample that made a particular offer. The right edge of the lightly shaded horizontal gray bar gives the mean offer for that group.

Source: Henrich and colleagues (2005).

sex, age, education, and wealth could not explain the variation. Instead, what mattered was how group-specific conditions such as social institutions or cultural fairness norms affected individual preferences or expectations. The researchers rank ordered the fifteen societies along two dimensions: (a) payoffs to cooperation and (b) market integration. *Payoffs to cooperation* refer to how important it is to cooperate with non-immediate kin in economic production. Market integration refers to how much the groups relied on market exchange in their everyday lives. At the low end of the "payoffs to cooperation" dimension were the Machiguenga and Tsimané, whose members rarely engaged in cooperative production with individuals outside of the family. At the high end of this dimension were the Lamelara, whose members hunted whales in large canoes manned by twelve or more people at a time. The researchers expected that groups in which the payoffs to cooperation were high would make high offers in situations like the Ultimatum Game. At the low end of the "market integration" dimension were the Hadza, whose members rarely engaged in market activity. At the high end of this dimension were the Orma, whose members often worked for wages and sold livestock. The researchers expected that groups with greater market integration would make high offers in situations like the Ultimatum Game. This is because the more frequently people experience market transactions, the more they should also experience abstract sharing principles concerning behavior toward strangers. As predicted, a statistical analysis revealed that higher values on both dimensions were, indeed, associated with higher mean offers in the Ultimatum Game. In fact, fully 68 percent of the variance in offers could be explained by these two variables alone.

How should we interpret these results? One interpretation is that the individuals in these societies looked for similar situations in their everyday lives when they were faced with the novel situations presented by the Ultimatum Game and the Dictator Game. Rather than reason through the logic of the game, it seems that they asked themselves the following question: "What familiar situation is this game like?" They then acted in a way appropriate for this analogous situation. Consider the hyperfair offers and the frequent rejections of these offers among the Au and Gnau in Papua New Guinea. This behavior can be explained by the culture of gift giving in these societies. Providing expensive gifts is a signal of prestige and importance in these societies. At the same time, it is recognized that accepting gifts commits one to reciprocate at some future time determined by the gift giver. Moreover, particularly generous gifts put you in a clearly subordinate position. The culture of gift giving not only explains the generous offers made by the Au and Gnau proposers but also explains why large offers were so readily rejected by the responders; these "excessively" large gifts tended to produce anxiety about the unspoken strings that were attached to them.

Consider now the low offers and high rejection rates of the Hadza. This behavior is entirely compatible with the fact that Hadza hunters often try to avoid sharing their meat. One ethnographer goes so far as to call this reluctance to share "tolerated theft." What about the Lamelara's tendency to divide the pie equally or to offer the respondent slightly more than a fair share? In real life, when a Lamelara whaling crew returns with a large catch, a designated person carefully divides the whale into predesignated parts allocated to the harpooner, crew members, and others participating in the hunt, as well as the sailmaker, members of the hunters' corporate group, and other community members. The Lamelara may well have seen dividing the large pie in the Ultimatum Game as similar to dividing up a whale. Similar stories to these could be told to explain the behavior of individuals from the other societies in the study.

By now, you're probably wondering what these experiments have to do with culture and democracy. The results from these experiments suggest that culture might be considered a shared way of playing everyday games that has evolved over many years (Bednar and Page 2007). It seems clear that individual choices are shaped by the economic and social interactions of everyday life. It appears that people often search for analogous situations when trying to figure out how to act in new situations. If this is true, then it seems reasonable to think that the shared way of playing games in some societies might be less compatible with the game of democracy than it is in other societies. For example, the game of democracy often requires cooperation, competition, and compromise. Societies that already require this type of behavior in their everyday "games" should find it easier to adopt and support democratic institutions. In contrast, societies in which individuals are engaged in games that do not encourage this type of behavior will find it much harder to consolidate democracy.

CONCLUSION

As we noted at the very beginning of this chapter, the notion that political institutions, such as democracy and dictatorship, are more suited to some cultures is not new. The rather vague claims made by scholars such as Montesquieu and Mill in the eighteenth and nineteenth centuries regarding the compatibility of democracy with particular cultures were later taken up in a more systematic fashion by cultural modernization theory. Cultural modernization theory argues that economic development produces certain cultural changes and that it is these cultural changes that lead to democratization (Inglehart and Welzel 2005). A key cultural change according to this line of reasoning is the emergence of what political scientists call a "civic culture."

For many, the existence of a civic culture is seen as a prerequisite for the successful emergence and survival of democracy (Almond and Verba [1963] 1989; Inglehart 1990; Inglehart and Welzel 2005). In addition to its importance for democracy, a civic culture is also seen by some as crucial for the good performance of government (Putnam 1993, 2000). Although there are strong proponents of the idea that democracy requires a civic culture, others question the direction of causality. Does a civic culture produce democracy, or does experience with democracy produce a civic culture? As we suggested earlier, the answer to both of these questions may well be "yes." Societal development may foster democratization by producing certain cultural changes, but it may also affect democratization through other channels such as those examined in Chapter 6. Similarly, it seems reasonable that experience with democracy can contribute to producing a civic culture that in turn reinforces democratic practice in the future. If we are correct, there may be a virtuous cycle linking social development, cultural change, and democratic outcomes.

More recently, the focus of cultural arguments regarding democracy has shifted to questions of whether certain religions are compatible with democratic institutions. Given the current state of world affairs, it is not surprising that particular attention has been paid to whether Islam is compatible with democracy. As we indicate in this chapter, though, a quick glance at the history of these types of arguments should make one very cautious of unthinkingly accepting that certain religions are incompatible with democracy. For example, some political scientists used to claim as recently as the 1970s that Catholicism was antithetical to democracy, but few do now, given how firmly established democracy has become in many Catholic countries around the world.

Many scholars point to particular doctrines to explain why such and such a religion is inimical to democracy. As we have sought to demonstrate, however, virtually all religions, including Islam, have some doctrinal elements that seem incompatible with democracy and others that seem compatible (Przeworski, Cheibub, and Limongi 1998). This hardly seems a firm basis on which to draw such strong conclusions about the incompatibility of certain religions with democracy. Moreover, there is growing empirical evidence that the stance of different religions toward various political institutions often depends less on the content of their doctrine and more on the interests and strategic concerns of religious leaders (Kalyvas 1996, 1998, 2000). When combined with a vast literature indicating how culture is constructed and malleable rather than primordial and inherited, this growing evidence helps to explain why all religions have historically been compatible with a broad range of political institutions, including democracy.

Despite the widely held belief by many that Islam is incompatible with democracy, the empirical analyses that we conducted in this chapter suggest that there is little reason to believe that majority Muslim countries cannot become and remain democratic once we take account of their wealth. To a large extent, our analyses indicate that the hurdle these majority Muslim countries need to overcome to be able to sustain democracy has less to do with the fact that they are Muslim and more to do with the fact that they are poor.

Many arguments about the cultural determinants of democracy implicitly assume that democracy is increasingly likely to arise and be sustained as more citizens come to appreciate the benefits of democracy. But "liking democracy" is almost certainly not a sufficient condition for democracy, and it may not even be a necessary one. Indeed, a more cynical view suggests that democracy is at best most people's second favorite form of government. Recall from the comparison of the behavior of individuals in the ultimatum and dictator games that most individuals might take most or all of the pie when they are confident that they can get away with it. Similarly, individuals might prefer monarchy if they were allowed to be the ruler, but they reluctantly accept democracy when they realize that they, or their chosen one, may not be permitted to rule. Such strategic calculations turn out to be important in the transition process from dictatorship to democracy. We focus on precisely that in the next chapter.

KEY CONCEPTS

civic culture *228*

constructivist arguments *224*

cultural modernization theory *226*

differential item functioning *234*

primordialist arguments *224*

social capital *229*

social desirability bias *233*

PROBLEMS

1. Consider the following argument.

Major premise: If Catholicism is incompatible with democracy, then Catholic countries are more likely to be dictatorships than democracies.

Minor premise: Catholic countries are more likely to be democracies than dictatorships.

Conclusion: Therefore, Catholicism is not incompatible with democracy.

    a. Is this a valid or an invalid argument?

    b. What form of categorical syllogism is this (affirming the antecedent/consequent or denying the antecedent/consequent)?

2. Consider the following argument.

Major premise: If Islam is incompatible with democracy, then Islamic countries are more likely to be dictatorships than democracies.

Minor premise: Most Islamic countries around the world today are dictatorships.

Conclusion: Therefore, Islam is incompatible with democracy.

    a. Is this a valid or an invalid argument?

    b. What form of categorical syllogism is this?

3. "If a democracy has a civic culture, then it will stay a democracy." In this statement, is "having a civic culture" an example of a sufficient condition or a necessary condition?

4. Obtain a copy of M. Steven Fish's (2002) article "Islam and Authoritarianism" from the journal *World Politics* (55:4–37), using your institution's library resources. Read the article and then answer the following questions.

    a. What is Fish's dependent variable? How is it measured? What is the primary source for the dependent variable? What is the main independent variable? How is it measured?

    b. What is the main hypothesis of this article? What evidence would falsify this hypothesis?

    c. Why does Fish believe that having a predominantly Islamic religious tradition might be detrimental to the level of democracy in a country? Fish examines four proposed causal mechanisms for why this might be the case. Describe each of these four causal mechanisms in a sentence or two.

    d. Fish tests his theory using statistical analyses. Given his dependent variable, what sign (positive or negative) does Fish predict for the coefficient on his primary explanatory variable? *Hint*: See your answers to parts a and b above. What sign does he find? Is the coefficient on this variable statistically significant? How do you know? *Hint*: The answer is in Table 3, column 1, page 13. Interpret these results in substantive terms. In other words, what does Fish find about the relationship between Islam and a country's level of democracy?

    e. Which of the four potential causal mechanisms does Fish find the most evidence for? How do you know?

    f. One of the conclusions that Fish reaches is that Islam is a hindrance to democracy because women are not treated equally in Islamic countries. He reaches this conclusion using Freedom House as his measure of democracy. Why might it be problematic to use Freedom House to examine the impact that the unequal treatment of women in Islamic countries has on democracy? Find the complete list of questions that are used to create a country's Freedom House score by going to https://freedomhouse.org/. Identify which questions make it problematic to use Freedom House scores to test Fish's statement that Islam is bad for democracy because of its unequal treatment of women. Explain why these questions make Fish's statement more of a tautology than a scientific statement.

    g. Fish (p. 6) recognizes that one of the limitations to his analysis is that it looks at the relationship between Islam and a country's level of democracy only at a fixed point in time. Based on our discussion in the chapter, why might this be problematic for drawing inferences about whether Islam is incompatible with the emergence and the survival of democracy?

5. Obtain a copy of Andrew Beath, Fotini Christia, and Ruben Enikolopov's (2013) article "Empowering Women: Evidence from a Field Experiment in Afghanistan" from the journal *American Political Science Review* (107:540–557) using your institution's library resources. Read the article and then answer the following questions.

    a. Based on the information in the article, describe the state of gender equality in Afghanistan.

    b. What is the National Solidarity Program (NSP), and how is it connected to gender equality?

    c. The researchers in the study used an experiment to conduct an "impact evaluation" of the NSP as it related to gender equality. Describe their experiment in your own words. Be sure to note the difference between a village in the "treatment" group and a village in the "control" group.

    d. What were the researchers' hypotheses? Explain these in your own words.

    e. What data did the researchers use to test their hypotheses?

    f. What conclusions did the researchers draw based on the experimental evidence? Which of the hypotheses, if any, were consistent with the empirical evidence?

    g. What do you think this experiment can tell us, more generally, about the link between culture and democracy?

6. In this chapter, we presented a question from the World Values Survey that is sometimes used as an indicator of a country's level of democratic stability.

    a. Reread the possible responses to this survey question on page 233. Does this survey question provide a nominal, ordinal, or interval measure of democratic stability?

b. Write down two questions that you think should be put on a survey to elicit useful information about a country's level of democratic stability. Include the possible responses that you would provide as well. Do your survey questions provide nominal, ordinal, or interval measures of democratic stability?

7. The World Values Survey website (http://www.worldvaluessurvey.org/wvs.jsp) allows you to conduct online analyses. Click on the *Data and Documentation* link in the left-hand column. At the top of the page, you'll be able to click on a link that allows you to "download a quick reference to using the site." Read this document.

a. Use the information in the quick reference document to identify three survey questions from the latest wave of the World Values Survey that you find interesting. Use the online analysis tools to produce a map of the world for each of these survey questions. The maps will visually show how the responses to your survey questions vary across countries. Do the countries exhibit much variation in their responses? Do the geographic patterns that you see align with what you expected? If so, why? If not, why not?

b. Now choose one survey question of particular interest. Choose three countries and produce a graph showing how the responses to your survey question have changed over time in each of your three countries. Are the patterns over time similar across your three countries? Do the trends across time align with what you expected? If so, why? If not, why not?

8. In this chapter, we discussed some limitations that surveys face when addressing sensitive topics.

a. Explain what we mean by "social desirability bias" and why it can cause problems for drawing inferences from surveys.

b. Examine the survey question below that seeks to measure the level of support for racial diversity on university campuses.

"There should be more racial diversity on university campuses. Do you strongly agree, agree, neither agree nor disagree, disagree, or strongly disagree?"

Do you think this is a good survey question, or do you think that it is problematic? If you think it is problematic, explain why. What do you think the researcher can do to get a more accurate measure of the level of support for racial diversity on university campuses?

c. In the chapter, we discussed several methods that researchers can use to mitigate problems with sensitive items on surveys: better survey administration, list experiments, randomized response techniques, and endorsement experiments. Think of a sensitive topic that researchers might want to examine. Explain why the topic is sensitive, and then show how one of the methods mentioned above can be utilized to examine it.

d. While better survey administration, list experiments, randomized response techniques, and endorsement experiments can often mitigate concerns with sensitive survey items, they are not a cure-all. Can you think of potential problems that remain even with these innovative techniques?

9. In this chapter, we discussed some limitations that surveys face when respondents come from different regions, countries, ethnic groups, or cultures.

   a. Explain what we mean by "differential item functioning" and why it can cause problems for surveys.

   b. Examine the survey question below that seeks to determine an individual's ideological preferences.

   "In politics people sometimes talk of left and right. Where would you place yourself on a scale from 0 to 10, where 0 means left and 10 means right?"

   Suppose that this question was asked in a cross-national survey like the World Values Survey. Do you think this is a good survey question, or do you think that it is problematic? If you think it is problematic, explain why. What do you think the researcher can do to get a more accurate measure of an individual's ideological preferences?

   c. In the chapter, we discussed how researchers sometimes use anchoring vignettes to help overcome differential item functioning. Explain how anchoring vignettes can be helpful. Can you think of potential problems that might occur when using anchoring vignettes?

10. Obtain a copy of Claire L. Adida, David D. Laitin, and Marie-Anne Valfort's (2010) article "Identifying Barriers to Muslim Integration in France" from the journal *Proceedings of the National Academy of Sciences* (107:22384–22390) using your institution's library resources. Read the article and then answer the following questions.

    a. When it comes to measuring discrimination, the authors refer to "correspondence tests." What is a correspondence test?

    b. Why is it hard to identify a "Muslim effect" when it comes to facing discrimination in France?

    c. What strategy did the authors use to isolate a Muslim effect? Explain how this strategy worked.

    d. What did the authors find in their correspondence test?

11. *Coordination and Democracy Game*

Some political scientists argue that democracy can be sustained only if citizens can coordinate their beliefs about (a) what types of government actions are unacceptable and (b) when they ought to take action against the government in response. Countries in which citizens have coordinated their beliefs on these matters might be said to be characterized by a "democratic culture." We now analyze a Coordination and Democracy Game inspired by Weingast (1997) to explore this argument further.

Our Coordination and Democracy Game has three actors—a state, S, and two groups of citizens, A and B. The state must decide whether to transgress or not. If the state decides to transgress, then the two groups of citizens, A and B, must simultaneously decide whether to acquiesce to the state's transgression or challenge it. Only if both citizen groups "coordinate" on challenging the state will their challenge be successful. The most preferred outcome for the state is the one in which it transgresses and the two groups of citizens fail to coordinate on challenging it. The state prefers not to transgress if a transgression produces a successful challenge from the two citizen groups. The most preferred outcome for both citizen groups is obviously the one in which the state does not transgress in the first place. If the state does transgress, though, then both citizen groups prefer the outcome in which they successfully challenge the state to outcomes in which they either do not challenge it or they challenge unsuccessfully. Both citizen groups would rather not challenge the state than participate in an unsuccessful challenge. Figure 7.4 illustrates the game tree for our Coordination and Democracy Game along with cardinal payoffs capturing how the three actors evaluate the different outcomes. The payoffs to the state are listed first, those to group A are listed second, and those to group B are listed third.

The dashed line in Figure 7.4 indicates that when group A has to choose whether to acquiesce or challenge, it does not know whether group B will acquiesce or challenge. In other words, group A and group B do not make their choices sequentially; they must make them simultaneously without knowing what the other is going to do. You are more familiar with seeing this sort of thing being captured by a strategic form game. As a result, let's rewrite this particular subgame (the part of the game tree in Figure 7.4 shown in gray) in its equivalent strategic form. This strategic form game is shown in Figure 7.5. The only thing that is unusual about this game is that the first payoff in each cell of the payoff table belongs to the state (even though it is not a player in this particular subgame).

FIGURE 7.4   Coordination and Democracy Game

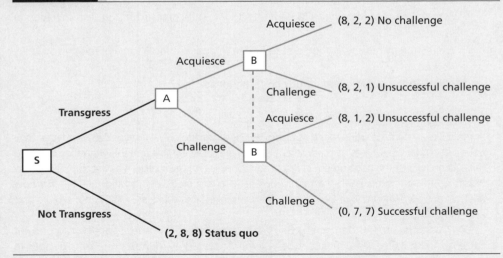

Note: A and B = citizen groups; S = state.

FIGURE 7.5	**Group Subgame**

		Group B	
		Acquiesce	Challenge
Group A	Acquiesce	8, 2, 2	8, 2, 1
	Challenge	8, 1, 2	0, 7, 7

a. Solve the strategic form game in Figure 7.5 for any Nash equilibria. *Hint:* Ignore the payoffs belonging to the state, because the state is not a player in this game. If you solve the game correctly, you will find two Nash equilibria.

b. What are the expected outcomes associated with the two Nash equilibria? What are the payoffs that each of the three players receive in the two Nash equilibria?

c. By solving the game in Figure 7.5, you have found out that the state can expect to receive one of two possible payoffs if it transgresses. Compare each of the state's potential payoffs from transgressing with the state's payoff from not transgressing. What can you say about the circumstances under which the state will or will not transgress against its citizens?

d. How does the Coordination and Democracy Game help illustrate the notion that the coordination of beliefs between different groups in society might be considered a "democratic culture"—something that is necessary for democracy to emerge and survive?

e. In the chapter, we note that some political scientists believe that democracy is hard to sustain in countries that are characterized by a large number of ethnic or cultural groups. How does the Coordination and Democracy Game that you have just examined help to explain why this might be the case?

f. Weingast (1997) extends the game in Figure 7.4 to allow the state to transgress against only one group while keeping the other one satisfied. Without constructing and solving such a game, what difference do you think this would make to the conclusions from our original Coordination and Democracy Game? Do you think that groups will find it easier or harder to coordinate their beliefs in this new setting? What difference do you think this new setting makes to the likelihood that democracy can survive?

8 Democratic Transitions

The most radical revolutionary will become a conservative the day after the revolution.

Hannah Arendt, quoted in *The New Yorker*, 1970

Those who make peaceful revolution impossible will make violent revolution inevitable.

John F. Kennedy, in a speech at the White House, 1962

- In this chapter, we examine bottom-up and top-down processes by which democratic transitions might occur. A bottom-up process is one in which the people rise up to overthrow an authoritarian regime in a popular revolution. A top-down process is one in which the dictatorial ruling elite introduces liberalizing reforms that ultimately lead to a democratic transition.

- Collective action theory throws light on why popular revolutions are so rare and why authoritarian regimes frequently appear incredibly stable. The prevalence of preference falsification under dictatorships helps to explain the puzzle as to why revolutions nearly always come as a surprise yet appear so inevitable in hindsight. Tipping models provide further insight into why revolutions are so unpredictable and why even small changes in people's preferences can sometimes rapidly transform previously subservient individuals into revolutionary protesters.

- Authoritarian elites occasionally introduce liberalization policies. The goal of these policies, though, is the stabilization of dictatorial rule in the form of a broadened dictatorship rather than a full democratic transition. We present a game-theoretic model of this liberalization process suggesting that top-down transitions cannot occur unless someone makes a mistake. Our analysis highlights the important role that information, beliefs, and uncertainty play in democratic transitions—and politics more generally.

The number of independent countries in the world grew from 70 in 1946 to 192 in 2008. This large increase in the number of independent countries was largely the result of the accelerated decolonization process forced upon European powers in the 1950s and 1960s and the breakup of the Soviet Union in the early 1990s. Figure 8.1 illustrates how the number of independent countries, dictatorships, and democracies in the world has changed since 1946. Despite the consensus that now exists in favor of democracy, it is only since 1992 that the number of democracies worldwide has actually been greater than the number of dictatorships. Of those countries that gained independence in the 1950s and 1960s, the vast majority soon became dictatorships. By 1977 there were 2.7 times as many dictatorships as there were democracies—only 27 percent of the countries in the world were democratic.

FIGURE 8.1 **Independent Countries, Democracies, and Dictatorships, 1946–2008**

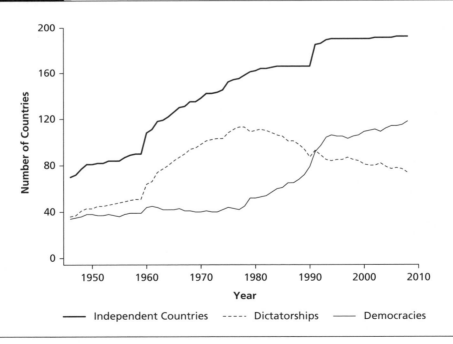

Source: Data are from Cheibub, Gandhi, and Vreeland (2010).

The mid-1970s, though, ushered in an era of democratization that Samuel Huntington (1991) has called the **"third wave of democratization."** On April 25, 1974, Portuguese military officers, unhappy with the ongoing

> The **third wave of democratization** refers to the surge in democratic transitions that have occurred around the world since 1974.

colonial conflicts in Mozambique and Angola, conducted a coup, triggering events that eventually led to the first democratic multiparty elections in Portugal since 1926. Although it was not foreseen at the time, the movement toward democracy in Portugal was soon to be followed by democratic stirrings elsewhere. For example, Greece returned to the democratic fold in 1974 following conflict with Turkey over the island of Cyprus, and Spain finally threw off four decades of dictatorial rule under General Francisco Franco in 1977. This reemergence of democracy in much of southern Europe in the 1970s was followed by a global wave of democratization over the next twenty or so years in Africa, Asia, Eastern Europe, and Latin America (see Box 8.1, "Three Waves of Democracy").

In the previous two chapters, we examined the economic and cultural determinants of the emergence and survival of democracy. Although those chapters were useful in giving us an aggregate view of democratization, you may be wondering how the democratic transition process actually plays out in practice. In this chapter, we flesh out two types of democratic transition processes—bottom-up and top-down processes—drawing on historical evidence primarily from Eastern Europe. A **bottom-up democratic transition** process is one in which the people rise up to overthrow an authoritarian regime in a popular revolution. In contrast, a **top-down democratic transition** process is one in which the dictatorial ruling elite introduces liberalizing

> A **bottom-up democratic transition** is one in which the people rise up to overthrow an authoritarian regime in a popular revolution. A **top-down democratic transition** is one in which the dictatorial ruling elite introduces liberalizing reforms that ultimately lead to a democratic transition.

ox 8.1   THREE WAVES OF DEMOCRACY

Samuel Huntington (1991, 15) has argued that the spread of democracy around the world has come in waves, where a wave "is a group of transitions from non-democratic to democratic regimes that occur within a specified period of time and that significantly outnumber transitions in the opposite direction during that period of time." Specifically, Huntington argues that there have been three waves of democracy in the modern world. The first "long" wave between 1828 and 1926 had its roots in the American and French Revolutions. Countries that transitioned to democracy during the first wave include Argentina, France, Great Britain, Iceland, Ireland, Italy, Switzerland, and the United States. The second "short" wave between 1943 and 1962 had its origins in World War II. Countries that became democratic during the second wave include Austria, Brazil, Costa Rica, India, Israel, Italy, Japan, Malaysia, Nigeria, Sri Lanka, Turkey, Uruguay, and West Germany. The third wave started with the end of the Portuguese dictatorship in 1974 and, arguably, continues to this day. Numerous authoritarian regimes have been replaced by democratic forms of government in Africa, Asia, Latin America, and southern and eastern Europe since the mid-1970s.

- First wave of democratization 1828–1926
- First reverse wave 1922–1942
- Second wave of democratization 1943–1962
- Second reverse wave 1958–1975
- Third wave of democratization 1974–

As with real waves, the three waves of democracy have experienced weaker undercurrents flowing in the opposite direction. Thus, between the three waves of democracy have been periods in which some, but not all, of the countries that had previously made the transition to democracy slipped back into dictatorship. For example, the 1920s and 1930s saw the collapse of democracy in much of Europe and a return to traditional forms of authoritarian rule. Transitions to dictatorship also predominated in the 1960s and early 1970s, with military intervention in much of Latin America—Peru (1962), Bolivia (1964), Brazil (1964), Argentina (1966), Ecuador (1972), Chile (1973), and Uruguay (1973). Numerous authoritarian regimes also emerged during the 1960s in Asia and Africa. Thus, Huntington's analysis suggests that the global spread of democracy over the last two centuries has been marked by an ebb and flow, largely characterized by a two-step-forward and one-step-back pattern.

reforms that ultimately lead to a democratic transition. Although most real-world cases are probably characterized by aspects of both types of transition process, it can be illuminating to examine these two transition processes separately.

BOTTOM-UP TRANSITIONS TO DEMOCRACY

We begin by examining bottom-up transitions to democracy.

East Germany 1989

One of the most dramatic examples of a bottom-up transition to democracy occurred in East Germany in November 1989 when protests on the streets of Leipzig and Berlin forced the Communist East German government to open up the Berlin Wall and allow free multiparty elections. The end result was the emergence of a democratic East Germany and the eventual reunification of Germany in 1990. Few alive at the time will forget the scenes of East and West German citizens happily dancing together on top of the Berlin Wall under the watchful eyes of the East German border guards—guards who until recently had been under strict orders to shoot anyone who attempted to cross the border.

Although the collapse of communism in East Germany, and Eastern Europe more generally, seems inevitable from our vantage point, it came as a complete surprise to most observers at the time. Until 1989, Communist regimes had proved to be remarkably stable. Indeed, there had been very few major uprisings or revolts in Eastern Europe during the entire postwar period. With the exception of revolts in East Germany in 1953, in Poland and Hungary in 1956, in Czechoslovakia in 1968, and in Poland in 1981, the Communist regimes of Eastern Europe had been relatively unchallenged for forty years or more. The revolts that did occur were put down by considerable force and direct Soviet military intervention, which only further discouraged Eastern Europeans from publicly opposing their Communist governments. Of all the governments in the Eastern bloc in 1989, the one in East Germany was arguably the most stable, prosperous, and hard-line. The East German secret police—the *Staatssicherheitsdienst,* or *Stasi* for short—were infamous for their ability to monitor and control the lives of ordinary citizens (Rosenberg 1996). In 1989 there were 85,000 full-time Stasi officers and more than 100,000 informers (Lohmann 1994, 59). With a population of slightly less than 17 million, these figures reveal the shocking fact that there was one Stasi officer or informer for every ninety East German citizens. To most observers, East Germany looked far from the brink of collapse in 1989.

The eventual collapse of communism in East Germany had much to do with the election of Mikhail Gorbachev to the position of general secretary of the Communist Party in the Soviet Union on March 11, 1985. To a large extent, Gorbachev inherited a Soviet Union in crisis. The economy that had seemed to perform so well during much of the postwar period had begun to stagnate by the mid-1980s, and the Soviet invasion of Afghanistan in 1979 to prop up a Communist government against Islamic rebels was increasingly taking up valuable resources. The 1986 Chernobyl disaster, in which a nuclear reactor exploded and spread radioactive fallout across much of Europe, revealed the dysfunctional nature of a deeply sclerotic and secretive Soviet state.

Gorbachev responded to these crises with two reform policies, called perestroika and glasnost. **Perestroika** was a policy aimed at liberalizing and regenerating the Soviet economy, whereas **glasnost** was a policy designed to increase political openness and encourage freedom of expression. We all know what happened to the Soviet Union and Eastern Europe, but it is important to recognize that Gorbachev was an ardent Communist who deeply believed in socialism. It was his hope that the policies of perestroika and glasnost would save the Soviet Union; he did not intend for them to facilitate its breakup, as they arguably did.

> **Perestroika**, or "economic restructuring," was a reform policy aimed at liberalizing and regenerating the Soviet economy. **Glasnost**, or "openness," was a reform policy aimed at increasing political openness.

The liberalizing reform policies introduced by Gorbachev in the Soviet Union had the effect of encouraging reformists and opposition groups in other countries in Eastern Europe. Following a big wave of strikes, the Polish government convened a conference in August 1988, known as the Roundtable Talks, with the main opposition group, Solidarity, to help reach a compromise on how to deal with the growing economic and political problems.

The result of these talks was the legalization of the independent trade union—Solidarity—and nationwide elections in 1989, which produced the first non-Communist prime minister in Eastern Europe in forty years. These changes in Poland served to encourage liberalizers in other Communist countries. For example, talks in Hungary, known as the Triangular Table Talks, which began about three months after those in Poland, resulted in cautious moves toward easing censorship and legalizing an independent trade union. When this brought little response from the Soviet Union, further reforms were introduced—the Communist Party renamed itself the Socialist Party, the country's name was changed from the Hungarian People's Republic to the Republic of Hungary, and multiparty elections were planned for 1990.

Although these changes in Eastern Europe were clearly significant, it should be noted that people at the time did not see them as signs of the imminent collapse of Communist control. The Chinese Communist Party's use of tanks and soldiers to violently disperse thousands of protesters in Tiananmen Square in June 1989 clearly illustrated that some Communist regimes were willing to use overwhelming force to retain power (see Box 8.2, "Tiananmen Square, Beijing, June 4, 1989").

| Box 8.2 | **TIANANMEN SQUARE, BEIJING, JUNE 4, 1989** |

Between April 15 and June 4, 1989, students, intellectuals, and labor activists held mass demonstrations against the Chinese Communist government in Tiananmen Square, Beijing. After the demonstrators refused to disperse, a hard-line faction in the Communist Party decided to use force against them. On May 20 the government declared martial law, and on June 4 army tanks and infantry troops were sent in to crush the protest. Estimates of civilian deaths vary from a low of 23 according to the

A Chinese man stands alone to block a line of tanks heading east on Beijing's Chang'an Boulevard in Tiananmen Square on June 4, 1989.

AP Photo/Jeff Widener

Chinese Communist Party to a high of 2,600 according to the Chinese Red Cross. The Chinese government then conducted widespread arrests to suppress remaining opposition groups.

Over the years, we have had dozens of Chinese students in our classes. Many have told us that they were unaware of the events that took place in Tiananmen Square in 1989. Our students are not unusual. In one study, only 15 out of 100 students at Beijing University were

The situation in East Germany began to change when Hungary decided to open its border with Austria in August 1989, thereby breaching the Iron Curtain for the first time. Although East Germans had always been relatively free to travel to other Communist countries in Eastern Europe, it had been all but impossible to get permission to travel to the West. In September 1989, 13,000 East Germans fled to the West across Hungary's open border. Thousands of other East Germans tried to reach the West by staging sit-ins at West German embassies in other Eastern European capitals, such as Prague. In response to these "refugees," the East German government eventually provided special trains to carry them to the West. Before doing so, East German officials took away their East German passports and claimed that they were expelling "irresponsible antisocial traitors and criminals." In a matter of weeks, thousands of East Germans had left their possessions and relatives behind to make a dash for freedom. The willingness of East Germans to leave so much behind is further evidence that few at the time foresaw the imminent collapse of the Communist system in East Germany.

Although tens of thousands of East Germans fled the country, a fledgling opposition group called Neues Forum (New Forum) surfaced in East Germany demanding reform.

able to recognize the "Tank Man" photo shown above (Lim 2015). This is despite the fact that this photo has become the international symbol for the Tiananmen Square protests.

The reason for this lack of awareness has to do with China's massive censorship apparatus. The events of Tiananmen Square are considered a political taboo and inappropriate for public conversations. Individuals in China are not allowed to make websites related to the events that took place in Tiananmen Square, and Internet searches, if they return anything, return only government mandated versions of the events. The system of censorship in China is massive. It is enforced by the government and by technology companies. "Internet content providers . . . may be fined or shut down if they fail to comply with government censorship guidelines. To comply with the government, each individual site privately employs up to 1,000 censors. Additionally, approximately 20,000–50,000 Internet police (*wang jing*) and Internet monitors (*wang guanban*) as well as an estimated 250,000–300,000 '50 cent party members' (*wumao dang*) at all levels of government—central, provincial, and local—participate in this huge effort" (King, Pan, and Roberts 2013, 1). Among other things, it is the job of censors to update the lists of sensitive words to take account of the new references and creative expressions that individuals have adopted to beat the censorship system (Hui and Rajagopalan 2013). *China Digital Times*, a news website based in the United States, has found that at least 262 different Tiananmen-related phrases have been censored since 2011 (Ser 2016).[1] The goal of the censorship system as it relates to the events of Tiananmen Square is to erase it from Chinese history, especially among the younger generation. Our experience with Chinese students suggests that it has been quite effective at achieving its goal.

---

1. You can find (more) examples of the censorship patterns at http://www.pri.org/stories/2016-06-03/how-china-has-censored-words-relating-tiananmen-square-anniversary.

Opposition protests began to take place on the streets of Leipzig and East Berlin. Initially, the crowds chanted, "Wir wollen raus!" (We want to leave!). Soon, however, they began to defiantly chant, "Wir bleiben hier!" (We are staying here!). It was the emergence of protesters demanding reform and refusing to leave that proved to be the real threat to the East German government's hold on power. The early protests were small, but they soon began to grow as the failure of the East German government to successfully intimidate and crack down on the initial demonstrators encouraged more and more people to participate. By October 1989 more than 250,000 people were regularly taking part in pro-democracy demonstrations. In a clear challenge to the Communist Party's claim to represent the East German people, the protesters famously chanted, "Wir sind das Volk!" (We are the People!).

Despite the protests, the East German government went ahead with celebrations on October 7 to mark the fortieth anniversary of the founding of the East German state (see Box 8.3, "A Brief History of East Germany, 1945–1990"). These celebrations included extravagant military parades, orchestrated pro-regime demonstrations, and a visit by Mikhail Gorbachev. To the embarrassment of the East German leadership, or politburo, the crowd at the parades, many of them handpicked by Communist Party officials, began chanting for Gorbachev to help them. In defiance of Gorbachev's advice that "Life will punish latecomers"—a clear reference to the necessity for reform—the hard-line East German leader, Erich Honecker, reacted within days of Gorbachev's departure by signing the *Schiessbefehl* (order to shoot) for a Chinese solution to the protests (Lohmann 1994, 69). East Germany was on the brink of civil war. As troops were being assembled and armed, the rest of the East German politburo rebelled, countermanded the order, and replaced Honecker with the more moderate Egon Krenz.

Despite the introduction of minor reforms, the mass protests continued and were emboldened when, on a trip to Finland, Gorbachev announced that the Soviets would no longer intervene militarily in Eastern Europe to prop up Communist governments. On November 4, more than one million East Germans took to the streets of East Berlin. In a final attempt to ward off ever larger protests, the East German government agreed on November 9 to remove all restrictions on travel to the West. The announcement of this decision on television led to tens of thousands of East Berliners rushing to the Berlin Wall, where surprised border guards eventually allowed them to pour through. In the following weeks, the whole socialist system in East Germany unraveled. Despite brief attempts to create a nonsocialist East Germany, elections on March 18, 1990, demonstrated that an overwhelming majority of East Germans wanted reunification with West Germany. By now, instead of shouting, "Wir sind das Volk!" (We are the People!), the protesters were shouting, "Wir sind ein Volk!" (We are one People!). Reunification finally took place on October 3, 1990, when the areas of the former German Democratic Republic were incorporated into the Federal Republic of Germany.

The transition to democracy that occurred in East Germany in 1989 represents but one case of a bottom-up transition, in which popular mobilization led to the overthrow ox 8.3

A BRIEF HISTORY OF EAST GERMANY, 1945–1990

At the Potsdam Conference in August 1945, the Allied powers divided Germany into four zones, to be occupied by France in the southwest, Britain in the northwest, the United States in the south, and the Soviet Union in the east. Berlin, which was more than 100 miles inside the eastern zone controlled by the Soviet Union, was also divided into four similar occupation zones. As the postwar rivalry between the Western powers and the Soviet Union increased, the Americans, French, and British signed the London Agreements in June 1948, joining their sectors together and introducing a new currency—the deutsche mark. In response to this

MAP 8.1   Divided Germany

perceived act of aggression, the Soviets responded by blocking all ground transportation between the western sectors and West Berlin on June 24, 1948. The next day, the Western powers began a massive airlift to supply West Berlin with essentials such as food and fuel. The Berlin Airlift, or the Berlin Blockade as it became known, finally ended ten months later when the Soviets realized that the West would not simply give up West Berlin. By now the division of Germany was almost inevitable. The Federal Republic of Germany (West Germany) was formally established on May 23, 1949, and the German Democratic Republic (East Germany) was established on October 7, 1949.

Between 1949 and 1961, 2.7 million people reacted to the increasingly dismal economic and political conditions in East Germany by emigrating to the West. It was in response to this that the East German government closed the borders to the West and began construction of the ninety-six-mile-long Berlin Wall during the night of August 12–13, 1961. The Berlin Wall split numerous families and separated many Berliners from their places of employment. Although the whole length of the border between East and West Germany was closed with chain-link fences, walls, minefields, and other installations, it was the Berlin Wall that arguably became the most iconic symbol of the Cold War. Over the years, thousands of attempts were

---

MAP 8.2   **The Division of Berlin**

made to breach the wall and reach the West. In all, about 200 people were killed trying to escape, with Chris Gueffroy being the last to be shot dead in February 1989.

During the summer and autumn of 1989, massive changes occurred in East Germany that eventually led to the reunification of Germany. Tens of thousands of East Germans fled to the West, taking advantage of the Hungarian government's decision to open its border to Austria. Increasingly, growing numbers of East Germans began protesting on the streets of Leipzig and Berlin, demanding reform within East Germany itself. Ongoing protests forced the East German government to allow free, multiparty elections in March 1990. These elections produced a victory for the pro-unification forces headed by West German chancellor Helmut Kohl. East Germany entered into an economic and monetary union with West Germany in July 1990. On September 12, 1990, East Germany, West Germany, and the four powers that occupied Germany at the end of World War II signed the Treaty on the Final Settlement with Respect to Germany. This treaty paved the way for German reunification on October 3, 1990.

of an authoritarian regime. There are numerous other examples. For instance, a few weeks after the fall of the Berlin Wall, mass protests forced the overthrow of the Communist government in Czechoslovakia in what became known as the Velvet Revolution because of its lack of violence (Garton Ash 1999). A few weeks after this, in December 1989, crowds played an integral role in removing the Communist dictator Nicolae Ceaușescu from power in Romania. Other examples include the EDSA Revolution, or the People Power Revolution, which saw massive demonstrations of up to three million people remove Ferdinand Marcos from power in the Philippines in 1986, or the June Resistance, which saw mass protests force South Korea's

East and West Germans stand on the Berlin Wall in front of the Brandenburg Gate the day after the wall opened on November 9, 1989.

General Roh Tae Woo to allow direct presidential elections in mid-1987. The list could go on and on.

As political scientists, we need to ask ourselves how we can explain these types of bottom-up transitions. How can we capture the surprise with which actual participants greeted the events that were unfolding around them? Why did the collapse of communism in Eastern Europe occur in 1989 and not any earlier or any later? Why did Eastern Europe, which in retrospect seems to have been filled with extremely fragile Communist regimes, seem so stable before 1989? Why are revolutions like those in Eastern Europe and elsewhere so rare? Why are they so hard to predict? We believe that collective action theory and tipping models provide answers to some of these questions. We begin by examining collective action theory.

Collective Action Theory

Collective action theory focuses on forms of mass action, or "collective action," such as the protests in East Germany in 1989. Other examples of **collective action** are revolutions, interest group activities, strikes, elections, some events organized by fraternities and sororities, and the like. Typically, collective action concerns the pursuit of public goods by groups of individuals. A **public good** has two characteristics: (a) **nonexcludability** and (b) **nonrivalry**. A good is nonexcludable if you cannot prevent those in the group who did not contribute to its supply from consuming it, and it is nonrivalrous if its consumption by one individual does not reduce the amount available for consumption by other individuals in the group.

> **Collective action** refers to the pursuit of some objective by groups of individuals. Typically, the objective is some form of public good.
>
> A **public good** is nonexcludable and nonrivalrous. **Nonexcludability** means that you cannot exclude people from enjoying the public good, and **nonrivalry** means that there is just as much public good for people to enjoy no matter how many people consume it.

Some examples should clarify the idea of a public good. One example of a public good is clean air. Clean air is nonexcludable in the sense that you cannot stop people from breathing it, and it is nonrivalrous in the sense that one person's consumption of it does not diminish the amount of clean air that others can consume. Another example of a public good is a lighthouse. A lighthouse is nonexcludable in that you cannot stop ships in the sea from seeing the light irrespective of whether they contribute to the building and upkeep of the lighthouse, and it is nonrivalrous in that there is just as much light for everyone to see no matter how many ships are taking advantage of it. Other examples of public goods include public parks, fire stations, public radio, and national defense. We can also think of democracy as a public good—it is nonexcludable in that anyone living in a democracy gets to enjoy living under democratic rule irrespective of whether they helped bring democracy about or whether they help to sustain it, and it is nonrivalrous because one person's enjoyment or consumption of democracy does not reduce the amount of democracy that others can consume.

Most people will recognize that the nature of public goods makes them quite desirable. This might lead you to think that individuals who expect to benefit from a public good would be enthusiastic contributors to the provision of that good—at least as long as the benefit from the good outweighed the cost of providing it. Put more starkly, you might expect that groups of individuals with common interests would act collectively to achieve those interests. Although this might seem reasonable, a famous economist, Mancur Olson ([1965] 1971), has shown that there are compelling reasons to doubt whether individuals will actually contribute to the provision of public goods or take collective action to achieve their common interests. The difficulty that groups of individuals have in providing public goods that all members of the group desire is commonly known as the **collective action, or free-rider, problem**. As we will see, the free-rider problem provides one explanation for why protests were so rare in Eastern Europe prior to 1989 and why the

> The **collective action, or free-rider, problem** refers to the fact that individual members of a group often have little incentive to contribute to the provision of a public good that will benefit all members of the group.

Communist regimes in that part of the world seemed stable for so long; in fact, it provides an explanation for why revolutions and public displays of opposition in dictatorships are so rare in general.

Start by asking yourself whether you would contribute to the provision of a public good that you value. Would you join a pro-democracy protest like those in East Germany in 1989, or would you stay at home? It is important to recognize that your *individual* decision to contribute to the public good or to participate in the pro-democracy protest is unlikely to be the decisive factor in determining whether the public good is provided or whether the protest is successful. What possible difference could one person make to the success of a mass protest? Given that you are individually unlikely to influence the outcome of the protest, why pay the costs that come with participation? The costs of participation include time, possibly expense, and perhaps even loss of life. It should be obvious that the potentially high costs associated with joining pro-democracy rallies in Communist Eastern Europe would have been only too clear to would-be participants at the time. All in all, the decision not to participate in a pro-democracy protest (or not to contribute to a public good more generally) is very appealing. If the pro-democracy rally fails, you will not have paid any costs or run the risk of incurring the dictatorship's wrath. And if the pro-democracy rally succeeds, you can "free ride" on the participation of others because everyone gets to benefit from the establishment of democracy irrespective of whether they participated in the rally or not. This is the basic logic underlying the collective action problem.

To better understand this logic, let's try to be a little more analytical. Imagine a group made up of N individuals. For example, we could think of the group as being the entire East German population. Now imagine that K individuals (where $K \leq N$) in the group must contribute or participate for the public good to be provided. We could think of the public good as being democracy and K as being the number of pro-democracy protesters that are necessary to make the Communist government in East Germany (or any other dictatorship) back down and allow democracy to emerge. If democracy is achieved, then everyone receives a benefit, B (where $B > 0$), irrespective of whether everyone participated in the pro-democracy rally or not. If you participate in the pro-democracy rally, you must pay a cost C (where $C > 0$). To capture the notion that the provision of the public good provides more benefits to you than the individual cost of participating in the protest, let's assume that $B > C$. If we did

TABLE 8.1	Pro-Democracy Protest: Do I Participate or Not?		
	Scenario 1 (Fewer than $K - 1$ participate)	Scenario 2 (Exactly $K - 1$ participate)	Scenario 3 (K or more participate)
Participate	$- C$	$\underline{B - C}$	$B - C$
Don't participate	$\underline{0}$	0	$\underline{B}$

Note: K = the number of individuals that must participate for the pro-democracy protest to be successful; C = cost associated with participating; B = benefit associated with a successful pro-democracy protest; underlined letters indicate the payoffs associated with the actor's best response—participate or don't participate—in each scenario. It is assumed that $B - C > 0$.

not make this assumption, then no one would ever have an incentive to contribute to the public good. Now ask yourself whether you would ever contribute to the public good under these circumstances. Would you participate in a pro-democracy protest? As Table 8.1 illustrates, your decision will depend on your conjecture or expectation about what other members of the group will do.

As you can see, if these payoffs capture your assessment of the situation, it makes no sense for you to participate in the pro-democracy protest if you expect that fewer than $K - 1$ others will participate (Scenario 1). This is because your individual participation will not make the protest successful, and you will only end up incurring the cost of participation; you'd be better off staying at home. It also makes no sense for you to participate if you conjecture that at least K others will participate (Scenario 3). This is because your participation is not necessary for a successful protest; you might as well stay at home and free ride on the successful participation of others without paying any costs. It makes sense for you to participate only if you expect that exactly $K - 1$ others will participate (Scenario 2). In this scenario, your participation is decisive because it turns an otherwise unsuccessful protest into a successful one; you get a payoff of $B - C$. By not participating, you condemn the protest to failure, and your payoff is 0. Given that $B - C > 0$, it is rational for you to participate. The rational choices in each of the three possible scenarios are underlined in Table 8.1.

The fact that the logic behind these choices applies to every individual in the group suggests that there are only two possible types of equilibria here—either no one participates in the pro-democracy rally, or exactly K individuals do. Think about it this way. If no one is participating in the rally, then no one will want to individually deviate by participating because he or she will pay the cost of participating, but the one-person rally will be a failure. As a result, "no participation" is an equilibrium. If K individuals are participating, none of the K participants will want to individually deviate by staying home because the rally will fail without their participation, and none of the other group members will want to protest because their participation is costly and not crucial to the rally's success. As a result, "exactly K participants" is also an equilibrium. Thus, for the pro-democracy rally (or any form of collective action) to succeed, exactly K individuals must believe that they, and only they, are likely to participate. This insight suggests that two factors in particular are crucial for determining the likely success of collective action: (a) the difference between K and N, and (b) the size of N.[2]

Why would the difference between K and N matter? Suppose that the number of people required for a successful pro-democracy protest, K, was equal to the size of the group, N. In this situation, all in the group know that their participation is crucial for the success of the protest and that they each prefer a successful protest to a failed one. As a result, there is no incentive for any member of the group to free ride by staying at home.[3] Suppose now that only some of the group members are required for a successful pro-democracy protest; that is, $K < N$. In this situation, group members know that a successful rally can take place without everyone's participation. It is this realization that creates the incentive to free ride. It does not take much of a leap to realize that the incentive to free ride becomes greater the larger the difference between K and N. For example, if K is only slightly smaller than N, then most group members are still going to think that their participation will be crucial to the success of the protest. The result of this is that participation rates and, hence, the likelihood of a successful protest will remain relatively high. If K is much smaller than N, however, then most group members are going to think that they are not crucial to the success of the protest and that they can get away with free riding on the participation of others. Given the increased level of free riding, the likelihood of a successful protest is going to decline in this situation.

The bottom line here is that forms of collective action, such as protests, strikes, revolutions, lobbying, and the like, are less likely to be successful when the number of group members required for success, K, is significantly smaller than the number of people who will benefit from the success, N. Somewhat counterintuitively, this means that group leaders interested in some form of collective action, such as a demonstration or a letter-writing campaign, will be more successful if they tell their members that success depends on the participation of nearly all of their members rather than just a few of them. The logic of collective action that we have just presented helps to explain why political parties try to convince their supporters that all of their votes are crucial to their electoral success or why pledge drives for public television or National Public Radio in the United States continually state that the contribution of all listeners is crucial to the ongoing existence of these

---

2. It seems reasonable to think that the likelihood of successful collective action also depends on (a) the costs of participation, C, and (b) the size of the benefit, B, at issue. As participation becomes more costly (holding N, K, and B fixed), it is likely that group members will be less willing to participate. Similarly, as the benefit to be obtained from successful collective action increases (holding N, K, and C fixed), it seems likely that the group members will be more willing to participate.

3. It turns out that it is also an equilibrium for no one to participate if $K = N$. For example, if everyone else is choosing not to participate, it makes no sense for one person to deviate and participate, because the protest will obviously fail with only one protester. In this situation, the group is stuck in an equilibrium trap in which no one is participating, even though everyone would be better off if they all participated. Shepsle and Bonchek (1997, 228) argue that this equilibrium is unlikely, because everyone "will realize that everyone else benefits from achieving the group goal, and that the only way for this to happen is if everyone" participates.

institutions even if this is not true—they are trying to persuade voters, listeners, and viewers to participate rather than to free ride.

Why would the size of the group matter? The size of N matters because it influences the likelihood that you will think of yourself as critical to the form of collective action under consideration. Should you run the risks associated with participating in a pro-democracy rally where N is large? Will it make a difference? If hardly anyone else participates, then the pro-democracy protest is unlikely to be successful. And if lots of people participate, it is unlikely that your individual participation will make much of a difference. Given this, why participate? The size of N also matters because it influences the ability of group members to monitor and punish free riders. The larger the group, the harder it is to monitor, identify, and punish those who do not participate in the protest. The result is that larger groups tend to be characterized by higher levels of free riding and a lower likelihood that collective action will be successful.

The relationship between group size and successful collective action has some important and counterintuitive implications. Most important, it suggests that small groups may be more effective than large groups because of the small group's increased ability to solve the free rider problem. In this sense, the relationship that we outline challenges the common concern in democratic theory that the majority will tyrannize and exploit the minority. In fact, the opposite may well occur in some circumstances. For example, the result about group size helps to explain why business groups (relatively small) seem to have greater lobbying power and influence over policy than, say, consumer groups or workers (relatively large). It also helps to explain why relatively small constituencies such as religious fundamentalists can have a significant influence on political outcomes compared with the much larger constituencies made up of religious moderates and secularists. In sum, the free-rider problem is likely to damage the ability of large groups to conduct forms of collective action much more than that of small groups.

Collective action theory provides a possible explanation for the apparent stability of communism in postwar East Germany and for why public demonstrations of regime opposition are so rare in dictatorships more generally. Collective action theory reminds us that the fact that many East Germans shared a common interest—in the overthrow of the Communist regime and the establishment of democracy—did not automatically translate into their taking collective action to bring this about. The public goods nature of democracy created an incentive for East Germans to avoid the potential costs of participating in pro-democracy rallies and to free ride on the participation of others. The incentives to free ride in East Germany were large because the number of people who would benefit from democracy, N—virtually the entire 17 million population—was huge and because the number of protesters necessary to bring democracy about, K—several hundred thousand in the end—was relatively small in comparison. The costs of participating in pro-democracy demonstrations were largely prohibitive as well. The violent and deadly outcome of the Berlin Uprising in 1953 was a stark reminder to potential protesters of the dangers that they faced if they publicly opposed the Communist government. It is important to recognize that the lack of public opposition in East Germany for most of the postwar period was not necessarily a sign that the Communist regime enjoyed widespread support; it may simply have been that the collective action problem made it difficult for the opposition to organize itself into a coherent force.

Tipping Models

Although collective action theory helps to explain why revolutions are so rare and why dictatorships often appear quite stable, it cannot explain the mass protests that eventually brought communism to its knees in 1989–1990. Participation now becomes the puzzle that needs to be explained. One explanation for the mass protests that occurred in East Germany in 1989 can be found in what political scientists call "tipping," or "threshold," models (DeNardo 1985; Ellis and Fender 2011; Ginkel and Smith 1999; Granovetter 1978; Kuran 1991; Lohmann 1994).

As in the model of collective action that we have just examined, we start with an individual who must decide whether to publicly support or oppose a dictatorship. The individual has a private preference and a revealed public preference. His private preference is his true attitude toward the dictatorship, and his public preference is the attitude toward the dictatorship that he reveals to the outside world. The dangers that come from publicly revealing one's opposition to a dictatorship often mean that individuals who oppose the regime falsify their true preferences; instead of opposing the dictatorship in public, they support it. In East Germany, as elsewhere in Eastern Europe, "people routinely applauded speakers whose message they disliked, joined organizations whose mission they opposed, and signed defamatory letters against people they admired" (Kuran 1991, 26).[4]

One consequence of **preference falsification** is that individuals do not know the true level of opposition in a dictatorship because they all seem to be publicly supporting it. The perception is that society is publicly behind the dictatorship and that there is no point in opposing it. As the political dissident Aleksandr Solzhenitsyn (1975, 275) wrote about the Soviet Union, "The lie has been incorporated into the state system as the vital link holding everything together."[5] Note that preference falsification provides an alternative, but complementary, explanation to that provided by collective action theory for the relative stability of Eastern Europe in the postwar period. It suggests that even if collective action could be effectively organized, individuals might still choose not to protest because they are not sure of the extent to which others really oppose the regime.

> **Preference falsification** means not revealing one's true preferences in public.

---

4. In addition to individual self-censorship, anticipation of government disapproval also leads to "regime-induced private censorship" by non-government actors (Crabtree, Fariss, and Kern 2016). In effect, newspapers, advertising agencies, and other private actors "choose" to censor the material that they produce.

5. The state itself, often through the use of state-controlled media, reinforces the "lie" referred to by Solzhenitsyn. State officials can use a combination of propaganda and censorship to provide the public with the version of information, both about contemporary and historical events, that helps the state maintain its authority. The combination of censorship and propaganda make it particularly difficult to know what other citizens believe.

Although many people may be engaged in preference falsification, there is probably some protest size at which they would be willing to publicly reveal their true preferences. In other words, an opponent of the regime might not wish to participate in a pro-democracy rally that comprises a few hundred people but may be willing to participate in one that comprises tens of thousands or hundreds of thousands of people. We will refer to the protest size at which an individual is willing to participate as his **revolutionary threshold**.

> A **revolutionary threshold** is the size of protest at which an individual is willing to participate.

The intuition behind the notion of a revolutionary threshold is relatively straightforward. As the size of a protest grows, it becomes harder for the state to identify and punish individuals for participating. In other words, the costs of participation decline in rough proportion to the number of protesters.

Individuals have different revolutionary thresholds. Some people are really brave and are quite happy to oppose dictatorial rule irrespective of whether others do. These people are commonly referred to as political dissidents and often include academics, writers, or religious figures. For example, Aleksandr Solzhenitsyn and Andrei Sakharov were both political dissidents who, between them, challenged the police state and nuclear weapons policy of the Soviet Union. Other people may be scared and unwilling to publicly show their opposition to a dictatorship unless lots of others also do so. Still others may actually support the regime; these people are unlikely to join in a pro-democracy protest under any circumstances. As you might expect, people's thresholds are likely to depend on many different factors, such as whether they have benefited or suffered under the regime, whether they have much to lose from participating in protests, and whether they believe that the regime is fragile or stable. The point is that revolutionary thresholds vary across individuals.

An example might make this concept clearer.[6] Below is an example of a ten-person society labeled A.

$$A = \{0, 2, 2, 3, 4, 5, 6, 7, 8, 10\}.$$

The numbers in the brackets indicate the revolutionary threshold of each of the ten people in society A. The first individual in this society has a revolutionary threshold of 0, meaning that he is willing to protest on his own. The second and third individuals in this society have a revolutionary threshold of 2, meaning that they need two other people to be protesting before they are willing to join in. In this example, the tenth individual has a revolutionary threshold of 10. Given that there are only ten people in this society, this means that the tenth individual will never participate in a protest, because there can never be ten people already protesting without his participation.

The distribution of revolutionary thresholds in a society is crucial for determining whether a revolution occurs or not. Consider the example of society A. In this society, only one person will protest. The individual with a revolutionary threshold of 0 will protest, but

---

6. Several of the examples that follow were provided by a former colleague, Marek Kaminski.

no one else will. It is unlikely that a one-person protest will be successful. Now consider a slightly different society, A':

$$A' = \{0, 1, 2, 3, 4, 5, 6, 7, 8, 10\}.$$

The only difference between society A and society A' is that the second individual's revolutionary threshold has dropped from 2 to 1. We can think of these two examples as the same society at two different points in time. For example, we can think that the government took some action or introduced some policy that made the second individual more willing to publicly oppose the government. Although this small change in one person's revolutionary threshold might appear inconsequential, it actually has quite a dramatic effect on the size and likely success of a protest. The reason for this is that the second individual is now willing to join the first individual who is protesting. Now that there are two people protesting, the third individual with a revolutionary threshold of 2 is willing to join in as well. This, in turn, causes the fourth individual to join in. Before you know it, there is a nine-person protest going on. The fact that fully 90 percent of the people in this society are now protesting is likely to mean that this protest is successful. In this example, the slight shift in the revolutionary threshold of one individual has caused what we call a **revolutionary cascade**. This example should make it clear why these types of models are referred to as "tipping," or "threshold," models.

> A **revolutionary cascade** is when one person's participation triggers the participation of another, which triggers the participation of another, and so on.

Note that a small shift in the revolutionary threshold like that in the previous example will not always produce a revolution or protest. Consider society B:

$$B = \{0, 2, 3, 3, 4, 5, 6, 7, 8, 10\}.$$

The only difference from society A is that the third individual now has a revolutionary threshold of 3 instead of 2. Notice, though, what happens when the government takes the same action or introduces the same policy as before, causing the second individual to reduce his threshold from 2 to 1.

$$B' = \{0, 1, 3, 3, 4, 5, 6, 7, 8, 10\}.$$

As you can see, the change of threshold produces only a two-person protest this time. In other words, there is a slight decline in the popularity of the regime but no revolution. Thus, a slightly different distribution of a society's revolutionary thresholds can mean the difference between a small, abortive, and ultimately unsuccessful protest (society B') and a revolutionary cascade (society A') that produces the overthrow of the dictatorship.

This result has implications for those who argue that revolutions and protests are caused by structural factors such as relative deprivation, grievances, or oppression (Gurr 1970). As the tipping model suggests, things like economic recession or the introduction of a repressive policy may cause private preferences and revolutionary thresholds to move against the regime without actually producing a revolution. For example, economic recession may cause the regime in some society C to become deeply unpopular (as exhibited by the relatively low revolutionary thresholds).

$$C = \{0, 2, 2, 2, 2, 2, 2, 2, 2, 10\}.$$

The low threshold of virtually every individual in this society indicates that it would not take much for a revolutionary cascade to occur. Despite this, though, the distribution of revolutionary thresholds indicates that the regime will not experience a revolution as things stand. Structural factors such as economic recession are not sufficient in and of themselves to produce revolutions. All we can say is that structural factors can make revolutions more likely by reducing individual thresholds; they do not make revolutions inevitable. In effect, structural factors may create an environment in which idiosyncratic events, such as Mohamed Bouazizi's ill treatment by local officials in Tunisia and his subsequent self-immolation in December 2010 (see Chapter 1), can turn an act of desperation into the start of a revolution.[7] But similar acts of desperation in situations where structural factors have not lowered the revolutionary thresholds of individuals in society might well be remembered as tragic, largely private, acts that have few consequences beyond those directly affected.

It is important to remember at this point that preference falsification means that a society's distribution of revolutionary thresholds is never known to the individuals of that society. Each individual knows his own revolutionary threshold, but not that of anyone else. This means that a society can come to the brink of revolution without anyone's ever knowing it. In effect, people may be ready to participate in a full-scale revolt as long as one more person goes out to protest. If that one extra person does not protest, however, then no revolution occurs, and the dictatorship appears entirely stable. Note that even if people know for sure that preference falsification is occurring (as they surely must), they cannot know if they live in a society like A or one like B. This implies that it is often impossible for observers to distinguish between very stable and very fragile dictatorships. Moreover, our inability to observe both private preferences and thresholds conceals potential revolutionary cascades and makes it impossible to predict when a revolution will occur. In effect, revolutions will always come as a surprise. This is why we talk about the "predictability of unpredictability" of revolutions (Kuran 1989, 1991). Note, though, that our inability to predict revolutions such as the fall of communism in Eastern Europe in 1989 or the overthrow of various dictators in the Arab Spring of 2011 (see Box 8.4, "Revolutionary Cascades, Social Media, and

---

7. In a recent study of Moroccan protesters during the Arab Spring, Lawrence finds that the people who were "first movers" tended to have family members who had previously suffered repression at the hands of the regime. She argues that the friends of these first movers are likely to increase their support for anti-regime activity if new repression occurs, suggesting that if "repression generates support among first movers' friends, all else equal, their probability of mobilizing is likely to increase. Once they join, the movement is one step closer to triggering cascades of participation" (Lawrence, forthcoming).

the Arab Spring") should not lead one to conclude that revolutions are somehow irrational. As the logic underlying the tipping model that we have just presented indicates, our failure to predict revolutions "is entirely consistent with calculated, purposeful human action" (Kuran 1991, 45).

Preference falsification helps explain why the Communist regimes in Eastern Europe were substantially more vulnerable than their subservient populations had made them seem prior to 1989. During the 1980s, a series of structural changes had the effect of lowering revolutionary thresholds in Eastern Europe to such an extent that they triggered a revolutionary cascade both within countries and between countries. For example, the appointment of Gorbachev to power in the Soviet Union and his introduction of reformist

---

ox 8.4

REVOLUTIONARY CASCADES, SOCIAL MEDIA, AND THE ARAB SPRING

In this chapter, we have focused on the revolutionary cascade that occurred across Eastern Europe in 1989. As we described in more detail in Chapter 1, though, another revolutionary cascade occurred more recently in the Middle East and North Africa. This particular revolutionary cascade began in December 2010 when Mohamed Bouazizi set himself on fire in Tunisia to protest his poor treatment by local officials. In the weeks that followed Mr. Bouazizi's self-immolation, mass protests spread from his hometown to the capital city, Tunis. On January 15, 2011, Tunisian president Zine al-Abidine Ben Ali fled to Saudi Arabia, making him the first Arab leader in generations to leave office in response to public protests. Over the next several months, protests spread beyond the Tunisian border to other countries such as Egypt, Libya, Syria, Yemen, and Bahrain. Protesters in one country after another began to emulate the rebellious actions of protesters in other countries, and belief began to spread that the dictatorial regimes in the region could be toppled. With the diffusion of protests across national borders, the Arab Spring was born.

Information is central to the success of a revolutionary cascade. For example, protesters need to know about events in other countries. They also need to be able to pass on various pieces of information such as where and when to meet so that they can coordinate their protests successfully. Some commentators have referred to the Arab Spring as the "Twitter Revolution," suggesting that new developments in information technology, such as Twitter, Facebook, and YouTube, which enable information to be shared quickly with others, are empowering citizens, weakening authoritarian elites, and helping to make revolutionary cascades more likely.

It is certainly true that protesters during the Arab Spring used these new technologies in various capacities. For example, they were used to spread the word about the location of government crackdowns and "flash" protests. Moreover, opposition leaders, like Nobel Peace Prize winner Mohamed ElBaradei, are known to have used things like Twitter to launch attacks on dictatorial rulers, such as Egyptian president Hosni Mubarak (Hammer 2010). Similarly, YouTube was used on numerous occasions to publicize government massacres, thereby building support among both domestic and foreign audiences for opposition movements. It is unclear, though, exactly how big a role these new technologies played in the Arab Spring. For example, no scholar has so far carefully matched up specific bursts of, say, Twitter communication with data on subsequent protests. Until this is done, we will not know the true magnitude, if any, of the causal effect of these new technologies (Voeten 2010).

It should be pointed out that these new forms of social media do not necessarily weaken the power of authoritarian elites to control their citizens. Indeed, there is growing evidence that dictatorial regimes may well be able to use these new forms of social media to their own advantage. Indeed, the British police demonstrated how this might be done during the August 2011 riots in London when they monitored social networks related to Twitter and BlackBerry Messenger to stay one step ahead of protesters. In the process, they prevented attacks on the Olympic site and the main shopping areas around Oxford Street ("Riots Thwarted" 2011). In 2009, China simply closed Twitter messaging sites and blocked access to websites that were reporting on the ethnic protests in Xinjiang province ("Scores Killed" 2009). Recognizing that people will often find alternative ways to reach the outside world if social network systems are simply shut down, some authoritarian regimes have adopted more ingenious strategies where they create state-controlled intranets and Internet providers that give people the "illusion" of access to the outside world. For example, Iran has established a "halal" Internet that has been described as "a stilted alternative reality of government-approved content on controlled national intranets" (US Department of State 2011). In many ways, traditional off-line surveillance can be difficult and expensive for authoritarian regimes. The emergence of new technologies actually makes it easier and cheaper for them to monitor their citizens. For instance, the government in China often forces companies to log social network users' Internet protocol (IP) addresses. Similarly, the Egyptian state security apparatus under Mubarak collected records of activists' text messages, e-mail exchanges, and Skype chats (Saletan 2011).

It should also be noted that the new social media are but the latest example of the way communications technologies may play a role in the diffusion and coordination of protest. Historians have pointed to the explosive growth of newspaper circulation during the revolutions of 1848 and the role increased readership played in the dissemination of information about revolutionary protests occurring across Europe. Similarly, some analysts have pointed to the role played by twenty-four-hour news networks in the spread of information across Eastern Europe in 1989.[8] The bottom line is that political scientists do not yet have a firm understanding of exactly how new forms of social media will influence the likelihood of protests and other forms of collective action. This is an area in which we expect to see a lot of new research in the coming years.

---

8. Although the idea of the media influencing protests is intuitively appealing, the empirical evidence is not always strong. One recent study looking at the events of 1989 in East Germany found no evidence to "support the widely accepted 'fact' that West German television served as a coordination device for antiregime protests during the East German revolution" (Crabtree, Darfomal, and Kern 2015, 269).

policies, such as perestroika and glasnost, reduced the perceived risk of challenging the political status quo, thereby reducing people's thresholds. Revolutionary thresholds were also lowered by the increasingly poor economic performance of many Eastern European countries from the mid-1980s on and Gorbachev's statement in 1989 that the Soviet Union would not intervene militarily to help sustain Communist rule in Eastern Europe. Once pro-democracy reforms were successfully introduced in one Eastern European country, they started to have demonstration effects in other countries, further reducing revolutionary thresholds. The end result was a democratic cascade with the diffusion of democracy from one country to another (Brinks and Coppedge 2006; O'Loughlin et al. 1998; Starr and Lindborg 2003). The democratic cascade that occurred in Eastern Europe is best summed up by a protest banner seen at a pro-democracy rally in Prague in 1989 stating simply, "Poland—10 years, Hungary—10 months, East Germany—10 weeks, Czechoslovakia—10 days" (Garton Ash 1999). The message of the banner was that a democratic transition had finally taken place roughly ten years since the rise of Solidarity in Poland, roughly ten months since the introduction of reforms in Hungary, roughly ten weeks since the start of mass protests in East Germany, and roughly ten days since pro-democracy rallies began in Czechoslovakia.

In hindsight, the collapse of communism in Eastern Europe has come to be seen by many as inevitable. Numerous historians, sociologists, and political scientists who interviewed individuals across Eastern Europe reported that there had been a huge pent-up pool of opposition to Communist rule and that this was bound to break out at some point in time. Almost all of the interviewees reported that they had opposed Communist rule and wanted it to end. These reports certainly make it seem that the collapse of communism was inevitable, but the notion of preference falsification should make us extremely wary of drawing this inference. For example, put yourself in the shoes of a Communist Party supporter. As the revolutionary cascade starts to snowball into an overwhelming majority, it becomes imprudent for you to remain a government supporter. You may even feel obliged to join the pro-democracy protests even though you would have preferred that they fail. We might call this a revolutionary *bandwagon* to distinguish it from a revolutionary *cascade*. Just as pro-democracy supporters falsify their preferences under dictatorship to avoid punishment, pro-dictatorship supporters will falsify their preferences under democracy for similar reasons. Supporters of the former Communist regime are likely to lie about their true preferences and indicate that they were long-standing opponents of the toppled government. In effect, the evidence from these people will make it seem as if the former dictatorship was much more unstable and unloved than it actually was. As Kuran (1991, 23) puts it, "Having misled everyone into seeing a revolution as highly unlikely, preference falsification now conceals the forces that were working against it. One of the consequences of post-revolutionary preference falsification is thus to make it even less comprehensible why the revolution was unforeseen." In other words, revolution will often seem inevitable in hindsight even though this is, in fact, far from the case at the time.

TOP-DOWN TRANSITIONS TO DEMOCRACY

Some transitions to democracy do not occur through a bottom-up process as occurred in East Germany. Instead, they result primarily from a policy of liberalization on the part of authoritarian elites themselves. This policy of liberalization is often designed to stabilize a dictatorship but sometimes inadvertently leads to democracy. Periods of liberalization have preceded numerous transitions to democracy throughout history. For example, Generals Ernesto Geisel and João Figueiredo introduced a period of liberalization (distensão) and opening (abertura) in Brazil between 1982 and 1985 as they tried to strengthen their position in relation to hard-liners like General Sylvio Frota. This period of liberalization ultimately led to an implicit pact between government soft-liners, the regime party, the military, and the opposition to name the opposition leader, Tancredo Neves, as president in 1985.

A similar period of liberalization preceded the democratic transition in Uruguay between 1983 and 1984. In this case, month-long discussions between soft-liners in the authoritarian regime and representatives of the opposition led to the Acuerdo del Club Naval (Naval Club Accord) and the reintroduction of presidential elections in 1984 (Colomer 1991, 1295). Chile, similarly, experienced a period of liberalization before its return to the democratic fold in 1988. Its transition to democracy began in 1980 with the introduction of a new constitution that contained provisions for the transfer of power from the military government of Augusto Pinochet to a civilian government within eight years. Chile's slow democratization process was tightly orchestrated, culminating in a defeat for Pinochet in a plebiscite on his leadership in October 1988 and the reintroduction of presidential elections later that year. As discussed in more detail a little later in this chapter, Poland's transition to democracy in 1989 was another case in which democracy was preceded by a period of liberalization introduced by authoritarian elites.

A Game-Theoretic Model of Top-Down Transitions

We now present a stylized story of top-down transitions.

The Story

Top-down transitions to democracy frequently result from a split between soft-liners and hard-liners in an authoritarian regime. Typically, the dictatorship has come under some sort of pressure, often having to do with declining economic conditions, and soft-liners have come to prominence. Whereas hard-liners tend to be satisfied with the political status quo, soft-liners may prefer to liberalize and broaden the social base of the dictatorship in an attempt to gain allies, strengthen their position in relation to the hard-liners, and manage opposition groups.[9] The soft-liners have a choice to make. Should they open up the political regime through a process of liberalization, or should they stick with the status quo?

---

9. The decision to liberalize is rarely taken in a vacuum. Instead, it often occurs after the authoritarian elites have come under some form of pressure from opposition groups in society. In this sense, it is hard to entirely disentangle bottom-up and top-down processes of democratization. As we noted at the beginning of the chapter, we believe that both processes typically interact with each other in the real world.

A **policy of liberalization** entails a controlled opening of the political space and might include the formation of political parties, holding elections, writing a constitution, establishing a judiciary, opening a legislature, and so on. It is important to recognize that the goal of any "opening" for the soft-liners is not to bring about

A **policy of liberalization** entails a controlled opening of the political space and might include the formation of political parties, holding elections, writing a constitution, establishing a judiciary, opening a legislature, and so on.

democracy but to incorporate various opposition groups into authoritarian institutions. As we discuss in more detail in Chapter 10, the liberalization process is typically an attempt by dictatorial elites to co-opt opposition groups or, at least, to divide and control them (Gandhi and Przeworski 2006; Przeworski 1991). The intended goal is not a democracy, but what we might call a "broadened dictatorship."[10] As an example, Lust-Okar (2005) uses evidence from Egypt, Jordan, and Morocco to illustrate how authoritarian elites have employed periods of liberalization and institutionalization to divide and control opposition groups. She shows how dictators in these countries have been able to influence the timing of when political opponents unite and divide, as well as when they emerge and dissolve, by creating rules and institutions that allow some groups to participate in the formal political sphere but not others. In taking these steps, the authoritarian elites in these Middle Eastern states have been able to lower the opposition's willingness and ability to challenge them. As the events of 2011 clearly demonstrate, however, this does not mean that even skillfully strategic authoritarians will always be able to contain the actions of opposition groups.

It is worth noting that broadened dictatorships characterized by seemingly democratic institutions such as elections and legislatures are increasingly common in the world today (Diamond 2002; Levitsky and Way 2002, 2003). Many people have championed the introduction of these types of institutions in several dictatorships as signs that these states are gradually moving toward democracy. The implication is that the liberalization process will eventually lead to a transition to full democracy. It is this belief that often encourages some scholars to label these regimes as "mixed," "hybrid," "partial democracies," or "partly free," as if they were some halfway house between dictatorship and democracy.[11] Strong, and growing, empirical evidence, however, shows that broadened dictatorships are not necessarily undergoing a prolonged democratic transition (Carothers 2002; Herbst 2001). Indeed, it appears that liberalization and institutionalization can, under many circumstances, significantly enhance the stability of dictatorial rule.

Given the potential benefits of liberalization, you might wonder why authoritarian elites do not always push for it. The problem is that the soft-liners cannot guarantee that liberalization will successfully produce a broadened dictatorship. As you might expect, the

---

10. Different terms have been used by political scientists to capture the concept of a "broadened dictatorship." For example, scholars have sometimes referred to these regimes as "competitive authoritarianism," "electoral authoritarianism," "soft-authoritarianism," "semi-authoritarianism," "pseudo-democracy," "illiberal democracy," "hybrid regimes," and other terms (Diamond 2002; Karl 1995; Levitsky and Way 2002, 2003; Schedler 2002; Zakaria 1997).

11. These broadened dictatorships frequently score somewhere in the middle of the continuum used by the continuous measures of democracy (Freedom House and Polity IV) that we examined in Chapter 5, thereby giving the impression that they are moving toward democracy and away from dictatorship.

Lech Walesa, head of the striking workers' delegation, stands in the Lenin shipyard in Gdansk, Poland, as he addresses striking workers after negotiations on August 26, 1980, that led to a preliminary contract between the striking workers and the Polish government.

liberalization process is inherently unstable. If the soft-liners do liberalize, then the democratic opposition has two options. On the one hand, it can accept the concessions offered by the authoritarian elites and enter the institutions of a broadened dictatorship. In this case, the democratic opposition essentially agrees to maintain the dictatorial rules of the game in return for entrance into the formal political sphere. The soft-liners would obviously see this as a success. On the other hand, however, the democratic opposition can take advantage of its new freedoms to further organize and mobilize against the dictatorship. In many cases around the world, this is precisely what happened. For example, the Polish Communist Party agreed to allow the formation of the independent trade union Solidarity in September 1980. Within just two weeks, Solidarity had three million members and was rapidly becoming a direct threat to ongoing Communist rule (Garton Ash 1999, 34). It is easy to see that the soft-liners in the authoritarian regime are playing a dangerous game—they could unleash forces that might escape them.

If the democratic opposition does choose to continue organizing and mobilizing against the regime, then this is evidence that the controlled opening initiated by the soft-liners has failed. As a consequence, the position of the soft-liners in the dictatorship is likely to be undermined. At this point, two choices are available to the authoritarian elites. The first choice is to use force in an attempt to repress popular mobilization and to restore order. If the repression is successful, then the result will be a "narrow dictatorship" in which the soft-liners pay the consequence for having introduced a failed policy of liberalization and are replaced by hard-liners. This particular scenario has played out quite frequently throughout history. For example, the experiment with liberalization attempted by King Hussein of Jordan in the 1950s and by King Hassan II of Morocco in the 1960s failed to appease their opponents, who simply demanded more significant reductions in, and even the elimination of, the monarchs' power. The two kings both responded to ongoing mobilization by imposing martial law, removing the men they had assigned to implement liberalization, and excluding all opposition groups from the formal political system (Lust-Okar 2005, 49–60). Periods of liberalization in Eastern Europe prior to 1989, such as the 1968 Prague Spring, also ended in repression and the establishment of narrow dictatorships led by hard-liners (see Box 8.5, "Prague Spring, 1968"). Of course, state repression may prove to be unsuccessful, at which point the dictatorship is likely to have an insurgency on its hands. Clearly, authoritarian elites must weigh the likelihood that repression will be successful before deciding to take this route.

ox 8.5

PRAGUE SPRING, 1968

By the mid-1960s, the Czechoslovak economy had stalled, and moderate Communists were increasingly calling for economic, social, and political reform. In January 1968 the soft-liner Alexander Dubček replaced the hard-liner Antonín Novotný as leader of the Czechoslovak Communist Party. The period from March to August 1968 is known as the Prague Spring and was a period in which Dubček tried to open up the political regime and introduce a policy of liberalization. The goal of these reforms was not the end of the socialist state but what Dubček called "socialism with a human face." Dubček wanted to overcome the disillusionment of the people with the previous two decades of Communist rule and breathe new life into socialism. He attempted to do this by increasing the freedom of the press, reducing censorship, and encouraging more participation in politics.

The introduction of these rather limited reforms encouraged further mobilization by the democratic opposition. Within weeks, the people were demanding still more reforms, and Communist control of the country faltered. Anti-Soviet statements appeared in the press, the Social Democrats began to form a separate party, and independent political clubs were created. At this point, the Soviet Union and its leader, Leonid Brezhnev, demanded that Dubček stop the reforms. Although Dubček had not originally intended for his policy of liberalization to go this far, he refused. The Soviets and their Warsaw Pact allies responded by invading Czechoslovakia. Dubček called on the people not to resist, but there were numerous acts of nonviolent resistance anyway. For example, one man, Jan Palach, set himself on fire in Prague's Wenceslas Square to protest the renewed suppression of free speech. Dubček was eventually replaced by the hard-liner Gustáv Husák, who introduced a period of "normalization." Husák reversed Dubček's reforms, purged the Communist Party of its soft-liners, and repressed remaining dissidents with the help of the secret police.

In 1987 Gorbachev acknowledged that his liberalizing policies of glasnost and perestroika owed a great deal to Dubček's vision of "socialism with a human face." When asked what the difference was between the Prague Spring and his own reforms, Gorbachev simply replied, "Nineteen years."

Given the renewed repression that followed the Prague Spring, it is bitterly ironic that observers quickly dubbed the events of early 2011 in the Middle East and North Africa (MENA) region the "Arab Spring." Gorbachev's willingness to link his reforms to those of his predecessor, Dubček, reminds us that the effects of political actions may be felt over decades and that current setbacks in the democracy movements in the MENA region may be masking long-run democratizing effects.

The second choice available to the soft-liners if the democratic opposition continues to mobilize is to accept its demands and allow the emergence of truly democratic institutions. This is essentially what happened in South Korea when pro-democracy rallies through the 1980s finally transformed the regime's soft-liners from liberalizers into democratizers; free elections were allowed in 1987. It is arguably what also happened in the Soviet Union under Gorbachev, and, as we will see, it is what happened in Poland in 1989. The argument that we have presented basically suggests that failed "liberalizations are either reversed, leading to grim periods euphemistically termed normalization, or continue to democratization" (Przeworski 1991, 60).

The Model

Under what conditions do authoritarian elites introduce a period of liberalization? When does liberalization succeed in producing an institutionalized and broadened dictatorship? When does it fail? Put differently, when do opposition groups agree to enter authoritarian institutions, and when do they choose to continue mobilizing independently of the regime? If liberalization fails, when do authoritarian elites respond with repression, and when do they allow a transition to full democracy? Clearly, the choice by the authoritarian elite to stick with the political status quo or to open up the regime depends on how it thinks the democratic opposition will respond to liberalization. Similarly, the choice by the democratic opposition to enter a broadened dictatorship or to continue mobilizing depends on how it thinks the dictatorship will respond to ongoing mobilization. As we have argued in previous chapters, strategic situations like this, in which the decisions of one actor depend on the choices of other actors, are usefully analyzed with the help of game theory. In Figure 8.2, we present one way to model the strategic interaction between authoritarian soft-liners and democratic opposition groups, using an extensive form game.[12]

The prehistory to the Transition Game is that a split has developed in the authoritarian elite between soft-liners and hard-liners. For some reason, the soft-liners have come to prominence and are in a position to open up the political space through a policy of liberalization if they so choose. The game illustrated in Figure 8.2 now begins. The soft-liners move first and must decide whether to do nothing or open up the regime. If the soft-liners do nothing, we are left with the political status quo (Outcome 1). If they decide to open up, then the democratic opposition groups must choose whether to enter the authoritarian institutions or to continue organizing. If they enter, the result is a broadened dictatorship (Outcome 2). If they organize, then the soft-liners must decide whether to repress or democratize. If they repress, there are two possible outcomes. If the repression is successful, there will be a narrow dictatorship in which the hard-liners return to prominence (Outcome 3). If the repression is unsuccessful, there will be an insurgency (Outcome 4). Whether state

---

12. Our Transition Game is based on an outline of a similar game provided by Przeworski (1991).

FIGURE 8.2 **Transition Game without Payoffs**

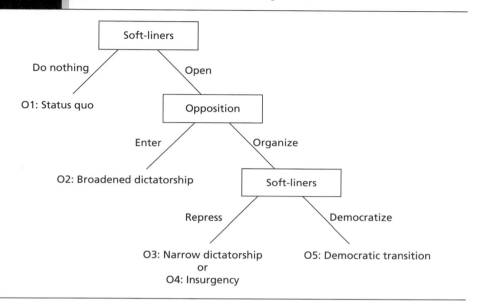

repression is successful or not is likely to depend, among other things, on the strength of the opposition groups. In what follows, we assume that state repression is successful and leads to a narrow dictatorship if the democratic opposition is weak but is unsuccessful and produces an insurgency if the democratic opposition is strong. Finally, if the soft-liners choose to democratize, the result is a democratic transition (Outcome 5).

Before we can determine what the players are likely to do in the Transition Game, we need to know how the players value the possible outcomes. Based on the argument that we have presented, we can provide a preference ordering for each player over the five possible outcomes; that is, we can determine how both players would rank the outcomes. The preference ordering for the soft-liners over the five outcomes is

Broadened dictatorship > Status quo > Narrow dictatorship >
Democratic transition > Insurgency,

where ">" means "is strictly preferred to." As this preference ordering illustrates, the ideal outcome for the soft-liners is a broadened dictatorship in which opposition groups are co-opted and their position in the dictatorship is strengthened relative to that of the hard-liners. If they cannot obtain this outcome, then they would prefer the political status quo—the dictatorship is maintained, and they are still in a position of power. If this outcome cannot be achieved, then they would prefer maintaining the dictatorship by handing power to the hard-liners in the form of a narrow dictatorship rather than having a democratic transition or an insurgency. If the dictatorship cannot be maintained in any form, we have assumed that the soft-liners would prefer a democratic transition to a potentially costly insurgency. We feel comfortable in making this assumption because the results of the Transition Game do not depend on whether the soft-liners prefer a democratic transition or an insurgency.

The preference ordering for the democratic opposition groups is

Democratic transition > Broadened dictatorship > Status quo > Insurgency
> Narrow dictatorship.

The ideal outcome for the opposition is a full transition to democracy. If this outcome is not possible, however, then it prefers a broadened dictatorship in which it gets to enjoy some concessions from the soft-liners. The political status quo is better than both an insurgency in which many people are likely to die and a narrow dictatorship in which the democratic opposition is repressed by hard-liners. We have assumed that the opposition will prefer an insurgency to a narrow dictatorship. Again, we are comfortable making this assumption because the results of the game do not depend on whether the opposition prefers an insurgency or a narrow dictatorship.

Given that there are five possible outcomes, we can assign the number 5 to each player's most preferred outcome, 4 to his or her second preferred outcome, 3 to his or her third preferred outcome, and so on. The players' payoffs are illustrated in Table 8.2. Recall from the discussion in Chapter 4 that these "ordinal payoffs" tell us about the order in which the players rank each of the outcomes but do not tell us how much more each player prefers one outcome to another.

We can now add these payoffs into the game tree shown earlier. To distinguish between the situation in which the soft-liners face a strong democratic opposition and the one in which they face a weak democratic opposition, we present two separate game trees in Figure 8.3. The only difference between the game trees is that repression produces a narrow dictatorship when the democratic opposition is weak but an insurgency if the democratic

TABLE 8.2	**Turning Outcomes into Payoffs in the Transition Game**		
Outcome	Description	Soft-liners	Opposition
O1	Status quo	4	3
O2	Broadened dictatorship	5	4
O3	Narrow dictatorship	3	1
O4	Insurgency	1	2
O5	Democratic transition	2	5

opposition is strong. As in previous game-theoretic models that we have presented, the soft-liners' payoffs are shown first because they are the first mover in the game; the opposition's payoffs are shown second. A comma separates the payoffs for each player. Just as an illustration, this means that the soft-liners receive a payoff of 4 and the democratic opposition receives a payoff of 3 if the outcome is the political status quo. Now that we have the payoffs, we can try to figure out what the players will do.

Let's start by looking at the situation in which the soft-liners are faced with a weak democratic opposition (left side, Figure 8.3a). As usual, we solve the game for subgame perfect equilibria using backward induction.[13] Recall that backward induction requires starting at the end of the game tree (at the final choice node) and working one's way back to the beginning of the game tree (initial node). The final choice node has the soft-liners deciding whether to repress or democratize. The soft-liners get a payoff of 3 if they repress and a payoff of 2 if they democratize. As a result, the soft-liners will choose to repress. We indicate this choice by making the repress branch at this final choice node bold in Figure 8.3a. Now we move backward to the choice node prior to the final choice node. At this choice node, the democratic opposition must decide whether to enter a broadened dictatorship or continue to organize. If the democratic opposition enters, it will get a payoff of 4. If it organizes, it can look down the game tree (follow the bold lines) and see that the soft-liners will repress and that its payoff will be 1. As a result, the democratic opposition will choose to enter. We indicate this choice by making the enter branch at this choice node bold. We now move back to the choice node prior to this one, which happens to be the initial node in the Transition Game. At this node the soft-liners must decide whether to do nothing and stick with the status quo or to open up the political regime. If the soft-liners do nothing, they will get a payoff of 4. If they open up, they can look down the game tree (follow the bold lines) and see that the democratic opposition will enter and that their payoff will be 5. It is easy to see that the soft-liners will choose to liberalize and open up in these circumstances.

We have now solved the Transition Game when the democratic opposition is weak using backward induction. So what is the subgame perfect equilibrium? Recall that the subgame perfect equilibrium (SPE) lists the actions chosen by each player at all of the choice nodes in the game. Thus, the SPE for this particular game is (Open, Repress; Enter). As before, we first list the choices made by the soft-liners (the first player) at each of the nodes at which they get to make a choice (Open, Repress), and then, we list the choices made by the democratic opposition (the second player) at each of the nodes at which it gets to make a choice (Enter). As a result, the SPE indicates that the soft-liners choose to open up and would choose to repress at the final choice node if the game arrived here; the democratic opposition chooses to enter at its one and only choice node. The expected outcome of the game is a broadened dictatorship, and the payoffs are 5 for the soft-liners and 4 for the opposition.

---

13. For a review of backward induction and subgame perfect equilibria, return to our initial and more detailed discussion of these concepts in Chapter 3.

FIGURE 8.3 **Transition Game with Payoffs**

a. Weak Opposition

b. Strong Opposition

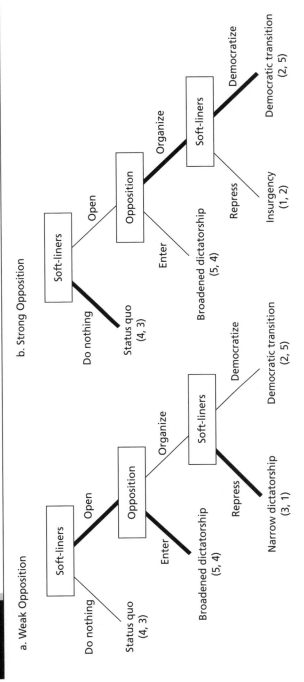

The subgame perfect equilibrium is (Open, Repress; Enter).

The subgame perfect equilibrium is (Do nothing, Democratize; Organize)

Now let's examine the situation in which the soft-liners are faced with a strong democratic opposition (right side, Figure 8.3b). The final choice node again has the soft-liners deciding whether to repress or democratize. This time, however, the soft-liners get a payoff of 1 if they repress and a payoff of 2 if they democratize. As a result, the soft-liners will choose to democratize. We indicate this choice by making the repress branch at this final choice node bold in Figure 8.3b. At the choice node prior to this, the democratic opposition must decide whether to enter a broadened dictatorship or continue to organize. If the democratic opposition enters, it will get a payoff of 4. If it organizes, it can look down the game tree and see that the soft-liners will democratize and that its payoff will be 5. As a result, the democratic opposition will choose to continue organizing. We indicate this choice by making the organize branch at this choice node bold. At the initial node, the soft-liners must decide whether to do nothing or open up the political regime. If the soft-liners do nothing, they will get a payoff of 4. If they open up, they can look down the game tree and see that the democratic opposition will organize. Given that the opposition organizes, the soft-liners will choose to democratize, and their payoff will be 2. It is easy to see, then, that the soft-liners will choose to do nothing at the initial node. We have now solved the Transition Game when the democratic opposition is strong using backward induction. The subgame perfect equilibrium is (Do nothing, Democratize; Organize). The expected outcome of the game is the political status quo, and the payoffs are 4 to the soft-liners and 3 to the opposition.

What can be learned from the Transition Game? The most important insight is that a transition to democracy is *not* possible as things stand. The only two possible outcomes are a broadened dictatorship or the political status quo. It is worth reexamining why these are the only two outcomes. When the democratic opposition is weak, the soft-liners can obtain their most preferred outcome—a broadened dictatorship. Why? A weak opposition chooses to accept the concessions of the soft-liners and enter the authoritarian institutions because this is better than the status quo and because it knows that it is not strong enough to prevent the soft-liners from successfully repressing it if it chooses to continue organizing against the regime. Knowing that a weak opposition will prefer to enter a broadened dictatorship rather than organize, the soft-liners are willing to liberalize, and the outcome is a broadened dictatorship.[14] When the democratic opposition is strong, though, the political status quo will prevail. Why? A strong opposition knows that if it organizes, then it is strong enough that the soft-liners will be unable to successfully repress it, and they will, therefore, prefer to democratize at this point. The soft-liners in turn know that a strong opposition will respond to liberalization by organizing and that, as a result, they will eventually be forced to democratize. To avoid being forced into a democratization they do not want, the soft-liners simply do nothing and stick with the political status quo.

---

14. If we think of the democratic opposition's strength as being determined by how unified or divided it is, then this result is consistent with one of the insights in Lust-Okar's (2005) study of authoritarian rule in Morocco, Egypt, and Jordan. She finds that political liberalization is more likely to be successful in situations in which the opposition is divided (weak) rather than in those in which it is unified (strong).

But we know that top-down transitions to democracy do occur. So what's going on? Is there something wrong with the Transition Game? All of the game-theoretic models that we have examined in this book up to this point are what we call complete information games. A **complete information game** is essentially one in which each player knows all the information that there is to know about the game—the identity and type of the players, the choices available to each player, the order of the choices, the possible outcomes, and the preferences of the players over the outcomes. The Transition Game shown in Figure 8.3 is also a complete information game. What we have shown to this point is that top-down transitions to democracy are not possible in situations in which the players know everything, or have complete information.

> A **complete information game** is one in which each player knows all the information that there is to know about the game.

One of the key assumptions underlying our analysis is that the soft-liners know what type of opposition they are dealing with—they know whether they are dealing with a strong democratic opposition or a weak democratic opposition. In effect, we have assumed that the soft-liners know whether they are playing the game outlined in Figure 8.3a (left) or the one shown in Figure 8.3b (right). What if this is not the case, though? What if we change our game into one of incomplete information, where the soft-liners are uncertain as to the type of opposition—weak or strong—that they are dealing with? What follows is an informal discussion of the consequences of adding this type of incomplete information into our Transition Game. After reading this informal discussion, we encourage you to read Box 8.6, "Transition Game with Incomplete Information," for a more formal elaboration of our argument.

Given our earlier discussion of preference falsification, it seems almost certain that authoritarian soft-liners will not always have complete information and that they will often be uncertain or misinformed about the true strength of the democratic opposition. Although citizens are likely to support the regime in public, they may well oppose it quite vehemently in private. Opposition groups are likely to take great care to keep their activities hidden from the prying eyes of the dictatorship and its secret police. Despite their best efforts, it is almost impossible for dictatorships to successfully shut down all forms of autonomous organizations that escape their control; there will nearly always be underground resistance networks of some sort.

It turns out that top-down transitions to democracy can occur if authoritarian soft-liners are incorrect about the type of opposition (weak or strong) they are facing. Suppose that the soft-liners think that the democratic opposition is weak, that is, that they are playing the Transition Game in Figure 8.3a. As we demonstrated earlier, the soft-liners will choose to liberalize and open up the political regime because they expect the opposition to enter into a broadened dictatorship. But what happens if the soft-liners are mistaken in their beliefs about the strength of the democratic opposition? What happens if the opposition is actually strong and the soft-liners are really playing the Transition Game in Figure 8.3b? If this is the case, then we have already seen that the strong democratic opposition will choose to continue organizing when the soft-liners open up. As soon as the soft-liners see the opposition organizing, they will immediately realize that they have made a dreadful mistake because they will know that only a strong opposition would take such an action; a weak opposition would enter a broadened dictatorship. Now that they know for sure that they are facing a strong democratic opposition, the soft-liners will realize that repression will be unsuccessful and that their best option is to democratize further. The end result is a top-down transition to democracy.

The central point to take away from this is that democratic transitions from above are not possible under complete information, that is, in situations in which everyone knows everything. They can occur only when there is some uncertainty or incomplete information. In effect, this type of transition occurs only because someone makes a mistake. In regard to our particular version of the Transition Game, the mistake is that the soft-liners think they are dealing with a weak democratic opposition when, in fact, they are facing a strong one.

---

ox 8.6   ## TRANSITION GAME WITH INCOMPLETE INFORMATION

In the main text of this chapter, we claim that top-down transitions are possible if authoritarian soft-liners are uncertain as to whether they face a weak democratic opposition or a strong democratic opposition. We now examine this claim more formally with the help of an **incomplete information game**.

> An **incomplete information game** is one in which a player does not know all of the relevant information about some other player's characteristics.

Recall that we previously analyzed two complete information Transition Games. In one, the soft-liners know for sure that the democratic opposition is strong, and in the other, they know for sure that it is weak (Figure 8.3). In our incomplete information Transition Game, we incorporate a new "actor" who determines whether we are playing the game with the strong opposition or the one with the weak opposition. We refer to this new actor as "Nature." Unfortunately for the soft-liners, they don't know which game Nature is going to choose. All they know is that Nature chooses the game in which the opposition is weak with some probability p and that it chooses the game in which the opposition is strong with some probability $1 - p$.

We now incorporate this information into a new game tree shown in Figure 8.4. The dashed line indicates that when the soft-liners choose to do nothing or open up at their first choice node, they don't know whether they are playing the game with the strong opposition or the weak opposition. One other change should be pointed out. Unlike with games of complete information, we cannot use ordinal payoffs with games of incomplete information. Instead, we have to use cardinal payoffs. Cardinal payoffs are different from ordinal payoffs in that they tell us exactly how much more a player values one outcome compared with another. In other words, a player values an outcome with a payoff of 4 four times as much as an outcome with a payoff of 1. To keep things as simple as possible, we have retained the same payoffs we used in our complete information Transition Game. Remember, however, these are now cardinal payoffs, not ordinal payoffs.

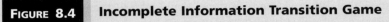

FIGURE 8.4   **Incomplete Information Transition Game**

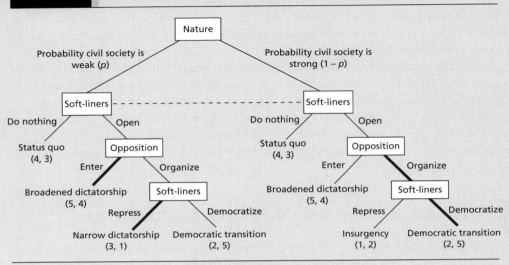

Now that we have specified the game, we can try to figure out what the players will do. We start with the usual method of backward induction. At the final two choice nodes, the soft-liners must choose whether to democratize or repress. As we saw earlier, the soft-liners will choose to repress in the left-hand side of the game tree (when they believe the democratic opposition is weak), and they will choose to democratize in the right-hand side of the game tree (when they believe the democratic opposition is strong). We indicate these choices by making the relevant branch at these final two choice nodes bold. We now move back to the two previous choice nodes where the democratic opposition must choose whether to continue organizing or enter a broadened dictatorship. As we saw earlier, a weak opposition will enter and a strong opposition will organize. As a result, we indicate these choices by making the relevant branch at these choice nodes bold as well.

We must now determine whether the soft-liners will choose to do nothing or open up at their initial choice nodes. Unfortunately, the method of backward induction no longer works. This is because the dashed line between these two choice nodes in Figure 8.4 indicates that the soft-liners don't know which side of the game tree they are on. Their uncertainty over the strength of the democratic opposition means that the soft-liners don't know for sure what their payoffs will be if they open up. On the one hand, if the soft-liners open up and the opposition is weak, they can look down the game tree (follow the bold lines on the left-hand side) and see that the outcome will be a broadened dictatorship with a payoff of 5. On the other hand, if they open up and the opposition is strong, they can again look down the game tree (follow the bold lines on the right-hand side) and see that the outcome will be a democratic transition with a payoff of 2. Whether the democratic opposition is weak or strong, the soft-liners will get a payoff of 4 if they do nothing; that is, the "do nothing" branch on either side of the game tree always gives the soft-liners a payoff of 4.

What should the soft-liners do? They know that they can get a payoff of 4 if they do nothing, and they know that they will get either a payoff of 5 or a payoff of 2 if they open up. What would you do? The way political scientists approach this problem is to ask whether the payoff the soft-liners *expect* to get if they open up is greater than the payoff they *know* they'll get if they do nothing. To answer this question, it is necessary to calculate the soft-liners' expected payoff from opening up. In general, the **expected payoff** of some choice (in this case to open up) is calculated by multiplying the payoff associated with each possible outcome by the probability that that

> An **expected payoff** is the sum of the payoffs associated with each outcome multiplied by the probability with which each outcome occurs.

outcome occurs and then summing these values. Thus, if there are two possible outcomes associated with some choice, as is the case here, then the expected payoff is calculated as follows:

$$\text{Expected payoff (Choice)} = (\text{Probability Outcome 1 occurs} \times \text{Payoff from Outcome 1})$$
$$+$$
$$(\text{Probability Outcome 2 occurs} \times \text{Payoff from Outcome 2}).$$

As some of you will no doubt have realized, an expected payoff essentially tells the players what they could expect their average payoff to be if they were able to make their choice over and over again.

What is the expected payoff for the soft-liners if they open up? With probability p, the soft-liners are on the left-hand side of the game tree with a weak democratic opposition, and we have already seen that the outcome is a broadened dictatorship with a payoff of 5. With probability $1 - p$, the soft-liners are on the right-hand side of the game tree with a strong democratic opposition, and we have already seen that the outcome is a democratic transition with a payoff of 2. Thus, their expected payoff from opening up is

$$\text{Expected payoff (Open)} = (p \times 5) + [(1 - p) \times 2]$$
$$= 5p + 2 - 2p$$
$$= 3p + 2.$$

Now that we know this, will the soft-liners choose to do nothing and receive a payoff of 4, or will they choose to open up with an expected payoff of $3p + 2$? It should be immediately obvious that the soft-liners' choice will depend on the value of p, that is, the probability with which the soft-liners believe the democratic opposition is weak. The soft-liners will choose to open up and liberalize when the expected payoff from opening up is greater than the payoff from doing nothing. This occurs when

$$\text{Expected payoff (Open)} > \text{Payoff (Do Nothing)}$$
$$\Rightarrow \qquad 3p + 2 > 4$$
$$\Rightarrow \qquad 3p > 2$$
$$\Rightarrow \qquad p > 2/3.$$

As you can see, the soft-liners will choose to open up and liberalize if and only if they believe that the probability that the opposition is weak is greater than 2/3. This is referred to as the "critical probability." If they believe that the opposition is weak with a probability less than this, then the soft-liners will choose to do nothing and the outcome will be the status quo.

Our analysis illustrates just how a top-down transition to democracy might occur. In effect, we have just demonstrated that authoritarian soft-liners will choose to open up and liberalize whenever they are sufficiently confident that the democratic opposition is weak.[15] The problem is that their beliefs about the strength of the opposition may be wrong; the democratic opposition may, in fact, be strong. As we saw earlier, the opposition will continue to organize and mobilize if it is strong. Because only a strong democratic opposition would organize, the soft-liners will realize that they have made a critical mistake and update their initial beliefs about the opposition's strength. Their updated beliefs will now be that the democratic opposition is strong for sure; that is, $p = 0$. Having realized that the opposition is strong, the soft-liners will then choose to democratize because they know that repression will be unsuccessful and will lead to an unwanted insurgency. In effect, the authoritarian soft-liners inadvertently become democratizers in this situation because of their mistaken beliefs.

Games of incomplete information highlight the important role that information and beliefs play in politics. One implication of these games is that political actors have incentives to take actions that influence the beliefs of other actors. For example, a strong democratic opposition in the prehistory of our incomplete information Transition Game will try to avoid taking actions that signal its strength to the authoritarian soft-liners if it thinks that they might liberalize; it will try to act just like a weak democratic opposition. By acting as if it were weak, a strong opposition makes it more likely that the soft-liners will choose to open up the regime. At this point, the democratic opposition can reveal that it is strong and push for a full transition to democracy. The incomplete information Transition Game that we have just presented is one in which the soft-liners don't know what type (weak or strong) of democratic opposition they are dealing with. We could, however, easily adapt our game to examine situations in which the democratic opposition doesn't know what type of dictatorship (repressive or liberal) it is dealing with. Indeed, we

---

15. Given the particular payoffs that we employed, the soft-liners had to believe that the democratic opposition was weak with a probability greater than 2/3.

16. Blaydes and Lo (2012) do exactly this, extending our incomplete information Transition Game such that the opposition doesn't know the type of dictatorship it faces, and the dictatorship doesn't know whether it faces a moderate opposition (that wants a democracy) or a radical opposition (that wants a theocracy). The game presented by Blaydes and Lo essentially combines the insights of our Transition Game with the insights of our Religious Party Game (Problem 6 at the end of this chapter).

could investigate the situation in which the opposition is unsure about the type of dictatorship it faces and the dictatorship is unsure about the type of opposition it faces.[16] As you can see, incomplete information games have the potential to capture situations in the world in which there are quite complicated informational asymmetries and where actors have strong incentives to try to deceive each other.

Our Transition Game has two further implications. The first has to do with when we are likely to see institutionalized dictatorships—those with legislatures, political parties, elections, and so on. If we conceive of a broadened dictatorship as an institutionalized one, then the results from our Transition Game indicate that dictatorial institutionalization is likely to occur only when the authoritarian soft-liners believe that the democratic opposition has moderate strength. The opposition has to be strong enough that the soft-liners feel they can benefit from making some liberalizing concessions, but not so strong that they think they won't be able to repress the opposition if it looks like they are about to lose control of the liberalization process. Although our Transition Game has something to say about the conditions under which we expect to see institutionalized dictatorships, it does not provide any firm predictions as to whether liberalization and institutionalization actually help the stability and survival of dictatorships. Dictators may well establish seemingly democratic institutions in the hope that they will improve their chances of staying in power. Our Transition Game illustrates that the effectiveness of the liberalization process in achieving this objective will depend heavily on whether the beliefs of the authoritarian elites about the strength or weakness of the democratic opposition are correct. If a dictatorship establishes institutions such as elections and legislatures under the mistaken belief that the democratic opposition is weak, then these institutions may, in fact, accelerate the dictatorship's collapse.

The second implication is that it is possible to have authoritarian soft-liners who would like to open up the political system by introducing liberalizing reforms but who choose to do nothing because they are not sure that the democratic opposition is sufficiently weak that they could control the liberalization process if they start it. This suggests that some people living in dictatorships are actually living under more repressive conditions than need be the case. If the democratic opposition could somehow commit to not taking advantage of the liberalization process by organizing and pushing for full democracy, then soft-liners might be willing to introduce some liberalizing reforms. The result would not be full democracy, but it may be a more palatable and less repressive form of broadened dictatorship. The difficulty facing a weak opposition is that they cannot simply tell the soft-liners they are weak, as a strong opposition would also say that they are weak in an attempt to trick the soft-liners into introducing a liberalization process that would eventually result in democratization.

Applying the Transition Game to Poland

We now illustrate the usefulness of our Transition Game for understanding top-down transitions by applying it to help explain the democratic transition that occurred in Poland in 1989. In the late 1970s, the Polish economy was in a state of crisis. The Communist government had borrowed money from the West that it then used to subsidize prices on things like food to keep its citizens satisfied. From 1975 to 1981, Poland's foreign debt increased from $700 million to $23 billion (Hitchcock 2004). When the repayment of this huge debt began to come due, the leader of Poland's Communist Party, Edward Gierek, was forced to raise prices. This led to strikes that started in the Gdansk shipyards. The strikers presented twenty-one demands to the government. These demands included things like freedom of expression, a right to strike, access to the media, and better housing, but the most important one was for a trade union independent of Communist Party control. Unsure of whether the Polish army would actually fire on its own people, Gierek backed down, and the independent trade union, Solidarity, was formed in September 1980. Within two weeks of its formation, three million Poles had joined Solidarity under the leadership of an electrician by the name of Lech Walesa. By 1981, Solidarity had ten million members and had come out in direct opposition to the Communist regime. At this point, Solidarity had become much more than just a trade union.

The Soviets were becoming increasingly worried about the situation in Poland, and there were rumors that they were drawing up invasion plans. By now, Gierek had been replaced by the hard-liner General Wojciech Jaruzelski. In December 1981, Jaruzelski declared martial law. Overnight, thousands were arrested, the army occupied factories and smashed strikes, Solidarity was banned, and a military dictatorship was established. Martial law remained in place until 1983. This particular episode in Polish history illustrates just how a period of liberalization could get out of control and eventually produce a repressive backlash resulting in the coming to power of hard-liners like Jaruzelski.

Despite attempts to solve the economic problems that plagued Poland, the economy did not significantly improve over the next few years. As a new wave of strikes threatened to get out of control and turn violent in mid-1988, the Polish Communist Party (PUWP) attempted to introduce a new period of liberalization. In December 1988 the government agreed to convene a conference with the banned trade union Solidarity to see if they could hammer out a compromise. These talks, which took place between February and April 1989, became known as the Roundtable Talks. At these talks, it was agreed, among other things, that Solidarity would be legalized and that nationwide legislative elections would occur in June. The goal of this liberalization process was to defuse social unrest, co-opt the democratic opposition, and get Solidarity to lend its moral authority to the electoral process. As Jaruzelski put it, "the game is about absorbing the opposition into our system" (Perzkowski 1994, 262).

Like most elections in dictatorships, the proposed legislative elections in Poland were not entirely open. All 100 seats in the Polish Senate were to be freely contested, but 65 percent of the seats in the lower house, or Sejm, were reserved for the Communists and their allies. With 65 percent of the seats in the Sejm, the Communists could expect to appoint the prime minister; they were already guaranteed the presidency because there were to be no presidential elections. The Polish Communist Party expected to do quite well in the legislative elections and did not believe that Solidarity was strong enough to realistically challenge its hold on power. Just after introducing martial law in 1981, General Jaruzelski had established a special Center for Public Opinion Research (CBOS; Kaminski 1999). CBOS was designed to provide information about the level of support enjoyed by the regime among the public and to reduce incentives for bureaucrats and administrators to paint an overly rosy picture of regime stability. Opinion polls since the mid-1980s had consistently shown that the Communist Party enjoyed more confidence than Solidarity.

Given the beliefs that the Communist Party had about the strength of Solidarity, the election results came as a complete surprise. Solidarity won all 35 percent of the Sejm seats that it was allowed to contest and 99 of the 100 seats in the Senate. Up until the time that the election results were announced, the process surrounding the Roundtable Talks had been understood as one designed to bring about a "big thaw" and not the end of Communist rule. The election results of June 4, 1989, and the overwhelming victory for Solidarity changed this understanding dramatically. That night, a popular Polish actress, Joanna Szczepkowska, announced on official television: "Friends, this is the end of communism in our country!" What happened next, though, also came as a surprise. The 65 percent of the guaranteed seats had "symbolically" been divided between the Communist Party (37.6 percent) and the so-called "deaf and speechless" puppet parties that were allied to it (26.9 percent). After the election, two of these previously loyal parties joined forces with Solidarity to give it more than 50 percent of the Sejm seats. With this legislative majority, Solidarity was able to appoint the first non-Communist prime minister in Eastern Europe in forty years. In contrast to 1981, the Soviets now made it abundantly clear that they would not intervene in Polish affairs, which meant that the Communists could not feasibly break the agreement they had reached with Solidarity and reverse the liberalization process. As we saw earlier in the chapter, the events in Poland had the effect of encouraging the democratic opposition in other East European countries to challenge their own Communist rulers. Within months, Communist control in Eastern Europe had essentially come to an end.

As our Transition Game predicted, one of the key elements in Poland's democratic transition was the Communist Party's incorrect beliefs about the strength of Solidarity. The opinion surveys conducted by CBOS turned out to be poor indicators of the political support enjoyed by Solidarity. Although they were carefully conducted, they were deeply flawed in many ways. For example, roughly 30 percent of respondents refused to complete the surveys. To a large extent, this high refusal rate was the result of Solidarity supporters not wanting to interact with Communist institutions. Many of those who opposed Communist rule but who actually agreed to complete the surveys would have falsified their preferences out of fear anyway. Much of the Solidarity organization remained underground, out of sight of the

Communist Party. The considerable strength of this underground Solidarity network is described by a former colleague, Marek Kaminski, who also spent time in a Polish jail as a political prisoner:

> In 1985, I was running an underground publishing house, STOP, that employed about twenty full-time workers and up to 100 moonlighters. Between 1982 and 1989, we published about thirty-five titles of more than 100,000 books combined. We were a part of a decentralized network that included about 100 underground publishing houses, hundreds of periodicals, thousands of trade union organizations with a hierarchically organized leadership structure, a few Nobel Prize winners, and even underground theaters, galleries, and video rentals. We called it an "independent society." (2004, 2)

It is worth noting that Kaminski was a twenty-two-year-old student at Warsaw University in 1985—probably not much older than most of you reading this book. It is easy to see from what Kaminski writes why the Polish Communist Party might have seriously overestimated its own strength relative to that of Solidarity. Mistaken beliefs were crucial to the Polish transition to democracy in 1989, and they are, in fact, central to top-down transitions to democracy more generally.

CONCLUSION

Democratic transitions tend to result from bottom-up processes, in which the people rise up to overthrow an authoritarian regime in a popular revolution, or from top-down processes, in which dictatorial elites introduce liberalizing reforms that inadvertently lead to democracy. In this chapter, we have examined bottom-up and top-down democratic transitions drawing on historical evidence from Eastern Europe.

Collective action theory throws light on why bottom-up democratic transitions like those that took place in East Germany, Czechoslovakia, and Romania in 1989 are so rare and why authoritarian regimes frequently appear stable. Because democracy is a form of public good, attempts at collective action to bring it about suffer from a free-rider problem. This means that individuals have strong incentives not to participate in mass protests or demonstrations calling for democratic reforms and instead free ride on the actions of others. The end result is that public displays of opposition are extremely rare in dictatorships. A consequence of this is that authoritarian elites usually seem, at least on the surface, to have a strong hold on power.

Because there can be significant dangers associated with publicly opposing dictatorships, individuals who dislike authoritarian regimes tend not to reveal their true preferences—instead of opposing the dictatorship in public, they support it. The prevalence of this type of preference falsification helps to explain the puzzle of why popular revolutions nearly always come as a surprise yet appear so inevitable in hindsight. Revolutions come as a surprise because nobody can be exactly sure about the true level of opposition in a dictatorship—societies can come to the brink of revolution without anyone's realizing it. Revolutions frequently appear inevitable in hindsight because few people will openly claim to have supported the old dictatorial regime, even if they did, once it has been overthrown and replaced by a democracy; the danger now comes from publicly opposing the democracy. The tipping models that we examined in this chapter provide further insight into why revolutions are so unpredictable and why even small changes in people's preferences can sometimes rapidly transform previously subservient individuals into revolutionary protesters. Because each society has a different distribution of revolutionary thresholds, policies or actions that lead to a revolutionary cascade in one dictatorship may have little, or at least appear to have little, effect in some other dictatorship.

Our analysis of top-down democratic transitions like the one that occurred in Poland in 1989 suggests that they can happen only when someone makes a mistake. Although authoritarian elites sometimes introduce periods of liberalization, the goal of liberalization policies is typically to strengthen and stabilize the dictatorship rather than produce a democratic transition. In effect, the objective of the dictatorship is to broaden its social base in an attempt to maintain its hold on power. According to the Transition Game that we presented in this chapter, top-down transitions will not occur if the relevant actors—the authoritarian elite and democratic opposition groups—know everything there is to know about each other. They *can* occur, however, if incomplete information leads actors to have mistaken beliefs about the types of actors with whom they are interacting. For example, a democratic transition can occur in our Transition Game if the authoritarian elite mistakenly believes that the opposition is weak when, in fact, it is strong. Our game-theoretic analysis highlights the important role that information, beliefs, and uncertainty can play in democratic transitions—and politics more generally.

We should remind readers that the distinction between top-down and bottom-up transitions that we have made in this chapter is, to some extent, an analytical convenience. Bottom-up transitions may *begin* with the largely autonomous actions of mass publics—like many of the demonstrations in the Middle East and North Africa (MENA) region in the spring of 2011—but once they do, opposition groups often become involved in a game of strategic interaction with elites. In some cases, elites may respond to pressures from below with liberalizing reforms, or at least the promise thereof. For example, Egypt's Hosni Mubarak responded to the first wave of protests in January 2011 with promises of a crackdown. But when his military seemed unwilling to engage in widespread repression, he promised to step down in six months after an election to choose his successor. This move—clearly in response to bottom-up pressures—could be thought of as the first node of the "top-down" Transition Game described in this chapter. Not surprisingly, however, since this offer came from a position of weakness relative to the opposition, it did not lead to a broadened dictatorship. Instead, the opposition organized another wave of protests and demanded that Mubarak step down immediately. A few weeks later Mubarak did, in fact, step down, and new elections were held in 2012. Within a year, though, the newly elected president, Mohammed Morsi, was ousted in a military coup, his supporters were attacked, and the constitution was suspended. Thus, opposition organizing has led to repression and a narrow dictatorship in Egypt, at least for now.

The bottom-up pressures for democracy expressed across the MENA region during the spring of 2011 have not, with the exception of Tunisia, led to democratic transitions. In many cases, the Arab Spring has resulted in authoritarian reactions similar to the "return to normalcy" that occurred following the 1968 Prague Spring (see Box 8.5, "Prague Spring, 1968"). In an analysis written shortly after the MENA protests, Way (2011) argued that there were reasons to be pessimistic about the probability of successful transitions to democracy in many of the countries that were experiencing pressures for change in the MENA region. He argued that a decade after the fall of communism, structural factors such as the level of economic development and the presence of natural resources turned out to be the best predictors of which Eastern European countries would experience successful democratic consolidations. As we suggested in Chapter 6, these factors do not provide the basis for optimism in most of the MENA countries. In addition, Way argued that external factors encouraging democracy in Eastern Europe, such as the hands-off approach adopted by the Soviet Union and the desire of the Eastern European countries to join the democratic club of the European Union, are also largely absent in the MENA region. In fact, concerns about radical Islam and access to oil resources have historically led the United States to support authoritarian regimes in the region. Nearly five years after the Arab Spring, it is clear that the early optimism felt by many participants was not warranted.

The last three chapters have examined the economic and cultural determinants of democracy and dictatorship, as well as the dynamics of regime transition. An implicit assumption throughout has been that democracy is good and something that should be promoted. In the next chapter, we ask if it really matters whether someone lives in a democracy or a dictatorship. Specifically, we focus on whether democracy makes a material difference in people's lives.

KEY CONCEPTS

bottom-up democratic transition *271*
collective action *280*
collective action, or free-rider, problem *281*
complete information game *302*
expected payoff *305*
glasnost *273*
incomplete information game *303*
nonexcludability *280*
nonrivalry *280*

perestroika *273*
policy of liberalization *293*
preference falsification *285*
public good *280*
revolutionary cascade *287*
revolutionary threshold *286*
third wave of democratization *271*
top-down democratic transition *271*

PROBLEMS

We start with five problems addressing issues to do with transitions, collective action, information, and democratic consolidation. We then go on to provide material to help prepare you for dealing with games of incomplete information. You will find this material extremely helpful for answering problems 6 and 7.

Part I: Problems 1–5

1. *Collective Action Problem*

   a. Give three examples—not already provided in the chapter—of public goods. Explain why they are public goods.

   b. Suppose that you are a leader of an interest group trying to get the government to change one of its policies by holding a street protest. According to collective action theory, would you prefer to live in a world where you need 20 percent of your members to march in the streets in order to be successful or a world in which you need 80 percent of your members to march in the streets to be successful? Explain your answer.

   c. Suppose that there are two interest groups, A and B, trying to get the government to change its policies by holding street protests. Group A has 5,000 members and group B has 10,000 members. Assume that each group's protest will be successful if it gets 20 percent of its members marching in the streets. According to collective action theory, which interest group is most likely to get the government to change its policies? Explain your answer.

2. *Top-Down versus Bottom-Up Transitions*

   a. There was a regime transition in Burkina Faso in 2014 when the long-lived dictatorship of Blaise Compaoré collapsed. Use the Internet and other sources to identify the key political actors in this transition. Do you think this transition is best characterized as "top-down" or "bottom-up"? Why? Provide the sources you used for this answer.

   b. Myanmar, formerly Burma, was under military rule from 1962 to 2010. In 2003, the ruling military junta, known as the State Peace and Development Council, announced a "Roadmap to Discipline-flourishing Democracy." Use the Internet and other sources to examine the political reforms that have taken place in Myanmar since the adoption of a new constitution in 2008. How does the material covered in this chapter help to throw light on recent developments in Myanmar?

3. *Controlling Information*

Authoritarian regimes find it useful to control certain kinds of information, either by punishing people who dissent publicly or by trying to influence public opinion using state-controlled media. Obtain a copy of Maja Adena and colleagues' 2015 article "Radio and the Rise of the Nazis in

Prewar Germany" from the journal *Quarterly Journal of Economics* (130:1885–1939) using your institution's library resources. Read the article and then answer the following questions.

   a. The authors distinguish between three distinct periods in the use of radio in interwar Germany. Prior to 1929, the use of radio was largely apolitical. From 1929 to January 1933, radio broadcasts were politically favorable to the Weimar governments and displayed a strong bias against the Nazi party. From January 1933, radio broadcasts exhibited considerable pro-Nazi propaganda. In each of these three periods, what effect do the authors expect radio broadcasts to have on citizen support for the democratic government? What effect do they expect them to have on the support for the Nazi party?

   b. How do the authors test the implications of their argument about the impact of radio broadcasts on political opinions? What do they find?

   c. Do the authors argue that the effects of radio propaganda were similar across the entire population? Explain what they find. Do you think this finding is compatible with the assumption in the tipping model that individuals have different revolutionary thresholds?

4. *Protesting in an Authoritarian Regime: The Mothers of the Plaza de Mayo*

In 1976, Argentina's armed forces launched a coup d'état and established a military dictatorship that was to last until 1983. This period of Argentinian history is commonly referred to as the "Dirty War." During the Dirty War, political and trade union activity was banned, detention centers were created, and special forces, including right-wing death squads, were established to kidnap, interrogate, torture, and kill political dissidents, opponents of the regime, and anyone believed to be associated with socialism. Those people who were taken by the military are commonly referred to as "the disappeared." As many as 30,000 Argentinians are reported to have disappeared during the Dirty War (Global Nonviolent Action Database, http://nvdatabase .swarthmore.edu/).

   During the military dictatorship, and in spite of the sometimes severe repercussions from the regime, a group of protesters known as the Mothers of the Plaza de Mayo would gather for weekly protests. Over time, the group grew larger and attracted international attention. As Bosco (2006, 348) notes,

> The Madres first encountered each other as they were looking for their sons and daughters in [official government offices.] [...] [T]he Madres decided to meet weekly in the Plaza de Mayo in downtown Buenos Aires to exchange the meager information they had been collecting in police stations and military facilities. The Madres' first meetings were not meant to be public demonstrations but they began functioning as such once the police threatened the women with arrests for loitering. This forced the Madres to begin walking many times on the perimeter of the square to avoid being arrested. Such was the origin of the Madres' weekly marches that were to become their signature public display of activism

and mobilization. [...] In remembering their beginning, the Madres are quick to point out that the majority of them had not met each other before their children were kidnapped. Although the women did not know one another, it was their participation in different kinds of neighborhood, family, friendship, political, ethnic, and workplace networks that allowed them access to information about other women in the same situation. Even those women who lived in the relative isolation of rural areas were able to meet other women like themselves through networks of acquaintances. Some of the Madres became activists even before their sons and daughters were disappeared by the military.[17]

a. What features of this situation make collective action unlikely?
b. What features of this situation might have led to an increase or a decrease in the revolutionary thresholds of the mothers? In your answer, consider their interactions with the regime as well as with each other.

5. *Democratic Consolidation Game*

Political scientists sometimes distinguish between democratic transitions and democratic consolidation (Svolik 2007). "Transition and consolidation are conceptually distinct aspects of [democratic development], although in practice they may temporally overlap or sometimes even coincide. Transition begins with the breakdown of the former [dictatorial] regime and ends with the establishment of a relatively stable configuration of political institutions within a democratic regime. Consolidation . . . refers to the achievement of substantial attitudinal support for and behavioral compliance with the new democratic institutions and the rules of the game which they establish. . . . [T]ransition results in the creation of a new regime; consolidation results in the stability and persistence of that regime, even in the face of severe challenges" (Gunther, Puhle, and Diamandouros 1995, 3).

One of the stated goals behind the US invasion of Iraq and the overthrow of Saddam Hussein in 2003 was to help establish a consolidated democracy in the Middle East. Although Iraq has undergone a transition that has seen the emergence of numerous political parties, elections, a new legislature, a new constitution, and so on, it is unclear that the end result will be a consolidated democracy. As with other democratic transitions that have occurred around the world, much depends on the types of agreement that are possible between the supporters of the former authoritarian regime (primarily Sunnis) and the supporters of the new regime (primarily Shiites).

One way to think about this is whether or not the two sides are willing to take moderate approaches toward each other. The supporters of the new regime can take a moderate approach and offer amnesty and concessions to Saddam Hussein's former supporters (Sunnis), *or* they can take a radical approach and refuse amnesty and any concessions. The authoritarian supporters (Sunnis) can take a moderate approach and agree to support the new regime, *or* they can take

17. For more information about the Mothers of the Plaza de Mayo, see the Global Nonviolent Action Database webpage at http://nvdatabase.swarthmore.edu/content/mothers-plaza-de-mayo-campaign-democracy-and-return-their-disappeared-family-members-1977-19. Note that many of the cases addressed in this database are based on research done by undergraduate students.

FIGURE 8.5	Democratic Consolidation Game

		Shiites (Supporters of new regime)	
		Radical approach (No amnesty)	Moderate approach (amnesty)
Sunnis (Authoritarian supporters)	Radical approach (Fight back)	Civil war	Civil war
	Moderate approach (Support new regime)	Full democracy	Limited democracy

a radical approach that involves taking up arms and fighting. If the Sunnis decide to fight back, there will be a civil war no matter whether the Shiites offer an amnesty or not. If the Sunnis agree to support the new regime and the Shiites offer no amnesty or concessions, then there will be a full democracy. If the Sunnis agree to democratic reforms and the Shiites offer an amnesty, however, there will be a limited democracy—democracy will be limited because the Shiites had to make concessions to the Sunnis that probably include retaining some legacy of the Saddam Hussein dictatorship. This strategic situation is shown in the normal form Democratic Consolidation Game shown in Figure 8.5.

Let's suppose that the Sunnis have the following preference ordering:

Limited democracy > Civil war (amnesty) > Civil war (no amnesty) > Full democracy

and that the Shiites have the following preference ordering:

Full democracy > Limited democracy > Civil war (no amnesty) > Civil war (amnesty).

a. Use the preference orderings shown above to fill in the matrix shown in Figure 8.5 with the payoffs for each player. Use the numbers 4, 3, 2, and 1 to indicate the preference ordering for the players. What is the Nash equilibrium? What is the expected outcome? What are the payoffs that each player receives?

b. Is there another outcome that both the Sunnis and the Shiites would prefer to the expected outcome? If so, what is it? Why isn't this outcome a Nash equilibrium?

Now let's suppose that the Shiites have a slightly different preference ordering from the one shown above. Specifically, let's assume that the Shiites have the following preference ordering, where "=" means "is indifferent between":

Full democracy = Limited democracy > Civil war (no amnesty) > Civil war (amnesty).

As you can see, the only difference is that the Shiites are now indifferent between having a full democracy and a limited democracy; before, they had strictly preferred a full democracy to a limited democracy.

    c. Use the new preference ordering for the Shiites and the same preference ordering as before for the Sunnis to fill in the matrix shown in Figure 8.5 with the payoffs for each player. (Note that if any of the players are indifferent between two outcomes, then they receive the same payoff from both outcomes.) List any Nash equilibria. List any expected outcomes. List the payoffs that each player receives from each expected outcome.

    d. Is some form of consolidated democracy—limited or full—a possible equilibrium in this modified version of the Democratic Consolidation Game?

    e. In May 2003 the US administrator of Iraq, L. Paul Bremer, issued two orders. One order outlawed Saddam Hussein's Sunni-dominated Baath Party and dismissed all its senior members from their government posts. This order led to the firing of about 30,000 ex-Baathists from various government ministries. The second order dissolved Iraq's 500,000-member military and intelligence services. All military officers above the rank of colonel were barred from returning to work, as were all 100,000 members of the various Iraqi intelligence agencies. In November 2003 Bremer established a Supreme National De-Baathification Commission to root out senior Baathists—primarily Sunnis—from Iraq's ministries. Imagine that you were an adviser to Bremer during this period and that your goal was to establish a consolidated democracy. Based on what you have learned from the two versions of the Democratic Consolidation Game that we examined, would you have advised Bremer to issue these two orders or not? Explain your answer.

    f. Nouri al-Maliki became the first prime minister appointed under the provisions of Iraq's new constitution. If you were one of Maliki's advisers, would you tell him to offer an amnesty to Sunnis involved in terrorist activities? Explain your answer.

    g. One problem with promises of amnesty has to do with their credibility. Can you think of how credible commitment problems (see Chapter 6) might affect the efficacy of amnesty promises? How might actors try to overcome these credible commitment problems?

    h. Between 1936 and 1975, Spain was a dictatorship under the rule of General Francisco Franco. Spain finally underwent a transition to democracy in 1976 following a series of negotiations between elites who wanted to continue the dictatorship (Francoists) and elites who wanted to introduce democratic reforms (Reformists). In 1976 King Juan Carlos appointed a Reformist, Adolfo Suárez, as president. Upon coming to power Suárez presented a bill for political reform. Although Suárez was a Reformist, his bill promised the Francoists the continuation of the monarchy in the person of King Juan Carlos, the maintenance of the unity of Spain, and the exclusion of the Communists. It also promised them an electoral system that rewarded representation in rural areas and a Senate in which a certain number of senators would be designated by the king (Colomer 1991). In effect, the newly democratic Spain was characterized by an institutional legacy from the dictatorial period under Franco. Based on what you have learned from the Democratic Consolidation Game, can you provide a potential reason why countries like Spain that are successfully able to consolidate democracy after a transition often have institutional legacies from the dictatorial period?

PREPARATION FOR PROBLEMS DEALING WITH INCOMPLETE INFORMATION GAMES

Important: You should read Box 8.6, "Transition Game with Incomplete Information," and the following section, which provides a step-by-step overview of how to deal with incomplete information games, before answering Problems 6 and 7.[18]

An incomplete information game is one in which a player does not know all of the relevant information about some other player's characteristics or type. For example, the soft-liners are unsure whether the democratic opposition is weak or strong in our incomplete information Transition Game. As a result, it becomes difficult for the soft-liners to know what to do at those nodes in the game tree where they have to make a choice. This is the essential problem facing actors in games of incomplete information.

As we can see with the incomplete information Transition Game in Figure 8.4, the key to dealing with incomplete information in game theory involves combining multiple games. In effect, we have to write alternative games to capture all of the possible ways that the world might look. This means that if some player has two possible types, say weak and strong, as in our Transition Game, then we have to write two games, one in which the player is weak and one in which the player is strong. We then figure out what the players will do in each of the two games and find some way to combine the answers. Ultimately, we are going to engage in the following sort of reasoning: "If the world is like this, then I would choose to do X and the following thing would happen. But if the world is like that, then I would choose to do Y and the following would happen. I believe that the world is *probably* like *this*, and so I will do (X or Y)" (Powner and Bennett 2005, 87; italics in original).

The basic steps for writing and analyzing incomplete information games are these:

1. Write out separate games for the different possible ways the world works.
2. Solve the separate games.

---

18. The overview of incomplete information games provided in this section draws on Powner and Bennett (2005, 87–89).

3. Put the games together with a dashed line that shows the uncertainty about the two games.
4. Compare the expected payoffs of the uncertain actor's choices in the combined game.

We will now walk you through an example of an incomplete information game by returning to the Terrorism Game that you first saw in the problems at the end of Chapter 3.

Example: Terrorism Game Revisited

If you recall, our Terrorism Game in Chapter 3 examines the interaction between a group of Reluctant Terrorists and a Government. Reluctant Terrorists are people who would prefer to solve problems through negotiation but who will engage in terrorist acts if they are repressed by the government. Let's assume that the Government with which the Reluctant Terrorists interact comes in one of two types: "Responsive" or "Repressive." A Responsive Government is willing to listen to the demands of opposition groups and enter good faith negotiations with them. In contrast, a Repressive Government wishes to repress all social groups that oppose it.

The strategic situation that we are interested in is one in which the Reluctant Terrorists must decide whether to request some policy concession from the government that will satisfy them politically or to engage in a violent terrorist act. If the Reluctant Terrorists choose violence, then the game ends with a terrorist act that fails to produce cooperative negotiations. If the Reluctant Terrorists request some policy concession, the government must decide whether to repress them or enter good faith negotiations with them. The Terrorism Game that we have just described has three possible outcomes: Terrorist act, Repression, or Good faith negotiations. Based on the story that we have just told, the preference ordering for the Reluctant Terrorists and the Government are

- Reluctant Terrorists: Good faith negotiations > Terrorist act > Repression
- Responsive Government: Good faith negotiations > Repression > Terrorist act
- Repressive Government: Repression > Good faith negotiations > Terrorist act

Let's assume that the Reluctant Terrorists do not know whether they are interacting with a Responsive Government or a Repressive Government. How can we use game theory to examine this strategic situation?

Step 1. Write Out the Separate Games

Figure 8.6 illustrates two versions of the Terrorism Game. Each game represents one of the two possible states of the world. The game at the top (Figure 8.6a) represents the situation in which the Reluctant Terrorists confront a Responsive Government, whereas the game at the

| FIGURE 8.6 | **Complete Information Terrorism Game** |

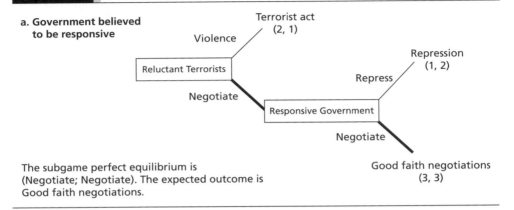

a. Government believed to be responsive

The subgame perfect equilibrium is (Negotiate; Negotiate). The expected outcome is Good faith negotiations.

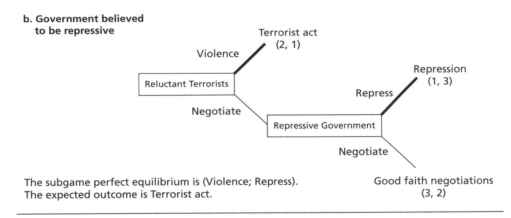

b. Government believed to be repressive

The subgame perfect equilibrium is (Violence; Repress). The expected outcome is Terrorist act.

bottom (Figure 8.6b) represents the situation in which they confront a Repressive Government. The payoffs shown in the two games are cardinal payoffs.

Step 2. Solve the Separate Games

If you solved these games correctly using backward induction in Chapter 3, you will know that the SPE when the Reluctant Terrorists are faced with a Responsive Government is (Negotiate; Negotiate) and the expected outcome is Good faith negotiations. When they are faced with a Repressive Government, the SPE is (Violence; Repress) and the expected outcome is Terrorist act. The problem is that the Reluctant Terrorists don't know which game they are actually playing.

Step 3. Connect the Games with a Dashed Line Showing the Uncertainty about the Two Games

Figure 8.7 represents the Terrorism Game with uncertainty. Basically, Figure 8.7 combines the two games illustrated in Figure 8.6 and makes two changes. The first change is that we add a move by "Nature" at the initial node of the game. The move by Nature indicates that there are two possible states of the world, each of which exists with some probability. There is some probability p that the Reluctant Terrorists are in the top subgame, in which they are facing a Responsive Government. And there is some probability $1 - p$ that they are in the bottom subgame, in which they are facing a Repressive Government. The second change is the dashed line connecting the choice nodes of the Reluctant Terrorists. This dashed line tells us that the Reluctant Terrorists do not know which node they are at—they might be playing

| FIGURE 8.7 | Incomplete Information Terrorism Game |

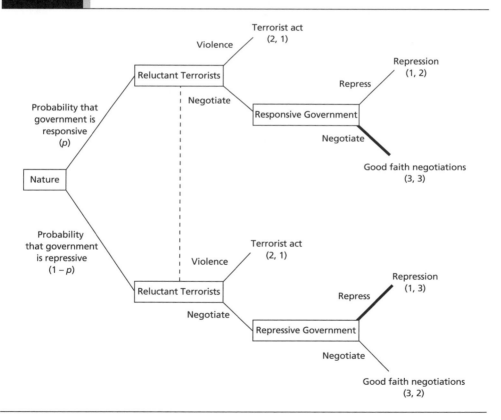

the top subgame, or they might be playing the bottom subgame. The dashed line is how uncertainty is introduced into our model.

Step 4. Compare the Expected Payoffs in the Combined Game

In order to solve the combined game, we must do two things. The first thing we must do is calculate the payoffs that the Reluctant Terrorists can expect to get from each of their two possible choices—Violence and Negotiate. In other words, we need to calculate expected payoffs. The second thing we must do is calculate the critical probability that will make the Reluctant Terrorists choose Violence or Negotiate.

a. *Expected payoff of the choices.* What is the expected payoff from choosing Violence for the Reluctant Terrorists? With probability p, the Reluctant Terrorists are in the top subgame with the Responsive Government; the decision to use violence here will give them a payoff of 2. With probability $1 - p$, they are in the bottom subgame with the Repressive Government; the decision to use violence here will also give them a payoff of 2. Thus, the Reluctant Terrorists' expected payoff from violence can be calculated as

$$\text{Expected payoff (Violence)} = (p \times 2) + [(1 - p) \times 2]$$
$$= 2p + 2 - 2p$$
$$= 2.$$

In other words, the Reluctant Terrorists can expect to get a payoff of 2 if they choose Violence at their choice node.

Now we must calculate the expected payoff from choosing Negotiate. With probability p, the Reluctant Terrorists are in the top subgame with the Responsive Government; the decision to negotiate here will give them a payoff of 3 because we know that the Responsive Government will negotiate at its choice node. With probability $1 - p$, they are in the bottom subgame with the Repressive Government; the decision to negotiate here will give them a payoff of 1 because we know that the Repressive Government will repress at its choice node. Thus, the Reluctant Terrorists' expected payoff from negotiating can be calculated as

$$\text{Expected payoff (Negotiate)} = (p \times 3) + [(1 - p) \times 1]$$
$$= 3p + 1 - 1p$$
$$= 2p + 1.$$

Now we must determine whether Violence or Negotiate gives the Reluctant Terrorists the larger expected payoff. If $2 > 2p + 1$, the Reluctant Terrorists will use violence. If $2 < 2p + 1$, they will negotiate. And if $2 = 2p + 1$, they will be indifferent. To determine what the Reluctant Terrorists will do, we need to calculate the critical probability p that determines which scenario we are in.

b. *Critical probability.* As we just noted, the Reluctant Terrorists will choose violence if $2 > 2p + 1$. We can calculate the critical probability at which the expected payoff from violence is larger than the expected payoff from negotiating in the following way:

$$\text{Expected payoff (Violence)} > \text{Expected payoff (Negotiate)}$$
$$2 > 2p + 1$$
$$1 > 2p$$
$$\tfrac{1}{2} > p.$$

This means that if $p < \tfrac{1}{2}$, then the Reluctant Terrorists will choose to use violence rather than negotiate.[19] What does this mean in the real world? Essentially, it means that if the Reluctant Terrorists believe that the probability that the government is responsive is sufficiently small (less than 0.5, given our payoffs), then they will choose to engage in violence. It is important to note that what we have calculated is not the actual or perceived beliefs that the Reluctant Terrorists have about the type of government that they are facing; rather, what we have calculated is the critical value of p that would make the Reluctant Terrorists prefer to use violence rather than negotiate. We have now solved the incomplete information version of the Terrorism Game introduced in Chapter 3.

It should be obvious from the incomplete information version of the Terrorism Game that a terrorist act can occur even if reluctant terrorists are interacting with responsive governments. It can happen, for example, if the reluctant terrorists mistakenly believe that they are facing a repressive government when they are in fact facing a responsive one. Note that a terrorist act cannot occur between reluctant terrorists and responsive governments if there is complete information. This suggests that responsive governments that are dealing with reluctant terrorists should not take actions that might lead the reluctant terrorists to perceive them as repressive.

PROBLEMS

Part II: Problems 6 and 7

6. Religious Party Game

In "Commitment Problems in Emerging Democracies: The Case of Religious Parties," Stathis Kalyvas (2000) examines whether religious parties are compatible with secular and liberal democratic institutions. He concludes that religious parties may be compatible with democracy as long as they can credibly commit not to impose a theocratic dictatorship when they come to power. He goes on to argue that some religions are better able to provide these credible commitments than others. We now provide a Religious Party Game that throws light on the credible commitment problem facing religious parties that Kalyvas describes.

---

19. It follows automatically that if $p > \tfrac{1}{2}$, then the Reluctant Terrorists will choose to negotiate rather than use violence, and if $p = \tfrac{1}{2}$, then they will be indifferent between negotiating and engaging in violence.

The two players in our game are a dictatorial regime (Regime) that has recently introduced a process of democratization and a religious party (Religious Party) that seeks to gain power through the newly proposed democratic elections. The Religious Party is expected to win the elections, and many fear that it will turn the country into a theocracy rather than continuing the process of democratic consolidation. The Regime has to decide whether to hold the elections as scheduled or to cancel them and retain power as a dictatorship. If elections are held and the Religious Party wins (which we are assuming will happen), then the Religious Party has to decide whether to pursue a moderate political agenda and support democratic consolidation or to subvert the democratization process and create a religious regime. The Religious Party comes in two types—moderate and radical. One way to think about these types is that religious parties have both moderate and radical factions, and that whichever faction is dominant determines the Religious Party's type. Moderate religious parties prefer democratic consolidation to establishing a theocracy, whereas radical religious parties prefer the opposite. There are three possible outcomes in this game: Continued dictatorship, Religious dictatorship, and Democratic consolidation. Figure 8.8 illustrates an incomplete information version of this game with cardinal payoffs in which the Regime does not know whether it is interacting with a moderate Religious Party or a radical Religious Party.

a. Based on the cardinal payoffs shown in Figure 8.8, write down the preference ordering for (a) the Regime, (b) the moderate Religious Party, and (c) the radical Religious Party over the three possible outcomes.

FIGURE 8.8 Religious Party Game

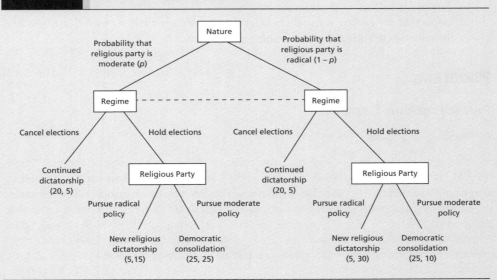

b. Solve the subgame on the left, where the Religious Party is moderate, as if there were no uncertainty. What is the subgame perfect equilibrium? What is the expected outcome? What are the payoffs that each player receives?

c. Solve the subgame on the right, where the Religious Party is radical, as if there were no uncertainty. What is the subgame perfect equilibrium? What is the expected outcome? What are the payoffs that each player receives?

d. What is the expected payoff for the Regime from "Cancel elections"?

e. What is the expected payoff for the Regime from "Hold elections"?

f. Use the expected payoffs from the two previous questions to calculate the critical probability at which the Regime will choose to hold elections rather than cancel them.

g. If the Regime believes that the Religious Party is moderate with a probability of 0.75, will it choose to hold elections, will it cancel elections, or will it be indifferent between these two actions? Explain.

h. If the Regime believes that the Religious Party is moderate with a probability of 0.8, will it choose to hold elections, will it cancel elections, or will it be indifferent between these two actions? Explain.

i. If the Regime believes that the Religious Party is moderate with a probability of 0.5, will it choose to hold elections, will it cancel elections, or will it be indifferent between these two actions? Explain.

j. If you represented a moderate religious party poised to win the elections, would you want the Regime to believe that your party was moderate or radical?

k. If you represented a radical religious party poised to win the elections, would you want the Regime to believe that your party was moderate or radical?

l. If you solved the game correctly, you will find that the Regime will hold elections as long as it believes that the Religious Party is moderate with a high enough probability. If there is some uncertainty on the part of the Regime and you are representing a moderate religious party that wants the elections to go ahead, why might it not be enough for you to simply announce to the Regime that your party is a moderate religious party and not a radical one?

In his article, Kalyvas (2000) claims that there have been only two cases in which religious parties won or were expected to win an electoral mandate—Belgium (1870–1884) and Algeria (1988–1992).[20] In January 1992 in Algeria, the Islamic Salvation Front (FIS) was deprived of a sweeping electoral victory when the military stepped in and aborted the country's electoral process. The result was a bloody civil war. In contrast, a Catholic party was able to come to power in Belgium

---

20. The electoral successes of religious parties in India, Jordan, Pakistan, and Turkey do not count as cases in which religious parties won an "electoral mandate" because, at the time of writing in 2000, these parties either were always in opposition or had been only in coalition governments—they never ruled on their own. Religious parties in Afghanistan, Iran, and Sudan have ruled on their own; however, they came to power through revolutions rather than an electoral process (Kalyvas 2000, 380).

in 1884 having won a large electoral victory on the basis of a religious program. The incumbent elites accepted the electoral outcome even though they had the power to abort it. In turn, the Catholic party did not apply its religious program in full, nor did it challenge Belgium's secular and liberal institutions.

Although the religious parties in both countries had moderate and radical factions, Kalyvas presents evidence that the moderate factions were dominant in each party. If our Religious Party Game is correct, the reason why the Catholic party in Belgium was allowed to come to power but the Islamic party in Algeria was not must have been because only the promises from the Catholic party to pursue a moderate policy once in power were seen as credible. This raises the question as to why the promises to adopt a moderate policy once in power were credible coming from the Catholic party but not coming from the Islamic party. After examining several potential answers to this question, Kalyvas argues that it has to do with the different organizational structures of the two religions. In effect, he claims that commitments to pursue moderate policies when in power are more credible when they come from hierarchical religions like Catholicism than when they come from more decentralized religions like Islam. The idea is that when someone at the top of a hierarchy orders its members to abide by liberal democratic rules, then this should be seen as a credible statement because that person actually has the ability to control the behavior of the members. This is exactly what Pope Leo XIII did in 1879 when he told Belgian Catholics to stop attacking the Belgian constitution and to purge prominent radical leaders (Kalyvas 2000, 389). In contrast, promises to pursue moderate policies are seen as less credible when there is no single religious leader who can speak for all believers. In Islam, different religious leaders compete with one another, and each claims to speak for the masses.

7. Private Censorship Game

In "Truth Replaced by Silence: A Field Experiment on Private Censorship in Russia," Charles Crabtree, Christopher J. Fariss, and Holger L. Kern (2016) distinguish between different types of censorship in authoritarian regimes. *State censorship* occurs when agents of the state engage in censorship activities. *Private censorship* occurs when private companies such as media firms choose to censor others. And *self-censorship* occurs when private individuals engage in preference falsification. The authors argue that the threat of state repression can encourage private censorship and self-censorship so that state agents don't have to engage in much state censorship at all. Here we provide a Private Censorship Game, inspired by their paper, which shows how anticipation of government repression can influence other actors—in this case, the media—to censor the news stories they produce.

The two players in our game are an independent newspaper (Newspaper), which has to decide whether or not to publish an article critical of the government, and an authoritarian regime (Regime), which has to decide whether or not to punish the Newspaper if it publishes a critical story. If the Newspaper refuses to run the negative story, then we have private censorship. If the Newspaper does publish a critical story, then the Regime has to decide whether to ignore this or to repress those in charge of the Newspaper, perhaps by firing or imprisoning them. Repression of the media can be costly if it attracts negative international attention. The Regime comes in two types—one type cares about its international reputation and the other does not. We can imagine that regimes that are reliant on foreign aid, military support, or international cooperation are likely to worry about their international reputation. The regime type that cares about its international reputation prefers to allow free speech, even if it is critical of the Regime, rather than engage in state repression of the media. In contrast, the regime type that doesn't care about its international reputation prefers to engage in state repression of the media rather than allow free speech.[21] One way to think about these types is that regimes vary in the extent to which they care about their international reputation over time. The media are not always sure about the extent to which the Regime values its international reputation and are therefore uncertain about what they can get away with publishing. There are three possible outcomes in the Private Censorship game: Private censorship, Free speech, and State repression. Figure 8.9 illustrates an incomplete information version of this game with cardinal payoffs.

a. Based on the cardinal payoffs shown in Figure 8.9, write down the preference ordering for (a) the Newspaper, (b) the Regime that doesn't value its international reputation, and (c) the Regime that does value its international reputation.

FIGURE 8.9 Private Censorship Game

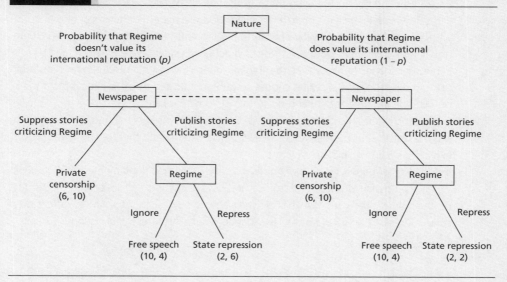

---

21. While we have focused here on whether regimes care about their international reputation, the Private Censorship Game could capture any situation in which authoritarian regimes differ in the costs of repression.

b. Solve the subgame on the left, where the Regime doesn't value its international reputation, as if there were no uncertainty. What is the subgame perfect equilibrium? What is the expected outcome? What are the payoffs that each player receives?

c. Solve the subgame on the right, where the Regime does value its international reputation, as if there were no uncertainty. What is the subgame perfect equilibrium? What is the expected outcome? What are the payoffs that each player receives?

d. In the two complete information versions of the Private Censorship Game, is it possible to see the Newspaper publish critical stories of the Regime and then be repressed? If yes, explain why? If not, explain why not?

e. What is the expected payoff for the Newspaper from "Suppress stories criticizing Regime"?

f. What is the expected payoff for the Newspaper from "Publish stories criticizing Regime"?

g. Use the expected payoffs from the two previous questions to calculate the critical probability at which the Newspaper will choose to publish stories criticizing the Regime rather than suppressing them.

h. If the Newspaper believes that the Regime doesn't value its international reputation with a probability of 0.5, will it choose to publish critical articles, will it suppress them, or will it be indifferent between these two actions? Explain.

i. If the Newspaper believes that the Regime doesn't value its international reputation with a probability of 0.7, will it choose to publish critical articles, will it suppress them, or will it be indifferent between these two actions? Explain.

j. If the Newspaper believes that the Regime doesn't value its international reputation with a probability of 0.4, will it choose to publish critical articles, will it suppress them, or will it be indifferent between these two actions? Explain.

k. In the incomplete information version of the Private Censorship Game, is it possible to see the Newspaper publish stories critical of the Regime and then be repressed? If yes, explain why. If not, explain why not.

l. In the original paper, the authors note that after they had implemented their study in 2014, the Russian legislature passed several laws restricting free speech. In the context of the game that you have just solved, how would such information affect your estimation of p? If you were the Newspaper, would this affect your actions? Explain.

9 Democracy or Dictatorship

Does It Make a Difference?

> In the terrible history of famines in the world, no substantial famine has ever occurred in any independent and democratic country with a relatively free press.
>
> Amartya Sen, 1999a

- We live in a world that tends to associate good outcomes with democracy and bad ones with dictatorships. In reality, the world is much more complex than this. Oftentimes, we have no compelling theoretical reason to expect that democracies will outperform dictatorships. Although the empirical evidence indicates that democracies tend to produce high levels of material well-being for their citizens, it also shows that they do not regularly outperform all dictatorships. In effect, some dictatorships perform quite well even though others perform extremely poorly. Classifying the world into democracies and dictatorships fails to explain this variation in the performance of dictatorships.

OVERVIEW

In previous chapters, we examined how political scientists distinguish between democracies and dictatorships, we explored economic and cultural explanations for the emergence and survival of democracy, and we investigated the dynamics of regime transition. Now we ask whether it really matters whether someone lives in a democracy or a dictatorship. We live in a world that tends to associate good outcomes with democracy and bad ones with dictatorships. But is this an accurate reflection of the real world? Although there may be many important normative arguments to justify democracy—that it protects certain freedoms, that it is fairer, or that it is more just—we focus our attention in this chapter on whether democracy makes a *material* difference in people's lives. Are government policies better for the average citizen in a democracy or in a dictatorship? For example, do economies grow faster in democracies or dictatorships? Do people live longer in democracies? Are they healthier? Are they more educated? Are they wealthier? It turns out that the answers to these types of questions are not as straightforward as you might imagine. It is not at all obvious, for example, that democracies experience lower levels of child mortality than dictatorships (Ross 2006) or that democracies produce better economic growth (Przeworski and Limongi 1993).

In this chapter, we examine the effect of regime type on various aspects of government performance. We begin by looking closely at the competing arguments concerning the effect of democracy on economic growth. Some of these arguments suggest that democracies should produce higher growth than dictatorships do, but others suggest the exact opposite. In other words, political scientists do not, as yet, have a clear theoretical prediction as to whether or when democracies will economically outperform dictatorships. We then report somewhat inconclusive results from tests in which we investigate the effect of regime type on a variety of indicators of material well-being, such as wealth, infant mortality, life expectancy, and health care spending. Overall, the empirical evidence suggests that although democracy is often sufficient for ensuring a high level of citizen material well-being, it is certainly not necessary; some dictatorships perform at relatively high levels as well.

THE EFFECT OF REGIME TYPE ON ECONOMIC GROWTH

Do democratic governments promote higher levels of economic growth than dictatorships? This question has generated an enormous literature in both political science and economics, but you'll perhaps be surprised to learn that there is, as yet, no strong consensus on what the answer is. Conflicting arguments abound. Some scholars suggest that democracy promotes economic growth (Acemoglu et al. 2014; Barro 1990; North 1990; Olson 1991), some that it hinders it (de Schweinitz 1959; Galenson 1959; Huntington 1968; Huntington and Dominguez 1975; Tavares and Wacziarg 2001), and some that it makes no difference (Barro 1997; Doucouliagos and Ulubaşoğlu 2008; Przeworski and Limongi 1993; Przeworski et al. 2000). Typically, theoretical arguments that attempt to link regime type to economic growth focus on three main factors: (a) the protection of property rights, (b) citizens' incentives to consume rather than invest, and (c) dictatorial autonomy. We look at all three in turn.

Property Rights

It is common today for scholars to argue that democracies will enjoy higher levels of economic growth than dictatorships because democracies are characterized by the rule of law and the protection of property rights (North 1990; North and Thomas 1973). According to these scholars, democracy places limits on the ability of governments to engage in the arbitrary seizure of private property. As a result, democracy encourages investment and, in turn, growth. In Chapter 6, one of the arguments for the emergence of democracy—or, at least, limited government—focused on the role that democratic institutions can play in providing a credible commitment mechanism to asset holders who wish to invest in the economy but who worry that the government will later seize their investments. As you'll recall, we illustrated this argument by examining the emergence of limited government in England during the seventeenth century. Although the emergence of a democratic form of government in England at this time was not originally brought about with the specific intention of promoting economic growth, it does appear to have had precisely this effect. Indeed, the fact that England had a limited government in early modern Europe but France did not offers a potential explanation for why the English economy grew so much faster during this period than the French one. In effect, the causal logic of this "property rights" argument (Figure 9.1)

FIGURE 9.1	**A Hypothesized Causal Path between Democracy and Economic Growth**

Democracy

↓

Rule of law

↓

Stable property rights

↓

Investment

↓

Growth

Photo by Keystone/Getty Images

Shah Mohammed Reza Pahlavi making a statement to the Iranian Senate about the Anglo-Iranian Oil Company on March 14, 1953. Control over Iranian oil was a contentious political issue, with many Iranians supporting the nationalization of their oil industry.

in favor of democracy is that democracy helps ensure the rule of law, that the rule of law then helps secure stable property rights, and that stable property rights then encourage growth-boosting investment.

This argument might seem extremely convincing at first, but Barro (2000) presents evidence that only parts of the causal chain outlined in Figure 9.1 actually work in the real world. As predicted, Barro finds that the rule of law does significantly encourage economic growth when he examines data from roughly one hundred countries between 1960 and 1995. Indeed, he claims that because a similar relationship exists between the rule of law and the ratio of investment to gross domestic product (GDP), then "one route by which better rule of law promotes growth is by encouraging investment" (Barro 2000, 40). So far, everything seems good for the property rights argument linking democracy to economic growth. The problem, though, is that Barro does not find democracy to be strongly associated with the rule of law. In effect, the initial step in the causal chain linking democracy to economic growth appears to be missing.

As illustrated in Table 9.1, some countries score high on a rule of law index but poor on an electoral rights (democracy) index.[1] These countries are typically run by dictators who promote property rights and a reliable legal system. Examples of such dictators include Augusto Pinochet in Chile (1973–1990), Lee Kuan Yew in Singapore (1959–1990), and Shah Mohammed Reza Pahlavi in Iran (1941–1979). It is perhaps important to note that the legal systems in these countries are reliable—meaning rules tend to be applied in a consistent manner—but not necessarily fair or just. Investors (especially international investors who, by definition, live outside the country), though, are typically more concerned with reliability than fairness. This is because reliable laws, whether fair or not, allow investors to make accurate predictions about their ability to earn a return on their investments. In contrast to these countries, there are others, like Colombia, Israel, and Venezuela (1980s), and Bolivia, Honduras, and South Africa (1990s), that score high on the electoral rights index but poor

---

1. Both indexes are compiled by a private firm, Political Risk Services, that monitors the investment climate in particular countries and sells its findings to international investors.

TABLE 9.1	Countries with Large Gaps between Rule of Law and Electoral Rights Indexes

a. High Rule of Law Relative to Electoral Rights in 1982

Country	Rule of Law Index	Electoral Rights Index
Burkina Faso	0.50	0.00
Chile	0.83	0.17
Ethiopia	0.50	0.00
Guinea	0.50	0.00
Hong Kong	1.00	0.50
Hungary[a]	0.83	0.33
Myanmar (Burma)	0.50	0.00
Niger	0.67	0.00
Poland[a]	0.67	0.17
Singapore	1.00	0.50
Somalia	0.50	0.00
Taiwan	1.00	0.33

b. High Rule of Law Relative to Electoral Rights in 1998

Bahrain	0.83	0.00
Cameroon	0.50	0.00
China	0.83	0.00
Egypt	0.67	0.17
Gambia	0.83	0.00
Hong Kong	0.83	0.33
Iran	0.83	0.17
Kuwait	0.83	0.33
Malaysia	0.83	0.33
Morocco	1.00	0.33
Myanmar (Burma)	0.50	0.00
Oman	0.83	0.17
Saudi Arabia	0.83	0.00
Singapore	1.00	0.33
Syria	0.83	0.00
Tanzania	0.83	0.33
Tunisia	0.83	0.17
United Arab Emirates	0.67	0.17
Yugoslavia	0.83	0.17

(Continued)

TABLE 9.1 **(Continued)**

c. Low Rule of Law Relative to Electoral Rights in 1982

Country	Rule of law index	Electoral rights index
Bolivia	0.17	0.83
Colombia	0.33	0.83
Cyprus[a]	0.33	1.00
Dominican Republic	0.50	1.00
Greece	0.50	1.00
Honduras	0.17	0.83
South Africa	0.50	1.00
Uruguay	0.50	1.00

a. Data are unavailable for 1982 and are shown for 1985.

Note: The indexes run from 0 to 1 with higher numbers indicating greater rule of law or greater electoral rights. The table shows observations for which the magnitude of the gap between the rule of law and electoral rights indexes was at least 0.5.

Source: Barro (2000).

on the rule of law index.[2] Whereas these countries have fairly advanced forms of electoral competition, they have little to no legal protection for property rights.

Barro's evidence indicates that breakdowns in the rule of law and the protection of property rights occur under both dictatorships and democracies. As a consequence, he concludes that "the electoral rights index has no predictive content for the rule of law index" and, therefore, that encouraging democracy on the grounds that it will lead to economic growth "sounds pleasant, but is simply false" (Barro 2000, 46, 47). Other scholars, however, disagree. For example, some have found that more democratic countries *are* more likely to protect property rights (Leblang 1996; Rigobon and Rodrik 2004) and, as a consequence, experience higher growth rates (Leblang 1996, 1997). The precise relationship between democracy and economic growth clearly remains a hotly contested issue.

---

2. In some other countries, property rights are protected in some sectors of the economy but not in others. For example, Haber, Razo, and Maurer (2003) detail how the Mexican government between 1876 and 1929 failed to protect property rights in many sectors of the economy but did protect them in sectors in which the technology of production was sophisticated and in which the government relied on actors with high levels of human capital. In effect, the Mexican government protected property rights in those sectors of the economy in which it depended on actors who had credible exit threats. Haber and colleagues go on to demonstrate that significant investment, industrial expansion, and economic growth occurred in precisely those sectors with protected property rights and that all of this occurred despite the tremendous social disorder and political instability that plagued Mexico during this period.

Why Democracy Might Hurt Property Rights

One reason why the relationship between democracy and economic growth is not clear-cut has to do with the fact that democratic governments appear to be more than capable of ignoring or abolishing property rights when they want. One explanation for why democracy might fail to protect property rights can be derived from an influential model of the size of government that political scientists refer to as the "Meltzer-Richard" model (Meltzer and Richard 1981). The model starts with a situation in which everyone in society is asked to pay a portion of his or her income as a tax, t. The government then takes this tax revenue and divides it equally among all members of society. Because government spending is divided equally among all members of society in this imaginary world but the amount of tax paid is a function of each individual's income, anyone with above-average income ends up paying above-average taxes and gets back government benefits equal only to those received by the average taxpayer. As a result, any individual with below-average income in this society stands to be a net beneficiary of the tax system. In contrast, anyone with above-average income stands to be a net contributor to the tax system.[3] Because the Meltzer-Richard model assumes a balanced budget, the amount of redistribution a government can engage in is constrained by the amount of taxes it can raise. As a result, individuals who stand to be net recipients of the government's "tax and transfer system" will prefer high taxes (and the ensuing high transfers), whereas individuals who are net contributors to the system will prefer low taxes and few transfers.

In a market economy, income is likely to be tied to productivity. Highly productive individuals have high incomes and less productive individuals have low incomes. Consequently, an individual's preferred tax rate is related to his or her level of productivity in a manner similar to that shown in Figure 9.2. If an individual's level of productivity is extremely low (say, below x_0), then he chooses not to work at all and he survives purely on government transfers. As a result, individuals in this category have a preferred level of taxation that is uniformly high (t_{max}). In contrast, individuals whose level of productivity is above the societal average, $\bar{x}$, and who, hence, have an above-average income pay more taxes than the average citizen but receive only the societal average of government transfers. As a result, such individuals are net contributors to the tax and transfer system and prefer a tax rate of zero. Between these two groups are individuals with productivity levels that are somewhat high but below the societal average. Because these individuals are net beneficiaries of the tax and transfer system, they prefer a nonzero tax rate. The precise level of their desired tax rate (on

3. Note that redistribution from the "rich" to the "poor" occurs in this society despite the fact that government spending is not targeted toward the poor and that both the poor and the rich pay exactly the same tax rate. "Means tested" welfare programs that restrict access to government benefits to low-income families (such as food stamp programs in the United States) and "progressive" income tax systems that apply higher tax rates to rich people than poor people would make the system even more "redistributive." All that is necessary to make a system redistributive, though, is to have the total tax paid by each person be an increasing function of income while making benefits independent of income.

FIGURE 9.2 **Individual Productivity and Desired Tax Rate According to the Meltzer-Richard Model**

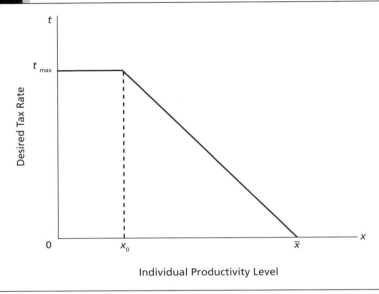

Individual Productivity Level

Note: x = an individual's level of productivity; $\bar{x}$ = the average level of individual productivity in society. Individuals with a productivity level below x_0 will choose not to work and to live entirely on government transfers. *t* = an individual's desired tax rate; t_{max} = the maximum desired tax rate.

the downward-sloping line), however, depends on the distance between their productivity level and the societal average. Those with productivity rates very close to the societal average want tax rates close to zero, because they expect to benefit only slightly from the tax and transfer system, whereas those with low productivity rates want tax rates almost as high as do individuals that have left the labor market altogether, because they expect to benefit from the tax and transfer system a lot.

So far, we have used the Meltzer-Richard model to explain why some individuals might prefer a higher tax rate than others. In order to make predictions about what the tax rate will be, however, we need to say something about how policy is actually chosen. In general, democracies tend to represent the interests of a wider portion of society than dictatorships. This means that the interests of poor (low-productivity) people are given more effective representation in democracies than in dictatorships. If we assume that dictatorships make tax policy to reflect the preferences of individuals with above-average incomes but that democracies make tax policy to reflect the preferences of individuals with below-average incomes, then a change from dictatorship to democracy can be expected to lead to an increase in the level of taxation and, therefore, an increase in the amount of redistribution from the rich to the poor. Indeed, this increase in the level of taxation and redistribution

Box 9.1

CONSUMPTION VERSUS INVESTMENT
The Trade-Off

For the sake of argument, let's say a potential investor has 100 units of after-tax income. Should she consume it immediately or invest it? If she consumes it, she can consume all of it. If she invests it, it may grow, and she will have more to consume in the future. Let's assume that she is confident that the return on her investment will be 10 percent per year. Her choice between consumption and investment, therefore, comes down to a choice between consuming 100 units this year and consuming 110 units next year. Clearly, 110 units are better than 100 units, but most people "discount" the future. That is, 100 units of consumption today are typically better than waiting a year to consume the same 100 units. Whether 100 units today will be better than 110 units a year from now, however, will depend on a person's discount factor. Suppose, for example, that a person thinks that 105 units next year is as good as 100 units today. Given the choice between consuming today and investing with an expected return of 10 percent, the person will choose to invest. This is because if the person believes that 105 units next year is as good as 100 units today, then she must think that 110 units next year is better than 100 units today. Now, imagine that the government imposes a 55 percent tax on any profits that come from investments. This means that 5.5 units of the 10-unit profit that she expects to make from investing will have to be given to the government. As a result, investing 100 units today will allow her to walk away with only 104.5 units next year. Suddenly, consuming today is preferred to investing.

when countries transition to democracy is likely to be quite large if there is widespread inequality in society.

How might this affect economic growth? Well, consider that potential investors—in this story, the rich—are always deciding whether to consume (spend) their after-tax income or invest it (see Box 9.1, "Consumption versus Investment: The Trade-Off"). If they think that the tax rate is too high, then they will prefer to consume rather than invest. In the absence of investment, economic growth can be expected to grind to a halt. Although democracy might be expected to offer property owners protection against seizures by the state, the Meltzer-Richard model illustrates that democracy introduces the possibility that the poor will seize the property of the rich through a redistributive tax scheme. When left-wing parties come to power in democracies promising to "expropriate" the rich—take their wealth and redistribute it to the poor—wealthy citizens often feel threatened and sometimes call on the military to step in and protect their property rights. This is a story commonly told about right-wing military coups that toppled left-wing democratic regimes in Latin American countries, such as Argentina (1976), Chile (1973), and Guatemala (1954; Drake 1996; O'Donnell 1973; Stepan 1985). The same theme can be found in the writings of the political elites setting up the American democracy in the late eighteenth century (Roemer 1998). Why else did the founding fathers extend the suffrage only to male property holders and spend so long trying to write a constitution that protected property?

Why Democracy Might Not Hurt Property Rights

There are, however, two criticisms of the Meltzer-Richard model. Both of these criticisms suggest that the model may overstate the extent to which democratic politics will lead to large-scale redistribution and, therefore, to growth-reducing disinvestment. First, political participation in democracies is typically inversely related to income—poor people are less likely to vote than rich people (Blais 2000; Leighley and Nagler 1992a, 1992b; Verba, Schlozman, and Brady 1995; Wolfinger and Rosenstone 1980). As a result, it is possible that, in reality, democracies implement tax and transfer policies that are not very different from the policies adopted in dictatorships. In fact, if the "decisive" voter in both systems has a level of productivity (and, therefore, income) higher than the societal average, $\bar{x}$, then there should be no difference in the tax and transfer system between the two regimes types.

The second criticism of the Meltzer-Richard model is related to a famous Marxist argument that highlights what political scientists call the "structural dependence of the state on capital" (Block 1977; Lindblom 1977; Przeworski and Wallerstein 1988). The important insight from this Marxist theory is clearly seen with the help of a model by Przeworski (1991, 9–10). The model starts with an economy comprising two groups: one group, P, derives its income from profits; the other group, W, derives it from wages. For any given level of technological development in society, there is a maximum level of output that the economy is capable of producing. We might think that the fruits of this output can be divided between profit takers and wage earners in any number of ways. The downward-sloping line in Figure 9.3 represents all of the feasible ways we could divide society's maximum output between profit takers and wage earners. At P^*, the profit takers receive all of the output and the wage earners receive nothing. At W^*, the wage earners receive all of the output and the profit takers receive nothing. In between these two points, there is a continuum of distributional possibilities that includes the perfectly egalitarian distribution, E, in which the profit takers and wage earners each receive half of society's maximum potential output. Political scientists sometimes refer to this downward-sloping line as the "technological possibility frontier" because it represents all the different divisions of what it is possible for society to technologically produce.

As just mentioned, there is a maximum level of output that an economy is capable of producing. It turns out that this level of output can be achieved only if profit takers and wage earners efficiently invest their resources—their capital and labor—in the economy. As we'll show, this will happen only if profit takers and wage earners receive a particular division of societal output whereby each group receives the entire return on the investments they make. In other words, only one of the points or divisions on the technological possibility frontier is actually consistent with the economy's producing the maximum that it is capable of

FIGURE 9.3	The Potential Trade-Off between Growth and Equality

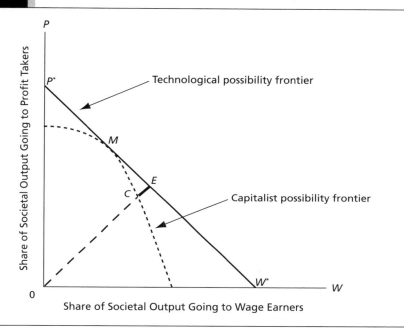

Figure axes: *P* (vertical), labeled "Share of Societal Output Going to Profit Takers"; *W* (horizontal), labeled "Share of Societal Output Going to Wage Earners." Points labeled P^*, M, E, C, W^*. Lines labeled "Technological possibility frontier" and "Capitalist possibility frontier."

producing. In Figure 9.3, this is point *M*. Because *M* is on the technological possibility frontier to the left of the egalitarian point, *E,* in this specific society, we are assuming that, in line with much of historical experience, profit takers will receive more of society's maximum output than wage earners.[4] But why, you might wonder, is there only one division of societal output between profit takers and wage earners that maximizes total economic output? Why wouldn't any of the other possible divisions on the technological possibility frontier also maximize output?

The answer to this question has to do with the fact that individuals in a capitalist economy always have a choice about how to allocate their resources. For example, profit takers are always comparing what they could get from investing their capital against the enjoyment

---

4. The precise position of point *M* on the technological possibility frontier depends on the relative rate of return on capital and labor. If the rate of return on capital is larger than the rate of return on labor, then the division of societal output will benefit capital and be on the technological possibility frontier to the left of the egalitarian point, *E*. If the rate of return on labor is greater, then the division of societal output will benefit labor and be to the right of the egalitarian point. What do we mean by "rate of return"? In everyday language, the rate of return on an investment is just the ratio of money gained on an investment relative to the amount of money invested. If capital and labor were measured in the same units, then the relative rate of return on capital would be higher than that on labor if one unit of capital produced more than one unit of labor.

they could get from simply consuming it. Similarly, wage earners are always comparing what they could get from an additional hour's work against the value they place on an additional hour of leisure. If profit takers or wage earners ever receive less than their entire return on their capital or labor investments—perhaps because the government taxes them—then profit takers will start consuming more of their capital rather than investing it and wage earners will start taking more leisure time rather than working. As a result, society's resources will be underutilized, and there will be a decline in societal output away from what is technologically possible. The logic here leads to what we might call a "capitalist possibility frontier"—the curved line in Figure 9.3—that is entirely inside the technological possibility frontier except for the point at which capital and labor receive the entire return on their investments, M. In other words, a capitalist economy will always produce less than is technologically possible unless profit takers and wage earners divide societal output between them in a manner indicated by point M.

To help illustrate how the model works, imagine a society in which the tax and transfer system has historically been controlled by an autocratic government representing the interests of profit takers. Over time and through experience, the autocratic government has discovered that societal output is maximized by returning a larger share of society's product to the profit takers than to the wage earners. Recall that this is point M in Figure 9.3. Now, imagine that the autocratic government is replaced by a democratic one in which there are at least as many wage earners as profit takers. This change in regime would, presumably, put pressure on the government to use its tax and transfer system to redistribute wealth in a more egalitarian fashion—say, to a point like E. So far, the predicted effect of a shift to democracy is essentially the same as that generated by the Meltzer-Richard model that we examined earlier—there will be pressure for redistribution.

But note, now, what happens if the government actually uses its tax and transfer capability in this way. Because profit takers are no longer receiving the full value of their investments, they will begin to remove their capital assets from the economy, either by consuming them or by shifting them to a different economy—a process known as "capital flight." As a result, societal output will decline from point E on the technological possibility frontier to point C on the capitalist possibility frontier that is associated with the new egalitarian distribution of income. The distance between points E and C (the short boldface line in Figure 9.3) constitutes the cost in lost societal output that results from the redistributive policy. In effect, Przeworski's model illustrates that there is a potential trade-off between equality and growth—increased equality can be obtained only by accepting reduced economic growth.

Structural Marxists argue that governments will recognize this trade-off and choose to promote growth over equality. They argue that whether the government is controlled by capitalists or by workers, the fact that resource allocation decisions are in the hands of private individuals in a capitalist economy means that policies will be adopted that protect the interests of the capitalist class. As Fred Block (1977, 15) notes,

Those who manage the state apparatus—regardless of their own political ideology—are dependent on the maintenance of some reasonable level of economic activity. This is true for two reasons. First, the capacity of the state to finance itself through taxation or borrowing depends on the state of the economy. If economic activity is in decline, the state will have difficulty maintaining its revenues at an adequate level. Second, public support for a regime will decline sharply if the regime presides over a serious drop in the level of economic activity, with a parallel rise in unemployment and shortages of key goods. Such a drop in support increases the likelihood that the state managers will be removed from power one way or another.

In other words, even if the tax and transfer system comes under the control of actors who want to increase redistribution from profit takers to wage earners, either for ideological reasons or simply because they think it politically expedient, they probably will not introduce such a redistributive scheme in practice. This is because they recognize that they will pay a large price in the form of (a) reduced societal output and, therefore, a smaller tax base in the future and (b) increased unemployment and, hence, increased opposition, for doing so. Ironically, the very people redistribution is supposed to help—the poor—are most likely to suffer first from any economic downturn because the least productive members in society are likely to be the first to become unemployed (Hibbs 1987). As a result, structural Marxists argue that strongly redistributive tax and transfer systems are likely to be self-defeating—they hurt those they are intended to help—and that the political benefits of such policies will be fleeting—state managers are likely to be punished for causing an economic downturn. In this sense, capitalists "have a veto over state policies in that their failure to invest at adequate levels can create major political problems for the state managers" (Block 1977, 15). It is precisely for this reason that some political scientists talk of the **structural dependence of the state on capital** (Przeworski and Wallerstein 1988). If structural Marxists are correct, then a change in "who governs" is not likely to have much of an effect on the tax and transfer system. Consequently, a change from dictatorship to democracy will *not* have the negative effect on economic growth suggested by the Meltzer-Richard model discussed earlier.

> The **structural dependence of the state on capital** is a theory suggesting that capitalists have a veto over state policies in that their failure to invest at adequate levels can create major problems for the state managers.

It is important to recognize that the predictions we have drawn from Przeworski's model depend on many implicit assumptions that may or may not be satisfied in any given situation. The first, and least problematic, assumption is that the distribution that maximizes societal output, *M,* returns a larger share of society's product to the profit takers than to the wage earners. Recall that it was this assumption that led us to place point *M* on the technological possibility frontier to the left of the egalitarian point in Figure 9.3. Historical experience tells us that this is probably a reasonable assumption. What happens, however, if the reverse is true and the distribution that maximizes societal output returns a larger share of society's product to the wage earners rather than the profit takers? In other words, what happens if point M is to the right of the egalitarian point? Well, it turns out that any attempt to reach a more egalitarian distribution from this point would still result in a decline in societal output. The difference is that the decline would now occur because workers choose to work less and not because capitalists decide to disinvest. In effect, we would be talking about the structural dependence of the state on labor in this scenario. The bottom line, though, is that there would be a drop in societal output and, as a result, there would be similar incentives not to implement a redistributive tax and transfer system; the potential trade-off between equality and growth remains.

The second assumption concerns the expected effect of capital flight on the amount of societal output going to wage earners. Although aggressive redistribution by wage earners in a democracy will reduce societal output, it is important to remember that wage earners will get a larger (more egalitarian) share of the "smaller" economic pie as a result of increased government transfers. Thus, there may be conditions under which wage earners are better off pushing for redistribution rather than opposing it.

Ultimately, aggressive redistribution will be deterred only if the threat of capital flight by profit takers is sufficiently large to shrink societal output to such an extent that wage earners end up worse off than if there were no redistribution. Whether this is the case depends on the alternatives that capitalists have. For example, if it is relatively easy for capitalists to direct their resources away from investment into consumption or from domestic investment into foreign investment, then aggressive redistribution is likely to result in a sharp and immediate economic decline that hurts wage earners. Thus, democracy is less likely to lead to aggressive redistribution and, hence, lower economic growth when the capitalists who influence the economy have what we referred to in Chapters 3 and 6 as "credible exit threats." In contrast, democracy is much more likely to lead to aggressive redistribution when there are constraints on international capital markets or when immobile asset holders dominate the economy. When capital markets are constrained or immobile asset holders dominate, the poor are relatively free to redistribute wealth from the rich to themselves, safe in the knowledge that it is hard for the rich to remove their assets from the economy. Evidence in support of this claim can be seen in the rapid expansion of redistributive tax and transfer systems that occurred when international capital markets collapsed between 1918 and 1939, and in the aggressive redistribution that occurs in a whole range of countries (the Persian Gulf states, Norway, Venezuela, and so on) whose economies are dominated by the "immobile" oil sector.

To this point, we have shown that any movement away from a distribution of resources that maximizes societal output, M, toward a more egalitarian division results in a reduction in output. We should note that *any* movement from point M, whether toward a more equal division of resources or a more unequal one, leads to a decline in output. For example, allocating a greater share of resources to profit takers—moving from M toward P^* in Figure 9.3—also leads to a decline in societal output. This is because workers no longer receive their full return on their labor and, therefore, decide to consume more leisure rather than work. At a certain point, this may even be involuntary—workers who receive less than subsistence will be too sick or malnourished to work. The Nobel Prize–winning economic historian Robert Fogel (2004) estimates that throughout most of human history the average person consumed enough food to work for only about two hours a day. As a result, even dictators are likely to try to move the distribution of societal output toward *M*, lest they "kill the goose that lays the golden eggs."

Conclusion

Tracing a link between democracy and economic growth through the protection of property rights and the rule of law is extremely difficult. The basic problem is that although effective property rights and the rule of law appear to promote economic growth, it is not at all clear that democracies are better at protecting property rights or implementing the rule of law than dictatorships. As a result, it is extremely difficult to tell a compelling story about the effect of regime type on economic growth if the causal mechanism has to do with the protection of property rights. On the one hand, does the state itself or do the poor pose the more important threat to investment and production? If it is the state, then democracies, in which the predatory powers of the state are limited, should experience higher economic growth. If it is the ability of the poor to expropriate the rich through a redistributive tax scheme, then dictatorships should experience higher economic growth. On the other hand, if the structural Marxists are correct and state managers—whatever their ideological stripe—are able to figure out that tax and transfer systems that produce income distributions that fail to maximize societal output are self-defeating, then who rules—democrats or dictators, the bourgeoisie or the proletariat—will have little effect on the amount of redistribution in society and, therefore, little effect (at least by the mechanism presently under consideration) on economic growth.

Consumption versus Investment

A second argument linking regime type and economic growth is based on the claim that democracy encourages workers to consume their assets immediately rather than invest them (de Schweinitz 1959; Galenson 1959). As a result of this consumption, democracies are expected to produce poor economic growth. Note that this story is different from the previous one in that we are now talking about investment by workers rather than investment by economic elites. The claim is that poor people (workers) tend to consume rather than invest. The intuition is that the poor cannot afford to direct their assets away from immediate consumption—they need to eat and pay the rent today—toward investment for the future. When workers can organize by forming political parties or trade unions, as they can in democracies, they have the ability to drive wages up, thereby reducing profits for business owners and, hence, overall investment. Because workers can vote in democracies, the government also has incentives to direct money toward them and away from investment in the economy, thereby slowing economic growth even further. If democratic governments fail to do this and instead promote saving and investment too heavily, they will likely be voted out of office. In contrast, if dictators are future oriented—they care about the future—then they can use their power to force people to save, thereby launching economic growth. As Rao (1984, 75) puts it,

> Economic development is a process for which huge investments in personnel and material are required. Such investment programs imply cuts in current consumption that would be painful at the low levels of living that exist in almost all developing societies. Governments must resort to strong measures and they must enforce them with an iron hand in order to marshal the surpluses needed for investment. If such measures were put to a popular vote, they would surely be defeated. No political party can hope to win a democratic election on a platform of current sacrifices for a *bright future*. (italics in original)

As you may have noticed, a lot of implicit assumptions underpin this story. For example, it is assumed that the poor have a higher propensity to consume than the rich and that economic growth is primarily driven by capital investment. Even if we were to accept these assumptions, it still does not follow that dictatorships will produce better economic growth than democracies unless we happen to also assume that dictators care more about the future than democratic leaders. But why would this necessarily be the case? In effect, without a clear set of expectations about the incentives and constraints facing both democratic leaders and dictators, it is difficult to tell a compelling story about how each will behave. As a result, this second argument also fails to provide clear predictions about whether democracies or dictatorships will produce higher economic growth.

ERIC PIERMONT/AFP/Getty Images

At the World Economic Forum attended by the world's economic and political elite in the Swiss Alps resort of Davos, on January 26, 2013, police keep protesters at bay.

A related story about the effects of regime type on economic outcomes comes from the study of what political scientists call "economic voting" and "political business cycles." This literature argues that voters tend to reward officeholders when the economy is performing well. Consequently, incumbent politicians have an incentive to try to stimulate economic activity as elections approach (Nordhaus 1975; Tufte 1978). The result is a series of pre-election economic "booms" followed by post-election "busts." In this way, elections can increase volatility in macroeconomic indicators, such as gross domestic product, unemployment, and inflation. Evidence that political business cycles occur is mixed (Franzese 2002a), but if they do occur, the increased volatility they cause is likely to be bad for the economy since risk-averse investors can be expected to respond to this volatility by consuming rather than investing. Since economic decision making in autocracies is less likely to be tied to the electoral calendar in this fashion (despite the fact that, as we will see in Chapter 10, elections occur in many authoritarian regimes), political business cycles are another way in which democracy might inhibit, rather than promote, economic performance. Note that in the classic formulation of the political business cycle, while voters are thought to reward politicians who engineer economic expansions, they appear to place little weight on the future consequences of such manipulations. In this way, the classic political business cycle argument can be thought of as another example of how democracy might encourage current consumption over the future benefits of investment.

Autonomy from Special Interests

A third argument linking regime type and economic growth has to do with the claim that dictators are not subjected to as many pressures from special interests as democratic leaders. This claim is based on the intuition that democratic leaders are more heavily influenced by special interests because they can so easily be voted out of office if they fail to retain the political and financial support of powerful interest groups. Unfortunately, some political scientists use the claim that dictators enjoy more autonomy from special interests than democratic leaders to argue that dictatorships are better for economic growth, and some use it to argue that dictatorships are worse for growth.

One story states that because dictators are insulated from the pressures of interest groups, they do not need to spend money in an inefficient manner to keep various electoral constituencies happy. In effect, dictators have the ability to make difficult short-term policy decisions that will have good long-term effects on the economy. As a result, dictatorships will produce better economic growth than democracies. We hope you have noticed the key assumption behind this story—the dictator *chooses* to promote economic growth. But why would the dictator necessarily choose to do this? As long as the dictator is satisfied with his own share of the annual revenue, why should the national level of economic growth matter? Do you think it is reasonable to assume that dictators are necessarily benevolent and that they behave in the national interest?

The second story states that dictators who are autonomous and insulated from pressure groups will be able to behave in a predatory way because there is no one to constrain their behavior. Economic elites will be less likely to invest because they will be worried that a predatory dictator will confiscate all of their wealth and profits. Given the lack of investment, economic growth is expected to be low. Political scientists who make this type of argument go one step further and claim that economic growth will be lower in dictatorships than in democracies. As you'll quickly realize, the implicit assumption necessary to make this final leap is that democracies protect property rights (limit state predation) better than dictatorships. We have already seen from our earlier discussion of economic growth and property rights, however, that this assumption is extremely hard to defend from both a theoretical and an empirical point of view.

Evidence

We suspect that you have not found the various causal arguments that we have presented linking regime type and economic growth entirely convincing. You almost certainly have noticed that they reach quite different predictions. But what does the empirical evidence say? Do democracies or dictatorships produce higher economic growth in the real world? In an overview of eighteen different studies examining the effect of regime type on economic growth, Przeworski and Limongi (1993) report that eight find that dictatorships grow faster, eight find that democracies grow faster, and five find that regime type has no effect on growth. They conclude that "we do not know whether democracy fosters or hinders economic growth. . . . Our own hunch is that politics does matter, but '*regimes' do not capture the relevant differences*" (Przeworski and Limongi 1993, 65; italics added).

So far, we have focused on the effect of regime type on economic growth. In this regard, we have found the theoretical and empirical results to be inconclusive. But what about the effect of regime type on other measures of government performance? We now briefly turn to some data on other indicators of material well-being.

THE EFFECT OF REGIME TYPE ON GOVERNMENT PERFORMANCE

How does a country's level of democracy affect the material well-being of its citizens? In Figure 9.4, we show how the average level of democracy in eighty-eight countries between 1960 and 1990 is associated with six different indicators of material well-being: (a) wealth as measured by GDP per capita, (b) the percentage of births attended by a physician, (c) the percentage of pregnant women receiving prenatal care, (d) the percentage of infants and children receiving vaccinations, (e) infant and child (under five years of age) mortality rates per thousand, and (f) life expectancy as measured in years. Given that we are interested in how the *level* of democracy influences material well-being, we employ Polity IV's continuous measure of democracy in our plots (Marshall, Jaggers, and Gurr 2016). As you will recall from our discussion of the democracy measures in Chapter 5, Polity IV codes a country's level of democracy on a scale that ranges from −10 (*most dictatorial*) to +10 (*most democratic*). Data on the various indicators of material well-being come from James McGuire (2002).

Before examining the information in Figure 9.4, let's first stop to think about what relationship we would expect to find between a country's level of democracy and material well-being. Several theories of regime type suggest that democracies are better than dictatorships at improving the material well-being of their citizens, especially that of their poorest citizens—the people who, arguably, need government assistance the most. One idea is that

FIGURE 9.4 The Effect of Democracy on Various Indicators of Material Well-Being

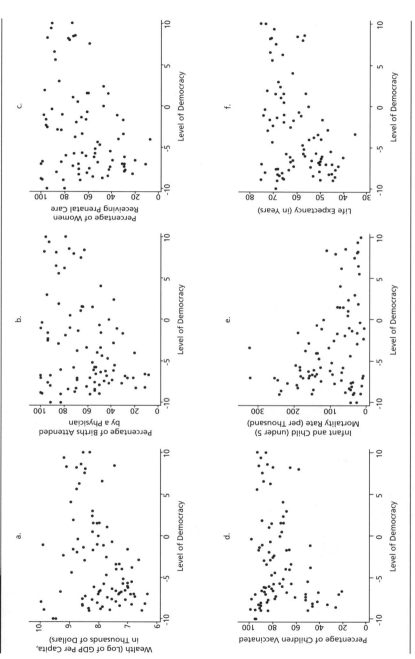

Note: The horizontal axes measure a country's average level of democracy from 1960 to 1990 as coded by Polity IV. The measure ranges from –10 (most dictatorial) to +10 (most democratic). The vertical axes vary by graph.

the poor are able to vote leaders out of office in a democracy if their political leaders do not implement policies aimed at improving their situation. As a result, democratic leaders have an incentive to help the poor. A second idea has to do with the fact that democratic regimes are typically characterized by a greater freedom of the press than dictatorships (Sen 1981, 1999a). This means that democratic governments—and their electorates—are more likely to be aware of the serious problems faced by the poor in the first place. Thus, democratic governments are in a position to act to alleviate the problems, and the voters are in a position to evaluate these efforts. In contrast, dictatorships are more likely to be able to censor embarrassing new stories. For example, it seems reasonable to think that a dictatorship might well have tried to suppress the diffusion of the shocking images that were broadcast from New Orleans in the wake of hurricane Katrina in the United States in 2005. The third idea is simply that democratic leaders provide more public goods and more redistribution from the rich to the poor than dictators. Some argue that democratic leaders do this because they expect it to help them win elections and stay in power (Lake and Baum 2001; M. McGuire and Olson 1996). Others argue that they do this because democratic governments have a broader range of supporters to appease, which creates incentives for democratic leaders to produce public, rather than private, goods (Bueno de Mesquita et al. 2003; Ghobarah, Huth, and Russett 2004).[5] If any of these arguments are correct, then we should see a clear trend in the data showing that government performance is better when countries are more democratic.

Students at the National University of Singapore record a partial solar eclipse on March 9, 2016. Over the past few decades, the Singapore government has been investing significantly in higher education.

A first glance at the information in Figure 9.4 might lead one to think that there is very little relationship between democracy and the various indicators of material well-being. Notice, however, the "triangular" nature of the data in each of the plots. This feature of the data indicates an interesting asymmetry suggesting that although democracies seldom perform poorly in terms of these indicators of material well-being, they frequently fail to outperform a substantial number of dictatorships. Put differently, although

---

5. Some have argued, however, that even if democracies do redistribute at higher levels than dictatorships and even if democracies do provide more public goods than dictatorships, these policies are not necessarily directed at the poor; rather, they are directed at the middle class (Ross 2006).

it appears that dictatorships often produce outcomes that are substantially worse than most democracies, some seem to perform every bit as well as democracies. In other words, democracy appears to be *sufficient* for ensuring some degree of success in these various areas of material well-being, but it is obviously not *necessary* for success.

Triangular data like those seen in Figure 9.4 are often a sign that the variables being captured are related through a process of complex causation. In this case, they suggest that there is greater variability in the performance of dictatorships than in that of democracies. As a result, attempts to gauge the differences in performance between democracies and dictatorships that fail to take account of the variation *among* dictatorships are likely to be misleading at best and wrong at worst. Making sense of the variability in performance among dictatorships, therefore, is crucial if we are to get a clear picture of the effects of democracy on material well-being. That said, it will not do to just remove the high-performing dictatorships, declare them "different," and estimate the difference in performance between democracies and the remaining dictatorships in an attempt to confirm our prejudices about bad dictatorial performance. Instead, it is important to understand *why* some dictatorships perform poorly and some do not.

Thus far, we have seen contradictory theoretical and empirical evidence suggesting that we don't really know if, how, or why regime type matters for economic growth or a host of other political outcomes that we generally think are important for ensuring a good quality of life. Does this mean that political institutions such as regime type have no effect on policy and outcomes? We believe that this is too quick and too pessimistic a conclusion to draw. As we are about to demonstrate in the following chapter, political institutions do, in fact, matter a great deal for determining the type of performance that governments have incentives to provide. Institutions do matter for government performance, but you will see that thinking about the world in terms of democracies and dictatorships is not always the most useful approach to explaining how or why. One reason for this has to do with the great variety of institutional arrangements that occur within the category of dictatorships. Consequently, we will devote the entire next chapter to examining the varieties of dictatorship that exist in the world. We will return at the end of that chapter to the question of why some dictatorships produce better outcomes than others, and how dictatorships compare with democracies.

CONCLUSION

As we noted at the beginning of this chapter, we live in a world that tends to clearly associate good outcomes with democracy and bad ones with dictatorships. As we have shown, the world, in reality, is much more complex than this. Oftentimes, we have no compelling theoretical reason to believe that democracies outperform dictatorships. For example, we presented several different stories linking regime type to economic growth. They all reached different conclusions. Some suggested that democracy is good for economic growth, whereas others suggested that dictatorship was better. When it comes to the empirical evidence, it does appear that democracies produce a relatively high level of material well-being for their citizens. It is not the case, however, that democracies regularly outperform all dictatorships. Although some dictatorships perform extremely poorly on many different indicators of material well-being, others perform relatively well. As a whole, the empirical evidence suggests that thinking of the world purely in terms of a democracy-dictatorship dichotomy may not be the best way to explain the variation in the performance levels of different countries.

KEY CONCEPTS

structural dependence of the state on capital *341*

PROBLEMS

The following problems address some of the more important concepts and theories introduced in this chapter.

The Effect of Regime Type on Economic Growth

1. On September 17, 2011, protesters occupied Zuccotti Park in the financial district of New York as part of a movement that became known as "Occupy Wall Street" (OWS). Many of the protesters had been inspired by the popular uprisings that had occurred in Egypt and Tunisia in early 2011. The OWS protesters were opposed to what they perceived to be the undue influence of banks and multinational corporations on the political system. They believed that the wealthiest 1 percent of society had a disproportionate share of capital and political influence, and they used the slogan "We are the 99%" to highlight the problem of social and economic inequality. The OWS led to the creation of the international Occupy Movement, which has organized protests in dozens of countries around the world. The occupation of Zuccotti Park ended on November 15, 2011, when the protesters were forcibly removed by the police. Imagine that you are discussing issues of inequality and the power of the financial sector with some of the "Occupy Wall Street" protesters in the fall of 2011. How would you explain the implications of the structural dependence of the state on capital to someone who doesn't understand why left-wing parties do not always "expropriate" the rich when they come to power?

2. On September 8, 2009, the *New York Times* columnist Thomas L. Friedman claimed that "One-party nondemocracy certainly has its drawbacks. But when it is led by a reasonably enlightened group of people, as China is today, it can also have great advantages. That one party can just impose the politically difficult but critically important policies needed to move a society forward in the 21st century" (Friedman 2009, Opinion section). Discuss Friedman's claim in the context of the material presented in this chapter.

3. Explain the logic behind the hypothesized causal path between regime type and economic growth shown in Figure 9.1, and then discuss what the empirical evidence tells us about each of the links in this path. Overall, what can you conclude about the connection between democracy and economic growth?

Empirical Evidence of the Effect of Regime Type on Government Performance

4. Explain what the "triangular" data shown in Figure 9.4 tell us about the relationship between regime type and various measures of material well-being. Then, speculate about the possible causes of the wide variability in performance among certain countries. What are some of the factors not captured in the Polity IV measure of democracy that might affect material well-being?

5. If your argument in question 4 (above) is correct, what empirical implications should you be able to observe? Present these implications as testable hypotheses.

10 Varieties of Dictatorship

A monarchy is the best kind of government because the King is the owner of the country. Like the owner of a house, when the wiring is wrong, he fixes it.

Italian peasant, quoted in Banfield and Banfield (1958, 26)

There can be no government without an army. No army without money. No money without prosperity. And no prosperity without justice and good administration.

Ibn Qutayba, ninth-century Muslim scholar

- In this chapter, we examine the wide variety of dictatorships around the world. One common way to distinguish between dictatorships is in terms of their "support coalitions." Such an approach indicates that there are three main types of dictatorship: (i) monarchic dictatorships, (ii) military dictatorships, and (iii) civilian dictatorships. Civilian dictatorships can be further classified into those that are personalist and those that have a dominant regime party.

- There are two fundamental problems of authoritarian rule. The *problem of authoritarian power-sharing* recognizes that authoritarian regimes face potential intra-elite conflict and that the dictator must satisfy those with whom he shares power. The *problem of authoritarian control* recognizes that authoritarian regimes face potential elite-mass conflict and that the dictator must deal with threats from below. The institutional structure, policies, and survival of authoritarian regimes are shaped by these two problems of authoritarian rule.

OVERVIEW

- Selectorate theory helps to explain why we observe tremendous variation in the economic performance of dictatorships. Rather than categorize governments as either democratic or dictatorial, selectorate theory characterizes all governments by their location in a two-dimensional institutional space. One dimension is the size of the selectorate—those with a say in selecting the leader—and the second is the size of the winning coalition—those in the selectorate whose support is essential for the leader to stay in office.

- Leaders in systems with large winning coalitions and large selectorates—democracies—have incentives to produce public goods. These leaders produce good government performance—high levels of wealth, efficient governance, and low rates of corruption and kleptocracy.

- Leaders in systems with small winning coalitions and large selectorates—personalist and dominant-party dictatorships—have incentives to provide private rewards to their winning coalition. These leaders produce poor government performance—low levels of wealth, inefficient governance, and high levels of corruption and kleptocracy.

- Leaders in systems with small winning coalitions and small selectorates—monarchic and military dictatorships—produce middling levels of government performance.

In the previous chapter, we saw that there is tremendous variation in the economic performance of dictatorial regimes. In this chapter, we take time to examine the wide variety of authoritarian regimes that exist around the world. We begin by discussing one common typology of authoritarian regimes that distinguishes between dictatorships based on the identity of their "support coalitions." This typology suggests that there are three basic types of authoritarian regime: (i) monarchic dictatorships, (ii) military dictatorships, and (iii) civilian dictatorships. Civilian dictatorships can be further classified into those that are personalist and those that have a dominant party.

There are two fundamental problems of authoritarian rule (Svolik 2012). The first problem is the *problem of authoritarian power-sharing*. Dictators never rule alone. Instead, they rely on support from key groups and allies within the authoritarian elite with whom they share power. Dictators must keep this support coalition satisfied in order to prevent them from challenging their rule. The second problem is the *problem of authoritarian control*. This problem focuses on the conflict that exists between the authoritarian elite and the masses over which it rules. These two problems of authoritarian rule indicate that dictatorial politics is fundamentally shaped by intra-elite conflict and elite-mass conflict. As we'll see, these two sources of conflict shape the institutional structure adopted by dictatorships and the prospects for authoritarian survival.

In terms of their economic performance, some dictatorships perform poorly, but others perform at least as well as the average democracy. In the remainder of this chapter, we explore why this might be the case with the help of selectorate theory. According to selectorate theory, the key to a country's material well-being has less to do with whether it is democratic or dictatorial and more to do with the size of its "winning coalition" and "selectorate," two terms that we'll define in more detail shortly. Once we start to think in terms of the size of the winning coalition and the selectorate, it becomes a lot easier to explain why some countries produce better economic policies and provide more public goods than others.

A COMMON TYPOLOGY OF AUTHORITARIAN REGIMES

Dictatorships are not all alike. Indeed, there is a wide variety of dictatorships, and many different ways in which they could be classified (Geddes, Wright, and Frantz 2014; Hadenius and Teorell 2007; Levitsky and Way 2002; Schedler 2002). Cheibub, Gandhi, and Vreeland (2010) provide one common typology of authoritarian regimes. They suggest that a useful way to distinguish between dictatorships is in terms of how authoritarian rulers are removed from office. As dictators are nearly always deposed by fellow members of the regime (Ezrow and Frantz 2011; Geddes 1999; Svolik 2009), this means classifying dictatorships based on the characteristics of their "inner sanctums" or "support coalitions."

A Three-Way Classification: Monarchy, Military, Civilian

According to this approach, there are three basic types of dictatorship: (i) monarchic dictatorships, (ii) military dictatorships, and (iii) civilian dictatorships. A **monarchic dictatorship** is an autocracy in which the executive comes to and maintains power on the basis of family and kin networks. A **military dictatorship** is an autocracy in which the executive relies on the armed forces to come to and stay in power. All other dictatorships are **civilian dictatorships**. In Figure 10.1, we illustrate the coding rules employed by Cheibub, Gandhi, and Vreeland (2010, 87) for identifying each type of authoritarian regime.

> A **monarchic dictatorship** is an autocracy in which the executive comes to and maintains power on the basis of family and kin networks. A **military dictatorship** is an autocracy in which the executive relies on the armed forces to come to and stay in power. All other autocracies are **civilian dictatorships**.

The first goal is to identify the effective head of the government. Although this is relatively straightforward in democracies (see Chapter 12), it is not always as easy in dictatorships. In most cases, the head of a dictatorial government will be a king, a president, or a prime minister. Occasionally, "an *eminence grise* lurks behind the scenes. . . . For example, Somoza and his sons installed figurehead presidents in Nicaragua to formally comply with term limits" (Cheibub, Gandhi, and Vreeland 2010, 88). The second goal is to identify whether the head of government bears the title of "king" *and* whether he has a hereditary successor or predecessor. If this is the case, then we have a monarchic dictatorship. The third goal is to identify whether the head of government is a current or past member of the armed forces. If this is the case, we have a military dictatorship. And if not, we have a civilian dictatorship. It is worth noting that leaders who come to power as part of a guerrilla movement or insurgency, such as Fidel Castro in Cuba (1959–2011), Yoweri Museveni in Uganda

FIGURE 10.1   Classifying Dictatorships

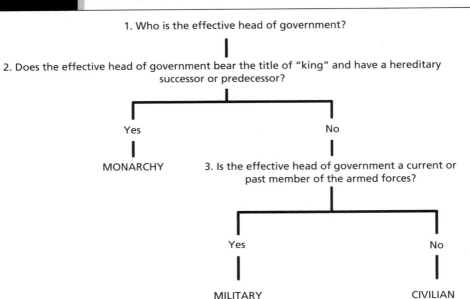

Source: Cheibub, Gandhi, and Vreeland (2010, 87).

(1986–), and Paul Kagame in Rwanda (2000–), are considered civilian, rather than military, dictators. Although these leaders often give themselves military titles, they cannot rely on the support of the military in the same way that former or current members of the military can. Indeed, the military are often one of the main threats to these types of dictators.

In Figure 10.2, we show how the number and percentages of monarchic, military, and civilian dictatorships in the world have changed from 1946 to 2008. The civilian form of dictatorship has always been the most common. In 2008, there were seventy-four dictatorships around the world. Of these, thirty-eight (51.4 percent) were civilian, twenty-four (32.4 percent) were military, and twelve (16.2 percent) were monarchies. The heyday for military dictatorships was in the late 1970s when almost 40 percent of dictatorships were run by the military. There has been a significant decline in the number of military dictatorships since the end of the Cold War. While the number of civilian and military dictatorships in the world has changed quite a bit over time, the same is not true of monarchies. This suggests that monarchies have been a particularly stable form of dictatorial regime.

To a large extent, the typology of authoritarian regimes that we have presented here is based on the idea that we can distinguish between different types of dictators in terms of the identity of their support coalitions or what we'll call a little later in the chapter their "winning

FIGURE 10.2 **Monarchic, Military, and Civilian Dictatorships, 1946–2008**

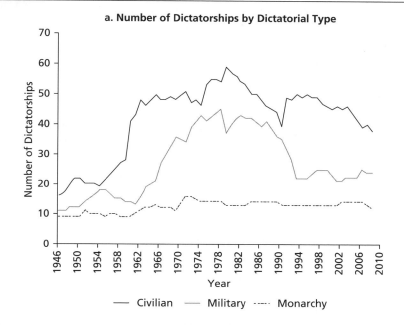

a. Number of Dictatorships by Dictatorial Type

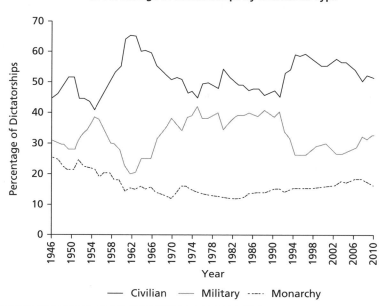

b. Percentage of Dictatorships by Dictatorial Type

Source: Data for Figure 10.2 come from Cheibub, Gandhi, and Vreeland (2010).

coalitions." Dictators need to keep their support coalitions happy if they are to stay in power. This is an important point. Although the term *dictator* often conjures up the image of an all-powerful individual, it is important to recognize that all dictators, like their democratic counterparts, rely on the support of a coalition to stay in power.

An implication of this is that when we see a dictator removed from power, we are likely to see him replaced by a defecting member of his own support coalition. As a result, we should frequently see dictators replaced by dictators of a similar type. In fact, there is considerable evidence that this is what happens. Three things can happen when a dictator leaves office (Geddes, Wright, and Frantz 2014). First, democratization may occur with the result that the authoritarian regime is replaced by a democratic regime. Second, the same authoritarian regime may survive but under new leadership. And third, the incumbent authoritarian regime may be replaced by a different type of authoritarian regime. In Table 10.1, we present data showing what happened when 388 authoritarian leaders left office for reasons other than natural death between 1945 and 1996. As we can see, dictatorial leaders are replaced by individuals from the same authoritarian regime about 50 percent of the time. Of the 22 monarchs, 11 (50 percent) were replaced by other monarchs. Of the 179 military leaders, 89 (49.7 percent) were replaced by other military leaders. And of the 187 civilian leaders, 103 (55 percent) were replaced by civilian leaders. If we ignore, for the moment, authoritarian leaders who are succeeded by democratic leaders, then the tendency for authoritarian leaders to be succeeded by leaders of the same type becomes even more pronounced—70 percent of military leaders were followed by a military leader, and 65 percent of civilian leaders were followed by civilian leaders. The persistence of an authoritarian leader's type when the particular authoritarian leader is removed is the reason why we often speak not just of individual dictatorial *leaders* but also of dictatorial *regimes*. This point emphasizes the fact that the survival of a dictatorial leader and the survival of a dictatorial regime are not the same thing.

TABLE 10.1 Leader Succession in Three Types of Dictatorial Regime, 1946–1996

Type of current dictator	Type of successor				Total
	Monarchy	Military	Civilian	Democrat	
Monarchy	11	6	4	1	22
Military	0	89	38	52	179
Civilian	2	53	103	29	187
Total	13	148	145	82	388

Note: Excludes dictators who died of natural causes while in office or who were still in office as of 1996.

Source: Gandhi and Przeworski (2007, 1289).

Monarchic Dictatorships

The first type of authoritarian regime comprises monarchies.[1] Dictatorial monarchs rely on their family and kin network to come to power and stay in power. As an example, Gandhi and Przeworski (2007, 1288) note how the emir of Qatar "reshuffled his cabinet in 1992, installing his sons as ministers of defense, finance and petroleum, interior, and economy and trade; his grandson in charge of defense affairs; and his nephews in public health and Islamic affairs." In general, the family and kin members in a monarchy play an important role when it comes to the issue of succession. Although the successor is typically a member of the royal family, he or she need not be the monarch's firstborn; that is, the system of succession need not be based on primogeniture. In fact, Herb (1999, 80) notes that "the most basic rule of the succession [in Kuwait] is that the family 'elects' the ruler by consensus, based on the perception by family leaders of their own best interests." Even if the established procedure for succession is violated in a monarchy, it is typically the case that the new leader must have the support of the royal family elite.

Swaziland is a contemporary monarchic dictatorship that highlights the important role that the royal family can play in choosing the monarch and the lengths that some monarchs will go to in order to stabilize their base of societal support (Woods 2012, forthcoming). Historically, the king (*Ngwenyama*, Lion) and "senior queen" (*Ndlovukati*, She-Elephant) of Swaziland have ruled together. The senior queen is typically the king's mother. When the king's mother is dead, the role of senior queen goes to one of the king's wives. The king and senior queen must come from different families, and they each have separate royal villages that act as their headquarters. No king can appoint his successor to the throne. In fact, the key role in the choice of a successor is played by the Royal Council (*Liqoqo*), a traditional advisory council made up of members of the royal family. The new king must be chosen from the royal family line, the Dlaminis. Although the exact rules of succession are shrouded in secrecy, it is thought that the Royal Council chooses someone who is unmarried and the only child of his mother; the mother, in turn, becomes the new senior queen. The king is expected to consolidate his position over time by choosing wives from every clan in Swaziland. The first two wives are chosen for the king from specific clans—the Matsebula clan and the Motsa clan—by the Royal Council, and their children cannot become king. According to custom, the king can only marry his fiancées once they have fallen pregnant, thereby proving that they can actually bear him heirs. The current king is Makhosetive Dlamini (Mswati III). He came to power in 1986 and has fifteen wives and twenty-five children. Other contemporary examples of dictatorial monarchies include Jordan, Bahrain, Kuwait, and Saudi Arabia.

---

1. As we will see in Chapter 12, some democracies—parliamentary democracies—can have a monarch as the head of state. Thus, the presence of a monarch is not necessarily a sign that a country is a dictatorship. We discussed the criteria for classifying democracies and dictatorships in Chapter 5.

As Figure 10.2 suggests, dictatorial monarchies are a particularly stable form of authoritarian regime. Empirically, monarchic dictatorships suffer from less violence and political instability than other forms of dictatorship, and monarchic leaders survive in office longer than other authoritarian leaders. There is also some evidence that monarchies have more stable property rights and experience faster economic growth than other types of dictatorships (Menaldo 2012). As Table 10.1 indicates, only one monarchic dictatorship (Nepal) has transitioned to democracy in the postwar period. In 1991, the Nepalese king, faced with societal opposition demanding multiparty elections, negotiated a transition to a parliamentary democracy in which he would remain as the head of state. In effect, he agreed to transform Nepal from an authoritarian monarchy to a constitutional monarchy in a parliamentary democracy. Not only are transitions to democracy quite rare among monarchic dictatorships, but when a dictatorial monarchy does collapse, it is often followed by periods of violence and the installation of an even more repressive authoritarian regime. As Geddes, Wright, and Frantz (2014, 326) point out, the overthrow of monarchic dictatorships has led to long and bloody civil wars in three countries—Yemen (1962–1970), Ethiopia (1974–1991), and Afghanistan (1978–). Similarly, the Libyan monarchy was replaced by a repressive civilian dictatorship led by Muammar al-Qaddafi (1969–2011), while the Shah of Iran was removed during the 1979 Iranian Revolution and replaced by the Islamist cleric Ayatollah Khomeini (1979–1989).

Why are monarchic dictatorships so stable? Menaldo (2012) argues that monarchic dictatorships have developed a political culture that allows them to solve credible commitment problems with respect to their support coalitions. To motivate his argument, Menaldo starts by contrasting the experience of monarchies in the Middle East and North Africa (MENA) during the Arab Spring of 2011 with the experience of other types of dictatorship in the region. He indicates that monarchies, such as Morocco, Jordan, Saudi Arabia, Bahrain, the United Arab Emirates, and Oman, were largely spared the sort of political violence that plagued dictatorial leaders in the rest of the region. As we noted in Chapter 6, some monarchies, like Saudi Arabia, did feel it necessary to pump billions of dollars into public programs to keep the populace on their side (Ross 2011). Indeed, Bahrain's king Hamad bin Isa al-Khalifa went further than this, imprisoning hundreds of protesters, imposing martial law, and calling in thousands of troops from Saudi Arabia to clamp down on emerging protest movements. Despite this, it seems clear that the level of political violence and instability in the region's monarchies was considerably less than that observed in non-monarchic dictatorships, such as those in Tunisia, Egypt, Syria, Yemen, and Libya. Why?

As we noted earlier, monarchs often seek to maintain the loyalty of their support coalition by allowing members of the royal family to colonize government posts that they can then use for their own material benefit. Obviously, other dictatorships distribute rents in a similar way to keep their own support coalitions happy. What's different in monarchies, at least according to Menaldo, is that they have generated a political culture where a leader's promise to distribute rents to his support coalition is more credible than in other types of dictatorship. This "monarchic culture" rests on three things. First, there are clear rules as to who the insiders and outsiders are. In general, monarchies tend to depend on tightly knit family structures that are reinforced through intermarriage. These rules allow insiders to know that their privileged position in the regime is relatively secure. Second, monarchies tend to have rules or norms that indicate exactly how regime rents are to be shared among the various members of the royal family. For example, there is a norm in Kuwait that succession alternates between the two branches of the Sabah family (Herb 1999). This creates a system in which members of the royal family all have a stake in maintaining the regime; in effect, regime collapse threatens access to the political and economic rents they have been promised. Third, monarchies tend to have institutions that allow members of the royal family to monitor the actions of the monarch and enforce the norms regarding the distribution of regime rents. As our earlier example from Swaziland indicates, most monarchies have royal courts or appointed legislatures that enforce rules relating to the succession of monarchs and that place limits on the actions that monarchs can take. These royal courts act as commitment devices, forcing monarchs to follow through on their promises relating to things like the distribution of regime rents. In many ways, these royal courts perform a role similar to the legislatures that were created by monarchs seeking to raise revenue in early modern Europe (see Chapter 6).

Military Dictatorships

The second type of authoritarian regime comprises military dictatorships. In most cases, military leaders rule as part of a "junta," or committee. High-ranking officers who take power on behalf of the military typically have small juntas that comprise the three or four heads of the various armed services. On the other hand, lower-ranked officers who come to power, perhaps as part of a military coup, often have larger juntas as they seek to build the support necessary to consolidate their hold on power. Military rulers often portray "themselves as 'guardians of the national interest,' saving the nation from the disaster wrought by corrupt and myopic civilian politicians" (Cheibub, Gandhi, and Vreeland 2010, 85). This helps to explain why these juntas frequently adopt titles such as the "Military Council of National Salvation," as occurred in Poland in 1981 when General Jaruzelski imposed martial law, or the "National Council for Peace and Order," as occurred in Thailand following the 2014 military coup.

Of course, it is not clear that military rulers actually have such altruistic motivations. Some scholars have argued, for instance, that military coups are more often than not motivated by class conflict or corporate interests (Finer 1988; Nordlinger 1977; Stepan 1971). For example, many of the military juntas in Latin American countries, such as Argentina (1976), Chile (1973), and Guatemala (1954), resulted from right-wing coups that toppled left-wing democratic governments that threatened to redistribute wealth from the rich to the poor (Drake 1996; O'Donnell 1973; Stepan 1985). Similarly, the military junta—the Supreme Council of Armed Forces (SCAF)—that came to power in Egypt after protests forced longtime president Hosni Mubarak to step down in the spring of 2011 was widely perceived to be acting in its own economic interests. The military controlled anywhere from 5 percent to 45 percent of the Egyptian economy (Fadel 2011). It is perhaps not surprising, then, that the military moved against Hosni Mubarak during the Arab Spring protests in 2011; the military saw the people camped out in Tahrir Square as "customers," and it no longer believed that Mubarak could protect its economic interests.

The most pressing threat to the stability of military dictatorships tends to come from within the military itself. Consider the history of military rule in the West African country of Guinea. A military junta, called the Military Committee of National Recovery (CMRN), was established in Guinea in April 1984 following a coup by Lieutenant-Colonel Lansana Conté. The coup had followed the death of independent Guinea's first president, Sékou Touré. The subsequent history of Guinea has seen numerous examples of military protests, coups, and countercoups, some successful and some not. President Conté, for example, had to suppress his first military revolt, led by his deputy Colonel Diarra Traoré, as early as 1985. In 1996 there was another attempted coup when the military mutinied over poor living conditions. The military junta responded by introducing various reforms aimed at appeasing the armed forces. Lansana Conté eventually died on December 23, 2008, after a long illness. According to the constitution, new presidential elections were supposed to be held within sixty days. However, within six hours of the announcement of Conté's death, there was another military coup, this time led by the head of the army, Captain Moussa Dadis Camara ("Military 'Seizes Power'" 2008). In December 2009, President Camara suffered a head wound in an attempted assassination and countercoup led by his aide-de-camp, Lieutenant Aboubacar Sidiki "Toumba" Diakité (Howden 2009). Camara was forced to leave the country for medical treatment in Morocco and eventually agreed not to return. The military junta then handed power over to Alpha Condé, who won the 2010 presidential elections. After several postponements due to security issues, legislative elections were finally held in 2013 amid ethnic violence and charges of election fraud from opposition groups.

Although we have focused here on military juntas within Guinea, the threat that factions within the military pose to stability is commonplace among all military dictatorships. Indeed, power has changed hands thirteen times between various military factions in Guatemala since 1945 (Gandhi and Przeworski 2007, 1288). Contemporary military dictatorships include Thailand and Chad.

Empirically, military dictatorships tend to have short durations and are more likely to end with negotiations as opposed to violence than other types of authoritarian regime (Geddes 2003). There is also some evidence that military dictatorships are more likely to leave behind competitive and democratic forms of government than other types of dictatorship. As Table 10.1 indicates, 29.1 percent of military dictatorships between 1946 and 1996 ended with democratic transitions; only 15.6 percent of civilian dictatorships and 4.5 percent of monarchic dictatorships ended with democratic transitions. What explains these empirical patterns?

The military tends to value discipline and cohesiveness, autonomy from civilian intervention, and military budgets large enough to attract recruits and buy weapons (Geddes 2003, 54). Officers tend to participate in coups only when a government threatens the interests, or the very existence, of the military (Nordlinger 1977; Stepan 1971). As we have seen, the decision of the Egyptian military to end its loyalty to the Mubarak regime following popular protests in 2011 and establish a military junta can be understood in this light. If militaries do come to power, though, they often carry with them "the seeds of their own destruction" (Geddes 2003, 63). Disagreements over, say, economic policy or the distribution of office benefits among senior officers can lead to factionalization. In these circumstances, many officers prefer to return to the barracks and allow elections rather than risk the unity of the military by trying to cling to power. Importantly, the value of the exit option—the value associated with giving up power—is considerably higher for military dictatorships than for other forms of dictatorship. The fact that the military has all the "guns" means that it retains a credible threat to re-intervene in politics in a way that other groups do not necessarily have. In other words, the military can step down from power with a greater sense of assurance that whoever wins the elections will still have to take account of the military's preferences due to the possibility of future coups. In many cases, the military will actually negotiate the handover of power to make sure that its interests are indeed protected.

Goemans and Marinov (2014) indicate that the shorter duration of military dictatorships and the propensity of military juntas to leave behind competitive elections are even more pronounced in the post–Cold War period. Some of their empirical evidence is presented graphically in Figure 10.3. There were 167 military coups between 1960 and 1990 in the Cold War period. Only 25 percent of these coups were followed by competitive elections within five years. In contrast, there were 43 military coups between 1991 and 2004 in the post–Cold

| FIGURE 10.3 | **The Timing of Elections after Military Coups** |

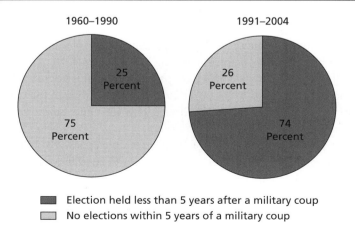

Source: Marinov and Goemans (2014).

War period. As we can see, military coups are less common in the post–Cold War period. More significant, though, is the fact that fully 74 percent of these coups were followed by competitive elections within five years.

What explains this dramatic difference between the Cold War and post–Cold War periods? Coup leaders are often very sensitive to how the international community will respond to their actions, particularly if they depend on the outside world for foreign aid. Marinov and Goemans (2014, 805) argue that foreign countries, particularly Western ones, exerted much less pressure on military dictatorships to hold elections during the Cold War period because they viewed the world as a "chessboard of West vs. East." Essentially, Western countries, like the United States, often preferred to support staunchly anti-Communist military juntas during the Cold War rather than encourage competitive elections that might produce left-leaning governments sympathetic to the Soviet Union.[2] According to Marinov and Goemans, the demise of the Soviet Union has enabled Western countries to push a more pro-democracy agenda. Since 1997, for example, US presidents have been bound by an act of Congress to suspend foreign aid to any recipient country that experiences a coup d'état. In line with their argument, Marinov and Goemans (2014) find that a country's dependence on Western aid increases the likelihood that a postcoup election will take place, but only in the post–Cold War period.

This line of reasoning has led some to wonder whether coups might even be "good" for democracy. Thyne and Powell (2014), for example, suggest that coups, by providing a "shock" to the system, can create opportunities for liberalization that would not otherwise exist. Along similar lines, Collier (2009, n.p.) argues that "coups and the threat of coups can be a significant weapon in fostering democracy" in Africa. As an example of a "good coup," we might consider the February 2010 coup in Niger when the military stepped in to remove the increasingly autocratic president, Mamadou Tandja (Armstrong 2010). Within a year, the military-led Supreme Council for the Restoration of Democracy had allowed free and fair legislative and presidential elections, which brought the former opposition leader Mahamadou Issoufou to power (Freedom House 2012). This optimistic view of military coups, though, is not consistent with the broader empirical evidence. For example, Derpanopoulos and colleagues (2016) find that although military coups in dictatorships are more likely to be followed by democratic transitions in the post–Cold War period than in the Cold War period, the most common outcome is the establishment of a new and more repressive form of authoritarian regime.

The apparent break in the behavior of Western countries toward military juntas, and dictatorships more generally, in the post–Cold War world should not be overstated either. It is true that the West is no longer in a global competition with a foe like the Soviet Union and that, therefore, there are fewer countries on which the West must rely to protect its

---

2. In some cases, Western countries even helped the military with its coup. For example, it is known that the Nixon administration and the CIA helped in the military overthrow of the left-leaning President Salvador Allende in Chile in 1973.

strategic interests. In certain regions of the world, though, Western influence continues to be challenged. In many places, this challenge comes from countries like China or radical Islamist groups like al-Qaida, ISIL, or the Taliban. It is not clear to us whether Western countries will support elections in these regions with the inherent uncertainties that they bring or whether they will prefer to prop up dictatorships that promise to protect Western interests. To support our concerns here, we point to the reaction of the United States toward the military coup that took place in Egypt in 2013. Following the ouster of the longtime dictator Hosni Mubarak during the Arab Spring, Mohamed Morsi, the candidate for the Islamist Muslim Brotherhood, became in 2012 the first democratically elected president in Egypt's history. The following year, the Egyptian military intervened to remove President Morsi from power. There was a mixed international reaction to these events, with the United States refusing to call them a "military coup" because the 1997 Congressional Act we mentioned earlier would have required it to freeze the substantial economic and military aid that it provided to Egypt.

Civilian Dictatorships

The third type of authoritarian regime comprises civilian dictatorships. Unlike monarchic and military dictatorships, which can rely on family and kin networks or the strength of the armed forces to stay in power, civilian dictators do not have an immediate institutional base of support; instead they have to create one. Many civilian dictators do this with the help of regime parties or personality cults. For this reason, some scholars distinguish between two subcategories of civilian dictatorships: (i) dominant-party dictatorships and (ii) personalist dictatorships (Geddes 1999).

Dominant-Party Dictatorships

In a **dominant-party dictatorship**, "one party dominates access to political office and control over policy, though other parties may exist and compete as minor players in elections" (Geddes 2003, 51). Just as political parties play an important role in recruiting and socializing the polit-

> A **dominant-party dictatorship** is one in which a single party dominates access to political office and control over policy, though other parties may exist and compete in elections.

ical elite in democracies (see Chapter 14), they can perform a similar function in civilian dictatorships. Consider the role played by the Communist Party in the former Soviet Union (CPSU). For all intents and purposes, membership in the CPSU was a necessary condition for becoming part of the political, economic, and academic ruling class—the *nomenklatura* (Gershenson and Grossman 2001). Describing the Soviet *nomenklatura* in the 1980s, Voslensky (1984, 98) wrote that "while a party card is of course no guarantee of success, lack of it is a guarantee that you will not have a career of any kind." Power and authority increased the higher one rose in the party, as did the monetary and nonmonetary benefits. For example, members of the *nomenklatura* were able to enjoy many of the things that were denied to the average citizen—they got to shop in well-stocked stores, they had access to foreign goods, and they were allowed to travel abroad. As George Orwell ([1949] 1977, 192) describes in his novel *1984*,

> By the standards of the early twentieth century, even a member of the Inner Party lives an austere, laborious kind of life. Nevertheless, the few luxuries that he does enjoy—his large well-appointed flat, the better texture of his clothes, the better quality of his food and drink and tobacco, his two or three servants, his private motorcar or helicopter—set him in a different world from a member of the Outer Party, and the members of the Outer Party have a similar advantage in comparison with the submerged masses.

As citizens gained membership into the CPSU and advanced up its ranks, they would be increasingly socialized into following the party line. Demonstrating loyalty to the party was crucial to gaining and retaining the benefits of power associated with membership in the *nomenklatura*.

A further illustration of how political parties can be used to control the masses comes from Gandhi and Przeworski (2006, 25).

> Consider communist Poland. Even though in 1948 communists forced their major rival, the Polish Socialist Party, into a "merger," thus creating the Polish United Workers Party (PUWP), they tolerated a pre-war left-wing United Peasant Party (ZSL), a small private business party (SD), and a Catholic group with direct ties to Moscow. After 1956, two other Catholic groups were allowed to organize. Even though these parties functioned under separate labels in the legislature, they were presented to the voters as a single list, with all candidates approved by the communists. Hence, elections only ratified the distribution of parliamentary seats and the specific appointees of the Communist Party. One way to think of this "multipartism" is that it represented a menu of contracts, allowing people characterized by different political attitudes (and differing degrees of opportunism) to sort themselves out. Membership in each party entailed a different degree of identification with the regime: highest for members of the PUWP, lower for those joining the Peasant Party, the lowest for the Catholic groups. In exchange, these memberships offered varying amounts of perks and privileges, in the same order. Someone not willing to join the Communist Party, with the social opprobrium this membership evoked among Catholic peasants, may have joined the Peasant Party. This choice entailed a less direct commitment and fewer perks, but it did signify identification with the regime, and it did furnish perks and privileges. This separating equilibrium maximized support for the regime and visibly isolated those who were not willing to make any gesture of support.

Hough (1980, 33) makes a similar point, claiming that "the Soviet government has thus far been skillful in the way it has tied the fate of many individuals in the country to the fate of the regime. By admitting such a broad range of the educated public into the party, it has provided full opportunities for upward social mobility for those who avoid dissidence, while giving everyone in the managerial class reason to wonder what the impact of an anti-Communist revolution would be on him or her personally."

We should note that the value of a regime party is not restricted to only Communist countries. For example, Magaloni (2006) provides a nice description of the types of mobilization techniques that the Institutional Revolutionary Party (PRI) used for many years in Mexico to signal its own strength and highlight the weakness of the opposition. For example, she describes how the PRI regime in Mexico put in place a series of policies that prevented peasants from rising out of poverty, thereby making them systematically dependent on state patronage through the PRI. Magaloni goes on to talk about the "tragic brilliance" of the regime, in which "citizens' choices are free, yet they are constrained by a series of strategic dilemmas that compel them to remain loyal to the regime" (2006, 19). She also describes how the PRI established various institutions to maintain the loyalty of its party members. For instance, the PRI imposed term limits, which increased the dependence of legislators on the party for future jobs, and at the same time kept ambitious politicians in check as they waited for their turn in power.

After authoritarian monarchies, dominant-party dictatorships are the longest-lived dictatorships (Brownlee 2009; Geddes 2003). Party cadres in a dominant-party dictatorship are similar to politicians in a democracy in that they want to hold office. The best strategy for maintaining access to office is to stay united. Although policy differences and competition for leadership positions are likely to produce factionalism in dominant-party regimes just like they do in other types of dictatorship, everyone is better off if they can stay united and maintain access to power (Geddes 2003, 59). Splits run the risk that an opposition party will come to power. And even if one of the factions is able to stay in office following a split, its grip on power is often significantly weakened. This is why majority factions within regime parties tend to try to co-opt minority factions rather than exclude them from power. When crises do emerge, the dominant faction usually responds by "granting modest increases in political participation, increasing opposition representation in the legislature, and granting some opposition demands for institutional change" (Geddes 2003, 68).

This logic helps to explain why regime parties often engage in widespread electoral fraud even when they know that they are going to win elections. Until recently, the traditional view of electoral fraud was that it is most likely to occur when elections are expected to be close, that is, when the incumbent feels that he needs to buy some votes to push him over the finish line. However, this view of electoral fraud is not consistent with the empirical record (Simpser 2008, 2013). Incumbents frequently engage in electoral fraud even when there is little chance that they will lose. As an example, consider Georgia's president, Eduard Shevardnadze. As Simpser (2008, 1) points out, Shevardnadze was expected to be reelected in the 2000 presidential elections by a very wide margin. One poll shortly before the election suggested he would win 52 percent of the vote compared with just 19 percent for his closest rival. Nevertheless, Shevardnadze engaged in widespread electoral manipulation and won with close to 80 percent of the vote. One reason for engaging in electoral fraud in this type of situation is that it can help deter regime party defections, discourage opponents in the future, and reduce the likelihood of protests against the dictatorship. In effect, lopsided electoral victories signal the strength of the regime party and the futility of challenging it.

The types of co-optation strategies employed in dominant-party dictatorships obviously require that the dominant faction have sufficient resources to buy off potential rivals and convince minority factions that they are better off sticking with the regime party than siding with the opposition. This suggests that economic downturns can create problems with stability for dominant-party regimes. Stability is also threatened when opposition parties or rival factions do better in elections than expected. Given the tools that dictatorial regimes have at their disposal to guarantee electoral victory, a close-run election can signal weakness in the regime, thereby encouraging opponents. When combined with an economic downturn or widespread protest, a close election result can trigger mass defection from the regime party. As Way (2011) writes, "If a crisis convinces ruling elites that continued loyalty threatens their future access to patronage, it may trigger a bandwagoning effect in which politicians defect en masse to the opposition. As one defecting member of the ruling UNIP party in Zambia that collapsed in 1991 put it, 'only a stupid fly . . . follows a dead body to the grave.'"[3] Arguably, this is the scenario that preceded many of the colored revolutions that occurred in Eastern Europe in the early 2000s.[4]

Personalist Dictatorships

In contrast to the leaders in dominant-party dictatorships who use regime parties to maintain their hold on power, some civilian dictators attempt to establish a more personalist form of rule. "Institutionally, what [these **personalist dictatorships**] have in common is that although they are often supported by parties and militaries, these particular organizations have not become sufficiently developed or autonomous to prevent the leader from taking personal control of policy decisions and the selection of regime personnel" (Geddes 2003, 53). Indeed, a personalist dictator often deliberately undermines these institutions so that they cannot act as a power base for a potential rival. For example, it is typical for regime personnel to be rotated frequently at the whim of the leader to prevent them from building independent bases of support. These dictatorships are also often characterized by a weak or nonexistent press, a strong secret police, and an arbitrary use of state violence that keeps the population living in constant fear.

> A **personalist dictatorship** is one in which the leader, although often supported by a party or the military, retains personal control of policy decisions and the selection of regime personnel.

Many of these dictators cultivate elaborate personality cults in an attempt to maintain the loyalty of their support coalition and the citizenry more generally. These personality cults often seem strange to outsiders. Consider Saparmurat Niyazov, who ruled Turkmenistan from 1985 to 2006. His book, the *Ruhnama* (Book of Souls), which was part spiritual and moral

---

3. Lucan Way, February 21, 2011 (blog post). "Some Thoughts on Authoritarian Durability in the Middle East." *Monkey Cage* blog (http://themonkeycage.org/blog/2011/02/21/some_thoughts_on_authoritarian/).

4. The phrase *colored revolutions* refers to revolutions, such as the Bulldozer Revolution in Serbia in 2000, the Rose Revolution in Georgia in 2003, the Orange Revolution in Ukraine in 2004, and the Tulip Revolution in Kyrgyzstan in 2005 (Tucker 2007).

guidance, part revisionist history, and part autobiography, served as the chief textbook for students at all levels of the education system from elementary schools to universities. The *Ruhnama's* influence extended well beyond the education system, with new government employees tested on the book during interviews and all citizens seeking a driving license required to take a sixteen-hour course on the book ("Turkmenistan Wrestles" 2004). Gurbangly Berdymukhammedov, who replaced Niyazov following his death in 2006, eventually removed the *Ruhnama* as a man-

Protesters ripping up Muammar al-Qaddafi's *The Green Book* in the Libyan town of Benghazi in February 2011.

datory subject in Turkmen schools. However, he appears to have simply replaced the *Ruhnama* in the school curriculum with several books of his own (Fitzpatrick 2011).

Kim Jong-il, who ruled North Korea from 1994 until his death in December 2011, inherited a similar personality cult from his father, Kim Il-sung, the "eternal president" ("Toughs at the Top" 2004). Kim Jong-il, who was referred to as the "Supreme Leader," "Dear Leader," "Our Father," and "the General," claimed to be able to control the weather with his mood and to be able to teleport from place to place (Hassig and Oh 2009; Kang and Rigoulot 2005). He was also known to issue various hairstyle guidelines as part of grooming and dress standards. These guidelines have in the past emphasized the negative effects of long hair on human intelligence, noting that long hair consumes a great deal of nutrition and thus robs the brain of energy ("N Korea Wages War on Long Hair" 2005).

Muammar al-Qaddafi is another dictator who also established a cult of personality before his death in 2011. In a similar way to Niyazov in Turkmenistan, al-Qaddafi forced a generation of Libyans to grow up studying his "*Green Book*" as a great work of social and political theory. Some have described the book as part Chairman Mao, who himself had written the "Red Book," and part Marx and Engels ("What Now for Colonel Gaddafi's Green Book?" 2011). It appears that tablet-like statues of its three volumes were erected in many Libyan towns. Al-Qaddafi often portrayed himself as a revolutionary against colonial powers who did not seek power for himself. In keeping with the precepts set out in *The Green Book*, "Colonel [al-Q]addafi eventually gave up any official title in the Libyan government, giving rise to one of the prime examples of Libyan doublespeak. While everyone in Libya regards Colonel [al-Q]addafi as the all-powerful ruler behind every decision of state, he often answers critics calling on him to surrender power by saying it is too late—he already has" (Kirkpatrick 2011). Al-Qaddafi's outlandish claims perhaps peaked during the Arab Spring in 2011 when he claimed that the people protesting his rule were high on drugs supplied by Osama bin Laden and al-Qaida ("Libya Protests" 2011).

Given how strange these personality cults seem to outsiders (and presumably insiders), it is perhaps worth thinking about exactly what role they play in keeping authoritarian leaders in power. Personality cults are often viewed in the media as the creation of narcissistic and megalomaniacal dictators who wish to be flattered and deified. However, this view, while almost certainly true in many respects, probably understates the role that personality cults play in maintaining dictatorial rule. The standard story with respect to personality cults is that they gradually alter the beliefs of the citizenry through a steady process of state indoctrination. By eliminating alternative sources of information, it is thought that personalist dictators are able to use their control of such things as the state media to persuade citizens of their amazing powers and leadership qualities, thereby generating support and loyalty. In effect, the standard story suggests that personality cults are designed to create citizen loyalty by producing false beliefs in the population.

The problem with this story, though, is that the personality cults are often ridiculously unbelievable. Did the North Koreans really believe that Kim Jong-il could control the weather with his mood and teleport from one place to another? Marquez (2011) suggests that although "cults of personality can sometimes 'persuade' people of the superhuman character of leaders . . . or . . . draw on people's gullibility in the absence of alternative sources of information and their need for identification with high status individuals, they are best understood in terms of how dictators can harness the dynamics of 'signaling' for the purposes of social control."[5] This alternative view of personality cults is premised on something that we discussed in Chapter 8, namely, that individuals living in dictatorships often engage in preference falsification. The **dictator's dilemma** is that he relies on repression to stay in power, but this repression creates incentives for everyone to lie so that the dictator never knows his true level of support in the country (Wintrobe 2001). In effect, a dictator is often confronted by two rather unsatisfactory choices. On the one hand, he can limit repression and allow free debate, thereby learning his true level of societal support. This often occurs when the dictator has insufficient resources to establish a reliable spy network to monitor the population (Egorov, Guriev, and Sonin 2009). On the

> The **dictator's dilemma** is that he relies on repression to stay in power, but this repression creates incentives for everyone to falsify their preferences so that the dictator never knows his true level of societal support.

---

5. The following discussion of personality cults is based on a very interesting blog post by Xavier Marquez, a political scientist at Victoria University in Wellington, New Zealand, on March 14, 2011 (http://abandonedfootnotes.blogspot.com/2011/03/simple-model-of-cults-of-personality.html).

other hand, he can use repression, but run the risk that he will be surprised by his lack of support at some future point in time.

This is where personality cults can be useful. As Marquez (2011, para. 7) notes, "The dictator wants a *credible* signal of your support; merely staying silent and not saying anything negative won't cut it. In order to be credible, the signal has to be costly: you have to be willing to say that the dictator is not merely OK, but a superhuman being, and you have to be willing to take some concrete actions showing your undying love for the leader." As we noted in Chapter 8, these actions often include things like denouncing others who lack sufficient faith in the leader and ostentatious displays of the dictator's image or ideology. This view of the role of personality cults helps to explain why dictators often make outlandish claims that strain credulity. By slowly raising the degree to which his claims are "over the top," a dictator can better gauge his true level of societal support by finding the point at which the population is no longer willing to publicly accept his "incredible" claims.

In effect, personality cults have three benefits from the perspective of the dictator, in addition to stroking his ego. First, they make it hard for opposition groups to organize and coordinate their actions. Citizens are unwilling to reveal their true preferences for fear of being denounced by others, thereby making it difficult for opposition groups to evaluate their true strength. Second, they help the dictator gain a better handle on his level of societal support. And third, they will, in fact, persuade some segments of society to become "true believers" in the dictator. Marquez (2011, para. 11) writes that personality cults can be difficult to establish in the first place but goes on to note that "once the cult of personality is in full swing, it practically runs itself, turning every person into a sycophant and basically destroying everyone's dignity. It creates an equilibrium of lies that can be hard to disrupt unless people get a credible signal that others basically hate the dictator as much as they do and are willing to do something about that."

To a large extent, we can think of intra-regime politics in a personalist dictatorship as involving the leader's faction and a minority rival faction, with the leader's faction having to decide how much of the spoils of office to share with the rival faction to keep it from defecting (Geddes 2003, 60). Whereas it is common for majority factions in dominant-party dictatorships to try to co-opt or buy off minority factions, this is much less the case in personalist dictatorships, where the leader's faction frequently keeps tight control over the spoils of office. The reason that the leader's faction can do this has to do with the huge risk that the minority faction faces if it defects. Recall that in a personalist dictatorship, all spoils from office come from remaining loyal to the leader. If the rival faction defects, it risks everything—life, liberty, and property. The payoff from successfully overthrowing the dictator may well be large, but so are the costs of failure. This, combined with a highly repressive security apparatus that limits the likelihood of a successful overthrow, explains why the leader's faction rarely shares the benefits of office with the rival faction. In effect, the leader's faction gives just enough benefits to the rival faction to prevent it from defecting and keeps the rest for itself.

As with dominant-party systems, the stability of personalist dictatorships rests on them having enough economic resources to keep their support coalitions satisfied. As a result, economic crises can have a destabilizing effect on both types of dictatorship. However, it is generally the case that the depth and duration of the economic crisis has to be greater in a personalist dictatorship than in a dominant-party dictatorship before it becomes unstable. There are at least three related reasons for this. First, the concentration of office benefits in the leader's faction means that a personalist dictator can more easily ride out periods of poor economic performance. Although ordinary citizens may well suffer in an economic downturn, it is often the case that the dictator will retain sufficient resources to keep his support coalition satisfied. Second, the highly repressive nature of the security apparatus in a personalist dictatorship means that the probability of successfully overthrowing the regime is quite low. And third, members of the leader's faction in a personalist dictatorship have much less valuable exit options than members of the regime party in a dominant-party dictatorship.

Box 10.1

ELECTORAL AUTHORITARIANISM: A NEW TYPE OF DICTATORSHIP?

Elections are increasingly common in dictatorships. Only Brunei, China, Eritrea, Qatar, and Saudi Arabia have failed to hold national-level elections at some point in the postwar period (Golder 2005). The increasing frequency with which elections are taking place in dictatorships has led some scholars to suggest that we are observing the emergence of a new type of dictatorship that goes under the heading of "electoral authoritarianism" (Schedler 2002, 2006). In an **electoral authoritarian regime**, leaders "hold elections and tolerate some pluralism and interparty competition, but at the same time violate minimal democratic norms so severely and systematically that it makes no sense to classify them as democracies" (Schedler 2002, 36). The extent to which competition is allowed in electoral authoritarian regimes varies (Diamond 2002). In some countries, the leader's party routinely wins with overwhelming majorities, and there is no meaningful contestation. These regimes are often called **hegemonic electoral regimes**. In other countries, though, competition is more real and opposition parties are able to win substantial minorities at election time. These latter regimes are often called **competitive authoritarian regimes** (Levitsky and Way 2002). Electoral authoritarian regimes can be contrasted with **politically closed authoritarian regimes** in which no opposition party is granted a legal space in the political arena.

An **electoral authoritarian regime** is one in which leaders hold elections and tolerate some pluralism and interparty competition but violate minimal democratic norms so severely and systematically that it makes no sense to classify them as democracies. A **hegemonic electoral regime** is one in which the leader's party routinely wins with overwhelming majorities. A **competitive authoritarian regime** is one in which opposition parties win substantial minorities at election time. Electoral authoritarian regimes can be contrasted with **politically closed authoritarian regimes** in which no opposition party is granted a legal space in the political arena.

Until recently, there were two rather divergent views about elections in dictatorships. For those who had hegemonic electoral dictatorships in mind, elections were often seen as forms of institutional window dressing with few political consequences. For those who had competitive authoritarian regimes in mind, elections were often seen as a prelude to further shifts toward democratization. Both of these views have been shown to be wrong. The overall consensus is that authoritarian elections have very significant political consequences, and that dictators use them to help stabilize their rule, not hasten their demise.

Elections can help dictators in at least three ways (Gandhi and Lust-Okar 2009). First, they can help them co-opt elites (Boix and Svolik 2008), party members (Magaloni 2006), or larger societal groups (Gandhi 2008; Gandhi and Przeworski 2006; Wright 2008). In effect, elections can be used as an arena for patronage distribution and as a means of recruiting and rewarding local political elites. Second, elections can help dictators co-opt opposition groups, as well as divide and control them. By allowing opposition groups to compete in elections, dictators provide access to political office and some decision-making authority. This provides these groups with a stake in maintaining the existing power structure. And by allowing only some, and not all, opposition groups to compete in elections, dictators sow the seeds of division within the opposition, thereby making it harder for opposition groups to overthrow them (Lust-Okar 2005). Third, elections can provide important information to the dictator. For example, dictators can use multiparty election results to identify their bases of support and opposition strongholds (Brownlee 2007; Magaloni 2006). In this way, dictators can use election results to identify which regions they should reward and which regions they should punish. Election results can also provide dictators with information about the performance of their local officials (Blaydes 2011). For example, dictatorial elites in China sometimes use low support at the polls in local elections to identify incompetent and poorly performing local officials (Birney 2007).

Although there is a growing literature on electoral authoritarian regimes, we have doubts about whether these regimes truly represent a new "type" of dictatorship. In our opinion, electoral competition is simply a dimension along which *all* dictatorships can be classified. Brownlee (2009) provides evidence in support of this when he maps data on the degree of electoral competition—politically closed, hegemonic electoral, and competitive authoritarian—onto our existing typology of authoritarian regimes. In Table 10.2, we use Brownlee's data to list the number of country-years that have occurred under each type of authoritarian regime for each category of electoral competition. The main point to note is that there is considerable variation in the degree of electoral competition across all forms of authoritarian regime. For example, all types of dictatorship come in both "politically closed" and "open" variants. A substantial minority of military, personalist, and dominant-party regimes can be classified as electoral authoritarian regimes, and in all three cases, the nature of electoral authoritarianism is fairly evenly split between hegemonic and competitive authoritarianism. Monarchic dictatorships, in contrast, have a strong tendency toward being politically closed.

Further evidence for our claim that electoral authoritarianism is not a separate category of dictatorship comes from the fact that the degree of electoral competition varies across time

TABLE 10.2	**Number of Country-Years by Authoritarian Regime and Degree of Electoral Competition, 1975–2004**

	Degree of electoral competition			
		Electoral authoritarianism		
Regime type	**Politically closed**	**Hegemonic electoral**	**Competitive authoritarian**	**Total**
Military	178	47	61	286 (14.2 percent)
Personalist	296	86	155	537 (26.7 percent)
Dominant party	586	165	187	938 (46.6 percent)
Monarchy	203	51	0	254 (12.6 percent)
Total	1,263 (62.6 percent)	349 (17.3 percent)	403 (20.0 percent)	2,015

Note: Numbers are based on data from Brownlee (2009).

within authoritarian regimes. Consider, for example, the authoritarian regime of Ferdinand Marcos, which ruled the Philippines from 1972 to 1986. In terms of its support coalition, the Marcos regime is generally considered a personalist dictatorship (Geddes 2003). But what about in terms of its degree of electoral competition? Prior to 1979, the Marcos regime is classified as "politically closed." From 1979 to 1983, though, it is classified as "hegemonic electoral" because Marcos won the 1981 presidential elections in a landslide. One reason for the landslide, and hence the "hegemonic electoral" classification, was that the major opposition parties boycotted these elections. From 1984 to its downfall in 1986, the Marcos regime is classified as "competitive authoritarian." This is because the major opposition parties decided to compete in the 1986 presidential election and unite behind the candidacy of Corazon Aquino. Corazon Aquino and the opposition parties registered such a strong showing in the 1986 presidential elections that when the National Assembly declared Marcos the winner, it set off the "People's Power Revolution" that ultimately led to Marcos's removal from power.

Note that although the degree of electoral competition varied significantly during the time that Marcos was in power, few scholars would argue that the Philippines experienced three different authoritarian regimes between 1972 and 1986. From his declaration of martial law in 1972 to his removal from office, there was one Marcos regime. What changed over time were the strategies of the incumbent leader and the opposition. At times the dictator found it helpful to allow elections, and at times the opposition found it useful to participate. While the literature on "electoral authoritarianism" points to an important source of variation across authoritarian regimes, the degree of electoral competition also constitutes an important source of variation *within* authoritarian regimes. The example of the Marcos regime also highlights that the degree of electoral competition at any given point in time is driven in large part by the strategic interaction of dictators and their opposition. For these reasons, we believe that it is best to consider the degree of electoral competition in a dictatorship to be an outcome or policy choice that varies within and across regime types rather than a defining feature of a particular authoritarian regime.

To some extent, our concerns with identifying electoral authoritarianism as a "type" of dictatorship also apply to the common typology of authoritarian regimes that we present in the main text. To what extent, for example, are military dictatorships really a distinct type of authoritarian regime? One could reasonably argue that civil-military relations represent a continuum and that all authoritarian (and democratic) regimes vary in the extent to which the military is willing and able to intervene in civil affairs. The same is true for personalist dictatorships. All authoritarian (and, again, democratic) regimes vary in the extent to which the leader has personal discretion over policy and personnel choices. We understand that many political scientists like typologies because they seem to simplify the complexity of the world into distinct categories, and students, like yourself, probably value this simplicity as it gives them an accessible way to talk about the diverse forms of authoritarian rule. However, it might be more useful to recognize that

AP Photo

During the 1986 presidential campaign, presidential candidate Corazon Aquino and running mate Salvador Laurel flash the thumbs down sign under an enormous bust of incumbent president Ferdinand Marcos at a campaign stop in La Union province in northern Philippines.

authoritarian regimes can be characterized on multiple different (and often continuous) dimensions. Rather than examine the causes and consequences of different discrete types of dictatorship, we could look at why some authoritarian regimes score high on some dimensions but low on others and what this means for their survival and how they behave. In fact, we examine one such approach a little later in the chapter when we discuss selectorate theory.

Due to the fact that personalist dictators retain personal control of policy decisions and the selection of personnel, members of their support coalition are very closely linked to the incumbent regime. As a result, it is often incredibly difficult for them to successfully defect to the opposition, and they typically have to go into exile if the regime is threatened. A consequence of this is that elites in personalist dictatorships often fight to the very end when their access to power is threatened. This helps to explain why personalist dictatorships are more likely to end in violence than other types of dictatorship. On the whole, then, personalist dictatorships tend to become unstable only when there is an economic catastrophe as opposed to a mild downturn, when the security apparatus and military defect, or when the leader dies and the system of patronage based around him collapses.

THE TWO FUNDAMENTAL PROBLEMS OF AUTHORITARIAN RULE

So far we have examined different types of authoritarian regimes separately. Political scientists, though, have identified two fundamental problems of authoritarian rule that exist in all dictatorships—the *problem of authoritarian power-sharing* and the *problem of authoritarian control* (Svolik 2012).[6] These two problems highlight the fact that threats to dictatorial rule can come either from within the authoritarian elite or from the masses. In this section, we take a brief look at each of these problems and examine some of the institutional solutions that authoritarian rulers have developed to mitigate them.

The Problem of Authoritarian Power-Sharing

The problem of authoritarian power-sharing focuses on intra-elite conflict. Dictators never come to power on their own, and they rarely control enough resources to govern alone. Instead, dictators rely on what we have so far called a support coalition. As we've seen, this support coalition might include members of the armed forces, key allies in the royal family, economic and religious elites, and so on. If the dictator retains the support of this support coalition, then the authoritarian regime stays in power. When the dictator first comes to power, there is an implicit, and possibly explicit, agreement on how to share economic and political rents among the members of the support coalition. The problem is that in a dictatorship there is no independent third-party actor to enforce this "power-sharing" agreement.

The members of the support coalition know that the dictator always has an incentive to alter the power-sharing agreement to his benefit. In effect, the dictator will want to acquire more power at the expense of his allies. The only thing stopping the dictator from grabbing more power is the ability of the support coalition to replace him. When the threat to remove the dictator is credible, we have a contested dictatorship where power is shared between the

---

6. In discussing the two fundamental problems of authoritarian rule we follow the theoretical framework outlined by Svolik (2009, 2012) and Boix and Svolik (2013).

dictator and his allies. Removing a dictator, perhaps via a coup, can be costly, though. There is a chance that the coup will fail, in which case the coup-plotters are likely to be imprisoned or killed. Even if the coup succeeds, it can leave lingering divisions that destabilize the authoritarian regime. Significantly, members of the support coalition have only limited information about exactly what actions the dictator is taking. After all, the dictator is unlikely to publicly announce his intention to usurp power. A consequence of this is that it can be difficult for the support coalition to distinguish between a situation in which the dictator is making a power grab and one in which he is allocating rents in the pre-agreed manner. This can result in "unnecessary" coups where the support coalition attempts to remove a dictator who is following the original power-sharing agreement and "missed opportunities" where the support coalition fails to act against a dictator who is concentrating power in his own hands.

This uncertainty about the dictator's actions and the reluctance of the support coalition to rebel creates incentives for the dictator "to try his luck and attempt to acquire power at their expense" (Svolik 2012, 55). If the dictator is able to make successive power grabs without being stopped, then it is possible for him to accumulate sufficient power that the "support" coalition no longer has the ability to credibly threaten to remove him. At this point, the authoritarian regime has shifted from a "contested" dictatorship in which the dictator is constrained by his allies to a "personalist" dictatorship in which the dictator has effectively monopolized power (Svolik 2012). In this account, personalist dictatorships arise when the support coalition repeatedly fails to act in response to a series of power grabs by the dictator. This is essentially the trajectory followed by all personalist dictators, including Mao Zedong in China, "Papa Doc" Duvalier in Haiti, and Joseph Stalin in the Soviet Union. In the case of Stalin, he rose from relative obscurity to become one of the most powerful dictators in the modern era (Suny 1998). He did not achieve this status immediately, though. Instead, he consolidated power gradually over many years, first eliminating rival factions headed by people like Leon Trotsky and Nikolai Bukharin and then subordinating the power of the Communist Party and the Red Army in what became known as the Great Purges (Svolik 2012, 53–54). The transformation of Stalin into a personalist dictator was possible only because members of his support coalition did not successfully step in early enough to prevent him from consolidating his hold on power.

What can the dictator do to solve this power-sharing problem? Dictators and their support coalitions clearly have an incentive to create a power-sharing agreement that allows the dictator to stay in power and the support coalition to benefit from the dictator being in power. However, when the members of the support coalition cannot fully monitor the dictator's actions and cannot be confident that the dictator is following the agreement rather than trying to surreptitiously consolidate power, they might either launch an unnecessary coup or, through inaction, find that they have been marginalized (or worse). For a stable power-sharing agreement to exist, the support coalition and the dictator must find a solution to this "monitoring problem" such that the support coalition receives credible information about

General Antonio Kebreau pins a cordon on Dr. François Duvalier, nicknamed "Papa Doc," at Duvalier's presidential inauguration ceremony in Port-au-Prince, Haiti, October 22, 1957. Following an attempted coup in 1958, Duvalier consolidated power, partly by purging military leaders and setting up his own militia (the Tonton Macoute). In 1964, he took the title of President for Life, remaining in office until his death in 1971.

the dictator's actions. Note that the dictator cannot simply promise to abide by the power-sharing agreement because such a promise is not credible.

Svolik (2012) suggests that the "monitoring problem" at the heart of intra-regime conflict can be solved, or at least minimized, with appropriate political institutions. In particular, decision-making bodies within legislatures or parties can provide a forum for exchanging information and deliberating about policy. These decision-making bodies, sometimes called ruling councils or politburos, "typically establish formal rules concerning membership, jurisdiction, protocol, and decision making that both facilitate the exchange of information among the ruling elite and provide for an easy assessment of compliance with those rules" (Svolik 2012, 7). These decision-making bodies are useful because they provide the members of the support coalition with information about the actions of the dictator, making it less likely that the dictator can stealthily consolidate power without being called to account for his actions. Having formal rules and protocols makes it easier to see when they have been violated. It is commonly thought that dictators adopt institutions such as legislatures and political parties to reward their allies in the support coalition or to co-opt members of the opposition (Gandhi 2008; Gandhi and Przeworski 2006; see also Chapter 8). The story here, though, is slightly different—dictatorships institutionalize to solve *informational problems* within the authoritarian elite.

Information on its own, though, is not sufficient to create a stable power-sharing arrangement (Svolik 2012). In addition to being able to detect power grabs, support coalitions must also have the ability to credibly punish the dictator if he reneges on their agreement. This raises the issue of whether support coalitions can overcome the collective action problems that arise when attempting to remove a dictator. Support coalitions will find it easier to overcome collective action problems and punish "rule-breaking" dictators when the distribution of power between the dictator and the support coalition is fairly even. A balance of power in the authoritarian regime means that it is feasible for the support coalition to punish the dictator. If the dictator is particularly powerful, there will be disagreement among the various factions in the support coalition as to whether they should, or are even able to, move against the dictator. Thus, stable power-sharing agreements in authoritarian regimes require institutionalization *and* a fairly even distribution of power between the dictator and his support coalition.

The argument here has implications both for when we will see institutionalization in dictatorships and for the effectiveness of authoritarian institutions (Boix and Svolik 2013). If authoritarian leaders have been able to consolidate their hold on power and establish a personalist dictatorship, then they have no need to institutionalize. If institutions, like parties or legislatures, exist in these circumstances, they will not have the power to constrain the dictator. If the dictator is relatively weak, then he has an incentive to institutionalize so as to establish a stable power-sharing agreement. In these circumstances, institutions will allow the support coalition to monitor the dictator's actions, and the dictator will choose not to violate the agreement because he knows that the support coalition can credibly punish him. If the dictator has middling levels of strength relative to his support coalition, then things are more complicated. Institutionalization will improve the monitoring capacity of the dictator's support coalition. If there is a sufficient balance of power between the dictator and his support coalition, then the dictator will abide by the power-sharing agreement. However, if there is an imbalance in the distribution of power that favors the dictator, we are likely to see the effectiveness of institutional constraints on the dictator gradually erode over time as the dictator successfully consolidates his hold on power.

The Problem of Authoritarian Control

In addition to facing threats from within the authoritarian elite, dictators also face threats from the masses over which they rule. This is referred to as the problem of authoritarian control. What is to stop the masses from rising up and overthrowing the dictator? To a large extent, dictators have two distinct strategies for solving the problem of authoritarian control—they can either repress the masses or co-opt them (Svolik 2012).

From the dictator's point of view, repression is somewhat of a double-edged sword. On the one hand, repression can keep the masses under control. On the other hand, the dictator must rely on other actors, typically the military, to do the actual repressing, and these actors may or may not share the same preferences as the dictator. By providing the military with the resources necessary to successfully repress the population, the dictator effectively empowers the military to act (if it wishes) against the dictator. If the dictator becomes sufficiently reliant on the military to stay in power, then the military can use this leverage to demand policy concessions and other rents from the authoritarian regime. As you can see, dictators face a trade-off. They can keep the military weak but run the risk that they will be overthrown in a revolution if the masses rise up, or they can maintain a strong military and expose themselves to threats from the military.

How this trade-off is ultimately resolved is likely to depend on the nature of societal opposition (Svolik 2012). When dictators are faced with ongoing large-scale, organized, and armed opposition, they will have little choice but to rely on the military to stay in power.

Whereas the internal security forces and secret police may be able to deal with small and irregular protests, only the military has the institutional capacity to put down more widespread and violent unrest. In return for services rendered to the dictator, the military will demand policy concessions, large budgets to buy weapons and attract recruits, and autonomy from authoritarian control (Geddes 2003). Importantly, both the dictator and the military recognize the pivotal role that the military play in sustaining the authoritarian regime in this type of situation. As a result, the military will not have to overtly intervene in the day-to-day running of the country. As Svolik (2012, 125) notes, "A politically pivotal military should be an *eminence grise* behind the throne," a situation he refers to as "military tutelage."

If dictators are faced only with small-scale intermittent protests, they are likely to side with keeping the military weak. In these circumstances, dictators will prefer to rely on internal security forces, such as the police, to repress societal opposition. In many cases, the dictator will provide only limited resources to the military writ large but generously reward a small "palace guard" that is loyal to the dictator. This was the general strategy adopted by Tunisian president Zine El Abidene Ben Ali (1987–2011). Historically, there had been few large-scale violent protests in Tunisia. Feeling relatively safe, Ben Ali kept the military small and under-equipped. This came back to haunt him during the Arab Spring in 2010–2011, though, when protests were so large and widespread that they overwhelmed the ability of the police to keep law and order, and the military refused to step in to save his regime. Given that the military is kept weak when the prospects for societal unrest are low, the military does not have the ability to openly intervene in the day-to-day running of the country; the civilian government has control over the military in this type of situation.

Svolik (2012) argues that direct military intervention in the political system is likely to occur only when the probability of mass unrest is moderately high. As we've seen, direct military intervention is unlikely to occur when the probability of mass unrest is high. This is because the dictator recognizes the pivotal role that the military plays in ensuring his regime's survival and will do whatever the military wants. Direct military intervention is also unlikely to occur when the probability of mass unrest is low. This is because the dictator will keep the military so weak that it is unable to successfully intervene in the political system even if it wants to. Direct military intervention will occur only when the probability of mass unrest is moderately high. This is because the dictator and the military are more likely to hold different beliefs about the probability of mass unrest in these circumstances, and hence, different beliefs about the importance of the military to the survival of the authoritarian regime. Svolik (2012) refers to these types of situations as "military brinksmanship."

In situations of military brinksmanship, the military has incentives to exaggerate or even promote evidence of social unrest in order to highlight its importance to the dictator. The military may also be sufficiently well resourced that it feels tempted to threaten the dictator with military intervention in order to obtain material and policy concessions. In contrast, the dictator may not believe that the military is critical to his regime's survival and may also be willing to call the military's bluff on its threat to intervene in the political system.

The concept of incomplete information, which we examined in our Transition Game in Chapter 8, is important here. If the military misjudges the resolve of the dictator to stand firm, or the dictator misjudges the military's resolve to intervene, then we can end up with a military coup that neither side really wants. In effect, the bargaining that occurs between the dictator and the military in situations of military brinksmanship can easily spiral out of control and lead to direct military intervention.

All of this raises an interesting point about how we judge the power of the military in civil-military relations. You might have thought that military coups or military dictatorships are a sign that the military is strong. In some sense they are. However, the framework that we have discussed here suggests that this is not quite correct. In cases where the military is truly strong, it has no need to conduct coups or directly hold the reins of power. As we noted back in Chapter 3, it is often difficult to identify who has power simply by observing the actions that different actors take. Truly powerful actors rarely need to use their power.

Rather than repress the masses, the dictator can try to co-opt them. You'll recall that we discussed this strategy to some extent in Chapter 8 when we discussed top-down transitions to democracy. In that discussion, we suggested that social unrest can produce a split in the authoritarian regime between soft-liners and hard-liners. If the soft-liners gain prominence, they might try to liberalize the regime and broaden the social base of the dictatorship. Liberalization policies typically entail a controlled opening of the political space and are associated with the formation of political parties, holding elections, writing a constitution, establishing a judiciary, opening a legislature, and so on. The goal of this "institutionalization," as we mentioned at the time, was to co-opt opposition groups (Blaydes 2011; Gandhi 2008; Gandhi and Przeworski 2006; Lust-Okar 2005; Malesky and Schuler 2010). As we have discussed in this chapter and elsewhere, elections, legislatures, and political parties give regime outsiders access to regime rents that they can distribute among their supporters, as well as a formal say in the policymaking process.

But why do dictatorships create institutions to co-opt opposition groups rather than just buy them off directly? Why, for example, don't dictatorships simply use cash transfers, land reform, programmatic redistribution, and other policies to co-opt opposition groups? Well, the answer to some extent is that they do. As Ross (2011, 3–4) notes, Saudi Arabia spent billions of dollars increasing public sector wages, unemployment benefits, and housing subsidies at the height of the Arab Spring protests. One issue with this type of strategy, though, is that dictators tend to make direct transfers when their survival is under threat from mobilized opposition groups but then reverse course once protesters have returned to their homes. If opposition groups recognize this, then direct transfers may not satisfy them and they will not be co-opted. In effect, the dictator's promise to provide direct transfers to opposition groups may not be viewed as credible. As you'll recall from Chapter 6, one solution to credible commitment problems is to create political institutions, such as legislatures, that enable opposition groups to maintain some influence over the dictator into the future, when protesters have left the streets.

Even if direct transfers are considered credible, institutions can provide additional advantages when it comes to co-opting opposition groups. Regime parties are often considered a key institution when it comes to co-opting the masses (Magaloni 2006; Svolik 2012). As we saw earlier in the chapter, members of dominant regime parties gain access to a more rewarding set of benefits as they work their way up the party hierarchy. Initial recruits to the party typically have to engage in costly activity on behalf of the party to prove themselves. The most lucrative benefits of party membership come only after working one's way up the party ranks. After exerting costly effort in the lower echelons of the party, party members develop a stake in seeing the regime survive as this is the only way that they can obtain the fruits of their labor. In effect, regime parties not only provide the masses with access to rents, something that can be achieved with direct transfers, but they also incentivize the masses to work on behalf of the regime's survival.

SELECTORATE THEORY

At the end of Chapter 9, we observed that there is tremendous variation in the economic experiences of authoritarian regimes. Whereas all democracies seem to perform quite well, some dictatorships perform poorly, while others appear to perform as well as, if not better than, the average democracy. In the remainder of this chapter, we'll explore why this might be the case with the help of something called *selectorate theory*. According to selectorate theory, the key to a country's material well-being has less to do with whether it is democratic or authoritarian and more to do with the size of its winning coalition and selectorate. As we'll see, the typology of dictatorships that we presented at the beginning of this chapter fits neatly into the theoretical framework provided by selectorate theory.

The basic assumption underpinning selectorate theory is that all political leaders are motivated by the desire to gain office. Of course, political leaders may have other goals as well, such as implementing particular policies or helping certain groups in society. Although selectorate theory does not deny this, it argues that the competitive nature of politics forces leaders in all regimes, democratic and authoritarian, to at least behave "as if" they desire to gain office. Political actors who fail to exert effort in an attempt to win power are likely to be replaced by competitors who do exert such effort. Knowing that they can achieve whatever goals motivate them only if they win, all political leaders are, therefore, forced to act as if they care about gaining office even if this is not their primary motivation.

A key part of this perspective is that there is a challenger willing, at any moment, to replace the incumbent leader. It is important to recognize that leaders always face political competition. It is often easier to identify political challengers in democracies than in dictatorships. Competitors who seek to replace a dictator are likely to face significant threats to their lives, and as a result, they tend to keep a low profile until they deem the moment right to challenge the dictator. The fact that we are not always able to identify who the competitors are in a dictatorship, though, should not lead us to think that there is no political competition or that the dictator is unchallenged. Someone else always wants to be the leader, and incumbent leaders must continually guard against losing power to these competitors.

The puzzle posed by the authors of selectorate theory, Bueno de Mesquita, Smith, Siverson, and Morrow (2003; hereafter referred to as BDM^2S^2), is the following: If all political leaders have the same (induced) goals—to gain office—why do we get so much variance in political outcomes? In other words, why do some leaders produce good economic outcomes and some leaders produce bad ones? Why do some leaders provide public goods but others do not? Why do some leaders engage in corruption but others do not? Why do some leaders adopt policies that lead to peace and prosperity but others adopt policies that lead to war and ruin?

Given that all political leaders wish to gain power and keep it, you might think that they would all want to produce good economic performance. It turns out, however, that good economic performance does not necessarily result in longevity in power. For example, BDM^2S^2 (2003, 273–276) provide both a list of the twenty-five "best" leaders in regard to their provision of peace and prosperity from 1955 to 2002 and a list of the top twenty-five longest-ruling leaders in the same period. It turns out that there is *no overlap* between the leaders on the two lists. The high-performing leaders, with an average economic growth rate of 7 percent, last just six years in office on average, whereas the longest-ruling leaders, with an average growth rate of 4.4 percent, last 35.1 years. These data would seem to suggest that producing good performance leads to short terms in office, whereas poor performance produces long stretches of time in office. Why, then, do some political leaders ever produce good performance? What explains the variation in the economic performance of political leaders?

Institutions

Selectorate theory argues that the variation in the performance of political leaders can be explained with regard to the institutional environment in which they operate. Some institutional environments encourage political leaders to behave in ways that benefit society, whereas other environments encourage them to behave in ways that benefit only themselves and a few others. Each country has a fundamental set of institutions or rules that govern interactions between residents within its borders. These include rules that define who is **disenfranchised**, who is part of the **selectorate**, and who is part of the **winning coalition**. The relationship between the disenfranchised, the selectorate, and the winning coalition in a country is shown graphically in Figure 10.4.

> **Selectorate theory** characterizes all governments by their location in a two-dimensional institutional space. One dimension is the size of the selectorate, and the second dimension is the size of the winning coalition.
>
> The **disenfranchised** are those residents who do not have the legal right to participate in choosing the government. The **selectorate** is the set of people who can play a role in selecting the leader. The **winning coalition** includes those people whose support is necessary for the leader to stay in power.

FIGURE 10.4   The Institutional Environment in Selectorate Theory

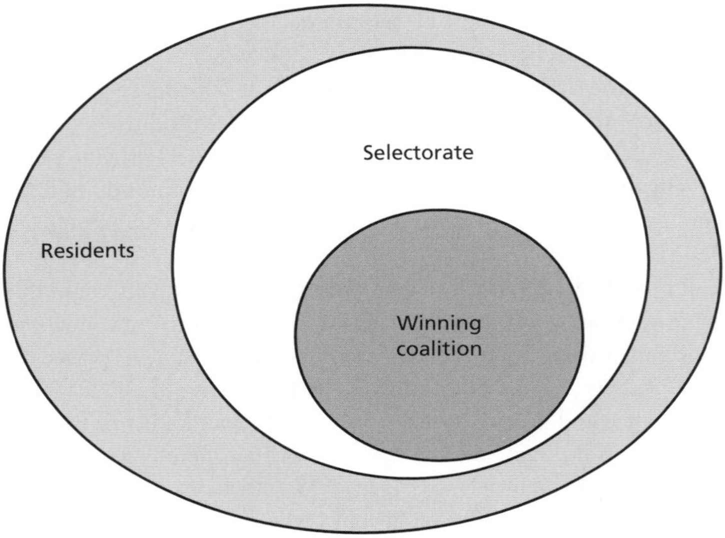

The disenfranchised are all those residents who do not have the legal right to participate in choosing the government. The selectorate (S), in contrast, is the set of people who have a legitimate say, if they so choose, in the selection of the leader. The term *selectorate* is chosen deliberately so as to indicate that the people "selecting" a leader do not necessarily have to do so by voting. In other words, the selectorate is not always the same as an electorate. In some forms of dictatorship, the selectorate is quite small. For example, the selectorate in a monarchy typically comprises only members of the royal family or, perhaps, the wider nobility and certain religious leaders. Similarly, the selectorate in a military junta usually consists only of members from the armed forces or, perhaps, the heads of each of the military branches. In other forms of dictatorship, though, the selectorate can be quite large. For example, the selectorate arguably consists of all adult citizens with the right to vote in dominant-party dictatorships that hold elections. Although the selectorate can be small or large in dictatorships, it is nearly always large in democracies. In a democracy, the selectorate comprises all those who are eligible to vote. In the past, certain groups such as women, nonwhites, and those without property were ineligible to vote in particular democracies. For example, nonwhites were banned from voting in apartheid South Africa between 1948 and 1994, and women did not get the right to vote until 1945 in France and until as late as 1971 in Switzerland. In most contemporary democracies, however, the selectorate means all adult citizens.

The winning coalition (W) consists of those members of the selectorate whose support is necessary for the leader to remain in power.[7] If the leader is ever unable to keep his winning coalition loyal, he will lose his position to a challenger. In democracies, the winning coalition is always quite large and comprises those voters who are required to elect the winning candidate or government. If there are only two candidates or parties at election time, then the winning coalition is as large as a majority of the electorate. In contrast, the winning coalition in a dictatorship is always quite small. For example, the winning coalition in a military junta might be a majority of the officers or a small group of colonels and generals who together control the armed forces. In Communist countries like China, the winning coalition is often just a small subset of the Communist Party. In a monarchy, the winning coalition might consist of a majority of the nobility. Earlier in the chapter, we classified dictatorships in terms of the identity of their "support coalitions," and we indicated that dictators needed to keep these support coalitions satisfied if they are to stay in power. It's now easy to see that these support coalitions are essentially the same as the winning coalitions in selectorate theory.

Mapping *W* and *S* onto a Typology of Regimes

Selectorate theory is able to differentiate various forms of government—monarchic dictatorships, military dictatorships, dominant-party dictatorships, personalist dictatorships, democracies, and so on—by the size of their selectorate and winning coalition. In Figure 10.5a, we plot the *theoretical* location of these various forms of government in a two-dimensional institutional space, where one dimension is the size of the selectorate and the other dimension is the size of the winning coalition. As you can see, selectorate theory differentiates between different types of dictatorships, as well as between dictatorships and democracies. The key factor that distinguishes democracies from dictatorships is the size of the winning coalition. Whereas all dictatorships have small winning coalitions, all democracies have large winning coalitions. And the key factor that distinguishes between the different types of dictatorship is the size of the selectorate. The selectorate is large in dominant-party and personalist dictatorships, particularly those that hold elections. BDM^{2}S^2 refer to these types of systems as "rigged election systems." In contrast, the selectorate tends to be small in military juntas and monarchies.

As you can imagine, measuring the size of a country's winning coalition and selectorate in the real world is extremely difficult. Nonetheless, BDM^{2}S^2 have attempted to do precisely this.[8] In Figure 10.5b, we plot the *actual* location of different forms of government by their average selectorate and winning coalition scores from 1946 to 2000. Even though BDM^{2}S^2

---

7. To make meaningful cross-national comparisons, the winning coalition and the selectorate are not conceptualized in terms of the absolute numbers of residents who belong to them; rather, they are conceptualized in terms of the proportion of residents that they represent.

8. For precise details on how the size of a country's selectorate and winning coalition are measured, see BDM^{2}S^2 (2003, 133–140).

FIGURE 10.5	Selectorate Theory and Regime-Type Locations

a. Theoretical regime-type locations

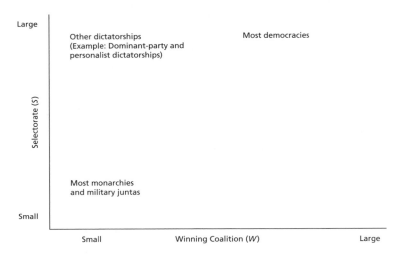

b. Actual regime-type locations (1946–2000)

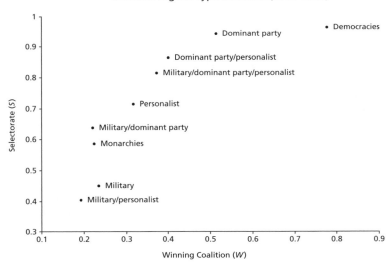

Note: W and S both range from a minimum of 0 to a maximum of 1. Geddes (2003) classifies dictatorships into four types: (a) personalist, (b) military, (c) dominant-party, or (d) hybrid mixtures of these pure types. Countries that are not classified as one of these four types of dictatorships are either monarchies or democracies; we employ data from Polity IV to determine which were monarchies and which were democracies.

Source: Data on the size of W and S are from Bueno de Mesquita and colleagues (2003); data on the different forms of dictatorships are from Geddes (2003).

do not use information about the form of government to measure the size of a country's selectorate and winning coalition, Figure 10.5b reveals that the scores for each country situate the different forms of government in the two-dimensional institutional space in a manner that is entirely consistent with the theoretical locations shown in Figure 10.5a. As expected, the average size of the winning coalition in a democracy is much larger than that in any of the various forms of dictatorship. Also as predicted, there is considerable variation in the average size of the selectorate among dictatorships. Monarchic and military dictatorships have small selectorates, whereas personalist and dominant-party dictatorships have large selectorates.

Government Performance

How does the institutional environment in which a leader operates influence government performance? According to selectorate theory, political leaders must keep members of their winning coalition happy to stay in power. They can do this by distributing public goods or private goods or both. As you will recall from Chapter 8, public goods benefit everyone in society regardless of whether they are in the winning coalition or not. This is because they are nonexcludable (once they are provided, anyone can enjoy them) and nonrivalrous (the amount of the good available to be consumed is not diminished by the number of people who consume it). Examples of public goods might be increased spending on education, health care, and infrastructure. In contrast, private goods benefit only some members of society and not others. In effect, private goods, such as business or export licenses, private jets, and villas in the South of France, can be given directly to members of the winning coalition. Those individuals who are not members of the winning coalition do not receive private goods. It is the job of an incumbent leader to figure out how many public and private goods to distribute in order to keep his winning coalition loyal.

In addition to deciding what mix of public and private goods to hand out to his winning coalition, the leader must pick a tax rate. This tax rate ultimately determines how much money the leader has at his disposal to pay for the provision of public and private goods. Depending on the tax rate chosen, residents decide how to allocate their time between economically productive activities and leisure. At the same time that the incumbent is deciding his tax rate and announcing his offer of public and private goods, a challenger also makes an offer to the selectorate (a combination of public goods, private goods, and a tax rate) in an attempt to put together an alternative winning coalition. The bottom line is that the political entrepreneur—the incumbent leader or challenger—who is best able to meet the needs of the winning coalition wins.

Loyalty Norm

Exactly how leaders distribute public and private goods depends on the size of the winning coalition and the size of the selectorate. Recall that the goal of the incumbent leader is to stay in power and that to do this he must keep the winning coalition happy. The key for the leader, then, is to stop members of the current winning coalition from defecting. Given this, let's start by thinking about the conditions under which a member of the current winning coalition might decide to defect and shift her loyalty to a challenger. Clearly, any disgruntled member of the winning coalition must weigh the potential risks and rewards from defecting. Oftentimes, there will be more than one potential defector in a winning coalition or multiple challengers to whom they can defect or both. Moreover, it is almost always the case that there will be members of the selectorate who are not in the winning coalition but who would like to be. As a result, individuals who defect from the current winning coalition have no guarantee that they will end up as part of the next leader's coalition. Indeed, any promise by a challenger to make them part of the future winning coalition if they defect and bring down the incumbent leader is not credible for obvious reasons. Thus, individuals who choose to defect risk losing access to the private goods that they presently enjoy as members of the current winning coalition.

The risk that members of the winning coalition face when they think about defecting is embodied in the ratio of the size of the winning coalition to the size of the selectorate (W/S). The ratio W/S essentially represents the probability that a member of the selectorate will be in any winning coalition. This is because S people could be in the winning coalition, but only (some portion) W of them will actually make it into the winning coalition. As you can see, W/S indicates the probability that someone who defects from the current winning coalition will be in the next winning coalition. Members of the selectorate have only a small chance of being in the winning coalition when W/S is small (when few people in the selectorate are needed to form a winning coalition), but they have a large chance when W/S is large (when many people in the selectorate are needed to form a winning coalition). As you can imagine, the size of W/S has important implications for the loyalty of members in the current winning coalition. If W/S is small, then members of the winning coalition are likely to be intensely loyal to the incumbent leader, because they realize that they are lucky to be part of the winning coalition and that they have a low probability of being in anyone else's winning coalition. As W/S gets larger and the probability of being in the next leader's winning coalition increases, this loyalty to the incumbent leader naturally declines.[9] In effect, W/S represents a sort of **loyalty norm**: there is a strong loyalty norm in small W/S systems and a weak loyalty norm in large W/S systems.

> The strength of the **loyalty norm** is determined by W/S—the probability that a member of the selectorate will be in the winning coalition. Members of the winning coalition are most loyal when W/S is small and least loyal when W/S is large.

The existence or absence of a strong loyalty norm has important implications for the performance of leaders in power. For example, political leaders in small W/S systems with

---

9. In the language of the Exit, Voice, and Loyalty Game examined in Chapters 3 and 6, a large W/S indicates that members of the winning coalition have credible exit threats; that is, they can defect and still have a high probability of being in the next leader's winning coalition.

strong loyalty norms have greater opportunities to engage in **kleptocracy** and **corruption** than leaders in large W/S systems with weak loyalty norms. Why? Consider two societies, A and B. In both societies, the political leader has $1 billion in tax revenue to distribute among the 1,000 members of his winning coalition and himself. The

> **Corruption** is when public officials take illegal payments (bribes) in exchange for providing benefits for particular individuals. **Kleptocracy** is when corruption is organized by political leaders with the goal of personal enrichment.

only difference between the two societies is that the selectorate is made up of 100,000 people in society A and just 10,000 people in society B. In effect, society A has a stronger loyalty norm (smaller W/S) than society B. It is easy to see that both of the leaders in societies A and B could pay each member of their winning coalitions up to $1 million in private goods to win over their support, that is, $1 billion divided equally among the 1,000 people in the winning coalition. As we'll see, though, neither leader has to actually pay out this much to ensure the loyalty of his winning coalition. In fact, it also turns out that the leader of society A, by taking advantage of the strong loyalty norm in his country, does not have to pay out as much as the leader of society B to keep his winning coalition happy. Ultimately, this means that the leader in society A can keep more of his tax revenue for his own discretionary use. How does all this work exactly?

Let's start with society A. The probability that a member of the current winning coalition will be a member of the next leader's coalition if she defects is just 1 percent; that is, $W/S = 1,000/100,000 = 0.01$. It is this low probability of being in the next leader's coalition that generates the strong loyalty norm we mentioned earlier. Anyone who defects from the current winning coalition in society A has a 1 percent chance of obtaining (at most) $1 million in private goods and a 99 percent chance of obtaining nothing.[10] As a result, the expected value of defecting in terms of private goods is just $10,000; that is, $1 million $\times$ 0.01 + $0 $\times$ 0.99 = $10,000.[11] All the incumbent leader, therefore, has to do to stay in power is to offer each member of his winning coalition slightly more than $10,000 in private goods and come close to matching the provision of public goods promised by any challenger. In effect, the incumbent can skim off for himself the difference between the $1 million per supporter that he could have distributed and the something over $10,000 per supporter that he needs to distribute to stay in power. If the incumbent's challenger offers a particularly attractive set of public goods, then the incumbent can give some of this "slush fund" to his supporters to purchase their continued loyalty (Bueno de Mesquita 2006, 421).

What about society B? Well, the probability that someone in the current winning coalition will be a member of the next leader's coalition if he defects is now 10 percent; that is, $W/S = 1,000/10,000 = 0.1$. This is somewhat higher than in society A, and as a result, the

---

10. A million dollars is the most that a defector can receive because that is the most that a challenger can offer to each member of the winning coalition if all tax revenue is spent on private goods.

11. For a review of how to calculate expected payoffs or expected values, see Box 8.6, "Transition Game with Incomplete Information," in Chapter 8.

loyalty norm in this society is weaker. The expected value of defecting from the current winning coalition in terms of private goods is $100,000; that is, $1,000,000 × 0.1 + $0 × 0.9 = $100,000. This means that the incumbent leader in society B has to pay a little more than $100,000 in private goods to each member of his winning coalition and come close to matching whatever provision of public goods a challenger has promised in order to stay in power. In society B, the incumbent gets to skim off for himself the difference between the $1 million per supporter that he could have distributed and the something over $100,000 per supporter that he needs to distribute to stay in power. This is still a lot of money, but it is considerably less than the leader in society A can skim off for himself.

Although we might think that all leaders want to engage in kleptocracy and corruption, the example that we have just provided illustrates that the institutional arrangements in a country influence their ability to do so without jeopardizing their hold on power. Specifically, leaders in small *W/S* systems (society A) have greater opportunities to "steal" from their citizens by skimming off tax revenue into their own pockets than do leaders of large *W/S* systems (society B). As an example of widespread kleptocracy and corruption, consider the small *W/S* system of Zaire under Mobutu Sese Seko (1965–1997). Mobutu was reportedly able to put as much as a third of the national budget under his personal control and skim off a quarter of all the profits from the country's vast copper mines. As Rose-Ackerman (1999, 116) notes, "Corruption and predation undermined the formal private sector, and grandiose infrastructure projects were used as sources of payoffs" for Mobutu and his supporters. Indeed, in the thirty-two years that Mobutu was in power, he is estimated to have stolen a staggering $4 billion. As another example, consider the small *W/S* system of the Philippines under Ferdinand Marcos (1965–1986). Marcos is thought to have stolen somewhere between $5 billion and $10 billion during the thirty-one years that he was in office (BDM^{2}S^2 2003, 167).

The strong loyalty norm that encourages leaders in small *W/S* systems, such as dominant-party and personalist dictatorships, to engage in kleptocracy also generates incentives for poor public policy more generally. Note that members of the winning coalition in these systems are loyal because (a) the leader provides them with more private goods than any challenger can and (b) they have to worry about being cut out of the next leader's coalition if they decide to defect. It follows from this that as long as members of the winning coalition are being sufficiently "bribed," they do not really care about the material well-being of the citizenry more generally (Bueno de Mesquita 2006, 423). As a result, leaders in small *W/S* systems have no incentive to produce good public policy—it does not help them stay in power. Leaders in small *W/S* systems recognize that they stay in power by keeping their supporters happy with private goods. "Just think of Saddam Hussein's success in holding on to power even after a worldwide trade embargo against Iraqi goods left his nation's economy in shambles. . . . As long as Saddam Hussein continued to pay the military well and keep his clansmen happy, he was unlikely to suffer an internal coup" (Bueno de Mesquita 2006, 424). We should note that not only does good public policy fail to help leaders in small *W/S* systems stay in power but it may actually get the leader ousted as well. This is because allocating resources to things like public goods that benefit the citizenry more widely opens up an opportunity for a challenger to credibly promise to provide more private goods to members of the winning coalition than are currently being provided by the incumbent.

In contrast to these types of systems, large *W/S* systems, such as democracies, do not have strong loyalty norms. For example, voters in a democracy are unlikely to lose access to private goods, such as particular tax policies or redistributive schemes that benefit them if they switch their support from the incumbent leader to the leader of an opposition party. As a result, leaders in large *W/S* systems have to work harder to keep their supporters happy and cannot afford to skim off too many resources if they want to stay in power. Moreover, because leaders in large *W/S* systems need more resources to keep their winning coalition loyal, they have a strong incentive to produce good overall economic performance. As a result, they are unlikely to tax or steal from their citizens too much lest this cause the citizens to spend more time relaxing and less time working. Remember that if the citizens do not work, then there will be a smaller economic pie with which the leader can win over the winning coalition. All in all, government performance should be better in large *W/S* systems than in small *W/S* systems—kleptocracy should be lower, taxation and state predation should be lower, economic growth should be higher, and so on.[12]

The Size of the Winning Coalition

In addition to the strength of the loyalty norm (*W/S*), selectorate theory indicates that the manner in which leaders distribute public and private goods also depends on the size of the winning coalition (*W*). Leaders always prefer to use private goods rather than public goods to satisfy their winning coalition. As our earlier example of leaders in societies A and B illustrates, an incumbent leader is always able to defeat a challenger if competition is restricted to the distribution of private goods. This inherent advantage comes from the simple fact that challengers cannot credibly guarantee to put would-be defectors in their own winning coalition. Recognizing the uneven playing field, challengers, therefore, attempt to defeat incumbents by emphasizing the provision of public goods. Not only does this help to explain why challengers spend considerable time criticizing incumbents for their poor performance in tackling corruption and providing food, health care, education, and the like, but it also helps to explain why these same challengers frequently maintain the preexisting system of corruption and do little to increase the provision of public goods when they finally come to power. In this regard, we can think of people like Jomo Kenyatta, who railed against corruption in Kenya before coming to power in 1963, but who then did little to stamp it out while in office (BDM^{2}S^2 2003, 374–375). Kenya has consistently ranked at the bottom of

---

12. Although large *W/S* systems encourage leaders to perform well in office, there is no guarantee that good performance will translate into longevity in office. Due to a weak loyalty norm, leaders in large *W/S* systems are likely to survive in office for shorter periods of time than leaders in small *W/S* systems even if they produce better government performance. This helps to explain why democratic leaders rarely last as long in office as even the poorest performing dictators in dominant-party or personalist dictatorships.

Transparency International's list of corrupt countries. Selectorate theory suggests that foreign countries that today promote and support seemingly public-minded opposition leaders should not necessarily expect government performance to significantly improve if these opposition leaders ever come to power.

Although incumbent leaders always prefer to use private goods to keep their winning coalition loyal, it turns out that this is not always a viable strategy. Much depends on the size of the winning coalition. As the size of the winning coalition increases, the share of private goods that can go to each member of the winning coalition shrinks. In our earlier example, the leaders in societies A and B had $1 billion in tax revenues to distribute to the winning coalition. Because the winning coalition comprised 1,000 members, the maximum amount of private goods that any one member could receive was $1 million. If the winning coalition in these societies had comprised one million members, then the maximum amount of private goods that any one member could have received would be just $1,000. Clearly, the private goods deal looks a lot better when the winning coalition is small than when it is large. It follows that the advantage the incumbent has over the challenger in regard to the provision of private goods shrinks as the winning coalition gets larger. At some point, the winning coalition is so large that it is no longer efficient or viable for the leader to buy the support of the winning coalition with just the help of private goods. In effect, the value of the private goods going to each member of the winning coalition becomes so small that the members would obtain more value if the leader provided public goods. An implication of this is that leaders in small W systems (dictatorships) will tend to use private goods to stay in power, whereas leaders in large W systems (democracies) will primarily use public goods. The fact that democratic leaders simply do not have sufficient resources to "bribe" all the people they need to win an election with private goods helps to explain why political competition in contemporary democracies is nearly always a contest over public goods—who has the best education policy, who has the best health care plan, and so on.

In Figure 10.6, we summarize how a leader's institutional environment (W and S) affects government performance and the material well-being of citizens. The dotted line indicates those positions where W/S is large; that is, the loyalty norm is low. Note that W/S can be large when both W and S are large, as in democracies, or when both W and S are small, as in monarchic and military dictatorships. As Figure 10.6 illustrates, we can think of three different levels of government performance—good, middling, and poor—depending on the institutional environment in place. Government performance is likely to be good when W and W/S are both large (democracies). This is because leaders are likely to provide public goods rather than private goods (W is large) and because the weak loyalty norm (W/S is large) forces leaders to work hard to stay in office.

In contrast, government performance is likely to be poor when W and W/S are both small (dominant-party and personalist dictatorships). In countries with this type of institutional environment, leaders have little incentive to care about the state of the national economy or the material well-being of the citizenry in general. Instead, they provide small amounts of

FIGURE 10.6   Selectorate Theory and Government Performance

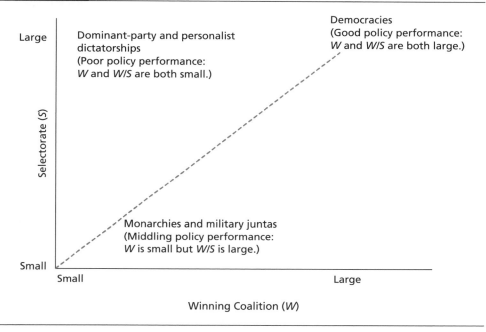

Note: W/S is large (and the loyalty norm is weak) along the dotted line.

private goods to members of their winning coalition and engage in highly kleptocratic and corrupt activities. The only thing keeping these types of leaders from excessive predation is the refusal of residents to work and therefore the lack of anything to prey on. This constraint is obviously much weaker if the country is rich in natural resources, such as oil and minerals, or if the leaders receive significant amounts of foreign aid.

Government performance is likely to be middling when W is small and W/S is large (monarchies and military juntas). Although leaders in these types of system provide few public goods to the general citizenry, they are forced to care about their overall performance in office because of the weak loyalty norm at work. For example, leaders have an incentive to produce reasonably good economic performance, because this is the only way of generating the necessary resources to pay off their not-so-loyal winning coalition. That these leaders are interested in good economic performance necessarily means that they also care, to some extent, about the material well-being of the residents who make up the workforce and thus have an incentive to provide some basic public goods.

As you'll no doubt have realized, the theoretical predictions about government performance shown in Figure 10.6 are entirely consistent with our earlier empirical results shown in Figure 9.4 in the previous chapter. Recall that those empirical results suggest that whereas democracies tend to produce relatively good government performance, the performance of dictatorships shows significant variation. Whereas some dictatorships perform quite well, others perform extremely poorly. As we can now see, selectorate theory offers a potential explanation for this variation in the performance of authoritarian regimes. On the one hand, dominant-party and personalist dictatorships are likely to produce poor government performance because they are characterized by small winning coalitions and strong loyalty norms. On the other hand, monarchies and military juntas are likely to produce reasonably good government performance because they are characterized by weak loyalty norms.

Before examining whether there is any empirical evidence to support selectorate theory, we should stop and ask ourselves what this all means for the *type* of leader necessary to generate good public policy. By now you should realize that implementing good public policy is not as simple as identifying decent human beings who genuinely want to improve their fellow citizens' lives and then ensuring that these people rise to political power. It turns out that having a civic-minded leader is neither necessary nor sufficient for successful public policies. Simply put, what is needed for good public policy is a set of institutions that creates a large W, large W/S system. If the political institutions in a country are such that a large proportion of the residents can participate in choosing their leader and the leader depends on a large proportion of that selectorate to remain in power, then only leaders who provide a sufficiently high level of government performance will be *able* to stay in power. It doesn't matter whether the leader cares about providing good government performance for its own sake or whether he cares about it only because it helps him stay in power; both goals dictate the same course of action. This results in competition to provide more, and better, public goods, as well as good economic policies designed to generate higher overall revenue. Under such conditions, residents have incentives to invest, and the economy is expected to grow.

The bottom line is that even if there are two types of leaders in the world—those that are civic minded and those that are not—all leaders are forced to govern well in large W, large W/S systems and poorly in small W, small W/S systems if they want to stay in power. This point is well illustrated by leaders who had the opportunity to rule over very different systems of government. Consider Leopold II (1835–1909), who was king of Belgium (large W, large W/S) and ruler of the Congo Free State (small W, small W/S). Consider also Chiang Kai-shek (1887–1975), who ruled China (small W, small W/S) for twenty years and then Taiwan (large W, large W/S) for another twenty-five. In both of these cases, the two leaders provided more public goods and better government performance in the large W, large W/S systems that they governed (BDM^{2}S^2 2003, 208–213). For more details, see Box 10.2, "The Tale of Two Leopolds."

It follows from this discussion that one's preference for the type of institutions in a country depends on one's position in the society. Leaders clearly prefer to set up institutions that encourage a small winning coalition and a large selectorate, because these institutions help them not only to stay in power but also to enrich themselves at the expense of their citizenry.

BOX 10.2   THE TALE OF TWO LEOPOLDS

Leopold II is remembered as an excellent king of Belgium (1865–1909) who provided his subjects with significant amounts of public goods. He instituted progressive reforms and promoted high levels of economic growth and industrial development. For example, he gave workers the right to strike, expanded the suffrage, set limits on child labor, introduced educational improvements, and supported massive public works projects designed to lower unemployment and enhance the economy.

King Leopold II of Belgium.

The Granger Collection, New York

While Leopold was presiding over this set of progressive policies in Belgium, he was taking a decidedly different approach in the Congo Free State (1885–1908), over which he also ruled. Leopold created a low-paid military force in the Congo, the Force Publique, and offered the soldiers additional wages based on commissions for goods such as rubber and ivory. Without laws to protect Congolese workers, the members of the Force Publique used slave labor, torture, and murder to meet its quotas. The soldiers were also given rewards for killing "antigovernment rebels," although more often than not these were villagers who simply did not want to be forced into slave labor. The soldiers would bring hands (or heads) to the Belgian commissioner as proof of the number of "rebels" that had been killed; eyewitness accounts report that some of these hands obviously belonged to women and children and

suggested that ordinary Congolese were being killed because doing so meant that soldiers could get higher wages. Leopold and the Force Publique gained incredible riches from the sale of ivory and rubber on the world market. This revenue was not returned to the Congo Free State in the form of public goods to benefit its residents. The only goods exported to the Congo, in fact, were weapons for the Force Publique to keep the flow of goods (the result of slave labor) headed toward Belgium. Thus, Leopold was allowing—even promoting—slave labor in the Congo at the same time as he was promoting laws protecting workers in Belgium.

What was different about the institutions in the two countries? Belgium was a constitutional monarchy, which means that Leopold's rule relied on the support of a popularly elected government. In effect, the winning coalition size in Belgium was reasonably large. By contrast, the Congo Free State was considered to be Leopold's personal property. Leopold's winning coalition in the Congo consisted of just himself and the members of the Force Publique. As selectorate theory predicts, Leopold worked hard to promote economic growth and provide significant amounts of public goods when his winning coalition was large

(Belgium) but provided small amounts of private goods for his supporters and stole the rest of the revenue for himself when the winning coalition was small (Congo).

Which was the real Leopold? BDM²S² (2003, 208–213), who provide the account of the two Leopolds that we have drawn on here, conclude that it must have been the "murderous ruler of the Congo" rather than the "civic-minded king of Belgium." Why? Well, Leopold simply inherited his institutions in Belgium and acted accordingly. In contrast, he had free rein to set up any type of government arrangement he wanted in the Congo. Leopold's actions in both countries were entirely consistent with the institutional incentives he faced.

Members of the winning coalition like institutions in which W is small but W/S is large. This is because a small W means that the leader will provide coalition members with private goods, and a large W/S guarantees that the leader will have to provide large quantities of these goods to counteract the weak loyalty norm. Members of the selectorate and the disenfranchised classes like institutions in which both W and W/S are large. This is because a large W forces the leader to provide coalition members with public goods, and the large W/S provides strong incentives for the leader to perform well in office to counteract the weak loyalty norm. In other words, leaders prefer to rule over dominant-party or personalist dictatorships, members of the winning coalition prefer to live in monarchic or military dictatorships, and everyone else prefers to live in democracies.

Some Empirical Evidence

We now put some of the implications derived from selectorate theory to the test. Specifically, we ask how the size of a country's W and the size of its W/S affect the material well-being of the citizenry. Recall that we expect better government performance as both W and W/S get larger. In Table 10.3, we show the effect of W and W/S on six different indicators of material well-being: economic growth, wealth as measured by gross domestic product (GDP) per capita, health care expenditures as a percentage of GDP, education expenditures as a percentage of GDP, infant mortality rates per thousand, and life expectancy in years. We control for the size of the selectorate (S) in each country.

Recall that it is the dependent variable that we want to explain—economic growth, life expectancy, and so on. Our independent or explanatory variables are what we hypothesize might affect the various dependent variables. In each table of results, our explanatory variables are W (and S) in Model 1 and W/S in Model 2. Next to each independent variable is a coefficient with a corresponding standard error beneath it in parentheses. As always, the coefficient tells us the slope of the relationship between the independent variable and the dependent variable. For example, a positive coefficient on W would indicate that an increase in the size of the winning coalition is associated with higher values of the dependent variable. A negative coefficient on W would indicate that an increase in the size of the winning

TABLE 10.3 — Effect of *W* and *W/S* on Six Indicators of Material Well-Being

a. Economic growth

Dependent variable: Economic growth rate

Independent Variables	Model 1	Model 2
W	0.02***	
	(0.005)	
S	−0.004	
	(0.005)	
W/S		0.02***
		(0.004)
Constant	0.01***	0.009***
	(0.004)	(0.003)
N	3,772	3,772
R^2	0.01	0.01

b. Wealth

Dependent variable: Log of GDP per capita

Independent Variables	Model 1	Model 2
W	2.30***	
	(0.22)	
S	−0.67***	
	(0.17)	
W/S		1.83***
		(0.19)
Constant	6.97***	6.66***
	(0.15)	(0.13)
N	3,813	3,813
R^2	0.35	0.32

c. Education

Dependent variable: Government spending on education as share of GDP

Independent Variables	Model 1	Model 2
W	2.07***	
	(0.37)	
S	−0.44	
	(0.27)	
W/S		1.8***
		(0.30)
Constant	2.86***	2.63***
	(0.23)	(0.21)
N	3,313	3,313
R^2	0.12	0.12

d. Health care

Dependent variable: Government spending on health care as share of GDP

Independent Variables	Model 1	Model 2
W	4.09***	
	(0.61)	
S	−0.35	
	(0.51)	
W/S		3.95***
		(0.49)
Constant	3.04***	2.80***
	(0.32)	(0.33)
N	1,204	1,204
R^2	0.22	0.22

(Continued)

TABLE 10.3	(Continued)

e. Infant mortality			f. Life expectancy		
Dependent variable: Infant mortality (deaths per 1,000 live births)			Dependent variable: Life expectancy at birth (in years)		
Independent Variables	Model 1	Model 2	Independent Variables	Model 1	Model 2
W	−101.5***		W	24.6***	
	(8.3)			(1.9)	
S	10.1		S	−2.6*	
	(6.3)			(1.4)	
W/S		−96.4***	W/S		23.1***
		(7.2)			(1.5)
Constant	113.1***	119.4***	Constant	49.0***	47.5***
	(6.7)	(6.4)		(1.3)	(1.3)
N	3,365	3,365	N	2,692	2,692
R^2	0.33	0.33	R^2	0.34	0.33

***$p < 0.01$

Note: W = winning coalition; S = selectorate; W/S = loyalty norm; data on W, S, and W/S cover all countries in the world averaged over the time period 1960–1999. Standard errors are shown in parentheses.

Source: Data are from Bueno de Mesquita and colleagues (2003) and McGuire (2002).

coalition is associated with lower values of the dependent variable. If the statistical analysis were to reveal that there is no relationship between W and the dependent variable, then the coefficient for W would be zero.

Recall also that the standard error beneath each coefficient helps us determine how confident we should be in our results. We tend to be confident that we have found a pattern in the data that is likely to be found more generally when the standard error is small relative to the size of its corresponding coefficient. Typically, as a rule of thumb, we say that we have found a statistically significant relationship when the coefficient is bigger than twice the size of the standard error. It is common practice for political scientists to place stars next to the coefficients of variables that are considered statistically significant; more stars signal higher statistical significance. Independent variables that do not have a coefficient with stars are not considered statistically significant. An independent variable is considered statistically insignificant if we don't feel confident ruling out the possibility that the observed pattern between this variable and the dependent variable arose by chance.[13]

---

13. For a more detailed discussion of how we determine whether an observed pattern in the data is "real" or not, see the material on significance tests covered in the Appendix at the end of Chapter 6, "An Intuitive Take on Statistical Analyses."

So what do the results in Table 10.3 tell us? We'll start by looking at the effect of W and W/S on economic growth in Table 10.3a. As predicted by selectorate theory, the coefficient on W in Model 1 is positive and statistically significant. This indicates that larger winning coalitions are associated with higher levels of economic growth. The coefficient on W/S in Model 2 is positive and statistically significant as well. This indicates that regimes with weaker loyalty norms (that is, higher W/S) are associated with higher levels of economic growth. This same pattern of results is repeated for all of the different indicators of material well-being shown in the other panels of Table 10.3. Wealth, education, health care expenditures, and life expectancy are all higher and infant mortality is lower when W and W/S are large. These results offer a great deal of support for two of the key implications derived from selectorate theory. Increasing the size of the winning coalition is associated with better outcomes from the point of view of the average citizen. Likewise, increasing the ratio of W/S, thereby making the loyalty norm weaker, is also associated with better outcomes. In other words, political institutions have a clear and marked effect on the kinds of government policies that are generally thought to be important for the material well-being of citizens around the world.

CONCLUSION

In this chapter, we have examined the wide variety of authoritarian regimes that exist around the world. In the first section of the chapter, we examined a common typology of dictatorships. In this typology, dictatorships are classified in terms of the identity of their "support coalitions." Such an approach indicates that there are three main types of authoritarian regime: (i) monarchic dictatorships, (ii) military dictatorships, and (iii) civilian dictatorships. Civilian dictatorships are sometimes further classified into those that are personalist and those that have a dominant regime party.

In the second section of the chapter, we focused on the two fundamental problems of authoritarian rule. The problem of authoritarian power-sharing focuses on potential conflict within the regime elite. Many authoritarian regimes create institutions such as legislatures to facilitate power-sharing agreements between the dictator and his support coalition. These institutions help the dictator credibly commit to not violating any power-sharing agreement as they enable the support coalition to better monitor his behavior. As we saw, though, these institutions are effective only if the support coalition can credibly threaten to remove the dictator, which requires power to be evenly distributed between the dictator and his support coalition. The problem of authoritarian control focuses on potential conflict between the dictatorial elite and the masses. Dictators have two strategies for controlling the masses, repression and co-optation. From the dictator's perspective, repression is often a dangerous strategy as the agents of repression, typically the military, may have different preferences from the dictator's and can turn their guns on the dictator rather than the masses. In these circumstances, the dictator can find himself as the figurehead of the regime, with true power lying in the hands of the military. Dictators often use institutions such as regime parties to co-opt the masses. In addition to being a vehicle for transferring regime rents to some opposition groups, these institutions give citizens a stake in promoting regime survival.

In the last part of the chapter, we examined selectorate theory. Selectorate theory provides a potential story both for why democracies produce a relatively high level of material well-being for their citizens and for why some dictatorships perform better than others. Starting from the simple assumption that all political leaders care about winning and retaining power, selectorate theory offers an explanation for the observed variation in the performance of different forms of government that focuses on the institutional structure surrounding political leaders. This "institutional structure" refers primarily to the size of a country's winning coalition and selectorate. As we saw, leaders in systems with large winning coalitions and weak loyalty norms like democracies have to provide public goods and a high level of overall government performance if they want to remain in office. In contrast, leaders in systems with small winning coalitions and strong loyalty norms, like dominant-party and personalist dictatorships, are "forced" to provide private goods and produce a poor level of overall government performance, because this is the best way to stay in power in these countries. In between these two ends of the performance spectrum are leaders in systems with small winning coalitions and weak loyalty norms, such as monarchies and military juntas. Although these leaders are more likely to provide private goods than public goods, they do have to care about their overall government performance because of the weak loyalty norm at work.

KEY CONCEPTS

civilian dictatorship *355*
competitive authoritarian regime *372*
corruption *389*
dictator's dilemma *370*
disenfranchised *383*
dominant-party dictatorship *365*
electoral authoritarian regime *372*
hegemonic electoral regime *372*
kleptocracy *389*

loyalty norm *388*
military dictatorship *355*
monarchic dictatorship *355*
personalist dictatorship *368*
politically closed authoritarian regimes *372*
selectorate *383*
selectorate theory *383*
winning coalition *383*

PROBLEMS

The following problems address some of the more important concepts and theories introduced in this chapter.

Game Theory and Dictatorial Regimes

1. Military Intervention Game

In the chapter, we suggested that professional soldiers often place a higher value on the unity and efficacy of the military than on anything else. If this is correct, then the most important concern for military officers thinking about joining a coup is their assessment of how many others will join. And the most important concern for military officers thinking about giving up power and returning to the barracks is their assessment of how many others will follow them. In effect, the military will want to move in and out of power as a cohesive whole.

From this perspective, Geddes (2003, 55) suggests that internal politics in military dictatorships can be modeled as an Asymmetric Coordination Game (see Chapter 4, Problem 7). Suppose that the military in some unidentified country is split between those who wish to intervene in the political system to overthrow the civilian government and those who wish to maintain their apolitical position as members of the armed forces. We can think of the faction that wants to "launch a coup" as the "Intervener Faction" and of the faction that wants to "stay out" as the "Professional Faction." We'll assume that a coup is unsuccessful if only one of the military factions participates. An unsuccessful coup is likely to be detrimental to both factions in the military. Members of the faction that launches an unsuccessful coup face possible demotion, court-martial, or execution. Members of the faction that stays out may also suffer as the civilian government increases its oversight of the military in an attempt to ensure its future loyalty. Although each faction holds different attitudes toward intervention in the political system, they both prefer that the military act as a cohesive unit above all else. This strategic situation can be modeled as a strategic form game. An empty payoff table is shown in Figure 10.7.

    a. Based on the strategic situation that we have described, write down the preference ordering for each faction over the four possible outcomes: (Launch Coup; Launch Coup), (Launch Coup; Stay Out), (Stay Out; Launch Coup), and (Stay Out; Stay Out).

    b. Use these preference orderings to fill in the payoff table shown in Figure 10.7. Use the numbers 4, 3, 2, and 1 to indicate the preference ordering over the four possible outcomes for each faction.

    c. Solve the game in Figure 10.7 for all Nash equilibria. What is the expected outcome of the game?

If you solve this game correctly, you'll see why it is a game of asymmetric coordination. There are often two ways to solve coordination problems like this. One is for the two players to negotiate ahead of time about what they should do. As Geddes (2003, 57) notes, "Some military decisions to seize power have been carefully negotiated over periods of months until rules for sharing power have been hammered out and the last legalist holdout has either given

FIGURE 10.7 Military Intervention Game

		Professional Faction	
		Launch coup	Stay out
Intervener Faction	Launch coup		
	Stay out		

in or retired. Such negotiated interventions occurred in Argentina in 1976, Brazil in 1964, and Chile in 1973." The second way to solve a coordination problem is for one player to move first. We're now going to look at how this might happen.

d. Draw an extensive form version of our Military Intervention Game in which the Intervener Faction moves first and the Professional Faction moves second.
e. What is the subgame perfect equilibrium? What is the expected outcome?
f. Based on your previous answers, does it make a difference whether the two factions in the military make their decision simultaneously or the Intervener Faction moves first?

As Geddes (2003, 57) notes, any first-mover strategy needs to be credible to work. In other words, the other faction must believe that the seizure of power is irreversible and that they must therefore go along with the coup or risk splitting the military. She cites the attempted Spanish coup of 1981 as an example of a case where the first-mover strategy turned out to be noncredible. With ongoing violence in the Basque region and political infighting in government, a faction in the Spanish military launched a coup. Colonel Antonio Molina marched into parliament, fired shots in the air, and announced that all of the legislators were under arrest. The coup-plotters had every reason to believe that garrison commanders in the rest of the country would go along with them. Instead of giving them his blessing as many of the coup-plotters expected, King Juan Carlos began telephoning the garrison commanders, telling them to oppose the coup and that they would be guilty of treason if they joined in. The king also went on television dressed in his full military uniform to denounce the plotters. "Once the [k]ing had taken such a strong stand, the first move lost its credibility, and most of the military refused to go along. Josep Colomer [a Spanish political scientist] reports that one of the coup conspirators, when interviewed later, said, 'Next time, cut the king's phone line' (1995, 121). Colomer suggests that had the king not been able to use television and the phone to rally support, the first-mover strategy might well have worked, because many in the officer corps sympathized with the goals of the conspirators" (Geddes 2003, 57).

g. In July 2016, there was a coup attempt in Turkey. Use Internet resources to find out what happened. How do the insights that you have gained from solving the Military Intervention Game help you to better understand what happened in Turkey? Does the aftermath of the coup attempt in Turkey match the predictions made by Geddes (2003)?

2. *Dictatorship Party Game*

In a paper titled "Why Parties and Elections in Authoritarian Regimes?" Barbara Geddes (2005) examines why dictators might choose to conduct elections and form political parties. Her basic argument is that dictators choose to establish these institutions because they help ward off potential coups from challengers within the authoritarian elite. Let's examine the logic of her "party" story a little more with the help of some game theory.

There are two different factions within the authoritarian elite—the "Regime" faction and the "Challenger" faction. The Regime is currently in charge. The Challenger is not in charge but would like to be. We can think that the Challenger comes in two types: weak and strong. At the beginning of the game, the Regime has to decide whether or not to form a political party (and hold elections). We will assume that forming a political party is costly for both factions in the authoritarian elite. Once the Regime has made its choice, the Challenger must decide whether to launch a coup against the Regime or not. We will assume that launching a coup is costly and that launching an unsuccessful coup is particularly costly. Whether a coup is successful depends on the strength of the Challenger and whether the Regime has created a political party. Political parties, as we have seen, often provide a means by which the Regime can mobilize supporters to counter a coup and stay in power. To keep things simple, we will assume that coup attempts by both types of Challenger fail if the Regime has created a party. If there is no party, though, then the Regime is able to counter coups by weak Challengers, but coups by strong Challengers will be successful. There are five possible outcomes in this game: Status Quo; Party and No Coup; Party and Failed Coup; No Party and Failed Coup; and No Party and Successful Coup. Figure 10.8 illustrates an incomplete information game with cardinal payoffs where the Regime does not know whether it is interacting with a weak Challenger or a strong Challenger.

a. Based on the cardinal payoffs shown in Figure 10.8, write down the preference ordering for the Regime and both types of Challenger over the five possible outcomes.
b. Solve the subgame on the left where the Challenger is weak as if there were no uncertainty. What is the subgame perfect equilibrium? What is the expected outcome? What are the payoffs that each player receives?
c. Solve the subgame on the right where the Challenger is strong as if there were no uncertainty. What is the subgame perfect equilibrium? What is the expected outcome? What are the payoffs that each player receives?
d. What is the expected payoff for the Regime from "Do Nothing"?
e. What is the expected payoff for the Regime from "Launch Party"?
f. Use the expected payoffs from the two previous questions to calculate the critical probability at which the Regime will choose to launch a party rather than do nothing.

FIGURE 10.8 **Dictatorship Party Game**

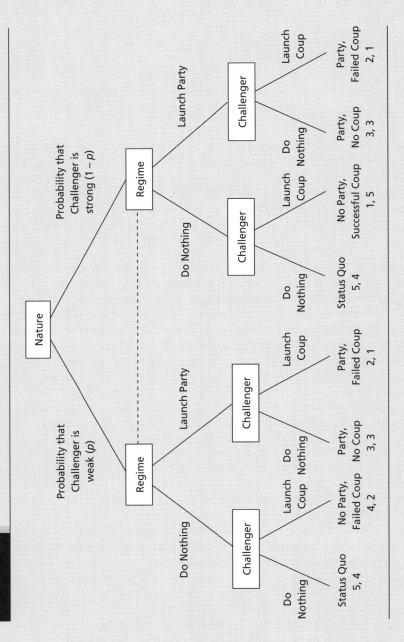

g. If the Regime believes that the Challenger is weak with a probability of 0.75, will it choose to do nothing, launch a party, or be indifferent between these two actions? Explain.

h. If the Regime believes that the Challenger is weak with a probability of 0.25, will it choose to do nothing, launch a party, or be indifferent between these two actions? Explain.

i. If the Regime believes that the Challenger is weak with a probability of 0.5, will it choose to do nothing, launch a party, or be indifferent between these two actions? Explain.

j. If you were the Regime, would you prefer to be in a world where you knew the strength of the Challenger or one in which you didn't? Would it make a difference? Explain your answer.

k. If you were the Challenger and you were weak, would you prefer to be in a world where the Regime knew your strength or one in which it didn't? Would it make a difference? Explain your answer.

l. If you were the Challenger and you were strong, would you prefer to be in a world where the Regime knew your strength or one in which it didn't? Would it make a difference? Explain your answer.

Selectorate Theory

3. Classifying Political Regimes

Rather than classify regimes as either democratic or dictatorial, selectorate theory characterizes all regimes in regard to their location in a two-dimensional institutional space. One dimension is the size of the selectorate (*S*), and the second dimension is the size of the winning coalition (*W*). These two dimensions are graphically shown in Figure 10.9 along with the types of regimes that fall into each cell. Use Internet and other resources to determine into which cell of the two-dimensional space in Figure 10.9 each of the following regimes should be placed. Explain your answers.

    a. Guinea Bissau
    b. Iraq under Saddam Hussein (pre-2003)
    c. United States in 1776
    d. United Arab Emirates
    e. Chile under Augusto Pinochet
    f. Argentina
    g. South Africa under apartheid (pre-1991)
    h. Mongolia
    i. Jordan

4. Public and Private Goods

In Chapter 8 we introduced the notion of public and private goods.

    a. Name at least three examples of private goods that leaders might use to stay in power. Explain why they are private goods.

    b. Name at least three examples of public goods that leaders might use to stay in power. Explain why they are public goods.

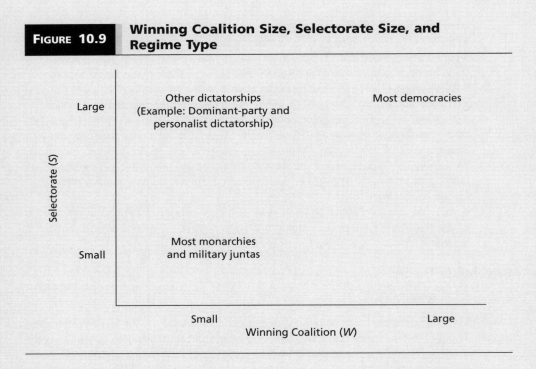

FIGURE 10.9 **Winning Coalition Size, Selectorate Size, and Regime Type**

5. *The Distribution of Public and Private Goods: The Size of the Winning Coalition*

Suppose that a political leader raises $1 billion in tax revenue. Assume that the leader can supply public goods worth $2,000 to each individual in society if he spends all of this tax revenue on providing public goods. Assume also that the size of the winning coalition is 250,000. With all of this in mind, answer the following questions.

    a. If the leader were to spend all of the tax revenue on providing private goods, what would the maximum value of the private goods be for each member of the winning coalition if we assume that they all receive the same amount?

    b. Would the leader prefer to provide only public goods or only private goods in this situation? Why?

Now suppose that the size of the winning coalition is 750,000. Keeping everything else the same, answer the following questions.

    c. If the leader were to spend all of the tax revenue on providing private goods, what would the maximum value of the private goods be for each member of the winning coalition if we assume that they all receive the same amount?

    d. Would the leader prefer to provide only public goods or only private goods in this new situation? Why?

    e. Based on the answers you have given and the description of selectorate theory in this chapter, why is providing public goods a more efficient way for leaders in democracies to stay in power?

    f. Based on the answers you have given and the description of selectorate theory in this chapter, why is providing private goods a more efficient way for leaders in dictatorships to stay in power?

6. *The Distribution of Public and Private Goods: The Loyalty Norm*

Suppose that a political leader raises $1 billion in tax revenue. Assume that the size of the winning coalition is 250,000 and that the size of the selectorate is 50 million.

    a. If the leader were to spend all of the tax revenue on providing private goods, what would the maximum value of the private goods be for each member of the winning coalition if we assume that they all receive the same amount?

    b. How much are private goods worth to someone who is not a member of the winning coalition?

    c. What is the probability that a member of the selectorate will be a member of the winning coalition?

    d. What is the probability that a member of the selectorate will not be a member of the winning coalition?

    e. Suppose that you, as a member of the winning coalition, are thinking of defecting to the challenger. What is the (maximum) expected value of defecting to the challenger in terms of private goods?

    f. Based on your answer to the previous question, how much does the political leader have to give each member of the winning coalition in terms of private goods in order to ensure that the member remains loyal?

    g. What is the difference between how much the political leader could give each member of the winning coalition and how much the political leader needs to give each member of the winning coalition to ensure the member's loyalty?

Now suppose that the size of the selectorate is just one million. Keeping everything else the same, answer the following questions.

    h. What is the probability that a member of the selectorate will be a member of the winning coalition?

    i. What is the probability that a member of the selectorate will not be a member of the winning coalition?

    j. Suppose that you, as a member of the winning coalition, are thinking of defecting to the challenger. What is the (maximum) expected value of defecting to the challenger in terms of private goods?

   k. Based on your answer to the previous question, how much does the political leader have to give each member of the winning coalition in terms of private goods in order to ensure that the member remains loyal?

   l. What is the difference between how much the political leader could give each member of the winning coalition and how much the political leader needs to give each member of the winning coalition to ensure the member's loyalty?

   m. Based on the answers you have given and the description of selectorate theory in this chapter, why are leaders in dominant-party and personalist dictatorships particularly well placed to steal the state's wealth for themselves?

7. International Organizations and Economic Development

Many international organizations such as the International Monetary Fund (IMF) and the World Bank (WB) have economic development and the alleviation of poverty as two of their central goals. Although international organizations frequently provide expertise and resources for economic development and poverty relief, these resources are often misappropriated. Consider the following description of events in Kenya in 2002.

> In December 2002 Mwai Kibaki was elected president following the retirement of the long-term incumbent Daniel Arap Moi. Billions of dollars were stolen under Moi's regime. Given worsening economic conditions, aid agencies such as the IMF agreed to the resumption of aid to Kenya. The Kenyan government promised to reduce corruption. Unfortunately, rather than being used to root out corruption, these funds have been largely stolen. The BBC reports that graft has cost Kenya $1 billion under Kibaki's increasingly autocratic regime. A majority of Kenyans believe they are worse off under Kibaki than Moi. (A. Smith 2005, 566)

   a. Would the ongoing corruption in Kenya come as a surprise to someone familiar with the selectorate theory? Explain your answer.

   b. What does selectorate theory have to say about the potential of international organizations such as the IMF and the WB to achieve their goals of economic development and poverty reduction in countries with small winning coalitions? Explain your answer.

11 Problems with Group Decision Making

Democracy is the recurrent suspicion that more than half of the people are right more than half of the time.

E. B. White, *The New Yorker,* July 3, 1944

- In this chapter, we look at whether the process by which democracies make decisions has appealing features that make it morally or normatively attractive compared with dictatorships, above and beyond any material benefits that it might produce.

- At its very heart, democracy is a system in which the majority is supposed to rule. Still, making decisions that reflect the preferences of a majority can be a lot more complicated and less fair than one might think. Even if all the members of a group have rational preferences, Condorcet's paradox shows that it might be impossible to reach a stable group decision using majority rule.

- The median voter theorem indicates that stable group decisions can be achieved if we are willing to rule certain preferences out of bounds and reduce the policy space to a single-issue dimension. Unfortunately, neither of these restrictions is uncontroversial.

- Arrow's theorem proves that no method of group decision making can guarantee a stable group decision while simultaneously satisfying minimal conditions of fairness. In effect, it proves that there is no perfect set of decision-making institutions; either fairness is compromised, or there will be potential for unstable group choices.

- The absence of an ideal decision-making mechanism means that institutional choice is an exercise in the choice of "second bests" and that trade-offs will need to be made. This helps to explain why we observe so many different types of democracy in the world.

OVERVIEW

What kinds of political institutions should we adopt when we have an opportunity to set up new institutions or change existing ones? One obvious way to begin answering this question is to see which sets of institutions produce good outcomes. For example, do democratic regimes produce better material outcomes, say, than dictatorial ones? If they do, then we should recommend adopting some set of democratic institutions. Although it is commonly believed that democracies outperform dictatorships in regard to providing material well-being, our analyses in Chapters 9 and 10 suggests that things are not this simple. As we demonstrated in those chapters, citizens living in certain types of dictatorship tend, on average, to enjoy a very high quality of life that easily rivals that of citizens in democracies, at least according to various measures of economic development and growth or the provision of government services, such as health care and education. Indeed, several dictatorships regularly outperform many democracies when it comes to the measures of material outcomes that we examined.

At this point, the philosophy students among you might point out that we are overlooking some important criteria with which to evaluate sets of political institutions. Political philosophers usually use one of two broad approaches for evaluating the moral or ethical value of adopting a given set of institutions. On the one hand, those inclined toward **consequentialist ethics** ask whether the institutions in question produce good outcomes. This is the approach that we adopted in the previous two chapters. On the other hand, those favoring **deontological ethics** attempt to evaluate institutions in a way that is independent of the outcomes that those institutions produce—they ask whether the institutions are good, fair, or just, in and of themselves. In this chapter, we consider democracy from a deontological perspective. In particular, we examine whether the process by which democratic governments make decisions for the entire country has appealing properties that make it morally or normatively attractive above and beyond any material benefits that it might produce. In other words, is the process by which decisions are made in democracies inherently good, fair, or just?

> **Consequentialist ethics** evaluate actions, policies, or institutions in regard to the outcomes they produce. **Deontological ethics** evaluate the intrinsic value of actions, policies, or institutions in light of the rights, duties, or obligations of the individuals involved.

People typically assume that a dictatorial decision-making process is inherently unfair, whereas a democratic decision-making process is inherently fair. In what follows, we explore this assumption in some detail and lay out several criteria for evaluating how groups of individuals make decisions.[1] Overall, we think that the results of our analysis will surprise many

---

1. The material in this chapter comes from a part of the political science literature called social choice theory. Social choice theory addresses the voting rules that govern and describe how individual preferences are aggregated to form a collective group preference. Much of this literature is highly mathematical. In this chapter, we focus on providing you with the intuition behind some of the more important ideas in social choice theory. For those of you interested in examining social choice theory in more depth, we suggest starting with Sen (1970), Riker (1982), Hinich and Munger (1997), and Patty and Penn (2014).

of you. As we demonstrate, there are no perfect decision-making processes—all institutional choices, including the decision to adopt democratic institutions, entail a set of significant trade-offs. It is the existence of these trade-offs that helps to explain why there are so many different types of democracies in the world. In effect, different countries choose to make different trade-offs when they decide to adopt democratic institutions.

PROBLEMS WITH GROUP DECISION MAKING

Many people say that they like democracy because they believe it to be a fair way to make group decisions. One commonsense notion of fairness is that group decisions should reflect the preferences of the majority of group members. We believe that most people would probably agree, for example, that a fair way to decide between two options is to choose the option that is preferred by the most people. When selecting among just two options, the option preferred by the most members of a group is necessarily the option preferred by a majority of the group.[2] At its very heart, democracy is a system in which the majority rules. In this section of the chapter, we show that there are many situations in which "majority rule" is a lot more complicated and less fair than our commonsense intuition about it would suggest. In effect, we demonstrate that allowing the majority to decide can be deeply problematic on many different dimensions.

Majority Rule and Condorcet's Paradox

If a group of people needs to choose between just two options, then majority rule can be quite straightforward, as we just saw. But what if a group needs to choose between more than two options? For example, imagine a city council deciding on the level of social services it should provide.[3] The proposed options are to increase (I), decrease (D), or maintain current (C) levels of social service provision. Assume that the council is made up of three members— a left-wing councillor, a right-wing councillor, and a centrist councillor—who all rank the proposed options differently. Specifically, the left-wing councillor prefers an increase in spending to current levels of spending and prefers current levels of spending to a decrease. The centrist councillor most prefers current levels of spending but would prefer a decrease in spending over any increase if it came to it. The right-wing councillor most prefers a decrease in spending. Because he views current levels of spending as unsustainable, however, the right-wing councillor would prefer to "break the bank" with an increase in spending in order to spur much-needed reforms than maintain the status quo. The preference ordering for each of the council members is summarized in Table 11.1.

---

2. A majority of a group is defined here as more than half. If we have a group of size N, and we assume that none of the members of the group are indifferent between the two options on offer, then a majority M of the group would be any subgroup, such that $M \geq (N + 1) / 2$. If indifference were allowed, then it is possible for the alternative receiving the most votes to win a plurality without winning a majority of the votes.

3. This example comes from Dixit, Skeath, and Reiley (2014).

TABLE 11.1 — City Council Preferences for the Level of Social Service Provision

Left-wing councillors	Centrist councillors	Right-wing councillors
$I > C > D$	$C > D > I$	$D > I > C$

Note: I = increased social service provision; D = decreased social service provision; C = maintenance of current levels of social service provision; $>$ = "is strictly preferred to."

Let's assume that the council employs majority rule to make its group decisions. In this particular example, this means that any policy alternative that enjoys the support of two or more councillors will be adopted. How should the councillors vote, though? It's not obvious how they should vote given that there are more than two alternatives. One way they might proceed is to hold a **round-robin tournament** that pits each alternative against every other alternative in a set of "pair-wise votes"—I versus D, I versus C, and C versus D—and designates as the winner whichever alternative wins the most contests. If we assume that the councillors all vote for their most preferred alternative in each pair-wise contest (or round), then we see that D defeats I, I defeats C, and C defeats D. The outcomes of these pair-wise contests and the majorities that produce them are summarized in Table 11.2. Notice that there is no alternative that wins most often—each alternative wins exactly one pair-wise contest. This multiplicity of "winners" does not provide the council with a clear policy direction. In other words, the council fails to reach a decision on whether to increase, decrease, or maintain current levels of social service provision.

A **round-robin tournament** pits each competing alternative against every other alternative an equal number of times in a series of pair-wise votes.

This simple example produces several interesting results that we now examine in more detail. The first is that a group of three *rational* actors (the councillors) make up a group (the council) that appears to be incapable of making a rational decision for the group as a whole. What do we mean by "rational"? When political scientists use the word *rational,* they have a very specific meaning in mind. An actor is said to be **rational** if she possesses a complete and

TABLE 11.2   Outcomes from the Round-Robin Tournament

Round	Contest	Winner	Majority that produced victory
1	Increase vs. decrease	D	Centrist and right
2	Current vs. increase	I	Left and right
3	Current vs. decrease	C	Left and centrist

transitive preference ordering over a set of outcomes.[4] An actor has a **complete preference ordering** if she can compare each pair of elements (call them x and y) in a set of feasible outcomes in one of the following ways—either the actor prefers x to y, she prefers y to x, or she is indifferent between x and y. The assumption of completeness essentially states that an individual can always make up her mind as to whether she prefers one option or is indifferent when presented with a pair of options. What about the assumption of transitivity? Before we get to this, we need to first make a distinction between strict and weak preferences. An actor is said to "strictly prefer" x to y if x is always better than y. And she is said to "weakly prefer" x to y if x is at least as good as y. An actor has a **transitive preference ordering** if for any x, y, and z in the set of outcomes it is the case that if x is weakly preferred to y, and y is weakly preferred to z, then

> An actor is **rational** if she possesses a complete and transitive preference ordering over a set of outcomes. An actor has a **complete preference ordering** if she can compare each pair of elements (call them x and y) in a set of outcomes in one of the following ways—either the actor prefers x to y or y to x, or she is indifferent between them. An actor has a **transitive preference ordering** if for any x, y, and z in the set of outcomes it is the case that if x is weakly preferred to y, and y is weakly preferred to z, then it must be the case that x is weakly preferred to z.

it must be the case that x is weakly preferred to z. Actors whose preference orderings do *not* meet these conditions—completeness and transitivity—are said to be irrational.

In the example we have been examining, each of the councillors is rational because each has a complete and transitive preference ordering over the three policy alternatives. For example, the left-wing councillor prefers I to C and C to D and also prefers I to D. The outcome of the round-robin tournament, however, reveals that this set of rational individuals becomes a group that acts like an individual with intransitive preferences. Recall that the group prefers D to I and I to C. Transitivity would require, therefore, that the group prefer D to C. Round 3 of the round-robin tournament reveals, however, that the group prefers C to D. This juxtaposition—of rational individuals forming a group that behaves irrationally—was first described in a paper in 1785 by Marie Jean Antoine Nicolas de Caritat, the Marquis de Condorcet, and is usually referred to as **Condorcet's paradox**.

> **Condorcet's paradox** illustrates that a group composed of individuals with rational preferences does not necessarily have rational preferences as a collectivity; individual rationality is not sufficient to ensure group rationality.

A second interesting aspect of our example is that a different majority supports the winning alternative or outcome in each round. In round 1, the majority that votes in favor of a decrease in social service provision is made up of the centrist and right-wing councillors. In round 2, the majority that votes in favor of an increase in social service provision is a coalition of "odd bedfellows" comprising the left- and right-wing councillors. Finally, in round 3, the majority that votes in favor of the status quo comprises the left-wing and centrist

---

4. Technically, a rational individual must also have a "reflexive" preference ordering. This means that any alternative in the set of outcomes can be thought of as at least as good as itself. As the Nobel Prize–winning economist Amartya Sen (1970, 2–3) has noted, the reflexivity "requirement is so mild that it is best looked at as a condition . . . of sanity rather than of rationality." Most political scientists focus on the conditions of completeness and transitivity as we do here.

councillors. Although "letting the majority decide" may sound fair and straightforward, our example here makes it very clear that "a majority" does not necessarily exist until the policy debate is framed in a certain way.

As we just noted, Condorcet's paradox points out that individual rationality is not sufficient to ensure group rationality. A set of actors, each with complete and transitive preference orderings, may behave in a way that reveals group intransitivity. When this occurs, there is no "majority" to speak of; instead, there is a cycle of different majorities. For example, suppose that we start with the current level of social service provision as the status quo. A council member who is unhappy with this status quo (say, the left-wing councillor) might propose a vote like that in round 2 of the round-robin tournament (C vs. I). In this vote, a majority would support an increase in social service provision over the maintenance of the status quo (see Table 11.2). But as soon as this vote ends, a disgruntled council member (say, the centrist) can propose a vote like that in round 1 of the round-robin tournament (I vs. D). In this vote, a majority would support a decrease in social service provision over an increase. But as soon as this vote ends, a different disgruntled council member—in this case, the left-wing councillor—can propose a vote like that in round 3 of the round-robin tournament (C vs. D). In this vote, a majority would support maintaining the current level of social service provision rather than decreasing it. Interestingly, the centrist who just one vote ago proposed decreasing the provision of social services now votes to maintain current levels of social service provision. Having arrived back where they began (C), and absent any institutional mechanism to end the succession of proposals and counterproposals, the scene is set for the cycle to begin anew—with no end in sight. This cycle through the different majorities is illustrated in Figure 11.1.

Some of you may feel that our example of cyclical majorities is unlikely ever to occur in practice. After all, we see deliberative bodies make decisions all the time and, although we may sometimes think they are far from efficient, they do not seem to be caught in the type of endless cycle suggested by our example. On the whole, there are two broad reasons for this. One has to do with preference orderings, and the other has to do with decision-making rules. Let's start with preference orderings. To some extent, our current example is special in the sense that it depends on the councillors having a particular set of preference orderings. For example, if the right-wing councillor's preferences were the mirror image of those of the left-wing councillor—that is, if the right-wing council member preferred a decrease to the current level but preferred the current level to an increase—then maintaining current levels of social service provision would win both rounds of the round-robin tournament in which it competes. In political science, we call an option like this—that is, one that beats all other options in a series of pair-wise contests—a **Condorcet winner**. Given the

> An option is a **Condorcet winner** if it beats all other options in a series of pair-wise contests.

decision-making process adopted by the council, and assuming that all councillors vote for their most preferred option, this would mean that maintaining current levels of social service provision is a stable outcome.

FIGURE 11.1   An Example of Cyclical Majorities

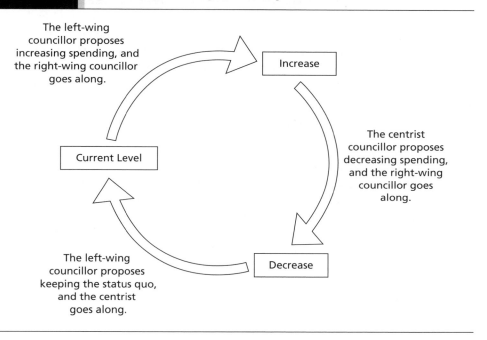

The left-wing councillor proposes increasing spending, and the right-wing councillor goes along.

Increase

The centrist councillor proposes decreasing spending, and the right-wing councillor goes along.

Current Level

Decrease

The left-wing councillor proposes keeping the status quo, and the centrist goes along.

To see why, imagine that maintaining current spending on social services is the status quo and ask yourself who would benefit from a change. The answer is that both the left- and right-wing councillors would like to propose a change. The right-wing council member prefers a decrease in social service provision to the status quo. If he proposed a decrease, however, both the centrist and left-wing councillors would vote against the proposal. Similarly, the left-wing council member prefers an increase in social service provision to the status quo. But if he proposed an increase, both the centrist and right-wing councillors would vote against the proposal. In other words, with this new profile of preferences in the group, there is no cycle of majorities, and as a result, current levels of spending constitute a stable outcome. In effect, the group now behaves as if it were an individual with transitive (and complete) preferences—it prefers current levels of social service provision to a decrease and a decrease to an increase.

The point here is that majority rule is not necessarily incompatible with rational group preferences. All that Condorcet showed was that it is *possible* for a group of individuals with transitive preferences to produce a group that behaves as if it has intransitive preferences. As a result, Condorcet's paradox erodes our confidence in the ability of majority rule to produce stable outcomes only to the extent that we expect actors to hold the preferences that cause group intransitivity. So how likely is it that transitive individual preferences will lead to group intransitivity? Modern scholars have analyzed this problem in detail and found, assuming that all preference orderings are equally likely, that the likelihood of group intransitivity increases with the number of alternatives under consideration or the number of voters or both. In Table 11.3, we show estimates of the share of all possible strict preference orderings that fail to produce a Condorcet winner (that is, that produce group intransitivity) as the numbers of voters and alternatives increase (Riker 1982, 122).

As Table 11.3 illustrates, the example of the city council that we started with, in which a Condorcet winner fails to emerge from a contest among three alternatives and three voters, is indeed a rarity. Nearly all (94.4 percent) of the logically possible strict preference orderings produce a Condorcet winner and, hence, a stable outcome. As the number of voters increases, however, the probability of group intransitivity rises to some limit. When the number of alternatives is relatively small, this limit is still small enough that most of the logically possible preference orderings will not lead to group intransitivity. In contrast, although an increase in the number of alternatives also increases the probability of group intransitivity, this process continues until the point at which group intransitivity is certain to occur. In other words, as the number of alternatives goes to infinity, the probability of group intransitivity converges to one—even when the number of voters is small. This is an extremely important result because many political decisions involve a choice from, essentially, an infinite number of alternatives.

TABLE 11.3	Proportion of Possible Strict Preference Orderings without a Condorcet Winner					
	Number of voters					
Number of alternatives	**3**	**5**	**7**	**9**	**11** ⟶	**Limit**
3	0.056	0.069	0.075	0.078	0.080	0.088
4	0.111	0.139	0.150	0.156	0.160	0.176
5	0.160	0.200	0.215			0.251
6	0.202					0.315
↓						↓
Limit	1.000	1.000	1.000	1.000	1.000	1.000

Source: Riker (1982, 122).

Imagine, for example, what would happen if we introduced a bit more realism into our example about a city council deciding on social welfare spending. Previously, we simplified the situation to one in which the councillors were deciding between three alternatives—increase, decrease, or maintain current spending. In reality, though, the councillors would normally be choosing an exact amount of money to spend on social services. In effect, they would be choosing a share of the budget to allocate to social service provision from 0 percent to 100 percent. Thus, there is an infinite number of choices that could be made in this interval (0–100).[5] As a consequence, if no restrictions are placed on the councillors' preferences, then group intransitivity is all but guaranteed. Significantly, all policy decisions that involve bargaining over some divisible resource—questions relating to things like the distribution of government resources, the allocation of the tax burden, the allocation of ministerial portfolios in the government, the amount of permissible greenhouse gas emissions, and the location of toxic waste—can be seen in a similar light.

To summarize, Condorcet's paradox makes it clear that restricting group decision making to sets of rational individuals is no guarantee that the group as a whole will exhibit rational tendencies. Group intransitivity is unlikely when the set of feasible options is small, but it is almost certain that majority rule applied to a pair-wise competition among alternatives will fail to produce a stable outcome when the set of feasible options gets large. As a result, it is impossible to say that the majority "decides" except in very restricted circumstances.

The analytical insight from Condorcet's paradox suggests that group intransitivity should be common, but, as we have already noted, we observe a surprising amount of stability in group decision making in the real world. Our discussion so far suggests that this must be the result of either of two factors. Either the number of decision makers or issues is kept small *and* the kinds of preferences that produce group intransitivity are rare, or a decision-making mechanism other than a simple pair-wise comparison of alternatives is being used. We have already seen that some of the most common types of political decisions involve a great number of alternatives, so it is likely that any stability we observe in the real world results from the use of alternative decision rules. It is to these alternative decision-making rules that we now turn.

The Borda Count and the Reversal Paradox

One alternative decision-making rule—the Borda count—was suggested by Jean-Charles de Borda, a compatriot of Condorcet, in 1770 (published in 1781). The Borda count asks individuals to rank potential alternatives from their most to least preferred and then assigns numbers to reflect this ranking. For instance, if there are three alternatives as in our city council example, then the Borda count might assign a 3 to each councillor's most preferred

---

5. This is true in abstract games in which players bargain over the share of a "pie." In real life, budgets are denominated in currency, and so the smallest accounting increment (like a penny) can place a limit on the divisibility of the pie. What is important here, though, is that there are many, many possible outcomes, and group intransitivity is therefore nearly certain to occur.

| TABLE 11.4 | Determining the Level of Social Service Provision Using the Borda Count | | | |

| | Points awarded | | | |
Alternative	Left-wing	Centrist	Right-wing	Borda count total
Increase spending	3	1	2	6
Decrease spending	1	2	3	6
Current spending	2	3	1	6

option, a 2 to his second-best option, and a 1 to his least preferred option. The weighted votes for each alternative are then summed, and the alternative with the largest score wins. Using the same preferences as shown earlier in Table 11.1, the Borda count would again be indecisive in determining whether to increase, decrease, or maintain current levels of social service provision. This is because each alternative would garner a score of 6. This is shown in Table 11.4.

Although the indecisiveness of the Borda count is once again an artifact of the particular preference ordering we are examining,[6] a more troubling aspect of this decision rule can be seen if we consider the introduction of a possible fourth alternative. Let's assume, for example, that the councillors consider a new alternative: maintain current spending levels for another year (perhaps it's an election year) but commit future governments to a decrease in spending of, say, 10 percent in each successive year.[7] Suppose that the left-wing councillor likes this new option the least, the right-wing councillor prefers it to all alternatives except an immediate decrease, and the centrist councillor prefers all options except an increase to this new alternative. The preference ordering for each of the council members over the four alternatives is summarized in Table 11.5.

If we apply the Borda count in this new situation by assigning a 3 to each councillor's most preferred alternative, a 2 to his second-best alternative, a 1 to his third-best alternative, and a 0 to his least preferred alternative, then we find that the vote tally looks like the one shown in Table 11.6. As you can see, the council now has a strict preference ordering over the alternatives. Based on the councillors' votes, the council would decrease the level of social service provision.

---

6. We could, of course, conclude that the group actually is indifferent between these alternatives, given this aggregation of citizen preferences. Doing so, however, requires us to make what political scientists call "interpersonal comparisons of utility." For example, we would have to believe that the welfare improvement that a left-wing councillor feels when a decrease in social service provision is replaced by an increase is exactly equal to the sum of the decline in welfare experienced by the centrist and left-wing councillors when this happens. Most modern scholars are reluctant to make these types of interpersonal comparisons of utility and so would be reluctant to make normative statements about the appropriateness of this outcome.

7. This example is not as fanciful as it might sound. In fact, it shares many qualities with the "balanced budget" proposals of politicians who are all too eager to be "fiscally conservative" tomorrow (when an election is no longer looming).

TABLE 11.5	**City Council Preferences for the Level of Social Service Provision (Four Alternatives)**

Left-wing	Centrist	Right-wing
$I > C > D > FC$	$C > D > FC > I$	$D > FC > I > C$

Note: I = an increase in social service provision; D = a decrease in social service provision; C = a maintenance of current levels of social service provision; FC = future cuts in social service provision; $> =$ "is strictly preferred to."

TABLE 11.6	**Determining the Level of Social Service Provision Using the Borda Count with a Fourth Alternative**

	Points awarded			
Alternative	Left-wing	Centrist	Right-wing	Borda count total
Increase spending	3	0	1	4
Decrease spending	1	2	3	6
Current spending	2	3	0	5
Future cuts in spending	0	1	2	3

You will immediately notice that something very strange has happened. Despite the fact that the new alternative receives a lower score than all of the original options and that it is not the first choice of any of the councillors, its addition as an active alternative for consideration changes how the councillors, as a collectivity, rank the three original options. In doing so, it changes the outcome of the vote. Whereas the group had previously been "indifferent" between the three original options, it now possesses a strict and transitive preference ordering over them, with "decreased spending" as the group's "most preferred" outcome. Note that this is the case despite the fact that none of the councillors has changed the way that he rank orders *I, D,* and *C.* In effect, the choice that the council now makes has been influenced by the introduction of what might be called an "irrelevant alternative." As this example illustrates, the Borda count does not demonstrate the property that political scientists refer to as "independence from irrelevant alternatives."[8]

---

8. Technically, the "independence from irrelevant alternatives" (IIA) property in the social choice literature refers to the independence from the "ranking" (and not the "presence") of an irrelevant alternative. This is the requirement that the ranking of an irrelevant alternative in a fixed set of alternatives should not affect the alternative that is chosen (Arrow 1963; Sen 1970). Our city council example can be understood in these terms too. For example, we can imagine that the city councillors all originally ranked the alternative of future spending cuts last but through some kind of deliberation process came to rank it in the way shown in Table 11.5. When the future spending cuts are ranked last, the council is indifferent between *D, I,* and *C.* But when the future spending cuts are ranked according to the preference orderings in Table 11.5, then the council has a strict preference ordering, $D > C > I.$

Many analysts find the susceptibility of the Borda count to the introduction of what they consider "irrelevant alternatives" disconcerting. Note that in our city council example, there was no change in the individual preference ordering of any of the actors over the original three alternatives, yet the introduction of an "irrelevant alternative" had a marked effect on the outcome of the decision-making process. The group is behaving like a customer at a restaurant whose choice for dinner is being influenced by the presence (or absence) on the menu of an item he is not going to consume. Another reason why we might like a decision rule to be "independent from irrelevant alternatives" is that if it is not, wily politicians can more easily manipulate the outcome of a decision process in order to produce their most preferred outcome. For example, instead of making persuasive arguments about the desirability of her preferred outcome or seeking compromise solutions that leave all parties better off, a politician might get her way by the imaginative introduction of an alternative that has no chance of winning, but that—by its sheer presence—changes the weights attached to other alternatives and, therefore, changes the alternative that is ultimately chosen.

Majority Rule with an Agenda Setter

An alternative decision-making mechanism that overcomes the potential instability of majority rule in round-robin tournaments requires actors to begin by considering only a subset of the available pair-wise alternatives. For instance, in our original city council example, we might require that both departures from the status quo (that is, increases and decreases in social service spending) first face each other in a pair-wise contest and that the winner then go on to compete in a vote against the status quo. Imposing a voting agenda such as this turns the voting process into a sequential game with three players—each player simultaneously chooses between increasing and decreasing social service provision, and then, each player simultaneously chooses between the winning alternative from the first round and the maintenance of current spending levels in the second round.

Let's assume for a moment that each council member votes for her preferred option when confronted with any two choices. In other words, let's assume that each councillor casts what is known as a sincere vote. In the first round, the councillors choose between increasing social service spending and decreasing it. Given the preferences of the councillors in our example, we know that both the centrist and the right-wing council members prefer a decrease in spending over an increase. As a result, the vote in the first round would be 2–1 in favor of a decrease. This means that the second (and final) round of voting is a choice between decreasing social service spending and maintaining current levels of spending. Because the left-wing and centrist councillors both prefer the current level of social service spending to a decrease, the outcome of this game is the status quo; that is, current spending levels are maintained. (Stop for a moment and ask yourself, which of the councillors is likely to have set this voting agenda.)

But should we expect all of the councillors to vote sincerely in our example? Consider that the councillors know that there are only two possible contests in the second round—either

D versus *C* or *I* versus *C*. Given the preference orderings in our example, the councillors know that these potential second-round contests will end up with either *C* defeating *D* or *I* defeating *C*. It follows from this that the councillors know that if *D* wins in the first round against *I*, then the final outcome will be the status quo, *C*. In other words, voting for *D* in the first round is essentially equivalent to voting for the status quo in the end. As a result, the first round of voting should, in reality, be seen as a contest between *I* and *C* (even if the councillors are actually voting between *I* and *D*).

Think about how the right-wing councillor might reason through the logic of this voting procedure. Recall that her favorite outcome is a decrease in social service spending, her second-best outcome is an increase in social service spending, and her least preferred outcome is maintaining the current level of social service spending. If she casts her vote in the first round for her most preferred outcome without thinking about the consequences for the rest of the game, then we have already seen that option *D* will be victorious in the first round but will go on to lose to *C* in the second and final round. This is, of course, the right-wing councillor's worst possible outcome. As a result, she has a strong incentive to change her vote in the first round from *D* to *I* even though this new vote does not conform to her sincere preferences. If she does this and votes for an increase in social service spending in the first round, then *I* will win and be pitted against *C* in the final round. In this final round, *I* will defeat *C*. In other words, the final outcome will be an increase in social service provision. Note that by deviating from her sincere preferences in the first round, the right-wing councillor is able to alter the final outcome from her least preferred outcome to her second-best one. In this example, the right-wing councillor casts what political scientists call a **strategic**, or **sophisticated, vote**—a vote in which an individual votes in favor of a less preferred option because she believes doing so will ultimately produce a more preferred outcome than would otherwise be the case. Some analysts find strategic voting lamentable and would prefer decision rules that induce **sincere voting**—voting that constitutes a sincere revelation of an individual's preferences.[9]

> A **strategic**, or **sophisticated, vote** is a vote in which an individual votes in favor of a less preferred option because she believes doing so will ultimately produce a more preferred outcome. A **sincere vote** is a vote for an individual's most preferred option.

The incentives to vote strategically are not the only thing that scholars find lamentable with voting agendas like the one that we just examined. Another thing that many scholars find disconcerting is that alternative agendas can produce very different outcomes even if we hold all of the actors' preferences constant. In fact, the three alternatives in our city council example can face each other in three different two-round tournaments, all of which produce a different outcome. The three different two-round tournaments and the outcomes that they produce are shown in Table 11.7. As you can see, choosing the agenda is essentially equivalent to choosing which outcome will win. For example, if you decide to have a first-round

---

9. We return to a more detailed discussion of sincere and strategic voting in Chapters 13 and 14.

contest between *I* and *D*, you know that the eventual outcome will be a victory for *C*. If you decide to have a first-round contest between *C* and *I*, you know that the eventual outcome will be *D*. And if you decide to have a first-round contest between *C* and *D*, you know that the eventual outcome will be *I*. Consequently, if one of the councillors is given the power to choose the agenda, she is, effectively, given the power to dictate the outcome of the decision-making process. This phenomenon, in which choosing the agenda is tantamount to choosing which alternative will win, is referred to as the "power of the agenda setter," and it exists in many institutional settings. In our example, the agenda setter can obtain her most preferred outcome simply by deciding what the order of pair-wise contests should be. For example, the centrist councillor would choose agenda 1 in Table 11.7 if she were the agenda setter; the right-wing councillor would choose agenda 2; and the left-wing councillor would choose agenda 3.

In sum, it is possible to avoid the potential for group intransitivity that arises in majority rule round-robin tournaments by imposing an agenda—by designating which outcomes will be voted on first and which outcome will, in effect, be granted entry into a second round, in which it will compete against the winner of the first round. Unfortunately, the outcome of such a process is extremely sensitive to the agenda chosen, and consequently, either of two things is likely to happen. Either the instability of group decision making shifts from votes on outcomes to votes on the agendas expected to produce those outcomes, or some subset of actors is given power to control the agenda and therefore given considerable influence over the outcome likely to be produced. Thus, one possible explanation for observed policy stability in democracies is that some subset of the decision makers is controlling the agenda in a manner that prevents its preferred outcome from being defeated as part of a cycle of majorities. While this set of events might introduce desired stability to the policymaking process, it does so by sacrificing the notion that democratic outcomes reflect the will of the majority.

TABLE 11.7   Pair-Wise Contests and Different Voting Agendas

Agenda	1st Round	1st-Round winner	2nd Round	2nd-Round winner	Councillor obtaining her most preferred outcome
1	*I* vs. *D*	*D*	*D* vs. *C*	*C*	Centrist councillor
2	*C* vs. *I*	*I*	*I* vs. *D*	*D*	Right-wing councillor
3	*C* vs. *D*	*C*	*C* vs. *I*	*I*	Left-wing councillor

Note: I = an increase in social service provision; *D* = a decrease in social service provision; *C* = a maintenance of current levels of social service provision.

Restrictions on Preferences: The Median Voter Theorem

As was the case with the Borda count, it appears that institutional factors restricting the agenda may produce stable outcomes, but only at the expense of creating incentives for actors to attempt to manipulate the decision-making process. This obviously raises questions about our ability to design our way around the instability of majority rule in such a way that the cure is not worse than the disease. In the next section of this chapter, we discuss important work that suggests it may be impossible to design a decision-making mechanism that ensures group transitivity while simultaneously meeting minimal criteria for fairness. But before we get there, let's pause briefly to consider the behavior of majority rule in one more special case.

Recall that group intransitivity in our original city council example seemed to stem from the fact that the right-wing councillor has a particular type of preference ordering. Specifically, the right-wing council member prefers both lower and higher levels of social service provision to the maintenance of current levels of social service provision. The right-wing councillor's most preferred option is to decrease social service spending. But if it came to it, she would rather increase spending in the hope that this would "break the bank" and force the city to adjust to lower levels of spending in the future than maintain current levels of spending (which she thinks are too high) that would slowly bleed the city dry.

It is possible to represent the right-wing councillor's preferences with what political scientists call a **utility function**. A utility function can be thought of as a numerical scale in which higher numbers stand for higher positions in an individual's preference ordering. It essentially indicates how satisfied an individual is with the available alternatives. In Figure 11.2, we display a utility function that is consistent with the preference ordering of the right-wing councillor over the level of social service provision in our example. The utility function is highest over the proposal to decrease social service provision (*D*), it is lowest over the proposal to maintain current levels of social service provision (*C*), and it is between these two extremes over the proposal to increase social service provision (*I*).

> A **utility function** is essentially a numerical scaling in which higher numbers stand for higher positions in an individual's preference ordering.

Let's now examine the utility function of the centrist councillor. This is shown in Figure 11.3. You will immediately notice that the centrist councillor's utility function looks very different from that of the right-wing councillor's in Figure 11.2. In particular, the centrist councillor's utility function captures what political scientists call a **single-peaked preference ordering**. In other words, the utility function reaches a "peak" above the centrist councillor's most preferred point. In this particular example, her most preferred point, sometimes called her "ideal point," is *C*. As proposals move away from this "ideal point" in either direction, the centrist councillor experiences a decline in her

> A **single-peaked preference ordering** is characterized by a utility function that reaches a maximum at some point and slopes away from this maximum on either side, such that a movement away from the maximum never raises the actor's utility.

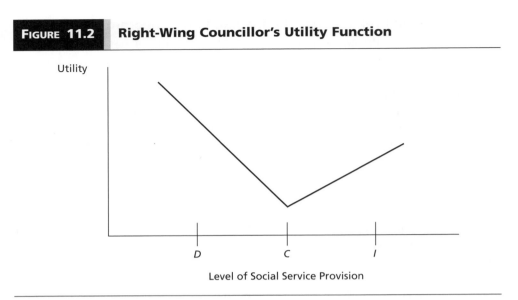

FIGURE 11.2 | **Right-Wing Councillor's Utility Function**

Note: D = decreased social service provision; *C* = maintenance of current levels of social service provision; *I* = increased social service provision.

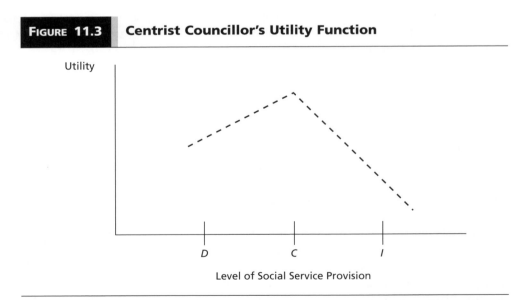

FIGURE 11.3 | **Centrist Councillor's Utility Function**

Note: D = decreased social service provision; *C* = maintenance of current levels of social service provision; *I* = increased social service provision.

utility function.[10] The basic intuition behind single peakedness is that individuals prefer outcomes that are closer to their ideal point than those that are farther away. A quick glance at Figure 11.2 again shows that the right-wing councillor's utility function is not single peaked. Although there is a point at which the right-wing councillor's utility function reaches a maximum (around *D*), the utility function does not continuously decline as it moves farther away from this point—it starts to go back up to the right of *C*. In other words, the right-wing councillor prefers some outcomes that are farther from her ideal point (say, *I*) than outcomes that are closer (say, *C*).

One of the most important results in all of political science is called the median voter theorem (see Box 11.1, "The Median Voter Theorem and Party Competition") (Black 1948). The **median voter theorem** (MVT) states that no alternative can beat the one preferred by the median voter in pair-wise majority-rule elections if the number of voters is odd, voter preferences are single-peaked over a single-policy dimension, and voters vote sincerely. When voters are arrayed along a single-issue dimension in terms of their ideal points, the **median voter** is the individual who has at least half of all the voters at his position or to his right and at least half of all the voters at his position or to his left.

> The **median voter theorem** (MVT) states that the ideal point of the median voter will win against any alternative in a pair-wise majority-rule election if the number of voters is odd, voter preferences are single-peaked over a single-policy dimension, and voters vote sincerely. When voters are arrayed along a single-policy dimension in terms of their ideal points, the **median voter** is the individual who has at least half of all the voters at his position or to his right and at least half of all the voters at his position or to his left.

Suppose that we placed a restriction on the preferences of the councillors in our city council example such that they all had single-peaked preference orderings. For example, we could restrict the preferences of the right-wing councillor such that her most preferred proposal is *D*, her second-best proposal is *C*, and her least preferred proposal is *I*. If we did this, then the preference orderings of all the councillors would be single peaked.[11] In Figure 11.4, we illustrate utility functions that are consistent with the single-peaked preferences of all three councillors. As we saw earlier in the chapter, maintaining current levels of social service provision (*C*) would win a round-robin tournament in which the councillors have preferences consistent with the utility functions shown in Figure 11.4.

Up to this point, we have allowed the city councillors to choose between only three alternatives—increase, decrease, and maintain current levels of social service provision. We are now in a position to consider what might happen if the councillors are free to propose any level of social service spending. In other words, we can now look at the situation in which

---

10. Note that the decline in utility may occur more rapidly when moving in one direction away from an individual's ideal point than the other.

11. We already showed in Figure 11.3 that the centrist councillor has a single-peaked preference ordering over the level of social service provision. You can check for yourself that the left-wing councillor also has a single-peaked preference ordering.

| **Box 11.1** | **THE MEDIAN VOTER THEOREM AND PARTY COMPETITION** |

The median voter theorem (MVT) was originally constructed in the context of committee voting (Black 1948). In his classic book, *An Economic Theory of Democracy,* Anthony Downs (1957) then extended the MVT to elections more generally. Building on an earlier model of economic competition presented by Harold Hotelling (1929), Downs shows that if we assume that there is a single-issue dimension, an odd number of voters with single-peaked preferences who vote sincerely, and only two parties, then both parties will converge to the ideal point of the median voter. Any other point in the policy space will lose in a pair-wise contest against the policy position preferred by the median voter. Thus, if one party is located at the median voter's ideal point and the competing party is not, then the first party will win a majority of the votes. The losing party, therefore, has an incentive to move to the median voter's ideal point as well. The consequence is that both parties will be located at the position of the median voter, resulting in a tied election in which each party wins with equal probability.

The logic of the MVT indicates that political parties have an incentive to converge to the position of the median voter and adopt similar policy positions in two-party systems. The fact that observers of two-party systems frequently criticize the dominant parties in these countries for being ideologically indistinguishable on the major issues provides some evidence that policy convergence does, indeed, occur. These observers complain that the parties are giving voters an "echo" rather than a "choice" (Monroe 1983; Page 1978). A common expression for the convergence of party platforms in these countries is "Tweedledee-Tweedledum politics" (Goodin and Pettit 1993, 6). For example, while campaigning in the midwestern states in 1968, third-party US presidential candidate George Wallace famously referred to the Democratic and Republican parties in a speech as "Tweedledum and Tweedledee." He argued that both were serving the interests of the "Eastern establishment" and that since around the time of the Civil War, "both parties have looked down their noses and called us rednecks down here in this part of the country. I'm sick and tired of it, and on November 5, they're goin' to find out there are a lot of rednecks in this country" ("Neither Tweedledum Nor Tweedledee," 1968). Similar criticisms are made by smaller parties or outsider candidates in nearly every country that has two large parties that dominate elections. Indeed, political discourse in Britain often refers explicitly to the Tweedledum-Tweedledee phrase. Non-English-speaking countries, of course, have their own expressions for this phenomenon.

the councillors can pick any point on the horizontal axis of Figure 11.4 as their proposed level of social service spending.

Let's look at what happens if we assume that all the councillors vote sincerely for whichever proposal is closest to their ideal point. We will look at two kinds of scenarios. First, suppose that the status quo level of social service spending is given by point *C*—the ideal point of the centrist councillor. Clearly, the left-wing councillor would like to move social service spending to the right, toward her own ideal point *I*. Any proposal to do this, however,

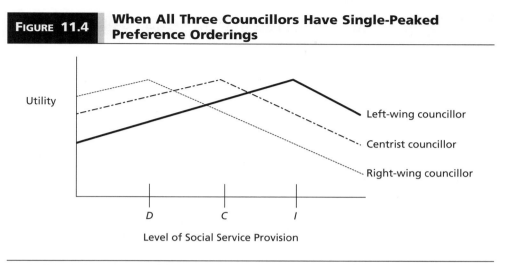

FIGURE 11.4 | **When All Three Councillors Have Single-Peaked Preference Orderings**

Note: I = the ideal point of the left-wing councillor; *C =* the ideal point of the centrist councillor; *D =* the ideal point of the right-wing councillor.

would be opposed by the centrist and right-wing councillors because any such proposal would be farther from their ideal points than the existing status quo. The right-wing councillor would like to move social spending to the left, toward her own ideal point *D*. Any proposal to do this would now be opposed by the centrist and the left-wing councillors because any such proposal would be farther from their ideal points than the existing status quo. As a result, if the status quo is at the centrist councillor's ideal point, then it is an equilibrium.

Second, suppose that the status quo level of social service spending is anywhere other than *C*—let's say somewhere to the left of *C*. This type of scenario is shown in Figure 11.5, with the status quo policy arbitrarily placed at *SQ* (status quo). In this type of situation, both the centrist and left-wing councillors are likely to propose moving social service spending closer to *C*. Let's suppose they propose *A*. Proposal *A* beats the *SQ* because the left-wing and centrist councillors vote for it and only the right-wing councillor votes against. But is policy *A* an equilibrium? The answer is no. The left-wing and centrist councillors would like to move social service provision farther to the right, closer to their ideal points. Let's suppose that they now propose *B*. Proposal *B* will be adopted because it is closer to the ideal points of both the left-wing and centrist councillors than proposal *A*; the right-wing councillor will vote against the new proposal but will lose. Is proposal *B* an equilibrium? Again, the answer is no. The right-wing and centrist councillors will now want to move social service provision to the left, closer to their ideal points. Any proposal that is closer to *C* than *B* will win with the support of the right-wing and centrist councillors. This process will continue until policy fully converges to the ideal point of the centrist councillor at *C*. Only then will the policy

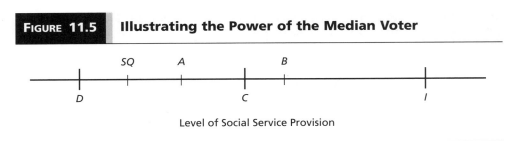

FIGURE 11.5 | **Illustrating the Power of the Median Voter**

Level of Social Service Provision

Note: D = the ideal point of the right-wing councillor; *C* = the ideal point of the centrist councillor; *I* = the ideal point of the left-wing councillor; *SQ* = status quo level of social service provision; *A* and *B* = proposals for a new level of social service provision.

outcome be stable. A similar process of convergence to the position of the centrist councillor would occur if the status quo started off to the right of *C* instead of to the left.

Even if the centrist councillor is never given the opportunity to propose a policy change, we would still expect to see alternative offers by the left- and right-wing council members that slowly converge to the most preferred policy of the centrist candidate. In fact, if making different policy proposals was sufficiently costly, farsighted councillors of the left and right might look to the end of this convergence process and simply propose a policy that matched the policy preferences of the centrist candidate from the very beginning. Whatever the process that produces the convergence to the centrist councillor's ideal point, once policy arrives there, there is no longer any impetus for change in the system. In other words, the policy that is most preferred by the centrist councillor is the only point on the policy continuum for which there is no policy alternative that is preferred by a majority of the councilors—it is the only equilibrium. This is so not because we have labeled the policymaker in the center a "centrist" but because the centrist happens to be the median voter.[12]

The median voter theorem essentially shows that the difficulties we encountered earlier with Condorcet's paradox, such as group intransitivity and cyclical majorities, can be avoided if we are willing to both rule certain preference orderings "out of bounds" and reduce the policy space to a single-issue dimension. Unfortunately, neither of these restrictions is uncontroversial. For example, there is nothing intrinsically troubling about individual preferences that are not single peaked. In fact, there is a whole host of issues for which voters might, like the right-wing councillor in our example, legitimately prefer a lot or a little of something to a moderate amount.[13] As a result, we might have moral objections to a

---

12. The median voter theorem does not assert that the equilibrium policy outcome will be centrist in terms of the underlying issue dimension. All it states is that the equilibrium policy will be the ideal point of the median voter. Whether it is centrist or not will, therefore, depend on the location of the median voter in the issue space.

13. We suspect that many of you probably have the following non-single-peaked preference ordering over coffee when the single dimension under consideration is the utility you derive from coffee served at different temperatures: you prefer both hot coffee and iced coffee to lukewarm coffee. We see nothing inherently wrong with a preference ordering like this.

decision-making procedure that prohibits individuals from holding preferences that are not single peaked.

The restriction of politics to a single-issue dimension can also be controversial. This is because many political questions are inherently multidimensional. As an example, consider a situation in which the representatives of three constituencies—labor, capital, and agriculture—are deciding how to divide a pot of subsidies from the government's budget. This decision-making situation can be represented by a two-dimensional policy space in which the percentage of subsidies going to labor is one dimension and the percentage of subsidies going to capital owners is the other; anything left over goes to agriculture. This decision-making situation is depicted in Figure 11.6. The downward-sloping dashed line sets an upper bound on all the possible distributions of subsidies. This limit is necessary because there is a finite amount of resources that can be spent on subsidies. In what follows, we assume that the entire pot of subsidies will be distributed between the three constituencies. At point L, all of the subsidies go to labor. At point C, all of the subsidies go to capital. And at point A, all of the subsidies go to agriculture. Any point along the sloping dashed line between L and C is some distribution of the subsidies between labor and capital; agriculture gets nothing. Any point along the solid vertical line between L and A is some distribution of

---

FIGURE 11.6 **Two-Dimensional Voting**

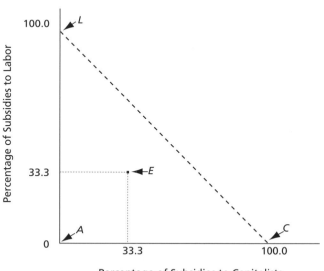

Note: At *L* all the subsidies go to labor; at *C* all the subsidies go to capital; at *A* all the subsidies go to agriculture; and at *E* the subsidies are divided equally between labor, capital, and agriculture.

the subsidies between labor and agriculture; capital gets nothing. And any point along the solid horizontal line between *A* and *C* is some distribution of the subsidies between agriculture and capital; labor gets nothing. Finally, any point within the triangle *LAC* is some distribution of the subsidies between all three constituencies. For example, at point *E*, the subsidies are divided equally between labor, capital, and agriculture.

Imagine that each constituency wants to maximize its share of the government subsidies but has no opinion about how the portion it does not receive is divided among the other constituencies. If each constituency votes to allocate the subsidies by majority rule and can propose a change in the division at any time, then the problem of cyclical majorities that we encountered with Condorcet's paradox will rear its ugly head again. To see why, imagine that someone, perhaps the national government, proposes to divide the subsidies equally between all three constituencies. This point can be thought of as the status quo proposal, and it is marked as *SQ* in Figure 11.7. Given the assumptions that we have made, the most preferred outcome for each constituency will be to get 100 percent of the subsidies for itself. Recall that these ideal points are given by points *L* (labor), *A* (agriculture), and *C* (capital) in Figure 11.6.

FIGURE 11.7 **Two-Dimensional Voting with Winsets**

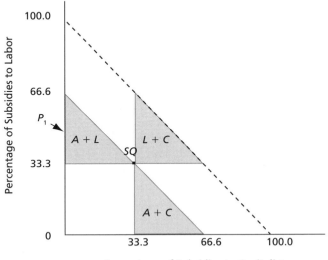

Note: The three solid gray lines going through *SQ* (status quo) are the indifference curves for labor (*L*), capital (*C*), and agriculture (*A*); P_1 = proposal 1. The shaded triangles are winsets that represent alternative divisions of the subsidies that are preferred by a majority to the status quo; the majority in question is shown in each winset.

The gray sloping line through the status quo proposal in Figure 11.7 indicates all of the ways that the pot of subsidies can be divided between labor and capital such that agriculture receives one third of the pot. Because agriculture cares only about how much it is getting, agriculture is essentially indifferent between any of the points on this line and the status quo proposal made by the national government. For this rea-son, the gray sloping line is called agriculture's **indiffer-ence curve** (with respect to the status quo).[14] Any point to the southwest of this indifference curve involves a division of subsidies in which agriculture receives more than one third of the pot. As a result, agriculture strictly prefers any point to the southwest

> An **indifference curve** is a set of points such that an individual is indifferent between any two points in the set.

of its indifference curve to any point on its indifference curve. The vertical gray line through the status quo proposal is capital's indifference curve because it indicates all of the ways that the pot of subsidies can be divided between labor and agriculture so that capital receives one third of the pot. Any point to the right of this indifference curve involves a division of sub-sidies in which capital receives more than one third of the pot. As a result, capital strictly prefers any point to the right of its indifference curve to any point on its indifference curve. Finally, the horizontal gray line through the status quo proposal is labor's indifference curve because it indicates all of the ways that the pot of subsidies can be divided between capital and agriculture so that labor receives one third of the pot. Although labor is indifferent among any of the points along this line, it strictly prefers any point above this line because it will receive more than one third of the pot.

Because labor prefers any point above the horizontal gray line to the status quo, capital prefers any point to the right of the vertical gray line, and agriculture prefers any point below the sloping gray line, each of the triangle-shaped petals radiating from the status quo repre-sents a set of alternative divisions of the subsidies that a majority of the constituency repre-sentatives prefer to the status quo. Such sets of alternatives that would win a majority vote if pitted against the status quo in a pair-wise contest are sometimes referred to as **winsets** of the status quo. The triangle to the northwest of the status quo, labeled $A + L$, represents outcomes that are preferred by labor and agriculture to the status quo.

> The **winset** of some alternative z is the set of alternatives that will defeat z in a pair-wise contest if everyone votes sincerely according to whatever voting rules are being used.

The triangle to the northeast of the status quo, labeled $L + C$, represents outcomes that are preferred by labor and capital to the status quo. Finally, the triangle to the southeast of the status quo, labeled $A + C$, represents outcomes that are preferred by capital and agriculture to the status quo.

The existence of these nonempty winsets indicates that if any of the three constituencies has an opportunity to propose a change in the division of subsidies, it will. For example, the labor representative might propose a 50–50 split of the subsidies with agriculture. This

---

14. This is despite the fact that, in this case, it is not actually a curve but a straight line.

proposal is denoted by P_1 in Figure 11.7. Because this proposal leaves both agriculture and labor better off vis-à-vis the status quo, the agriculture and labor representatives will vote to accept this proposal; the capital representative will vote against the proposal because capital would be worse off. Hence, proposal P_1 will defeat the original status quo 2–1 and become the new status quo proposal. Are there any alternative divisions of the subsidies that a majority of representatives prefer to the new status quo proposal P_1? To answer this question, we must draw the indifference curves of the three constituencies with respect to P_1 and see if there are any nonempty winsets. We do this in Figure 11.8.

As before, the indifference curves for each constituency are shown by the gray lines going through the new status quo proposal P_1. As Figure 11.8 illustrates, there are two winsets. The winset labeled $L + C$ contains alternatives that are preferred to P_1 by both labor and capital. The winset labeled $A + C$ contains alternatives that are preferred to P_1 by both agriculture and capital. In other words, there are several alternative divisions of the subsidies that are preferred by a majority to the new status quo proposal P_1. For example, the capital representative might propose to give two thirds of the subsidies to labor and one third of the subsidies to capital. This proposal is denoted by P_2 in Figure 11.8. Because this proposal leaves labor better off (labor receives 66.6 percent instead of 50 percent) and

FIGURE 11.8	**Two-Dimensional Voting with a New Status Quo (P_1)**

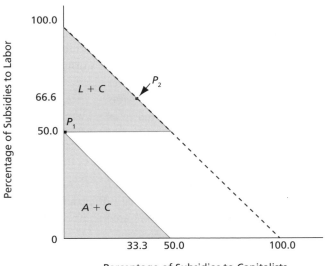

Note: The three solid gray lines going through P_1 are the indifference curves for labor (*L*), capital (*C*), and agriculture (*A*). The shaded triangles are winsets that represent alternative divisions of the subsidies that are preferred by a majority to the status quo; the majority in question is shown in each winset.

capital better off (capital gets 33.3 percent instead of 0 percent), the labor and capital representatives will vote to accept proposal P_2; the agriculture representative will vote against the proposal because agriculture will be worse off (agriculture receives 0 percent instead of 50 percent). Hence, proposal P_2 will defeat proposal P_1 2–1 and become the new status quo proposal.

Is P_2 a stable division of subsidies? The answer is no. Agriculture, which is not getting any share of the subsidies under proposal P_2, could propose a 50–50 division of the subsidies between itself and capital. This is proposal P_3 in Figure 11.9. This proposal would defeat P_2 because agriculture would vote for it (agriculture receives 50 percent instead of 0 percent), and capital would also vote for it (capital receives 50 percent instead of 33 percent). Thus, proposal P_3 would dislodge proposal P_2 as the new status quo proposal. Because there is always some division of the subsidies that gives the excluded constituency a share of the pot while giving one of the other constituencies a bigger share of the pot than it is receiving with the status quo proposal, this process of ever-shifting divisions of the subsidy pot can be expected to go on forever. This is illustrated in Figure 11.9.

The process of cyclical majorities highlighted in Figure 11.9 exemplifies a famously unsettling theorem about politics relating to majority rule in multidimensional settings

---

FIGURE 11.9 | **Two-Dimensional Voting with Cyclical Majorities**

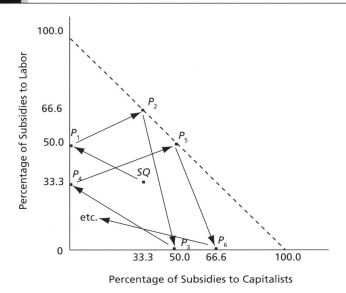

Note: SQ = original status quo; P_1 = proposal that beats SQ; P_2 = proposal that beats P_1; P_3 = proposal that beats P_2; P_4 = proposal that beats P_3, and so on.

The **chaos theorem** states that if there are two or more issue dimensions and three or more voters with preferences in the issue space who all vote sincerely, then except in the case of a rare distribution of ideal points, there will be no Condorcet winner.

(McKelvey 1976; Plott 1967; Schofield 1978). According to the **chaos theorem**, if there are two or more issue dimensions and three or more voters with preferences in the issue space who all vote sincerely, then except in the case of a rare distribution of ideal points, there will be no Condorcet winner. As a result, whoever controls the order of voting can determine the final outcome.

Like Condorcet's paradox, the chaos theorem suggests that unless we are lucky enough to have a set of actors who hold preferences that do not lead to cyclical majorities, either of two things will happen: (a) the decision-making process will be indeterminate and policy outcomes hopelessly unstable; or (b) there will exist an actor—the agenda setter—with the power to determine the order of votes in such a way that she can produce her most favored outcome.

In the absence of institutions that provide an actor with agenda-setting powers, stable outcomes are even less likely to occur in the circumstances covered by the chaos theorem than those covered by Condorcet's paradox. This is because the set of preferences that prevent majority cycling in two or more dimensions is extremely rare and special. Students who are interested in learning more about the conditions for stable outcomes in multidimensional policy spaces are referred to the Appendix, "Stability in Two-Dimensional Majority-Rule Voting," at the end of this chapter (pp. 442–444).

The important lesson to draw from the chaos theorem is that if politics cannot be reduced to a single-issue dimension, then there is a wide set of circumstances under which either (a) stable outcomes will not occur, or (b) stable outcomes will be imposed by whichever actor controls the agenda. The results of the chaos theorem highlight "the importance of investigating the effects of the political institutions within which collective choices are made" (McCarty and Meirowitz 2007, 80), because it is likely that it is these institutions that play a significant role in alleviating the "chaos" that might otherwise reign.

ARROW'S THEOREM

Up to this point, we have seen that thinking about democracy as simply a matter of allowing the majority to make decisions runs into difficulties on several fronts. First, Condorcet's paradox shows that a set of rational individuals can form a group that is incapable of choosing rationally in round-robin tournaments. Specifically, situations might arise in which majorities cycle indefinitely, rendering the group incapable of reaching a decision. We learned that although voting schemes, like the Borda count, that allow voters to rank order all possible alternatives might allow clear winners to emerge under some conditions, the outcomes that are produced by such decision-making processes are not robust. In particular, altering rankings over irrelevant alternatives could change the way votes are counted and therefore change the outcome. Next, we learned that if round-robin tournaments are replaced by "single elimination" tournaments that form a voting agenda, then cyclical majorities may be avoided and a stable outcome achieved. Unfortunately, we also saw that whoever controls the agenda—the order by which alternatives are pitted against each other and submitted to a vote—could dictate the outcome of such procedures.

We saw, though, that the problem of instability could be overcome if the political question to be decided can be thought of as a single-issue dimension *and* if each voter has single-peaked preferences over that dimension. When these and other conditions are met, the alternative that is most preferred by the median voter is a stable outcome in the sense that no other alternative exists that can defeat it in a majority-rule pair-wise contest. Unfortunately, the median voter theorem is, at best, cold comfort for a couple of reasons. First, it requires restrictions on the types of preferences that individuals can have. If some voters have non-single-peaked preferences, it is possible for a cycle of majorities to arise—just as in round-robin tournaments. Consequently, the median voter theorem tells us only that we can avoid the potential for decision-making instability if certain preference orderings do not occur, either because we are lucky or because we are willing to rule them out of bounds. This is problematic because it seems reasonable that an individual's preferences should be treated as sacrosanct. It seems to us that a "democratic" decision-making process that works reliably only when we restrict participation to those with the "right kind" of preferences loses much of its ethical appeal. Second, it is likely that many crucial political questions involve more than one dimension. We presented an example of distributional bargaining between three groups as an illustration of a two-dimensional political question that is, in many ways, the very essence of politics. In this example, the decision-making process was unstable and "chaotic." As we noted at the time, the stability implied by the median voter theorem occurs in situations in which there are two or more dimensions to a political problem only in exceedingly rare circumstances. Worse still, in the absence of such stability, outcomes in two dimensions can vacillate.

Each of these complications with majority rule raises fundamental questions about the ethical appeal of democracy—understood as majority rule—as a mechanism for making group decisions. Specifically, we have seen that it is difficult to guarantee that majority rule will produce a stable group choice without either granting someone agenda-setting power or restricting the kinds of preferences that individuals may hold. In a famous book, Kenneth Arrow (1963) put forth a theorem that shows that these problems with majority rule are, in some ways, special cases of a more fundamental problem. Arrow's theorem demonstrates that it is impossible to design any decision-making system—not just majority rule—for aggregating the preferences of a set of individuals that can guarantee producing a rational outcome while simultaneously meeting what he argued was a minimal standard of fairness.[15] When deciding which set of conditions a fair decision-making procedure should meet,

---

15. It is common to see Arrow's theorem referred to as Arrow's "impossibility" theorem. In fact, Arrow himself labeled it the "possibility theorem."

Arrow sought a minimal set in the sense that violations of these fairness conditions would lead to a procedure that is unfair in a way that would be evident to all.

Arrow's Fairness Conditions

Arrow presented four fairness conditions that he believed all decision-making processes should meet. Each of these four conditions is related to issues that have already arisen during our examination of majority rule and can reasonably be argued to be a part of any conception of democracy that meets minimal ethical standards. We will discuss each of the four conditions in turn.

Nondictatorship

The **nondictatorship condition** states that there must be no individual who fully determines the outcome of the group decision-making process in disregard of the preferences of the other group members. In fact, this condition is an extremely minimal fairness condition because it only says that there can be no individual who, if she prefers x to y, forces the group choice to be x instead of y, irrespective of the preferences of everyone else. A group decision-making process that pays attention to only one member of the group and disregards the preferences of all the other members is clearly not democratic. Although it is possible that a dictator would be benevolent and choose an outcome that benefits the group, it is clear that a mechanism that allows a single individual to determine group outcomes for everyone else is inherently unfair.

> The **nondictatorship condition** states that there must be no individual who fully determines the outcome of the group decision-making process in disregard of the preferences of the other group members.

Universal Admissibility

The **universal admissibility condition** states that any fair group decision-making rule must work with any logically possible set of individual preference orderings. This allows actors to adopt any rational preference ordering they want. This condition is closely related to the philosophical doctrine of individualism. According to this perspective, individuals should be free to formulate their own desires. Although it may be appropriate under some conditions to prohibit individuals from acting on those desires, it is inappropriate to comment on the intrinsic social desirability of another's desires per se. It is on this basis that Arrow believed it inappropriate to exclude individuals from group decision-making processes simply on the basis of the types of preferences that they happen to hold. Riker (1982, 117) defends the universal admissibility condition by stating that "if social outcomes are to be based exclusively on individual judgments—as seems implicit in any interpretation of democratic methods—then to restrict individual persons' judgments in any way means that the social outcome is based as much on the restriction as it is on individual judgments." In the context of voting, this condition states that every voter may vote as she pleases.

> The **universal admissibility condition** states that individuals can adopt any rational preference ordering over the available alternatives.

Unanimity, or Pareto Optimality

The **unanimity**, or **pareto optimality, condition** states that if all individuals in a group prefer x to y, then the group preference must reflect a preference for x to y as well. A decision-making process that fails to meet this condition is not only unfair; it is perverse. Imagine pressing the Coke button on a vending machine and having a Sprite come out. The unanimity condition is extremely minimal in that it merely states that if everybody in the group is unanimous in sharing a preference for x to y, then the group must not choose y when x is available.

> The **unanimity**, or **pareto optimality, condition** states that if all individuals in a group prefer x to y, then the group preference must reflect a preference for x to y as well.

Independence from Irrelevant Alternatives

The **independence from irrelevant alternatives condition** states that when groups are choosing between alternatives in a subset, the group choice should be influenced only by the rankings of these alternatives and not by the rankings of any (irrelevant) alternatives that are not in the subset. Suppose that, when confronted with a choice between x, y, and z, a group prefers x to y. The independence from irrelevant alternatives condition states that if one or more individuals alter their ranking of z, the group must still prefer x to y. Or as Varian (1993, 535) puts it, the group's preference "between x and y should depend only on how people rank x versus y, and not on how they rank other alternatives." We saw earlier that the Borda count can violate this condition. A decision rule respects the independence from irrelevant alternatives condition whenever the group's ranking of any two alternatives, x and y, depends only on the relative ranking of these alternatives by every individual in the group (Geanakoplos 2005). Some scholars have, therefore, interpreted this condition to mean that the decision rule should be reliable in the sense that it always returns the same decision if the way individuals rank relevant alternatives remains unchanged (Riker 1982). In this respect, the independence from irrelevant alternatives condition is as much a condition about the reliability of the preference aggregation technology as it is a condition about the fairness of the decision-making mechanism.

> The **independence from irrelevant alternatives condition** states that group choice should be unperturbed by changes in the rankings of irrelevant alternatives.

In sum, Arrow's four conditions suggest that any fair group decision-making mechanism must prevent dictatorship (nondictatorship), must not restrict the type of preferences that individuals can hold (universal admissibility), and must link group choice, in at least some rudimentary sense, to individual preferences (unanimity and independence from irrelevant alternatives). We have already seen examples of how particular majority-rule decision-making mechanisms must violate at least one of these requirements if we wish to guarantee that the group's preference ordering will be transitive. As we have seen, group transitivity is necessary in order for the group decision-making process to produce stable outcomes in the absence of manipulation by powerful minorities acting as agenda setters. The real power of

Arrow's theorem states that every decision-making process that we could possibly design must sacrifice at least one of Arrow's fairness conditions—nondictatorship, universal admissibility, unanimity, or independence from irrelevant alternatives—if it is to guarantee group transitivity and, hence, stable outcomes.

Arrow's theorem, though, comes from demonstrating that *every* decision-making process that we could possibly design, including any majority-rule one, must sacrifice at least one of Arrow's fairness conditions if it is to guarantee group transitivity and, hence, stable outcomes. Put differently, if we insist that Arrow's four fairness conditions be met, we must accept the possibility of group intransitivity—there is no way around it.

The implications of Arrow's theorem are far-reaching. Suppose that we take Arrow's conditions of unanimity and independence from irrelevant alternatives as uncontroversial and given. If we do this, Arrow's theorem tells us that we face an institutional "trilemma" between stable outcomes, universal admissibility, and nondictatorship. In other words, we can design decision-making institutions that have at most two of these three desirable attributes. In Figure 11.10, we illustrate Arrow's institutional trilemma with the help of a triangle.

Basically, Arrow's theorem states that when we design decision-making institutions, we can choose one and only one side of the triangle shown in Figure 11.10. If we want decision-making institutions that guarantee group transitivity and stable outcomes (*A*), then we must give up either nondictatorship (*B*) or universal admissibility (*C*). If, on the other hand, we want to avoid dictatorship (*B*), then we must give up either transitivity (*A*) or universal admissibility (*C*). Finally, if we hold individual preferences as inviolable (*C*), then we must

---

FIGURE 11.10 **Arrow's Institutional Trilemma**

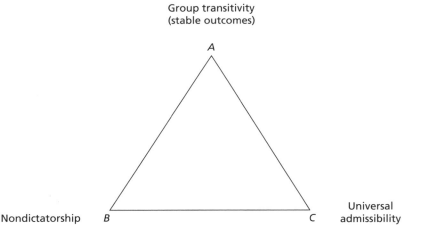

Note: Arrow's conditions of unanimity and independence from irrelevant alternatives are assumed as given here.

give up either transitivity (*A*) or nondictatorship (*B*). To summarize, Arrow's theorem proves that if the independence from irrelevant alternatives and the unanimity conditions are assumed, then designers of group decision-making institutions will be forced to choose their poison from the following set: restrictions on individual preferences, dictatorship, and the possibility of group intransitivity.

In addition, Arrow's theorem shows that it is, at the very least, difficult to interpret the outcome of any group decision-making process as *necessarily* reflecting the will of the group (Shepsle 1992). When a group comes to a clear decision, it *may* mean that individual preferences lined up in a way that allowed for a clear outcome that represented, in some meaningful way, the desires of a large portion of the group. But it may also mean that individuals with inconvenient preferences were excluded from the process, or that some actor(s) exercised agenda control. In such cases, outcomes may reflect the interest of some powerful subset of the group rather than the preferences of the group as a whole, or even some majority of the individuals in the group. Put differently, when choosing between alternative institutional arrangements that are decisive—that is, they do not display intransitivity—we are essentially engaged in a discussion about *which* minority we will allow to influence outcomes through the control of the agenda.

Blair and Pollack (1982a, 1982b) extend Arrow's work by demonstrating that if the assumption of group transitivity is replaced by a less restrictive condition known as *acyclicality* (the absence of cycles based on strict preferences), then collective decision rules that meet Arrow's other conditions do exist. But these authors go on to show that if the number of alternatives exceeds the number of individuals in the group, then there must exist an individual who can veto some proposals. Further, as the number of alternatives being decided over increases without limit, as we have argued it does in many important policy areas, then the share of alternatives an individual can veto approaches 100 percent. This suggests that stable outcomes produced by (otherwise) fair decision rules occur because some subset of actors, which Blair and Pollack refer to as an "oligarchy," is able to veto challenges to the status quo that are preferred by a majority of individuals. Choosing decisive democratic institutions, therefore, comes down to choosing which oligarchy to empower to protect their preferred status quo. In other words, the design of institutions is a fundamentally political, rather than technocratic, exercise.

CONCLUSION

Most people associate democracy with majority rule. In this chapter we have examined various problems with majority-rule decision-making procedures. We have shown, for example, that there is a fundamental tension between the desire to guarantee that a group of individuals will be able to make coherent and stable choices on the one hand and the ability to guarantee the freedom of these individuals to form their own preferences and have those preferences influence group decisions on the other. Arrow's theorem shows that these tensions extend far beyond majority rule to encompass a wide set of minimally fair group decision-making methods. Because most conceptions of democracy would probably be even more ambitious than Arrow's fairness criteria, these results have important and profound implications for democracy.

It is important to note at this point that the most direct implications of Arrow's theorem concern particular mechanisms for group decision making. Arrow's theorem is not in any direct sense about *collections* of decision-making procedures. Consider constitutions. A constitution does not typically stipulate *a* decision-making procedure to be used in a country but rather stipulates an entire set of decision-making procedures. For example, a constitution may stipulate how the head of the executive branch will be chosen, how legislators are chosen, how legislators choose laws, how the executive and legislative branches interact, how and if courts decide whether legislation is constitutional, which laws are under the jurisdiction of the national government and which are under local control, and the like. Arrow's theorem applies to each and every one of these decision-making mechanisms, and the way the trilemma that Arrow's theorem poses is resolved may vary from mechanism to mechanism within a particular constitution.[16] Some mechanisms or institutions may privilege group transitivity by reducing the number of alternatives from which people can choose—the two-party system used for electing presidents in the United States can be seen as an example of this. Other mechanisms or institutions may avoid group intransitivity by granting agenda-setting powers to an individual. A large literature on the US Congress argues that committee chairs play this role in the legislative process. Cabinet ministers play a similar role in many parliamentary systems.

The key point is that *every* decision-making mechanism must grapple with the trade-offs posed by Arrow's theorem, and *every* system of government represents a collection of such decision-making mechanisms. Consequently, we can think of a system of government in terms of how its decision-making mechanisms tend to resolve the trade-offs between group transitivity and Arrow's fairness criteria. And to the extent that a set of decision-making mechanisms privileges group transitivity, it is useful to think about *which* of Arrow's fairness criteria tends to be sacrificed. For example, is stability produced because strong agenda setters are present or because restrictions are placed on the preferences that actors hold? If it is the latter, we might ask whether this is achieved because some actors are excluded from deliberations or because strong mechanisms are in place to socialize participants so that they adopt the preferences that are compatible with stable group choice.

---

16. Arrow's theorem also applies to decision-making bodies we are involved with on a day-to-day basis—student organizations, faculties, labor unions, religious congregations, corporate boards, families, and groups of friends deciding which movie to see.

It should be clear by now that the most basic implication of Arrow's theorem is this: there is no perfect set of decision-making institutions. Every set of institutions either runs the risk of group intransitivity or compromises a fairness condition. As such, democracy must in some sense be imperfect—either fairness is compromised, or there will be a potential for instability.[17] Perhaps this is what inspired former British prime minister Winston Churchill to say, "Democracy is the worst form of government, except for all those other forms that have been tried from time to time."[18] In the following chapters, we examine the immense variety of democratic forms of government, focusing specifically on different configurations and their consequences.

In the next chapter, we examine the different ways we can choose the head of government and structure the relationship between the head of government and the legislative branch. In Chapter 13 we look at the myriad ways in which legislators are elected around the world. In Chapter 14 we investigate the ways in which group preferences interact with electoral laws to shape party systems. From the perspective of Arrow's theorem, party systems can be thought of as a way of encouraging stability by reducing the number of alternatives to be considered in an election. In Chapter 15 we examine a whole host of other institutional mechanisms, such as the division of powers between national and subnational governments (federalism), the division of powers between different houses of the legislature (bicameralism), and the division of powers between the legislative and judicial branches (constitutional review). From the standpoint of Arrow's theorem, these institutional mechanisms can be thought of as attempts to limit the control of powerful agenda setters by pitting them against each other.

The immense variety of democratic institutions observed in the world is itself implied by Arrow's theorem. Because there is no ideal decision-making mechanism, institutional choice is an exercise in the choice of "second bests," and which institution (or set of institutions) is adopted in any given time or place is going to be dictated by context—some situations make instability sufficiently threatening to make the sacrifice of fairness conditions reasonable, whereas others may permit individuals to accept a certain degree of instability in exchange for protecting the fairness of the decision-making process. Of course, the suggestion that we, as a society, may "choose" optimal institutions is itself in tension with Arrow's theorem. Perhaps the institutions we confront today are the product of choices by agenda setters in the past, or inherited from times when actors with certain preferences were restricted from participating in the constitutional deliberations.

---

17. Patty and Penn (2014) argue that while, for the reasons outlined in this chapter, democratic institutions are not likely to yield a single "best choice," they may be able to arrive at a set of legitimate choices.

18. House of Commons speech, November 11, 1947.

APPENDIX: STABILITY IN TWO-DIMENSIONAL MAJORITY-RULE VOTING

Earlier in this chapter, we argued that multidimensional voting was almost always going to be characterized by instability and cyclical majorities. Recall that this was the central insight gleaned from the chaos theorem. Only in extremely rare circumstances can stability be achieved. At the time, we did not present any evidence for why the conditions necessary to achieve stability in multidimensional voting were likely to be so rare. Although a full treatment of this subject exceeds the space and technical limits of this book, we now present some informal evidence to support this assertion. To keep things simple, we focus on two-dimensional voting. The logic of our argument, though, applies equally well to multidimensional scenarios in general.

One way instability is avoided in two-dimensional voting is if the individuals in a group have radially symmetric preferences (Plott 1967). This involves having a single individual be the median voter in both dimensions and aligning all of the other voters symmetrically around this person. In Figure 11.11, we present a situation in which three individuals (voters *A, B,* and *C*) must make decisions on two issue dimensions simultaneously. For example, perhaps issue 1 is the amount of money spent on education and issue 2 is the amount of money spent on health care. As you can see, the voters in Figure 11.11 have radially symmetric preferences. Voter *B* is the median voter on both issue 1 and issue 2. For example, voter *B* has one voter to her left and one to her right on issue 2, and one voter above her and one below her on issue 1. As the dashed line indicates, the two other voters, *A* and *C,* are aligned symmetrically around voter *B*; that is, they are exactly opposite each other with voter *B* in between. Given this arrangement of voter preferences, if voter *B*'s ideal point were ever to become the status quo, there would be no majority that could displace it. In effect, voter *B*'s ideal point is an equilibrium in this two-dimensional majority-rule voting scenario.

To see why, we must examine the indifference curves of voters *A* and *C* with respect to voter *B*'s ideal point (the status quo)—these are the circles that surround the ideal points of voters *A* and *C*. These circles show all of the policy outcomes for which voters *A* and *C* would

FIGURE 11.11   Stability in Two-Dimensional Voting

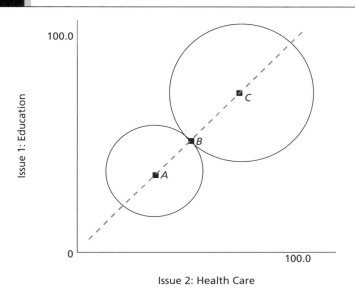

Note: Voter B's position = the status quo policy; the two circles = the indifference curves for voters A and C with respect to the status quo policy B.

be indifferent between that policy and the status quo. Note that each indifference curve goes through B. Consequently, any point inside a circle is closer (and, therefore, preferred) to the relevant voter's ideal point than the status quo (represented by voter B's ideal point). There is no circle with B as its center because there are no alternatives that voter B prefers to her own ideal point. The two circles in Figure 11.11, therefore, represent the set of policy proposals that A and C prefer to the status quo. Majority rule means that two out of the three voters would have to prefer an alternative to B's position for a policy proposal to dislodge C. The fact that the two circles never overlap, though, means that A and C cannot agree on an alternative to replace the status quo. If C proposed an alternative closer to his ideal point, A and B would vote against it. Similarly, if A proposed an alternative closer to his ideal point, B and C would vote against it. In other words, any alternative to B's position would never get more than one vote and would, therefore, lose. As this example illustrates, it is possible to obtain a stable outcome—in this case B's position—in two-dimensional majority-rule voting.

Although stability is possible in two-dimensional majority-rule voting games, is it likely? Many scholars think not. To see why, imagine what happens if one of the voters' ideal points moves just a little. In Figure 11.12, we shift voter C's ideal point by an arbitrary amount off of the dashed line to the southeast. You will immediately notice that there is now a lens-shaped area south of B in which the indifference curves of voters A and C overlap. This lens-shaped area is the winset of B and contains all of the alternative policy outcomes that both voters A and C prefer to B. This

FIGURE 11.12 | **Instability in Two-Dimensional Voting**

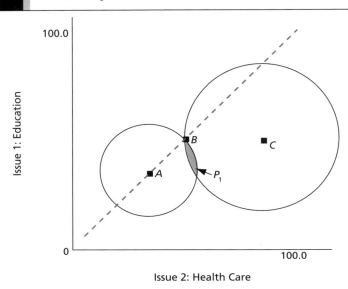

Note: Voter *B*'s position = the status quo policy; the two circles = the indifference curves for voters *A* and *C* with respect to the status quo policy; the shaded oval area = the winset of *B* and represents the alternative policy outcomes that voters *A* and *C* prefer to voter *B*'s position. P_1 = a policy proposal that would defeat the status quo policy (*B*) in a majority rule vote.

means that if either voter *A* or voter *C* has an opportunity to propose a change in policy to a point in the winset, say P_1, she will do so, and the new policy proposal will win a majority vote. Once this happens, all the indifference curves will need to be redrawn so that they go through this new status quo point. If we were to do this, we would find another lens-shaped area, thereby demonstrating that at least two voters will prefer yet another policy combination to this new status quo. At this point we will be off to the races, and the instability of the chaos theorem will ensue because the condition that had previously made *B* a stable outcome no longer pertains.

Recall what made *B* stable in the first place. First, there was a voter whose ideal point made her a median voter in both issue dimensions. Second, all of the other voters' ideal points radiated from *B* in just the right way. Specifically, *A* and *C* were aligned on a straight line with *B* (the dashed line in Figure 11.11). Charles Plott (1967) proved that such "radial symmetry" is sufficient to guarantee the existence of a stable outcome in a two-dimensional majority-rule voting scenario. Radial symmetry, however, is not strictly necessary, and subsequent scholars have identified other conditions that are sufficient to produce stability.[19] These further conditions, like Plott's condition, though, are quite restrictive. As a result, it is reasonable to conclude that majority rule is unstable in multidimensional situations except under very unusual circumstances in which voter preferences line up in just the right way.

---

19. Hinich and Munger's *Analytical Politics* (1997) is a good resource for ambitious students who would like to pursue this topic further.

PROBLEMS

The following problems address some of the more important concepts, theories, and methods introduced in this chapter.

Individual Preferences

1. What does it mean for an individual to be "rational"? Give a brief definition of the concept in your own words. If you use terms like *complete* and *transitive* to define the concept, be sure to define those terms as well.

2. In the problems at the end of Chapter 4, you were asked to consider the children's game of Rock, Paper, Scissors. In this game, two children simultaneously choose "rock," "paper," or "scissors." Rock beats scissors, paper beats rock, and scissors beats paper. Let's say that you prefer the winner in each of these pair-wise comparisons. That is, you prefer rock to scissors, scissors to paper, and paper to rock. Is your preference ordering complete? Explain your answer. Is your preference ordering transitive? Explain your answer. Are you rational? Explain your answer.

3. Construct a complete and transitive preference ordering between three or more alternatives that you think some people might hold (or that you yourself hold). Now construct another (reasonable) preference ordering that does not satisfy completeness or transitivity.

4. Choose some issue dimension. With the help of a diagram, construct one preference ordering over the issue dimension that is single peaked and one that is not. Explain what single-peaked preferences are in your own words.

5. In your own words, explain Condorcet's paradox. Provide an example that illustrates Condorcet's paradox and is different from the one used in the chapter.

Agenda Setting

6. Imagine that you are one of three judges for a singing competition. You need to decide which of three finalists should win. You have no qualifications to evaluate actual singing ability, so you plan to make your choice based entirely on your preferences for the style of music that each performer chose: a sappy ballad, a traditional Irish folk song, and a heavy metal song. Luckily for you, you happened to see the notes written by the other judges, and so you know how your fellow judges ranked the finalists. One judge had the following preference ordering: ballad > Irish folk song > heavy metal. The other judge had the following preference ordering: heavy metal > ballad > Irish folk song. Your preference ordering, however, is the following: Irish folk song > heavy metal > ballad. The rules of the competition do not specify how the judges are to reach their decision.

   a. Let's suppose that you suggest a round-robin tournament in which everyone votes on the finalists in a series of pair-wise contests. How many pair-wise contests does each of the finalists win? Is there a Condorcet winner? Explain. Does this decision-making process identify a clear winner? Explain.

b. Now let's suppose that you propose a decision-making procedure by which all of the judges begin by considering only a subset of the available pair-wise contests. The specific decision-making procedure that you propose is that two finalists should compete in a pair-wise contest with the winner competing in a second and final round against the remaining finalist. Given your preference ordering, which finalist do you want to win? If you were in charge of setting the voting agenda and could determine the order in which the pair-wise contests took place, what order would you pick and why?

7. Imagine that you participated in a study group comprising some of the members of your comparative politics class. After spending several hours studying for the second midterm, you are all ready for a break but can't decide what to do. Shannon suggests a CrossFit workout, Brandon suggests joining a battle reenactment over at the military museum, and Katie suggests hanging out with food and drink, while watching a *Friends* marathon on her giant TV. Based on what you know of your classmates' interests, you expect that the following would be true: (i) a majority would prefer CrossFit to the battle reenactment; (ii) a majority would prefer the battle reenactment to the *Friends* marathon; and (iii) a majority would prefer the *Friends* marathon to CrossFit.

a. Specify which of the three outcomes you prefer the most (if you can't decide, pick one for the sake of this example).

b. Given your choice above, explain how you would set the agenda to arrive at this outcome, if you were all going to vote sincerely using a sequence of pair-wise contests.

Median Voter Theorem and Party Competition

8. In Figure 11.13, we illustrate an election in which there are seven voters (*A, B, C, D, E, F, G*) arrayed along a single left-right issue dimension that runs from 0 (*most left*) to 10 (*most right*). Each voter is assumed to have single-peaked utility functions and to vote for the party that is located closest to her ideal point. The voters are participating in a majority-rule election in which there are two parties, P_1 and P_2, competing for office.

a. Which voter is the median voter? What is her ideological position?

Part I: Office-Seeking Parties vs. Policy-Seeking Parties

Suppose that parties P_1 and P_2 are office-seeking parties in that they care only about winning the election and getting into office.

FIGURE 11.13   Illustrating the Median Voter Theorem

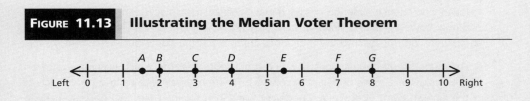

b. Suppose that P_1 locates at position 2 on the left-right issue dimension and that P_2 locates at position 7. How many votes does P_1 win? How many votes does P_2 win? Who wins the election? Where does the winner implement policy on the left-right issue dimension? Will P_1 and P_2 want to stay at these policy positions for the next election? If not, what policy positions do you think they will adopt and why?

c. Now let's suppose that P_1 locates at position 4 and P_2 locates at position 4. What is the outcome of this election? Does P_1 or P_2 want to change policy positions given where the other party is located? If so, why? If not, why not?

Now suppose that instead of having two office-seeking parties, P_1 and P_2, we have two "policy-seeking" parties, L and R. L is a left-wing party whose ideal point is 2, and R is a right-wing party whose ideal point is 7. Policy-seeking parties care about where policy is implemented.

d. Suppose that L locates at its ideal point (2) on the left-right issue dimension and that R locates at its ideal point (7). How many votes does L win? How many votes does R win? Who wins the election? Where does the winner implement policy on the left-right issue dimension? Will L and R want to stay at their ideal points for the next election? If not, what policy positions do you think they will adopt and why?

e. Now suppose that L locates at position 4 and R locates at position 4. What is the outcome of this election? Where will policy be implemented on the left-right issue dimension? Does L or R want to change policy positions given where the other party is located? If so, why? If not, why not?

f. Based on your answers so far, does the result from the median voter theorem stating that parties will converge to the position of the median voter depend on whether political parties are office seeking or policy seeking? Explain.

Part II: Voter Distribution

Suppose that some event occurs that causes several voters to adopt more centrist positions on the left-right issue dimension. The new distribution of voters is shown in Figure 11.14.

FIGURE 11.14   **Illustrating the Median Voter Theorem: A Centrist Electorate**

g. Where will parties P_1 and P_2 locate in the left-right space, given the centrist nature of the electorate? Why?

Suppose now that some polarizing event occurs that causes several voters to adopt more extreme positions on the left-right issue dimension. The new distribution of voters is shown in Figure 11.15.

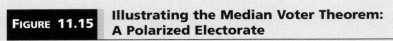

FIGURE 11.15 **Illustrating the Median Voter Theorem: A Polarized Electorate**

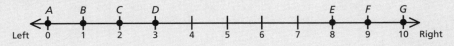

h. Where will parties P_1 and P_2 locate in the left-right space, given the polarized nature of the electorate? Why?

i. Based on your answers to the two previous questions, does the result from the median voter theorem stating that parties will converge to the position of the median voter depend on the distribution of voter ideal points? Explain.

Part III: Number of Parties

Suppose now that three parties instead of just two are competing in the election. Imagine that all three of the parties locate at the position of the median voter.

j. Would any of the parties want to change their position? If so, why? If not, why not? If it helps, you can think of all three parties locating at the position of the median voter in any of the three figures (11.13, 11.14, or 11.15).

k. Based on your answer to the previous question, does the result from the median voter theorem stating that parties will converge to the position of the median voter depend on there being only two parties? Explain.

Spatial Models

9. The median voter theorem is an example of a larger class of models known as spatial models. The primary characteristic of spatial models is that the preferences of actors can usefully be conceived as points in some kind of policy "space" (Hinich and Munger 1997, 5). Political scientists have employed spatial models to examine a diverse array of political situations, from leaders of countries negotiating territorial conflicts; to the relations between Congress, the president, and the Supreme Court in the United States; to party factions choosing a policy platform; to a policy adviser making recommendations to an elected official; and so on.

We now employ a simple spatial model to examine a situation in which a president (*P*) and a legislature (*L*) are considering whether to change the current level of public goods provision in a country. We can think of the level of public goods provision in a country as a single-issue dimension ranging from low public goods provision (0) to high public goods provision (10). The current level of public goods provision is referred to as the status quo (*SQ*). Both the president and the legislature have preferences over what the level of public goods provision should be. We will assume that the legislature gets to make proposals on what the level of public goods provision should be and that the president can either accept or veto these proposals. If the president vetoes the legislature's proposal, then the status quo policy is maintained. If the president approves the legislature's proposal, then the proposal is implemented and becomes the new status quo.

In Figure 11.16, we illustrate one possible scenario in which a president and a legislature could find themselves. The status quo level of public goods provision is 2. The president's most preferred level of public goods provision is 7, and the legislature's most preferred level is 4. Recall that in spatial models, actors are assumed to prefer policy outcomes that are closer to their ideal points than ones that are farther away. In other words, if an actor has to vote over two alternatives, she will choose the one that is closer to her ideal point. If an actor has to choose between two policy outcomes that are equidistant from her ideal point, she is indifferent between them and could choose either as a best response. For instance, the president would be indifferent between having public goods provision at 6 or 8 because both of these outcomes are one unit away from her ideal point, 7. *To keep the following examples simple, you can assume that if an actor is indifferent between the status quo point and an alternative point, the actor will choose the alternative point.*

FIGURE 11.16 | Choosing a Level of Public Goods Provision: Scenario 1

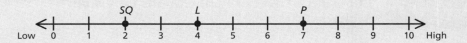

Note: SQ = the current level of public goods provision; *L* = the ideal point of the legislature; *P* = the ideal point of the president.

Part I: Scenario 1

Suppose that the *SQ* and the ideal points of the legislature and president are aligned as in Scenario 1 in Figure 11.16.

  a. Given that the status quo is at 2, what is the range of policy outcomes that the president prefers to the status quo? Recall that the president prefers any policy that is closer to her ideal point than the status quo.

  b. Given that the status quo is at 2, what is the range of policy outcomes that the legislature prefers to the status quo? Recall that the legislature prefers any policy that is closer to its ideal point than the status quo.

  c. Do the ranges of policy outcomes that the president and legislature prefer to the status quo overlap? If they do overlap, how would you interpret the set of points where they overlap?

d. If the legislature proposes a new policy, and if it needs the president's approval for the new policy to be implemented, what level of public goods provision do you think the legislature will propose? Why? *Hint:* If the legislature proposes a new policy, it will want to choose the level of public goods provision that is closest to its ideal point and that is acceptable to the president.

Part II: Scenario 2

Now imagine that the ideal points of the president and the legislature are reversed. In other words, the president's ideal point is now 4 and the legislature's ideal point is now 7. This scenario is illustrated in Figure 11.17.

e. Given that the status quo is at 2, what is the range of policy outcomes that the president prefers to the status quo?

f. Given that the status quo is at 2, what is the range of policy outcomes that the legislature prefers to the status quo?

g. Do the ranges of policy outcomes that the president and legislature prefer to the status quo overlap? If they do overlap, how would you interpret the set of points where they overlap?

h. If the legislature proposes a new policy, and its implementation needs the president's approval, what level of public goods provision do you think the legislature will propose? Why?

FIGURE 11.17 **Choosing a Level of Public Goods Provision: Scenario 2**

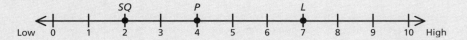

Note: SQ = the current level of public goods provision; *L* = the ideal point of the legislature; *P* = the ideal point of the president.

Part III: Scenario 3

Now suppose that the ideal points of the president and the legislature are on opposite sides of the status quo. Let's assume that the president's ideal point is now 1 and the legislature's ideal point is now 4. This scenario is illustrated in Figure 11.18.

i. Given that the status quo is at 2, what is the range of policy outcomes that the president prefers to the status quo?

j. Given that the status quo is at 2, what is the range of policy outcomes that the legislature prefers to the status quo?

k. Do the ranges of policy outcomes that the president and legislature prefer to the status quo overlap? If they do overlap, how would you interpret the set of points where they overlap? If they do not overlap, what does this mean?

l. Can the legislature make a successful proposal to change the status quo? If so, why? If not, why not?

| FIGURE 11.18 | **Choosing a Level of Public Goods Provision: Scenario 3** |

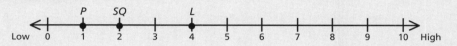

Note: SQ = the current level of public goods provision; L = the ideal point of the legislature; P = the ideal point of the president.

Part IV: Conclusion

m. Given your analysis of the three scenarios above (Parts I–III), what can you say about the conditions under which policy will change versus when it will be stable?

Arrow's Theorem

10. What is the fundamental implication of Arrow's Theorem? Describe this in your own words.

11. Two of the authors of this book presented a lesson on Condorcet's paradox to a third grade math class at a local Friends (Quaker) school. The eight-year-old children were assigned preferences over three flavors of ice cream and asked to vote for the kind of ice cream that would be (hypothetically) provided to the class. One girl immediately raised her hand and said, "Voting isn't Quaker-like." Indeed, in Quaker meetings, decisions are made only after the members of the meeting have come to a consensus. In terms of Arrow's conditions of fairness, what are the trade-offs involved when choosing to make group decisions by majority rule versus by consensus (unanimity)?

12 Parliamentary, Presidential, and Semi-Presidential Democracies

The essence of pure parliamentarism is mutual dependence. . . . The essence of pure presidentialism is mutual independence.

Alfred Stepan and Cindy Skach, "Constitutional Frameworks and Democratic Consolidation"

A cabinet is a combining committee—a hyphen which joins, a buckle which fastens, the legislative part of the state to the executive part of the state. In its origin it belongs to the one, in its functions it belongs to the other.

Walter Bagehot, The English Constitution

OVERVIEW

- Political scientists often classify democracies as parliamentary, presidential, or semi-presidential. Whether a democracy is parliamentary, presidential, or semi-presidential depends on the relationship between the government, the legislature, and (if there is one) the president.

- The government formation process in parliamentary democracies can be quite complicated and take a long time. Several different types of government can form: single-party majority governments, minimal winning coalitions, minority governments, surplus majority governments, and so on. The type of government that forms depends on many factors, including whether the political actors in a country are office seeking or policy seeking. Although some governments in parliamentary democracies last several years, others last just a few days.

- The government formation process in presidential democracies is different in many ways from that in parliamentary democracies. Presidential democracies have more minority governments but fewer coalition governments on average than parliamentary ones. They also have more nonpartisan ministers and a lower proportionality in the allocation of ministerial posts. Governments in presidential democracies look more like those in parliamentary democracies if the president is weak.

- The government formation process in semi-presidential democracies is relatively understudied. There is evidence, however, that governments in semi-presidential democracies share characteristics from governments in both parliamentary and presidential democracies.

- To a large extent, parliamentary, presidential, and semi-presidential democracies can be viewed as different systems of delegation.

In Chapter 10 we looked at the different types of dictatorships in the world. Our focus now turns to examining the institutional variation among democracies. As you can imagine, we could distinguish between democracies in many different ways. Most political scientists, however, tend to classify democracies according to the form of government they have, that is, according to the rules that define who the government is, how the government comes to power, and how the government remains in power (Cheibub 2007). According to this classification scheme, there are three basic types of democracy: parliamentary, presidential, and semi-presidential. In this chapter, we examine how scholars distinguish between these three types of democracy. We then take a close look at how governments form and survive in these different systems. And finally, we look at how principal-agent, or delegation, models provide a unifying framework for thinking about parliamentary, presidential, and semi-presidential democracies.

CLASSIFYING DEMOCRACIES

Whether a democracy is parliamentary, presidential, or semi-presidential depends on the relationship between (a) the government, which comprises the political chief executive and the ministers that head the various government departments, (b) the legislature, and (c) the president (if there is one). In effect, we must ask two basic questions if we want to classify democracies as parliamentary, presidential, or semi-presidential.[1] These questions are shown in Figure 12.1.

Is the Government Responsible to the Elected Legislature?

The first question is whether the government is responsible to the elected legislature. Recall that the government is made up of the political chief executive and the ministers that head

---

1. Some political scientists employ slightly different criteria for classifying the three different types of democracy (Cheibub 2007; Elgie 2011; Lijphart 1984, 1999; Sartori 1997; Shugart and Carey 1992). In what follows, we employ the classification scheme presented in Cheibub, Gandhi, and Vreeland (2010).

| FIGURE 12.1 | **Classifying Parliamentary, Presidential, and Semi-Presidential Democracies** |

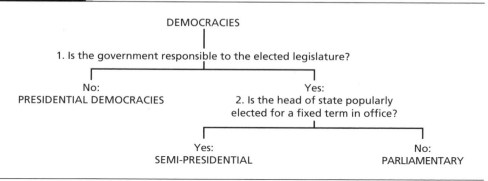

Source: Cheibub, Gandhi, and Vreeland (2010).

the various government departments. **Legislative responsibility** means that a legislative majority has the constitutional power to remove the government from office without cause. In those democracies that are characterized by legislative responsibility, the mechanism

> **Legislative responsibility** refers to a situation in which a legislative majority has the constitutional power—a vote of no confidence—to remove a government from office without cause.

that the legislature can initiate to remove a government is called the **vote of no confidence**. Basically, a vote of no confidence involves a vote in the legislature on whether the government should remain in office. If a majority of legislators vote against the government, then the government must resign.[2]

Some countries, such as Belgium, Germany, Israel, and Spain, adopt a slightly different version of this procedure called a ***constructive* vote of no confidence**. A constructive vote of no confidence requires that those who oppose the government also indicate who should replace the government if the incumbent loses. In effect, a successful constructive vote of no confidence removes one government from office and replaces it with another in a single step. One of the reasons for adopting a constructive vote of no confidence is that it tends to reduce government instability. As you can imagine, it is often easier to get people to vote against a government than it is to get them to agree on who should replace it. During the interwar period in Weimar Germany, it was relatively easy to build legislative majorities who opposed the incumbent government. It was extremely difficult, however, to construct and maintain majorities in favor of a particular alternative. As a result, governments tended to be extremely short-lived. It was in response to this that the postwar German constitution adopted the

2. Germany represents a slight exception. Article 81 of the German constitution allows a government that has lost a vote of no confidence in the lower house (Bundestag) to retain power for six months if it continues to enjoy the support of a majority in the upper house (Bundesrat).

A vote of no confidence is initiated by the legislature; if the government does not obtain a legislative majority in this vote, it must resign. A **constructive vote of no confidence** must indicate who will replace the government if the incumbent loses a vote of no confidence. A **vote of confidence** is initiated by the government; if the government does not obtain a legislative majority in this vote, it must resign.

constructive vote of no confidence. With this new provision, an incumbent German government can be brought down only if a legislative majority can also agree on an alternative government to replace it.

In addition to votes of no confidence, some countries have what is known as a **vote of confidence** (Huber 1996). A vote of confidence is similar to a vote of no confidence in that governments who do not obtain a legislative majority must resign. The difference is that votes of confidence are initiated by governments, whereas votes of no confidence are initiated by the legislature. You might be wondering why a government would ever call for a vote of confidence on itself. There are a number of reasons. For example, one has to do with the fact that votes of confidence can be attached to pieces of legislation in many countries. If a government is unsure about its ability to gain sufficient legislative support to pass some piece of legislation, then it can choose to make the vote on this legislation a vote on the continued existence of the government. Oftentimes, legislators who do not like the particular piece of legislation that the government is trying to pass may nonetheless decide to vote for it under these circumstances because they do not actually wish to bring the government down over it. This is particularly the case if bringing the government down means new elections and the possibility of losing their seats. Similarly, governments can employ votes of confidence in an attempt to unite a divided party or to humiliate critics who publicly criticize the government but who are unwilling to actually vote the government out of office. Of course, these tactical uses of the vote of confidence can backfire against those who use them if the government misjudges the willingness of its opponents to call its bluff and vote against the motion.

In sum, legislatures in democracies that exhibit legislative responsibility can remove governments by successfully passing a vote of no confidence, or by defeating a government-initiated vote of confidence. As Figure 12.1 illustrates, presidential democracies are not defined by the presence of a president. Instead, they are defined by the absence of legislative responsibility—the legislature in a presidential democracy cannot remove the government *without cause*.[3] Democracies that do have legislative responsibility—a vote of no confidence—are either parliamentary or semi-presidential. To help determine which, we must ask a second question.

Is the Head of State Popularly Elected for a Fixed Term?

To determine whether a democracy with legislative responsibility is parliamentary or semi-presidential, we need to know whether it has a popularly elected head of state who serves a fixed term in office. If it does, then it is semi-presidential. And if it doesn't, then it is

---

3. It is true that legislatures can sometimes remove members of the government in presidential democracies. However, this is only "for cause"—typically incapacitation or criminal behavior.

parliamentary. But what does it mean to have a popularly elected head of state who serves a fixed term in office?

A head of state is *popularly elected* if she is elected through a process where voters either (i) cast ballots directly for the candidate they wish to elect (as in Benin, Mexico, and the Philippines) or (ii) cast ballots to elect an assembly, sometimes called an electoral college, whose sole role it is to elect the head of state (as in the United States). Note that it is possible for a democracy to have an elected head of state who is not "popularly elected." For example, the German head of state is elected by the regional legislatures in Germany and is, therefore, not popularly elected by the voters. To *serve a fixed term* means that the head of state serves for a fixed period of time before she needs to be reappointed and cannot be removed from office in the meantime.[4] For example, Irish presidents serve a fixed term of seven years. In a democracy, the head of state is either a monarch or a president.[5] It should be clear by now that the presence of a presidential head of state is neither necessary nor sufficient for distinguishing between the three types of democracy—presidents can exist in presidential, semi-presidential, and parliamentary democracies. In contrast, the presence of a monarchic head of state in a democracy automatically indicates that we are dealing with a parliamentary democracy. This is because monarchs do not serve fixed terms and are not popularly elected.

As our discussion indicates, we can classify the three basic types of democracy in the following way:

- **Presidential democracy**: Democracies in which the government does not depend on a legislative majority to exist are presidential.
- **Parliamentary democracy**: Democracies in which the government depends on a legislative majority to exist and in which the head of state is not popularly elected for a fixed term are parliamentary.
- **Semi-presidential democracy**: Democracies in which the government depends on a legislative majority to exist and in which the head of state is popularly elected for a fixed term are semi-presidential.

> A **presidential democracy** is one in which the government does not depend on a legislative majority to exist.
>
> A **parliamentary democracy** is one in which the government depends on a legislative majority to exist and the head of state is not popularly elected for a fixed term.
>
> A **semi-presidential democracy** is one in which the government depends on a legislative majority to exist and the head of state is popularly elected for a fixed term.

---

4. Some democracies allow for the possibility of removing the head of state before his or her term is up but only through the extraordinary and costly procedure of impeachment or incapacitation.

5. It is worth noting that simply bestowing the title of president on a political actor does not necessarily make that actor a presidential head of state. For example, Kiribati, the Marshall Islands, and South Africa all have political actors that are called "presidents." The fact that these actors can all be removed from office through a vote of no confidence, though, means that they are not presidential heads of state. In effect, these actors are prime ministers, even though they go by the title of president (Cheibub 2007, 39–40).

An Overview

In Map 12.1 we show the geographic distribution of parliamentary, presidential, and semi-presidential democracies in the world as of 2015. Presidential democracies are shown in black, semi-presidential democracies in dark gray, parliamentary democracies in medium gray, and dictatorships in light gray. As you can see, presidential democracies tend to predominate in the Americas, particularly in South America. In contrast, presidential democracies are, with the exception of Switzerland, entirely absent in Europe, where there is a mixture of parliamentary and semi-presidential democracies. In Africa, democracies tend to be either presidential or semi-presidential.

As Map 12.1 indicates, the parliamentary form of democracy is the most common in the world. Just over 41 percent (51 out of 123) of the world's democracies in 2015 were parliamentary. The percentage of parliamentary democracies in the world has been much higher in the past, though, with fully 74 percent of democracies being parliamentary in 1978. Nearly 30 percent (36 out of 123) of the world's democracies were presidential in 2015, and the same percentage were semi-presidential. A striking change has been the rapid increase in the number and percentage of semi-presidential democracies in the world from 1946 to 2015. For example, out of the world's 34 democracies in 1946, only Austria, Finland, Ireland, and Iceland (11.8 percent) were semi-presidential. By 2015, though, fully 29.3 percent of the world's democracies were semi-presidential. In Table 12.1, we list those democracies that were parliamentary, presidential, and semi-presidential in 2015.

MAKING AND BREAKING GOVERNMENTS IN PARLIAMENTARY DEMOCRACIES

Having addressed the criteria for classifying democracies, we now try to give a more in-depth insight into how these different types of democracy operate in the real world. We do so by carefully examining how their governments form and survive. We start with parliamentary democracies.

The **government in a parliamentary democracy** comprises a prime minister and the cabinet. The **prime minister** is the political chief executive and head of the government in a parliamentary democracy. The **cabinet** is composed of ministers whose job it is to be in the cabinet and head the various government departments. In a parliamentary democracy, the executive branch and the government are the same thing.

The Government

The **government in a parliamentary democracy** is essentially made up of a **prime minister** and a **cabinet**. As an example, we show the 2015 Canadian government in Table 12.2. The prime minister (PM) in a parliamentary democracy is the political chief executive and head of the government. The position of prime minister goes under a number of different titles in various countries—"prime minister" in the United Kingdom, "chancellor" in Germany, and even "president" in the Marshall Islands. Here, and throughout, we will follow convention and refer to the political chief executive in a parliamentary system as prime minister.

Map 12.1

**Parliamentary, Presidential, and Semi-Presidential
Democracies around the World in 2015**

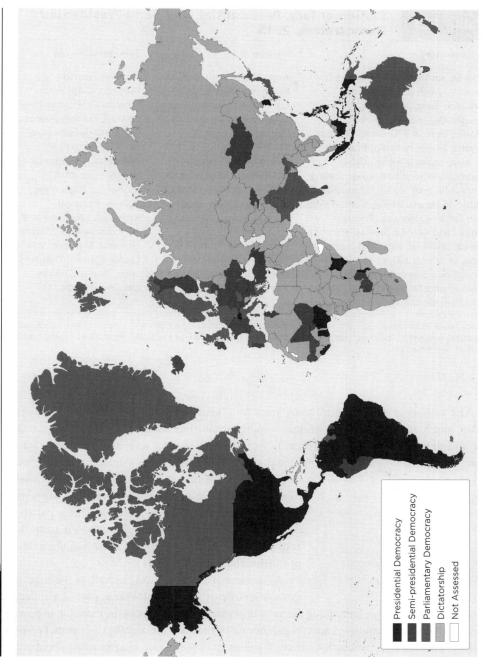

Presidential Democracy
Semi-presidential Democracy
Parliamentary Democracy
Dictatorship
Not Assessed

Source: Data for Map 12.1 come from Robert Elgie (http://www.semipresidentialism.com/?p=3097) and various country constitutions. Countries are classified as democracies or dictatorships using the criteria employed in the DD measure of regime type (see Chapter 5).

Table 12.1	**Parliamentary, Presidential, and Semi-Presidential Democracies, 2015**		
Parliamentary	**Presidential**	**Semi-Presidential**	

Parliamentary

Albania, Andorra, Antigua and Barbuda, Australia, Bahamas, Barbados, Belgium, Belize, Bhutan, Canada, Denmark, Dominica, Estonia, Germany, Greece, Grenada, Guyana, Hungary, India, Israel, Italy, Jamaica, Japan, Kiribati, Latvia, Lesotho, Liechtenstein, Luxembourg, Malta, Marshall Islands, Mauritius, Moldova, Nauru, Nepal, Netherlands, New Zealand, Norway, Pakistan, Papua New Guinea, Samoa, Solomon Islands, Spain, St. Kitts and Nevis, St. Lucia, St. Vincent and the Grenadines, Sweden, Thailand, Trinidad and Tobago, Tuvalu, United Kingdom, Vanuatu

Presidential

Argentina, Benin, Bolivia, Brazil, Burundi, Chile, Colombia, Comoros, Costa Rica, Cyprus, Dominican Republic, Ecuador, El Salvador, Ghana, Guatemala, Honduras, Indonesia, Kenya, Liberia, Malawi, Maldives, Mexico, Micronesia, Nicaragua, Nigeria, Palau, Panama, Paraguay, Philippines, Sierra Leone, South Korea, Suriname, Switzerland, United States, Uruguay, Venezuela

Semi-Presidential

Armenia, Austria, Bulgaria, Cape Verde, Croatia, Czech Republic, Finland, France, Georgia, Guinea-Bissau, Iceland, Ireland, Kyrgyzstan, Lithuania, Macedonia, Madagascar, Mali, Mongolia, Niger, Peru, Poland, Portugal, Romania, São Tomé and Príncipe, Senegal, Serbia, Slovakia, Slovenia, Sri Lanka, Taiwan, Timor-Leste, Tunisia, Turkey, Ukraine, Zambia

Source: Data from Robert Elgie (http://www.semipresidentialism.com/?p=3097) and various country constitutions. Countries considered to be dictatorships based on the criteria employed in the DD measure of regime type (see Chapter 5) are excluded.

The cabinet is equivalent in many ways to a "country's board of directors" (Gallagher, Laver, and Mair 2006, 40). The cabinet comprises ministers whose job it is to be in the cabinet and to head one of the government's various departments, such as Education, Finance, Foreign Affairs, and Social Policy. The department of which the minister is head is often referred to as the minister's portfolio. Each minister is directly responsible to the cabinet for what happens in her department. If a problem arises in a particular department, then the minister is supposed to be held responsible for it. This practice is known as the doctrine of **ministerial responsibility**.

As a member of the cabinet, as well as the head of a government department, a minister is part of a collective entity that is responsible for making the most important decisions about the direction of government policy. Cabinet ministers are typically bound by the doctrine of **collective cabinet responsibility**. This doctrine means that, although ministers may air their disagreements about policy

Ministerial responsibility refers to the idea that cabinet ministers should bear ultimate responsibility for what happens in their ministry.

Collective cabinet responsibility refers to the doctrine by which ministers must publicly support collective cabinet decisions or resign.

Table 12.2	Canadian Government in November 2015

Minister	Department	Minister	Department
Justin Trudeau	Prime Minister/Minister of Intergovernmental Affairs and Youth	Marie-Claude Bibeau	International Development and La Francophonie
Ralph Goodale	Public Safety and Emergency Preparedness	James Gordon Carr	Natural Resources
		Mélanie Joly	Canadian Heritage
Lawrence MacAulay	Agriculture and Agri-Food	Diane Lebouthillier	National Revenue
Stéphane Dion	Foreign Affairs	Kent Hehr	Veterans Affairs / Associate Minister of National Defence
John McCallum	Immigration, Refugees and Citizenship		
Carolyn Bennett	Indigenous and Northern Affairs	Catherine McKenna	Environment and Climate Change
Scott Brison	President of the Treasury Board	Harjit Singh Sajjan	National Defence
Dominic LeBlanc	Leader of the Government in the House of Commons	MaryAnn Mihychuk	Employment, Workforce Development and Labour
Navdeep Bains	Innovation, Science and Economic Development	Amarjeet Sohi	Infrastructure and Communities
William Francis Morneau	Finance	Maryam Monsef	Democratic Institutions
Jody Wilson-Raybould	Justice / Attorney General of Canada	Carla Qualtrough	Sport and Persons with Disabilities
Judy Foote	Public Services and Procurement	Hunter Tootoo	Fisheries and Oceans / Canadian Coast Guard
Chrystia Freeland	International Trade	Kirsty Duncan	Science
Jane Philpott	Health	Patricia L. Hajdu	Status of Women
Jean-Yves Duclos	Families, Children and Social Development	Bardish Chagger	Small Business and Tourism
Marc Garneau	Transport		

Source: "Full List of Justin Trudeau's Cabinet" (2015).

freely in cabinet meetings, once a cabinet decision has been made, each minister must defend the government policy in public. Cabinet ministers who feel that they cannot do this must resign, as Robin Cook did as foreign minister in the United Kingdom in 2003 when he disagreed with the government's decision to go to war over Iraq. This notion of collective cabinet responsibility stands in stark contrast to the behavior and expectations about cabinet ministers in presidential democracies. This is because cabinet members in presidential democracies are in charge of particular policy areas and are not responsible for, or expected to influence, the overall direction of government policy; that is the domain of the president and his staff.

Government Formation Process

In parliamentary democracies, citizens do not elect the prime minister or cabinet members; they elect only members of the legislature. So how, you might wonder, do governments actually form? Consider the results from the 1987 West German legislative elections shown in Table 12.3. Can you figure out what German government formed after these elections just by looking at the table? It's not obvious, right?

When thinking about the government formation process, it is important to remember that any proposed government must enjoy the "confidence" of the legislature, both to come to power and to stay in power. As we saw earlier, this is a defining characteristic of parliamentary democracies—governments must always enjoy the support of a legislative majority. In some countries, a potential government may have to demonstrate that it has such support before it can take office by holding what's known as an investiture vote (see Box 12.1, "Investiture Votes"). If the proposed government does not win a majority in this vote, it cannot take office. Even if there is no formal investiture vote, though, a potential government in a parliamentary democracy must still have the *implicit* support of a legislative majority at all times. This is because of the ability of the legislature to call a vote of no confidence in the government at any time. If the government ever loses such a vote because it cannot garner the support of a legislative majority, then it must resign. Ultimately, a parliamentary government can be removed from office any time a majority of legislators decides that this is what should happen. As a result, governments that come to power in parliamentary systems must always enjoy the implicit support of a legislative majority even if they never have to explicitly demonstrate this in an investiture vote or a vote of no confidence.

Table 12.3	West German Legislative Elections in 1987	
Party	**Seats**	**Percentage**
Christian Democrats (CDU/CSU)	223	44.9
Social Democrats (SPD)	186	37.4
Free Democrats (FDP)	46	9.3
Greens	42	8.5
Total	497	100

Notes: Data are from Adam Carr's webpage at http://psephos.adam-carr.net/.

Box 12.1   **INVESTITURE VOTES**

An **investiture vote** is a formal vote in the legislature to determine whether a proposed government can take office. The precise

> An **investiture vote** is a formal vote in the legislature to determine whether a proposed government can take office.

rules governing investiture votes vary from country to country (Rasch, Martin, and Cheibub 2015). Some constitutions require an absolute majority—more than half of all legislative members must vote for the proposed government. Other constitutions require only a plurality—more people should vote for the proposed government than vote against it. In Germany and Spain, a proposed government must win an absolute majority in a first vote of investiture but only a plurality if a second vote is needed. In Belgium and Italy, a new government requires only a plurality. If abstentions are allowed, they may count for or against the government, depending on the country. For example, abstentions count in favor of the government in Italy. As Strøm (1995, 75) reports, "Giulio Andreotti's famous [1976] government of *non sfiducia* ('non-no confidence') was supported by no more than 258 deputies out of 630. Yet Andreotti comfortably gained office, since all but 44 of the remaining members abstained."

If a single party controls a majority of the seats in the legislature, then one might expect that party to form a single-party majority government. In fact, this is typically what happens. Data from the Comparative Parliamentary Democracy (CPD) project, for example, show that a single party controlling a majority of legislative seats formed a government on its own 40 (85 percent) out of a possible 47 times that such a party existed in eleven West European parliamentary democracies from 1945 to 1998.[6]

But what happens when no single party commands a legislative majority, as in our West German example? This is, in fact, the normal situation in most parliamentary democracies. As the CPD data reveal, fully 219 of the 266 governments (82 percent) that formed in the eleven West European parliamentary democracies in the sample emerged from political situations in which no single party controlled a majority of legislative seats. As we shall see in more detail when we examine electoral rules in the next two chapters, the frequent use of proportional representation electoral systems in Europe helps to explain why so few parties ever win a majority of votes or seats. Only countries like the United Kingdom that employ disproportional electoral rules regularly produce single parties that control a legislative majority.

---

6. The countries included here are Belgium, Denmark, Germany, Greece, Italy, Luxembourg, the Netherlands, Norway, Spain, Sweden, and the United Kingdom. The Comparative Parliamentary Democracy project can be found at http://www.erdda.se/cpd/index.html (Müller and Strøm 2000; Strøm, Müller, and Bergman 2003). Data are from the March 2006 release.

We know that any potential government must implicitly control a legislative majority before coming to office. There are no rules about who should be in this legislative majority though. As a result, any legislator could conceivably be a part of the government's majority support and, hence, play a role in appointing the government. In practice, however, the tight discipline of political parties in many countries means that the actual business of forming a government tends to be done by a small group of senior politicians in each party (Gallagher, Laver, and Mair 2006, 49). These politicians typically include party leaders and potential cabinet members. After an election or the fall of a previous government, these party leaders bargain with one another, and a government forms as soon as enough party leaders have committed their support (and that of their party) for it to command a legislative majority. But can we say anything more about the government formation process and the type of government that these actors are likely to choose?

Table 12.4 illustrates all of the potential governments that could have formed in West Germany in 1987. It also indicates the number of surplus seats controlled by each potential

Table 12.4   Potential West German Governments in 1987

Party	Seats	Percentage	Surplus seats
CDU/CSU + SPD + Greens + FDP	497	100	248
CDU/CSU + SPD + Greens	451	90.7	202
CDU/CSU + SPD + FDP	455	91.5	206
CDU/CSU + FDP + Greens	311	62.6	62
SPD + FDP + Greens	274	55.1	25
CDU/CSU + SPD	409	82.2	160
CDU/CSU + FDP	269	54.1	20
CDU/CSU + Greens	265	53.3	16
SPD + FDP	232	46.7	−17
SPD + Greens	228	45.9	−21
FDP + Greens	88	17.7	−161
SPD	186	37.4	−63
CDU/CSU	223	44.9	−26
Greens	42	8.5	−207
FDP	46	9.3	−203

Note: "Surplus seats" indicate the number of seats controlled by each potential government that were not required for obtaining a legislative majority.

government that were not required for obtaining a legislative majority. For example, a coalition between the Social Democrats (SPD), the Free Democrats (FDP), and the Greens would have 25 "surplus" seats more than it actually needed to guarantee a legislative majority. In contrast, a coalition between just the SPD and the Greens would be 21 seats shy of a majority. One question you should ask yourself is whether all of these potential governments are equally plausible. To answer this question, you really need to know more about the exact process by which governments form in parliamentary democracies.

In principle, the head of state, either a monarch or a president, presides over the government formation process, and it is she who ultimately invests a government with the constitutional authority to take office.[7] The extent to which the head of state actively becomes involved in the actual bargaining varies from country to country. In some countries, the head of state is limited to simply swearing in the government proposed by the party elites. If there is an investiture vote, then the proposed government must demonstrate that it has a legislative majority. Once this is done, the head of state simply appoints the government. This government stays in power until the next election, until it loses in a vote of no confidence, or until it resigns. In other countries, the head of state plays a more active role by choosing a particular politician to initiate the government formation process. This politician is known as a **formateur**. It is her job to construct a government.

> A **formateur** is the person designated to form the government in a parliamentary regime. The formateur is often the PM designate.

In some countries, the constitution explicitly states who the formateur will be. For example, the Greek and Bulgarian constitutions state that the head of state must appoint the leader of the largest party as the formateur. If this person fails to form a government, then the head of state allows the leader of the second largest party to try to build a government by making her the new formateur. This process continues until a formateur successfully forms a government. Obviously, the head of state has little discretion in these countries because the election results determine the order in which parties get to try to form the government.

In other countries, the head of state is less constrained and can actually "choose" the formateur in a more meaningful sense. For example, choosing the formateur has been one of the more important duties belonging to the head of state in countries like the Czech Republic. Following legislative elections in June 2006, the Czech president, Václav Klaus, was able to influence the government formation process in a starkly partisan way because of his power to appoint the formateur. The Czech elections resulted in a dead heat in the 200-seat legislature: a coalition of left-wing parties won 100 seats, and a coalition of right-wing parties won 100 seats. The Czech president, who belonged to a right-wing party, appointed a member of his own party—Mirek Topolánek—to be the first formateur. When his nominated formateur failed to get his proposed government passed in an investiture vote that saw all

---

7. Our description of the government formation process in parliamentary democracies builds on Gallagher, Laver, and Mair (2006, 47–54).

100 legislators from the right vote for it and all 100 legislators from the left vote against it, the Czech president simply renominated the same person to be the next formateur. In somewhat dubious circumstances, Topolánek managed to win a second investiture vote even though he proposed the same government as before—he won the vote 100 to 98 when two left-wing legislators surprisingly decided to abstain rather than vote against the proposed government (S. Golder 2010).

In other countries, the ability of the head of state to engage in partisan politics is seen as inappropriate. This is typically the case when a monarch is the head of state. As a result, such countries have limited the power of the head of state to appointing an **informateur**. An informateur is someone

An **informateur** examines politically feasible coalitions and nominates a formateur.

who is supposed to lack personal political ambition and whose job it is to look at politically feasible coalitions and recommend people who would make good formateurs. The existence of an informateur means that the head of state is, at least theoretically, one step removed from the partisan nature of the government formation process. However, this has not always stopped monarchs, such as the Dutch Queen or Belgian King, from intervening more directly in the government formation process in an attempt to influence the final outcome (Andeweg and Irwin 2009; S. Golder 2010).

Despite the discretion enjoyed by some heads of state, it turns out that the first person appointed formateur is usually the leader of the largest party in the legislature (Bäck and Dumont 2008). In almost all cases, the formateur is also the prime minister designate.[8] All of this is to be expected, given that the leader of the largest party can often credibly threaten to veto any proposal by other possible formateurs. Once the formateur has been chosen, she has to put a cabinet together that is acceptable to a legislative majority.

The ability to nominate cabinet members is one of the most important powers held by the prime minister (formateur). In single-party majority cabinets, the prime minister has enormous discretion when it comes to making appointments to the cabinet and she is constrained only by the internal politics of her party. Politicians might be rewarded with cabinet appointments because they have demonstrated loyalty to the party or the prime minister, because they represent a particular ideological faction within the party, or because they have useful administrative skills. In some cases, a prime minister might feel that internal party politics require her to appoint internal party opponents to the cabinet. In fact, British Prime Minister Margaret Thatcher, later to be called the "Iron Lady," felt compelled to appoint a cabinet in which her own party supporters were in a distinct minority on first being elected in 1979 (Young 1990, 138). Still, even at this initial moment of relative weakness, Thatcher

---

8. A rare exception to this rule is the leader of India's Congress Party, Sonia Gandhi. Although the Italy-born party leader was the formateur during the government formation process that followed the 2004 legislative elections in India, she declined the prime ministership when it was offered to her.

(1993, 26) later recalled, "I made sure that the key economic ministers would be true believers in our economic strategy."

In coalition cabinets, the discretion that the prime minister has in nominating cabinet members is more constrained. Typically, party leaders in the proposed cabinet will nominate particular ministers to the subset of portfolios that have been allocated to their party during the initial stages of the government formation process. Although possible, it is rare to see the prime minister or party leaders veto a nomination by another party leader. On the face of it, this would seem to suggest that the leaders of each government party are generally free to pick the people they want for "their" portfolios. The fact that we do not see nominations vetoed, though, does not necessarily mean that party leaders have full discretion over who they nominate. It might simply be the case that objectionable ministerial choices are not proposed in the first place (Indriðason and Kam 2005). Given the considerable influence that cabinet members have over policy in their respective portfolios, party leaders will bargain hard, first over how many ministerial portfolios they get, and second over who should be appointed to these posts, before deciding whether to support the proposed cabinet.[9]

Once a cabinet has been formed, the support of a legislative majority may or may not have to be demonstrated by a formal investiture vote. If the investiture vote is unsuccessful, then the government formation process starts all over again; there may or may not be a new election before this happens. If the investiture vote is successful (or there is no required vote), however, then the head of state simply appoints the cabinet nominated by the formateur to office. At this point, the government is free to rule until it is defeated in a vote of no confidence or until a new election is necessary. If the government is defeated in a vote of no confidence or a new election is called, then the incumbent government remains in office to run the country as a **caretaker government**.[10] This caretaker government remains in office until the next round of the government formation process is complete and a new government is ready to take its place. In most countries, there is a strong

> A **caretaker government** occurs when an election is called or when an incumbent government either resigns or is defeated in a vote of no confidence. It rules the country for an interim period until a new government is formed.

constitutional convention that caretaker governments will not make any important policy changes to those in place when the outgoing government loses its parliamentary basis (Boston et al. 1998). As you can imagine, the fact that caretaker governments generally have no authority to make major policy initiatives can be problematic if the government formation process takes a long time. This is particularly the case if the government has collapsed as the result of some sort of political, economic, or military crisis.

---

9. In this chapter, we focus primarily on the parties that enter government, and not the individual politicians. However, scholars do examine how individual characteristics affect who gets appointed to the cabinet. For an example of the role that gender plays in ministerial appointments, see O'Brien and colleagues (2015) and Escobar-Lemmon and Taylor-Robinson (2016).

10. In Germany, the "constructive" vote of no confidence means that an alternative government must be proposed as part of a no confidence motion. As a result, there is no caretaker government in Germany if the legislature ever passes such a motion, because there is no interim period between governments.

A Simple Model of Government Formation

Now that we know more details about the government formation process in parliamentary democracies, we can return to our West German example from 1987. All of the potential governments were listed in Table 12.4. Given what you now know about the government formation process, ask yourself whether all of these governments are equally plausible. Who is likely to be the formateur? Helmut Kohl, the leader of the Christian Democrats (CDU/CSU), was appointed formateur as he controlled the largest party in the Bundestag. If you were Helmut Kohl, would you form a government that did not include your own party? The obvious answer is no. As a result, we can immediately eliminate those potential governments in Table 12.4 that do not include the CDU/CSU.

Now ask yourself whether any of the remaining potential governments are more plausible than others. The fact that a government must have the support of a legislative majority in order to come to power suggests that the government formation process may be easier if the proposed government actually controls a majority of legislative seats. As a result, you might think to eliminate those potential governments that do not have a positive number of surplus seats, that is, those governments that do not control a legislative majority.[11] Table 12.5 lists the remaining potential governments. Which of the seven remaining possibilities do you think is most likely to become the government? To answer this question, you should start to think about the goals of the political actors engaged in the government formation process. What do they want?

We can think about two types of politicians: those who are "office seeking" and those who are "policy seeking." When forming a government, an office-seeking politician will want to secure as many ministerial portfolios as he can. After the position of prime minister, cabinet positions represent the highest political posts in a parliamentary democracy. In effect,

Table 12.5	Potential Majority West German Governments Containing the CSU/CDU in 1987		
Party	Seats	Percentage	Surplus seats
CDU/CSU + SPD + Greens + FDP	497	100	248
CDU/CSU + SPD + Greens	451	90.7	202
CDU/CSU + SPD + FDP	455	91.5	206
CDU/CSU + FDP + Greens	311	62.6	62
CDU/CSU + SPD	409	82.2	160
CDU/CSU + FDP	269	54.1	20
CDU/CSU + Greens	265	53.3	16

---

11. As we'll see shortly, governments that do not explicitly control a legislative majority do sometimes come to power. You should start to think about how and why this might happen.

landing a cabinet portfolio is often a signal of a successful political career and is a prize that many politicians seek. Being in the cabinet brings power and fame. An **office-seeking politician** is interested in the "intrinsic" benefits of office. In contrast, a **policy-seeking politician** will, when forming a government, want to secure ministerial portfolios in order to be able to influence public policy. This type of politician is not interested in the "intrinsic" benefits of office; she does not want to be a minister simply for the sake of being a minister. Instead, a policy-seeking politician wants ministerial portfolios so that she can make a difference in how the country is run.

> An **office-seeking politician** is interested in the intrinsic benefits of office; he wants as much office as possible. A **policy-seeking politician** only wants to shape policy.

A Purely Office-Seeking World

Imagine again that you are Helmut Kohl, the CDU/CSU leader, in West Germany in 1987. If you lived in a purely office-seeking world, what government would you propose? To control a legislative majority, you know that you have to get the support of other party leaders because your party controls only a minority of the legislative seats. Because you live in a purely office-seeking world, you can win their support only by giving them offices. In effect, you say to them, "I will give you X ministerial posts in the government in exchange for your legislative support." You will obviously want to give them as few portfolios as possible, however, so that you can keep the rest for yourself. In order to win their support, you will probably have to give up more cabinet positions to a party leader who controls a large number of legislative seats than to a party leader who controls a small number of seats. In fact, there is strong empirical evidence that a prime minister must give portfolios to other parties in proportion to the number of seats that each party contributes to the government's total number of legislative seats (Laver, de Marchi, and Mutlu 2011; Warwick and Druckman 2001, 2006). This empirical regularity is known as **Gamson's law** (see "Portfolio Allocation and Gamson's Law" in Box 12.2).

> **Gamson's law** states that cabinet portfolios will be distributed among government parties in strict proportion to the number of seats that each party contributes to the government's legislative seat total.

One of the implications of the office-seeking logic that we have just outlined is that you will not want more parties in government than are strictly necessary to obtain a legislative majority. Thus, you will want to form a particular type of coalition government called a **minimal winning coalition** (MWC). A minimal winning coalition is one in which there are just enough parties (and no more) to control a legislative majority. Of the seven remaining potential governments in Table 12.5, there are three MWCs: (CDU/CSU + SPD), (CDU/CSU + FDP), and (CDU/CSU + Greens). In none of these coalitions is it possible to remove a party without, at the same time, giving up your legislative majority. A second implication of the purely office-seeking logic is that you will choose the smallest MWC, or the **least minimal winning coalition**.

> A **minimal winning coalition** (MWC) is one in which there are no parties that are not required to control a legislative majority. A **least minimal winning coalition** is the MWC with the lowest number of surplus seats.

| **Box 12.2** | **PORTFOLIO ALLOCATION AND GAMSON'S LAW** |

Gamson's law: *Cabinet portfolios will be distributed among government parties in strict proportion to the number of seats that each party contributes to the government's legislative seat total (Gamson 1961).*

Gamson's law predicts that if parties *A* and *B* form a government together, and party *A* has 80 legislative seats, and party *B* has 40 legislative seats, then party *A* will receive two-thirds of the ministerial portfolios because it provides 80/120 of the government's legislative seats, and party *B* will receive one-third of the ministerial portfolios because it provides 40/120 of the government's legislative seats. But what is the empirical evidence in support of Gamson's law?

In Figure 12.2, we plot the share of cabinet portfolios controlled by a government party against its share of the government's legislative seats, using data from fourteen Western European countries from 1945 to 2000. It should be immediately obvious that there is a strong positive relationship between the share of seats that a party contributes to a government's legislative seat total and the share of portfolios that it controls. This positive relationship, which is one of the most robust empirical patterns in all of political science,

| **FIGURE 12.2** | **Portfolio Allocation in Western Europe, 1945–2000** |

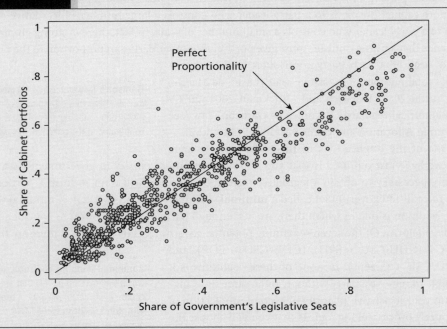

Note: Based on data from Warwick and Druckman (2006).

represents strong evidence for Gamson's law. Note, though, that this relationship is not *perfectly* proportional (Golder and Thomas 2014; Indriðason 2015). The solid black line in Figure 12.2 indicates the 1:1 relationship that would exist if portfolios were allocated proportionally. The gray circles tend to be above this line when a government party is small but below it when a government party is large, indicating that smaller parties tend to be slightly overrepresented in parliamentary cabinets and larger parties tend to be slightly underrepresented.

The fact that there is a slight bias in favor of smaller parties when it comes to portfolio allocation turns out to be a puzzle for political scientists. Most bargaining models that have been developed to explain government formation predict that large parties, not small parties, will do better when ministerial portfolios are allocated (Austen-Smith and Banks 1988; Baron and Ferejohn 1989). So, what is going on?

One possible answer is that although larger parties may be receiving slightly fewer ministerial portfolios than their size would predict, they are getting the more powerful ones such as the prime minister, the finance minister, the foreign minister, or the defense minister. In fact, there is some evidence that this is the case (Warwick and Druckman 2001). Another possible answer, though, has to do with the existence of the vote of no confidence in parliamentary democracies (Indriðason 2015). Rather than give their smaller coalition partners just enough portfolios to make them willing to join the government, large formateur parties may well see it in their interests to give them slightly more portfolios so that they will be less likely to leave the cabinet and trigger a vote of no confidence at a later point in time. By doing this, large formateur parties can expect to receive a slightly smaller share of the overall cabinet pie, but for a longer period of time (Penn 2009).

Evidence for this line of reasoning comes from a study by Golder and Thomas (2014) that began as an undergraduate honors thesis. The study looks at portfolio allocation at the national and subnational level in France. Although the vote of no confidence exists for governments at the national level in France, this is not the case for governments at the regional level. In line with their predictions, Golder and Thomas find that smaller parties received a greater share of portfolios at the national level (where the existence of the vote of no confidence leads large formateur parties to worry about government survival) than at the regional level (where the vote of no confidence is absent and formateur parties do not need to worry about government survival). The logic here also suggests that large formateur parties in presidential democracies, where votes of no confidence are absent, should, all else being equal, receive a greater share of portfolios than their counterparts in parliamentary democracies. This is precisely what Ariotti and Golder (2016) find when comparing ministerial portfolio allocation across Africa's presidential and parliamentary democracies.

The least MWC is the one with the lowest number of surplus seats. You want the least MWC because you do not want to "buy" more legislative seats by giving more cabinet posts to others than you strictly have to. This leads to the hypothesis that if the world is purely office seeking, then we should observe the formation of least minimal winning coalitions. In terms of our 1987 West German example, this means that we should expect the leader of the CDU/CSU to form a minimal winning coalition with the Greens because this MWC has the fewest surplus seats.

A Purely Policy-Seeking World

Imagine that you are Helmut Kohl again, but that you now live in a purely policy-seeking world. Which of the remaining potential governments in Table 12.5 would you propose? To answer that question, you will need to know something about the policy positions of the parties along the salient issue dimensions in West Germany in 1987. Figure 12.3 illustrates the policy positions, or "ideal points," of the four German parties with legislative seats on the left-right dimension of economic policy. As the leader of the CDU/CSU, you know that you must get the support of other party leaders in order to control a legislative majority. Because you now live in a purely policy-seeking world, you can win their support only by giving them policy concessions. This means that instead of being able to implement policy at your own ideal point, you will have to implement a coalition policy that lies somewhere between the ideal points of all your coalition partners. It is likely that you will have to make more policy concessions to win the support of a party leader who controls a large number of legislative seats than you will to win the support of a party leader who controls a small number of legislative seats. In other words, large parties will tend to be able to pull policy more toward their ideal point than small parties.

> A **connected coalition** is one in which the member parties are located directly next to each other in the policy space.

One of the implications of this logic is that you will want to form governments with parties that are located close to you in the policy space. Political scientists often refer to this type of coalition as a "compact coalition," or "connected coalition." A **connected coalition** is one in which all members of the coalition are located next to each other in the policy space. For example, a coalition between the CDU/CSU and the FDP is a connected coalition. A coalition between the CDU/CSU and the Greens, however, is not a connected coalition because a noncoalition party (the SPD) lies between them in the policy space. Of the seven remaining potential governments in Table 12.5, there are five connected coalitions: (CDU/CSU + SPD

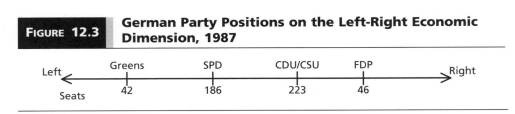

	German Party Positions on the Left-Right Economic
FIGURE 12.3	**Dimension, 1987**

+ Greens + FDP), (CDU/CSU + SPD + Greens), (CDU/CSU + SPD + FDP), (CDU/CSU + SPD), and (CDU/CSU + FDP). The parties in all of these coalitions are located directly next to each other in the policy space. A second implication of the purely policy-seeking logic is that you will choose the connected least minimal winning coalition. You want the connected least MWC because you do not want to "buy" more legislative seats with policy than you strictly have to. This leads to the hypothesis that if the world is purely policy seeking, then we should observe the formation of connected least minimal winning coalitions. In our West German example, this means that we should expect the leader of the CDU/CSU to form a coalition government with the FDP.

The Trade-Off between Office and Policy

The actual government formed by Helmut Kohl in 1987 was a coalition between the CDU/CSU and the FDP. This was the prediction from the purely policy-seeking logic. Does this mean that policy seeking dominates office seeking in Germany? There is a vast literature in political science that seeks to answer questions like this, but we believe that this sort of question is hard to answer empirically. Consider our example again. It is difficult to know if policy seeking really dominated office seeking in Germany, because the CDU/CSU did not have to give up too much extra office in order to get a coalition policy closer to its ideal point. In effect, the CDU/CSU preferred to give up slightly more office by forming a government coalition with the FDP (four extra surplus seats) in exchange for a coalition policy that was likely to be much closer to its ideal point than if it had formed a coalition with the Greens. In practice, we believe that politicians probably care about both office and policy and are, therefore, always making trade-offs. They are always asking how much extra office they should give up to get policy closer to their ideal point, or how much policy they should give up to get more office. If this is the case, then it probably makes little sense to categorize real-world politicians into purely policy-seeking or purely office-seeking types.

Even if politicians were purely office seekers or purely policy seekers, we believe that the reality of political competition would force them to act *as if* they cared about both policy and office. For example, a politician who wishes to affect policy must win office in order to be in a position to change policy. As a result, a purely policy-seeking politician will have to care about office, if only as a means to affect policy. Similarly, an office-seeking politician will realize that voters are unlikely to elect her if she cares only about office and being famous. A consequence is that an office-seeking politician will have to care about policy, if only to make sure that she wins election. Ultimately, this suggests that all politicians will act *as if* they care about both office and policy to some extent, which suggests that it probably makes slightly more sense to think that government coalitions are likely to be connected least MWCs rather than just least MWCs.[12]

---

12. Alexiadou (2016) theoretically and empirically distinguishes between three different types of cabinet ministers: ideologues, partisans, and loyalists. Although all care about policy and office, ideologues care more about policy, loyalists care mostly about supporting their party, and partisans prioritize office (that is, their own political success). She finds that partisans and ideologues (but not loyalists) are necessary to implement major policy reforms.

Different Types of Government

We know that a government in a parliamentary democracy must control an implicit legislative majority in order to come to power and remain in office. Up to this point, we have assumed that governments must contain enough parties that they *explicitly* control a majority of the legislative seats. In fact, the logic presented in the previous section suggests that governments should contain just enough parties to obtain this legislative majority and no more. It is for this reason that we have focused up to now on single-party majority governments and various forms of minimal winning coalitions. When we look around the world, however, we sometimes observe other types of government in parliamentary democracies—minority governments and surplus majority governments. Table 12.6 provides information on 266 cabinets that formed in eleven West European parliamentary democracies from 1945 to 1998. Figure 12.4 illustrates the percentage of cabinets of each government type and the percentage of time spent under each government type.

Table 12.6	Government Types in Western Europe, 1945–1998					
Country	Single party majority	Minimal winning coalition	Single party minority	Minority coalition	Surplus majority	Total
Belgium	3	16	2	1	11	33
Denmark	0	4	14	13	0	31
Germany	1	17	3	0	5	26
Greece	7	1	1	0	1	10
Italy	0	3	14	9	22	48
Luxembourg	0	15	0	0	1	16
Netherlands	0	9	0	3	10	22
Norway	6	3	12	5	0	26
Spain	2	0	6	0	0	8
Sweden	2	5	17	2	0	26
United Kingdom	19	0	1	0	0	20
Total	40	73	70	33	50	266

Source: Data are from the Comparative Parliamentary Democracy (CPD) project (Müller and Strøm 2000; Strøm, Müller, and Bergman 2003).

Note: Data do not include caretaker or nonpartisan governments.

FIGURE 12.4	**Government Types in Eleven Western European Parliamentary Democracies, 1945–1998**

a. Proportion of Governments of Different Cabinet Types, 1945–1998

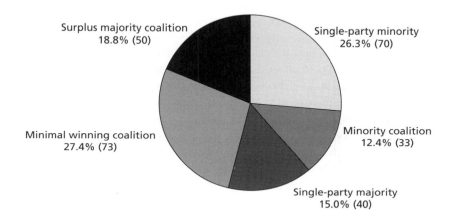

Surplus majority coalition
18.8% (50)

Single-party minority
26.3% (70)

Minimal winning coalition
27.4% (73)

Minority coalition
12.4% (33)

Single-party majority
15.0% (40)

b. Proportion of Time under Different Cabinet Types, 1945–1998

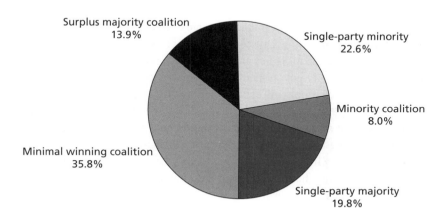

Surplus majority coalition
13.9%

Single-party minority
22.6%

Minority coalition
8.0%

Minimal winning coalition
35.8%

Single-party majority
19.8%

Source: Data are from the Comparative Parliamentary Democracy (CPD) project (Müller and Strøm 2000; Strøm, Müller, and Bergman 2003).

Note: Data do not include caretaker or nonpartisan governments. The numbers in parentheses indicate the number of governments of different cabinet types.

Minority Governments

A **minority government** is one in which the party or parties in power do not explicitly command a majority of legislative seats. Minority governments may be single-party minority gov-

> A **minority government** is one in which the governmental parties do not together command a majority of legislative seats.

ernments or minority coalition governments. You are probably wondering how a minority government could come to power and why it would stay in power in a parliamentary democracy. After all, the opposition in parliament controls enough seats that it could remove the government through a vote of no confidence whenever it wants to do so. A minority government can exist only as long as the opposition chooses not to bring it down. This means that whenever we observe a minority government, we know that there must be an implicit majority in the legislature that supports it.

In some countries, we know precisely who makes up this implicit majority because some nongovernmental party or parties publicly state that they will sustain the government against votes to overthrow it but that they do not want to actually be in the cabinet. In exchange, the government usually agrees to consult these "support parties" on various policy matters. This occurred in Britain in 1977 when the Liberals agreed to support the Labour Party when it lost its majority. This also occurred more recently after the 2010 legislative elections in the Netherlands when a populist far right party—the Freedom Party (PVV)—publicly agreed to support a minority coalition government made up of the People's Party for Freedom and Democracy (VVD) and the Christian Democratic Alliance (CDA). In other countries, the government does not rely on specific support parties but instead builds legislative majorities on an ad hoc basis. In effect, the government builds different majorities for each piece of legislation that it wants to pass. In these countries, it is not always easy to figure out exactly who in the legislature is keeping the minority government in power; all we know is that at least one of the nongovernmental parties must be helping it at any given point in time. One consequence of this is that it becomes difficult for voters to know who is responsible for policy and to hold them accountable for it.

For a long time, minority governments were seen as undemocratic. They were seen as something that should occur only infrequently and something that, if they did occur, should be short-lived. Strøm (1990) was one of the first political scientists to challenge this accepted wisdom. He argued that minority governments should be seen as a normal and "democratic" outcome of party competition in parliamentary democracies. One thing he illustrated was the high frequency with which minority governments formed in West European democracies and the relative stability that characterized these cabinets. As Figure 12.4a indicates, over a third (38.7 percent) of all governments that formed in West European parliamentary democracies from 1945 to 1998 were minority governments. In countries like Denmark (82 percent), Sweden (81 percent), and Norway (65 percent), minority governments were the norm in this period. In addition to their numerical frequency, minority governments have also been in power for long stretches of time. For example, minority cabinets have ruled in West European parliamentary democracies for more than a quarter (30.6 percent) of the postwar period (Figure 12.4b). Each minority government that formed remained in power for well over a year (539 days) on average.

Several theories have been proposed to explain the apparent puzzle of why minority governments exist. All of these theories point to the importance of policy in the government formation process. If politicians cared only about office, then it is hard to understand why any nongovernmental party would ever choose not to be in the cabinet when it has the power to force its way into it. In other words, why would nongovernmental parties ever allow a minority government to enjoy all the benefits of office without controlling a legislative majority? The simple answer is that they wouldn't. If politicians care about policy, however, then we can think of situations in which a party might decide that it can better achieve its policy objectives by remaining outside the cabinet.

Minority governments are more likely in countries where nongovernmental (opposition) parties have a strong say over policy. In some countries, the legislative committee system is structured to disperse policymaking influence to many groups, including nongovernmental parties. We would expect minority governments to be more likely when opposition parties can influence policy through legislative committees—because they don't need to be in the government to affect policy (Strøm 1990). A related explanation for the existence of minority governments comes from Luebbert (1984), who argues that the ability of opposition groups to influence policy depends heavily on whether a country provides a formal institutional role for key social and economic actors in making policy. For example, ministries in Norway and Sweden that contemplate legislative or administrative action that might affect a particular interest group are obliged to consult with that interest group before proceeding. Thus, the cabinet is only *one* of the sites in which fundamental social and economic decisions are made. As a result, we should see more minority governments in such countries because of the lower incentive for parties to enter government in order to influence policy.

You might be wondering why a party would ever choose to influence policy from outside the government rather than from inside it. Why not be in the government and enjoy the benefits of office while making policy? There are several reasons why a party might prefer to shape policy from outside the government. First, parties may be reluctant to take responsibility for the policies that will be implemented. Governing parties are much more likely to be held responsible for failed policies than opposition parties. By remaining in the opposition, parties can often achieve some of their policy objectives while being held less accountable if things go wrong. These types of concerns are particularly strong during periods of economic crisis when governments may have to introduce unpopular austerity policies. Second, a party may have made an election pledge not to go into government with certain parties. Breaking this promise might be electoral suicide at the next election. Third, opposition parties have more flexibility in choosing their campaign strategies in future elections because they do not have a past record in office to constrain them. These are all possible reasons why parties might choose not to be in government in countries that allow them to influence policy from the opposition benches.

Minority governments are less likely in countries that require a formal investiture vote (Strøm 1990). This is because potential minority governments face a higher hurdle to taking office than in countries in which no investiture vote is required. If a formal investiture vote is required, then opposition parties must choose to openly support a minority government, something that might be difficult to justify to their constituents. Some parties that would not necessarily support a particular minority government in a public vote, though, may find it acceptable to tacitly lend their support to a government if no investiture vote is required.

Policy divisions within the opposition also affect the formation of minority governments (Laver and Shepsle 1996). Minority governments can survive and be relatively stable when opposition parties are ideologically divided and cannot reach an agreement on a replacement. For example, the Congress Party was able to dominate Indian politics as a minority government for many years because the opposition parties on each side of it could not agree on a suitable replacement. A similar situation occurred with the Social Democrats in Sweden and the Christian Democrats in Italy. These parties were consistently able to form minority governments by being relatively large parties located in the middle of the ideological spectrum with opposition parties on either side.

Surplus Majority Governments

Although governments that appear "too small" (minority) often form, cabinets that appear "too large" (surplus majority) also emerge from time to time. A **surplus majority government** is one in which the cabinet contains more parties than are strictly necessary to control a legislative majority. In effect, the government could lose or remove a party and still control a majority of the seats in the legislature.

> A **surplus majority government** is one in which the cabinet includes more parties than are strictly necessary to control a majority of legislative seats.

Like minority governments, it is often thought that surplus majority cabinets are rare. The data do not support this view, however. As Figure 12.4a indicates, a little under a fifth (18.8 percent) of all governments that formed in West European parliamentary democracies from 1945 to 1998 were surplus majority governments. In fact, surplus majority governments have made up almost half the governments in Italy (46 percent) and the Netherlands (45 percent). In addition to their numerical frequency, surplus majority governments have also been in power for reasonably long stretches of time. For example, surplus majority cabinets have ruled in Western Europe for about 13.9 percent of the postwar period (Figure 12.4b). Moreover, surplus majority governments remain in power for well over a year (505 days) on average.

Several arguments have been proposed to explain the apparent puzzle as to why surplus majority governments form. Just as with minority governments, these arguments emphasize the importance of policy in the government formation process. If politicians were purely office seekers, then it is hard to see why surplus majority governments would ever form, because they require political actors to give up office when they do not have to. This implies that the existence of surplus majority governments must be a signal that policy matters.

Surplus majority governments often form in times of political, economic, or military crisis. These crisis governments are sometimes referred to as "national unity" governments. For example, national unity governments formed in Belgium, Germany, Italy, Luxembourg, and the Netherlands immediately after World War II. They also formed in several East European countries following the collapse of communism in 1989. A national unity government also formed in Iraq following the 2006 legislative elections. The belief is that only by bringing together parties from across the ideological spectrum and giving them a reason to be invested in the existing political system is it possible to resolve whatever crisis is afflicting the country. The goal is to put the everyday partisan, ethnic, or religious nature of politics on hold for the sake of the country's immediate future. Although governments of national unity often have strong popular support, this particular type of surplus majority government tends to be short-lived in practice. Political parties that are not required to sustain a legislative majority are often quickly pushed into opposition. The desire on the part of politicians to enjoy as much office and policy influence as possible essentially overrides the wishes of the electorate that parties work together to rescue a country from whatever ails it.

In some circumstances, the formation of a surplus majority government may actually be necessary to pass particular pieces of legislation. For example, constitutional amendments often require "supermajorities," which are made up of more than a legislative majority. If a government wants to pass a constitutional amendment that requires a supermajority, then it might choose to have more parties in the cabinet than are strictly necessary just to remain in power. Of course, the surplus majority government in this case does not actually contain more parties than are strictly necessary to pass the constitutional amendment. In fact, you might say that this type of government is "oversized" in name only and that in practice it is no different from a minimal winning coalition given its policy objectives. A country that often produces this type of surplus majority government is Belgium (Gallagher, Laver, and Mair 2006, 392). The Belgian constitution requires that laws affecting the relationship between different language groups in the country require the support of two-thirds of the legislators and a majority of each language group. This has led to several surplus majority governments in Belgium.

Another explanation for the formation of surplus majority governments focuses on the strategic interaction between coalition partners or between actors within parties. If a minimal winning coalition takes office, any party in the cabinet, no matter how small, can bring the government down simply by resigning. This situation allows for the possibility of blackmail by a single dissatisfied party (Luebbert 1984, 254). In particular, it allows a small party to extract significant policy concessions from its coalition partners in vast disproportion to its size simply because its votes are critical to the government's continued existence. To prevent this scenario from occurring, larger parties in the coalition may decide to form surplus majority coalitions so that the government is not automatically brought down if a single party decides to resign. Parties that lack party discipline and suffer from high levels of internal dissent may also choose to form surplus majority governments for similar reasons. In addition, the fact that parties typically agree on a set of coalition policies prior to forming the government—but ultimately have to implement these policies in some order—also creates incentives for surplus majority governments (Carrubba and Volden 2000). Consider two parties that agree on a set of coalition policies prior to coming to power. As soon as one of the parties has managed to implement the policies that it wants, it will have an incentive to defect from the government and bring it down if it does not like any of the policies still to be introduced. This incentive is reduced with a surplus majority coalition, because the defection of one party will not prevent the government from implementing the remaining policies.

Finally, parties may sometimes form surplus coalitions because they had formed a preelectoral coalition, publicly announcing their coalition intentions to voters (see Box 12.3, "Preelectoral Coalitions"). To avoid reneging on their campaign promise, even if one of the parties turns out to be unnecessary to maintain a majority, they form a surplus coalition.

Box 12.3   PREELECTORAL COALITIONS

So far we have assumed that parties in parliamentary democracies wait until after elections before thinking about what government to form. This, however, is not necessarily the case. The fact that single parties are unable to command a majority of support in the legislature in most democracies typically means that parties who wish to be in the government have to form some sort of coalition. In effect, parties can either form a **preelectoral coalition** with another party (or parties) prior to election in hopes of governing together afterward if successful at the polls, or they can compete independently and hope to form a **government coalition** after the election. Historically, political scientists have focused almost exclusively on the government coalitions that form after elections. Recently, however, scholars have begun to examine preelectoral coalitions as well (Blais and Indriðason 2007; S. Golder 2005; Gschwend and Hooge 2008; Ibenskas 2016b). In an analysis of twenty-three advanced industrial democracies, S. Golder (2006) shows not only that preelectoral coalitions are common but also that they affect election outcomes, have a strong impact on the government formation process, and have significant policy and normative implications.

A **preelectoral coalition** is a collection of parties that do not compete independently at election time. A **government coalition** is a coalition that forms after the election.

As with the governments that form after elections, the emergence of preelectoral coalitions is the result of a bargaining process among party leaders. For example, party leaders who wish to form a preelectoral coalition must reach agreement over a joint electoral strategy and the distribution of office benefits that might accrue to them. This may involve outlining a common coalition platform, choosing which party's candidates should step down in favor of candidates from their coalition partners in particular districts, or determining which leader is to become prime minister. But why form such a coalition before the election? Why not wait until afterward? The main reason is that forming a preelectoral coalition can sometimes be electorally advantageous, especially in countries with disproportional electoral systems that punish small parties.

Preelectoral coalitions can have a significant impact on election outcomes and government policies. Consider the following simple example. Imagine a legislative election with single-member districts in which there are two blocs of parties, one on the left and one on the right.

The left-wing bloc has more electoral support than the right. Suppose that the parties on the right form a preelectoral coalition and field a common candidate in each district but that the parties on the left compete independently. The left would most likely lose. In this example, the possibility arises that a majority of voters could vote for a group of left-wing politicians who support similar policies but that these politicians might still lose the election by failing to coordinate sufficiently. The result is that a right-wing coalition is elected to implement policies that a majority of the voters do not want.

This simple example might be considered a good description of what happened in the 2002 French presidential elections. It had been widely expected that Jacques Chirac, the president and leader of the mainstream right, would make it through to the second round of voting along with Lionel Jospin, the Socialist prime minister and leader of the mainstream left. The real question for months had been which of the two men would win the second round. Then, unexpectedly, the left vote was split among so many candidates in the first round that the Socialist leader came in third, behind the populist far-right politician Jean-Marie Le Pen. The French press described the event as an earthquake, and the French elections were for a couple of weeks the subject of worldwide speculation. In reality, there was little chance that Le Pen would be elected president, and Chirac easily won the runoff election two weeks later. Most analyses of this particular election focus on the disturbing success of the far right. This political "earthquake," however, had as much to do with the inability of the French left to form a coherent preelectoral coalition as it did with an increase in the strength of the far right. The result of the left's failure to form a preelectoral coalition was that the French electorate got a right-wing government implementing right-wing policies even though there was good reason to think that a relative majority of the voters wanted a left-wing cabinet—opinion polls at the time suggested that Jospin may well have won a head-to-head contest with Chirac if he could have just made it to the second round. Ironically, the popularity of the left-wing parties among the electorate may have emboldened their leaders to run alone rather than in a coalition—a decision that, in the end, led to their electoral failure.

Preelectoral coalitions also have important normative implications. One would like to think that voters choose their governments through the electoral process. A government, however, forms beyond the scrutiny of the electorate whenever the election does not produce a single-party majority government or whenever parties begin the government formation process after the election. In countries that employ proportional electoral rules, elections frequently serve "as devices for electing representative agents in postelection bargaining processes, rather than as devices for choosing a specific executive" (Huber 1996, 185). Voters often end up voting for a single, unaligned party, not knowing what, if any, government it would join. This disconnect between the voters and the government formation process in these countries is a problem, because it is not always clear whether the final coalition that takes office has the support of the electorate in a meaningful sense. Preelectoral coalitions can help to alleviate this problem by helping voters to identify government alternatives and to register their support for one of them (Powell 2000). By providing a direct link between the voters and the cabinet that proposes and implements policy, preelectoral coalitions help to undermine the criticism of parliamentary democracies that employ proportional representation electoral rules, namely, that governments lack a convincing mandate from the voters. We return to some of these normative issues in Chapter 16.

Duration of Governments: Formation and Survival

The government formation process in parliamentary democracies can be quite complex. Even if parties agree to go into government together, they still have to haggle over who gets which portfolio and what the government policy should be. This bargaining process can sometimes last a long time. In Table 12.7, we present information about the length of time in days that it typically takes governments to form after an election in eleven West European parliamentary democracies from 1945 to 1998.

As Table 12.7 indicates, there is considerable cross-national variation in the length of time that it takes to form a government following an election. If a single party obtains a majority of the legislative seats, then it is normally understood that this party will form a cabinet on its own, and the only question is who from this party will get which portfolio. This explains why it takes only about a week (8.7 days) on average for a cabinet to form in the United Kingdom, because it usually has a majority party. In countries in which many parties gain legislative representation, it can take much longer to form a cabinet, because it is not always obvious which combination of parties will be able to form the government, how these parties will allocate portfolios among themselves, and what the coalition policy will be. For example, the average length of the government formation process in the Netherlands is about three

Table 12.7	Duration of Government Formation Process after Elections, 1945–1998 (Days)			
Country	Minimum	Maximum	Average	N
Belgium	2	148	59.7	17
Denmark	0	35	9.4	22
Germany	23	73	36.4	14
Greece	3	19	7.5	8
Italy	11	126	47.3	14
Luxembourg	19	52	31.2	12
Netherlands	31	208	85.7	16
Norway	0	16	2.5	14
Spain	2	58	28.6	7
Sweden	0	25	5.7	17
United Kingdom	1	21	8.7	15
All	0	208	29.9	156

Notes: Data come from the Comparative Parliamentary Democracy (CPD) project (Müller and Strom 2000; Strom, Müller, and Bergman 2003) and cover governments that formed after an election between 1945 and 1998. Bargaining duration measures the number of days between the election and the day on which the new government is officially inaugurated.

months (85.7 days). For many years, the Netherlands held the record for the longest delay in government formation in Europe at 208 days. This record was recently broken by Belgium, though. Elections took place in Belgium in June 2010, and a new government did not enter office until the beginning of December 2011, more than 500 days later! This government formation process in Belgium is clearly an outlier. As Table 12.7 indicates, it takes, on average, about a month (29.9 days) for a government to form after an election in Western Europe.

Delays in the government formation process can have important implications for governance. You may recall that caretaker governments, which administer the affairs of state while negotiations are proceeding, do not generally have the authority to make major policy initiatives. This means that delays in the government formation process can be quite problematic, particularly if the previous cabinet has fallen because of some sort of crisis. Until a cabinet is finally formed, the identity of government parties, the allocation of portfolios to particular politicians, and the content of policy compromises among coalition partners have yet to be determined. The uncertainty that surrounds the future direction of government policy can have serious consequences on the behavior of economic and political actors, both domestic and international. For example, consider the seven-month delay in forming a government that followed the June 2006 elections in the Czech Republic (S. Golder 2010). By August, the Czech media were already reporting on the deleterious consequences of the prolonged period under a caretaker government. The *Prague Post Online* (Alda 2006, n.p.) wrote, "Lawmakers are getting nothing done, while legislation and important reforms rest in a state of limbo, including long awaited pension reform, the privatization of many state-owned companies, an overhaul of the country's Criminal Code, and the fate of the controversial flat tax. A nonfunctioning parliament costs taxpayers as much as 3 million Kč ($136,500) a day." A number of empirical studies paint a similar picture, finding that uncertainty over the government formation process affects exchange rate markets (Leblang 2002) and the types of assets that market actors choose to invest in (Bernhard and Leblang 2006). Delays in government formation have real consequences for many people.

Not only is there considerable variation in the length of time that it takes to form governments but there are also large differences in the amount of time that various governments stay in power. Of the governments that formed in eleven West European parliamentary democracies from 1945 to 1998, less than a quarter actually stayed in office for their maximum permitted term. On average, governments lasted only 60 percent of their permitted time in office. In Figure 12.5, we illustrate the average duration of governments in days by cabinet type. As one might expect, single-party majority governments last the longest at 910 days on average. Minimal winning coalitions last only slightly less time at 893 days. Both of these types of government last considerably longer (about a year in all) than minority or surplus majority governments.

In Figure 12.6, we illustrate the minimum and average duration of governments by country in days. As you can see, there is considerable cross-national variation in the length of time that a government stays in office. Governments last longest on average in Luxembourg

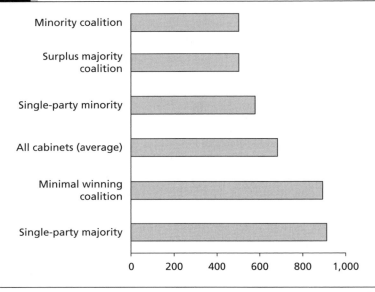

FIGURE 12.5 | **Average Parliamentary Government Duration by Cabinet Type, 1945–1998 (Days)**

Source: Data are from the Comparative Parliamentary Democracy (CPD) project (Müller and Strøm 2000; Strøm, Müller, and Bergman 2003).

Note: Data cover eleven Western European parliamentary democracies.

(1,170 days), the United Kingdom (981 days), and Spain (957 days). They last much less time in Italy (354 days) and Belgium (520 days).

Governments end for both "technical" and "discretionary" reasons (Müller and Strøm 2000, 25–27). Technical reasons are things that are beyond the control of the government. For example, a government might end because the prime minister dies or resigns due to ill health or because there is a constitutionally mandated election. In our sample of eleven West European parliamentary democracies from 1945 to 1998, 39 percent of governments ended for technical reasons. Discretionary reasons are political acts on the part of the government or opposition. For instance, a government might end because the government dissolves the parliament and calls early elections, because the opposition defeats the government in a vote of no confidence, or because conflicts between or within the coalition parties force the government to resign. These discretionary reasons are obviously not mutually exclusive. Of the governments in our sample, 61 percent ended for discretionary reasons. A quarter of the cabinets ended because the government called early elections (see Box 12.4, "Endogenous Election Timing"). Only 31 governments ended as a result of a parliamentary defeat. Still, not too much should be read into this relatively low number, because governments often resign in order to avoid being defeated in a vote of no confidence.

FIGURE 12.6	**Minimum and Average Duration of Governments, 1945–1998 (Days)**

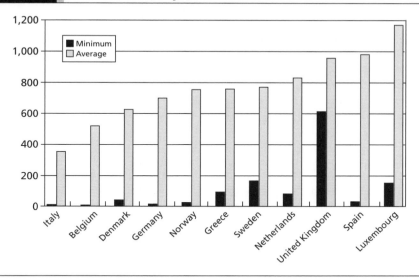

Source: Data are from the Comparative Parliamentary Democracy (CPD) project (Müller and Strøm 2000; Strøm, Müller, and Bergman 2003).

Box 12.4	**ENDOGENOUS ELECTION TIMING**

In some countries, the government gets to choose when it wants to hold elections. For example, governments in Sweden are constrained to hold an election at least once every four years but can choose exactly when to hold the election in this four-year window. We refer to this possibility as endogenous election timing. Three different stories have been proposed to explain the timing of elections. All three stories assume that politicians want to win elections and that voters hold governments accountable for their past economic performance.

1. *Political surfing*: The government waits until the economic conditions are right before calling an election. The government does not actively manipulate the economy but waits until the economy, for whatever reason, is at a high point before announcing the election (Kayser 2005).
2. *Political business cycle*: The government actively manipulates the economy to engineer a short-term economic high and then calls an election. The election is then followed by an economic decline. Thus, the economy goes through cycles of boom and bust that are politically driven (Clark 2003).

3. *Signaling*: The government is better informed about future economic performance than the voters and so can time elections to occur prior to any expected economic decline. In other words, the government calls early elections in order to cash in on its past successes by censoring the public's ability to observe the future decline. The very act of calling an early election, however, effectively sends a signal to voters that the future performance of the economy looks bad. If voters are naive or have short-term memories, or if the opposition is unprepared, the government may prefer to call an early election. Otherwise, governments might be reluctant to take advantage of good economic times by calling an early election because they want to avoid sending voters a signal that they don't expect the good times to last (A. Smith 2003).

Several different predictions can be derived from these stories. First, let's consider predictions about economic performance. Both the political surfing and political business cycle stories predict that elections are called when the economy is doing well, whereas the signaling story says that current economic conditions should not matter. Both the political business cycle and signaling stories predict that calls for early elections should be followed by economic declines (if for different reasons), but the political surfing story makes no prediction about future economic performance. The signaling story predicts that the support of the government in the opinion polls will fall if it calls early elections because voters learn that the government is about to produce bad economic outcomes; the other stories have nothing to say about the electoral support of the government. The signaling story predicts that the earlier an election is called, the greater the economic decline to come—why else risk losing office? The other stories make no such prediction.

Alastair Smith (2004) has tested these predictions on data from the United Kingdom and finds strongest support for the signaling story. He finds that when elections are called early relative to expectations, support for the government in opinion polls declines, stock market indexes fall, and postelection economic performance worsens. When elections are called especially early, he finds that postelection economic performance is particularly bad. There was little evidence that the current performance of the economy affected the probability that a government would call an early election. All of these findings are consistent with the signaling story but not the other stories.

Does it really matter whether or not a government survives for a long time? It is perhaps a natural reaction to think that cabinet instability is a bad thing, but why exactly might this be the case? You might think that governments that do not survive long result in policy instability and cabinet ministers who lack experience. It has long been known, however, that cabinet instability does not automatically imply ministerial instability. For example, Allum (1973, 119) found that a set of politicians had been "in office almost continuously for over twenty years" during the heyday of cabinet instability in Italy. Huber and Martinez-Gallardo (2004) also find that cabinet instability is not necessarily associated with high levels of turnover in cabinet membership. They measured cabinet duration, portfolio experience (the average amount of experience in days that ministers have in the specific cabinet portfolio that they hold), and political experience (the average amount of experience in days that ministers have in *any* significant cabinet portfolio) in nineteen democracies from 1945 to 1999. What they find is that cabinet duration is not necessarily the same thing as political or portfolio experience. For example, cabinets in the United Kingdom, Canada, and the Netherlands last quite a long time but have low levels of portfolio and political experience because of the frequent cabinet reshuffles in these countries (Indriðason and Kam 2005). In contrast, cabinets in Germany, Sweden, and Belgium do not last a long time, but they have relatively high levels of portfolio and political experience because the same individuals are often returned to the cabinet and their former ministries. Huber and Martinez-Gallardo's (2004) analysis suggests that we should, perhaps, be less concerned about what affects cabinet duration and more interested in discovering what influences the degree of portfolio and political experience in a country. Political scientists are only now beginning to look at this (Dowding and Dumont 2009).

MAKING AND BREAKING GOVERNMENTS IN PRESIDENTIAL DEMOCRACIES

While the literature on the government formation process in parliamentary democracies is vast and much has been learned, relatively little is known about government formation in presidential democracies. This situation has recently begun to change, though. A growing number of scholars are contributing to a promising and ambitious research agenda examining various aspects of governments in presidential democracies (Amorim Neto 2006; Amorim Neto and Strøm 2006; Chaisty, Cheeseman, and Power 2014; Cheibub and Limongi 2002; Cheibub, Przeworski, and Saiegh 2004; Escobar-Lemmon and Taylor-Robinson 2016; Martinez-Gallardo 2012; Martinez-Gallardo and Schleiter 2015). In this section, we summarize some of the principal lines of research that have been followed so far.

Government Formation Process

The **government in a presidential democracy** comprises the president and her cabinet. The **president** is the political chief executive and head of the government; she is also the head of state. The government formation process in presidential democracies is different in many important ways from that in parliamentary ones. First, and most fundamentally, legislative responsibility does not exist in presidential democracies. As a result, governments in presidential systems do not have to maintain majority legislative support to stay in office as they do in parliamentary systems. Second, unlike in most parliamentary democracies, there is no uncertainty about the identity of the formateur in

> The **government in a presidential democracy** comprises the president and the cabinet. The **president** is the political chief executive and head of state. In a presidential democracy, the executive branch and the government are the same thing.

presidential democracies. This is because the president is *always* the formateur, irrespective of whether her party does well or poorly in legislative elections. Coupled with the absence of legislative responsibility, this means that the president appoints whomever she wants to the cabinet (and dismisses them as she wishes). Third, the fact that the president is always the formateur means that the president's party must be included in each cabinet regardless of its legislative size. Note that this does not necessarily mean that the cabinet will exclude all other parties, just that it must include the president's party.

Finally, the "reversion point" of the government formation process is different in presidential democracies. A "reversion point" here refers to what happens when a minority formateur fails to form a coalition. In a parliamentary system, the failure of a minority prime minister to obtain an implicit legislative majority results in—or causes the actors to "revert" to—an early election, a new round of bargaining, or a caretaker government. In a presidential system, though, the failure of a minority president to win the support of opposition parties simply results in the president's party ruling alone. Recall also that elections occur at fixed intervals in presidential democracies; the president cannot simply dissolve the legislature when she wishes. As a consequence, members of the legislative delegation of a government party can often vote against cabinet-sponsored bills without the fear of forcing new elections (which they may lose). Consequently, a **portfolio coalition** (government) does not imply a **legislative coalition** in presidential democracies to the extent that it does in parliamentary democracies.

> A **portfolio coalition** is composed of those legislators belonging to parties in the cabinet. A **legislative coalition** is a voting bloc composed of legislators who support a piece of legislation.

These differences create particular incentives and opportunities that help to distinguish presidential governments from parliamentary ones. We will focus here on differences in the type and composition of presidential governments.

Types of Presidential Cabinets

In a parliamentary system, the prime minister must appoint a cabinet that enjoys an implicit legislative majority. We have seen that this does not necessarily imply that she must appoint a cabinet that controls a majority of legislative seats—opposition parties in the legislature may be willing to support minority cabinets on policy grounds. Clearly, presidents will form majority cabinets whenever their party controls a majority of the legislative seats. But what happens when the president's party is not a majority party? Presidents have no constitutional imperative to form majority cabinets—they are free to form minority cabinets whenever they want. Some of these minority presidential governments will rule with the support of an implicit legislative majority, just like minority governments in parliamentary systems; that is, some opposition party or parties in the legislature will support the government without receiving posts in the cabinet. Other minority presidential governments, however, will rule without this kind of support. This second type of minority government is not possible in a parliamentary system because of the existence of legislative responsibility. This difference suggests that, all things being equal, minority governments will be more frequent in presidential systems than in parliamentary ones.

The empirical evidence supports this claim. It is widely recognized that about a third of all parliamentary governments are minority governments (Strøm 1990). In contrast, Amorim Neto (2006) finds that 46 percent (49) of the governments in presidential regimes in Latin America from the late 1970s to 2000 were minority governments. This information is shown in Table 12.8. This difference in the frequency of minority governments in presidential and parliamentary systems is even more marked if we focus explicitly on minority situations, that is, situations in which the party of the president or prime minister does not control a majority of legislative seats. Data from Cheibub, Przeworski, and Saiegh (2004, 574) on minority situations in the world from 1946 to 1999 indicate that 65 percent of these situations resulted in minority governments in presidential democracies compared with just 35 percent in parliamentary ones.

The fact that presidents can appoint whomever they like to the cabinet might lead you to think that they would rarely form coalition governments. Indeed, Linz (1994, 19) predicts

Table 12.8	**Government Types in Presidential Systems (Late 1970s–2000)**				
Country	**Single party majority**	**Majority coalition**	**Single party minority**	**Minority coalition**	**Total**
Argentina	1	0	3	2	6
Bolivia	0	4	1	3	8
Brazil	0	11	0	4	15
Chile	0	5	0	0	5
Colombia	0	10	1	0	11
Costa Rica	3	0	3	0	6
Ecuador	0	1	4	15	20
Mexico	2	0	0	0	2
Panama	0	3	0	4	7
Peru	2	4	1	2	9
United States	2	1	2	0	5
Uruguay	0	6	0	0	6
Venezuela	1	1	3	1	6
Total	11	46	18	31	106

Source: Data are from Amorim Neto (2006).

that coalition governments in presidential democracies will be "exceptional."[13] Coalition governments would certainly be unexpected if political actors lived in a purely office-seeking world—why would they form a coalition and give up cabinet seats if they didn't have to? As we noted earlier, however, political actors are likely to care to some extent about policy or, at least, to act as if they care about policy. If this is the case, then it is easy to see why presidents might have an incentive to form coalition governments. The extent to which this incentive is felt will depend to a large extent on the legislative powers of the president.

> A **presidential decree** is an order by the president that has the force of law. The scope and extent of these decrees vary from country to country.

All presidents have the ability to issue a **decree**—a presidential order that has the force of law. The scope and strength of these decrees, however, vary from country to country (Shugart and Carey 1992). For example, decrees in the United States, known as executive orders, allow the president only to regulate and interpret statutes already enacted by the legislature and give orders to the public administration; the president cannot enact *new* laws. In other countries, though, presidents can issue "decree-laws"—decrees that immediately become law—even when faced with a hostile legislature. Presidents who have relatively weak decree power and whose party does not control a majority of legislative seats need support from other parties if they are to achieve any of their policy goals. As a result, these presidents will have an incentive to try to form coalitions. The bottom line is that coalition governments should not be exceptional in presidential systems for this reason. In fact, the empirical evidence suggests that coalition governments occur quite frequently in presidential democracies. Ariotti and Golder (2016) find that 49 percent of the governments that formed in Africa's presidential democracies between 1990 and 2014 were coalition governments. As Table 12.8 indicates, fully 73 percent (77) of the Latin American governments studied by Amorim Neto (2006) were coalition governments.

The frequency with which coalition governments form in presidential systems has led some scholars to conclude that "it is not true that incentives for coalition formation are any different in presidential than in parliamentary democracies" (Cheibub and Limongi 2002, 168). This conclusion is probably an exaggeration, however. Why? Much has to do with the "reversion point" that we mentioned earlier. If negotiations over the formation of a coalition government break down in a presidential democracy, the result is that the president's party gets to rule on its own. This implies that the president ultimately has the last word over policy in a way that is not true of a prime minister (Samuels 2007). In a parliamentary system, we have seen that the prime minister may have to concede control over particular ministries to her cabinet partners in order to be able to form a government (Laver and Shepsle 1996). In a presidential system, the president does not face the same need to make such policy concessions. This is particularly the case if he can use presidential decrees or

---

13. This kind of assumption, which used to be widespread, helps to explain why the study of government formation in presidential contexts is less well developed than in parliamentary ones.

vetoes to achieve his policy goals. Even if the president does make policy concessions in order to get opposition parties to join his cabinet, these policy promises lack a certain amount of credibility because the president has the right to dismiss these parties without losing office whenever he wants. Even presidential preelectoral coalition agreements are less binding than their counterparts in parliamentary democracies (Kellam, forthcoming). The ability of some presidents to use decrees and the inability of opposition parties to bring the government down therefore reduce the expected benefits (in regard to both office and policy) of opposition parties that are thinking about joining the government. The fact that legislators belonging to coalition parties can vote against government-sponsored bills without running the risk of causing the government to fall, however, implies that the costs (in regard to committing support to the government's legislative agenda) of belonging to a coalition may also be lower. Thus, although presidents may want to form coalition governments in some circumstances, it is not clear that they will always find willing coalition partners; if they do find coalition partners, they are likely to be less reliable.

Two implications follow from this logic. First, although coalition governments should not be exceptional in presidential democracies, they should be less common than in parliamentary ones. Again, there is some empirical evidence to support this. When examining minority situations in the world between 1946 and 1999, Cheibub, Przeworski, and Saiegh (2004) found that coalitions formed 78 percent of the time in parliamentary democracies but only 54 percent of the time in presidential ones. The second implication is that coalition governments in presidential systems may be more unstable and survive a shorter amount of time, all things being equal, than coalition governments in parliamentary countries. Alternatively, coalitions in presidential regimes may survive as long as coalitions in parliamentary regimes, but they may not govern as effectively because it is possible for a portfolio coalition to outlive the legislative coalition implied by its membership. To our knowledge, these last two hypotheses have not been tested. Can you think of how someone might test them?

The Composition of Presidential Cabinets

We have just illustrated that presidential democracies tend to be characterized by more minority governments and fewer coalition governments than parliamentary ones. It turns out that the composition of presidential cabinets also differs systematically from parliamentary cabinets. On average, presidents appoint cabinets that contain a higher proportion of nonpartisan ministers. A nonpartisan minister is someone who does not come from the legislature; he might be someone like a technocrat, a crony, or a representative of an interest group. On average, presidents also allocate cabinet portfolios in a less proportional way than prime ministers (Amorim Neto and Samuels 2006; Ariotti and Golder 2016). Table 12.9 provides empirical evidence in support of these claims from 30 parliamentary and 13 presidential democracies from 1980 to 2000.

In general, the composition of cabinets in any type of democracy will reflect the extent to which formateurs must negotiate with political parties. Although political parties exert

Table 12.9	Government Composition in Presidential and Parliamentary Democracies	
Democratic system	Average percentage of nonpartisan ministers	Average proportionality of cabinet portfolio allocation
Parliamentary	2.12	0.90
Presidential	29.17	0.65

Notes: Numbers are based on data from Amorim Neto and Samuels (2006). Proportionality is measured from 0 to 1, with 1 being perfect proportionality.

a relatively strong impact over the allocation of cabinet seats in parliamentary systems, this is not necessarily the case in presidential democracies. Prime ministers almost always appoint partisan ministers—individuals from political parties in the legislature—to the cabinet as a way of building the legislative majority that they need to stay in power. As we saw earlier, it is for precisely the same reason that prime ministers tend to allocate cabinet seats in proportion to the seats each party provides to the government coalition. Recall that this was the basis for Gamson's law. Because presidents do not depend on having a legislative majority to stay in office, they do not have to negotiate with political parties to the same extent as prime ministers. As a result, they are much freer to vary both the partisan nature and the proportionality of their cabinets. The policy positions and types of parties in the legislature also affect the degree of flexibility that presidents have in making cabinet appointments. Kellam (2015) distinguishes between programmatic parties that have strong policy interests and particularistic or clientelistic parties that simply want resources for their supporters. She finds that presidents who need support to pass their legislation tend to form coalition governments when confronted with programmatic parties, but they head minority cabinets and use government transfers when confronted with particularistic parties.

On the whole, presidential democracies have fewer partisan ministers and lower cabinet proportionality than parliamentary ones. Some presidential cabinets, however, look more like parliamentary ones than others. This is because of the variation in the legislative powers of presidents that we mentioned earlier. Presidents can choose to achieve their policy goals either through the legislature or through decrees. Those presidents who have relatively weak decree power, whose parties in the legislature are quite small and whose parties exhibit low levels of party discipline, appoint cabinets that look more like those found in parliamentary democracies—more partisan ministers and a more proportional allocation of cabinet portfolios—because they rely on winning the support of opposition parties to pass their policies. As Table 12.10 illustrates, there is considerable variation in the extent to which presidents appoint partisan and proportional cabinets. Cabinets tend to be very partisan and highly proportional in countries like Costa Rica, Mexico, and the United States but much less so in countries like Brazil, Peru, and Venezuela. Amorim Neto (2006) has shown that this

Table 12.10	**Government Composition in Presidential Systems (Late 1970s–2000)**	
Country	Average percentage of nonpartisan ministers	Average proportionality of cabinet portfolio allocation[†]
Argentina	7.2	0.89
Bolivia	20.5	0.73
Brazil	46.9	0.50
Chile	6.7	0.85
Colombia	5.6	0.87
Costa Rica	1.8	0.98
Ecuador	65.3	0.27
Mexico	3.6	0.96
Panama	17.8	0.71
Peru	40.8	0.54
Uruguay	1.5	0.77
United States	0	0.91
Venezuela	43.7	0.56
Total	29.2	0.64

Source: Data are from Amorim Neto (2006).

[†]The proportionality of cabinet portfolio allocation refers to the extent to which government parties receive the same percentage of cabinet posts as the percentage of legislative seats they provide to the government's seat total.

variation is systematically related to the need of presidents to negotiate with opposition parties to achieve their policy objectives.

MAKING AND BREAKING GOVERNMENTS IN SEMI-PRESIDENTIAL DEMOCRACIES

A semi-presidential democracy is one in which the government depends on the legislature to stay in power and in which the head of state is popularly elected for a fixed term. As with presidential democracies, there has been relatively little research that addresses government formation in specifically semi-presidential democracies. This is likely to change with the growing number of countries that have become semi-presidential democracies in recent years. In Eastern Europe, Armenia, Bulgaria, Croatia, Georgia, Kyrgyzstan, Lithuania, Macedonia, Poland, Romania, Russia, Serbia, Slovakia, and Ukraine all adopted semi-presidential forms of democracy following their democratic transitions in the late 1980s and early 1990s.

There are two basic types of semi-presidential democracy. In both types, the government comprises a prime minister and a cabinet. In a **premier-presidential system**, the government is responsible to the legislature but not the president. In a **president-parliamentary system**, the government is responsible to the legislature and the president.

It turns out that there are actually two different types of semi-presidential democracy: **premier-presidential systems** and **president-parliamentary systems** (Elgie 2011; Shugart and Carey 1992). In both types of semi-presidential system, the government, which comprises a prime minister and a cabinet, is responsible to the legislature. The distinction between the systems comes with respect to whether the government is also responsible to the president or not. In a premier-presidential system, the presidential head of state has no power to remove the government; that is, there is no "presidential responsibility." To a large extent, premier-presidential systems look and function like parliamentary democracies with a presidential head of state. The only difference is that the presidential head of state is popularly elected in a premier-presidential democracy but not in a parliamentary one. In fact, the similarity between the two systems has led some scholars to classify premier-presidential systems as parliamentary democracies rather than as their own separate category (Cheibub 2007). As the name *premier-presidential* suggests, the reins of power are firmly with the "premier" or prime minister in these systems, and the president is not considered part of the executive; the executive comprises just the government, that is, the prime minister and the cabinet. Examples of premier-presidential democracies include Ireland, Armenia, Portugal, Mali, Mongolia, and Cape Verde.

In contrast, the presidential head of state in a president-parliamentary system does have the power to remove the government. In other words, these systems are characterized by both legislative responsibility *and* presidential responsibility. As the name *president-parliamentary* might suggest, the president is a much more powerful figure in this type of semi-presidential democracy, and the government must take greater account of her policy preferences. Although the president is not part of the government itself, she is part of the executive—the executive comprises the government and the president. On the whole, both the president and the prime minister are involved in the day-to-day administration of the state. The precise way in which executive power is divided between the president and the prime minister varies from one president-parliamentary democracy to another. It is often the case, however, that the president has more influence in matters of foreign policy, whereas the prime minister is more powerful in domestic politics. For example, a political convention has evolved to some extent in France in that the president is responsible for foreign policy and the prime minister for domestic policy. In other countries, this type of division of power is more clearly stated in the constitution. Examples of president-parliamentary democracies include France, Taiwan, Senegal, and Kyrgyzstan. Table 12.11 summarizes the responsibility of the government in both kinds of semi-presidential democracies, compared with the responsibility of the government in parliamentary and presidential ones.

Given that premier-presidential systems effectively function like parliamentary democracies, we focus our attention in the rest of this section on president-parliamentary systems. It is worth noting that it is common for scholars to equate semi-presidentialism with its

Table 12.11	Responsibility of Government in Each Type of Democracy			
	Parliamentary	Semi-presidential		Presidential
Responsible to:		Premier-presidential	President-parliamentary	
Legislature	YES	YES	YES	NO
President	NO	NO	YES	YES

president-parliamentary version. As a result, debates about the advantages and disadvantages of semi-presidentialism are often ones about the virtues and vices of president-parliamentary systems, not premier-presidential systems.

Given that presidents in president-parliamentary systems are popularly elected, there is nothing to guarantee that the president and the prime minister will come from the same political party. Periods in which politicians from different political parties or blocs hold the presidency and prime ministership are often referred to as **cohabitation**. During cohabitation, the president's party is in the legislative opposition rather than the cabinet. Given that the president nearly always gets to appoint the prime minister in semi-presidential democracies, you might wonder why the president would ever appoint a prime minister from an opposing political party. The answer has to do with the fact that the government (prime minister and cabinet) must enjoy the support of a legislative majority to remain in office. Thus, a president may need to appoint a prime minister from an opposition party when the president's party or political bloc does not control a majority of legislative seats. In effect, the potential for cohabitation results from the duality of the executive—a president who is not elected by the legislature, and a prime minister who must enjoy a legislative majority.

> **Cohabitation**—a president from one political bloc and a prime minister from another—occurs when the party of the president does not control a majority in the legislature and is not represented in the cabinet.

At first glance, cohabitation sounds very similar to divided government in the context of presidential democracies. Cohabitation, though, is not the same as divided government. Indeed, cohabitation is effectively impossible in a presidential democracy. The reason for this is that unlike in a semi-presidential democracy, a president in a presidential system is free to appoint whomever she likes to the cabinet (and the legislature is able to appoint whomever it wants as its presiding officers). To make things a little clearer, consider the United States in 2011 after the Republicans had regained control of the House of Representatives from the Democrats. If the United States had allowed for cohabitation, then the new Republican speaker of the House, John Boehner, would have been able to remove the cabinet appointed by the Democratic president, Barack Obama, and replace it with a cabinet of his own choosing. This was not possible, though. The United States of 2011 had divided government, not cohabitation.

France has experienced three periods of cohabitation since 1986. Cohabitation could have occurred even earlier, in 1981, when a Socialist president, François Mitterrand, was voted into office (for a seven-year term) by the French electorate; at that time the legislature was controlled by a right-wing coalition. On coming to office, though, Mitterrand used his constitutional power to dissolve the legislature and call new legislative elections. In these elections, Mitterrand's Socialist Party won an absolute majority of seats (for a five-year term), thereby preempting a period of cohabitation. France's first experience with cohabitation came just five years later when a right-wing coalition won a two-seat majority in the constitutionally mandated legislative elections in 1986. Despite the small size of the legislative majority, Mitterrand was forced to appoint Jacques Chirac, the leader of the main right-wing party, as prime minister because a left-wing prime minister would have been unacceptable to the right-wing majority in the legislature. An uneasy two-year period of cohabitation ensued in which each leader felt constrained by the powers of the other. This initial period of cohabitation came to an end in 1988 when Mitterrand defeated Chirac in presidential elections. Mitterrand immediately dissolved the legislature, and the Socialist Party won a sufficient number of legislative seats for him to be able, with the help of some centrist legislators, to appoint a left-wing prime minister.

In 1993 President Mitterrand found himself in a similar position to that in 1986, when a right-wing coalition won an 80 percent majority of the seats in the legislative elections. Mitterrand was again forced to appoint a right-wing politician, Édouard Balladur, to be prime minister. This second period of cohabitation ended when the right-wing candidate Jacques Chirac was elected president in 1995. Because the right already controlled a legislative majority, Chirac was able to appoint a right-wing prime minister. This alignment of a right-wing president and a right-wing legislature should have lasted until the normally scheduled legislative elections in 1998. President Chirac made the ill-fated decision, however, to dissolve the legislature and call early elections in a strategic attempt to build more support for his reform policies. Chirac's plan backfired, and the left won the 1997 legislative elections. As a result, Chirac was forced to appoint the leader of the Socialist Party, Lionel Jospin, as prime minister. Jospin remained prime minister until 2002, when Chirac was reelected president. On winning the presidential elections, Chirac immediately dissolved the legislature. Chirac's right-wing party won an overwhelming majority in the legislative elections that followed, allowing Chirac to appoint a right-wing prime minister and end France's third period of cohabitation after five years.

For much of the history of the French Fifth Republic, it was thought that the president was the dominant political figure in French politics. The constitution provides the president with significant powers, such as the power to appoint the prime minister, the authority to dissolve the legislature (not more than once a year), and the ability to take on emergency powers if the integrity of France's territory is under threat. Until 1986, the president seemed to dominate both domestic and foreign policy in France. The first period of cohabitation, though, quickly revealed that the dominance of the French president prior to 1986 was not automatic but was, in fact, contingent on the president's controlling a majority in the legislature. Without a legislative majority, the president is forced to defer on domestic politics and, to some extent, on foreign policy, to the prime minister. In periods of cohabitation, France functions very much like a parliamentary democracy with executive power in the hands of the prime minister and the cabinet. This has led some to claim that the president-parliamentary version of semi-presidentialism is, at least in the case of France, just an alternation between presidential and parliamentary forms of government, depending on whether the president controls a legislative majority or not (Duverger 1980).

Other semi-presidential democracies, such as Ukraine's, have also experienced cohabitation. In 2006 President Viktor Yushchenko was forced to appoint his political rival, Viktor Yanukovych, as prime minister. The rivalry between these two men dates back at least as far as the 2004 presidential elections, when the pro-Western Yushchenko eventually defeated the pro-Russian Yanukovych in rather controversial circumstances. During the bitter and often violent presidential electoral campaign, Yushchenko became extremely ill, and it was later alleged that he had been poisoned with dioxin, possibly by elements associated with the Russian Federal Security Service. Neither candidate won the required majority in the first round of voting to be elected president. The second round of voting, which was marred by significant electoral fraud, saw Yanukovych declared president. Due to electoral irregularities, Yushchenko and his supporters refused to recognize the results. Following thirteen days of protest that became known as the Orange Revolution, the Ukrainian Supreme Court overturned the election results and ordered a rerun of the second round runoff, which Yushchenko eventually won. A year and a half later, the Party of Regions, led by Yanukovych, won the most seats in the 2006 legislative elections.

Despite the obvious personal hostility between the two men, the election results forced Yushchenko and Yanukovych to reach a compromise. Yushchenko eventually appointed Yanukovych to be prime minister in a coalition government that included both men's parties. Relations between the president and the prime minister were not smooth during this period of cohabitation, with both actors involved in an apparent power struggle. In April 2007, President Yushchenko dissolved parliament and called for new elections

AP Photo/RTR Russian Channel

Viktor Yushchenko, a Western-leaning reformer (*right*), and Prime Minister Viktor Yanukovych, seen as an ally of Russia (*left*), appear in a television debate in Ukraine's capital, Kiev, on Monday, November 15, 2004, between the first and second rounds of the presidential elections. Due to allegations of voter fraud following the second round, an unprecedented third round was held, and Yushchenko eventually took office in January 2005.

that he hoped would reduce the power of Yanukovych. This decision plunged Ukraine into a political crisis, with legislators calling it a coup d'état. Eventually, both the president and the prime minister agreed to hold new elections in an attempt to end weeks of political deadlock. Parties aligned with President Yushchenko won these elections, and the period of cohabitation came to an end. Although periods of cohabitation in semi-presidential democracies can often be characterized as an effective system of checks and balances, this example from Ukraine illustrates that cohabitation can also be characterized by bitter and violent conflict when the political actors involved share starkly different ideologies and goals.[14]

Few studies have examined the composition of governments in president-parliamentary democracies. One study, though, comes from Amorim Neto and Strøm (2006). They argue that, although the government formation process varies across president-parliamentary democracies, it is perhaps appropriate to think that both the president and the prime minister have de facto vetoes over cabinet appointments. Thus, the president is not as strong as he would be in a presidential democracy, and the prime minister is not as strong as she would be in a parliamentary one. This suggests that we might expect president-parliamentary democracies to possess both parliamentary and presidential characteristics when it comes to the composition of cabinets. An implication of this is that cabinets in president-parliamentary democracies should be characterized by fewer partisan ministers and a lower proportionality in the allocation of portfolios than in parliamentary regimes but more partisan ministers and a higher proportionality in the allocation of portfolios than in presidential regimes. In fact, this is precisely what Amorim Neto and Strøm find in their study of parliamentary and semi-presidential democracies in Europe during the 1990s. As with presidential democracies, we would expect there to be variation in cabinet partisanship and proportionality across different president-parliamentary democracies. For example, when the president's party controls a legislative majority, we would expect cabinets in a president-parliamentary democracy to look more like those commonly found in a presidential democracy. In contrast, when the president is faced by a legislature dominated by an opposition party, we would expect cabinets in a president-parliamentary democracy to look more like those commonly found in a parliamentary democracy. The historical experience of the government formation process in France seems to bear this out.

Scholars are beginning to explore the duration and stability of president-parliamentary democracies as well. The conventional wisdom has held that president-parliamentary institutional arrangements are a dangerous choice for new democracies, and the struggles

---

14. The political situation in Ukraine remains tense today. Yanukovych finally became president after winning the 2010 presidential elections. In 2014, large crowds of Ukrainians took to the streets to protest Yanukovych's pro-Russian policies and his decision to renege on an association agreement with the European Union. These protests, known as the Euromaidan protests, turned violent and President Yanukovych was forced to flee the country and seek sanctuary in Russia. Russia, which called the overthrow of Yanukovych a coup d'état, refused to recognize the new Ukrainian government and annexed Ukraine's Crimean Peninsula. The Ukrainian government is currently engaged in armed conflict with pro-Russian forces in the east of the country.

between the president and the prime minister during cohabitation in Ukraine, mentioned above, help to explain why this would be the case (Elgie 2011). Some recent work, though, suggests that we do not yet have a complete understanding of how executive-legislative relations in president-parliamentary democracies affect government and regime stability. For example, Schleiter and Morgan-Jones (2009) find that if we take account of government attributes and the constitutional rules surrounding the dissolution of the legislature, then governments in president-parliamentary democracies are no less stable than governments in parliamentary democracies. Given the recent proliferation of semi-presidential democracies, additional research on the consequences of this set of institutions will be important for scholars and policymakers alike.

A UNIFYING FRAMEWORK: PRINCIPAL-AGENT AND DELEGATION PROBLEMS

To a large extent, parliamentary, presidential, and semi-presidential democracies can be viewed as different systems of delegation. **Delegation** occurs when one person or group, called the **principal**, relies on another person or group, called an **agent**, to act on the principal's behalf. Delegation is ubiquitous in both political and nonpolitical settings. In our private lives, we often delegate tasks to agents with specialized knowledge, such as when we go to a doctor to solve a medical issue or a mechanic to fix a car. In this setting, the patient or customer is the principal, and the doctor or mechanic is the agent. In the political sphere (at least in democracies), we, the voters, are the ultimate principals, and we delegate the task of making public policy to our agents, our political representatives. It may have been possible in Ancient Greece for citizens to participate directly in the making of public policy. However, as populations have grown and the complexity of governing has increased, it has been necessary to shift away from **direct democracy** to **representative democracy** where citizens delegate policymaking powers to their representatives. Citizens simply do not have the time or expertise to make all of the necessary policy decisions in a country anymore.

> **Delegation** occurs when one person or group, called the **principal**, relies on another person or group, called an **agent**, to act on the principal's behalf.
>
> **Direct democracy** is a form of government in which people collectively make decisions for themselves. **Representative democracy** is a form of government where citizens delegate power to elected individuals to represent them and act on their behalf.

Consider the form of delegation adopted by parliamentary democracies. At election time, voters (principal) delegate policymaking power to their representatives (agents) in the legislature. At this point, the government formation process begins, and the legislators, who can be thought of as the new principal, delegate policymaking power to a prime minister (agent). Within the cabinet, the prime minister (principal) then delegates policymaking power in particular areas to individual cabinet ministers (agents). This process of delegation continues, with cabinet ministers (principal) then delegating policymaking and policy-implementing power to civil servants or bureaucrats (agents) within their government departments. In effect, parliamentary democracy represents a long chain of delegation going from the voters, the original principal, to civil servants, the ultimate agents. This "single-chain" delegation model of parliamentary democracy is illustrated in Figure 12.7a. In each link of the chain, a principal, in whom authority is placed, delegates to an agent, whom the principal has conditionally authorized to act on her behalf (Strøm, Müller, and Bergman 2003). At each step of the delegation chain, the agent is accountable to the principal to the extent that the principal exerts some control over the agent. For example, voters can refuse to vote for an incumbent legislator if the politician did not perform well in office, the legislature can oust a government with a vote of no confidence if the government is performing poorly, and the doctrine of ministerial responsibility may require a minister to resign if something goes seriously wrong in her ministry. Note that this chain of delegation is indirect in that voters get to directly choose their legislators, but all of the other agents are only indirectly chosen and therefore only indirectly accountable to the voters.

In a presidential system, voters delegate policymaking power to a legislature *and* a president. The legislature and the president are then required to bargain, or transact, with each other in order to govern and produce policy. Scholars sometimes refer to this type of executive-legislative relation as "transactional" and contrast it with the more "hierarchical" form of executive-legislative relation found in parliamentary democracies (Shugart 2006). Once the voters have delegated power to the legislature and the president, power is then delegated to the secretaries (ministers) in the president's cabinet and to the civil servants in the bureaucracy. This "multiple-chain" delegation model of presidential democracy is illustrated in Figure 12.7b for a country like the United States. Note the link in Figure 12.7b between the Upper House and the Secretaries. This reflects the role of the US Senate in the president's choice of cabinet members. Once the cabinet members are confirmed, however, the delegation relationship is purely between the president and the minister; that is, the cabinet members are only responsible to the president, not the legislature. It is easy to see that the delegation chain in presidential democracies is much more complex than that in parliamentary democracies.

Delegation, like that observed in a parliamentary or presidential democracy, offers a number of potential advantages for the principal. For example, it allows the principal to benefit from the expertise and abilities of others. It also allows the principal to accomplish her desired goals with reduced personal effort and cost. At the same time, though, delegation also poses some significant risks. This is because delegation involves a transfer of power from the principal to the agent, and there is always a danger that the people to whom power is transferred will not do what the principal wants (Lupia 2003, 34). In such cases, the agent is said to be "shirking." Agents can shirk for different reasons. For example, the agent may not be capable of carrying out the assigned task, or she may have preferences that conflict with those of the principal. These potential problems are known generally as

FIGURE 12.7	**Delegation and Accountability in Parliamentary and Presidential Democracies**

a. Single-Chain Delegation Model of a Parliamentary System

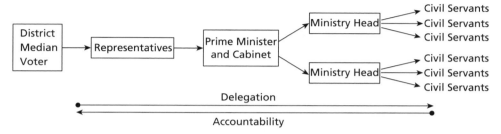

b. Multiple-Chain Delegation Model of a US-style Presidential System

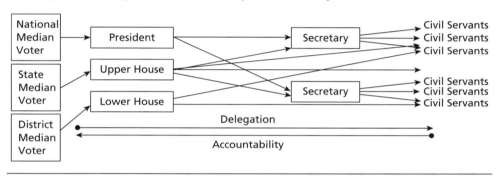

Source: Figure taken from Strøm (2003, 65). By permission of Oxford University Press.

principal-agent, or **delegation, problems**. One of the Founding Fathers in the United States, James Madison (1788), famously recognized these problems in the *Federalist Papers,* Number 51, when he noted, "In framing a government to be administered by men over men, the great difficulty lies in this: you must first enable the government to control the governed; and in the next place oblige it to control itself."

We can think of the outcomes produced by delegation in terms of (i) agency loss or (ii) whether delegation is successful. **Agency loss** is the difference between the actual consequence of delegation and what the consequence would have been had the agent been perfect. A **perfect agent** is one that

A **principal-agent**, or **delegation, problem** refers to the difficulties that arise when a principal delegates authority to an agent who (a) potentially has different goals from the principal and (b) cannot be perfectly monitored.

Agency loss is the difference between the actual consequence of delegation and what the consequence would have been had the agent been perfect. A **perfect agent** is one that does what a principal would have done had the principal been the agent.

does what a principal would have done had the principal been the agent. In effect, agency loss describes the delegation outcome from the principal's perspective. In addition to thinking of delegation in terms of agency loss, we can also think of it in terms of whether it is "successful." Delegation is considered successful if the delegation outcome improves the principal's welfare relative to what would have happened if the principal had chosen not to delegate. The outcome that would have occurred had the principal not delegated is often called the status quo or reversion point. Delegation is considered successful whenever it makes the principal better off compared with the status quo. To better comprehend these ideas, it is useful to examine a simple Principal-Agent Game.

In the following Principal-Agent Game, we have two actors: (i) a principal and (ii) an agent. The principal has delegated policymaking powers to the agent. Each actor has single-peaked preferences on a one-dimensional policy space that runs from 0 to 10. In other words, each has an ideal point in some policy space, indicated by A for the agent and P for the principal, and each prefers policy outcomes that are closer to this point than those that are farther away. There is also a status quo point indicated by SQ. In the game, the agent moves first and proposes a policy on the 0–10 scale to implement. The principal must then choose to accept the new policy proposal or reject it. If she accepts it, then the new policy is implemented and replaces the status quo. If she rejects it, then the status quo remains in place.

In Figure 12.8, we illustrate various principal-agent scenarios. In the first scenario (Figure 12.8a), the status quo is located at 5, and the principal and agent share the same ideal point of 3. In a Principal-Agent Game, it is often useful to determine the set of policy proposals that the principal prefers to the status quo. In this particular example, the status quo is two units away from the principal's ideal point. The principal will accept any policy proposal from the agent that is closer to her ideal point than this. In effect, the set of policies that the principal prefers to the status quo, and will therefore find acceptable if proposed by the agent, runs from $3 - 2 = 1$ to $3 + 2 = 5$.[15] Since the agent's ideal point is within the principal's "region of acceptability," it is easy to see that the agent will propose his ideal point of 3 and the principal will accept it. This is the ideal scenario for the principal since the agent proposes exactly what the principal wants and there is no agency loss at all.

The second scenario (Figure 12.8b) is quite different. The status quo is located at 1. Although the principal and the agent both want to move policy in the same direction, they have conflicting preferences about how far to move it. The principal's ideal point is 7, and the agent's ideal point is 3. The principal is currently 6 units away from the status quo and will therefore accept any proposal from the agent that is closer to her ideal point than this. Thus, the principal's region of acceptability, not shown in Figure 12.8b, runs from 1 to 13. Since the agent's ideal point falls in this region of acceptability, it is easy to see that the agent

---

15. To keep things simple, we assume that the principal prefers, and will accept, any policy proposal that does not make her worse off than the status quo.

FIGURE 12.8 **Various Principal-Agent Scenarios**

a. The Principal and Agent Share the Same Preferences

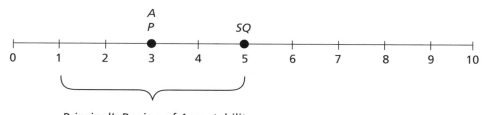

Principal's Region of Acceptability

b. The Principal and Agent Have Different Preferences I

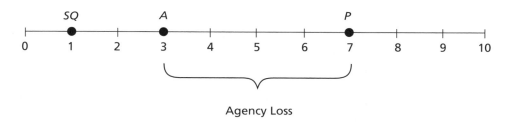

Agency Loss

c. The Principal and Agent Have Different Preferences II

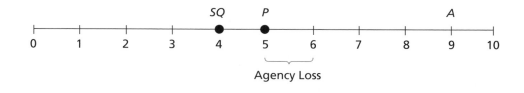

Agency Loss

will propose her ideal point of 3 and that the principal will accept this. In other words, policy will shift from the status quo of 1 to a new position of 3. While delegation has been "successful"—the principal is better off than she was with the status quo—the principal does suffer some agency loss. Specifically, the agency loss is equal to 4, that is, the difference between the principal's ideal point (7) and the delegation outcome (3).

In the third scenario (Figure 12.8c), the status quo is located at 4. Once again, the principal and the agent want to move policy in the same direction, but they have different preferences about how far to move it. The principal's ideal point is 5, and the agent's ideal point is 9. The principal is currently 1 unit away from the status quo and will therefore accept any proposal from the agent that is closer to her ideal point than this. Thus, the principal's region of acceptability, not shown in Figure 12.8c, runs from 4 to 6. Unlike in the previous two scenarios, the agent's ideal point is not in the principal's region of acceptability. If the agent were to propose his ideal point, the principal would reject it, and the status quo would remain in place. The agent would obviously like to move policy as close to his ideal point as possible. As a result, the agent will propose a policy that is as close to his ideal point as possible but that is also in the principal's region of acceptability. In effect, the agent will propose a policy of 6, and the principal will accept this. Again, delegation is successful—the principal is better off than she was with the status quo—but she suffers an agency loss of 1.

As these hypothetical scenarios illustrate, the principal may suffer varying amounts of agency loss when policymaking power is delegated to an agent. From this perspective, the examples illustrate the potential dangers of delegating policymaking power to an agent rather than making policy oneself. From another perspective, though, they illustrate that the principal is often better off by delegating to an agent than she would be if she just maintained the status quo. Finally, the examples also highlight that the power of the agent in a principal-agent relationship is not unconditional; in some situations, the agent gets to implement his own ideal point, but in others he can't.

Note that principal-agent problems often arise due to incomplete and asymmetric information. In effect, principals often delegate to agents because they do not have the requisite skills or knowledge to undertake certain actions, but the agents do. This can put the principal at a significant disadvantage in any principal-agent relationship. Two particular problems arise if the agent has more information than the principal: **adverse selection** and **moral hazard**. Adverse selection occurs when the principal can't observe the agent's "type" (Akerlof 1970). In other words, she can't observe whether the agent shares the right preferences, or whether she possesses the required skills or motivation to carry out the task to be delegated. The information gap is one-sided; the agent knows whether she is the type sought by the principal, but the principal does not. As an illustration, think about voters who are presented with candidates who all claim to be interested in public service at election time. The problem is that voters can't always tell the difference between candidates who truly are public-spirited and those who merely pretend to be public-spirited while secretly intending to use their elected position for personal gain (Lupia 2003, 42). Similarly, think about voters who are presented with candidates who all claim that they will be competent at governing. Even if the candidates have an accurate knowledge of their own abilities, the problem is that the principal (the electorate)

> **Adverse selection** occurs when the agent has attributes that are hidden from the principal.
>
> **Moral hazard** occurs when the agent has the opportunity to take actions that are hidden from the principal.

does not. If the principal does not know whether an agent has the desired skills or preferences, it is very difficult for the principal to delegate successfully. This helps explain why voters sometimes elect politicians who are corrupt, inept, or both.

Moral hazard occurs when the principal does not have complete information about the agent's actions. This allows the agent to act in ways that are not in the principal's best interest. The standard example comes not from political science but from insurance. Insurance companies face a moral hazard problem because once they insure their clients against certain risks, these clients may begin engaging in riskier behavior than they would have done without insurance. The financial problems in countries within the Euro zone (Ireland, Portugal, and Greece) have generated a great deal of discussion about the moral hazard problem with respect to debates over whether other European Union countries, or organizations like the International Monetary Fund, should step in to "bail out" the troubled countries. Similar discussions about the moral hazard problems created by government bailouts and government guarantees to the financial sector occurred in the United States during the 2008 financial crisis as well. The worry is that financial institutions will engage in riskier behavior than they otherwise might if they expect to be saved by the government. In the political setting we address in this chapter, the potential for moral hazard problems arises whenever the principal, such as the electorate, lacks information about what the agent, such as the government, is doing. Some issues are widely reported in the media, and the public pays close attention to them. In such cases, the agent will be constrained to hew more closely to the guidelines set out by the principal. However, there are many political issues that do not attract much attention, are too complicated to understand easily, and may be affected by international events that the

agents cannot control. In these cases, the principal is either uninterested or unable to determine exactly what the agent *is* doing compared with what she *ought* to be doing. This frees the agent to do whatever she wants rather than what the principal wants (assuming their preferences are not perfectly aligned).

Moral hazard and adverse selection problems can be mitigated if the principal can gather more information about the agent. Principals generally

AP Photo/Kostas Tsironis

Protestors in Athens, Greece, chant slogans in front of the Greek Parliament during an anti-austerity protest in November 2011.

An **ex ante mechanism** helps principals to learn about their agents before these agents are chosen.

An **ex post mechanism** is used to learn about agents' actions after they have occurred. There are two basic types of ex post mechanism. In a **fire alarm system**, the principal relies on information from others to learn about what the agent is doing. In a **police patrol system**, principals monitor the actions of their agents themselves.

adopt two types of mechanisms to gain more information about their agents: **ex ante mechanisms** and **ex post mechanisms**. Ex ante mechanisms help principals to learn about their agents before they act, typically as they select particular individuals to serve as their agents. These mechanisms are useful if the principal anticipates adverse selection problems. Ex post mechanisms help principals to learn about their agents' actions after the fact. These mechanisms are useful if the principal anticipates moral hazard problems.

Ex ante mechanisms tend to fall into two categories: (a) screening and (b) selection. A screening mechanism is one that sets up a competition among potential candidates for the agent position. For example, political campaigns typically generate information about which candidate has the most preferred policy position or the highest level of competence. Even if candidates all claim to be committed public servants and try to avoid making specific policy promises, the back-and-forth of the election campaign and things like debates between the competing candidates force the candidates to reveal some information that should say something about their "type."

The screening process for the executive is quite different in a typical presidential system versus a typical parliamentary one. The necessary skills to campaign effectively in a nationwide presidential contest are not necessarily the same as those that are important for governing effectively. In a presidential system, voters will probably take competence into account in a presidential election, but usually they will have more information about how the candidate campaigns than how the candidate governs. In a parliamentary setting, by contrast, politicians work their way up through the party hierarchy, showing their ability to master the intricacies of different policy areas, before they are given even low-level positions in the cabinet. Only by performing well at each stage does a politician get considered for a higher position. The prime ministerial post, then, normally goes to a politician who has been thoroughly screened by the rest of the political elite over a period of decades. This political elite has more detailed information about the policy preferences as well as the competence and motivations of the potential agents than is the case for an ordinary voter in a presidential election. We will return to this point in Chapter 16 when we discuss patterns of executive recruitment in parliamentary versus presidential democracies.

A selection process is another way for principals to gain information about potential agents. In this case, agents are put in a position to choose an action that reveals information about their type. The classic example is of education as a signal of a job applicant's skills. The original signaling model for this example comes from Spence (1974), and it focuses on the dilemma of an employer who wishes to hire a highly skilled worker but is not sure how to distinguish among the many job applicants because the skill level of the applicants cannot be observed directly. What can be observed? Well, one easily observed characteristic of each applicant is his or her level of education. Spence shows that if it is the case that skilled applicants can more easily attain a high level of education—say, a university degree—than unskilled applicants and if skill levels are correlated with education levels, then employers can use education as a good "signal" of an individual's skill level. The insights of Spence's signaling model can be applied directly to things like portfolio allocation. When ministerial portfolios are allocated in parliamentary, semi-presidential, and presidential democracies, some are handed out for purely political reasons, but others are awarded to people with highly distinguished backgrounds in the relevant policy area. For example, finance ministers tend to have an unusually strong background in economics and/or finance, because the position is thought to require a high level of technical knowledge. Given that elections are often won or lost based on how the economy is doing, this is one position where delegating to an unskilled agent can be extremely costly. We might also think that political candidates are trying to signal the types of policies that they will pursue if they are elected when they choose which party to join. As we will discuss in Chapter 14, the political party is one of the primary ways in a representative democracy of ensuring that the preferences of voters are reflected in government policy.

Once agents have been chosen, though, principals shift their concern from adverse selection issues to moral hazard issues. As a result, they try to establish ex post mechanisms to gather information about their agents' actions. Ex post mechanisms come in two basic types, commonly referred to as "police patrols" and "fire alarms" (McCubbins and Schwartz 1984). In a **police patrol system**, principals directly and actively monitor the actions of their agents. For example, legislators and governments might decide to hold public hearings where they bring in organized interest groups or experts in particular policy areas to learn about the actions of their bureaucratic agencies. In a **fire alarm system**, the principal does not monitor her agents herself but instead relies on information from others to learn about what the agent is doing. For example, governments might establish a system of rules or procedures that enable individual citizens and organized interest groups to charge bureaucratic agencies with violating government policy and to seek remedies from agencies, courts, and sometimes the government itself. For voters, a free and vibrant media can act as a fire alarm system, providing important information about the behavior of their elected officials.

In general, it is thought that the types of delegation problems that we have examined here are greater in presidential democracies than in parliamentary ones. This is due to the increased complexity of the multiple-chain delegation process and the transactional executive-legislative relations found in presidential democracies when compared with the simpler and more transparent single-chain delegation process and hierarchical executive-legislative relations found in parliamentary democracies (see Figure 12.7).

Box 12.5   **DELEGATION PROBLEMS IN COALITION CABINETS**

Coalition cabinets pose an interesting moral hazard problem. Each party in government (principal) delegates the discretion and resources to make policy in a particular ministry to a cabinet minister (agent). The key problem is that parties nearly always have distinct preferences on at least some issues. It is often the case that party leaders will agree to a coalition policy that is some mix of each party's preferred policy during the government formation process. But what's to stop cabinet ministers from implementing their own party's preferred policy in the ministries that they control rather than the coalition policy that they had agreed to before coming to power? The problem is that the cabinet minister has more information about the available policy options in her ministry than the rest of the cabinet and can take advantage of this informational asymmetry if she wants.

Müller and Strøm (2000) suggest that problems of delegation that arise in the context of coalition governments can be resolved simply by writing very detailed coalition agreements in an attempt to bind the relevant parties to an agreed-upon government policy. In effect, parties promise, in writing, to implement the coalition policy. But what makes these promises credible? Political parties have recognized that there is a moral hazard problem when forming a cabinet and have come up with a couple of institutional solutions to help monitor and keep tabs on what their coalition partners are doing.

One solution is to use what are known as "junior ministers." These ministers are also sometimes known as ministers of state or undersecretaries. The use of junior ministers is effectively a police patrol system. Although it is rare for government parties to veto cabinet nominations by another party, Michael Thies (2001) has argued that they often appoint their own junior ministers to cabinet portfolios controlled by their coalition partners in order to monitor them and ensure that they do not stray too far from the agreed-upon government policy. The appointment of junior ministers is part of the deal that sets up the cabinet, but these junior ministers are not actually full members of the cabinet—they generally do not vote in the cabinet, and they only occasionally participate in cabinet meetings. Nonetheless, the cabinet minister to whom they have been

AP Photo/Jockel Finck

Lawmakers in the German parliament in Berlin cast their ballots for a confidence vote on July 1, 2005. German chancellor Gerhard Schroeder called the confidence vote, which he intentionally lost, in order to enable early elections to be held that fall.

appointed cannot unilaterally dismiss them. Thies finds that parties purposely assign their own junior ministers to ministries headed by their partners in Italy, Japan, and the Netherlands, but not in Germany.

A second solution that helps to resolve Thies's "German anomaly" focuses on legislative committees. Martin and Vanberg (2004) show that the legislative committees in the Dutch and German parliaments scrutinize government bills more extensively when the ideological divergence between coalition partners on the issues addressed in the bill is large. Kim and Loewenberg (2005) examine the importance of legislative committees further and show that government parties in the German Bundestag from 1961 to 1998 have appointed members of their own party to chair legislative committees that oversee ministries controlled by their coalition partners. In effect, German parties use legislative committees, not junior ministers, to monitor the actions of their coalition partners.

A study by Lipsmeyer and Pierce (2011) seems to confirm the idea that junior ministers and legislative committees are substitutes when it comes to monitoring coalition partners. Using data from twelve parliamentary and semi-presidential countries, they show that junior ministers are more likely to be assigned in important ministries when coalition partners have large policy differences *and* when other methods of oversight (such as strong legislative committees) are not available.

CONCLUSION

One way to classify democracies is in terms of whether they are parliamentary, presidential, or semi-presidential. As we have seen, whether a democracy is parliamentary, presidential, or semi-presidential basically depends on the relationship between three "actors"—the president, the government, and the legislature. In effect, the different institutional forms of democracy examined in this chapter represent three alternative ways to structure the relationship between the executive and legislative branches of government.

The defining feature of presidentialism is the absence of legislative responsibility—the government serves at the pleasure of the president, not the legislature. Consequently, even when members of the president's own party call for the resignation of one of her cabinet appointees, the most the legislature can do when faced with a president who fails to heed its council is to hold a *symbolic* "no confidence vote" to register its disapproval. These forms of symbolic no confidence votes are rare in presidential systems, in part because they are not binding. During President George W. Bush's second term in office, a Democratic-led Senate in the United States had scheduled a no confidence vote to register its disapproval of the activities of Attorney General Alberto Gonzales (Johnston and Lewis 2007). Although such a measure might convey the "sense of the Senate," any successful vote would have no legal status to compel Gonzales's removal from the government. For example, the Senate passed a similar vote in 1950 when it determined that Secretary of State Dean Acheson was not doing enough to combat the spread of communism; despite the vote, Acheson retained his post for the remainder of the Truman administration (Tsai 2007). The ability of a cabinet member to stay in office despite the explicit disapproval of a legislative majority demonstrates a key feature of presidential systems—a separation of powers between the executive and legislative branches.

In stark contrast, the defining feature of parliamentary systems is that the composition of the government is directly controlled by the legislature. In this chapter, we have outlined the negotiations among party elites that result in the appointment of prime ministers and cabinets in parliamentary systems in some detail. The prime minister—typically the head of the largest legislative party—will, de facto, play a central role in the appointment of the heads of the ministries. Nevertheless, the members of the cabinet—including the prime minister herself—ultimately serve at the pleasure of the legislature in parliamentary systems. Consequently, in 1990 when the United Kingdom's Margaret Thatcher—who had been elected prime minister three times, most recently in 1987 with a 102-seat majority for the Conservative Party—lost the support of party members in the cabinet and in the House of Commons, she stepped down, thereby avoiding a vote of no confidence that had been proposed by Neil Kinnock, the leader of the opposition Labour Party. Before a vote of no confidence occurred, Thatcher was subjected to a leadership challenge from within her own party. After Thatcher's longtime supporter Deputy Prime Minister Sir Geoffrey Howe resigned in frustration with her opposition to agreeing to a single European currency, Michael Heseltine (who had resigned from the cabinet four years earlier) challenged her in a Conservative Party leadership vote. Although Thatcher managed to win more votes than Heseltine, she fell short of the supermajority needed under Conservative Party rules to prevent a second-round election. She agreed to step down before the second ballot, which was eventually won by John Major.

Although the intricacies of party leadership elections vary from country to country and from party to party, this dramatic episode highlights important characteristics of parliamentary systems. Ministers serve at the pleasure of the legislature. Shifts in opinion or circumstances in the legislature can remove the head of government—oftentimes without recourse to the voting public. Margaret Thatcher was elected to the House of Commons as a representative of a London suburb and was elevated to the head of the government by a vote of her fellow Conservative members of Parliament. Eleven years later a similar vote, in which she garnered support from 204 of the 362 valid votes cast by Conservative members of Parliament, led to her removal from the position of prime minister. For students familiar with the workings of the US government, a simple (but fairly accurate) way to think about parliamentary government is to imagine a US government in which the Speaker of the House, rather than the president, is the head of government.

Semi-presidential systems are as they sound. Cabinets require the support of a majority of the legislature, but the head of state is a popularly elected president. In some semi-presidential democracies—president-parliamentary ones—the government can be formed and reformed by either presidential or legislative initiative. Earlier in the chapter, we described how France's Socialist president François Mitterrand decided to dismiss the right-wing-dominated cabinet in 1981 by dissolving the legislature to which it was responsible. The ensuing election returned a Socialist majority in the National Assembly, and as a result, Mitterrand was free to appoint a Socialist as prime minister. The 1986 legislative elections, however, produced a slight majority for a coalition of right-wing parties, and, as a consequence, the cabinet was changed to reflect the new parliamentary reality—most visibly in the form of a new right-wing prime minister, Jacques Chirac. In the president-parliamentary version of semi-presidentialism, therefore, governments can be said to have two masters—the president and the legislature. Which one dictates at any given time, though, depends on the electoral fortunes of the political parties involved.

Thus, the relationship between the country's chief executive officer (whatever her title), the cabinet, and the legislature is fundamentally different in presidential and parliamentary democracies. Some political scientists have used these differences to conclude that presidentialism is a system of governance based on the division of executive and legislative powers, whereas parliamentarism is a system based on the fusion of these powers. There is, indeed, a good deal of truth in Stepan and Skach's (1993) assertion that the essence of parliamentarism is "mutual dependence" and that the essence of presidentialism is "mutual independence." These differences are obvious in the different chains of delegation that link voters with policymakers in presidential and parliamentary democracies as well. In Chapter 16, we will examine the strategic dynamic between the executive and legislative branches in more detail when we explore how the decision to adopt parliamentary or presidential systems of government affects the survival of democracy.

KEY CONCEPTS

adverse selection *504*

agency loss *501*

agent *499*

cabinet *458*

caretaker government *467*

cohabitation *495*

collective cabinet responsibility *460*

connected coalition *472*

constructive vote of no confidence *456*

delegation *499*

direct democracy *499*

ex ante mechanism *506*

ex post mechanism *506*

fire alarm system *506*

formateur *465*

Gamson's law *469*

government coalition *480*

government in a parliamentary
    democracy *458*

government in a presidential democracy *487*

informateur *466*

investiture vote *463*

least minimal winning coalition *469*

legislative coalition *488*

legislative responsibility *455*

minimal winning coalition *469*

ministerial responsibility *460*

minority government *476*

moral hazard *504*

office-seeking politician *469*

PROBLEMS

The problems that follow address some of the more important concepts and ideas introduced in this chapter.

Classifying Democracies

1. In this chapter, we discussed the rules for classifying democracies as parliamentary, presidential, or semi-presidential. Look at the information from the following constitutions and decide whether these democracies are parliamentary, presidential, or semi-presidential. Explain your decision.

    a. 1991 Burkina Faso Constitution

    - Article 37: The President of Faso is elected for five years by universal, direct, equal and secret suffrage. He is re-eligible one time.
    - Article 46: The President of Faso appoints the Prime Minister from among the majority of the National Assembly and terminates his functions, either on the presentation by him of his resignation, or on his own authority in the superior interest of the Nation. On the proposal of the Prime Minister, he appoints the other members of the Government and terminates their functions.
    - Article 62: The Government is responsible before the Parliament in the conditions and following the procedures specified by this Constitution.
    - Article 114: The reciprocal relations of the National Assembly and of the Government are expressed equally by: the motion of censure; the question of confidence; the dissolution of the National Assembly; the procedure of parliamentary discussion.
    - Article 115: The National Assembly can present a motion of censure with regard to the Government. The motion of censure is signed by at least one-third of the Deputies of the Assembly. To be adopted, it must be voted by an absolute majority of the members composing the Assembly. In case of rejection of the motion of censure, its signatories may not present another before the time period of one year.

b. 1937 Irish Constitution

- Article 12: There shall be a President of Ireland (Uachtarán na hÉireann), hereinafter called the President, who shall take precedence over all other persons in the State and who shall exercise and perform the powers and functions conferred on the President by this Constitution and by law. The President shall be elected by direct vote of the people.
- Article 13: The President shall, on the nomination of the Dáil Éireann, appoint the Taoiseach, that is, the head of the Government or Prime Minister. The president shall, on the nomination of the Taoiseach with the previous approval of Dáil Éireann, appoint the other members of the Government. The President shall, on the advice of the Taoiseach, accept the resignation or terminate the appointment of any member of the Government. Dáil Éireann shall be summoned and dissolved by the President on the advice of the Taoiseach. The President may in his absolute discretion refuse to dissolve Dáil Éireann on the advice of a Taoiseach who has ceased to retain the support of a majority in Dáil Éireann. . . . The President shall not be answerable to either House of the Oireachtas or to any court for the exercise and performance of the powers and functions of his office or for any act done or purporting to be done by him in the exercise and performance of these powers and functions.
- Article 15: The National Parliament shall be called and known, and is in this Constitution generally referred to, as the Oireachtas. The Oireachtas shall consist of the President and two Houses, viz.: a House of Representatives to be called Dáil Éireann and a Senate to be called Seanad Éireann.
- Article 28: The Government shall consist of not less than seven and not more than fifteen members who shall be appointed by the President in accordance with the provisions of this Constitution. . . . The Government shall be responsible to the Dáil Éireann. The head of the government, or Prime Minister, shall be called, and is in this Constitution referred to as, the Taoiseach.

c. 1980 Chilean Constitution

- Article 4: Chile is a democratic republic.
- Article 24: The government and administration of the State are vested in the President of the Republic, who is the Chief of the State.
- Article 25: The President of the Republic shall hold office for a term of eight years and may not be reelected for the consecutive period.
- Article 26: The President shall be elected by direct ballot, with an absolute majority of the votes validly cast.
- Article 32: The special powers vested in the President of the Republic are the following: . . . To appoint, and remove at will, Ministers of State, Undersecretaries, Intendants, Governors and Mayors appointed by him.

- Article 33: The Ministers of State are the direct and immediate collaborators of the President of the Republic in governing and administering the State.

d. 1947 Japanese Constitution

- Article 1: The Emperor shall be the symbol of the State and of the unit of the People, deriving his position from the will of the people with whom resides sovereign power.
- Article 4: The Emperor shall perform only such acts in matters of state as are provided in the Constitution, and he shall not have powers related to government.
- Article 6: The Emperor shall appoint the Prime Minister as designated by the Diet.
- Article 41: The Diet shall be the highest organ of state power, and shall be the sole law-making organ of the State.
- Article 42: The Diet shall consist of two Houses, namely the House of Representatives and the House of Councillors.
- Article 65: Executive power shall be vested in the Cabinet.
- Article 66: The Cabinet shall consist of the Prime Minister, who shall be its head, and other Ministers of State, as provided for by law. The Prime Minister and other Ministers of State must be civilians. The Cabinet, in the exercise of executive power, shall be collectively responsible to the Diet.
- Article 69: If the House of Representatives passes a non-confidence resolution, or rejects a confidence resolution, the Cabinet shall resign en masse, unless the House of Representatives is dissolved within ten (10) days.

2. On June 16, 2016, *Al Jazeera* reported that "Croatia's parliament has overwhelmingly voted to oust technocrat Prime Minister Tihomir Oreskovic, who took office just five months ago, triggering the fall of the government and raising the prospect of a snap election. The vote on Thursday in the 151-seat assembly was 125 for the ouster, 15 against, and two abstentions. The no-confidence vote was put forward by the ruling coalition's biggest party, the conservative HDZ, which had helped to install Oreskovic but then fell out with him and accused him of being incapable of leading the country amid deep economic and social problems" ("Croatia Government Falls" 2016, para. 1–3). Note that the current president, Kolinda Grabar Kitarović, was directly elected in 2015. Based on this information, is Croatia a presidential, parliamentary, or semi-presidential democracy? Explain your answer.

3. If a democracy has a popularly elected president, then we automatically consider it to be a presidential democracy. True or false? Explain your answer.

Institutions

4. A constructive vote of no confidence is essentially a vote of no confidence and an investiture vote rolled into one. What does this mean?

5. Which of the following statements best describes a vote of confidence?

   a. A new government must pass a vote (on the cabinet's composition and proposed policies) in the legislature before it can take office.

   b. A government declares that a vote on a particular piece of legislation is also a vote on support for the government itself; if the legislators do not support the legislation, then the government will resign (and new elections might result).

   c. A group of legislators propose a vote on support for the incumbent government. If the government passes the vote, then it stays in office. If it fails the vote, then it must resign (and new elections might result).

Government Formation

6. A story in the The *New York Times* from 2006 stated the following: "Dutch political parties began the complicated task of forming a new government on Thursday, one day after national elections thrust the Netherlands into the same kind of inconclusive terrain that Austria and Germany experienced in their votes. Austria has yet to form a government after its election two months ago, and in Germany last year, it took six weeks of grueling negotiations to form a coalition government under Angela Merkel" ("Dutch Parties Seek Alliances after Vote" 2006, para. 1–2). How would you explain what this means to a roommate or family member who has no idea what a parliamentary government is? Your explanation should include what the government is, how it forms, what factors affect how long this formation process takes, who gets into government, and so on.

7. Legislative elections were held in Sweden on September 17, 2006, and seven parties won seats. Although the left-wing Social Democratic Party won more seats than any other party, the leader of the largest right-wing party was appointed to be the first formateur. Which of the following statements might explain this choice?

   a. The choice of formateur is random. As a result, the leader of the largest right-wing party had the same chance of being chosen as did each of the other party leaders.

   b. In this particular election, four right-wing parties ran as a preelectoral coalition and together won a majority of the seats. Because they had pledged to govern together if successful, it made sense to give the leader of the largest coalition party the position of formateur.

   c. The position of formateur is always offered first to a party on the right; if the first attempt to form a government fails, the second formateur will be chosen from a left-wing party, and so on.

8. Legislative elections were held in Israel on March 17, 2015. Ten parties won seats in parliament. Based on what you have learned in this chapter and the information in Table 12.12, the leader of which party is likely to be appointed formateur? Explain.

TABLE 12.12	Legislative Election Results in Israel, 2015	
Party	**Seats (no.)**	**Seats (%)**
Likud	30	25.0
Zionist Union	24	20.0
Joint List	13	10.8
Yesh Atid	11	9.2
Kulanu	10	8.3
The Jewish Home	8	6.7
Shas	7	5.8
Yisrael Beiteinu	6	5.0
United Torah Judaism	6	5.0
Meretz	5	4.2
Total	120	100

Source: Inter-Parliamentary Union Database (2015).

9. In Table 12.13, we show the results from the 2016 legislative elections in South Korea.

   a. Based on the results in Table 12.13, from which party would you expect the formateur to come if South Korea were a parliamentary democracy?

   b. South Korea is in fact a presidential democracy. In the 2012 presidential elections, Park Geun-hye of the Saenuri Party (SP) was elected president, and following the 2016 legislative elections, she still had nearly two years left in her term. Based on this new information, from which party would you now expect the formateur to come? Why is this?

TABLE 12.13	Legislative Election Results in South Korea, 2016	
Party	**Seats (no.)**	**Seats (%)**
Minjoo Party of Korea (MPK)	123	41.0
Saenuri Party (SP)	122	40.7
People's Party (PP)	38	12.7
Justice Party (JP)	6	0.02
Independents	11	0.04
Total	300	100

Source: Inter-Parliamentary Union Database (2015).

Government Types

10. Look back at the information about the 2015 Israeli elections in Table 12.12. Based on the information in this table, indicate five of the possible minimal winning coalitions that could form. What is the least minimal winning coalition out of this set of five MWCs?

11. In Table 12.14, we show the results from the 2002 legislative elections in Germany. Answer the following questions.

    a. If a government formed between the Christian Democratic Party and the Free Democratic Party, what type of government would it be?

    b. If a government formed between the Social Democratic Party and the Greens, what type of government would it be?

    c. If a government formed between the Social Democratic Party, the Greens, and the Party of Democratic Socialism, what type of government would it be?

TABLE 12.14	**Legislative Election Results in Germany, 2002**	
Party	**Seats**	**Ideology**
Party of Democratic Socialism (PDS)	2	Most left
Greens (G)	55	
Social Democratic Party (SPD)	251	
Christian Democratic Party (CDU/CSU)	248	
Free Democratic Party (FDP)	47	Most right
Total	603	

Source: Inter-Parliamentary Union Database (2015).

12. Angela Merkel, leader of the Christian Democratic Party, has been chancellor (prime minister) of Germany since 2005. As of the writing of this chapter, she is still in office. Her first government, formed in 2005, was a coalition between the CDU/CSU and the SPD. (See Table 12.14 for the policy positions of the parties.) Her second government, formed in 2009, was a coalition between the CDU/CSU and the FDP. Her third government, formed in 2013, was once again a coalition between the CDU/CSU and the SPD. Using Internet or other resources, explain why Merkel's government coalitions took the form that they did following the 2005, 2009, and 2013 legislative elections.

13. Minority governments are more likely to form in parliamentary democracies when opposition parties have a significant role in the policymaking process. True or false? Explain your answer.

14. Explain why minority governments should be more frequent on average in presidential democracies than parliamentary ones.

15. Explain, in your own words, the three different stories that have been proposed to explain endogenous election timing.

Delegation Problems

16. Below are various scenarios for our Principal-Agent Game.

    a. After each scenario, indicate (i) the range of policies acceptable to the principal, (ii) the policy proposed by the agent, (iii) the final policy outcome, (iv) the agency loss, and (v) whether delegation was "successful."

    Scenario 1: The principal and the agent have the same ideal point.

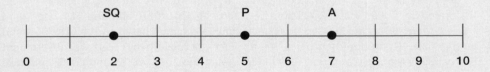

    Scenario 2a: The principal and the agent do not have identical ideal policies, but they agree on the direction in which policy should be moved.

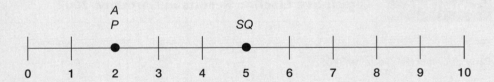

    Scenario 2b: The principal and the agent do not have identical ideal policies, but they agree on the direction in which policy should be moved.

Scenario 2c: The principal and the agent do not have identical ideal policies, but they agree on the direction in which policy should be moved.

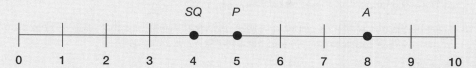

Scenario 3: The principal and the agent do not have identical ideal policies, and they do not agree on the direction in which policy should be moved.

b. Think about the power of the agenda setter. In this set of examples, the agenda setter is the agent (*A*). Her power is not unconditional—sometimes she has no power to move the status quo, sometimes she has unlimited power to choose her own preferred policy, and sometimes she has only limited power. Looking at the scenarios above, when is each the case?

c. The principal (*P*) suffers varying amounts of agency loss in each situation. Under what circumstances is the agency loss likely to be low (or high)? Is the amount of agency loss suffered ever greater than what he was subjected to under the status quo policy? Why or why not?

17. Examine the two scenarios below, and then answer the questions that follow. The principal in this case is a cabinet minister, and the agent is a civil servant.

Scenario 1

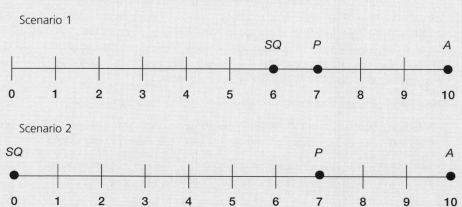

Scenario 2

a. What is the final policy outcome in each scenario?

b. Does delegation seem to work better (from the point of view of the principal) in one of these scenarios than the other? Why or why not?

18. Examine the two scenarios below, and then answer the questions that follow. The principal in this case is a cabinet minister, and the agent is a civil servant.

Scenario 1

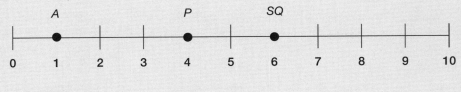

Scenario 2

a. What will the policy outcome be in the two scenarios above?

b. Which scenario better represents a situation in which the principal used a screening mechanism to alleviate the problem of adverse selection? Explain your answer (and include an explanation of adverse selection).

19. In Box 12.5, "Delegation Problems in Coalition Cabinets," we discussed how coalition governments use junior ministers and legislative committees to solve moral hazard problems with respect to their coalition partners. Indicate whether junior ministers and legislative committees are examples of ex ante or ex post mechanisms for dealing with delegation problems. If they are ex ante mechanisms, indicate whether they are screening or selection mechanisms. If they are ex post mechanisms, indicate whether they are fire alarm or police patrol systems. Explain your answers. Would the delegation problems with coalition governments increase, decrease, or stay the same if the parties in government have similar policy positions versus dissimilar ones? Why?

20. Think about principal-agent relationships in your own experience.

a. Describe a situation in which you were the principal. Discuss any potential adverse selection and moral hazard issues and how these were addressed (if they were).

b. Describe a situation in which you were the agent. Discuss any potential adverse selection and moral hazard issues and how these were addressed (if they were).

13 Elections and Electoral Systems

It's not the voting that's democracy; it's the counting.

Tom Stoppard, *Jumpers*

The most important choice facing constitution writers is that of a legislative electoral system.

Arend Lijphart, "Constitutional Design for Divided Societies"

- Elections are one of the defining characteristics of democracies and provide the primary mechanism by which democratic governments obtain the authority to rule.

- Although there is a great deal of variety in the types of electoral systems that are employed around the world, most political scientists categorize them into three main families based on the electoral formula that is used to translate votes into seats: majoritarian, proportional, and mixed.

- After discussing issues related to electoral integrity, we take a close look at how different electoral systems work in practice. We also discuss the effect of these electoral systems on things like proportionality, ethnic accommodation, accountability, minority representation, and the revelation of sincere preferences. Finally, we provide an overview of electoral systems by geographic region and regime type.

OVERVIEW

n the previous chapter, we described how political scientists often classify democracies in terms of the form of government that they have: parliamentary, presidential, or semi-presidential. We also noted, however, that there are many other ways that one can distinguish between different types of democracy. One of the key elements of any democracy is the use of elections. It is perhaps no surprise, then, that political scientists sometimes distinguish between democracies by the type of electoral system employed in these elections. An **electoral system** is a set of laws and regulations that govern the electoral competition between candidates or parties or both (Cox 1997, 38). These laws and regulations relate to a whole host of things such as the **electoral formula** (how votes are translated into seats), the **ballot structure** (whether individuals vote for candidates or parties or both, and whether they cast a single vote or express a series of preferences), and the **district magnitude** (the number of representatives elected in a district). Despite the different dimensions along which electoral systems can vary, most political scientists categorize electoral systems into three main families based on the electoral formula that they use to translate votes into seats: majoritarian, proportional, and mixed. Indeed, it is partly on this basis that some political scientists talk of majoritarian and proportional democracies (M. Golder and Stramski 2010; Lijphart 1999; Powell 2000).

> An **electoral system** is a set of laws that regulates electoral competition between candidates or parties or both. An **electoral formula** determines how votes are translated into seats. The **ballot structure** is how electoral choices are presented on the ballot paper. **District magnitude** is the number of representatives elected in a district.

In this chapter, we explore how various forms of majoritarian, proportional, and mixed electoral systems work in some detail. We also discuss some of the advantages and disadvantages associated with each of these systems. Before we address these issues, though, we provide a brief overview of elections around the world.

ELECTIONS AND ELECTORAL INTEGRITY

Elections are increasingly being used to fill legislative and executive offices around the world. Indeed, 185 of the world's 193 independent states now use direct elections to elect people to their lower house of parliament (Norris et al. 2016a, 19). In democracies, elections serve both a practical and a symbolic role. In a practical sense, elections provide the primary means by which citizens select their representatives. As such, they provide citizens with an opportunity to influence the government formation process, to reward or punish politicians for their time in power, and to shape the direction of future policy. In a symbolic sense, the legitimacy of a democratic government comes from the fact that it was chosen through an electoral process—citizens have an equal and relatively low-cost opportunity to participate in selecting the people who rule over them and hence the types of policy that should be implemented. Democratic elections provide the primary mechanism by which the people's consent is translated into the authority to rule.

In Figure 13.1, we show how the number of legislative and presidential elections in democracies has increased over the last six decades. There were more legislative and presidential elections in the last decade than at any other point in the postwar period (or, indeed, ever). Two hundred ninety-nine legislative and 133 presidential elections were held in 120 different democracies between 2001 and 2010 (Bormann and Golder 2013). Seven countries held democratic elections for the first time: East Timor (2002), Georgia (2004), Kyrgyzstan (2005), Liberia (2005), Mauritania (2006), Bhutan (2008), and the Maldives (2008). The increase in the number of democratic elections since the 1970s is largely a consequence of the third wave of democratization (see Chapter 8) in Eastern Europe, Latin America, Asia, and Africa. As you can see, presidential elections now make up a larger share of all democratic elections than they did in the past. To a large extent, this has to do with the increasing proportion of semi-presidential democracies in the world (see Chapter 12), as these regimes have popularly elected presidents.

Elections do not occur only in democracies. As we saw in Chapter 10, elections are also increasingly common in dictatorships. Only Brunei, China, Eritrea, Qatar, and Saudi Arabia have failed to hold national-level elections at some point in the postwar period (M. Golder 2005). The increasing frequency with which elections are taking place in dictatorships has

| **FIGURE 13.1** | **Legislative and Presidential Elections by Decade in Democracies** |

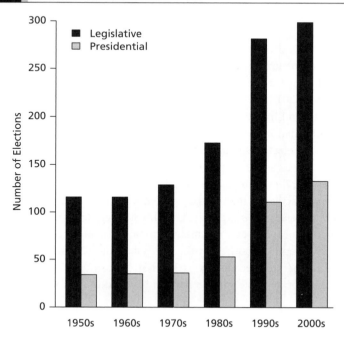

Source: Bormann and Golder (2013, 361).

led some scholars to talk about the rise of "electoral authoritarianism" (Schedler 2002, 2006). Of course, elections are not a defining characteristic of dictatorships in the same way that they are of democracies. More significantly, elections tend to serve very different purposes in a dictatorship than in a democracy. Among other things, dictatorial elections are often used to co-opt elites and larger societal groups, to gain good favor with foreign aid donors, as a safety valve for public discontent, or to gather information about the strength of the opposition (Gandhi and Lust-Okar 2009). Dictatorial elections are almost never used as a mechanism for translating the people's consent into the authority to govern.

Electoral Integrity: An Overview

The increasing use of legislative and presidential elections around the world has been accompanied by growing concerns about **electoral integrity**. The concept of electoral integrity is somewhat vague and remains contested in both academic and policy circles. Here we follow the definition provided by the Electoral Integrity Project (EIP, n.d.).[1] According to the EIP, electoral integrity refers to the extent to which the conduct of elections meets international standards and global norms concerning "good" elections as set out in various treaties, conventions, and guidelines issued by organizations such as the UN General Assembly, the Organization for Security and Cooperation in Europe, the Organization of American States, and the African Union (Norris et al. 2016a, 13). Electoral integrity has to do with the conduct of elections at all stages of the electoral cycle, including the preelection period, the campaign, the polling day, and the election aftermath (Norris 2013).

Electoral integrity refers to the extent to which the conduct of elections meets international standards and global norms concerning "good" elections. These norms and standards are usually set out in treaties, conventions, and guidelines issued by international and regional organizations. Violations of electoral integrity are referred to as **electoral malpractice**.

Violations of electoral integrity, which include things like ballot stuffing, electoral violence and voter intimidation, pro-government media bias, and restrictive ballot access are generally referred to as **electoral malpractice**. Although you might think that electoral malpractice is restricted to underdeveloped countries, authoritarian regimes, or new democracies, evidence of electoral malpractice also exists in established democracies like the United States. Electoral malpractice in these settings often has to do with political interference in how district boundaries are drawn, problems with voter registration, technical failures with online or early voting procedures, and unfair campaign finance rules. The authors of *The Year in Elections 2015* report produced by the EIP stated that 12 percent of the elections that have taken place in the last decade have triggered opposition boycotts, 17 percent have experienced postelection protests, and 18 percent have led to electoral violence in which at

---

1. The Electoral Integrity Project is run by Pippa Norris and is based at the University of Sydney and Harvard's Kennedy School of Government. The project is designed to look at three questions: (i) when do elections meet international standards of electoral integrity? (ii) what happens when elections fail to do so? and (iii) what can be done to mitigate these problems? For more information about The Electoral Integrity Project, visit its website at www.electoralintegrityproject.com.

least one citizen has died.[2] Electoral integrity matters because flawed elections can reduce trust in the political system, fuel social instability, undermine recent democratic gains, discourage voter participation and other forms of civic activism, and exacerbate ethnic, religious, and other grievances that can in extreme circumstances lead to civil war (Norris 2014).

To date, the Electoral Integrity Project has measured electoral integrity in 213 legislative and presidential elections in 153 countries from 2012 to 2016. To measure electoral integrity, the EIP has surveyed more than 2,000 country experts to ask about their perceptions of forty-nine electoral integrity issues, grouped into eleven categories that relate to the whole electoral cycle. In terms of the preelection period, the country experts are asked to evaluate electoral integrity as it relates to (1) the electoral laws, (2) the electoral procedures, (3) district boundaries, (4) voter registration, and (5) party registration. In terms of the election campaign, they are asked to consider (6) the campaign media environment and (7) campaign finance regulations. With respect to the election day itself, they focus on (8) the voting process. And with respect to the postelection period, they consider (9) the vote counting process, (10) the response to the election results, and (11) the role played by the electoral authorities. Based on expert responses to the forty-nine electoral integrity indicators, each election in a country is given an overall Perceptions of Electoral Integrity (PEI) score that runs from 0 to 100, with higher scores indicating higher electoral integrity ("Perceptions" 2016).[3]

In Map 13.1, we show how electoral integrity varies across the world in 2016. Darker colors indicate higher levels of electoral integrity. Countries in white do not currently have electoral integrity scores, either because they do not hold national-level elections or because their elections have yet to be evaluated. As you can see, there is considerable variation in the level of electoral integrity across countries. The ten countries with the highest electoral integrity scores are Denmark, Finland, Norway, Iceland, Costa Rica, Sweden, Germany, Estonia, the Netherlands, and Switzerland. The ten countries with the lowest electoral integrity scores are Ethiopia, Burundi, Syria, Equatorial Guinea, the Republic of Congo, Haiti, Djibouti, Chad, Cambodia, and Afghanistan. The highest scores tend to occur in the established democracies of Western Europe, whereas the lowest scores are concentrated in the authoritarian regimes found in Africa and parts of Asia.

Electoral Integrity in Four Countries

We now take a closer look at electoral integrity in four specific countries: the United States, Turkey, Belarus, and Egypt. Whereas the United States and Turkey are democracies, Belarus and Egypt are dictatorships. The "star-plots" in Figure 13.2 show how these countries do on

---

2. These numbers are based on data from the National Elections Across Democracy and Autocracy (NELDA) data set (Hyde and Marinov 2012). For more information, the NELDA data set can be found at http://www.nelda.co/.

3. Additional information about how the PEI scores are calculated, along with the data itself, can be found online ("Perceptions" 2016). At the time of writing this chapter, the latest release of the data was PEI 4.5.

MAP 13.1 Electoral Integrity across the World in 2016

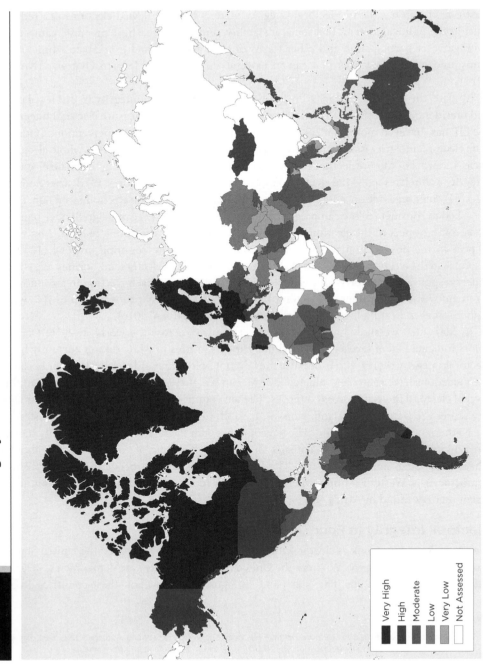

Very High
High
Moderate
Low
Very Low
Not Assessed

Source: Data come from the Perceptions of Electoral Integrity expert survey (PEI 4.5) and are based on national-level elections that have taken place between July 1, 2012, and June 30, 2016 ("Perceptions" 2016). Darker colors indicate higher levels of electoral integrity.

FIGURE 13.2 Electoral Integrity in Four Countries

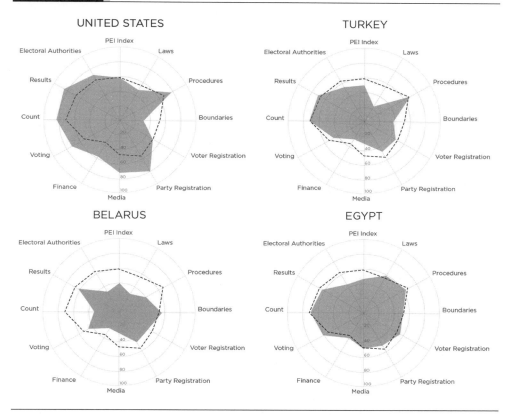

Source: Data for the star-plots come from the Perceptions of Electoral Integrity expert survey (PEI 4.5; "Perceptions" 2016). The gray star-plots indicate how the four countries score on each of the eleven categories of electoral integrity. They also show each country's overall PEI score. The black dashed line indicates the average global score across the same categories of electoral integrity.

each of the eleven categories of electoral integrity as well as their overall PEI score. The shaded gray area in the star-plot is large when a country scores highly on each of the eleven categories in the PEI measure. To help provide context, we overlay each country's star-plot (filled, gray) with a star-plot (black dashed line) showing the average *global* score on each of the eleven categories in the PEI measure. This allows us to see where the countries are doing better or worse than the global average when it comes to electoral integrity.

Although established democracies tend to have high PEI scores, there is some variation. It turns out that the United States has the lowest overall PEI score among established democracies (62), leaving it ranked 52nd worldwide in 2016 (Norris et al. 2016b, 12). As the top left panel of the star-plot in Figure 13.2 indicates, the low PEI score for the United States is primarily driven by concerns about the quality of voter registration, the process of drawing district boundaries, campaign finance regulations, and the electoral rules. Long-standing issues related to voter registration have been politically salient since the US Supreme Court intervened in the recount of the votes cast in Florida during the 2000 presidential elections. Republicans have repeatedly raised concerns about voter fraud and have sought to pass voter identification laws that critics claim will suppress turnout, particularly among minority voters and the poor. The highly politicized way in which district boundaries are drawn in the United States sees it receive the second lowest PEI score on this dimension, just ahead of Malaysia (Norris et al. 2016a, 24). The PEI score for the United States is also negatively affected by the partisan and decentralized nature of the electoral administrative bodies that oversee American elections and by the majoritarian electoral system that makes it difficult for small parties to win legislative representation. At the time of writing this chapter, concerns about electoral malpractice are rife in the 2016 presidential election campaign. Among other things, Republican candidate Donald Trump has claimed that election results in swing states, such as Pennsylvania, may be rigged (Haberman and Flegenheimer 2016). His call for partisan election observers to monitor polling stations has raised fears of voter intimidation and possible violence in some quarters (Grinspan 2016).

There were Turkey is widely considered a democracy, its 2016 PEI score of 48 means that its most recent elections have been characterized by low levels of electoral integrity. According to the constitution, Turkey is a secular democracy. The Turkish military has historically seen itself as the defender of the country's secular democracy and has intervened in politics on several occasions to keep religion out of politics ("Timeline" 2016). Turkey has been ruled by the Justice and Development Party (AKP) since 2002 when it won a legislative majority with just 34.3 percent of the vote. Although the AKP is popular among large segments of the population, critics claim that the AKP is weakening Turkey's secularism and has a hidden agenda to make the country more Islamist. In 2013 a wave of demonstrations known as the Gezi Park protests, in which large numbers of Turks criticized restrictions on the freedom of the press and attacked the perceived authoritarianism of the government, was violently suppressed by the police (Letsch 2013).

There were two legislative elections in Turkey in 2015. In the June elections, the AKP remained the largest party but lost its legislative majority, forcing it to begin coalition negotiations with other legislative parties. When these negotiations failed, the AKP called for new elections in December. In these elections, the AKP regained its legislative majority and was able to form a government without any coalition partners. As the top right panel of the star-plot in Figure 13.2 indicates, the low PEI score for Turkey is driven by several factors. The Turkish electoral threshold requires that parties must win 10 percent of the vote before they can receive any legislative seats. This is the largest threshold in the world and makes it very difficult for small parties to win legislative representation. The government has significant control of the national media, and journalists critical of the regime have faced considerable intimidation. There were reports during the 2015 elections of the improper use by the AKP of state resources for campaigning. Between the two elections, the AKP also ramped up its attacks on the minority Kurdish population, hoping to evoke a nationalist response and a demand for political stability.

The political situation in Turkey has become more polarized since the 2015 legislative elections. Shortly after the elections, the AKP renewed its call to alter the constitution so that Turkey becomes a presidential democracy. This attempt to increase the power of the executive relative to the legislature is not new. In 2007, the AKP made changes to the constitution that transformed Turkey from a parliamentary democracy to a semi-presidential democracy, with the AKP's Recep Tayyip Erdoğan winning the first direct presidential elections in 2014. In July 2016, a section of the Turkish military conducted a failed coup in which it claimed that the AKP was eroding the tradition of secularism, violating human rights, and becoming more authoritarian. According to some sources, President Erdoğan has used the failure of the coup as an opportunity to conduct a "counter-coup" and purge tens of thousands of his rivals in the military and the civil service, including judges, teachers, and academics ("After the Coup" 2016). These events do not bode well for electoral integrity in future Turkish elections.

Belarus is an authoritarian former Soviet republic in Eastern Europe. It has been referred to as Europe's last dictatorship (Wilson 2012). Belarus's 2016 PEI score is very low (36) and leaves it ranked 138 out of 153 countries in the data set. Belarus has been ruled by President Alexander Lukashenko since 1994. Lukashenko is the longest-serving leader among post-Soviet heads of state, and he regularly wins presidential elections with massive majorities. The bottom left panel of the star-plot in Figure 13.2 indicates that there are many reasons for Belarus's low PEI score. Over his time in office, Lukashenko has expanded executive control over the legislature, consolidated state control of the media, and built the largest security apparatus in Europe (Crabtree, Fariss, and Schuler, forthcoming). There were four candidates in the October 2015 presidential elections. At least two of these candidates were considered "shadow" candidates who ran only to create the impression of political competition (Wilson 2015). During the campaign, Lukashenko played on Belarusians' fear that if he were to lose, then Russia would intervene in Belarus as it had done in Ukraine. Fear of Russian intervention limited the extent to which the other candidates were willing to attack Lukashenko. Lukashenko easily won reelection with 83.49 percent of the vote, with more voters casting a ballot marked "against all" than for any of the other three candidates (Crabtree, Fariss, and Schuler, forthcoming). Election observers and human rights organizations have reported evidence of widespread voter coercion, incorrect ballot counting, and election fraud.

Egypt is a dictatorship in North Africa. Its 2016 PEI score is only 42. Many observers had high hopes for democracy in Egypt, following the overthrow of the longtime dictator Hosni Mubarak during the Arab Spring in February 2011. In 2012, Mohamed Morsi, the Muslim Brotherhood candidate, became the first democratically elected president in Egypt's history. After a year of divisive rule, though, the Egyptian military, led by General Abdel Fattah el-Sisi, intervened to remove President Morsi from power in July 2013. There was a mixed international reaction to these events, with the United States refusing to call the events a "military coup" as this would have required freezing the substantial economic and military aid that it provided to Egypt. A new Egyptian constitution, which critics claim gives too much power to the military, was passed in a January 2014 referendum. Shortly afterward, General Sisi was elected president in May 2014. The October–December legislative elections in 2015, which form the basis for Egypt's PEI scores shown in the bottom right panel of Figure 13.2, were supposed to mark the final step in the restoration of democracy. Following the military coup, the Muslim Brotherhood was banned and labeled a terrorist organization, and many of its members were arrested and sentenced to death. Dissidents and journalists critical of the regime have been repressed. Indeed, the regime rejected several political parties who sought to place candidates on the ballot for the 2015 elections. Many of those candidates who were allowed to run were supporters of President Sisi, and a number were closely tied to the ousted dictator, Hosni Mubarak. Secular and leftist parties, many of whom had helped to organize the protests during the Arab Spring, chose to boycott the elections. The boycott and the banning of the Muslim Brotherhood depressed turnout, with some reports putting it as low as 10 percent ("Low Turnout" 2015). The Carter Center, which monitors elections for electoral malpractice, closed its Cairo office ahead of the election and stated "that the political space has narrowed for Egyptian political parties, civil society, and the media. As a result, the upcoming elections are unlikely to advance a genuine democratic transition in Egypt" ("Carter Center Closes Egypt Office" 2014).

The Determinants of Electoral Integrity

Experts tend to perceive democratic elections as displaying more electoral integrity than dictatorial elections. This is not surprising given that elections tend to serve different purposes in democracies and dictatorships. However, this observation does not help us explain the variation we see in electoral integrity among democracies or among dictatorships. We now take a quick look at why elections in some countries have higher levels of electoral integrity than others.

Norris (2015) identifies a number of factors that influence electoral integrity. One factor concerns domestic structural constraints such as the level of economic development, a country's dependence on natural resources, a legacy of conflict, or inhospitable geography. Wealthy countries are more likely to be democratic (see Chapter 6), and they have more resources that they can devote to the electoral process. A salient issue for many poor countries is the cost of actually holding elections. As we'll see shortly, electoral systems vary in the costs that they impose on a political system. The political resource curse suggests that countries that depend on natural resources will exhibit high levels of corruption and that ruling elites will use natural resource revenue to manipulate elections, intimidate opponents, and suppress opposition. This helps to explain the low levels of electoral integrity in countries like Equatorial Guinea, Iraq, and the Democratic Republic of Congo. Countries that have a legacy of conflict, such as Afghanistan, Rwanda, Sri Lanka, and Burundi, typically have deep divisions and high levels of mistrust that can also hinder electoral integrity. As one might expect, the logistical, financial, and technical difficulties of running a well-functioning election are harder in large states with mountainous and other difficult-to-reach areas. For example, the 2014 legislative elections in India took place over nine phases of voting, cost $5 billion, and involved 930,000 polling stations and 814 million eligible voters (Norris 2015, 78).

A second factor concerns the international community. One claim is that countries that are more integrated into the global system will be more likely to adopt international norms and practices that encourage electoral integrity. Regional intergovernmental organizations can also play a role. For example, those European countries seeking membership in the European Union have strong incentives to respect human rights and produce free and fair elections. In contrast, countries associated with regional organizations where member states tend to be authoritarian are less likely to feel pressure to produce high levels of electoral integrity. It is often claimed that donor countries can use foreign aid to encourage recipient countries to increase human rights protections, strengthen civil society associations, and increase media independence. Elections in developing countries frequently receive considerable financial aid and technical assistance from a variety of international organizations and donor countries. As we discussed in Chapter 6, though, there are many reasons to doubt the ability and willingness of donor countries to bring about meaningful democratic and electoral reforms in recipient countries.

A particular international factor that has received growing attention in recent years has been the role played by nonpartisan international organizations that monitor elections. Election observer missions have become increasingly common over the last three decades (Hyde 2011). Organizations such as the Carter Center, the Organization for Security and Cooperation in Europe (OSCE), the African Union (AU), the Organization of American States (OAS), and the European Union (EU) have deployed thousands of international and domestic observers in numerous countries in an attempt to deter incumbents from committing electoral fraud. Very few elections these days have no international observers.

The effectiveness of these observer missions remains open to debate, though. Although some studies find that electoral irregularities are lower in polling stations that have observers (Hyde 2007a, b), others suggest that election monitors simply displace irregularites from the places they visit to surrounding areas they do not visit (Ichino and Schündeln 2012). Observer missions are not always perceived as impartial, and reports can sometimes be politicized and reach contradictory conclusions. For example, the OSCE reported significant irregularities in Azerbaijan's 2013 presidential election, but the delegation of former members of the US House of Representatives declared that the elections had been free, fair, and transparent (Norris 2014, 9). In some cases, observer missions have incentives to understate the degree of electoral malfeasance so that they are invited back to monitor the next elections or because they wish to prevent postelection violence that might result from charges of electoral fraud. Partly in response to these concerns, some political scientists have begun to develop a science of electoral forensics that allows one to detect electoral fraud from the reported election results themselves and does not rely on having "boots on the ground" (see Box 13.1 "The Science of Election Forensics").

THE SCIENCE OF ELECTION FORENSICS

Political scientists have begun to develop tests to identify election fraud. The underlying idea is that human attempts to manipulate election results leave telltale signs that can be picked up by statistical tests (Hicken and Mebane 2015). Many of these tests focus on the frequency distribution of digits in reported vote totals. Benford's law describes a pattern for the frequency distribution of digits in numbers that occurs in many settings (Mebane 2013, 9). Although we might think that each digit from 1 to 9 has an equal probability of appearing as the first digit in a number, this is often not the case. It turns out that in a wide variety of settings, smaller digits are more common than larger digits. To illustrate why this might be the case, Deckert, Myagkov, and Ordeshook (2011, 246) give the example of collecting house street numbers at random from a telephone book. As street numbers tend to begin with 1 (or 10 or 100) and restart at 1 after crossing a boundary or end before higher numbers are reached, addresses that start with the number 1 will be more common than those that start with the number 2, and those that start with a 2 will be more common than those that start with a 3, and so on. According to Benford's law, the first and second digits in a number will follow the frequency distributions shown in Table 13.1. For example, the probability that the first digit in a number will be a 3 is 0.125, and the probability that it will be a 6 is 0.067. Similarly, the probability that the second digit in a number will be a 0 is 0.120, and the probability that it will be a 6 is 0.093. The mean or expected value of the first digit is 3.441, whereas it is 4.187 for the second digit.

Benford's law has been used to detect financial and accounting fraud (Cho and Gaines 2007). The general idea is that individuals who fabricate numbers have a tendency to do so uniformly. As a result, one can compare the frequencies with which different digits appear as the first number in financial accounts with the expected probabilities for those digits from Benford's law. Significant deviations would indicate "suspicious" numbers and possible fraud. Scholars have adopted the same basic idea to try to identify electoral fraud in voting returns (Cantu and Saiegh 2011), though they tend to focus on the distribution of the second digit rather than the first digit (Mebane 2006, 2008; Pericchi and Torres 2011). For example, Mebane (2013) examined electoral returns from 45,692 ballot boxes in the 2009 presidential elections in Iran and found that the frequency distribution of the second digits in the vote totals for the incumbent president, Ahmadinejad, was suspicious. Rather than focus on Benford's law, other scholars have argued that fair elections should produce voting returns that have uniformly distributed 0–9 last digits. Using this method, Beber and Scacco (2012)

| TABLE 13.1 | **Benford's Law: The Frequency Distribution of First and Second Digits** | | | | | | | | | |

0	1	2	3	4	5	6	7	8	9	Mean
—	0.301	0.176	0.125	0.097	0.079	0.067	0.058	0.051	0.046	3.441
0.120	0.114	0.109	0.104	0.100	0.097	0.093	0.090	0.088	0.085	4.187

found evidence of electoral manipulation in the 2007 presidential elections in Nigeria and Senegal.

The use of digit-based methods to identify electoral fraud is not without its critics (Deckert, Myagkov, and Ordeshook 2011; Mebane 2014), and there is evidence that "anomalous" vote counts can be the result of normal behavior such as strategic voting rather than human manipulation (Hicken and Mebane 2015). Researchers are beginning to look at how one might distinguish between suspicious vote totals that arise from strategic voting and those that arise from human manipulation. One possibility is to combine digit-based methods with other methods to identify electoral fraud. In his analysis of electoral fraud in Iran, Mebane (2013) also examined the proportion of invalid votes in a ballot box. One would expect that the proportion of invalid ballots would be particularly low in cases where ballot boxes have been stuffed, that is, where valid votes have been artificially added for one particular candidate. If there is a relationship between the proportion of invalid votes in a ballot box and the second digits of the ballot box vote totals, then this would be evidence in favor of electoral fraud rather than strategic voting. This is precisely what Mebane found with respect to President Ahmadinejad's vote totals. He also found that Ahmadinejad's vote share increased sharply as the proportion of invalid votes in a ballot box declined, providing further evidence of ballot box stuffing. These types of tests obviously cannot provide conclusive evidence of electoral fraud. What they can do, though, is highlight suspicious activity and indicate which elections require further investigation.

Two other factors influence electoral integrity—institutional design and electoral management bodies. Some scholars argue that countries with power-sharing institutions exhibit higher levels of electoral integrity than countries with institutions that concentrate power in the hands of the majority (Lijphart 2004; Norris 2015). This is because power-sharing institutions create checks and balances that limit the ability of incumbents to abuse their power and encourage minority groups to "buy in" to the political system. Other scholars, though, argue that power-sharing institutions make it harder to hold political actors accountable and that they tend to reify social divisions in the political system. We will revisit the relative benefits and costs of power-sharing institutions in more detail in Chapters 15 and 16. Electoral management bodies refer to the institutions and authorities that administer elections. Electoral management bodies that are independent of the executive branch and have functional capacity (technical expertise, trained officials, adequate budgets, and so on) are often key to holding high-quality elections. Strengthening these bodies would seem to be an easy step to improve electoral integrity. It is often the case, though, that those actors who have an incentive to strengthen these institutions (opposition and minority groups) are not the actors who have the ability to strengthen them (incumbents and majority groups).

ELECTORAL SYSTEMS

Although elections always involve citizens casting votes for candidates or political parties or both, there is a great deal of variation in the precise set of rules employed by the world's electoral systems. Some allow citizens to vote for candidates, whereas others allow them to vote only for political parties; some allow citizens to cast only one vote, whereas others allow them to cast multiple votes; some allow for only one round of voting, whereas others allow for two or more; some involve electing only one representative in each district, whereas others involve electing many. The list of differences could go on and on. Despite the many different ways in which one might think to distinguish among the world's electoral systems, most political scientists categorize electoral systems into three main families—majoritarian, proportional, and mixed—based on the electoral formula that they use to translate votes into seats. In Figure 13.3, we illustrate these electoral system families along with the names of the various electoral systems they include. The electoral systems shown in Figure 13.3 are all those that are currently employed in national-level legislative elections around the world. In what follows, we examine how some of the more common majoritarian, proportional, and mixed electoral systems work.[4]

Majoritarian Electoral Systems

A **majoritarian electoral system** is one in which the candidates or parties that receive the most votes win. We should note that the word *majoritarian* is somewhat misleading.

> A **majoritarian electoral system** is one in which the candidates or parties that receive the most votes win.

Although some majoritarian electoral systems require the winning candidate or party to obtain an absolute majority of the votes (absolute majority systems), others require only that the candidate or party win more votes than anyone else (plurality systems). In other words, not all majoritarian electoral systems actually require the winning candidates or parties to obtain an absolute majority of the votes. Probably the main reason why majoritarian electoral systems are referred to as "majoritarian" is, as we will see, that they frequently produce outcomes in which the largest party wins a majority of the legislative seats even if the party does not win a majority of the votes. In effect, majoritarian electoral systems tend to help the largest party obtain a legislative majority. As Figure 13.3 indicates, there are many different types of majoritarian electoral systems.

Single-Member District Plurality System

A **single-member district plurality (SMDP) system** is the simplest and most commonly used majoritarian electoral system in the world. It is employed primarily in the United

> A **single-member district plurality (SMDP) system** is one in which individuals cast a single vote for a candidate in a single-member district. The candidate with the most votes is elected.

Kingdom and in former British colonies, such as Belize, Canada, India, Nigeria, and the United States. In an SMDP system, voters cast a single candidate-centered vote in single-member districts. The candidate with the

---

4. For information on how each of the electoral systems shown in Figure 13.3 works, see Bormann and Golder (2013).

FIGURE 13.3 **Electoral System Families**

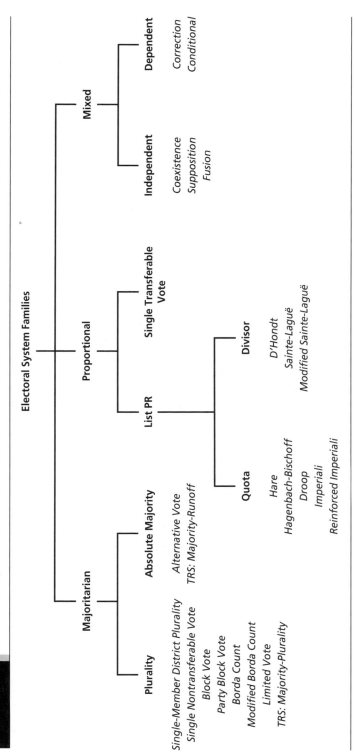

Note: These are all of the electoral systems used in national-level legislative elections around the world (Bormann and Golder 2013, 362). TRS refers to "two-round systems."

most votes, even if this is not a majority of the votes, is elected from the district. SMDP systems are sometimes referred to as "first-past-the-post." This name, though, is misleading as it suggests that a candidate is elected once she gets past a certain vote total. In theory, a candidate can win in an SMDP system with as few as two votes if all the other candidates win only one vote each. An example of the operation of an SMDP system in the Bath constituency in the United Kingdom in the 2015 legislative elections is shown in Table 13.2. Ben Howlett of the Conservative Party won the most votes and was, therefore, elected as the Member of Parliament for this district.

SMDP electoral systems have both strengths and weaknesses. Perhaps the greatest strength of SMDP systems is their simplicity. This means that they are easy for voters to understand. It also means that they are easy and relatively inexpensive to administer. A second strength of SMDP systems has to do with the fact that only one representative is elected in each district. Having only one representative per constituency means that responsibility for what happens in the district lies squarely with that person. In other words, SMDP systems make it easy for voters to identify who is responsible for policies in their district and therefore to hold them accountable in the next election. By making it easier for voters to hold representatives accountable, SMDP systems create incentives for representatives to perform well in office. As a result, SMDP systems tend to produce high levels of constituency service and close bonds between constituents and their representatives.

Despite these strengths, SMDP electoral systems have many critics. Some critics point to the fact that SMDP systems have the potential to produce unrepresentative outcomes. As our example in Table 13.2 illustrates, it is possible for a candidate to win without obtaining a majority of the votes; in fact, 62.2 percent of Bath voters did not support the winning candidate. It is worth noting that candidates can win in SMDP systems with even lower vote shares than that obtained by the winning candidate in Bath. As an example, the winning candidate in the Kerowagi constituency in Papua New Guinea won with just 7.9 percent of the vote in the 1987 legislative elections (Cox 1997, 85).

TABLE 13.2   Election Results from the Bath Constituency, UK Legislative Elections, 2015

Candidate	Party	Votes	Percentage
Ben Howlett	Conservative	17,833	37.8
Steve Bradley	Liberal Democrat	14,000	29.7
Ollie Middleton	Labour	6,216	13.2
Dominic Tristram	Green	5,634	11.9
Julian Deverell	UKIP	2,922	6.2
Lorraine Morgan-Brinkhurst	Independent	499	1.1
Jenny Knight	Independent	63	0.1

Not only are SMDP systems criticized for producing unrepresentative outcomes at the district level, but they are frequently criticized for their potential to produce unrepresentative outcomes at the national level as well. Under an SMDP system, it is entirely possible for a party that wins a significant percentage of the overall national vote to obtain very few legislative seats because it fails to come first in many constituencies. For instance, consider the 1983 legislative elections in the United Kingdom. In these elections, the coalition between the Social Democratic Party and the Liberal Party, which was known as the Alliance, won 25.4 percent of the national vote but received just 3.5 percent of the seats. In fact, the Alliance won only 675,985 votes (out of 30,661,309 votes) fewer than the Labour Party but received 186 fewer legislative seats. In stark contrast to the Alliance, the Conservative Party won 61.1 percent of the seats and formed a single-party government even though it had won only 42.4 percent of the votes. As this example demonstrates, SMDP systems can produce a highly disproportionate translation of votes into seats that tends to favor larger parties at the expense of smaller ones.

SMDP systems are also criticized by some for encouraging individuals to vote strategically rather than in accordance with their true preferences. Sincere voting means voting for your most preferred candidate or party. In contrast, strategic voting means voting for your most preferred candidate *who has a realistic chance of winning.*[5] To see how the SMDP system creates an incentive to vote strategically, consider the Bath example in Table 13.2 again. Imagine an individual who prefers the Labour candidate to the Liberal Democrat candidate and the Liberal Democrat candidate to the Conservative candidate; that is, $L > LD > C$. If this individual votes for the Labour candidate, she will be voting sincerely. However, this individual has an incentive to vote strategically because opinion polls are likely to show that the Labour candidate is going to finish in third place and has little to no chance of coming in first. Thus, a vote for the Labour candidate is likely to be "wasted." As a result, the individual may decide to vote strategically for the Liberal Democrat candidate (who has a more realistic chance of winning) in an attempt to stop the Conservative candidate (the least-preferred candidate) from winning. Clearly, we prefer democratic electoral systems that encourage voters to express their sincere preferences. Unfortunately, though, scholars have shown that *all* reasonable electoral systems create incentives for individuals to act strategically; there are no "strategy-proof" systems (Gibbard 1973; Satterthwaite 1975). Nonetheless, some electoral systems, such as SMDP, create stronger incentives to act strategically than others. We address these incentives to vote strategically and their effects in more detail in the next chapter.

Another criticism of SMDP systems is that they can encourage the creation of ethnic parties in countries in which ethnic groups are regionally concentrated. This can result in regional fiefdoms or party strongholds in which there is little electoral competition, the party of the majority ethnic group is dominant, and minorities have little sway over public policy or the allocation of private goods. This type of situation frequently occurs in African countries like Malawi and

---

5. For more detailed definitions of sincere and strategic voting, see Chapter 11.

Kenya, where ethnic groups are geographically concentrated in particular regions (Barkan 1995; Posner 2005). In effect, the use of SMDP electoral systems in Africa has helped produce countries that are "divided into geographically separate party strongholds, with little incentive for parties to make appeals outside their home region and cultural-political base" (Reynolds, Reilly, and Ellis 2005, 43). Similarly, the use of SMDP probably helped segregationist Democrats maintain single-party dominance in the southern United States for almost a century (Mickey 2015).

Single Nontransferable Vote

The **single nontransferable vote (SNTV)** is a second type of majoritarian electoral system. SNTV is essentially the same as an SMDP electoral system except that it works in multimember districts instead of single-member districts. Basically, each party competing in a district puts up a list of candidates, and individuals vote for one of them. The candidates that win the most votes are elected. For example, in a three-seat district, the top three vote-getters are elected. In a four-seat district, the top four vote-getters are elected, and so on. One advantage of SNTV systems over SMDP ones is that they tend to produce more proportional outcomes and greater representation for smaller parties and minority ethnic groups. This is because candidates from smaller parties and minority ethnic groups can now get elected even though they do not win the most votes in a district.

> The **single nontransferable vote (SNTV)** is a system in which voters cast a single candidate-centered vote in a multimember district. The candidates with the highest number of votes are elected.

Interestingly, candidates in an SNTV system know exactly how many votes they need to win in order to guarantee their election. For example, if there are n district seats to be filled, then any candidate A can guarantee being elected by receiving one more than $1 / (n + 1)$ of the votes. This is because n other candidates cannot all receive more than candidate A. Thus, in a four-seat district, a candidate can guarantee winning one of the seats by winning more than 20 percent of the vote. An SNTV system was employed for legislative elections in Japan until 1994 and in Taiwan until 2005. It is currently employed for legislative elections in Afghanistan and Vanuatu.

SNTV electoral systems are often considered problematic. First, they tend to weaken political parties by creating incentives for intraparty fighting and factionalization. This is because candidates are competing against candidates not only from other parties in their district but also against candidates from their own party. The result is that electoral campaigns are often centered on candidate characteristics rather than policy differences, with candidates going to great lengths to cultivate personal reputations. SNTV systems may even impede the emergence of fully fledged parties. In 2005, for example, Afghan president Hamid Karzai adopted an SNTV electoral system and pronounced that candidates could not show party affiliation on the ballot (Reynolds 2006).[6] The system has produced a great deal

---

6. That the SNTV system can work without fully fledged parties was one of the reasons why it was adopted (Reynolds 2006). As the *New York Times* reported, Afghans "associate parties with both the Communists who brought the Soviet invaders and the ethnic militias that pillaged the country after the Communists' downfall" ("Afghanistan: The Wrong Voting System" 2016). A law introduced in 2009 allows candidates to have their party's symbol on the ballot. However, only 34 candidates had their party's name added to the ballot in the 2010 legislative elections (Reynolds and Carey 2012).

of voter confusion. Voters in Kabul, for example, were confronted with more than four hundred candidates on the ballot, all vying for the thirty-three seats up for election. Over two-thirds of the votes were cast for losing candidates and therefore wasted. The end result was a highly fragmented legislature containing more than thirty factions with shifting loyalties (Reynolds 2011, 9–10). The 2010 legislative elections produced even higher levels of fragmentation. With weak or nonexistent parties in the legislature, it can be difficult for governments to build legislative coalitions to keep them in power and support their policy objectives.

Election workers and donkeys carry voting material to remote villages on September 17, 2010 (the day before the election), in the Panjshir province, Afghanistan. More than 2,500 candidates contested 249 seats in the lower house of the Afghan parliament, using the single nontransferable vote electoral system.

Second, the fact that candidates can guarantee their own election with a specific percentage of votes encourages clientelistic behavior and the development of patronage systems, in which candidates target electoral bribes at well-defined interest groups. For example, candidates of the Liberal Democratic Party (LDP) in Japan were notorious for engaging in constituency service and targeting subsidy (pork) allocations toward their districts (Hirano 2011; see also Box 14.2, "One-Party Dominant Systems," in Chapter 14). Clientelism is likely to be particularly prevalent when candidates do not need to win many votes to guarantee themselves a seat. This will be the case when the SNTV system is combined with a large multimember district. Recall that a candidate in an SNTV system can guarantee election if they receive one more than $1 / (n + 1)$ of the votes, where n refers to the number of district seats to be filled. It is perhaps worth noting that Japan, which was infamous for its system of political clientelism, employed an SNTV system in relatively small multimember districts comprising three to five seats. In contrast, the SNTV system in Afghanistan is being employed in districts where the magnitude ranges from a low of two to a high of thirty-three. This means that Afghan candidates in some districts can *guarantee* winning seats with less than 3 percent of the vote. Indeed, several candidates in the provinces of Helmand, Kandahar, and Zabul were able to win seats in the 2010 legislative elections with just a few hundred votes. As one would expect, the "cheapness" of an Afghan seat encourages vote buying. As the *New York Times* reported in 2010, political candidates were literally buying Afghan votes for anywhere from a high of about $18 in Ghazni province to a low of about $1 in Kandahar (Nordlan 2010). This is a small price for Afghan candidates to pay given that legislative seats come with a high monthly salary and the opportunity to exploit the corrupt patron-client political system.

Third, the SNTV system tends to favor both incumbent and well-organized parties. As we have seen, SNTV systems encourage the development of political systems that are based on patronage and other particularistic connections. Incumbent parties are advantaged in these systems because they have greater access to state resources and can more credibly commit to allocating those resources to their supporters. Parties that are well organized are not only better equipped to make sure that sufficient goods are distributed to their voters but are also better placed to deal with the strategic quandaries that political parties and voters face in an SNTV system. Although all parties in an SNTV system want to win as many seats as they can in each multimember district, they do not want to put up too many candidates in case their party supporters split their vote between these candidates to such an extent that none, or only a few, of the candidates actually finish among the top vote winners. In the extreme, it is possible in an SNTV system for a party whose candidates together obtain a substantial percentage of the votes, even an absolute majority, to win no seats. This suggests that political parties have to be very careful in choosing how many candidates to run in each district. Similarly, supporters of each party must think hard about which candidate from their party most needs their vote to be elected; if they give their vote to a candidate who is already likely to obtain a sufficient number of votes, then their vote will be wasted. Well-organized parties are better able to deal with these issues because they can often coordinate their nominations and distribute their supporters' votes in a way that maximizes the number of their candidates elected in each district. For example, the Kuomintang in Taiwan used to assign its candidates to particular geographic zones in a district and send party members a letter telling them which candidate to vote for (Liu 1999; Patterson and Stockton 2010).

Finally, the fact that candidates under an SNTV system can win with only a small fraction of the vote share means that they do not have to moderate their political message and can instead espouse a more extremist rhetoric that appeals to a specific segment of the electorate. As such, some believe that the SNTV system increases the likelihood that extremists will be elected, potentially destabilizing the political system in the process.

The **alternative vote (AV)** is a candidate-centered preference voting system used in single-member districts where voters rank order the candidates. A candidate who receives an absolute majority is elected. If no candidate wins an absolute majority, then the candidate with the fewest votes is eliminated, and her votes are reallocated until one candidate has an absolute majority of the valid votes remaining.

Preference, or preferential, voting involves voters ranking one or more candidates or parties in order of preference on the ballots.

Alternative Vote

Whereas SMDP and SNTV are both "plurality" majoritarian systems, the **alternative vote (AV)** is an "absolute majority" majoritarian system. Candidates cannot win without obtaining a majority of the votes. The alternative vote is a candidate-centered **preference, or preferential, voting** system used in single-member districts where voters rank order the candidates. Voters typically have to place numbers next to the names of the candidates on the ballot to indicate whether each is the voter's first choice, second choice, third choice, and so on. AV systems in which voters have to rank order all of the candidates are called "full preference" systems, whereas AV systems in which voters have to rank order only some candidates are called "optional preference" systems. If a candidate wins an absolute majority of first-preference votes, he is immediately elected. If no candidate wins an absolute majority, then the candidate with the fewest first-preference votes is eliminated, and her votes are reallocated among the remaining candidates based on the designated second preferences. This process is repeated until one candidate has obtained an absolute majority of the votes cast (full preferential system) or an absolute majority of the valid votes remaining (optional preferential system). The alternative vote is sometimes referred to as an instant-runoff vote (IRV) because it is much like holding a series of runoff elections in which the candidate with the fewest votes is eliminated in each round until someone receives an absolute majority of the vote.

Australia uses the AV system for its legislative elections. Australian voters must rank order all of the candidates on the ballot because they employ a full preference AV system. In Table 13.3, we show how the AV system worked in the Richmond constituency of New South Wales in the 1990 elections. When the first-preference votes from all the voters were initially tallied up, Charles Blunt came first with 40.9 percent of the vote. Because no candidate won an absolute majority, the candidate with the lowest number of votes (Gavin Baillie) was eliminated. As Table 13.3 illustrates, Baillie was ranked first on 187 ballots. These 187 ballots were then reallocated to whichever of the remaining candidates the voters ranked second after Gavin Baillie. For example, the fact that Ian Paterson received 445 votes in the first count but 480 votes in the second count indicates that thirty-five of the people who had listed Gavin Baillie as their most preferred candidate had listed Ian Paterson as their second-choice candidate. Because there was still no candidate with an absolute majority after this second count, the new candidate with the lowest number of votes (Dudley Leggett) was eliminated, and his ballots were reallocated among the remaining candidates in the same manner as before. This process continued until the seventh round of counting, when Neville Newell became the first candidate to finally obtain an absolute majority of the votes. The overall result, then, was that Neville Newell became the representative elected from the Richmond constituency of New South Wales.

It is worth noting that Charles Blunt had won by far the most votes in the first round and had been leading on all of the counts up until the very last one. It was only when the last votes were reallocated according to the preferences of the voters that it became clear that an absolute majority of those who voted in Richmond preferred Neville Newell to Charles Blunt. As this example illustrates, the reallocation of votes from eliminated candidates to remaining candidates can play an important role in determining the outcome of elections in AV systems. It is for this reason that political parties in Australia often give voters "how-to-vote" cards outside polling stations with clear instructions on how to rank candidates so that the flow of preferences will benefit them either directly or, by helping any allied parties, indirectly. An example of a how-to-vote card for the Liberal Party is illustrated in Figure 13.4.

TABLE 13.3 Richmond Constituency, New South Wales, Australian Legislative Elections, 1990

Candidate	First count (no.)	(%)	Second count (no.)	(%)	Third count (no.)	(%)	Fourth count (no.)	(%)	Fifth count (no.)	(%)	Sixth count (no.)	(%)	Seventh count (no.)	(%)
Stan Gibbs	4,346	6.3	4,380	6.3	4,420	6.4	4,504	6.5	4,683	6.8				
Neville Newell	18,423	26.7	18,467	26.7	18,484	26.8	18,544	26.9	18,683	27.1	20,238	29.4	34,664	50.5
Gavin Baillie	187	0.3												
Alan Sims	1,032	1.5	1,053	1.5	1,059	1.5	1,116	1.6						
Ian Paterson	445	0.6	480	0.7	530	0.8								
Dudley Leggett	279	0.4	294	0.4										
Charles Blunt	28,257	40.9	28,274	41.0	28,303	41.0	28,416	41.2	28,978	42	29,778	43.2	33,980	49.5
Helen Caldicott	16,072	23.3	16,091	23.3	16,237	23.5	16,438	23.8	16,658	24.1	18,903	27.4		

Note: Blank cells indicate that a candidate was eliminated.

FIGURE 13.4	**Australian "How-to-Vote" Card from the 2001 Legislative Elections**

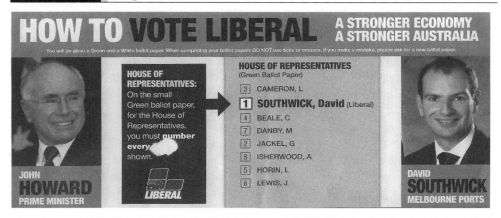

Source: http://australianpolitics.com/elections/htv/htv-cards-pictures.shtml

To a large extent, AV systems retain many of the strengths associated with SMDP electoral systems. For example, the fact that there is only one representative elected per constituency means that it is easy for voters to identify who is responsible for district policy and hold them accountable. As a result, we can expect high levels of constituency service and strong bonds between citizens and their representatives. AV systems have several additional strengths, though. One is that voters have a greater opportunity to convey information about their preferences than they have under an SMDP system. This is because they get to rank order the candidates rather than simply vote "yes" and "no" for one of them. A second strength is that there is less of an incentive for voters to engage in strategic voting because they know that their vote will not be wasted if the candidate they most prefer is unpopular and unlikely to win; their vote is simply transferred to the candidate they prefer next. We should note, though, that strategic incentives do not disappear entirely. For example, voters may decide not to rank the candidates according to their sincere preferences because they want to influence the order in which candidates are eliminated and hence who ultimately wins in a district. That this type of strategic concern matters is one explanation for why Australian parties hand out how-to-vote cards at the polling stations.

A third strength is that AV systems encourage candidates and parties to win the votes from not only their base supporters but also the "second preferences" of others. This is because these second preferences may end up being crucial to their election. To attract these votes, candidates are likely to have to make broadly based centrist appeals to all interests rather than focus on narrow sectarian or extremist issues. Some evidence for this comes from Australia, where the major parties frequently attempt to negotiate deals with smaller parties for their second preferences prior to an election in a process known as "preference swapping" (Reilly 2001, 45). The incentive to build broadly based support helps to explain why the AV system is often advocated for elections in deeply divided societies, such as the ethnically fragmented Bosnia and Herzegovina, Fiji, Papua New Guinea, and South Africa (Horowitz 1991; Reilly 2001).

Recall that one of the most common criticisms made of SMDP electoral systems is that they allow candidates to win who do not obtain majority support. This problem is addressed by AV systems because candidates are eliminated one at a time until one has an overall majority. Although this would appear to be one of the main strengths of AV systems, some critics claim that the winning candidate does not necessarily obtain a "genuine" majority. By this, they mean that it is possible for a majority of the voters in a district to prefer some other candidate to the one who actually wins. The reason why this possibility exists is that a candidate who is preferred to all the other candidates in a series of head-to-head races can be eliminated early on in an AV system because he or she receives an insufficient number of first-place votes. A clear weakness of the AV system is that it is rather complicated. From the point of view of the voters, it requires a reasonable degree of literacy and numeracy. And from the point of view of the election authorities, the counting process can be costly and drawn out.

Majority-Runoff Two-Round System

Another "absolute majority" majoritarian electoral system is the majority-runoff two-round system. A **two-round system (TRS)** has the potential for two rounds of elections. The **majority-runoff TRS** is a system in which voters cast a single candidate-centered vote in a single-member district. Any candidate who obtains an absolute majority of the votes in the first round is elected. If no candidate wins an absolute majority, then the top two vote winners go on to compete in a runoff election one or two weeks later. Whoever wins the most votes in this runoff election—necessarily an absolute majority as there are only two candidates—is elected.

A **two-round system (TRS)** is an electoral system that has the potential for two rounds of elections.

The **majority-runoff TRS** is a system in which voters cast a single candidate-centered vote in a single-member district. Any candidate who obtains an absolute majority in the first round of elections is elected. If no one obtains an absolute majority, then the top two vote winners go on to compete in a runoff election in the second round.

The majority-runoff TRS is by far the most common method for electing presidents around the world. While the majority-runoff TRS was used in just 6 percent of the presidential elections that occurred in the 1950s, it has been used in more than 65 percent of the presidential elections that have occurred since 2000 (Bormann and Golder 2013, 368). In Tables 13.4 and 13.5 we show the results from the Burkina Faso presidential elections in 2015 and the Benin presidential elections in 2016. Roch Christian Kaboré won an absolute majority of the votes (53.49 percent) in the first round of the Burkina Faso presidential elections and was therefore elected without the need for a second round runoff. In the Benin presidential elections, no candidate obtained an absolute majority in the first round. Patrice Talon was eventually elected president after winning

TABLE 13.4	**Burkina Faso Presidential Elections 2015**

First round

Candidate	Party	Vote share (%)
Roch Christian Kaboré	People's Movement for Progress	53.49
Zéphirin Diabré	Union for Progress and Reform	29.65
Tahirou Barry	National Rebirth Party	3.09
Bénéwendé Stanislas Sankara	Union for Rebirth	2.77
Ablassé Ouedraogo	Alternative Faso	1.93
Saran Sérémé	Party for Development and Reform	1.73
Others		7.33

TABLE 13.5	**Benin Presidential Elections 2016**

First round

Candidate	Party	Vote share (%)
Lionel A. L. Zinsou-Derlin	Cowry Forces for an Emerging Benin	28.4
Patrice A. G. Talon		24.8
Sébastien G. M. A. Adjavon		23.0
Abdoulaye B. Bio-Tchane	Alliance for a Triumphant Benin	8.8
Pascal J. I. Koupaki	New Consciousness Rally	5.9
Robert Gbian		1.6
Fernand M. Amoussou		1.2
Salifou Issa		1.0
Others		5.3

Second round

Patrice A. G. Talon		65.4
Lionel A. L. Zinsou-Derlin	Cowry Forces for an Emerging Benin	34.6

65.4 percent of the vote in the second round runoff. A few countries such as Haiti and Comoros use the majority-runoff TRS for their legislative elections.

The majority-runoff TRS has a number of strengths, particularly when compared with SMDP systems. The first is that it gives voters more choice than they enjoy in SMDP systems. For example, individuals who vote for a candidate who "loses" in the first round get a second opportunity to influence who gets elected in the second round. The majority-runoff TRS also allows voters to change their mind and switch their votes even if the candidate they supported in the first round actually makes it into the second round. Voters might want to change their mind as a result of new information that emerges between the first and second rounds. It is worth noting that changing one's ranking of candidates in this way is not possible in a preference voting system, such as the alternative vote.

A second strength is that voters have less incentive to behave strategically than they do in SMDP systems because they have two opportunities to affect the election outcome. Individuals can vote for their most preferred candidate in the first round even if this candidate has little chance of winning in the end and then switch their support to a more well-placed candidate in the second round. Of course, strategic incentives do not disappear entirely, and things can go wrong if individuals vote sincerely in this way. Voters need to think about whether their decision to vote sincerely in the first round positively affects the likelihood that a candidate whom they do not like will win either the first or the second round. For example, consider the 2002 presidential elections in France. The second round of these elections involved a candidate from the mainstream right, Jacques Chirac, and a candidate from the extreme right, Jean-Marie Le Pen. One reason why there was no left-wing candidate was that the left-wing electorate split its vote among so many left-wing candidates in the first round that none made it into the second round. As a result, the only choice that left-wing voters had in this second round was between a candidate whom they disliked (Chirac) and a candidate whom they really disliked (Le Pen). It is arguable that France's left-wing voters would have been better off had they voted more strategically in the first round.

A third strength of the majority-runoff TRS is that it creates incentives for candidates who make it into the second round to look beyond their own electoral base and reach compromises with the leaders of parties who are already eliminated in an attempt to win over their supporters. In addition, because voters are not required to rank order candidates with numbers to express their second choice, some have argued that the majority-runoff TRS is more suitable for countries with widespread illiteracy and low levels of education than preference voting systems, such as the alternative vote (Reynolds, Reilly, and Ellis 2005, 53). A final strength of the majority-runoff TRS is that the winning candidate can claim to have won the support of a majority of the voters.

The majority-runoff TRS also has a number of weaknesses. One is that it imposes significant costs on the electoral administration. After all, the electoral administration has to conduct two sets of elections instead of one. Indeed, these additional costs have led some countries such as Sri Lanka that were initially interested in a majority-runoff TRS to adopt a different electoral system (see Box 13.2, "The Supplementary Vote and Sri Lanka"). The majority-runoff TRS also imposes significant costs on individuals, who potentially have to vote in two elections. Empirical evidence suggests that there is a considerable drop-off in the level of turnout between the two rounds of elections. A second weakness is that, like SMDP electoral systems, the majority-runoff TRS often produces a disproportional translation of votes into seats. Indeed, there is some evidence that it produces the most disproportional results of any electoral system used in Western democracies (Reynolds, Reilly, and Ellis 2005, 53). According to some critics, a third weakness of the majority-runoff TRS is that it hurts minority representation. For example, Guinier (1994) has argued that, on extending the right to vote to African Americans, several southern states in the United States adopted the majority-runoff TRS in an attempt to reduce the ability of African American candidates to win. Evidence that the majority-runoff TRS does, indeed, hurt minority candidates comes from a series of elections conducted in the laboratory by Morton and Rietz (2008).

Box 13.2

THE SUPPLEMENTARY VOTE AND SRI LANKA

One of the disadvantages of the majority-runoff TRS is that it is costly. A similar electoral system but with lower costs is the **supplementary vote (SV)**. The supplementary vote is a candidate-centered electoral system used in single-member districts, in which voters are required to rank at least one and at most two candidates in order of preference. Typically, voters are presented with a ballot with two columns alongside a list of names. Voters place an X in the first column to indicate their most preferred candidate and, if they wish, an X in the second column to indicate their second choice. A candidate who wins an absolute majority of the first-preference votes is automatically elected. If no candidate wins an absolute majority, however, all but the two leading candidates are eliminated. The second-preference votes of those who voted for eliminated candidates are then reallocated to determine the winner. The SV is, in many ways, like a majority-runoff TRS except that there is only one round of voting. It is this characteristic that makes the SV less costly. As you will have noticed, the supplementary vote is also a special variant of the alternative vote (AV) in which voters are restricted to expressing only a first and second choice and in which there can be at most two counts of the votes. This means that, unlike in an AV system, voters affect the outcome of the election only if they indicate a preference for at least one of the top two candidates; if individuals vote for candidates who finish outside the top two, then their votes are wasted. The SV system is currently used to elect the mayor of London.

The **supplementary vote (SV)** is a candidate-centered system used in single-member districts, where voters are required to rank at least one and at most two candidates in order of preference. A candidate who wins an absolute majority is elected. If no candidate wins an absolute majority, then all but the two leading candidates are eliminated. The second-preference votes of those who voted for eliminated candidates are then reallocated to determine the winner.

A slight variant of the SV system is used to elect the Sri Lankan president (Reilly 2002). The only difference with the SV system described above is that voters can mark their preferences for the top three, instead of the top two, candidates. If no candidate wins an absolute majority of the first-preference votes, then all but the top two candidates are eliminated, and the second- and third-preference votes of the eliminated candidates are reallocated to determine the winner.

Maithripala Sirisena is sworn in as the new president on January 9, 2015, at Independence Square in Colombo, Sri Lanka.

In 1978, Sri Lanka adopted a new constitution that included an elected president (Reilly 2001, 112–115). The need to elect a president raised particular concerns given that Sri Lanka had a long history of bitter ethnic conflict between the majority Sinhalese and the minority Tamil communities. The goal was to have a president who would be a national figure capable of representing all the groups in society and who could encourage different factions to compromise and reach a consensus. But what was the best way to elect such a president?

Two objectives were seen as being particularly important. One was that the minority Tamil community should have a meaningful role in electing the president. The other was that the president should have the explicit support of an absolute majority of the voters. Political actors were initially interested in adopting a majority-runoff TRS similar to that used in France. "However, the extreme costs and security issues associated with holding two separate elections within a two-week period was seen as being a major defect, particularly since Sri Lanka was in the midst of a violent civil war at the time" (Reilly 2002, 115). These concerns ultimately led to the adoption of the supplementary vote system that combines the two rounds of voting into one election.

In addition to ensuring that the president is elected with majority support, the SV system creates incentives for candidates to look beyond their own political party or ethnic constituency to win over the second- and third-preference votes from other groups. Sri Lanka has conducted seven presidential elections—1982, 1988, 1994, 1999, 2005, 2010, and 2015—since adopting the supplementary vote. So far, the winning presidential candidate has won an absolute majority (if only just) in the first round and has had no need to rely on the transfer of preference votes to be elected. Despite this, some scholars have argued that the possibility that winning candidates might have to rely on these preference votes has led presidential candidates to pay more attention to minority groups during their campaigning than they otherwise might (Reilly 2001, 119–120). For example, Chandrika Kumaratunga, the winning candidate in the 1994 presidential elections, made formal coalition arrangements with the major Muslim party in Sri Lanka. In addition, her moderate approach to ethnic matters led parties representing Sri Lankan and Indian Tamils to support her as well (Schaffer 1995, 423).

Proportional Electoral Systems

The rationale behind **proportional**, or **proportional representation (PR), electoral systems** is to consciously reduce the disparity between a party's share of the vote and its share of the seats. In other words, the goal of proportional representation systems is to produce proportional outcomes—if a party wins 10 percent of the vote, it should win 10 percent of the seats; if it wins 20 percent of the vote, it should win 20 percent of the seats; and so on. This proportionality should exist both within districts and in the nation as a whole. All PR systems share two things in common. One is that they employ multimember districts. This is because it is impossible to divide a single seat proportionally. The second is that they use either a quota or a divisor to determine who is elected in each district. As we will see, a quota or a divisor essentially determines the number of votes that a candidate or party needs in order to win a seat. Given this, we define a proportional electoral system as a quota- or divisor-based system that is employed in multimember districts. Although there are important variations among proportional systems, they are typically divided into the two main types illustrated in Figure 13.3: list proportional representation (list PR) systems and the single transferable vote (STV).

> A **proportional**, or **proportional representation (PR), electoral system** is a quota- or divisor-based electoral system employed in multimember districts.

Many scholars have argued that proportional electoral systems have a number of strengths when compared with majoritarian ones (Lijphart 1999). Perhaps the main strength of PR systems is that they tend to produce a more accurate translation of votes into seats. This means that PR systems avoid the possibility that a party wins a large percentage of the vote but only a few legislative seats. Recall that this was one of the possible anomalies with majoritarian systems. It also means that small parties are able to win representation in proportion to their size. As a result, minorities are likely to be better represented in a PR system than in a majoritarian one. The fact that small parties have a greater chance of winning seats means that individuals face weaker incentives to vote strategically. As a consequence, electoral outcomes in PR systems should be a more accurate reflection of voters' sincere preferences. Arguably, it is also the case that individuals are more likely to turn out and vote in PR systems because they know that their votes are less likely to be wasted (Blais and Carty 1990; Blais and Dobrzynska 1998).

Some have argued that PR systems are all but essential for maintaining stability in ethnically and religiously divided societies (Lijphart 1990, 1991; Norris 2008). The claim is that the stakes of the game are often high in a divided society and that the risk of state instability is simply too great for parties to view elections and control of the executive branch as a winner-take-all contest (Reynolds 2011, 19). PR makes it easy for social groups to organize into ethnic and religious parties that can obtain legislative representation in proportion to their size. This, in turn, produces legislatures that reflect all the significant segments of society and leads to coalition governments based on power-sharing arrangements. The implicit assumption here, of course, is that the different ethnic groups will ultimately choose to work together in the legislature and the government.

The notion that PR systems are essential for stability and democratic rule in divided societies is widely, but not universally, accepted. A few scholars, for example, argue that preferential voting systems, such as the alternative vote, are superior (Horowitz 1985, 1991; Reilly 1997, 2001). These scholars note that PR systems may simply replicate bitter societal divisions in the legislature without creating incentives for cooperation and accommodation across the different ethnic parties. In contrast, they argue that preferential voting systems encourage political parties to run moderate broad-based campaigns that are appealing beyond their core set of supporters because they know that their electoral success is likely to depend on the transfer of preference votes from other ethnic groups. Of course, this is likely to happen only if ethnic groups are not geographically concentrated in such a way that parties can win a majority by appealing to a single ethnic or religious group.[7] In effect, when it comes to dealing with divided societies, one can think of the choice of electoral system as being between replicating ethnic divisions in the legislature and hoping that political leaders will cooperate after the election, and creating institutional incentives that seek to weaken or even transcend the political salience of ethnicity altogether. One common complaint made of preferential voting systems like the alternative vote is that they are majoritarian and produce disproportional outcomes (Lijphart 1997). As we will see, though, an alternative preferential voting system that works in multimember districts and produces relatively proportional outcomes is the single transferable vote. We will return to the discussion of electoral system choice in divided societies in Chapter 16.

Other scholars have offered more general criticisms of proportional electoral systems. One of the most common is that they tend to produce coalition governments. As we noted earlier, it is often difficult to hold political parties accountable in coalition governments because it is hard to identify who is responsible for policy and hence whom to hold accountable at election time. Even if those responsible for policy could be identified, it is still difficult to hold them accountable because parties that lose significant numbers of votes frequently make it back into coalition governments anyway. As the empirical evidence we presented in Chapter 12 indicates, coalition governments are also more unstable than the single-party majority governments that are typically produced by majoritarian electoral systems. A second criticism of PR systems is that they allow small, extremist parties to win representation. This is frequently seen as problematic. For example, some have argued that the existence of extremist parties, such as the Nazi Party in the Weimar Republic, undermines democracy. A third criticism is that small parties in PR systems frequently have a strong role in the government formation process and receive concessions that are disproportionate to their actual level of support in the electorate. It is rare for parties to obtain a majority of the legislative

---

7. Fiji introduced the alternative vote in 1997 in hopes of encouraging political parties to make appeals across ethnic groups. However, things did not work out entirely as planned because the small size of the electoral districts and the geographic concentration of indigenous and Indo-Fijians meant that there were too few constituencies with a sufficient mix of ethnic groups to make a strategy of appealing across ethnic group lines worthwhile. Some have argued that the choice of an AV system in this setting actually precipitated the collapse of Fijian democracy following a coup in 2000 (Reynolds 2011, 27–28).

seats in PR systems, so large parties often rely on the support of some smaller party to get into government. These smaller parties can often use their leverage to wring concessions from the larger party. Some of these concessions may be quite radical and lack the support of an electoral majority. In Israel, for example, small ultrareligious parties have won support for many of their policies by threatening to pull out of the government. A fourth criticism is that PR systems create a weak link between constituents and their representatives, because no single representative is responsible for policy in a given district. Voters might also wonder which of the elected representatives from their districts actually represent them.

List PR Systems

How do proportional electoral systems actually work? We start by looking at list PR systems. In a **list PR system,** each party presents a list of candidates to voters in each multimember district. Parties then receive seats in proportion to their overall share of the votes. Despite obvious similarities, list PR systems differ in important ways. In particular, they differ with respect to the precise electoral formula used to allocate seats to parties, the district magnitude, the use of electoral thresholds, and the type of party list. We discuss each of these in turn.

> In a **list PR system**, each party presents a list of candidates to voters in each multimember district. Parties receive seats in proportion to their overall share of the votes.

All proportional electoral systems employ either quotas or divisors to determine how many seats are won by each party. In a quota system, the **quota** is essentially the "price" in terms of votes that a party must "pay" to guarantee themselves a seat in a particular electoral district. Five different quotas are in common use around the world: Hare, Hagenbach-Bischoff, Imperiali, Reinforced Imperiali, and Droop. A quota, Q(n), is defined as

> A **quota** is the "price" in terms of votes that a party must pay to guarantee themselves a seat in a particular electoral district.

$$Q(n) = \frac{V_d}{M_d + n},$$

where V_d is the total number of valid votes in district d, M_d is the number of seats available in district d, and n is the modifier of the quota. When $n = 0$, the system employs the Hare quota. When $n = 1$, the system employs the Hagenbach-Bischoff quota. When $n = 2$, the system employs the Imperiali quota. When $n = 3$, the system employs the Reinforced Imperiali quota. The Droop quota is equal to the Hagenbach-Bischoff (H-B) plus one with any "decimal part" removed.

To see how the various quotas are calculated, suppose that we have an electoral district with 10 seats and 100,000 valid votes. The Hare quota for this district would be 100,000 / 10 = 10,000. This means that a political party can guarantee itself a seat for every 10,000 votes that it wins. The Hagenbach-Bischoff quota for the same district would be 100,000 / (10 + 1) = 9,090.9 votes. With the Hagenbach-Bischoff quota, a political party can guarantee itself a seat for every 9,090.9 votes that it wins. The Imperiali quota for the same district would be 100,000 / (10 + 2) = 8,333 votes, and the Reinforced Imperiali quota would be 100,000 / (10 + 3) = 7,692 votes. The Droop quota is simply the Hagenbach-Bischoff quota (9,090.9), plus one (9,091.9), minus the "decimal part," that is, 9,091.

We now provide an example of how seats are allocated to parties in a list PR system that employs the Hare quota system. Table 13.6 illustrates the election results for a ten-seat district in which 100,000 valid votes are split among six parties, A through F. How many seats does each party win? As we have already seen, the Hare quota in this case is 10,000. Because Party A has 47,000 votes, it can "buy" four seats at the cost of 10,000 votes each. After receiving these seats, Party A has 7,000 votes or 0.7 of a quota left over. Following the same logic, Parties B, C, and D can all "buy" one seat each, and they each have a different number of votes left over. You'll have noticed that we have allocated only seven of the ten seats available in this district so far. The seats that we have allocated so far are often called "automatic" seats. What happens to the three "remainder" seats? How are these seats allocated?

The issue of remainder seats occurs in all list PR systems that use quotas to allocate seats. The most common method for allocating remainder seats is called the "largest remainder method." Table 13.7 illustrates how the largest remainder method works in our ten-seat district. Remainder seats arise when some district seats are left unallocated and none of the parties have a sufficient number of votes left to "buy" them at the "full price" set out by the quota. The largest remainder method essentially allocates the remaining seats to those parties that can "pay" the most for them. To determine who can pay the most for the remainder seats, we calculate the fraction of a Hare quota that was left unused (remainder) by each party. The first remainder seat is then allocated to the party with the largest remainder. In our example, Party A wins the first remainder seat because its remainder (0.7 quotas) is the largest. In effect, Party A can pay 7,000 votes for the first remainder seat. The second remainder seat is then allocated to the party with the next largest remainder. Party E is the party with the second largest remainder (0.61 quotas); it can pay 6,100 votes for the second

TABLE 13.6	Allocating Seats to Parties Using the Hare Quota						
	Party A	Party B	Party C	Party D	Party E	Party F	Total
Votes	47,000	16,000	15,800	12,000	6,100	3,100	100,000
Seats							10
Quota							10,000
Votes ÷ Quota	4.7	1.6	1.58	1.2	0.61	0.31	
Automatic seats	4	1	1	1	0	0	7
Remainder seats							3

		Allocating Seats to Parties Using the Hare Quota with Largest Remainders						
TABLE 13.7								
	Party A	**Party B**	**Party C**	**Party D**	**Party E**	**Party F**	**Total**	
Votes	47,000	16,000	15,800	12,000	6,100	3,100	100,000	
Seats							10	
Quota							10,000	
Votes ÷ Quota	4.7	1.6	1.58	1.2	0.61	0.31		
Automatic seats	4	1	1	1	0	0	7	
Remainder	0.7	0.6	0.58	0.2	0.61	0.31		
Remainder seats	1	1	0	0	1	0	3	
Total seats	5	2	1	1	1	0	10	

remainder seat. The party with the third largest remainder (0.6 quotas) is Party B; it can pay 6,000 votes for the third and final remainder seat. The total number of seats won by each party in a district is just the sum of its automatic seats and its remainder seats. As Table 13.7 illustrates, Party A wins five seats in our ten-seat district, Party B wins two seats, and Parties C, D, and E each win one seat.

A list PR system that does not employ quotas to allocate seats to parties is known as a **divisor**, or **highest average**, **system**. Three divisor systems are commonly employed around the world: d'Hondt, Sainte-Laguë, and modified Sainte-Laguë. In divisor systems, the total number of votes won by each party in a district is divided by a series of numbers called divisors to give quotients. District seats are then allocated according to which parties have the highest quotients.

> A **divisor**, or **highest average**, **system** divides the total number of votes won by each party in a district by a series of numbers (divisors) to obtain quotients. District seats are then allocated according to which parties have the highest quotients.

To illustrate how these systems work, we apply the d'Hondt method, which is the most common divisor system, to the same ten-seat district that we used to examine quota systems. The results are shown in Table 13.8. Under the d'Hondt system, we divide the total number of votes won by each party by 1, 2, 3, 4, 5, 6, and so on to obtain a series of quotients. The ten largest quotients are shown in boldface type. The exact order in which the ten district seats are allocated among these ten quotients is shown by the numbers in parentheses next to them. For example, Party A receives the first and second seat, Party B wins the third seat, Party C wins the fourth seat, Party A the fifth seat, and so on. Unlike quota systems, divisor systems do not leave any remainder seats. The final allocation of the ten district seats is five to Party A, two each to Party B and Party C, and one to Party D. As you can see, this is a slightly different allocation of seats across the parties than what we obtained when we applied the Hare quota with largest remainders in this district (Table 13.7). The other divisor

TABLE 13.8	Allocating Seats to Parties Using the d'Hondt System						
	Party A	Party B	Party C	Party D	Party E	Party F	Total
Votes	47,000	16,000	15,800	12,000	6,100	3,100	100,000
Seats							10
Votes ÷ 1	47,000 (1)	16,000 (3)	15,800 (4)	12,000 (6)	6,100	3,100	
Votes ÷ 2	23,500 (2)	8,000 (9)	7,900 (10)	6,000	3,050	1,550	
Votes ÷ 3	15,666 (5)	5,333	5,266	4,000	2,033	1,033	
Votes ÷ 4	11,750 (7)	4,000	3,950	3,000	1,525	775	
Votes ÷ 5	9,400 (8)	3,200	3,160	2,400	1,220	620	
Votes ÷ 6	7,833	2,667	2,633	2,000	1,017	517	
Total seats	5	2	2	1	0	0	10

Note: The numbers in parentheses indicate the order in which the ten seats in the district are allocated among the parties.

systems work in exactly the same way except that the divisors are different. With the Sainte-Laguë system, the votes of each party are divided by 1, 3, 5, 7, 9, and so on to obtain the quotients. With the modified Sainte-Laguë system, the votes of each party are divided by 1.4, 3, 5, 7, 9, and so on.

District Magnitude The different formulas used to translate votes into seats affect the proportionality of an electoral system. However, the most important factor influencing the proportionality of an electoral system is the district magnitude (Cox 1997). Recall that the district magnitude refers to the number of representatives that are elected in a district. Electoral systems are more proportional when the district magnitude is large, as smaller parties are much more likely to win seats in these circumstances. For example, a party would need to win more than 25 percent of the vote to guarantee winning a seat in a three-seat district, but it would need to win only a little more than 10 percent of the vote to guarantee winning a seat in a nine-seat district. One thing to note is that the electoral outcome is likely to be disproportional whenever the district magnitude is small, irrespective of the particular formula used to translate votes into seats. It is for this reason that political scientists argue that the district magnitude is the most important factor for the proportionality of the electoral system.

Although all PR systems use multimember districts, the average size of these districts—the average district magnitude—can vary quite a lot from one country to another. At one extreme is Serbia, which elects all 250 of its legislators in a single national district. In fact,

Ukraine had a district magnitude of 450 in its 2006 and 2007 legislative elections. At the other extreme is Chile, which has historically had an average district magnitude of 2. In 2015, though, Chile adopted a new electoral system that will see its average district magnitude rise to 5.5 in the next scheduled legislative elections in 2017. Other countries have district magnitudes of varying size between these two extremes. In addition to the proportionality of the electoral system, a country's district magnitude also affects the strength of the linkage between elected representatives and their constituents. As district magnitude increases and with it the geographical size of the district, the linkage between representatives and their voters is likely to weaken.

Electoral Thresholds All proportional electoral systems have an **electoral threshold** that stipulates the minimum percentage of votes that a party must win, either nationally or in a particular district, to gain legislative representation. Either this threshold is legally imposed (**formal threshold**) or it exists as a mathematical property of the electoral system (**natural threshold**). The size of the electoral threshold has a strong effect on the proportionality of the electoral system.

> An **electoral threshold** is the minimum level of support a party needs to obtain legislative representation. A **natural threshold** is a mathematical by-product of the electoral system. A **formal threshold** is explicitly written into the electoral law.

Natural thresholds are not written into electoral laws; instead, they are a mathematical by-product of certain features of the electoral system, such as the district magnitude. For example, any candidate in the Netherlands must win more than 0.67 percent of the national vote, not because this is legally stipulated, but simply because there are 150 legislative seats allocated in a single national district; that is, 100 percent / 150 = 0.67 percent. All electoral systems have a natural threshold. In contrast to natural thresholds, formal thresholds are explicitly written into the electoral law. For example, political parties in Israel have to win 3.25 percent of the national vote before they can win seats in the Knesset (the natural threshold in Israel is only 0.83 percent). In Turkey, political parties must win more than 10 percent of the national vote before they can gain representation in parliament. Formal thresholds always increase the disproportionality of an electoral system because the votes for parties that might otherwise have won representation are wasted.

Formal thresholds are often introduced in an attempt to reduce party system fragmentation by preventing very small parties from gaining representation. For example, the adoption of a formal electoral threshold in Germany after World War II was largely a response to the fractious and unstable party system of Weimar Germany in the interwar period. Similarly, many Eastern European countries have imposed high formal thresholds in an attempt to reduce the number of parties and encourage the consolidation of a stable party system. Although some countries would like to prevent all small parties from winning seats, others want to prevent only small *extremist* parties from gaining representation. One potential way to do this is to combine a formal threshold with a provision known as

Apparentement is the provision in a list PR system for two or more separate parties to reach an agreement that their votes will be combined for the purposes of seat allocation.

apparentement. Apparentement allows small parties to group together to contest elections. The parties remain as separate entities on the ballot and campaign independently; however, the votes gained by each party are counted as if they belong to a single group for the purposes of surpassing the threshold. To the extent that getting other parties to join a group will be more difficult for extremist parties, apparentement helps nonextremist small parties win a share of seats proportional to their support, while making it difficult for extremist parties to win any representation.

Formal thresholds can have a significant effect on election outcomes. For example, there were so many parties that did not surpass the 10 percent threshold in the Turkish legislative elections of 2002 that fully 46 percent of all votes cast in these elections were wasted. Similarly, 34 percent of the votes cast in the Polish legislative elections of 1993 were wasted because of the 5 percent threshold for parties and 8 percent threshold for electoral coalitions. In the Polish case, these wasted votes were crucial in allowing the former Communists to return to power only a few years after the collapse of communism in that country (Kaminski, Lissowski, and Swistak 1998). These examples from Turkey and Poland force us to think about whether the problems arising from formal thresholds (wasted votes and increased disproportionality) are more or less acceptable than the problems they are designed to solve (fragmented party systems).

Types of Party List To this point we have discussed how seats are allocated to parties competing in multimember districts. However, we know that parties present lists of candidates in each district. You may be wondering which candidates on the lists actually get the seats that their party wins. This depends on which of the three types of party list is being used: **closed party lists**, **open party lists**, or **free party lists**.

In a **closed party list**, the order of candidates elected is determined by the party itself, and voters are not able to express a preference for a particular candidate. In an **open party list**, voters can indicate not just their preferred party but also their favored candidate within that party. In a **free party list**, voters have multiple votes that they can allocate either within a single party list or across different party lists.

In a closed party list, which is the most common type of party list, the order of candidates elected is determined by the party, and voters are not able to express a preference for a particular candidate. In a closed list system, political parties receive seats in proportion to the number of votes that they obtain using one of the formulas described earlier. The first seat won by the party goes to the candidate listed first on the party's list, the second seat goes to the second candidate on the list, and so on. Thus, if a party wins four seats in a district, then the top four candidates on the list obtain seats, and the remaining candidates do not win any. In some cases, the ballot paper in a closed list system will contain the names of the individual candidates and their positions on the list. More frequently, though, ballot papers in closed list systems do not contain the names of individual candidates. Instead, the only information on the list is the party names and symbols, and perhaps a photograph of the party leader. As Figure 13.5 illustrates, this type of ballot paper was used in South Africa's 1994 legislative elections.

One of the potential advantages of closed party lists is that parties can more easily include minority or women candidates who might otherwise have had difficulty getting elected. Of course, some voters may consider this potential advantage a disadvantage in that they are unable to choose the candidates that they most desire and may have to elect unpopular and undesirable candidates if they wish to vote for their preferred party.

Closed party lists are often preferred by the leaders of political parties because they provide a useful way of disciplining and rewarding candidates. Candidates that are important in the party hierarchy can be guaranteed relatively safe seats by being placed toward the top of the party list, whereas candidates who fail to toe the party line can be placed toward the bottom of the party list. Political parties tend to be more important than individual candidates in closed list systems for this reason.

In an open party list, voters can indicate not just their preferred party but their favored candidate within that party. In most open list systems, it is up to the voter to choose whether to indicate her preferred candidate as well as her preferred party. If individuals simply vote for a party and do not indicate a preferred candidate, then the candidate-choice option of the ballot paper will obviously have little effect. If we look at Sweden and its open list system, we find that over 25 percent of Swedish voters regularly choose an individual candidate within a party list; many of these candidates would not have been elected had the party list been closed (Reynolds, Reilly, and Ellis 2005, 84).

Figure 13.6 illustrates an open list ballot from the 1994 legislative elections in Denmark. In Danish elections, voters cast a single vote either for their preferred party (party vote) or for their preferred candidate from among that party's list of candidates (personal vote). The total number of seats won by a party is determined by its total number of votes, which is just the sum of its party votes and its personal votes. Each individual candidate is credited with all of the personal votes given to him plus a share of the votes cast for his party. The order in which the party's seats are allocated among the individual candidates is determined by the number of total votes (personal and party) that are credited to them.

Although voters normally have a choice in open list systems as to whether to vote for a particular candidate, this is not the case in all open list PR systems. For example, individuals have to vote for a party candidate in countries like Brazil and the Netherlands. The total number of seats won by each party in these countries is determined by the total number of votes given to its candidates, and the order in which each party's candidates receive these seats is determined by the number of individual votes that they receive.

Open list systems clearly give voters greater freedom over their choice of candidates and weaken the control of party leaders over their party's candidates compared with closed list systems. A frequent consequence of open lists, though, is that they generate internal party fighting, because candidates from the same party are effectively competing with each other

FIGURE 13.5   South African Closed List PR Ballot Paper

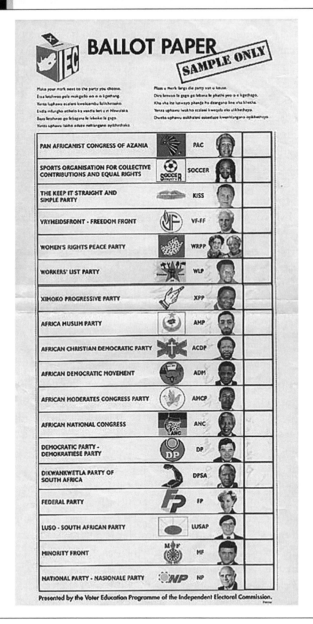

Source: http://www.unc.edu/~asreynol/ballot_pages/south_africa.html

FIGURE 13.6 Danish Open List PR Ballot Paper

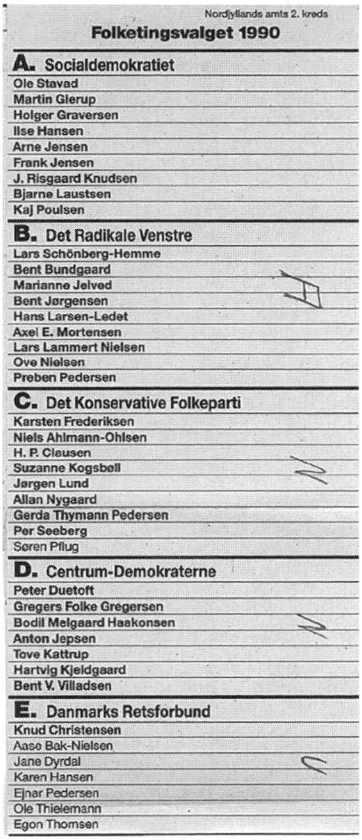

Nordjyllands amts 2. kreds
Folketingsvalget 1990

A. Socialdemokratiet
Ole Stavad
Martin Glerup
Holger Graversen
Ilse Hansen
Arne Jensen
Frank Jensen
J. Risgaard Knudsen
Bjarne Laustsen
Kaj Poulsen

B. Det Radikale Venstre
Lars Schönberg-Hemme
Bent Bundgaard
Marianne Jelved
Bent Jørgensen
Hans Larsen-Ledet
Axel E. Mortensen
Lars Lammert Nielsen
Ove Nielsen
Preben Pedersen

C. Det Konservative Folkeparti
Karsten Frederiksen
Niels Ahlmann-Ohlsen
H. P. Clausen
Suzanne Kogsbøll
Jørgen Lund
Allan Nygaard
Gerda Thymann Pedersen
Per Seeberg
Søren Pflug

D. Centrum-Demokraterne
Peter Duetoft
Gregers Folke Gregersen
Bodil Melgaard Haakonsen
Anton Jepsen
Tove Kattrup
Hartvig Kjeldgaard
Bent V. Villadsen

E. Danmarks Retsforbund
Knud Christensen
Aase Bak-Nielsen
Jane Dyrdal
Karen Hansen
Ejnar Pedersen
Ole Thielemann
Egon Thomsen

Source: http://www.unc.edu/~asreynol/ballot_pages/denmark.html

for the same votes. A result of this is that political candidates in open list systems have incentives to cultivate a personal vote rather than a party vote (Carey and Shugart 1995). A personal vote occurs when an individual votes based on the characteristics of a particular candidate rather than the characteristics of the party to which the candidate belongs. Building a personal vote is frequently associated in the United States with legislators bringing back pork-barrel projects to their single-member districts. As you can see, though, incentives to build personal votes also exist in multimember districts, where the election of candidates can depend on personal reputations in open list systems. In addition to internal party fighting, some scholars worry that open lists make it less likely that minority candidates will be elected. In Sri Lanka, for instance, majority Sinhalese parties tried to place minority Tamil candidates in winnable positions on their open party lists. These efforts at improving minority representation were rendered ineffective, however, when many voters deliberately voted for lower-placed Sinhalese candidates instead (Reynolds, Reilly, and Ellis 2005, 90).

Voters have even more flexibility in free party lists. This is because voters in free list systems have multiple votes, typically as many as there are seats available in the district, that they can allocate to candidates either within a single party list or across different party lists. The capacity to vote for candidates from different party lists is known as **panachage**. Panachage is attractive if there are particular types of candidates that you would like to support, say women candidates or candidates who share the same position on some policy, that appear across different party lists. Some countries, like Switzerland, allow voters to give more than one vote to the same candidate. The capacity to give more than one vote to a single highly favored candidate is known as **cumulation**. Some scholars have argued that cumulation can help boost minority representation (Guinier 1994). This is because minority groups can cumulate their votes on a single minority candidate while majority groups spread theirs across multiple candidates.

> **Panachage** is the ability to vote for candidates from different party lists. **Cumulation** is the capacity to give more than one vote to a single candidate.

Single Transferable Vote

The only proportional electoral system that does not employ a party list is the **single transferable vote (STV)**. STV is a candidate-centered preferential voting system used in multi-member districts where voters rank order the candidates. Candidates must obtain a particular quota, often the Droop quota, in order to win a seat. Votes go initially to each voter's most preferred candidate. If an insufficient number of candidates obtain the quota to fill all of the district seats, then the candidate with the lowest number of first-choice votes is eliminated. The votes from the eliminated candidate, as well as any surplus votes from candidates that are already elected, are then reallocated to the remaining candidates according to the designated second preferences. This process continues until enough candidates meet the quota to fill all of the district seats. If you think that the STV system sounds familiar, you would be right: it is essentially the same as the alternative vote but applied in multimember districts.

> The **single transferable vote (STV)** is a candidate-centered preferential voting system used in multimember districts. Candidates that surpass a specified quota of first-preference votes are immediately elected. In successive counts, votes from eliminated candidates and surplus votes from elected candidates are reallocated to the remaining candidates until all the seats are filled.

STV is quite a complicated electoral system, so an example of how it works might help. Our specific example illustrates how STV works when a Droop quota is used with the Clarke method for reallocating surplus votes.[8] This is the STV system employed to elect the Australian Senate. Imagine that there are five candidates—Bruce, Shane, Sheila, Glen, and

---

8. There are a variety of different ways of reallocating surplus votes (Tideman and Richardson 2000, 248–258).

TABLE 13.9	**Results from Twenty Ballots in an STV Election**				

Voting round	🧑🧑🧑🧑	🧑🧑	🧑🧑🧑🧑 🧑🧑🧑🧑	🧑🧑🧑🧑	🧑	🧑
1st	Bruce	Shane	Sheila	Sheila	Glen	Ella
2nd	Shane	Bruce	Glen	Ella		
3rd			Ella	Glen		

Note: Each icon represents a ballot, and each type of icon reflects a particular rank ordering of the candidates.

Ella—competing in a three-seat district containing twenty voters. Table 13.9 illustrates how the twenty voters marked their preferences on their ballots; each icon represents a ballot, and each type of icon reflects a particular preference ordering. Thus, four people [🧑] placed Bruce first and Shane second, two people [🧑] placed Shane first and Bruce second, and so on. One thing to note is that not everybody provided a complete preference ordering of all the candidates. For example, two people [🧑 and 🧑] marked only their first preferences.[9] The Droop quota in our three-seat district with twenty voters is calculated as [20 / (3 + 1)] + 1 = 6. In other words, each candidate must win six votes in order to be elected. We can now begin examining how votes are translated into seats in an STV system. The whole process is outlined in Table 13.10.

The first thing to do is to see if any candidates obtained a Droop quota in the first-choice votes. If they did, they are automatically elected. Because Sheila has twelve first-choice votes, she is elected in the first round. Next, it is necessary to reallocate any surplus votes from already elected candidates to the remaining candidates. In the example, Sheila has six surplus votes; that is, she received six votes more than she needed to be elected. As we noted at the beginning, we are going to use the Clarke method for reallocating these six surplus votes to the remaining candidates. To do this, it is necessary to separate Sheila's ballots into bundles based on who the second-choice candidates are. Because those who voted for Sheila list either Glen [🧑] or Ella [🧑] as their second choice, there would be two bundles. Because the eight 🧑 votes make up two-thirds of Sheila's twelve total votes, two-thirds of Sheila's surplus votes (four) go to Glen. Because the four 🧑 votes make up one-third of Sheila's total votes, one-third of Sheila's surplus votes (two) go to Ella.

After reallocating the surplus votes to Glen and Ella, votes are recounted a second time to see if any new candidate has now obtained the Droop quota. In our example, no candidate meets the Droop quota in the second count. As a result, the next step is to eliminate the

9. In the actual elections to the Australian Senate, individuals must rank order all of the candidates if they want their vote to count.

TABLE 13.10	The STV in a Three-Seat District with Twenty Voters

Voting round	Candidates					Result
	Bruce	Shane	Sheila	Glen	Ella	
1st						Sheila is elected, and Sheila's surplus votes are reallocated
2nd						Shane is eliminated
3rd						Bruce is elected
4th						Ella is eliminated, and Glen is elected

Note: Each icon represents a ballot, and each type of icon reflects a particular rank ordering of the candidates. See Table 13.9 to see the particular rank ordering of the candidates associated with each icon.

candidate with the lowest number of votes (Shane) and reallocate his votes to the remaining candidates. Because the second choice of Shane's voters is Bruce, Shane's two votes are reallocated to Bruce. Votes are now recounted a third time to see if any candidate now meets the Droop quota. As you can see, Bruce meets the Droop quota on the third count because he has six votes, and he is therefore elected. If there were any surplus votes for Bruce, then we would reallocate them among the remaining candidates. In this case, though, Bruce has no surplus votes. To this point, we have filled two of the three district seats. No one else meets the Droop quota, so the candidate with the next lowest number of votes (Ella) is eliminated. Because there is only one candidate left, there is no need for a fourth recount; Glen is the third and last candidate to be elected. Thus, the STV with the Droop quota and the Clarke method for reallocating surplus votes results in the election of Sheila, Bruce, and Glen in this three-seat district.

How does the STV system compare with other electoral systems? One of the strengths of STV systems is that they provide voters with an opportunity to convey a lot of information about their preferences (Bowler and Grofman 2000). Like other preferential voting systems, individuals in STV systems have the opportunity to rank order all of the candidates rather than simply voting "yes" or "no" to one of the candidates as in most majoritarian and list PR systems. Because an individual's preferences end up being reallocated whenever a candidate is elected or eliminated, the STV system minimizes wasted votes. STV systems also allow individuals to vote for candidates from different parties. This means that individuals can vote for candidates who share a similar policy stance even though the candidates may come from different parties. This might be useful in cases in which an issue cuts across traditional party lines such as abortion. With the exception of those systems that allow for panachage, the vast majority of list PR systems do not allow for this type of cross-party voting. It is worth noting that STV is a proportional electoral system that does not require the existence of political parties—individuals vote for candidates, not parties. This could be important in countries in which political parties are yet to organize or political elites do not wish to allow the formation of political parties (see Box 13.3, "Strategic Miscalculation: Electoral System Choice in Poland in 1989").

Like other preferential voting systems, an additional strength of STV systems is that they create incentives for candidates to appeal to groups outside their core set of supporters and campaign on broad-based centrist platforms. This is because a candidate's election may well depend on the transfer of votes from different social groups. Recall that this is why some scholars advocate the use of preferential voting systems in divided societies (Horowitz 1985, 1991; Reilly 1997, 2001). One criticism of the preferential voting systems that we have examined to this point, such as the alternative vote, is that they are majoritarian and can produce highly disproportional outcomes. An advantage of the STV system is that it works in multi-member districts and typically produces more proportional outcomes than majoritarian systems. Thus, the STV holds out the possibility of combining relatively proportional outcomes with incentives for candidates to make cross-cleavage appeals and build electorates that bridge religious and ethnic lines.

Another strength of STV highlighted by its supporters is that it tends to create a strong link between representatives and their constituents. Since the STV is a candidate- rather than a party-centered system, candidates have an incentive to build personal votes and engage in constituency service. For example, there is evidence that the STV system in Ireland leads to an emphasis on local campaigning, a focus on district work and local concerns, and a low importance attached to ideology and national issues (Katz 1980). In this respect, STV "involves a notion of the connection between the individual representative and his or her constituency that is much closer to the notion of representation implicit in the [SMDP] system than to the notion of representation of parties underlying list systems" (Sinnott 1992, 68). A further strength of STV systems is that they reduce the incentive for voters to behave strategically because their votes are less likely to be wasted. As with any electoral system, though, strategic concerns are never entirely absent. In an attempt to strategically channel the transfer of votes in an STV system so as to benefit their candidates as much as possible, parties in Ireland hand out "candidate cards" in a similar way to how parties hand out how-to-vote cards in the alternative vote system used in Australia.

Despite these strengths, the STV system has its critics. One criticism is that it tends to weaken the internal unity of parties and make them less cohesive. Because voters are allowed to rank order candidates from the same party, these candidates have incentives to criticize and campaign against one another. As Farrell and McAllister (2000, 18) note, "[T]he problems of intraparty factionalism and excessive attention to localist, particularistic concerns [in Ireland] are attributed to politicians who must compete with each other for votes on ordinally ranked STV ballots." You will perhaps recall that the single nontransferable vote (SNTV) also creates incentives for intraparty factionalism. It is worth noting, though, that the incentives for factionalism are weaker under the STV system because candidates can expect to receive votes from fellow party members who are eliminated. This means that candidates from the same party in an STV system do not want to harm each other too much.

A second criticism of STV is that it is hard to operate when district magnitude is large. This is because the ballot paper could contain a large number of candidate names. In fact, the ballot for the Australian Senate elections in New South Wales in 1995 contained the names of ninety-nine candidates and was several feet long (Farrell and McAllister 2000, 29). It is not unknown for Australian electoral officials to order thousands of magnifying glasses just so that voters can read the candidate names on the ballot ("Magnifying Glasses" 2013). It is difficult to believe that voters would have sufficient information to rank candidates beyond the first ten or so names on a ballot. For this reason, constituencies in STV systems tend to be relatively small. For example, the largest district magnitude in Ireland and Malta is five. These small district magnitudes limit the proportionality with which votes are translated into seats.

Mixed Electoral Systems

A **mixed electoral system** is one in which voters elect representatives through two different systems, one majoritarian and one proportional. In effect, some legislative representatives are elected using a majoritarian system and some are elected using a proportional system.

> A **mixed electoral system** is one in which voters elect representatives through two different systems, one majoritarian and one proportional.
>
> An **electoral tier** is a level at which votes are translated into seats. The lowest tier is the district or constituency level. Higher tiers are constituted by grouping together different lower-tier constituencies, typically at the regional or national level.

Most mixed systems employ multiple electoral tiers. An **electoral tier** is a level at which votes are translated into seats. The lowest electoral tier is the district or constituency level. Higher tiers are constituted by grouping together different lower-tier constituencies, typically at the regional or national level. A majoritarian electoral system is used in the lowest tier (district level) and a proportional electoral system is used in the upper tier (regional or national level).[10] Mixed systems differ in terms of whether they are independent or dependent (see Figure 13.3).

---

10. It is possible, though rare, to have a mixed system with only one electoral tier (Bormann and Golder 2013). For example, representatives in some districts could be elected via a proportional representation system while representatives in other districts could be elected via a majoritarian system. It is also possible for mixed systems to have more than two electoral tiers. For example, legislative seats might be allocated at the district level, the regional level, and the national level.

Independent Mixed Electoral Systems

An **independent mixed electoral system,** often referred to as a mixed parallel system, is one in which the majoritarian and proportional components of the electoral system are implemented independently of one another. Ukraine used an independent mixed electoral system with two electoral tiers for its 2014 legislative elections. Two hundred twenty five legislators were elected using the majoritarian SMDP electoral system in single-member districts at the constituency level, and 225 legislators were elected using an open party list proportional representation system in a single district at the national level. The precise balance between "proportional" and "majoritarian" seats varies from country to country. For example, 253 (84 percent) of the legislators in South Korea's 2016 elections were elected using majoritarian rules and 47 (16 percent) were elected using proportional rules. Although in some countries such as South Korea individuals have only one vote, which is used for both parts of the electoral system, in other countries such as Japan, they have two votes—one for the majoritarian component at the constituency level and one for the proportional component at the regional or national level.

> An **independent mixed electoral system** is one in which the majoritarian and proportional components of the electoral system are implemented independently of one another.

Table 13.11 illustrates how votes are translated into seats in an independent mixed electoral system with two electoral tiers. Two parties, A and B, are competing over ten seats. Five seats are allocated at the constituency level using an SMDP system, and five seats are allocated in a single district at the national level using some type of list PR system. Given the distribution of votes shown in Table 13.11, Party A wins eight seats. Why? First, it wins all five constituency seats because it came first in each constituency. Second, because Party A wins 60 percent of the party list vote, it wins 60 percent of the five seats allocated in the national tier, that is, three seats. As a result, Party A wins eight seats altogether. Party B wins two seats—it gets no constituency seats, but it gets 40 percent of the five party list seats in the national tier, or two seats.

| **TABLE 13.11** | **Translating Votes into Seats in an Independent Mixed Electoral System** |

	Votes won in each electoral district						Seats won			
	1	**2**	**3**	**4**	**5**	**National district votes won**	**% of votes won**	**SMDP**	**List PR**	**Total**
Party A	3,000	3,000	3,000	3,000	3,000	15,000	60	5	3	8
Party B	2,000	2,000	2,000	2,000	2,000	10,000	40	0	2	2
Total	5,000	5,000	5,000	5,000	5,000	25,000	100	5	5	10

Dependent Mixed Electoral Systems

A **dependent mixed electoral system**, often referred to as a mixed member proportional (MMP) system, is one in which the application of the proportional formula is dependent on

A **dependent mixed electoral system** is one in which the application of the proportional formula is dependent on the distribution of seats or votes produced by the majoritarian formula.

the distribution of seats or votes produced by the majoritarian formula. In these systems, the proportional component of the electoral system is used to compensate for any disproportionality produced by the majoritarian formula at the constituency level. New Zealand used a dependent mixed electoral system with two electoral tiers for its 2014 elections. Seventy-one legislators were elected using the majoritarian SMDP electoral system in single-member districts, and forty-nine legislators were elected using a closed party list proportional representation system in a single district at the national level. In most dependent mixed systems, such as the one used in New Zealand, individuals have two votes. They cast their first vote for a representative at the constituency level (candidate vote) and their second vote for a party list in a higher electoral tier (party vote). These types of mixed dependent systems allow individuals to give their first vote to a constituency candidate from one party and to give their second vote to a different party if they wish. This is called split-ticket voting. Figure 13.7 shows a sample ballot used in New Zealand. In systems in which voters have only one vote, the vote for the constituency candidate also counts as a vote for that candidate's party in the higher electoral tier.

Table 13.12 illustrates how votes are translated into seats in a dependent mixed electoral system with two electoral tiers. Two parties, A and B, are competing over ten seats. This example is identical to the one shown in Table 13.11 except that our mixed system is now dependent rather than independent. The first thing that happens is that each party receives legislative seats in proportion to the total number of votes that it obtained nationally. This means that because Party A won 60 percent of the vote overall, it receives 60 percent of the seats, that is, six seats. And since Party B won 40 percent of the vote overall, it receives 40 percent of the seats, that is, four seats. Once we know the total number of seats that go to each party, we must determine whether they will be constituency seats or party list seats.

| **TABLE 13.12** | **Translating Votes into Seats in a Dependent Mixed Electoral System** |

	Votes won in each electoral district						Seats won			
	1	2	3	4	5	National district votes won	% of votes won	SMDP	List PR	Total
Party A	3,000	3,000	3,000	3,000	3,000	15,000	60	5	1	6
Party B	2,000	2,000	2,000	2,000	2,000	10,000	40	0	4	4
Total	5,000	5,000	5,000	5,000	5,000	25,000	100	5	5	10

FIGURE 13.7 A Sample Ballot Used in New Zealand's Dependent Mixed Electoral System

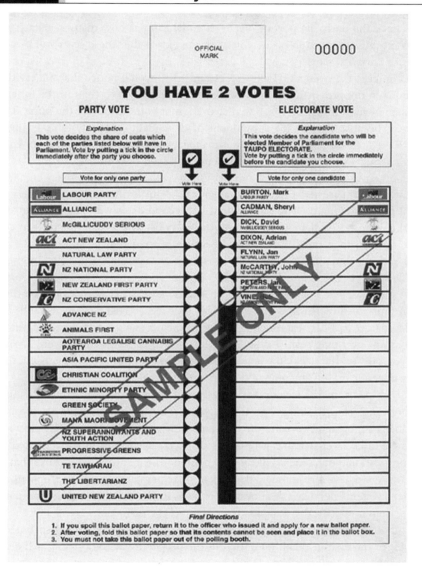

We do this by looking to see how many constituencies each party won. As Party A won all five constituency seats, its six seats will comprise five constituency seats and one party list seat. As Party B did not win any constituency seats, its four seats comprise only party list seats. In effect, the party list portion of the vote determines how many seats a party gets, whereas the candidate portion of the vote determines whether these seats will be constituency seats or party list seats.

If you compare the results in Tables 13.11 and 13.12, you'll notice that the election outcome is much more proportional in the dependent mixed system than in the independent mixed system, even though the starting distribution of votes is exactly the same. This is to be expected, because the list PR component of dependent mixed systems is specifically designed to reduce the disproportionality created by the majoritarian component of the electoral system; this is not the case in independent mixed systems.

Two issues crop up in dependent mixed systems. First, some candidates compete for a constituency seat but are also placed on the party list. This is often done as a "safety net" for influential party candidates. The hope is that these candidates will win their constituency seat and their names can then be crossed off the party list. If they fail to win their constituency seat, though, they can still be elected because of their high position on the (closed) party list. Second, some parties win more constituency seats than is justified by their party list vote. This happened in New Zealand's 2005 legislative elections. The Maori Party won 2.1 percent of the vote, which entitled it to three legislative seats. However, because the Maori Party won four constituencies, it ended up with four legislative seats. As a result, the New Zealand legislature had 121 seats in 2005 instead of the normal 120. This extra legislative seat is known as an "overhang seat." In the 2009 elections in Germany there were 24 overhang seats. As you can see, the size of the legislature in a dependent mixed system is not fixed and ultimately depends on the outcome of the election.

In many respects, mixed electoral systems are an attempt to combine the positive attributes of both majoritarian and proportional systems. In particular, mixed electoral systems help produce proportional outcomes at the same time as ensuring that some elected representatives are linked to particular geographic districts. The extent to which mixed systems produce proportional outcomes is likely to depend on the institutional features that characterize them. As we have already seen, dependent mixed systems are more proportional than independent systems because the allocation of seats in the proportional component of the electoral system is specifically designed to counteract the distortions created by the majoritarian component. Institutional features, such as the percentage of seats distributed by list PR, the size of the district magnitude used in the proportional component of the electoral system, and the proportional formula itself affect the degree of proportionality in independent mixed systems (M. Golder 2005).

Dependent mixed systems produce outcomes as proportional as those found in pure list PR systems. As a result, they share many of the advantages and disadvantages of list PR systems that we have already discussed. Some issues arise that are specific to dependent mixed systems, though. One is that dependent mixed systems can create two classes of legislators—one that is responsible and accountable to a geographic constituency, and one that is more beholden to the party. This can influence the cohesiveness of political parties (Reynolds, Reilly, and Ellis 2005). In addition, there is some concern that individuals who have two votes in dependent mixed systems are unaware that it is their party vote rather than their candidate vote that ultimately determines the number of seats that each party wins in the legislature.

LEGISLATIVE ELECTORAL SYSTEM CHOICE

In Map 13.2, we illustrate the global distribution of majoritarian, proportional, and mixed electoral systems around the world. As you can see, some regions are relatively homogeneous in the type of electoral systems that they use. The vast majority of countries in Latin America and Western Europe, for example, use a proportional electoral system. In contrast, other regions such as Oceana, North Africa and the Middle East, and sub-Saharan Africa display much more heterogeneity in their choice of electoral system. When looking at democracies and dictatorships together, we find that 80 countries use a proportional system, 78 countries use a majoritarian system, and 29 countries use a mixed system. There are distinct differences, though, when we distinguish between the electoral system choices of democracies and dictatorships. In terms of democracies, 23 percent use majoritarian systems, 59 percent use proportional representation, and 18 percent use mixed systems. In contrast, 61 percent of dictatorships use majoritarian systems, 25 percent use proportional systems, and 14 percent use mixed systems. In effect, dictatorships are much more likely to use majoritarian systems than democracies.

There has been relatively little work on the choice of electoral systems under dictatorship. However, we can throw out some conjectures for why dictatorships might favor majoritarian electoral systems. First, most proportional systems other than the single transferable vote use party lists and hence require the existence of political parties. As we discussed in Chapter 10, dictatorships vary in the extent to which political parties are allowed to exist. Second, there is some evidence that majoritarian systems may be easier to manipulate than proportional ones. Evidence for this comes from a study of twenty-four Communist countries in which the author finds that elections using the majoritarian SMDP system were much more likely to be the object of manipulation than those using a list proportional representation system (Birch 2007). Third, many dictatorships are poor with low levels of education. The simplicity of majoritarian electoral systems, such as SMDP, may be helpful in these conditions as they impose lower cognitive costs on voters.

A final conjecture focuses on the fact that majoritarian systems tend to produce disproportional outcomes that reward large parties and punish small parties. This may well appeal to large incumbent parties in dictatorships. Of course, the disproportionality of majoritarian systems creates incentives for opposition groups to coalesce, whereas proportional systems

MAP 13.2

Legislative Electoral System Choice around the World in 2016

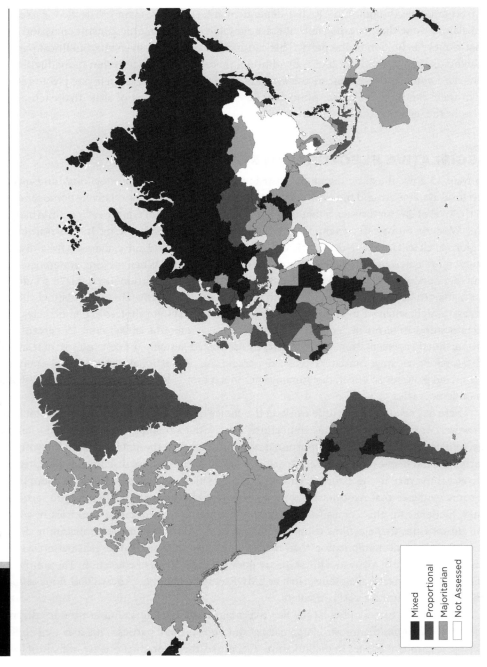

Mixed
Proportional
Majoritarian
Not Assessed

Note: The data for this map come from the Inter-Parliamentary Union at http://www.ipu.org/english/home.htm.

may help keep the opposition divided. In this respect, dictatorial incumbents face a trade-off between benefiting from disproportional majoritarian systems and hindering opposition coordination with proportional systems (Barberá 2013). Lust-Okar and Jamal (2002) suggest that this trade-off plays out differently depending on dictatorial type. Specifically, they claim that majoritarian systems are more likely to be adopted by dominant-party dictatorships, whereas proportional systems are more likely to be adopted by monarchic dictatorships. The idea is that leaders in these two types of dictatorship have divergent preferences. Monarchs are political arbitrators whose legitimacy typically comes from things like the royal family, religious authorities, or historical tradition rather than popular support. "For the monarch, then, political division and competition in popular politics, not unity, is the basis of stability. Kings have no interest in creating a single contender who could vie with them for power" (Lust-Okar and Jamal 2002, 253). As a result, monarchs prefer proportional systems that allow for the representation of competing political parties while they maintain their role as chief arbiter. In contrast, leaders in states dominated by a regime party are forced to enter politics to maintain their rule. For this reason, they want majoritarian systems that disproportionately favor their (large) political party. Lust-Okar and Jamal support this line of reasoning with empirical evidence from the Middle East.

Studies of electoral system choice in democracies are much more common. Various explanations have been proposed for why democracies have the electoral systems that they do. These explanations focus on the self-interest of political parties, general interest concerns, historical precedent, external pressures, and idiosyncratic occurrences (Benoit 2004, 2007). Self-interest explanations examine the preferences that political parties have for various electoral systems. Because electoral systems are basically distribution mechanisms that reward one party at the expense of another, parties are likely to have conflicting preferences for alternative electoral rules. The adoption of an electoral system is ultimately a struggle between political parties with competing interests. In one study, Boix (1999) sets out to explain the spread of proportional electoral systems at the beginning of the twentieth century. He argues that conservative ruling elites who were historically elected using some kind of majoritarian system began to take an interest in proportional systems when suffrage was being extended to the poor and the level of support for socialist parties was growing. The interest in proportional systems was particularly strong in those countries in which conservative parties on the right were fragmented and the presence of a strong socialist party posed a threat to their continued rule. In effect, Boix claims that conservative parties, faced with the rise of socialism, chose to adopt proportional systems as a preemptive strategy to guarantee their strong representation in the legislature even if they remained divided.

Rather than argue that electoral systems are adopted because they are in the interest of particular parties, some people claim that they are chosen because they serve some kind of general interest like promoting legitimacy, ethnic accommodation, or accountability. As we saw earlier, the adoption of the supplementary vote to elect the Sri Lankan president was driven by a desire to allow the minority Tamil community to have a meaningful role in presidential elections to

Box 13.3 **STRATEGIC MISCALCULATION: ELECTORAL SYSTEM CHOICE IN POLAND IN 1989**

As we note in the text, one explanation for why countries adopt the electoral systems that they do focuses on the strategic calculations of political parties. In effect, parties in power choose to adopt electoral rules that benefit them at the expense of their rivals. Although the stakes involved in choosing an electoral system can often be extremely high, history has shown us that political parties frequently make strategic miscalculations.

In a 1999 article titled "How Communism Could Have Been Saved," Marek Kaminski describes the bargaining that took place between the opposition movement, Solidarity, and the Communist Party over the electoral law to be used for the 1989 legislative elections in Poland. At the time, these elections were to be the first semi-free elections held in the Soviet bloc. During these negotiations, the Communist Polish United Workers' Party (PUWP) made two strategic miscalculations.

Mistake 1: The first mistake was that the PUWP overestimated its support in the electorate. Following the imposition of martial law in 1981, the PUWP under General Jaruzelski set up a Center for Public Opinion Research (CBOS) to keep better track of public opinion and support for the Communist regime. If you recall from our discussion of democratic transitions in Chapter 8, preference falsification is likely to be rampant in dictatorships because members of opposition groups are unwilling to publicly reveal their opposition for fear of punishment. This was certainly the case in Poland, where roughly 30 percent of respondents simply refused to complete surveys conducted by CBOS. Much of the opposition in Poland essentially remained underground and out of the sight of the PUWP. The result was that the PUWP went into the negotiations over the electoral law with Solidarity in 1989 with an overly optimistic belief about its electoral strength.

Mistake 2: The second mistake was that the PUWP did not adopt a proportional electoral system. As you may recall from our discussion in Chapter 8, the 1989 legislative elections turned into an electoral disaster for the PUWP with Solidarity winning all 35 percent of the legislative seats for which it was able to compete. The size of Solidarity's victory and the subsequent divisions that appeared between the PUWP and its supporters eventually led to the appointment of the first non-Communist prime minister in Eastern Europe. The reason that Solidarity won all the seats in these elections had a lot to do with the electoral system that was chosen—a majority-runoff TRS. Because Solidarity turned out to have the largest support in each district, this electoral system translated the 70 percent of the vote won by Solidarity into 100 percent of the seats and the roughly 25 percent of the vote won by the PUWP into zero seats. Had the PUWP adopted a proportional electoral system, though, the outcome of the elections would have been very different.

So why did the PUWP not adopt a proportional system? One reason has to do with the PUWP's belief that it had sufficient support to win seats in a majoritarian system. A second reason, however, has to do with the fact that the PUWP did not want to legalize any additional political parties. The maximum concession the PUWP was willing to make during the negotiations was to legalize Solidarity as a trade union; Poland was to remain a one-party state. As a result, the PUWP refused to consider adopting any electoral system that required individuals to vote for parties rather than candidates. At the time, the PUWP believed that all proportional systems required the presence of political parties. As you now know from reading this chapter, this is not true. The STV is a proportional electoral system in which individuals vote for candidates. It appears that the PUWP was simply unaware that the STV system existed. In his article, Kaminski indicates that had the option of the STV come up, it would have been acceptable to both Solidarity and the PUWP. The STV would have guaranteed a significant representation for Solidarity in the legislature and provided a greater margin of safety for the PUWP. It seems likely that with a more proportional allocation of seats, as would have occurred under an STV system, the PUWP may have been able to hold on to power and not had to appoint a prime minister from Solidarity.

This leads to an interesting counterfactual question that one might ask. What would have happened to communism in Eastern Europe had the PUWP adopted a proportional STV system in 1989 rather than the majoritarian TRS? What we know is that the collapse of communism in Poland had a snowball effect on the rest of the Eastern bloc. A different course of events in Poland could perhaps have prevented the breakdown of the Communist system. This leads one to wonder whether communism in Eastern Europe could have been saved if the political leaders in Poland had only been more aware of the information on electoral systems presented in this chapter.

After the Polish version of Kaminski's 1999 article was published, he received several letters from Premier Tadeusz Mazowiecki and other Solidarity leaders. Below, we list some of the responses he received from former Communist dignitaries.

Jerzy Urban (former Communist spokesman, number 4 in Poland in the 1980s):

> You are absolutely right that we did not read the surveys properly . . . we were ignorant about various electoral laws . . . probably nobody knew STV. . . . I distributed copies of your paper among General Jaruzelski, Premier Rakowski, and [the present] President Kwasniewski.

Hieronim Kubiak (former Politburo member, top political adviser):

> The negative heroes of Kaminski's article are the "ignoramus"—we, communist experts. . . . [He thinks that the communist regime could have survived] if General Jaruzelski had known the STV electoral law and if he had chosen differently!

Janusz Reykowski (former Politburo member, the designer of the 1989 electoral law):

> [The value of Kaminski's work] is in showing that technical political decisions [that is, the choice of the electoral law] may have fundamental importance for a historical process.

Maria Teresa Kiszczak (the wife of General Czeslaw Kiszczak, number 2 in Poland in the 1980s):

> You based your story on the bourgeois literature. . . . [C]ommunists did not really want to keep power. . . . [My husband] resisted a temptation to cancel the 1989 elections and to seize power.

ensure that the president would enjoy majority support, and to keep the administrative costs of running the election low (Reilly 2001). With respect to Eastern Europe, Birch and colleagues (2002) argue that the choice of electoral rules after the collapse of communism was driven by a desire to maximize legitimacy and promote the development of political parties.

External pressures and historical precedent can also affect the choice of electoral system. The choice of electoral system in many countries has been heavily influenced by their former colonial ruler (Blais and Massicotte 1997). For example, nearly every African country that employs an SMDP system is a former British colony. Similarly, many former French colonies, such as the Central African Republic, Comoros, and Mali, have adopted the same majoritarian two-round system used in France. Other countries seem to have adopted a particular electoral system for the simple reason that they have had some experience with it in the past. For example, there is some evidence that the newly democratic Czechoslovakia chose a proportional electoral system in 1990 because it had used a similar system in the interwar period. Similarly, France's adoption of a two-round system in 1958 can perhaps be traced back to its use in the Second Empire (1852–1870) and much of the Third Republic (1870–1940; Benoit 2004, 370).

It appears that some electoral systems are even chosen by accident. As an example, consider the following description from Benoit (2007, 376–377) of how New Zealand came to adopt a mixed electoral system in 1993.

> In a now famous incident of electoral reform through accident, ruling parties in New Zealand found themselves bound to implement a sweeping electoral reform that traced back in essence to a chance remark, later described as a gaffe, by Prime Minister David Lange during a televised debate. In New Zealand, the use of first-past-the-post [SMDP] had virtually guaranteed a two-party duopoly of the Labor Party and the National

Party, producing continuous single-party majority governments since 1914—often cited as the textbook example of the "majoritarian" or Westminster type of democracy (Nagel 2004). Grassroots dissatisfaction with the electoral system began in the 1970s among Maori and minor-party supporters who consistently found it difficult to obtain any representation, and increased with the 1978 and 1981 elections, in which Labor received a plurality of the vote yet National won a majority of the seats. This led Labor to pledge in the 1980s to establish a Royal Commission to reappraise the electoral law. The commission compared many options and finally recommended the "mixed-member plurality" (MMP) system combining single-member districts with lists, although the majority of Labor's Members of Parliament opposed this system. Because the commission was politically independent and had very broad terms of reference, its considerations were disconnected from the strategic considerations of any particular party. After the commission's report, "horrified politicians of both parties attempted to put the genie of reform back in the bottle" (Nagel 2004, 534). This succeeded for six years, until the televised leaders' debate in which Labor Prime Minister David Lange inadvertently promised to hold a binding referendum on electoral reform in response to a question from the leader of the Electoral Reform Coalition. Labor initially refused to honor this pledge when elected in 1987, but after the National Party politically exploited the incident as a broken promise, both parties promised a referendum in their 1990s manifestos. The National Party elected in 1990 finally held a referendum on electoral system reform in 1992, in which voters rejected the existing first-past-the-post system by 84.7 percent in favor of an MMP alternative (70.5 percent) (Roberts 1997). New Zealand's long-standing first-past-the-post system owes its changeover to the mixed-member system not so much to "a revolution from below [as to] an accident from above." (Rudd and Taichi 1994, p. 11, quoted in Nagel 2004)

A second referendum was held in 2011 when a majority of New Zealanders reaffirmed their support for the dependent mixed (MMP) electoral system.

CONCLUSION

Elections are increasingly being used by both democracies and dictatorships to fill political offices. The growing use of elections around the world has fostered a concern with electoral integrity. Flawed and contested elections can have significant negative consequences. They can produce social instability, undermine democratic consolidation, reduce trust in the political system, and exacerbate ethnic and religious grievances. As we have seen in this chapter, there is significant variation in electoral integrity across countries, both democracies and dictatorships. How can we promote "good" electoral practice? Unfortunately, many of the factors that influence the level of electoral integrity relate to domestic structural constraints such as a country's level of development or its dependence on natural resources that are difficult to change, at least in the short term. One possibility is to strengthen the electoral management bodies that oversee and administer the elections. The problem here is that the set of actors who have the strongest incentive to strengthen these organizations are often not the same set of actors who have the power to actually do this. Some people are optimistic that international donors can help promote free and fair elections in recipient elections by making their foreign aid conditional on electoral and democratic reform. This optimism must be tempered, though, by the fact that foreign aid donors are not always willing or able to follow through on their threats to withdraw aid if their conditions are not met.

In the second half of this chapter, we examined the different types of electoral system that are used in elections around the world. Most political scientists classify electoral systems into three main families, depending on the electoral formula that is used to translate votes into seats: majoritarian, proportional, and mixed. We are often asked whether there is a single electoral system that is better than all the others. As our discussion indicates, though, each electoral system has its strengths and weaknesses. For example, some electoral systems promote proportionality but lower the ability of voters to hold representatives accountable. Others allow voters to more accurately convey their sincere preferences but are complicated for individuals to understand and costly for electoral agencies to administer. In an echo of our comments from Chapter 11, there is no perfect electoral system—there are always trade-offs to be made.

Of course, you may be more willing to make certain trade-offs than others. Perhaps you think proportionality is the key criterion for evaluating different electoral systems and are less concerned with having a close link between the representative and his constituents. When we think about the actual adoption of an electoral system, though, we need to stop and ask what is in the interests of the actors involved in choosing the electoral system. Rather than thinking about which electoral system is best at meeting some objective criteria that we might care about, such as proportionality, we now need to think of which electoral systems are politically feasible, given the preferences of the actors involved. We can then try to choose the "best" electoral system from within the set of politically feasible electoral systems.

As we noted earlier, electoral systems are distributive mechanisms that reward one set of actors at the expense of another. This means that no electoral system is a winning situation for everyone involved. This has important consequences for any budding electoral reformers among you. It is nearly always the case that the political actors who won under the existing electoral system are the ones who are in a position to determine whether electoral reform should take place. Given that these actors won under the existing system, they are unlikely to be willing to reform the electoral system except in ways that solidify their ability to win in the future. Only when there is some impending threat to their continued electoral success, as was the case with conservative parties at the beginning of the twentieth century when the right to vote was extended to the working class, are they likely to consider major electoral reform. Although many people in the United States complain about the existing SMDP electoral system and advocate for the adoption of a more proportional one, we suggest that they not hold their breath. Why would either the Democratic or Republican party choose to adopt a more proportional electoral system that would hurt their chances to be reelected and help smaller political parties? Of course, as the New Zealand case that we just described illustrates, electoral reform can happen "by accident."

In the next chapter, we discuss how electoral systems affect the size of the party system. Why do some countries have few parties but others have many? As we will demonstrate, whether a country has a small or large party system depends to a great extent on the proportionality of the electoral system. It also depends on the social and ethnic makeup of a country. This last point forces us to think about which social and ethnic differences in a country become politicized.

KEY CONCEPTS

alternative vote (AV) *540*
apparentement *556*
ballot structure *522*
closed party list *556*
cumulation *560*
dependent mixed electoral system *566*
district magnitude *522*
divisor, or highest average, system *553*
electoral formula *522*
electoral integrity *524*
electoral malpractice *524*
electoral system *522*
electoral threshold *555*
electoral tier *564*
formal threshold *555*
free party list *556*
independent mixed electoral system *565*

list PR system *551*
majoritarian electoral system *534*
majority-runoff TRS *544*
mixed electoral system *564*
natural threshold *555*
open party list *556*
panachage *560*
preference, or preferential, voting *540*
proportional, or proportional representation
    (PR), electoral system *549*
quota *551*
single-member district plurality (SMDP)
    system *534*
single nontransferable vote (SNTV) *538*
single transferable vote (STV) *560*
supplementary vote (SV) *547*
two-round system (TRS) *544*

PROBLEMS

The following problems address various issues relating to electoral systems that were raised in this chapter.

Electoral System Design

1. What criteria do you think are important for evaluating electoral systems? Explain and justify your answer.

2. Electoral formulas are rules that allow us to translate votes into seats. As we note in the chapter, the rationale behind proportional representation (PR) electoral systems is that they produce highly proportional outcomes. In other words, the percentage of seats that a party

TABLE 13.13	Legislative Elections in Oslo, Norway, 2005		
Party	**Votes (no.)**	**Votes (%)**	**Seats (no.)**
Center Party (SP)	3,270	1.1	
Christian People's Party (KrF)	11,168	3.6	
Coast Party (Kyst)	551	0.2	
Conservative Party (H)	61,130	19.8	
Labour Party (Ap)	97,246	31.5	
Left Party (V)	28,639	9.3	
Socialist Left Party (SV)	41,434	13.4	
Progress Party (FrP)	53,280	17.3	
Others	12,116	3.9	
Total	308,834	100	17

wins should accurately reflect the percentage of votes it receives. Proportionality is often taken as a criterion of an electoral system's "fairness." However, it is not always clear how to design a system that produces "fair" results even when we employ multimember districts. We now provide an example in which you can try it for yourself. In Table 13.13, we present actual results from the 2005 Norwegian legislative elections for the Oslo district. There are seventeen seats available in this district. Note that the "others" category in Table 13.13 refers to all those parties whose vote totals are too small to list separately. You should ignore this category when allocating seats to parties. Answer the following questions (based on a modified series of questions asked by Professor Kaare Strøm, University of California, San Diego).

a. Copy Table 13.13. How would you allocate the seventeen seats among the parties? Put the number of seats you give to each party in your table.

b. Explain your method and attempt to justify how you arrived at your distribution of seats among the parties. Are there any problems with fairness that would arise from the seat allocation that you suggest?

c. How would your choice be affected if there were only three seats in Oslo instead of seventeen? What if there were thirty seats instead of fifteen? Under what conditions would it be easier to produce a "fairer" outcome?

3. Iraq is an ethnically and religiously diverse country. See Map 13.3, which illustrates the geographic location and size of Iraq's different ethnic groups. Answer the following questions.

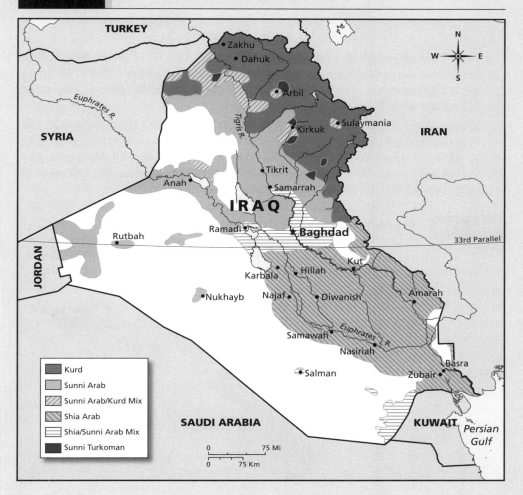

MAP 13.3   **Ethnoreligious Groups of Iraq**

a. The electoral system used for the 2014 legislative elections in Iraq was a list PR system. Use Internet resources to find out more detailed information about the electoral system. For example, how many districts and electoral tiers were there? How many legislators were elected in each district? What was the average district magnitude? What type of party list was employed? Did the Iraqis use a quota or divisor system? What type of quota and remainder system or what type of divisor method was employed? Were there any other special features of the Iraqi electoral system?

b. Given the ethnically diverse character of Iraq, what are the strengths and weaknesses of the electoral system that was adopted?

c. If you were in charge of designing an electoral system for Iraq, what would it be and why?

4. Afghanistan is another ethnically diverse country. See Map 13.4, which illustrates the geographic location of Afghanistan's different ethnic groups. In September 2010, voters elected 249 legislators to the Afghan House of the People (Wolesi Jirga). Answer the following questions.

a. The electoral system used for the 2010 legislative elections in Afghanistan was the single nontransferable vote. Use Internet resources to find out more detailed information about the electoral system. For example, how many districts and electoral tiers were there? How many legislators were elected in each district? Were there any special features of the Afghan electoral system with respect to women candidates?

MAP 13.4   **Ethnic Groups in Afghanistan**

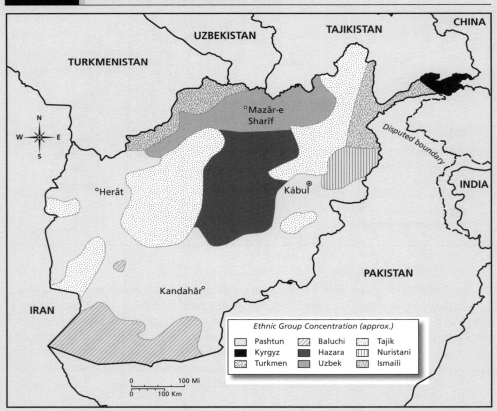

b. The Afghan electoral system has been heavily criticized by numerous actors. In a 2012 briefing paper written for an independent research institute based in Afghanistan, political scientists Andrew Reynolds and John Carey wrote that "The SNTV electoral system came about by a path of missteps and was a disservice to the millions of Afghans who deserved a clear and transparent tool to craft their first truly democratic parliament. If the system is retained for subsequent elections, there is every reason to believe that the fragmentation and parochialism of the legislature will continue, that the parliament as a whole will be ineffective in articulating and representing broad national interests, and that incumbents who strong-arm and bribe their way into office will thrive" (2012, 17). Explain the basis for Reynolds and Carey's criticisms, focusing on the problems typically associated with SNTV electoral systems.

c. If you were designing an electoral system for Afghanistan, what would it be and why?

How Do Electoral Systems Work?

5. In Table 13.14 we again show the results from the Oslo district in the 2005 Norwegian elections. Answer the following questions. In all of these questions, you should ignore the "others" category.

a. Copy Table 13.14. Imagine that the seventeen seats in Oslo are to be allocated according to the Hare quota with largest remainders. Fill in your table and indicate how Oslo's seventeen seats are allocated among the parties. How many automatic, remainder, and total seats does each party obtain?

TABLE 13.14 **Legislative Elections in Oslo, Norway, 2005 (Using Quota Systems)**

	Party									
	SP	KrF	Kyst	H	Ap	V	SV	FrP	Others	Total
Votes	3,270	11,168	551	61,130	97,246	28,639	41,434	53,280	12,116	308,834
Seats										17
Quota										
Votes ÷ Quota										
Automatic seats										
Remainder										
Remainder seats										
Total seats										

b. Now make another table like Table 13.14 and repeat the process using the Droop quota with largest remainders. Does the allocation of seats change?

6. In Table 13.15, we again show the same results from the Oslo district in the 2005 Norwegian elections. Answer the following questions. As before, you should ignore the "others" category.

a. Copy Table 13.15. Imagine that the seventeen seats in Oslo are to be allocated according to the d'Hondt divisor method. Show the different quotients that are calculated when you divide each party's vote total by the d'Hondt divisors in your table. How many seats does each party obtain?

b. Now repeat the process using the Sainte-Laguë divisor method and then the modified Sainte-Laguë divisor method. Note that you will need to change the integers used to estimate the quotients. How many seats does each party obtain under these divisor systems?

c. Are there any differences if you examine the seat allocations from the two quota systems and the three divisor systems? Does one method produce a more proportional or fairer outcome in your opinion than another?

TABLE 13.15 Legislative Elections in Oslo, Norway, 2005 (Using Divisor Systems)

	SP	KrF	Kyst	H	Ap	V	SV	FrP	Others	Total
					Votes					
	3,270	11,168	551	61,130	97,246	28,639	41,434	53,280	12,116	308,834
Divisors					**Quotients**					
Votes ÷ 1										
Votes ÷ 2										
Votes ÷ 3										
Votes ÷ 4										
Votes ÷ 5										
Votes ÷ 6										
Total seats										

Gender Quotas

7. At http://www.quotaproject.org/ you will find the Global Database of Quotas for Women (2015), a joint project of International IDEA, Inter-Parliamentary Union, and Stockholm University. The goal of the project is to provide information on quota provisions for women in parliaments around the world. After accessing the project website, answer the following questions.

   a. What are the three main types of gender quotas? Explain how each works, and for each provide an example of a country that employs it.

   b. What are the advantages and disadvantages of the different kinds of gender quotas?

   c. For the three countries you chose in part (a), use Internet resources to find out the current gender composition of their legislatures. In other words, what is the percentage of women legislators? Is the ratio of men and women in the legislature what you might expect given the quota provisions in that country? Why or why not?

14 Social Cleavages and Party Systems

Party is organized opinion.

Benjamin Disraeli

- Political scientists sometimes categorize democracies in terms of the type of party system that they exhibit. When they do this, they typically distinguish between party systems based on the number and size of the parties that they contain.

- A political party is an organization that includes officials who hold office and people who help get and keep them there. Parties help to structure the political world, recruit and socialize the political elite, mobilize the masses, and provide a link between rulers and the ruled.

- In this chapter, we examine why some party systems are divided primarily along ethnic lines, whereas others are divided mainly along class, religious, linguistic, or regional ones. We also investigate why some countries have few parties and others have many. As we will see, the general structure of a country's party system results from the complex interplay of both social and institutional forces.

OVERVIEW

In addition to classifying democracies according to the type of government they have or the type of electoral system they employ, political scientists sometimes categorize democracies by the type of party system they exhibit. Although there are obviously many facets to a party system that one might examine, political scientists often focus on the number and size of the parties in a country. As a result, you will frequently see scholars distinguish between democracies that have a two-party system, like the United States, and democracies that have a multiparty system, like the Netherlands. Although the type of government and electoral system in a country is nearly always enshrined in a constitution or some other legal document, this is not the case for the type of party system (Stokes 1999, 245). Rather than something that is intentionally designed by particular individuals, the structure of a party system is shaped by the changing nature of political competition in a country. We will suggest in this chapter that socioeconomic forces largely drive the structure of a country's party system, but we will also demonstrate that these forces are channeled in powerful and important ways by the kinds of political institutions that we have examined in the last two chapters. In effect, the structure of a country's party system results from the complex interplay of both social and institutional forces.

We begin this chapter by asking what a party is and what a party does. After briefly describing the different types of party systems that exist around the world, we then explore the social and institutional factors that interact to influence both the number and types of parties that exist in a country. As such, our goal is to help explain why some countries have few parties but others have many, and why some party systems are divided primarily along ethnic lines and others are divided mainly along class, religious, linguistic, or regional ones.

POLITICAL PARTIES: WHAT ARE THEY, AND WHAT DO THEY DO?

A **political party** "is a group of officials or would-be officials who are linked with a sizeable group of citizens into an organization; a chief object of this organization is to ensure that its officials attain power or are maintained in power" (Shively 2001, 234). As this definition suggests, a political party comprises a broad collection of actors that can range from officials who actually attain power to individuals who regularly vote for the party and people who contribute money or time to campaign for a party member. In other words, a party can be thought of as a group of people that includes those who hold office and those who help get and keep them there. One of the primary goals of political parties is to attain power; it is this goal that differentiates them from interest groups. In contrast to political parties, interest groups, such as the National Rifle Association, the American Medical Association, and Greenpeace, are organizations that attempt to influence policy without actually taking power.

One thing to note about the definition that we have just given is that political parties are not restricted to democracies or electoral activity. As we saw in Chapter 10, political parties

> A **political party** can be thought of as a group of people that includes those who hold office and those who help get and keep them there.

exist in many dictatorships around the world. Some of these parties, such as the Communist Party in China, control the levers of power without holding national-level elections. That some dictatorships have chosen to have political parties even in the absence of elections should immediately alert you to the fact that political parties can serve important purposes beyond simply helping officials get elected to power.

Political parties perform many important functions that are crucial to the operation of modern political systems in both democracies and dictatorships. In what follows, we focus on how political parties (a) structure the political world, (b) recruit and socialize the political elite, (c) mobilize the masses, and (d) provide a link between the rulers and the ruled (Shively 2001).

Political Parties Structure the Political World

Political parties help to structure the political world for both political elites and the masses. For the elites, political parties provide some kind of order to the policymaking process. Imagine, for a moment, a world in which there are no political parties. In other words, imagine a world in which every legislator is an independent with no institutionalized link to other legislators. Given that legislators must make policy decisions in numerous issue areas and that there is likely to be disagreement over which policies are most appropriate, the outcome of the policymaking process in this type of environment is probably going to be highly chaotic and unstable. You will no doubt recall that this is precisely the prediction we saw in Chapter 11 when we examined the chaos theorem and Arrow's (1963) impossibility theorem. Political parties help to overcome some of these problems by coordinating the actions of individual legislators and simplifying the issue space. In effect, parties help to provide structure to an otherwise unstable policymaking process. Aldrich (1995) argues that the need to coordinate votes on many issues among congressional representatives with similar, but not identical, preferences is precisely the explanation for why political parties were formed in the United States in the eighteenth century.

Just as for elites, political parties also structure the political world for voters. One way in which they do this is by providing "information shortcuts" to voters (Downs 1957; Fiorina 1981). Voters seldom have the opportunity, time, energy, or even inclination to gather information about particular political issues. For these uninformed voters, party labels and party attachments can be an information shortcut in the sense that these things tell voters how to feel about certain issues. In effect, voters might decide that they are against a particular piece of legislation not because they have read up on it and realized that it is not in their interests but simply because the party to which they feel attached dislikes it. In many ways, one's political identity is frequently tied up with one's **party identification** (Campbell et al. 1960).

> **Party identification** is an attachment to a party that helps citizens locate themselves on the political landscape.

Campbell and colleagues (1986, 100) note this when they describe "party identification [as] an attachment to a party that helps the citizen locate him/herself and others on the political landscape." For example, simply admitting to being a Democrat or a Republican in the United States or a Labour or Conservative supporter in the United Kingdom can convey a lot of information about a person's likely stance on a whole host of different issues. All of this helps to explain why so many people seem to view politics in terms of the fortunes of political parties rather than the fate of political issues.

Recruitment and Socialization of the Political Elite

In addition to structuring the political world, parties play an important role in recruiting and socializing the political elite. In many countries, it is extremely difficult to get elected as an independent. In other words, being selected as a party's candidate is often a necessary condition for a successful run for office. Similarly, cabinet positions are frequently restricted to senior members of a political party. In effect, "gaining access to political power requires being accepted by a party, and usually being a leading figure in it. Parties also socialize the political elite; most government ministers have spent a number of years as party members, working with other party members and learning to see the political world from the party's perspective" (Gallagher, Laver, and Mair 2006, 308). To see a more concrete example of this, consider the description Shively (2001, 238) gives of how an ambitious young woman interested in entering politics in Britain might behave.

> [She] might work for a while at lesser tasks for one of the major parties, such as the Conservative Party. Before too long, if she were interested in standing for Parliament, she might be nominated from a district. To get the nomination, she would have to convince the local selection committee of the Conservative Party in that district that she was their best nominee. As a beginner, she would probably be selected in a hopeless district, where no Conservative had much of a chance; but once she had proved she could campaign well in one or two lost causes, she might get the nomination from a decent district, win, and enter the House. In the House, she would continue to be molded and guided by the party. If she were the sort that party leaders like—witty in debate, hard working, and above all a faithful party voter—she might advance into positions of real responsibility, such as party spokesperson on defense or on health. Eventually, she might aim so high as to be prime minister. To be selected for this position, she would have to win an internal election at which all the Conservative members of Parliament vote to choose their leader. Throughout this career, her advancement would have been primarily due to her support from her party organization, and she would have risen to the top only because she was the sort of person her party wanted and because, in each position she held, she had learned from the rest of the party how to behave in ways they preferred. This is essentially the only way to make a political career in Great Britain.

To some extent, the role played by parties in recruiting and socializing the political elite is more important in parliamentary democracies than in presidential ones. Although it is true that much of the political elite in presidential democracies will have worked their way into place through the apparatus of one political party or another, parties are not the monopolistic gatekeepers to power that they frequently are in parliamentary systems. For example, our discussion of the government formation process in presidential democracies in Chapter 12 indicated that presidents are much more likely to appoint nonpartisan ministers to their cabinets than prime ministers are in parliamentary systems. If you recall, the reason for this is that the president has less need to negotiate with political parties in the legislature over the composition of the cabinet because the vote of no confidence is absent in presidential systems.

Presidential regimes that allow for primaries, like the United States and, increasingly, many Latin American countries (Carey and Polga-Hecimovich 2006, 2008), further weaken the role that political parties play in recruiting and socializing the political elite. By allowing candidates to appeal directly to the voters rather than rely on party leaders, primaries can allow candidates with little political or party experience to win elections. This has been illustrated most recently by the success of Donald Trump in winning the nomination of the Republican Party in the 2016 US presidential primaries. Indeed, Trump won the nomination, and then the presidency, despite considerable opposition from within the Republican Party itself. The existence of primary elections is a key reason for the organizational weakness of political parties and the dominance of candidate-centered, rather than party-centered, election campaigns in the United States (Aldrich 1995). In presidential democracies, it is even possible for complete political outsiders to win the presidency. This is precisely what happened when the academic and TV presenter Alberto Fujimori surprisingly won the 1990 presidential elections in Peru. The election of such a candidate to a position equivalent to that of prime minister in a parliamentary democracy is almost unthinkable.

That political parties do not exert the same degree of control over the recruitment and socialization of the political elite across different types of democracy suggests that the political direction of leaders in presidential democracies is inclined to be inherently less stable and more unpredictable than that of political leaders in parliamentary democracies (Gallagher, Laver, and Mair 2006, 308).

Mobilization of the Masses

Political parties are also key tools for mobilizing the masses. This is particularly important at election time when ordinary citizens must be encouraged to vote. A large literature in political science suggests that people will not necessarily choose to vote given that turning out to vote is costly—it takes time, they could be doing something else, it might be raining, and so on—and that the likelihood of anyone's individual vote determining the outcome of the election is incredibly small (Aldrich 1993; Gomez, Hansford, and Krause 2007). This suggests that organizations such as political parties have a significant role to play in getting people to the polls (Morton 1991; Uhlaner 1989). Political parties are well placed to carry out this role because they are likely to have membership and organizational structures that extend deeply into each constituency. Moreover, they have a strong incentive to get people (at least particular people) to the polls—they want to win elections.

The ability of political parties to mobilize the masses can be important even when elections are not being held. As an example, French president Charles de Gaulle used his Gaullist Party to mobilize his supporters against student and worker protests in 1968 (Lacouture 1986, 719–720). To many observers at the time, these protests, which had grown in size over several weeks, threatened the very existence of the French Fifth Republic. After initially keeping a low profile as events developed, de Gaulle eventually delivered a radio address that preyed on the French people's fears of a Communist revolution. He said that he would dissolve the National Assembly, that he would hold new elections, and that the country was "threatened with dictatorship, that of totalitarian communism." He also called on the people to come to the defense of the republic against the "Communist" students and workers. As Hitchcock (2004, 251) notes, "Within an hour of de Gaulle's address, crowds began to form on the place de la Concorde. . . . Perhaps as many as half a million people poured out of their homes into the streets, and marched up the Champs-Elysées behind the major political leaders of the Gaullist and right-wing parties." In the new elections that took place about a month later, the electorate gave a huge majority to the Gaullist candidates.

Although this particular example from France illustrates how political parties can be used to mobilize the masses in *support* of a regime, there are numerous other cases in which parties have been used to mobilize the people *against* the ruling order. For example, the Ukrainian political party known as Our Ukraine played an important role in organizing protests in Kiev that led to the Orange Revolution in 2004. Other examples of political parties mobilizing the masses against the ruling regime include the Congress Party in India and the National Front for Liberation in Algeria. Both of these parties were originally established as a means to mobilize the masses against British and French colonial rule (Shively 2001, 237).

A Link between the Rulers and the Ruled

Political parties also provide a link between the rulers and the ruled. According to most democratic theorists, democratic governments are supposed to reflect the preferences of their citizens (Dahl 1956; Mill [1861] 1991; Pitkin 1967). As discussed in Chapter 12 in our examination of the government formation process, the political party is the primary vehicle ensuring that citizen preferences are reflected in government policy. In fact, it is probably the central function of a political party in a democracy to represent, articulate, and champion the interests of its membership. Political parties are also the main means by which democracies can be induced to be responsive. In democracies, the people should be able to hold elected leaders accountable for their actions in office. The problem is that government policy is frequently determined by the collective actions of many officeholders. As a collective group, the political party provides the main means by which voters can hold elected officials responsible for what they do collectively. Fiorina (1980, 26) goes so far as to write that "the only way collective responsibility has ever existed, and can exist . . . is through the agency of the political party."

It is important to recognize that the link that parties create between officials and citizens runs both ways. We have just described the political party as an organization that citizens can use to control the actions of officials and hold them responsible for what they do in office. However, we should recognize that political parties can also help officials exert control over other political actors and citizens as well. Party leaders have many carrots and sticks at their disposal that they can use to deliberately enforce the obedience of legislators when it comes to voting in the legislature. For example, they can use promotion within the party, promises of campaign resources, threats of expulsion, and the like to induce legislators to vote the "right" way on pieces of legislation. Most political parties have an individual called a **whip**, whose job it is to ensure that members of the party attend legislative sessions and vote as the party leadership desires.

> A **whip** is an individual whose job it is to ensure that members of the party attend legislative sessions and vote as the party leadership desires.

Although the power of whips varies from country to country, whips are frequently some of the most important political actors in a country (see Box 14.1, "Party Whips in the United Kingdom"). The importance of whips often goes unrecognized by the public because these actors rarely appear in the media, at least in their capacity as whips.

Box 14.1   PARTY WHIPS IN THE UNITED KINGDOM

The term *whip* to describe someone who ensures that party members attend legislative sessions and vote as the party leadership desires originated in the English Parliament in the 1880s. The term derives from the "whipper-in" at a fox hunt, whose job it is to keep the pack of hounds together and under control. As you can imagine, the role of a whip is particularly important when the voting strengths of the government and the opposition are close. The duties of a whip include (a) keeping legislators informed of forthcoming parliamentary business, (b) maintaining the party's voting strength by ensuring that members attend important debates and vote as the party leadership desires, and (c) passing on the opinions of legislators to the party leadership. Each of the three major parties in the United Kingdom—the Conservatives, Labour, and the Liberals—have a chief whip, a deputy chief whip, and a varying number of junior whips. The government chief whip has the formal title of Parliamentary Secretary to the Treasury; she is directly answerable to the prime minister, attends cabinet meetings, and makes the day-to-day arrangements for the government's program of business.

The term *whip* also applies to a weekly circular sent out by each party's whips to all their Members of Parliament (MPs), notifying them of parliamentary business and the schedule for the days ahead. This circular includes the sentence "Your attendance is absolutely essential" next to each debate in which there will be a vote. The degree of importance of each debate is indicated by the number of times this sentence is underlined. Sentences that are underlined once are considered routine, and attendance is optional. Those that are underlined twice are more important, and attendance is required unless a "pair"—a member from the opposing side who also intends to be absent from the debate—has been arranged. Those that are underlined three times are highly important, and pairing is not normally allowed. The number of underlines determines whether there is a one-line, two-line, or three-line whip on a vote.

Three-line whips are imposed on important occasions such as for votes of no confidence and the second reading of significant bills.

The consequences of defying the party leadership depend on the circumstances surrounding a vote and are usually negotiated with the party whips in advance. Cabinet ministers who defy the whips are immediately dismissed. The consequences for defying the party whip for a backbencher—someone who is not in the cabinet or the "shadow" cabinet of the Opposition—can include being overlooked for future promotions to a cabinet post; being given little support by the party organization when seeking reelection; being deselected by local party activists or moved to a different, and less safe, constituency seat; or being expelled from the party altogether. Failure by MPs to attend a vote with a three-line whip is usually treated as a rebellion against the party and, theoretically, leads to suspension from the party. As an example, nine Conservative MPs were suspended from the party in 1994 when they voted against the position of John Major's government regarding the European Union.

Party whips can be extremely forceful in obtaining the votes of their backbenchers, even engaging in "blackmail, verbal intimidation, sexual harassment and physical aggression" from time to time to force some unpopular votes (Dixon 1996, 160). Occasionally, whips bring in very sick MPs for important votes. A former MP, Joe Ashton, describes such a case from the final days of James Callaghan's Labour government (1976–1979).

> I remember the famous case of Leslie Spriggs, the then [Labour] Member for St. Helens. We had a tied vote and he was brought to the House in an ambulance having suffered a severe heart attack. The two Whips went out to look in the ambulance and there was Leslie Spriggs laid there as though he was dead. I believe that John Stradling Thomas [Conservative whip] said to Joe Harper [Labour whip], "How do we know that he is alive?" So he leaned forward, turned the knob on the heart machine, the green light went around, and he said, "There, you've lost—it's 311." [The vote had been tied 310–310.] That is an absolutely true story. It is the sort of nonsense that used to happen. No one believes it, but it is true. (Hansard 1997, Column 507)

As we saw in Chapter 10, political parties can also be used to control and co-opt the masses, though the most egregious examples of this typically occur under authoritarian regimes. Having examined what it is that political parties do, we now briefly describe the different types of party systems that are observed around the world.

PARTY SYSTEMS

As we noted at the beginning of the chapter, political scientists sometimes categorize democracies in terms of their party system. When they do this, they typically classify party systems based on the number and size of the parties they contain. In what follows, we identify five different types of party system: **nonpartisan system, single-party system, one-party dominant system, two-party system**, and **multiparty system**. Single-party systems exist only in dictatorships, and nonpartisan and one-party dominant systems are relatively rare in democracies. It is for this reason that political scientists usually distinguish between democracies on the basis of whether they have a two-party system, like the United States, or a multiparty system, like the Netherlands.

> A **nonpartisan system** is one with no official political parties. A **single-party system** is one in which only one political party is legally allowed to hold power. A **one-party dominant system** is one in which multiple parties may legally operate but in which only one particular party has a realistic chance of gaining power. A **two-party system** is one in which only two major political parties have a realistic chance of holding power. A **multiparty system** is one in which more than two parties have a realistic chance of holding power.

The existence of political parties is often seen as a necessary condition for the existence of modern democracy. For example, scholars have claimed that "parties are the core institution of democratic politics" (Lipset 1996), that "democracy is unthinkable save in terms of parties" (Schattschneider 1942), and that "modern democracy is party democracy" (Katz 1980). Despite these claims, though, a small handful of democracies can be considered nonpartisan, that is, ones in which there are no official political parties. The absence of political parties may be because a law prohibits their existence or simply because they have yet to form. Historically, the administration of George Washington and the first few sessions of the US Congress were nonpartisan. Today, the only democracies that can be considered nonpartisan are the small Pacific islands of Kiribati, the Marshall Islands, Micronesia, Nauru, Palau, and Tuvalu (Veenendaal 2016).[1] These islands have extremely small populations; Nauru, Palau, and Tuvalu all have fewer than 20,000 residents. Although nonpartisan democracies at the national level are extremely rare, a few countries have some nonpartisan governments at the subnational level. For example, the unicameral legislature of Nebraska is nonpartisan, as are some Swiss cantons and some Canadian territories.

In single-party systems, only one political party is legally allowed to hold power. Liberia is generally considered the first single-party state in the world. The True Whig Party ruled Liberia from 1878 to 1980, when it was ousted by a military coup. Current single-party states include such countries as China, Cuba, Laos, North Korea, and Vietnam. Although these party systems are called single-party systems, minor parties are sometimes allowed to exist. These minor parties, however, are always legally required to accept the leadership of the dominant party. For example, consider Communist Poland. The Polish United Workers' Party (PUWP) allowed a prewar left-wing United Peasant Party (ZSL), a small private business party (SD), and a Catholic group with direct ties to Moscow to coexist with it under separate labels in the legislature (Gandhi and Przeworski 2006). During elections, though, these small parties had to present their legislative candidates on a single PUWP party list.

---

1. Of these six countries, it is widely accepted that Micronesia, Palau, and Tuvalu are nonpartisan democracies. There is some disagreement, however, as to whether political parties have existed in certain periods in the other countries, particularly in Kiribati. Much depends on how exactly one defines a political party.

Cuban president Raul Castro (*left*) and Botswana's president Ian Khama (*right*) attend the welcoming ceremony in Havana for Khama's June 2010 visit to Cuba. Khama's Botswana Democratic Party has ruled Botswana since independence in 1966. Ian Khama's father, Seretse Khama, founded the Botswana Democratic Party in 1961 and was himself president from 1966 to 1980.

In other words, the candidates of these minor parties had to be approved by the PUWP ahead of time. All single-party systems occur in dictatorships.

In some countries, multiple parties are legally allowed to exist, but only one party has a realistic chance of gaining power. States in which this is the case are said to have one-party dominant systems. Many of these one-party dominant systems occur in dictatorships. In these countries, the dictatorship might allow certain opposition parties to legally operate, but they then use various means to prevent them from actually coming to power (Lust-Okar 2005). Examples of one-party dominant systems in dictatorships include the Patriotic Salvation Movement (MPS) of Idriss Déby in Chad and the Cameroon People's Democratic Movement (CPDM) of Paul Biya in Cameroon. Not all one-party dominant systems are necessarily undemocratic, though. For example, there are several cases of democracies in which a single party is dominant for long periods of time. This dominance is normally attributed to things like long-running popularity, a divided opposition, the efficient use of patronage systems, and, occasionally, electoral fraud. Examples of one-party dominant systems in states that many consider democratic include the African National Congress in South Africa since 1994, the Botswana Democratic Party in Botswana since 1966, the Democratic Party in the southern United States from the 1880s to the 1960s, the Liberal Democratic Party in Japan from 1955 to 1993 (see Box 14.2, "One-Party Dominant Systems: Japan and the Case of the LDP"), and the Congress Party in India from 1947 to 1977. Although a one-party dominant system is similar in many ways to a single-party system, "the availability of other active parties does guarantee that there will be fairly open discussion and debate, and it also provides for possible long-term flexibility and adjustment in the system" (Shively 2001, 249).

A two-party system is one in which only two major political parties have a realistic chance of holding power. In democracies with this type of party system, nearly all elected offices are held by candidates endorsed by one of the two major parties; electoral success under the label of some third party, although not impossible, is extremely difficult. Examples of two-party systems include the systems in Jamaica, the United Kingdom, and the United States. As of 2016, all 435 seats in the US House of Representatives and 98 of the 100 seats in

ONE-PARTY DOMINANT SYSTEMS: JAPAN AND THE CASE OF THE LDP

The Liberal Democratic Party (LDP) was the dominant political force in Japan from 1955 to 1993, regularly winning more than 50 percent of the vote and managing to form single-party majority governments throughout this period. The LDP officially came into existence in 1955 when the Liberal Party and the Japan Democratic Party merged to form a united front against the popular Japan Socialist Party. Given the emerging Cold War, the merger that created the LDP was strongly supported by the United States. Indeed, the Central Intelligence Agency (CIA) spent millions over the following two decades to help the LDP win elections (Weiner 1994).

Since its formation, the LDP has represented a broad spectrum of interests. The party has failed to espouse a well-defined ideology, however, which has led many to claim that the LDP might more accurately be considered a coalition of factions rather than a party. Throughout its history, there have been between six and thirteen different factions in the LDP. Every LDP legislator is typically associated with one of these factions, and each faction is headed by a senior party figure. Among other things, faction leaders provide their followers with financial support and business contacts during election campaigns. Without these funds and contacts, it is extremely difficult for LDP legislators to survive politically. To a large extent, the primary thing that kept all of these factions together within the LDP was the desire to win elections and share in the spoils of office. Given the electoral dominance of the LDP from 1955 to 1993, much of the real struggle for political power in Japan has occurred between factions within the LDP rather than among the different Japanese parties. The central role of these factions has led some to joke that the LDP is neither liberal, nor democratic, nor even a party.

If you recall from our discussion of electoral systems in Chapter 13, Japan employed the single nontransferable vote (SNTV) to elect its legislators during the period of LDP dominance. As we noted at the time, SNTV creates incentives for intraparty fighting and factionalization because candidates from one party are competing not only against candidates from other parties in their district but also against candidates from their own party. One consequence of this was that LDP legislators went to enormous lengths to cultivate personal reputations in their districts to differentiate themselves from competing LDP candidates (Cox and Niou 1994). This led scholars to conclude that Japan was characterized by the most candidate-centered politics of any democracy in the world (Reed and Thies 2000).

As Hirano (2011, 57) notes, LDP legislators were notorious for engaging in constituency service and targeting subsidy (pork) allocations to their districts. "The constituency services, which are organized through the candidates' personal support networks (*koenkai*), provide a wide range of events for the constituents, such as local fund raisers, study groups, cultural events (such as sumo matches), tours of the Diet [parliament], and in some cases trips to hot springs. LDP candidates were also expected to perform personal favors for their constituents, such as providing monetary gifts at weddings and funerals, helping with job or school placement, and mediating disputes between constituents." Hirano goes on to describe Tanaka Kakuei as the most extreme example of a candidate who used services and pork provisions to cater to his electorate. For example, he writes (58) that "one of Tanaka's final activities while in office was to take eleven thousand people to Nukumi hot springs in Yamagata prefecture at a cost of $1.4 million (Richardson 1997, 28). He is also known for bringing Japan's high speed rail line to his home prefecture, a project that took 11 years to build at a cost of millions of dollars per kilometer. Four of the eight bullet train stops are in Tanaka's home prefecture, and two of the stops are less than 14 miles apart (Schlesinger 1997, 104)."

The importance and pervasiveness of personal ties between LDP legislators and their faction leaders, as well as between LDP legislators and their constituents, created a strong patronage structure in which many people had incentives to preserve the LDP's political dominance. The success of the LDP's system "depended less on generalized mass appeals than on the three 'bans': *jiban* (a strong, well-organized constituency), *kaban* (a briefcase full of money), and *kanban* (prestigious appointments, particularly on the cabinet level)" (Dolan and Worden 1994). The LDP's modus operandi led to numerous corruption and bribery scandals over the years. For example, several members of Japan's political and business elite were involved in the 1976 Lockheed bribery scandal, when Japanese Prime Minister Tanaka Kakuei was arrested for taking $3 million in bribes from the US aerospace company Lockheed during negotiations over the sale of aircraft.

In the wake of further corruption scandals and a strong downturn in the Japanese economy, the LDP's hold on power finally ended in the 1993 elections. Although the LDP remained the largest party following these elections, it did not have a legislative majority and was unable to form a coalition government. Instead, a coalition of eight opposition parties entered government, marking the first time since 1956 that the Japanese government did not include the LDP. In 1994 a package of reform laws was introduced that was specifically designed to reduce corruption. Not only did these laws create a new electoral system, but they also introduced a public subsidy program to fund political parties and stricter regulations for political donations. Despite these changes, it was not long before the LDP was back in power. When several parties withdrew from the government in 1994, the Japan Socialist Party decided to form a coalition government with the LDP, its former archrival.

In the last two decades, the LDP has remained the most powerful political force in Japanese politics. Unlike the earlier period, though, when the LDP almost always formed a single-party majority government, in the post-1993 period, the LDP has always formed a coalition government when it has come to power. Moreover, from 2009 to 2012, the LDP was in the opposition after it lost its status as the largest party in the legislature for the first time since its formation in 1955. This suggests that, to some extent, the Japanese party system has transitioned from a one-party dominant system to a multiparty system.

the US Senate were controlled by either the Democratic Party or the Republican Party. The 2016 elections in Jamaica resulted in all 63 legislative seats going to either the Jamaica Labour Party or the People's National Party. Although the United Kingdom has recently seen some electoral success for third parties, the two major parties—the Conservatives and Labour—still managed to win 86 percent of the legislatives seats in the most recent elections in 2015. Despite their name, virtually all two-party systems have many more than two parties competing for office. As of 2016, for instance, there were 432 registered political parties in the United Kingdom (394 in Great Britain and 38 in Northern Ireland) and at least 50 national-level parties in the United States. Both the United Kingdom and the United States, however, are traditionally seen as two-party systems because only the two major parties usually have any expectation of controlling the government.

A multiparty system is one in which more than two political parties have a realistic chance of holding power, either separately or as part of a coalition. Most democracies have multiparty systems. Examples include France, Israel, and the Netherlands. In Table 14.1, we list those parties holding legislative seats in the Israeli Knesset following the 2015 elections. As you can see, the seats in the legislature are split among numerous political parties, with no single party coming close to obtaining a legislative majority. The coalition government formed by Israeli Prime Minister Benjamin Netanyahu after the 2015 elections included his own Likud Party, Kulanu, Shas, United Torah Judaism, and Habayit Hayehudi.

We have just described how political scientists frequently distinguish between democracies based on the number and size of the parties that exist. In general, they tend to distinguish between two-party and multiparty democracies. Rather than lump democracies into just these two categories, however, we might want to know how many parties there are in each country. This requires us to think about how we count political parties. It turns out that the most appropriate way of doing this is not as obvious as you might think.

You might think to count every party that contests national elections. If you did this, though, the number of parties in many countries would be extremely large and include

| TABLE 14.1 | Political Parties with Seats in the Israeli Knesset, 2015 |

Political party	No. of seats
Likud	30
Zionist Union	24
Joint List	13
Yesh Atid	11
Kulanu	10
Habayit Hayehudi	8
Shas	7
United Torah Judaism	6
Yisrael Beiteinu	6
Meretz	5
Total	120

"joke" parties, such as the "The True English (Poetry) Party" and the "Monster Raving Loony Party" in the United Kingdom, the "Guns and Dope Party"—which advocates replacing one-third of Congress with ostriches—in the United States, and the "Beer Drinkers Party" in many countries. The problem is that a party system in which votes are divided evenly among ten parties is quite different from a system in which two parties get 90 percent of the votes with eight parties splitting the rest; this difference would be lost if we simply described both systems as "ten-party" systems.

To take account of this, political scientists have frequently used a measure called the **effective number of parties** to count political parties (Laakso and Taagepera 1979). This measure counts each party that wins votes or seats, but it attaches to each party a weight that is related to the share of votes or seats that it wins. The precise formula for the effective number of parties in a system in which four parties receive votes would be

$$\text{effective number of parties} = \frac{1}{v_1^2 + v_2^2 + v_3^2 + v_4^2},$$

where v_1 is the vote share of party 1, v_2 is the vote share of party 2, and so on. If all four parties received the same percentage of votes (0.25), then the effective number of parties would be 4, that is,

$$\text{effective number of parties} = \frac{1}{0.25^2 + 0.25^2 + 0.25^2 + 0.25^2} = \frac{1}{0.25} = 4.$$

Contrast this with the situation in which two parties split 90 percent of the vote equally and the two other parties split the remaining 10 percent equally. In this situation, the effective number of parties would be 2.44, that is,

$$\text{effective number of parties} = \frac{1}{0.45^2 + 0.45^2 + 0.05^2 + 0.05^2} = \frac{1}{0.41} = 2.44.$$

The "effective number of parties" is a desirable measure if we think that this latter situation is more like a two-party system than a four-party one.

If we use the "vote share" of political parties to weight each party, as we did in the example above, then we are measuring what political scientists call the **effective number of *electoral* parties**. This gives us a sense of how many parties earned votes and how the electorate's votes were distributed across the parties. If we use the "seat share" of political parties to weight each party, then we are measuring what political scientists call the **effective number of *legislative* parties**. This gives us

> The **effective number of parties** is a measure that captures both the number and the size of parties in a country. The **effective number of electoral parties** is a measure of the number of parties that win votes. The **effective number of legislative parties** is a measure of the number of parties that win seats.

a sense of how many parties won seats in the legislature and how those seats were distributed across the parties. In effect, both measures of the effective number of parties take account of not only the number but also the size of the parties in a country. Note that we can use the effective number of parties in a country to classify democracies as having two-party or multiparty systems. One common way to do this is to classify democracies as having a two-party system if the effective number of parties is less than three and a multiparty system if the effective number of parties is three or more.

In Table 14.2, we list the effective number of electoral and legislative parties in thirty democracies in the late 2000s (Bormann and Golder 2013). The country with the lowest effective number of electoral (2.03) and legislative (1.45) parties is Belize. The reason why the effective number of parties is so low in Belize is that the United Democratic Party won 56.6 percent of the vote and 80.6 percent of the legislative seats in the 2008 elections. In effect, one party dominated the Belizean elections, at least with respect to obtaining legislative seats. The country with the highest effective number of electoral (11.26) and legislative (10.44) parties is Brazil. The high effective number of parties in Brazil reflects the fact that votes and seats were shared fairly evenly among a very large number of parties.

WHERE DO PARTIES COME FROM?

You might be wondering at this stage why democracies have the types of party systems that they do. To answer this question, we need to understand where parties come from. Political scientists have two basic views—primordial and instrumental—on this. The primordial view treats parties as the natural representatives of people who share common interests. In effect, this view takes it as given that there are "natural" divisions, or cleavages, in society. As groups of individuals form around these cleavages, political parties emerge and evolve to represent these interests. This is sometimes referred to as the "bottom-up" approach to party formation. In contrast, the instrumental view of party formation treats parties as teams of office seekers and focuses on the role played by political elites and entrepreneurs. According to this "top-down" approach, political parties are created by individuals who, perhaps because of certain informational advantages and additional resources, are able to discern an opportunity to represent a previously unrepresented interest. Indeed, the instrumental approach recognizes that political entrepreneurs may even help citizens become aware that such an interest exists; in other words, they can even "create" divisions or cleavages in society.

These two views of party formation are similar to what economists would call supply and demand factors. The primordial view takes the social demand for the representation of particular interests as given and explains the existence of political parties as a response to those demands. In contrast, the instrumental view holds that "supply creates its own demand." Just as advertising and marketing firms can shape the tastes of consumers, savvy political entrepreneurs might help create the demand for particular policies and ideologies. As in the case with supply and demand, it turns out that understanding the origins of political parties

TABLE 14.2	Party Systems in Thirty Democracies in the late 2000s		
Country	Year	Effective number of electoral parties	Effective number of legislative parties
Albania	2009	3.28	2.6
Belgium	2010	10.22	8.42
Belize	2008	2.03	1.45
Bangladesh	2008	2.8	1.65
Bolivia	2009	2.06	1.85
Brazil	2010	11.26	10.44
Colombia	2010	5.97	4.95
Costa Rica	2010	4.78	3.9
Czech Republic	2010	6.8	4.51
Ecuador	2009	3.86	3.46
Estonia	2007	5.03	4.37
France	2007	4.35	2.5
Ghana	2008	2.4	1.74
Guinea-Bissau	2008	3.13	1.89
Guatemala	2007	7.74	4.78
Honduras	2009	2.46	2.3
India	2009	8.76	5.01
Indonesia	2009	10.48	6.13
Japan	2009	3.15	2.1
Mexico	2009	3.78	2.75
Mongolia	2008	2.26	2.05
New Zealand	2008	3.08	2.78
Nigeria	2007	2.09	1.75
Netherlands	2010	6.97	6.74
Panama	2009	4.18	3.66
South Korea	2008	4.33	2.92
Sierra Leone	2007	3.04	2.54
Taiwan	2008	2.41	1.75
United Kingdom	2010	3.71	2.57
United States	2010	2.15	1.97

Source: Bormann and Golder (2013).

Note: The effective number of parties is a measure that captures both the number and the size of parties in a country. The effective number of *electoral* parties is a measure of the number of parties that wins votes, and the effective number of *legislative* parties is a measure of the number of parties that wins seats.

involves recognizing the interaction of both primordial and instrumental forces. To a large extent, social demands for representation drive the formation of political parties. These demands, however, are channeled in powerful and important ways by political institutions that structure the environment of would-be political entrepreneurs and voters. In what follows, we examine how social (primordial) and institutional (instrumental) forces interact to determine both the *type* and the *number* of political parties that form in a democracy. We begin by looking at the types of parties that form. This requires us to examine societal cleavages and the process of political identity formation.

TYPES OF PARTIES: SOCIAL CLEAVAGES AND POLITICAL IDENTITY FORMATION

As we noted earlier, perhaps the central function of a political party in a democracy is to represent, articulate, and champion the interests of its membership. These interests are, by their very nature, shared by only a part of the overall population. The *Oxford English Dictionary* recognizes this when it defines a party as "a division of a whole; a part, portion, or share." By this definition, political parties arise when officials or would-be officials seek office to pursue goals that are shared by a *part,* but not all, of society. The origins of the British party system can be understood from this perspective.

Origins of the British Party System

The British party system first emerged in the seventeenth century out of a conflict in Parliament over the appropriate relationship between church and state. In 1679 the first Earl of Shaftesbury introduced an Exclusion Bill to Parliament with the goal of preventing King Charles II's Catholic brother, James, the Duke of York, from succeeding him. Supporters of the Exclusion Bill were known as Whigs, whereas opponents of the bill were known as Tories. Although these names were originally meant to be insults (one meaning of Whigs being "Scottish horse thieves" and one meaning of Tories being "Irish outlaws"), parliamentary leaders embraced the terms—probably because the insults gave them a sense of shared offense that could be mobilized to create a sense of group loyalty. These group identities survived even after the resolution of the Exclusion Crisis in 1681 because they helped parliamentarians who shared similar views on several issue dimensions to organize their work. Compared with most modern political parties, "Tories" and "Whigs" stood for loose groupings of men. Nonetheless, they captured important dispositional, confessional, and professional distinctions.

According to Ivor Bulmer-Thomas (1965), Tories and Whigs were divided most fundamentally in regard to their attitudes toward change. Forged in a time of revolution, with epic struggles between the Crown and Parliament, town and country, commerce and agriculture, capitalism and the remnants of feudalism, religious tradition and religious toleration—in short, tradition and modernity—Tories were associated with the status quo and Whigs with change or, as they would say, "progress." Although not fully determined by material relations, people's attitudes toward change were not entirely unrelated to their position in society. For example, Tories tended to come from the landed agricultural elite that had been long dominant in England, whereas the Whigs were more likely to come from the rising commercial elite. Tories and Whigs also differed in their attitudes toward the relationship between church and state. The Tories tended to support the Church of England's attempt to monopolize religious and political life by barring people who did not belong to the Church of England from holding public office, whereas the Whigs tended to support religious toleration. These differences in social and economic background also influenced foreign policy preferences. Because Whigs were more associated with commerce, they tended to be more "internationalist" in their outlook. For instance, they were willing to finance Queen Anne's military efforts because they saw such actions as important for protecting their commercial interests. Tories, by contrast, tended toward isolationism—they supported only those claimants to the Crown who came from the British line of succession and sought to avoid continental royalty that might bring foreign entanglements.

As you can see, the embryonic parties at the end of the seventeenth and beginning of the eighteenth centuries tended to sort members of Parliament into two distinct camps that were cleaved along several dimensions. The correlation or mapping across these dimensions was not entirely perfect. For example, there were nonconformist Tories as well as Whigs representing rural districts. Similarly, some Tories joined with the Whigs in inviting William of Orange and, later, George of Hanover to pursue the British Crown. As is the case with modern political parties, some members toed the "party line" more comfortably on some issues than on others. On the whole, though, the Whigs and Tories comprised parliamentarians who shared views across different policy dimensions. It is (only) at this point that these "like-minded" parliamentarians began to resemble what we would call a political party. Some of the policy dimensions along which Tories and Whigs competed at the beginning of the eighteenth century are shown in Table 14.3. As we will see, some of these same issue dimensions have been central to party systems in other times and places as well.

TABLE 14.3   Some Dimensions of Whig-Tory Conflict

Whigs		Tories
"Progress"		"Tradition"
Limited government		Monarchy
Gentry		Nobility
Nonconformity and toleration	⬅➡	High Church orthodoxy
Commerce		Agriculture
Urban		Rural
Internationalism		Isolationism

The Tories and Whigs went from groups of like-minded parliamentarians to competing teams of office seekers during the early eighteenth century. By excluding Tories from his ministry, George I was the first king (1714–1727) to compose his inner circle of advisers from a single party. One consequence of this "party ministry" was that gaining office now meant a party had greater control over policy and a greater control over public resources for the purpose of furthering the party's interests than before. Not only did this shift power from the Crown to the parliamentary elite, but it also raised the utility and benefit of holding office. Thus, what appeared to be differences of opinion within a bipartisan administration now became congealed into competing teams that had incentives to help get their fellow party members elected and an increased capacity to use patronage to further a party's electoral goals.

Social Cleavages

As we just noted, some of the dimensions of political conflict between Tories and Whigs have been salient in other political systems as well. These cleavages have been used by political scientists to analyze the structure of party systems around the world. Before we begin to discuss why certain cleavages have become salient in some countries but not others, it is worthwhile to list a few of the more common cleavages that occur and talk about the evolution of their salience over time.

The Urban-Rural Cleavage

The conflict between rural and urban interests is one of the oldest political conflicts in the world. Moreover, it remains salient in many countries to this day. The conflict in early modern Europe between feudal lords on the one hand and town dwellers—freemen, burghers, or the bourgeoisie—on the other had both an economic and a cultural dimension. Economically, rural dwellers were typically associated with agricultural production and city dwellers with trade, crafts, and commerce. The most basic point of conflict between rural and urban interests, therefore, involved the price of food. Town dwellers were consumers, not producers, of food, and as a result, they typically experienced an increase in their living standards when food prices dropped. Rural dwellers were more likely to be producers of food and, so, benefited from increased food prices. In addition, much of rural life took place through a barter system that involved the trading of goods and services. Reputation was an important element in making the complex set of commitments surrounding such trades "credible," and reputation typically rested upon ties of kinship. In contrast, economic exchange in towns tended to be monetized and to take place between relatively anonymous actors. Consequently, urban commitment problems often surrounded the credibility of the money used to buy goods or the weights and measures employed to apportion them. It was because of this that the development of contract law, clearly defined property rights, and financial innovation became more of a priority in towns than in rural areas. Culturally, rural actors tended to value tradition, whereas town dwellers favored change.

The Confessional Cleavage

Another important conflict in many countries centers on confessional, or religious, differences. Conflict over religious differences emerged in European countries during the Protestant Reformation in the early sixteenth century. At this time, the authority of the Roman Catholic Church was challenged by the rise of Protestantism and men like Martin Luther in Germany and John Calvin in Geneva. For several decades, Europe was thrown into tumult as struggles between Protestants and Catholics, which would later become known as the Wars of Religion, tore apart countries, principalities, and the Holy Roman Empire. Religious conflict also fueled war between various political entities that lasted well into the seventeenth century. When the Peace of Westphalia (1648) ended both the Thirty Years' War and the Eighty Years' War (or Dutch Revolt), it also reinvigorated the norm of *cuius regio, eius religio*. This Latin phrase means "whose region, his religion" and is used to describe the notion that the leader of a country, city-state, or principality is entitled to choose the religion for those who live under his or her rule. Although the Peace of Westphalia may have led to a reduction in religious conflict between jurisdictions and helped create the modern state by rendering the Holy Roman Empire irrelevant, it did little to resolve religious conflicts within states. In fact, by empowering leaders to declare a state religion, it all but dictated religious intolerance. The result was that individuals who confessed a commitment to a particular brand of Christianity often found themselves in conflict with devotees of other denominations.

The continued salience of the Protestant-Catholic cleavage depends largely on whether or not one or the other side was able to establish its dominance. In some places, the division led to two different countries. For example, the Eighty Years' War split the Low Countries into the Protestant (mostly Calvinist) dominated Dutch Republic (now the Netherlands) and the Catholic-dominated southern Netherlands (today's Belgium). In some places such as Germany, Catholics and Protestants eventually formed an uneasy truce, and in other countries such as Sweden (Lutheran) or France (Catholic), one or the other church became dominant. Finally, it is worth mentioning that in some countries such as Italy and Spain, the Protestant Reformation never made any significant inroads. Whatever the settlement, many European party systems bear the imprint of the now centuries-old conflict between Protestants and Catholics.

Confessional cleavages continue to be salient in many non-European countries as well. For example, conflict between Hindus and Muslims led to the partition of India into a predominantly Hindu India and a Muslim-dominated Pakistan in 1947. Following the creation of Pakistan, millions of Muslims moved from India to Pakistan, and millions of Hindus and Sikhs moved from Pakistan to India. The conflict between Hindus and Muslims continues to be salient in this region today, particularly in the disputed region of Kashmir. Deep divisions between Sunni and Shia Muslims have been central to the politics of many Middle Eastern countries for centuries. The removal of Saddam Hussein by US forces in 2003 exacerbated these divisions in Iraq and beyond. Nigeria and Sudan are two other countries with historically deep confessional divisions, this time between a predominantly Muslim north and a predominantly Christian south. Indeed, the divisions in Sudan played an instrumental role in the establishment of South Sudan as an independent country in July 2011; an internationally recognized referendum in January 2011 saw 98 percent of southerners vote to break away from what is now North Sudan. Finally, nowhere is the confessional cleavage more institutionalized than in Lebanon, where high political offices are explicitly reserved for representatives of different religious groups. For example, the president, prime minister, and speaker of the parliament are constitutionally mandated to be held by a Maronite Christian, Sunni Muslim, and Shia Muslim, respectively.

The Secular-Clerical Cleavage

In the last two centuries, political competition around religious issues in European democracies has taken place primarily along a church-state axis (Lipset and Rokkan 1967). The conflict "between the growing state, which sought to dominate, and the church, which tried to maintain its historic corporate rights," had been growing for some time (Lipset 2001, 6). This conflict was particularly pronounced in France, where close cooperation between the nobility and the Catholic clergy had helped maintain the Bourbon monarchy in power since the sixteenth century. The Roman Catholic Church was the largest landowner in the country and had, since A.D. 585, the right to exact a tax of 10 percent (or *la dîme*) on all agricultural products. These church taxes fueled resentment among many French people, in part because these resources, which were originally meant to provide for local parishes, were often siphoned off by the church hierarchy to support remote monasteries and bishops. Consequently, when the French Revolution was launched in 1789 against Louis XVI, the popular uprising was, to a large extent, aimed at the church as much as the monarchy. Legislation that was passed in 1790 abolished the church's authority to levy *la dîme*, confiscated church property, and canceled special privileges for the clergy. The 1790 Civil Constitution of the Clergy turned clergy into employees of the state, thereby subordinating the Roman Catholic Church to the French government and removing it from the authority of the pope.

In order to solidify his hold on power after a coup d'état in 1799, though, Napoleon Bonaparte reached an agreement with the Roman Catholic Church—the Concordat of 1801—to restore some of the church's power. With the brief restoration of the monarchy in 1814, the Catholic Church regained even more of its former status, and the clergy continued to enjoy privileges into the late nineteenth century. French **anticlericalism**—opposition to religious institutional power and influence in public and political life—once again grew stronger as the nineteenth century drew to a close. In the 1880s, religious figures began to be expelled from public schools, and the Jules Ferry laws mandated that the French state provide a free and *lay* education for its citizens. Numerous conflicts broke out at this time between supporters of the Catholic Church and supporters of a secular state.

> **Anticlericalism** is opposition to religious institutional power and influence in public and political life. **Laïcité** is the notion that there is a division between private life, where religion belongs, and public life, where it does not; it does not necessarily imply any hostility to religion.

In 1905 France passed a law requiring the complete separation of church and state. The law states, "The Republic neither recognizes, nor salaries, nor subsidizes any religion." In effect, this law established state secularism in France and is the backbone of the current French principle of **laïcité**. *Laïcité* refers to the division between private life, where religion belongs, and public life, where religion does not. To a large extent, this principle rests on the belief that citizens should be treated equally in the public sphere and that things like religion (and ethnicity), which might distinguish between individuals and lead to unequal treatment by the state, should be ignored. *Laïcité* is distinct from anticlericalism in that it does not necessarily imply any hostility on the part of the state toward religion; it is simply the idea that the state and political issues should be kept separate from religious organizations and religious issues.

Although the secular state is now well established and *laïcité* is overwhelmingly supported by the French people, religion remains a source of political conflict in contemporary France. In the 1990s, for example, it led to a political conflict that has come to be known as the Headscarf Debate. This debate was primarily about whether Muslim girls wearing headscarves in public schools were violating the principle of *laïcité* by wearing a religious symbol (the headscarf) in a state-funded institution (public school). After several years without a clear policy, the French National Assembly overwhelmingly passed a law against pupils wearing "conspicuous" or "ostentatious" symbols of belonging to a religion in 2005. Although the law does not mention any particular religious symbol, the prohibited items are generally recognized to include headscarves for Muslim girls, yarmulkes for Jewish boys, turbans for Sikhs, and large Christian crosses. In April 2011, the French government enacted an even more controversial law banning people from covering their faces in public. It is widely recognized that this law is targeted at Muslim women who wear full-face veils, or the niqab. In September 2011, the French government responded to growing public unease about street prayers in Paris by banning them. At that time, many Muslims in parts of northern Paris had taken to the streets to conduct their daily prayers due to a lack of mosque space in the French capital. Marine Le Pen, the leader of the

AP Images

Friday prayers in Paris, September 2011. Muslims pray in the Paris streets due to the lack of mosques, while French authorities have sought to find unoccupied state-owned buildings that can be converted into prayer halls.

far-right National Front, sparked outrage when she called these street prayers a "political act of fundamentalists" and likened them to the Nazi occupation of Paris in the Second World War "without the tanks or soldiers" (Samuel 2011, para. 5). Debate is ongoing as to whether these laws and the strict implementation of *laïcité* is actually encouraging the integration of religious groups, mainly Muslims, into mainstream French society or alienating them.[2]

The specifics of the French case should not distract us from a broader trend toward secularism in Europe from the dawn of the Enlightenment in the eighteenth century into the twenty-first century. Although the degree of secularization in terms of individual piety is the subject of considerable debate (Gaskins, Golder, and Siegel 2013a, b; Norris and Inglehart 2004; Stark and Finke 2000), there is little question that this period saw a persistent retreat by religious institutions from the public square. Modernizing elites around the world argued persuasively that state and church should be separated. Much of the popular appeal of this argument stemmed from the frequent association of the church with the unpopular ancien régime—conservative, monarchist forces seeking to protect aristocratic privilege.

Church officials and some believers resisted the separation of church and state, arguing that Christian values of charity for the poor, protection of the family, and the like needed to be protected against what they saw as the corrosive effects of secularism. As a consequence, religious parties formed in many countries. For example, the Tories in Britain originally rallied around the slogan "For Church and King." Separate Protestant and Catholic parties competed in the Netherlands, although by the late nineteenth century, they were typically making common cause against "secular" parties. Indeed, political conflicts between Catholics and Protestants subsided in many countries as the cleavage between confessional and secular groups became increasingly salient. For example, the Christian Democratic Appeal (CDA) in the Netherlands is explicitly nondenominational and seeks to unite Catholics and Protestants. In many countries in Europe and Latin America, Christian Democratic parties combine a conservative position on social issues like abortion and same-sex marriage with an activist position on economic policy. Although staunchly anti-Communist, many Christian Democratic parties take an organic or corporatist view of the economy that emphasizes individuals' obligation to serve their community. This stands in stark contrast to the economic position of Liberal parties in Europe, which derive their identity from the defense of individual, rather than group, rights. European liberals are staunchly secular in their social orientation and champion free-market capitalism in the economic world.

The Class Cleavage

Lipset and Rokkan (1967) refer to the preceding cleavages as "pre-industrial cleavages." This is in marked contrast to the class cleavage, which is said to have become salient during the Industrial Revolution at the end of the eighteenth century. Like the urban-rural cleavage, the

---

2. We encourage those of you who are interested in the integration of Muslims into French society to look at Question 10 in the Problems section at the end of Chapter 7.

class cleavage pits actors against each other over conflicting economic interests. Whereas the urban-rural cleavage involves horizontal conflicts between different sectors in society, however, the class cleavage involves vertical conflicts within sectors between actors who derive their livelihood from the use of their labor and those who derive their livelihood from the use of their property or capital. Class conflict takes place most fundamentally between workers and capitalists in industrial sectors of the economy, but it takes place primarily between peasants (or, later, agricultural workers) and large landowners in the agricultural sectors. Class conflict typically involves attempts to use the state to redistribute wealth from the rich to the poor. Capitalists tend to favor the free market, a small state, and a restricted franchise; in contrast, workers support greater state intervention in the economy and an expansion of the franchise.

The class cleavage became increasingly salient in most European countries during the nineteenth century as demands for franchise expansion, particularly from the working class, grew. At the beginning of the nineteenth century, the right to vote was typically restricted to adult male citizens who owned large amounts of property. Although the Great Reform Act of 1832 expanded the franchise in Great Britain, it still allowed only about one in five male adults to vote. The 1867 Reform Act expanded the suffrage further to include all working-class males. Through this process, and analogous processes in other European states, workers became relevant at the ballot box, and the state was set for full-scale competition between parties claiming to represent the industrial working class and parties that represented economic elites.

For the next hundred years, politics in Europe revolved around the "left-right" divide. The terms *left* and *right* were first used to describe the seating location of competing factions in the French National Assembly in 1791. From the viewpoint of the speaker's chair, monarchists sat to the right and bourgeois reformers sat to the left. This pattern was replicated in other continental parliaments: protectors of aristocratic and clerical interests sat on the right, and middle-class reformers sat on the left. At the time, people sitting on the left—the "left-wingers"—were advocating laissez-faire capitalism and democratization. Through the nineteenth century, though, the political center of gravity shifted further leftward throughout Europe so that by the beginning of the twentieth century, protectors of free markets and democracy were considered "right-wing," and those in favor of workers' rights and socialist revolution were considered "left-wing." Eventually the "Left" came to be represented by Communist, Social Democratic, and Labor parties and the "Right" by Christian Democratic, Conservative, and Liberal parties.

In the nineteenth century, many socialists were in favor of democracy and the socialist transformation of society. Marxist theory predicted the expansion of the industrial working class (proletariat) as capitalism expanded. Under such conditions it was thought that the expansion of the franchise and the natural course of economic development would in short order produce huge Socialist majorities that would then implement the transition to a socialist society by legislative means (Przeworski and Sprague 1988, 22–25). Several factors, however, conspired to inhibit the unfolding of this set of historical developments that many Marxists had once thought inevitable.

First, not all actors voted according to their class interests. In his book *The Poverty of Philosophy*, Karl Marx ([1847] 1995) makes the distinction between a class "in itself" and a class "for itself." Individuals are members of a class "in itself" simply by virtue of their objective "relation to the means of production." In other words, individuals who sell their labor for a wage are workers, and those who earn a profit are capitalists. In contrast, individuals are members of a "class for itself" only if they are actually conscious of their status as a member of that class. Thus, the socialist project can be thought of as a process of class formation. In effect, the goal was to make workers realize that they were workers and to transform the proletariat from a "class in itself" into a "class for itself." Marxist orthodoxy held that this process of class formation was a historical inevitability. When the radicalization of workers did not occur as quickly as many Marxist theorists hoped, scholars put the continued commitment of some workers to bourgeois parties and institutions down to a form of "false consciousness" (Engels [1893] 1968). Whether workers perceived their interests differently from the way that Marxist theorists suggested they should, or whether they were, in fact, suffering from "false consciousness," it is a historical fact across a wide range of countries and time periods that a nontrivial portion of manual laborers voted *against* left-wing parties and that a substantial share of managers and professionals voted *for* left-wing parties.

Second, workers "never were and never would become a numerical majority in their respective societies" (Przeworski and Sprague 1988, 31). As a consequence, Socialist parties found it necessary either to broaden their appeals to attract salaried workers and other members of the bourgeoisie or to govern in coalition with bourgeois parties. Przeworski and Sprague (1988) note how these strategies, which were designed to help win elections and gain office, ultimately ended up diluting the salience of class as a basis for individual behavior in some countries.

Finally, even where Socialist parties were electorally successful, there were structural factors at work to limit the extent to which they could bring about a socialist transformation. As we discussed in Chapters 6 and 9, part of the reason why Socialist parties did not institute a socialist transformation had to do with the disciplining effects that investors can play in deterring radical policies. As you will recall, this disciplining effect is referred to as the "structural dependence of the state on capital." In addition to this pressure from external actors, scholars have identified organizational factors that helped to moderate the policy positions of Socialist parties. With some irony, German sociologist Robert Michels ([1911] 2001, 13) noted that "[i]n theory, the principal aim of social and democratic parties is the struggle against oligarchy in all its forms. The question therefore arises how we are to explain the development in such parties of the very tendencies against which they have declared war." Michels responded to this puzzle by arguing that in all sufficiently complex organizations, including political parties, a division of labor arises between rank-and-file members and professional managers. Because the leaders of the organization develop lifestyles, skills, and interests that are different from those of the rank and file, the organization will inevitably begin to pursue goals that are different from those it was originally formed to pursue. In the case of labor unions and Socialist parties, the leadership exists to represent the "ruled" but is inevitably transformed into part of the ruling class by virtue of its position at the head of the organization. This notion that the leadership of an organization will develop goals that are distinct from those of the organization's rank and file, and that because they *are* leaders their goals will become dominant, is known as **Michels's iron law of oligarchy**.

> **Michels's iron law of oligarchy** states that the leadership of organizations such as political parties will never be faithful to the program and constituency that gave rise to the organization in the first place.

Michels's iron law of oligarchy has been used to explain organizational dynamics in many different social settings, from trade unions and political parties to religious denominations, corporations, and nonprofit organizations.

The Post-Material Cleavage

Lipset and Rokkan (1967) observed that European party systems were remarkably stable during most of the twentieth century. They observed that the cleavages we have examined so far were all activated during a period when new groups were in the process of being politically mobilized. For example, the urban-rural cleavage and the various religious cleavages became salient at the same time that new elites (the landed gentry and commercial elites in urban areas) were being incorporated into national politics in competition with traditional elites (the nobility and the clergy). The class cleavage became salient during a period when the franchise was expanded to include male workers and eventually women. As these cleavages were activated, new parties could be formed to capture segments of the population that had not previously been active in electoral politics. Lipset and Rokkan argued that European party systems became "frozen" with the achievement of universal suffrage during the 1920s. Social structures might change, as they had in the past, but there was no longer any untapped electoral base for new parties to mobilize. According to this argument, the barriers to successful entry for new parties seeking to represent emerging interests became too high after the 1920s. Either political positions associated with new cleavages would go unrepresented or existing parties would alter their positions to capture "unrepresented" voters. Lipset and Rokkan's famous **freezing hypothesis** was used to explain why the ideological dimensions of most European party systems were so similar. Although there was some interesting variety across cases, the modal European party system in the middle of the twentieth century had two parties on the left (Socialist and Communist, with Socialists being more hostile to Soviet influence than the Communists) and a Conservative Party (often Christian Democratic) and a Liberal Party on the right.

> Lipset and Rokkan's **freezing hypothesis** states that Western European party systems became frozen following the extension of universal suffrage in most countries during the 1920s.

European party systems began to "thaw" in the 1960s as societies underwent what Inglehart (1977, 1997) calls a post-materialist value shift. Having been raised in an environment of plenty in which their existential security was taken for granted, new generations of European voters began to prioritize the expansion of human freedom. This new generation of voters was more concerned with issues relating to multiculturalism, gender and racial equality, reproductive choice, and sexual freedom than the standard bread-and-butter issues of the past. In effect, the transition to a postindustrial society was accompanied by a decline in the salience of the economic cleavage and the emergence of a new post-materialist cleavage. When existing parties were slow to adapt to this, a niche emerged that new parties were able to exploit (Rydgren 2005).

The first parties to exploit this opportunity emerged on the left in the 1970s. These parties, which Kitschelt (1988) calls left-libertarian parties, differed from the "Old Left" in that they were less closely tied to the industrial working class and were likely to privilege issues such as environmentalism and immigration that can be perceived to run against working-class interests. According to Kitschelt (1988, 195), left-libertarian parties, such as the Greens, "are critical of the logic of societal development and the institutions that underlie the post-war compromise between capital and labor in industrial societies." They oppose the priority that economic growth has on the political agenda, the patterns of policymaking that restrict democratic participation to elite bargaining among centralized interest groups and party leaders, and the bureaucratic welfare state. Their political alternatives conform neither to traditional conservative nor to socialist programs but rather link libertarian commitments to individual autonomy and popular participation, with a leftist concern for equality.

The second set of parties to exploit the new post-materialist cleavage appeared on the far right. In many ways, the emergence of these new parties on the far right can be seen as a direct reaction to the post-materialist agenda of the libertarian left (Ignazi 1992). In contrast

Far right parties in Europe often campaign on anti-immigrant policies. The poster on the left, put up by the Swiss People's Party for the 2007 federal elections, was criticized for its exclusionary message. On the right, UK Independence Party leader Nigel Farage poses in front of a poster in London, June 2016, urging voters to vote to leave the European Union in an upcoming referendum. Many condemned the poster, which showed a largely non-white group of migrants crossing the Croatia-Slovenia border in 2015, for stoking anti-immigrant and racist sentiments.

to the libertarian left, populist parties on the far right emphasize traditional values and highlight how immigration is threatening national identity and culture as well as the jobs and economic welfare of native workers (Bustikova 2014; Dancygier 2010; M. Golder 2016; Ivarsflaten 2008; Mudde 2007). These parties see themselves as the true representatives of "the people" and in conflict with corrupt and immoral elites, a group that typically includes political parties, intellectuals, and the "liberal" media among others (Mudde 2004). The populism they espouse is exclusionary in that certain groups, such as immigrants and homosexuals, are not considered part of "the pure people" (Mudde and Kaltwasser 2013).[3] These parties also espouse nativist policies whereby welfare benefits, public housing, and jobs are to be reserved for the native population. While these parties are not antidemocratic per se, their radicalism comes in their opposition to *liberal* democracy and their desire for a fundamental reform of the political and economic system. The combination of radicalism, populism, and nativism has been referred to as the "master frame" of European far-right parties (Rydgren 2004, 2005).

Ethnic and Linguistic Cleavages

In various countries around the world, ethnic or linguistic cleavages are another important source of conflict. Exactly what counts as an "ethnic" cleavage is not obvious because there are many different definitions of what makes a group an "ethnic" group. One common characteristic in definitions of an **ethnic group**, though, is an emphasis on the role of "descent" (Chandra 2006). In effect, members of ethnic groups share some characteristic more closely with fellow group members than with nongroup members, and this characteristic is inherited in some way from their parents. What scholars tend to differ with one another about is what the particular characteristic or trait is that is shared by the ethnic group members. Thus, an individual's eligibility for membership in an ethnic group is based on the possession of certain attributes that are at least believed to be related to descent. We say "believed to be" because

> An **ethnic group** is one in which members possess some attributes, believed to be related to descent, which are shared more closely with fellow group members than with nongroup members.

the claims of many ethnic groups to having a common ancestry or common place of origin are simply myths. Chandra (2006, 400) notes that "descent-based attributes" shared by ethnic group members can be "acquired genetically (e.g., skin color, gender, hair type, eye color, height, and physical features), through cultural and historical inheritance (e.g., the names, languages, places of birth and origin of one's parents and ancestors), or in the course of one's lifetime as markers of such an inheritance (e.g., last name or tribal markings)."

Eligibility in an ethnic group does not mean the same thing as "membership." As with class, there is a natural tension between ethnic groups "in themselves" and ethnic groups "for themselves." On the one hand, there are circumstances in which individuals can choose the

---

3. Populism and its emphasis on an antagonistic conflict between "the pure people" and "the corrupt elite" have become increasingly salient in party systems around the world (Golder and Golder 2016).

extent to which they identify with an ethnic group. For example, one of the authors of this book (Clark) might embrace his Irish American heritage at a Celtic music performance or poetry reading but shy away from that same heritage when confronted with particularly crass and distasteful "St. Paddy's Day" debauchery. On the other hand, there are circumstances in which individuals might be classified by others (such as in-group "gatekeepers" or government officials) as belonging or not belonging to a particular ethnic group.

As with class, social scientists have differed on the extent to which they see ethnic group membership as based on objective or subjective traits. Scholars who emphasize the objective nature of ethnic identification have been termed "primordialists," and those who emphasize the subjective nature of ethnic identification have been called "constructivists" or "instrumentalists." Briefly, primordialists believe that ethnic attachments are transmitted automatically and that group composition is naturally and externally determined. Constructivists, in contrast, believe that group attachments are socially constructed. In other words, they believe that group identities today are the result of choices made by social actors in the past; social groups do not fall from heaven, nor do they spring from some primordial ooze. "Instrumentalism" might be thought of as a subcategory of constructivism in that instrumentalists believe that group attachments result from the intentional acts of social actors who see group attachments as *serving some other purpose,* such as aiding their political survival or giving them access to state resources.

Given the salience of various ethnic cleavages around the world, it is little surprise that ethnic parties exist in many countries. An **ethnic party** "appeals to voters as the champion of the interests of one ethnic category or set of categories to the exclusion of others, and makes such an appeal central to its mobilizing strategy. The key aspect of this definition is *exclusion.* An ethnic party may champion the interests of more than one ethnic category, but only by identifying the common ethnic enemy to be excluded" (Chandra 2005, 236). Although most people probably think of Africa when they think of ethnic parties, ethnic parties exist and do well in most regions of the world. In fact, probably the first ethnic parties were Jewish parties in the Russian and Austro-Hungarian empires and the Swedish Party in Finland, all founded in the nineteenth century or the first decade of the twentieth century. Relatively successful ethnic parties exist today in countries as far afield as Canada, Fiji, India, Ireland, Israel, Macedonia, New Zealand, Romania, Russia, Spain, Sri Lanka, and Turkey. One continent where there have historically been few ethnic parties is Latin America. This has begun to change, however, with the emergence of various ethnic parties in countries such as Bolivia, Colombia, Ecuador, and Venezuela to represent indigenous populations (Van Cott 2005).

> An **ethnic party** champions the interests of one ethnic category or set of categories to the exclusion of others, and it does so as a central component of its mobilizing strategy.

Theorizing about Politicized Cleavages

So far we have identified a number of salient social cleavages that define political conflict in party systems around the world. But why are some party systems divided primarily along ethnic lines, whereas others are divided mainly along class, religious, linguistic, or regional ones? What determines which social cleavages become politicized and salient? In sum, what explains why we get the types of parties that we do? Unfortunately, comparative political scientists have only just begun to examine these sorts of questions in any great detail. As yet, they have not developed a fully worked-out theory of politicized cleavages. Nonetheless, recent research suggests that the distribution of individual attributes in society and the electoral institutions in a country are likely to be key parts of any such theory (Chandra 2004, 2006; Chandra and Boulet 2012; Posner 2004, 2005).[4] In what follows, we present the general contours of this research, drawing heavily on insights from Chandra and Boulet (2012).

The basic premise in this new research is that individuals are multifaceted and have a repertoire of **attributes**, such as religion, language, class, gender, skin color, and so on, that makes them eligible for membership in some **identity category** or social group. The attributes of individuals can obviously take on different values. For example, consider the attribute of religion. An individual might be Catholic, Protestant, Jewish, Muslim, Hindu, atheist, or something else. In Table 14.4, we list some attributes that individuals might have and possible values that these attributes can take on. Chandra and Boulet (2012) take an individual's attributes as given, self-evident, and sticky (hard to change). In contrast, they assume that identity categories are socially constructed. In other words, whether identity categories or social groups form around all workers, just black workers, just male workers, or just black male workers who are tall and who happen to be political scientists, and so on, is not something that is natural or objective but something that is determined by the choices of social actors over time (and the institutional context in which they make those choices). By taking

> An **attribute** is a characteristic that qualifies an individual for membership in an identity category. An **identity category** is a social group in which an individual can place herself.

TABLE 14.4	Individual Attributes and Possible Attribute Values
Attribute	**Possible attribute values**
Class	Worker, bourgeoisie
Skin color	Black, white
Nationality	English, American, Nigerian
Profession	Political scientist, plumber, doctor
Region	North, south, east, west
Origin	Foreign, native
Height	Tall, short

---

4. The roots of this recent research can be traced to Laitin (1986, 1992, 1998).

attributes as given but identity categories as socially constructed, Chandra and Boulet (2012) provide a "thinly constructivist" approach to political identity formation.

Assignment to an identity category or social group, either by oneself or by someone else, will involve a shared understanding about the ways in which possession of certain attributes corresponds to membership in particular groups. This shared understanding is likely to have been built up over many years, decades, centuries, or even longer. As an example, suppose that a country's population is divided according to the region (North or South) and language (French or Dutch) associated with one's parents and that a social understanding has developed over the years that "who you are" is related to your ancestral language and region. Potential identity categories in this country would, therefore, be drawn from the possible combinations of these two attributes. The attributes of individuals in this country will obviously be distributed in a particular way. In Table 14.5, we list the two attributes in our hypothetical country and the proportion of the population (a, b, c, d) embodying each possible combination of attributes.

TABLE 14.5	**Attributes and Possible Combinations of Attributes in a Hypothetical Country**	
	French speaker	**Dutch speaker**
Northerner	a	b
Southerner	c	d

Note: Letters indicate the proportion of the population embodying each possible combination of attributes.

In Table 14.6, we list all nine of the potential identity categories (social groups) that could be formed (socially constructed) in our hypothetical country. These "potential" identity categories are sometimes referred to as "latent" identity categories. But which of the potential identity categories shown in Table 14.6 will be "activated" or "politicized"? The answer to this question is not immediately obvious.

To some extent, how attributes map onto actual identity categories is likely to depend on the distribution and correlation of those attributes. For example, if the attributes are uncorrelated (not associated) with each other and fairly evenly distributed across the population, then there may be a propensity for each combination of attributes to be thought of as a separate identity group and activated as such. For example, suppose that the attributes in our hypothetical country are uncorrelated and that the population is evenly distributed as in Table 14.7. In this scenario, our hypothetical country is said to have **cross-cutting attributes**. All other things being equal, the identity categories (northerner, southerner, French speaker, Dutch speaker) are equally distinctive and, presumably, equally likely to be activated. Indeed, either of these cleavages—North versus South or French speaking versus Dutch speaking—is as likely to be activated and politicized as the four-way cleavage (French-speaking northerner, Dutch-speaking northerner, French-speaking southerner, Dutch-speaking southerner).

TABLE 14.6	**Potential Identity Categories in a Hypothetical Country**
Potential identity category	**Size**
Northerner	a + b
Southerner	c + d
French speaker	a + c
Dutch speaker	b + d
Northerner and French speaker	a
Northerner and Dutch speaker	b
Southerner and French speaker	c
Southerner and Dutch speaker	d
Everyone	a + b + c + d

Note: Letters indicate the proportion of the population embodying the potential identity category shown.

TABLE 14.7	**Cross-Cutting Attributes**	
	French speaker	**Dutch speaker**
Northerner	0.25	0.25
Southerner	0.25	0.25

Now suppose that the attributes in our hypothetical country are highly correlated as in Table 14.8. When attributes are highly correlated like this, then the effective number of attribute repertoires is likely to be smaller. A country with highly correlated attributes is said to have **reinforcing attributes**. In regard to our hypothetical country in Table 14.8, this is because knowing that a person's family is from the North allows one to predict with a fair amount of confidence that his or her ancestral language is Dutch; similarly, knowing that a person's family is from the South allows one to predict that his or her ancestral language is likely to be French. In such circumstances it seems plausible, all other things being equal, to predict that the identity categories that will be activated or politicized will be "French-speaking southerners" and "Dutch-speaking northerners." In fact, a similar distribution of attributes to that shown in Table 14.8 is found in contemporary Belgium. Belgium is a country that is profoundly cleaved along ethnolinguistic and regional lines. Indeed, Belgians are constitutionally divided into three communities: a French-speaking community that lives primarily in the South (Wallonia), a Dutch-speaking community that lives primarily in the

> A country with uncorrelated attributes has **cross-cutting attributes** (cleavages), whereas a country with correlated attributes has **reinforcing attributes** (cleavages).

TABLE 14.8	**Reinforcing Attributes**	
	French speaker	**Dutch speaker**
Northerner	0.03	0.57
Southerner	0.36	0.04

North (Flanders), and a small German-speaking community that lives primarily in the East in a region that was part of Germany before World War I.

Clearly, the division of the people of Belgium into separate ethnic "communities" is the product of deep-seated historical processes. For example, the East-West line dividing French-speaking Wallonia from Dutch-speaking Flanders has been said to mark the northernmost reaches of the Roman province of Gaul in the fourth century. Thus, the line represents, in many ways, a historic dividing line between Frankish and Germanic cultures. If one drives through the region, one can immediately sense the change as one travels between towns such as Lille and Charleroi on the southern side of the line and Ghent and Leuven on the northern side. It is hard to overstate the cultural and political salience of such a boundary—a boundary, we should note, that is centuries older than the Mason-Dixon Line that is said to divide the North and South in the United States.

Although it is hard to overstate the salience of these types of boundaries, it is important to recognize that many such divisions exist around the world, and their salience rises and falls in different periods and different places. This variation in salience suggests that we should look for other factors that might influence which potential identity categories in a society get activated or politicized. The electoral rules that we examined in the previous chapter are one such factor. Different electoral rules can lead to the activation of different identity categories in countries that have identical distributions of attributes. For example, imagine that we have two countries, A and B, in which attributes are identically distributed as shown in Table 14.9. The only difference between the two countries is that the electoral institutions in country A are such that gaining national office requires 50 percent of the vote and the electoral institutions in country B are such that gaining national office requires 60 percent of the vote. How do you think this difference in electoral rules will influence which identity categories will get activated or politicized in the two countries? If you were a political

TABLE 14.9	**A Hypothetical Distribution of Attributes**	
	French speaker	**Dutch speaker**
Northerner	0.40	0.10
Southerner	0.40	0.10

entrepreneur, which identity categories would you try to politicize if you wanted to gain national office?

One way to think about this is to recall the logic of building government coalitions that we presented in Chapter 12. Let's start by thinking about country A. According to the logic of "least minimal winning coalitions," French-speaking northerners in country A have strong incentives to form a coalition with Dutch-speaking northerners; similarly, French-speaking southerners have strong incentives to form a coalition with Dutch-speaking southerners. Both coalitions could expect to win the required 50 percent of the vote to win national office.[5] In this scenario, each national election would effectively be decided by a flip of a coin. In fact, whoever was more effective out of the French-speaking northerners and French-speaking southerners at building ties with the Dutch speakers could expect to win every national election. This means that political parties in country A are likely to compete on the basis of how effective they are at generating interlinguistic cooperation. By doing this, though, the political parties would, in effect, be reinforcing regional divisions. As a result, the main politicized cleavage in country A is likely to be regional, and the party system is likely to be characterized by regional parties.[6]

What about country B? Recall that gaining national office in country B requires 60 percent of the vote. One possible scenario in country B is that a coalition will form between northern French speakers and southern French speakers. Such a coalition could expect to win 80 percent of the vote. In these circumstances, Dutch speakers would be a permanent minority.[7] In this case, the main politicized cleavage (and the party system) would be linguistic rather than regional. The only thing that has changed between country A, where interlinguistic cooperation is likely, and country B, where the exclusion of linguistic outgroups is likely, is the electoral threshold.

The importance of electoral institutions to the politicization of social cleavages can also be seen if we examine how identity categories might be activated in countries that share the same electoral rules but differ in their distribution of attributes. For example, imagine that two countries, C and D, have the same electoral institutions such that gaining national office requires 60 percent of the vote. The only difference between the two countries is that the attributes in country C are distributed as shown in Table 14.9 and the attributes in country D are distributed as shown in Table 14.10. Following the same logic as before, we might expect the identity categories that will be activated or politicized to be linguistic in country C and regional in country D. Posner (2004) employs a similar argument to help explain why Chewas and Tumbukas are political allies in Zambia but rivals in Malawi (see Box 14.3, "Allies or Adversaries? Chewas and Tumbukas in Zambia and Malawi").

---

5. You might think that French-speaking northerners and French-speaking southerners would form a coalition together. However, this coalition would require that government resources and offices be split among 80 percent of the population rather than among 50 percent of the population. The lower average "payoffs" associated with this coalition help to explain why political entrepreneurs have incentives to form least minimal winning coalitions rather than just minimal winning coalitions.

6. Readers who see the United States as being divided between the "Blue coasts" and the "Red heartland" might see something familiar in this example.

7. We explore the potentially disastrous consequences of such a situation in Chapter 16.

TABLE 14.10	An Alternative Hypothetical Distribution of Attributes	
	French speaker	**Dutch speaker**
Northerner	0.25	0.35
Southerner	0.25	0.15

Box 14.3

ALLIES OR ADVERSARIES? CHEWAS AND TUMBUKAS IN ZAMBIA AND MALAWI

In a 2004 article in the *American Political Science Review*, Daniel Posner examines why cultural differences become politicized in some contexts but not others. Specifically, he tries to explain why two ethnic groups, Chewas and Tumbukas, are allies in Zambia but adversaries in Malawi. Zambia and Malawi are two neighboring countries in sub-Saharan Africa. The border between the two countries was arbitrarily drawn by the British South Africa Company in 1891. No attention was paid to the distribution of ethnic groups when the border was drawn, so roughly two-thirds of all Chewas and Tumbukas found themselves living in Malawi, whereas the remaining third found themselves living in Zambia.

In his study of the Chewas and Tumbukas, Posner examined life in four villages along the Malawi-Zambia border. Two of the four villages were Chewa villages—one was just inside Malawi, and the other was just a few miles away across the border in Zambia. The other two villages were Tumbuka villages—again, one was just inside Malawi, and the other was just a few miles away in Zambia. Using survey questions, Posner first attempted to see if the Chewas and Tumbukas really were distinct cultural and ethnic groups. On numerous important dimensions, he found that they were. For example, he found that Chewas speak Chichewa and dance the nyau, whereas Tumbukas speak Chitumbuka and dance the vinbuza. In addition, he found that although Tumbuka parents must pay seven cows to have their daughters married, Chewa parents need pay only one chicken. These cultural and ethnic differences between Chewas and Tumbukas were equally strong in Malawi and Zambia. In other words, Chewas and Tumbukas represented distinct identity categories in both countries.

To examine whether these identity categories were actually salient and politicized, Posner asked other survey questions. One question asked whether the respondent would vote for a presidential candidate from the other ethnic group. Sixty-one percent of Chewas and Tumbukas in Malawi said that they would not vote for a presidential candidate from the other ethnic group; in contrast, just 21 percent of Chewas and Tumbukas in Zambia made a similar statement. A second survey question asked whether the respondent would marry a member of the other ethnic group. Fifty-five percent of the Chewas and Tumbukas in Malawi said that they would not marry a member of the other ethnic group; in contrast, just 24 percent of those in Zambia made a similar statement. These (and other) survey results clearly indicate that the cultural and ethnic differences between Chewas and Tumbukas were more salient in Malawi than in Zambia.

But why would these cultural differences be more salient in one country than the other? Perhaps it has something to do with the electoral system, the colonial history, or the party systems in the two countries. As Posner notes, though, both countries employ a single-member district plurality (SMDP) electoral system, both countries are former British colonies, and both countries have experienced one-party and multiparty rule. As a result, Posner argues that we must look elsewhere for an explanation for why Chewa-Tumbuka relations are so different in Malawi and Zambia.

Specifically, Posner argues that we must look to the different distribution of Chewas and Tumbukas in the two countries. Chewas and Tumbukas represent relatively large ethnic groups in Malawi. For example, Chewas compose roughly 57 percent of the population, whereas Tumbukas account for about 12 percent. Because groups of this size have a realistic chance of winning Malawi's SMDP elections, especially the Chewas, it made sense for political entrepreneurs to politicize the Chewa-Tumbuka cleavage and form political parties around the two different groups. In fact, this is precisely what happened. The Malawi Congress Party (MCP) was widely recognized as the Chewa party and the Alliance for Democracy (AFORD) was seen as the Tumbuka party.

Contrast this situation to the one in Zambia, where Chewas and Tumbukas represent only very small segments of the overall population. For instance, Chewas compose about 7 percent of the population, and the Tumbukas compose just 4 percent. These relatively small ethnic groups in Zambia do not represent good political vehicles for winning office because such small groups have little realistic chance of winning SMDP elections. As a result, political entrepreneurs in Zambia have had to look for other cleavages to politicize rather than the Chewa-Tumbuka cleavage. The main politicized cleavage in Zambia is a regional one, pitting easterners (Chewas and Tumbukas together) against northerners, westerners, and southerners. In this political environment, Chewas and Tumbukas (easterners) have to work together, rather than against one another, if they are to have any hope of winning political power.

Posner's story illustrates how the logic of political competition focuses the attention of both voters and political entrepreneurs on some cleavages rather than others. His story also recognizes that political actors need to build winning coalitions to achieve their goals. If they are going to emphasize cultural or ethnic differences, they will choose divisions that define the most usefully sized building blocks. As a result, not all latent cultural and ethnic differences will become politicized. Which differences become politicized will ultimately depend on the interaction between institutions like electoral rules and the distribution of latent social cleavages.

What these examples illustrate is that politicized cleavages are likely to be the result of an interaction between latent social cleavages and electoral (and other) institutions. In other words, each country has a certain set of latent social cleavages that is determined by its distribution of individual attributes. Which of these latent social cleavages become politicized, though, is going to be influenced by the electoral institutions employed in that country. This causal story is illustrated in Figure 14.1. An implication of this story is that the cleavages that are politicized and, hence, the types of parties that exist in a country can change either because the underlying set of latent social cleavages changes or because the electoral rules change or both.

| FIGURE 14.1 | **Politicized Cleavages and the Role of Electoral Institutions** |

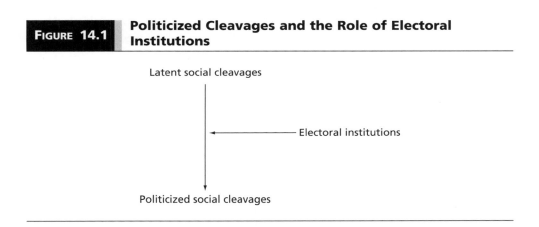

NUMBER OF PARTIES: DUVERGER'S THEORY

Although comparative political scientists currently lack a strong understanding of *which* parties will form in a country, we know a fair amount about *how many* parties will form.

Social Cleavages

Our current understanding of the factors influencing the size of party systems is due, in large part, to the seminal work of a French political scientist, Maurice Duverger ([1954] 1963). Duverger argued that the primary engine behind the formation of political parties can be found in social divisions—the more divisions there are, the greater the demand for political parties to form (Afonso Da Silva 2006; Clark and Golder 2006). In effect, he believed that there is some natural tendency for cleavages within society, such as those discussed earlier, to be represented in the party system. We should recall from our earlier discussion, though, that it is not just the number of cleavages per se but the way in which membership in society is distributed across those divisions that determines the pressures for distinctive representation.

For example, imagine that two societies, *A* and *B*, have the same number of identity attributes as each other. Let's suppose that the identity attributes are income, place of origin, and religion. Our two hypothetical countries might be from Latin America, where divisions between the rich and poor, European and indigenous populations, and Catholics and Protestants are common. In both of our hypothetical countries, let's imagine that exactly half the citizens are rich and half are poor, half have European ancestry and half have indigenous ancestry, and half are Catholic and half are Protestant.

In country *A*, we will assume that exactly half of the rich people are European and half are indigenous; half of the rich European people and half of the poor indigenous people are Catholic. The full distribution of identity attributes in country *A* is shown in Table 14.11. As you can see, the attributes that might contribute to the formation of identity categories are evenly distributed. This means that country *A* is entirely characterized by cross-cutting cleavages—there is no correlation between one's income level, one's place of origin, and one's religion. As a result, this means that there is a whole host of identity categories—rich, rich Catholic, rich Protestant, rich European, rich indigenous, rich Catholic European, rich Protestant European, and so on—that are equally distinctive and, presumably, equally likely to be activated.[8] According to Duverger, and assuming that policy preferences are associated with wealth, place of origin, and religious confession, the "engine" of social forces in country *A* is propelling the party system toward a large multiparty system.

| TABLE 14.11 | **The Distribution of Identity Attributes in Hypothetical Country *A* (Percentages)** | | | | |

| | European | | Indigenous | | |
	Catholic	Protestant	Catholic	Protestant	Total
Rich	12.5	12.5	12.5	12.5	50.0
Poor	12.5	12.5	12.5	12.5	50.0
Total	25.0	25.0	25.0	25.0	

In contrast to country *A*, let's assume that some of the attributes that might map onto identity categories are perfectly correlated in country *B*. Specifically, we'll imagine that although exactly half of the rich and poor people are of European descent as in country *A*, all rich people are Catholic, and all poor people are Protestant. The full distribution of identity attributes in country *B* is shown in Table 14.12. As you can see, the distribution of attributes reveals a mixture of both cross-cutting and reinforcing cleavages. As in country *A*, the

---

8. We are deliberately ignoring the effect of the country's electoral system at this point.

TABLE 14.12	**The Distribution of Identity Attributes in Hypothetical Country *B* (Percentages)**

| | European | | Indigenous | | |
	Catholic	Protestant	Catholic	Protestant	Total
Rich	25.0	0.0	25.0	0.0	50.0
Poor	0.0	25.0	0.0	25.0	50.0
Total	25.0	25.0	25.0	25.0	

income and place of origin cleavages are cross-cutting—knowing someone's place of origin is of no help in predicting that person's income. Unlike in country *A*, though, the income and religious cleavages are now reinforcing—knowing someone's religion allows one to predict which income group he or she is from. As the distribution of attributes in Table 14.12 indicates, there are now, in some sense, only four latent identity categories to be represented by the party system: rich Catholic Europeans, rich Catholic indigenous people, poor Protestant Europeans, and poor Protestant indigenous people. In other words, the total number of latent identity categories is considerably lower in country *B* than in country *A* even though both countries have the same three cleavages—income, place of origin, and religion. It should be clear that if one's place of origin was also perfectly correlated with income—for example, if all rich citizens had European ancestry and all poor citizens had indigenous ancestry—then there would be only two latent groups needing representation: rich Catholic Europeans and poor Protestant indigenous people.

The key aspect of a country's social structure influencing the demand for the number of parties, therefore, is not necessarily the total number of cleavages in a country but rather the total number of *cross-cutting* cleavages. As you might suspect, most cleavages in a country will not be perfectly cross-cutting or perfectly reinforcing as in our example. The same logic as that outlined above, however, suggests that the social pressure for distinctive representation (and a large party system) depends on the number of cleavages in a country and increases with the degree to which these cleavages are cross-cutting rather than reinforcing.

Electoral Institutions

Although Duverger believed that social divisions create the demand for political parties, he argued that electoral institutions play an important role in determining whether this latent demand for representation actually leads to the existence of new political parties. Recall the earlier claim that European societies have seen the emergence of a new post-materialist cleavage since the 1960s (Inglehart 1977). If social cleavages were the only factor influencing the size of party systems, then all European countries should have experienced an increase in the number of parties competing for office. However, Kitschelt (1988) finds that the share of votes going to "left-libertarian parties" increased only in some countries. The existence and electoral fortunes of populist far-right parties has also varied across European countries (M. Golder 2003). This should make one wonder why an increase in the number of cleavages would have a different effect on the size of party systems in different countries.

Although one explanation for this might be that the shift to post-materialist values was more pronounced in some countries than others, Duverger claims that it is likely to have something to do with the electoral institutions used in each country. In other words, he argues that the same value change can have a significant effect on the party structure of one country but not on that of another due to differences in electoral rules. The reason for this is that nonproportional electoral systems, such as the single-member district plurality system, act as a "brake" on the tendency for social cleavages to be translated into new parties. Put differently, Duverger's theory states that increasing the number of social cleavages in a country has less of an effect on party system size if the electoral system is nonproportional than if it is proportional. There are two reasons, commonly known as the "mechanical" and "strategic" effects of electoral laws, for why nonproportional electoral systems have this moderating effect. We now examine each of these effects in turn.

The Mechanical Effect of Electoral Laws

The **mechanical effect of electoral laws** refers to the way that votes are translated into seats.

> The **mechanical effect of electoral laws** refers to the way votes are translated into seats. When electoral systems are disproportional, the mechanical effect punishes small parties and rewards large parties.

As we discussed in Chapter 13, the mechanical effect of all electoral systems systematically punishes small parties and rewards large parties. The extent to which small parties are punished and large parties are rewarded, however, depends on the proportionality of the electoral system. Specifically, small parties will find it harder to win seats and large parties are more likely to be rewarded when the electoral system is highly disproportional, as in an SMDP system. To illustrate how the mechanical effect of electoral laws affects parties of different sizes, consider the following two examples. One is based on a hypothetical country called "Duvergerland" and the other is based on real-world electoral returns from the United Kingdom.

Duvergerland is a country that has historically been divided by a single class cleavage—the electorate has been divided fairly evenly between supporters of a workers' party and supporters of a party that represents the interests of the business class. The one hundred-person legislature in Duvergerland is elected using an SMDP electoral system. Recently, social transformation has led to an increase in the number of voters holding post-materialist values. In recent elections, 20 percent of voters cast ballots for the newly formed Green Party, with the rest split in different ways between the Business and Labor parties in each district. In Figure 14.2, we illustrate the distribution of electoral results across twenty of the one hundred districts using a "doughnut" graph. Although the Green Party wins 20 percent of the vote in each

| FIGURE 14.2 | **Duvergerland: A Hypothetical Country Using an SMDP Electoral System** |

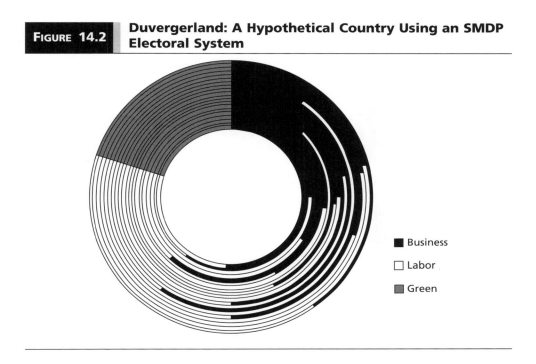

Business
Labor
Green

district, at least one of the other parties always wins more votes than this. As a result, the Green Party does not win a single legislative seat under the SMDP electoral system.

In Figure 14.3a, we illustrate the distribution of legislative seats if the pattern in the twenty districts shown in Figure 14.2 is reproduced throughout Duvergerland. The Labor and Business parties each get close to 50 percent of the seats in the legislature and the Green Party goes completely unrepresented even though it won 20 percent of the vote. Simply as a result of the way in which votes are translated into seats—the mechanical effect of the SMDP system—a party in Duvergerland that receives 20 percent of the population's support receives 0 percent of the legislative seats being contested. Moreover, although there is clearly support for three parties in the electorate, there are only two parties in the legislature.

Now contrast the way this same distribution of votes would have been translated into seats if Duvergerland had used a proportional representation system in a single national district. Given that the Green Party won 20 percent of the vote, it now obtains twenty legislative seats. This distribution of seats in this new legislature is shown in Figure 14.3b. As you can see, the fate of the small party—the Green Party—is substantially different under the two different electoral systems. The Green Party goes from controlling 20 percent of the legislative seats under PR to being excluded entirely from the legislature under SMDP. This reductive effect in the representation of the small party, as well as the electoral bonus given to the

FIGURE 14.3 | **Distribution of Seats in Duvergerland under SMDP and PR Electoral Rules**

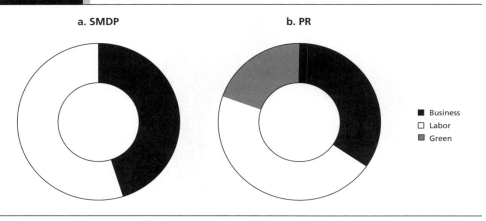

a. SMDP   b. PR

- ■ Business
- □ Labor
- ▨ Green

two large parties, is a direct result of the mechanical effect of the majoritarian SMDP electoral system employed in Duvergerland.

The mechanical effect of the SMDP electoral system that reduces the number of parties in the legislature by penalizing parties that win smaller shares of the vote is not just a matter of theoretical interest. In Table 14.13 we report the electoral returns for the St. Ives constituency during the 1992 legislative elections in the United Kingdom. In these elections, the Conservative Party candidate, David Harris, edges out the Liberal Democrat candidate, Andrew George, by fewer than 2,000 votes. Harris, who won just under 43 percent of the vote, becomes the sole representative of the St. Ives constituency. In contrast, Andrew George, who was supported by 40 percent of the voters in his constituency, is awarded nothing.

If the type of situation that occurred in the St. Ives constituency is repeated in a large number of constituencies, the "winner-take-all" logic of SMDP systems can lead to the introduction of a large gap between the share of votes that a party obtains and the share of seats

TABLE 14.13 | **Legislative Elections Results, St. Ives Constituency, United Kingdom, 1992**

	Votes	% of Vote
David Harris (Conservative)	24,528	42.9
Andrew George (Liberal Democrat)	22,883	40.1
Stephen Warr (Labour)	9,144	16.0
Graham Stevens (Liberal)	577	1.0
Harris is elected		

TABLE 14.14 Legislative Elections Results, National Totals, United Kingdom, 1992 (Percentages)		
	Votes	Seats
Conservative	41.9	51.6
Labour	34.9	41.6
Liberal Democrats	17.8	3.1
Others	5.4	3.7
Total	100	100

that it ultimately wins. In Table 14.14 we show some fairly typical national election results from the United Kingdom. One thing to notice about these results is that both of the two larger parties—the Conservatives and Labour—won about 20 percent more seats than their percentage of votes would suggest that they should have won. In the case of the Conservative Party, this "electoral bonus," which resulted from the mechanical way in which the SMDP system translates votes into seats, was enough to turn an electoral plurality into a legislative majority.[9] This type of legislative majority is sometimes referred to as a "manufactured" majority. The other thing to notice is that the smaller party—the Liberal Democrats—won only 3.1 percent of the legislative seats even though it won 17.8 percent of the vote. In Figure 14.4 we illustrate graphically how the mechanical effect of the SMDP electoral system

FIGURE 14.4 Distribution of Votes and Seats in Legislative Elections in the United Kingdom, 1992

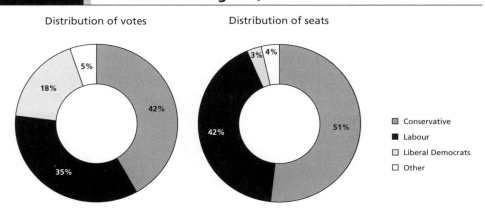

Distribution of votes

Distribution of seats

■ Conservative
■ Labour
□ Liberal Democrats
□ Other

9. The tendency for this to happen is the reason why some scholars refer to SMDP systems as "majoritarian" systems despite the fact that only a plurality of the votes in a district, not a majority, is needed to win a seat.

used in the 1992 UK legislative elections rewarded the larger parties and punished the smaller ones.

A quick comparison of the hypothetical case of Duvergerland and the real-world example from the 1992 UK legislative elections reveals that the extent to which nonproportional electoral systems, such as SMDP, punish small parties depends on the way that the votes for these parties are distributed across electoral districts. In Duvergerland, we assumed that the support for the Green Party was evenly distributed across all of the electoral districts. This particular distribution of support resulted in the Green Party's failing to win a single seat. Contrast this with the fact that the Liberal Democrats managed to win twenty seats (3.1 percent) in the 1992 UK elections even though they won a smaller share of the national vote than what the Greens won in Duvergerland. The reason for this difference is that the size of the support for the Liberal Democrats varied across different districts. Although the support for the Liberal Democrats was not sufficient to produce victory in the St. Ives constituency, it was big enough to win seats in twenty other districts. This indicates that the extent to which the mechanical effect of the SMDP system punishes small parties is directly related to how geographically dispersed their electoral support is.

The Liberal Democratic Party in the United Kingdom has generally been penalized quite heavily by the UK's SMDP electoral system because its support tends to be broadly distributed across many electoral districts. In contrast, small regional parties, such as Plaid Cymru in Wales, the Scottish National Party in Scotland, and Sinn Féin and the Ulster Unionists in Northern Ireland, which garner a much smaller share of the national vote, have experienced very little disadvantage from the way in which the UK's SMDP system translates votes into seats. This is because the support for these parties is heavily concentrated in a small number of districts. In fact, in the 2015 legislative elections in the United Kingdom, the Scottish National Party won 8.6 percent of the legislative seats (56 of the 59 seats available in Scotland) even though it won only 4.7 percent of the national (England, Scotland, Wales, Northern Ireland) vote.

The Strategic Effect of Electoral Laws

As we have just seen, the mechanical way in which votes are translated into seats in nonproportional systems tends to penalize small parties and reward large parties. The benefits that majoritarian systems like SMDP bestow on large parties are further enhanced by a second institutional effect called the **strategic effect of electoral laws**. To this point, we have isolated the mechanical effect of electoral laws by taking the way votes are distributed as given.

The **strategic effect of electoral laws** refers to how the way in which votes are translated into seats influences the "strategic" behavior of voters and political elites.

Now we must ask how voters and party elites are likely to respond to the mechanical effect of electoral systems. The strategic effect of electoral laws refers to how the way in which votes are translated into seats influences the "strategic" behavior of voters and political elites. When electoral systems are disproportional, their mechanical effect can be expected to reward large parties and punish small parties. Recognizing that this is going to happen, voters in these systems have an incentive to engage in *strategic voting*, and political elites have an incentive to engage in *strategic entry*. As we will see, both of these actions—strategic voting and strategic entry—bestow even more benefits on large parties and further penalize small parties.

Strategic Voting

As you will recall, we discussed strategic and sincere voting in Chapters 11 and 13. Strategic voting essentially means voting for your most preferred candidate *who has a realistic chance of winning*. In contrast, sincere voting means voting for your most preferred candidate or party. To help refresh your mind about the logic of strategic voting in nonproportional electoral systems, such as SMDP, take a look again at the election results from the St. Ives constituency in the 1992 UK elections (Table 14.13). Imagine that you preferred the Labour candidate to the Liberal Democrat candidate and the Liberal Democrat candidate to the Conservative candidate; that is, L > LD > C. Imagine also that you had reliable polling data indicating that the Labour candidate was trailing the Conservative and Liberal Democrat candidates by a wide margin. If you cast a sincere vote, then you would vote for the Labour candidate. However, a sincere vote is likely to be "wasted" in the sense that it has little chance of affecting the outcome of the election given how far the Labour candidate trails behind the other candidates. As a result, you have an incentive to vote strategically for the Liberal Democrat candidate (who has a more realistic chance of winning) in order to try to stop the Conservative candidate (who is your least-preferred candidate) from winning.

As this example illustrates, supporters of small parties that have little realistic chance of winning seats due to the way that votes are translated into seats have an incentive to vote strategically. In other words, they have an incentive not to vote for their most preferred party—a small party—and, instead, give their support to one of the larger parties that they like. This incentive to vote strategically increases as the electoral system becomes more disproportional. As a result, small parties are penalized in nonproportional systems not only because of the way that votes are translated into seats but also because voters in these systems have an incentive not to vote for them in the first place. Similarly, large parties benefit in nonproportional systems not only due to the electoral bonus that they receive from the way that votes are translated into seats but also because voters who prefer other parties often have an incentive to strategically vote for them.

Strategic Entry

Although nonproportional electoral systems create incentives for voters to engage in strategic voting, they also create similar incentives for political elites to engage in what is called **strategic entry**. Strategic entry refers to the decision by political elites about whether to enter the political scene under the label of their most preferred

> **Strategic entry** refers to the decision by political elites about whether to enter the political scene under the label of their most preferred party or under the label of their most preferred party that has a realistic chance of winning.

party or under the label of their most preferred party *that has a realistic chance of winning*. Imagine that you are an aspiring political entrepreneur in Duvergerland who has an interest in environmental politics. If this is the case, then you confront a dilemma. On the one hand, you could run as a candidate for the Green Party. The Green Party is your most preferred party because it will likely share your attitudes on environmental policy. The problem is that you will not get elected as a candidate for the Green Party given the use of an SMDP electoral system and the way that the party's support is distributed across Duvergerland. On the other hand, you could decide to run in the "lesser of two evils" from among those parties that you estimate to have a realistic chance of winning seats. Furthermore, even if the party that reflects your policy preference (Green Party) is able to gain a few seats in the legislature, you must consider whether you can better further your policy agenda by representing that party or by working within a different party that actually stands a chance of commanding a legislative majority.

In contrast to political elites who compete under an SMDP electoral system, political entrepreneurs in proportional systems do not face such a stark trade-off. This is because even a small amount of electoral success in garnering votes can often allow one to win legislative seats. Indeed, if there are many parties in the legislature, leaders of small parties might even find themselves in the enviable position of being a kingmaker in the government formation process and a highly sought-after junior coalition partner. The difference in opportunities for small party leaders between the SMDP and PR systems is evident if we compare the postwar experience of leaders of the Liberal Party in the United Kingdom (under the SMDP system) with that of leaders of the Free Democratic Party (FDP) in Germany (under the proportional dependent mixed system). Although these two parties have historically shared similar ideological positions in their respective party systems, the FDP was a near constant fixture in German cabinets, whereas the Liberal Party in the United Kingdom was, until the 2010 legislative elections, always consigned to watch from the sidelines as the Conservative and Labour parties rotated in and out of office. The different trajectories of these two parties would have to enter the calculations of ambitious young politicians. This suggests that small parties in SMDP systems will find it more difficult to attract and retain high-quality leaders than small parties in more proportional systems. For similar reasons, small parties in SMDP systems will also find it harder to attract private financial support. The lack of high-quality candidates and other resources in small parties that compete in SMDP systems will, in turn, make it harder for these parties to win votes.

Note that the example we have just presented assumes that the Green Party actually existed in Duvergerland. Now imagine that you are the same political entrepreneur as before with a strong interest in environmental politics. The social transformation that has seen an increase in the number of voters holding post-materialist values has just taken place. You must decide whether to form a Green Party to represent this new constituency or try to represent it within one of the established parties. Given that a Green Party is unlikely to win any seats in Duvergerland, you will have a strong incentive to work within one of the existing parties to achieve your political and policy goals. As this example illustrates, not only do disproportional electoral systems mean that small parties will receive a lower percentage of the vote because they are less likely to attract high-quality candidates and other resources, but they also mean that these small parties are less likely to exist in the first place.

The dilemma confronting political elites in an SMDP system can be demonstrated in another way with the help of the following Strategic Entry Game. Suppose that there are two left-wing parties (L_1 and L_2) and one right-wing party (R). Let's assume that if both left-wing parties compete in the election, then the right-wing party will win for sure, because the vote of the left-wing electorate will be split between two "small" parties. Let's also assume that the right-wing party will be defeated if only one left-wing party runs. Because each left-wing party prefers that the right-wing party be defeated for ideological reasons, its worst possible outcome occurs if both left-wing parties run. Note, though, that if only one of the left-wing parties is going to run, then each left-wing party would prefer that its own party be it. This is because not only would an electoral victory allow it to implement left-wing policies, but it would also allow the party to consume the benefits that come with holding office. Without any loss of generality, we can assign to each party a value of 0 for its worst outcome (both left-wing parties run and the right-wing party wins) and a value of 1 to its most preferred outcome (the other left-wing party drops out and it, the remaining one, wins). We can use a parameter λ (lambda) to represent the value that each left-wing party places on seeing its fellow left-wing party run instead of it. Because having the other left-wing party win is better than having the right-wing party win but not as good as winning itself, it follows that $0 < \lambda < 1$. Ultimately, the two left-wing parties must decide whether to run or not run. The normal form of this Strategic Entry Game is shown in Figure 14.5.

Notice that the two left-wing parties face a coordination dilemma. They share a common goal—defeat the right-wing party. They differ, however, on how that goal should be met—each

| FIGURE 14.5 | **Strategic Entry Game: Coordination between Competing Left-Wing Parties** |

| | | Left Party L_2 | |
		Run	Don't Run
Left Party L_1	Run	0, 0	1, λ
	Don't run	λ, 1	0, 0

party wants to be the party that rules in the event of a right-wing defeat.[10] If you solve the Strategic Entry Game, you will find that there are two Nash equilibria: (Run; Don't run) and (Don't run; Run). In other words, each party has an incentive to drop out of the race if the other player does not drop out. Such mixed-motive games present a dilemma that is often difficult for the actors involved to solve. In some countries, parties on the left (or right) realize that they have an incentive to withdraw from an electoral contest but cannot coordinate on which one should do it. As a result, parties that do not "drop out" wind up contributing to the election of their most bitter rivals. A good example of this occurred in the 2002 French presidential elections (S. Golder 2006, 56–57). It had widely been expected that Jacques Chirac, the president and leader of the mainstream right, would make it through to the second round, along with Lionel Jospin, the Socialist prime minister and leader of the mainstream left. The real question for months had been which of the two men would win the second round. Then, unexpectedly, the left vote was split among so many candidates that the Socialist leader came in third behind the extreme-right politician, Jean-Marie Le Pen. Although many people have naturally focused on the disturbing success of the extreme right, this political earthquake, as it became known, had as much to do with the inability of the French left to solve its coordination problems as it did with an increase in the strength of the extreme right. A similar example occurred in the 2000 US presidential elections when the presence of Ralph Nader on the ballot split the left-wing vote, particularly in Florida, to such an extent that the right-wing Republican George W. Bush was able to defeat the left-wing Democrat, Al Gore, in the Electoral College.

One way to prevent this type of worst-case scenario is for the parties splitting the vote to merge into a single party.[11] This is exactly what the Liberal Party and the Social Democratic Party did to create the Liberal Democratic Party in the United Kingdom in 1988. As several scholars have noted, the more disproportional the electoral system, the greater the incentive that small parties have to merge or form coalitions rather than compete as independent entities at election time (Cox 1997; S. Golder 2005, 2006).[12] It is worth noting that this incentive not only encourages mergers between small parties but can also even deter the entry of small parties in the first place. Even when disgruntled by the current direction of their party, forward-looking political entrepreneurs may decide that it is better to work within an

---

10. As you will recall from the problems at the end of Chapter 4, this sort of game is commonly referred to as an asymmetric coordination game.

11. An alternative strategy for avoiding this type of "worst-case scenario" is for the parties splitting the vote to form a pre-electoral coalition at election time rather than compete as independent entities (Blais and Indridason 2007; S. Golder 2005, 2006).

12. Determining when and why some small political parties retain their separate identities rather than merge or coalesce into a larger party is a complex question (Ibenskas 2016a). As we have already seen, it will depend to a large extent on the disproportionality of the electoral system. However, a number of other institutions are known to influence how likely it is that parties retain their separate identities. One such institution is the use of fusion candidates, where multiple parties can nominate the same candidate (S. Golder 2005, 2006). Fusion candidates were employed in many US states in the nineteenth century. Although this practice continues in New York State, it was stopped in most other states more than a century ago. The end of fusion candidates contributed quite markedly to the evolution of a party system in which the Democratic and Republican parties were the only viable parties outside of New York State (Argersinger 1980).

existing party rather than break away to form a new party and risk contributing to the election of a party that they find less desirable than their current one. As all of these examples illustrate, small parties that represent relatively small segments of the population will be less likely to form or be successful in disproportional electoral systems because of the strategic incentives that these electoral rules create for both voters and political elites.

Summarizing Duverger's Theory

To sum up, **Duverger's theory** states that the size of a country's party system depends on the complex interplay of both social and institutional forces. The precise causal story underlying Duverger's theory is illustrated in Figure 14.6. Characteristics of a country's social structure provide the driving force behind the formation of parties. When there are many cross-cutting cleavages, there are many distinct positions that, in some sense,

> **Duverger's theory** states that the size of a country's party system depends on the complex interplay of both social and institutional factors. Social divisions create the "demand" for political parties, and electoral institutions then determine the extent to which this demand is translated into parties that win votes (electoral parties) and parties that win seats (legislative parties).

need to be represented. Whether these distinct positions are ultimately translated into distinct parties, however, will depend on the proportionality of the electoral system.

Disproportional electoral systems translate votes into seats in such a way that small parties are penalized and large parties are rewarded. In other words, the "input-output" ratio by which votes are turned into seats in disproportional systems is smaller for small parties than it is for large parties. In contrast, proportional electoral systems translate votes into seats at a relatively constant rate. The way in which the mechanical effect of disproportional systems helps large parties and hurts small parties creates incentives for voters and political elites in these systems to engage in strategic voting and strategic entry. Supporters of small parties are more likely to see a vote for their most preferred party as a "wasted vote" in disproportional systems than in more proportional ones. Consequently, these voters are more likely to transfer their support to a larger party that is lower ranked in their preference ordering but that has a realistic chance of winning. Similarly, political entrepreneurs connected to policy positions that are not represented by existing parties or are associated with small parties have strong incentives to work within existing large parties if the electoral system is disproportional. As a result, disproportional electoral systems discourage the formation and electoral success of new parties in two related ways. First, the mechanical effect of these systems leaves small parties with fewer seats in the legislature than the votes cast for them would have produced in a PR system. Second, the strategic effect of these systems leaves small parties with fewer votes than the latent support for their policies in the electorate would suggest they could attract.

Duverger succinctly summed up the observational implications of his theory in two statements that have become known as **Duverger's law** and **Duverger's hypothesis**:

> **Duverger's law** states that single-member district plurality systems encourage two-party systems. **Duverger's hypothesis** states that proportional representation electoral rules favor multiparty systems.

FIGURE 14.6	**Party Systems: Social Cleavages and the Modifying Effect of Electoral Institutions**

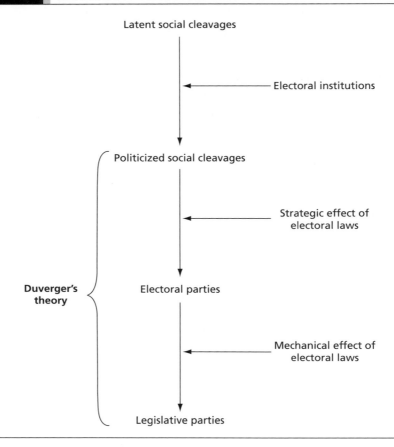

Duverger's law: Single-member district plurality systems encourage two-party systems.

Duverger's hypothesis: Proportional representation electoral rules favor multiparty systems.

Unfortunately, it turns out that the simple prediction that we should expect to find two-party systems when SMDP electoral laws are employed is a valid inference from Duverger's broader theory only when some auxiliary assumptions are satisfied. As Duverger himself noted, the logic by which the mechanical and strategic effects of SMDP electoral systems produce two-party systems works only at the district, and not the national, level (see Box 14.4, "Nationalizing Party Systems"). To see why, recall our example from the St. Ives constituency in the United Kingdom. If voters know that the Labour Party has no chance of

NATIONALIZING PARTY SYSTEMS

Duverger's law states that countries with SMDP electoral systems will be characterized by two-party systems. However, the logic by which the mechanical and strategic effects of SMDP electoral rules produce two-party systems really works only at the district level (Cox 1997; Duverger [1954] 1963). Because the SMDP system is a winner-take-all system, it is often the case that only the two largest parties in a district have a realistic chance of winning the seat. That two parties are likely to predominate in each district, though, does not necessarily mean that there is a two-party system at the national level. Whether this is the case or not depends on whether the same two parties predominate across the lion's share of the districts. In other words, there can be a discrepancy between the size of local party systems and the size of the national party system. In effect, there can be more parties competing nationally than there are, on average, competing in each district. Political scientists say that a country's party system has been nationalized if the local and national party systems are of a similar size.

Several factors have been found to influence the extent to which party systems are nationalized. For example, party systems are more likely to be nationalized when political and economic power is centralized in the national government (Chhibber and Kollman 1998, 2004). The logic is that as power is centralized, it becomes increasingly important to gain control of the national government. As a result, parties that have little chance of gaining control of the national government, even if they are one of the two largest parties in their district, are likely to find themselves abandoned by both voters and political entrepreneurs at election time. Parties that are able to compete nationally, rather than in just one or two districts, are likely to benefit from this strategic behavior. To illustrate this point, Chhibber and Kollman (1998) examine the size of local and national party systems in the United States from 1790 to 1990. Their data are shown in Figure 14.7.

As you can see, the average number of parties at the district level has been about two, as Duverger's theory predicts, throughout US history. The size of the national party system has varied quite considerably over this 200-year period, however. Prior to the New Deal in the 1930s, the number of parties at the national level was frequently much larger than two. This reflects the fact that several minor parties were able to enjoy regional success throughout this period. For example, a minor party, such as Labor, the Progressives, the Socialists, the Prohibitionists, or Farmers, was one of the two locally dominant political parties in certain regions and time periods. Ever since the 1930s, though, there has been little difference in how many parties compete at the local and national level in the United States. In effect, the US party system became nationalized in the 1930s with the same two parties—Democrats and Republicans—dominating both local and national party systems. Minor parties have enjoyed relatively little success since this time.

Chhibber and Kollman argue that this dramatic change was the result of the increased centralization of political and economic power in the US national government that occurred in the 1930s. As they note, national government spending as a percentage of total government spending (including state and local spending) more than doubled in this period; national

FIGURE 14.7 | **Number of Parties at the National and District Levels in the United States, 1790–1990**

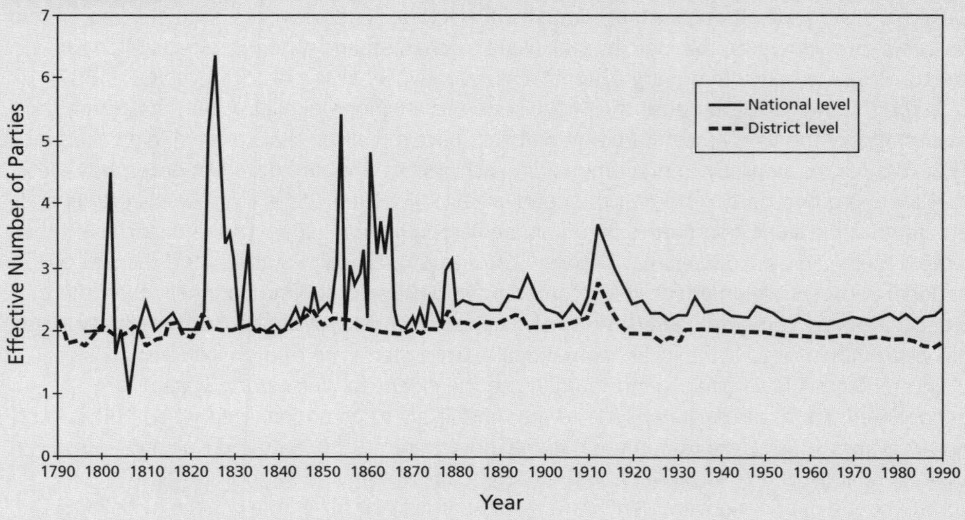

Source: Chhibber and Kollman (1998, 331).

government spending increased almost tenfold as a proportion of gross national product as well. In effect, holding national office became increasingly important in the 1930s. Minor parties that were unable to credibly compete for national office were therefore at a strategic disadvantage, and the party system became nationalized.

Hicken (2009) has built on this argument to suggest that the extent to which power is shared between different branches of the national government also matters. If political power is centralized in the national government and this power is not shared between different branches of government, the value of holding national office is especially high. This creates even greater incentives for political parties to solve cross-district coordination problems, such as those highlighted in our Strategic Entry Game. The result is a party system in which Duvergerian dynamics are reflected at both the national and the district level.

Another factor that influences the nationalization of party systems is the presence of presidential elections (M. Golder 2006; Stoll 2015). The presidency is nearly always the most important electoral prize in a presidential democracy. There is typically, however, only a small number of viable presidential candidates because only one person can become the president. Given the importance of the presidency, parties that do not have a viable presidential candidate, even if they are electorally strong in their local regions, are likely to find themselves abandoned by both voters and political entrepreneurs at election time. Parties that have a national base and hence viable presidential candidates will naturally benefit from this strategic behavior. The end result is a nationalized party system where regionally based parties can struggle to compete. The extent to which presidential elections exert nationalizing pressures on a country's party system depends on how important it is to win the presidency and the temporal proximity between presidential and legislative elections. Specifically, party systems in presidential democracies are more likely to be nationalized if the president's power is large relative to that of other political actors and if presidential elections occur at the same time as legislative ones.

Another obvious factor influencing the extent to which party systems are nationalized has to do with the distribution of politicized cleavages in a country. If these cleavages are national in the sense that the same cleavages dominate political competition in each region, then the party system as a whole is likely to be national in character. If a country's politicized cleavages vary from region to region, however, the party system is likely to be less nationalized. As our discussion in this chapter makes clear, though, the extent to which regional cleavages are actually translated into distinct parties still depends on the permissiveness of the electoral system.

winning *in this district*, then the benefits of strategic voting accrue to the Conservatives and the Liberal Democrats *in this district*. In other districts—indeed, in most districts in the UK—it is the Liberal Democrats who are the "also ran" party. As a result, it is the Conservative and Labour parties that benefit in most districts from the strategic voting induced by the mechanical effect of the SMDP electoral system.

As you can see, the logic of Duverger's argument leads us to expect a national two-party system in SMDP countries only to the extent that the same two parties are favored by strategic voting across the lion's share of the electoral districts. It is possible, for example, for some parties to be favored by SMDP in some regions of the country and other parties to receive an electoral boost from SMDP in other parts of the country. The net effect of these offsetting distortions may leave the country with different two-party systems at the district level and hence a multiparty system at the national level. In short, if the party system is not fully nationalized with the same parties advantaged in each district, SMDP electoral systems could very well have more than two parties nationally. As Box 14.4 explains, the extent to which a party system is nationalized also depends on a host of other factors, including whether economic and political power is centralized in the national government, how this power is shared between the different branches of government, and whether there are presidential elections (Chhibber and Kollman 1998, 2004; M. Golder 2006; Hicken 2009; Stoll 2015).

These cautions, however, do little damage to Duverger's broader theory. This is because his theory is more concerned with how *changes* in social conditions or electoral laws result in *changes* in the number of parties, and there is considerable evidence consistent with his predictions in this area (Amorim Neto and Cox 1997; Brambor, Clark, and Golder 2007; Clark, Gilligan, and Golder 2006; Clark and Golder 2006; Cox 1997; Ordeshook and Shvetsova 1994).

Duverger used the metaphor of a car to explain why some countries have many parties and other countries have few. Social structure is the "engine" that drives the multiplication of parties, whereas electoral laws serve as the brake pedal. Disproportional electoral systems, such as SMDP, depress the brake pedal and therefore prevent the engine of social division from producing multiparty systems. Another metaphor that describes this process focuses on how social divisions create a storm of policy demands and how the electoral system determines if those demands will be permitted to flow downstream and be translated into distinctive parties. Just as a dam in a river moderates the flow of water, electoral laws *moderate* the way social divisions get turned into parties (see Figure 14.6). When the dam is closed, it prevents some of the water from flowing downstream; when the dam is open, it permits more of the water to flow downstream. SMDP electoral systems are like a closed dam that, for the reasons described above, prevents some societal demands from being transformed into political parties. Proportional electoral systems are like an open dam in that they permit *more* of these demands to be translated into parties. It is for this reason that political scientists frequently say that proportional electoral systems are permissive and disproportional ones are nonpermissive.

As we have seen, the effect of social structure on the size of a country's party system depends on the permissiveness of the electoral system. Similarly, the effect of the electoral system on party system size depends on a country's social structure. Consider the four different scenarios shown in Table 14.15. The case in which there are many social divisions—high social heterogeneity—and a permissive electoral system (top right) is like a river filled with storm water meeting an open dam. Because the dam is open, it has little effect on the current of the river, and most, if not all, of the water flows unimpeded downstream. In other words, social heterogeneity is expected to result in the formation of many parties when a PR electoral system *permits* it to. Contrast this with the case in which there are many social divisions and a nonpermissive electoral system (top left). This situation is like having a storm-filled river confront a closed dam—some of the water will not get to flow downriver and, instead, will form a reservoir on the upstream side of the dam. In other words, some of the societal demands in a socially heterogeneous country that employs a nonpermissive electoral system will not be translated into political parties.

TABLE 14.15 | **The Interplay of Social Heterogeneity and Electoral System Permissiveness on Party System Size**

| | | Electoral System Permissiveness | |
		Low (SMDP)	High (PR)
Social Heterogeneity	High	Few parties	Many parties
	Low	Few parties	Few parties

Now consider the two cases in which there are few social divisions—social heterogeneity is low (bottom left and bottom right). This situation is equivalent to having a dry season that results in an almost entirely dry river. We can imagine that the river is so low that water cannot reach the gates or valves in the dam. Clearly, little water will be getting downstream in this situation, irrespective of whether the dam is open or closed. In other words, when social heterogeneity is low, we do not expect much of a demand for political parties. As a result, few parties will be formed whether or not the electoral system is permissive.

A key implication of Duverger's theory, then, is that there are two reasons why a party system may have few parties. Some countries may have few parties, despite the fact that they are socially heterogeneous, because they have a nonpermissive electoral system that prevents this heterogeneity from being reflected in the party system. Alternatively, some countries may have few parties regardless of how permissive their electoral system is because they have few social divisions. In contrast, there is only one way, according to Duverger's theory, to end up with many parties—you need a heterogeneous society and a permissive electoral system.

CONCLUSION

Political scientists sometimes categorize democracies in terms of the type of party system that they employ. When they do this, they tend to focus on the number and size of the parties in a country. But what explains why some countries have many parties and others have few? As we have seen, party system size is shaped by the interaction between social heterogeneity and the permissiveness of electoral institutions. Social divisions provide the demand for distinctive representation and, hence, the driving force behind the multiplication of political parties. However, electoral laws modify the way that these social divisions are translated into parties that win votes (electoral parties) and parties that win seats (legislative parties). According to Duverger's theory, countries will only have a large multiparty system if they are characterized both by high levels of social heterogeneity *and* by permissive electoral systems.

When electoral systems are permissive (high district magnitude), social heterogeneity is translated into electoral and legislative parties with very little distortion. In contrast, nonpermissive (low district magnitude) electoral institutions are likely to produce party systems that are much smaller than the number of social cleavages in a country might lead us to imagine. In effect, nonpermissive electoral laws introduce a large amount of distortion in how social heterogeneity is translated into parties at the electoral and legislative levels. It is important to remember, though, that the precise amount of distortion that is introduced by nonpermissive electoral rules depends on the way that social heterogeneity is geographically distributed in a country. For example, if the supporters of small parties are distributed fairly evenly across electoral districts, then we should expect nonpermissive electoral laws to produce legislatures with many fewer parties than social cleavages. If the supporters of small parties are geographically concentrated, however, the reductive effect that nonpermissive electoral rules exercise on the number of parties will be greatly curtailed.

In this chapter, we also examined why it is that some party systems are divided primarily along ethnic lines, whereas others are divided mainly along class, religious, or linguistic ones. In other words, we looked at why countries have the types of parties that they do. As with party system size, we argued that the types of parties in a country are determined by the complex interplay of social and institutional forces. At some basic level, the patterns of social cleavages in a country provide the potential lines of conflict that could underpin the existence of distinct political parties. We also saw that institutions, such as electoral rules, are likely to determine which of these cleavages become activated or politicized. Overall, comparative politics scholars have made much greater progress in understanding the number of parties that exist in a country than in understanding the likely ideological or programmatic orientation of the parties. Given this, we hope that readers of this text will contribute to the construction and testing of theories relating to the types of parties found in different countries.

KEY CONCEPTS

anticlericalism *605*
attribute *614*
cross-cutting attributes *616*
Duverger's hypothesis *633*
Duverger's law *633*
Duverger's theory *633*
effective number of electoral parties *598*
effective number of legislative parties *598*
effective number of parties *598*
ethnic group *612*
ethnic party *613*
freezing hypothesis *610*
identity category *614*
laïcité *605*

mechanical effect of electoral laws *624*
Michels's iron law of oligarchy *610*
multiparty system *593*
nonpartisan system *593*
one-party dominant system *593*
party identification *587*
political party *586*
reinforcing attributes *616*
single-party system *593*
strategic effect of electoral laws *628*
strategic entry *629*
two-party system *593*
whip *591*

PROBLEMS

The problems that follow address some of the more important concepts and ideas introduced in this chapter.

Party System Size

1. As we note in the chapter, the actual number of parties competing in an election or winning seats is not necessarily a good reflection of "how big" a country's party system is. As a result, political scientists often prefer to use a measure of the effective number of parties in a country to capture party system size. If you recall, the effective number of electoral parties when there are four actual parties is calculated as

$$\text{effective number of electoral parties} = \frac{1}{v_1^2 + v_2^2 + v_3^2 + v_4^2}$$

where v_1 is the vote share of party 1, v_2 is the vote share of party 2, and so on. The effective number of legislative parties when there are four actual parties is calculated as

$$\text{effective number of legislative parties} = \frac{1}{s_1^2 + s_2^2 + s_3^2 + s_4^2}$$

where s_1 is the seat share of party 1, s_2 is the seat share of party 2, and so on. These measures can easily be adapted to cases in which there are more parties or fewer parties. For example, the general formulas for the effective number of parties are

$$\text{effective number of electoral parties} = \frac{1}{\sum_{i=1}^{P} v_i^2},$$

and

$$\text{effective number of legislative parties} = \frac{1}{\sum_{i=1}^{P} s_i^2},$$

where P is the total number of actual parties. In Table 14.16, we show the results from the 2014 legislative elections in South Africa. As you can see, thirty parties won votes and thirteen parties won seats. This would seem to suggest that South Africa has a large multiparty system. Answer the following questions.

a. What is the effective number of electoral parties in the 2014 South African elections? What is the effective number of legislative parties? (You will probably want to use a calculator for this.)

b. Compare the effective numbers of electoral and legislative parties in these elections with the actual number of parties winning votes and seats. Which measure—the actual or effective number of parties—does a better job, in your opinion, of capturing the size of the South African party system? Why? Are there circumstances in which you would be more likely to use the actual number of parties as the measure of party system size? Are there circumstances in which you would be more likely to use the effective number of parties?

c. Based on your answers to the previous questions and the information in Table 14.16, what do you think is the most accurate classification of the South African party system: nonpartisan, single party, one-party dominant, two party, or multiparty?

d. Based on the effective numbers of electoral and legislative parties that you calculated, does the mechanical effect of South Africa's electoral system introduce much distortion in the way that votes are translated into seats? Based on your answer to this question,

TABLE 14.16	Legislative Election Results in the Republic of South Africa, 2014		
Party name	**Votes (%)**	**Seats (no.)**	**Seats (%)**
African National Congress (ANC)	62.15	249	62.25
Democratic Alliance (DA)	22.23	89	22.25
Economic Freedom Fighters	6.35	25	6.25
Inkatha Freedom Party	2.40	10	2.50
National Freedom Party	1.57	6	1.50
United Democratic Movement	1.00	4	1.00
Freedom Front Plus	0.90	4	1.00
Congress of the People	0.67	3	0.75
African Christian Democratic Party	0.57	3	0.75
African Independent Congress	0.53	3	0.75
Agang South Africa	0.28	2	0.50
Pan Africanist Congress	0.21	1	0.25
African People's Convention	0.17	1	0.25
Al Jama-ah	0.14	0	0.00
Minority Front	0.12	0	0.00
United Christian Democratic Party	0.12	0	0.00
Azanian People's Organisation	0.11	0	0.00
Bushbuckridge Residents Association	0.08	0	0.00
Independent Civic Organization	0.08	0	0.00
Patriotic Alliance	0.07	0	0.00
Workers and Socialist Party	0.05	0	0.00
Ubuntu Party	0.04	0	0.00
Kingdom Governance Movement	0.03	0	0.00
Front National	0.03	0	0.00
Keep It Straight and Simple	0.02	0	0.00
Pan Africanist Movement	0.02	0	0.00
First National Liberation Alliance	0.02	0	0.00
United Congress	0.02	0	0.00
National Party South Africa	0.01	0	0.00
People's Alliance	0.01	0	0.00

what type of electoral system do you think South Africa employs—a permissive or nonpermissive one? Use Internet resources to find out whether South Africa really does use a permissive or a nonpermissive electoral system.

Party System Nationalization

2. India uses an SMDP electoral system to elect its legislators to the Lok Sabha, the Indian lower house of parliament. In the 2009 elections, thirty-five different political parties won seats. As the data in Table 14.2 indicate, the effective number of electoral parties was 8.76 and the effective number of legislative parties was 5.01.

   a. Given that India employs the highly nonpermissive SMDP electoral system, can you think of reasons why we do not see a two-party system similar to the ones found in the United States or Belize?

   b. In Figure 14.8, we illustrate the effective number of parties at the district and national level in India from 1957 to 1995. As you can see, the effective number of parties at the district level always hovers around two. Explain why this is the case with reference to the mechanical and strategic effects of electoral laws.

   c. Although the effective number of parties at the district level in India always hovers around two, the number of parties at the national level exhibits a considerable amount of variation, ranging from a low of about three in the mid-1970s to a high of over six in the 1990s. One thing that is noticeable in Figure 14.8 is that the size of the national party system in India was lower in the 1970s than in the 1960s or in the 1980s and

| FIGURE 14.8 | **Number of Parties at the National and District Levels in India, 1957–1995** |

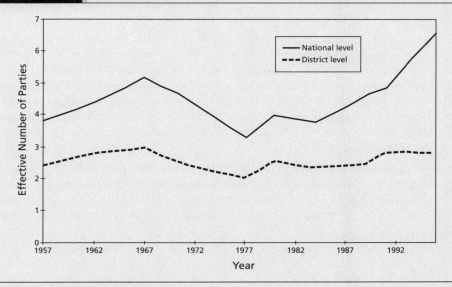

Source: Chhibber and Kollman (1998).

1990s. In effect, there is evidence that the Indian party system was more nationalized in the 1970s than in other periods. Without knowing anything in particular about Indian politics, can you try to explain this variation over time?

Political Identity Formation

3. In Table 14.17, we illustrate the distribution of attributes in a hypothetical Los Angeles community that is divided along language and race lines.

TABLE 14.17   **Distribution of Attributes in a Hypothetical Los Angeles Community (Percentages)**

	English speaker	Spanish speaker	Korean speaker
Latino	20	31	0
Asian	17	0	14
Black	10	0	0
White	8	0	0

a. If you know that someone is an English speaker, can you predict with much certainty what racial group he or she belongs to? If you know that someone is a Latino, can you predict with much certainty what language he or she speaks? If you know that someone is Asian, can you predict with much certainty what language he or she speaks? Based on your answers to these questions, would you say that the attributes in this hypothetical Los Angeles community are cross-cutting or reinforcing?

b. Let's assume that in order to win political office in this Los Angeles community, a candidate needs to win 50 percent of the vote. Let's also assume that political entrepreneurs will try to mobilize voters along either racial or linguistic lines. If this is the case, what identity categories could be activated or politicized to win the election? In other words, what identity categories (racial or linguistic) form minimal winning coalitions? If you have answered this question correctly, you will find that there are two identity categories that form minimal winning coalitions. Which of these two identity categories do you think is most likely to be politicized and why?

c. In the previous question, you found that there were two identity categories that could form minimal winning coalitions in this Los Angeles community. Are there any groups of individuals that are members of both minimal winning coalitions? If so, who are they? Do you think that being in both potential winning coalitions is politically advantageous? If so, why?

15 Institutional Veto Players

The accumulation of all powers, legislative, executive, and judiciary, in the same hands, whether of one, a few, or many, and whether hereditary, self appointed, or elective, may justly be pronounced the very definition of tyranny.

James Madison, *The Federalist Papers,* No. 47

It is very dangerous to allow the nation as a whole to decide on matters which concern only a small section, whether that section be geographical or industrial or defined in any other way. The best cure for this evil, so far as can be seen at present, lies in allowing self-government to every important group within a nation in all matters that affect that group much more than they affect the rest of the community.

Bertrand Russell, *Proposed Roads to Freedom*, 1919

[In government] the constant aim is to divide and arrange the several offices in such a manner as that each may be a check on the other; that the private interest of every individual may be a sentinel over the public rights.

James Madison, *The Federalist Papers,* No. 51

OVERVIEW

- In this chapter, we examine the origins and consequences of federalism, bicameralism, and constitutionalism.

- A federal state is one in which sovereignty is constitutionally split between at least two territorial levels so that independent governmental units at each level have final authority in at least one policy realm. It is important to distinguish between "federalism in structure" and "federalism in practice."

- A bicameral state is one in which legislative deliberations occur in two distinct assemblies. Although bicameral legislatures were originally designed to represent different social classes, they are now more closely associated with the representation of different territorial units.

- Constitutionalism refers to the commitment of governments to be governed by a set of authoritative rules and principles that are laid out in a constitution. Constitutionalism requires a codified constitution, a bill of rights, and constitutional review.

- Rather than view the world in terms of institutional dichotomies, comparative scholars are increasingly recognizing that institutions such as federalism, bicameralism, and constitutionalism are conceptually the same. In effect, all three of these institutions act as checks and balances, thereby influencing how easy it is to change the political status quo. This new approach to understanding political institutions is called veto player theory.

As we noted in Chapter 11, there are many, many different types of democracy in the world. In subsequent chapters, we looked at how political scientists sometimes distinguish between democracies in terms of the type of government that they have (Chapter 12), the type of electoral system that they employ (Chapter 13), and the type of party system that they have (Chapter 14). In this chapter, we focus on other institutional dimensions of democracy. Specifically, we examine federalism, bicameralism, and constitutionalism. All three of these institutions can be thought of as forms of checks and balances on the political system. In effect, they can all be conceptualized as "institutional veto players" that influence the ease with which the political status quo in a country can be changed. As such, their causes and consequences are closely related. It is for this reason that we consider these different institutions in a single chapter.

FEDERALISM

Political scientists sometimes distinguish between states according to whether they are federal or unitary. Unfortunately, scholars do not all agree on exactly what it is that makes a state federal (Bednar 2009). The result is that there are different lists of federal states. Although almost everyone agrees that countries such as Argentina, Canada, Germany, and the United States are federal, there is considerable disagreement over the federal-unitary status of many other countries. For example, countries like China, India, Italy, Russia, Spain, the United Kingdom, and Venezuela are considered federal by some political scientists but not by others. Part of the problem has to do with whether a country needs to be both federal *in structure* (de jure) and federal *in practice* (de facto) to be considered truly federal. For our part, we believe that it is useful to retain a conceptual distinction between de jure federalism and de facto federalism (Bednar 2009). Only by making this distinction can we examine why some states that are federal on paper actually *behave* federally but others do not. In what follows, we refer to de jure federalism (federalism in structure) as federalism and de facto federalism (federalism in practice) as decentralization.

Federalism: Federalism in Structure

To be classified as federal, a country must satisfy three structural criteria: (a) geopolitical division, (b) independence, and (c) direct governance (Bednar 2009, 18–19). Typically we can determine whether a country satisfies these criteria for **federalism** by looking at its constitution.

1. *Geopolitical division* requires that the country be divided into mutually exclusive regional governments that are recognized in the constitution and that cannot be unilaterally abolished by the national government.
2. *Independence* requires that the regional and national governments must have independent bases of authority. This is typically ensured by having them elected independently of one another.
3. *Direct governance* requires that authority be shared between the regional governments and the national government such that each citizen is governed by at least two authorities. Each level of government must have the authority to act independently of the other in at least one policy realm, and this authority must be protected by the constitution.

The regional units in a federal country go under different names. For example, they are called states in Australia, the United States, and Venezuela; provinces in Canada; *Länder* in Germany and Austria; cantons in Switzerland; and regions in Belgium. Taken together, the three criteria outlined above indicate that a **federal state** is one in which sovereignty is constitutionally split between at least two territorial levels so that independent governmental units at each level have final authority in at least one policy realm.

In Table 15.1, we list all twenty-four countries that could be considered federal at some point between 1990 and 2000 (Bednar 2009). We also list whether these countries are democratic or authoritarian based on their Polity IV scores (Marshall, Gurr, and Jaggers 2016). All countries that do not appear in Table 15.1 are **unitary states**. As the information in Table 15.1 indicates, federalism is relatively rare in the world. As of 2000, only about 10 percent of the world's independent countries were federal; slightly less than 20 percent of the world's population lived in a federal country. On the whole, those countries that are federal tend to be either relatively large countries, such as Australia, Brazil, the former Soviet Union, and the United States, or relatively heterogeneous and diverse countries, such as Belgium, Ethiopia, Malaysia, Switzerland, and Yugoslavia.

> **Federalism** has three structural components: (a) geopolitical division, (b) independence, and (c) direct governance. A **federal state** is one in which sovereignty is constitutionally split between at least two territorial levels so that independent governmental units at each level have final authority in at least one policy realm. States that are not federal are known as **unitary states**.

TABLE 15.1   Federal Countries, 1990–2000

	Country	Regime	Years
1	Argentina	Democracy	1990–2000
2	Australia	Democracy	1990–2000
3	Austria	Democracy	1990–2000
4	Belgium	Democracy	1994–2000
5	Bosnia & Herzegovina	Dictatorship	1990–2000
6	Brazil	Democracy	1990–2000
7	Canada	Democracy	1990–2000
8	Czechoslovakia	Democracy	1990–1992
9	Ethiopia	Dictatorship	1995–2000
10	Germany	Democracy	1990–2000
11	Malaysia	Dictatorship	1990–2000
12	Mexico	Dictatorship	1990–1995
		Democracy	1996–2000
13	Micronesia	Democracy	1990–2000
14	Nigeria	Democracy	1999–2000
15	Pakistan	Democracy	1990–1999
16	Russia	Democracy	1992–2000
17	South Africa	Democracy	1993–2000
18	Switzerland	Democracy	1990–2000
19	USSR	Dictatorship	1990–1991
20	United Arab Emirates	Dictatorship	1990–2000
21	United States of America	Democracy	1990–2000
22	Venezuela	Democracy	1990–2000
23	Yugoslavia	Dictatorship	1990–1991
24	Yugoslavia (Serbia & Montenegro)	Dictatorship	1992–2000

Source: Data are from Bednar (2009); the coding for regime type is from the Polity IV data set (Marshall, Gurr, and Jaggers 2016).

Note: All of these countries satisfy the criteria of (a) geopolitical division, (b) independence, and (c) direct governance.

The United Arab Emirates (UAE) is an example of a federal dictatorship. The UAE comprises seven emirates in the Middle East—Abu Dhabi, Ajman, Dubai, Fujairah, Ra's al-Khaimah, Sharjah, and Umm al-Quwain. The seven emirates are shown in Map 15.1. Originally, the seven emirates were known as the Trucial States, and they formed part of a

| MAP 15.1 | **The Federal States of the United Arab Emirates** |

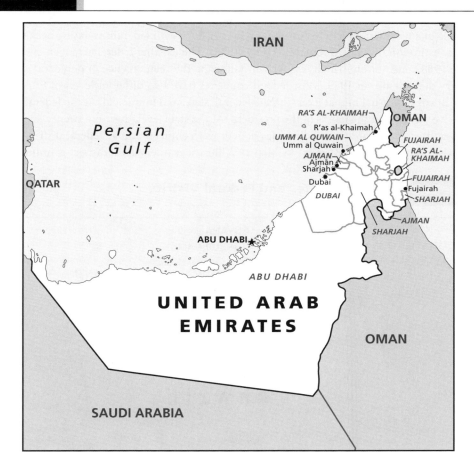

British protectorate along with Bahrain and Qatar. Following Britain's decision to withdraw from the Gulf in 1968, the seven Trucial States, along with Bahrain and Qatar, began negotiations to form a federation of Arab Emirates. Bahrain and Qatar ultimately decided to go their separate ways, but six Trucial States went on to form the United Arab Emirates in December 1971; the seventh Trucial State—Ra's al-Khaimah—joined in February 1972 (Peterson 1988). The provisional constitution of the UAE, which only became permanent in 1996, established a federal form of government (Peck 2001). This essentially involved constructing federal authorities above the preexisting local governments in each of the seven emirates. The federal nature of the UAE is guaranteed in Articles 116 and 122 of the constitution. These articles state that all powers that are not explicitly given to the federal authorities in the constitution belong to the individual emirates.

Whereas the United Arab Emirates is an example of a federal dictatorship, Brazil is an example of a federal democracy. Brazil has a long history with federalism dating back to the 1891 constitution of the Old Republic (1889–1930). The existing federal arrangements date to the 1988 constitution, which was written following the reemergence of democracy from military dictatorship in 1985. Most federal countries have two different levels of territorial units. Brazil is unusual in that it has three—federal, state, and municipal. At the federal level, executive power is in the hands of the president. At the state level, there are twenty-six states based on historical borders that have developed over centuries and a "federal district" that comprises Brazil's capital, Brasília. As Map 15.2 illustrates, the federal district is in the state

MAP 15.2   Brazil's States and Federal District

of Goiás. Executive power at the state level is in the hands of governors. At the municipal level, there are 5,570 different municipalities with their own legislative council; executive power is in the hands of mayors. Each of the municipalities has its own "little constitution."

The federal nature of Brazil's government is guaranteed in Article 1 of the constitution, which states that Brazil is formed by "the indissoluble union of the states and municipalities and of the federal district." Political authority is constitutionally shared among all three levels of government. In effect, state governments are allowed to pass legislation in any area that is not explicitly prohibited to them in the constitution (Article 25). Similarly, municipal governments are permitted to pass laws on any matter that does not contradict either the state or national constitutions (Article 30). Brazil is one of four federal states in Latin America, the others being Argentina, Mexico, and Venezuela.

Although all of the states shown in Table 15.1 can be considered federal, there is a great deal of variation in the precise form that federalism takes in these countries. When it comes to distinguishing between different forms of federalism, political scientists frequently focus on whether a federal system is (a) congruent or incongruent and (b) symmetric or asymmetric (Lijphart 1999).

Congruent federalism exists when the territorial units of a federal state share a similar demographic (ethnic, cultural, linguistic, religious, and so on) makeup. In a perfectly congruent federal state, each of the territorial units would be a precise miniature reflection of the country as a whole. Examples of a congruent federal state include the United States and Brazil. In both of these countries, the demographic composition of the

> **Congruent federalism** exists when the territorial units of a federal state share a similar demographic makeup with one another and the country as a whole. **Incongruent federalism** exists when the demographic makeup of territorial units differs among the units and the country as a whole.

territorial units does not vary significantly along ethnic, linguistic, cultural, or religious lines. In contrast, **incongruent federalism** exists when the demographic makeup of the territorial units differs among the units and the country as a whole. Examples of an incongruent federal state include Switzerland and Belgium. In both of these countries, the territorial units differ from one another along linguistic lines.

One way to think about congruent and incongruent federalism is in regard to whether the political boundaries of the territorial units line up with the geographic boundaries of ethnic, linguistic, cultural, or religious groups in a country. In an incongruent federal state, political boundaries tend to be aligned with the geographic boundaries of these social groups, whereas they tend to cut across them in congruent federal systems (Lijphart 1999, 196). One of the purported advantages of incongruent federalism is that it can transform highly diverse and heterogeneous countries that have geographically concentrated social groups into a federation of relatively homogeneous territorial units. As an example, consider Switzerland. Although Switzerland has four official language groups—German, French, Italian, and Romansch—the way that the territorial boundaries are drawn in the Swiss system of incongruent federalism means that twenty-two of the twenty-six cantons officially

Box 15.1 **DEVOLUTION VERSUS FEDERALISM**

Although only twenty-four countries satisfied all three structural criteria for federalism at some point during the 1990s, several other countries such as Comoros, India, Italy, Spain, Sudan, St. Kitts and Nevis, Tanzania, Ukraine, and the United Kingdom satisfied two of them (Bednar 2009). On the whole, the criterion that most of these unitary countries failed to meet was that of geopolitical division. Recall that this criterion requires that a country be divided into mutually exclusive regional governments that are constitutionally recognized and that cannot be unilaterally abolished by the national government. Many of the aforementioned countries, like India, Spain, and the United Kingdom, have transferred a considerable amount of power from the central government to regional governments. In all of these countries, however, the central government retains the right to unilaterally recall or reshape the powers given to the regional governments. Ultimately, political power resides in the central government of these countries; regional governments do not have a constitutional right to any of their powers. This type of situation is known as **devolution**, not federalism. To further illustrate this point, consider the United Kingdom and India.

Devolution occurs when a unitary state grants powers to subnational governments but retains the right to unilaterally recall or reshape those powers.

Although the United Kingdom has historically had a very powerful central government, things have begun to change in the last two decades. Following successful referenda on the establishment of regional parliaments in 1997, elections were held for a Scottish parliament and a Welsh senate in 1999. In accordance with the 1998 Good Friday Agreement, a provincial assembly was also established in Northern Ireland in 1999. These regional governments have had the legal right to act independently of the central government in London in numerous policy areas. As a result of these developments, the United Kingdom has come to satisfy two of the criteria for a federal state: independence and direct governance. The United Kingdom is not a federal state, however, because it fails to satisfy the criterion of geopolitical division—the UK central government retains the unilateral right to recall or reshape the powers that it has delegated to the regional governments. Indeed, the history of the Northern Ireland Assembly clearly illustrates this point. On four separate occasions since the establishment of the assembly in 1999, the central government in London has suspended it; the fourth suspension lasted for more than four years, from October 14, 2002, to May 7, 2007.

The relationship between the regional parliaments and the UK central government could change, however, if a region were to hold a successful referendum on seceding from the UK. In 2014, a Scottish referendum on independence resulted in 55 percent of voters choosing to remain a part of the UK. This result was thought to end speculation about an independent Scotland. However, the June 2016 "Brexit" referendum has reopened the debate on Scottish independence. In the Brexit referendum, a majority of UK voters, though only a minority of voters in Scotland and Northern Ireland, voted in favor of withdrawing from the European Union. This result has prompted speculation that Scotland might again try to secede so that it could (re)join the European Union as an independent state.

Like the UK, India also has many characteristics of a federal state. For example, it has two different levels of government—national and state. At present, twenty-nine states have their own local governments. There are also seven union territories, which differ from states in that they do not have their own local governments and are, instead, governed directly by the national government. Map 15.3 shows the states and union territories of India. Article 246 of the Indian constitution divides political authority between policy areas that are the exclusive concern of the national government (Union List) and policy areas that are the exclusive concern of the state governments. India clearly satisfies two of the criteria for a federal state:

MAP 15.3　　**India's States and Union Territories**

independence and direct governance. Like the United Kingdom, however, India is not a federal state because it fails to satisfy the criterion of geopolitical division.

Two articles in the Indian constitution are of particular relevance here. The first is Article 3, which states that the national legislature has the power to change the boundaries of individual states and to create new states by separating territories from existing ones. The newest Indian state was created in June 2014 when the Indian legislature voted to create Telangana by bifurcating the existing state of Andhra Pradesh. This action reversed a 1956 legislative decision that had merged Telangana with Pradesh to form Andhra Pradesh. The second is Article 356, which allows for the imposition of emergency presidential rule in a state that cannot be governed "in accordance with the provisions of the Constitution." This article is commonly known as "President's Rule." Article 356 was originally designed to allow the central government to take control of a state in the event of civil unrest. There have been numerous criticisms, though, that its use has been politically motivated—Indian presidents have often invoked Article 356 to dissolve state governments ruled by political opponents.

Despite sharing some of the features of a federal state, both the United Kingdom and India remain unitary states in structure even though they have devolved significant power to the regions.

have only one language; three cantons—Bern, Fribourg, and Valais—are bilingual; and only one—Graubünden—is trilingual (McRae 1983, 172–179). In effect, Switzerland comprises a collection of homogeneous cantons within a relatively diverse country.

Symmetric federalism exists when the territorial units of a federal state possess equal powers relative to the central government. This is the case in the United States—the Constitution gives each state equal standing and power vis-à-vis the central government. In contrast, **asymmetric federalism** exists when some territorial units of a federal state enjoy more extensive powers than others relative to the central government. On the whole, asymmetries in the division of power are designed to satisfy the different needs and demands that arise from ethnic, linguistic, demographic, or cultural differences between the separate subnational units. Examples of asymmetric federal states include Belgium, Canada, Malaysia, Russia, and Switzerland.[1] In Canada, the French-speaking province of Quebec enjoys significantly more autonomy in relation to the central government than the other nine English-speaking provinces. In addition to having special powers to promote and protect its French-Canadian

> **Symmetric federalism** exists when the territorial units of a federal state possess equal powers relative to the central government. **Asymmetric federalism** exists when some territorial units enjoy more extensive powers than others relative to the central government.

---

1. Unitary states can devolve power in an asymmetric manner as well. For example, the Navarra and Basque communities have more extensive tax and spending powers than the other "autonomous communities" in Spain; Galicia and Catalonia enjoy special authority in the areas of education, language, and culture (Congleton 2006). In the United Kingdom the Scottish parliament enjoys more power, particularly in the area of taxation, than the Welsh senate.

culture, Quebec has considerable authority over employment and immigration issues within its borders; it is also the only Canadian province to have its own pension plan.

Decentralization: Federalism in Practice

As we noted earlier, it is possible to make a conceptual distinction between federalism in structure (federalism) and federalism in practice (**decentralization**). As we have just seen, whether a state is federal or unitary is ultimately a constitutional issue. It depends on whether a country has certain structural characteristics written into its consti-
tution. Note, though, that whether a country is federal or unitary says very little about exactly *where* policy is made in practice. Knowing that a state is federal does not immediately imply that significant policymaking power is in the hands of regional governments. Similarly, knowing that a state is unitary does not necessarily mean that all policymaking power is in the hands of the national government. The degree to which actual policymaking power lies with the national or regional governments in both federal and unitary states determines the extent to which political sci-
entists view these states as centralized or decentralized.

> **Decentralization** refers to the extent to which actual policymaking power lies with the central or regional governments in a country. Most political scientists see decentralization as a revenue issue: the greater the share of all tax revenues going to the central government, the less decentralized the state.

Determining the extent to which a state is centralized or decentralized can be quite dif-
ficult. You might think that we need only look at what a state's constitution has to say about the division of power between different levels of government. This, however, can be problematic for several reasons. Consider unitary states. In almost all unitary states, policymak-
ing authority constitutionally resides with the central government. Still, as indicated in Box 15.1, "Devolution versus Federalism," significant amounts of policymaking power can be devolved to regional governments in unitary countries. In other words, subnational governments can play an important policymaking role even when they derive no explicit authority to do so from the constitution.

Now consider federal states. Oftentimes, the constitution of a federal country will delin-
eate the specific policy realms in which the central or regional governments can act. Although this is somewhat informative, it is important to remember that having the *author-
ity to act* in a policy realm can be very different from having the practical *ability to act* in that area. Consider, for example, a country in which the regional governments have the authority to make health or education policy. Unless these regional governments also have the ability to raise their own tax revenue, they may find it difficult to actually implement policy in these areas. Put another way, regional governments in a federal state may have a much weaker role in the policymaking process than a reading of the state's constitution might suggest, because they do not have the financial wherewithal to implement their policy choices. The bottom line is that looking at a constitution, whether in a federal or unitary country, can be misleading if one wants to know the extent to which that country is centralized or decentralized in practice.

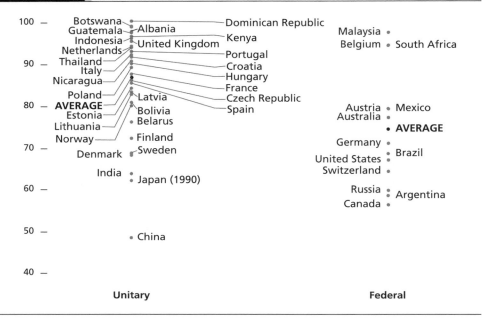

| FIGURE 15.1 | **Revenue Centralization: Central Government's Share of Tax Revenue** |

Source: Data are from Yusuf and the World Bank (1999, 216–217).

Note: With the exception of Japan, all data points are for 1997; Japan's data point is for 1990. Tax revenue that is legally mandated to be transferred to regional governments through a revenue-sharing scheme is treated as belonging to the regional governments even if it is first collected by the central government. The names of some unitary countries have been omitted for visual clarity.

In recognition of these difficulties, political scientists frequently use the percentage of all tax revenue that is collected by the central government as a measure of state centralization.[2] This is often referred to as "fiscal (de)centralization." The basic assumption underlying this measure is that governments need tax revenue in order to implement policies. Thus, the scope of policymaking activities at any one level of government will ultimately depend on the share of tax revenues that it collects. The higher the share of all tax revenues collected by the central government, the more centralized the state. The lower the share of all tax revenues collected by the central government, the more decentralized the state. In sum, although political scientists tend to see federalism as a constitutional issue, they tend to see decentralization as a budgetary one.

In Figure 15.1, we illustrate the share of tax revenue collected by the central government out of the total tax revenue collected by all levels of government for fifty-three

---

2. For a good discussion of various measures of federalism and decentralization, see Rodden (2004).

countries in 1997. Of these fifty-three countries, thirteen are federal and forty are unitary. As we might expect, the average degree of revenue centralization is lower in federal states (74.6 percent) than in unitary ones (87.95 percent). In other words, federalism and decentralization tend to go together. It should be noted, however, that there is a substantial amount of variation in revenue centralization in both unitary and federal countries (Arzaghi and Henderson 2005). For example, some unitary states (China, Denmark, Finland, India, Japan, Sweden) are more decentralized than the average federal state. Indeed, China, where the central government collects only 48.6 percent of the country's tax revenue, is the most decentralized state in the whole sample. Similarly, some federal states (Belgium, Malaysia, South Africa) are much more centralized than the average unitary state. Fully 97.6 percent of the tax revenue collected in federal Malaysia is collected by the central government.

To summarize, federalism can be distinguished along two dimensions: federalism in structure (federal versus unitary) and federalism in practice (decentralized versus centralized). Whereas federalism in structure is a dichotomy—a country is either federal or unitary—decentralization is best thought of as a continuum, with some states being more decentralized than others. In Figure 15.2, we simplify the world somewhat and show

FIGURE 15.2   Two Dimensions of Federalism

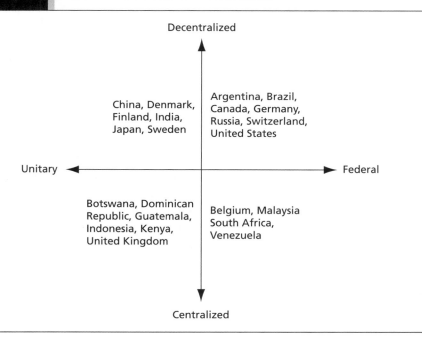

the names of various countries in a two-dimensional plot. Those countries in the top right quadrant, such as Brazil, Canada, and Germany, are federal both in structure and in practice. Those countries in the bottom left quadrant, such as Botswana, the Dominican Republic, and Kenya, are unitary both in structure and in practice. Those countries in the top left quadrant, such as China, India, and Sweden, are unitary in structure but federal in practice. Finally, those countries in the bottom right quadrant, such as Belgium, Malaysia, and Venezuela, are federal in structure but unitary in practice.

Why Federalism?

Why do some states adopt federal arrangements?[3] Political scientists often distinguish between "coming-together" federalism and "holding-together" federalism (Stepan 1999, 21–22). **Coming-together federalism** results from a bottom-up bargaining process in which previously sovereign polities come together and voluntarily agree to pool their resources in order to improve their collective security and achieve other, typically economic, goals, such as a common currency and increased trade (Riker 1964). Australia, Switzerland, and the United States are examples of coming-together federal states. Although there is some variation, coming-together federations are typically characterized by a symmetric form of federalism.

Coming-together federalism is the result of a bargaining process in which previously sovereign polities voluntarily agree to pool their resources in order to improve their collective security or achieve other economic goals. **Holding-together federalism** is the result of a process in which the central government chooses to decentralize its power to subnational governments in order to diffuse secessionist pressures.

In contrast, **holding-together federalism** is the result of a top-down process in which the central government of a polity chooses to decentralize its power to subnational governments. This process typically occurs in multiethnic states in which the central government fears that the continued existence of the state is threatened by one or more territorially based "ethnic" groups that wish to secede. In order to appease these secessionist groups and keep the country together, the central government decentralizes power to those subnational units in which the aggrieved ethnic group is dominant, thereby making the group more content to live within a unified state. For example, Belgium adopted federal arrangements in the 1990s to placate the demands of its different linguistic groups. Although they remain unitary states in their constitutional structure, India, Spain, and the United Kingdom are also examples of states that have engaged in "holding-together federalism"—they have all devolved significant policymaking power to regional governments in an attempt to defuse secessionist pressures. In general, holding-together federations are characterized by both incongruent and asymmetric federalism. These federations are incongruent because their whole reason for existing is to decentralize power to territorially based ethnic

---

3. In this section, we use the term *federalism* quite broadly to capture both dimensions of federalism—"federalism in structure" and "federalism in practice."

groups; they tend to be asymmetric because they are trying to satisfy the different needs and preferences of the various ethnic groups in the country.

Over the years, supporters of federalism have sought to highlight its advantages over other forms of government. For example, some scholars have argued that decentralized forms of government are best for satisfying popular preferences in democratic countries in which individuals hold heterogeneous preferences (Alesina and Spolaore 1997; Buchanan and Tullock 1962; Tiebout 1956; Tullock 1969). On the whole, it seems reasonable to expect that fewer citizens will be dissatisfied with public policy in a federal state than in a unitary one. Consider the following example. Suppose that sixty citizens in a unitary state prefer policy *A*, and forty citizens prefer policy *B*. In this situation, policy *A* will be adopted, and forty citizens will be unhappy. Suppose now that we have a federal state with two regions. Imagine that fifty citizens prefer policy *A* and ten prefer policy *B* in the first region, whereas thirty citizens prefer policy *B* and ten prefer policy *A* in the second region. In this scenario, policy *A* will be adopted in one region, and policy *B* will be adopted in another. Only twenty citizens will now be dissatisfied with government policy in our federal state. Obviously, if citizens are free to move from one region to another, then even greater citizen satisfaction can be achieved—citizens can simply "sort" themselves by moving to the region that best satisfies their policy preferences. As this example suggests, government policy is more likely to match citizen preferences in a federal state than in a unitary one. This is particularly the case in large countries in which individuals hold diverse policy preferences.

Another purported advantage of federalism is that it brings the "government" closer to the people. Some have claimed that this leads to an increase in the amount of information that is available to both citizens and governments (Hayek [1939] 1948; Oates 1972). By being closer to the people, subnational governments in federal systems should have better information about exactly what it is that their citizens want. This means that they will be able to tailor policies to the specific needs of their citizens. By being closer to the government, citizens in federal systems should have better information about exactly what it is that their government is doing. This means that they will be better placed to hold their government accountable. As a result, federalism is frequently linked to increased government accountability and responsiveness to citizen preferences (Lijphart 1999). By bringing the government closer to the people, federalism is also thought to encourage political participation and enhance perceived levels of legitimacy in the democratic process.

It is commonly claimed that subnational governments in federal systems have a strong incentive to perform well in office if citizens and investors have the ability to move from one region to another. This is because poor performance is expected to cause citizens and investors to move to better performing regions, taking their tax dollars and other assets with them. This is sometimes referred to as "voting with one's feet" (Tiebout 1956) and is a prime example of the power that comes from having an exit option (see Chapters 3 and 6). The competition between subnational governments for investment and citizens that is engendered by federalism is often expected to result in smaller, more efficient, and less corrupt government (Buchanan 1995). This competition is also at the heart of arguments suggesting that federalism enhances market economies and produces higher economic growth (Weingast 1995).[4]

Advocates of federalism also point to its ability to encourage policy experimentation and innovation. For example, subnational governments in federal systems have the opportunity to experiment with, and evaluate, different policies for tackling social, economic, and political problems. As US Supreme Court Justice Louis D. Brandeis put it in 1932, subnational governments in federal systems are "laboratories" for democracy and innovative government action. The ability to experiment with different policies is important because it means that policymakers can learn more quickly about which policies work and which ones do not. In effect, federalism allows subnational governments to quickly learn from the experimentation of others without putting the whole country at risk of a single failed policy.

Ever since Montesquieu expressed his views, numerous individuals have also promoted federalism as a bulwark against tyranny. For instance, many of the Founding Fathers in the United States believed that the interlocking arrangements of federalism reduced the risk of tyranny because the subnational governments could, and would, check each other. As James Madison put it, "A rage for paper money, for an abolition of debts, for an equal division of property, or for any improper or wicked project, will be less likely to pervade the whole body of the Union than a particular member of it" (Madison, 1787–1788, *The Federalist Papers,* No. 10). Alexander Hamilton also believed that the interlocking nature of federalism protected individual rights against abuse by authorities at both the national and the subnational level (Hamilton 1787). Others have argued that federalism also has the ability to protect territorially based groups whose preferences diverge from those of the majority population from being subject to majority decisions that run counter to their preferences (Horowitz 1985). As such, federalism can be thought to minimize citizen coercion.

Although federalism has many supporters, several scholars have questioned its purported benefits (Rose-Ackerman 2000). Rather than leading to a more efficient form of government as the proponents of federalism maintain, critics claim that the different layers of federalism can lead to the unnecessary duplication of government and the inefficient overlapping of potentially contradictory policies. Critics also argue that federalism exacerbates collective action problems in the formulation and implementation of economic and other politics,

---

4. The free movement of labor should not be taken for granted in federal systems, though. In the 1950s, China, a country that is highly federal in practice, introduced a household registration system (*hukou*) that classifies citizens as rural or urban and assigns them to a particular administrative unit. The goal of this registration system is to control and limit the free movement of citizens. From the start, urban citizens had access to more government services than did rural citizens. Migration to an urban area legally requires converting one's registration status from rural to urban, but this is difficult and rarely successful. Rural citizens who move to cities, referred to as "non-*hukou* migrants" in their new urban environment, cannot access government services such as health care, pensions, or education beyond middle school. The children of non-*hukou* migrants are also considered rural even if they are born in the city. According to one scholar, "the denial of local urban *hukou* to migrant workers, combined with their plentiful supply and lack of access to legal information and support, has created a large, easily exploitable, highly mobile, and flexible industrial workforce for China's export economy" (Chan 2010, 359).

particularly in developing countries. For example, Rodden and Wibbels (2002, 500) argue that "[f]ederalism empowers regional politicians who face incentives to undermine macro-economic management, market reforms, and other policies that have characteristics of national public goods. Self-interested regional elites do this either through autonomous policies made at the local level or through their [ability to block] the policy-making process at the center." Because provincial politicians ultimately care about their own political success, they face only weak incentives to make economic and other decisions in the interests of the federal system as a whole. For example, regional governments often block attempts at fiscal reform by the central government, particularly if these reforms are expected to be painful for their constituents. Regional governments also have incentives to spend beyond their means if there is an expectation that the central government will come to their rescue and bail them out. Evidence in support of this line of reasoning comes from several scholars who have found that federal systems are more prone to economic mismanagement than unitary systems (Rodden 2002, 2006; Treisman 2000; Wibbels 2000).

Although supporters of federalism regularly point to the benefits that accrue from having competition between different subnational governments, critics point to the possible deleterious consequences that such competition can have. For example, in attempting to attract investment and retain their citizens, competition between subnational governments may lead to "downward harmonization" or a "race to the bottom" in which levels of regulation, welfare, taxes, and trade barriers are continuously lowered (Hallerberg 1996). One consequence of downward harmonization is that it becomes difficult to implement local redistributive tax systems because the wealthy simply move to those regions with the lowest tax rates. Another potential consequence is increased poverty, with the poor migrating to those regions that still maintain some form of welfare protection; these regions will, in turn, be forced to lower their welfare protection as a result of the added fiscal strain of dealing with the arrival of poor immigrants from other regions.

Competition, particularly in asymmetric federations in which some regions enjoy more power and discretion than others, may also lead to the amplification of preexisting inequalities in population, wealth, and political power (Congleton 2006; Peterson 1995). If favored regional governments can take advantage of their additional authority to attract residents and enlarge their tax base, then they will likely prosper relative to other regional governments. The expectation of greater regional inequality is, in turn, likely to create conflict and political instability, with advantaged communities demanding increased autonomy and disadvantaged communities attempting to reverse asymmetries in the regional distribution of power.

Far from enhancing government accountability, as its supporters claim, critics argue that federalism is just as likely to undermine it. By adding layers of government and expanding areas of shared responsibility, federalism facilitates blame shifting and credit claiming (Rodden 2004, 494). This is because federalism can make it difficult for citizens to know which level of government is responsible for policy successes and which is to blame for policy failures. For example, if the regional economy performs poorly, is this the result of policies adopted by the subnational government or those implemented by the national government? In this type of situation, neither the subnational nor the national government will want to take responsibility for the poor economic performance and will likely try to blame the other. If federalism does lower government accountability, as critics maintain, it may actually increase, rather than reduce, levels of corruption (Rose-Ackerman 1978; Schleifer and Vishny 1993). Indeed, this is precisely what Treisman (2002) finds in a study examining the effect of decentralization on the quality of government. He concludes that countries with higher levels of decentralization have higher levels of corruption and lower levels of public goods provision.

BICAMERALISM

In addition to distinguishing states according to whether they are federal or unitary, political scientists sometimes distinguish them according to whether they have a unicameral or bicameral legislature.[5] Whereas a **unicameral legislature** is one in which legislative deliberations occur in a single assembly, a **bicameral legislature** is one in which legislative deliberations occur in two distinct assemblies (Tsebelis and Money 1997, 15). According to the Inter-Parliamentary Union (IPU 2016), 77 (39.9 percent) of the 193 independent states in existence as of 2016 have a bicameral legislature (http://www.ipu.org/english/home.htm).

> A **unicameral legislature** is one in which legislative deliberation occurs in a single assembly. A **bicameral legislature** is one in which legislative deliberation occurs in two distinct assemblies.

We should note from the beginning that whether a country has a unicameral or bicameral legislature does not affect the relationship between the legislature and the executive. Recall from Chapter 12 that governments depend on a legislative majority to exist in parliamentary and semi-presidential (though not presidential) democracies. In almost every non-presidential democracy, legislative responsibility refers exclusively to having a legislative majority in the popularly elected lower house.[6] As a result, there is no inherent conflict between bicameralism and the parliamentary form of government.

As we will see, though, having a second assembly can have a significant effect on a country's legislative process. This is fairly obvious when the upper chamber is powerful. In the United States, the House of Representatives and the Senate are equal partners in the legislative process. Both chambers have the power to veto bills proposed by the other chamber. The equal power of the two chambers in the United States opens up a range of strategic possibilities that are not always available to legislators in unicameral systems (Tsebelis and Money

---

5. Surprisingly little has been written on the causes and consequences of unicameral versus bicameral legislatures. Much of the information in this section comes from Tsebelis and Money (1997) and Lijphart (1999).

6. The two most notable exceptions to this are Italy and Germany. Article 94 of the Italian constitution requires that the government must retain the support of *both* Houses of Parliament—the Chamber of Deputies and the Senate—to stay in power. Article 81 of the German constitution allows a government that has lost a vote of confidence in the lower house (Bundestag) to retain power for six months if it continues to enjoy the support of a majority in the upper house (Bundesrat).

1997). For example, US legislators in one chamber can often get away with voting for a politically popular but ideologically unpalatable bill if they know that the other chamber is going to reject it. It is much harder for legislators in a unicameral legislature to engage in this type of position taking or credit claiming.

Bicameral systems can also have a significant impact on the legislative process even when the upper chamber is relatively weak, as in the United Kingdom. Ever since the Parliament Acts of 1911 and 1949, the lower house in the United Kingdom, the House of Commons, has had the power to make legislative decisions. The only real power that the upper house, the House of Lords, has in the legislative process is the ability to delay the passage of nonfinancial legislation for two parliamentary sessions or one calendar year. Although this power might seem relatively inconsequential, it can be very important in the year leading up to an election when delaying a bill may mean killing it. As Tsebelis and Money (1997, 2) point out, the ability to delay legislation in the year prior to an election has enabled the House of Lords to kill several pieces of significant legislation proposed by both Conservative and Labour governments.

Types of Bicameralism

Although 77 states had a bicameral legislature in 2016, there is a great deal of variation in the precise form that bicameralism takes in these countries. When it comes to distinguishing between different forms of bicameralism, political scientists frequently focus on whether a bicameral system is (a) congruent or incongruent and (b) symmetric or asymmetric (Lijphart 1999). Congruence and incongruence refer to the political composition of the two chambers, whereas symmetry and asymmetry refer to the relative power of the two chambers.

Congruent and Incongruent Bicameralism

Congruent bicameralism occurs when the two chambers have a similar political composition, whereas **incongruent bicameralism** occurs when they have a different political composition. Whether bicameralism is congruent or incongruent depends on how the two chambers are elected and whom they are supposed to represent. If the same methods are used to elect the members of each legislative chamber and both chambers represent the same set of citizens, then the political composition of each chamber will be congruent. When this is the case, the policy preferences of the two chambers will be identical or, at least, very similar.

> **Congruent bicameralism** occurs when the two legislative chambers have a similar political composition. **Incongruent bicameralism** occurs when the two legislative chambers differ in their political composition. The level of congruence depends on how the membership of the two chambers is selected and whom that membership is supposed to represent.

When it comes to electing bicameral legislatures, it is almost always the case that members of the lower chamber are directly elected through systems in which all eligible voters are given equal weight. This is not necessarily the case with members of the upper chamber, though. Members of the upper chamber usually owe their position to heredity, political appointment, indirect elections, or direct elections (Tsebelis and Money 1997). Historically, it was quite common for monarchs to grant seats in the upper chamber to members of the aristocracy, which would be passed down from generation to generation. Since the 1999 House of Lords Act in the United Kingdom, though, which significantly reduced the number of hereditary positions in the upper chamber, there are no longer any contemporary bicameral systems that use heredity as the predominant means for selecting members of the upper chamber.

Appointment is a common method for selecting members to an upper chamber. A whole host of countries such as Belize, Germany, Ireland, Jordan, Madagascar, Russia, and Thailand have fully or partially appointed upper chambers. Although a monarch appoints the members of the upper chamber in a few countries (Jordan, Malaysia, Thailand), it is much more common for an elected government to make these appointments. Germany is somewhat unusual in that the members of the upper chamber are appointed by regional governments. In almost every other case, it is the national government that appoints individuals to serve in the upper chamber. One of the rationales behind appointing, rather than electing, members of the upper chamber is that it facilitates the selection of individuals who have particular skills, knowledge, or experience that might be useful when debating particular pieces of legislation.

Like hereditary methods, though, appointing individuals to an upper chamber is often perceived as undemocratic. As a result, many countries allow their citizens to *indirectly* or *directly* elect the members of the upper chamber. Austria, France, India, Madagascar, Mauritania, the Netherlands, and Swaziland, for example, all employ indirect elections. In most of these countries, citizens directly elect the members of local or regional governments, and it is these local or regional representatives who elect the members of the upper chamber. Many more countries allow their citizens to directly elect individuals to the upper chamber. This is the case in countries such as Argentina, Australia, Bolivia, Brazil, Chile, Colombia, Japan, Malaysia, Mexico, Norway, Poland, Romania, the United States, and Venezuela. Some countries such as Spain employ a mix of both indirect and direct elections. In 2016, the Spanish Senate comprised

Japan's opposition Democratic Party leader Katsuya Okada shakes hands with a voter on the last day of campaigning for the July 2016 upper house election.

266 members, of whom 208 were directly elected by popular vote and 58 were appointed by regional legislatures.

Whether a bicameral legislature is congruent or not depends not only on whether the members of the two chambers are selected in the same way but also on whether they represent the same set of citizens. In almost all countries, the members of the lower legislative chamber are supposed to represent all citizens equally under the general principle of "one person, one vote." In a few countries such as Italy and Japan this is also the case for members of the upper chamber. In these countries, the political composition of the upper house tends to mimic that of the lower house. On the whole, though, this type of situation is quite rare. In the vast majority of bicameral systems, the upper chamber is not designed to represent the entire population equally. For example, the Irish Senate provides representation for certain professional occupations—most Irish senators are elected by five vocational panels representing culture and education, labor, industry and commerce, agriculture, and administration. In other countries, the upper chamber is supposed to ensure that minorities (Venezuela) or linguistic communities (Belgium) are represented.

By far the most common role for the upper chamber in a bicameral system is to represent the citizens of subnational geographic units. Although this is always the case in federal systems, such as Austria, Germany, Mexico, Switzerland, and the United States, it is also the case in some unitary countries, such as Bolivia, the Netherlands, and Spain. The fact that citizens are not distributed equally across different subnational geographic units often leads to **malapportionment** in territorially based upper chambers, with the result that some citizens receive significantly more representation than others (Monroe 1994; Samuels and Snyder 2001). This is easily seen in countries such as Australia,

> **Malapportionment** occurs when the distribution of political representation between constituencies is not based on the size of each constituency's population. In a malapportioned system, the votes of some citizens weigh more than the votes of others.

Switzerland, Venezuela, and the United States, where the different geographic units all receive the same level of representation irrespective of how many residents they have. For example, each of the fifty US states is represented by two senators. This means that California, with its 38 million residents, receives the same level of representation in the US Senate as Wyoming, with its approximately 0.6 million residents. Other countries, such as Canada and Germany, do not give equal representation to each of their subnational regions but still tend to overrepresent less populous regions and underrepresent more populous ones. Austria is unusual in that the allocation of upper chamber representatives to each subnational unit is roughly proportional to the size of each unit's population.

To get a better idea of the level of malapportionment found in upper chambers that are designed to represent subnational geographic units, consider Table 15.2. Here we illustrate the percentage of seats in the upper chamber going to the most favorably represented citizens in nine countries in 1996 (Lijphart 1999, 208). To see where these numbers come from, imagine that all of the subnational units in a country are lined up from left to right based on the size of their populations, with smaller units to the left and larger units to the right. Starting with

TABLE 15.2	**Malapportionment in Upper Chambers, 1996**			
	Seats held by the percentages of the most favorably represented citizens (percentages)			
	10	**20**	**30**	**50**
United States	39.7	55.0	67.7	83.8
Switzerland	38.4	53.2	64.7	80.6
Venezuela	31.6	47.2	60.0	77.5
Australia	28.7	47.8	58.7	74.0
Canada	33.4	46.3	55.6	71.3
Germany	24.0	41.7	54.3	72.6
India	15.4	26.9	37.4	56.8
Austria	11.9	22.5	32.8	52.9
Belgium	10.8	20.9	31.0	50.9

Source: Data are from Lijphart (1999, 208).

the smallest unit and working our way to the right, we identify those units that together comprise 10 percent, 20 percent, 30 percent, and 50 percent of the country's overall population. We then determine the percentage of upper chamber seats that are allocated to these regions. These are the percentages shown in Table 15.2. As an example, consider the case of the United States. Table 15.2 indicates that the smallest states that together comprise 10 percent of the national population control 39.7 percent of the seats in the US Senate. In other words, these states receive almost four times the amount of representation in the Senate as their population sizes would imply they should. The smallest states, which together constitute 20 percent of the overall US population, control 55 percent of the Senate seats—an overall majority. The other percentages in Table 15.2 can be interpreted in a similar way. As you can see, there is a great deal of variation in the level of malapportionment seen in upper chambers around the world. Countries like the United States and Switzerland exhibit very high levels of malapportionment, whereas countries like Austria and Belgium exhibit low levels.

In sum, the degree of congruence in a bicameral system depends on whether the two legislative chambers employ similar methods for selecting their members and on whether the two chambers represent the same set of citizens. On the whole, congruent bicameralism is relatively rare (Lijphart 1999).

Symmetric and Asymmetric Bicameralism

Symmetric bicameralism occurs when the two legislative chambers have equal or near equal constitutional power (Lijphart 1999, 206). Total symmetry exists when the agreement of both chambers is needed to enact a law. In practice, symmetric bicameralism is extremely rare. Countries in which the upper chamber has formally equal powers with the lower chamber include Colombia, Italy, Switzerland, and the United States. Countries in which the two chambers enjoy similar, but not quite equal, power include Australia, Germany, Japan, and the Netherlands. **Asymmetric bicameralism** is much more common and occurs when the two legislative chambers have unequal constitutional power. Total asymmetry exists when one chamber is granted ultimate decision-making power. In all cases of asymmetric bicameralism, it is the lower house that has more power.

> **Symmetric bicameralism** occurs when the two legislative chambers have equal or near equal constitutional power. **Asymmetric bicameralism** occurs when the two legislative chambers have unequal constitutional powers.

To a large extent, the degree of symmetry in the powers of the two chambers is related to how the members of the upper chamber are selected. Upper chambers are much more likely to have coequal power with the lower house when citizens play a direct role in electing upper chamber representatives (Mastias and Grangé 1987). This is likely due to the increased democratic legitimacy that these upper chambers are perceived to have from being directly (or indirectly) elected as opposed to appointed. Of the four countries we just mentioned in which the upper chamber enjoys formally equal power with the lower chamber, Colombia, Italy, and the United States all have directly elected upper chambers; most of the members of the Swiss upper chamber are also popularly elected.

Overview

To summarize, it is possible to distinguish bicameral systems based on their level of congruence and symmetry. In Figure 15.3, we simplify the world somewhat and plot the names of various countries along these two dimensions. Countries such as those in the upper right quadrant—Australia, Germany, Switzerland, and the United States—exhibit a strong form of bicameralism. In a strong bicameral system, the upper house is likely to be an important political actor because it enjoys similar constitutional powers to the lower house (symmetric) and because the different political composition of the upper chamber (incongruent) tends to mean that it has different policy preferences to the lower chamber. Countries such as those in the lower left quadrant—Austria, the Bahamas, and Jamaica—exhibit what might be thought of as an insignificant form of bicameralism. In an insignificant bicameral system, the upper chamber is unlikely to be an important political actor because its constitutional powers are extremely weak (asymmetric) and because its political composition tends to mirror that of the lower chamber (congruent).

Countries in the upper left and lower right quadrants exhibit a weak form of bicameralism. In weak bicameral systems, the upper chamber is likely to be a weak political actor. Although such countries as those in the upper left quadrant—Italy and Japan—have a powerful upper chamber (symmetric), the upper chamber is not expected to significantly affect the policymaking process given its political makeup, which is similar to that in the lower chamber (congruent). Similarly, although such countries as those in the lower right quadrant—Canada, France, India, and the United Kingdom—have an upper chamber that is

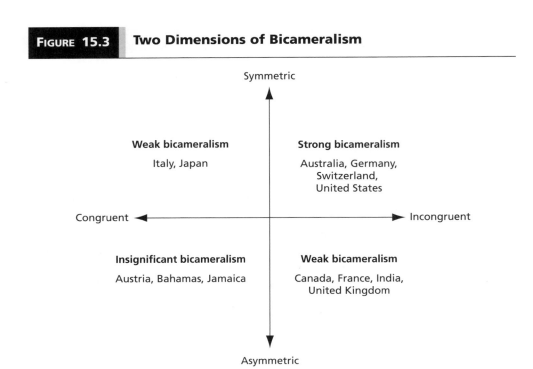

FIGURE 15.3 | **Two Dimensions of Bicameralism**

Symmetric

Weak bicameralism
Italy, Japan

Strong bicameralism
Australia, Germany,
Switzerland,
United States

Congruent ◄─────────────────────► Incongruent

Insignificant bicameralism
Austria, Bahamas, Jamaica

Weak bicameralism
Canada, France, India,
United Kingdom

Asymmetric

Source: Based on information in Lijphart (1999, 212).

likely to conflict with the lower chamber as a result of its differing political composition (incongruent), the upper chamber is not expected to play a significant role in the policymaking process because its constitutional powers are weak (asymmetric).

Why Bicameralism?

As Tsebelis and Money (1997, 17) explain, the origins of bicameralism can be traced back to ancient Greece. Rather than a "simple government" in which the interests of only one social class—the one (monarchy), the few (aristocracy), or the many (people)—would be represented, many Greek philosophers, such as Aristotle and Plato, preferred a "mixed government" that would represent all social classes. In practice, mixed governments in ancient Greece saw the aristocracy and the people represented in separate adviser-legislative councils. One of the purported benefits of a mixed government was that it would maintain a balance of power in which no single social class could gain control of the state for itself. By the eighteenth century, most people had come to see the Greek notion of mixed government as entailing a bicameral legislature in which the aristocracy would deliberate in one chamber and the common people in another. A class-based bicameral legislature, along with a monarch as the executive, was seen as an efficient system of checks and balances that helped ensure political stability.

At the end of the eighteenth century, the legitimacy of class-based bicameral legislatures was challenged by the rise of republicanism and the belief that the people should be represented as a whole rather than as a set of competing social classes. In this new environment, bicameralism increasingly came to be associated with federal states that used the upper chamber to guarantee the representation of their constituent territorial units. This new view of bicameralism was first seen in the United States where the "Great Compromise" of 1787 led to the creation of a House of Representatives that was elected on the basis of a state's population and a Senate that granted equal representation to each state. Essentially, the House of Representatives was to represent the popular dimension of the people's will, whereas the Senate was to represent its territorial dimension. This particular form of "incongruent bicameralism" was justified on the grounds that the different territorial units were likely to have distinct needs from the population as a whole. To fully protect the specific needs of the states and federalism as a whole, the Founding Fathers in the United States promoted a symmetric form of bicameralism in which the agreement of both legislative chambers was needed to change the status quo. The distinct interests of constituent territorial units eventually came to replace the differing interests of social classes as the justification for powerful upper chambers (Tsebelis and Money 1997). It is perhaps no surprise then that all of the examples of "strong"—symmetric and incongruent—bicameral systems illustrated in Figure 15.3 are in federal countries.

Strong bicameral systems like the ones that emerged in the United States and Switzerland were harder to justify in unitary countries with no constituent territorial units to represent. Some unitary countries with bicameral systems chose to reduce the power of their upper chambers. For example, the 1911 and 1949 Parliament Acts in the United Kingdom asserted the legislative supremacy of the House of Commons and limited the maximum amount of time that the House of Lords could delay legislation to one year. A much more recent example concerns Italy. As of writing this chapter, debates are ongoing about reducing the power of the Italian Senate by shrinking its size, removing the Senate's ability to veto legislation from the lower house, and eliminating the requirement that Italian governments enjoy the support of a legislative majority in the Senate (Damiani 2015).

Why keep these weak upper chambers in unitary states rather than just get rid of them? One argument is that members of the upper chamber have characteristics of value, such as wisdom, age, and training, that are often absent among members of the popularly elected lower chamber. Another argument is that the upper chamber's ability to delay legislation can help prevent the production of "bad" laws that are made in haste. In effect, the argument for keeping weak upper chambers in unitary countries rests on the belief that they improve the overall quality of legislation. This line of reasoning obviously requires that the political composition of the upper chamber be different from that of the lower chamber. In many countries, bicameral incongruence is achieved by having an appointed upper chamber in which members are selected on the basis of some special skill, expertise, or experience. This might involve appointing, say, teachers, engineers, scientists, businesspeople, farmers, or religious leaders. An implicit assumption is that individuals such as these may not be elected in sufficient numbers or on a regular enough basis in the popular elections to the lower chamber and must therefore be appointed to the upper chamber.

Whereas some unitary countries, like the United Kingdom, responded to the spread of democratic values by establishing asymmetric, but still incongruent, forms of bicameralism, a few, like Denmark and Sweden, responded by trying to "democratize" the selection procedures used in the upper chamber. This typically involved adopting a similar selection procedure for the upper chamber to the one employed in the popularly elected lower chamber. The result, as one would expect, was that the political composition of the upper chamber in these countries came to increasingly mirror that of the lower chamber. In many places, this congruence between the upper and lower chambers raised questions as to the actual utility of having an upper chamber. As Tsebelis and Money (1997, 35) point out, the general thrust of these questions is best summed up in the famous words of the seventeenth-century philosopher Abbé Sieyès: "If the second chamber agrees with the first, it is useless, and if not, it is bad." Like several other countries that initially decided to establish congruent upper chambers, Denmark (in 1953) and Sweden (in 1959) eventually resolved the debate over the utility of the upper chamber by abolishing it and establishing a unicameral legislature.

Contemporary debates over bicameralism largely mirror those that have driven the evolution and justification of bicameral systems in the past. In effect, there are two basic arguments in favor of bicameralism. In federal countries, bicameralism is primarily defended as an institutional means for protecting the federal system and promoting the distinct preferences of different territorial units. In unitary countries, bicameralism is primarily defended as an institutional means for improving the quality of legislation.

CONSTITUTIONALISM

Political scientists also distinguish between states based on the extent to which they accept **constitutionalism**. Constitutionalism refers to a commitment to be governed by a set of overarching rules and principles that are laid out in a constitution (Stone Sweet 2000, 20). A central part of any commitment to constitutionalism is the establishment of a set of institutions and procedures to protect constitutional rules and principles. These institutions and procedures are known as **systems of constitutional justice** (Stone Sweet 2008). Historically, few countries have had any system of constitutional justice. Until relatively recently, most countries have followed a norm of legislative supremacy. According to this norm, the laws created by the people's elected representatives in the legislature should not be constrained by other

> **Constitutionalism** refers to a commitment to be governed by a set of authoritative rules and principles that are laid out in a constitution. A **system of constitutional justice** comprises the set of institutions and procedures that are established to protect constitutional rules and principles.

authorities, including the constitution. Looking around the world today, though, we see that the norm of legislative supremacy has been replaced by what Shapiro and Stone Sweet (1994) call a "new constitutionalism." This new constitutionalism describes a situation in which virtually all countries now have constitutions containing a charter of human rights that is protected by institutions such as constitutional courts. These institutions can use the power of constitutional review to invalidate legislation that is deemed to violate individual rights and can thereby constrain legislative authority.

Although there has been a general shift toward this new constitutionalism since 1945, there is considerable variation in the extent to which states have delegated constitutional control over their actions to judges. In this section we briefly describe the historical shift from a norm of legislative supremacy to a situation in which most states now agree to live within the constraints imposed by a constitution. This shift toward a new constitutionalism has increasingly involved judges in the legislative process, leading some to worry about "activist judges" and a possible "government of judges." Following this, we outline some of the distinctive features of the different systems of constitutional justice that have been adopted around the world. As we will see, there are two basic systems of constitutional justice—the American model and the European model.

The Shift to a New Constitutionalism

A **constitution**, in a very general sense, provides the formal source of state authority. For example, a constitution establishes governmental institutions, such as legislatures, executives, and courts, and then gives these institutions the power to make, enforce, and interpret laws. Recent constitutions, such as those adopted in the last seventy years or so, also tend to contain a list of guaranteed rights that are protected by some kind of constitutional body. This list of rights, and the constitutional body protecting them, places substantive constraints on what governments can and cannot do.

> A **constitution** provides the formal source of state authority. In addition to establishing the structure, procedures, powers, and duties of governmental institutions, more recent constitutions also contain a list of guaranteed rights.

Almost all current constitutions are **codified constitutions** in that they are written in a single document. An **uncodified constitution** is one that has several sources, which may be written or unwritten. As of 2016, only three countries—Israel, New Zealand, and the United Kingdom—had uncodified constitutions. Some of the United Kingdom's uncodified constitution is written and some of it is not. The written part includes constitutional statutes passed by the legislature, such as the 1998 Scotland Act and the 1998 Human Rights Act, whereas the unwritten part includes things like constitutional conventions, royal prerogatives, customs and traditions, and observations of precedents.

> A **codified constitution** is one that is written in a single document. An **uncodified constitution** is one that has several sources, which may be written or unwritten.

In addition to whether constitutions are codified or not, constitutions also differ in regard to whether they are entrenched or not. An **entrenched constitution** can be modified only through a procedure of constitutional amendment. Constitutional amendments require more than the approval of a legislative majority. Exactly what is required to pass a constitutional amendment varies from country to country. In federal systems, for example, it is often the case that constitutional amendments require the support of a majority of the regional legislatures. Some countries require a popular referendum. Australia and Switzerland both require that a successful amendment win not only a majority of votes nationwide in a popular referendum but also a majority of the votes in every state or canton. Other countries require legislative supermajorities. Successful amendments in Japan must obtain a two-thirds supermajority in both legislative chambers and a majority in a popular referendum (Article 96, Japanese Constitution). By requiring a special constitutional amendment procedure to be modified, entrenched constitutions recognize that constitutional law has a higher legal status than ordinary statute law. **Unentrenched constitutions** have no special amendment procedures—they can be modified at any point in time by a simple legislative majority just like any other law. As a result, it makes no sense to talk of constitutional amendments in countries like the United Kingdom that have unentrenched constitutions. By their very nature, unentrenched constitutions do not recognize that constitutions have a higher or different legal status from ordinary statutes. Almost all contemporary constitutions are entrenched.

> An **entrenched constitution** can be modified only through a special procedure of constitutional amendment. An **unentrenched constitution** has no special amendment procedure and can be modified at any point in time with the support of a legislative majority.
>
> A **legislative supremacy constitution** has no constitutional review, has no bill of rights, and is not entrenched. A **higher law constitution** has constitutional review, has a bill of rights, and is entrenched.

Historically, we can identify two ideal types of constitutions: the **legislative supremacy constitution** and the **higher law constitution**.

Legislative Supremacy Constitution

The core principle behind legislative supremacy constitutions is that "elections legitimize legislative authority, and legislative majorities legitimize statutory authority" (Stone Sweet 2000, 20). According to legislative supremacy constitutions, legislatures can do no legal wrong as they derive their legitimacy from being elected by the people. Legislative supremacy constitutions have three basic features. One is that they are not entrenched and can be revised at the discretion of the legislature. Legislative supremacy constitutions have no special legal status and are the same as ordinary laws in that they can be modified or replaced without recourse to special amendment procedures. The second distinctive feature is that there is no institution with the power to review the constitutional legality of statutes. The authority to make law resides only with the legislature. As a result, statutes cannot be challenged once they are promulgated, and they can be replaced or modified only if the legislature passes a new statute. Any perceived conflict between a statute and some constitutional rule or principle must be resolved in favor of the statute. The third distinctive feature of legislative supremacy constitutions is that they do not contain a bill of rights that might constrain legislative authority. The rights that are protected in countries with legislative supremacy constitutions have their source in the ordinary statutes passed by the legislature, not in the constitution. The constitutions of the United Kingdom and New Zealand are examples of legislative supremacy constitutions.

Higher Law Constitution

According to higher law constitutions, the state *can* do legal wrong and must therefore be constrained in what it can and cannot do. The notion of legislative supremacy is rejected. Higher law constitutions typically contain a bill of rights that allows nonstate actors to challenge state actions that violate individual and minority rights. They also establish a mechanism—**constitutional review**—for defending the supremacy of the constitution and the rights that it contains. Constitutional review is the authority of an institution to invalidate acts of government, such as legislation, administrative decisions, and judicial rulings that violate constitutional rules (Stone Sweet 2000, 21). As we will see, constitutional review can be exercised by judges sitting on special tribunals—constitutional courts—that are not part of the regular judicial system, as in most European countries, or by ordinary judges in the regular judicial system, as in the United States. When constitutional review is conducted by ordinary judges from the regular judicial system, it is more commonly referred to as **judicial review**. By allowing constitutional review, higher law constitutions signal that constitutional laws are superior to "ordinary" laws passed by the legislature. In recognition of the special status of constitutional law, higher law constitutions are entrenched and stipulate special amendment procedures for modifying constitutional provisions. The differences between legislative supremacy constitutions and higher law constitutions are summarized in Table 15.3.

> **Constitutional review** is the authority of an institution to invalidate legislation, administrative decisions, judicial rulings, and other acts of government that violate constitutional rules and rights. When constitutional review is conducted by ordinary judges from the regular judicial system, it is more commonly referred to as **judicial review**.

Table 15.3	Legislative Supremacy Constitution versus Higher Law Constitution	
Characteristic	**Legislative supremacy**	**Higher law**
Entrenched	No	Yes
Constitutional review	No	Yes
Bill of rights	No	Yes

The New Constitutionalism

Legislative supremacy constitutions were historically quite common but are relatively rare now. Virtually all new constitutions—both democratic and authoritarian—are higher law constitutions that establish constitutional review and include an extensive list of political and social rights. For example, all 106 constitutions that were adopted between 1985 and 2007 contained a bill of rights, and only 5—Iraq (1990), Laos, North Korea, Saudi Arabia, and Vietnam—failed to establish provisions for constitutional review (Stone Sweet 2008, 233–234). As we noted earlier, this convergence around the idea that higher law constitutions are somehow better than legislative supremacy constitutions has been called the **new constitutionalism** (Shapiro and Stone 1994). But why did this shift to the new constitutionalism happen?

> The **new constitutionalism** describes a situation in which almost all countries now have an entrenched constitution, a bill of rights, and a procedure of constitutional review to protect rights.

The shift toward this new constitutionalism began in Europe after 1945 with the creation of constitutional courts in Austria (1945), Italy (1948), and West Germany (1949). The adoption of higher law constitutions in these countries was partly a response to the experience with fascism in the interwar period (Stone Sweet 2000, 37). The experience of fascist governments in Italy and Germany clearly illustrated that states could do considerable wrong and that individuals sometimes needed protection from the state. In effect, Europe's experience with fascism undermined much of Europe's faith in a powerful and unconstrained state and highlighted the need to protect individual and minority rights. To a large extent, the subsequent adoption of higher law constitutions in other countries has coincided with democratic transitions. For example, both Portugal (1976) and Spain (1978) adopted constitutional courts following their democratic transitions in the 1970s. Central and eastern European countries, such as the Czech Republic, Hungary, Poland, Romania, Russia, Slovakia, the Baltic states, and the states of the former Yugoslavia, adopted constitutional courts following the collapse of Communist rule in 1989 (Ludwikowski 1996; Schwartz 1999). The strengthening of constitutional courts in Latin America and Asia during the 1980s and 1990s has also been seen as part of a concerted effort to consolidate democracy in these regions of the world (Ginsburg 2003; Helmke 2002; Navia and Ríos-Figueroa 2005). In all of these cases, the adoption of higher law constitutions can, in part, be viewed as an attempt to prevent a repetition of the individual abuses inflicted by the state in the recent past (see Box 15.2 for a discussion of judicial power).

Different Systems of Constitutional Justice

That higher law constitutions have increasingly been adopted around the world in the last seventy years does not mean that countries have embraced the exact same system of constitutional justice. Systems of constitutional justice vary along many different dimensions (Epstein, Knight, and Shvetsova 2001; Murphy, Pritchett, and Epstein 2001). In what follows, we focus on three aspects of constitutional review: (a) the type of constitutional review, (b) the timing of constitutional review, and (c) the jurisdiction of constitutional review.

> **Abstract constitutional review** involves the constitutional review of legislation in the absence of a concrete legal case. **Concrete constitutional review** involves the constitutional review of legislation with respect to a specific legal case.

The two basic types of constitutional review are **abstract constitutional review** and **concrete constitutional review**. Abstract review is "abstract" in that it involves the constitutional review of legislation in the absence of a concrete legal case. In contrast, concrete review is "concrete" in that it involves the constitutional

Box 15.2   JUDICIAL POWER AND THE JUDICIALIZATION OF POLITICS

The spread of constitutional review around the world has raised fears about the power of constitutional judges and the possible judicialization of politics. This raises the question of exactly how powerful courts really are in practice. Here we outline what we mean by judicial power and examine the conditions under which courts can effectively influence policy outcomes.

Traditionally, there have been two main approaches to understanding judicial power. One approach looks at the formal, or de jure, powers given to courts. Under this notion of judicial power, a court is powerful whenever it is granted significant legal authority. One obvious problem with this approach is that it does not take into account whether courts use their legal authority or whether their decisions are actually implemented. As several political scientists have pointed out, there is ample empirical evidence of courts that appear to be powerful on paper being ignored (Staton 2004). For example, local governments in the United States and Germany have refused to implement various constitutional decisions relating to equal protection and religious establishment (G. Rosenberg 1991; Vanberg 2005). There is also plenty of evidence to suggest that courts strategically try to avoid conflict by not making decisions that they know will be opposed by the other branches of government (Clinton 1994; Epstein and Knight 1998a; Volcansek 1991).

The problem with simply looking at judicial power in terms of the jurisdiction that courts are granted on paper has led most political scientists to focus on the de facto power of courts. In other words, they focus on whether courts have the power to change policy outcomes in practice, not in theory. In this sense, political scientists define judicial power as the ability of courts to bring about policy outcomes that they prefer (Cameron 2002). This definition, along with empirical evidence that courts act strategically, necessarily implies that courts are not always the impartial interpreters of laws that legal scholars and judges frequently claim them to be. Just like other political actors, judges have their own policy preferences that influence how they make legal decisions.

Judges are constrained in their ability to make legal decisions in line with their own preferences. The central difficulty faced by all courts is that they are inherently weak institutions that must rely on others to implement and enforce their decisions. As you might expect, this "implementation problem" can be particularly constraining when courts are required to make decisions against the very actors on whom they rely to implement their decisions (Vanberg 2001). It is the existence of this implementation problem that drives the strategic behavior of courts. Given their inability to independently enforce their decisions, it is hardly surprising that judges sometimes rule that constitutionally suspect policies are constitutional in order to avoid conflict with elected officials (Carrubba 2005; Epstein and Knight 1998b; Helmke 2005; Ramseyer and Rasmusen 2003; Rogers 2001).

The fundamental insight from the "implementation problem" and strategic models of judicial politics would seem to be that judicial power is inherently constrained. However, we do sometimes see courts acting powerfully. What explains this? Why is it that courts can act powerfully in some situations but not others?

Two conditions need to be met for courts to exert judicial power (Vanberg 2001, 2005). The first condition is that courts must enjoy public support. If courts enjoy public support and, hence, high levels of legitimacy, then elected officials can expect to suffer a negative electoral backlash if they do not comply with court decisions (Gibson and Caldeira 1992; Gibson, Caldeira, and Baird 1998). The fear of such a backlash creates a powerful incentive for legislative majorities to respect judicial decisions (Vanberg 2000). Of course, this "electoral connection" mechanism works only if voters know about court decisions and can identify noncompliance by elected officials. Thus, the second condition needed for a court to exert judicial power is that voters be able to monitor legislative responses to judicial rulings. At a minimum, this requires that court decisions be transparent and available to the public. Without this information, voters cannot hold elected representatives accountable for noncompliance.

These conditions for exercising judicial power create strong incentives for courts to act strategically when publicizing their decisions (Staton 2006, 2010). Courts can expect to gain public support and legitimacy by publicizing their work if their decisions show them to be impartial interpreters of the constitution. We have already seen, however, that judges sometimes act politically and seek to impose their own personal preferences on the legislative process. It is likely that publicizing these types of decisions will not increase public support for the judicial system. As a result, courts will have a strong incentive to publicize only some of their decisions—the impartial-looking ones.

That constitutional judges regularly engage in public relations exercises suggests that they are well aware of the role that public support plays in their ability to assert judicial power. For example, virtually all constitutional courts throughout the world maintain a website on which they provide information on pending and completed cases, descriptions of their jurisdiction, and biographical summaries of their membership. Constitutional judges also give university lectures and media interviews to publicize their decisions and explain their legal reasoning (Staton 2010). Although this type of behavior is to be expected of legislative representatives, who can be held electorally accountable, it is sometimes seen as puzzling as to why unelected and unaccountable constitutional judges would engage in these types of public relations activities. This kind of behavior becomes understandable, though, once we recognize that public support is necessary for courts to exert judicial power.

review of legislation with respect to a specific case before the court. These two types of constitutional review are not mutually exclusive in that countries can allow both types of review.

Constitutional review can take place at two points in time during the legislative process. If constitutional review occurs before a law is formally enacted, then it is referred to as **a priori constitutional review**. If constitutional review occurs after a law is formally enacted, then we speak of **a posteriori constitutional review**. Again, a priori and a posteriori reviews are not mutually exclusive in that countries can allow constitutional review to take place both before and after a law is enacted.

A priori constitutional review occurs before a law is formally enacted, whereas **a posteriori constitutional review** occurs only after a law is formally enacted.

The jurisdiction of constitutional review can be centralized or decentralized. **Centralized constitutional review** refers to a situation in which only one court is responsible for conducting constitutional review. This single court, called a constitutional court, exists entirely outside of the normal judicial system. It considers only constitutional disputes and does not get involved in normal litigation. As such, we might want to think of it more as a special tribunal than a court. **Decentralized constitutional review** refers to a situation in which more than one court can interpret the constitution and declare laws, decrees, and administrative decisions to be unconstitutional. These courts and the judges that sit on them are part of the regular judicial system. The highest court in a decentralized jurisdiction system, typically called a Supreme Court, has general jurisdiction in that it can settle all legal disputes and not just constitutional ones.

> **Centralized constitutional review** refers to a situation in which only one court can conduct constitutional review. **Decentralized constitutional review** refers to a situation in which more than one court can interpret the constitution.

Although it is possible to distinguish between different systems of constitutional justice, most political scientists focus on the distinction between centralized and decentralized systems. They refer to decentralized systems as the American model of constitutional justice and to centralized systems as the European model of constitutional justice.

The American Model

In the United States, "any judge of any court, in any case, at any time, at the behest of any litigating party, has the power to declare a law unconstitutional" (Shapiro and Stone Sweet 1994, 400). As this quotation makes clear, constitutional review in the United States is decentralized and carried out by ordinary judges in the regular judicial system. Constitutional review in the United States is, as a result, judicial review. The American separation-of-powers system, in which the executive, legislature, and judiciary are separate but equal branches of government, attempts to mark a clear distinction between what we can think of as the "judicial function"—resolving legal cases—and the "political function"—legislating. American courts are supposed to avoid legislating as that is the function of the people's elected representatives in the legislature. Still, it is recognized that a constitutional issue that needs resolving might arise in the course of a legal case. It is for this reason that ordinary judges in the United States have the right to conduct concrete a posteriori constitutional review—they need it to do their prescribed job. Courts in the American model are prohibited, though, from engaging in abstract review or giving advisory opinions on the constitutionality of legislative bills because this is not part of their job and would be usurping the rightful role of the legislature.

The European Model

The judiciary has traditionally been seen as subordinate to the legislature in Europe. In other words, the judiciary has never been seen as a coequal branch of the government as it is in the United States. Indeed, judicial review has been explicitly prohibited in French and German constitutions since the end of the eighteenth century. This view of the judiciary helps to explain why American-style judicial review has faced so much hostility in much of Europe. From a European perspective, "American-style judicial review, rather than corresponding to a separation of powers, actually establishes a permanent confusion of powers, because it enables the judiciary to participate in the legislative function" (Stone Sweet 2000, 33). To avoid judicial review and a "government of judges" that might ensue, Europeans invented a completely new institution, the constitutional court, to conduct constitutional review.

Constitutional courts have several defining characteristics. First, they have a monopoly on conducting constitutional review. Ordinary courts cannot engage in constitutional review and cannot appeal any of the decisions made by a constitutional court. Second, constitutional courts are formally detached from the regular judicial system. A constitutional court is, therefore, not a "judicial" institution. These two defining characteristics mean that judicial review remains prohibited in the European model. Third, constitutional courts have jurisdiction only over constitutional matters. They cannot oversee judicial disputes or litigation as, say, the US Supreme Court can. Fourth, most constitutional courts can engage in abstract constitutional review. In other words, they can evaluate legislative initiatives to see if they are unconstitutional before they actually have the opportunity to harm anyone. This is the only type of constitutional review that is allowed in France. Many constitutional courts can also exercise concrete constitutional review. The main characteristics of the American and European models of constitutional justice are shown in Table 15.4.

TABLE 15.4	**American and European Models of Constitutional Justice**	
Characteristic	**American model**	**European model**
Jurisdiction: Who has the power to engage in constitutional review?	Decentralized; ordinary courts can engage in constitutional review.	Centralized; only a single constitutional court can engage in constitutional review; other courts are barred from doing so, although they may refer to the constitutional court.
Timing: When can constitutional review occur?	A posteriori	A priori or a posteriori or both; some courts have a priori review over treaties or government acts; others have both; and some have either but not both.
Type: Can constitutional review occur in the absence of a real case or controversy?	Concrete	Abstract and concrete; most constitutional courts can exercise review in the absence of a real case, and many can also exercise concrete review.

Source: Adapted from Navia and Ríos-Figueroa (2005, 192).

TABLE 15.5	**The Geographic Distribution of Different Models of Constitutional Justice, 2010**				
Region	American model	European model	Mixed	Other	None
Europe	5	33	3	1	2
Africa	13	28	1	7	2
Middle East	2	5	0	3	0
Asia and Southeast Asia	19	15	2	10	0
North America	2	0	0	0	0
Central America and South America	13	8	8	1	0
Total	54	89	14	22	4

Source: Data are from Dr. Arne Mavčič and are available at http://www.concourts.net.

Note: "Mixed" means some combination of the American and European models; "Other" means that the system of constitutional justice is unique or unclassifiable; "None" means that there are no mechanisms for constitutional review. Systems based on France are coded as European.

In Table 15.5, we illustrate the geographic distribution of the American and European models of constitutional justice around the world as of 2010. As you can see, the European model of constitutional justice is more popular than the American one, although there are clear regional differences. For example, the American model is predominant in Asia, North America, and Central and South America, whereas the European model is predominant everywhere else.

VETO PLAYERS

As we have noted in this chapter, political scientists sometimes distinguish between democracies by whether they are federal or unitary, bicameral or unicameral, and whether they accept constitutionalism or not. In effect, these political scientists see the world in terms of different institutional dichotomies. Recently, though, comparative scholars have begun to move away from this position and to recognize that these institutions are conceptually the same in that they all act as checks and balances on the political system. Put differently, they all affect the ease with which the political status quo in a country can be changed. This new approach to understanding political institutions is called **veto player theory** (Tsebelis 1995, 1999, 2002).

Veto player theory offers a way to think about political institutions in a consistent way across countries. In effect, veto player theory conceptualizes the institutional structure of a given country in terms of its configuration of veto players. A **veto player** is an individual or collective actor whose agreement is necessary for a change in the political status quo. There are two types of veto player. An **institutional veto player** is generated by a country's constitution. A **partisan veto player** is generated by the way the political game is played.

Veto player theory argues that important characteristics of any country's institutional structure are determined by its configuration of veto players. A **veto player** is an individual (such as a president) or collective actor (such as a legislative chamber) whose agreement is necessary for a change of the political status quo.[7] In any given country, there are two types of veto player. First, there is the **institutional veto player**. Institutional veto players are those generated by a country's constitution. For example, the US Constitution identifies actors like the president, the Congress, and the Senate as institutional veto players because it gives these actors the right to block legislative changes to the status quo. Second, there is the **partisan veto player**. Partisan veto players are those generated by the political game. In other words, partisan veto players are not specified in a constitution but are determined by the way political competition plays out in a given country. For example, particular parties in a legislature or a coalition government might be considered partisan veto players if they are in a position to block changes to the status quo. Such parties are veto players not because they have been identified as such in some document but rather because of the way that citizens vote, how votes are translated into seats, how governments form, and so on. Whereas the identity of institutional veto players is essentially fixed across time as long as the constitution remains the same, the identity of partisan veto players changes with the vagaries of political competition.

Rather than see federalism, bicameralism, and constitutional review as entirely different institutions that need to be studied separately, as most political scientists have traditionally done, veto player theory suggests that we might constructively view them as just different types of the same thing—that is, as different types of institutional veto players.[8] All three institutions place hurdles on the ability of political actors to change the status quo. For example, a legislative majority in the lower chamber may require the support of a powerful upper chamber to change some policy status quo. As we saw earlier, this is the case in the United States, where the agreement of both legislative chambers is required to pass legislation. Courts are not veto players when they interpret ordinary statutes, because their decisions can be overridden by subsequent legislation. They are veto players, however, when they engage in constitutional review (Tsebelis 2002, 226). The French Constitutional Council has the ability to invalidate laws on constitutional grounds before they are applied. This suggests that, in many ways, we can think of constitutional courts like the French Constitutional Council as a third legislative chamber (Stone Sweet 1992). Similarly, the support of a subnational government in a federal system may be necessary for political actors to change

---

7. Note that veto player theory is not restricted to democracies. In dictatorships, veto players might include the military or particular religious leaders and so on. The key to applying veto player theory in any given setting involves identifying which actors are in a position to block changes to the political status quo. This will vary across countries, across time, and potentially across policy areas.

8. In previous chapters, we looked at whether countries have single-party or coalition governments and whether they have two-party or multiparty systems. Just as federalism, bicameralism, and constitutional review can be reconceptualized in terms of institutional veto players, the type of government and the size of the party system in a country can be reconceptualized in terms of partisan veto players. If we do this, then we can think of countries with coalition governments as having more partisan veto players than countries with single-party majority governments.

the status quo. This is particularly the case for those policy areas that are constitutionally delegated to subnational governments. In this framework, then, adopting federalism, bicameralism, or constitutional review can be thought of as equivalent to increasing the number of institutional veto players in a country.

As we will see, veto player theory shows that the number of veto players in a country, as well as the ideological distance between them, has important consequences for policy stability. Specifically, veto player theory indicates that countries in which there are many veto players with conflicting policy preferences are likely to be characterized by (a) greater policy stability, (b) smaller shifts in policy, (c) less variation in the size of policy shifts, and (d) weaker agenda-setting powers. This, in turn, has important consequences for things like judicial and bureaucratic activism, government stability, and regime stability.

To see where these results come from, let's start with the basic building blocks of veto player theory. Veto players can be represented by their preferred policy positions or ideal points in some issue space.[9] In Figure 15.4, we have three veto players, A, B, and C, who are located in a two-dimensional issue space on the basis of their most preferred position on two different policies. To give our example some substance, we can think of one issue dimension as being about the appropriate level of state intervention in the economy and the other issue dimension as being about the appropriate amount of money to be spent on education. The status quo policy in the two-dimensional policy space is given by the point SQ. In Figure 15.4, we illustrate the indifference curves for each veto player with respect to the status quo—these are the circles that surround the ideal points of the three veto players and go through the status quo point. These indifference curves, as you will remember, indicate all of the policy outcomes that are equally distant from each veto player's ideal point as the status quo. As a result, each veto player is indifferent between any point on her indifference curve and the status quo. More important, each veto player will prefer any policy outcome inside her indifference curve to the status quo because this policy outcome will necessarily be closer to her ideal point.

A central concept in veto player theory is the winset. Recall that a winset is the set of policy alternatives that would defeat the status quo in a pair-wise contest under whatever voting rules are being employed. Given the very definition of a veto player, unanimity is required to change the status quo. As a result, the winset in a veto player setting is the set of policy alternatives that falls within the indifference circle of *every* veto player. In Figure 15.4, this winset is represented by the shaded petal-shaped area coming from the status quo. Any policy alternative in this shaded area will win the support of all veto players in a pair-wise vote against the status quo.

According to veto player theory, the size of the winset has a significant impact on policy outcomes. First, the size of the winset affects policy stability. When the winset is large, policy is less stable, because there are many policy alternatives that can defeat the status quo.

---

9. At this point, readers may well benefit from rereading the material on spatial models first presented in Chapter 11.

FIGURE 15.4	An Application of Veto Player Theory

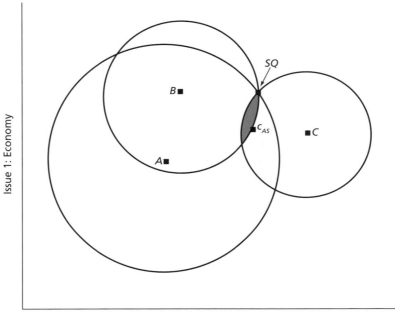

Note: A, B, and *C* = three veto players; *SQ* = the status quo policy; c_{AS} = the policy alternative that *C* would propose if she were the agenda setter; the three circles = the indifference curves of *A, B,* and *C* with respect to the status quo; the shaded area = the winset, assuming decisions are made by unanimity rule.

In contrast, when the winset is small, policy is more stable, because there are few policy alternatives that can defeat the status quo. Second, the size of the winset determines the likely size of policy shifts. When the winset is small, policy shifts must necessarily be small; it is impossible to move policy very far from the status quo. When the winset is large, though, the possibility arises for more radical policy shifts. If we think that every policy alternative in a winset is equally possible, then it follows that the average size of policy shifts will increase with the size of the winset. Third, the size of the winset influences how much variation we are likely to see in the size of policy shifts. As we have already noted, policy shifts must be small when the winset is small. When the winset is large, however, policy shifts may be small or large. As a result, we are likely to observe more variation in the size of policy shifts the larger the size of the winset.

Fourth, the size of the winset affects the power of an agenda-setting veto player to influence the policy outcome. So far, we have assumed that all veto players are created equal.

Although this assumption allows us to identify the feasible set of policy alternatives that can defeat the status quo (the winset), it does not permit us to identify a specific policy outcome. In reality, it is often the case that some veto players are also agenda setters in that they get to make take-it-or-leave-it policy proposals to the other veto players. Clearly, any veto player who is an agenda setter is at an advantage because he can view the winset as his constraint and select the outcome within it that is closest to his ideal point. For example, if veto player C were the agenda setter in Figure 15.4, then she would propose shifting policy to c_{AS} because this is the closest point in the winset to her ideal point. The size of the winset affects the importance of agenda setting. When the winset is small, the agenda setter cannot move policy far from where the other veto players would want to move it if they were the agenda setter. In contrast, agenda setting becomes much more important when the winset is large because the agenda setter now has the possibility to move policy far from where the other veto players would choose if they were the agenda setters.

We now know that the size of the winset has a significant impact on policy outcomes. But how do the number of veto players in a country and the ideological distance between them affect the size of the winset? Let's start by examining how the number of veto players influences the size of the winset with the help of Figure 15.5. In panel (a) there are two veto players, and in panel (b) there are three veto players. In this particular comparison, increasing the number of veto players shrinks the size of the winset; that is, the winset in the second panel is smaller than the winset in the first one. But does this mean that increasing the number of veto players *always* shrinks the size of the winset? The answer to this question is no. To see why, let's now compare the second and third panels (b and c). In the third panel there are two veto players, and in the second panel there are three veto players. As this comparison indicates, increasing the number of veto players does not shrink the size of the winset; the size of the winset in the second panel is exactly the same as the size of the winset in the third one. The reason for this is that the new veto player (B) is ideologically located in such a way that if we were to draw a line connecting the two existing veto players (A and C), she would be on it.[10] What this means, practically speaking, is that it is impossible for veto players A and C to jointly prefer alternatives to the status quo that veto player B will not also prefer. In the language of veto player theory, we say that veto player B is "absorbed" by the existing veto players. It is because of this that the winset remains the same size as we move from the third panel (c) to the second panel (b). The bottom line is that veto player theory shows that an increase in the number of veto players decreases the size of the winset or leaves it the same; it never increases the size of the winset.

Let's now examine how the ideological distance between veto players influences the size of the winset with the help of Figure 15.6. The two veto players in the first panel (a) have

---

10. In this particular example, the line connecting the two existing veto players (A and C) is known as the "unanimity core." Whenever an additional veto player is added to the unanimity core, the size of the winset remains unchanged. We discuss the unanimity core in more detail in problems 13 and 14 at the end of this chapter.

| FIGURE 15.5 | The Number of Veto Players and the Size of the Winset |

a. Two veto players, *A* and *B*

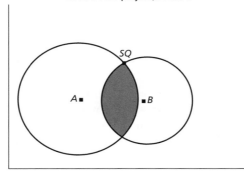

b. Three veto players, *A*, *B*, and *C*

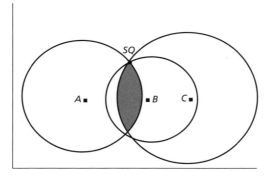

c. Two veto players, *A* and *C*

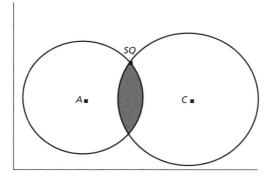

Note: A, B, C = veto players; *SQ* = the status quo policy; the shaded area = the winset, assuming decisions are made by unanimity rule.

| FIGURE 15.6 | **The Ideological Distance between Veto Players and the Size of the Winset** |

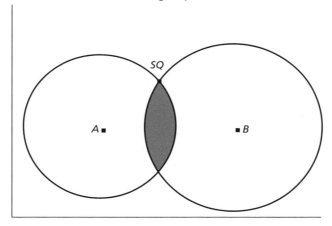

a. Similar ideological positions

b. Dissimilar ideological positions

Note: A, B = veto players; *SQ* = the status quo policy; the shaded area = the winset, assuming decisions are made by unanimity rule.

more similar ideal points than the two veto players in the second panel (b). As you can see, increasing the ideological distance between veto players—moving from the first panel (a) to the second panel (b)—shrinks the size of the winset, which makes policy change less likely. This is a general result from veto player theory that always holds. Interestingly, this result sheds light on the alleged dangers of "ideological polarization." Many commentators have lamented the rise of ideological polarization on the ground that political actors are holding more extreme policy positions. As veto player theory indicates, though, ideological polarization actually increases the probability that the status quo will remain in place.

As Figures 15.5 and 15.6 illustrate, the size of the winset in any particular situation is determined jointly by the number of veto players and the ideological distance between these veto players. In general, we can expect the size of the winset to shrink as we increase the number of veto players or the ideological distance between veto players or both. As we noted earlier, federalism, bicameralism, and constitutional review are all institutions that can be reconceptualized as institutional veto players. In regard to policy outcomes, this means that we can expect countries with these types of institutions to be characterized by (a) policy stability, (b) small policy shifts, (c) little variation in the size of policy shifts, and (d) weak agenda-setting powers. These characteristics are likely to be particularly prevalent if the institutional veto players have dissimilar policy preferences. For example, we would expect policy output to be lower and less radical during periods of divided government or cohabitation (Binder 1999, 2003; Erikson, MacKuen, and Stimson 2002; Mayhew 1991) and when coalition governments are ideologically diverse (Tsebelis 2002, 173). We would also expect greater policy stability when the two legislative chambers in a bicameral system or the central and subnational governments in a federal system are controlled by different political parties.

Consider the United States. Many on the left of the political spectrum were disappointed with the legislative achievements of President Barack Obama after he came to power in January 2009. Obama had run on a platform of "hope" and "change," and many believed that he would push the status quo in a distinctly progressive direction. Obama had proposed radical changes in many areas. For example, he had supported the introduction of a single-payer health care system, strong regulations on the financial and banking sectors, the closure of Guantanamo Bay, an end to the Bush-era tax cuts for the wealthy, and a large economic stimulus program. In all of these cases, any change, if it occurred at all, did not lead to dramatic shifts in the status quo. Although many of Obama's supporters felt disappointed, the fact that there has been so little change to the status quo did not come as a surprise to those political scientists familiar with veto player theory. With its support for constitutionalism, and its bicameral and federal system of government, the US political system is full of veto players. Moreover, the ideological distance between these veto players increased significantly following the 2010 midterm elections when Obama and the Democrats lost control of Congress to the Republicans; the Republicans had a quite different vision for the future of America. Given this situation, changes to the status quo, and in particular radical changes to the status quo, were always going to be extremely unlikely. Note that this lack of radicalism is not something unique to the Obama presidency. American politicians frequently run for office on a platform of "shaking things up" and breaking with the Washington establishment. However, the institutional structure of the United States, with its wide range of institutional veto players, all but guarantees that this is not going to happen. To a large extent, this is precisely what the Founding Fathers intended when they wrote the constitution—they specifically designed a constitution with a set of institutions that would protect the status quo and, with it, their privileges and power.

We should note at this point that there is nothing inherently good or bad about policy stability. After all, policy stability is typically viewed as a good thing by those who like the status quo but a bad thing by those who do not. Policy stability, though, can have important consequences for various aspects of a political system, such as government stability, regime stability, and judicial or bureaucratic activism. Let's first briefly consider the effect of policy stability on government and regime stability. Imagine that a government comes to power in a country with the promise to shake up some policy area. Perhaps some crisis requires radical reform. If the configuration of veto players in the country is such that the status quo cannot be changed or can be altered only a little, the government will likely appear ineffective and immobilized. If we are in a parliamentary democracy, political and social actors who want to resolve the

The Barack Obama "Hope" poster became synonymous with the 2008 Obama presidential campaign.

crisis will likely push for a vote of no confidence in the government. As a result, veto player theory predicts a connection between policy stability and the likelihood of *government* instability in parliamentary democracies. If we are in a presidential democracy, though, there is no institutional mechanism, such as a vote of no confidence, to remove an ineffective government from office. This may lead political and social actors who want to resolve the crisis to look to extraconstitutional means, such as a military coup, to replace the government. As a result, veto player theory predicts that policy stability will increase the likelihood of *regime* instability in presidential democracies. We return to the connection between policy stability and regime instability in Chapter 16, where we examine the effect of institutions on the survival of democracy in more detail.

Let's now briefly consider the effect of policy stability on judicial and bureaucratic activism. Veto player theory suggests that policy stability leads to high levels of judicial and bureaucratic activism (Tsebelis 2002, 222–247). Why? In many situations, judges have the opportunity to make policy through their ability to interpret statutes. Similarly, bureaucrats get to make policy by virtue of actually implementing policy. Obviously, if the members of the legislature do not like policies made by the judges and bureaucrats, they can write new legislation that will effectively overrule the judiciary or bureaucracy. When policy is stable because there are many legislative veto players with dissimilar policy preferences, however, judges and bureaucrats get to interpret and implement laws close to their own ideal points, safe in the knowledge that the legislature will not be able to reach an agreement on overriding them. This suggests that we should expect to see higher levels of judicial and bureaucratic activism in federal and bicameral countries than in unitary and unicameral ones.

CONCLUSION

In Chapter 11, we examined some theoretical results suggesting that constitutional designers necessarily face trade-offs when designing democratic institutions. In particular, Arrow's theorem demonstrates that stable outcomes (group transitivity) can be guaranteed only if the freedom of individuals to form their own preferences (universal admissibility) or the ability of individuals to have their preferences influence group decisions (nondictatorship) is compromised.[11] If we accept universal admissibility as inalienable, then the basic tension that exists in democratic regimes is between instability and dictatorship. As we have noted before, increased stability of outcomes is likely to be the result of someone's having been given agenda power.

In this and the three preceding chapters, we have examined many of the dimensions along which democratic institutions vary. For example, in Chapter 12 we looked at the ways in which the relationship between the executive and legislative branches can be organized. In Chapter 13, we examined the tremendous variety of ways in which elections have been organized. And in Chapter 14, we investigated the structure of party systems. In this chapter, we looked at three more ways in which institutions might vary from democracy to democracy—federalism, bicameralism, and constitutionalism. We suggested that these three institutional forms have a common feature—they create political actors capable of blocking a change in the political status quo. Federalism, for instance, has the potential to create powerful regional actors capable of blocking the implementation of national law. Bicameralism creates a second legislative body capable of blocking legislation. And constitutionalism creates the possibility that judges might overturn laws that the legislature approves of. Each of these institutions, therefore, has the effect of creating an institutional veto player.[12]

---

11. As we note in Chapter 11, this trade-off—something we called the "institutional trilemma"—assumes that the independence from irrelevant alternatives and unanimity conditions are met.

12. Presidentialism (see Chapter 12) also creates an institutional veto player—the president—who can check the power of the legislature.

Veto player theory can be thought of as a modern-day version of arguments about the effects of mixed government and checks and balances that can be traced back to political theorists such as Aristotle. As we have demonstrated, countries with many veto players with conflicting preferences are expected to be characterized by great policy stability, smaller shifts in policy, less variation in the size of policy shifts, and weaker agenda-setting powers. As a result, systems with many veto players may, in some sense, overcome the instability of democratic institutions without creating a single powerful agenda setter. Unfortunately, the existence of multiple veto players doesn't fully overcome the dilemmas posed by Arrow's theorem, because complex veto structures necessarily mean that current policy decisions are profoundly influenced by the status quo policy. In this sense, they grant something like dictatorial power to the policymakers who chose those policies in the past. As a consequence, circumstances or tastes may change in such a way that a large share of the populace might desire policy change but be unable to achieve it. As implied by Arrow's theorem, then, there appears to be some trade-off between policy stability and the responsiveness of decisions to voters' preferences.

In the next chapter, we have more to say about how democratic institutions influence the way voters' preferences are translated into policy decisions. We will also have more to say about the potentially explosive effects that can be produced by policy stability in presidential democracies—policy stability, it seems, may come at the expense of regime instability. A comprehensive examination of the varieties of democracy observed in the world is well beyond the scope of our book, but in the next chapter we attempt to highlight some prominent findings in the comparative politics literature regarding the consequences of the varieties of democracy. Specifically, we look at how variations in democratic institutions influence four sets of important outcomes—the quality of representation, the size of the welfare state, the propensity for ethnic conflict, and the survival of democracy.

KEY CONCEPTS

PROBLEMS

The problems that follow address some of the more important concepts and ideas introduced in this chapter.

1. Describe the difference between coming-together federalism and holding-together federalism.

2. What are some of the advantages and disadvantages of federalism?

3. What are some of the advantages and disadvantages of bicameral legislatures? Does your answer depend on whether a country has a federal system? Why or why not?

4. Higher law constitutions are based on the premise that legislatures can do no legal wrong, because they derive their legitimacy from the fact that they are popularly elected. True or false? Explain your answer.

5. Use the Constitute website (https://www.constituteproject.org/) to find the constitutions from at least three countries. What are some of the rights explicitly delineated in each constitution? What are some of the duties expected of citizens? What are some of the duties expected of the state?

6. Use the hyperlinks maintained by the Venice Commission of the Council of Europe (http://www.venice.coe.int/webforms/courts/?lang=EN) to find out information about three constitutional or supreme courts around the world. For example, what is the composition of the courts? How are judges appointed? What is the competency of the court? How are decisions made? What are some of the recent decisions?

7. Explain the difference between institutional veto players and partisan veto players, providing examples of each.

8. If a country reforms its institutions so that it has fewer veto players, would it be easier or more difficult for political actors to change existing policy? Why?

The next two problems use spatial models to examine the effect of bicameralism and judicial review. When determining which policies are acceptable to an actor, you should assume that any policy that is *not worse* than the status quo is acceptable. If an actor is indifferent between the status quo and a new policy, you should assume, to keep things simple, that the actor will choose the new policy.

Spatial Model of Bicameralism

9. In Figure 15.7, we illustrate a situation in which we have a unicameral legislature that includes a median voter (*MV*) and a status quo policy (*SQ*) arrayed along a single left-right issue dimension that runs from 0 (*most left*) to 10 (*most right*). The median voter is assumed to have a single-peaked utility function and to vote for the policy that is located closest to her ideal point.

FIGURE 15.7	**Illustrating a Unicameral Legislature**

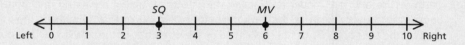

Note: *MV* = the median voter in the legislature; *SQ* = the policy status quo.

a. What is the range of policies that the median voter prefers to the status quo? If the median voter in the legislature gets to propose a new policy, what would she propose? What would the outcome be?

In Figure 15.8, we illustrate a situation in which we have a bicameral legislature. The location of the status quo policy is *SQ*, the location of the median voter in the lower chamber is *LC*, and the location of the median voter in the upper chamber is *UC*. Assume that both median voters have a single-peaked utility function and that the support of both chambers is needed to pass a new policy.

FIGURE 15.8	**Illustrating a Bicameral Legislature**

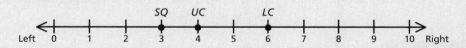

Note: *UC* = the median voter in the upper chamber; *LC* = the median voter in the lower chamber; *SQ* = the policy status quo.

b. What is the range of policies preferred to the status quo by the median voter in the lower chamber? What is the range of policies preferred to the status quo by the median voter in the upper chamber? What is the overlapping range of policies preferred by both chambers to the status quo?

c. If the lower chamber is the agenda setter and can make take-it-or-leave-it proposals, where on the left-right issue dimension will the lower chamber make its policy proposal? Would your answer change if the upper chamber is the agenda setter instead? If so, how and why?

Now imagine that the status quo policy is located at 5 instead of 3 on the left-right issue dimension and that the ideal points of the two median voters remain the same as in Figure 15.8.

d. Answer parts (b) and (c) again for this new situation. What changes? That is, how do the expected policy outcomes compare across these different scenarios?

Spatial Model of Judicial Review

10. We now use a spatial model to examine the effects of judicial review. In our model, a bureaucratic agency, such as the Environmental Protection Agency (EPA), sets the initial policy. If the agency's policy is not challenged by the legislature or the courts, then the policy prevails. Our model is loosely based on one by Ferejohn and Shipan (1990, 3), who argue that policymaking by bureaucratic agencies is the typical decision-making practice throughout modern government. Relatively few governmental decisions are directly mandated by government acts. For the most part, statutes serve as constraints on what bureaucrats can do rather than as detailed directives. Thus, while not denying the importance of the classical statutory model of democratic government—in which a democratically elected legislature instructs its delegates in public action—it seems likely that a model of administrative action that puts agency actions at the front is more relevant for explaining government action most of the time.

To start with, imagine that we have three actors: a legislature, a legislative committee, and a regulatory agency (we will add a court shortly). We will call this the Agency Policymaking Model. Suppose that the legislature has delegated supervision of the regulatory agency to the legislative committee. In Figure 15.9, we show the ideal points of the median member of the legislature (L), the median member of the legislative committee (LC), and the regulatory agency (A). The agency makes the first move by choosing a policy position. If it wishes, the legislative committee can initiate legislation to alter the agency's policy. If it does

| FIGURE 15.9 | **Agency Policymaking Model** |

Note: A = the regulatory agency; LC = the median voter on the legislative committee; L = the median voter in the legislature.

so, legislation is sent to the floor of the legislature, where it can be amended freely. If the committee does not wish to initiate legislation, then the policy chosen by the agency stands. As always, you should assume that all actors have single-peaked preferences and that they will vote over alternatives sincerely.

a. If the legislature gets a chance to amend a proposal from the legislative committee, what will the outcome of the amendment process be? In other words, where will the legislature set policy if it gets the chance?

b. What is the range of policies that the legislative committee would prefer to the policy outcome that the legislature would choose in an amendment process?

c. Given your previous answer, when will the legislative committee initiate legislation to alter the agency's policy? When will the legislative committee not initiate legislation to alter the agency's policy? In your own words, explain your answers.

d. Given your previous answer, where do you think the agency should initiate policy so that it will not be overturned?

Now imagine that we add a fourth actor: a court. Assume that the court has the ability to review agency actions and can strike them down if it wants to. If this happens, policy reverts to some status quo policy that we will label *SQ*. Ferejohn and Shipan (1990) refer to this as the Statutory Review Model. After the court has decided whether to strike down the agency's policy, the committee can choose to initiate new legislation if it wants to. If it does so, legislation is sent to the floor of the legislature, where it can be amended freely, as in the Agency Policymaking Model that we just examined. In Figure 15.10, we show the status quo reversion point (*SQ*) and the ideal points of the median member of the legislature (*L*), the median member of the legislative committee (*LC*), the regulatory agency (*A*), and the median judge on the court (*C*).

FIGURE 15.10	**Statutory Review Model, Scenario 1**

Note: A = the regulatory agency; *LC* = the median voter in the legislative committee; *L* = the median voter in the legislature; *C* = the median judge on the court; *SQ* = the reversion status quo.

e. Imagine for some reason that the court decides to strike down the agency's policy (wherever it might be). If this happens, policy will revert to the status quo point shown in Figure 15.10. How do you think the legislative committee will react? Will it initiate legislation to change the status quo policy? If the legislative committee does initiate legislation to change the status quo policy, what will the legislature do? What will the final policy position be in this situation if the court decides to strike down the agency's policy?

f. In the previous question, we did not specify where the agency would implement policy. Let's suppose that the agency chooses to implement its policy at 3.1 on the left-right issue dimension. Would the court prefer to have policy at 3.1 or at the final policy position you found in the previous question (e)? In other words, if the agency chooses to implement policy at 3.1, will the court want to strike it down? Explain your answer.

g. If the agency chooses to implement its policy at 3.1, the legislative committee will not bother to initiate legislation to change the agency's policy. Explain, in your own words, why this is the case.

h. Given your answers to the last three questions (e, f, g), what will the final policy outcome be if the agency initially sets policy at 3.1? Explain your answer.

Imagine now that we change the ideal point of the median judge on the court. The new scenario is shown in Figure 15.11.

FIGURE 15.11   **Statutory Review Model, Scenario 2**

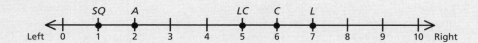

Note: SQ = the reversion status quo; A = the regulatory agency; LC = the median voter on the legislative committee; C = the median judge on the court; L = the median voter in the legislature.

i. What is the range of policies that the court prefers to the ideal point of the median voter in the legislature?

j. If the court strikes down the agency's policy (wherever it might be), it is easy to see that the legislative committee will initiate legislation to try to change the status quo policy (make sure that you understand why). We also know that policy will end up at the ideal point of the median voter in the legislature if the legislative committee initiates legislation to change the status quo. Given this, where should the agency implement policy in order to keep the court from striking down its policy in the first place? Will this be the final policy outcome? Explain your answers.

Imagine that we now change the ideal point of the median judge on the court one more time. The new scenario is shown in Figure 15.12.

Note: SQ = the reversion status quo; *A* = the regulatory agency; *LC* = the median voter on the legislative committee; *L* = the median voter in the legislature; *C* = the median judge on the court.

k. What is the range of policies that the court prefers to the ideal point of the median voter in the legislature?

l. As before, if the court strikes down the agency's policy, it is easy to see that the legislative committee will initiate legislation to try to change the status quo policy. We also know that policy will end up at the ideal point of the median voter in the legislature if the legislative committee initiates legislation to change the status quo. Given this, where should the agency implement policy in order to keep the court from striking down its policy in the first place? Will this be the final policy outcome? Explain your answers.

m. Does the effect of having a court that can engage in judicial review affect policy outcomes? To answer this question, compare the final policy outcome from the Agency Policymaking Model and the final outcome(s) across the three Statutory Review Scenarios. Does the court actually have to do anything, such as make rulings, to affect policy outcomes?

n. In the particular scenarios that we have evaluated, does the presence of a court with the power of judicial review move policy toward or away from the ideal point of the median voter in the legislature? Again, compare the final policy outcome from the Agency Policymaking Model without a court and the final outcome(s) across the three Statutory Review Scenarios with a court.

o. Many people worry that judicial review is antidemocratic because judges are making policy instead of the people's elected representatives in the legislature. In the particular model of judicial review that we have examined, should people be worried by the antidemocratic nature of judicial activism? Explain your answer.

Veto Player Theory

The remaining questions evaluate your understanding of veto player theory.

11. In Figure 15.13, we have two veto players, *A* and *B*, who are located in a two-dimensional issue space. The status quo policy is given by the point *SQ*.

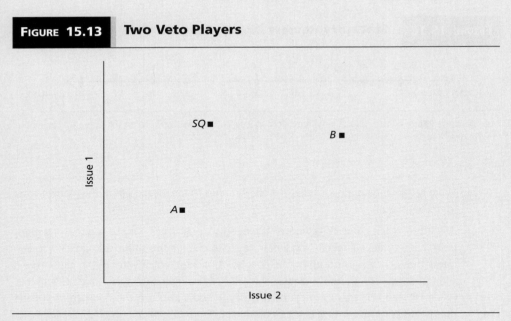

| FIGURE 15.13 | Two Veto Players |

Note: SQ = a status quo policy; A, B = veto players.

a. Using Figure 15.13, draw indifference curves for each veto player with respect to the status quo. Shade in the winset if there is one.

b. In your own words, describe what a winset is in the context of veto player theory.

12. In Figure 15.14, we have three veto players, A, B, and C, who are located in a two-dimensional issue space. The status quo policy is given by the point SQ.

a. Using Figure 15.14, draw indifference curves for each veto player with respect to the status quo. Shade in the winset if there is one.

b. Is the winset in Figure 15.14 smaller than the winset in Figure 15.13? What does this mean for policy outcomes?

13. In the chapter, we argued that a central concept in veto player theory is the winset. Recall that in the context of veto player theory, the winset is the set of policy alternatives that would defeat the status quo in a pair-wise contest by unanimity rule. In fact, there is another important concept in veto player theory called the **unanimity core**. The unanimity core is the set of policy alternatives that *cannot* be defeated in a pair-wise contest by unanimity rule. In other words, the unanimity core can be thought of as a region of policy stability—if policy ever gets into the unanimity core, it cannot be moved. It turns out that the size of the

The **unanimity core** is the set of policy alternatives that cannot be defeated in a pair-wise contest by unanimity rule.

| FIGURE 15.14 | **Three Veto Players** |

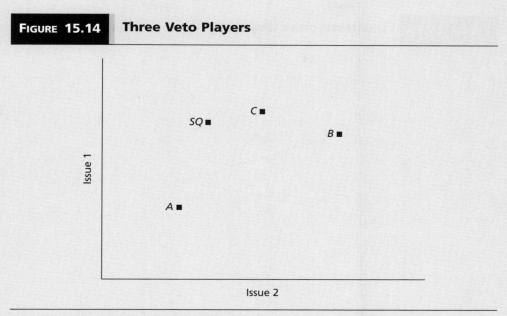

Notes: SQ = a status quo policy; *A, B, C* = veto players.

unanimity core is directly related to the size of the winset. Specifically, whatever makes the winset smaller makes the unanimity core bigger. And whatever makes the winset bigger makes the unanimity core smaller. This means that all of the results from veto player theory that we presented in the chapter in the context of the winset can also be presented in the context of the unanimity core. For example, whereas policy stability is associated with having a small winset, it is associated with having a large unanimity core. The following questions examine veto player theory in the context of the unanimity core.

Finding the unanimity core is relatively simple. Imagine that the ideal points of the veto players are pins sticking up out of a board. Now imagine that you take an elastic band and stretch it so that you can place it over all of the pins at once. If you were to let go of the elastic band at this point, it would snap into place around the pins and identify the location of the unanimity core. For example, the unanimity core for the situation in Figure 15.15 is given by the triangle connecting the three veto players, *A, B,* and *C.*

a. Demonstrate that a policy inside the unanimity core in Figure 15.15 cannot be defeated by an alternative policy in a pair-wise vote under unanimity rule. To do this, choose some point inside the triangle and label it the status quo. Now draw indifference curves for each veto player with respect to the status quo policy. Is there a winset? What does it mean if you find one? What does it mean if you do not find one?

FIGURE 15.15   Illustrating the Unanimity Core

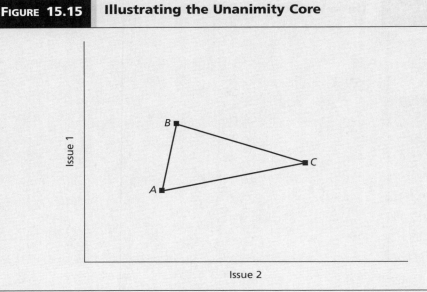

Note: A, B, C = veto players; the triangle outlines the unanimity core.

b. Now demonstrate that a policy outside the unanimity core in Figure 15.15 can be defeated by an alternative policy in a pair-wise vote under unanimity rule. To do this, choose some point outside the triangle and label it the status quo. Now draw indifference curves for each veto player with respect to the status quo policy. Is there a winset? What does it mean if you find one? What does it mean if you do not find one?

c. What would happen to the size of the unanimity core if the ideal points of the veto players were further apart? What do you think the relationship is between the size of the unanimity core and policy stability? Why?

d. Suppose that we were to add an additional veto player within the area captured by the triangle in Figure 15.15. Would the size of the unanimity core change? Explain your answer.

e. Suppose that we were to add an additional veto player outside of the area captured by the triangle in Figure 15.15. Would the size of the unanimity core change?

f. Based on your answers to questions (d) and (e), does increasing the number of veto players always increase policy stability by increasing the size of the unanimity core?

14. Imagine a set of institutional arrangements in which judges have the opportunity to make policy through their ability to interpret statutes. If the members of the legislature don't like the policy made by the judges, they can write new legislation to change it, effectively overruling the judiciary. In this scenario, the judge moves first and sets policy by interpreting

the law. The legislature then moves and decides whether to change the law by overruling the judge. Consider the situation outlined in Figure 15.16, where we have three legislative veto players, L_1, L_2, and L_3, located in a two-dimensional policy space. We are going to examine two scenarios with two different judges ruling on separate laws. The ideal points of the two judges are shown in Figure 15.16 as J_1 and J_2.

| FIGURE 15.16 | **Activist Judges with Agenda-Setting Power** |

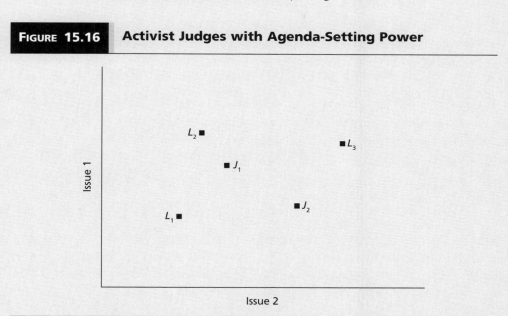

Note: L_1, L_2, L_3 = legislative veto players; J_1, J_2 = judicial agenda setters.

a. Draw the unanimity core for this situation.

b. First consider judge J_1. If she interprets statutes so that the new policy is exactly at her ideal point, will the legislative veto players be able to overturn it and move it someplace else? If so, where could they move it? If not, why not? Where should judge J_1 set policy?

c. Now consider judge J_2. If she interprets statutes so that the new policy is exactly at her ideal point, will the legislative veto players be able to overturn it and move it someplace else? If so, where could they move it? If not, why not? Where should judge J_2 set policy?

d. What do you think would happen to the agenda-setting power of judges if the ideal points of the legislative veto players were further apart? What do you think the relationship is between the size of the unanimity core and the amount of discretion judicial activists can exercise over policy outcomes? Why?

e. Based on your answers to question (d), do you think that we should expect to see more judicial activism in federal and bicameral countries or in unitary and unicameral ones? Why?

16 Consequences of Democratic Institutions

Proportional representation will thus create a situation where everyone has his will represented exactly but where no one's will is carried out.

Dankwart A. Rustow, "Some Observations on Proportional Representation," 1950

OVERVIEW

- Democratic institutions reflect the interests of voters in different ways. Two fundamentally different perspectives on how democracy should work are known as the majoritarian and consensus visions of democracy. These two visions of democracy have important implications for things like accountability, government mandates, and representation.

- Political institutions influence economic policy and outcomes in different ways too. Research suggests that the choice of electoral institutions in a country has an important influence on who gets to govern and what types of economic policies they are likely to implement when given the chance.

- Electoral laws and federalism affect the likelihood of ethnic conflict. Comparative politics may have advice to offer constitutional designers in ethnically or religiously diverse societies.

- Particular institutional choices might influence the survival of democracy. In this chapter, we look at whether the prospects for democratic consolidation are greater in countries that adopt parliamentarism or in countries that adopt presidentialism.

As we have seen over the last four chapters, there is what sometimes appears to be a dizzying array of different democratic institutions around the world. For example, democracies can be presidential, parliamentary, or semi-presidential. They can employ majoritarian, proportional, or mixed electoral rules. They can have many parties or just a few, they can be federal or unitary, they can be bicameral or unicameral, and they can allow constitutional review or not. Democracies can also have very different types of government: single-party majority, minimal winning coalition, surplus majority, minority coalition, or single-party minority. Indeed, the list of democratic features presented here barely scratches the surface of the set of institutional choices that are available to designers of new constitutions. For instance, the decision to establish a parliamentary democracy with proportional electoral rules simply opens up a whole new round of institutional choices that need to be made: whether to require an investiture vote, whether to employ a constructive vote of no confidence, what district magnitude to use, whether to employ an electoral threshold, whether to use the single transferable vote or some party list system, and so on.

The immense variety of democratic institutions observed in the world should come as no surprise. As our discussion of Arrow's theorem in Chapter 11 illustrates, there is no ideal decision-making mechanism, and institutional choice is ultimately an exercise in the choice of "second bests." This does not mean, however, that constitutional designers mix and match institutions with reckless abandon. In practice, constitutional designers choose particular sets of institutions to bring about the political, social, and economic outcomes they desire. This presumes, of course, that they have a good idea about how different democratic institutions affect these outcomes. It is to the effects of particular democratic institutions that we now turn.

In this chapter, we introduce you to four different literatures, each of which examines the effect of particular democratic institutions on important political, social, and economic outcomes. In the first section of this chapter, we examine the way in which various democratic institutions reflect the interests of voters. Democracy gets much of its moral authority from being a form of government "of the people, for the people, and by the people." In Chapter 11, we examined the theoretical reasons why such a notion of democracy is complicated. In this chapter, we evaluate the extent to which different institutions facilitate this notion *in practice*. We then examine some of the ways in which the institutions that vary across democracies influence economic policy and economic outcomes. As we will see, the choice of electoral rules has a strong impact on who gets to govern and the types of economic policies they implement when given the chance. Later, we consider the effects of electoral laws and federalism on the likelihood of ethnic conflict in an attempt to discover whether comparative politics has any advice to offer constitutional designers in ethnically or religiously diverse societies. In the final section of this chapter, we use the knowledge we have learned in the second half of this book about institutions to supplement some of the answers we gave in the first half of the book about the economic and cultural determinants of democracy. In particular, we examine how parliamentarism and presidentialism affect democratic survival.

MAJORITARIAN OR CONSENSUS DEMOCRACY?

As Arrow's theorem makes clear, there is a fundamental tension when designing institutions between the desire to guarantee that a group of individuals will be able to make coherent and stable choices (group transitivity) on the one hand and the ability to guarantee the freedom of these individuals to form their own preferences (universal admissibility) and have those preferences influence group decisions (nondictatorship) on the other. In effect, constitutional designers face an institutional "trilemma" (see Figure 11.10) in that they are only able to design institutions that satisfy at most two of these three desirable attributes—group transitivity, universal admissibility, and nondictatorship. There is no way around it— constitutional designers have to make trade-offs.

Although constitutional designers could theoretically make different trade-offs for each individual institution they create, a look at the real world suggests that they frequently make a particular trade-off for the system of government as a whole. In practice, constitutional designers have (implicitly) responded to Arrow's institutional "trilemma" in one of two ways—by creating institutions that disperse power or by creating institutions that concentrate it. Democracies in which power is concentrated are referred to as majoritarian democracies, whereas democracies in which power is dispersed are referred to as consensus democracies (Lijphart 1984). Thus, although there are theoretically many possible combinations of democratic institutions that could occur in the world, political scientists often think in terms of two basic types of democracy: majoritarian or consensus (Lijphart 1999; Powell 2000; Steiner 1971). We now describe these two types of democracy and examine what they mean for political representation.

Two Visions of Democracy

Policy decisions in contemporary democracies are not made by citizens but by their elected representatives. If democracy is understood as a system in which citizens should be able to influence policy decisions, then it follows that elections must play an important role in any well-functioning democracy. Indeed, to the extent that elections allow citizens to participate in the policymaking process, they can be considered the primary "instruments of democracy" (Powell 2000). The influence that the citizens should be able to exert over the policy decisions made by their elected representatives can be thought of from two distinct perspectives, each of which has a long tradition in democratic theory. These two perspectives can be thought of as two different visions of how democracy should work (Powell 2000). As we will see, these two visions of democracy view the role that elections play in giving citizens influence over the policymaking process in very different ways.

Majoritarian Vision

According to the majoritarian vision of democracy, elections are supposed to be events in which citizens get to choose between two alternative teams of politicians that are competing to form the government. Whichever team wins an electoral majority gets to form the

In the **trustee model of representation**, representatives are free to use their own judgement when making policy. They are supposed to promote the collective good and act in the national interest rather than in the interest of any particular constituency. In the **delegate model of representation**, representatives have little autonomy and are mandated to act as faithful agents of their particular constituents.

government and is supposed to implement the policies that it ran on during the election campaign. The majoritarian vision takes a particular stance when it comes to a central debate in democratic theory, namely, whether representatives should be independent trustees or mandated delegates (Pitkin 1967; Rehfeld 2009). In the **trustee model of representation**, representatives are free to use their own judgement when making policy. They are supposed to promote the collective good and act in the national interest rather than in the interests of any particular constituency. In contrast, in the **delegate model of representation**, representatives have little autonomy and are mandated to act as faithful agents of their particular constituents. The majoritarian vision of democracy adopts the delegate model of representation—governments are supposed to faithfully implement the policy platform chosen by the majority of the people.

In the majoritarian vision, citizens know that whichever team forms the government is responsible for the policies that get implemented during its tenure. As a result, citizens can use their evaluations of the policy record when deciding whether to reward or punish the incumbent in the following election. If citizens wish to reward the government for its performance in office, then they vote for the incumbent at election time. And if citizens wish to punish the government, then they vote for the opposition team. As this description of the majoritarian vision suggests, citizens get to exert influence over policy decisions only at election time. In effect, citizens choose a team of politicians at election time to implement the set of policies outlined in the team's campaign manifesto. Only when the next election rolls around do citizens get another opportunity to assert their influence over the policymaking process—they get to assert their influence by deciding whether the policies of the incumbent government should continue or whether they should be replaced by the policy proposals of the opposition. Citizens are not expected to exert influence over policy decisions between elections.

One of the central ideas of the majoritarian vision is, as its name suggests, that policy should be determined by the majority; citizens who hold minority preferences should have no influence in the policymaking process. As Tocqueville ([1835] 1945, 264), an early proponent of this view, puts it, "The very essence of democratic government consists in the absolute sovereignty of the majority." To make sure that only the majority rule, policymaking power is to be concentrated in the hands of a majority government. Power is not to be dispersed among different political actors or institutions as this will almost certainly require the involvement of minority opposition members in the policymaking process; this is something that is seen as illegitimate. In fact, according to the majoritarian vision of democracy, the citizenry's ability to control its elected representatives and, hence, policy decisions through the electoral process is possible only if there is a clear concentration of power in the hands of a single majority team of politicians.

Consensus Vision

According to the consensus vision of democracy, elections are supposed to be events in which citizens choose representatives from as wide a range of social groups as possible. These agents are then entrusted to bargain over policy on behalf of the citizens in the legislature. Elections are not designed to serve as some sort of referendum on the set of policies implemented by the government as they are in the majoritarian vision of democracy. Instead, elections are there to provide citizens with the opportunity to choose representatives who they believe will be effective advocates for their interests when bargaining over policy finally begins after the election. With this in mind, one of the central goals of elections in the consensus vision is to produce a legislature that is a miniature reflection of society as a whole. As John Stuart Mill ([1859] 1991, 116) put it, the legislature is supposed to be "an arena in which not only the general opinion of the nation, but that of every section of it . . . can produce itself in full light."

The consensus vision of democracy adopts a trustee model of representation. Representatives are not elected to enact a precise set of policies demanded by their particular constituents; rather, they are elected to bargain freely with each other over the policies they think will promote the common good. A consequence of this is that majorities frequently shift as representatives build different legislative coalitions, depending on the specific policy that is under consideration. Whereas the ability of citizens to influence policy decisions begins and ends at election time in the majoritarian vision, citizens in the consensus vision are able, through the ongoing bargaining of their elected representatives, to exert influence over the policymaking process *between* elections. In effect, the consensus vision of democracy demands that policy decisions continuously respond to changes in the preferences of the citizens.

One of the central ideas of the consensus vision of democracy is, as its name suggests, that policy should be determined by as many citizens (and their representatives) as possible. Unlike in the majoritarian vision, citizens with majority preferences are not to be given any privileged status in the policymaking process; instead, all groups of citizens, including minorities, should have the power to influence policy decisions in direct proportion to their electoral size. One obvious objective of the consensus vision of democracy, then, is to prevent the majority from riding roughshod over the preferences of the minority. As proponents of the consensus vision note, the best way to guarantee that the majority takes account of minority preferences is to disperse power in such a way that the minority has some valuable policymaking influence with which to defend its interests. If power becomes too concentrated, there is always the risk that the majority will capture it and use it against the minority; this is something that is seen as illegitimate.

According to Lijphart (1999, 1–2), the key difference between the two visions of democracy has to do with how they each answer this question: "Who should govern and to whose interests should the government be responsive?" For the majoritarian vision, the answer is a majority of the people. And for the consensus vision, the answer is as many people as

The **majoritarian vision of democracy** is based on the idea that power should be concentrated in the hands of the majority. The **consensus vision of democracy** is based on the idea that power should be dispersed among as many political actors as possible.

possible. In effect, the **majoritarian vision of democracy** demands that political power be concentrated in the hands of the majority, whereas the **consensus vision of democracy** demands that it be dispersed among as many actors as possible.

Why might political actors wish to privilege one vision of democracy over another? Theoretically, one could argue that the majoritarian vision of democracy would be better in some circumstances and the consensus vision in others. Powell (2000, 8–9) notes:

> Where the issues are clear-cut and a unified citizenry has an overwhelmingly clear set of preferences, voters might well prefer to take most of the choices out of the hands of the negotiators and be sure that the election results are in themselves decisive. But where the issues are complex, the citizens divided, and problems that the citizens cannot anticipate arise, each group of citizens may well prefer to be represented by trustworthy agents who can be relied upon to negotiate for their constituents. Citizens who fear being in the minority on the issues that dominate a single election outcome, but anticipate being part of a majority on other issues, may especially prefer to have representative agents bargaining for them anew on each separate issue.

Practically speaking, for a democracy to function efficiently it needs relatively stable rules, so key institutions cannot be continuously restructured depending on whether the most important issues of the day are "clear-cut" or "complex." As a result, a choice needs to be made about whether to set up a majoritarian- or consensus-style democracy, and this choice is likely to endure. But how does one go about making this choice? Which institutions, or sets of institutions, create systems of government that most closely resemble one or the other of the two different visions of democracy?

Majoritarian and Consensus Institutions

Every democracy has a set of rules that specify how policy gets made and who gets to make it. As we saw in Chapter 15, many of these rules are explicitly written down in a country's constitution. If a constitution encourages the election of single-party legislative majorities that can control the executive and concentrates power in the hands of a single-party government, then it can be considered majoritarian in nature. If the constitution encourages the equitable representation of multiple parties and the dispersal of policymaking power among these parties, however, then it can be considered consensual in nature (Powell 2000, 21). It is possible to think of the two visions of democracy as representing opposing end points of a majoritarian-consensus dimension that captures how widely power is dispersed. To a large extent, the different institutions we have examined in the last four chapters can be thought of in terms of whether they concentrate or disperse power. In effect, they determine the extent to which a constitution is majoritarian or consensual.

In Table 16.1, we illustrate when a particular "institution" can be considered more majoritarian or more consensual.[1] As will become clear, the decisions to adopt majoritarian or consensus institutions are not entirely independent of one another. Choosing to adopt certain majoritarian institutions can virtually guarantee having to live with other majoritarian institutions. Similarly, choosing to adopt certain consensus institutions virtually guarantees having to live with other consensus institutions. This is because many of these institutions are causally related. Indeed, it is this causal interdependence among institutions that explains why constitutional designers are not mixing and matching institutions with reckless abandon and why democracies, despite their great institutional variety, tend to come in just two main types—majoritarian and consensus (Lijphart 1999; Powell 2000).

It is easy to see how electoral systems fit onto a majoritarian-consensus dimension. As our discussion of electoral systems in Chapter 13 indicates, majoritarian electoral systems tend to concentrate power in that only those candidates or parties with the most votes win; indeed, in most majoritarian systems only one candidate wins. In contrast, proportional electoral systems tend to disperse power among candidates or parties in proportion to the share of electoral support they win. As a result, even candidates winning minority support obtain some policymaking power. The more proportional the electoral system, the more it disperses power and the more it approximates the consensus vision of democracy. The size of the party system can also be conceptualized along a majoritarian-consensus dimension in a fairly straightforward manner. For example, power is concentrated in two-party systems in that there are two dominant political parties in the legislature and only these parties have a

TABLE 16.1	**Institutions and the Majoritarian-Consensus Dimension**

Institution	Majoritarian	Consensus
Electoral system	Majoritarian	Proportional
Party system	Two parties	Many parties
Government type	Single-party majority	Coalition/minority
Federalism	Unitary	Federal
Bicameralism	Unicameral	Bicameral
Constitutionalism	Legislative supremacy constitution	Higher law constitution
Regime type	Parliamentary	Presidential

---

1. The information in Table 16.1 gives the impression that institutions are either majoritarian or consensus. This, however, is somewhat misleading because the extent to which institutions disperse or concentrate power is best thought of as a continuum rather than a dichotomy. For example, some forms of bicameralism disperse power more than others. Similarly, some electoral systems are more proportional than others. The point here is that the extent to which particular institutions, such as the electoral system, bicameralism, federalism, and so on, disperse power depends crucially on exactly what form they take.

realistic chance of holding power. In contrast, power is dispersed in multiparty systems in that there are multiple parties in the legislature and more than two parties have a realistic chance of holding power. The more parties there are in the party system, the more that power is dispersed. The type of government in a country also fits neatly into a majoritarian-consensus continuum. For instance, power is concentrated in the hands of a single party in single-party majority governments but dispersed more widely among multiple parties in coalition or minority governments.[2]

These three institutions—the electoral system, the party system, and the type of government—are all causally related. As our discussion of Duverger's theory in Chapter 14 illustrates, majoritarian electoral systems tend to be associated with small party systems, whereas proportional electoral systems tend to be associated with large party systems (at least in countries with sufficiently high levels of social heterogeneity). And as our discussion of the government formation process in Chapter 12 illustrates, the size of the party system, in turn, influences the type of government that forms. Specifically, single-party majority governments are much more likely to form when there are few political parties, because concentrated party systems increase the likelihood that a single party will win a legislative majority. In contrast, coalition and minority governments are much more likely to form when there are many political parties, because fractionalized party systems reduce the likelihood that a single party will win a legislative majority. As this indicates, the choice of a constitutional designer to adopt a particular type of electoral system—majoritarian or proportional—tends also to be a choice to have a particular type of party system and government. This is why we tend to see either (a) countries with a majoritarian electoral system, a small party system, and a high frequency of single-party majority governments, or (b) countries with a proportional electoral system, a large party system, and a high frequency of coalition or minority governments.

Federalism, bicameralism, and constitutionalism are three other institutions that can easily be conceptualized in terms of a majoritarian-consensus dimension. For example, federal states disperse power between at least two territorial levels of government; in contrast, unitary states concentrate power in the national government. Bicameral states disperse power between two legislative chambers; in contrast, unicameral states concentrate power in a single legislative chamber. Higher law constitutions disperse power by giving certain institutions, like constitutional courts, the authority to invalidate acts of government. They also contain a bill of rights that protects minority rights. In contrast, legislative supremacy constitutions concentrate power in the hands of legislative majorities and do not allow for constitutional review.

---

2. That power is dispersed in coalition governments is largely self-evident in that there are multiple parties in the cabinet. It is important to recognize, however, that power is also dispersed in minority governments. This is even true of single-party minority governments, at least in parliamentary democracies. Although there is only one cabinet party in a single-party minority government, we know from our discussion of minority governments in parliamentary democracies (Chapter 12) that some other party or parties in the legislature must be supporting the government for it to remain in power. The ability of these "support" parties to bring the government down means that the government will have to share policymaking power with them if it wants to stay in office.

Federalism, bicameralism, and constitutionalism often occur together. Why? Imagine that you are a constitutional designer for a country and that you see significant advantages to setting up a decentralized form of government to better take account of regional disparities in preferences. A problem, though, is that for decentralized forms of government to be stable and credible, it must be the case that regional governments do not try to take advantage of each other and, more important, that the central government does not try to usurp power from the regions. If these conditions do not hold, then some constituent regional units might decide that it is preferable to withdraw from the system of government altogether. But how can these conditions be achieved? One thing you can do is to explicitly write into the constitution that sovereignty is to be divided between governments from different territorial levels. In other words, you might think to write a federal constitution, thereby constitutionally protecting the decentralized system of government. Although this could help, you should ask yourself why actors would necessarily act in accordance with the federal system merely because it is written down somewhere in the constitution. Why, for example, would a central government interested in centralizing power comply with federal provisions in a constitution?

Concerns about compliance might lead you to create an institution like a constitutional court with the authority to punish attempts by political actors to violate federal provisions in the constitution. But would the creation of something like a constitutional court be sufficient to make the federal system stable and credible? Not necessarily. For example, a legislative majority at the national level may emerge that wishes to amend the constitution so as to create a more centralized and unitary form of government.[3] To prevent this from happening, you might decide to create a system of checks and balances that makes it harder for national majorities to form that wish to centralize power. One way to do this is to establish a bicameral legislature in which the upper legislative chamber is specifically designed to represent the interests of the different regions. This upper chamber would obviously have a stake in maintaining the federal system. By combining these institutions—federalism, bicameralism, and constitutionalism—it is possible to enhance the stability and credibility of decentralized systems of government (Bednar 2009; Bednar, Eskridge, and Ferejohn 2001). This line of reasoning explains why constitutional designers who wish to disperse power in the form of a decentralized system of government frequently choose to adopt all three of these institutions.

Although perhaps less obvious, the choice of whether to adopt a parliamentary or presidential form of democracy can also be thought of in terms of a majoritarian-consensus continuum. Presidential systems fall at the consensus end of the spectrum because power is dispersed between the executive and the legislature. Indeed, presidential systems are often

---

3. You might also wonder whether a constitutional court would be sufficiently independent of the national government to check its attempts at centralizing power. As we saw in Chapter 15, this concern arises because a constitutional court has to rely on other institutions to enforce its decisions (see Box 15.2, "Judicial Power and the Judicialization of Politics"). To the extent that a constitutional court is institutionally dependent on other national institutions to enforce its decisions, it may act like a creature of the national government and be reluctant to check its powers (Bednar, Eskridge, and Ferejohn 2001).

referred to as "separation of powers" systems for precisely this reason. In contrast, parliamentary systems fall at the majoritarian end of the spectrum because power is concentrated in the hands of an executive that is supported by a legislative majority. Where, you might wonder, do semi-presidential regimes fall on the majoritarian-consensus dimension? As you might expect, the premier-presidential type of semi-presidential democracies fall at the majoritarian end of the spectrum with the parliamentary democracies. Exactly where the president-parliamentary type of semi-presidential democracies fit on the spectrum depends to a large extent on whether there is cohabitation or not. Recall from Chapter 12 that periods of cohabitation occur when the president is from one political bloc and the prime minister is from another. President-parliamentary democracies fall at the consensus end of the spectrum during periods of cohabitation, because power is dispersed and divided between the president and the prime minister. However, they fall at the majoritarian end of the spectrum when there is no cohabitation, because power is concentrated in the hands of the president, who effectively runs the entire show.

Unlike many of the other institutional choices in Table 16.1, the choice to have a parliamentary or presidential system does not necessarily imply the adoption of other majoritarian or consensus institutions. For example, parliamentary democracies can have many consensus institutions. Belgium is parliamentary but has proportional electoral rules, a large party system, coalition governments, federalism, bicameralism, and a higher law constitution. Similarly, presidential democracies can have many majoritarian institutions. For example, the United States is presidential but has majoritarian electoral rules, a small party system, and single-party governments. With the exception of parliamentarism and presidentialism, though, the majoritarian institutions shown in Table 16.1 tend to occur together, as do the consensus institutions that are shown. This is what allows us to speak of majoritarian and consensus democracies.

Historically, the prototype for majoritarian democracies has been the United Kingdom (UK). Indeed, majoritarian democracies are sometimes referred to as Westminster-style democracies because the British House of Commons meets in the Palace of Westminster in the heart of London. With its majoritarian single-member district plurality electoral system, the UK has traditionally had two dominant parties in the legislature and single-party majority governments. In addition to a legislative supremacy constitution, the UK is unitary and has tended to make policy in a very centralized manner. Although the UK is bicameral, the upper house, the House of Lords, is very weak. Several changes in recent years mean that the UK is no longer the model of a majoritarian system that it once was. These changes include policies promoting devolution to regional legislative bodies in Scotland, Wales, and Northern Ireland; the increasing legislative strength of third parties such as the Liberal Democrats or the Scottish National Party; and the formation of a coalition government between the Conservatives and Liberal Democrats, following the 2010 legislative elections. New Zealand has also historically been seen as a prototype of a majoritarian democracy (Lijphart 1999). Like the United Kingdom, though, it has recently adopted more consensus-oriented institutions.

Specifically, it replaced its SMDP electoral system with a more proportional mixed system in 1996. This has led to an increase in the size of the party system and an increase in the frequency of coalition, as opposed to single-party majority, governments. With these changes in the UK and New Zealand, the most prototypical majoritarian democracies now exist in the Caribbean in places like Barbados, the Bahamas, Jamaica, and Trinidad and Tobago.

The prototype for consensus democracies is Belgium. Belgium is federal (since 1993) and bicameral (since 1995) and employs constitutional review (since 1984). Its proportional representation electoral system encourages a large party system, which in turn generates broad coalition governments. Belgian cabinets are required to have an equal number of French- and Flemish-speaking ministers (not including the prime minister). Because the parties are split along linguistic lines, the language-parity requirement has the effect of increasing the number of parties in a typical Belgian cabinet. In order to implement any new policies in Belgium, many different actors must agree to the change. The positive spin on this state of affairs would be that politicians must build broad coalitions. This typically involves compromising with many different political actors and taking minority views into account. The negative spin would be to simply point out the difficulties that political actors in Belgium sometimes face in reaching agreements on any policy changes. After the June 2007 legislative elections for the lower house, for example, eleven different parties won seats. A new government did not enter office until December of that year, eight months after the election (S. Golder 2010). In the meantime, Belgian citizens had descended onto the streets to protest the absence of an effective government, with some questioning whether their country should simply cease to exist, splitting along linguistic lines into Wallonia and Flanders. The government collapsed less than two and a half years later, and early elections were held in June 2010. The policy disagreements that had delayed government formation in 2007 had not been resolved, however, and the eleven parties reelected to parliament now hold the record for the longest delay ever in government formation. A government was finally sworn in on December 6, 2011, fully 541 days after the election.

Given our discussion of the government formation process in Chapter 12, it should come as

GEORGES GOBET/AFP/Getty Images

After 541 days of a caretaker government in Belgium, a new government takes office as Prime Minister Elio Di Rupo (*left*) takes an oath beside King Albert II (*right*) on December 6, 2011, at the royal castle of Laeken in Brussels.

no surprise that a country with a large number of parties would experience delays in the length of time that it takes to form a government. Nor should it come as a surprise that the coalition governments that do form in such a country tend to be unstable and short-lived. All institutional choices present trade-offs. We can have a broad representation of social groups, but this may lead to instability in the government. Or we can have a stable and efficient government, but at the cost of dramatically limiting citizens' choices at the ballot box. Whether you prefer the majoritarian vision or the consensus vision of democracy depends on how you value political representation and meaningful choices versus efficiency and accountability. We now examine in more detail what the two visions of democracy mean for political representation.

Political Representation

In her famous 1967 book, *The Concept of Representation*, Hanna Pitkin distinguishes between four different views of political representation.[4] **Formalistic representation** has to do with how representatives are authorized and held accountable. **Descriptive representation** addresses the extent to which representatives resemble and "stand for" their constituents. **Symbolic representation** focuses on the symbolic ways that representatives "stand for" their constituents. **Substantive representation** emphasizes how representatives "act for" the people and promote their interests. Whereas descriptive and symbolic representation focus on *who* is being represented, either literally or symbolically, substantive representation focuses on the *actions* taken by representatives. In what follows, we examine how majoritarian and consensus institutions influence these different forms of representation.

> Hanna Pitkin (1967) distinguishes between four different views of political representation. **Formalistic representation** has to do with how representatives are authorized and held accountable. **Descriptive representation** addresses the extent to which representatives resemble and "stand for" their constituents. **Symbolic representation** focuses on the symbolic ways that representatives "stand for" the citizens. **Substantive representation** emphasizes how representatives "act for" the people and promote their interests.

Formalistic Representation

Rather than focus on how a representative behaves, formalistic representation has to do with the formal procedures by which representatives are authorized to act and held accountable for their actions. Authorization and accountability are treated differently in the majoritarian and consensus visions of democracy. According to the majoritarian vision, power is to be concentrated in the hands of the majority. It is majority support that authorizes representatives (legislators, parties, governments) to wield power. Policymaking power in the hands of representatives with only minority support is considered illegitimate. Majoritarian democracies do not always live up to this ideal in practice. As we saw in Chapter 13, the most common majoritarian electoral system, the single-member district plurality system, does not

---

4. For alternative views of representation, see Mansbridge (2003), Saward (2006, 2014), Disch (2011), and Kuyper (2016).

require the winning candidate to obtain majority electoral support. Candidates can win and obtain 100 percent of the representation in their district with minority support. In line with the majoritarian vision, most governments in majoritarian democracies are single-party majority governments that dominate the policymaking process. The problem, as we saw in Chapters 12 and 14, is that many of these single-party majority governments do not actually enjoy majority support in the electorate. In many cases, the party in power has won only a plurality of votes but has seen the mechanical effect of the disproportional electoral system transform its plurality electoral support into a "manufactured" legislative majority.

According to the consensus vision, power is to be dispersed among as many people as possible. Majority support is not necessary to authorize representatives to wield power. Instead, power is supposed to be distributed among political actors in direct proportion to their electoral size. As a result, there should be a close connection between the percentage of votes that representatives receive and the percentage of policymaking power they enjoy. In practice, consensus democracies approximate this ideal in some respects but not others. On the one hand, the fact that consensus democracies employ proportional electoral systems means that there is a close connection between the percentage of votes that a party wins at election time and the percentage of legislative seats that it obtains. That proportional electoral rules typically produce multiparty systems also means that it is rare for a single party to control a legislative majority. As a result, power is almost never concentrated in the hands of a single-party majority government in a consensus democracy. On the other hand, the complicated nature of the government formation process means that there is only a weak connection between the percentage of seats (and votes) that a party wins and its share of government power. Some parties can control a significant share of the legislative seats, for example, but not be in the government. It is important to remember, though, that consensus democracies do not concentrate power entirely in the hands of the government. Instead, they disperse it (to differing degrees) among both governmental and nongovernmental parties. One way in which they do this is by having legislative committees on which opposition parties receive representation and play a significant role in the policymaking process.

Not only do majoritarian and consensus visions of democracy differ when it comes to authorizing representatives but they also differ when it comes to holding representatives accountable. **Accountability** refers to the extent to which it is possible for voters to sanction parties for the actions they take while in office. Put slightly differently, accountability is about how easy it is for citizens "to throw the rascals out." Accountability is often considered desirable, because it provides incentives for politicians to pursue policies that will keep the voters—or, at least, a winning coalition of the voters—satisfied. Accountability basically requires that citizens look at how an incumbent party has behaved in the past in order to decide whether to reward or punish it at the next election. Such behavior on the part of voters is referred to as **retrospective voting** (Erikson,

> **Accountability** is the extent to which voters are able to sanction parties for their behavior in office.
> **Retrospective voting** occurs when voters look at the past performance of incumbent parties to decide how to vote in the current election.

MacKuen, and Stimson 2002; Fiorina 1981). If citizens decide that an incumbent party has performed sufficiently well in office, they will reward it by voting for it. In contrast, if citizens decide that an incumbent party has not performed sufficiently well, they will punish it by voting for another party. If accountability works well, incumbent parties that perform well are reelected into office, and incumbent parties that perform poorly are removed from office.

The extent to which citizens can hold their governments accountable through elections varies from country to country. Majoritarian democracies typically have high levels of accountability as it is relatively easy to throw the rascals out when you have single-party majority governments and two-party systems. If the citizens in a majoritarian democracy are dissatisfied with the performance of the party in power, they simply vote for the opposition party to replace it.

In contrast, accountability tends to be much lower in consensus democracies. One reason for this is that voters in these countries are rarely in a position to directly choose the government. As we have already noted, it is relatively unusual for a single party to win a legislative majority when there are many parties. As a result, elections in consensus-style democracies almost never determine the identity of the government. Instead, elections usher in periods of negotiations in which party leaders bargain over the identity of the future government. The choices of these party leaders may or may not accurately reflect the preferences of the citizens. As we saw in Chapter 12, it is also common for governments in these types of countries to be removed from office in interelection periods without the electorate being directly consulted. This clearly diminishes the ability of voters to sanction their elected officials (Hellwig and Samuels 2007). A second reason why consensus democracies tend to have low levels of accountability is that citizens may vote against a particular incumbent party at election time and yet find that this party is still a member of the next coalition government because the other parties could not form a cabinet without it. There are numerous examples of parties losing votes and seats in consensus democracies but nonetheless finding themselves in the next government. Perhaps the most egregious case of this is Switzerland, where the four main parties have agreed since 1959 to form governments together irrespective of how the citizens vote. This arrangement is commonly known as the "magic formula" (Caramani 1996; Kerr 1987).

Clarity of responsibility is the extent to which voters can identify exactly who it is that is responsible for the policies that are implemented.

A concept that is closely related to accountability is **clarity of responsibility**. Whereas accountability refers to the ability to "throw the rascals out," clarity of responsibility refers to the ability to identify "who the rascals are." Clarity of responsibility is a necessary condition for voters to be able to hold their government accountable. If citizens cannot identify who is responsible for the policies that get implemented (or don't get implemented), they will not be able to appropriately sanction those parties for their behavior.

As with accountability, clarity of responsibility varies from country to country. The more that power is concentrated, the greater the clarity of responsibility. One factor that affects clarity of responsibility is the type of government in a country. For example, clarity of responsibility is very high in those countries in which power is concentrated in the hands of a single-party majority government. In such countries, citizens know exactly whom to reward or blame—the party in power—at election time. Clarity of responsibility is less high in countries in which power is dispersed among multiple parties in a coalition government, because it is not always obvious which coalition party is responsible for the policies that get implemented (Duch, Przepiorka, and Stevenson 2015; Hobolt, Tilley, and Banducci 2013; Powell and Whitten 1993).[5] Clarity of responsibility is even lower in minority governments, in which citizens may not know who is keeping the government in power and, hence, who is responsible for the policies that get implemented. Indeed, different parties in the legislature may be keeping the minority government in office at different points in time. The reason for this, as we saw in Chapter 12, is that minority governments frequently build shifting legislative majorities on different issues to stay in power.

Other institutions that disperse power, such as bicameralism and federalism, also reduce clarity of responsibility. As we noted in Chapter 15, federalism can make it difficult for citizens to know which level of government is responsible for policy successes and which is to blame for policy failures (Arceneaux 2005; Gomez and Wilson 2008; Maestas et al. 2008; Malhotra and Kuo 2008). For example, is the poor performance of the regional economy the result of policies adopted by the subnational government or of those implemented by the national government? In this type of situation, neither the subnational nor the national government will want to take responsibility for the poor economic performance, and each will likely try to blame the other. In this way, federalism facilitates blame shifting (and credit claiming), thereby making it difficult for citizens to know exactly who is responsible for what. Bicameral systems can have a similar effect, particularly if the two legislative chambers are equally powerful and controlled by opposing political sides.

In sum, by concentrating power, majoritarian democracies tend to produce high levels of both accountability and clarity of responsibility. Not only do majoritarian institutions make it easy for voters to identify which political actors are responsible for the policies that get implemented, but they make it easy also for voters to sanction these actors for their performance in office. By dispersing power, consensus democracies tend to produce relatively low levels of accountability and clarity of responsibility. Consensus-style institutions make it hard for voters to know exactly which political actors are responsible for the policies that a government enacts. And even if voters can figure this out, consensus-style institutions make it hard for voters to reward or punish these actors for their performance in office.

---

5. Some studies suggest voters hold the prime ministerial party most responsible for policy at election time (Crabtree et al. 2016). This is because the prime minister is often the most visible member of the government and someone who is widely recognized as the agenda setter (Duch and Stevenson 2013). Indeed, there is empirical evidence that the electoral fortunes of the prime ministerial party are more strongly affected by the state of the economy than those of other governmental parties (Duch and Stevenson 2008). Some scholars suggest that the party in charge of the finance ministry is also held more responsible for policy than other cabinet parties (Williams, Seki, and Whitten 2016).

Substantive Representation

Substantive representation occurs when representatives take actions in line with the substantive and ideological interests of those they represent. For many democratic theorists, substantive representation is the most important form of representation as it focuses on what representatives actually do in office. Substantive representation has typically been studied in terms of either **ideological congruence** (Huber and Powell 1994) or **ideological responsiveness** (Page and Shapiro 1983). Ideological congruence has to do with the extent to which the actions of the representatives are in line with the interests of the people at a fixed point in time, whereas ideological responsiveness has to do with how representatives change their behavior to become more congruent with the interests of the people over time (Golder and Ferland, forthcoming). One way to think about this is that congruence captures a static or distance form of representation, whereas responsiveness captures a dynamic or directional form of representation.

> **Ideological congruence** has to do with the extent to which the actions of the representatives are in line with the interests of the people at a fixed point in time. **Ideological responsiveness** has to do with how representatives change their behavior to become more congruent with the interests of the people over time.

To highlight the conceptual distinction between ideological congruence and ideological responsiveness, consider the three different scenarios in Figure 16.1. Each scenario depicts a representative R and a citizen C in some policy space. The dashed gray lines indicate how a fully responsive representative would move in each scenario. Scenario (a) shows a situation of perfect ideological congruence with the representative sharing the same policy position as

---

FIGURE 16.1   Ideological Congruence and Responsiveness

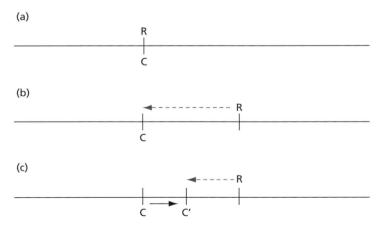

Source: Golder and Ferland (forthcoming).

the citizen. In scenario (b), we start from a situation of ideological incongruence. The representative demonstrates responsiveness by moving leftward to the citizen's policy position, thereby establishing perfect congruence. In scenario (c), we again start from a situation of ideological incongruence. The citizen changes his position by moving rightward from C to C′. The representative demonstrates responsiveness by moving leftward to the citizen's new position, C′, thereby establishing perfect congruence. As this last scenario indicates, responsiveness does not necessarily imply that the representative will always move in the same direction that the citizen moves (Ferland 2015).

The majoritarian and consensus visions of democracy differ in how they think about ideological congruence. The majoritarian vision demands that representatives (parties, legislatures, governments) are congruent with the preferences of the majority. As we saw in Chapter 11, the policy position of the median citizen (voter) is the only one that cannot be defeated in a pair-wise contest (if we have a one-dimensional policy space). In practice, therefore, the ideological position of the median citizen is taken as indicative of the majority's preferred policy position. Rather than demand ideological congruence with the median citizen, the consensus vision demands that representatives be congruent with as many citizens as possible.

Majoritarian and consensus institutions produce very different types of party systems and legislatures. Majoritarian electoral rules produce few parties where each party tends to adopt centrist positions close to the median voter. There are two reasons for this. First, majoritarian electoral rules reward large parties. To the extent that there are more voters in the center of the policy space, they incentivize parties to adopt centrist positions. Second, majoritarian electoral rules tend to produce few parties. Models of spatial competition suggest that small party systems create centripetal tendencies where parties converge on the center of the policy space (Cox 1990; Matakos, Troumpounis, and Xefteris, forthcoming). Indeed, the median voter theorem we examined in Chapter 11 predicts that both parties in a majoritarian two-party system have incentives to converge on the position of the median voter. In sum, majoritarian rules are associated with party systems and legislatures that are dominated by a small number of large parties that adopt similar centrist policy positions. These large parties are typically "umbrella" parties that represent a broad coalition of diverse voters. Although parties tend to be congruent with the median voter, the diversity of their bases of support means that there is often a large degree of incongruence between a party's policy position and the preferences of many of its voters. As an example, many Democratic and Republican voters in the United States hold preferences that are quite distant from their party's policy platform, something that can produce voter dissatisfaction. That parties in majoritarian systems often hold similar policy positions limits the extent to which voters have meaningful choices at election time.

Party systems and legislatures in consensus democracies tend to be quite different. Proportional electoral rules are typically associated with a large number of small parties that disperse throughout the policy space. These parties compete in a permissive environment where they can win legislative seats even if they are not the largest party and even if they do not adopt centrist positions. Parties are able to adopt a wide range of policy positions and carve out niche electorates. This means not only that the diversity of citizen preferences is reflected in the party system but also that the policy platforms of the individual parties are congruent with the preferences of their specific voters. Proportional systems provide voters with more meaningful choices at election time. Although an individual who holds "green" policy preferences may have little choice but to vote for a center-left party in a majoritarian system, she is likely to have the option of voting for a green party that is more congruent with her preferences in a proportional system. Because proportional systems accurately translate votes into seats, they also produce legislatures that are congruent with the full range of diversity in society (Golder and Stramski 2010).

In most parliamentary democracies, governments play the dominant role in the policy-making process.[6] As a result, the degree of ideological congruence between citizen preferences and the government's policy position is particularly important. Government congruence is typically conceptualized as the ideological distance between the government's policy position and the preferences of the median voter, and it is something that is valued in both visions of democracy. From a theoretical point of view, government congruence can be achieved in both majoritarian and consensus democracies. Government congruence is expected to be high in majoritarian systems due to the fact that party system size tends to be small and parties typically adopt centrist positions. Whichever party forms a single-party majority government is likely to implement policies that align closely with the preferences of the median voter. Proportional systems, as we have seen, usually produce coalition governments. The median legislative party, which will usually be ideologically close to the median voter, plays a pivotal role in the coalition formation process as governments in parliamentary democracies must enjoy the support of a legislative majority. In effect, the median legislative party in a proportional system can be expected to pull government policy toward the ideological position of the median voter. In line with these theoretical predictions, most recent empirical studies find that there is no significant difference in the level of government congruence between majoritarian and consensus democracies (Blais and Bodet 2006; Ferland 2016; Golder and Lloyd 2014; Golder and Stramski 2010).

What about ideological *responsiveness*? Recall that a responsive representative is one who changes her behavior to become more congruent with the ideological preferences of those she represents. Two conditions are necessary for responsiveness (Golder and Ferland, forthcoming; Soroka and Wlezien 2015). Representatives must want to become more congruent *and* they must be able to act on those desires. If there are weak incentives to be responsive, responsiveness will be low irrespective of whether representatives have the ability to be responsive. If there are strong incentives to be responsive but representatives are constrained

---

6. We focus on government congruence in parliamentary democracies as there are few studies of government congruence in presidential democracies (Golder and Ferland, forthcoming).

in their ability to act on those incentives, then responsiveness will also be low. Responsiveness will be high only if representatives have both the desire and ability to be responsive.

Given this theoretical framework, we would expect responsiveness to be higher in majoritarian democracies than consensus ones. Why? First, the incentives to be responsive are higher in majoritarian systems. Single-party majority governments, which typically form in majoritarian systems, have strong incentives to follow the preferences of the median voter. As Golder and Ferland (forthcoming) note, things are more complicated in the coalition governments that form in consensus democracies. This is because only some government parties are likely to be responsive to the preferences of the median voter. Government parties that hold non-centrist policy positions are much more likely to be responsive to the preferences of their own niche electorates. The incentives to be responsive are likely to depend on the ability of voters to punish unresponsive representatives. Government responsiveness should be lower in consensus democracies, because clarity of responsibility—a necessary condition for accountability—is lower in these countries. Second, the ability to be responsive is higher in majoritarian systems. Veto player theory, which we examined in Chapter 15, indicates that the ability of governments to be responsive will be low if the number of ideologically diverse veto players is large (Tsebelis 2002). As the institutions listed in Table 16.1 indicate, consensus democracies are likely to have significantly more veto players than majoritarian democracies. Theory, therefore, would suggest that ideological responsiveness will be greater in majoritarian democracies. Unfortunately, we have few empirical studies that have examined this prediction.

Descriptive Representation

Descriptive representation has to do with whether representatives resemble and therefore "stand for" their constituents. It calls for representatives who share the same characteristics, such as race, gender, religion, and class, as those they represent. In effect, descriptive representation calls for women representatives to represent women constituents, minority representatives to represent minority constituents, and so on. Descriptive representation requires that parties, legislatures, and governments accurately reflect the full range of diversity that exists in society. As such, descriptive representation is valued more highly in the consensus vision of democracy than the majoritarian vision.

On the whole, democratic theorists generally consider descriptive representation as inferior to substantive representation because it focuses on "who" representatives are as opposed to what representatives "do" (Celis et al. 2008). It seems unreasonable, after all, to hold representatives accountable for their descriptive characteristics, which they cannot change, as opposed to what they do, which they can change. Nonetheless, many believe that descriptive representation is important, especially in situations where there are high levels of mistrust between groups or a history of discrimination, or when new issues have emerged on which parties and other representatives have yet to take a clear stance (Mansbridge 1999; Phillips 1998).

Some scholars claim that descriptive representation is important in its own right, either because it signals a policy of recognition and acceptance or because it promotes a sense of fairness and legitimacy. The existence of minority representatives, for example, can challenge social hierarchies and change the social understanding of who gets to rule (Mansbridge 1999). In effect, it can signal, to both the minority group and the larger community, that minorities are accepted as equal members in society and that they can play a legitimate role in determining how the political system is to be run. In doing so, descriptive representation may enhance a sense of fairness and strengthen the attachment that minorities or other groups feel toward the political system. Women and minority representatives can also act as role models, demonstrating to women and minorities that particular careers and positions are not closed off to them.

Other scholars promote descriptive representation not for its own sake but because they see it as a pathway to improving substantive representation. Here the general idea is that individuals who share similar descriptive characteristics, such as their gender, race, or religion, are likely to have shared experiences and developed a sense of linked fate that generate a common set of perspectives and substantive interests (Phillips 1998; Tate 1994, 1995; Young 2002). According to these scholars, it is important to have, say, female representatives in the legislature, not because of some reason related to their biology but because they are likely to have a common set of experiences that are not shared by male representatives. These common experiences result from many factors, including the fact that women typically share similar, often subordinate, positions in most societies. These shared experiences are likely to mean that there are issues that are particularly salient to women or on which women take distinctive positions. Although men could advocate on behalf of these issue positions, the argument is that women are likely to receive greater substantive representation, on average, from a woman representative than a man representative. One reason for this is that women representatives are likely to have an informational advantage with respect to these issues as a result of their personal experience.

Critics of descriptive representation argue that it can promote group essentialism, the idea that all members of a group share an essential identity that only they can have and understand. Among other things, group essentialism implies that all members of a group share a common interest that overrides any interests that divide them. This is what allows people to talk about "women's issues" or "minority issues." In effect, proponents of descriptive representation have been criticized both for ignoring the diversity that exists within particular groups and for failing to recognize that individuals who are not members of the group, such as men, can usefully advocate on behalf of group members, such as women (Celis 2009; Childs and Krook 2006). One response to this criticism has been the increasing focus on "intersectional" identities in which individuals have overlapping or intersecting social identities related to gender, class, religion, ethnicity, and so on (Crenshaw 1989; Hancock 2007; Hughes 2011; Weldon 2006). Rather than treat women as a single group, for example, scholars of intersectionality might distinguish between the representation of black women and white women. Scholars who adopt this approach have demonstrated, among other things, that much of the women's movement in the United States has been driven by middle-class white women and their concerns, whereas little attention has been paid to black women and the representation of their interests (Junn and Brown 2008). Concerns about intersectional identities, though, do not necessarily undermine the importance of descriptive representation; rather, they highlight the necessity of adopting a more fine-grained approach to achieving descriptive representation.

If you value descriptive representation, you might wonder whether majoritarian or consensus institutions are better at bringing it about. In what follows, we briefly look at the descriptive representation of women. In Map 16.1, we show the proportion of legislative seats held by women in national parliaments around the world in 2014 using data from the Inter-Parliamentary Union (see "Proportion of Legislative Seats" 2016).[7] Darker colors indicate higher levels of women's legislative representation. The average level of women's legislative representation in the world in 2016 is just 20.9 percent. The average level of women's legislative representation is lower in dictatorships (18.8 percent) than in democracies (22.3 percent). The ten countries with the highest levels of women's legislative representation are Rwanda (63.8 percent), Bolivia (53.1 percent), Cuba (48.9 percent), Sweden (44.7 percent), Senegal (43.3 percent), Finland (42.5 percent), Nicaragua (42.4 percent), Ecuador (41.6 percent), South Africa (41.5 percent), and Spain (39.7 percent). In only two countries—Rwanda and Bolivia—do women make up the majority of legislative representatives. The ten countries with the lowest levels of women's legislative representation are Qatar (0 percent), Yemen (0.3 percent), Oman (1.2 percent), Kuwait (1.5 percent), the Solomon Islands (2 percent), Papua New Guinea (2.7 percent), Comoros (3 percent), Lebanon (3.1 percent), Iran (3.1 percent), and Haiti (4.2 percent). Women representatives hold less than 20 percent of the legislative seats in more than half of the world's countries.

What explains the variation in the level of women's legislative representation? To answer this question, we might begin by considering the steps someone must go through to be elected to the legislature (Krook and Norris 2014). The political recruitment process begins with the set of people who are eligible to run for office. Only a subset of eligible candidates aspire to compete for office, however, and of this group, only some are nominated by a political party to run. Finally, of those candidates who do compete for office, only some are elected. If we assume that women and men place the same value on achieving office and if there are no gender "distortions" at any of these stages, then we should see a roughly equal proportion of men and women representatives in the legislature. As the information in Map 16.1 clearly indicates, some distortion is occurring somewhere in the political recruitment process in most countries. In what follows, we focus on the final step in the political recruitment process, and in particular on the role that electoral rules play in the election of women candidates.

---

7. The data on women's legislative representation can be found at http://data.worldbank.org/indicator/SG.GEN.PARL.ZS.

MAP 16.1

Women's Legislative Representation in 2014

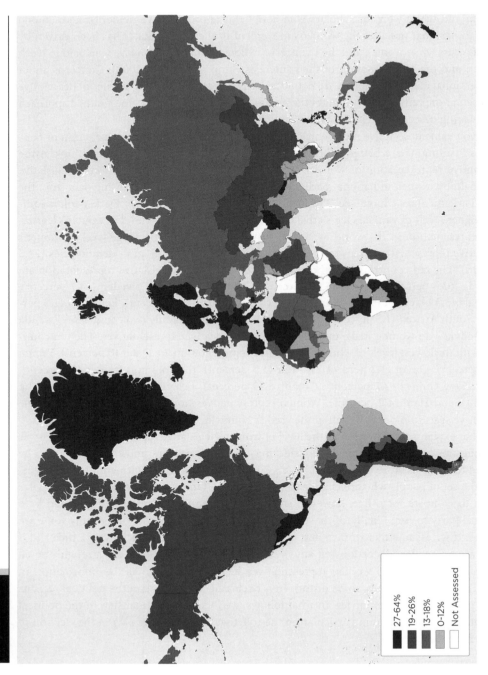

27–64%

19–26%

13–18%

0–12%

Not Assessed

Source: Data are from the Inter-Parliamentary Union and can be found at http://data.worldbank.org/indicator/SG.GEN.PARL.ZS ("Proportion of Legislative Seats" 2016).

Note: The map shows the proportion of legislative seats held by women in national parliaments in 2014.

Most empirical studies find that proportional electoral systems with large district magnitudes are associated with greater descriptive representation of women than majoritarian systems (Kittilson and Schwindt-Bayer 2012). The precise reason for this, though, is not entirely clear. At least two explanations have been proposed for this result. One is that majoritarian electoral systems tend to favor incumbents, and incumbents have traditionally been men (Fréchette, Maniquet, and Morelli 2008). A second has to do with the fact that left-wing parties tend to perform better under proportional electoral rules than under majoritarian ones.[8] This is important because left-wing parties typically have more women candidates than right-wing parties (Kittilson 2006).

Three members of the Alianza Pais party in Ecuador assumed leadership positions in the legislature during the first session of the new parliament in Quito on May 14, 2013, with Gabriela Rivadeneira (*center*) as president of the National Assembly, Rosana Alvarado (*right*) as first vice president, and Marcela Aguinaga as second vice president. Parties in Ecuador are required to place men and women in alternating positions on the ballot for legislative elections; in the 2013 election, Rivadeneira was placed in the first position on the Alianza Pais party list.

Some scholars have also looked at whether the *type* of proportional electoral system matters. In particular, they have looked at whether open party lists or closed party lists produce higher levels of women's legislative representation. The results, though, are mixed. This is not entirely surprising. Assuming that there are women candidates running for office, the type of party list is unlikely to matter in countries where the demand for women representatives is high. If party lists are open, then voters can give their support directly to the women candidates. And if party lists are closed, then there is a good chance that the parties will respond to voter preferences by placing women candidates toward the top of the list. In either case, the level of women's representation should be high in these countries. It is unclear, however, whether the type of party list will matter in countries where the demand for women representatives is low. If party lists are open, it does not matter much whether there are many or only a few women candidates on the party list as voters will not select them. If party lists are closed, parties can "force" voters to elect women candidates by placing them toward the top of the list. This, though, raises the question of why parties would want to increase the number of women representatives when this would run counter to voter preferences. Depending

---

8. The reason why left-wing parties do better in proportional systems is something that we will address in the next section.

on the demand from voters and party elites for women candidates, the effect of different types of party lists might be either negligible or substantial.

Gender quotas are an increasingly popular tool for parties or countries that want to increase the number of women elected to office (Dahlerup 2006; Krook 2009). There are three general types of gender quotas. First, there are reserved seats where legislative seats are set aside for women candidates only. According to the Global Database of Quotas for Women, twenty-three countries have reserved seats for women, including Burundi, Iraq, Uganda, Kenya, and Tanzania ("Quota Database" 2015). Tanzania has the highest percentage of reserved seats for women (36 percent). Reserved seats are particularly common in Arab countries, South Asia, and parts of Africa. Second, there are legislated candidate quotas that specify the percentage of women candidates that must appear on party lists. These quotas differ on whether they include placement mandates that indicate where women candidates must be placed on party lists. Fifty-four countries, including Argentina, Bolivia, Ecuador, Nicaragua, and Rwanda, have legislated candidate quotas. The common use of legislated candidate quotas in Latin America helps to explain the relatively high levels of women's legislative representation seen in this region in Map 16.1. Third, there are voluntary political party quotas where individual parties agree to have women candidates make up a certain percentage of all their candidates. These are the most common type of gender quotas in Western Europe. Although not a necessity, gender quotas are often easier to implement in proportional representation systems.

It is worth noting that elections held in post-conflict situations often result in more women being elected than elections held prior to the conflict. This is because post-conflict power-sharing agreements frequently include gender quotas and because incumbents are often killed or exiled during the conflict, leading to more open seats (Tripp and Kang 2008). The particularly high levels of women's legislative representation in Rwanda is partly due to Rwanda's use of gender quotas but also partly due to the fact that the perpetrators of the Rwandan genocide in 1994 targeted men and left the country with a huge gender imbalance. It turns out that although Rwanda has the highest level of women's legislative representation in the world (63.8 percent), women are still underrepresented as they compose 70 percent of the population (Bennett 2014).

Does the descriptive representation of women lead to the substantive representation of women? Although there is some evidence linking the descriptive representation of women to the improved substantive representation of women, the strength of the empirical evidence is contested (Wängnerud 2009). For example, Schwindt-Bayer and Mishler (2005) find that increased descriptive representation of women in legislatures does lead to greater responsiveness to women's interests but that the effect is smaller than anticipated. Moreover, there is no compelling evidence for the prediction from critical mass theory (Kanter 1977; Dahlerup 1988) that the substantive representation of women would increase significantly once the level of women's legislative representation passed some threshold, frequently thought to be 30 percent (Childs and Krook 2006). In her study of women's representation in Latin America, Htun (2016) notes that the increased levels of descriptive representation brought about by gender quotas in this region has not significantly increased the substantive representation of women; she refers to this as "inclusion without representation." The low substantive representation of women, even in countries with high levels of women's legislative representation, is often attributed to the fact that women legislators have limited legislative experience, that they are rarely given powerful positions, and that they are constrained in what they can do by their party affiliations (Beckwith 2007; Celis et al. 2008; Celis 2009). Many scholars have argued that critical actors, both men and women, who have been "critical" in initiating women-friendly policies are more important to women's substantive representation than high levels of women's legislative representation (Celis et al. 2008; Childs and Krook 2006; Htun 2016).

Symbolic Representation

Symbolic representation focuses on the symbolic ways that representatives "stand for" the citizens. To get a better sense of what this means, it is useful to start by thinking about particular symbols that we are familiar with in our everyday lives. Two common symbols are flags and company logos. Flags like the Star Spangled Banner in the United States symbolize certain ideals, beliefs, or norms that are associated with the thing they are representing. Flags evoke meaning, and often emotions; they tell us what it means to be American, British, Chinese, and so on. Similarly, a company's logo, such as the Apple or BMW logos, can evoke images and feelings about the types of products that the company sells—high quality, reliable, quirky, stylish, and so on. In both of these cases, the symbol is not the thing being represented and as such is not a form of descriptive representation. Nor does the symbol— the flag or company logo—take action on behalf of what is being represented; it is not a form of substantive representation. Instead, the symbol "stands for" and symbolizes what is being represented. Political representatives can also perform this function.

As many scholars have pointed out, the act of giving meaning to something is a constitutive act. Symbolic representation constructs boundaries that allow us to see who and what is being represented. For the Star Spangled Banner to symbolically represent Americans, we first have to construct what it means to be American—we have to create a boundary between what is American and what is un-American. According to symbolic representation, political representatives do not just passively represent some constituency; indeed, constituencies are not out there waiting to be represented. Instead, representatives must create constituencies for them to represent through the symbolic claims they make about their constituents (Saward 2006, 2009). If constituencies are constructed, then symbolic representation is a process by which certain groups or identities are deemed worthy of representation and others are not. In addition to identifying who is worthy of representation, the constitutive process of symbolic representation also identifies who can appropriately represent particular groups; that is, it identifies who would be a "good" representative for a particular constituency. The process of constructing constituencies, and hence symbolic representation, is not unidirectional or fixed in time. The symbolic claims made by representatives about the "represented" must be accepted by those being represented for them to have meaning, and they can evolve over time in response to new events and changing values. Thus, symbolic representation is a "dynamic, performative, and constitutive" process that involves a back-and-forth claims-making process between the representative and the represented (Celis et al. 2008, 101–102).

Consider symbolic representation in the context of populist parties. Populism is an ideology that portrays society as divided into two homogeneous and antagonistic groups, "the pure people" and "the corrupt elite" (Mudde 2004, 2007). Many commentators have wondered how a populist candidate like Donald Trump in the recent 2016 US presidential election could plausibly claim to represent ordinary people given his privileged background. What many of these commentators failed to realize is that Trump was attempting to provide symbolic representation, not descriptive or substantive representation. When Trump referred to America's "forgotten men and women" during his acceptance speech as the Republican nominee for president and said "I am your voice," he was not claiming to be one of the forgotten people; instead, he was claiming to symbolically "stand for" them. Other populist leaders have also emphasized their symbolic representation of the people. For example, Venezuelan president Hugo Chávez stated that "I demand absolute loyalty to me. I am not an individual, I am the people" in a clear reference to his perceived role as the embodiment of the Venezuelan people (de la Torre 2016, 43).

Compared with formalistic, descriptive, and substantive representation, symbolic representation is relatively understudied. To our knowledge, there is no research examining the effects of majoritarian or consensus institutions on different forms of symbolic representation. That said, our discussion of political identity formation in Chapter 14 suggests that majoritarian institutions incentivize political representatives to construct larger, and therefore potentially more inclusive, constituencies than proportional institutions. This is because political representatives require greater electoral support to win office in majoritarian systems than in proportional ones.

From a normative standpoint with respect to political representation, you probably have your own preferences by now for whether a country should adopt majoritarian or consensus institutions. If you are having trouble deciding which type of democracy you would recommend to the framers of a new constitution, however, perhaps you need some information about the substantive consequences that are likely to follow from the institutional choices that you would make. In the following three sections, we examine the effects of different institutional choices on economic policy, ethnic conflict, and democratic stability.

THE EFFECT OF POLITICAL INSTITUTIONS ON FISCAL POLICY

There is an extremely large and expanding literature on the effect of institutions on economic policies and economic outcomes. Anything like an adequate review of this important topic would cover at least a whole book. Thus, we focus our attention in this section on understanding how the political institutions that we examined in Chapters 12 through 15 influence fiscal policy. **Fiscal policy** refers to the set of government policies related to the raising of revenues through taxation and to the set of policies accomplished through government spending.

> **Fiscal policy** involves the manipulation of tax and spending decisions to accomplish governmental goals.

In what follows, we examine the political sources of economic policy from a *political economy* perspective. A political economy approach to understanding economic policy is based on two fundamental assumptions: (a) economic policy is typically made by elected officials (or technocrats appointed by elected officials) who may have goals other than the provision of "stable growth," and (b) economic policies tend to have distributional consequences; that is, they do not affect all citizens in the same way. In contrast to the political economy perspective, traditional, or "welfare," economics typically assumes that economic policy is made by a "benevolent social planner"—a hypothetical policymaker who weighs the interests of all members of society and chooses the policies that best meet the needs of society as a whole. Because the benevolent social planner is a single individual, the problems that arise from group decision making, such as those we examined in Chapter 11, are assumed away. According to the political economy perspective adopted here, though, economic policy is fraught with conflicts of interest—between the government and citizens, between citizens themselves, and between members of the government representing different groups of citizens—that should not be assumed away. Although these conflicts of interest arise in all areas of macroeconomic policymaking, we restrict our attention to fiscal policy. We do this partly because of space limitations but also because fiscal policy is often explicitly used for the purpose of redistribution; because the raising of revenues is central to what it means to be a state, as we saw in Chapter 4; and because fiscal policy is frequently used as a measure of the overall size of government.

It turns out that there is a tremendous amount of cross-national variation in fiscal policy. In Figure 16.2, we present a "box and whiskers plot" showing how total public fiscal activity—central government revenue and expenditures as a percentage of gross domestic product (GDP)—varies both within and between twenty-one advanced industrialized countries from 1947 to 1997 (Franzese 2002b, 16). The black dots indicate the average level of fiscal activity for each country. The "boxes" and "whiskers" display how the level of fiscal activity varied within each country during the postwar period. When the boxes stay close to the country average, as in the United States and Switzerland, it means that fiscal policy varied little during the postwar period. In contrast, when the boxes are large, as in Belgium, the Netherlands, and Sweden, it means that fiscal activity varied quite a bit in that country. The "whiskers," or vertical black lines, indicate the maximum and minimum levels of fiscal activity in each country during the postwar period. The main thing to note from Figure 16.2 is that there is considerable cross-national variation in the level of fiscal activity. For example, in many countries, such as the United States, Japan, Canada, Spain, and Switzerland, fiscal activity is relatively low, near or below 50 percent of GDP. And in many other countries, such

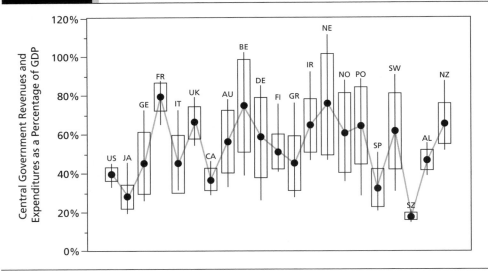

FIGURE 16.2 | **Total Public Fiscal Activity in Twenty-One OECD Countries, 1947–1997**

Source: Franzese (2002b, 16).

Note: AL = Australia; AU = Austria; BE = Belgium; CA = Canada; DE = Denmark; FI = Finland; FR = France; GE = Germany; GR = Greece; IR = Ireland; IT = Italy; JA = Japan; NE = Netherlands; NO = Norway; NZ = New Zealand; PO = Portugal; SP = Spain; SW = Sweden; SZ = Switzerland; UK = United Kingdom; US = United States. The black dots indicate the mean level of total public fiscal activity for each country; the vertical black lines indicate the maximum and minimum levels of total public fiscal activity in each country; the vertical size of each box indicates one standard deviation above and below the mean in each country.

as France, Belgium, and the Netherlands, fiscal activity is relatively high, above 75 percent of GDP. What explains this cross-national variation in fiscal policy? It is this question that we address in the remainder of this section. We begin by examining economic and cultural determinants of fiscal policy. We then turn to our primary task, which is to examine the ways in which political institutions influence fiscal policy.

Economic and Cultural Determinants of Fiscal Policy

Total public fiscal activity is interpreted by many economists as the "size of government" because it gives an indication of the ratio of total government economic activity to overall economic activity within a country. The traditional explanation for the size of the government is "Wagner's law," named after the German economist Adolph Wagner (1835–1917), who predicted that the size of government would grow as countries became more industrialized. Wagner's law is often interpreted to mean that the size of government increases as countries become wealthier. In the broadest sense, Wagner's law seems consistent with the facts—as European countries became richer and more industrialized, the role of the government in the economy did increase as predicted. As Figure 16.3 illustrates, there was an

FIGURE 16.3	**Total Public Fiscal Activity by Year in Twenty-One OECD Countries, 1947–1997**

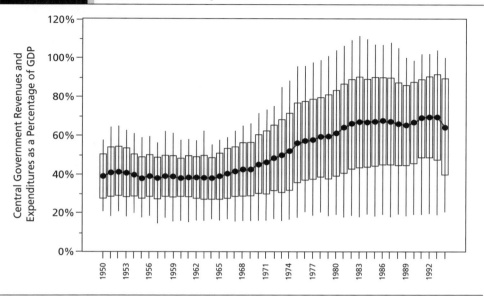

Source: Franzese (2002b, 17).

Note: The black dots indicate the mean level of total public fiscal activity in the OECD countries; the vertical black lines indicate the maximum and minimum levels of total public fiscal activity in the OECD countries; the vertical size of each box indicates one standard deviation above and below the mean in the OECD countries.

upward trend in fiscal activity among countries in the Organisation for Economic Co-operation and Development (OECD) during the postwar period, a period generally considered a time of economic growth and increased industrialization. This can be seen by looking at how the black dots, which represent the OECD average level of fiscal activity in each year, rise over time. Note, though, that not only do the black dots rise over time, but the "boxes" and "whiskers" lengthen too. This indicates not only that the mean level of government fiscal activity among OECD countries increased during the postwar period but also that the cross-national variation in the level of government fiscal activity increased as well. Wagner's law does not provide a straightforward explanation for this continued and increasing variation in the level of fiscal activity across countries that, in regard to wealth and industrialization, were probably becoming increasingly similar over time (Le Pen 2005; Li and Papell 1999).

What might explain this cross-national variation in the level of fiscal activity? One explanation that has been offered as an improvement over Wagner's law emphasizes the conflicting preferences that citizens have with regard to fiscal policy. As our discussion of the Meltzer-Richard model in Chapter 9 indicated, there are good reasons to believe that citizens will systematically differ in their views about fiscal policy (Meltzer and Richard 1981). One way to think about this is to consider what would happen in a hypothetical world in which the government taxed every citizen at the same rate ($0 < t < 1$) and then turned around and transferred all tax revenues in the form of an equal subsidy (s) to every citizen. You can think of the subsidy that each citizen (i) receives as the dollar value that the citizen places on the public goods provided by the state. Because taxes are taken from citizens as a rate, the tax bill of each citizen (T) will be an increasing function of her gross income (y_i):

$$T = y_i t.$$

That is, although all citizens pay the same *share* of their income in taxes, those with large incomes will have larger tax bills than those with low incomes. This means that the overall benefit (B) of living under a particular tax and transfer system for citizen i will be

$$B_i = y_i + s - y_i t.$$

If an individual's income is unrelated to the tax rate, by which we mean that taxes are *non-distortionary* in that they do not change an individual's level of income by affecting the trade-offs one makes between work and leisure, then the citizen will be concerned only with the net effect of the government's tax and transfer regime ($s - y_i t$).

If we assume, for the purposes of illustration, that the government budget must be balanced over the medium run (that is, that the total subsidies paid out to the citizens must equal the total taxes collected from the citizens), then some citizens will be net recipients with respect to the government's tax and transfer system and some will be net contributors. In Figure 16.4, we plot the tax bill paid and the subsidy received by citizens at different levels of income for a given tax rate and subsidy size.[9] In this economy, the citizen earning slightly more than \$20,000, which is the average income in our hypothetical example, is indifferent with respect to the tax and transfer regime—her tax bill is exactly equal to the subsidy she receives from the government.[10] All citizens with below-average incomes are net recipients—they receive more in subsidies than they pay in taxes. And all citizens with above-average incomes are net contributors to the tax and transfer scheme—they pay more in taxes than they receive in subsidies.

The distributional implications of this particular tax and transfer system are clear. Low-income citizens (to the left of the vertical dotted line in Figure 16.4) are net recipients of the tax and transfer system, and high-income citizens (to the right of the vertical dotted line) are net contributors. Consequently, citizens with high incomes would prefer a system with a tax

---

9. In our specific hypothetical example, the tax rate is 20 percent, and the subsidy is \$4,100. We should note, however, that any numbers would produce similar figures as long as (a) subsidies weren't so high compared with revenues that everyone was a net recipient, which would produce unsustainable deficits, or (b) tax rates weren't so high that everyone was a net contributor, which might lead to either a tax revolt or costly repression (Levi 1988).

10. The fact that the average earner breaks even in our example is a result of the assumption that the budget must balance.

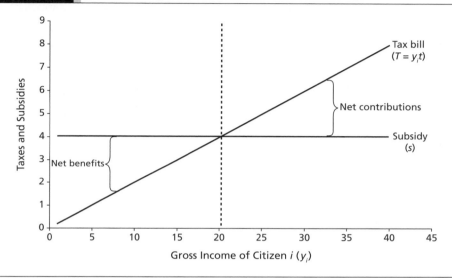

FIGURE 16.4 — The Relationship between Income, Taxes, and Government Subsidies in a Hypothetical Tax and Transfer System (Thousands of Dollars)

Note: Subsidy (s) = the total subsidy awarded to citizen *i*; tax bill (*T* = *y*ᵢ*t*) = the total tax paid by citizen *i*.

rate of zero and no subsidies. In contrast, citizens with low incomes are quite happy with this tax and transfer system; in fact, low-income citizens can be expected to support even higher tax rates because they would get the full benefit (*B*) of a more aggressive tax and transfer system but pay only a fraction of the cost (*y*ᵢ*t*). Put differently, the tax rate in our economy determines the slope of the line in Figure 16.4. If the tax rate goes up, then the slope of the "Tax bill" line increases (gets steeper). This results in an increase in the size of the net *benefits* going to citizens who have an income below the national average but an increase in the size of the net *contributions* paid by citizens who have an income above the national average.

The analysis so far helps to show that fiscal policy preferences are likely to be related to one's income. High-income voters are likely to be less enthusiastic about increased taxation and spending than low-income voters. Some readers may be concerned that this result is derived from a model that differs in substantial ways from most observed tax and transfer systems in the real world. For example, real-world taxation systems do not apply a single tax rate to all earners. Similarly, governments do not spend equally on all members of society—some individuals receive more government services, subsidies, and so on, than others. These observations, however, do not challenge the usefulness of the analysis presented here unless it can be shown that changing our assumptions to reflect these realities changes our conclusions in a fundamental fashion. Although it is true that governments tend to choose different tax rates and subsidies for voters at different levels of income, the standard pattern is for tax rates to be progressive—that is, high-income earners typically face higher tax rates than low-income earners. This insight would have the consequence of causing the line plotting individual tax bills in Figure 16.4 to curve upward as income increases. Similarly, many government-spending programs are aimed at citizens with below-average income. This insight would have the consequence of causing the line plotting subsidies awarded to citizens to slope downward as income increases. Neither of these changes would alter the central result of our analysis that tax and transfer systems necessarily divide the population into net contributors and net recipients, and that rich voters tend to fall in the former category and poor voters tend to fall in the latter category. The only tax and transfer systems that would not have this characteristic would be ones in which the tax system was regressive (the rich were taxed at a lower rate than the poor), subsidies went disproportionately to the rich, or there was no budget constraint so that subsidies could be so large that all citizens were "net recipients." Nothing like these systems is observed in modern polities.

One possible exception was raised by the "Occupy Wall Street" movement in the United States. You may have heard that rich financiers sometimes exploit tax loopholes that allow them to pay fewer taxes than "middle-income" earners. It is undeniable that differential access to tax lawyers allows upper-income earners an advantage in the search for loopholes. These loopholes may lower the "effective tax rate" of upper-income earners and, therefore, reduce the de facto progressivity of the tax code in the sense that they pay a lower tax *rate* than the tax code suggests. But it is unlikely that the *amount* of tax they pay is smaller than that paid by middle-income earners. As a result, it is still likely that they are net contributors—indeed, earners in the highest 1 percent of the income distribution are responsible for a very large share of government revenue. One might wonder why the government does not aggressively close such loopholes. At least part of the explanation comes from the fact that these actors typically control extremely liquid assets that the government wants them to continue to invest in the economy (see Chapters 6 and 9).[11]

The Meltzer-Richard model predicts that the greater the income inequality in society, the greater the demand from citizens for a large tax and transfer system. In the context of the current setup, we can better understand the Meltzer-Richard model by asking what would happen if actors at different income levels could dictate fiscal policy. The voter with the average income would be indifferent between the existing tax and transfer system and one in which the tax rate and subsidies are both zero. Voters with more income than the average-income earner would be increasingly anxious to *lower* taxes and subsidies. And voters with less income than the average-income earner would be increasingly anxious to *raise* taxes and subsidies. The Meltzer-Richard model shows why preferences over tax rates will be a function

---

11. Another possible exception is that some oil-rich countries give out large subsidies to all citizens, thereby making large portions of the citizenry net recipients. But even here the subsidy given to all citizens is likely to be smaller than the tax bill of the richest citizens, and so the point of intersection of the lines in Figure 16.4 would move upward and to the right, but the general pattern of the lines would probably remain the same.

of a voter's income, and it assumes that the median voter, who is the citizen with the *median* income, will get to dictate fiscal policy. Because every country in the world has some degree of income inequality—there is a relatively small number of citizens at the top end of the income scale and a relatively large number of individuals at the bottom end of the income scale—the *median* voter always has less income than the *average*-income earner (he is always to the left of the vertical dashed line in Figure 16.4). As a result, the median voter is always a net recipient of redistributive taxation and is, therefore, enthusiastic about increased spending and the taxes that make such spending possible. The more income inequality there is in society (the greater the income gap between the median voter and the average income earner), the more enthusiastic the median voter will be for a large tax and transfer system.

As you can see, the Meltzer-Richard model helps us move toward an explanation of the cross-national variation in fiscal policy activity. According to the Meltzer-Richard model, fiscal activity should be larger in countries characterized by a high level of income inequality. Like Wagner's law, however, the explanation provided by the Meltzer-Richard model is incomplete. Although there is a growing consensus that voter preferences over fiscal policy are likely to be tied to their income levels, as the Meltzer-Richard model shows, it is important to recognize that these preferences affect policy only after they are filtered through political institutions.

Consider the implicit assumption in the Meltzer-Richard model that all income earners vote. This assumption is contradicted by numerous empirical studies showing that high-income earners are much more likely to vote than low-income earners (Leighley and Nagler 1992b; Wolfinger and Rosenstone 1980). Some studies have found little evidence linking income inequality to larger tax and transfer systems (Iversen and Soskice 2006). However, this may be because high-income earners are much more likely to turn out to vote than low-income earners and because voter turnout varies across countries. The fact that high-income earners are more likely to turn out than low-income earners means that the income gap between the average-income *earner* and the median *voter* is likely to be smaller than the income gap between the average-income earner and the median-income earner. As a result, the demand for redistribution in the real world is likely to be smaller than that predicted in the Meltzer-Richard model. In addition, since voter turnout is known to vary systematically across countries, the Meltzer-Richard model can be expected to fit the data better in high-turnout countries than in low-turnout countries. In fact, Franzese (2002b, 62–125) finds support for exactly this in his analysis of fiscal activity in OECD countries. Specifically, he finds that the effect of income inequality on the size of the tax and transfer system is largest when voter participation is high. This suggests that institutional factors that influence voter turnout, such as compulsory voting, voter registration rules, and the proportionality of the electoral system, should also have an influence on fiscal policy.

The connection between the proportionality of the electoral system and voter turnout might require a word of explanation. As we saw in Chapters 13 and 14, single-member district plurality (SMDP) electoral systems tend to reward candidates from large parties and punish candidates from small parties. As a result, voters who support a party that is unpopular in their district are likely to either vote strategically for a second-choice party or abstain from voting altogether. Consequently, voter participation rates tend to be higher in PR systems than in SMDP systems (Powell 1982). It is for this reason that we might expect fiscal activity to be larger in countries with PR systems than in countries with plurality electoral laws. Although there is a growing consensus that proportional electoral systems are linked with higher fiscal activity, there is little scholarly agreement, as we will see, on exactly why this is the case.

So far, we have examined an argument that says that voters will differ in their evaluation of fiscal policy based on their incomes. High-income voters will seek to reduce the size of government and low-income voters will seek to expand it. The Meltzer-Richard model, in essence, predicts that the size of the state will vary across countries and time as the size of these groups varies. Where income inequality is high, there are many more poor voters than rich voters, and as a result, the state will be large. Conversely, where income inequality is low, there are relatively few poor voters compared with rich voters, and as a result, the state will be small. One problem with this approach is that it implicitly assumes that voter preferences are automatically and directly translated into fiscal policy. If, however, voter preferences are refracted through political institutions in complex ways, fiscal policy may have as much to do with cross-national differences in political institutions as it does with the distribution of

> The **partisan model of macroeconomic policy** argues that left-wing parties represent the interests of low-income voters and that right-wing parties represent the interests of high-income voters. The main prediction of the partisan model is that changes in the partisan control of the government produce predictable changes in fiscal policy.

voter preferences. As we learned in Chapter 14, voter preferences are typically aggregated through political parties. So one way to put a little bit of institutional structure on the Meltzer-Richard model is to ask what would happen if there were competing teams of candidates (political parties) that claimed to represent different segments of

the income spectrum. This is exactly the approach taken by the **partisan model of macroeconomic policy**.

According to the partisan model of macroeconomic policy, left-wing parties represent the interests of low-income voters and right-wing parties represent the interests of high-income voters. The main prediction of the partisan model is that changes in the partisan control of the government produce predictable changes in fiscal policy. Specifically, left-wing governments are expected to engage in more fiscal activity than right wing governments. In particular, left-wing governments are expected to adopt "expansionary" fiscal policies that are thought to favor left-wing voters (Hibbs 1977).[12] Although this sounds plausible, it turns out that there is only mixed empirical support for the idea that left- and right-wing governments in the same country adopt different

---

12. For a critical review of the partisan model of fiscal policy, see Clark (2003, 41–84).

fiscal policies. Some scholars find that left-wing governments do, indeed, adopt more expansionary fiscal policies than right-wing governments; some find no relationship between the partisan orientation of the government and fiscal policy; and some find evidence that, if anything, right-wing governments are more expansionary than left-wing governments. Of course, the fact that it is difficult to identify a difference in the fiscal policies of left- and right-wing governments in the same country is not evidence in and of itself that these parties—and the voters they represent—do not wish to implement different policies. It may very well be the case that they would like to implement different fiscal policies but that incentives to court the median voter (see Chapter 11) or the "structural dependence of the state on capital" (see Chapter 9) prevent them from effectively acting on these desires.

There is also the possibility that the policy preferences (income position) of the median voter differ across countries. If the median voter is further to the left in some countries than others, then these countries are likely to have a high frequency of left-wing governments. In such a scenario, we might expect to see evidence for a *cross-national* version of the partisan model. In fact, this is precisely what David Cameron (1978) found in his seminal study of the politics of macroeconomic policy. In Figure 16.5, we reproduce a scatter plot from Cameron's article, showing a positive relationship between the percentage of the government's electoral base composed of left-wing parties in a country and the growth of government revenues as a share of GDP. As you can see, Sweden and the United States represent polar extremes. Sweden was ruled by a left-wing party during the whole period (1960–1975), and it experienced a 20-percentage-point increase in government revenues as a share of GDP. In contrast, the United States was ruled by a right-wing party during the whole period, and it experienced almost no growth in government revenues as a share of GDP.[13] Between these two extremes in fiscal policy, there is a fairly close relationship between the percentage of time that a country experiences left-wing rule and increases in the size of government.[14]

The *cross-national* version of the partisan model rests on the idea that cross-national differences in the partisan composition of governments reflect cross-national differences in voter preferences. So far, we have not presented much evidence that voter preferences vary across countries. Some scholars have suggested that the absence of a "European style" welfare state in the United States can be explained by differing attitudes toward the poor in Europe and the United States. Alesina, Glaeser, and Sacerdote (2001), for example, use data from the World Values Survey to show that Europeans are twice as likely as Americans to say they believe the poor are trapped in poverty and almost twice as likely to say that

---

13. Like many comparativists, Cameron (1978, 1248 n. 12) considers both the Republican and Democratic parties in the United States to be "center-right" parties compared with the parties in other developed democracies.

14. Canada, Ireland, and the Netherlands don't quite fit the pattern—they experienced a larger growth in the size of the government than the partisan composition of their governments would predict.

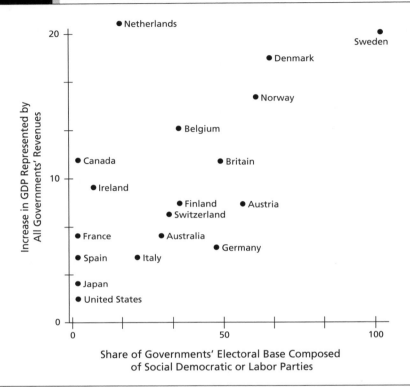

FIGURE 16.5 — The Partisan Composition of Government and the Expansion of the Public Economy, 1960–1975 (Percentages)

Source: Cameron (1978, 1255, fig. 1).

luck determines income. Americans are twice as likely as Europeans to say that the poor are lazy. And Europeans are twice as likely as Americans to self-identify as leftists. To some extent, these data, which are shown in Table 16.2, suggest that differences in attitudes toward the poor might be what is driving broad differences in the left-right policy preferences of citizens between the United States and Europe. Although there is some truth to this, Alesina, Glaeser, and Sacerdote note that things are more complicated when we look at the individual level rather than the national level. It appears that many Europeans who are not leftists hold what might be thought of as charitable views toward the poor; indeed, the number of people holding these views is about twice as large as the number identifying as leftists.

There are at least two possible explanations for the lack of a close link at the individual level between attitudes toward the poor and self-identification as a leftist. One is that the

TABLE 16.2	**European and American Attitudes toward the Poor (Percentages)**	
Item	European Union	United States
Believe poor are trapped in poverty	60	29
Believe luck determines income	54	30
Believe the poor are lazy	26	60
Identify themselves as on the left of the political spectrum	30	17

Source: World Values Survey data from 1981–1997 as reported in Alesina, Glaeser, and Sacerdote (2001, table 13).

presence of a large number of leftists in a country may shift the terms of debate about welfare in such a way that the attitudes they hold about the poor come to be accepted by some non-leftists as well. The second is that leftists may not have a monopoly on these attitudes about the poor. In most European countries, for example, there are parties and substantial numbers of voters that ascribe to what are sometimes called "Christian democratic" attitudes. Christian democrats often espouse a form of conservatism, not often articulated in the United States, that combines interventionist social welfare attitudes with morally conservative views on social issues. Thus, it may be that the large number of non-leftist Europeans expressing "charitable" views to the poor are Christian democrats. For this reason, some careful studies of the partisan sources of fiscal policy divide parties into three categories—right-wing, left-wing, and Christian democratic— and typically expect parties of the last two varieties to act alike (E. Huber, Ragin, and Stephens 1993).

There is also some empirical evidence that attitudes toward the poor are related to fiscal policy that goes beyond the United States–Europe comparison that we have just presented. In Figure 16.6, we reproduce a scatter plot from Alesina, Glaeser, and Sacerdote (2001) showing the relationship between the national average response concerning the belief that luck determines income and the national average share of GDP devoted to social spending. Although there is considerable variation in social spending for any given set of beliefs, countries in which relatively few people believe that income is determined by luck have substantially lower levels of social spending, and, with the exception of Portugal and Brazil, countries in which most people believe income is determined by luck have substantially higher levels of social spending. Overall, the data presented by Alesina, Glaeser, and Sacerdote suggest that fiscal policy is influenced not only by economic factors, such as income inequality, but also by cultural factors, such as attitudes toward the poor and beliefs about the extent to which luck determines income.

We now turn to an examination of how political institutions influence fiscal policy. In particular, we focus on the relationship between electoral laws and fiscal policy.

FIGURE 16.6 | Relationship between Social Spending and the Belief That Luck Determines Income

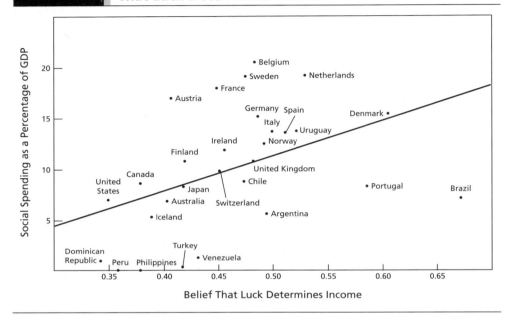

Source: Alesina, Glaeser, and Sacerdote (2001, 244).

Note: Social spending as a percentage of GDP is the average for the 1960–1998 period; the belief that luck determines income is the mean value for a country, measured as an index from 0 to 1, for the 1981–1997 period.

Electoral Laws and Fiscal Policy

Over the last two decades, a steady stream of research has shown that proportional electoral systems are associated with more public goods, larger and more redistributive social welfare programs, and a larger overall size of government than majoritarian electoral systems (Iversen and Soskice 2006; Persson and Tabellini 2004). Although there is a growing consensus that fiscal policy activity is higher in countries that employ proportional electoral rules, there is little agreement as to exactly why this is the case. In what follows, we present three sets of arguments linking fiscal policy to a country's electoral system.

Proportional Representation Leads to More Redistribution by Facilitating the Election of Left-Wing Governments

Although it is important, as we saw earlier, to look at the way cross-national differences in attitudes affect the propensity to elect left-wing governments, many scholars have suggested that electoral laws also play an important role in determining the partisan composition of governments. Specifically, several studies have argued that proportional electoral systems encourage the election of left-wing governments and that majoritarian systems encourage the election of right-wing governments (Iversen and Soskice 2006; Kedar, Harsgor, and Scheinerman 2016; Rodden 2006).

Rodden (2006) argues that electoral institutions influence "who rules" because of the geographic distribution of support for left-wing parties and the way electoral laws overlay this geographic distribution. He points out that left-wing parties have traditionally drawn their electoral support from concentrated pockets of voters in urban industrial areas and mining centers. This geographic concentration of support for left-wing parties is the product of industrialization in an era when transportation costs were sufficiently high that workers needed to live close to where they worked. This pattern of left-wing support has persisted, even after such large-scale social changes in recent decades as deindustrialization and gentrification. As Rodden (2006, 2) puts it, "Densely populated manufacturing and mining regions vote overwhelmingly for parties of the left and less industrial and rural areas for parties of the right . . . , even in many settings where cities are affluent and rural areas are mired in poverty." Right-wing parties, in contrast, tend to draw their voters from a much broader geographic base.

According to Rodden, the higher geographic concentration of left-wing support is a liability in majoritarian single-member district plurality (SMDP) systems. This is because of the distortionary effects of SMDP systems that we examined in Chapter 14. In Chapter 14, we emphasized that votes for a losing party in a district were, in a sense, wasted because they contributed nothing to the party's representation in the legislature. Rodden's argument emphasizes that votes can also be wasted in districts where parties succeed. In SMDP systems, the best a party can do in a particular district is to elect a single representative, and to do so, it merely needs to win more votes than any other party. Any additional votes are "surplus," and they contribute nothing to enhancing the party's control of the legislature; in effect, these surplus votes are wasted votes. The geographic concentration of left-wing support means that left-wing parties will be electorally competitive in a smaller number of districts than right-wing parties, and a larger number of left-wing votes will be wasted than right-wing votes. In contrast, legislative seats in proportional representation (PR) systems are distributed in a manner that reflects a party's underlying electoral support, and so fewer votes are wasted. The result is that the bias for right-wing parties caused by the geographic concentration of left-wing support is reduced (or even disappears) in proportional electoral systems.

There is, in fact, a strong association between the type of electoral system in a country and the propensity for left-wing parties to win enough seats in the legislature to control the government. In Table 16.3, we present data from seventeen advanced industrialized democracies between 1945 and 1998 showing that a left-wing government was in power about three-quarters of the time in countries with proportional electoral systems but only one-quarter of the time in countries with majoritarian systems (Iversen and Soskice 2006). Note that we are not necessarily claiming that proportional electoral rules *cause* left-wing electoral success but merely that the two go together. This is important because several scholars have pointed out that ruling elites in European countries in which left-wing parties were strong replaced their majoritarian electoral systems at the

TABLE 16.3	Electoral Systems and the Number of Years with Left and Right Governments, 1945–1998		
	Government partisanship		
Electoral system	Left	Right	Proportion of left governments
Proportional	342	120	0.74
Majoritarian	86	256	0.25

Source: Iversen and Soskice (2006, fig. 1).

Note: Data are from seventeen advanced industrialized democracies; centrist governments have not been included.

beginning of the twentieth century with proportional ones (Boix 1999). This suggests that the causal relationship between proportional representation and left-wing electoral success may run in both directions—countries in which left-wing parties are strong have tended to adopt PR, and PR, in turn, is likely to reinforce the representation of left-wing parties in government.

Rodden (2006) argues that the electoral system affects not only the probability of left-wing parties gaining power but also the way that left-wing parties behave once in power. Specifically, he claims that left-wing parties in SMDP systems are less aggressive in pressing for redistributive fiscal policies than they are in PR systems. The reason is that, to the extent that parties have incentives to court the median voter, parties have incentives to court the *national* median voter in PR systems but the *marginal constituency* median voter in SMDP systems. Marginal constituencies are basically constituencies in which the electoral support for the two biggest parties is evenly split. In SMDP systems, national parties have incentives to ignore voters in "safe districts"—ones where they are likely to win and ones that are "safe" for their competitors where they are likely to lose. Elections in SMDP systems are won and lost in marginal constituencies because that is where the "swing voters" are. Because of the geographic concentration of support for left parties mentioned earlier, the median voter in marginal constituencies is likely to be far to the right of the average supporter of the left-wing party. As a result, left-wing parties in SMDP systems have an incentive not to be as redistributive in regard to fiscal policy as those same parties would be in PR systems.

Iversen and Soskice (2006) agree that left-wing parties are likely to participate in government more frequently in PR systems than in SMDP systems. They argue, however, that this is because of the difference in coalitional bargaining across the two systems and not because of the geographic distribution of left-wing support. Iversen and Soskice present a model in which there are three equal-size groups in society based on income level (*Low, Middle,* and *High*). According to their model, the low-income voters want to tax the high- and middle-income groups at the highest possible rate and redistribute this wealth to themselves. The middle-income voters want to tax the high-income group and divide this wealth between themselves and low-income voters. Finally, as in the Meltzer-Richard model, the high-income voters want zero taxes and no redistribution.

Following the logic behind Duverger's theory, which we examined in Chapter 14, Iversen and Soskice assume that there will be only two parties in the legislature of SMDP systems, with the middle-income group splitting its vote between the two other income groups. In effect, some middle-income voters will form a center-left party with low-income voters and some will form a center-right party with high-income voters. Median voter dynamics lead both the center-left and center-right parties to campaign on the policies preferred by middle-income voters. The problem is that neither the center-left party nor the center-right party can credibly commit to implement these policies once the election is over. The problem arises from the fact that if middle-income voters split their support between the center-left and center-right parties, then they will be only a minority faction within each party. The middle-income voters must therefore worry that after the election each party will implement the preferences of its majority faction. If you were a middle-income voter in this situation, how would you vote? If the center-right party comes to power, there is a good chance that it will implement a zero tax, zero subsidy policy—the preferred policy of the high-income group. If the center-left party comes to power, there is a good chance that it will implement a policy that redistributes income from the high- and middle-income groups to the low-income group—the preferred policy of the low-income group. Given these possibilities, middle-income voters are likely to have a greater tendency to vote for center-right parties in SMDP systems than center-left parties.

How do things change in a PR system? According to Duverger's theory, we would expect a PR system to produce three parties, one for each of the different income groups. In effect, we would have a left party, a center party, and a right party. As all three income groups have the same size, no single party will control a legislative majority, so a coalition government is likely to form. Once again, the middle-income voters will be pivotal. The middle-income voters do not have to worry that the center party will deviate to the left or right, as the center party exists to represent the middle-income group. Iversen and Soskice (2006) predict that the center party is likely to form a coalition with the left party in these circumstances. Why? A center-left coalition government will want to redistribute income away from the high-income group. While the left party would like all of this redistribution to go to the low-income group, the fact that the center party is pivotal in the coalition formation process means that this will not happen. In effect, the low-income and middle-income groups will both benefit from the redistribution that occurs under a center-left coalition government. A center-right coalition government does not offer such benefits to the middle-income group. Although the center party would want to redistribute from the high-income group to the middle-income group, the right party in the coalition will veto this. The fact that the tax and redistribution system is, by assumption, non-regressive (low-income voters cannot do worse than middle-income voters, who cannot do worse than high-income voters) means that the center-right coalition cannot redistribute up the income scale from the poor. As a result, the middle-income group cannot benefit from a center-right coalition. According to this argument, center-left coalition governments are more likely to form in PR systems than center-right coalition governments.

We have already seen that a country's electoral system has a strong impact on the partisan orientation of its governments as Iversen and Soskice's model predicts (Table 16.3). Their model also predicts that the electoral system will influence the level of redistribution in society. This is exactly what they find in their empirical analyses. Among other things, they find that right-wing governments are associated with less redistribution than left-wing governments. More importantly, however, they also show that fiscal policy is more redistributive in countries with PR systems irrespective of the government's partisan orientation. Thus, PR systems do not lead to more redistribution just because they produce more left-wing governments (although they show that this is, in fact, the case). For the reasons outlined above, should a left-wing government come to power in an SMDP system, it is likely to engage in less redistribution than it would if it came to power in a PR system.

Proportional Representation Leads to More Redistribution through Its Effect on the Size of Electoral Districts

Persson and Tabellini (1999, 2000, 2004) provide an alternative explanation for why countries with PR systems experience more redistribution than countries with SMDP electoral systems. They argue that political competition is fiercer in SMDP systems and that party leaders have to focus on winning the votes of ideologically flexible swing voters through the use of targeted transfers. As a result, fewer government resources will be available for the provision of broader public goods, which, they assume, tend to be more redistributive.

The notion that government spending will be focused on public goods in PR systems but on "pork-barrel projects" that favor local interests at the expense of broader national interests in majoritarian systems is expressed in many different ways in the political economy literature. Since Weingast, Shepsle, and Johnsen's (1981) article, this argument has been known as the "law of $1/n$." If individual legislators care only about spending projects in their district but taxes are not directly linked to those spending projects (because, for example,

> A **common pool resource problem** exists when actors can consume some commonly held resource and pay only a share of its cost. As a result, they consume more of the resource than is socially optimal; that is, they consume more than they would if they had to pay the full social cost of the resource.

taxes are proportional to income, as we have been assuming in this section), then taxing and spending decisions take on aspects of what is known as a **common pool resource problem**. A common pool resource problem exists if each legislator has an incentive to maximize government spending in his own district in order to please voters, but the costs of that spending are spread across society as a whole. If there are n districts in a country, the people in each district get the full benefit of a spending project but pay only $1/n$ of the cost.

Because there tends to be a large number of small districts in SMDP systems and a small number of large districts in PR ones, this argument has important implications for the effect of electoral laws on fiscal policy. Specifically, legislators in SMDP systems can be expected to vote for lavish spending projects in their own districts and shift the cost of paying for such projects onto the legislature as a whole. If legislators adopt a norm called "universalism" in which each legislator is expected to support the spending proposed for her colleagues' districts in exchange for her colleagues' support for spending in her own district, then the result is a level of national spending that is higher than each of the legislator's desires (Weingast 1979). The legislators are, in effect, trapped in a Prisoner's Dilemma that is played out among hundreds of legislators. In contrast, if fiscal policy were controlled by a single actor that answered to a national constituency (such as a president), then that actor would pay the total cost of spending projects, and only projects that yielded a national benefit greater than their total cost would be approved. Because legislators in PR systems are elected from a small number of larger districts, they bear a larger share of the total cost of spending projects and therefore refuse to pay for at least some projects that have little national benefit. As a result, we might expect legislators in SMDP systems to push for a large number of costly projects with concentrated benefits and legislators in PR systems to limit the overall level of government spending and to have a tendency to adopt only spending projects that produce broader benefits. To the extent that projects producing broader benefits are more redistributive than projects producing concentrated benefits, PR systems will therefore be associated with higher levels of redistribution.

It should be noted that the selectorate model of politics discussed in Chapter 10 is related to this line of research (Bueno de Mesquita et al. 2003). In a parliamentary democracy with SMDP electoral rules, such as the United Kingdom, a government needs to win a little more than half the votes in a little more than half the districts to stay in power. In other words, the winning coalition in an SMDP system like this is roughly 25 percent of the electorate. In contrast, in the archetypical PR system that has one nationwide electoral district, such as the Netherlands, the government needs to win about half the votes in the country to stay in power. In other words, the winning coalition in a PR system like this is roughly 50 percent of the electorate. As this comparison indicates, PR systems generally have larger winning coalitions than SMDP systems. As we saw in Chapter 10, this means that they should provide more public goods and spend fewer government resources targeted at narrow minority groups than SMDP systems.

Proportional Representation Affects Government Spending and Debt through Its Effect on the Composition of Governments

The common pool resource problem that we have just described has also been used to explain a related question—the overall size of government spending and, by extension, the size of government debt and deficits. Once again, many different arguments link electoral rules to overall levels of government spending and debt, each of which highlights a slightly different causal process.

One argument emphasizes the incentives that electoral rules create for legislators to cultivate a "personal vote." A personal vote occurs when an individual votes based on the characteristics of a particular candidate rather than the characteristics of the party to which the candidate belongs. As we briefly mentioned in Chapter 13, there are many factors in addition to district magnitude that influence the propensity for candidates to put the concerns of their district over their party and, therefore, cultivate a personal vote (Carey and Shugart 1995). The most important of these factors may be the type of ballot used in PR systems. In a closed list system, voters can only express a preference for a party, leaving party leaders with the power to determine which candidates will fill the seats that the party wins. In contrast, in an open list system, voters can indicate the particular candidates they support, and these votes determine which candidates fill the seats won by the party. Clearly, candidates in closed list systems have an incentive to curry favor with the party leadership. In contrast, candidates in open list systems have an incentive to cultivate a personal vote by making direct appeals and distributing resources to voters in their own district. Hallerberg and Marier (2004) argue that the common pool resource problem in fiscal policy will be most severe where legislative candidates have strong incentives to cultivate a personal vote.

An alternative argument states that the relevant common pool resource problem in relation to fiscal policy occurs not in the legislature, as we have suggested up to this point, but in the cabinet. According to this argument, each minister seeks to maximize the size of her own ministry's budget while shifting the costs of such spending onto the government as a whole (Bawn and Rosenbluth 2006; Hallerberg and von Hagen 1999). As a consequence, any factor that reinforces "fiscal centralization"—that is, spending decisions that encourage policymakers to consider the full cost, rather than a fraction, of spending—is expected to lead to lower levels of government spending, smaller deficits, and less government debt. The literature that makes this argument typically assumes that political parties have mechanisms to discipline only their own ministers, and so the severity of the common pool resource problem is really an increasing function of the number of parties in government. For example, single-party majority governments often delegate power to a strong finance minister who is able to discipline overspending ministers (Hallerberg 2004). In contrast, coalition governments tend to find it much more difficult to rein in cabinet ministers, because some of them belong to different parties. Neither the prime minister nor the finance minister will necessarily control instruments to discipline cabinet ministers from outside his party. As a result, we would expect that countries with a larger number of parties in government would be associated with higher spending levels, larger deficits, and bigger debt levels. Because we expect SMDP systems to have a reductive effect on the number of parties in the legislature (see Chapter 14) and to encourage the formation of single-party governments (see Chapter 12), this amounts to a specific argument about the way electoral laws influence fiscal policy. Many papers have explored the causal connections that we have just outlined, but perhaps the clearest evidence in support of this line of reasoning comes from an article by Persson, Roland, and Tabellini (2007). This article finds positive associations between PR systems and party system fragmentation, between party system fragmentation and coalition government, and between coalition government and higher levels of government spending.

George Tsebelis (2002) offers an interesting rejoinder to those studies that find evidence of a link between the number of parties in government and high levels of government spending or debt. As we saw in Chapter 15, veto player theory predicts that policy change occurs more slowly when there are a large number of veto players. Because each party in the cabinet can be thought of as a veto player, we should expect fiscal policy to change more slowly when the number of cabinet parties is large. But can veto player theory explain the *level* of spending in addition to explaining the rate at which spending levels change? Tsebelis argues that we ought to consider the fact that almost all of the countries included in studies that find a relationship between the number of cabinet parties and the level of government spending were greatly affected by the oil crises of the 1970s. Because of the oil crises, these countries were saddled with extremely high levels of spending and debt that were, in effect, exogenously determined. Countries with few veto players were able to reduce debt levels relatively quickly after the oil crises eased, whereas countries with a large number of veto players took longer to turn fiscal policy around and reduce debt levels. Consequently, the positive association found in many studies between fiscal policy and the number of cabinet parties may be the result of a historical accident (oil crises) that produced high levels of debt in many countries and the fact that the number of partisan veto players in a country determines the amount of fiscal policy inertia. This suggests that if analysts were to examine a different time period, one that did not include the effects of the 1970s oil crises, they might not find any association between the number of cabinet parties and the level of government spending and debt.

Summary

As we have demonstrated, there are good reasons to believe that political institutions have an important influence on macroeconomic policies. We presented evidence, for example, that PR electoral laws are associated with coalition governments and with left-wing parties entering government more frequently. Both of these factors were, in turn, shown to be associated with more extensive government redistribution and higher levels of spending, larger deficits, and higher debt levels. Although there remains considerable debate about the particular causal mechanisms at work here, there is little question that constitutional choices have important effects on the way that governments manage their economies. Central to our perspective throughout this section has been the idea that macroeconomic outcomes are distributional in nature; that is, they tend to help some citizens and harm others. It is not, therefore, possible to suggest on the basis of this literature what the best institutions for encouraging good macroeconomic performance would be. Our goal, rather, is to show that there are trade-offs to be made and that a knowledge of comparative politics can be useful in helping citizens and policymakers evaluate some of these trade-offs.

In the next section, we explore the effects of different democratic institutions on the likelihood of ethnic conflict. Because it is hard to find supporters of ethnic conflict, it might seem that comparative politics will be able to offer unqualified recommendations in this area. As you may have come to suspect, however, reality is a bit more complicated than that.

ELECTORAL LAWS, FEDERALISM, AND ETHNIC CONFLICT

In recent decades, a debate has raged between political scientists regarding the effect of institutional choice, including the choice of electoral laws and federalism, on ethnic conflict. In the last fifteen years or so, the debate has taken on a great deal of urgency as the United States and various international organizations have become increasingly ambitious about nation building. Are there constitutional choices that might encourage successful democratic consolidation in ethnically divided countries, such as Iraq or Afghanistan? More recently, the 2011 Arab Spring in the Middle East and North Africa saw the toppling of dictators in Tunisia, Egypt, and Libya. All three of these countries have adopted new constitutions and political institutions in the last few years. Will these institutions solidify moves toward democracy and encourage democratic consolidation? Or will they simply lead to a new dictatorship and possible civil war? A firm understanding of the way the institutions that we studied in Chapters 12 through 15 operate will be essential for answering these questions. But before examining whether there is an "institutional fix" for ethnic conflict, it is important to ask a prior question: are ethnically diverse societies inclined toward conflict in the first place?

Ethnic Diversity and Conflict

Although large-scale ethnic or religious conflict can be devastating, we should recognize that such conflict is the exception and that interethnic peace is the rule. This may be surprising because when such conflict occurs, the memory of its horror tends to stay with us. Indeed, when asked, it may be easy for people to provide a list of tragically violent interactions between ethnic or religious groups. For example, you might think of the conflicts during the 1990s between Hutus and Tutsis in Rwanda or between Serbs, Croats, and Bosnians in the former Yugoslavia. Or you might think of the more recent conflicts between Africans and Arabs in Sudan; between Shias, Sunnis, and Kurds in Iraq; between Uighurs and the Han-dominated Chinese government in China's Xinjiang province; or between various ethnic groups in post-Communist states, such as Azerbaijan, Georgia, Moldova, and Russia. There are two problems, however, with simply enumerating ethnic conflicts in this way. First, it tends to ignore the even larger list of "nonevents"—incidents in which groups of people with ethnic or religious differences live in relatively peaceful coexistence. Second, such enumerations frequently fail to ask the question, "Compared with what?" That is, if we say groups with ethnic differences tend to be conflict prone, we are implicitly arguing that they are *more* conflict prone than relations within an ethnic group or between nonethnic groups. That may be the case, but a list of conflicts between groups is not enough to establish this claim.

James Fearon and David Laitin (1996) argue that once we address these concerns, ethnic conflict can be seen as a relatively rare event. Table 16.4 reproduces their analysis of data from thirty-six countries in sub-Saharan Africa, an area of the world often thought to be particularly prone to ethnic violence. Fearon and Laitin examine four different forms of what might be considered ethnic violence: ethnic violence, irredentism, rebellion, and

| TABLE 16.4 | **Actual and Potential Communal Violence in Thirty-Six Sub-Saharan African Countries, 1960–1979** |

Type of communal violence	Number of incidents for all countries and years[a]	Country mean of incidents per year[b]	Number of potential incidents for all countries and years[c]	Country mean of potential incidents per year[d]	Ratio of all actual incidents to all potential incidents[e]
Ethnic violence	20	0.03	38,383	59	0.0005
Irredentism	29	0.04	18,757	26	0.0015
Rebellion	27	0.04	18,757	26	0.0014
Civil war	52	0.10	18,757	26	0.0028

Source: Fearon and Laitin (1996, 717), based on data from Morrison, Mitchell, and Paden (1989).

Note: See Fearon and Laitin (1996) for how the number of ethnic groups is determined.

a. Cases of communal violence that persist for three years are counted three times, once for each year. Two independent conflicts in the same year are coded as two incidents for that year.

b. The mean for all countries is all incidents in a country divided by the number of full years since independence through 1979; countries that became independent before 1960 are treated as if they became independent in 1960.

c. For irredentism, rebellion, and civil war, potential cases per year in each country are estimated as the number of ethnic groups in the country less one ($N - 1$), under the assumption that typically one group holds power and potential challengers come from all other groups. These numbers are then summed across countries and years to get the figures in this column. For potential cases of ethnic violence, a conservative estimate of the number of ethnic groups engaged in interactions, namely, the smaller of $2N$ and $N(N - 1) / 2$, is summed across countries and years. If there are N groups, then the total number of dyads is $N(N - 1) / 2$.

d. The mean for all countries of potential incidents per year.

e. Computed by dividing the number of incidents for all years and all countries by the number of potential incidents per year for all years and all countries.

civil war. *Ethnic violence* is defined as a conflict of short duration between two identifiable communal groups. The other three forms of violence are also ethnically based in that they involve a conflict between an identifiable communal group and the state. *Irredentism* occurs when a communal group attempts to change its allegiance from the government of its current territorial unit to a government in which the ruling authorities share the communal identification of the irredentist group. *Rebellion* involves the use of violence by a communal group in an effort to gain greater autonomy from state authorities. *Civil war* occurs when a communal group uses violence in an attempt to form a new political system based on the geographic boundaries of the ethnic community. Fearon and Laitin summarize the data in such a way that we can compare the number of actual incidents of ethnic violence with an estimate of the number of potential incidents of ethnic violence, yielding a ratio of actual incidents of violence to all potential incidents of violence. The summary data are shown in Table 16.4.

The comparison of actual to potential events is achieved by moving across the rows of Table 16.4. Beginning with the row "Ethnic violence," we see that there were 20 incidents of ethnic violence in these thirty-six countries between 1960 and 1979. Although we would never seek to minimize the human suffering caused by such violence, it is important to keep these incidents in perspective. Because the sample includes thirty-six countries observed over nineteen years, there are approximately 680 country-years in the data set.[15] One way to estimate the frequency of ethnic conflict, therefore, is to take the ratio of the number of conflicts to the number of country-years in the data set. The third column shows that this figure is 0.03. This means that there have been 3 incidents of ethnic conflict for every 100 country-years in this group of countries. This is, however, still an overestimate of the frequency of ethnic conflict because it assumes that each country-year represents just 1 potential incident of ethnic group conflict. In reality, because the typical country in this sub-Saharan sample has more than two dozen ethnic groups, the potential is there for far more than 1 ethnic conflict per country-year. Consequently, Fearon and Laitin (1996) estimate the number of potential incidents of ethnic conflict based on the number of ethnic groups in a country and find that the ratio of actual incidents of ethnic violence to potential incidents of ethnic violence is lower still (last column): there were just 5 incidents of ethnic conflict for every 10,000 potential incidents (roughly, ethnic group-years).

Similar calculations can be conducted to gauge the frequency of the other three forms of violence. We see from the last column, for example, that although communal violence aimed at the state occurs with a greater frequency than group-on-group violence, it is still quite rare. Actual communal-based irredentism and rebellion occur about 1 to 5 times for every 1,000 potential incidents. Although communally based civil wars occur about twice as often as this, they are still quite rare—only 2.8 civil wars for every 1,000 potential civil wars. One could, of course, say that Fearon and Laitin (1996) have made these phenomena seem rare by dividing them into separate categories, but even if we combine all types of communal violence against the state, they are still a tiny fraction of the number of potential events—just 5.8 actual incidents for every 1,000 potential incidents.

One thing is clear from Fearon and Laitin's analysis—even in very poor countries where the state has little capacity to rule effectively and the society is reeling from decades of colonialism that left a legacy of externally imposed borders, such as sub-Saharan Africa, ethnic heterogeneity does not lead inexorably to ethnic conflict—either between ethnic groups or between ethnic groups and the state. Simply looking at these data of violent incidents and thinking about how many incidents could have occurred if different ethnic groups were to engage in conflict should lead you to question popular notions about the nature of the link between ethnic diversity and violence.

The above conclusion can be arrived at even before we begin to answer the question of whether ethnic violence is more common than other forms of violence. One way to judge

---

15. There are actually somewhat fewer observations because some countries did not become independent until after 1960.

whether ethnic conflicts are more common than other forms of conflict is to examine whether ethnic diversity—having large numbers of ethnic groups—increases the likelihood of civil war. In a different article, Fearon and Laitin (2003) find that, after taking account of wealth and a battery of other variables, countries that experience civil wars are no more ethnically or religiously diverse than countries that do not. Instead, what Fearon and Laitin find to matter most for civil war onset are factors that favor insurgency, such as poverty, oil-dependent export sectors, political instability, and rough terrain. These factors increase the probability of civil war by creating bureaucratically weak states and by creating environments favorable to rebel recruitment.[16]

Although the study by Fearon and Laitin challenges the popular belief that having more ethnic groups in a country increases the likelihood of civil war, it is possible that ethnic diversity does increase the risk of civil war—but through an indirect effect that goes undetected in their study. Several economists, for example, have argued that ethnic heterogeneity has a deleterious effect on economic growth (Easterly and Levine 1997). If this is true, ethnic heterogeneity might contribute to the risk of civil war by helping to keep countries poor. Indeed, an analysis using Fearon and Laitin's own data finds that (a) ethnic diversity is positively associated with the onset of civil war when wealth (measured by GDP per capita) is removed from their statistical model, and (b) there is a negative association between ethnic heterogeneity and wealth. Taken together, these results suggest that ethnic heterogeneity may not have a direct effect on civil war onset but that it might have an indirect effect by reducing wealth, which, in turn, increases the likelihood of civil war. This causal story is graphically illustrated in Figure 16.7.

Considerable disagreement remains among economists and political scientists as to the exact causal connection between ethnic heterogeneity and economic growth, which somewhat complicates the above discussion. Some economists maintain that ethnic heterogeneity and economic growth are not causally related. And even those that accept that there is a causal relationship often disagree about the exact process by which ethnic heterogeneity inhibits economic growth. Easterly and Levine (1997) show that ethnically heterogeneous African countries experience lower economic growth rates than more ethnically homogeneous African countries. They argue that this is the case because governments in ethnically diverse countries are often politically unstable and tend to choose policies that lead to low levels of schooling, underdeveloped financial systems, distorted financial exchange markets, and insufficient infrastructure. Easterly and Levine suggest that when various ethnic groups in a country have different preferences, they may derive less satisfaction from providing

---

16. Poverty, which lowers tax revenue, and political instability weaken the state, thereby making it easier for rebel groups to challenge it successfully. Rough terrain, like mountainous regions, gives rebel groups hiding places and strongholds that hinder attempts by the state to crush them. Thus, poverty, political instability, and rough terrain increase the likelihood of civil war by increasing the probability that a challenge to the state will be successful. In contrast, the presence of oil increases the likelihood of civil war by increasing the value of gaining control of the state. All of these factors together increase the expected value of civil war on the part of rebel groups.

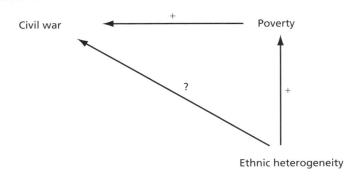

FIGURE 16.7 **Possible Causal Paths by Which Ethnic Heterogeneity Encourages Civil War**

Note: The positive signs indicate the direction of the causal effect. Thus, high levels of ethnic heterogeneity increase poverty, and high levels of poverty increase the likelihood of civil wars. It is unclear whether ethnic heterogeneity has a direct effect on civil war.

public goods than would be the case in a more homogeneous society. For instance, a public good like a school might lead to lower satisfaction in an ethnically diverse setting if the groups cannot agree on the main language of instruction, location, or general curriculum. The result is that the ethnically diverse society is less likely to end up building the school. Part of the problem is also that members of one ethnic group may not be willing to spend resources on providing public goods that members of other ethnic groups will get to consume. Whatever the reason behind the low level of investment in public goods, economic growth is likely to be inhibited. Evidence supporting this argument linking ethnic heterogeneity with lower levels of public goods provision can be found in a variety of settings, including advanced industrialized democracies. For example, Alesina, Baqir, and Easterly (1999) compare US cities and find that governments in ethnically diverse cities tend to provide fewer public goods than governments in more ethnically homogeneous cities.

Significantly, given our upcoming discussion of institutions, Easterly (2001) notes that what economists call "good institutions" (those that reduce bureaucratic delay, enforce contracts, reduce the risk of nationalization, and provide sound infrastructure) can help to alleviate the negative effects of ethnic heterogeneity on economic growth. In other words, if a country's institutions are of a sufficiently high quality, then ethnic heterogeneity may have no effect on the provision of public goods or on conflict.

The arguments that we have examined so far focus on the claim that it is the number of ethnic groups in a country that increases the risk of conflict and violence. Some scholars, though, argue that it is not the number of ethnic groups per se that matters for conflict but rather the distribution of ethnic group memberships. For example, some studies have suggested that it is *ethnic polarization* and not ethnic heterogeneity that increases the likelihood of things like civil wars (Esteban and Ray 1999, 2008; Esteban and Schneider 2008; Montalvo and Reynal-Querol 2005; Reynal-Querol 2002). This literature suggests that the risk of civil war is higher when there are a few large ethnic groups with opposing interests than when there are many small ethnic groups. Along similar lines, Chandra and Boulet (2012) argue that democratic stability is put at risk not by ethnic heterogeneity but by the existence of a permanently excluded ethnic minority. The reasoning is that an ethnic minority that sees no democratic means by which it can ever come to power is more likely to break with democracy than one that foresees coming to power from time to time through the electoral process. Chandra and Boulet go on to claim that far from hurting democratic stability, having a large number of evenly sized ethnic groups in a country can help to stabilize democracy by making a variety of shifting ruling coalitions possible, something that lowers the likelihood that particular ethnic groups will be permanently excluded from power. Empirical evidence for a corollary of this theory comes from Collier and Hoeffler (2004), who show that the risk of civil war is highest when one ethnic group composes between 45 and 90 percent of the population. That is, they provide evidence that civil war is more likely when a single ethnic group is in a position to act as a permanent *majority*—presumably because for every permanent majority, there is at least one potentially disgruntled permanent minority.

As we will see, arguments about the effect of electoral laws on ethnic conflict are closely tied to arguments about the existence of permanent ethnic minorities. The main dispute is whether these minorities should receive a guarantee of permanent representation or whether they should be encouraged to form coalitions with other groups and, thereby, avoid being placed in the position of permanent opposition. But before we examine the effect of electoral laws on ethnic conflict in detail, it is important to recognize that other factors influence how responsive voters are to ethnic-based appeals from politicians and, hence, how likely it is that there will be group-based conflict in the first place.

Varshney (2001, 2002), for example, argues that the pattern of social ties between citizens is an important factor influencing the probability of group-based conflict. Specifically, he argues that peace is promoted when citizens form interethnic social ties. Interethnic civic engagement, he finds, promotes peace, and its "absence or weakness opens up space for ethnic violence" (Varshney 2001, 363). As he notes, though, not all forms of interethnic civic engagement are equally effective at promoting peace. For example, he argues that joining formal associations, such as interethnic business associations, sports teams, reading or film clubs, and labor unions, is more effective in promoting ethnic peace than more everyday forms of interethnic contact, such as regularly eating together or allowing children to play together. Although both forms of interethnic civic engagement promote peace, Varshney finds that the associational form is sturdier than everyday engagement, especially when politicians attempt to polarize people along ethnic lines. This evidence suggests that vigorous associational life, if it has an interethnic aspect, acts as a serious constraint on the ability of politicians to mobilize voters along ethnic lines, even when ethnic polarization is in their political interest. The more the associational networks cut across ethnic boundaries, the harder it is for politicians to achieve such polarization (Varshney 2001, 363).

Most of the studies on ethnic politics that we have examined so far take ethnic identities and how these identities are manifested in associational life as given. As we saw in Chapter 14, however, institutions, such as electoral laws, are likely to influence the type of ethnic identities that become politicized in the first place (Chandra 2004, 2005; Chandra and Boulet 2012; Posner 2004, 2005). Chandra (2005) argues that one reason why so many studies find an inherent tension between ethnic heterogeneity and things like democratic stability is that they treat ethnic identity as given rather than as something that is socially constructed. To demonstrate this point, Chandra presents a model of electoral competition under a single-member district plurality electoral system in which party leaders are free to define ethnic groups strategically. The results of the model show that there are conditions in which party leaders will choose to redefine group identity in order to attract voters across ethnic lines. In other words, it is not always the case

that party leaders will choose to mobilize voters along ethnic lines. This is an important result because it suggests that the conflict and extremism predicted by traditional models of **ethnic outbidding**, in which the

Ethnic outbidding is a process in which ethnic divisions are politicized and the result is the formation of increasingly polarized ethnic parties.

politicization of ethnic divisions inevitably gives rise to one or more competing ethnic parties (Horowitz 1985; Rabushka and Shepsle 1972), are the result of assuming that ethnic identities are fixed.

According to models of ethnic outbidding, once a single ethnic party emerges, it "infects" the political system because it results in a new and more extreme ethnic party emerging to oppose the first one. This, in turn, leads the first ethnic party to become more extreme, and so on, producing a downward spiral in which nonethnically based competitive politics is destroyed altogether. Essentially what Chandra (2005) shows is that this ethnic outbidding process need not occur if ethnic identities are not fixed. Interestingly, Chandra's study suggests that far from being a cause of concern, ethnic heterogeneity may actually help ensure democratic stability by increasing the number of dimensions along which interethnic alliances can form. In effect, majorities that are constructed along one dimension are unlikely to be permanent and, hence, dangerous when there is ethnic diversity, because politicians from groups that comprise a minority on that dimension can try to mobilize voters along a different dimension, one in which they will be part of a majority.

We should note at this point, though, that Chandra has analyzed these dynamics under only one type of electoral system—single-member district plurality rule. Further analysis is required to support her conclusion that "some institutional contexts produce benign forms of ethnic politics, while others produce malign forms" (Chandra 2005, 245). Fortunately, there is a large literature that we can draw on that looks at how electoral laws affect the link between ethnic conflict and democratic stability. It is to this debate that we now turn.

Electoral Laws and Ethnic Conflict

We learned in Chapter 14 that electoral laws influence whether or not social cleavages are reflected in a country's party system. Proportional representation (PR) electoral laws with a high district magnitude allow social cleavages to be translated directly into the party system. In contrast, less permissive electoral systems, such as SMDP rule, create incentives for political entrepreneurs and voters to put aside some of their differences in an attempt to capture a difficult-to-obtain electoral prize. Anticipating the effect of electoral rules, members of ethnic groups are likely to engage in what Chandra (2004) refers to as an "ethnic head count"—they will look around to see if there are enough members of their ethnic group, given the electoral rules in place, to make a plausible ethnic-specific bid for a legislative seat. If there are, they will be encouraged to support a party that appeals mainly to their specific ethnic group. But if the perceived electoral threshold exceeds their subjective assessment of the size of their ethnic group, then they will likely support a more broadly based party— either a nonethnic party or an ethnic party that defines the ethnic group in a more inclusive manner. Political entrepreneurs play an important role in all of this. For example, political entrepreneurs may try to influence voters' perceptions about the presence of their coethnics by organizing cultural, religious, sporting, and sometimes even explicitly political events that encourage ethnics to reveal their group membership. But political entrepreneurs will also be aware of how electoral thresholds interact with group size to determine the likelihood that such strategies will succeed. Because electoral thresholds are directly affected by electoral laws, the propensity for elites to make ethnic-specific appeals or make interethnic alliances, and the likelihood that voters will respond to such appeals or eschew them and support more broadly based parties, will be a function of the interaction between group size and electoral laws.[17]

Scholars wishing to influence the design of constitutions in societies characterized by ethnic heterogeneity do not disagree about the role played by electoral institutions. They all recognize that, given high levels of social heterogeneity, the choice of electoral laws will play an important role in determining whether many ethnically homogeneous parties or a smaller number of broadly based parties, each drawing support from multiple ethnic groups, will form. Rather, the debate is whether democratic stability is best ensured by taking ethnic groups as given and ensuring that minorities are guaranteed adequate representation, or by assuming that group identities are malleable and can be successfully channeled into regime-supporting, rather than regime-challenging, behaviors.

---

17. Suggesting that actors condition their behavior on the probability of success in achieving their goals is controversial for some. An alternative view is that actors sometimes choose behaviors because they see such behaviors as the "right thing to do," independently of expected consequences (Varshney 2004). This is, to some extent, true. The difficulty, though, comes in determining ex ante when individuals will and will not make such sacrifices. Work on suicide bombings has demonstrated that even these acts of self-sacrifice can be understood from within a standard rational actor framework (Berman and Laitin 2006).

Arend Lijphart is the most recognized champion of the view that we should take ethnic groups as given and ensure that minorities receive adequate representation. His approach to dealing with ethnic heterogeneity has come to be known as **consociationalism**. According to Lijphart (2004), ethnic minorities pose an acute danger to democratic stability when they are excluded from participation in formal political institutions. But if ethnic minorities are able to gain access to formal institutions and those institutions are designed to reflect the interests of as broad a set of the population as possible, then these minorities will have a stake in the continued survival of the democratic system. According to Lijphart, it is important that there also be multiple checks on governmental power so as to minimize the likelihood that the state can be used to systematically abuse minority rights. As you can see, consociationalism is closely related to the consensus vision of democracy. As outlined earlier in this chapter, the consensus vision of democracy envisions the adoption of institutional mechanisms that divide power and make it necessary for the government to seek input from as wide a range of citizens as possible. In effect, consociationalism is a particular strategy for implementing the consensus vision of democracy that involves the adoption of institutions guaranteeing the representation of minority groups.

> **Consociationalism** is a form of government that emphasizes power sharing through guaranteed group representation.

Consociationalism has its roots in the religious and social conflicts experienced by the Netherlands in the late nineteenth and early twentieth centuries. These conflicts eventually resulted in the division of Dutch society into four "pillars," representing Calvinist, Catholic, Socialist, and liberal citizens. Each pillar had its own schools, hospitals, university, newspapers, political parties, and institutional guarantees of representation. Another famous example of consociationalism is Lebanon. In 1943, Lebanon adopted an unwritten agreement—the National Pact—that guaranteed political representation to Maronite Christians, Sunni Muslims, and Shia Muslims. The National Pact stipulated that the president was to be a Maronite Christian, the prime minister a Sunni Muslim, and the speaker of parliament a Shia Muslim. In addition, the Christian and Muslim communities were each to be allotted a specific number of legislative seats.[18] Ministerial portfolios, as well as many government positions in the executive, legislative, and judicial branches, were also allocated along religious lines. Even positions such as those of judges and teachers were divided up, with some attention paid toward sectarian quotas (Bannerman 2002). Lebanese **confessionalism**, as consociationalism is known when it is applied to religious groups, was initially thought to be highly successful. Demographic changes, the inflow of

> **Confessionalism** is a form of government that emphasizes power sharing by different religious communities through guaranteed group representation.

---

18. Originally, the allocation of legislative seats reflected a 6:5 ratio between Christians and Muslims. Since 1989, legislative seats have been allocated evenly across these two religious groups. The sixty-four seats currently allocated to the Christian community are further divided among Maronite (34), Orthodox (14), Catholic (8), Armenian (6), Protestant (1), and other groups (1). The sixty-four seats currently allocated to the Muslim community are also further divided among Sunni (27), Shiite (27), Alawite (2), and Druze (8) groups.

Palestinian refugees starting in 1948, and conflicts over regional politics, however, led to a protracted and violent civil war in Lebanon that started in 1975 and ended in 1990.

You will probably have noticed that consociationalism's goal of institutionalizing ethnic (religious) groups is precisely the type of policy that Chandra (2005, 245) argues against on the grounds that it tends to "impose an artificial fixity on ethnic identities." In what follows, we do not engage in a protracted examination of the pros and cons of consociationalism per se. Instead, we focus on the effect of two institutional choices—PR and federalism—

The Lebanese parliament elected Michel Aoun (*center*) as president of Lebanon, breaking the deadlock caused by political infighting that had left Lebanon without a head of state for two years. On November 3, 2016, the new president met Lebanese Parliament Speaker Nabih Berri (*left*) and newly appointed Prime Minister Saad Hariri (*right*) at Baabda Presidential Palace in Beirut. Under Lebanon's confessional system, the president is a Maronite Christian, the prime minister is a Sunni Muslim, and the Speaker of parliament is a Shiite Muslim.

that are typically part of consociational arrangements. We begin by examining the effect of electoral laws on ethnic divisions and conflict. We then examine the use of federalism for guaranteeing minority rights and preventing conflict.

Lijphart (2004, 99) states that "the most important choice facing constitution writers is that of a legislative electoral system." He goes on to state that "for divided societies, ensuring the election of a broadly representative legislature should be the crucial consideration" and that PR is "undoubtedly the optimal way of doing so" (100). To demonstrate his point, Lijphart claims that there is a scholarly consensus in the literature against the use of majoritarian electoral laws in deeply divided societies on the ground that they can lead to the indefinite exclusion of significant societal groups. Not only are PR electoral systems better in divided societies than majoritarian systems, according to Lijphart, but they are also better than the mixed electoral systems that are increasingly being adopted around the world. As you will recall from Chapter 13, mixed electoral systems combine both majoritarian and proportional components. The extent to which mixed systems yield minority representation depends on the extent to which the proportional component is compensatory, that is, the extent to which the PR component is specifically designed to counteract the disproportionality produced by the majoritarian component. If the PR component is not compensatory, "the results will necessarily be less than fully proportional—and minority representation less accurate and secure" (Lijphart 2004, 100). If the PR component does override the majoritarian component, though, these mixed systems are, according to Lijphart, essentially proportional with the same benefits as straight PR systems. Some countries such as Bolivia, Colombia, Croatia, India, and Pakistan seek to deal with ethnic diversity by providing reserved legislative seats for specified minorities. For Lijphart, however, guaranteed minority representation is inferior to simply using PR electoral rules because it requires governments to address the difficult and politically incendiary question of which minorities require special representation guarantees and which do not. PR, in contrast, treats all groups the same and, if done correctly, produces the desired minority representation.

The basic assumptions behind Lijphart's argument are that ethnic and other deep-seated conflicts can be mitigated as long as all the relevant parties to a dispute receive adequate legislative representation and that proportional electoral rules are the best way to achieve this representation. As we saw in Chapter 13, though, scholars have pointed to several drawbacks to proportional electoral systems. For example, some point to how PR electoral rules sometimes facilitate the election of small antisystem parties that become locked in cycles of legislative conflict, which can then spill over into violent social conflict. The most dramatic and troubling example of this occurred in Weimar Germany, whose highly proportional electoral system helped Hitler's Nazi Party come to power. Others point to how PR systems frequently wind up giving small parties a disproportionate influence in the government formation process. Because it is rare for parties to obtain a legislative majority in PR systems, large parties often rely on the support of smaller parties to get into government. These smaller parties can frequently use their leverage to wring concessions from the larger party. Some of these concessions can be quite radical and lack the support of an electoral majority. In Israel, for example, small ultrareligious parties have won support for many of their policies by threatening to pull out of the government. Recently, some scholars have argued that these particular issues can be mitigated by employing a proportional electoral system with a relatively small district magnitude (about six seats per district). In a study of 609 elections in eighty-one countries from 1945 to 2006, for example, Carey and Hix (2011) find that low-magnitude PR systems produce similar levels of proportionality as large-magnitude systems but without high levels of legislative fragmentation. They refer to these low-magnitude PR systems as the "electoral sweet spot."

Some political scientists claim that the representation of distinct groups is neither necessary, nor sufficient, to bring about intergroup peace (Barry 1975). For instance, Horowitz (1991, 119) argues that even if proportional systems guarantee that ethnic minorities win seats in parliament, this is not the same as saying that "minority interests will receive attention in the legislative process." Indeed, if conflicts exist in divided societies, one might wonder why simply using PR systems to replicate the societal divisions that led to these conflicts in the legislature will be of any help if there are no incentives for cross-party cooperation and accommodation. What is needed, according to these critics, is an institutional mechanism that encourages compromise and moderation. Many of these scholars believe that some majoritarian electoral laws provide such a mechanism.

Donald Horowitz (1985, 1991) presents the most widely recognized alternative to PR for deeply divided societies: the alternative vote (AV). Recall from Chapter 13 that the alternative vote is, essentially, an "instant-runoff" system in which one legislator is elected from each district and voters have the opportunity to rank order all the candidates. The candidate who wins an absolute majority of the first-preference votes is elected. If no candidate wins an absolute majority, the candidate with the lowest number of first-preference votes is eliminated, and her ballots are reallocated among the remaining candidates according to the indicated second preferences. This process continues until a candidate receives an absolute majority of votes.

Unlike with SMDP systems, voters in an AV system have little incentive to vote strategically because they know that their vote will not be wasted if their most preferred candidate is unlikely to win; their vote is simply transferred to the next candidate. This means that voters motivated by ethnic identity are likely to indicate a coethnic as their first preference and the least unsavory candidate from an alternative ethnic group as their second preference. In highly diverse districts, candidates realize that their electoral success will likely depend on the transfer of second preferences from other ethnic groups. Consequently, successful candidates will typically be those who are effective at making broad-based centrist appeals that cross ethnic lines. It is for this reason that many scholars believe that the alternative vote encourages moderation and compromise across ethnic groups (Horowitz 1985, 1991; Reilly 1997, 2001). Empirical evidence to support this belief comes from Australia, where the major parties frequently attempt to negotiate deals with smaller parties for their second preferences prior to an election (Reilly 2001, 55–56). Additional evidence that the alternative vote encourages the building of coalitions across ethnic groups comes from Papua New Guinea and, to some extent, Fiji (Horowitz 2004, 513–514).

It is important to recognize that the potential benefits of the AV system will be realized only if electoral districts are sufficiently diverse that no single ethnic group is large enough to win based on first preference votes alone. If ethnic groups are geographically concentrated in distinct parts of a country, it is unlikely that an AV system will promote cross-ethnic appeals, because each party knows that it can win simply by appealing to its own ethnic group. As a result, the success of the AV system in reducing ethnic conflict depends on the geographic distribution of ethnic groups and the ethnic makeup of individual districts.

To sum up, you can think of the choice between PR and AV as being a choice between replicating ethnic divisions in the legislature hoping that political leaders will cooperate after the election (PR) and creating institutional incentives that seek to weaken or even transcend the political salience of ethnicity altogether (AV). Given the centrality of the above debate to questions of institutional design, it is surprising that so few attempts have been made to use systematic empirical evidence to adjudicate the competing claims put forward by Lijphart and Horowitz. On the whole, the literature is full of evidence from a small number of cases presented by partisans of one view or the other to support their claims. Systematic evaluations of the purported benefits of PR or the majoritarian alternative vote for divided societies are relatively rare.

It is true that some studies find support for the claim that PR systems reduce the likelihood of violent conflict (F. Cohen 1997; Reynal-Querol 2002; Saideman et al. 2002). There are, however, several reasons to be cautious about these results. First, these studies rarely make a direct comparison between PR and majoritarian democracies. For example, many of the studies cited above combine both democratic and undemocratic countries. As a result, PR democracies are being compared with a heterogeneous mixture of majoritarian democracies and dictatorships in the sample. The study by Reynal-Querol (2002, 37) appears to compare parliamentary democracies that use either proportional or majoritarian electoral rules with presidential and mixed democracies as well as dictatorships. Again, this is not the appropriate comparison to evaluate the competing claims put forward by Lijphart and Horowitz. Second, although various scholars have looked at the association between PR and conflict, none has examined whether PR systems *modify* the way that ethnic heterogeneity influences the probability of conflict. In other words, none of them are testing the precise causal story put forward by Lijphart, which is that ethnic heterogeneity leads to conflict in majoritarian democracies but less so or not at all in proportional democracies.[19] Finally, it should be noted that none of these studies distinguishes among the variety of majoritarian electoral systems that exists. As a result, we have little to no systematic evidence as to whether the alternative vote produces the sort of moderating effects that reduce violence in divided societies that Horowitz claims that it does. An obvious reason why so few studies have focused specifically on the impact of the alternative vote is that only a small number of countries around the world actually use this electoral system—this makes conducting statistical analyses problematic.

In a recent article, Selway and Templeman (2012) attempt to correct some of the shortcomings of prior studies. Most important, the authors examine whether proportional representation electoral rules mitigate the link between high levels of ethnic fractionalization and political violence. They find that they do not; indeed, if anything, proportional representation appears to exacerbate political violence when ethnic fractionalization is high. They find similar results for the effect of parliamentary, as opposed to presidential, rule. These results cast serious doubt on the benefits of consociationalism for mitigating conflict in ethnically divided societies. We expect that this is but the first of a series of future studies on the impact of electoral rules on ethnic conflict and democratic stability—perhaps some that begin as undergraduate research projects. These studies will hopefully result in clearer policy recommendations for constitutional designers. It is likely that such recommendations will have to take account of how electoral rules might interact with other institutions. It is to one of these institutions—federalism—that we now turn.

---

19. The study by Reynal-Querol (2002) represents a partial exception. Reynal-Querol finds evidence that "inclusive democracy"—by which she appears to mean parliamentary systems that use PR—reduces the likelihood that "religious polarization" will lead to civil war.

Federalism and Ethnic Conflict

Recent history in Iraq and Afghanistan has led to a renewed debate among political scientists about the role that federalism can play in stabilizing democracy in divided societies. Traditionally, comparative political scientists have seen incongruent and asymmetric federalism as a particularly appealing form of government for those countries in which policy preferences differ in significant ways across geographically concentrated ethnic groups.[20] By bringing the government closer to the people, increasing opportunities to participate in government, and giving groups discretion over their political, social, and economic affairs, incongruent and asymmetric federalism is thought to reduce ethnic conflict and dampen secessionist demands, thereby stabilizing democracy. In effect, federalism helps ethnic groups to protect their interests and concerns—such as language, education, culture, security, and economic development—at the regional level. By providing increased autonomy to regional governments in which national minorities might constitute majorities, federalism effectively shifts power to minorities, thereby making them more content to live within a unified state despite being permanent minorities in the national electorate. These purported advantages have led many scholars to view federalism as the most promising means for holding heterogeneous and conflict-ridden countries together (Horowitz 1991; Lijphart 1977, 1996, 1999; Lustik, Miodownik, and Eidelson 2004; Riker 1964; Stepan 1999; Tsebelis 1990). In support of this line of reasoning, it is commonly accepted that federalism has played an important role in stabilizing democracies in ethnically diverse countries, such as Belgium, Canada, India, Spain, and Switzerland.

Several scholars have called for the adoption of federalism in Iraq as an institutional means for dealing with the ethnic conflict between Kurds, Sunnis, and Shias. For example, Brancati (2004, 7–8) states:

> [B]y dividing power between two levels of government—giving groups greater control over their own political, social, and economic affairs while making them feel less exploited as well as more secure—federalism offers the only viable possibility for preventing ethnic conflict and secessionism as well as establishing a stable democracy in Iraq. . . . [A federal] system will help the United States not only to build democracy in Iraq but also to prevent the emergence of a Shi'a-dominated government in the country. Without this form of federalism, an Iraq rife with internal conflict and dominated by one ethnic or religious group is more likely to emerge, undermining US efforts towards establishing democracy in Iraq as well as the greater Middle East.

Although federalism has historically been seen as helpful in dampening the flames of ethnic conflict and secessionism, several studies have challenged this view. Some of these studies even go so far as to suggest that federalism might actually intensify, rather than

---

20. Recall from Chapter 15 that incongruent and asymmetric federalism occurs when the political boundaries of the subnational units are specifically aligned with the geographic boundaries of social groups and when some territorial units enjoy more extensive powers than others relative to the central government.

reduce, ethnic conflict. One way in which federalism is thought to do this is by reinforcing regionally based ethnic identities (Hardgrave 1994; Kymlicka 1998). Rather than encouraging the construction of political coalitions across ethnic lines, federalism creates incentives for the politicization of ethnic identities by officially recognizing particular ethnic groups and giving them a sense of legitimacy. In this way, federalism leads to the strengthening, rather than the weakening, of ethnic divisions. A second way that federalism is thought to intensify ethnic conflict is by providing access to political and economic resources that ethnic leaders can then use to bring pressure against the state. In other words, decentralizing power to the regional level may have the unfortunate consequence of supplying groups with the necessary resources—regional legislatures, regional police forces, and regional forms of media—to more effectively engage in ethnic conflict and secessionism in the first place (Bunce 1999; Hechter 2000; Kymlicka 1998; Leff 1999; Roeder 1991; Snyder 2000). Indeed, leaders of multiethnic states like Sri Lanka and Indonesia have historically opposed federalism on precisely these grounds, seeing political decentralization as a slippery slope that is only likely to strengthen secessionist groups and generate demands for additional autonomy. A third way in which federalism is thought to encourage ethnic conflict is by making it easier for ethnic groups at the subnational level to produce legislation that discriminates against regional minorities (Horowitz 1991; Nordlinger 1972).

Several recent cross-national studies that support this line of reasoning present suggestive evidence that federalism may not be the panacea for ethnic conflict in divided societies that it is traditionally thought to be. For example, some studies find that although federalism tends to decrease outright rebellion, it increases protest activity among minority groups (Hechter 2000; Lustik, Miodownik, and Eidelson 2004). Another study finds that federalism has no effect on the level of attachment that minority (or majority) groups feel toward the state (Elkins and Sides 2007).

To a large extent, scholars have viewed the impact of federalism on ethnic conflict in black-and-white terms—it either always reduces the likelihood of ethnic conflict or always increases it. In reality, though, we believe that most political scientists would accept that political decentralization has been helpful in curbing ethnic conflict and secessionism in some countries, such as Belgium and India, but that it has proved to be a failure in other countries, such as Nigeria and the former Yugoslavia. This suggests that the question we really need to ask ourselves is why federalism seems to be helpful in some contexts but not in others.

Brancati (2006) provides one potential answer to this question. She suggests that much has to do with the strength of regional parties in a country. Specifically, she argues that political decentralization reduces ethnic conflict when regional parties are weak but that it can increase ethnic conflict when regional parties are strong. Her causal story is graphically illustrated in Figure 16.8. On the one hand, Brancati believes that political decentralization reduces ethnic conflict by bringing the government closer to the people, by increasing opportunities to participate in government, and by giving groups discretion over their

FIGURE 16.8 | Political Decentralization and Ethnic Conflict

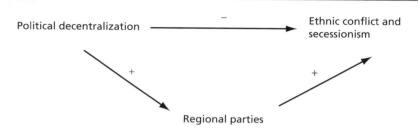

Note: Causal story posited by Brancati (2006).

political, social, and economic affairs. On the other hand, though, she claims that political decentralization increases ethnic conflict by strengthening regional identity-based parties.

As we saw in Chapter 14 (see Box 14.4, "Nationalizing Party Systems"), political decentralization increases the strength of regional parties through the opportunities it provides these parties to win elections and influence policy in regional legislatures (Chhibber and Kollman 1998, 2004). According to Brancati, this strengthening of regional parties has a detrimental effect on ethnic conflict because these parties frequently reinforce regionally based ethnic identities, they produce legislation that favors certain groups over others, and they mobilize groups to engage in ethnic conflict and secessionism or support terrorist organizations that participate in these activities. Regional parties, by their very nature, tend to reinforce regional and ethnic identities by making people who share certain attributes think of themselves as a group with shared needs and goals. For example, the Northern League, a regional party in Italy, has gone to great lengths to make the people of northern Italy think of themselves as Northern Italians rather than simply as Italians. Regional parties also frequently attempt to pass laws that discriminate against regional minorities. As an example, regional parties in Moldova exacerbated ethnic tensions with minority Romanians in Transnistria in 2004 when they passed a law closing schools that did not use the Cyrillic alphabet, thereby preventing Romanians in this region from being educated in their language. Regional parties also sometimes help violent insurgent groups in their activities against the state. For instance, regional parties in Northern Ireland and Spain, such as Sinn Féin and Herri Batasuna, have helped such organizations as the Irish Republican Army (IRA) and the Basque Euskadi Ta Askatasuna (ETA) in their secessionist campaigns against the state.

In sum, Brancati (2006) argues that whether federalism is helpful in reducing ethnic conflict or not depends on the extent to which decentralization leads to the strengthening of regional parties. If she is correct, then the key for policymakers interested in reducing ethnic conflict and stabilizing democracy is to combine incongruent and asymmetric federalism with other institutional features that lower the likelihood that regional parties will form and do well. As we saw in Chapter 14, one factor influencing the success of regional parties is the presence and timing of presidential elections (M. Golder 2006; Hicken and Stoll 2013). As we noted then, the presidency is nearly always the most important electoral prize in a presidential democracy. Typically, however, there are only a small number of viable presidential candidates, because only one person can become the president. Given the importance of the presidency, parties that do not have a viable presidential candidate, even if they are electorally strong in particular regions, are likely to find themselves abandoned by both voters and political entrepreneurs at election time. Parties that have a national base and, hence, a viable presidential candidate will naturally benefit from this strategic behavior. The end result is a nationalized party system in which regionally based parties will struggle to compete. The extent to which presidential elections exert nationalizing pressures on a country's party system will depend on how important it is to win the presidency and the temporal proximity between presidential and legislative elections. Specifically, party systems in presidential democracies are more likely to be stacked against regional parties if the president's power is large relative to that of other political actors and if presidential elections occur at the same time as regional ones (Hicken 2009; Hicken and Stoll 2011).

Electoral laws can also be written to discourage the emergence and success of regional identity-based parties. As we saw in Chapter 13 and as we noted earlier in this section, preferential voting systems, such as the alternative vote, should encourage political parties to make broad-based centrist appeals beyond their core set of supporters, because their electoral success is likely to depend on the transfer of preference votes from other groups. In effect, preferential voting systems attempt to weaken or even transcend the political salience of regional as well as ethnic identities (Horowitz 1985, 1991; Reilly 1997, 2001). As a result, they are likely to discourage the emergence and success of parties that focus their campaigning on a particular identity (regional or ethnic) group. An alternative strategy to penalize regional parties would be to impose cross-regional vote requirements that force parties to compete in a certain number of regions and to win a certain percentage of the vote in these regions to be elected to the federal government. Russia, Indonesia, and Nigeria have explicitly adopted such cross-regional voting laws in an attempt to prevent identity-based parties from forming (Brancati 2004). Overall, it appears that incongruent and asymmetric federalism can help reduce ethnic conflict and stabilize democracy in countries with geographically concentrated ethnic groups. But this might be the case only if it is combined with institutional mechanisms designed to prevent regionally based identity parties from dominating the subnational governments.

PRESIDENTIALISM AND DEMOCRATIC SURVIVAL

To finish this chapter, we bring our discussion back to the question that dominated Part II of this book: why are some countries democratic, whereas others are not? In Chapters 6 and 7, we examined economic and cultural explanations for the emergence and survival of democracy. Having studied at some length the different institutions that democracies can adopt, we are now in a position to look at a third set of explanations for the survival of democracy: institutional explanations. Institutionalist approaches to democracy ask the following question: if democracy emerges, are there institutions, or combinations of institutions, that make the survival of democracy more or less likely? Although many institutional choices are thought to affect the prospects of democratic survival, one that has generated an enormous literature in comparative politics is the choice of whether to adopt a presidential or parliamentary form of democracy (Bernhard, Nordstrom, and Reenock 2001; Cheibub 2002, 2007; Gasiorowski 1995; Jones 1995; Linz 1990, 1994; Mainwaring 1993; Mainwaring and Shugart 1997; Przeworski et al. 2000; Shugart and Carey 1992; Stepan and Skach 1993; Valenzuela 2004). It is on this institutional choice that we focus in this section.

Considerable historical evidence suggests that democracy is less stable in presidential regimes than in parliamentary ones. Indeed, Przeworski and colleagues (2000, 129) present evidence showing that the expected life of democracy under presidentialism (twenty-one years) is about three to five times shorter than it is under parliamentarism (seventy-three years). This type of evidence has led some to talk of the "perils of presidentialism" (Linz 1990). For many years, comparative politics scholars have debated whether the fragility of democracy in presidential regimes is really due to something inherent in the structure of presidentialism itself, and, if so, what this might be. Answers to these questions are important because, despite the historical pattern showing that democracy is less likely to survive in presidential regimes, many new democracies have adopted presidential constitutions. If the survival of democracy is inherently problematic in presidential regimes, this does not bode well for some of these newly democratic countries. In what follows, we suggest that some presidential democracies, specifically those with multiparty systems, are more unstable than others. As we go on to note, though, ongoing economic development around the world is making all presidential democracies more stable than they were in the past.

The Perils of Presidentialism

Presidentialism is often thought to have a number of negative consequences (Shively 2001). First, presidentialism is thought to make it difficult for citizens to identify who is responsible for policies; that is, it is thought to produce low clarity of responsibility. In effect, the separation of powers between the executive and legislative branches in presidential democracies allows each to blame the other when outcomes are bad and each to engage in credit claiming when outcomes are good. This low clarity of responsibility makes it difficult for voters in presidential democracies to hold their government accountable.

Second, presidentialism is thought to slow the policymaking process. In presidential democracies, new legislation must work its way through the legislature and be accepted by the president before it can be enacted. Such negotiations are often protracted because, unlike in parliamentary democracies where governments must have the support of a legislative majority, a presidential government can face a legislature controlled by parties that do not support the president's legislative goals. Divided government is possible in presidential democracies but not parliamentary ones.

Third, presidentialism is thought to produce a pattern of executive recruitment that is very different from what is seen in parliamentarism. In many parliamentary democracies, prime ministers are selected from the leadership of a party's legislative delegation. As we illustrated in Chapter 14, membership in that leadership is typically restricted to parliamentarians who have worked their way up from lowly "backbench" positions by gaining policy expertise, honing their debating skills, and demonstrating their loyalty to the party. In contrast, presidential candidates are often drawn from outsiders who are seen to be free from commitments to the party elite. Significantly, this means that presidential candidates are also frequently free of legislative experience and policymaking expertise. As an example, Alberto Fujimori, an academic and TV presenter, won the 1990 presidential elections in Peru. In 2016, political outsider Donald Trump became the president of the United States. The election of such candidates to the "equivalent" position of prime minister in a parliamentary democracy is almost unthinkable.

Fourth, presidentialism is thought to make it difficult to produce comprehensive policy. As we have already mentioned, the policymaking process in presidential democracies typically involves complex bargaining between the executive and legislative branches of government. A result is that some policies in presidential systems get adopted simply because they are crucial to gaining acquiescence from another branch of government on an unrelated matter. In contrast, because, by definition, the cabinet in a parliamentary democracy enjoys the confidence of the legislature, it is thought that parliamentary governments have a better chance of putting together comprehensive, rationalized, legislative programs.

It should be noted that many of these "perils of presidentialism" actually occur in some parliamentary democracies as well. In particular, parliamentary democracies that have coalition governments are also likely to experience difficulty in (a) making policy quickly, (b) locating responsibility for policy, and (c) making comprehensive policy. Indeed, we often hear some people make the case that presidentialism, far from being a cause for concern, is, in fact, the solution to these problems in parliamentary democracies. Rather than talk about the "perils of presidentialism," some scholars choose to focus on the "problems of parliamentarism."

The problems of parliamentarism are, perhaps, best illustrated by the French Fourth Republic (1946–1958). As many scholars have noted, the French Fourth Republic was characterized by high levels of **immobilism** and government instability (Rioux 1989). In the twelve years of its existence, the French Fourth Republic witnessed twenty-four different governments under sixteen different prime ministers (Huber and Martinez-Gallardo 2004).

> **Immobilism** describes a situation in parliamentary democracies in which government coalitions are so weak and unstable that they are incapable of reaching an agreement on new policy.

A consequence of this instability was that French governments were unable to deal with the main issues of the day, particularly those having to do with its colonies in Indochina and Algeria. Much of the problem lay with the Fourth Republic's proportional electoral system that helped to produce a highly fragmented and polarized legislature. For example, roughly 30 percent of the seats in the National Assembly regularly went to parties on the extreme right (Gaullists and Poujadists) and the extreme left (Communists) that were not viewed as viable government coalition partners. This meant that the five or six small moderate parties that existed in the center of the policy space were forced to try to build legislative majorities from the remaining 70 percent of seats, something that proved extremely difficult. Governments typically had to choose between immobility—doing nothing and remaining in power—and attempting to push forward with their legislative program, which normally resulted in their quick removal from office. In May 1958, a majority of legislators in the National Assembly eventually voted themselves and the constitution out of existence and delegated power to General Charles de Gaulle to write a new constitution. One of the goals of de Gaulle's new constitution was to concentrate power in the hands of a president so that he could override the stalemates that dogged the Fourth Republic and rule in the interest of the nation at large. For de Gaulle, a stronger president was the solution to the problems of parliamentarism as exhibited in the Fourth Republic.

Other parliamentary systems have experienced the same sort of chronic government instability and immobilism that plagued the French Fourth Republic. For example, another well-known case of a country characterized by endemic cabinet instability is postwar Italy. As we noted in Chapter 12, the average duration of an Italian cabinet from 1945 to 1998 was about a year. As with the French Fourth Republic, many scholars put this cabinet instability down to a proportional electoral system that helped to create highly fragmented and polarized legislatures. These legislatures, in turn, made it difficult for party leaders to form stable government coalitions or get much done. Explanations of immobilism nearly always start with the use of proportional electoral systems. As Rustow (1950, 116) put it, proportional representation, "by facilitating cabinet crises, parliamentary stalemates, and legislative inaction, will tend to prevent any exercise of power whatever."

We should recall at this point, though, that a focus on government instability can often lead us to overstate the actual amount of political instability in a country. As we noted in Chapter 12, for example, government instability need not imply a lack of political or portfolio experience among cabinet ministers (Huber and Martinez-Gallardo 2004, 2008). Consider the case of Italy again. Although postwar Italy has been ruled by shifting and unstable government coalitions, there has always been a great deal of political continuity just below the surface. For example, the Christian Democratic Party, the largest party in parliament for most of the postwar period, participated in every cabinet from 1948 to 1992 in coalition with a rotating set of junior partners comprising the Liberal, Republican, Social Democratic, and Socialist parties. As several scholars have noted, each new cabinet was essentially composed of the exact same people from the previous cabinet. According to P. A. Allum (1973, 119), "behind the façade of continuous cabinet crises, there [was] a significant continuity of party, persons, and posts" in postwar Italy. Scholars of French politics make an almost identical argument in regard to the government instability in the French Fourth

Republic. In short, it is important to remember that cabinet instability in parliamentary democracies need not imply ministerial instability. More significantly, *cabinet* instability, as we will see, does not imply *democratic* instability either.

So where does this leave us? Are the "problems of parliamentarism" greater than the "perils of presidentialism," or vice versa? Although the examples of immobilism in the parliamentary democracies of postwar Italy and the French Fourth Republic are somewhat illustrative, ransacking history for supportive cases in favor of one's favorite or most hated institution is not good scientific practice. As a result, we will now turn our attention to a more systematic analysis of how presidentialism and parliamentarism affect democratic survival.

Stepan and Skach (1993) claim that the prospects for the survival of democracy are worse under presidentialism than under parliamentarism. They argue that the reason for this can be traced to the fact that the essence of parliamentarism is *mutual dependence,* whereas the essence of presidentialism is *mutual independence.* In a parliamentary democracy, the legislative and executive branches are mutually dependent. On the one hand, the government needs the support of a legislative majority to stay in power. On the other hand, the government can dissolve the legislature by calling new elections. In other words, the government and the legislature cannot continue to exist without the support of the other in a parliamentary democracy. In a presidential democracy, in contrast, the executive and legislative branches are mutually independent. Both the legislature and the president have their own independent sources of legitimacy and their own fixed electoral mandates. The legislature cannot remove the president from office, and the president cannot remove the legislature.

Stepan and Skach (1993) argue that the mutual dependence of parliamentarism encourages *reconciliation* between the executive and legislative branches, whereas the mutual independence of presidentialism encourages *antagonism* between them. In presidential democracies, this antagonism, which can arise when the president is faced by a legislature dominated by opposition parties, can lead to legislative deadlock. With no constitutional mechanism to resolve the deadlock, politicians and citizens in presidential democracies may look to the military to break the stalemate. In contrast, if deadlock occurs between the executive and legislative branches in a parliamentary democracy, there are constitutional means for resolving the crisis. Either the legislature can pass a vote of no confidence and remove the government, or the prime minister can dissolve the parliament and call for new elections. It is the existence of these constitutional means in parliamentary democracies for resolving deadlock situations that is thought to be at the heart of why democratic stability is greater in parliamentary democracies than in presidential ones.

Stepan and Skach (1993) present an impressive array of facts to support their claim that democratic consolidation is more likely in parliamentary democracies than in presidential ones. They begin by asking how many of the countries that became independent democracies between 1945 and 1979 were able to sustain democracy throughout the 1980s. In Table 16.5a, we list the names of all eighty countries that became independent democracies

TABLE 16.5 — Democratic Survival in Newly Independent States after World War II

a. Form of Democracy Adopted

Parliamentary N = 41		Presidential N = 36		Semi-Presidential N = 3
Bahamas	Mauritius	Algeria	Madagascar	Lebanon
Bangladesh	Nauru	Angola	Malawi	Senegal
Barbados	Nigeria	Benin	Mali	Zaire
Botswana	Pakistan	Burkina Faso	Mauritania	
Burma	Papua New Guinea	Cameroon	Mozambique	
Chad	St. Lucia	Cape Verde	Niger	
Dominica	St. Vincent	Central African	Philippines	
Fiji	Sierra Leone	Republic	Rwanda	
The Gambia	Singapore	Comoros	São Tomé	
Ghana	Solomon Islands	Congo	Seychelles	
Grenada	Somalia	Cyprus	Syria	
Guyana	Sri Lanka	Djibouti	Taiwan	
India	Sudan	Equatorial Guinea	Togo	
Indonesia	Suriname	Gabon	Tunisia	
Israel	Swaziland	Guinea	Vietnam (N)	
Jamaica	Tanzania	Guinea Bissau	Vietnam (S)	
Kenya	Trinidad and Tobago	Ivory Coast	Yemen (S)	
Kiribati	Tuvalu	Korea (N)	Zambia	
Laos	Uganda	Korea (S)		
Malaysia	Western Samoa			
Malta				

b. Continuously Democratic Countries, 1979–1989

Parliamentary N = 15/41		Presidential N = 0	Semi-Presidential N = 0
Bahamas	Nauru		
Barbados	Papua New Guinea		
Botswana	St. Lucia		
Dominica	St. Vincent		
India	Solomon Islands		
Israel	Trinidad and Tobago		
Jamaica	Tuvalu		
Kiribati			

Source: Data are from Stepan and Skach (1993, 8–9).

between 1945 and 1979. We also list whether they adopted a parliamentary, presidential, or semi-presidential form of democracy. As you can see, countries that became independent in the post–World War II period were about as likely to adopt parliamentarism (forty-one) as they were to adopt presidentialism (thirty-six). In Table 16.5b, we list the names of those countries that were continuously democratic from 1979 to 1989 and the form of democracy that they had. Of the eighty countries that became independent democracies in the postwar period, only fifteen were continuously democratic through the 1980s. Incredibly, all fifteen of these countries had adopted parliamentarism; none of the thirty-six countries that adopted presidentialism managed to sustain democracy during the 1980s.

Lest a focus on newly independent countries be a source of bias, Stepan and Skach next present evidence from all countries that experienced democracy between 1973 and 1989 but that were not members of the Organisation for Economic Co-operation and Development (OECD).[21] They wanted to know how many non-OECD countries that experienced democracy for at least a year between 1973 and 1989 were able to sustain it for a continuous ten-year period. Their data are shown in Table 16.6. As you can see, countries that experienced democracy for at least a year between 1973 and 1989 were about as likely to adopt parliamentarism (twenty-eight) as they were to adopt presidentialism (twenty-five). Of those countries that managed to sustain democracy for a continuous ten-year period, though, almost none had a presidential form of democracy. By comparing "democratic experimenters" with "democratic survivors," we can calculate a "democratic survival rate." As Table 16.6 illustrates, the democratic survival rate for parliamentary regimes is three times that for presidential regimes.

TABLE 16.6	**Democratic Survival in Fifty-Three Non-OECD Countries, 1973–1989**	
	Parliamentary	**Presidential**
Democratic for at least one year	28	25
Democratic for ten consecutive years	17	5
Democratic survival rate	61%	20%

Source: Data are from Stepan and Skach (1993, 11).

Although these simple comparisons suggest that there is something to the notion that presidentialism imperils democratic survival, they say almost nothing about why this might be the case. In other words, they say very little about the causal link between regime type and

---

21. The Organisation for Economic Co-operation and Development is essentially a club of rich democracies set up by the Allied powers after World War II. Stepan and Skach focus on non-OECD countries because it is in poor countries that democracy is most unstable and that institutional choice is arguably most important for the survival of democracy. This last point is one that we return to at the end of this section.

democratic survival. Recall, though, that Stepan and Skach do provide a potential causal story for the results in Tables 16.5 and 16.6. Specifically, they argue that presidentialism is more likely to lead to the kind of deadlock between the executive and legislative branches that invites extraconstitutional behavior. Thus, an observable implication of their theory is that military coups should be more common in presidential democracies than in parliamentary ones. Is this actually the case in the real world? In Table 16.7, we present data on the frequency of military coups collected by Stepan and Skach in the same fifty-three non-OECD countries as before. As you can see, military coups are more than twice as likely in presidential democracies as they are in parliamentary ones. Whereas 40 percent of the non-OECD countries that adopted presidentialism experienced a military coup between 1973 and 1989, just 18 percent of the countries that adopted parliamentarism did. This higher coup rate in presidential regimes is exactly as Stepan and Skach (1993) predict.

TABLE 16.7	**Military Coups in Fifty-Three Non-OECD Countries, 1973–1989**	
	Parliamentary	**Presidential**
Democratic for at least one year	28	25
Number that experienced a coup	5	10
Coup susceptibility rate	18%	40%

Source: Data are from Stepan and Skach (1993, 12).

Although these simple statistics are quite illustrative, it is probably the case that some factors that cause democracies to fail are also associated with the choice to adopt parliamentarism or presidentialism in the first place. This raises the concern that it may be these other factors, and not presidentialism per se, that lead to the collapse of democracy. In other words, the failure to take account of these other factors might lead us to overestimate the true effect of regime type on democratic survival. Recognizing this concern, Stepan and Skach attempt to deal with it by leaning on the work of a Finnish political scientist named Tatu Vanhanen.

Recall from Chapter 6 that modernization theory predicts a strong association between democracy and societal development. In an attempt to evaluate modernization theory, Vanhanen (1991) constructed an index of democratization—a measure capturing the level of democracy in a country—and what he calls an index of power resources—a measure capturing the level of societal development in a country.[22] If modernization theory is accurate, then countries with a high score on the power resource index should also have a high score

---

22. Vanhanen's (1991) index of power resources combines six factors related to modernization: the percentage of the population that is urban, the percentage of the population in nonagricultural occupations, the percentage of students in the population, the literacy rate, the percentage of land in family-owned farms, and the degree of decentralization of nonagricultural economic resources.

on the democratization index. Indeed, this is exactly what Vanhanen finds. Although Vanhanen finds a strong association between the power resource index and the democratization index, the fit is certainly not perfect. Some countries, for example, score significantly higher on the democratization index than their level of modernization, as revealed by the power resource index, would predict. Similarly, some countries score significantly lower on the democratization index than their level of modernization would predict. Stepan and Skach label those countries that score surprisingly high on the democratization index as "democratic overachievers." And they label those countries that score surprisingly low on the democratization index as "democratic underachievers." In Table 16.8, we present data from Stepan and Skach (1993) showing whether the democratic overachievers and underachievers are presidential or parliamentary democracies.

TABLE 16.8	Democratic Underachievers and Overachievers by Regime Type

	Parliamentary	Presidential
Overachievers	31	10
Underachievers	6	12
Ratio of overachievers to underachievers	5.17	0.83

Source: Data are from Stepan and Skach (1993, 10).

Stepan and Skach interpret the comparison of democratic overachievers and underachievers in Table 16.8 to mean that, after taking account of a set of modernization variables thought to influence democratic survival, parliamentary systems are five times more likely to be democratic overachievers than they are to be democratic underachievers. In contrast, presidential systems are slightly more likely to be democratic underachievers than they are to be democratic overachievers. A different way to look at the data is that democratic overachievers are about three times more likely to be parliamentary regimes than they are to be presidential ones. In contrast, democratic underachievers are about twice as likely to be presidential regimes as they are to be parliamentary ones. Overall, the evidence in Table 16.8 provides strong support for the claim that the prospects of democratic survival are lower in presidential systems than they are in parliamentary systems even after controlling for other factors that affect the survival of democracy.

We now briefly present some new statistical evidence to further support this conclusion. In Chapter 6, we used data from Przeworski and colleagues (2000) on 135 countries from 1950 to 1990 to examine how economic factors, such as a country's status as an oil producer, its wealth, and its economic growth, affect the survival of democracy. We can use the same data to examine whether the choice of parliamentarism or presidentialism also affects the probability of democratic survival. The results of our analysis are shown in Table 16.9.

TABLE 16.9	Effect of Regime Type on Democratic Survival, 1946–1990	
	Dependent variable: Probability that a country will be a democracy this year if it was a democracy last year	
Independent variables	Model 1	Model 2
Presidentialism	−0.58***	−0.32*
	(0.14)	(0.16)
GDP per capita		0.0002***
		(0.00005)
Growth in GDP per capita		0.04***
		(0.01)
Oil producer		−0.12
		(0.28)
Constant	2.22***	1.29***
	(0.10)	(0.18)
Number of observations	1,584	1,576
Log-likelihood	−170.85	−142.15

$*p < 0.10$; $**p < 0.05$; $***p < 0.01$

Note: Standard errors are in parentheses.

Source: Data are from Przeworski and colleagues (2000).

Recall that the sign of a coefficient is important because it tells us the slope of the relationship between some independent variable in the left column and the dependent variable, democratic survival. A positive coefficient indicates that an increase in the independent variable is associated with an increase in the probability of democratic survival. A negative coefficient indicates that an increase in the independent variable is associated with a reduction in the probability of democratic survival. If the statistical analysis reveals that there is no relationship between an independent variable and the probability of democratic survival, then the coefficient will be zero. Recall also that the standard error beneath the coefficient helps us to determine how confident we should be in our results. We tend to be confident that we have found a pattern in the data that is likely to be found more generally when the standard error is small relative to the size of its corresponding coefficient. Typically, as a rule of thumb, we say that we have found a statistically significant relationship whenever the coefficient is bigger than twice the size of the standard error. It is common practice for political scientists to place stars next to the coefficients that are considered statistically significant; more stars signal higher statistical significance. Independent variables that do not have a coefficient with stars—where the size of the coefficient is not sufficiently large relative to the size of the standard error—are considered statistically insignificant. An independent variable is considered statistically insignificant if we don't feel confident ruling out the possibility that the observed pattern between this variable and the dependent variable arose by chance.[23]

So what do the results in Table 16.9 tell us? In line with the evidence presented by Stepan and Skach (1993), the coefficient on presidentialism is negative and statistically significant. This indicates that presidential democracies are less likely to remain democratic than non-presidential democracies. This is the case even when we take account of the economic factors thought to affect democratic survival that we examined in Chapter 6.

The Difficult Combination: Presidentialism and Multipartism

So far, the empirical evidence suggests that the prospects for democratic survival are greater in parliamentary democracies than in presidential ones. But recall our earlier discussion of immobilism in the French Fourth Republic. As you will remember, de Gaulle argued that concentrating power in the hands of a president was the key to solving the problems of highly fragmented legislatures, government instability, and immobilism in the French Fourth Republic. De Gaulle's belief that we should call upon a "strong man," such as a president, who can bring the country together in moments of crisis is quite widespread. As we now suggest, this has important implications for any causal connection between presidentialism and democratic survival. Specifically, if presidentialism is adopted in moments of crisis, then presidential regimes may fail at a higher rate than parliamentary regimes, not because there is something inherently problematic about presidentialism, but simply because presidentialism tends to be adopted in difficult circumstances.[24] One way to think about this is that presidentialism is like a hospital for ailing polities. We would not want to say that "hospitals kill people" just because large numbers of people die in hospitals. If people who go to the hospital are, on average, in poorer health than those who do not, then the explanation for high mortality rates in hospitals is likely to have more to do with the fact that people in a hospital are very sick than it does with the fact that they are in a hospital. Maybe the same is true for presidentialism. Until we can convince ourselves that countries that adopt presidentialism are the same as countries that adopt parliamentarism, studies such as Stepan and Skach's run the risk of overstating the deleterious effects of presidentialism.

The standard way to address this issue is, to continue our metaphor, to find a measure of "poor health" and include it as a control variable in an analysis of the relationship between mortality and being in a hospital. With one exception, we know of no empirical analysis that has adopted this approach when examining the relationship between presidentialism and

---

23. For a reminder of how we determine whether an observed pattern in the data is "real" or not, see the material on significance tests covered in the Appendix at the end of Chapter 6, "An Intuitive Take on Statistical Analyses."

24. Shugart (1999) makes a similar argument claiming that presidentialism tends to be adopted in large and complex societies with highly unequal income distributions and great regional disparities. Shugart argues that it is these inhospitable conditions rather than presidentialism itself that makes it difficult to sustain democracy.

democratic survival.[25] This may, in part, be because the analytical problem before us is probably more complicated than the one suggested by our hospital metaphor. For example, the factors that cause death in humans—cardiovascular diseases, parasitic diseases, respiratory diseases, and so on—affect those in a hospital and those not in a hospital the same way. But it may be the case that some factors that are "dangerous" for democracy are dangerous only in parliamentary regimes or only in presidential ones. If this is true, and presidential and parliamentary regimes are different sorts of organisms that process factors such as legislative fragmentation in fundamentally different ways, then it may prove extremely difficult to measure the underlying health of a regime independently of its status as a presidential or parliamentary system.

The work of one political scientist, Scott Mainwaring, suggests that presidential and parliamentary democracies *do* process political factors differently. In particular, it suggests that they process legislative fragmentation differently. Whereas legislative fragmentation always increases the likelihood of instability, the instability that is produced in parliamentary democracies is different from that produced in presidential ones. Specifically, legislative fragmentation increases the likelihood of *cabinet instability* in parliamentary systems, whereas it increases the likelihood of *democratic instability* in presidential systems. The work by Mainwaring (1993) ultimately suggests that if legislative fragmentation is viewed as a political ailment in parliamentary democracies, as, say, critics of the French Fourth Republic like de Gaulle and others claim, then presidentialism could well be a form of medicine that is worse than the disease.

Why is legislative fragmentation likely to lead to such different outcomes in parliamentary and presidential democracies? One reason is that legislative fragmentation is more likely to lead to legislative deadlock in a presidential regime than in a parliamentary one. Legislative deadlock in a presidential democracy occurs when a legislative majority opposed to the president is large enough to pass bills in the legislature but not large enough to override a presidential veto. As we have already seen, legislative fragmentation increases the chances that the president's party will not command a legislative majority and, hence, the chances that legislative deadlock will occur. But why is legislative fragmentation more likely to lead to legislative deadlock in presidential systems than in parliamentary systems? The answer is that in a parliamentary democracy, the head of government, the prime minister, serves at the pleasure of the legislature and is, therefore, obliged to form a cabinet made up

---

25. The exception is Cheibub's (2007) analysis of presidentialism and democracy. He argues that what has made presidential regimes more fragile than parliamentary ones is that presidential regimes are more likely to emerge in countries in which the military has traditionally had a strong political role. As Cheibub demonstrates, any democratic regime, parliamentary or presidential, is more likely to fail in countries with a strong military tradition than in countries without such a tradition. This leads him to conclude that presidential democracies are more likely to fail not because they are presidential but because they are more likely to be adopted in difficult circumstances—when the military has a strong political presence. Przeworski and colleagues (2000, 136) argue, however, that "parliamentary democracies . . . are still more stable regardless of their origins. . . . Thus, again, the stability of democracies seems to be an effect of their institutional frameworks, not only of their origins."

of a coalition of parties that *does* command a legislative majority. As we saw in Chapter 12, presidents do sometimes form coalitions (Amorim Neto 2006; Cheibub 2007; Cheibub, Przeworski, and Saiegh 2004).[26] The key difference, though, between parliamentary and presidential democracies is that when legislators vote against a president's legislation in sufficient numbers, the legislation is blocked, but when legislators vote against a prime minister's legislation, there is a good chance that the government will fall. In other words, a coalition government in a parliamentary democracy implies a legislative coalition, whereas this presumption is not the case in presidential democracies.[27] A consequence of this is that legislative fragmentation is more likely to produce deadlock in a presidential democracy than it is to produce immobilism in a parliamentary democracy.

The problem of legislative deadlock created by legislative fragmentation in presidential democracies tends to be exacerbated by the way presidents are recruited to office. As we noted earlier, presidential candidates are often political outsiders who have relatively little policymaking expertise or experience dealing with the legislature. One of the main reasons for this is that presidents tend to be directly elected by the people and, therefore, have less need to build links with legislative actors than prime ministers do. A consequence of this, though, is that presidents tend to lack the necessary skills or experience to build legislative coalitions to resolve deadlock situations when they arise. Even when they do manage to build a coalition, it has been argued that coalition partners in presidential regimes have acute incentives to distance themselves from the president's policy goals. One reason for this is that they expect to run against the president in a winner-take-all contest in the next election and they want to be able to criticize his policies (Coppedge 1994, 168). In contrast, prime ministers tend to be individuals who have worked in the legislature for many years, who have gained enormous amounts of policy expertise, and who have been schooled in the art of coalition building. A result of this is that prime ministers are often better placed than presidents to build legislative coalitions to resolve deadlock situations when they emerge. Thus, according to Mainwaring (1993), not only are presidential democracies more apt than parliamentary democracies to have executives whose policy programs will be consistently blocked by the legislature but they are also more apt to have executives who are less capable of dealing with problems when they arise.

When legislative deadlock does occur, it is much more likely to lead to democratic instability in presidential democracies than in parliamentary ones. If legislative deadlock occurs between the executive and legislative branches in a parliamentary regime, then there are constitutional means for resolving the crisis. Either the legislature can pass a vote of no confidence and remove the government, or the prime minister can dissolve the parliament and call new

---

26. Although presidents do sometimes form coalitions, coalition governments are less common and minority governments are more common in presidential democracies than in parliamentary ones (Amorim Neto 2006; Cheibub 2007; Cheibub, Przeworski, and Saiegh 2004).

27. As Mainwaring (1993, 221) puts it, "The existence of a cabinet portfolio does not necessarily imply party support for the president, as it does in a parliamentary system."

elections. As Mainwaring (1993, 208) notes, though, in presidential democracies "there are no neat means of replacing a president who is enormously unpopular in the society at large and has lost most of his/her support in the legislature." Thus, the absence of a vote of no confidence may ensure the stability of the head of government in presidential regimes, but it introduces a rigidity that can threaten democratic stability by encouraging frustrated elites or masses to call for the removal of the president, or the dissolution of parliament, as a way to break the deadlock (Linz 1994). Although there are some circumstances under which political actors can accomplish this within the bounds of

La Moneda, the Chilean presidential residence, under ground and air attack by Chilean armed forces during the September 11, 1973, coup d'état that led to the ruthless dictatorship of General Augusto Pinochet. The democratically elected Socialist president Salvador Allende is thought to have committed suicide during the palace siege.

some presidential constitutions, the solution to deadlock is more likely to be extraconstitutional in presidential regimes than in parliamentary ones. To be clear, the claim is not that deadlock situations will always lead to democratic collapse in presidential systems, just that deadlock situations are more likely to produce a democratic collapse in a presidential system than a parliamentary one. To sum up, legislative deadlock is likely to be associated with *democratic* instability in presidential democracies; if and when immobilism occurs in parliamentary democracies, it is more likely to be associated with *cabinet* instability.

Earlier, we presented evidence suggesting that democracy was more fragile in presidential regimes than in parliamentary ones. An important implication of Mainwaring's argument, though, is that democracy should be more fragile in some presidential regimes than in others. Specifically, his argument implies that democracy should be more fragile in (perhaps only in) presidential democracies that are characterized by high levels of legislative fragmentation than in those characterized by low levels of legislative fragmentation, because legislative fragmentation increases the likelihood of deadlock, which, in turn, increases the likelihood of democratic instability. When legislative fragmentation is low, the likelihood of deadlock and, hence, democratic instability will also be low.

To evaluate his claim that presidential democracies will be unstable particularly (or only) when legislative fragmentation is high, Mainwaring (1993) examines all countries that experienced uninterrupted democracy for the twenty-five-year period between 1967 and 1992. Although twenty-four parliamentary regimes were able to sustain democracy during this period, just four presidential regimes were able to do so: Colombia, Costa Rica, the United States, and Venezuela. Mainwaring wanted to know what made these presidential regimes different from other presidential regimes. His answer was that they all effectively had two-party systems, as illustrated in Table 16.10; none of them had multiparty systems. At the time of his writing in 1993, Mainwaring argued that only one multiparty presidential regime had historically managed to sustain democracy for a twenty-five-year period. And this exception was Chile, a democracy, begun in 1932, that experienced a dramatic "death" in 1973 when a military coup overthrew the Socialist president Salvador Allende and replaced him with the dictator General Augusto Pinochet. Allende had been elected in 1970 with a slim plurality of the vote (35.3 percent) and was immediately beset with problems from every side in the country's highly fragmented and deeply polarized legislature.[28]

TABLE 16.10	Presidential Regimes That Sustained Democracy from 1967 to 1992 and Their Party System Size
Country (Year)	Effective number of legislative parties
Colombia (1986)	2.45
Costa Rica (1986)	2.21
United States (1984)	1.95
Venezuela (1983)	2.42

Source: Amorim Neto and Cox (1997, 169–170).

In Table 16.11, we use data from Mainwaring (1993, 205–207) to calculate the democratic success rate for parliamentary regimes, multiparty presidential regimes, and two-party presidential regimes. Democratic success is defined here as a sustaining of democracy for an uninterrupted twenty-five-year period at any time between 1945 and 1992. The information in Table 16.11 suggests that democratic consolidation is possible in two-party presidential regimes but not in multiparty presidential regimes. Interestingly, the democratic success rate for two-party presidential regimes (0.50) is almost as high as the democratic success rate for parliamentary regimes (0.57). These results provide strong evidence that it is the combination of presidentialism and multipartism rather than just presidentialism that is inimical to democracy. Indeed, Mainwaring refers to the combination of presidentialism and multipartism as "the difficult combination" for precisely this reason.

---

28. We are generally reluctant to invoke the "exception that proves the rule," but if this hackneyed phrase ever applies, this seems to be the case.

TABLE 16.11	Regime Type, Party System Size, and Democratic Consolidation, 1945–1992
Regime type	Democratic success rate
Multiparty presidentialism	1/15, or 0.07
Two-party presidentialism	5/10, or 0.5
Parliamentarism	25/44, or 0.57

Source: Data are from Mainwaring (1993, 205–207).

Note: The democratic success rate refers to the proportion of countries that were able to sustain democracy for an uninterrupted twenty-five-year period at any time between 1945 and 1992.

It is worth noting that Stepan and Skach (1993) also provide evidence in support of Mainwaring's conjecture in their own analysis of presidentialism and democratic survival. Although they do not make too much of it, they provide data on the size of party systems in those countries that became independent after 1945 and that managed to sustain democracy during the 1980s. These data are shown in Table 16.12. As you can see, long-lived multiparty parliamentary regimes are not particularly rare, but long-lived multiparty presidential regimes are.

TABLE 16.12	Consolidated Democracies by Regime Type and Party System Size	
	Effective number of legislative parties	
Constitution	Fewer than three	Three or more
Parliamentary	23	11
Semi-presidential	0	2
Presidential	5	0

Source: Data are from Stepan and Skach (1993, 8–9).

Note: The numbers in the table refer to those countries that became independent after 1945 and that sustained democracy for a continuous ten-year period from 1979 to 1989.

Summary

In this section we examined, and found considerable support for, an argument that says that presidential constitutions make successful democratic consolidation more difficult than parliamentary constitutions, particularly when the legislature is highly fragmented. The key weakness of presidentialism appears to be its inability to find legal ways out of executive-legislative deadlock, something that is more likely to occur when the legislature is highly fragmented. It is possible to put this finding in a broader perspective by comparing it with the analysis of veto players that we did in the last chapter. In Chapter 15, we discussed various arguments about the effect of multiple veto players on policy stability. All else being equal, it was argued, an increase in the number of veto players is expected to make it more difficult to change the status quo policy. This was particularly true if the veto players held diverse policy preferences. What we characterized in the last chapter as policy stability induced by veto players is equivalent in many ways to what we have referred to in this chapter as deadlock or immobilism. The father of modern veto player theory, George Tsebelis, has conjectured that although large numbers of veto players with diverse preferences may encourage policy stability, they may also encourage political instability (Tsebelis 1995, 322). The Mainwaring claim that multipartism and presidentialism form a "difficult combination" for democratic consolidation can be interpreted in light of veto player theory. If Tsebelis is correct that an increased number of veto players leads to policy stability, which in its extreme form manifests itself as "deadlock," then we should expect presidentialism and parliamentarism to affect the type of political instability that ensues.

In other words, multiple veto players lead to policy stability (deadlock), but the form of political instability that results depends on a country's constitution. As we have already argued, if the constitution is presidential, then policy stability or deadlock is likely to encourage a coup or some other form of democratic instability. If, however, the constitution is parliamentary, the policy stability or immobilism is likely to lead to a vote of no confidence, a cabinet reshuffle, or elections leading to the formation of a new cabinet—that is, cabinet instability. This causal argument is presented in Figure 16.9.[29]

At this point, we would like to point out one last subtlety that involves our discussion of democratic survival in this section and our discussion of the effects of wealth on democratic survival from Chapter 6. Recall that Przeworski and colleagues (2000) argue that wealth is, essentially, a sufficient condition for democratic survival. As they indicate, countries above a certain wealth threshold (about $6,055 per capita in 1985 purchasing power parity [PPP] US dollars) are likely to stay democratic forever, should they, for whatever reason, become democratic in the first place (see Chapter 6, Box 6.1, "Comparing Income Across Countries," for a discussion of PPP). The claim that wealth is sufficient to ensure democratic consolidation leads to a surprising result—the choice of political institutions, say, the combination of multipartism and presidentialism, is likely to have a bigger effect on the chances that democracy will survive in poor countries than in rich ones. This is because, according to Przeworski and colleagues (2000), democracy is likely to survive in rich countries whether they have chosen felicitous institutions or not. In other words, institutional choice matters much more in poor countries than in rich ones, at least when it comes to democratic consolidation.[30] This result is somewhat surprising because traditional approaches in this area predict that

---

29. We should note that we have simplified matters throughout this section by ignoring semi-presidential democracies.

30. Evidence consistent with this line of reasoning comes from Boix (2003, 153–154). In a study of democratic survival from 1850 to 1990, for example, he finds that presidential democracies are more likely than parliamentary democracies to fail only in underdeveloped countries; he finds no difference in the democratic survival rates of parliamentary and presidential regimes in developed countries.

Veto Players, Policy Stability, and Different Types of Political Instability

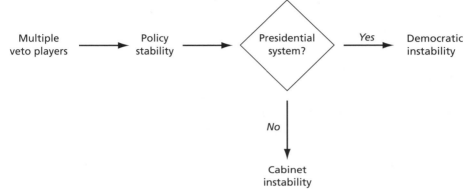

formal institutions are more important in rich countries, where they are more likely to be accompanied by the rule of law, than in poor countries.[31] One of our former students tested this implication in her undergraduate honors thesis at New York University (Ferrer 2003). Her findings, consistent with a veto player interpretation of the Mainwaring argument, show that the probability of democratic regime failure increases as the number of veto players increases *but only in poor countries*.[32]

Finally, we would like to point out that whereas the choice between presidentialism and parliamentarism is typically addressed explicitly by constitution writers, the size of the party system is not entirely under their direct control. As we saw in Chapter 14, though, comparative politics scholars know quite a bit about why some countries have many parties and some have few. Specifically, we can expect a country with high levels of social heterogeneity to produce a highly fragmented legislature unless specific electoral institutions (majoritarian ones) are adopted with the goal of reducing the number of parties. Consequently, the results in this section suggest that if a presidential constitution is chosen for some reason, then adopting permissive electoral laws, such as PR, with a high district magnitude has the potential to cause problems. In the presence of social heterogeneity, permissive electoral laws can be expected to produce multipartism, which, combined with presidentialism, is likely to inhibit democratic consolidation. Of course, the finding of Przeworski and colleagues (2000) on the apparent sufficiency of wealth may suggest that relatively rich countries have a greater

---

31. Recent studies in this area strongly suggest that the importance of rule of law and other legal institutions for democratic consolidation itself varies across different levels of societal development (Reenock and Staton 2010; Reenock, Staton, and Radean 2013).

32. In this case, "poor" is defined as $6,055 per capita GDP, Przeworski and colleagues' (2000) cutoff point.

margin of error in choosing their institutions than poor countries. This may explain why some multiparty presidential regimes in Latin America have managed to stay democratic since the wave of transitions to democracy that began there in the mid-1980s. For some time now, many of these countries have exceeded Przeworski and colleagues' "magical" threshold of wealth at which democracy is immune to breakdown.

CONCLUSION

We have, perhaps, gone on long enough. We hope, however, that this chapter has convinced you that contemporary comparative politics has a great deal to say that is of vital interest to citizens and policymakers who would like to know how the institutions they choose are likely to affect the political, social, and economic outcomes they will experience. Let us briefly summarize the basic results that we have presented in this chapter. First, we have shown patterned differences in the way that majoritarian and consensus democracies represent the interests of voters. Second, we have demonstrated that electoral laws influence both who is chosen to rule and how they are likely to wield that power—at least with respect to redistributive fiscal policy. Third, we have highlighted the ways in which constitutional elements, such as electoral laws and federalism, are likely to affect the probability of ethnic conflict. And finally, we have reported results suggesting that the choice of electoral laws and the decision about whether to adopt presidentialism or parliamentarism are likely to strongly influence the survival of new democracies—especially if the country's level of wealth is not sufficiently high, by itself, to make democratic survival likely.

Many questions remain about how these results interact with each other. We invite students to speculate about such matters and to develop the tools necessary to evaluate their answers. Comparative politics raises and attempts to answer questions with life-and-death implications. We hope that as you finish this book, your development as a student of comparative politics is just beginning.

KEY CONCEPTS

accountability *713*
clarity of responsibility *714*
common pool resource problem *742*
confessionalism *754*
consensus vision of democracy *706*
consociationalism *754*
delegate model of representation *704*
descriptive representation *712*
ethnic outbidding *752*
fiscal policy *727*

formalistic representation *712*
ideological congruence *716*
ideological responsiveness *716*
immobilism *764*
majoritarian vision of democracy *706*
partisan model of macroeconomic policy *734*
retrospective voting *713*
substantive representation *712*
symbolic representation *712*
trustee model of representation *704*

PROBLEMS

1. What is the difference between descriptive and substantive representation? In your opinion, which form of representation is more important and why?

2. Obtain a copy of Jane Mansbridge's 1999 article, "Should Blacks Represent Blacks and Women Represent Women? A Contingent 'Yes,'" from the *Journal of Politics* (61:628–657), using your institution's library resources. Read the article and then answer the following questions.

   a. Mansbridge considers several arguments against promoting descriptive representation. Describe these arguments in your own words.

   b. Mansbridge argues that descriptive representation may be valuable in contexts of distrust and in contexts when interests are uncrystallized. Describe these arguments in your own words.

   c. What other arguments does Mansbridge make in support of descriptive representation?

   d. Ultimately, Mansbridge gives a "contingent 'Yes'" to descriptive representation. What is your opinion of descriptive representation now that you have read some of the pros and cons?

3. As we mentioned in this chapter, several countries use gender quotas—reserved seats, legislated candidate quotas, and voluntary political party quotas—to promote women's descriptive representation in the legislature. In your opinion, what are the pros and cons of using gender quotas in this way?

4. Obtain a copy of James Habyarimana, Macartan Humphreys, Daniel N. Posner, and Jeremy M. Weinstein's 2007 article, "Why Does Ethnic Diversity Undermine Public Goods Provision?" from the *American Political Science Review* (101:709–725), using your institution's library resources. Read the article and then answer the following questions.

   a. As we mention in the chapter, there is empirical evidence that ethnic diversity undermines economic growth and public goods provision. The article that you have just read tests "three families of mechanisms" for why this relationship might exist. What are these three families of mechanisms, and why do they predict that economic diversity undermines public goods provision?

   b. The authors test each of the "three families of mechanisms" using field experiments. Explain how each of the experiments works.

   c. Based on their experimental results, which mechanism or mechanisms explains why ethnic diversity undermines public goods provision?

5. Consider the statistical results in Model 2 in Table 16.9 on page 771. Interpret the coefficients on "GDP per capita," "Growth in GDP per capita," and "Oil producer."

6. In this chapter, we described the majoritarian and consensus visions of democracy. Which vision of democracy do you prefer and why? If you preferred a majoritarian vision of democracy, what institutions would you adopt and why? If you preferred a consensus vision of democracy, what institutions would you adopt?

The final two problems are designed to incorporate material covered in the earlier sections of the book with the material presented in this final chapter, and to encourage you to synthesize what you have learned so that you can make practical policy recommendations.

7. After a long experience with authoritarianism, a new democracy is looking to adopt a constitution that will maximize its chances of survival. As an expert in comparative institutions, you have been hired as a consultant by the transitional government. Government leaders have asked you to develop a proposal in which you are to make recommendations on specific institutions that you believe will enhance their chances of never returning to authoritarianism. To aid in their selection, they have asked you to rank your reform recommendations according to their likely impact on regime survival. What are your recommendations? Be sure to support your claims with evidence from the literature (both theoretical and empirical). Is there information about the country such as its wealth and ethnic heterogeneity that would shape your recommendations?

8. You have received a telephone call from the new interim leadership in Burkina Faso, following the collapse of the military dictatorship. The caller, a policymaker, asks you to explain the pros and cons of parliamentarism versus presidentialism and to advise whether a semi-presidential form of democracy would capture the benefits of both parliamentary and presidential systems while taming the problems commonly associated with each of them. In your reply, you should draw on both theory and empirics. Be sure to discuss what other institutions the caller needs to consider and under what conditions some sets of institutions might be preferable to others. (In answering part of this question, it might be useful to refer back to the section on the making and breaking of governments in semi-presidential democracies in Chapter 12.)

References

Abootalebi, Ali. 1999. "Islam, Islamists, and Democracy." *Middle East Review of International Affairs* 3:14–24.

Acemoglu, Daron, Suresh Naidu, Pascual Restrepol, and James A. Robinson. 2014. "Democracy Does Cause Growth." National Bureau of Economic Research Working Paper 2004, Cambridge, MA.

Acemoglu, Daron, and James A. Robinson. 2000. "Why Did the West Extend the Franchise? Democracy, Inequality, and Growth in Historical Perspective." *Quarterly Journal of Economics* 115:1167–1199.

———. 2001. "A Theory of Political Transitions." *American Economic Review* 91:938–963.

———. 2006. *Economic Origins of Dictatorship and Democracy.* New York: Cambridge University Press.

Adena, Maja, Ruben Enikolopov, Maria Petrova, Veronica Santarosa, and Ekaterina Zhuravskaya. 2015. "Radio and the Rise of the Nazis in Prewar Germany." *Quarterly Journal of Economics* 130:1885–1939.

Adcock, Robert, and David Collier. 2001. "Measurement Validity: A Shared Standard for Qualitative and Quantitative Research." *American Political Science Review* 95:529–546.

Adida, Claire L., Karen E. Ferree, Daniel N. Posner, and Amanda Lea Robinson. 2016. "Who's Asking? Interviewer Coethnicity Effects in African Survey Data." *Comparative Political Studies* 40: 1630–1660.

Adida, Claire L., David D. Laitin, and Marie-Anne Valfort. 2010. "Identifying Barriers to Muslim Integration in France." *Proceedings of the National Academy of Sciences* 107:22384–22390.

"Afghanistan: The Wrong Voting System." 2016. *The New York Times,* March 16. http://www.nytimes .com/2005/03/16/opinion/afghanistan-the-wrong-voting-system.html.

Afonso Da Silva, Virgílio. 2006. "Duverger's Laws: Between Social and Institutional Determinism." *European Journal of Political Research* 45:31–41.

"After the Coup, the Counter-Coup." 2016. *The Economist,* July 23. http://www.economist.com/news/ briefing/21702511-failed-putsch-was-bloodiest-turkey-has-seen-backlash-worrying-after-coup.

Ahmed, Faisal Z. 2012. "The Perils of Unearned Foreign Income: Aid, Remittances, and Government Survival." *American Political Science Review* 106:146–165.

Ahmad, Zakaria Haji. 1988. "Malaysia: Quasi Democracy in a Divided Society." In *Democracy in Developing Countries: Asia,* ed. Larry Diamond, Juan J. Linz, and Seymour Martin Lipset. Boulder, CO: Lynne Rienner.

Akerlof, George A. 1970. "The Market for 'Lemons': Quality Uncertainty and the Market Mechanism." *The Quarterly Journal of Economics* 84:488–500.

Alda, K. 2006. "Legislative Limbo." *The Prague Post,* August 24. Accessed 2007 at http://www.theprague post.com/articles/2006/08/23/legislative-limbo.php.

Aldrich, John H. 1993. "Rational Choice and Turnout." *American Journal of Political Science* 37:246–278.

———. 1995. *Why Parties? The Origin and Transformation of Political Parties in America.* Chicago: University of Chicago Press.

Alesina, Alberto, Reza Baqir, and William Easterly. 1999. "Public Goods and Ethnic Divisions." *Quarterly Journal of Economics* 114:1243–1284.

Alesina, Alberto, Edward Glaeser, and Bruce Sacerdote. 2001. "Why Doesn't the United States Have a European-Style Welfare State?" *Brookings Papers on Economic Activity* 2:187–277.

Alesina, Alberto, and Roberto Perotti. 1994. "The Political Economy of Growth: A Critical Survey of the Recent Literature." *The World Bank Economic Review* 8:351–371.

Alesina, Alberto, and Enrico Spolaore. 1997. "On the Number and Size of Nations." *Quarterly Journal of Economics* 112:1027–1056.

Alexiadou, Despina. 2016. *Ideologues, Partisans, and Loyalists: Ministers and Policymaking in Parliamentary Cabinets.* Oxford: Oxford University Press.

Allum, P. A. 1973. *Italy—Republic without Government?* New York: Norton.

Almond, Gabriel A., and Sydney Verba. [1963] 1989. *The Civic Culture: Political Attitudes and Democracy in Five Nations.* London: Sage.

"Al Shabaab: Narrative Summary." 2010–2016. Mapping Militants Organization. Stanford University. http://web.stanford.edu/group/mappingmilitants/cgi-bin/groups/view/61.

Althusser, Louis. 1969. *For Marx.* London: Penguin Books.

Altincekic, Ceren, and David H. Bearce. 2014. "Why There Should Be No Political Foreign Aid Curse." *World Development* 64:18–32.

Al-Ubaydli, Omar. 2012. "Natural Resources and the Tradeoff between Authoritarianism and Development." *Journal of Economic Behavior & Organization* 81:137–152.

Alvarez, Michael E., José Cheibub, Fernando Limongi, and Adam Przeworski. 1996. "Classifying Political Regimes." *Studies in Comparative International Development* 31:1–37.

Amorim Neto, Octavio. 2006. "The Presidential Calculus: Executive Policy Making and Cabinet Formation in the Americas." *Comparative Political Studies* 39:415–440.

Amorim Neto, Octavio, and Gary Cox. 1997. "Electoral Institutions, Cleavage Structures, and the Number of Parties." *American Journal of Political Science* 41:149–174.

Amorim Neto, Octavio, and David Samuels. 2006. "Democratic Regimes and Cabinet Politics: A Global Perspective." Paper presented at the Annual Meeting of the Midwest Political Science Association, Chicago, April 20–23.

Amorim Neto, Octavio, and Kaare Strøm. 2006. "Breaking the Parliamentary Chain of Delegation: Presidents and Non-partisan Cabinet Members in European Democracies." *British Journal of Political Science* 36:619–643.

Anderson, Jon Lee. 2009. "The Most Failed State: Is Somalia's New President a Viable Ally?" *The New Yorker*, December 14. http://www.newyorker.com/magazine/2009/12/14/the-most-failed-state.

Andeweg, Rudy B., and Galen A. Irwin. 2009. *Governance and Politics of the Netherlands*, 3rd ed. New York: Palgrave Macmillan.

Ansell, Ben W., and David J. Samuels. 2014. *Inequality and Democratization: An Elite-Competition Approach.* New York: Cambridge University Press.

Arce, Daniel G., and Todd Sandler. 2005. "Counterterrorism: A Game-Theoretic Analysis." *Journal of Conflict Resolution* 49:183–200.

Arceneaux, Kevin. 2005. "Does Federalism Weaken Democratic Representation in the United States?" *Publius: The Journal of Federalism* 35:297–311.

Argersinger, Peter H. 1980. "'A Place on the Ballot': Fusion Politics and Antifusion Laws." *American Historical Review* 85:287–306.

Ariotti, Margaret H., and Sona N. Golder. "Partisan Portfolio Allocation in African Democracies." Unpublished manuscript, 2016.

Aristotle. [350 BCE] 1996. *The Politics and the Constitution of Athens*, edited by Stephen Everson. New York: Cambridge University Press.

Armstrong, Hannah. 2010. "Niger Coup: Can Africa Use Military Power for Good?" *The Christian Science Monitor*, March 25. http://www.csmonitor.com/World/Africa/2010/0325/Niger-coup-Can-Africa-use-military-power-for-good.

Arrow, Kenneth. 1963. *Social Choices and Individual Values*. New Haven, CT: Yale University Press.

Arzaghi, Mohammad, and J. Vernon Henderson. 2005. "Why Countries Are Fiscally Decentralizing." *Journal of Public Economics* 89:1157–1189.

Austen-Smith, David, and Jeffrey Banks. 1988. "Elections, Coalitions, and Legislative Outcomes." *American Political Science Review* 82:405–422.

Axelrod, Robert. 1981. "Emergence of Cooperation among Egoists." *American Political Science Review* 75:306–318.

———. 1984. *The Evolution of Cooperation*. New York: Basic Books.

Bäck, Hanna, and Patrick Dumont. 2008. "Making the First Move: A Two-Stage Analysis of the Role of Formateurs in Parliamentary Government Formation." *Public Choice* 135:353–373.

Bagehot, Walter. 1867. *The English Constitution*. Available from http://www.gutenberg.org/ebooks/4351.

Balmer, Randall. 2006. *Thy Kingdom Come: An Evangelical's Lament*. New York: Basic Books.

Banfield, Edward C., and Laura Fasano Banfield. 1958. *The Moral Basis of a Backward Society*. Glencoe, IL: Free Press.

Bannerman, M. Graeme. 2002. "Republic of Lebanon." In *Government and Politics in the Middle East and North Africa*, 4th ed., ed. David E. Long and Bernard Reich. Boulder, CO: Westview Press.

Baradat, Leon P. 2006. *Political Ideologies: Their Origins and Impact*. Englewood Cliffs, NJ: Prentice Hall.

Barberá, Pablo. "When Duverger Becomes Autocratic: Electoral Systems and Opposition Fragmentation in Non-democratic Regimes." Unpublished manuscript, New York University, 2013.

Barkan, Joel D. 1995. "Elections in Agrarian Societies." *Journal of Democracy* 6:106–116.

Barnes, Cedric, and Harun Hassan. 2007. "The Rise and Fall of Mogadishu's Islamic Courts." *Journal of Eastern African Studies* 1:151–160.

Baron, David, and John Ferejohn. 1989. "Bargaining in Legislatures." *American Political Science Review* 83:1181–1206.

Barro, Robert J. 1990. "Government Spending in a Simple Model of Endogenous Growth." *Journal of Political Economy* 98:S103–S125.

———. 1997. *Determinants of Economic Growth*. Cambridge, MA: MIT Press.

———. 1999. "Determinants of Democracy." *Journal of Political Economy* 107:158–183.

———. 2000. "Rule of Law, Democracy, and Economic Performance." In *Index of Economic Freedom*, 31–51. Washington, DC: Heritage Foundation.

Barry, Brian. 1970. *Sociology, Economists, and Democracy*. Chicago: University of Chicago Press.

———. 1975. "Political Accommodation and Consociational Democracy." *British Journal of Political Science* 5:477–505.

Bartlett, Robert. 1993. *The Making of Europe: Conquest, Colonization and Cultural Change 950–1350*. London: Penguin Books.

Bates, Robert H., and Da-Hsiang Donald Lien. 1985. "A Note on Taxation, Development, and Representative Government." *Politics and Society* 14:53–70.

Bawn, Kathleen, and Frances Rosenbluth. 2006. "Short versus Long Coalitions: Electoral Accountability and the Size of the Public Sector." *American Journal of Political Science* 50:251–265.

Bearce, David H., and Daniel C. Tirone. 2010. "Foreign Aid Effectiveness and the Strategic Goals of Donor Governments." *Journal of Politics* 72:837–851.

Beath, Andrew, Fotini Christia, and Ruben Enikolopov. 2013. "Empowering Women: Evidence from a Field Experiment in Afghanistan." *American Political Science Review* 107:540–557.

Beber, Bernd, and Alexandra Scacco. 2012. "What the Numbers Say: A Digit-Based Test for Electoral Fraud." *Political Analysis* 20:211–234.

Beblawi, Hazem. 1987. "The Rentier State in the Arab World." In *The Rentier State: Nation, State, and the Integration of the Arab World,* ed. Hazem Beblawi and Giacomo Luciani. London: Croom Helm.

Beckwith, Karen. 2007. "Numbers and Newness: The Descriptive and Substantive Representation of Women." *Canadian Journal of Political Science* 40:27–49.

Bednar, Jenna. 2009. *The Robust Federation.* New York: Cambridge University Press.

Bednar, Jenna, William N. Eskridge, Jr., and John Ferejohn. 2001. "A Political Theory of Federalism." In *Constitutional Culture and Democratic Rule,* ed. John Ferejohn, John Riley, and Jack N. Rakove. New York: Cambridge University Press.

Bednar, Jenna, and Scott Page. 2007. "Can Game(s) Theory Explain Culture? The Emergence of Cultural Behavior within Multiple Games." *Rationality and Society* 19:65–97.

Bennett, Elizabeth. 2014. "Rwanda Strives towards Gender Equality in Government." August 15. http://harvardkennedyschoolreview.com/rwanda-strides-towards-gender-equality-in-government/.

Benoit, Kenneth. 2004. "Models of Electoral System Change." *Electoral Studies* 23:363–389.

———. 2007. "Electoral Laws as Political Consequences: Explaining the Origins and Change of Electoral Institutions." *Annual Review of Political Science* 10:363–390.

Berman, Eli, and David Laitin. 2006. "Hard Targets: Theory and Evidence on Suicide Attacks." University of California, San Diego. Available from http://econ.ucsd.edu/~elib/.

Bermeo, Sarah Blodgett. 2016. "Aid Is Not Oil: Donor Utility, Heterogeneous Aid, and the Aid-Democratization Relationship." *International Organization* 70:1–32.

Bernhard, Michael, Timothy Nordstrom, and Christopher Reenock. 2001. "Economic Performance, Institutional Intermediation, and Democratic Survival." *Journal of Politics* 63:775–803.

Bernhard, William, and David Leblang. 2006. *Pricing Politics: Democratic Processes and Financial Markets.* New York: Cambridge University Press.

Binder, Sarah. 1999. "The Dynamics of Legislative Gridlock, 1947–1996." *American Political Science Review* 93:519–533.

———. 2003. *Stalemate: Causes and Consequences of Legislative Gridlock.* Washington, DC: Brookings Institution Press.

Birch, Sarah. 2007. "Electoral Systems and Electoral Misconduct." *Comparative Political Studies* 40:1533–1556.

Birch, Sarah, Frances Millard, Kieran Williams, and Marina Popescu, eds. 2002. *Embodying Democracy: Electoral System Design in Post-Communist Europe.* Basingstoke, England: Palgrave-Macmillan.

Birney, Mayling. 2007. "Can Local Elections Contribute to Democratic Progress in Authoritarian Regimes? Exploring the Political Ramifications of China's Village Elections." PhD thesis, Department of Political Science, Yale University.

Black, Duncan. 1948. "On the Rationale of Group Decision-Making." *Journal of Political Economy* 56:23–34.

Blair, Douglas H., and Robert A. Pollak. 1982a. "Acyclic Collective Choice Rules." *Econometrica* 50:931–943.

———. 1982b. "Rational Collective Choice." *Scientific American* 249:88–95.

Blair, Graeme. 2015. "Survey Methods for Sensitive Topics." In Symposium: Studying Sensitive Political Phenomena, eds. Matt Golder and Sona N. Golder. *CP: Newsletter of the Comparative Politics Organized Section of the American Political Science Association*, 25(1):12–16.

Blair, Graeme, Christine Fair, Neil Malhotra, and Jacob N. Shapiro. 2013. "Poverty and Support for Militant Politics: Evidence from Pakistan." *American Journal of Political Science* 57:30–48.

Blair, Graeme, Kosuke Imai, and Jason Lyall. 2014. "Comparing and Combining List and Endorsement Experiments: Evidence from Afghanistan." *American Journal of Political Science* 58(4):1043–1063.

Blair, Graeme, Kosuke Imai, and Yang-Yang Zhou. 2015. "Design and Analysis of the Randomized Response Technique." *Journal of the American Statistical Association* 110(511):1304–1319.

Blais, André. 2000. *To Vote or Not to Vote: The Merits and Limits of Rational Choice Theory*. Pittsburgh: University of Pittsburgh Press.

Blais, André, and Marc André Bodet. 2006. "Does Proportional Representation Foster Closer Congruence between Citizens and Policymakers?" *Comparative Political Studies* 39:1243–1262.

Blais, André, and R. K. Carty. 1990. "Does Proportional Representation Foster Voter Turnout?" *European Journal of Political Research* 18:167–181.

Blais, André, and Agnieszka Dobrzynska. 1998. "Turnout in Electoral Democracies." *European Journal of Political Research* 33:239–261.

Blais, André, and Indriði Indriðason. 2007. "Making Candidates Count: The Logic of Electoral Alliances in Two-Round Legislative Elections." *Journal of Politics* 69:193–205.

Blais, André, and Louis Massicotte. 1997. "Electoral Formulas: A Macroscopic Perspective." *European Journal of Political Research* 32:107–129.

Blaydes, Lisa. 2011. *Elections and Distributive Politics in Mubarak's Egypt*. New York: Cambridge University Press.

Blaydes, Lisa, and James Lo. 2012. "One Man, One Vote, One Time? A Model of Democratization in the Middle East." *Journal of Theoretical Politics* 24:110-146.

Block, Fred. 1977. "The Ruling Class Does Not Rule: Notes on the Marxist Theory of the State." *Socialist Revolution* 33:6–27.

Boix, Carles. 1999. "Setting the Rules of the Game: The Choice of Electoral Systems in Advanced Democracies." *American Political Science Review* 93:609–624.

———. 2003. *Democracy and Redistribution*. New York: Cambridge University Press.

———. 2011. "Democracy, Development, and the International System." *American Political Science Review* 105:809–828.

Boix, Carles, and Daniel N. Posner. 1996. "Making Social Capital Work: A Review of Robert Putnam's *Making Democracy Work: Civic Traditions in Modern Italy*." Working Paper 96-4, Harvard University, Cambridge, MA.

Boix, Carles, and Susan Carol Stokes. 2003. "Endogenous Democratization." *World Politics* 55:517–549.

Boix, Carles, and Milan Svolik. 2013. "The Foundations of Limited Authoritarian Government: Institutions, Commitment, and Power-Sharing in Dictatorships." *Journal of Politics* 75:300–316.

Bollen, Kenneth A., and Robert W. Jackman. 1985. "Political Democracy and the Size Distribution of Income." *American Sociological Review* 50:438–457.

———. 1989. "Democracy, Stability, and Dichotomies." *American Sociological Review* 54:612–621.

———. 1995. "Income Inequality and Democratization Revisited: A Comment on Muller." *American Sociological Review* 60:983–989.

Borda, Jean-Charles de. 1781. "Mémoire sur les élections au scrutin." *Mémoires de l'Académie Royale des Sciences,* 657–665.

Bormann, Nils-Christian, and Matt Golder. 2013. "Democratic Elections around the World, 1946–2011." *Electoral Studies* 32:360–369.

Bosco, Fernando J. 2006. "The Madres de Plaza de Mayo and Three Decades of Human Rights' Activism: Embeddedness, Emotions, and Social Movements." *Annals of the Association of American Geographers* 96(2):342–365.

Boston, Jonathan, Stephen Levine, Elizabeth McLeay, Nigel S. Roberts, and Hannah Schmidt. 1998. "Caretaker Government and the Evolution of Caretaker Conventions in New Zealand." *Victoria University of Wellington Law Review* 28:629–648.

Bowler, Shaun, and Bernard Grofman, eds. 2000. *Elections in Australia, Ireland, and Malta under the Single Transferable Vote: Reflections on an Embedded Institution.* Ann Arbor: University of Michigan Press.

Brambor, Thomas, William Roberts Clark, and Matt Golder. 2006. "Understanding Interaction Models: Improving Empirical Analyses." *Political Analysis* 14:63–82.

———. 2007. "Are African Party Systems Different?" *Electoral Studies* 26:315–323.

Brancati, Dawn. 2004. "Can Federalism Stabilize Iraq?" *Washington Quarterly* 27:7–21.

———. 2006. "Decentralization: Fueling the Fire or Dampening the Flames of Ethnic Conflict and Secessionism?" *International Organization* 60:651–685.

Bräutigam, Deborah A., and Stephen Knack. 2004. "Foreign Aid, Institutions, and Governance in Sub-Saharan Africa." *Economic Development and Cultural Change* 52:255–285.

Breunig, Charles. 1971. "Part IV: The Age of Revolution and Reaction, 1789–1850." In *The Norton History of Modern Europe,* ed. Felix Gilbert. New York: Norton.

Brinks, Daniel, and Michael Coppedge. 2006. "Diffusion Is No Illusion: Neighbor Emulation in the Third Wave of Democracy." *Comparative Political Studies* 39:463–489.

Brownlee, Jason. 2007. *Authoritarianism in the Age of Democratization.* New York: Cambridge University Press.

———. 2009. "Portents of Pluralism: How Hybrid Regimes Affect Democratic Transitions." *American Journal of Political Science* 53:515–532.

Brownlee, Jason, Tarek Masoud, and Andrew Reynolds. 2015. *The Arab Spring: Pathways of Repression and Reform.* Oxford: Oxford University Press.

Bryden, Matt. 2013. "Somalia Redux? Assessing the New Somali Federal Government." Report of the Center for Strategic and International Studies (CSIS) Africa Program. Washington, DC: CSIS.

Buchanan, James. 1995. "Federalism as an Ideal Political Order and an Objective for Constitutional Reform." *Publius: The Journal of Federalism* 25:19–28.

Buchanan, James, and Gordon Tullock. 1962. *The Calculus of Consent: Logical Foundations of Constitutional Democracy.* Ann Arbor: University of Michigan Press.

Bueno de Mesquita, Bruce. 2006. *Principles of International Politics: People's Power, Preferences, and Perceptions.* Washington, DC: CQ Press.

Bueno de Mesquita, Bruce, and Alastair Smith. 2009. "Political Survival and Endogenous Institutional Change." *Comparative Political Studies* 42:167–197.

Bueno de Mesquita, Bruce, Alastair Smith, Randolph M. Siverson, and James D. Morrow (BDM^{2}S^2). 2003. *The Logic of Political Survival*. Cambridge, MA: MIT Press.

Bulmer-Thomas, Ivor. 1965. *The Growth of the British Party System I, 1640–1923*. London: John Bake.

Bunce, Valerie. 1999. *Subversive Institutions: The Design and the Destruction of Socialism and the State*. New York: Cambridge University Press.

Bustikova, Lenka. 2014. "Revenge of the Radical Right." *Comparative Political Studies* 47:1738–1765.

Büthe, Tim, and Alan M. Jacobs. 2015. "Symposium: Transparency in Qualitative and Multi-Method Research." *Newsletter of the American Political Science Association Organized Section for Qualitative and Multi-Method Research* 13:2–64.

Camerer, Colin. 2003a. *Behavioral Game Theory: Experiments on Strategic Interaction*. Princeton, NJ: Princeton University Press.

Cameron, Charles M. 2000. *Veto Bargaining: Presidents and the Politics of Negative Power*. New York: Cambridge University Press.

———. 2002. "Judicial Independence: How Can You Tell It When You See It?" In *Judicial Independence at the Crossroads: An Interdisciplinary Approach,* ed. Stephen B. Burbank and Barry Friedman. Thousand Oaks, CA: Sage.

Cameron, David R. 1978. "The Expansion of the Public Economy: A Comparative Analysis." *American Political Science Review* 72:1243–1261.

Campbell, Angus, Philip E. Converse, Warren Miller, and Donald Stokes. 1960. *The American Voter*. New York: Wiley.

Campbell, James E., Mary Munro, John R. Alford, and Bruce A. Campbell. 1986. "Partisanship and Voting." In *Research in Micropolitics,* ed. Samuel Long. Greenwich, CT: JAI Press.

Cantu, Francisco, and Sebastien M. Saiegh. 2011. "Fraudulent Democracy? An Analysis of Argentina's Infamous Decade Using Supervised Machine Learning." *Political Analysis* 19:409–433.

Caramani, Daniele. 1996. "The Swiss Parliamentary Election of 1995." *Electoral Studies* 15:128–137.

Carey, John M., and Simon Hix. 2011. "The Electoral Sweet Spot: Low-Magnitude Proportional Electoral Systems." *American Journal of Political Science* 55:383–397.

Carey, John M., and John Polga-Hecimovich. 2006. "Primary Elections and Candidate Strength in Latin America." *Journal of Politics* 68:530–543.

———. 2008. "The Primary Elections 'Bonus' in Latin America." *Designing Democratic Government,* 227–247.

Carey, John M., and Matthew Soberg Shugart. 1995. "Incentives to Cultivate a Personal Vote: A Rank Ordering of Electoral Formulas." *Electoral Studies* 14:417–439.

Carothers, Thomas. 2002. "The End of the Transition Paradigm." *Journal of Democracy* 13:5–21.

Carroll, Susan J. and Linda M. G. Zerilli. 1993. "Feminist Challenges to Political Science." In *Political Science: The State of the Discipline II,* ed. Ada W. Finifter, 55–76. Washington, DC: American Political Science Association.

Carrubba, Clifford J., 2005. "Courts and Compliance in International Regulatory Regimes." *Journal of Politics* 67:669–689.

Carrubba, Clifford J., and Craig Volden. 2000. "Coalitional Politics and Logrolling in Legislative Institutions." *American Journal of Political Science* 44:521–537.

"Carter Center Closes Egypt Office." 2014. Carter Center. October 14. https://www.cartercenter.org/news/pr/egypt-101514.html.

Casper, Gretchen, and Claudiu Tufts. 2003. "Correlation versus Interchangeability: The Limited Robustness of Empirical Findings on Democracy Using Highly Correlated Datasets." *Political Analysis* 11:196–203.

Celis, Karen. 2009. "Substantive Representation of Women (and Improving It): What It Is and Should Be About." *Comparative European Politics* 7:95–113.

Celis, Karen, Sarah Childs, Johanna Kantola, and Mona Lena Krook. 2008. "Rethinking Women's Substantive Representation." *Representation* 44:99–110.

Central Intelligence Agency. 2011. *The World Factbook.* Available from https://www.cia.gov/library/publications/the-world-factbook/.

Chaisty, Paul, Nic Cheeseman, and Timothy Power. 2014. "Rethinking the 'Presidentialism Debate': Conceptualizing Coalitional Politics in Cross-Regional Perspective." *Democratization* 21(1):72–94.

Chan, Kam Wing. 2010. "The Household Registration System and Migrant Labor in China: Notes on a Debate." *Population and Development Review* 36(2):357–364.

Chandra, Kanchan. 2004. *Why Ethnic Parties Succeed.* London: Cambridge University Press.

———. 2005. "Ethnic Parties and Democratic Stability." *Perspectives on Politics* 3:235–252.

———. 2006. "What Is Ethnic Identity and Does It Matter?" *Annual Review of Political Science* 9:397–424.

Chandra, Kanchan, and Cillane Boulet. 2012. "A Language for Thinking about Ethnic Identity Change." In *Constructivist Theories of Ethnic Politics*, ed. Kanchan Chandra. New York: Oxford University Press.

Chauchard, Simon. 2013. "Using MP3 Players in Surveys: The Impact of a Low-Tech Self-Administration Mode on Reporting of Sensitive Attitudes." *Public Opinion Quarterly* 77:220–231.

Cheibub, José Antonio. 2002. "Minority Governments, Deadlock Situations, and the Survival of Presidential Democracies." *Comparative Political Studies* 35:284–312.

Cheibub, José Antonio. 2007. *Presidentialism, Parliamentarism, and Democracy.* New York: Cambridge University Press.

Cheibub, José Antonio, Jennifer Gandhi, and James Raymond Vreeland. 2010. "Democracy and Dictatorship Revisited." *Public Choice* 143:67–101.

Cheibub, José Antonio, and Fernando Limongi. 2002. "Modes of Government Formation and the Survival of Democratic Regimes: Presidentialism and Parliamentarism Reconsidered." *Annual Review of Political Science* 5:151–179.

Cheibub, José Antonio, Adam Przeworski, and Sebastian Saiegh. 2004. "Government Coalitions and Legislative Success under Presidentialism and Parliamentarism." *British Journal of Political Science* 34:565–587.

Chhibber, Pradeep, and Ken Kollman. 1998. "Party Aggregation and the Number of Parties in India and the United States." *American Political Science Review* 92:329–342.

———. 2004. *The Formation of National Party Systems: Federalism and Party Competition in Canada, Great Britain, India, and the United States.* Princeton, NJ: Princeton University Press.

Childs, Sarah, and Mona Lena Krook. 2006. "Should Feminists Give Up on Critical Mass? A Contingent 'Yes.'" *Politics and Gender* 2:522–530.

Cho, Wendy K. Tam, and Brian Gaines. 2007. "Breaking the (Benford) Law: Statistical Fraud Detection in Campaign Finance." *The American Statistician* 61:218–223.

Clark, William Roberts. 2003. *Capitalism, Not Globalism: Capital Mobility, Central Bank Independence, and the Political Control of the Economy.* Ann Arbor: University of Michigan Press.

Clark, William Roberts, Michael Gilligan, and Matt Golder. 2006. "A Simple Multivariate Test for Asymmetric Hypotheses." *Political Analysis* 14:311–331.

Clark, William Roberts, and Matt Golder. 2006. "Rehabilitating Duverger's Theory: Testing the Mechanical and Strategic Modifying Effects of Electoral Laws." *Comparative Political Studies* 39:679–708.

Clark, William Roberts, Sona N. Golder, and Matt Golder. Forthcoming. "An Exit, Voice, and Loyalty Model of Politics." *British Journal of Political Science.*

Clark, William Roberts, and Usha Nair Reichert (with Sandra Lynn Lomas and Kevin L. Parker). 1998. "International and Domestic Constraints on Political Business Cycle Behavior in OECD Economies." *International Organization* 52:87–120.

Clinton, Robert Lowry. 1994. "Game Theory, Legal History, and the Origins of Judicial Review: A Revisionist Analysis of *Marbury v. Madison.*" *American Journal of Political Science* 38:285–302.

Cohen, Frank. 1997. "Proportional versus Majoritarian Ethnic Conflict Management in Democracies." *Comparative Political Studies* 30:607–630.

Collier, David. 1993. "The Comparative Method." In *Political Science: The State of the Discipline II,* ed. Ada W. Finifter. Washington, DC: American Political Science Association.

Collier, David, and Robert Adcock. 1999. "Democracy and Dichotomies: A Pragmatic Approach to Choices about Concepts." *Annual Review of Political Science* 2:537–565.

Collier, David, and Steven Levitsky. 1997. "Democracy with Adjectives: Conceptual Innovation in Comparative Research." *World Politics* 49:430–451.

Collier, Paul. 2009. "In Praise of the Coup: Military Takeovers Can Be a Good Thing for African Democracy." *New Humanist,* March 4. https://newhumanist.org.uk/articles/1997/in-praise-of-the-coup.

Collier, Paul, and Anke Hoeffler. 2002. "On the Incidence of Civil War in Africa." *Journal of Conflict Resolution* 46:13–28.

———. 2004. "Greed and Grievance in Civil War." *Oxford Economic Papers* 56:563–595.

———. 2005. "Resource Rents, Governance, and Conflict." *Journal of Conflict Resolution* 49:625–633.

Collins, Patricia Hill. 1986. "Learning from the Outsider Within: The Sociological Significance of Black Feminist Thought." *Social Problems* 33(6):S14–S32.

———. 1989. "The Social Construction of Black Feminist Thought." *Signs* 14(4):745–773.

Colomer, Josep M. 1991. "Transitions by Agreement: Modeling the Spanish Way." *American Political Science Review* 85:1283–1302.

Congleton, Roger D. 2006. "Asymmetric Federalism and the Political Economy of Decentralization." In *Handbook of Fiscal Federalism,* ed. Ehtisham Ahmad and Giorgio Brosio. Northampton, MA: Edward Elgar.

Coppedge, Michael. 1994. *Strong Parties and Lame Ducks: Presidential Partyarchy and Factionalism in Venezuela.* Stanford, CA: Stanford University Press.

———. 1997. "Modernization and Thresholds of Democracy: Evidence for a Common Path and Process." In *Inequality, Democracy, and Economic Development,* ed. Manus I. Midlarsky. New York: Cambridge University Press.

Coppedge, Michael, and John Gerring (with David Altman, Michael Bernhard, Steven Fish, Allen Hicken, Matthew Kroenig, Staffan I. Lindberg, Kelly McMann, Pamela Paxton, Holli A. Semetko,

Svend-Erik Skaaning, Jeffrey K. Staton, and Jan Teorell). 2011. "Conceptualizing and Measuring Democracy: A New Approach." *Perspectives on Politics* 9:247–267.

Cox, Gary W. 1990. "Centripetal and Centrifugal Incentives in Electoral Systems." *American Journal of Political Science* 34:903–935.

———. 1997. *Making Votes Count: Strategic Coordination in the World's Electoral Systems.* New York: Cambridge University Press.

Cox, Gary, and Emerson Niou. 1994. "Seat Bonus under the Single Nontransferable Vote System: Evidence from Japan and Taiwan." *Comparative Politics* 26:221–236.

Crabtree, Charles, David Darfomal, and Holger L. Kern. 2015. "A Spatial Analysis of the Impact of West German Television on Protest Mobilization during the East German Revolution." *Journal of Peace Research* 52(3):269–284.

Crabtree, Charles, Christopher J. Fariss, and Holger L. Kern. 2016. "Truth Replaced by Silence: An Internet Experiment on Private Censorship in Russia." Unpublished manuscript, University of Michigan.

Crabtree, Charles, Christopher J. Fariss, and Paul Schuler. Forthcoming. "The Presidential Election in Belarus, October 2015." *Electoral Studies.*

Crabtree, Charles, Matt Golder, Thomas Gschwend, and Indridi Indridason. "Campaign Sentiment in European Party Manifestos." Unpublished manuscript, Pennsylvania State University, 2016.

Crenshaw, Kimberlé. 1989. "Demarginalizing the Intersection of Race and Sex: A Black Feminist Critique of Antidiscrimination Doctrine, Feminist Theory and Antiracist Politics," University of Chicago Legal Forum 1989: 139–167.

"Croatia Government Falls as PM Loses No-Confidence Vote." 2016. *Al Jazeera*, June 17. http://www.aljazeera.com/news/2016/06/croatia-government-falls-pm-loses-confidence-vote-160616202143562.html.

Dahl, Robert A. 1956. *A Preface to Democratic Theory.* Chicago: University of Chicago Press.

———. 1971. *Polyarchy: Participation and Opposition.* New Haven, CT: Yale University Press.

Dahlerup, Drude. 1988. "From a Small to a Large Minority: Women in Scandinavian Politics." *Scandinavian Political Studies* 4:275–298.

Dahlerup, Drude, ed. 2006. *Women, Quotas and Politics.* New York: Routledge.

Dalton, Russell J., and Nhu-Ngoc T. Ong. "Authority Orientations and Democratic Attitudes: A Test of the 'Asian Values' Hypothesis." Unpublished manuscript, University of California, Irvine, 2004.

Damiani, Roberta. 2015. "Reforming the Italian Senate." The Constitution Unit, November 17. https://constitution-unit.com/2015/11/17/reforming-the-italian-senate.

Dancygier, Rafaela M. 2010. *Immigration and Conflict in Europe.* New York: Cambridge University Press.

Deckert, Joseph, Mikhail Myagkov, and Peter C. Ordeshook. 2011. "Benford's Law and the Detection of Election Fraud." *Political Analysis* 19:245–268.

De la Torre, Carlos. 2016. "What Went Wrong? Leftwing Populist Democratic Promises and Autocratic Practices." In Symposium: Populism in Comparative Perspective, eds. Matt Golder and Sona N. Golder. *CP: Newsletter of the Comparative Politics Organized Section of the American Political Science Association* 26(2):40–45.

DeNardo, James. 1985. *Power in Numbers.* Princeton, NJ: Princeton University Press.

Derry, Gregory. 1999. *What Science Is and How It Works.* Princeton, NJ: Princeton University Press.

De Jong, Martijn G., Rik Pieters, and Stefan Stremersch. 2012. "Analysis of Sensitive Questions across Cultures: An Application of Multigroup Item Randomized Response Theory to Sexual Attitudes and Behavior." *Journal of Personality and Social Psychology* 103:543.

Derpanopoulos, George, Eric Frantz, Barbara Geddes, and Joseph Wright. 2016. "Are Coups Good for Democracy?" *Research & Politics* 3:1–7.

De Schweinitz, Karl, Jr. 1959. "Industrialization, Labor Controls, and Democracy." *Economic Development and Cultural Change* 7:385–404.

Diamond, Larry. 2002. "Thinking about Hybrid Regimes." *Journal of Democracy* 13:21–35.

Dietrich, Simone, and Joseph Wright. 2014. "Foreign Aid Allocation Tactics and Democratic Change in Africa." *Journal of Politics* 77:216–234.

Disch, Lisa. 2011. "Toward a Mobilization Conception of Democratic Representation." *American Political Science Review* 105:100–114.

Dixit, Avinash K., Susan Skeath, and David Reiley. 2015. *Games of Strategy,* 4th ed. rev. New York: Norton.

Dixit, Avinash K., and Susan Skeath. 1999. *Games of Strategy.* New York: Norton.

Dixon, Patrick. 1996. *The Truth about Westminster.* London: Hodder.

Djankov, Simeon, Jose G. Montalvo, and Marta Reynal-Querol. 2008. "The Curse of Aid." *Journal of Economic Growth* 13:169–194.

Dolan, Ronald E., and Robert L. Worden, eds. 1994. *Japan: A Country Study.* Washington, DC: Library of Congress.

Doucouliagos, Hristos, and Mehmet Ali Ulubaşoğlu. 2008. "Democracy and Economic Growth: A Meta-Analysis." *American Journal of Political Science* 52:61–83.

Dowding, Keith, and Patrick Dumont, eds. 2009. *The Selection of Ministers in Europe: Hiring and Firing.* New York: Routledge.

Downs, Anthony. 1957. *An Economic Theory of Democracy.* New York: Harper and Row.

Drake, Paul W. 1996. *Labor Movements and Dictatorships: The Southern Cone in Comparative Perspective.* Baltimore: Johns Hopkins University Press.

Duch, Raymond M., Wojtek Przepiorka, and Randolph T. Stevenson. 2015. "Responsibility Attribution for Collective Decision Makers." *American Journal of Political Science* 59:372–389.

Duch, Raymond M., and Randolph T. Stevenson. 2008. *The Economic Vote: How Political and Economic Institutions Condition Election Results.* New York: Cambridge University Press.

———. 2013. "Voter Perceptions of Agenda Power and Attribution of Responsibility for Economic Performance." *Electoral Studies* 32:512–516.

Dunning, Thad. 2005. "Resource Dependence, Economic Performance, and Political Stability." *Journal of Conflict Resolution* 49:451–482.

———. 2008. *Crude Democracy: Natural Resource Wealth and Political Regimes.* New York: Cambridge University Press.

"Dutch Parties Seek Alliances after Vote." 2006. *The New York Times,* October 23. http://www.nytimes.com/2006/11/23/world/europe/23iht-dutch.3648222.html.

Dutta, Prajit K. 1999. *Strategies and Games: Theory and Practice.* Cambridge, MA: MIT Press.

Duverger, Maurice. [1954] 1963. *Political Parties.* London: Methuen.

———. 1980. "A New Political System Model: Semi-Presidential Government." *European Journal of Political Research* 8:165–187.

Easterly, William. 2001. "Can Institutions Resolve Ethnic Conflict?" *Economic Development and Cultural Change* 49:687–706.

Easterly, William, and Ross Levine. 1997. "Africa's Growth Tragedy: Policies and Ethnic Divisions." *Quarterly Journal of Economics* 112:1201–1250.

Egorov, Georgy, Sergei Guriev, and Konstantin Sonin. 2009. "Why Resource-Poor Dictators Allow Freer Media: A Theory and Evidence from Panel Data." *American Political Science Review* 103:645–668.

Eickelman, Dale F., and James P. Piscatori. 1996. *Muslim Politics*. Princeton, NJ: Princeton University Press.

Electoral Integrity Project, The (EIP). n.d. https://sites.google.com/site/electoralintegrityproject4/home.

Elgie, Robert. 2011. *Semi-Presidentialism: Sub-types and Democratic Performance*. Oxford: Oxford University Press.

Elkins, Zachary. 2000. "Gradations of Democracy? Empirical Tests of Alternative Conceptualizations." *American Journal of Political Science* 44:287–294.

Elkins, Zachary, and John Sides. 2007. "Can Institutions Build Unity in Multiethnic States?" *American Political Science Review* 101:693–708.

Emmerson, Donald K. 1995. "Singapore and the 'Asian Values' Debate." *Journal of Democracy* 6:95–105.

Enders, Walter, and Todd Sandler. 1993. "Effectiveness of Anti-Terrorism Policies: Vector-Autoregression-Intervention Analysis." *American Political Science Review* 87:829–844.

Engels, Friedrich. [1893] 1968. "Letter to Mehring." In *Marx-Engels Correspondence*. Geneva, Switzerland: International Publishers.

Epstein, David L., Robert Bates, Jack Goldstone, Ida Kristensen, and Sharyn O'Halloran. 2006. "Democratic Transitions." *American Journal of Political Science* 50:551–569.

Epstein, David, and Peter Zemsky. 1995. "Money Talks: Deterring Quality Challengers in Congressional Elections." *American Political Science Review* 89:295–308.

Epstein, Lee, and Jack Knight. 1998a. *The Choices Justices Make*. Washington, DC: CQ Press.

———. 1998b. "On the Struggle for Judicial Supremacy." *Law and Society Review* 30:87–120.

Epstein, Lee, Jack Knight, and Olga Shvetsova. 2001. "The Role of Constitutional Courts in the Establishment of Democratic Systems of Government." *Law and Society Review* 35:117–167.

Erikson, Robert S., Michael B. MacKuen, and James A. Stimson. 2002. *The Macro Polity*. New York: Cambridge University Press.

Escobar-Lemmon, Maria C., and Michelle M. Taylor-Robinson. 2016. *Women in Presidential Cabinets: Power Players or Abundant Tokens?* New York: Oxford University Press.

Esposito, John L. 2003. "Practice and Theory: A Response to 'Islam and the Challenge of Democracy.'" *Boston Review,* April–May.

Esposito, John L., and John O. Voll. 1996. *Islam and Democracy*. New York: Oxford University Press.

Esteban, Joan, and Debraj Ray. 1999. "Conflict and Distribution." *Journal of Economic Theory* 87:379–415.

———. 2008. "Polarization, Fractionalization, and Conflict." *Journal of Peace Research* 45:163–182.

Esteban, Joan, and Gerald Schneider. 2008. "Polarization and Conflict: Theoretical and Empirical Issues." *Journal of Peace Research* 45:131–141.

"Ethiopian Troops on Somali Soil." 2006. BBC News, July 20. http://news.bbc.co.uk/2/hi/africa/5198338.stm.

Ezrow, Natasha M., and Erica Frantz. 2011. *Dictators and Dictatorships: Understanding Authoritarian Regimes and Their Leaders*. New York: Continuum.

Fadel, Laila. 2011. "Egypt's Military Guards Its Own Power." *The Washington Post,* November 12. http://www.washingtonpost.com/world/middle_east/egypts-military-guards-its-own-power/2011/11/10/gIQA7QVVFN_story.html.

Fahim, Kareem, and Hwaida Saad. 2013. "A Faceless Teenage Refugee Who Helped Ignite Syria's War." *The New York Times,* February 8. http://www.nytimes.com/2013/02/09/world/middleeast/a-faceless-teenage-refugee-who-helped-ignite-syrias-war.html?_r=1)

Fantz, Ashley, and Ben Brumfield. 2015. "More Than Half the Nation's Governors Say Syrian Refugees Not Welcome." CNN, November 19. http://www.cnn.com/2015/11/16/world/paris-attacks-syrian-refugees-backlash/index.html.

Farrell, David M., and Ian McAllister. 2000. "Through a Glass Darkly: Understanding the World of STV." In *Elections in Australia, Ireland, and Malta under the Single Transferable Vote: Reflections on an Embedded Institution,* ed. Shaun Bowler and Bernard Grofman. Ann Arbor: University of Michigan Press.

Fearon, James D. 2003. "Ethnic and Cultural Diversity by Country." *Journal of Economic Growth* 8:195–222.

———. 2005. "Primary Commodity Exports and Civil War." *Journal of Conflict Resolution* 49:483–507.

Fearon, James D., and David D. Laitin. 1996. "Explaining Interethnic Cooperation." *American Political Science Review* 90:715–735.

Ferejohn, John, and Charles Shipan. 1990. "Congressional Influence on Bureaucracy." *Journal of Law, Economics, and Organization* 6:1–20.

Ferland, Benjamin. 2015. *Electoral Systems, Veto Players, and Substantive Representation: When Majoritarian Electoral Systems Strengthen the Citizen-Policy Nexus.* Montreal: McGill University.

———. 2016. "Revisiting the Ideological Congruence Controversy." *European Journal of Political Research* 55:358–373.

Ferrer, Meghan. 2003. "The Impact of Institutions: Do Veto Players Influence Regime Duration." Honors thesis, Department of Politics, College of Arts and Sciences, New York University. Available from http://politics.as.nyu.edu/object/politics.undergrad.honorstheses.html.

Feynman, Richard. 1967. *The Character of Physical Law: The 1964 Messenger Lectures.* Cambridge, MA: MIT Press.

Filali-Ansary, Abdou. 1999. "Muslims and Democracy." *Journal of Democracy* 10:18–32.

Finer, S. E. 1988. *The Man on Horseback: The Role of the Military in Politics.* Boulder, CO: Westview Press.

Fitzpatrick, Catherine A. 2011. "Turkmen Government Removes Ruhnama as Required Subject." Eurasianet, April 26. http://www.eurasianet.org/node/63365.

Fiorina, Morris. 1980. "The Decline of Collective Responsibility in American Politics." *Daedalus* 109:25–45.

———. 1981. *Retrospective Voting in American National Elections.* New Haven, CT: Yale University Press.

Fish, M. Steven. 2002. "Islam and Authoritarianism." *World Politics* 55:4–37.

Fogel, Robert. 2004. *The Escape from Hunger and Premature Death, 1700–2100: Europe, America and the Third World.* New York: Cambridge University Press.

Ford, Caroline. 1993. *Creating the Nation in Provincial France: Religion and Political Identity in Brittany.* Princeton, NJ: Princeton University Press.

Fox, Jean-Paul, and Rob R. Meijer. 2008. "Using Item Response Theory to Obtain Individual Information from Randomized Response Data: An Application Using Cheating Data." *Applied Psychological Measurement* 32:595–610.

Franzese, Robert J., Jr. 2002a. "Electoral and Partisan Cycles in Economic Policies and Outcomes." *Annual Review of Political Science* 5(1):369–421.

———. 2002b. *Macroeconomic Policies of Developed Democracies.* New York: Cambridge University Press.

Fréchette, Guillaume R., François Maniquet, and Massimo Morelli. 2008. "Incumbents' Interests and Gender Quotas." *American Journal of Political Science* 52:891–909.

Freedom House. 2011. "Freedom in the World 2011: The Authoritarian Challenge to Democracy." http://www.freedomhouse.org/.

———. 2012. *Freedom in the World: Niger.* https://freedomhouse.org/report/freedom-world/2012/niger.

———. 2016. Home page. http://www.freedomhouse.org.

Freeman, John R., and Dennis P. Quinn. 2010. "The Economic Origins of Democracy Reconsidered." *American Political Science Review* 106:58–80.

Friedman, Edward. 2002. "On Alien Western Democracy." In *Globalization and Democratization in Asia,* eds. Catarina Kinnvall and Kristina Jonsson. New York: Routledge.

Friedman, Thomas L. 2009. "Our One-Party Democracy." *The New York Times,* September 8. http://www.nytimes.com/2009/09/09/opinion/09friedman.html?_r=0.

Fukuyama, Francis. 1992. *The End of History and the Last Man.* New York: Penguin.

———. 1995a. "Confucianism and Democracy." *Journal of Democracy* 6:20–33.

———. 1995b. "The Primacy of Culture." *Journal of Democracy* 6:7–14.

"Full List of Justin Trudeau's Cabinet." 2015. CBC News. http://www.cbc.ca/news/politics/full-list-of-justin-trudeau-s-cabinet-1.3300699.

Galenson, Walter. 1959. *Labor and Economic Development.* New York: Wiley.

Gallagher, Michael, Michael Laver, and Peter Mair. 2006. *Representative Government in Modern Europe: Institutions, Parties, and Government.* New York: McGraw-Hill.

Gamson, W. A. 1961. "A Theory of Coalition Formation." *American Sociological Review* 26:373–382.

Gandhi, Jennifer. 2008. *Political Institutions under Dictatorship.* New York: Cambridge University Press.

Gandhi, Jennifer, and Ellen Lust-Okar. 2009. "Elections under Authoritarianism." *Annual Review of Political Science* 12:403–422.

Gandhi, Jennifer, and Adam Przeworski. 2006. "Cooperation, Cooptation, and Rebellion under Dictatorships." *Economics and Politics* 18:1–26.

———. 2007. "Authoritarian Institutions and the Survival of Autocrats." *Comparative Political Studies* 40:1279–1301.

Garton Ash, Timothy. 1999. *The Magic Lantern: The Revolution of '89 Witnessed in Warsaw, Budapest, Berlin and Prague.* New York: Vintage Books.

Gasiorowski, Mark J. 1995. "Economic Crisis and Political Regime Change: An Event History Analysis." *American History Analysis* 89:882–897.

Gaskins, Ben, Matt Golder, and David Siegel. 2013a. "Religious Participation and Economic Conservatism." *American Journal of Political Science* 57:823–840.

Gaskins, Ben, Matt Golder, and David Siegel. 2013b. "Religious Participation, Social Conservatism, and Human Development." *Journal of Politics* 75:1125–1141.

Gat, Azar. 2006. *War in Human Civilization.* Oxford: Oxford University Press.

Geanakoplos, John. 2005. "Three Brief Proofs of Arrow's Impossibility Theorem." *Economic Theory* 26:211–215.

Geddes, Barbara. 1999. "Authoritarian Breakdown: Empirical Test of a Game Theoretic Argument." Paper presented at the Annual Meeting of American Political Science Association Atlanta, September.

———. 2003. *Paradigms and Sand Castles: Theory Building and Research Design in Comparative Politics.* Ann Arbor: University of Michigan Press.

———. 2005. "Why Parties and Elections in Authoritarian Regimes?" Paper presented at the Annual Meeting of the American Political Science Association, Washington, DC, September 1–4.

Geddes, Barbara, Joseph Wright, and Erica Frantz. 2014. "Autocratic Breakdown and Regime Transitions: A New Data Set." *Perspectives on Politics* 12(2):313–331.

Geertz, Clifford. 1973. *The Interpretation of Cultures.* New York: Basic Books.

Gerges, Fawaz. 2013. "Saudi Arabia and Iran Must End Their Proxy War in Syria." *The Guardian,* December 15. http://www.theguardian.com/commentisfree/2013/dec/15/saudia-arabia-iran-proxy-war-syria.

Gerschenkron, Alexander. 1962. *Economic Backwardness in Historical Perspective: A Book of Essays.* Cambridge, MA: Harvard University Press.

Gershenson, Dmitriy, and Hershel I. Grossman. 2001. "Cooption and Repression in the Soviet Union." *Economics and Politics* 13:31–47.

Ghobarah, Hazem Adam, Paul Huth, and Bruce Russett. 2004. "Comparative Public Health: The Political Economy of Human Misery and Well-Being." *International Studies Quarterly* 48:73–94.

Gibbard, Allan. 1973. "Manipulation of Voting Schemes: A General Result." *Econometrica* 41:587–601.

Gibson, James, and Gregory Caldeira. 1992. "The Etiology of Public Support for the Supreme Court." *American Journal of Political Science* 36:459–489.

Gibson, James, Gregory Caldeira, and Vanessa Baird. 1998. "On the Legitimacy of National High Courts." *American Political Science Review* 92:343–358.

Gingerich, Daniel W. 2010. "Understanding off-the-Books Politics: Conducting Inference on the Determinants of Sensitive Behavior with Randomized Response Surveys." *Political Analysis* 18:349–380.

———. 2013. *Political Institutions and Party-Directed Corruption in South America: Stealing from the Team.* New York: Cambridge University Press.

Ginkel, John, and Alastair Smith. 1999. "So You Say You Want a Revolution? A Game Theoretic Explanation of Revolution in Repressive Regimes." *Journal of Conflict Resolution* 43:291–316.

Ginsburg, Tom. 2003. *Judicial Review in New Democracies: Constitutional Courts in Asian Cases.* New York: Cambridge University Press.

Gintis, Herbert. 2003. "Towards a Unity of the Human Behavioral Sciences." Working Paper 03-02-015, Santa Fe Institute.

Gleditsch, Kristian S., and Michael D. Ward. 1997. "Double Take: A Re-examination of Democracy and Autocracy in Modern Polities." *Journal of Conflict Resolution* 41:361–382.

Global Database of Quotas for Women. 2015. "Quota Database." http://www.quotaproject.org/.

Golder, Matt. 2003. "Explaining Variation in the Electoral Success of Extreme Right Parties in Western Europe." *Comparative Political Studies* 36:432–466.

———. 2005. "Democratic Electoral Systems around the World, 1946–2000." *Electoral Studies* 24:103–121.

———. 2006. "Presidential Coattails and Legislative Fragmentation." *American Journal of Political Science* 50:34–48.

———. 2016. "Far Right Parties in Europe." *Annual Review of Political Science* 19:477–497.

Golder, Matt, and Benjamin Ferland. Forthcoming. "Electoral Systems and Citizen-Elite Ideological Congruence." In *The Oxford Handbook of Electoral Systems*, eds. Erik Herron, Robert Pekkanen, and Matthew Soberg Shugart. New York: Oxford University Press.

Golder, Matt, and Sona N. Golder. 2016. "Symposium: Data Access and Research Transparency." *CP: Newsletter of the Comparative Politics Organized Section of the American Political Science Association* 26(1):1–108.

Golder, Matt, and Gabriella Lloyd. 2014. "Re-evaluating the Relationship between Electoral Rules and Ideological Congruence." *European Journal of Political Research* 53:200–212.

Golder, Matt, and Jacek Stramski. 2010. "Ideological Congruence and Electoral Institutions." *American Journal of Political Science* 54:90–106.

Golder, Sona N. 2005. "Pre-electoral Coalitions in Comparative Perspective: A Test of Existing Hypotheses." *Electoral Studies* 24:643–663.

———. 2006. *The Logic of Pre-electoral Coalition Formation.* Columbus: Ohio State University Press.

———. 2010. "Bargaining Delays in the Government Formation Process." *Comparative Political Studies* 43:3–32.

Golder, Sona N., and Jacquelyn A. Thomas. 2014. "Portfolio Allocation and the Vote of No Confidence." *British Journal of Political Science* 44(1):29–39.

Gomez, Brad T., Thomas G. Hansford, and George A. Krause. 2007. "The Republicans Should Pray for Rain: Weather, Turnout, and Voting in U.S. Presidential Elections." *Journal of Politics* 69:649–663.

Gomez, Brad T., and J. Matthew Wilson. 2008. "Political Sophistication and Attributions of Blame in the Wake of Hurricane Katrina." *Publius: The Journal of Federalism* 38.

Gonzalez-Ocantos, Ezequiel, Chad Kiewiet De Jonge, Carlos Meléndez, Javier Osorio, and David W. Nickerson. 2012. "Vote Buying and Social Desirability Bias: Experimental Evidence from Nicaragua." *American Journal of Political Science* 56:202–217.

Goodin, Robert E., and Philip Pettit, eds. 1993. *A Companion to Contemporary Political Philosophy.* Oxford: Blackwell.

Gourevitch, Philip. 1998. *We Wish to Inform You That Tomorrow We Will Be Killed with Our Families: Stories from Rwanda.* New York: Picador.

Granovetter, Mark. 1978. "Threshold Models of Collective Behavior." *American Journal of Sociology* 83:1420–1443.

Grinspan, Jon. 2016. "Why Donald Trump's Election Observers Are a Bad Idea." *The New York Times*, August 24. http://www.nytimes.com/2016/08/24/opinion/why-donald-trumps-election-observers-are-a-bad-idea.html.

Gschwend, Thomas, and Marc Hooghe. 2008. "Should I Stay or Should I Go? An Experimental Study on Voter Responses to Pre-electoral Coalitions." *European Journal of Political Research* 47:555–577.

Guinier, Lani. 1994. *The Tyranny of the Majority.* New York: Free Press.

Gunther, Richard, Hans-Jürgen Puhle, and P. Nikiforos Diamandouros, eds. 1995. *The Politics of Democratic Consolidation: Southern Europe in Comparative Perspective.* Baltimore: Johns Hopkins University Press.

Gurr, Ted Robert. 1970. *Why Men Rebel.* Princeton, NJ: Princeton University Press.

Haber, Stephen, Armando Razo, and Noel Maurer. 2003. *The Politics of Property Rights: Political Instability, Credible Commitments, and Economic Growth in Mexico, 1876–1929.* New York: Cambridge University Press.

Haberman, Maggie, and Matt Flegenheimer. 2016. "Donald Trump, a 'Rigged' Election and the Politics of Race." *The New York Times,* August 21. http://www.nytimes.com/2016/08/22/us/politics/donald-trump-a-rigged-election-and-the-politics-of-race.html?_r=0.

Habyarimana, James, Macartan Humphreys, Daniel Posner, and Jeremy Weinstein. 2007. "Why Does Ethnic Diversity Undermine Public Goods Provision?" *American Political Science Review* 101: 709–725.

Hadenius, Axel, and Jan Teorell. 2007. "Pathways from Authoritarianism." *Journal of Democracy* 18:143–157.

Haggard, Stephen, and Robert K. Kaufman. 2012. "Inequality and Regime Transition: Democratic Transitions and the Stability of Democratic Rule." *American Political Science Review* 106:495–516.

Hallerberg, Mark. 1996. "Tax Competition in Wilhelmine Germany and Its Implications for the European Union." *World Politics* 48:324–357.

———. 2004. *Domestic Budgets in a United Europe: Fiscal Governance from the End of Bretton Woods to EMU.* Ithaca, NY: Cornell University Press.

Hallerberg, Mark, and Patrik Marier. 2004. "Executive Authority, the Personal Vote, and Budget Discipline in Latin American and Caribbean Countries." *American Journal of Political Science* 48:571–587.

Hallerberg, Mark, and Jürgen von Hagen. 1999. "Electoral Institutions, Cabinet Negotiations, and Budget Deficits in the European Union." In *Fiscal Institutions and Fiscal Performance,* eds. James Poterba and Jürgen von Hagen. Chicago: University of Chicago Press.

Hamilton, Alexander. 1787. "The Union as a Safeguard against Domestic Faction and Insurrection for the Independent Journal." *The Federalist Papers: No. 9.* http://avalon.law.yale.edu/18th_century/fed09.asp.

Hammer, Joshua. 2010. "The Contenders: Is Egypt's Presidential Race Becoming a Real Contest." *The New Yorker,* April 5. http://www.newyorker.com/reporting/2010/04/05/100405fa_fact_hammer.

Hancock, Ange-Marie. 2007. "Intersectionality as a Normative and Empirical Paradigm." *Politics and Gender* 3:248–254.

Hansard. 1997. "Modernisation of the House of Commons" (House of Commons Debate). Vol. 295 Column 507 (4 June 1997). http://hansard.millbanksystems.com/commons/1997/jun/04/modernisation-of-the-house-of-commons#column_506.

Hanson, Russell L. 1989. "Democracy." In *Political Innovation and Conceptual Change*, eds. Terence Ball, James Farr, and Russell L. Hanson. New York: Cambridge University Press.

Haraway, Donna. 1988. "Situated Knowledges: The Science Question in Feminism and the Privilege of Partial Perspective." *Feminist Studies* 14(3):575–599.

Hardgrave, Robert, Jr. 1994. "India: The Dilemma of Diversity." In *Nationalism, Ethnic Conflict, and Democracy,* eds. Larry Diamond and Marc F. Plattner. Baltimore: Johns Hopkins University Press.

Hardin, Garrett. 1968. "The Tragedy of the Commons." *Science* 162:1243–1248.

Hardin, Russell. 1982. *Collective Action.* Baltimore: Johns Hopkins University Press.

Hassig, Ralph, and Kongdan Oh. 2009. *The Hidden People of North Korea: Everyday Life in the Hermit Kingdom.* New York: Rowman and Littlefield.

Hayek, Friedrich von. [1939] 1948. "The Economic Conditions of Interstate Federalism." Repr. in *Individualism and the Economic Order.* Chicago: University of Chicago Press.

Heard, Stephen. 2015. "Why Do We Make Statistics So Hard for Our Students?" October 6. https://scientistseessquirrel.wordpress.com/2015/10/06/why-do-we-make-statistics-so-hard-for-our-students/.

Hechter, Michael. 2000. *Containing Nationalism*. New York: Oxford University Press.

Hefner, Robert W. 2000. *Civil Islam: Muslims and Democratization in India*. Princeton, NJ: Princeton University Press.

Hellwig, Timothy, and David Samuels. 2007. "Electoral Accountability and the Variety of Democratic Regimes." *British Journal of Political Science* 38:65–90.

Helmke, Gretchen. 2002. "The Logic of Strategic Defection: Court-Executive Relations in Argentina under Dictatorship and Democracy." *American Political Science Review* 96:305–320.

———. 2005. *Courts under Constraints: Judges, Generals, and Presidents in Argentina*. New York: Cambridge University Press.

Henrich, Joseph, Robert Boyd, Samuel Bowles, Colin Camerer, Ernst Fehr, Herbert Gintis, and Richard McElreath. 2001. "In Search of Homo Economicus: Behavioral Experiments in 15 Small-Scale Societies." *American Economic Review* 91:73–78.

Henrich, Joseph, Robert Boyd, Samuel Bowles, Colin Camerer, Ernst Fehr, Herbert Gintis, Richard McElreath et al. 2005. "Economic Man in Cross-Cultural Perspective: Behavioral Experiments in 15 Small-Scale Societies." *Behavior and Brain Sciences* 28:795–815.

Herb, Michael. 1999. *All in the Family: Absolutism, Revolution and Democracy in the Middle East*. Albany: State University of New York Press.

Herbst, Jeffrey. 2000. *States and Power in Africa: Comparative Lessons in Authority and Control*. Princeton, NJ: Princeton University Press.

———. 2001. "Political Liberalization in Africa after Ten Years." *Comparative Politics* 33:357–375.

Herodotus. [440 BCE] 2005. *The Histories*, trans. G. C. Macaulay. New York: Barnes and Noble Classics.

Hibbs, Douglas A., Jr. 1977. "Political Parties and Macroeconomic Policy." *American Political Science Review* 71:1467–1487.

———. 1987. *The Political Economy of Industrial Democracies*. Cambridge, MA: Harvard University Press.

Hicken, Allen. 2009. *Building Party Systems in Developing Countries*. New York: Cambridge University Press.

Hicken, Allen, and Walter R. Mebane Jr. 2015. "A Guide to Election Forensics." Working Paper, University of Michigan.

Hicken, Allen, and Heather Stoll. 2011. "Presidents and Parties: How Presidential Elections Shape Coordination in Legislative Elections." *Comparative Political Studies* 44(7):854–883.

———. 2013. "Are All Presidents Created Equal? Presidential Powers and the Shadow of Presidential Elections." *Comparative Political Studies* 46(3):291–319.

Hinich, Melvin J., and Michael C. Munger. 1997. *Analytical Politics*. New York: Cambridge University Press.

Hirano, Shigeo. 2011. "Electoral Institutions, Hometowns, and Favored Minorities: Evidence from Japanese Electoral Reforms." *World Politics* 59:51–82.

Hirschman, Albert. 1970. *Exit, Voice, and Loyalty: Responses to Decline in Firms, Organizations, and States*. Cambridge, MA: Harvard University Press.

Hitchcock, William I. 2004. *The Struggle for Europe: The Turbulent History of a Divided Continent, 1945 to the Present*. New York: Anchor Books.

Hobbes, Thomas. [1651] 1994. *Leviathan*, ed. Edwin Curley. Indianapolis, IN: Hackett.

Hobolt, Sarah B., James Tilley, and Susan Banducci. 2013. "Clarity of Responsibility: How Government Cohesion Conditions Performance Voting." *European Journal of Political Research* 52:164–187.

Horowitz, Donald L. 1985. *Ethnic Groups in Conflict*. Berkeley: University of California Press.

———. 1991. *A Democratic South Africa? Constitutional Engineering in a Divided Society*. Berkeley: University of California Press.

———. 1993. "Democracy in Divided Societies." *Journal of Democracy* 4:18–38.

———. 2004. "The Alternative Vote and Interethnic Moderation: A Reply to Fraenkel and Grofman." *Public Choice* 121:507–516.

Hotelling, Harold. 1929. "Stability in Competition." *Economic Journal* 39:41–57.

Hough, Jerry F. 1980. *Soviet Leadership in Transition*. Washington, DC: Brookings Institution.

Houle, Christian. 2009. "Inequality and Democracy: Why Inequality Harms Consolidation but Does Not Affect Democratization." *World Politics* 61:589–622.

Howden, Daniel. 2009. "From Coup to Counter-Coup? Guinea Plunged into Chaos." *Independent*, December 4. http://www.independent.co.uk/news/world/africa/from-coup-to-countercoup-guinea-plunged-into-chaos-1834644.html.

Htun, Mala. 2016. *Inclusion without Representation in Latin America: Gender Quotas and Ethnic Reservations*. New York: Cambridge University Press.

Huber, Evelyne, Charles Ragin, and John D. Stephens. 1993. "Social Democracy, Christian Democracy, Constitutional Structure, and the Welfare State." *American Journal of Sociology* 99:711–749.

Huber, John D. 1996. *Rationalizing Parliament*. New York: Cambridge University Press.

Huber, John D., and Cecilia Martínez-Gallardo. 2004. "Cabinet Instability and the Accumulation of Experience in the Cabinet: The French Fourth and Fifth Republics in Comparative Perspective." *British Journal of Political Science* 34:27–48.

———. 2008. "Replacing Cabinet Ministers: Patterns of Ministerial Stability in Parliamentary Democracies." *American Political Science Review* 102:169–180.

Huber, John D., and G. Bingham Powell. 1994. "Congruence between Citizens and Policymakers in Two Visions of Liberal Democracy." *World Politics* 46:291–326.

Hughes, Melanie. 2011. "Intersectionality, Quotas, and Minority Women's Political Representation Worldwide." *American Political Science Review* 105:604–620.

Hui, Li, and Magha Rajagopalan. 2013. "At Sina Weibo's Censorship Hub, China's Little Brothers Cleanse Online Chatter." Reuters, September 11. http://www.reuters.com/article/us-china-internet-idUSBRE98A18Z20130912.

Humphreys, Macartan. 2005. "Natural Resources, Conflict, and Conflict Resolution: Uncovering the Mechanisms." *Journal of Conflict Resolution* 49:508–537.

Huntington, Samuel P. 1968. *Political Order in Changing Societies*. New Haven, CT: Yale University Press.

———. 1991. *The Third Wave: Democratization in the Late Twentieth Century*. Norman: University of Oklahoma Press.

———. 1993. "The Clash of Civilizations?" *Foreign Affairs* 72:22–49.

———. 1996. *The Clash of Civilizations and the Remaking of World Order*. New York: Simon and Schuster.

Huntington, Samuel P., and Jorge I. Domínguez. 1975. "Political Development." In *Macropolitical Theory*, eds. Fred I. Greenstein and Nelson W. Polsby, 1–114. Reading, MA: Addison-Wesley.

Hyde, Susan. 2007a. "Experimenting in Democracy Promotion: International Observers and the 2004 Presidential Elections in Indonesia." *Perspectives on Politics* 8:511–527.

———. 2007b. "The Observer Effect in International Politics: Evidence from a Natural Experiment." *World Politics* 60:37–63.

———. 2011. *The Pseudo-Democrat's Dilemma: Why Election Observation Became an International Norm.* Ithaca, NY: Cornell University Press.

Hyde, Susan, and Nicolay Marinov. 2012. "Which Elections Can Be Lost?" *Political Analysis* 20: 191–210.

Ibenskas, Raimondas. 2016a. "Marriages of Convenience: Explaining Party Mergers in Europe." *The Journal of Politics* 78(2):343–356.

———. 2016b. "Understanding Pre-electoral Coalitions in Central and Eastern Europe." *British Journal of Political Science* 46:743–761.

Ibrahim, Mohamed. 2010. "Somalia and Global Terrorism: A Growing Connection?" *Journal of Contemporary African Studies* 28:283–295.

Ichino, Nahomi, and Matthias Schündeln. 2012. "Deterring or Displacing Electoral Irregularities? Spillover Effects of Observers in a Randomized Field Experiment in Ghana." *Journal of Politics* 74:292–307.

Ignazi, Piero. 1992. "The Silent Counter-Revolution: Hypotheses on the Emergence of Extreme Right-Wing Parties in Europe." *European Journal of Political Research* 22:3–34.

Im, H. B. 1997. *The Compatibility of Confucianism and Democratic Civil Society in Korea.* Paper presented at the International Political Science Association Seventeenth World Congress, Seoul, Republic of Korea, August 17–21.

Indriðason, Indriði. 2015. "Live for Today, Hope for Tomorrow? Rethinking Gamson's Law." Working Paper, University of California, Riverside.

Indriðason, Indriði, and Christopher Kam. 2005. "The Timing of Cabinet Reshuffles in Five Westminster Parliamentary Systems." *Legislative Studies Quarterly,* 327–363.

Inglehart, Ronald. 1977. *The Silent Revolution: Changing Values and Political Styles among Western Publics.* Princeton, NJ: Princeton University Press.

———. 1990. *Culture Shift in Advanced Industrial Society.* Princeton, NJ: Princeton University Press.

———. 1997. *Modernization and Postmodernization: Cultural, Economic and Political Change in 43 Societies.* Princeton, NJ: Princeton University Press.

Inglehart, Ronald, and Christian Welzel. 2003. "Political Culture and Democracy: Analyzing Cross-Level Linkages." *Comparative Politics* 36:61–79.

———. 2005. *Modernization, Cultural Change, and Democracy: The Human Development Sequence.* New York: Cambridge University Press.

International Crisis Group. 2006. "Can the Somali Crisis Be Contained?" Africa Report no. 116.

Inter-Parliamentary Union (IPU). 2016. "Home." http://www.ipu.org/english/home.htm.

Ivarsflaten, Elisabeth. 2008. "What Unites Right-Wing Populists in Western Europe? Re-examining Grievance Mobilization Models in Seven Successful Cases." *Comparative Political Studies* 41:3–23.

Iversen, Torben, and David Soskice. 2006. "Electoral Institutions and the Politics of Coalitions: Why Some Democracies Redistribute More than Others." *American Political Science Review* 100:165–181.

Jacobson, Gary C. 2001. *The Politics of Congressional Elections.* New York: Longman.

Jensen, Nathan, and Leonard Wantchekon. 2004. "Resource Wealth and Political Regimes in Africa." *Comparative Political Studies* 37:816–841.

Johnston, David, and Neil A. Lewis. 2007. "Senate Democrats Plan a Resolution on Gonzales." *The New York Times,* May 18. http://www.nytimes.com/2007/05/18/washington/18gonzales.html.

Jones, Mark P. 1995. "Presidential Election Laws and Multipartism in Latin America." *Political Research Quarterly* 47:41–57.

Junn, Jane, and Nadia Brown. 2008. "What Revolution? Incorporating Intersectionality in Women and Politics." In *Political Women and American Democracy*, eds. Christina Wolbrecht, Karen Beckwith, and Lisa Baldez, 64–78. New York: Cambridge University Press.

Kalyvas, Stathis. 1996. *The Rise of Christian Democracy in Europe*. Ithaca, NY: Cornell University Press.

———. 1998. "Democracy and Religious Politics: Evidence from Belgium." *Comparative Political Studies* 31:291–319.

———. 2000. "Commitment Problems in Emerging Democracies: The Case of Religious Parties." *Comparative Politics* 32:379–399.

Kaminski, Marek M. 1999. "How Communism Could Have Been Saved: Formal Analysis of Electoral Bargaining in Poland in 1989." *Public Choice* 98:83–109.

———. 2004. *Games Prisoners Play*. Princeton, NJ: Princeton University Press.

Kaminski, Marek M., Grzegorz Lissowski, and Piotr Swistak. 1998. "The 'Revival of Communism' or the Effect of Institutions? The 1993 Polish Parliamentary Elections." *Public Choice* 3:429–449.

Kang, Chol-hwan, and Pierre Rigoulot. 2005. *The Aquariums of Pyongyang: Ten Years in the North Korean Gulag*. New York: Basic Books.

Kanter, Rosabeth Moss. 1977. "Some Effects of Proportions on Group Life." *American Journal of Sociology* 82:965–990.

Karatnycky, Adrian. 2002. "Muslim Countries and the Democracy Gap." *Journal of Democracy* 13:99–112.

Karl, Terry Lynn. 1995. "The Hybrid Regimes of Central America." *Journal of Democracy* 6:72–87.

———. 1997. *The Paradox of Plenty: Oil Booms and Petro-States*. Berkeley: University of California Press.

Kasaija, Apuuli Phillip. 2010. "The UN-Led Djibouti Peace Process for Somalia 2008–2009: Results and Problems." *Journal of Contemporary African Studies* 28:261–282.

Katz, Richard S. 1980. *A Theory of Parties and Electoral Systems*. Baltimore: Johns Hopkins University Press.

Katznelson, Ira. 1985. "Working-Class Formation and the State: Nineteenth-Century England in American Perspective." In *Bringing the State Back In,* eds. Peter B. Evans, Dietrich Rueschmeyer, and Theda Skocpol. New York: Cambridge University Press.

Kayser, Mark Andreas. 2005. "Who Surfs, Who Manipulates? The Determinants of Opportunistic Election Timing and Electorally Motivated Economic Intervention." *American Political Science Review* 99:17–28.

Kedar, Orit, Liran Harsgor, and Raz A. Scheinerman. 2016. "Are Voters Equal under Proportional Representation?" *American Journal of Political Science* 60:676–691.

Kellam, Marisa. 2015. "Parties for Hire: How Particularistic Parties Influence Presidents' Governing Strategies." *Party Politics* 21(4):511–526.

Kellam, Marisa. Forthcoming. "Why Pre-electoral Coalitions in Presidential Systems?" *British Journal of Political Science*.

"Kenya al-Shabab Attack: Security Questions as Dead Mourned." 2015. BBC News, April 4. http://www.bbc.com/news/world-africa-32177123.

Kerr, Henry H. 1987. "The Swiss Party System: Steadfast and Changing." In *Party Systems in Denmark, Austria, Switzerland, the Netherlands, and Belgium,* ed. Hans Daalder. New York: St. Martin's Press.

Khan, Ali. 2006. "The Medina Constitution." Unpublished manuscript, Washburn University, Topeka, KS.

Khan, Amjad Mahmood. 2010. "Religious Freedom in America." Paper presented at the 62nd Annual Jalsa Salana USA, Los Angeles, California.

Khan, Muqtedar. 2001. "The Compact of Medina: A Constitutional Theory of the Islamic State." May 30. http://www.ijtihad.org/compact.htm.

Kim, Dong-Hun, and Gerhard Loewenberg. 2005. "The Role of Parliamentary Committees in Coalition Governments: Keeping Tabs on Coalition Partners in the German Bundestag." *Comparative Political Studies* 38:1104–1129.

Kim, Yung-Myung. 1997. "Asian-Style Democracy: A Critique from East Asia." *Asian Survey* 37: 1119–1134.

King, Gary. 1995. "Replication, Replication." *PS: Political Science and Politics* 28:443–499.

———. 2003. "The Future of Replication." *International Studies Perspectives* 4:72–107.

King, Gary, Christopher J. L. Murray, Joshua A. Salomon, and Ajay Tandon. 2004. "Enhancing the Validity and Cross-Cultural Comparability of Measurement in Survey Research." *American Political Science Review* 98:191–207.

King, Gary, Jennifer Pan, and Margaret Roberts. 2013. "How Censorship in China Allows Government Criticism but Silences Collective Expression." *American Political Science Review* 107:1–18.

King, Gary, and Jonathan Wand. 2007. "Comparing Incomparable Survey Responses: Evaluating and Selecting Anchoring Vignettes." *Political Analysis* 15:46–66.

King, Gary, and Langche Zeng. 2001. "Improving Forecasts of State Failure." *World Politics* 53:623–658.

Kirkpatrick, David D. 2011. "A Libyan Leader at War With Rebels, and Reality." *The New York Times,* March 6. http://www.nytimes.com/2011/03/07/world/middleeast/07qaddafi.html?_r=1&pagewanted=all.

Kitschelt, Herbert P. 1988. "Left-Libertarian Parties: Explaining Innovation in Competitive Party Systems." *World Politics* 40:194–234.

Kittilson, Miki Caul. 2006. *Challenging Parties, Changing Parliaments: Women and Elected Office in Contemporary Western Europe.* Columbus: Ohio State University Press.

Kittilson, Miki Caul, and Leslie Schwindt-Bayer. 2012. *The Gendered Effects of Electoral Institutions: Political Engagement and Participation.* New York: Oxford University Press.

Knack, Stephen. 2004. "Does Foreign Aid Promote Democracy?" *International Studies Quarterly* 48:251–266.

Kono, Daniel Yuichi, and Gabriella R. Montinola. 2009. "Does Foreign Aid Support Autocrats, Democrats or Both?" *Journal of Politics* 71(2):704–718.

Krook, Mona Lena. 2009. *Quotas for Women in Politics: Gender and Candidate Selection Reform Worldwide.* New York: Oxford University Press.

Krook, Mona Lena, and Pippa Norris. 2014. "Beyond Quotas: Strategies to Promote Gender Equality in Elected Office." *Political Studies* 62:2–20.

Krumpal, Ivar. 2012. "Estimating the Prevalence of Xenophobia and Anti-Semitism in Germany: A Comparison of Randomized Response and Direct Questioning." *Social Science Research* 41:1387–1403.

Krysan, Maria. 1998. "Privacy and the Expression of White Racial Attitudes." *Public Opinion Quarterly* 62:506–544.

Krysan, Maria, and Mick Couper. 2003. "Race in Live and Virtual Interviews: Racial Deference, Social Desirability, and Activation Effects in Attitude Surveys." *Social Psychology Quarterly* 66:364–383.

Kuran, Timur. 1989. "Sparks and Prairie Fires: A Theory of Unanticipated Political Revolution." *Public Choice* 61:41–74.

———. 1991. "Now Out of Never: The Element of Surprise in the East European Revolution of 1989." *World Politics* 44:7–48.

Kuyper, Jonathan W. 2016. "Systemic Representation: Democracy, Deliberation, and Nonelectoral Representatives." *American Political Science Review* 110:308–324.

Kymlicka, Will. 1998. "Is Federalism a Viable Alternative to Secessionism?" In *Theories of Secessionism*, ed. Percy B. Lehning. New York: Routledge Press.

Laakso, Markku, and Rein Taagepera. 1979. "'Effective' Number of Parties: A Measure with Application to West Europe." *Comparative Political Studies* 12:3–27.

Lacouture, Jean. 1986. *De Gaulle: Le Souverain, 1959–1970.* Paris: Seuil.

Laitin, David D. 1983. "Rational Choice and Culture: A Thick Description of Abner Cohen's Hausa Migrants." In *Constitutional Democracy: Essays in Comparative Politics: A Festschrift for Henry W. Ehrmann*, ed. Fred Eidlin. Boulder, CO: Westview Press.

———. 1986. *Hegemony and Culture: Politics and Religious Change among the Yoruba.* Chicago: University of Chicago Press.

———. 1992. *Language Repertoires and State Construction in Africa.* New York: Cambridge University Press.

———. 1998. *Identity in Formation: The Russian-Speaking Populations in the Near Abroad.* Ithaca, NY: Cornell University Press.

Lake, David A., and Matthew Baum. 2001. "The Invisible Hand of Democracy: Political Control and the Provision of Public Services." *Comparative Political Studies* 34:587–621.

Lane, Frederick C. 1958. "Economic Consequences of Organized Violence." *Journal of Economic History* 18:401–410.

LaPalombara, Joseph. 1974. *Politics within Nations.* Englewood Cliffs, NJ: Prentice Hall.

Lasser, William. 1988. *The Limits of Judicial Power: The Supreme Court in American Politics.* Chapel Hill: University of North Carolina Press.

Lave, Charles, and James March. 1975. *An Introduction to Models in the Social Sciences.* New York: Harper and Row.

Laver, Michael, Scott de Marchi, and Hande Mutlu. 2011. "Negotiation in Legislatures over Government Formation." *Public Choice* 147:285–304.

Laver, Michael, and Kenneth A. Shepsle. 1996. *Making and Breaking Governments: Cabinets and Legislatures in Parliamentary Democracies.* New York: Cambridge University Press.

Lawrence, Adria K. Forthcoming. "Repression and Activism among the Arab Spring's First Movers: Evidence from Morocco's February 20th Movement." *British Journal of Political Science.*

Leblang, David A. 1996. "Property Rights, Democracy, and Economic Growth." *Political Research Quarterly* 49:5–26.

———. 1997. "Political Democracy and Economic Growth: Pooled Cross-Sectional and Time-Series Evidence." *British Journal of Political Science* 27:453–466.

———. 2002. "Political Uncertainty and Speculative Attacks." In *Coping with Globalization: Cross-National Patterns in Domestic Governance and Policy Performance*, eds. Steve Chan and James Scarritt. London: Frank Cass.

Leff, Carol Skalnick. 1999. "Democratization and Disintegration in Multi-national States: The Breakup of the Communist Federations." *World Politics* 51:205–235.

Leighley, Jan E., and Jonathan Nagler. 1992a. "Individual and Systemic Influences on Turnout—Who Votes? 1984." *Journal of Politics* 54:718–740.

———. 1992b. "Socioeconomic Class Bias in Turnout, 1964–1988—The Voters Remain the Same." *American Political Science Review* 86:725–736.

Le Pen, Yannick. 2005. "Convergence among Five Industrial Countries (1870–1994): Results from a Time Varying Cointegration Approach." *Empirical Economics* 30:23–35.

Letsch, Constanze. 2013. "Turkey Protests Spread after Violence in Istanbul over Park Demolition." *The Guardian*, May 31. https://www.theguardian.com/world/2013/may/31/istanbul-protesters-violent-clashes-police.

Levi, Margaret. 1988. *Of Rule and Revenue.* Berkeley: University of California Press.

Levitsky, Steven, and Lucan A. Way. 2002. "The Rise of Competitive Authoritarianism." *Journal of Democracy* 13:51–65.

———. 2003. "Autocracy by Democratic Rules: The Dynamics of Competitive Authoritarianism in the Post–Cold War Era." Paper presented at the Conference on Mapping the Great Zone: Clientelism and the Boundary between Democratic and Democratizing, Columbia University, New York, April 4–5.

Lewis, Bernard. 1993. "Islam and Liberal Democracy." *Atlantic Monthly.*

Lewis, I. M. 2002. *A Modern History of the Somali: Nation and State in the Horn of Africa,* 4th ed. Athens: Ohio University Press.

"Libya Protests: Gaddafi Says 'All My People Love Me.'" 2011. BBC News, February 28. http://www.bbc.co.uk/news/world-africa-12603259.

Li, Qing, and David Papell. 1999. "Convergence of International Output: Time Series Evidence for 16 OECD Countries." *International Review of Economics and Finance* 8:267–280.

Lieberson, Stanley. 1991. "Small N's and Big Conclusions: An Examination of the Reasoning in Comparative Studies Based on a Small Number of Cases." *Social Forces* 70:307–320.

———. 1994. "More on the Uneasy Case for Using Mill-Type Methods in Small-N Comparative Studies." *Social Forces* 72:1225–1237.

Lijphart, Arend. 1971. Comparative Politics and the Comparative Method. *American Political Science Review* 65:682–693.

———. 1977. *Democracy in Plural Societies.* New Haven, CT: Yale University Press.

———. 1984. *Democracies: Patterns of Majoritarian and Consensus Government.* New Haven, CT: Yale University Press.

———. 1990. "Electoral Systems, Party Systems, and Conflict Management in Segmented Societies." In *Critical Choices for South Africa: An Agenda for the 1990s,* ed. Robert A. Schreirer. Cape Town, South Africa: Oxford University Press.

———. 1991. "The Power-Sharing Approach." In *Conflict and Peacemaking in Multi-ethnic Societies,* ed. J. V. Montville. New York: Lexington Books.

———. 1996. "Puzzle of Indian Democracy." *American Political Science Review* 90:258–268.

———. 1999. *Patterns of Democracy: Government Forms and Performance in Thirty-Six Countries.* New Haven, CT: Yale University Press.

———. 2004. "Constitutional Design for Divided Societies." *Journal of Democracy* 15(2):96–109.

Lim, Louisa. 2015. *The People's Republic of Amnesia: Tiananmen Revisited.* New York: Oxford University Press.

Lindblom, Charles. 1977. *Politics and Markets.* New York: Basic Books.

Linz, Juan J. 1990. "Virtues of Parliamentarism." *Journal of Democracy* 4:84–91.

———. 1994. "Democracy: Presidential or Parliamentary: Does It Make a Difference?" In *The Failure of Presidential Democracy?* eds. J. J. Linz and A. Valenzuela. Baltimore: Johns Hopkins University Press.

Lipset, Seymour Martin. 1959. "Some Social Requisites of Democracy: Economic Development and Political Legitimacy." *American Political Science Review* 53:69–105.

———. 1960. *Political Man: The Social Bases of Politics.* New York: Doubleday.

———. [1960] 1994. *Political Man: The Social Bases of Politics.* Baltimore: Johns Hopkins University Press.

———. 1996. "What Are Parties For?" *Journal of Democracy* 7:169–175.

———. 2001. "Cleavages, Parties, and Democracy." In *Party Systems and Voter Alignments Revisited,* eds. Lauri Karvonen and Stein Kuhnle, 3–10. London: Routledge.

Lipset, Seymour Martin, and Stein Rokkan. 1967. "Cleavage Structures, Party Systems, and Voter Alignments: An Introduction." In *Party Systems and Voter Alignments: Cross-National Perspectives,* eds. Seymour M. Lipset and Stein Rokkan. New York: Free Press.

Lipsmeyer, Christine S., and Heather N. Pierce. 2011. "The Eyes That Bind: Junior Ministers as Oversight Mechanisms in Coalition Governments." *Journal of Politics* 73(4):1152–1164.

Liu, I-Chou. 1999. "Campaigning in an SNTV System: The Case of the Kuomintang in Taiwan." In *Elections in Japan, Korea, and Taiwan under the Single Non-transferable Vote: The Comparative Study of an Embedded Institution,* eds. Bernard Grofman, Sung-Chull Lee, Edwin Winckler, and Brian Woodall. Ann Arbor: University of Michigan Press.

Locke, John. [1690] 1980. *Second Treatise of Government,* ed. C. B. Macpherson. Indianapolis, IN: Hackett.

Lohmann, Susanne. 1994. "The Dynamics of Informational Cascades: The Monday Demonstrations in Leipzig, East Germany, 1989–91." *World Politics* 47:42–101.

Londregan, John B., and Keith T. Poole. 1996. "Does High Income Promote Democracy?" *World Politics* 49:1–30.

Longino, Helen E. 1987. "Can There Be a Feminist Science?" *Hypatia* 2(3):51–64.

"Low Turnout as Egyptians Shun Elections Designed to Shore up Sisi." 2015. *The Guardian,* October 18. https://www.theguardian.com/world/2015/oct/18/egypt-parliamentary-elections-shore-up-sisi.

Ludwikowski, Rett R. 1996. *Constitution-Making in the Region of Former Soviet Dominance.* Durham, NC: Duke University Press.

Luebbert, Gregory M. 1984. "A Theory of Government Formation." *Comparative Political Studies* 17:229–264.

Lupia, Arthur. 2003. "Delegation and Its Perils." In *Delegation and Accountability in Parliamentary Democracies,* eds. Kaare Strøm, Wolfgang C. Müller, and Torbjörn Bergman, 33–54. Oxford: Oxford University Press.

Lupia, Arthur, and Colin Elman. 2014. "Symposium: Openness in Political Science: Data Access and Research Transparency." *PS: Political Science and Politics* 47(1):19–83.

Lust-Okar, Ellen. 2005. *Structuring Conflict in the Arab World: Incumbents, Opponents, and Institutions.* New York: Cambridge University Press.

Lust-Okar, Ellen, and Amaney Ahmad Jamal. 2002. "Rulers and Rules: Reassessing the Influence of Regime Type on Electoral Law Formation." *Comparative Political Studies* 35:337–366.

Lustik, Ian S., Dan Miodownik, and Roy J. Eidelson. 2004. "Secessionism in Multicultural States: Does Sharing Power Prevent or Encourage It?" *American Political Science Review* 98:209–229.

Lyall, Jason, Graeme Blair, and Kosuke Imai. 2013. "Explaining Support for Combatants during Wartime: A Survey Experiment in Afghanistan." *American Political Science Review* 107:679–705.

Machiavelli, Niccolò. [1531] 1998. *The Discourses*, trans. Leslie J. Walker. New York: Penguin Books.

Madison, James. 1787–1788. *The Federalist Papers Authored by James Madison* (nos. 10–63). Founding Fathers Info. http://www.foundingfathers.info/federalistpapers/madison.htm.

Madison, James. 1788. "The Structure of the Government Must Furnish the Proper Checks and Balances between the Different Departments." *The Federalist Papers No. 51.* https://en.wikipedia.org/wiki/Federalist_No._51.

Macpherson, C. B. 1966. *The Real World of Democracy*. Oxford: Clarendon Press.

Maestas, Cherie, Lonna Rae Atkeson, Thomas Croom, and Lisa Bryant. 2008. "Shifting the Blame: Federalism, Media, and Public Assignment of Blame Following Hurricane Katrina." *Publius: The Journal of Federalism* 38(4):609–632.

Magaloni, Beatriz. 2006. *Voting for Autocracy: The Politics of Party Hegemony and Its Demise*. New York: Cambridge University.

"Magnifying Glasses on Order for Victoria's Metre-Long Senate Ballot Paper." 2014. ABC news, July 8. http://www.abc.net.au/news/2013-07-09/magnifying-glasses-on-order-for-vic-senate-ballot-paper/4807956.

Mahdavy, Hussein. 1970. "The Patterns and Problems of Economic Development in Rentier States: The Case of Iran." In *Studies in the Economic History of the Middle East*, ed. M. A. Cook. London: Oxford University Press.

Mainwaring, Scott. 1993. "Presidentialism, Multipartism, and Democracy: The Difficult Combination." *Comparative Political Studies* 26:198–228.

Mainwaring, Scott, and Matthew Sobert Shugart, eds. 1997. *Presidentialism and Democracy in Latin America*. New York: Cambridge University Press.

Malesky, Edmund, and Paul Schuler. 2010. "Nodding or Needling: Analyzing Delegate Responsiveness in an Authoritarian Parliament." *American Political Science Review* 104:482–502.

Malhotra, Neil, and Alexander G. Kuo. 2008. "Assigning Blame: The Public's Response to Hurricane Katrina." *Journal of Politics* 70:120–135.

Mansbridge, Jane. 1999. "Should Blacks Represent Blacks and Women Represent Women? A Contingent 'Yes.'" *Journal of Politics* 61:628–657.

———. 2003. "Rethinking Representation." *American Political Science Review* 97:515–528.

Mapping Militant Organizations. 2010–2016. Stanford University. https://web.stanford.edu/group/mappingmilitants/cgi-bin/.

Marinov, Nikolay, and Hein Goemans. 2014. "Coups and Democracy." *British Journal of Political Science* 44:799–825.

Marquez, Xavier. 2011. "A Simple Model of Cults of Personality." In *Abandoned Footnotes* [blog], March 14. http://abandonedfootnotes.blogspot.com/2011/03/simple-model-of-cults-of-personality.html.

Marshall, Monty G., Ted Robert Gurr, and Keith Jaggers. 2016. *Polity IV Project: Political Regime Characteristics and Transitions, 1800–2015. Dataset Users' Manual.* http://www.systemicpeace.org/inscr/p4manualv2015.pdf.

Martin, Lanny W., and Georg Vanberg. 2004. "Policing the Bargain: Coalition Government and Parliamentary Scrutiny." *American Journal of Political Science* 48:13–27.

Martínez-Gallardo, Cecilia. 2012. "Out of the Cabinet: What Drives Defections from the Government in Presidential Systems?" *Comparative Political Studies* 45(1):62–90.

Martínez-Gallardo, Cecilia, and Petra Schleiter. 2015. "Choosing Whom to Trust: Agency Risks and Cabinet Partisanship in Presidential Democracies." *Comparative Political Studies* 48(2):231–264.

Marx, Karl. [1850] 1952. *The Class Struggle in France, 1848 to 1850.* Moscow: Progress.

———. [1847] 1995. *The Poverty of Philosophy.* Amherst, NY: Prometheus Books.

Mastias, Jean, and Jean Grangé. 1987. *Les secondes chambres du parlement en europe occidentale.* Paris: Economica.

Matakos, Konstantinos, Orestis Troumpounis, and Dimitrios Xefteris. Forthcoming. "Electoral Rule Disproportionality and Platform Polarization." *American Journal of Political Science.*

Matharu, Hardeep. 2015. "Doctors, Veterans, and Students Tweet Donald Trump Photos of Their 'Muslim IDs' Following His Calls for a Database." *Independent,* November 25. http://www.independent.co.uk/news/world/americas/doctors-veterans-and-students-tweet-donald-trump-photos-of-their-muslim-ids-following-his-call-for-a6746236.html.

Mayhew, David R. 1991. *Divided We Govern: Party Control, Lawmaking, and Investigations, 1946–1990.* New Haven, CT: Yale University Press.

Mazower, Mark. 2000. *Dark Continent: Europe's Twentieth Century.* New York: Vintage Books.

McCarty, Nolan, and Adam Meirowitz. 2007. *Political Game Theory: An Introduction.* New York: Cambridge University Press.

McCubbins, Mathew D., and Thomas Schwartz. 1984. "Congressional Oversight Overlooked: Police Patrols versus Fire Alarms." *American Journal of Political Science* 28:165–179.

McGuire, James. 2002. "Democracy, Social Provisioning, and Child Mortality in Developing Countries." Wesleyan University.

McGuire, M. C., and Mancur Olson. 1996. "The Economics of Autocracy and Majority Rule: The Invisible Hand and the Use of Force." *Journal of Economic Literature* 34:72–96.

McKelvey, Richard D. 1976. "Intransitivities in Multidimensional Voting Models and Some Implications for Agenda Control." *Journal of Economic Theory* 12:472.

McRae, Kenneth D. 1983. *Conflict and Compromise in Multilingual Societies: Switzerland.* Waterloo, Ontario: Wilfrid Laurier University Press.

Mebane, Walter R., Jr. 2006. "Election Forensics: Vote Counts and Benford's law." Paper prepared for the 2006 Summer Meeting of the Political Methodology Society, UC-Davis, Davis, CA, July 20–22.

———. 2008. "Elections Forensics: The Second-Digit Benford Law's Test and Recent American Presidential Elections." In *Election Fraud,* eds. R. Michael Alvarez, Thad E. Hall, and Susan D. Hyde, 162–181. Washington, DC: The Brookings Institutions.

———. 2013. "Fraud in the 2009 Presidential Election in Iran?" *Chance* 23:6–15.

———. 2014. "Can Votes Counts' Digits and Benford's Law Diagnose Election?" In *The Theory and Application of Benford's Law,* ed. Steven J. Miller, 212–222. Princeton: Princeton University Press.

Meltzer, Allan H., and Scott F. Richard. 1981. "A Rational Theory of the Size of Government." *Journal of Political Economy* 89:914–927.

Menaldo, Victor. 2012. "The Middle East and North Africa's Resilient Monarchs." *Journal of Politics* 74:707–722.

Mendelsohn, Ezra. 1983. *The Jews of East Central Europe: Between the World Wars*. Bloomington: Indiana University Press.

Meng, Tianguang, Jennifer Pan, and Ping Yang. Forthcoming. "Conditional Receptivity to Citizen Participation: Evidence from a Survey Experiment in China." *Comparative Political Studies*.

Michels, Robert. [1911] 2001. *Political Parties: A Sociological Study of the Oligarchical Tendencies of Modern Democracy*. Kitchener, Ontario: Batoche Books.

Mickey, Robert W. 2015. *Paths Out of Dixie: The Democratization of Authoritarian Enclaves in America's Deep South, 1944–1972*. Princeton, NJ: Princeton University Press.

"Migrant Crisis: Migration to Europe Explained in Seven Charts." 2016. BBC News, March 4. http://www.bbc.com/news/world-europe-34131911.

"Military 'Seizes Power' in Guinea." 2008. BBC News, December 23. http://news.bbc.co.uk/2/hi/africa/7796902.stm.

Mill, John Stuart. [1859] 1991. "On Liberty." In *J. S. Mill: On Liberty*, eds. John Gray and G. W. Smith, 23–130. London: Routledge.

———. [1861] 1991. *Considerations on Representative Government*. Buffalo, NY: Prometheus Books.

———. [1861] 2001. *Representative Government*. Ontario: Bartoche Books. Available from http://socserv2. socsci.mcmaster.ca/~econ/ugcm/3ll3/mill/repgovt.pdf.

———. 1872. *A System of Logic, Ratiocinative and Inductive: Being a Connected View of the Principles of Evidence and the Methods of Scientific Investigation,* 8th ed. New York: Harper and Brothers.

Milliken, Jennifer, ed. 2003. *State Failure, Collapse and Reconstruction*. Oxford: Blackwell.

Mohamud, Hassan Sheikh, and Catherine Ashton. 2013. "Somalia is no longer a failed state." Hiiraan Online, February 11. http://hiiraan.com/op4/2013/feb/28062/somalia_is_no_longer_a_failed_state.aspx.

Monroe, Alan. 1983. "American Party Platforms and Public Opinion." *American Journal of Political Science* 27:27–42.

Monroe, Burt L. 1994. "Disproportionality and Malapportionment: Measuring Electoral Inequity." *Electoral Studies* 13:132–149.

Montalvo, José G., and Marta Reynal-Querol. 2005. "Ethnic Polarization, Potential Conflict, and Civil Wars." *American Economic Review* 95:796–816.

Montesquieu. [1721] 1899. *The Persian Letters*. London: Gibbings. Available from http://fsweb.wm.edu/plp/.

———. [1752] 1914. *The Spirit of the Laws*. London: Bell & Sons. Available from http://www.constitution.org/cm/sol.htm.

Moore, Barrington, Jr. [1966] 1999. *Social Origins of Dictatorship and Democracy: Lord and Peasant in the Making of the Modern World*. Boston: Beacon Press.

Morgenthau, Hans. 1948. *Politics among Nations*. New York: Knopf.

Morrison, Donald, Robert Mitchell, and John Paden. 1989. *Black Africa: A Comparative Handbook*. New York: Paragon House.

Morrison, Kevin M. 2007. "Natural Resources, Aid, and Democratization: A Best-Case Scenario." *Public Choice* 131:365–386.

———. 2009. "Oil, Nontax Revenue, and the Redistributional Foundations of Regime Stability." *International Organization* 63:107–138.

———. 2012. "What Can We Learn about the 'Resource Curse' from Foreign Aid?" *The World Bank Research Observer* 27:52–73.

Morton, Rebecca B. 1991. "Groups in Rational Turnout Models." *American Journal of Political Science* 35:758–776.

Morton, Rebecca B., and Thomas A. Rietz. 2008. "Majority Requirements and Minority Representation." *New York University Law Review* 63:691–726.

Mosley, Jason. 2015. "Somalia's Federal Future: Layered Agendas, Risks, and Opportunities." Research Paper, Chatham House, The Royal Institute of International Affairs.

Moss-Racusin, Corinne A., John F. Dovidio, Victoria L. Brescoll, Mark J. Graham, and Jo Handelsman. 2012. "Science Faculty's Subtle Gender Biases Favor Male Students." *Proceedings of the National Academy of Sciences* 109(41):16474–16479.

Moyo, Dambisa. 2009. *Dead Aid: Why Aid Is Not Working and How There Is Another Way for Africa.* New York: Farrar, Straus, and Giroux.

Mudde, Cas. 2004. "The Populist Zeitgeist." *Government and Opposition* 39:541–563.

———. 2007. *Populist Radical Right Parties in Europe.* New York: Cambridge University Press.

Mudde, Cas, and Cristóbal Rovira Kaltwasser. 2013. "Exclusionary versus Inclusionary Populism: Comparing Contemporary Europe and Latin America." *Government and Opposition* 48:147–174.

Müller, Wolfgang C., and Kaare Strøm, eds. 2000. *Coalition Governments in Western Europe.* Oxford: Oxford University Press.

Muhlberger, Steve, and Phil Paine 1993. "Democracy's Place in World History." *Journal of World History* 4:23–45.

Muller, Edward N., and Mitchell A. Seligson. 1994. "Civic Culture and Democracy: The Question of Causal Relationships." *American Political Science Review* 88:635–652.

Munck, Gerardo L., and Jay Verkuilen. 2002. "Conceptualizing and Measuring Democracy: Evaluating Alternative Indices." *Comparative Political Studies* 35:5–34.

Murphy, Walter F., C. Hermann Pritchett, and Lee Epstein. 2001. *Courts, Judges, and Politics: An Introduction to the Judicial Process.* New York: McGraw-Hill.

Nagel, Jack H. 2004. "New Zealand: Reform by (Nearly) Immaculate Design." In *Handbook of Electoral System Design,* ed. Josep Colomer, 530–543. London: Palgrave.

Navia, Patricio, and Julio Ríos-Figueroa. 2005. "The Constitutional Adjudication Mosaic of Latin America." *Comparative Political Studies* 38:189–217.

Nest, Michael W. 2002. *The Evolution of a Fragmented State: The Case of the Democratic Republic of Congo.* PhD diss., New York University.

Newton, Kenneth, and Pippa Norris. 2000. "Confidence in Political Institutions: Faith, Culture, or Performance?" In *Disaffected Democracies: What's Troubling the Trilateral Countries?* eds. Susan Pharr and Robert Putnam, 52–73. Princeton, NJ: Princeton University Press.

"N Korea Wages War on Long Hair." 2005. BBC News, January 8. http://news.bbc.co.uk/2/hi/asia-pacific/4157121.stm.

Nordhaus, William. 1975. "The Political Business Cycle." *The Review of Economic Studies* 42(2): 169–190.

Nordlan, Rod. 2010. "Afghan Votes Come Cheap, and Often in Bulk." *The New York Times*, September 17. http://www.nytimes.com/2010/09/18/world/asia/18vote.html.

Nordlinger, Eric. 1972. *Conflict Regulation in Divided Societies.* Cambridge, MA: Harvard University Center for International Affairs.

———. 1977. *Soldiers in Politics: Military Coups and Governments.* Englewood Cliffs, NJ: Prentice Hall.

Norris, Pippa. 2008. *Driving Democracy: Do Power-Sharing Institutions Work?* New York: Cambridge University Press.

———. 2013. "The New Research Agenda Studying Electoral Integrity." *Electoral Studies* 32:563–575.

———. 2014. *Why Do We Care about Electoral Integrity.* New York: Cambridge University Press.

———. 2015. *Why Elections Fail.* New York: Cambridge University Press.

Norris, Pippa, and Ronald Inglehart. 2004. *Sacred and Secular: Religion and Politics Worldwide.* New York: Cambridge University Press.

Norris, Pippa, Ferran Martínez i Coma, Allesandro Nai, and Max Grömping. 2016a. "The Year in Elections 2015: The Expert Survey on Perceptions of Electoral Integrity (PEI-4.0)." www.electoralintegrityproject.com.

———. 2016b. "The Year in Elections, Mid-2016 Update." www.electoralintegrityproject.com.

North, Douglass C. 1981. *Structure and Change in Economic History.* New York: Norton.

———. 1990. *Institutions, Institutional Change, and Economic Performance.* New York: Cambridge University Press.

North, Douglass C., and Robert Paul Thomas. 1971. "The Rise and Fall of the Manorial System: A Theoretical Model." *Journal of Economic History* 31(4):777–803.

———. 1973. *The Rise of the Western World: A New Economic History.* New York: Cambridge University Press.

North, Douglass C., and Barry R. Weingast. 1989. "Constitutions and Commitment: The Evolution of Institutions Governing Public Choice in Seventeenth Century England." *Journal of Economic History* 49:803–832.

Oates, Wallace. 1972. *Fiscal Federalism.* New York: Harcourt Brace Jovanovich.

O'Brien, Diana Z., Matthew Mendez, Jordan Carr Peterson, and Jihyun Shin. 2015. "Letting Down the Ladder or Shutting the Door: Female Prime Ministers, Party Leaders, and Cabinet Members." *Politics & Gender* 11(4):689–717.

O'Donnell, Guillermo. 1973. *Modernization and Bureaucratic Authoritarianism: Studies in South American Politics.* Berkeley: University of California, Institute for International Studies.

Offe, Claus. 1983. "Competitive Party Democracy and the Keynesian Welfare State: Factors of Stability and Disorganization." *Policy Sciences* 15:225–246.

O'Loughlin, John, Michael D. Ward, Corey L. Lofdahl, Jordin S. Cohen, David S. Brown, David Reilly, Kristian S. Gleditsch, and Michael Shin. 1998. "The Diffusion of Democracy, 1946–1994." *Annals of the Association of American Geographers* 88:545–574.

Olson, Mancur C. [1965] 1971. *The Logic of Collective Action: Public Goods and the Theory of Groups,* revised ed. Harvard University Press.

———. 1991. "Autocracy, Democracy, and Prosperity." In *Strategy and Choice,* ed. R. J. Zeckhauser, Chapt. 6, 131–158. Cambridge, MA: MIT Press.

Ordeshook, Peter, and Olga Shvetsova. 1994. "Ethnic Heterogeneity, District Magnitude, and the Number of Parties." *American Journal of Political Science* 38:100–123.

Orwell, George. [1949] 1977. *1984: A Novel.* New York: Harcourt, Brace and World.

Osborne, Martin J. 2004. *An Introduction to Game Theory.* New York: Oxford University Press.

Page, Benjamin I. 1978. *Choices and Echoes in Presidential Elections: Rational Man and Electoral Democracy*. Chicago: University of Chicago Press.

Page, Benjamin I., and Robert Y. Shapiro. 1983. "Effects of Public Opinion on Policy." *American Political Science Review* 77:175–190.

Paler, Laura. 2013. "Keeping the Public Purse: An Experiment in Windfalls, Taxes, and the Incentives to Restrain Government." *American Political Science Review* 104:706–725.

Patterson, Dennis, and Hans Stockton. 2010. "Strategies, Institutions, and Outcomes under SNTV in Taiwan, 1992–2004." *Journal of East Asian Studies* 10:31–59.

Patty, John W., and Elizabeth Maggie Penn. 2014. *Social Choice and Legitimacy: The Possibilities of Impossibility*. New York: Cambridge University Press.

Peçanha, Sergio, Sarah Almukhtar, and K. K. Rebecca Lai. 2015. "Untangling the Overlapping Conflicts in the Syrian War." *The New York Times*, October 18. http://www.nytimes.com/interactive/2015/10/16/world/middleeast/untangling-the-overlapping-conflicts-in-the-syrian-war.html?hp&action=click&pgtype=Homepage&module=photo-spot-region&region=top-news&WT.nav=top-news&_r=0.

Peck, Malcolm C. 2001. "Formation and Evolution of the Federation and Its Institutions." In *United Arab Emirates: A New Perspective*, eds. Ibrahim al Abed and Peter Hellyer. London: Trident Press.

"Perceptions of Electoral Integrity Dataverse." 2016. PEI. https://dataverse.harvard.edu/dataverse/PEI.

Pemstein, Daniel, Stephen A. Meserve, and James Melton. 2010. "Democratic Compromise: A Latent Variable Analysis of Ten Measures of Regime Type." *Political Analysis* 18:426–449.

Penn, Elizabeth Maggie. 2009. "A Model of Farsighted Voting." *American Journal of Political Science* 53:36–54.

Pericchi, Luis Raúl, and David Torres. 2011. "Quick Anomaly Detection by the Newcomb-Benford Law, with Applications to Electoral Processes Data from the USA, Puerto Rico, and Venezuela." *Statistical Science* 26:502–516.

Persson, Torsten, Gerard Roland, and Guido Tabellini. 2007. "Electoral Rules and Government Spending in Parliamentary Democracies." *Quarterly Journal of Political Science* 2:155–188.

Persson, Torsten, and Guido Tabellini. 1999. "The Size and Scope of Government: Comparative Politics with Rational Politicians." *European Economy Review* 43:699–735.

———. 2000. *Political Economics: Explaining Economic Policy*. Cambridge, MA: MIT Press.

———. 2004. "Constitutional Rules and Fiscal Policy Outcomes." *American Economic Review* 94:24–45.

Perzkowski, S., ed. 1994. *Secret Documents of the Politburo and the Secretariat of the Central Committee: The Last Year, 1988–89*. London: Aneks.

Peterson, J. E. 1988. "The Future of Federalism in the United Arab Emirates." In *Crosscurrents in the Gulf: Arab Regional and Global Interests*, eds. H. Richard Sindelar III and J. E. Peterson, 198–230. London: Routledge.

Peterson, Paul. 1995. *The Price of Federalism*. Washington, DC: Brookings Institution.

Phillips, Anne. 1998. *The Politics of Presence: The Political Representation of Gender, Ethnicity, and Race*. New York: Oxford University Press.

Pilkington, Ed. 2015. "Donald Trump: Ban All Muslims Entering US." *The Guardian*, December 7. https://www.theguardian.com/us-news/2015/dec/07/donald-trump-ban-all-muslims-entering-us-san-bernardino-shooting.

Pitkin, Hanna Fenichel. 1967. *The Concept of Representation*. Berkeley: University of California Press.

Piven, Frances Fox, and Richard A. Cloward. 1988. *Why Americans Don't Vote.* New York: Pantheon Books.

———. 2000. *Why Americans Still Don't Vote: And Why Politicians Want It That Way.* Boston: Beacon Press.

Plato. [360 BCE] 1991. *The Republic of Plato,* trans. Allan Bloom. New York: Basic Books.

———. 1871. "Apology." In *The Dialogues of Plato, Volume 1,* transl. by Benjamin Jowett, 319–356. Oxford University: Clarendon. https://books.google.com/books?id=hbUNAAAAQAAJ&source=gbs_navlinks_s.

Plott, Charles. 1967. "A Notion of Equilibrium and Its Possibility under Majoritarian Rule." *American Economic Review* 57:787–806.

Popper, Sir Karl. [1959] 2003. *The Logic of Scientific Discovery.* New York: Routledge.

———. 1962. *Conjectures and Refutations: The Growth of Scientific Knowledge.* New York: Basic Books.

Posner, Daniel N. 2004. "The Political Salience of Cultural Difference: Why Chewas and Tumbukas Are Allies in Zambia and Adversaries in Malawi." *American Political Science Review* 98:529–545.

———. 2005. *Institutions and Ethnic Politics in Africa.* New York: Cambridge University Press.

Poulantzas, Nicos. 1975. *Political Power and Social Class.* London: Verso.

———. 1980. *State, Power and Socialism.* London: Verso.

Powell, G. Bingham. 1982. *Contemporary Democracies: Participation, Stability, and Violence.* Cambridge, MA: Harvard University Press.

———. 2000. *Elections as Instruments of Democracy: Majoritarian and Proportional Visions.* New Haven, CT: Yale University Press.

Powell, G. Bingham, and Guy D. Whitten. 1993. "A Cross-National Analysis of Economic Voting: Taking Account of the Political Context." *American Journal of Political Science* 37:391–414.

Powell, Robert. 1999. *In the Shadow of Power: States and Strategies in International Politics.* Princeton, NJ: Princeton University Press.

Powner, Leanne C., and D. Scott Bennett. 2005. *Applying the Strategic Perspective: Problems and Models.* Washington, DC: CQ Press.

Price, Daniel E. 1999. *Islamic Political Culture, Democracy, and Human Rights: A Comparative Study.* New York: Praeger.

"Proportion of Legislative Seats Held by Women in National Parliaments" (Map). 2016. World Bank. http://data.worldbank.org/indicator/SG.GEN.PARL.ZS.

Przeworski, Adam. 1985. *Capitalism and Social Democracy.* New York: Cambridge University Press.

———. 1991. *Democracy and the Market: Political and Economic Reforms in Eastern Europe and Latin America.* New York: Cambridge University Press.

———. 2001. "Why Democracy Survives in Affluent Societies." Unpublished manuscript, New York University.

———. 2005. "Democracy as an Equilibrium." *Public Choice* 123:253–273.

———. 2006. "Self-Enforcing Democracy." In *The Oxford Handbook of Political Economy,* ed. Donald Wittman and Barry Weingast. New York: Oxford University Press.

Przeworski, Adam, Michael E. Alvarez, José Antonio Cheibub, and Fernando Limongi. 1996. "Classifying Political Regimes." *Studies in Comparative International Development* 31:3–36.

———. 2000. *Democracy and Development: Political Institutions and Well-Being in the World, 1950–1990.* New York: Cambridge University Press.

Przeworksi, Adam, José Antonio Cheibub, and Fernando Limongi. 1998. "Culture and Democracy." In *Culture and Development*. Paris: UNESCO.

Przeworski, Adam, and Fernando Limongi. 1993. "Political Regimes and Economic Growth." *Journal of Economic Perspectives* 7:51–69.

———. 1997. "Modernization: Theories and Facts." *World Politics* 49:155–183.

Przeworski, Adam, and John Sprague. 1988. *Paper Stones: A History of Electoral Socialism*. Chicago: University of Chicago Press.

Przeworski, Adam, and Henry Teune. 1970. *The Logic of Comparative and Social Inquiry*. New York: Wiley-Interscience.

Przeworski, Adam, and Michael Wallerstein. 1988. "Structural Dependence of the State on Capital." *American Political Science Review* 82:11–19.

Putnam, Robert D. 1993. *Making Democracy Work: Civic Traditions in Modern Italy*. Princeton, NJ: Princeton University Press.

———. 2000. *Bowling Alone: The Collapse and Revival of American Community*. New York: Simon and Schuster.

Pye, Lucian W. 1985. *Asian Power and Politics*. Cambridge, MA: Harvard University Press.

Rabushka, Alvin, and Kenneth A. Shepsle. 1972. *Politics in Plural Societies*. Columbus, Ohio: Merrill.

Rahman, Fazlur. 1979. *Islam*. Chicago: University of Chicago Press.

Ramseyer, J. Mark, and Eric B. Rasmusen. 2003. *Measuring Judicial Independence: The Political Economy of Judging in Japan*. Chicago: University of Chicago Press.

Rao, Vaman. 1984. "Democracy and Economic Development." *Studies in Comparative International Development* 19:67–81.

Rasch, Bjørn Erik, Shane Martin, and José Antonio Cheibub, eds. 2015. *Unpacking Parliamentarism: How Investiture Rules Shape Government Formation*. New York: Oxford University Press.

Rauch, Jonathan. 1993. *Kindly Inquisitors: The New Attacks on Free Thought*. Chicago: University of Chicago Press.

Reed, Steven, and Michael F. Thies. 2000. *The Causes of Electoral Reform in Japan*. Oxford: Oxford University Press.

Reenock, Christopher, Michael Bernhard, and David Sobek. 2007. "Regressive Socioeconomic Distribution and Democratic Survival." *International Studies Quarterly* 51:677–699.

Reenock, Christopher, and Jeffrey K. Staton. 2010. "Substitutable Protections: Credible Commitment Devices and Socioeconomic Insulation." *Political Research Quarterly* 63:115–128.

Reenock, Christopher, Jeffrey K. Staton, and Marius Radean. 2013. "Legal Institutions and Democratic Survival." *Journal of Politics* 75(2):491–505.

Rehfeld, Andrew. 2009. "Representation Rethought: On Trustees, Delegates, and Gyroscopes in the Study of Political Representation and Democracy." *American Political Science Review* 103:214–230.

Reilly, Ben. 1997. "Preferential Voting and Political Engineering: A Comparative Study." *Journal of Commonwealth and Comparative Politics* 35:1–19.

———. 2001. *Democracy in Divided Societies: Electoral Engineering for Conflict Management*. New York: Cambridge University Press.

———. 2002. "Sri Lanka: Changes to Accommodate Diversity." In *The International IDEA Handbook of Electoral System Design*, ed. Andrew Reynolds and Ben Reilly. Stockholm, Sweden: International Institute for Democracy and Electoral Assistance.

Remmer, Karen. 2004. "Does Foreign Aid Promote the Expansion of Government?" *American Journal of Political Science* 48:77–92.

Reynal-Querol, Marta. 2002. "Ethnicity, Political Systems, and Civil Wars." *Journal of Conflict Resolution* 46:29–54.

Reynolds, Andrew. 2006. "The Curious Case of Afghanistan." *Journal of Democracy* 17:104–117.

———. 2011. *Designing Democracy in a Dangerous World*. Oxford: Oxford University Press.

Reynolds, Andrew, and John Carey. 2012. "Fixing Afghanistan's Electoral System: Arguments and Options for Reform." Afghanistan Research and Evaluation Unit, July. http://www.areu.org.af/EditionDetails.aspx?EditionId=593&ContentId=7&ParentId=7&Lang=en-US.

Reynolds, Andrew, Ben Reilly, and Andrew Ellis. 2005. *Electoral System Design: The New International IDEA Handbook*. Stockholm, Sweden: International Institute for Democracy and Electoral Assistance.

Rhodes, P. J. 2003. *Ancient Democracy and Modern Ideology*. London: Duckworth.

Richardson, Bradley. 1997. *Japanese Democracy: Power, Coordination, and Performance*. New Haven, CT: Yale University Press.

Rigobon, Roberto, and Dani Rodrik. 2004. "Rule of Law, Democracy, Openness, and Income: Estimating the Interrelationships." NBER Working Paper 10750, National Bureau of Economic Research, Cambridge, MA.

Riker, William. 1964. *Federalism: Origin, Operation, Significance*. Boston: Little, Brown.

———. 1982. *Liberalism against Populism: A Confrontation between the Theory of Democracy and the Theory of Social Choice*. San Francisco: Freeman.

"Riots Thwarted by Blackberry and Twitter Chat—Police." 2011. BBC News, August 16. http://www.bbc.co.uk/news/uk-politics-14542588.

Rioux, Jean-Pierre. 1989. *The Fourth Republic, 1944–1958*. New York: Cambridge University Press.

Roberts, N. S. 1997. "A Period of Enhanced Surprise, Disappointment, and Frustration? The Introduction of a New Electoral System in New Zealand." In *Electoral Systems for Emerging Democracies: Experiences and Suggestions*, ed. Jørgen Elklit. Copenhagen, Denmark: Danida.

Rodden, Jonathan. 2002. "The Dilemma of Fiscal Federalism: Grants and Fiscal Performance around the World." *American Journal of Political Science* 46:670–687.

———. 2004. "Comparative Federalism and Decentralization: On Meaning and Measurement." *Comparative Politics* 36:481–500.

———. 2006. *Hamilton's Paradox: The Promise and Peril of Fiscal Federalism*. New York: Cambridge University Press.

Rodden, Jonathan, and Erik Wibbels. 2002. "Beyond the Fiction of Federalism: Macroeconomic Management in Multitiered Systems." *World Politics* 54:494–531.

Roeder, Philip. 1991. "Soviet Federalism and Ethnic Mobilization." *World Politics* 43:196–232.

Roemer, John E. 1998. "Why the Poor Do Not Expropriate the Rich: An Old Argument in New Garb." *Journal of Public Economics* 70:399–424.

Rogers, James R. 2001. "Information and Judicial Review: A Signaling Game of Legislative-Judicial Interaction." *American Journal of Political Science* 45:84–99.

Romm, Cari. 2014. "Where Are All the Female Test Subjects?" *The Atlantic*, September 4. http://www.theatlantic.com/health/archive/2014/09/where-are-all-the-female-test-subjects/379641/

Rosanvallon, Pierre. 1995. "The History of the Word 'Democracy' in France." *Journal of Democracy* 6:140–154.

Rose-Ackerman, Susan. 1978. *Corruption: A Study in Political Economy.* New York: Academic Press.

———. 1999. *Corruption and Government: Causes, Consequences, and Reform.* New York: Cambridge University Press.

———. 2000. "The Economics and Politics of Federalism: Tensions and Complementarities." *APSA-CP Newsletter* 11:17–19.

Rosenberg, Gerald. 1991. *The Hollow Hope: Can Courts Bring About Social Change?* Chicago: University of Chicago Press.

Rosenberg, Tina. 1996. *The Haunted Land: Facing Europe's Ghosts after Communism.* New York: Vintage Books.

Rosendorff, B. Peter. 2001. "Choosing Democracy." *Economics and Politics* 13:1–29.

Ross, Michael Lewin. 1999. "The Political Economy of the Resource Curse." *World Politics* 51:297–322.

———. 2001. "Does Oil Hinder Democracy?" *World Politics* 53:325–361.

———. 2004. "Does Taxation Lead to Representation?" *British Journal of Political Science* 34:229–249.

———. 2006. "Is Democracy Good for the Poor?" *American Journal of Political Science* 50:860–874.

———. 2011. "Will Oil Drown the Arab Spring?" *Foreign Affairs* 90(5):2–7.

———. 2012. *The Oil Curse.* Princeton, NJ: Princeton University Press.

Rostow, W. W. 1960. *The Stages of Economic Growth: A Non-communist Manifesto.* Cambridge: Cambridge University Press.

Rotberg, Robert I. 2002. "Failed States in a World of Terror." *Foreign Affairs* 81:127–140.

———, ed. 2005. *Battling Terrorism in the Horn of Africa.* Washington, DC: Brookings Institution Press and the World Peace Foundation.

Rousseau, Jean-Jacques. 1762. *The Social Contract, or Principles of Political Right.* Available from http://www.constitution.org/jjr/socon.htm.

———. [1762] 1987. *The Social Contract,* trans. Maurice Cranston. New York: Penguin Books.

———. [1755] 1997. "Discourse on the Origin and Foundations of Inequality among Men." In *The Discourses and Other Political Writings,* ed. Victor Gourevitch. New York: Cambridge University Press.

Rudd, C., and I. Taichi. 1994. *Electoral Reform in New Zealand and Japan: A Shared Experience?* Palmerston North, New Zealand: Massey University Press.

Rueschemeyer, Dietrich, Evelyne Huber Stephens, and John D. Stephens. 1992. *Capitalist Development and Democracy.* Chicago: University of Chicago Press.

Russell, Bertrand. [1919] 2004. *The Proposed Roads to Freedom.* New York, NY: Cosimo.

Rustow, Dankwart A. 1950. "Some Observations on Proportional Representation." *Journal of Politics* 12:107–127.

Rydgren, Jens. 2004. *The Populist Challenge: Political Protest and Ethno-nationalist Mobilization in France.* New York: Berghahn Books.

———. 2005. "Is Extreme Right-Wing Populism Contagious? Explaining the Emergence of a New Party Family." *European Journal of Political Research* 44:413–437.

Sachedina, Abdulaziz. 2000. *The Islamic Roots of Democratic Pluralism.* New York: Oxford University Press.

Sahlins, Peter. 1991. *Boundaries: The Making of France and Spain in the Pyrenees.* Berkeley: University of California Press.

Saideman, Stephen M., David J. Lanoue, Michael Campenni, and Samuel Stanon. 2002. "Democratization, Political Institutions, and Ethnic Conflict: A Pooled Time-Series Analysis, 1985–1998." *Comparative Political Studies* 35:103–129.

Saletan, William. 2011. "Springtime for Twitter: Is the Internet Driving the Revolutions of the Arab Spring." *Slate*, July 18. http://www.slate.com/articles/technology/future_tense/2011/07/springtime_for_twitter.html.

Samuel, Henry. 2011. "Praying in Paris Streets Outlawed." *The Telegraph*, September 15. http://www.telegraph.co.uk/news/worldnews/europe/france/8766169/Praying-in-Paris-streets-outlawed.html.

Samuels, David. 2007. "Separation of Powers." In *The Oxford Handbook of Comparative Politics,* eds. Carles Boix and Susan C. Stokes. New York: Oxford University Press.

Samuels, David, and Richard Snyder. 2001. "The Value of a Vote: Malapportionment in Comparative Perspective." *British Journal of Political Science* 31:651–671.

Sandler, Todd, and Walter Enders. 2004. "An Economic Perspective on Transnational Terrorism." *European Journal of Political Economy* 20:301–316.

Sartori, Giovanni. 1997. *Comparative Constitutional Engineering: An Inquiry into Structures, Incentives, and Outcomes.* New York: NYU Press.

Satterthwaite, Mark A. 1975. "Strategy-Proofness and Arrow's Conditions: Existence and Correspondence Theorems for Voting Procedures and Social Welfare Functions." *Journal of Economic Theory* 10:187–217.

Saward, Michael. 2006. "The Representative Claim." *Contemporary Political Theory* 5:297–318.

———. 2009. "Authorisation and Authenticity: Representation and the Unelected." *Journal of Political Philosophy* 17:1–22.

———. 2014. "Shape-Shifting Representation." *American Political Science Review* 108:723–736.

Scalapino, Robert. 1989. *The Politics of Development: Perspectives on Twentieth Century Asia.* Cambridge, MA: Harvard University Press.

Schaffer, Howard B. 1995. "The Sri Lankan Elections of 1994: The Chandrika Factor." *Asian Survey* 35:409–425.

Schattschneider, Elmer E. 1942. *Party Government.* New York: Rinehart.

Schedler, Andreas. 2002. "Elections without Democracy: The Menu of Manipulation." *Journal of Democracy* 13(2):36–50.

———, ed. 2006. *Electoral Authoritarianism: The Dynamics of Unfree Competition.* Boulder, CO: Lynne Rienner.

Schelling, Thomas C. 1978. *Micromotives and Macrobehavior.* New York: Norton.

Scheve, Kenneth, and David Stasavage. 2009. "Institutions, Partisanship, and Inequality in the Long Run." *World Politics* 61:215–253.

Schleifer, Andrei, and Robert Vishny. 1993. "Corruption." *Quarterly Journal of Economics* 108:599–617.

Schleiter, Petra, and Edward Morgan-Jones. 2009. "Constitutional Power and Competing Risks: Monarchs, Presidents, Prime Ministers, and the Termination of East and West European Cabinets." *American Political Science Review* 103:496–512.

Schlesinger, Jacob M. 1997. *Shadow Shoguns: The Rise and Fall of Japan's Postwar Political Machine.* New York: Simon and Schuster.

Schofield, Norman J. 1978. "Instability of Simple Dynamic Games." *Review of Economic Studies* 45:575–594.

Schumpeter, Joseph. [1942] 1962. *Capitalism, Socialism, and Democracy.* New York: Harper Perennial.

———. 1947. *Capitalism, Socialism, and Democracy*. New York: Harper.

Schwartz, Hermann. 1999. "Surprising Success: The New Eastern European Constitutional Courts." In *The Self-Restraining State*, eds. Andreas Schedler, Larry Diamand, and Marc Plattner. Boulder, CO: Lynne Rienner.

Schwindt-Bayer, Leslie A., and William Mishler. 2005. "An Integrated Model of Women's Representation." *Journal of Politics* 67:407–428.

"Scores Killed in China Protests." 2009. BBC News, July 6. http://news.bbc.co.uk/2/hi/asia-pacific/8135203.stm.

Sekhon, Jasjeet. 2004. "Quality Meets Quantity: Case Studies, Conditional Probability, and Counterfactuals." *Perspectives on Politics* 2:281–293.

Seligson, Mitchell A. 2002. "The Renaissance of Political Culture or the Renaissance of the Ecological Fallacy?" *Comparative Politics* 34:273–292.

Selway, Joel, and Kharis Templeman. 2012. "The Myth of Consociationalism? Conflict Reduction in Divided Societies." *Comparative Political Studies* 45(12):1542–1571.

Sen, Amartya K. 1970. *Collective Choice and Social Welfare*. San Francisco: Holden-Day.

———. 1981. *Poverty and Famines: An Essay on Entitlement and Deprivation*. New York: Oxford University Press.

———. 1999. "Democracy as a Universal Value." *Journal of Democracy* 10:3–17.

———. 2002. "Health: Perception versus Observation." *British Medical Journal* 324:860–861.

Ser, Kuang Keng Kuek. 2016. "How China Has Censored Words Relating to the Tiananmen Square Anniversary." PRI's *The World*, June 4. http://www.pri.org/stories/2016-06-03/how-china-has-censored-words-relating-tiananmen-square-anniversary.

Shafer, D. Michael. 1994. *Winners and Losers: How Sectors Shape the Developmental Prospects of States*. Ithaca, NY: Cornell University Press.

Shah, Zia H. 2012. "The Constitution of Medina: A Symbol of Pluralism in Islam." *The Muslim Times*, November 9. https://themuslimtimes.info/2012/11/09/the-constitution-of-medina-a-symbol-of-pluralism-in-islam/.

Shapiro, Martin, and Alec Stone Sweet. 1994. "Introduction: The New Constitutional Politics." *Comparative Political Studies* 26:397–420.

Shelton, Cameron A. 2007. "The Size and Composition of Government Expenditure." *Journal of Public Economics* 91:2230–2260.

Shepsle, Kenneth A. 1992. "Congress Is a 'They' Not an 'It': Legislative Intent as Oxymoron." *International Review of Law and Economics* 12:239–257.

Shepsle, Kenneth A., and Mark S. Bonchek. 1997. *Analyzing Politics: Rationality, Behavior, and Institutions*. New York: Norton.

Shively, W. Phillips. 1990. *The Craft of Political Research*. Englewood Cliffs, NJ: Prentice Hall.

———. 2001. *Power and Choice: An Introduction to Political Science*. New York: McGraw-Hill.

Shugart, Matthew Soberg. 1999. "Presidentialism, Parliamentarism, and the Provision of Collective Goods in Less-Developed Countries." *Constitutional Political Economy* 10:53–88.

———. 2006. "Comparative Executive-Legislative Relations." In *The Oxford Handbook of Political Institutions*, eds. R. A. W. Rhodes, Sarah A. Binder, and Bert A. Rockman. New York: Oxford University Press.

Shugart, Matthew Soberg, and John M. Carey. 1992. *Presidents and Assemblies: Constitutional Design and Electoral Dynamics*. New York: Cambridge University Press.

Simpser, Alberto. 2013. *Why Governments and Parties Manipulate Elections: Theory, Practice, and Implications.* New York: Cambridge University Press.

Sinnott, Richard. 1992. "The Electoral System." In *Politics in the Republic of Ireland,* eds. John Coakley and Michael Gallagher. Dublin: Folens and PSAI.

Sirowy, Larry, and Alex Inkeles. 1991. "The Effects of Democracy on Economic Growth and Inequality." In *On Measuring Democracy,* ed. Alex Inkeles. New Brunswick, NJ: Transaction.

Smith, Alastair. 2003. "Election Timing in Majoritarian Parliamentary Systems." *British Journal of Political Science* 33:397–418.

———. 2004. *Election Timing.* New York: Cambridge University Press.

———. 2005. "Why International Organizations Will Continue to Fail Their Development Goals." *Perspectives on Politics* 3:565–567.

———. 2008. "The Perils of Unearned Income." *Journal of Politics* 70(3):780–793.

Smith, Benjamin. 2006. "The Wrong Kind of Crisis: Why Oil Booms and Busts Rarely Lead to Authoritarian Breakdown." *Studies in Comparative International Development* 40:55–76.

Smith, Dorothy E. 1974. "Women's Perspective as a Radical Critique of Sociology." *Sociological Inquiry* 44(1):7–13.

Snyder, Jack. 2000. *From Voting to Violence: Democratization and Nationalist Conflict.* New York: Norton.

Solzhenitsyn, Aleksandr Isaevich. 1975. "The Smatterers." In *From under the Rubble,* eds. Aleksandr Isaevich Solzhenitsyn, Mikhail Agursky, and Evgeny Barabanov, 275. Boston: Little, Brown.

"Somali Peace Process: The Djibouti Process." (n.d.). African Union Mission in Somalia (AMISOM). http://amisom-au.org/about-somalia/somali-peace-process/.

Soroka, Stuart N., and Christopher Wlezien. 2015. "The Majoritarian and Proportional Visions of Democratic Responsiveness." *Electoral Studies* 40:539–547.

Spence, A. Michael. 1974. *Market Signaling: Informational Transfer in Hiring and Related Screening Processes.* Cambridge, MA: Harvard University Press.

Stark, Rodney. 2004a. "SSRC Presidential Address: Putting an End to Ancestor Worship." *Journal for the Scientific Study of Religion* 43:465–475.

———. 2004b. *The Victory of Reason: How Christianity Led to Freedom, Capitalism, and Western Success.* New York: Random House.

Stark, Rodney, and Roger Finke. 2000. *Acts of Faith: Exploring the Human Side of Religion.* Berkeley: University of California Press.

Starr, Harvey, and Christina Lindborg. 2003. "Democratic Dominoes Revisited: The Hazards of Governmental Transitions, 1974–1996." *Journal of Conflict Resolution* 47:490–519.

Stasavage, David. 2002. "Credible Commitment in Early Modern Europe: North and Weingast Revisited." *Journal of Law, Economics, and Organization* 18:155–186.

Staton, Jeffrey K. 2004. "Judicial Policy Implementation in Mexico City and Mérida." *Comparative Politics* 37:41–60.

———. 2006. "Constitutional Review and the Selective Promotion of Case Results." *American Journal of Political Science* 50:98–112.

———. 2010. *Judicial Power and Strategic Communication in Mexico.* New York: Cambridge University Press.

Steiner, Jürg. 1971. "The Principles of Majority and Proportionality." *British Journal of Political Science* 1:63–70.

Stepan, Alfred. 1971. *The Military in Politics: Changing Patterns in Brazil.* Princeton, NJ: Princeton University Press.

———. 1985. "State Power and the Strength of Civil Society in the Southern Cone of Latin America." In *Bringing the State Back In,* eds. Peter B. Evans, Dietrich Rueschemeyer, and Theda Skocpol. New York: Cambridge University Press.

———. 1999. "Federalism and Democracy: Beyond the U.S. Model." *Journal of Democracy* 10:19–34.

———. 2000. "Religion, Democracy, and the 'Twin Tolerations.'" *Journal of Democracy* 11:37–57.

Stepan, Alfred, and Cindy Skach. 1993. "Constitutional Frameworks and Democratic Consolidation: Parliamentarism versus Presidentialism." *World Politics* 46:1–22.

Stokes, Susan C. 1999. "Political Parties and Democracy." *Annual Review of Political Science* 2:243–267.

Stoll, Heather. 2015. "Presidential Coat-tails: A Closer Look." *Party Politics* 21:417–427.

Stone Sweet, Alec. 1992. *The Birth of Judicial Politics in France: The Constitutional Council in Comparative Perspective.* Oxford: Oxford University Press.

———. 2000. *Governing with Judges: Constitutional Politics in Europe.* New York: Oxford University Press.

———. 2008. "Constitutions and Judicial Power." In *Comparative Politics,* ed. Daniele Caramani. New York: Oxford University Press.

Strøm, Kaare. 1984. "Minority Governments in Parliamentary Democracies." *Comparative Political Studies* 17:199–227.

———. 1990. *Minority Government and Majority Rule.* Cambridge: Cambridge University Press.

———. 1995. "Parliamentary Government and Legislative Organization." In *Parliaments and Majority Rule in Western Europe,* ed. Herbert Döring. New York: St. Martin's Press.

———. 2003. "Parliamentary Democracy as Delegation and Accountability." In *Delegation and Accountability in Parliamentary Democracies,* eds. Kaare Strøm, Wolfgang C. Müller, and Torbjörn Bergman, 55–106. Oxford: Oxford University Press.

Strøm, Kaare, Wolfgang C. Müller, and Torbjörn Bergman, eds. 2003. "Parliamentary Democracy and Delegation." In *Delegation and Accountability in Parliamentary Democracies,* eds. Kaare Strøm, Wolfgang C. Müller, and Torbjörn Bergman, 55–106. Oxford: Oxford University Press.

Suny, Ronald Grigor. 1998. *The Soviet Experiment: Russia, the USSR, and the Successor States.* New York: Oxford University Press.

Svensson, Jakob. 2003. "Why Conditional Aid Does Not Work and What Can Be Done about It." *Journal of Development Economics* 70:381–402.

Svolik, Milan W. 2008. "Authoritarian Reversals and Democratic Consolidation." *American Political Science Review* 102:153–168.

———. 2009. "Power Sharing and Leadership Dynamics in Authoritarian Regimes." *American Journal of Political Science* 53:477–494.

———. 2012. *The Politics of Authoritarian Rule.* New York: Cambridge University Press.

"Syria: The Story of the Conflict." 2016. BBC News, March 11. http://www.bbc.com/news/world-middle-east-26116868.

Tate, Katherine. 1994. *From Protest to Politics: The New Black Voters in American Politics.* Cambridge, MA: Harvard University Press.

———. 1995. *Behind the Mule: Race and Class in African-American Politics*. Princeton, NJ: Princeton University Press.

Tavares, José, and Romain Wacziarg. 2001. "How Democracy Affects Growth." *European Economic Review* 45:1341–1378.

Taylor, Michael. 1976. *Anarchy and Cooperation*. New York: Wiley.

Thatcher, Margaret. 1993. *Margaret Thatcher: The Downing Street Years*. London: HarperCollins.

Theil, Henri. 1971. *Principles of Econometrics*. New York: Wiley.

Thies, Michael F. 2001. "Keeping Tabs on Partners: The Logic of Delegation in Coalition Governments." *American Journal of Political Science* 45:580–598.

Thyne, Clayton L., and Jonathan M. Powell. 2014. "Coup d'état or Coup d'autocracy? How Coups Impact Democratization, 1950–2008." *Foreign Policy Analysis* 12:192–213.

Tideman, Nicolaus, and Daniel Richardson. 2000. "A Comparison of Improved STV Methods." In *Elections in Australia, Ireland, and Malta under the Single Transferable Vote: Reflections on an Embedded Institution*, eds. Shaun Bowler and Bernard Grofman. Ann Arbor: University of Michigan Press.

Tiebout, Charles M. 1956. "A Pure Theory of Local Expenditures." *Journal of Political Economy* 64: 416–424.

Tilly, Charles. 1985. "War Making and State Making as Organized Crime." In *Bringing the State Back In*, eds. Peter Evans, Dietrich Rueschmeyer, and Theda Skocpol, 169–191. New York: Cambridge University Press.

"Timeline: A History of Turkish Coups." 2016. *Al Jazeera*, July 15. http://www.aljazeera.com/news/europe/2012/04/20124472814687973.html.

Tocqueville, Alexis de. [1835] 1988. *Democracy in America*. New York: HarperCollins.

———. [1835] 1945. *Democracy in America*, trans. Henry Reeve, Francis Bowen, and Phillips Bradley. New York: Random House.

"Toughs at the Top." 2004. *The Economist*, December 16. http://www.economist.com/node/3445136.

Treier, Shawn, and Simon Jackman. 2008. "Democracy as a Latent Variable." *American Journal of Political Science* 52:201–217.

Treisman, Daniel. 2000. "Decentralization and Inflation: Commitment, Collective Action, or Continuity?" *American Political Science Review* 94:837–857.

———. 2002. "Decentralization and the Quality of Government." University of California, Los Angeles.

Tripp, Aili Mari, and Alice Kang. 2008. "The Global Impact of Quotas: On the Fast Track to Increased Female Legislative Representation." *Comparative Political Studies* 41:338–361.

Tsai, Michelle. "Vote of No Consequence." 2007. *Slate*, May 21. http://www.slate.com/articles/news_and_politics/explainer/2007/05/vote_of_no_consequence.html.

Tsebelis, George. 1990. "Elite Interaction and Constitution Building in Consociational Societies." *Journal of Theoretical Politics* 2:5–29.

———. 1995. "Decision Making in Political Systems: Veto Players in Presidentialism, Multicameralism, and Multipartyism." *British Journal of Political Science* 25:289–326.

———. 1999. "Veto Players and Law Production in Parliamentary Democracies: An Empirical Analysis." *American Political Science Review* 93:591–608.

———. 2002. *Veto Players: How Political Institutions Work*. Princeton, NJ: Princeton University Press.

Tsebelis, George, and Jeannette Money. 1997. *Bicameralism*. New York: Cambridge University Press.

Tufte, Edward R. 1978. *The Political Control of the Economy*. Princeton, NJ: Princeton University Press.

Tullock, Gordon. 1969. "Federalism: Problems of Scale." *Public Choice* 6:19–29.

"Turkmenistan Wrestles with Child Labor Issue as Cotton Harvest Approaches." 2004. Eurasianet, August 31. http://www.eurasianet.org/departments/rights/articles/eav090104.shtml/.

Uhlaner, Carole. 1989. "Rational Turnout: The Neglected Role of Groups." *American Journal of Political Science* 33:390–422.

Uhlfelder, Jay. 2007. "Natural-Resource Wealth and the Survival of Autocracy." *Comparative Political Studies* 40:995–1018.

United Nations High Commissioner for Human Rights. 2013. "Periodic Update." December 20. http://www.ohchr.org/Documents/Countries/SY/ColSyriaDecember2012.pdf.

US Congress. 2006. House of Representatives. Committee on International Relations, Subcommittee on Africa, Global Human Rights, and International Operations and the Subcommittee on International Terrorism and Nonproliferation. *Somalia: Expanding Crisis in the Horn of Africa*: Joint hearing. 109th Congress, 2nd Session, June 29. Available from http://democrats.foreignaffairs.house.gov/archives/afhear.htm.

US Department of State. 2011. "Internet Freedom and Human Rights: The Obama Administration's Perspective." July 13. http://www.state.gov/j/drl/rls/rm/2011/168475.htm.

Uzonyi, Gary J., Mark Souva, and Sona N. Golder. 2012. "Domestic Institutions and Credible Signals." *International Studies Quarterly* 56(4):765–776.

Valenzuela, Arturo. 2004. "Latin America Presidencies Interrupted." *Journal of Democracy* 15:5–19.

Van Cott, Donna Lee. 2005. *From Movements to Parties in Latin America: The Evolution of Ethnic Politics*. New York: Cambridge University Press.

Vanberg, Georg. 2000. "Establishing Judicial Independence in Germany: The Impact of Opinion Leadership and the Separation of Powers." *Comparative Politics* 32:333–353.

———. 2001. "Legislative-Judicial Relations: A Game-Theoretic Approach to Constitutional Review." *American Journal of Political Science* 45:346–361.

———. 2005. *The Politics of Constitutional Review in Germany*. New York: Cambridge University Press.

Vanhanen, Tatu. 1991. *The Process of Democratization: A Comparative Study of 147 States, 1980–1988*. New York: Crane Russak.

Varian, Hal R. 1993. *Intermediate Economics: A Modern Approach*. New York: Norton.

Varshney, Ashutosh. 2001. "Ethnic Conflict and Civil Society: India and Beyond." *World Politics* 53:362–398.

———. 2002. *Ethnic Conflict and Civic Life: Hindus and Muslims in India*. New Haven, CT: Yale University Press.

———. 2004. "Nationalism, Ethnic Conflict, and Rationality." *Perspectives on Politics* 1:85–99.

"V-Dem: Global Standards, Local Knowledge." 2016. V-DEM. https://www.v-dem.net/en/.

Veenendaal, Wouter P. 2016. "How Democracy Functions without Parties: The Republic of Palau." *Party Politics* 22(1):27–36.

Verba, Sidney, Kay Schlozman, and Henry Brady. 1995. *Voice and Equality: Civic Voluntarism in American Politics*. Cambridge, MA: Harvard University Press.

Vlasic, Bill, and David M. Herszenshorn. 2008. "Detroit Chiefs Plead for Aid." *The New York Times*, November 19. http://www.nytimes.com/2008/11/19/business/19auto.html? pagewanted=print.

Voeten, Erik. 2010. "A New Twittered Revolution." April 7. http://themonkeycage.org/blog/2010/04/07/a_new_twittered_revolution/.

Volcansek, Mary L. 1991. "Judicial Activism in Italy." In *Judicial Activism in Comparative Perspective*, ed. Kenneth Holland. New York: St. Martin's Press.

Voslensky, Michael. 1984. *Nomenklatura: The Soviet Ruling Class*. Garden City, NY: Doubleday.

Waltz, Kenneth N. 1979. *Theory of International Politics*. New York: McGraw-Hill.

Wängnerud, Lena. 2009. "Women in Parliaments: Descriptive and Substantive Representation." *Annual Review of Sociology* 12:51–69.

Wantchekon, Leonard. 2001. "Why Do Resource Abundant Countries Have Authoritarian Governments?" *Journal of African Finance and Development* 5:57–77.

Warwick, Paul V., and Jamie Druckman. 2001. "Portfolio Salience and the Proportionality of Payoffs in Coalition Governments." *British Journal of Political Science* 31:627–649.

———. 2006. "The Paradox of Portfolio Allocation: An Investigation into the Nature of a Very Strong but Puzzling Relationship." *European Journal of Political Research* 45:635–665.

Way, Lucan. 2011. "Comparing the Arab Revolts: The Lessons of 1989." *Journal of Democracy* 232(4):17–27.

Weber, Max. [1918] 1958. "Politics as a Vocation." In *From Max Weber: Essays in Sociology*, eds. H. H. Gerth and C. Wright Mills, Chapt. IV: 77–128. New York: Oxford University Press.

———. [1930] 1992. *The Protestant Ethic and the Spirit of Capitalism*. New York: Routledge.

Weiner, Tim. 1994. "C.I.A. Spent Millions to Support the Japanese Right in 50's and 60's." *The New York Times,* October 9. Available from http://www.nytimes.com/1994/10/09/world/cia-spent-millions-to-support-japanese-right-in-50-s-and-60-s.html.

Weingast, Barry R. 1979. "A Rational Choice Perspective on Congressional Norms." *American Journal of Political Science* 23:245–262.

———. 1995. "The Economic Role of Political Institutions: Market-Preserving Federalism and Economic Development." *Journal of Law, Economics, and Organization* 11:1–31.

———. 1997. "The Political Foundations of Democracy and the Rule of Law." *American Political Science Review* 91:245–263.

Weingast, Barry R., Kenneth A. Shepsle, and Christopher Johnsen. 1981. "The Political Economy of Benefits and Costs: A Neoclassical Approach to Distributive Politics." *Journal of Political Economy* 89:642–664.

Weldon, S. Laurel. 2006. "The Structure of Intersectionality: A Comparative Politics of Gender." *Politics and Gender* 2:235–248.

Whaples, Robert. 2006. "Do Economists Agree on Anything? Yes!" *The Economists' Voice* 3, art. 1.

"What Now for Colonel Gaddafi's Green Book?" 2011. BBC News, April 29. http://www.bbc.com/news/world-africa-13235981.

Wibbels, Erik. 2000. "Federalism and the Politics of Macroeconomic Policy and Performance." *American Journal of Political Science* 44:687–702.

Wiens, David, Paul Poast, and William Roberts Clark. 2014. "The Political Resource Curse: An Empirical Re-evaluation." *Political Research Quarterly* 67:783–794.

Williams, Laron K., Katsunori Seki, and Guy D. Whitten. 2016. "You've Got Some Explaining to Do: The Influence of Economic Conditions and Spatial Competition on Party Strategy." *Political Science Research and Methods* 4(1):47–63.

Wilson, Andrew. 2012. *Belarus: The Last European Dictatorship*. New Haven, CT: Yale University Press.

———. 2015. "Belarus Votes—And this time it matters." European Council on Foreign Relations, October 9. http://www.ecfr.eu/article/commentary_belarus_votes_and_this_time_it_matters4068.

Wintrobe, Ronald. 2001. "How to Understand, and Deal with Dictatorship: An Economist's View." *Economics of Governance* 2:35–58.

Wolfinger, Raymond E., and Steven J. Rosenstone. 1980. *Who Votes?* New Haven, CT: Yale University Press.

Wood, Elisabeth J. 2000. *Forging Democracy from Below: Contested Transitions in Oligarchic Societies.* New York: Cambridge University Press.

Woodberry, Robert D. 2004. "The Shadow of Empire: Christian Missions, Colonial Policy, and Democracy in Postcolonial Societies." PhD dissertation, Department of Sociology, University of North Carolina.

———. 2012. "The Missionary Roots of Liberal Democracy." *American Political Science Review* 106(2):244–274.

Woodberry, Robert D., and Timothy S. Shah. 2004. "The Pioneering Protestants." *Journal of Democracy* 15:47–60.

Woods, Dwayne. 2012. "Patrimonialism (neo) and the Kingdom of Swaziland: Employing a Case-Study to Rescale a Concept." *Journal of Commonwealth and Comparative Politics* 50:344–366.

———. Forthcoming. "Monarchical Rule in Swaziland: Power Is Absolute but Patronage Is (for) Relative(s)." *Journal of African and Asian Studies.*

World Bank. 2000. "Decentralization: Rethinking Government." In *World Development Report 1999/2000.* New York: Oxford University Press.

"World Report 2015, Somalia." 2015. Human Rights Watch. https://www.hrw.org/world-report/2015/country-chapters/somalia.

Wright, Joseph. 2009. "How Foreign Aid Can Foster Democratization in Authoritarian Regimes." *American Journal of Political Science* 53:552–571.

Wright, Joseph, and Matthew Winters. 2010. "The Politics of Effective Foreign Aid." *Annual Review of Political Science* 13:61–80.

Yan, Holly. 2015. "Refugee Crisis: Pressure Builds for U.S. to Welcome More Syrians." CNN, September 9. http://www.cnn.com/2015/09/09/politics/us-syrian-refugees-pressure/.

Yazdi, Ibrahim. 1995. "A Seminar with Ibrahim Yazdi." *Middle East Policy* 3:15–28.

Yew, Lee Kuan. 1994. "Culture Is Destiny." An interview with Fareed Zakaria. *Foreign Affairs* 73:109–126.

Young, Hugo. 1990. *One of Us: Life of Margaret Thatcher.* London: Pan.

Young, Iris Marion. 2002. *Inclusion and Democracy.* New York: Oxford University Press.

Yusuf, Shahid, and World Bank. 1999. *Entering the 21st Century: World Development Report, 1999/2000.* New York: World Bank.

Zakaria, Fareed. 1997. "The Rise of Illiberal Democracy." *Foreign Affairs* 76:22–41.

Index